Practical
Business
Statistics
WITH STATPAD

The Irwin Series in Quantitative Analysis for Business
Consulting Editor   Robert B. Fetter   Yale University

Practical
Business
Statistics

WITH STATPAD

ANDREW F. SIEGEL

Department of Management
Science
Department of Finance
Department of Statistics
University of Washington

Homewood, IL 60430
Boston, MA 02116

Cover image © FourByFive
StatPad is a trademark of Skyline Technologies, Inc.
IBM® is a registered trademark of International Business Machines Corporation.
1-2-3® and Lotus® are registered trademarks of Lotus Development Corporation.
© Andrew F. Siegel, 1990

Sponsoring editor: Richard T. Hercher, Jr.
Senior developmental editor: Ann M. Granacki
Project editor: Margaret S. Haywood
Production manager: Carma W. Fazio
Designer: Diane Beasley Design
Artists: Jill Smith/Alice Thiede
Compositor: Beacon Graphics Corporation
Typeface: 10/12 Baskerville
Printer: R. R. Donnelley & Sons Company

Library of Congress Cataloging-in-Publication Data

Siegel, Andrew F.
    Practical business statistics with StatPad/Andrew F. Siegel.
       p.   cm.
    ISBN 0-256-07313-9
    1. Commercial statistics.   2. Industrial management—Statistical methods.   3. StatPad (Computer program) I. Title.
HF1017.S525 1990
519.5′028′55369—dc20   89–38365
                                                        CIP

Printed in the United States of America

1 2 3 4 5 6 7 8 9 0 DO 7 6 5 4 3 2 1 0

■
To Ann, Bonnie, Clara, Mildred, and Armand

Preface

The traditional business statistics course is changing. Now that computers are so widely available for number crunching, many old-fashioned topics are no longer worth covering in complete detail. This creates a tremendous opportunity for using new material during class time that will be more useful to a business manager—new material that solidifies the *concepts* and the *applications* of statistics to business and economics. For example, managers do not need to know how to derive the formulas for the least-squares regression coefficients, but they need to know how to interpret these regression coefficients so that appropriate decisions can be made based on these important summaries of relationships in complex situations.

Practical Business Statistics was written with this change in mind. Business students can excel at statistics when they are motivated by real-world examples and clear, direct explanations that show them why it is worthwhile to learn the statistical view of the world. Business students are different from other students and deserve a book created especially for their needs and interests.

Although *Practical Business Statistics* is aimed primarily at students in MBA and executive MBA–level statistics courses, it can also work well with undergraduate business majors.

Extensive Development: Reviews and Class Testing

This project began as a collection of readings I handed out to my students as a supplement to the assigned textbook. All of the available books seemed to make statistics seem unnecessarily difficult, and I wanted to present the straightforward, easy ways to think about the subject. I also wanted to add more of a modern, real-world business flavor to the topic. All of the helpful feedback I have received from students over the years has been acted on and has improved the book.

Practical Business Statistics has gone through several stages of reviews and has been class-tested in several MBA and executive MBA classes. Lots of good comments and recommendations about the material were made during this process, and further reviewing helped to incorporate these changes.

Writing Style

I enjoyed writing this book. I have presented the "inside scoop" wherever possible, explaining how we statisticians *really* think about a topic, what it implies, and how it is useful. This approach helps bring some sorely needed life to a subject that unfortunately suffers from dreadfu! public relations. Of course, the traditional explanations are also given here so that you can see it both ways: here is what they say, and here is what it means.

It thrilled me to hear even some of my more quantitative-phobic students tell me that the text is actually *enjoyable to read!* And this was *after* the final grades were in!

Examples

Examples bring statistics to life, making each topic relevant and useful. There are many real-world examples used throughout *Practical Business Statistics,* chosen from a wide variety of business sources. The stock market crash of October 1987 is used in Chapter 5 to illustrate market volatility and risk as measured by the standard deviation. Quality control is used throughout the book to illustrate individual topics and is also covered in its own Chapter (18). Prices of magazine advertisements are used in Chapter 12 to show how multiple regression can uncover relationships in complex data sets. Unemployment rates are used in Chapter 14 to demonstrate what goes on "behind the scenes" in time-series forecasting. Students learn better through the use of examples and applications.

Statistical Graphics

To help show what is going on in the data sets, *Practical Business Statistics* includes over 200 figures to illustrate important features and relationships. The graphs are exact because they were initially drawn with the help of a computer. For example, the bell-shaped normal curves here are accurate, unlike those in many books, which are distorted because they appear to be an artist's enhancement of a casual, hand-drawn sketch. There is no substitute for accuracy! This helps the student grasp the concepts more clearly.

Organization

A student should always know *why* the current material is important. For this reason, each part begins with a brief look at the subject of that part and the chapters to come. Each chapter begins with an overview of its topic, showing why the subject is important to business, before proceeding to the details and examples.

Key words, the most important terms and phrases, are presented in bold in the sentence of the text where they are defined. They are collected in the Key Words list at the end of each chapter and also included in the glossary at the back of the book. This makes it easy to study by focusing attention on the main ideas. An extensive index helps you find main topics as well as small details. Try looking up "example", "definition", "unpaired *t*-test" or even "microprocessor".

Extensive end-of-chapter materials are included, beginning with a *summary* of the important material covered. Next is the list of *key words*. The *questions* provide a review of the main topics, indicating why they are important. The *problems* give the student a chance to apply statistics to new situations. The *database exercises* (included in most chapters) give further practice problems based on the employee database in Appendix A. Finally, the *projects* bring statistics closer to the students' needs and interests by allowing them to help define the problem and choose the data set from their work experience or interests.

Several relatively new topics are covered in addition to the foundations of statistics and their applications to business. Because communication is so important in the business world, Chapter 13 shows how to gather statistical material in a report. Chapter 14 includes an intuitive discussion of the Box-Jenkins forecasting approach to time series using ARIMA models. Chapter 18 shows how statistical methods can help you achieve and improve quality; discussion of quality control techniques is also interspersed throughout the text.

Practical Business Statistics is organized into five parts, plus appendices, as follows:

Part I, Chapters 1 through 5, is "Introduction and Descriptive Statistics." Chapter 1 motivates the student by showing how statistics provides a competitive edge in business. Chapter 2 surveys the various types of data sets (quantitative, qualitative, ordinal, nominal, bivariate, time-series, etc.). Chapter 3 shows how the histogram lets you see what's in the data set, which may be difficult to determine just from staring at a list of numbers. Chapter 4 covers the basic landmark summaries, including the average, median, mode, and percentiles, which are displayed in box plots and cumulative distribution functions. Chapter 5 discusses variability, which often translates to *risk* in business terms, featuring the standard deviation as well as the range and coefficient of variation.

Part II, including Chapters 6 and 7, is "Probability." Chapter 6 covers probabilities of events and their combinations, using probability trees both as a way of visualizing the situation and as a way of computing probabilities. Conditional probabilities are interpreted as a way of making the best use of the information you have. Chapter 7 covers random variables (numerical outcomes), which basically represent those numbers that are important to your business but are not yet available. Details are provided concerning general discrete distributions, the binomial distribution, the normal distribution, and (briefly) the Poisson and exponential distributions.

Part III, Chapters 8 through 10, is "Statistical Inference." These chapters pull together the descriptive summaries of Part I and the formal probability assessments of Part II. Chapter 8 covers random sampling, which forms the basis for the exact probability statements of statistical inference, and introduces the all-important notion of the standard error of a statistic. Chapter 9 shows how confidence intervals lead to an exact probability statement about an unknown quantity based on statistical data. Both two-sided and one-sided confidence intervals are covered. Chapter 10 covers hypothesis testing, often from the point of view of determining the presence of a real pattern versus coincidence. By building on the intuitive process of constructing confidence intervals from Chapter 9, hypothesis testing can be performed in a relatively painless manner while ensuring strict statistical correctness.

Part IV, Chapters 11 through 14, is "Regression and Time Series." These chapters apply the concepts and methods of the previous parts to more complex and more realistic situations. Chapter 11 shows how relationships can be studied using correlation and regression methods on bivariate data. Chapter 12 extends these ideas to multiple regression, perhaps the most important method in statistics. Chapter 13 provides a guide to report writing to help the student communicate the results of a multiple regression analysis to other business people. Chapter 14 shows how new and different methods are required for time-series analysis. The trend-seasonal approach is used to give an intuitive feeling for the basic features of a time series. Box-Jenkins methods are covered to show how these complex, modern methods can handle more difficult situations.

Part V, Chapters 15–18, is "Methods and Applications," basically a grab bag of optional, special topics that extend the basic material covered so far. Chapter 15 shows how the analysis of variance allows hypothesis testing in more complex situations. Chapter 16 covers nonparametric methods to be used when the basic assumptions are not satisfied, that is, for cases where the distributions might not be normal or the data set might be merely ordinal. Chapter 17 shows how chi-squared analysis can be used to test relationships among the categories of nominal data. Finally, Chapter 18 shows how quality control relies heavily on statistical methods such as Pareto diagrams and control charts.

Appendix A is the "Employee Database," consisting of information on salary, experience, age, gender, and training level for a number of administrative employees. This data set is used in the *database exercises* section at the end of most chapters. Appendix B gives answers to some of the problems. Appendix C collects all of the statistical tables used throughout the text. Appendix D is the manual for *StatPad*[1] statistical software, which is included with every copy of *Practical Business Statistics*. *StatPad* is used with Lotus® 1-2-3®[2], enhancing the spreadsheet by adding extensive statistical capabilities.

Instructor's Manual with Data Disk

The instructor's manual is designed to help save time in preparing lectures. A brief discussion of teaching objectives, how to motivate students, and the summary and key words are provided for each chapter. The data sets from chapter examples and problems are provided on the data disk, which is included with the instructor's manual. Files are provided in both Lotus 1-2-3 format and standard text (ASCII) format. The instructor's manual was written by Mildred Siegel, Armand Siegel, and Andrew F. Siegel.

StatPad

One solution to the computer problem is to give students software that works in a processing environment they are already familiar with. In addition to making computing more accessible, this approach ensures that the students will still have convenient access to statistical methods after the course is over, and even after graduation! *StatPad,* a statistical program that adds statistical capabilities to Lotus 1-2-3 release 2.01, is provided with every copy of *Practical Business Statistics*. The manual is included in the text as Appendix D.

StatPad was developed by Skyline Technologies, Inc. with the assistance of Andrew F. Siegel. The package has been extensively tested in MBA and executive MBA classes at the University of Washington. Through the use of familiar Lotus-style menus, with the results placed back into the spreadsheet, statistics operations essentially become part of the worksheet, just like any other spreadsheet command.

Practical Business Statistics with *StatPad* is a good choice even if your course requires the use of other computer programs because the text is not tied to any particular computing environment. Think of *StatPad* as an "extra" that can be used by students who wish to augment the other resources of the class.

By breaking down barriers to the effective use of computers, statistical concepts can be learned more quickly and painlessly!

---

[1]*StatPad* is a trademark of Skyline Technologies, Inc.
[2]Lotus® and 1-2-3® are registered trademarks of Lotus Development Corporation.

Acknowledgments

Many thanks to all of the reviewers and students who have read and commented on drafts of *Practical Business Statistics*. I was lucky to have dedicated, careful readers at a variety of institutions who were not afraid to say what it would take to meet their needs.

I am fortunate (and proud) to have been able to keep in touch with my parents, Mildred and Armand Siegel, who worked extensively on the instructor's manual. In addition, Mildred did much of the writing for the *StatPad* manual, and Armand provided many careful and detailed suggestions for the text.

Warm thanks go to Michael Antonucci, my local sales rep, who started this whole thing by stopping by my office to talk about computers and see what I was up to. Mike put me in touch with lots of good people at Irwin. By now I've met many of them, and I still don't know how Irwin managed to find so many excellent and nice people to work with!

Thank goodness I had editors like Richard T. Hercher, Ann Granacki (special projects editor), and Margaret Haywood (project editor) to watch over this entire project. It's a big job producing a work like this, and I was lucky to have people with so much knowledge, dedication, and organizational skill.

The creative design of the text and cover is due to Diane Beasley. She was able to come up with an aesthetically pleasing layout that invites you into the book and makes it easy to locate the material you need. Tara Bazata directed the art and design programs, ensuring that the various style elements came together to form an attractive as well as functional book.

Additional thanks for helpful comments go to Eric Russell, Dayton Robinson, Eric J. Bean, Michael R. Rancher, Susan Stapleton, Sara S. Hemphill, Nancy J. Silberg, A. Ronald Hauver, Hirokuni Tamura, John Chiu, Brian McMullen, David B. Foster, Pablo Ferrero, Rolf R. Anderson, Gordon Klug, Reed Hunt, E. N. Funk, Rob Gullette, David Hartnett, Mickey Lass, Judyann Morgan, Richard Richings, Mark Roellig, Scott H. Pattison, Thomas J. Virgin, Carl Stork, Gerald Bernstein, and Jeremiah J. Sullivan.

To the Student

As you begin this course, you may have some preconceived notions of what statistics is all about. If you have positive notions, please keep them and share them with your classmates. But if you have negative notions, please set them aside and remain open-minded. Because this subject is not yet taught routinely in grade schools in many countries, relatively few university students have developed a statistical view of the world that helps them deal with mountains of data when decisions must be made in the face of uncertainty.

In some ways, statistics is easier for your generation than for those of the past. Now that computers can do the messy numerical work, you are free to develop a deeper understanding of the concepts and how they can help you beat out the competition in your business career.

Make good use of the introductory material so that you will always know *why* statistics is worth the effort. Take advantage of the summary, key words, and other materials at the ends of the chapters. Don't forget about the glossary at the back when you need a quick reminder. And don't worry. Once you realize how much statistics can help you in business, the things you need to learn will fall into place much more easily.

Keep this book as a reference. You'll be glad you did when the Boss needs a memo drafted immediately that requires a quick look at some data or a response to an adversary's analysis. With the help of *Practical Business Statistics* on your bookshelf and *StatPad* on your computer, you'll be able to finish early and still go out to dinner. *Bon appetit!*

ANDREW F. SIEGEL

About the Author

Andrew F. Siegel is Professor, Departments of Management Science and Finance, School of Business, University of Washington, Seattle. He holds an adjunct faculty appointment in the Department of Statistics and also serves as President and Chairman of the Board of Skyline Technologies, Inc. He has a Ph.D. in Statistics from Stanford University (1977), an MS in Mathematics from Stanford University (1975), and a BA in Mathematics and Physics summa cum laude with distinction from Boston University (1973). Before settling in Seattle, he held teaching and/or research positions at Harvard University, the University of Wisconsin, the RAND Corporation, the Smithsonian Institution, and Princeton University. The very first time he taught statistics in a business school (University of Washington, 1983) he was granted the "Professor of the Quarter" award by the MBA students. Other honors and awards include Research Associate, Center for the Study of Futures Markets, Columbia University, 1988; Excellence in Teaching Awards, Executive MBA Program, University of Washington, 1986 and 1988; Research Opportunities in Auditing Award, Peat Marwick Foundation, 1987; Burlington Northern Foundation Faculty Achievement Award for Scholarship, 1986; and Phi Beta Kappa, 1973. He belongs to the American Statistical Association, the American Finance Association, the Institute of Management Sciences, and the Western Finance Association. He has written three other books: *Statistics and Data Analysis: An Introduction* (1988, Wiley), *Counterexamples in Probability and Statistics* (1986, Wadsworth, with Joseph P. Romano), and *Modern Data Analysis* (1982, Academic Press, co-edited with Robert L. Launer). His articles have appeared in many publications, including the *Journal of the American Statistical Association*, the *Journal of Business*, the *Journal of Finance*, the *Encyclopedia of Statistical Sciences*, the *American Statistician*, the *Journal of Financial and Quantitative Analysis*, the *American Mathematical Monthly*, the *Journal of the Royal Statistical Society*, the *Annals of Statistics*, the *Annals of Probability*, the *Society for Industrial and Applied*

Mathematics Journal on Scientific and Statistical Computing, Biometrika, and the *Journal of Applied Probability.* He has consulted in a variety of business areas, including election predictions for a major television network, statistical algorithms in speech recognition for a prominent research laboratory, television advertisement testing for an active marketing firm, and computer design automation for a growing Silicon Valley startup company.

Contents

Practical
Business
Statistics
WITH STATPAD

Introduction and Descriptive Statistics

Welcome to the world of statistics. You will want to get comfortable with it because you will make better management decisions when you know how to assess the available information and how to ask for additional facts as needed. How else can you expect to manage 12 divisions, 683 products, and 5,809 employees? And even a small business will need to understand the larger business environment of potential customers and competitors it operates within. These first five chapters will begin by introducing you to the role of statistics in business management (in Chapter 1) and to the various types of data sets (in Chapter 2). Summaries help you see the "big picture" that might otherwise remain obscured in a collection of data. Chapter 3 will show you a good way to see the basic facts about a list of numbers by looking at a *histogram*. Fundamental summary numbers (such as the average, median, percentiles, etc.) will be explained in Chapter 4. One reason statistical methods are so important is because there is so much *variability* out there that gets in the way of the message in the data. Chapter 5 will show you how to measure the extent of this diversity problem.

Introduction
Defining the Role of Statistics in Business

A business executive must constantly make decisions under pressure, often with only incomplete and imperfect information available. Naturally, whatever information is available must be utilized to the fullest extent possible. *Statistical analysis* helps extract information from data and provides an indication of the reliability of that information. *Probability* helps you understand risky and random events and provides a way of evaluating the likelihoods of various potential outcomes.

Even those who would argue that business decision making should be based on expert intuition and experience (and therefore should not be overly quantified) must admit that all available relevant information should be considered. Thus, statistical techniques should be viewed as an important part of the decision process, allowing informed strategic decisions to be made that combine executive intuition with a thorough understanding of the facts available. This is a powerful combination.

We will begin with an overview of the competitive advantage provided by a knowledge of statistical methods, followed by some basic facts about statistics and probability and their role in business.

■ 1.1 Why Statistics?

Is knowledge of statistics really necessary to be successful in business? Or is it enough to rely on intuition, experience, and hunches? Let's put it another way: Do you really want to ignore much of the vast potentially useful information out there that comes in the form of data?

Why Should You Learn Statistics?

If you don't learn statistics, you will be at a competitive disadvantage compared to those who are basically like you but are also comfortable with statistics. A great deal of skill goes into creating strategy from knowledge, experience, and intuition. Statistics helps you deal with the knowledge component, especially when this knowledge is in the form of numbers, by answering questions such as, To what extent should you *really* believe these figures and their implications?

You won't be able to avoid statistics. These methods are already used routinely throughout the corporate world, and the lower cost of computers is increasing your need to be able to make decisions based on quantitative information.

Is Statistics Difficult?

Statistics is no more difficult than any other field of study. Naturally, some hard work is needed to achieve understanding of the general ideas and concepts. Although some attention to details and computations is necessary, it is much easier to become an expert *user* of statistics than it is to become an expert statistician trained in all of the fine details. Statistics is easier than it used to be because personal computers can do the repetitive number crunching tasks, allowing you to concentrate on interpreting the results and their meaning. Although a few die-hard purists may bemoan the decline of technical detail in statistics teaching, it is good to see that these details are now in their proper place; life is too short for all human beings to work out the intricate details of techniques such as long division and matrix inversion.

Does Learning Statistics Decrease Your Decision-Making Flexibility?

Knowledge of statistics *enhances* your ability to make good decisions. Statistics is not a rigid, exact science and should not get in the way of your experience and intuition. By learning about data and the basic properties of uncertain events, you will help solidify the information on which your decisions are based, and you will add a new dimension to your intuition. Think of statistical methods as a component of decision making, but not the whole story. You want to supplement—not replace—business experience, common sense, and intuition.

■ 1.2 What Is Statistics?

Statistics is the art and science of collecting and understanding data. Since *data* refers to any kind of recorded information, statistics plays an important role in many human endeavors.

Statistics Looks at the Big Picture

When you have a large, complex assemblage of many small pieces of information, statistics can help you classify and analyze the situation, providing a useful overview and summary of the fundamental features in the data. If you don't yet have the data, then statistics can help you collect them, ensuring that your questions can be answered and that you spend enough (but not too much) effort in the process.

Statistics Doesn't Ignore the Individual

If used carefully, statistics pays appropriate attention to all individuals. A complete and careful statistical analysis will summarize the general facts that apply to everyone and *will also alert you to any exceptions.* If there are special cases in the data that are not adequately summarized in the "big picture," the statistician's job is not yet complete. For example, you may read that in 1986 the average U.S. household size was 2.67 people.[1] Although this is a useful statistic, it doesn't come close to giving a complete picture of the size of all households in the United States. As you will see, statistical methods can easily be used to describe the entire distribution of household sizes.

EXAMPLE

Data in Management

Data sets are very common in management. Here is a short list of kinds of everyday managerial information that are, in fact, data:

1 Financial statements (and other accounting numbers).
2 Security prices and volumes and interest rates (and other investment information).
3 Money supply figures (and other government announcements).
4 Sales reports (and other internal records).
5 Market survey results (and other marketing data).
6 Production quality measures (and other manufacturing records).
7 Personnel records (and other internal databases).

Think about it. Probably much of what you do depends at least indirectly on data. Perhaps someone works for you and advises you on these matters, but you

---

[1] Bureau of the Census, *Statistical Abstract of the United States, 1987* (Washington, 1986), p.42.

rarely see the actual data. From time to time you might ask to see the "raw data" in order to keep some perspective. Looking at data and asking some questions about them may reveal surprises: You may find out that the quality of the data is not as high as you had thought (you mean that's what we base our forecasts on?), or you may find out otherwise and be reassured. Either way, it's worthwhile.

Looking at Data

What do you see when you look hard at tables of data (for example, the back pages of *The Wall Street Journal*)? What does a professional statistician see? The surprising answer to both of these questions is, often, Not much. You've got to go to work on the numbers — draw pictures of them, compute summaries from them, and so on — before the message will come through. This is what professional statisticians do; they find this much easier and more rewarding than staring at large lists of numbers for long periods of time. So don't be discouraged if a list of numbers looks to you like, well, a list of numbers.

Statistics in Management

What should a manager know about statistics? Your knowledge should include a broad overview of the basic concepts of statistics, with some (but not necessarily all) details. You should be aware that the world is random and uncertain in many aspects. Furthermore, you should be able to effectively perform two important activities:

1 Understand and use the results of statistical analysis as background information in your work.
2 Play the appropriate leadership role during the course of a statistical study if you are responsible for the actual data collection and/or analysis.

To fulfill these roles, it is not necessary for you to be able to perform a complex statistical analysis by yourself. However, some experience with actual statistical analysis is essential for you to obtain the perspective that leads to effective interpretation. Experience with actual analysis will also help you to lead others to sound results and to understand what they are going through. Moreover, there may be times when it will be most convenient for you to do some analysis on your own. Thus, we will concentrate on the ideas and concepts of statistics, reinforcing these with practical examples.

■ 1.3 The Four Basic Activities of Statistics

In the beginning stages of a statistical study, either there are not yet any data or else it has not yet been decided what data to look closely at. The *design* phase will resolve these issues so that useful data will result. Once data are available, an initial inspection is called for, provided by the *exploratory* phase. A numerical summary of an unknown quantity, based on data, is the result of the *estimation* process. The last of these basic activities is *hypothesis testing,* which uses the data to help you decide what the world is really like in some respect. We will now consider these four activities in turn.

Designing a Plan for Data Collection

Designing a plan for data collection might be called *sample survey design* for a marketing study or *experimental design* for a chemical manufacturing process optimization study. This phase of **designing the study** involves planning the details of data gathering. A careful design can avoid the costs and disappointment of finding out — too late — that the data collected are not adequate to answer the important questions. A good design will also collect just the right amount of data: enough to be useful, but not so much as to be wasteful. Thus, by planning ahead, you can help ensure that the analysis phase will go smoothly and hold down the cost of the project.

The *random sample* is one of the best ways to select a practical sample, to be studied in detail, from a population that is too large to be examined in its entirety.[2] By selecting randomly, two goals are accomplished:

1 You are guaranteed that the selection process is fair and proceeds without bias; that is, all items have an equal chance of being selected. This assures you that, on average, the sample will be representative of the population.
2 The randomness introduced in a controlled way during the design phase of the project will help ensure validity of the statistical inferences drawn later.

Exploring the Data

As soon as you have a set of data, you will want to check it out. **Exploring the data** involves looking at your data set from many angles, describing it, and summarizing it. In this way you will be able to make sure that the data are really what they are claimed to be and that there are no obvious problems. But good exploration also prepares you for the formal analysis in either of two ways:

1 By verifying that the expected relationships actually exist in the data, thereby validating the planned techniques of analysis.
2 By finding some unexpected structure in the data that must be taken into account, thereby suggesting some changes in the planned analysis.

This is the first phase. It is often not enough to rely on a formal, automated analysis, which can only be as good as the data that go into the computer and which assumes that the data set is "well behaved." Whenever

---

[2]Details of random sampling will be presented in Chapter 8.

possible, examine the data directly to make sure they look OK; that is, there are no large errors, and the relationships observable in the data are appropriate to the kind of analysis to be performed. This phase can help in (1) editing the data for errors, (2) selecting an appropriate analysis, and (3) validating the statistical techniques that are to be used in further analysis.

Estimating an Unknown Quantity

Estimating an unknown quantity produces the best educated guess possible based on the available data. We all want (and often need) estimates of things that are just plain impossible to know exactly. Here are some examples of unknowns to be estimated:

1 Next quarter's sales.
2 What the government will do next to our tax code.
3 How the population of Seattle will react to a new product.
4 How your portfolio of investments will fare next year.
5 The productivity gains of a change in strategy.
6 The defect rate in a manufacturing process.
7 The winners in the next election.
8 The long-term health effects of computer screens.

Statistics can shed light on some of these situations by producing a good, educated guess when reliable data are available. Keep in mind that all statistical estimates are just guesses and are, consequently, often wrong. However, they will serve their purpose when they are close enough to the unknown truth to be useful. If you knew how accurate these estimates were (approximately), you could decide how much attention to give them.

Statistical estimation also provides an indication of the amount of uncertainty or error involved in the guess, accounting for the consequences of random selection of a sample from a large population. The *confidence interval* gives probable upper and lower bounds on the unknown quantity being estimated, as if to say, I'm not sure exactly what the answer is, but I'm quite confident it's between these two numbers.

You should routinely expect to see confidence intervals (and ask for them if you don't) because they show you how reliable an estimated value actually is. For example, there is certainly some information in the statement that sales next quarter are expected to be

$11.3 million

However, additional and deeper understanding comes from also being told that you are 95% confident that next quarter's sales will be

between $5.9 million and $16.7 million

The confidence interval puts the estimate in perspective and helps you avoid the tendency to treat a single number as very precise when, in fact, it might not be precise at all.[3]

Hypothesis Testing

Statistical **hypothesis testing** is the use of data in deciding between two (or more) different possibilities in order to resolve an issue in an ambiguous situation. Hypothesis testing produces a definite decision about which of the possibilities is correct, based on data. The procedure is to collect data that will help decide among the possibilities and to use careful statistical analysis for extra power when the answer is not obvious from just glancing at the data.[4]

Here are some examples of hypotheses that might be tested using data:

1 The average New Yorker plans to spend at least $10 on your product next month.

2 You will win tomorrow's election.

3 A new medical treatment is safe and effective.

4 Brand X produces a whiter, brighter wash.

5 The error in a financial statement is smaller than some material amount.

6 It is possible to predict the stock market based on careful analysis of the past.

7 The manufacturing defect rate is below that expected by customers.

Note that each hypothesis makes a definite statement, and it may be either true or false. The result of a statistical hypothesis test is the conclusion that either the data support the hypothesis or they don't.

Often, statistical methods are used to decide whether or not you can rule out "pure randomness" as a possibility. For example, if a poll of 300 people shows that 53% plan to vote for you tomorrow, can you conclude that the election will go in your favor? Although many issues are involved here, we will (for the moment) ignore details, such as the (real) possibility that some people will change their minds between now and tomorrow, and instead concentrate only on the element of randomness (due to the fact that you can't call and ask every voter's preference). In this example, a careful analysis would reveal that it is a real possibility that less than 50% of voters prefer you and that the 53% observed is within the range of the expected random variation.

EXAMPLE

Statistical Quality Control

Your manufacturing processes are not perfect (nobody's are), and every now and then a product has to be reworked or tossed out. Thank goodness for your in-

---

[3]Details of confidence intervals will be presented in Chapter 9.

[4]Details of hypothesis testing are presented in Chapter 10.

spection team, which keeps these bad pieces from reaching the public. Meanwhile, however, you're losing lots of money manufacturing, inspecting, fixing, and disposing of these problems. This is why so many firms have begun using statistical quality control.

To simplify the situation, consider your assembly line to be *in control* if it produces similar results over time that are within the required specifications. Otherwise, your line will be considered to be *out of control.* Statistical methods help you monitor the production process so that you can save money in three ways: (1) keep the monitoring costs down, (2) detect problems quickly so that waste is minimized, and (3) whenever possible, don't spend time fixing it if it's not broken. Following is an outline of how the four basic activities of statistics apply to this situation.

During the design phase, you have to decide *what* to measure and *how often* to measure it. You might decide to select a random sample of 5 products to represent every batch of 500 produced. For each one sampled, you might have someone (or something) measure its length and width as well as inspect it visually for any obvious flaws. The result of the design phase is a plan for the early detection of problems. The plan must work in *real time* so that problems are discovered immediately, not next week.

Data exploration is accomplished by plotting the measured data on *quality control charts* and looking for patterns that suggest trouble. By spotting trends in the data, you may even be able to anticipate and fix a problem before any production is lost!

Statistical estimation can provide management with useful answers to questions about how the production process is going. You might assign a higher grade of quality to the production when it is well controlled within precise limits; such high-grade items command a higher price. Estimates of the quality grade of the current production will be needed to meet current orders, and forecasting of future quality grades will help with strategic planning and pricing decisions.

Statistical hypothesis testing can be used to answer the important question: Is this process in control, or has it gone out of control? Because a production process can be large, long, and complicated, you can't always tell just by looking at a few machines. By making the best use of the statistical information in your data, you hope to achieve two goals. First, you want to detect when the system has gone out of control even before the quality has become unacceptable. Second, you want to minimize the "false alarm" rate so that you're not always spending time and money trying to fix a process that is really still in control.

■ 1.4 What Is Probability?

✓   Probability is a *what if* tool for understanding risk and uncertainty. **Probability** shows you the likelihood, or chances, for each of the various potential future outcomes, based on a set of assumptions about how the world works. For example, you might assume that you know basically how the world works (i.e., all of the details of the process that will produce success or failure or payoffs in between). Probabilities of various outcomes would then be computed for each of several strategies to indicate how successful each strategy would be.

Probability is the inverse of statistics. That is, whereas statistics helps you go from observed data to generalizations about how the world works, probability goes the other direction: if you assume you know how the world works, then you can figure out what kinds of data you are likely to see and the likelihood for each. Here is a picture showing this inverse relation:

Probability

✓   How the world works ⟶ What will happen

Statistical inference

✓   What happened ⟶ How the world works

1.5 General Advice

Statistical results should be explainable in a straightforward way (even though their theory may be much more complicated). Here are some general words of advice:

✓ **1** Trust your judgment; common sense counts.
✓ **2** Maintain a healthy skepticism.
✓ **3** Don't be snowed by a seemingly ingenious statistical analysis (it may well rely on unrealistic and inappropriate assumptions).

Because of the vast flexibility available to the analyst in each phase of a study, one of the most important factors to consider in evaluating the results of a statistical study is: *Who funded it?* Remember that the analyst made many choices along the way—in defining the problems, designing the plan to select the data, choosing a framework or model for analysis, and interpreting the results.

1.6 End-of-Chapter-Materials

Summary

Statistics is the art and science of collecting and understanding data. Statistical techniques should be viewed as an important part of the decision process, allowing informed strategic decisions to be made that combine intuition and expertise with a thorough (statistical) understanding of the facts available. Use of statistics is becoming increasingly important in maintaining a competitive edge.

The basic activities of statistics are as follows:

1 The phase of **designing the study** involves planning the details of data gathering, perhaps using a random sample from a larger population.

2 **Exploring the data** involves looking at your data set from many angles, describing it, and summarizing it. This helps you make sure that the planned analysis is appropriate and allows you to modify the analysis if necessary.

3 **Estimating an unknown quantity** produces the best educated guess possible based on the available data. You will also want to have some indication of the size of the error involved by using this estimated value in place of the actual unknown value.

4 Statistical **hypothesis testing** uses data to decide between two (or more) different possibilities in order to resolve an issue in an ambiguous situation. This is often done to see if some apparent interesting feature of the data is really there as opposed to being an artifact of "pure randomness," which is basically uninteresting.

Probability shows you the likelihood, or chances, for each of the various potential future outcomes, based on a set of assumptions about how the world works. Probability is the inverse of statistics: probability tells you what the data will be like when you know how the world is, whereas statistics helps you figure out what the world is like after you have seen some data that it generated.

Statistics works best when you combine it with your own expert judgment and common sense. When statistical results go against your intuition, be prepared to work hard to find the reason why. The statistical analysis may well be incorrect due to wrong assumptions, or your intuition may be wrong because it was not based on facts.

Key Words

statistics 7
designing the study 9
exploring the data 9

estimating an unknown quantity 10
hypothesis testing 11
probability 12

Questions

1 Why is it worth the effort to learn about statistics?
   a. Answer for management in general.
   b. Answer for one particular area of business of special interest to you.
2 Choose a business firm, and list the ways in which statistical analysis could be used in decision-making activities within that firm.
3 How should statistical analysis and business experience interact with each other?
4 What is statistics?

5 What is the design phase of a statistical study?

6 Why is random sampling a good method to use for selecting items for study?

7 What can you gain by exploring data in addition to looking at summary results from an automated analysis?

8 Are statistical estimates always correct? If not, what else will you need (in addition to the estimated values) in order to use them effectively?

9 Why is a confidence interval more useful than an estimated value?

10 Give two examples of hypothesis testing situations that a business firm would be interested in.

11 Differentiate between probability and statistics.

12 A consultant has just presented a very complicated statistical analysis, complete with lots of mathematical symbols and equations. The results of this impressive analysis go against your intuition and experience. What should you do?

13 Why is it important to identify the source of funding when evaluating the results of a statistical study?

Problems

1 Describe a recent decision you made that depended, in part, on information that came from data. Identify the underlying data set, and tell how a deeper understanding of statistics might have helped you use these data.

2 Name three numerical quantities a firm might be concerned with for which exact values are unavailable. For each quantity, describe an estimate that might be useful. In general terms, how reliable would you expect these estimates to be?

3 Reconsider the three estimates from the previous problem. Are confidence intervals readily available? If so, how would they be useful?

4 List two kinds of routine decisions that you make in which statistical hypothesis testing could play a helpful role.

5 Look through a recent copy of *The Wall Street Journal*. Identify an article that relies directly or indirectly on statistics. Briefly describe the article (also be sure to give the title, date, and page number), and attach a copy. Which of the four activities of statistics is represented here?

6 Which of the four basic activities of statistics is represented by each of the following situations?

　a. A factory's quality control division is examining detailed quantitative information about recent productivity in order to identify possible trouble spots.

　b. A focus group is discussing the audience that would best be targeted by advertising, with the goal of drawing up and administering a questionnaire to this group.

　c. A firm is being sued for gender discrimination. Data that show salaries for men and women are presented to the jury to convince them that there is a consistent pattern of discrimination and that such a disparity could not be due to randomness alone.

　d. The size of next quarter's gross national product must be known so that a firm's sales can be forecast. Since it is unavailable at this time, an educated guess is used.

Project

Find the results of an opinion poll in a newspaper or magazine. Discuss how each of the four basic activities of statistics was applied (if it is clear from the article) or might have been applied to the problem of understanding what people are thinking. Attach a copy of the article to your discussion.

2 Data Structures
Classifying the Various Types of Data Sets

Data can come to you in several different forms. It will be useful to have a basic catalog of the different kinds of data so that you can recognize them and use appropriate techniques for each. For now, let's assume that data sets consist of measurements of individual items or things called **elementary units,** which may be people, households, firms, cities, TV sets, or just about anything of interest. A **data set** consists of some basic measurement or measurements for each item, with the same piece or pieces of information being recorded for each one. Data sets can be classified in three basic ways:

1 By the number of pieces of information (variables) there are for each elementary unit.
2 By the kind of measurement (numbers or categories) recorded in each case.
3 By whether or not the time sequence of recording is relevant.

■ 2.1 How Many Variables?

A piece of information recorded for every item (its cost, for example) is called a **variable**. The number of variables, or pieces of information, recorded for each item indicates the complexity of the data set and will guide you toward the proper kinds of analysis. Depending upon whether there is one, two, or many variables present, you have *univariate, bivariate,* or *multivariate* data, respectively.

Univariate Data

Univariate (one-variable) data sets have just one piece of information recorded for each item. Statistical methods would be used to summarize the basic properties of this single piece of information, answering such questions as:

1 What is a typical (summary) value?
2 How diverse are these items?
3 Are there any individuals or groups that require special attention?

Here are some examples of univariate data sets:

1 The incomes of subjects in a marketing survey. Statistical analysis would reveal the profile (or distribution) of incomes, indicating a typical income level, the extent of variation in incomes, and the percentage of people within any given income range.
2 The number of defects in each TV set in a sample of 50 manufactured this morning. Statistical analysis could be used to keep tabs on quality (estimate) and to see if things are getting out of control (hypothesis testing).
3 The interest rate forecasts of 25 experts. Analysis would reveal, as you might suspect, that the experts don't all agree and (if you check up on them later) that they can all be wrong. Although statistics can't combine these 25 forecasts into an exact, accurate prediction, it at least enables you to explore the data for the extent of consensus.
4 The colors chosen by members of a focus group. Analysis could be used to help in choosing an agreeable selection for a product line.
5 The bond ratings of the firms in an investment portfolio. Analysis would indicate the risk of the portfolio.

Bivariate Data

Bivariate (two-variable) data sets have exactly two pieces of information recorded for each item. In addition to summarizing each of these two variables separately as univariate data sets, statistical methods would also be used to explore the relationship between the two factors being measured in the following ways:

1 Is there a simple relationship between the two?
2 How strongly are they related?
3 Can you predict one from the other? If so, with what degree of reliability?
4 Are there any individuals or groups that require special attention?

Here are some examples of bivariate data sets:

1 The cost of production (first variable) and the number produced (second variable) for each of seven factories (items, or elementary units) producing integrated circuits, for the past quarter. A bivariate statistical analysis would indicate the basic relationship between cost and number produced. In particular, the analysis might identify a *fixed cost* of setting up production facilities and a *variable cost*[1] of producing one extra circuit. An analyst might then look at individual factories to see how efficient each is compared with the others.

2 The price of one share of your firm's common stock (first variable) and the date (second variable), recorded every day for the past six months. The relationship between price and time would show you any recent trends in the value of your investment. Whether or not you could then forecast future value is a subject of some controversy (is it an unpredictable "random walk," or are those apparent patterns real?).

3 The purchase or nonpurchase of an item (first variable, recorded as yes/no or as 1/0) and whether an advertisement for the item is recalled (second variable, recorded similarly) for each of 100 people in a shopping mall. Such data (as well as data from more careful studies) help shed light on the effectiveness of advertising: what is the relationship between advertising recall and purchase?

Multivariate Data

Multivariate (many-variable) data sets have three or more pieces of information recorded for each item. In addition to summarizing each of these variables separately (as a univariate data set), and in addition to looking at the relationship between any two variables (as a bivariate data set), statistical methods would also be used to look at the interrelationships among all the items, addressing the following questions:

1 Is there a simple relationship among them?
2 How strongly are they related?
3 Can you predict one (a "special variable") from the others? With what degree of reliability?
4 Are there any individuals or groups that require special attention?

---

[1]*Variable cost* refers to the cost that varies according to the number of units produced; it is not related to the concept of a *statistical variable*.

Here are some examples of multivariate data sets:

1 The growth rate (special variable) and a collection of measures of strategy (the other variables), such as type of equipment, extent of investment, and management style, for each of a number of new entrepreneurial firms. The analysis would give an indication of which combinations have been successful and which have not.

2 Salary (special variable) and gender (recorded as male/female or as 0/1), number of years of experience, job category, and performance record, for each employee. Situations such as this come up in litigation about whether women are discriminated against by being paid less than men on the average. A key question, which a multivariate analysis can help answer, is, Can this discrepancy be explained by factors other than gender? Statistical methods can remove the effects of these other factors and then measure the average salary differential between a man and a woman who are equal in all other respects.

3 The price of a house (special variable) and a collection of variables that contribute to the value of real estate, such as lot size, square footage, number of rooms, presence or absence of swimming pool, and age of house, for each of a collection of houses in a neighborhood. Results of the analysis would give a picture of how real estate is valued in this neighborhood. It might be used as part of an appraisal to determine fair market value of a house in that neighborhood, or it might be used by builders to decide which combination of features will best serve to enhance the value of a new home.

2.2 Quantitative Data: Numbers

If the data come to you as meaningful numbers, you have **quantitative** data (i.e., they represent quantities). With quantitative data, you can do all of the usual number-crunching tasks, such as finding the average (see Chapter 4) and measuring the variability (see Chapter 5). It is straightforward to compute directly with numerical data. There are two kinds of quantitative data: *discrete* and *continuous*, depending on the values potentially observable.

Discrete Quantitative Data

A **discrete**[2] variable can assume values only from a list of specific numbers. For example, the number of children in a household is a discrete variable. Since the possible values can be listed, it is relatively simple to work with discrete data sets. Here are some examples of discrete variables:

1 The number of computer shutdowns in a factory in the past 24 hours.

---

[2]Note the difference between a *discrete* variable (as defined here) and a *discreet* variable, which would be much more careful and quiet about its activities.

2 The number of contracts, out of the 18 for which you submitted bids, that were awarded.

3 The number of foreign tankers docked at a certain port today.

4 The gender of an employee, if this is recorded using the number 0 or 1.

Continuous Quantitative Data

We will consider any numerical variable that is not discrete to be **continuous**.[3] This word is used because the possible values form a "continuum," such as the set of all positive numbers, all numbers, or all values between 0 and 100%. For example, the actual weight of a candy bar marked "net weight 1.7 oz." is a continuous random variable; the actual weight might be 1.70235 or 1.69481 ounces instead of exactly 1.7. If you're not yet thinking statistically, you might have assumed that the actual weight was 1.7 ounces exactly; in fact, when you measure in the real world, there are invariably small (and sometimes large) deviations from expected values.

Here are some examples of continuous variables:

1 The price of an ounce of gold, in dollars, right now. You might think that this is discrete (and you would be technically correct, since a number such as $390.79 is part of a list of discrete numbers of pennies: 0.00, 0.01, 0.02, . . .). However, try to view such cases as examples of continuous data because the discrete divisions are so small as to be unimportant to the analysis. Should it ever happen that gold began trading at a few cents per ounce, it would become important to view it as a case of discrete data (however, it is more likely that the price would be quoted in thousandths of a cent at that point, again essentially a continuous quantity).

2 Investment and accounting ratios such as earnings per share, rate of return on investment, current ratio, and beta.

3 The amount of energy used per item in a production process.

Watch Out for Meaningless Numbers

One warning is necessary before you begin analyzing quantitative data: Make sure that the numbers are meaningful! Unfortunately, numbers can be used to record anything at all. If the coding is arbitrary, the results of analysis will be meaningless.

---

[3] Although this definition is suitable for many business applications, the mathematical theory is more complex and requires a more elaborate definition involving integral calculus (not presented here). We will also refrain from discussing *hybrid* variables, which are neither discrete nor continuous.

Alphabetical Order of States

Suppose the states of the United States are listed in alphabetical order and coded as 1, 2, 3, . . . , as follows:

1	Alabama
2	Alaska
3	Arizona
4	Arkansas
.	.
.	.
.	.

Now suppose you ask for the average of the states of residence for all employees in your firm's database. The answer is certainly computable. However, the result would be absurd because the numbers assigned to states are not numerically meaningful (although they are convenient for other purposes). To know that the average is 28.35, or somewhere between Nevada and New Hampshire, is not likely to be of use to anybody. The moral is: Be sure that your numbers have meaningful magnitudes before computing with them.

■ 2.3 Qualitative Data: Categories

If the data set tells you which one of several nonnumerical categories each item falls into, then the data are **qualitative** (because they record some quality that the item possesses). As you have just seen, care must be taken to avoid the temptation to assign numbers to the categories and then compute with them. If there are just a few categories, then you might work with the percentage of cases in each category (effectively creating something numerical from categorical data). If there are exactly two categories, you can assign the number 0 or 1 to each item and then (for many purposes) continue as if you had quantitative data. But let us first consider the general case in which there are three or more categories.

There are two kinds of qualitative data: *ordinal* (for which there is a meaningful ordering but no meaningful numerical assignment) and *nominal* (for which there is no meaningful order).

Ordinal Qualitative Data

A data set is **ordinal** if there is a meaningful ordering: you can speak of the first (perhaps the "best"), the second, the third, and so on. You can rank the data according to this ordering, and this ranking will probably play a role in the analysis, particularly if it is relevant to the questions being addressed. The *median* value (the middle one, once the data are put in order) will be defined in Chapter 4 as an example of a statistical summary.

Here are some examples of ordinal data:

1 Job classifications such as president, vice president, department head, and associate department head, recorded for each of a group of executives. Although there are no numbers involved here, and no clear way to assign them, there is certainly a standard way of ordering items by rank.

2 Bond ratings such as AA+, AA, AA−, A+, A, A−, B+, B, and B−, recorded for a collection of debt issues. These are clearly ordinal categorical data because the ordering is meaningful in terms of the risk involved in the investment, which is certainly relevant to investment analysis.

3 Questionnaire answers to a question such as "Please rate your feelings about working with your firm on a scale from 1 to 5, where 1 represents 'can hardly wait to get home each day' and 5 represents 'all my dreams have been fulfilled through my work.'" Although the answers are numbers, these results are better thought of as ordinal qualitative data because the scale is so subjective. It is really not clear if the difference between answers of 5 and 4 is of the same magnitude as the difference between a 2 and a 1. Nor do we assume that 2 is twice as good as 1. But at least the notion of ranking and ordering is present here.[4]

Nominal Qualitative Data

For **nominal** data there are only categories, with no meaningful ordering. There are no meaningful numbers to compute with, and no basis to use for ranking. About all that can be done is to count and work with the percentage of cases falling into each category, using the *mode* (the category occurring the most often, to be formally defined in Chapter 4) as a summary measure.

Here are some examples of qualitative data:

1 The states of residence for all employees in a database. As observed earlier, these are really just categories. Any ordering of states that might be done would actually involve some other variable (such as population or per-capita income), which might better be used directly.

2 The primary product of each of several manufacturing plants owned by a diversified business, such as plastics, electronics, and lumber. These are

---

[4]A very careful reader might validly question whether a 4 for one person is necessarily higher than a 3 for another. Thus, due to the lack of standardization among human perceptions, we may not even have a truly ordinal scale here. This is just one of the many complications involved in statistical analysis that we cannot give a complete account of.

really unordered categories; although they might be put into a sensible ordering, this would require some other factor (such as growth potential in the industry) not intrinsic to these categories themselves.

3 The names of all firms mentioned on the front page of today's issue of *The Wall Street Journal.*

■ 2.4 Time-Series and Cross-Sectional Data

If the data values are recorded in a meaningful sequence, such as daily stock market prices, then you have **time-series** data. If the sequence in which the data are recorded is irrelevant, such as the first-quarter 1987 earnings of eight aerospace firms, you have **cross-sectional** data. *Cross-sectional* is just a fancy way of saying that no time sequence is involved; you simply have a cross section, or snapshot, of how things are at one particular time.

Analysis of time-series data is generally more complex than cross-sectional data analysis because the ordering of the observations must be carefully taken into account. For this reason, in coming chapters we will initially concentrate on cross-sectional data. Time-series analysis will be covered in Chapter 14.

Here are some examples of time-series data:

1 The price of wheat each year for the past 50 years, adjusted for inflation. These time trends might be useful for long-range planning, to the extent that the variation in future events follows the patterns of the past.

2 Retail sales, recorded monthly for the past 20 years. This data set has a structure showing generally increasing activity over time as well as a distinct seasonal pattern, with peaks around the December holiday season.

3 The thickness of paper as it emerges from a rolling machine, measured once each minute. This kind of data might be important to quality control. The time sequence is important because small variations in thickness may either "drift" steadily toward an unacceptable level or "oscillate," becoming wider and narrower within fairly stable limits.

Following are some examples of cross-sectional data:

1 The number of hours of sleep last night, measured for 30 people being examined to test the effectiveness of a new over-the-counter drug.

2 Today's book values of a random sample of a bank's savings certificates.

3 The number of phone calls processed yesterday by each of a firm's order-taking employees.

■ 2.5 End-of-Chapter Materials

Summary

A **data set** consists of some basic measurement or measurements of individual items or things called **elementary units,** which may be people, households, firms, cities, TV sets, or just about anything of interest. The same piece or pieces of information are recorded for each one. A piece of information recorded for every item (its cost, for example) is called a **variable**.

There are three basic ways of classifying a data set: (1) by the number of variables (univariate, bivariate, or multivariate), (2) by the kind of information (numbers or categories) represented by each variable, and (3) by whether the data set is a time sequence or comprises cross-sectional data.

Univariate (one-variable) data sets have just one piece of information recorded for each item. For univariate data, you can identify a typical summary value and get an indication of diversity, as well as note any special features or problems with the data.

Bivariate (two-variable) data sets have exactly two pieces of information recorded for each item. For bivariate data, in addition to looking at each variable as a univariate data set, you can study the relationship between the two variables and predict one variable from the other.

Multivariate (many-variable) data sets have three or more pieces of information recorded for each item. Also with multivariate data, you can look at each variable individually, as well as examine the relationship among the variables and predict one variable from the others.

Values of a variable that are recorded as meaningful numbers are called **quantitative** data. A **discrete** quantitative variable can assume values only from a list of specific numbers (such as 0 or 1, or the list $0, 1, 2, 3, \ldots$, for example). Any quantitative variable that is not discrete is, for our purposes, **continuous**. A continuous quantity is not restricted to a simple list of possible values.

If a variable indicates which of several nonnumerical categories an item falls into, it is a **qualitative** variable. If the categories have a natural, meaningful order, then it is an **ordinal** qualitative variable. If there is no such order, it is a **nominal** qualitative variable. Although it is often possible to record a qualitative variable using numbers, the variable remains qualitative; it is not quantitative because the numbers are not inherently meaningful.

With quantitative data, you have available all of the operations that can be used for numbers: counting, ranking, and arithmetic. With ordinal data, you have counting and ranking only. With nominal data, you have only counting.

If the data values are recorded in a meaningful sequence, then the data set is a **time series.** If the order of recording is not relevant, then the data set is **cross-sectional**. Time-series analysis is more complex than that of cross-sectional data.

Key Words

elementary units 17	discrete 20
data set 17	continuous 21
variable 18	qualitative 22
univariate 18	ordinal 22
bivariate 18	nominal 23
multivariate 19	time series 24
quantitative 20	cross-sectional 24

Questions

1 What is a data set?
2 What is a variable?
3 What is an elementary unit?
4 What are the three basic ways in which data sets can be classified? (*Hint:* The answer is not "univariate, bivariate, and multivariate" but is at a higher level.)
5 What general questions can be answered by analysis of:
   a. Univariate data?
   b. Bivariate data?
   c. Multivariate data?
6 In what way do bivariate data represent more than just two separate univariate data sets?
7 What can be done with multivariate data?
8 What is the difference between quantitative and qualitative data?
9 What is the difference between discrete and continuous quantitative variables?
10 What are qualitative data?
11 What is the difference between ordinal and nominal qualitative data?
12 Differentiate between time-series data and cross-sectional data.
13 Which are simpler to analyze, time-series or cross-sectional data?

Problems

1 Name two different bivariate data sets that relate directly or indirectly to your responsibilities. In each case, identify the meaning of the relationship between the two factors, and indicate whether or not it would be useful to be able to predict one from the other.
2 Repeat the previous problem, but for multivariate data.
3 Choose a firm, and name two quantitative variables that might be important to that firm. For each variable, indicate whether it is discrete or continuous.
4 Choose a firm, and name two qualitative variables that might be important to that firm. For each variable, indicate whether it is nominal or ordinal.

5 Identify three time-series data sets of interest to you. For each one:
   a. Is there a definite time trend?
   b. Are there seasonal effects?
6 Choose a firm, and identify a database (in general terms) that would be important to it. Identify three different kinds of data sets contained within this database. For each of these three data sets, identify the elementary unit, and indicate what might be learned from an appropriate analysis.
7 Your firm has decided to sue an unreliable supplier. What kind of analysis would be used to estimate the foregone profit opportunities based on the performance of competitors, the overall state of the economy, and the time of year?
8 Following are some items from a human resources database, representing the status of five people on July 3, 1990:

Gender	Salary	Education*	Years of Experience
M	$42,300	HS	9
F	31,800	BA	4
M	29,500	MBA	2
F	58,100	MBA	15
F	36,000	BA	7

*HS = High school diploma, BA = College degree, MBA = Master's degree in business administration.

a. What is an elementary unit for this data set? *People/employee*
b. What kind of data set is this, univariate or multivariate? *– Multi.*
c. Which of these four variables are quantitative? Which are qualitative? *S+E. G+Ed.*
d. Which variables, if any, are ordinal qualitative? Why? *Ed,*
e. Is this a time series, or are these cross-sectional data? *cross-sect*

9 Here is a data set consisting of sales and income, both in hundred thousands of dollars, for the first six months of 1988:

Sales	Income (loss)
350	30
270	23
140	(2)
280	14
410	53
390	47

a. What is an "elementary unit" for this data set?
b. What kind of data set is this: univariate or multivariate?
c. Which of these two variables are quantitative? Which are qualitative?
d. Are these time-series or cross-sectional data?

10 Here is an excerpt from a salesperson's database of customers:

Level of Interest in New Products	Last Year's Total Purchases	Geographical Region
Weak	$ 88,906	West
Moderate	396,808	South
Very strong	438,442	South
Weak	2,486	Midwest
Weak	37,375	West
Very strong	2,314	Northeast
Moderate	1,244,096	Midwest
Weak	857,248	South
Strong	119,650	Northeast
Moderate	711,514	West
Weak	22,616	West

a. What is an elementary unit for this data set?
b. What kind of data set is this: univariate, bivariate, or multivariate?
c. Which of these variables are quantitative? Which are qualitative?
d. Which of these variables are nominal? Which are ordinal?
e. Are these time-series or cross-sectional data?

Database Exercises

Refer to the employee database in Appendix A.

1 Describe and classify this data base and its parts:
a. Is this a univariate, bivariate, or multivariate data set?
b. What are the elementary units?
c. Which variables are qualitative and which are quantitative?
d. Is "training level" ordinal or nominal? Why?
e. Would you ever want to do arithmetic on "employee number"? What does this tell you about whether or not this is truly a quantitative variable?
f. Is this a time series, or are these cross-sectional data?

2 For each variable in this database, tell which of the following operations would be appropriate:
a. Arithmetic (adding, subtracting, etc.).
b. Counting the number of employees in each category.
c. Rank ordering.
d. Finding the percentage of employees in each category.

Projects

1 Find a table of data used in an article in a business magazine or newspaper, and copy the article and table.

   a. Classify the data set according to the number of variables.

   b. What are the elementary units?

   c. Are the data time-series or cross-sectional?

   d. Classify each variable according to its type.

   e. For each variable, tell which operations are appropriate.

   f. Discuss (in general terms) some questions of interest in business that might be answered by close examination of this kind of data set.

2 Find a table of data in one of your firm's internal reports or record one from your own experience. Answer each part of project 1 for this data table.

Histograms
Looking at the Distribution of the Data

In this chapter, you will learn how to make sense of a list of numbers. A *histogram* is a picture that gives you a visual impression of many of the basic properties of the data set as a whole, answering the following kinds of questions:

1 What values are typical in this data set?
2 How different are the numbers from one another?
3 Are the data values strongly concentrated near some typical value?
4 What is the pattern of concentration? In particular, do data values "trail off" at the same rate at lower values as they do at higher values?
5 Are there any special data values, very different from the rest, that might require special treatment?
6 Do you basically have a single, homogeneous collection, or are there distinct groupings within the data that might require separate analysis?

Many standard methods of statistical analysis require that the data be approximately *normally distributed*. You will learn how to recognize this basic bell-shaped pattern and see how to transform the data if they do not already satisfy this assumption.

■ 3.1 A List of Data

The simplest kind of data set is a **list of numbers** representing some kind of information (a single statistical variable) measured on each item of interest (each elementary unit). A list of numbers can show up in several forms that may look very different at first. It may help you to ask yourself, What are the elementary units being measured here? to distinguish the actual measurements from their frequencies.

EXAMPLE

Performance of Regional Sales Managers

Here is an example of a very short list (only three observations), for which the variable is "last quarter sales" and the elementary units are "regional sales managers":

Name	Sales (ten thousands)
Bill	28
Jennifer	32
Henry	18

This data set contains information for interpretation (i.e., the first name of the sales manager responsible, indicating the elementary unit in each case) in addition to the list of three numbers.

EXAMPLE

Household Size

Sometimes a list of numbers is given as a table of frequencies, as in this example of family sizes from a sample of 17 households:

Household Size (number of people)	Number of Households (frequency)
1	3
2	5
3	6
4	2
5	0
6	1

The key to interpreting a table like this is to observe that it represents a list of numbers in which each number on the left (household size) is repeated according to the number to its right (the frequency—in this case, the number of households). The resulting list of numbers represents the number of people in each household:

$$1, 1, 1, 2, 2, 2, 2, 2, 3, 3, 3, 3, 3, 3, 4, 4, 6$$

Note that 1 is repeated three times (as indicated by the first row in the data table), 2 is repeated five times (as indicated by the second row), and so on.

The frequency table is especially useful for representing a very long list of numbers with relatively few values. Thus, for a large sample, you might summarize household size as follows:

Household Size (number of people)	Number of Households (frequency)
1	342
2	581
3	847
4	265
5	23
6	11
7	2

This table represents a lot of data! The corresponding list of numbers would begin by listing 1 a total of 342 times, 2 a total of 581 times, and so on. The table represents the sizes of all 2,071 households in this large sample.[1]

The Number Line

In order to visualize the relative magnitudes of a list of numbers, we will use locations along a line to represent numbers. The **number line** is a straight line, usually horizontal, with the scale indicated by numbers below it:

It is important that the numbers be equally spaced on a number line so that there is no distortion.[2] You can show the location of each number in the list by placing a mark at its location on the number line. For example, the list of sales figures

$$28, 32, 18$$

---

[1]The number 2,071 is the total frequency, the sum of the right-hand column.

[2]When it is necessary to distort the line, for example by skipping over some uninteresting intermediate values, you should show a break in the line. In this way you won't give the misleading impression of a regular, continuous line.

could be displayed on the number line as follows:

This diagram gives you a very clear impression of how these numbers relate to one another. In particular, you immediately see that the top two are relatively close to one another and are a good deal higher than the lowest number.

Using graphs such as the number line and others that you will study is more informative than looking at lists of numbers. Although numbers do a good job of recording information, they do not provide you with an appropriate visual hint as to their magnitudes. For example, the sequence

$$0\ 1\ 2\ 3\ 4\ 5\ 6\ 7\ 8\ 9$$

gives no particular *visual* indication of progressively larger magnitudes; the numerals do not get larger in size or darker as you move through the list. The number line, in contrast, does a nice job of showing you these important magnitudes.

■ 3.2 Using a Histogram to Display the Frequencies

The **histogram** displays the frequencies as a bar chart rising above the number line, indicating how often the various values occur in the data set. The horizontal axis represents the measurements of the data set (in dollars, number of people, miles per gallon, or whatever), and the vertical axis represents how often these values occur. An especially high bar indicates that many cases had data values at this position on the horizontal number line, while a shorter bar indicates a less common value.

EXAMPLE   **Mortgage Interest Rates**

Consider the interest rate for 30-year fixed home mortgages charged by lending institutions in Seattle in late 1986, shown in Table 3.2.1. The histogram for these institutions is shown in Figure 3.2.1. We will now describe how to interpret a histogram in general, and at the same time will see what this particular picture tells you about interest rates.

The horizontal number line at the bottom of the figure indicates mortgage rates, in percent. The vertical line at the left indicates the frequency of occurrence of a mortgage rate. For example, the bar just to the right of mortgage rate 9.2 has a frequency (height) of 12, indicating that there are 12 financial in-

TABLE 3.2.1   Home Mortgage Rates

Lender	Interest Rate	Lender	Interest Rate
Arcs Mortgage Inc.	9.250%	Metropolitan Federal Savings	9.500%
American Mortgage Corp.	9.125	Old National Bank	9.500
AmeriStar Financial Corp.	9.000	Old Stone Mortgage	9.125
Bankshares	9.250	Olympic Savings Bank	9.375
Bay Mortgage	9.250	Pacific R.E. Mortgage	9.000
Benjamin Franklin	9.125	Pacific First Federal	9.250
Capital Savings	9.500	Peoples Mortgage Co.	9.500
Cascade Pacific Mortgage	9.250	Pioneer Federal Savings	9.125
Cascade Savings	9.375	Principal Financial Group	9.375
Center Mortgage	9.250	Puget Sound Mortgage	9.250
CenTrust Mortgage	9.125	Puget Sound National Bank	9.750
Citicorp Home Owners	9.750	Rainier Financial Services	9.500
City Federal Mortgage	9.000	Redmond Mortgage	9.000
Columbia Services	9.000	Savings Bank of Puget Sound	9.375
Continental Inc.	9.250	Seafirst Bank	9.200
Countrywide Funding	9.000	Seattle Mortgage	9.375
First Interstate	9.500	Seattle Trust	9.750
First Mutual	9.250	Shelter Mortgage	9.125
Firstwest Mortgage	9.500	Shoreline Savings	9.375
Gibralter Savings	9.500	Summit Savings	9.375
GMAC Mortgage Co.	8.875	Tallman Home Mortgage	8.875
Great Western Savings Bank	9.400	United Bank	9.375
Heritage Mortgage	9.500	University Federal Savings	9.250
Home Savings & Loan	9.000	University Mortgage	9.375
ICA Mortgage Corp.	9.000	U.S. Bankcorp Mortgage	8.875
Lomas & Nettleton	9.500	Washington Mutual	9.375
Mason-McDuffie	9.000	Williamsburg Mortgage	9.250

Data are from "How the Winter Rates," *The Seattle Times,* December 21, 1986, p. D1.

FIGURE 3.2.1   A histogram of mortgage interest rates.

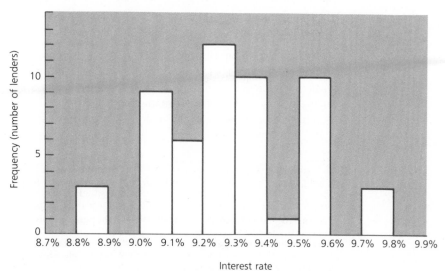

stitutions offering a mortgage rate between 9.2% and 9.3%.[3] Thus, you have a picture of the pattern of interest rates, indicating which values are most common, which are less common, and which are not offered at all.

What can you learn about interest rates from this histogram?

1 The *range*. Interest rates range a full percentage point, from a low of about 8.8% to a high of about 9.8% (this is where the histogram sits on the number line).

2 The *typical values*. Rates around 9.2% or 9.3% are most common (there is a concentration of high bars in this region).

3 The *diversity*. It is quite typical for institutions to differ from one another by 0.3%, more or less (there are high bars separated by about this distance).

4 The *overall pattern*. Most institutions are concentrated near the middle of the range, with a few institutions daring to offer especially low or high rates. Don't pay too much attention to the slightly bumpy nature of the bars; this is how you should expect real data to look, revealing both a message and some randomness.[4]

Histograms and Bar Charts

A histogram is a bar chart of the frequencies, not of the data. The height of each bar in the histogram indicates how frequently the values on the horizontal axis occur in the data set. This gives you a visual indication of where data values are concentrated and where they are scarce. Each bar of the histogram may represent many data values (in fact, the height of the bar shows you exactly how many data values are included in the corresponding range). This is different from a bar chart of the actual data, where there is one bar for each data value. Also note that the horizontal axis is always meaningful for a histogram but not necessarily so for a bar chart.

EXAMPLE   **Asian Immigrants**

Consider the number of people originally from selected Asian countries who live in the United States, shown in Table 3.2.2. Compare the histogram of these data values in Figure 3.2.2 to the bar chart shown in Figure 3.2.3. Note that the bars in the histogram show how many *countries* there are corresponding to each number of Asian people in the United States. Note that the bars in the bar chart show how many *people* from each country are in the United States.

---

[3]It is conventional to count all data values that fall exactly on the boundary between two bars of a histogram as belonging to the bar on the right. In the particular case of Figure 3.2.1, the bar above the range from 9.2% to 9.3% includes all institutions whose mortgage rate is equal to or greater than the left endpoint (9.2%) but less than the right endpoint (9.3%).

[4]Perhaps the dip just to the right of 9.4% has caught your eye; this one is actually a bit too large to be just randomness. Perhaps it occurs because 9.5% is a nice round number, so that institutions thinking of setting a rate *near* 9.5% will choose to set it at *exactly* 9.5%. Thus, the bar to the right of 9.5% (which includes rates of exactly 9.5%) is high, whereas those to the right of 9.4% and 9.6% are low (in fact, nonexistent in the latter case).

TABLE 3.2.2   Asian Immigrants

Country	Number in United States
China	286,100
Hong Kong	80,400
India	206,100
Iran	121,500
Israel	67,000
Japan	221,800
Korea	289,900
Philippines	501,400
Vietnam	231,100

Data are from Bureau of the Census, *Statistical Abstract of the United States, 1987* (Washington, 1986), p. 37.

FIGURE 3.2.2   A histogram of the number of people in the United States from selected Asian countries. Note that each bar may represent more than one country. The bars show which numbers are most and least typical in this data set.

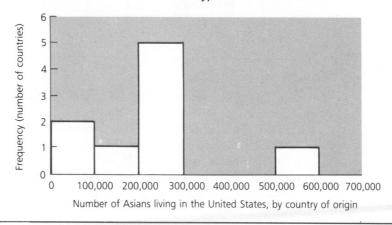

A bar chart of the data is most useful when you want to see all of the details of the individual data values. However, the histogram is far superior for visualizing the data set as a whole, especially a large data set.

■ 3.3 Normal Distributions

A **normal distribution** is an idealized, smooth, bell-shaped histogram with all of the randomness removed. It represents an ideal data set that has lots of numbers concentrated in the middle of the range, with the remaining num-

FIGURE 3.2.3   A bar chart of the number of people in the United States from selected Asian countries. Note that each bar represents one country.

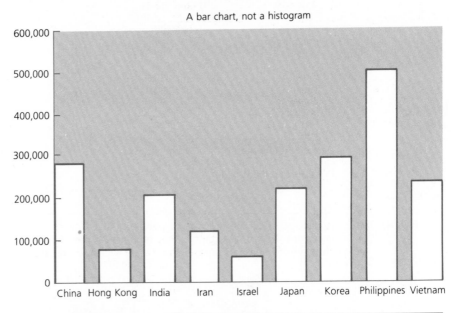

A bar chart, not a histogram

bers trailing off symmetrically on both sides. This degree of smoothness is not attainable by real data. Figure 3.3.1 is a picture of a normal distribution.[5]

There are actually many different normal distributions, all symmetrically bell-shaped. They differ in that the center can be anywhere and the scale (the width of the bell) can have any size.[6] Think of these operations as taking the basic bell shape and sliding it horizontally to wherever you'd like the center to be, then stretching it out (or compressing it) so that it extends outward just the right amount. Figure 3.3.2 shows a few normal distributions.

Why is the normal distribution so important? It is common for statistical procedures to assume that the data set is reasonably approximated by a normal distribution.[7] Statisticians know a lot about properties of normal distributions; this knowledge can be exploited whenever the histogram resembles a normal distribution.

---

[5]In case you are curious, the formula for this particular bell-shaped curve is $\dfrac{1}{\sqrt{2\pi}\sigma}e^{-[(x-\mu)/\sigma]^2/2}$ where μ (the center, presented in Chapter 4) gives the horizontal location of the highest point and σ (the variability or scale, presented in Chapter 5) controls the width of the bell.

[6]These concepts will be discussed in detail in Chapters 4 and 5.

[7]In particular, many standard methods for computing confidence intervals and hypothesis tests (which you will learn later on) require a normal distribution, at least approximately, for the data.

FIGURE 3.3.1   A normal distribution, in its idealized form. Actual data sets that follow a normal distribution will show some random variations from this perfectly smooth curve.

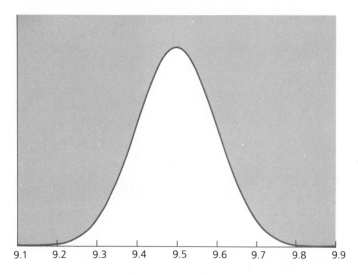

FIGURE 3.3.2   Some normal distributions with various centers and scales.

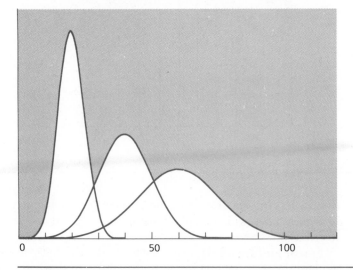

How do you tell if a data set is normally distributed? One good way is to look at the histogram. Figure 3.3.3 shows different histograms for a sample of 100 data values from a normal distribution. From these, you can see how random the shape of the distribution can be when you have only a finite amount of data. Fewer data values means more randomness because

FIGURE 3.3.3   Histograms of data drawn from an ideal normal distribution. In each case, there are 100 data values. Comparing the three histograms, you can see how much randomness to expect.

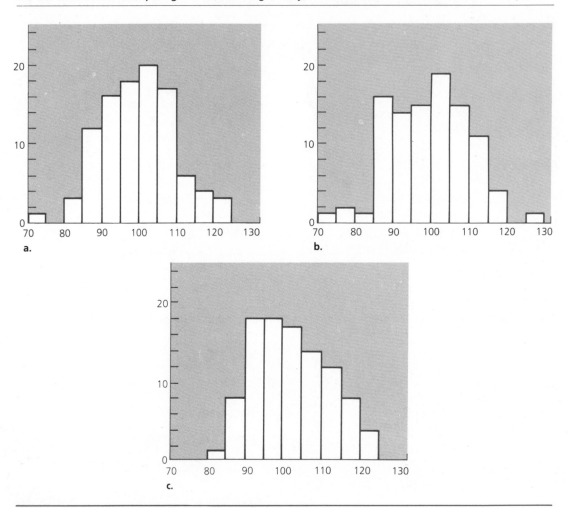

there is less information available to show you the big picture. This is shown in Figure 3.3.4, which displays histograms of 20 data values from a normal distribution.

In real life, are all data sets normally distributed? No. It is important to explore the data, by looking at a histogram, to determine whether or not it is normally distributed. This is especially important if, later on in the analysis, a standard statistical calculation will be used that requires a normal distribution. The next section shows one way in which many data sets in business deviate from a normal distribution and suggests a way to deal with the problem.

FIGURE 3.3.4   Data drawn from a normal distribution. In each case, there are 20 data values. Comparing the histograms, you can see how much randomness to expect.

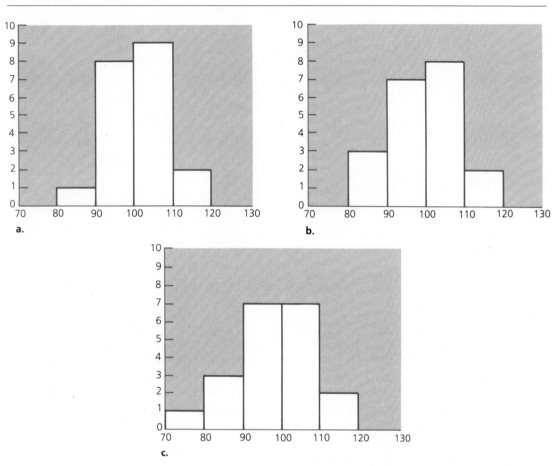

3.4 Skewed Distributions and Data Transformation

A **skewed distribution** is neither symmetric nor normal because the data values trail off more sharply on one side than on the other. In business you often find skewness in data sets that represent sizes using positive numbers (for example, sales or assets). This is because data values cannot be less than zero (imposing a boundary on one side) but are not restricted by a definite upper boundary. The result is that there are lots of data values concentrated near zero, and they become systematically fewer and fewer as you move to the right in the histogram. Figure 3.4.1 gives some examples of idealized shapes of skewed distributions.

FIGURE 3.4.1 Some examples of skewed distributions, in smooth, idealized form. Actual data sets that follow skewed distributions will show some random differences from this kind of perfectly smooth curve.

a.

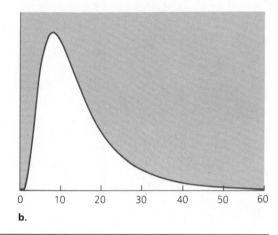

b.

EXAMPLE **Assets of Commercial Banks**

An example of a highly skewed distribution is provided by the assets of the 100 largest commercial banking companies, shown in Table 3.4.1. A histogram of this data set is shown in Figure 3.4.2. This is not at all like a normal distribution because of the lack of symmetry. The very high bar at the left represents the majority of these banks, which have less than $20 billion in assets. The next few bars to the right represent the relatively few banks that are larger. The very short bar at the far right represents a single bank: Citicorp, the largest, with assets of $174 billion.

EXAMPLE **Populations of States**

Another example of a skewed distribution is the populations of the states of the United States, viewed as a list of numbers.[8] The skewness reflects the fact that there are many states with small or medium populations and a few states with very large populations (the three largest are California, New York, and Texas). A histogram is shown in Figure 3.4.3.

The Trouble with Skewness

One of the problems with skewness in data is that, as mentioned earlier, many of the most common statistical methods (which you will learn more about in future chapters) require at least an approximately normal distribu-

---

[8]Bureau of the Census, *Statistical Abstract of the United States, 1984* (Washington, 1983), p. 11.

TABLE 3.4.1   The 100 Largest Commercial Banking Companies

Institution	Assets ($ millions)	Institution	Assets ($ millions)
Citicorp	$173,597	U.S. Bancorp	$8,349
BankAmerica	118,541	Rainier Bancorp	8,348
Chase Manhattan	87,685	Hartford National	8,342
Manufacturers Hanover	76,525	United Virginia Bankshares	8,099
J. P. Morgan	69,375	Shawmut	7,822
Chemical New York	56,990	Maryland National	7,791
Security Pacific	53,503	AmeriTrust	7,787
Bankers Trust New York	50,581	Bank of Virginia	7,744
First Interstate	48,991	Northern Trust	7,500
First Chicago	38,892	Michigan National	7,251
Mellon Bank	33,406	KeyCorp	7,122
Continental Illinois	30,528	Boatmen's Bancshares	7,054
Wells Fargo	29,429	Manufacturers National	6,980
Bank of Boston	28,296	Mercantile Bancorp	6,762
First Bank System	25,484	Fidelcor	6,760
Marine Midland Banks	23,385	European American Bancorp	6,654
RepublicBank	23,205	State Street Boston	6,652
MCorp	22,586	First Wisconsin	6,477
InterFirst	22,071	Texas American Bancshares	6,413
Irving Bank	21,650	BayBanks	6,269
Norwest	21,418	Huntington Bancshares	6,240
Texas Commerce Bancshares	20,076	Meridian Bancorp	6,229
NCNB	19,754	Florida National Banks of Florida	5,980
SunTrust Banks	19,405	First American Bankshares	5,725
Crocker National	19,208	First Pennsylvania	5,652
PNC Financial	18,777	Riggs National	5,434
Bank of New York	18,486	California First Bank	5,401
Bank of New England	17,804	Bank of Tokyo Trust	5,379
First Wachovia	17,706	First of America Bank	5,326
First City Bancorp of Texas	16,819	First Security	5,293
NBD Bancorp	16,675	First Tennessee National	5,248
First Union	16,567	AmSouth Bancorp	5,227
Republic New York	15,323	Centerre Bancorp	5,171
Barnett Banks of Florida	14,829	Third National	5,045
Citizens & Southern Georgia	13,590	Commerce Bancshares	4,923
First Fidelity Bancorp	12,620	United Banks of Colorado	4,849
National City	12,505	First American	4,789
CoreStates Financial	11,080	Marshall & Ilsley	4,741
Southeast Banking	11,052	Continental Bancorp	4,717
Banc One	10,823	Dominion Bankshares	4,688
Midlantic Banks	10,354	First Maryland Bancorp	4,493
Allied Bancshares	10,245	Bancorp Hawaii	4,438
Valley National	9,930	United Jersey Banks	4,428
National Westminster Bank USA	9,796	Indiana National	4,391
Comerica	9,769	Old Kent Financial	4,323
Sovran Financial	9,671	Louisiana Bancshares	4,293
Union Bancorp	9,559	South Carolina National	4,212
Harris Bankcorp	9,245	SouthTrust	4,210
Norstar Bancorp	8,998	American Security	4,154
Society	8,749	First Kentucky National	4,141

Data are from "The Service 500." *Fortune,* June 9, 1986, pp. 126–29.

FIGURE 3.4.2   A histogram of the assets (in billions of dollars) of the 100 largest commercial banks. This is a skewed distribution, not a normal distribution.

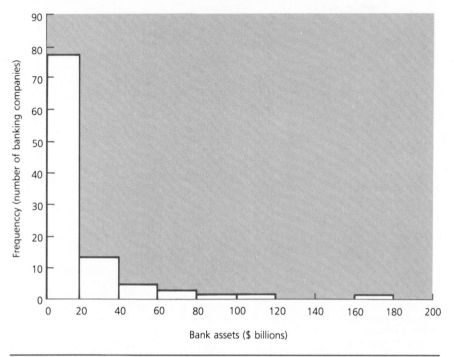

Bank assets ($ billions)

tion. When these methods are used on skewed data, the answers may well be misleading or just plain wrong. Even when the answers are basically correct, there is often some efficiency lost, essentially by not making the best use of all of the information in the data set.

Transformation to the Rescue

One solution to this dilemma of skewness is to use *transformation* to make a skewed distribution more symmetric. **Transformation** is replacing each data value by a different number (such as its logarithm) to facilitate statistical analysis. The most common transformation in business and economics is the logarithm, which can only be used on positive numbers (i.e., if your data include negative numbers or zero, this technique cannot be used). Using the **logarithm** often transforms skewness into symmetry because it stretches the scale near zero, spreading out all of the small values, which had been bunched together. It also pulls together the very large data values, which had been thinly spread out at the high end. Both types of logarithms (base 10 "common logs" and base *e* "natural logs") work equally well for this purpose. In this section, base 10 logs will be used.

FIGURE 3.4.3   A histogram of the 1981 populations of the states of the United States: a skewed distribution.

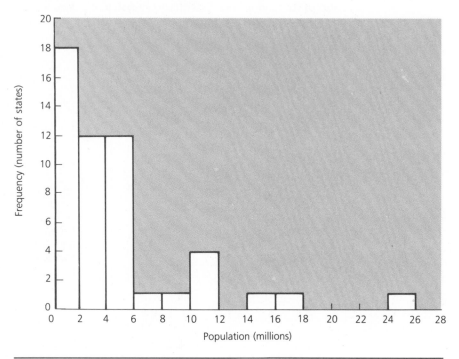

EXAMPLE   Transforming State Populations

Comparing the histogram of state populations in Figure 3.4.3 to the histogram of the logarithms of these numbers in Figure 3.4.4, you can see that the skewness vanishes when these numbers are viewed on the logarithmic scale. Although there is some randomness here, and the result is not perfectly symmetric, there is no longer the combination of a sharp drop on one side and a slow decline on the other, as there was in Figure 3.4.3.

The logarithmic scale may be interpreted as a *multiplicative* or *percentage* scale rather than an additive one. On the logarithmic scale, as displayed in Figure 3.4.4, the distance of 0.2 across each bar corresponds to a 58% increase in population from the left to the right side of the bar.[9] A span of five bars—for example, from points 6 to 7 on the horizontal axis—indicates a 10-fold increase in state population.[10] On the original scale (i.e., displaying actual numbers of people instead of logarithms) it is difficult to make a percentage comparison.

---

[9]This is because $10^{0.2}$ is 1.58, which is 58% larger than 1.
[10]This is because 10^1 is 10.

FIGURE 3.4.4   Transformation can turn skewness into symmetry. A histogram of the logarithms of the 1981 populations of the states of the United States is basically symmetric, except for randomness. Essentially no systematic skewness remains.

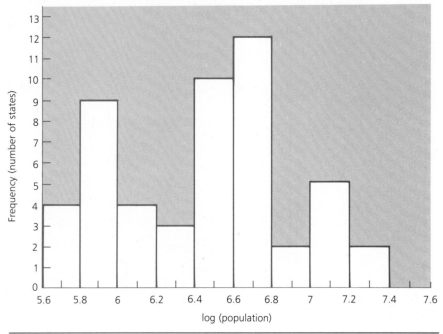

Instead, in Figure 3.4.3, you see a difference of 2 million people as you move from left to right across one bar, and a difference of 2 million people is a much larger percentage on the left side than on the right side of the figure.

Interpreting the Logarithm

A difference of 1 in the logarithm (to the base 10) corresponds to a factor of 10 in the original data. For example, the data values 392.1 and 3,921 (a ratio of 1 to 10) have logarithms of 2.5934 and 3.5934 (a difference of 1), respectively. Table 3.4.2 gives some examples of numbers and their logarithms.

From this you can see how the logarithm pulls in the very large numbers, minimizing their difference from other values in the set (changing 100 million to 8, for example). Also note how the logarithm shows roughly how many digits are in the nondecimal part of a number. A state population of 24,000,000, for example, has a logarithm of 7.380 (corresponding to the bar on the far right side of Figures 3.4.3 and 3.4.4).

There are two kinds of logarithms. We have looked at the base 10 logarithms. The other kind is the *natural logarithm,* abbreviated ln, which uses base e (=2.71828...) and is important in computing compound interest and other applications. For the purpose of transforming data, both kinds of loga-

TABLE 3.4.2   Some Examples of Logarithms to the Base 10

Number	Logarithm
0.001	−3
0.01	−2
0.1	−1
1	0
2	0.301
5	0.699
9	0.954
10	1
100	2
10,000	4
20,000	4.301
100,000,000	8

rithms have the same effect, pulling in high values and stretching out the low values.

Your calculator may have a logarithm key, denoted LOG.[11] Simply key in the number and hit the LOG key. Many spreadsheets, such as Lotus® 1-2-3®, have a @LOG function. You might enter @LOG(5) in a cell to observe the value 0.69897. To find the logarithms of a data set in a column, you can use the "Copy" command to copy the log formula down the entire column, greatly shortening the task of finding the logs of a list of numbers.

■ 3.5 Bimodal Distributions

It is important to be able to recognize when a data set consists of two or more distinct groups so that they may be analyzed separately, if appropriate. This can be seen in a histogram as a distinct gap between two cohesive groups of bars. When two clearly separate groups are visible in a histogram, you have a **bimodal distribution.** Literally, a bimodal distribution has *two modes,* or two distinct clusters of data.[12]

A bimodal distribution may be an indication that the situation is more complex than you had thought, and that extra care is required. At the very least, you should find out the reason for the two groups. Perhaps only one group is of interest to you, and you should exclude the other as irrelevant to the situation you are studying. Or perhaps both groups are needed, but some adjustment has to be done to account for the fact that they are so different.

---

[11]Some calculators do not have a LOG key to compute the base 10 logarithm, but instead have only an LN key to compute the natural logarithm (base *e*). To find the common logarithm on such a calculator, divide the result of LN by 2.302585, the natural log of 10.

[12]The *mode* as a summary measure will be presented in Chapter 4.

EXAMPLE **Money Market Yields**

Consider yields of money market funds expressed as an annualized percentage return on investment. Table 3.5.1 shows part of this data set. A histogram of the complete data set, as shown in Figure 3.5.1, looks like two separate histograms. One group indicates yields from about 3.2% to 4.2%, and the other

TABLE 3.5.1   Yields of Money Market Funds: Partial Listing

Fund	Yield
Alex. Brown Govt. Series	5.7%
Alex. Brown Prime	5.4
Alliance Group Capital Reserves	5.3
Alliance Group Government Reserves	5.4
Alliance Tax-Exempt Reserves	3.9
American Capital Reserve	5.7
Benham CA Tax-Free Trust	3.3
Boston Company Cash Mgt.	5.4
Boston Company Mass. T-F M.F.	3.6
Capital Preservation	4.8
Capital Preservation Fund II	5.3
CMA Tax-Exempt	3.5

These are the seven-day compound yields as reported by *Barron's*, December 1, 1986, p. 143.

FIGURE 3.5.1   Yields of money market funds. This is a highly bimodal distribution, with two clear and separate groups, probably not due to chance alone.

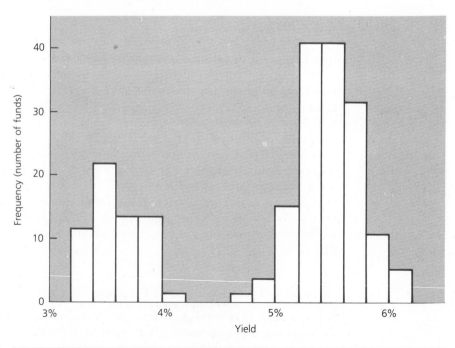

extends from 4.6% to 6.2%. This kind of separation is highly unlikely to be due to pure randomness from a single cohesive data set. There must be some other reason (perhaps you'd like to try to guess the reason before consulting the footnote below for the answer).[13]

Is It Really Bimodal?

Don't get carried away and start seeing bimodal distributions when they aren't there. The two groups must be large enough, be individually cohesive, and have a fair gap between them. It may take judgment to distinguish a "random" gap within a single group from a true gap separating two distinct groups.

EXAMPLE

Return on Equity for Banks

Consider the return on equity (ROE) of a group of major banks, reported as part of a study of executive compensation, as shown in Table 3.5.2. A histogram of this data set is shown in Figure 3.5.2. This is a fairly symmetric distribu-

TABLE 3.5.2   Return on Equity for Major Banks

Bank	ROE
Bank of Boston	13.7%
Bank of New York	15.2
Bankers Trust New York	15.2
Barnett Banks of Florida	16.0
Chase Manhattan	11.5
Chemical New York	13.7
Citicorp	13.8
First Bank System	13.6
First Chicago	8.0
First Interstate Bancorp	12.3
Fleet Financial Group	17.3
Irving Bank	12.1
Manufacturers Hanover	11.4
Marine Midland Banks	10.1
J. P. Morgan	16.4
Norwest	7.8
Security Pacific	14.5
Texas Commerce Bancshares	7.3
Wells Fargo	13.2

Data are from "Executive Compensation Scoreboard," *Business Week*, May 4, 1987, p. 59.

---

[13]The list of yields is in alphabetical order and includes ordinary taxable funds along with those that invest only in tax-free securities. Since no tax is ordinarily due on interest earnings paid by a tax-free fund, the effective (i.e., tax-adjusted) yield is higher than the amount usually reported. Thus, the group on the left in the histogram (Figure 3.5.1), with lower yields, consists of the tax-free money market funds. If you want to summarize current market interest rates, for example, it would be important to recognize that the tax-free yields require special treatment. You might disregard the tax-free yields and summarize only the taxable ones. Alternatively, you might first adjust the tax-free yields to make them comparable to the others for a representative tax bracket, and then continue to analyze the adjusted combined data set.

FIGURE 3.5.2   Return on equity for a group of banks. This is a fairly normal distribution, forming just one cohesive group.

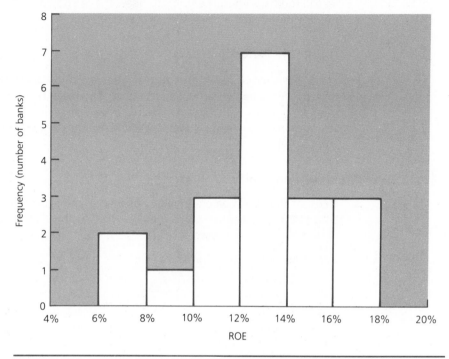

tion ("fairly symmetric" implies that it may not be perfectly symmetric, but at least it's not very skewed). The distribution is basically normal, and you see one single group.

However, if you display the histogram on a finer scale, with smaller bars, as in Figure 3.5.3, the extra detail suggests that there might be two groups: the three banks with the smallest ROE (on the left) and all other banks (on the right). However, this is not really bimodal for two reasons. First, the gap is a small one compared to the diversity among ROE values. Second, and more important, the histogram bars are really too small because many represent just one bank. Remember that one of the main goals of statistical summaries (such as the histogram) is to see the *big picture* and not get lost by reading too much into the details.

3.6 Outliers

Sometimes you will find **outliers,** which are data values that don't seem to belong with the others because they are either far too big or far too small.

FIGURE 3.5.3   Return on equity for banks (same data as in previous figure, but displayed with smaller bars). Since too much detail is shown here, it appears (probably wrongly) that there might be two groups: the three banks at the left are slightly separated from the others. This is probably just randomness and not true bimodality.

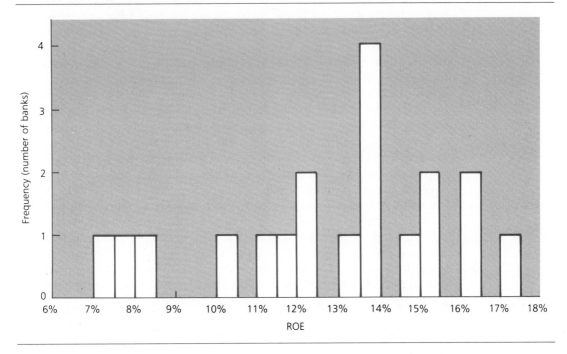

How you deal with outliers depends on what caused them. There are two main kinds of outliers: (1) mistakes and (2) correct but "different" data values.

Dealing with Outliers

Mistakes are easy to deal with: Simply change the data value to the number it should have been in the first place. For example, if a sales figure of $1,597.00 was wrongly recorded as $159,700 because of a misplaced decimal point, it might show up as being far too big compared to other sales figures in a histogram. Having been alerted to the existence of this strange data value, you should investigate and find the error. The situation would be resolved by correcting the figure to $1,597, the value it should have been originally.

Unfortunately, the correct outliers are more difficult to deal with. If it can be argued convincingly that the outliers do not belong to the general case under study, they may then be set aside so that the analysis can proceed with only the coherent data. For example, a few tax-free money market funds may appear as outliers in a data set of yields. If the purpose of the study is to summarize the marketplace for general-purpose funds, it may be appropriate to leave these special tax-free funds out of the picture. For another example, suppose your company is evaluating a new pharmaceutical product. In one of the trials, the laboratory technician sneezed into the sample before it was analyzed. If you are not studying laboratory accidents, it might be appropriate to omit this outlier.

If you wish to set aside some outliers in this way, you must be prepared to convince not just yourself that it is appropriate, but any person (possibly hostile) for whom your report is intended. Thus, the issue of exactly when it is or isn't OK to omit outliers may not have a single, objective answer. For an internal initial feasibility study, for example, it may be appropriate to delete some outliers. However, if the study were intended for public release or for governmental scrutiny, then you would want to be much more careful about omitting outliers.

One compromise solution, which can be used even when you don't have a strong argument for omitting the outlier, is to perform *two different analyses:* one with the outlier included and one with it omitted. By reporting the results of both analyses, you have not unfairly slanted the results. In the happiest case, should it turn out that the conclusions are identical for both analyses, you may conclude that the outlier makes no difference. In the more problematic case, where the two analyses produce different results, your interpretation and recommendations are more difficult. Unfortunately, there is no complete solution to this subtle problem.[14]

There is an important rule to be followed whenever any outlier is omitted, in order to inform others and protect yourself from any possible accusations:

■ **Whenever an Outlier is Omitted:**
Explain what you did and why!

That is, explain clearly somewhere in your report (perhaps a footnote would suffice) that there is an outlier problem with the data. Describe the outlier and tell what you did about it. Be sure to justify your actions.

Why should you deal with outliers at all? There are two main ways in which they cause trouble. First, it is difficult to interpret the detailed structure in a data set when one value dominates the scene and calls too much attention to itself. Second, as also occurs with skewness, many of the most common statistical methods can fail when used on a data set that doesn't ap-

---

[14]There is a branch of modern statistics called *robustness* that seeks to use computing power to adjust for the presence of outliers, and robust methods are available for many (but not all) kinds of data sets. For more detail, see D. C. Hoaglin, F. Mosteller, and J. W. Tukey, *Understanding Robust and Exploratory Data Analysis* (New York: Wiley, 1983); and V. Barnett and T. Lewis, *Outliers in Statistical Data* (New York: Wiley, 1978).

pear to have a normal distribution. Normal distributions aren't skewed and don't produce outliers. Consequently, you will have to deal with any outliers in your data before relying heavily on statistical inference.

EXAMPLE

Research and Development Expenses

The chemical industry is driven, in part, by new discoveries. Consequently, we would expect research and development (R&D) to be an important part of the budget of a modern chemical company. Consider the amounts spent on R&D in 1986, expressed as a percentage of pretax profits, for major chemical firms, as shown in Table 3.6.1. You can see just two bars in the corresponding histogram in Figure 3.6.1. The high bar on the left represents all of the firms except one. The short bar on the right represents the outlier, Air Products & Chemicals, which spent $61.1 million on R&D although it had only $4.7 million in pretax profits.

Because of the outlier on the right, you can't see any detail in the distribution of R&D expenditures of the other 41 firms. To produce a meaningful histogram,

TABLE 3.6.1   Research and Development Expenses

Chemical Firm	R&D Expense (percent of pretax profits)	Chemical Firm	R&D Expense (percent of pretax profits)
Air Products & Chemicals	805.0%	Lawter International	11.1
American Cyanamid	95.9	LeaRonal	16.4
Betz Laboratories	19.6	Liquid Air	10.1
Crompton & Knowles	27.3	Loctite	29.5
Detrex	55.5	Lubrizol	39.8
Dexter	48.8	MacDermid	60.1
Dow Chemical	48.9	Monsanto	82.2
Du Pont	38.7	Morton Thiokol	16.7
Ecolab	15.0	Nalco Chemical	29.2
Engelhard	36.5	Oil Dri Corp. of America	9.9
Essex Chemical	45.6	Olin	48.7
Ethyl	16.2	Pennwalt	54.4
Ferro	26.0	Petrolite	43.0
Fuller (H.B.)	31.3	Products Research & Chemical	41.3
GAF	9.1	Quaker Chemical	49.3
Great American Management	79.5	Reichhold Chemicals	47.8
Great Lakes Chemical	30.9	Rohm & Haas	60.6
Grow Group	29.5	Sequa	39.3
Hercules	23.1	Stepan	67.4
HIMONT	9.0	Union Carbide	65.5
Koppers	16.4	Witco	20.2

Data are from "R&D Scoreboard," *Business Week*, June 22, 1987, p. 144. By expressing R&D expenditures as a percentage of pretax profits, you can perform a more meaningful comparison of small and large firms. Naturally, you would expect small firms to spend less than large firms. However, their percentages would tend to be similar if they tend to follow similar R&D strategies.

FIGURE 3.6.1   Histogram of research and development expenses, as a precentage of pretax profits, for major chemical firms. Note how the outlier (805%) prevents you from seeing any detail in the other 41 firms in this data set.

FIGURE 3.6.2   Histogram of R&D expenses as a percentage of pretax profits, omitting the outlier (Air Products & Chemicals). Now you can see some of the structure in the more typical firms, which was obscured by the presence of the outlier.

let's set aside the outlier and produce a histogram of the remaining firms, shown in Figure 3.6.2. Now you have a much more informative picture of typical R&D expenses in the chemical industry. They cluster primarily in the 10% to 50% range, with some slightly lower and moderately higher values, and with a typical value around 30% or 40%. This is a slightly skewed distribution, trailing off more slowly on the right than on the left. None of these details are visible in the earlier histogram because the outlier did not allow you to see the structure in the rest of the data.

It is interesting to note that the outlier does not appear in a histogram of R&D expenses when they are expressed as a percentage of sales (instead of as a percentage of pretax profits), as shown in Figure 3.6.3 (data not listed here.) This suggests that R&D expenses for Air Products & Chemicals are entirely appropriate in terms of sales (3.1%, actually), but that profits were particularly low in 1986. In fact, their profits were down 44% from the previous year, further supporting this explanation.

EXAMPLE   **Growth of Liquor Brands**

Consider the five-year growth rate for an assortment of major liquor brands, shown in Table 3.6.2. The effects of outliers are shown in the histogram in Fig-

FIGURE 3.6.3 Histogram of R&D expenses as a percentage of sales rather than profits. Air Products & Chemicals, previously an outlier, falls in line with the other firms on this basis.

FIGURE 3.6.4 Histogram of five-year growth rate for liquor brands. Note the presence of two outliers with exceptionally high growth rates (Dekuyper Peachtree liqueur, 123.1%, and Absolut vodka, 60%), which obscure the details of the majority of brands by forcing them into just two bars from −20% to 20%.

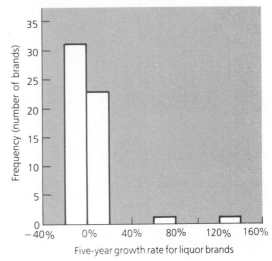

ure 3.6.4. The presence of two outliers (Dekuyper Peachtree liqueur at 123.1% and Absolut vodka at 60%) forces all other brands into just two bars around 0% and obscures the details of the distribution of growth rates.

Omitting the largest outlier, Dekuyper Peachtree liqueur at 123.1%, you can see a little more structure in the histogram for the other brands in Figure 3.6.5. The distribution is beginning to look like a normal distribution with a symmetric bell shape, trailing off quickly on each side, except for the outlier that still remains on the far right.

Omitting both outliers, you can see that the distribution of growth rates for the remaining brands follows a normal distribution centered around 0%, as shown in Figure 3.6.6.

Based on this analysis of growth in the liquor market, a basic assessment of the situation is as follows:

1 There are two wild success stories of exceptionally high growth, namely, the outliers Dekuyper Peachtree liqueur at 123.1% and Absolut vodka at 60%.

2 For the others, the typical case is either a growth or a loss of 5% to 10% (perhaps slightly more).

FIGURE 3.6.5 Histogram of five-year growth rate for liquor brands, with the largest outlier (Dekuyper Peachtree liqueur, 123.1%) omitted. You can begin to see some of the details for the other brands.

FIGURE 3.6.6 Histogram of five-year growth rate for liquor brands with both outliers removed. Now you can see an informative picture of the pattern of growth rates.

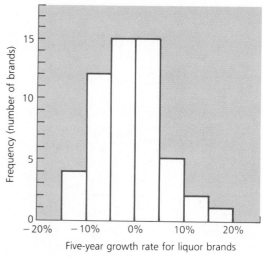

Five-year growth rate for liquor brands

Five-year growth rate for liquor brands

TABLE 3.6.2 Growth Rates for Liquor Brands

Brand	Growth Rate	Brand	Growth Rate	Brand	Growth Rate
Bacardi	−2.1%	Kahlua	−0.3	Chivas Regal	4.2
Smirnoff	1.6	Early Times	−3.6	Bailey's	4.4
Seagram's 7 Crown	−6.2	J&B	−10.7	Absolut	60.0
Canadian Mist	4.9	Gilbey's (vodka)	−1.8	Castillo	−2.7
Popov	5.8	Crown Royal	5.7	Calvert Extra	−9.5
Jim Beam	0.2	Jose Cuervo	10.3	Hennessy	7.8
Jack Daniel's	−1.8	Kessler	−2.3	Evan Williams	6.1
Seagram's	3.1	Southern Comfort	−0.3	Stolichnaya	13.6
Dekuyper Peachtree	123.1	Johnnie Walker Red	−5.7	Old Crow	−4.2
Windsor Supreme	0.9	Tanqueray	2.1	Canadian Ltd.	0.8
Seagram's V.O.	−8.9	Lord Calvert Canadian	0.6	Ronrico	−2.6
Dewar's	1.9	Christian Bros.	−10.2	Old Grand-dad	−7.4
Kamchatka	2.1	Beefeater	−4.1	Relska	0.7
Canadian Club	−12.1	Ten High	−8.9	Fleischmann's (gin)	−5.6
Black Velvet	−1.1	Ancient Age	−8.2	McCormick	9.1
Gordon's (gin)	−6.7	Wolfschmidt	−2.6	Old Smuggler	−6.6
E&J	17.2	Skol	0.9	Crown Russe	−5.4
Gordon's (vodka)	−1.8	Cutty Sark	−10.9	Usher's	0.0
Gilbey's (gin)	−6.4%	Fleischmann's (vodka)	−3.5		

Data are from "Liquor Industry Scoreboard," *Business Week*, June 22, 1987, p. 121.

The data in this analysis indicate the maturity of the market. Since the growth rates tend to cluster around 0%, this suggests that the market as a whole did not grow very much. Instead, there were some winners and some losers as many brands competed for essentially the same pool of consumers.

■ 3.7 Histograms by Hand: Stem-and-Leaf

These days, the most effective way to construct a histogram is probably to use a statistical software package on a computer. However, there are times when you might want to construct a histogram by hand. For example, there might not be a computer available before the deadline on the project, and you might want to check just one more possibility by examining a histogram. Also, for a small list of numbers it is actually faster to scratch down a histogram on paper than it would be to operate the computer and type the data into it. Finally, by drawing a histogram yourself, you end up "closer to the data," with an intuitive feel for the numbers that cannot be obtained by letting the computer do the work.

The easiest way to construct a histogram by hand is to use the **stem-and-leaf** style, in which the histogram bars are constructed by stacking numbers one on top of the other. Doing it in this way has the advantage of letting the histogram grow before your eyes, showing you useful information from the very start and making your efforts worthwhile.

Begin by identifying the initial digits to be included in the scale underneath the figure, ignoring the fine details. For example, you might include the millions and hundred thousands digits, but leave the ten thousands (and smaller digits) out of the scale. Then use the *next-level digit* (ten thousands) to record each data value, building columns upward to be interpreted as the columns of a histogram.

EXAMPLE **CEO Salaries in Food Processing**

Consider the 1986 compensations of the chief executive officers (CEOs) for food processing firms, including salary and bonus, as shown in Table 3.7.1. Using millions and hundred thousands to construct the scale, you would begin with the horizontal scale indicating the range 0 to 12. Thus, 1,200,000 would be represented at the far right in your initial drawing:

(in $100,000s)

TABLE 3.7.1   CEO Compensation for Food Processing Firms

Firm	CEO Compensation
Pillsbury	$ 698,000
Wm. Wrigley Jr.	507,000
Kraft	1,037,000
CPC International	647,000
Campbell Soup	646,000
Archer Daniels-Midland	885,000
General Mills	1,164,000
Pioneer Hi-Bred International	393,000
Hershey Foods	573,000
Quaker Oats	872,000
Sara Lee	1,180,000
Ralston Purina	750,000
Kellogg	950,000
Conagra	1,050,000
Borden	1,200,000

Data are from "Executive Compensation Scoreboard," *Business Week*, May 4, 1987, p. 72.

How should you record the first data value, representing compensation of $698,000 for the CEO of Pillsbury? This number has 6 in the hundred thousands place, so place the next digit, 9, above the 6 along the horizontal scale. Since the next digit (8, in the thousands place) is much less important, you need not trouble yourself with it for now. The result so far is as follows:

(in $100,000s)

The next data value, $507,000 for Wrigley, will be recorded as a 0 (the ten thousands digit) over the 5 (the hundred thousands digit). Next is Kraft at $1,037,000, which has a 10 (not just a 1) for its hundred thousands. Thus, Kraft will be represented by a 3 (the ten thousands digit) over the 10. Recording these two values produces:

(in $100,000s)

As you record more and more numbers, place them in columns. In this way, you get to watch the histogram grow before your eyes. This is much more satisfying (and informative) than having to calculate and count for a while before getting to see any results. The finished histogram in the stem-and-leaf style looks like this:

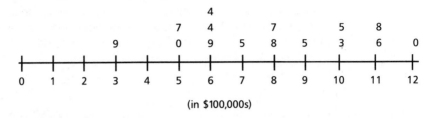

To represent this stem-and-leaf histogram in the more traditional style, simply replace the columns of numbers with bars of the same height, as shown in Figure 3.7.1.

Looking at either display (stem-and-leaf or traditional histogram), you can see the basic information in the data set. CEO compensation at major food processing firms ranged from about a third of a million to slightly over a million dollars.

FIGURE 3.7.1 A traditional histogram, using bars with the same heights as the columns of numbers in the stem-and-leaf histogram.

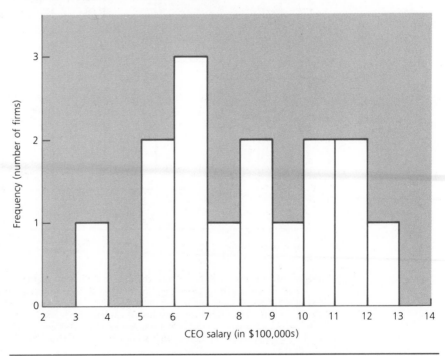

Although it's difficult to say with precision, due to the relatively small amount of data, it appears that the distribution is fairly symmetric and normal.[15]

It is possible to draw the histogram with fewer but wider bars in order to see the big picture. Note in Figure 3.7.2 that you are no longer paying attention to just one or two data values most of the time, and you can concentrate on the overall features of the distribution of CEO compensation figures. This confirms your judgment that the distribution is fairly normal.

FIGURE 3.7.2   A traditional histogram, also for the food industry CEO compensation data, with fewer and wider bars than the previous displays. This lets you see the big picture more effectively.

---

[15]Judging exactly when you have "enough" data is a difficult matter and often more of an art than a science. One guiding principle, which works here, is to recognize that whenever you are working at the level of just one or two individual data points, you should be very cautious about drawing conclusions. In this case, most histogram bars reach just 1 or 2 in height, indicating just one or two observations. Thus, unless you saw extreme skewness or distant outliers, you would give the distribution the benefit of the doubt and declare that it might be symmetric and normally distributed.

■ 3.8 End-of-Chapter-Materials

Summary

The simplest kind of data set is a **list of numbers** representing some kind of information (a single statistical variable) measured on each item of interest (each elementary unit). A list of numbers may come to you either as a list or as a table showing how many times each number should be repeated to form a list.

The first step toward understanding a list of numbers is to view its *histogram* in order to see its basic properties, such as typical values, special values, concentration, spread, the general pattern, and any separate groupings. The **histogram** displays the frequencies as a bar chart rising above the number line, indicating how often the various values occur in the data set. The **number line** is a straight line, usually horizontal, with the scale indicated by numbers below it.

A **normal distribution** is a particular idealized, smooth, bell-shaped histogram with all of the randomness removed. It represents an ideal data set that has lots of numbers concentrated in the middle of the range and trails off symmetrically on both sides. A data set follows a normal distribution if it resembles the smooth, symmetric, bell-shaped normal curve, except for some randomness. The normal distribution plays an important role in statistical theory and practice.

A **skewed distribution** is neither symmetric nor normal because the data values trail off more sharply on one side than on the other. Skewed distributions are very common in business. Unfortunately, many standard statistical methods do not work properly if your data set is very skewed.

Transformation means replacing each data value by a different number (such as its logarithm) to facilitate statistical analysis. The **logarithm** often transforms skewness into symmetry because it stretches the scale near zero, spreading out all of the small values that had been bunched together. The logarithm also pulls together the very large data values, which had been thinly scattered at the high end of the scale. The logarithm can only be computed for positive numbers. To interpret the logarithm, note that equal distances on the logarithmic scale correspond to equal percent increases instead of equal value increases (dollar amounts, for example).

When two clear and separate groups are visible in a histogram, you have a **bimodal distribution.** It is important to recognize when you have a bimodal distribution so that you can take appropriate action. You might find that only one of the groups is actually of interest to you, and that the other should be omitted. Or, you might decide to make some changes in the analysis in order to cope with this more complex situation.

Sometimes you will find **outliers**, which are one or more data values that just don't seem to belong with the others because they are either far too big or far too small. Outliers can cause trouble with statistical analysis, so they should be identified and acted on. If the outlier is a mistake, correct it and continue with the analysis. If it is correct but different, you might or might not omit it from the analysis. If you can convince yourself and others that the outlier is not part of the system you wish to study, you may continue without the outlier. If you cannot justify omitting the outlier, you may proceed with two projects: analyze the data with and without the outlier. In any case, be sure to state clearly somewhere in your report the existence of an outlier and the action taken.

The most efficient way to draw a histogram is with a computer, using a statistical software package. However, there are times when it is necessary (and even desirable) to construct a histogram by hand. The **stem-and-leaf** histogram constructs the bars of a histogram by stacking numbers one on top of another. Because data values are recorded successively, you can build intuition about the data set by watching the histogram grow.

Key Words

list of numbers 32	transformation 44
histogram 31	logarithm 44
number line 33	bimodal distribution 47
normal distribution 37	outlier 50
skewed distribution 41	stem-and-leaf 57

Questions

1 What is a list of numbers?
2 Name six properties of a data set that are displayed by a histogram.
3 What is a number line?
4 What is the difference between a histogram and a bar chart?
5 What is a normal distribution?
6 Why is the normal distribution important in statistics?
7 When a real data set is normally distributed, should you expect the histogram to be a perfectly smooth bell-shaped curve? Why or why not?
8 Are all data sets normally distributed?
9 What is a skewed distribution?
10 What is the main problem with skewness? How can it be solved in many cases?
11 How can you interpret the logarithm of a number?
12 What is a bimodal distribution? What should you do if you find one?
13 What is an outlier?
14 Why is it important in a report to explain how you dealt with an outlier?
15 What kinds of trouble do outliers cause?

16 When is it appropriate to set aside an outlier and analyze only the rest of the data?

17 Suppose there is an outlier in your data. You plan to analyze the data twice: once with and once without the outlier. What result would you be most pleased with? Why?

18 What is a stem-and-leaf histogram?

19 What are the advantages of a stem-and-leaf histogram?

Problems

1 Consider the yields (as an interest rate, in percent per year) of tax-exempt bonds, as shown in Table 3.8.1.

TABLE 3.8.1   Yields of Tax-Exempt Bonds

Issue	Yield	Issue	Yield
Austin TX Util Sys Rev	8.97%	NYC MAC	8.60
Cal Pub Works Board	8.37	NYS Dorm Auth	8.59
Camden City, NJ Util Auth	8.40	NYS Energy Res Dev	8.91
Cuyahoga County Ohio	8.70	NYS Med Care Fac Fin	8.51
Fla Bd Ed Cap Out Ser C	8.58	NYS Med Care Finance Ag	8.54
Fulton Cty Ga Sch Dist	8.38	NYS Power Auth GenPur	8.51
Ga Muni El Au Gn Pw	8.84	Ocean City NJ Util Auth	8.41
Ga Muni Electric Auth	8.84	Orange County Calif	8.70
Grand Rv Dam Auth Okla	8.89	Palm Beach Sch Dist Fla	8.54
Harris County Texas	9.08	Palm Beach Waste Auth	8.87
Houston, Texas	8.68	Penn Higher Ed Facil Au	8.47
Ill Health Facs Auth	8.52	Philadelphia, Pa	8.79
Intrmtn Pwr Agcy Utah	8.65	Piedmont Mun Pwr Rev	8.85
Jacksonville El Auth Ref	8.74	Platte Rv Pwr Auth Colo	8.66
Lower Colo Riv Auth Tex	8.89	Puerto Rico Bldgs Auth	8.62
Mass Hlth & Ed Facil Au	8.44	Rutgers State Univ NJ	8.52
NC Eastrn Muni Pwr Agcy	8.93	Tex Coastal Wtr Auth	8.61
NC Eastrn MPA Rev Ser87A	8.98	Texas Muni Pwr Agency	9.06

Data are from *The Wall Street Journal,* September 18, 1987, p. 30. Their source is *The Bond Buyer.*

   a. Construct a histogram of this data set.

   b. Based on the histogram, what values appear to be typical for this group of tax-exempt bonds?

   c. Describe the shape of the distribution.

2 Business firms occasionally buy back their own stock for various reasons, sometimes when they view the market price as a "bargain" compared to their view of its true worth. It has been observed that the market price of stock often increases around the time of the announcement of such a buy-back. Consider the data on actual percent changes over three months in stock prices for firms announcing stock buy-backs shown in Table 3.8.2.

TABLE 3.8.2 Market Response to Stock Buy-Back Announcements

Company	Three-Month Price Change
Tektronix	17.0%
General Motors	12.7
Firestone	26.2
GAF Corp.	14.3
Rockwell Intl.	−1.1
ITT Corp.	−7.5
Ohio Casualty	13.9
Kimberly-Clark	14.0
Anheuser-Busch	19.2
Hewlett-Packard	10.2

Data are from *The Wall Street Journal,* September 18, 1987, p. 17. Their source is Salomon Brothers.

a. Construct a histogram of this data set.

b. Construct a stem-and leaf style histogram of this data set using pen and paper. Your horizontal axis might include four columns of numbers (−0, 0, 1, and 2) representing the 10s place.[16]

c. Based on these histograms, what can you say to summarize typical behavior of these stock prices following a buy-back announcement?

d. Describe the shape of the distribution.

3 Consider the daily percentage change in stock price of the most active issues traded on the New York Stock Exchange, as shown in Table 3.8.3.

TABLE 3.8.3 Active Stock Market Issues

Firm	Percent Change
Citicorp	−1.3%
Amer T&T	0.4
IBM	0.8
HCA	−1.4
Exxon	−0.5
Gen Elct	1.3
Mobil	−0.3
Phillip Pet	−0.8
Storage Tch	0.0
Est Kodak	0.5
S Fe Sou Pac	2.0
Chevron	−1.5
Brockway	32.8
Nwmnt Mng	1.5
Fed Express	5.4

Data are from *The Wall Street Journal,* September 18, 1987, p. 33.

---

[16]The data value −7.5 would be recorded as a 7 placed over the −0 column (the number −7.5 has a negative 0 for its tens place, and the next digit, 7, is placed above it).

a. Construct a histogram of this data set.
b. Describe the distribution.
c. Identify the outlier.
d. Interpret the outlier in view of the fact that traders had just learned that Owens-Illinois might be willing to acquire Brockway for $60 per share. Brockway's share price increased 19 1/8 to 58 3/8.
e. Suppose you are conducting a study of price changes of heavily traded stocks. Discuss the different ways you might deal with this outlier. In particular, would it be appropriate to omit it from the analysis?

4 Consider TIAA, the Teachers Insurance & Annuity Association, which manages retirement pensions for college professors. TIAA manages a very large and highly diversified portfolio, somewhere around $28 billion. Investment in broadcasting companies represents 0.59% of this portfolio. Data on the market value of TIAA's investment in broadcasting companies is shown in Table 3.8.4.

TABLE 3.8.4   TIAA's Investments

Firm	Portfolio Market Value ($000)
Barris	$ 976
Capital Cities	44,026
CBS	30,267
Comcast	1,840
Comcast (new shares)	900
Financial News Network	987
King World Productions	1,624
LIN Broadcasting	13,068
Multimedia	2,092
Park Communications	2,779
Scripps Howard Broadcasting	1,777
Standard Shares	2,664
Taft Broadcasting	9,027
Tele-Communications	20,381
Turner Broadcasting System	1,172
United Cable Television	5,737
United Television	2,778
Westwood One	2,572

Source: TIAA/CREF 1986 Investment Supplement, p. 14.

a. Construct a histogram of this data set.
b. Based on this histogram, describe the distribution of TIAA's investment in broadcasting companies.
c. Describe the shape of the distribution. In particular, is it skewed or symmetric?
d. Find the logarithm of each data value.
e. Construct a histogram of these logarithms.
f. Describe the distribution of the logarithms. In particular, is it skewed or symmetric?

TABLE 3.8.5 Return on Equity for Conglomerates

Firm	ROE
Alco Standard	16.0%
Allied-Signal	8.7
Gulf & Western	11.6
Household International	13.1
IC Industries	7.1
ITT	5.9
Rockwell International	19.8
Teledyne	22.8
Tenneco	1.2
Textron	11.9

Data are from "Executive Compensation Scoreboard," *Business Week,* May 2, 1988, p. 62.

5 Consider the return on equity (ROE) for selected large conglomerates, as shown in Table 3.8.5.

a. Construct a histogram for this data set.

b. Describe the distribution.

c. Tenneco's ROE is the very smallest, just 1.2%, and appears at first glance to be quite different from the others. Based on the perspective given by your histogram from part a, is Tenneco an outlier? Why or why not?

6 Draw a stem-and-leaf histogram for the data set in problem 5.

7 Consider the price of perfume around the world, as shown in Table 3.8.6.

TABLE 3.8.6 Price of One-Half Ounce of Chanel No. 5 Perfume

City	Price
Paris	$ 76.26
Frankfurt	64.50
London	57.33
Milan	84.00
Amsterdam	76.00
Zurich	60.69
Singapore	42.87
Hong Kong	53.30
Tokyo	126.50
New York	92.01
Los Angeles	85.20

Data are from "Prices of Typical Items, Airports vs. Downtowns," *Fortune,* March 31, 1986, p. 160.

a. Construct a histogram for this data set.

b. Describe the distribution.

TABLE 3.8.7   Special Exemptions to the 1986 Revision of the IRS Tax Code

Firm	Estimated Government Revenue Loss ($ millions)
Paramount Cards	$ 7
Banks of Iowa	7
Ideal Basic Industries	0
Goldrus Drilling	13
Original Appalachian Artworks	6
Candle Corp.	13
S.A. Horvitz Testamentary Trust	1
Green Bay Packaging	2
New England Patriots	6
Ireton Coal	18
Ala-Tenn Resources	0
Metropolitan-First Minnesota Merger	9
Texas Air/Eastern Merger	47
Brunswick	61
Liberty Bell Park	5
Beneficial Corp.	67

Data are from "Special Exemptions in the Tax Bill, as Disclosed by the Senate," *New York Times*, September 27, 1986, p. 33. These particular firms are grouped under the heading "Transition Rules for Corporate Provisions." Don't you wish you could have qualified for some of these?

8 When the IRS tax code was revised in 1986, congress granted some special exemptions to specific corporations. The U.S. government's revenue losses due to some of these special transition rules for corporate provisions are shown in Table 3.8.7.
   a. Construct a histogram for this data set.
   b. Describe the distribution.

9 Continuing with the revenue loss data of Table 3.8.7:
   a. Find the logarithm for each data value. Omit the two firms with zero revenue loss from your answers to this problem.
   b. Construct a histogram for this data set.
   c. Describe the distribution.
   d. Compare this analysis of the transformed data to your analysis of the original data in problem 8.

10 The number of small electric motors rejected for poor quality, per batch of 250, were recorded for recent batches. The results were as follows:

   3, 2, 7, 5, 1, 3, 1, 7, 0, 6, 2, 3, 4, 1, 2, 25, 2, 4, 5, 0, 5, 3, 5, 3, 1, 2, 3, 1, 3, 0, 1, 6, 3, 5,

   41, 1, 0, 6, 4, 1, 3

   a. Construct a histogram for this data set.
   b. Describe the distribution.

c. Identify the outlier(s).

d. Remove the outlier(s), and construct a histogram for the remaining batches.

e. Summarize this firm's recent experience with quality of production.

Database Exercises

Refer to the employee database in Appendix A.

1 For the salary numbers:
  a. Construct a histogram.
  b. Describe the shape of the distribution.
  c. Summarize the distribution in general terms by giving the smallest salary, the largest salary, and the range that includes all salaries.
2 For the age numbers:
  a. Construct a histogram.
  b. Describe the shape of the distribution.
  c. Summarize the distribution in general terms.
3 For the experience numbers:
  a. Construct a histogram.
  b. Describe the shape of the distribution.
  c. Summarize the distribution in general terms.
4 For the salary numbers, separated according to gender:
  a. Construct a histogram for just the males.
  b. Construct a histogram for just the females using the same scale as in part a to facilitate comparison of male and female salaries.
  c. Compare these two salary distributions, and write a paragraph describing any gender differences in salary that you see from comparing these two histograms.[17]

Project

Draw a histogram for each of three data sets related to your business interests. Choose your own business data from sources such as *The Wall Street Journal* or your firm. Each data set should contain at least 15 numbers. Write a page (including the histogram) for each data set, commenting on the histogram as follows:

a. What is the distribution shape?

b. Are there any outliers? What might you do if there are?

c. Summarize the distribution in general terms.

d. What have you learned from examining the histogram?

---

[17]Statistical methods for comparing two groups such as these will be presented in Chapter 10.

Landmark Summaries
Interpreting Typical Values and Percentiles

One of the most effective ways to "see the big picture" in complex situations is through **summarization**, that is, using one or more selected or computed values to represent the data set. Studying each individual case in detail is not, in itself, a statistical activity,[1] but discovering and identifying the features that the cases have in common *is* a statistical activity because it treats the information as a whole.

In statistics, one goal is to condense a data set down to one number (or two, or a few numbers) that expresses the most fundamental characteristics of the data. The methods most appropriate for a single list of numbers (i.e., univariate data) include the following:

1 The *average, median,* and *mode* are different ways of selecting a single number that closely describes all the numbers in a data set. Such a single-number summary is referred to as a *typical value, center,* or *location.*

2 A *percentile* summarizes information about *ranks,* characterizing the value attained by a given percentage of the data after they have been ordered from smallest to largest.

3 The *standard deviation* is an indication of how different the numbers in the data set are from one another. This concept is also referred to as *diversity* or *variability* and will be deferred to Chapter 5.

What if there are individuals that are not adequately described by these summaries? Such outliers may simply be described separately. Thus, you can summarize a large group of data by (1) summarizing the basic structure of most of its elements, and then (2) making a list of any special exceptions. In this way, you can achieve the statistical goal of efficiently describing a large data set and still take account of the special nature of the of the individual.

---

[1]However, it may be a worthwhile activity, if there is time enough to study every one!

■ 4.1 What Is the Most Typical Value?

The ultimate summary of any data set is a single number that best represents all of the data values. You might call such a number *a typical value* for the data set. Unless all numbers in the data set are the same, you should expect some differences of opinion regarding exactly which number is "most typical" of the entire data set. There are three different ways to obtain such a summary measure:

1 The *average* or *mean*, which can be computed only for meaningful numbers (quantitative data).
2 The *median*, or halfway point, which can be computed either for ordered categories (ordinal data) or for numbers.
3 The *mode*, or most common category, which can be computed for unordered categories (nominal data), ordered categories, or numbers.

The Average: A Typical Value for Quantitative Data

The **average** (also called the **mean**) is the most common method for finding a typical value for a list of numbers, found by adding up all the values and then dividing by the number of items.[2] Here is the sample average expressed as a formula:

■ **The Sample Average**

$$\text{Sample average} = \frac{\text{Sum of data items}}{\text{Number of data items}}$$

$$\overline{X} = \frac{X_1 + X_2 + \cdots + X_n}{n}$$

$$= \frac{1}{n}\sum_{i=1}^{n} X_i$$

---

where n is the number of items in the list of data and $X_1, X_2, \ldots, X_n$ stand for the values themselves. The capital Greek letter sigma, Σ, tells you to add up the symbols that follow it, substituting the values 1 through n in turn for i. The symbol for the average, $\overline{X}$, is read aloud as "X bar."

For example, the average of the three-number data set 4, 9, 8 is

$$\frac{4 + 9 + 8}{3} = \frac{21}{3} = 7$$

---

[2]The words *average* and *mean* may be used interchangeably. However, in this text we will tend to use the word *average* for a sample of data and reserve the word *mean* for later on, when we deal with populations.

The idea is the same whether you view your list of numbers as a complete *population* or as a representative *sample* from a larger population.[3] However, the notation differs slightly. For an entire population, the convention is to use N to represent the number of items and to let μ (the Greek letter "mu") represent the population mean value. Here is the population mean expressed as a formula:

■ The Population Mean

$$\text{Population Mean} = \frac{\text{Sum of population values}}{\text{Number of population items}}$$

$$\mu = \frac{X_1 + X_2 + \cdots + X_N}{N}$$

$$= \frac{1}{N} \sum_{i=1}^{N} X_i$$

Since the data values must be added together as part of the process of finding the average, it is clear that this method cannot apply to qualitative data (how would you add colors or bond ratings together?).

The average may be interpreted as spreading the total evenly among the participants. For example, from an employee database you could compute the average salary for all employees in Houston. The resulting average would have the following interpretation: If we were to pay all Houston employees the same salary, without changing the total salary for all of Houston, it would be this average amount. Note that you don't have to be contemplating the institution of such a level salary structure to use the average as an indication of typical salary (particularly when you are concerned with the total payroll amount as a budget item).

Since the average preserves the total while spreading amounts out evenly, it is most useful as a summary when there are no extreme values (outliers) present and the data set is a more-or-less homogeneous group with randomness. If one employee earns vastly more than the others, then the average will not be useful as a summary measure. Although it will still preserve the total salary amount, it will not give as useful an indication of the salaries of individuals since the average will be too high for most employees and too low for the exceptional worker.

The average is the only summary measure capable of preserving the total. This makes it particularly useful in situations where a total amount is to be projected for a large group. First the average would be found for a smaller sample of data representing the larger group. Then this average would be

---

[3]The concept of sampling from a population is crucial to statistical inference and will be covered in detail in Chapters 8–10.

scaled up by multiplying it by the number of individuals in the larger group. The result gives an estimate, or forecast, of the total for the larger population. Generally, when a total is to be determined, the average should be used.

EXAMPLE   **How Much Will Consumers Spend?**

A firm is interested in total consumer expenditures on personal health items in the city of Cleveland. It has obtained the results of a random sample of 300 individuals in the area, showing that an average of $6.58 was spent last month by each one.

Naturally, some spent more and others spent less than this average amount. Rather than working with all 300 numbers, we use the average to summarize the typical amount each spent. More importantly, when you multiply it by the population of Cleveland, you obtain a reasonable estimate of the total personal health expenditures for the entire city:[4]

> Estimated Cleveland personal health expenditures
> = (Average per person from sample) (Population of Cleveland)
> = ($6.58) (573,822)
> = $3,775,748.76

This projection of total sales of nearly $4 million is reasonable and probably useful. However, it is almost certainly wrong (in the sense that it does not represent the exact amount spent). Later on, when you study confidence intervals (in Chapter 9), you will see how to account for the statistical error arising from the projection from a sample of 300 to a population of 573,822 individuals.

EXAMPLE   **How Many Defective Parts?**

The Globular Ball Bearing Company manufactures 1,000 items per lot. From the day's production of 253 lots, a sample of 10 lots was chosen randomly for quality control inspection. The number of defective items in each of these lots was

$$3, 8, 2, 5, 0, 7, 14, 7, 4, 1$$

The average of this data set is

$$\frac{3 + 8 + 2 + 5 + 0 + 7 + 14 + 7 + 4 + 1}{10} = \frac{51}{10}$$
$$= 5.1$$

which tells you that there were 5.1 defects per lot, on the average. This represents a defect rate of 5.1 per 1,000, or 0.51% (about half of a percent). Scaling up to the day's production of 253 lots, you would expect there to be about

$$5.1 \times 253 = 1,290.3$$

---

[4]This is the 1984 population estimate from Bureau of the Census, *Statistical Abstract of the United States, 1987* (Washington, 1986), p. 31.

defective items in the entire day's production, out of the total of 253,000 items produced.

To show how the average is indeed a reasonable summary of a list of numbers, Figure 4.1.1 shows a histogram of the 10 numbers in this data set with the average value indicated. Note how the average is nicely in the middle, reasonably close to all of the data values.

The Weighted Average: Adjusting for Importance

The **weighted average** is like the average, except that it allows you to give a different importance or "weight" to each data item. The weighted average gives you the flexibility to define your own system of importance when it is not appropriate to treat each item equally.

If a firm has three plants and the employee pension expenses for each plant are being analyzed, it may not make sense to take a simple average of these three numbers as a summary of typical pension expense, especially if the plants are very different in size. If one plant has twice as many employees as another, it seems reasonable that its pension expense should

---

FIGURE 4.1.1 A histogram of the number of defective items in each of 10 lots of 1,000 items, with the average (5.1) indicated.

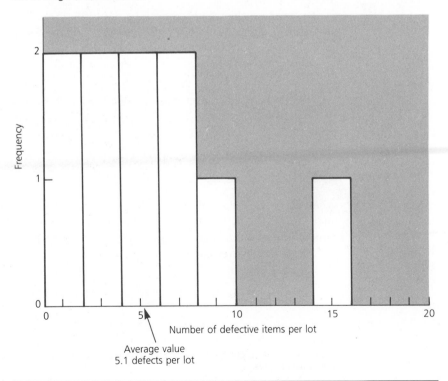

count double in the summarization process. The weighted average allows you to do this by using weights defined according to the size of each plant.

The weights are usually positive numbers that sum to 1, expressing the relative importance of each data item. Don't worry if your initial weights don't add up to 1. You can always force them to do this by dividing each weight by the sum of all of the weights. Your initial weights might be determined by number of employees, market value, or some other objective measure, or by a subjective method (i.e., using someone's personal or expert opinion). Sometimes it's easier to set initial weights without worrying about whether they add up to 1, and then convert later by dividing by the total.

Suppose you decide to compute a weighted average of pension expenses for the three plants using weights determined by the number of employees at each plant. If the three plants have 182, 386, and 697 employees, you would use respective weights of

$$182/1{,}265 = 0.144$$

$$386/1{,}265 = 0.305$$

$$697/1{,}265 = 0.551$$

Note that in each case, weights were obtained by dividing by the sum $182 + 386 + 697 = 1{,}265$. The resulting weights add to 1, as they must:[5] $0.144 + 0.305 + 0.551 = 1$.

To compute the weighted average, multiply each data item by its weight and sum these results. That's all there is to it. The formula looks like this:

■ **The Weighted Average**

Weighted average = Sum of (weight times data item)

$$= w_1 X_1 + w_2 X_2 + \cdots + w_n X_n$$

$$= \sum_{i=1}^{n} w_i X_i$$

---

where $w_1, w_2, \ldots, w_n$ stand for the respective weights, which add up to 1. You may think of the regular (unweighted) average as a weighted average in which all data items have the same weight, namely $1/n$.

The weighted average of 63, 47, and 98, with respective weights of 0.144, 0.305, and 0.551, is

$$(0.144 \times 63) + (0.305 \times 47) + (0.551 \times 98) = 9.072 + 14.335 + 53.998$$

$$= 77.405$$

---

[5]The actual sum might be 0.999 or 1.001 due to round-off error. You need not be concerned when this happens.

Note that this differs from the regular (unweighted) average value of (63 + 47 + 98)/3 = 69.333, as you might expect. The weighted average gives the largest number extra emphasis, namely, weight 0.551, which is more than one third of the weight. It is therefore reasonable that the weighted average should be larger than the unweighted average in this case.

The weighted average may best be interpreted as an average to be used when some items have more importance than others; the items with greater importance have more of a say in the value of the weighted average.

EXAMPLE

Your Grade Point Average

A grade point average, or GPA, computed for your university program is a weighted average. This is necessary because some courses have more credit hours, and therefore more importance, than others. It seems reasonable that a course that meets twice as often as another should have twice the impact, and the GPA reflects this.

Different schools have different systems. Suppose your system involves grades from 0.0 (flunking) to 4.0 (perfect), and your report card for the term looks like this:

Course	Credits	Grade
Statistics	5	3.7
Economics	5	3.3
Marketing	4	3.5
Track	1	2.8
Total	15	

The weights will be computed by dividing each of the credits by 15, the total number of credits. Your GPA will then be computed as a weighted average of your grades, weighted according to the number of credits:

$$\left(\frac{5}{15} \times 3.7\right) + \left(\frac{5}{15} \times 3.3\right) + \left(\frac{4}{15} \times 3.5\right) + \left(\frac{1}{15} \times 2.8\right) = 3.45$$

Your GPA, 3.45, fortunately was not greatly affected by the low grade (for track) due to its small weight (just 1 credit). Had these four grades simply been averaged, the result would have been lower (3.33). Thank goodness you didn't hurt your grades very much by concentrating on your business courses when the end-of-term crunch hit and letting the other one slide!

EXAMPLE

The Firm's Cost of Capital

The firm's cost of capital, a concept from corporate finance, is computed as a weighted average. The idea is that a firm has raised money by selling a variety of financial instruments: stocks, bonds, commercial paper, and so forth. Since each of these securities has its own rate of return (a cost of capital to the firm), it would be useful to combine and summarize the different rates as a single number representing the aggregate cost to the firm of raising money with this selection of securities.

The firm's cost of capital is a simple weighted average of the cost of capital of each security (this is its rate of return, or interest rate), where the weights are determined according to the total market value of that security. For example, if preferred stock represents only 3% of the market value of a firm's outstanding securities, then its cost should be given that low weight.

Consider the situation for Leveraged Industries, Inc., a hypothetical firm with lots of debt resulting from recent merger and acquisition activity:[6]

Security	Market value	Rate of return
Common stock	$100,000	18.5%
Preferred stock	15,000	14.9
Bonds (9% coupon)	225,000	11.2
Bonds (8.5% coupon)	115,000	11.2
Total	$455,000	

Divide each market value by the total to find the weights, which express the market's assessment of the proportion of each type of security:[7]

Security	Weight
Common stock	0.220
Preferred stock	0.033
Bonds (9% coupon)	0.495
Bonds (8.5% coupon)	0.253

Since the weight of common stock is 0.220, it follows that 22% of the firm is financed with common stock, in terms of market value. The cost of capital is then computed by multiplying market rates of return by these weights and summing:

$$(0.220 \times 18.5) + (0.033 \times 14.9) + (0.495 \times 11.2)$$
$$+ (0.253 \times 11.2) = 12.94$$

---

[6] In cost of capital computations, we always use current market values (rather than book values) due to the fact that market values indicate the likely cost to the firm of raising additional capital. Thus, in the case of bonds, you would use the current market yield (interest rate) rather than the coupon rate based on the face value because the bond is probably not trading at its face value. You would also use the market value per bond times the number of bonds outstanding to derive the total market value of outstanding bonds. Estimating the return demanded by the market for common stock is a challenging exercise you are likely to learn about in your finance course.

[7] For example, the first weight is $100,000/455,000 = 0.220$. The weights do not sum to 1 here due to round-off error. This is not a concern. If greater accuracy were needed or desired, you could work with four, five, or more decimal places for the weight and thereby increase the accuracy of the result.

The cost of capital for Leveraged Industries, Inc. is therefore 12.9%. This weighted average has combined the individual costs of capital (18.5%, 14.9%, and 11.2%) into a single number.

There would have been no change in this result (12.9) if you had combined the two bond issues into one line item, with a combined market value of $340,000 and 11.2% rate of return, as may be verified by performing the calculation. This is as it should be, since such a distinction should have no practical consequences: the two bond issues have different coupons because they were issued at different times, and since that time their market prices have adjusted so that their yields (rates of return) are identical.

This weighted average cost of capital may be interpreted as follows. If Leveraged Industries decided to raise additional capital without changing its basic business strategy (i.e., type of projects, risk of projects) and keeping the same relative mix of securities, then it will have to pay a return of 12.9% or $129 per $1,000 raised per year. This $129 will be paid to the different types of securities according to the weights given.

EXAMPLE   **Adjusting for Misrepresentation**

Another use of the weighted average is to correct for known misrepresentation in a sample as compared to the population you wish to know about. Since the average of the sample treats all individuals the same, but you know that (compared to the population) some groups of individuals are overrepresented and others underrepresented, by reweighting the average you can obtain a better result. A weighted average is better because it combines the known information about each group (from the sample) with better information about each group's representation (from the population rather than the sample). Since the best information of each type is used, the result is improved.

Reconsider the sample of 300 individuals from Cleveland analyzed in the earlier example of consumer personal health expenditures. Suppose that the percentage of young people (under 18 years old) in the sample (21.7%) did not match the known percentage for the entire population (27.8%) and that the average expenditures were computed separately for each group:[8]

Average expenditure for people under 18 = $4.86
Average expenditure for people 18 or over = $7.06

The weighted average of these expenditures will use the population (rather than the sample) weights, namely, 27.8% younger and 72.2% (which is 100% − 27.8%) older people since you know that these are the correct percentages to use. Of course, if you had expenditure information for the entire city, you would use that too, but you don't; you have it only for the 300 people in the sample.

---

[8]The figure 27.8% is the 1980 estimate from Bureau of the Census, *Statistical Abstract of the United States, 1987* (Washington, 1986), p. 31.

Converting the percentages to weights, the weighted average may be computed as follows:

$$\text{Weighted average expenditure} = (0.278 \times \$4.86) + (0.722 \times \$7.06)$$
$$= \$6.45$$

This weighted average, $6.45, gives a better estimate of average personal health expenditures in Cleveland than the regular (unweighted) average value ($6.58) found earlier. The weighted average is better because it has *corrected for* the fact that there were too many older people in the sample of 300.[9] Since these older people tend to spend more, without this adjustment, the estimate would have been too large ($6.58 compared to $6.45).

Of course, even this new weighted estimate is probably wrong. But it is based on better information and has a smaller expected error, as can be proven using mathematical models. The new estimate is not necessarily better in every case (that is, the truth may actually be closer to the regular, unweighted average in this example) but the weighted procedure will give an answer that is *more likely* to be closer to the truth.

The Median: A Typical Value for Quantitative and Ordinal Data

The **median** is the middle value; half of the items in the set are larger and half are smaller. Thus, it must be in the *center* of the data and provide an effective summary of the list of data. You find it by first putting the data in order and then locating the middle value. To be precise, you have to pay attention to some details; for example, you might have to average the two middle values if there is no single value in the middle.

One way to define the median is in terms of *ranks*. **Ranks** associate the numbers $1, 2, 3, \ldots, n$ with the data values so that the smallest has rank 1, the next smallest has rank 2, and so forth up to largest, which has rank n[10]. One basic principle involved in finding the median is as follows:

■ **The Rank of the Median**

The median has rank $(1 + n)/2$.

Paying attention to all of the special cases, you find the median for a list of n items as follows:

1 Put the data items in order from smallest to largest (or largest to smallest; it doesn't matter).

---

[9]Statisticians often speak of "correcting for" or "adjusting for" one factor or another. This is one way to do it; later on you will learn about multiple regression as another powerful way to correct for the influences of factors not under your control.

[10]The ranks form the basis for *nonparametric methods*, which will be presented in Chapter 16.

2 Find the middle value. There are two cases to consider:
    a. If n is an odd number, the median is the middle data value, which is located $(1 + n)/2$ steps in from either end of the ordered data list.

        For example, the median of the list 15, 27, 14, 18, 21, with $n = 5$ items, is

$$\text{Median } (15, 27, 14, 18, 21) = \text{Median } (14, 15, 18, 21, 27)$$
$$= 18$$

Note that to find the median, 18, you counted three steps into the ordered list, which is as the formula suggested, since $(1 + n)/2 = (1 + 5)/2 = 3$.

    For an ordinal data example, consider the list of bond ratings AAA, A, B, AA, A. The median is

$$\text{Median (AAA, A, B, AA, A)} = \text{Median (B, A, A, AA, AAA)}$$
$$= A$$

    b. If n is an even number, there are two middle values instead of just one. They are located $(1 + n)/2$ steps in from either end of the ordered data list.
       i If the data set is *quantitative* (i.e., consists of numbers), the median is the average of these two middle values.

          For example, the median of the list 15, 27, 18, 14, with $n = 4$ items, is

$$\text{Median (15, 27, 18, 14)} = \text{Median (14, 15, 18, 27)}$$
$$= (15 + 18)/2$$
$$= 16.5$$

The formula $(1 + n)/2$ gives $(1 + 4)/2 = 2.5$ in this case, which tells you to go halfway between the second and third number in the ordered list by averaging them.

       ii If the data set is *ordinal* (i.e., contains ordered categories) and if the two middle values represent the same category, this category is the median. If they represent different categories, you would have to report them both as defining the median.

          For example, the median of bond ratings A, B, AA, A is

$$\text{Median (A, B, AA, A)} = \text{Median (B, A, A, AA)}$$
$$= A$$

since both middle values are rated A.

    For another example, the median of bond ratings A, AAA, B, AA, AAA, B is

$$\text{Median (A, AAA, B, AA, AAA, B)} = \text{Median (B, B, A, AA, AAA, AAA)}$$
$$= A \text{ and } AA$$

This is the best you can do because you cannot find the average of two values with ordinal data.

How does the median compare to the average? When the data set is normally distributed, they will be close to one another since the normal distribution is so symmetric and has such a clear middle point. However, the average and median will usually be a little different even for a normal distribution because each is summarizing in a different way, and there is nearly always some randomness in real data. When the data set is not normally distributed, the median and average can be very different because a skewed distribution does not have a well-defined center point. Typically the average is more in the direction of the longer tail or of the outlier than the median is because the average "knows" the actual values of these extreme observations whereas the median knows only that each value is either on one side or on the other.

EXAMPLE

The Crash of October 19, 1987: Stocks Drop at Opening

Consider the percentage of value lost by 29 of the Dow Industrial stocks between the close of trading on Friday, October 16, and the opening of trading on Monday, October 19, 1987, the day of the crash. Even at the opening, these stocks had lost substantial value, as is shown in Table 4.1.1.

TABLE 4.1.1   Loss at Opening on the Day of the Stock Market Crash of 1987

Firm	Change in Value
Union Carbide	−4.1%
USX	−5.1
Bethlehem Steel	−4.5
AT&T	−5.4
Boeing	−4.0
International Paper	−11.6
Chevron	−4.0
Woolworth	−3.0
United Technologies	−4.4
Allied-Signal	−9.3
General Motors	−0.9
Procter & Gamble	−3.5
Coca-Cola	−10.5
McDonald's	−7.2
Minnesota Mining	−8.9
Primerica	−6.8
Navistar	−2.1
General Electric	−17.2
Westinghouse	−15.7
Alcoa	−8.9
Kodak	−15.7
Texaco	−12.3
IBM	−9.6
Merck	−12.0
Philip Morris	−12.4
Du Pont	−8.6
Sears Roebuck	−11.4
Goodyear Tire	−10.9
Exxon	−8.6

Data are from "Trading in the 30 Dow Industrials Shows Wide Damage of Oct. 19 Crash," *The Wall Street Journal*, December 16, 1987, p. 20. This source included only the 29 securities listed here. Negative numbers indicate a loss in value. All are negative, indicating that none of these 29 industrial stocks opened "up" from its previous close.

The histogram in Figure 4.1.2 shows that the distribution is fairly normal. There is a hint of skewness toward low values (that is, the tail is slightly longer on the left than on the right), but the distribution is still essentially normal except for randomness. The average percentage change, −8.2%, and the median percentage change, −8.6%, are close to one another. Indeed, this histogram has a clear central region, and any reasonable summary measure must be near this middle region.

The average percentage change, −8.2%, may be interpreted as follows. If you had invested in a portfolio at the close of trading on Friday, with the same dollar amount invested in each of these 30 stock securities (in terms of their value at the close of trading on Friday), then your portfolio would have lost 8.2% of its worth when it was sold at the start of trading on Monday. Different stocks clearly lost different percentages of their worth, but an equally weighted portfolio would have lost this average amount. What if you had invested different amounts in the different stocks? Then the portfolio loss could be computed as a weighted average using the initial investment values to define the weights.

The median percentage change, −8.6%, may be interpreted as follows. If you arrange these percentages in order, then about half of the securities fell by 8.6% or more and about half fell by 8.6% or less. Thus, a drop of 8.6% in value repre-

---

FIGURE 4.1.2   The distribution of the percentage of value lost by 29 industrial stocks at the opening of trading on the day of the crash of October 19, 1987.

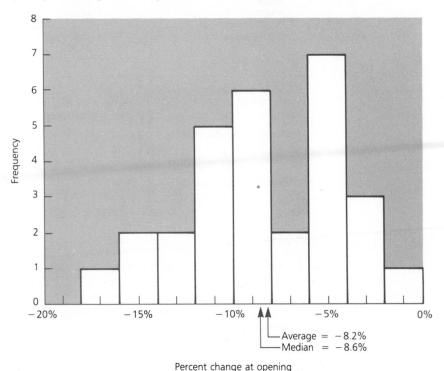

Percent change at opening

TABLE 4.1.2   Stocks Ranked by Loss at Opening, Stock Market Crash of 1987

Firm	Change in Value (sorted)	Rank
General Motors	−0.9%	1
Navistar	−2.1	2
Woolworth	−3.0	3
Procter & Gamble	−3.5	4
Boeing	−4.0	5
Chevron	−4.0	6
Union Carbide	−4.1	7
United Technologies	−4.4	8
Bethlehem Steel	−4.5	9
USX	−5.1	10
AT&T	−5.4	11
Primerica	−6.8	12
McDonald's	−7.2	13
Du Pont	−8.6	14
Exxon	−8.6	15
Minnesota Mining	−8.9	16
Alcoa	−8.9	17
Allied-Signal	−9.3	18
IBM	−9.6	19
Coca-Cola	−10.5	20
Goodyear Tire	−10.9	21
Sears Roebuck	−11.4	22
International Paper	−11.6	23
Merck	−12.0	24
Texaco	−12.3	25
Philip Morris	−12.4	26
Westinghouse	−15.7	27
Kodak	−15.7	28
General Electric	−17.2	29

sents the middle experience of this group of stocks. Table 4.1.2 shows the ordered list; note that Exxon is at the middle, at 15th, since (29 + 1)/2 = 15.

Whenever stocks lose more than a few percentage points of their value, it is noticed. For them to lose as much as 8% at the beginning of the day, just at the start of trading, was clearly an ominous signal. The Dow Jones Industrial Average lost 508 points that day—a record—representing a loss for the day of 22.6%, a tragedy for many people and institutions.[11]

EXAMPLE

Personal Incomes

The distribution of amounts such as incomes of individuals and families (as well as the distribution of sales, expenses, prices, etc.) is often skewed toward high values. This is because such data sets often contain many small values, some moderate values, and a few large and very large values. The usual result is that the average will be larger than the median. This is because the average, by sum-

---

[11]The figure 22.6% was reported in *The Wall Street Journal*, October 20, 1987, p. 1.

FIGURE 4.1.3   A histogram showing the distribution of incomes for 100 random people. This is a skewed distribution, and the average is substantially larger than the median.

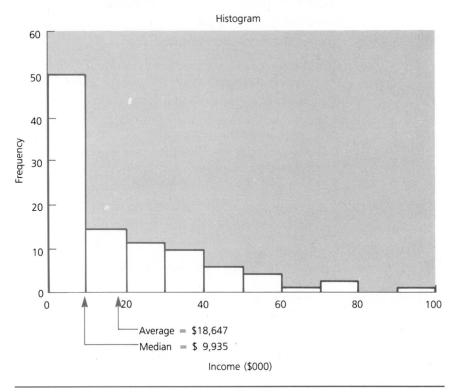

ming all data items, pays more attention to the large values. Consider the incomes of all households in the United States in 1984:[12]

Average household income: $27,464
Median household income: $22,415

The average income is higher than the median because the average has paid more attention to the relatively few very well-off households. Remember that these high incomes are added in when the average is found, but they are merely "high incomes" to the median (which allows these very high incomes to offset the low incomes on a household-by-household basis).

The histogram in Figure 4.1.3 shows how the distribution of incomes might look for a sample of 100 people. It is strongly skewed toward high values, since there are many low-income people (indicated by the high bar at the left) together with some moderate-income and high-income people (the shorter bars in the middle and on the right). The average income of $18,647 is nearly double the

────────────

[12]From *Statistical Abstract of the United States, 1987* (Washington, U.S. Bureau of the Census, 1986), pp. 431, 433.

median income of $9,935. Evidently the median (the halfway point) is low because most people are lower-income here, and the existence of some higher incomes has boosted the average substantially.

EXAMPLE

Stages of Completion of Inventory

Consider a computer manufacturer's inventory of work in progress, consisting of the following stages of production for each unit:

A The basic motherboard (the main circuit board) is produced.
B Sockets are installed on the motherboard.
C Chips are installed in the sockets.
D The resulting populated motherboard is tested.
E The populated motherboard is installed in the system unit.
F The completed system unit is tested.

If you are given a data set consisting of the production stage for each unit in the factory, the univariate ordinal data set might look like this:

$$A, C, E, F, C, C, D, C, A, E, E, \ldots$$

This data set is ordinal since there is a natural ordering for each category, namely, the order in which a unit proceeds through production from beginning to end. You might use a frequency listing for such a data set, which would look something like this:

Stage of Production	Number of Units
A	57
B	38
C	86
D	45
E	119
F	42
Total	387

Since these are ordinal data, you can compute the median but not the average. The median will be found as unit $(1 + 387)/2 = 194$ after units have been placed in order by stage of production. Here's how you might find the median here:

The units at ranks 1 through 57 are in stage A. Thus, the median (at rank 194) is beyond stage A.
The units at ranks 58 $(57 + 1)$ through 95 $(57 + 38)$ are in stage B. Thus, the median is beyond stage B.
The units at ranks 96 $(95 + 1)$ through 181 $(95 + 86)$ are in stage C. Thus, the median is beyond stage C.
The units at ranks 182 $(181 + 1)$ through 226 $(181 + 45)$ are in stage D. Thus, the median is stage D because the median's rank (194) is between ranks 182 and 226.

Thus about half of the units are less finished and half are more finished than units in stage D. Thus, stage D summarizes the middle point, in terms of completion, of all of the units currently in production.

The Mode: A Typical Value Even for Nominal Data

The **mode** is the most common category, the one listed most often in the data set. It is the only summary measure available for nominal qualitative data because unordered categories cannot be summed (as for the average) and cannot be ranked (as for the median). The mode is easily found for ordinal data by ignoring the ordering of the categories and proceeding as if you had a nominal data set with unordered categories.

The mode is also defined for quantitative data (numbers), although it can get a little ambiguous in this case. For quantitative data, the mode may be defined as the value at the highest point of the histogram, perhaps at the midpoint of the highest bar. The ambiguity enters in several ways. There may be two "tallest" bars. Or, even worse, the definition of the mode will depend on how the histogram was constructed; changing the bar width and location will make small (or medium) changes in the shape of the distribution, and the mode can change as a result. The mode is a slightly imprecise general concept when used with quantitative data.

It's easy to find the mode. Looking at either the number of items or at the percentage of items in each category, select the category with the largest number or percentage. If two or more categories tie for first place, you would report all of them as sharing the title of "mode" for that data set.

EXAMPLE   Voting

As votes come in to be counted during an election, they may be thought of as a nominal qualitative data set. Although you may have your own personal preference for the ordering of the candidates, since this is not universally agreed on, you will have to regard the data set as unordered. The list of data might begin as follows:

Smith, Jones, Buttersworth, Smith, Smith, Buttersworth, Smith, . . .

The results of the election could be summarized as follows:

Name	Votes	Percent
Buttersworth	7,175	15.1%
Jones	18,956	39.9
Harvey	502	1.1
Smith	20,817	43.9
Total	47,450	100.0

The mode is clearly Smith, with the most votes (20,817) as well as the largest percentage (43.9%). Note that the mode need not represent more than half (a majority) of the items, although it certainly could in some cases. It just needs to represent more items than any of the other categories.

EXAMPLE   **Quality Control: Controlling Variation in Manufacturing**

One of the important activities involved in creating quality products is the understanding of *variation* in manufacturing processes. Some variations are unavoidable and small enough to be tolerable, and other variations result from a process being "out of control" and producing inferior products. The subject of quality control will be covered in more detail in Chapter 18.

W. Edwards Deming brought quality control to the Japanese in the 1950s. Some of his methods may be summarized as follows:

> The heart of Deming's method for achieving high quality is statistical. Every process, whether it be on the factory floor or in the office, has variations from the ideal. Deming shows clients a systematic method for measuring these variations, finding out what causes them, reducing them, and so steadily improving the process and thereby the product.[13]

Gathering data and then analyzing them is a key component of good quality control. Consider a factory that has recorded the cause of failure each time an item emerges that is not of acceptable quality:

Cause of Problem	Number of Cases
Solder joint	37
Plastic case	86
Power supply	194
Dirt	8
Shock (was dropped)	1

The mode for this data set is clearly "power supply," since this cause accounted for more quality problems than any other.

The mode helps you focus on the most important category (in terms of its rate of occurrence). There would be little need to create a campaign to educate workers in cleanliness or the need to avoid dropping the boxes, since these causes were responsible for only a few of the problems. The mode, on the other hand, is the best candidate for immediate attention.

In this case, the firm would try to identify the problem with the power supplies and then take appropriate action. Perhaps it is the wrong power supply for the product, and one with larger capacity is needed. Or perhaps a more reliable supplier should be found. In any case, the mode has helped pinpoint the trouble.

---

[13]"The Curmudgeon Who Talks Tough on Quality," *Fortune*, June 25, 1984, p. 119.

EXAMPLE

Inventory Completion Stages Revisited

Reconsider the earlier example of a computer manufacturer's inventory of work in progress. The data set is:

Stage of Production	Number of Units
A	57
B	38
C	86
D	45
E	119
F	42
Total	387

The median was found to be at stage D of production, since this stage divides the more primitive half of the items in production from the more advanced half. However, the median is not the mode in this case (although the median and the mode might well be the same in other examples).

The mode here is clearly stage E, with 119 units, more than any other stage. Management may well wish to be aware of the mode in a case like this, because if a troublesome "bottleneck" were to develop in the production process, it would likely show up as the mode.

In this example, stage E represents the installation of the motherboard in the system unit. It could be the natural result of a large order that has now reached this stage. On the other hand, those responsible for installation may be having trouble (perhaps they are understaffed or have had excessive absences), causing items to pile up at stage E. In a case like this, management attention and action may be warranted.

Which Summary Should You Use?

Given these three summaries (average, median, and mode), which one should be used in a given circumstance? There are two kinds of answers. The first depends on which ones can be computed, and the second depends on which ones are most useful.

The mode can be computed for any univariate data set (although it does suffer from some ambiguity with quantitative data). However, the average can be computed only from quantitative data (meaningful numbers), and the median can be computed for anything except nominal data (unordered categories). Thus, sometimes your choices are restricted, and, in the case of nominal data, you have no choice at all and can only use the mode. Here is a guide to which summaries may be used with each type of data:

	Quantitative	Ordinal	Nominal
Average	Yes		
Median	Yes	Yes	
Mode	Yes	Yes	Yes

In the case of quantitative data, where all three summaries can be computed, how are they different? For a normal distribution, there is very little difference among the measures since each is trying to find the well-defined middle of that bell-shaped distribution, as illustrated in Figure 4.1.4. However, with skewed data, there can be noticeable differences among them (as we noted earlier for the average and median). Figure 4.1.5 contrasts these summaries for skewed data.

The average should be used when the data set is (at least approximately) normally distributed since it is known to be the most efficient in this case. The average should also be seriously considered in other cases where the need to preserve or forecast total amounts is important, since the other summaries do not do this as well.

The median can be a good summary for skewed distributions since it is not "distracted" by a few very large data items. It therefore summarizes most of the data better than the average does in cases of extreme skewness. The median is also useful when outliers are present because of its ability to resist their effects. The median is useful with ordinal data (ordered categories)

FIGURE 4.1.4 The average, median, and mode are identical in the case of a perfect normal distribution. With the randomness of real data, they would be approximately but not exactly equal.

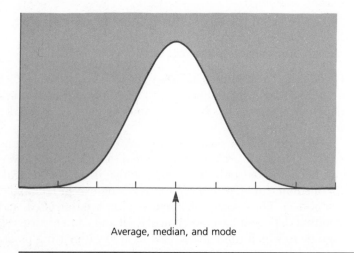

Average, median, and mode

FIGURE 4.1.5   The average, median, and mode are different in the case of a skewed distribution. The mode corresponds to the highest part of the distribution. The median has half of the area on each side. The average is where the distribution would balance, as if on a seesaw.

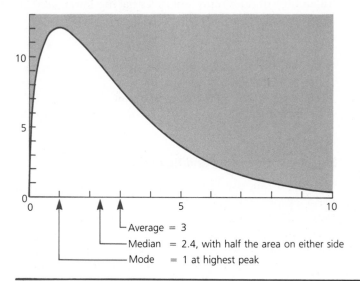

Average = 3
Median = 2.4, with half the area on either side
Mode = 1 at highest peak

although the mode should be considered also, depending on the questions to be addressed.

The mode must be used with nominal data (unordered categories) since the others cannot be computed. It is also useful with ordinal data (ordered categories) when the most represented category is important.

There are many more summaries than these three. One promising kind of estimator is the *biweight,* a "robust" estimator, which manages to combine the best features of the average and the median.[14] It is a fairly efficient choice when the data set is normally distributed but shares the ability of the median to resist the effects of outliers.

■ 4.2 What Percentile Is It?

Percentiles are summary measures expressing ranks as percentages from 0% to 100% rather than from 1 to n so that the 0th percentile is the smallest number, the 100th percentile is the largest, the 50th percentile is the median, and so on. Percentiles are available for quantitative and ordinal data.

---

[14]Further details about robust estimators may be found in D.C. Hoaglin, F. Mosteller, and J.W. Tukey, *Understanding Robust and Exploratory Data Analysis* (New York: Wiley, 1983).

Note that a percentile is a number, in the same units as the data set, at a given rank. For example, the 60th percentile of sales performance might be $385,062 (a dollar amount, like the items in the data set, *not* a percentage). This 60th percentile of $385,062 might represent Mary's performance, with about 60% of sales representatives having lower sales and about 40% having higher sales.

Percentiles are used in two ways:

1 To indicate the data value at a given percentage (as in "the 10th percentile is $156,293").
2 To indicate the percentage ranking of a given data value (as in "John's performance, $296,994, was in the 55th percentile").

Extremes, Quartiles, and Box Plots

One important use of percentiles is as landmark summary values. You can use a few percentiles to summarize important features of the entire distribution. You have already seen the median, which is the 50th percentile since it is ranked halfway between the smallest and largest. The **extremes**, the *smallest* and *largest* values, are often interesting. These are the 0th and 100th percentiles, respectively. To complete a small set of landmark summaries, you could also use the **quartiles**, defined as the 25th and 75th percentiles.

It may come as a surprise to learn that statisticians cannot agree on exactly what a quartile is; they can be computed in many different ways. The idea is clear: Quartiles are the data values ranked one fourth of the way in from the smallest and largest values; however, there is ambiguity as to exactly how to find them. John Tukey, who created exploratory data analysis, defines quartiles as follows:[15]

1 Find the median rank, $(1 + n)/2$, and discard any fraction. For example, with $n = 13$, use $(1 + 13)/2 = 7$. However, with $n = 24$, you would drop the decimal part of $(1 + 24)/2 = 12.5$ and use 12.
2 Add 1 to this, and divide by 2. This gives the *rank of the lower quartile*. For example, with $n = 13$, you find $(1 + 7)/2 = 4$. With $n = 24$, you find $(1 + 12)/2 = 6.5$, which tells you to average the data values with ranks 6 and 7.
3 Subtract this rank from $(n + 1)$. This gives the *rank of the upper quartile*. For example, with $n = 13$, you have $(13 + 1) - 4 = 10$. With $n = 24$, you have $(1 + 24) - 6.5 = 18.5$, which tells you to average the data values with ranks 18 and 19.

---

[15]J.W. Tukey, *Exploratory Data Analysis* (Reading, Mass.: Addison-Wesley, 1977). Tukey refers to quartiles as *hinges* and defines them on page 33.

The quartiles themselves may then be found based on these ranks. A general formula for the ranks of the quartiles, expressing the steps just given, may be written as follows:

■ Ranks for the Quartiles

$$\text{Rank of lower quartile} = \frac{1 + \text{int}[(1 + n)/2]}{2}$$

$$\text{Rank of upper quartile} = n + 1 - \text{Rank of lower quartile}$$

where *int* refers to the integer part function, which discards any decimal portion.

The **five-number summary** is defined as the following set of five landmark summaries: smallest, lower quartile, median, upper quartile, and largest.

■ The Five-Number Summary

The *smallest data value* (the 0th percentile).
The *lower quartile* (the 25th percentile, 1/4 of the way in from the smallest).
The *median* (the 50th percentile, in the middle).
The *upper quartile* (the 75th percentile, 3/4 of the way in from the smallest and 1/4 of the way in from the largest).
The *largest data value* (the 100th percentile).

These five numbers taken together give a clear look at many features of the unprocessed data. The two extremes indicate the range spanned by the data, the median indicates the center, the two quartiles indicate the edges of the "middle half of the data," and the position of the median between the quartiles gives a rough indication of skewness or symmetry.

The **box plot** is a picture of the five-number summary, as shown in Figure 4.2.1. The box plot serves the same purpose as a histogram, namely, to provide a visual impression of the distribution, but it does this in a different way. Box plots show less detail and are therefore more useful for seeing the big picture and comparing several groups of numbers without the distraction of every detail of each group. The histogram is still preferable for a more detailed look at the shape of the distribution.

You may want the box plot to show extreme outliers individually. For this purpose, **outliers** are defined as those data points (if any) that are far out with respect to the values near the middle of the data set. Specifically, large data values will be declared outliers if they are bigger than

Upper quartile + 1.5 × (Upper quartile − Lower quartile)

FIGURE 4.2.1   A box plot displays the five-number summary for a univariate data set, giving a quick impression of the distribution.

Small data values will be declared outliers if they are smaller than

Lower quartile − 1.5 × (Upper quartile − Lower quartile)

This definition of outliers is due to Tukey.[16] In addition to displaying and labeling outliers, you may also label the most extreme cases that are *not* outliers since these are also interesting. The **detailed box plot** displays the outliers and labels them along with the most extreme observations that are not outliers.

EXAMPLE   **International Profit Margins**

Consider the 1986 profit margins of major Swedish firms, sorted and ranked, with the five-number summary values indicated, as shown in Table 4.2.1. There are $n = 47$ firms listed; hence, the median has rank $(1 + 47)/2 = 24$. The lower quartile has rank $(1 + 24)/2 = 12.5$, so the lower quartile will average the profit margins at ranks 12 and 13. The upper quartile has rank $47 + 1 − 12.5 = 35.5$, so the upper quartile will average the profit margins at ranks 35 and 36. The five-number summary of profit margin for these 47 Swedish firms is therefore:

Smallest	0.1 %
Lower quartile	1.65
Median	3.4
Upper quartile	5.9
Largest	19.6

[16]J. W. Tukey, *Exploratory Data Analysis*, p. 44. Also, see Chapter 3 of Hoaglin et al., *Understanding Robust and Exploratory Data Analysis*.

TABLE 4.2.1   Profit Margins of Swedish Firms

Firm	Profit Margin	Rank	Five-Number Summary
Carnegie Group	0.1%	1	Smallest = 0.1%
Vattenfall	0.3	2	
Svenska Mejeriernas Riks.	0.6	3	
ABV group	0.6	4	
Swedyards	0.7	5	
KF	0.9	6	
SIAB	1.0	7	
Astra	1.1	8	
Flakt	1.1	9	
Euroc	1.2	10	
Nordstjernan	1.5	11	
Swedbank	1.6	12	Lower quartile = 1.65%
ASSAB	1.7	13	
PLM	2.0	14	
Pripps	2.1	15	
Sorda Skogsagarna	2.1	16	
Ericsson	2.1	17	
Marabou	2.5	18	
Alfa-Laval	2.8	19	
SKF Group	2.9	20	
Skanska	3.0	21	
Svenska Tandsticks	3.2	22	
Nobel Industries Sweden	3.3	23	
Kanthal Hoganas	3.4	24	Median = 3.4%
Volvo Group	3.5	25	
Atlas Copco	3.5	26	
Electrolux	3.6	27	
Esselte	3.6	28	
Nordbanken	4.5	29	
Procordia	4.7	30	
ASEA	4.8	31	
Mo och Domsjo	4.9	32	
Saab-Scania Group	5.4	33	
Sydkraft	5.7	34	
Papyrus	5.9	35	
Stora Kopparbergs Bergslags	5.9	36	Upper quartile = 5.9%
Sandvik	6.4	37	
Svenska Cellulosa	7.0	38	
AGA	7.0	39	
Scandinavian Airline System	7.0	40	
Investment AB Cardo	8.1	41	
Investment AB Beijer	9.2	42	
Svenska Handelbanken	9.6	43	
Incentive	10.2	44	
Forsta SparBanken	11.2	45	
Skandinaviska Enskilda Banken*	12.4	46	
Iggesunds Bruk*	19.6	47	Largest = 19.6%

*This is an outlier.

Data are from "International Corporate Scoreboard," *Business Week,* July 20, 1987, pp. 139–76.

Are there any outliers? If we compute using the quartiles, at the high end any profit margin larger than $5.9 + 1.5 \times (5.9 - 1.65) = 12.275\%$ will be an outlier. Thus, the two largest data values (Skandinaviska Enskilda Banken and Iggesunds Bruk) are outliers. At the low end, any profit margin smaller than

FIGURE 4.2.2   Box plots for profit margins of Swedish firms. Both display the five-number summary, but the detailed plot provides further important information about outliers (and the largest value that is not an outlier). In this example, outliers represent firms with exceptionally strong profit margins.

1.65 − 1.5 × (5.9 − 1.65) = −4.725% would be an outlier. Since the smallest profit margin is 0.1%, there are no outliers at the low end of the distribution.

Box plots for these 47 Swedish firms are displayed in Figure 4.2.2. Although ordinarily you would use only one of the two shown (probably the one with the extra detail), we show both here for comparison.

One of the strengths of box plots is their ability to help you concentrate on the important overall features of several data sets at once, without being overwhelmed by the details. Consider the 1986 profit margins of major firms in Britain, Germany, and Japan as well as Sweden.[17] This consists of four individual data sets, a univariate data set (a group of numbers) for each of the four countries. Thus, there is a five-number summary and, hence, a box plot for each country.

By placing box plots side by side on the same scale in Figure 4.2.3, we facilitate the comparison of typical profit margins from one country to another.[18]

---

[17]Data are from "International Corporate Scoreboard," *Business Week*, July 20, 1987, pp. 139–76.

[18]It is common to position box plots vertically, as has been done here, although it is also correct to position them horizontally.

FIGURE 4.2.3　Box plots for profit margins of major international firms, arranged on the same scale so that you may easily compare one country to another. The top figure gives details about the outliers and extremes, and the bottom figure shows only the five-number summaries.

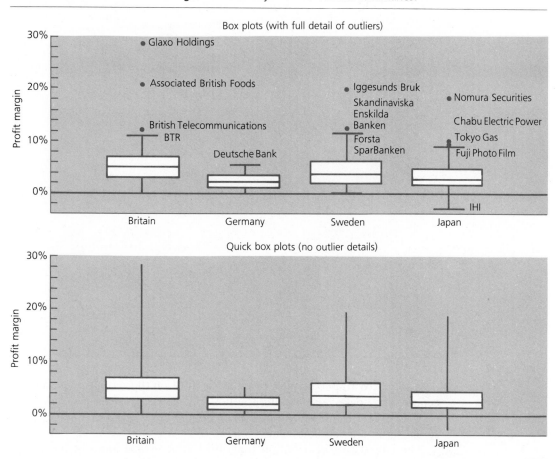

Note in the top figure how helpful it is to have exceptional firms labeled, compared to the bottom figure, which displays only the five-number summaries.

Which kind of box plot is the best? A cost-benefit analysis suggests balancing the extra time and energy involved in making the detailed box plots (showing the individual outliers) against their clear benefits in terms of added information. A good strategy might be to begin by quickly completing displays of the five-number summaries and then decide whether the additional detail is worth the time and trouble. Naturally, when the computer is doing the work, you would (nearly) always prefer the detailed display.

The Cumulative Distribution Function Displays the Percentiles

The **cumulative distribution function** is a plot of the data specifically designed to display the percentiles by plotting the percentages against the

FIGURE 4.2.4   The cumulative distribution function for the data set 1, 4, 3, 7, 3. Note the jump of size $1/n = 20\%$ at each data value, and the double jump at 3 (since there are two such data values).

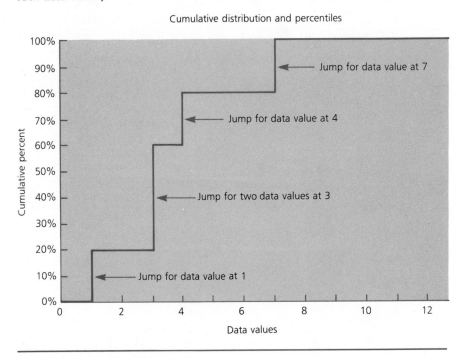

Cumulative distribution and percentiles

data values. With percentages from 0% to 100% on the vertical axis and percentiles (i.e., data values) along the horizontal axis, it is easy to find either (1) the percentile value for a given percentage, or (2) the percentage corresponding to a given data value.

The cumulative distribution function has a vertical jump of height $1/n$ at each of the n data values and continues horizontally between data points. Figure 4.2.4 shows the cumulative distribution function for a small data set consisting of $n = 5$ data values (1, 4, 3, 7, 3), with one of them (3) occurring twice.

If you are given a number and wish to find its percentile ranking, proceed as follows:

■ **Finding the Percentile Ranking for a Given Number**

1 Find the data value along the horizontal axis in the cumulative distribution function.
2 Move vertically up to the cumulative distribution function. If you hit a vertical portion, move halfway up.
3 Move horizontally to the left and read the percentile ranking.

FIGURE 4.2.5 The data value 4 represents the 70th percentile. Move vertically up from 4. Since you hit a vertical region, move halfway up. Then move across to read the answer 70%.

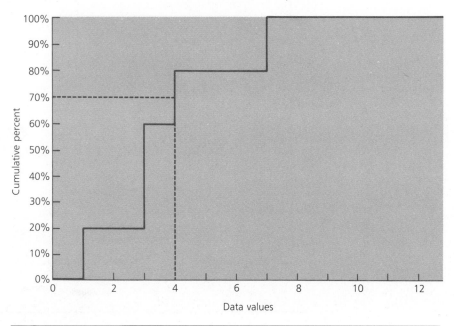

In this example, the number 4 is the 70th percentile, since its percentile ranking is halfway between 60% and 80%, as shown in Figure 4.2.5.

If you are given a percentage and wish to find the corresponding percentile, proceed as follows:

> ■ **Finding the Percentile for a Given Percentage**
>
> **1** Find the percentage along the vertical axis in the cumulative distribution function.
> **2** Move right horizontally to the cumulative distribution function. If you hit a horizontal portion, move halfway across it.
> **3** Move down and read the percentile on the data axis.

In this example, the 44th percentile is 3, as shown in Figure 4.2.6.

EXAMPLE   **Business Failures**

Consider business failures per million people, by state, for the United States, sorted in order from least to most failures per capita and shown in Table 4.2.3. The cumulative distribution function for this data set is displayed in Figure 4.2.7.

FIGURE 4.2.6   To find the 44th percentile, move across to the right from 44% and then down to read the answer, 3.

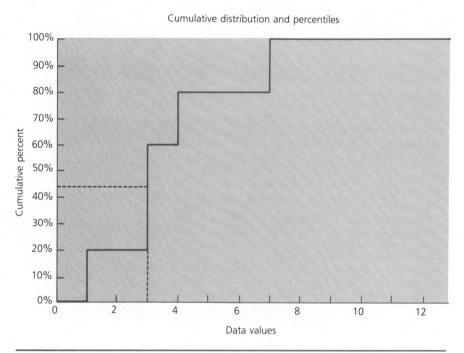

Cumulative distribution and percentiles

You can see that the experience of most states (say, from 10% through 90%) was around 50 to 100 failures per million population, that a few lucky states had very low failure rates, and that a few others had exceptionally high failure rates.

Figure 4.2.8 shows how to find percentiles from the cumulative distribution function. The 50th percentile is 63.4 (for Illinois, as may be seen from the data table), corresponding to the median value of 63.4 business failures per million people. The 90th percentile is 102.2 (for Utah), and the 95th percentile is 194.3 (for the state of Washington).

You actually have the choice of three different graphs to display a group of numbers: the histogram, the box plot, and the cumulative distribution function. Each technique displays the same information (the data values) in a different way. For this example of business failures, all three representations are displayed in Figure 4.2.9, arranged vertically so that the relationships are clear.

Regions of high data concentration (i.e., lots of data) correspond to high peaks of the histogram and to *steepness* in the cumulative distribution. Usually, a high concentration of data is found near the middle, as is the case here. Regions of low data concentration (i.e., just a few data values) correspond to low histogram bars and to *flatness* in the cumulative distribution.

TABLE 4.2.3   Business Failures by State, Sorted

State	Business Failures per Million People	State	Business Failures per Million People
Wyoming	4.1	Pennsylvania	67.3
New Hampshire	11.7	Maine	68.1
South Carolina	12.9	Oklahoma	69.6
Arizona	32.6	Virginia	69.7
Missouri	35.6	West Virginia	69.9
Rhode Island	37.7	New Jersey	70.2
Alabama	37.8	Texas	70.6
District of Columbia	37.9	Wisconsin	74.5
Massachusetts	39.1	Colorado	75.3
Indiana	39.9	North Dakota	77.3
Maryland	41.6	Kansas	78.4
New York	46.8	Delaware	80.4
Louisiana	47.7	Montana	80.5
Vermont	48.5	Minnesota	83.4
Georgia	50.9	Nebraska	84.3
North Carolina	51.2	Iowa	86.5
Florida	54.2	Michigan	94.1
Alaska	55.2	Nevada	96.9
Connecticut	56.8	South Dakota	97.1
New Mexico	60.0	Utah	102.2
Arkansas	60.2	California	117.7
Kentucky	60.8	Tennessee	130.4
Ohio	61.2	Washington	194.3
Idaho	61.6	Hawaii	213.9
Mississippi	63.1	Oregon	307.9
Illinois	63.4		

Data are from Table 897, "Industrial and Commercial Failures, Number and Liabilities, by States" for 1981, Bureau of the Census, *Statistical Abstract of the United States, 1984* (Washington, 1983), p. 535.

The box plot shows you the five-number summary, which may be read off from the cumulative distribution as the smallest (at 0%), lower quartile (at 25%), median (at 50%), upper quartile (75%), and largest (at 100%).

Note that the cumulative distribution function is the only display here that actually shows all of the data. The histogram has lost information because it displays only the number of states within each group (for example, from 50 to 100 failures). The box plot also has lost information because it preserves only the five landmark summaries. Only the cumulative distribution shows enough information to let you reconstruct each number from the original data set.

4.3 End-of-Chapter Materials

Summary

Summarization is using one or more selected or computed values to represent the data set. To completely summarize, you would first describe the basic structure of most of the data and then list any exceptions or outliers.

FIGURE 4.2.7 Cumulative distribution function for business failures per million people, by state, for 1981.

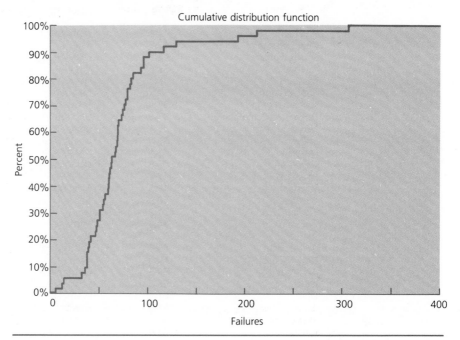

FIGURE 4.2.8 Cumulative distribution function for business failures, with 50th, 90th, and 95th percentiles indicated.

FIGURE 4.2.9   Three graphs of the business failures data: histogram, box plot, and cumulative distribution. Note that the cumulative distribution function is steepest in regions of high concentration of data.

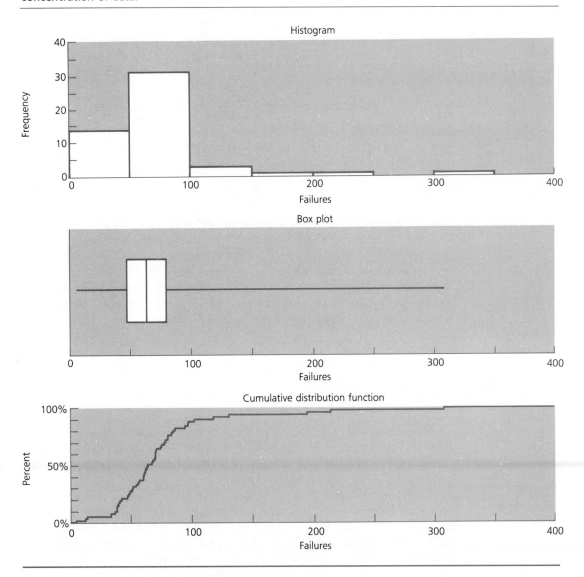

The **average** (also called the **mean**) is the most common method for finding a typical value for a list of numbers, found by adding all the values and then dividing by the number of items. Although the terms *average* and *mean* can be used interchangeably, in this text we will speak of *sample average* and *population mean*. The formulas for these are as follows:

$$\text{Sample average} = \frac{\text{Sum of data items}}{\text{Number of data items}}$$

$$\overline{X} = \frac{X_1 + X_2 + \cdots + X_n}{n}$$

$$= \frac{1}{n} \sum_{i=1}^{n} X_i$$

$$\text{Population mean} = \frac{\text{Sum of population values}}{\text{Number of population items}}$$

$$\mu = \frac{X_1 + X_2 + \cdots + X_N}{N}$$

$$= \frac{1}{N} \sum_{i=1}^{N} X_i$$

The average spreads the total equally among all of the cases and is most useful when there are no extreme outliers and total amounts are relevant. The data set must be quantitative in order for the average to be computed.

The **weighted average** is like the average, except that it allows you to give a different importance, or weight, to each data item. This extends the average to the case in which some data values are more important than others and need to be counted more heavily. The formula is:

$$\text{Weighted average} = \text{Sum of (weight times data item)}$$

$$= w_1 X_1 + w_2 X_2 + \cdots + w_n X_n$$

$$= \sum_{i=1}^{n} w_i X_i$$

The weights usually add up to 1 (you might divide them by their sum if they do not). The weighted average can be computed only for quantitative data.

The **median** is the *middle value;* half of the data items are larger, and half are smaller. **Ranks** associate the numbers $1, 2, 3, \ldots, n$ with the data values so that the smallest has rank 1, the next to smallest has rank 2, and so forth up to the largest, which has rank n. The rank of the median is $(1 + n)/2$, indicating how many cases to count in from the smallest (or largest) in order to find the median data value; if this rank contains a decimal portion (for example, 13.5 for $n = 26$), then average the two data values at either side of this value (for example, the values at ranks 13 and 14). The median may be computed for either quantitative data or ordinal data (ordered categories).

The median summarizes the "typical" value in a different way than the average; however, the two values will be similar when the data distribution is symmetric, as is the normal distribution. For a skewed distribution or in the presence of outliers, the average and median can give very different summaries.

The **mode** is the most common category, the one listed most often in the data set. It may be computed for any data set: quantitative, ordinal, or nominal (unordered categories), and it is the only summary available for nominal data. In the case of quantitative data, the mode is often defined as the midpoint of the tallest histogram bar; however, this can be ambiguous since it can vary depending on the choice of scale for the histogram.

To decide which of these summaries to use, proceed as follows. If the data set is *nominal,* then only the mode is available. If the data set is *ordinal,* then either the mode or the median can be used; the mode expresses the most popular category, and the median finds the central category with respect to the ordering. For *quantitative* data, all three methods may be used. For a normal distribution, all three methods give similar answers, and the average is best. For a skewed distribution, all three methods usually give different answers; the median is generally a good summary in this case since it is less sensitive to the extreme values in the longer tail of the distribution. However, if totals are important, the average would be preferred.

Percentiles are summary measures expressing ranks as percentages from 0% to 100% rather than from 1 to n; the 0th percentile is the smallest number, the 100th percentile is the largest, the 50th percentile is the median, and so on. Note that a percentile is a number in the same units as the data set (such as dollars, gallons, etc.). Percentiles can be used either to find the data value at a given percentage ranking or to find the percentage ranking of a given value. The **extremes**, the *smallest* and *largest* values, are often interesting. The **quartiles** are the 25th and 75th percentiles, whose ranks are determined as follows:

$$\text{Rank of lower quartile} = \frac{1 + \text{int}[(1 + n)/2]}{2}$$

$$\text{Rank of upper quartile} = n + 1 - \text{Rank of lower quartile}$$

where *int* refers to the integer part function, which discards any decimal portion.

The **five-number summary** gives special landmark summaries of a data set: the smallest, lower quartile, median, upper quartile, and largest. The **box plot** displays the five-number summary as a graph. **Outliers** are defined as those data points (if any) that are far out with respect to the data values near the middle of the data set. A **detailed box plot** displays the outliers and labels them separately along with the most extreme observations that are not outliers. Several data sets measured in the same units may be compared by placing their box plots alongside one another on the same scale.

The **cumulative distribution function** is a plot of the data specifically designed to display the percentiles by plotting the percentages against the data values. This graph has a jump of height $1/n$ at each data value. Given a percentage, the percentile may be found by reading across and then down. Given a number, the percentile ranking (percentage) may be found by reading up and then across. Thus, the cumulative distribution function displays the percentiles and helps you compute them. It is the only display that "archives" the data by preserving enough information for you to reconstruct the data values. The cumulative distribution function is steep in regions of high data concentration (i.e., where histogram bars are tall).

Key Words

summarization 71

average 72

mean 72

weighted average 75

median 80

rank 80

mode 87

percentile 91

extremes 92

quartiles 92

five-number summary 93

box plot 93

outlier 93

detailed box plot 94

cumulative distribution function 97

Questions

1 What is summarization of a data set? Why is it important?

2 List and briefly describe the different methods for summarizing a data set.

3 How should you deal with exceptions when summarizing a set of data?

4 What is meant by a typical value for a list of numbers? Name three different ways of finding one.

5 What is the average? Interpret it in terms of the total of all values in the data set.

6 What is a weighted average? When should it be used instead of a simple average?

7 What is the median? How can it be found from its rank?

8 How do you find the median for a data set:
   a. With an odd number of values?
   b. With an even number of values?

9 What is the mode?

10 How do you usually define the mode for a quantitative data set? Why is this definition ambiguous?

11 Which summary measure(s) may be used on:
   a. Nominal data?
   b. Ordinal data?
   c. Quantitative data?

12 Which summary measure is best for:
   a. A normal distribution?
   b. Projecting total amounts?
   c. A skewed distribution when totals are not important?

13 What is a percentile? In particular, is it a percentage (e.g., 23%), or is it specified in the same units as the data (e.g., $35.62)?

14 Name two ways in which percentiles are used.

15 What are the quartiles?

16 What is the five-number summary?

17 What is a box plot? What additional detail is often included in a box plot?

18 What is an outlier? How do you decide if a data point is an outlier or not?

19 Consider the cumulative distribution function:
  a. What is it?
  b. How is it drawn?
  c. What is it used for?
  d. How is it related to the histogram and box plot?

Problems

  1 Consider the quality of cars, as measured by the number of cars requiring extra work after assembly, in each day's production for 15 days:

$$30, 34, 9, 14, 28, 9, 23, 0, 5, 23, 25, 7, 0, 3, 24$$

  a. Find the average number of defects per day.
  b. Find the median number of defects per day.
  c. Draw a histogram of the data.
  d. Find the mode number of defects per day for your histogram in part c.
  e. Find the quartiles.
  f. Find the extremes (the smallest and largest).
  g. Draw a quick box plot of the data.
  h. Draw a cumulative distribution function of the data.
  i. Find the 90th percentile for this data set.
  j. Find the percentile ranking for the next day's value of 29 defects.
  2 Here is a list of the amounts that your regular customers spent on your products last month:

Customer	Sales ($000)
Consolidated, Inc.	$142
International, Ltd.	23
Business Corp.	41
Computer Corp.	10
Information Corp.	7
Associated, Inc.	93
Structural, Inc.	17
Communications Co.	174
Technologies, Inc.	420
Complexity, Ltd.	13

  a. Find the average sales per regular customer.
  b. Find the median and quartiles.
  c. Draw the quick box plot.
  d. Find the outliers, if any.
  e. Draw the detailed box plot.
  f. Comment briefly on the differences between these two box plots.
  g. If you could expand your list of regular customers to include 3 more, and if their purchasing patterns were like those of these firms, what would you expect total monthly sales for all 13 regular customers to be?
  h. Write a paragraph telling what you have learned about these customers using these statistical methods.

TABLE 4.3.1   Research and Development in the Food and Beverage Industry

Firm	R&D Expense ($ millions)	Firm	R&D Expense ($ millions)
Amalgamated Sugar	$ 1.1	Kellogg	38.2
American Maize	2.3	Kraft	66.7
Archer Daniels Midland	5.9	McCormick	6.6
Borden	22.7	PepsiCo	82.0
CPC International	45.4	Pillsbury	41.4
Campbell Soup	42.2	Pioneer Hi-Bred	
Coors	23.4	International	45.6
DEKALB	22.8	Quaker Oats	35.1
General Mills	41.7	Ralston Purina	51.4
Golden Valley		Shaklee	4.0
Microwave Foods	0.7	U.S. Sugar	2.0
Hershey Foods	13.2	Universal Foods	10.5
Hormel	3.9		
International			
Multifoods	1.7		

Data are from "R&D Scoreboard," *Business Week*, June 22, 1987, p. 147.

3 Consider the amounts spent on research and development in the food and beverage industry, as shown in Table 4.3.1.

a. Draw a histogram of this data set, and briefly describe the shape of the distribution.

b. Find the R&D expense for the average firm.

c. Find the median R&D expense.

d. Compare the average and median; in particular, which is larger? Is this what you would expect for a distribution with this shape?

e. Draw the cumulative distribution function.

f. Your firm has a strategic plan that includes moving into the high-tech food market. The business plan indicates that the R&D budget will soon reach $5,000,000. What percentile would this budget represent, with respect to this data set?

g. Your firm's strategic plan indicates that the R&D budget will reach the 40th percentile in the following year. Ignoring inflation, find the required budget level.

4 The *beta* of a firm's stock indicates the degree to which changes in stock price track changes in the stock market as a whole and is interpreted as the *market risk* of the portfolio. A beta of 1.0 indicates that, on average, the stock rises (or falls) the same percentage as does the market. A beta of 2.0 indicates a stock that rises or falls at twice the percentage of the market. The beta of a stock portfolio is the weighted average of the betas of the individual stock securities, weighted by the current market values (market value is share price times number of shares). Consider the following portfolio:

100 shares Speculative Computer at $35 per share, beta = 2.4
200 shares Conservative Industries at $88 per share, beta = 0.6
150 shares Dependable Conglomerate at $53 per share, beta = 1.2

a. Find the beta of this portfolio.

b. To decrease the risk of the portfolio, you have decided to sell all shares of Speculative Computer and use the money to buy as many shares of Dependable Conglomerate as you can.[19] Describe the new portfolio, find its beta, and verify that the market risk has indeed decreased.

5 Your firm has the following securities outstanding: common stock (market value $4,500,000; investors demand 17% annual rate of return), preferred stock (market value $1,700,000; current annual yield is 13%), and 20-year bonds (market value $2,200,000; current annual yield is 11%). Find your cost of capital.

6 A survey of 613 representative people within your current area indicates that they plan to spend a total of $2,135 on your products next year. You are considering expansion to a new city with 2.1 million people.

a. Find the average expenditure per person based on the survey of your current area.

b. If you can gain the same market presence in the new city that you have in your current area, what annual sales level do you expect?

c. If you expect to gain in the new city only 60% of the market presence in your current area, what annual sales level do you expect?

7 You have begun a quality improvement campaign in your paper mill, and, as a result, lots of pieces of paper come to your desk. Each one describes a recent problem with customers according to the following codes: A = paper unavailable, B = paper too thick, C = paper too thin, D = paper width too uneven, E = paper color not correct, F = paper edges too rough. Here are the results:

A, A, E, A, A, A, B, A, A, A, B, A, B, F, F, A, A, A, A, A, B, A, A, A, A, C, D, F, A, A, E, A, C, A, A, A, F, F

a. Summarize this data set by finding the percentage that each problem represents out of all problems.

b. Summarize this data set by finding the mode.

c. Write a brief (one-paragraph) memo to management recommending the most effective action to improve the situation.

d. Could the median or average be computed here? Why or why not?

8 Consider the loan fees charged for granting home mortgages, as shown in Table 4.3.2. These are given as a percentage of the loan amount and are one-time fees paid when the loan is closed.

TABLE 4.3.2   Home Mortgage Loan Fees

Institution	Loan Fee
Alaska USA FCU	2.00 %
Amco Mortgage	1.95
American Builders	2.00
ARCS Mortgage	2.00
Bay Mortgage	2.00
Bay Mortgage East	2.00
Benjamin Franklin	1.50
Cambelco Mortgage	2.00
Cascade Pacific Mortgage	2.00
Cascade S & L	1.50
Center Mortgage	2.50
Centrust Mortgage	1.125
Chase Manhattan	2.00

From "How the Summer Rates," *Seattle Times,* July 3, 1988, p. D1.

[19]You may assume that it's OK to trade any number of shares. For now, please ignore real-life problems with "odd lots" of less than 100 shares.

a. Find the average loan fee.

b. Find the median loan fee.

c. Find the mode.

d. Which summary is more useful as a description of the "typical" loan fee, the average or mode? Why?

9 A mail-order sales company sent its new catalog initially to a representative sample of 10,000 people from its mailing list and received orders totaling $36,851.

a. Find the average dollar amount ordered per person in this initial mailing.

b. What total dollar amount in orders should the company expect when the catalog is sent to everyone on the mailing list of 563,000 people?

c. From the sample of 10,000 people generating $36,851 in orders, only 973 people actually placed an order. Find the average dollar amount ordered per person who placed an order.

d. Given the information in part c, how many orders should the company expect when the catalog is sent to everyone on the mailing list of 563,000 people?

10 Consider the strength of cotton yarn used in a weaving factory, in pounds of force at breakage, measured from a sample of yarn from the supplies room:

117, 135, 94, 79, 90, 85, 173, 102, 78, 85, 100, 205, 93, 93, 177, 148, 107

a. Find the average breaking strength.

b. Find the median breaking strength.

c. Draw a histogram indicating the average and median values, and briefly comment on their relationship. Are they the same? Why or why not?

d. Draw a cumulative distribution.

e. Find the 10th and the 90th percentiles.

f. Management would like its supplies to provide a breakage value of 100 pounds or more at least 90% of the time. Based on this data set, do these supplies qualify? In particular, which percentile will you compare to?

11 For the yields of tax-exempt bonds (Problem 1 in Chapter 3):

a. Find the average yield.

b. Find the median yield.

c. Find the quartiles.

d. Find the five-number summary.

e. Draw a box plot of these yields.

12 Using the data from Problem 2 of Chapter 3, find the average and median to summarize the typical size of the market response to stock buy-back announcements.

13 Using the data from Problem 4 of Chapter 3, for the portfolio investments of Teachers Insurance & Annuity Association in broadcasting companies:

a. Find the average market value for each firm's stock in TIAA's portfolio.

b. Find the median of these market values.

c. Compare the average to the median.

d. Find the five-number summary.

e. Draw a box plot, and comment on the distribution shape. In particular, are there any signs of skewness?

f. Is the relationship between the average and median consistent with the distribution shape? Why or why not?

14 Summarize the price of perfume in major European cities using the average and median, based on the data in Problem 7 of Chapter 3.

15 Use the data set from Problem 10 of Chapter 3 on poor quality in the production of electric motors.

a. Find the average and median to summarize the typical level of problems with quality of production.
b. Remove the two outliers, and recompute the average and median.
c. Compare the average and median values with and without the outliers. In particular, how sensitive is each of these summary measures to the presence of outliers?

Database Exercises

Please refer to the employee database in Appendix A.

1 For the annual salary levels:
  a. Find the average.
  b. Find the median.
  c. Construct a histogram, and give an approximate value for the mode.
  d. Compare these three summary measures. What do they tell you about typical salaries in this administrative division?
2 For the annual salary levels:
  a. Construct a cumulative distribution function.
  b. Find the median, quartiles, and extremes.
  c. Construct a box plot, and comment on its appearance.
  d. Find the 10th percentile and the 90th percentile.
  e. What is the percentile ranking for employee number 6?
3 For the genders:
  a. Summarize by finding the percent of each category.
  b. Find the mode. What does this tell you?
4 For the ages: Answer the parts of Exercise 1.
5 For the ages: Answer the parts of Exercise 2.
6 For the experience variable: Answer the parts of Exercise 1.
7 For the experience variable: Answer the parts of Exercise 2.
8 For the training level: Answer the parts of Exercise 3.

Projects

1 Find a data set consisting of at least 25 numbers relating to a firm or an industry group of interest to you. Summarize the data using all of the techniques you have learned so far that are appropriate to your data. Be sure to use both numerical and graphical methods. Present your results as a two-page report to management, with an executive summary as the first paragraph. (You may find it helpful to use a reducing copy machine to produce graphs that will fit in the report.)
2 Find statistical summaries for two quantitative univariate data sets of your own choosing, related to your work, firm, or industry group. For each data set:
  a. Compute the average, the median, and a mode.
  b. For each of these summaries, explain what it tells you about the data set and the business situation.
  c. Construct a histogram, and indicate these three summary measures on the horizontal axis. Comment on the distribution shape and the relationship between the histogram and the summaries.
  d. Construct the box plot, and comment on the costs and benefits of having details (the histogram) as compared to having a bigger picture (the box plot.)

Variability
Dealing with Diversity

One reason we need statistical analysis is that there is variability in data. If there were no variability, many answers would be obvious, and there would be no need for statistical methods.[1] Following are some situations in which variability is important.

1 Consider the variability of worker productivity. Certainly, the average productivity of workers summarizes a department's overall performance. However, any efforts to improve that productivity would probably have to take into account individual differences among workers. For example, some programs may be aimed at improving all workers, whereas others may specifically target the quickest or slowest people. A measure of variability in productivity would summarize the extent of these individual differences and provide helpful information in your quest for improved performance.

2 The stock market provides a higher return on your money, on average, than do safer securities such as money market funds. However, the stock market is riskier and you can actually *lose* money by investing in stocks. Thus, the average or "expected" return does not tell the whole story. Variability in returns could be summarized for each investment and would indicate the level of risk you would be taking on with any particular investment.

3 You compare your firm's marketing expenditures to those of similar firms in your industry group, and you find that your firm spends less than is typical for this industry. To put your number in perspective, you might wish to take into account the extent of diversity within your industry group. Taking the difference between your firm and the group average and comparing it to a measure of variability for the industry group will indicate whether you are slightly low or are a special exception compared to these other firms. This information would help with strategic planning in setting next year's marketing budget.

---

[1] Some statisticians have commented informally that it is variability that keeps them in business!

Variability may be defined as the extent to which the data values differ from each other. Other terms that have a similar meaning include **diversity, uncertainty, dispersion,** and **spread**. You will see three different ways of summarizing the amount of the variability in a data set, all of which require numerical data:

1 The *standard deviation* is the traditional choice and is the most widely used. It summarizes how far an observation typically is from the average.

2 The *range* is quick and superficial and is of limited use. It summarizes the extent of the entire data set, using the distance from the smallest to the largest data value.

3 The *coefficient of variation* is the traditional choice for a *relative* (as opposed to an *absolute*) variability measure and is used moderately often. It summarizes how far an observation typically is from the average as a percentage of the average value, using the ratio of standard deviation to average.

Finally, you will learn how rescaling the data (for example, converting from Japanese yen to U.S. dollars or from units produced to monetary cost) changes the variability.

■ 5.1 The Standard Deviation: The Traditional Choice

The **standard deviation** is a number that summarizes *how far away from the average* the data values typically are. The standard deviation is a very important concept in statistics since it is the basic tool for summarizing the amount of randomness in a situation. Specifically, it measures the extent of randomness of individuals about their average.

If all numbers are the same, such as the simple data set

$$4, 4, 4, 4, 4, 4, 4, 4, 4, 4$$

the average will be $\overline{X} = 4$ and the standard deviation will be $S = 0$, expressing the fact that this trivial data set shows no variability whatsoever.

In reality, most data sets do have some variability. Each data value will be some distance away from the average, and the standard deviation will summarize the extent of this variability. Consider another simple data set with some variability:

$$7, 2, 1, 5, 5, 7, 2, 1, 7, 3$$

The average value again is $\overline{X} = 4$. The first data value, 7, is at a distance $X_1 - \overline{X} = 7 - 4 = 3$ away from the average. The second data value, 2, is at a distance $X_2 - \overline{X} = 2 - 4 = -2$ away from the average. Table 5.1.1 shows how far each data value is from the average. These distances from the average are called **deviations**, and they indicate how far above the average (if positive) or below the average (if negative) each data value is. The deviations form a data set centered around zero that is much like the original data set, which is centered around the average.

TABLE 5.1.1 Finding the Deviations from the Average

Data Value	Distance from Average $(X_i - \bar{X})$
7	$7 - 4 = 3$
2	$2 - 4 = -2$
1	$1 - 4 = -3$
5	1
5	1
7	3
2	-2
1	-3
7	3
3	-1

The standard deviation summarizes the deviations. Unfortunately, you can't just average them since some are negative and some are positive, and the end result is always an unhelpful zero.[2] Instead, first square each number (that is, multiply it by itself) to eliminate the minus sign, sum, divide by $n - 1$, and finally take the square root (which undoes the squaring you did earlier).[3]

Definition and Formula for the Standard Deviation

The standard deviation is defined as the result of the following procedure. Note that, along the way, the **variance** (the square of the standard deviation) is computed.[4]

■ Finding the Sample Standard Deviation

1 Find the deviations by subtracting the average from each data value.
2 Square these deviations, add them up, and divide the resulting sum by $n - 1$. This is the variance.
3 Take the square root. This is the standard deviation.

---

[2]In fact, using algebra it is possible to prove that the sum of the deviations from average will *always* be zero for any data set. You might suspect that you could simply discard the minus signs and then average, *but nooooo*. Unfortunately, such a simple solution is too mathematically complex to be the standard way of doing things in statistics. However, it is a topic of research interest in the field of robust statistics.

[3]Dividing by $n - 1$ instead of n (as you would usually do to find an average) is a way of adjusting for the technical fact that when you have a *sample*, you do not know the true population mean. It may also be thought of as an adjustment for the fact that you have lost one piece of information (a *degree of freedom*, in statistics jargon) in computing the deviations. This lost piece of information may be identified as an indication of the true sizes of the data values (since they are now centered around zero instead of around the average).

[4]The variance is sometimes used as a variability measure in statistics, but the standard deviation is a better choice. The variance contains no extra information and is more difficult to interpret than the standard deviation. For example, for a data set consisting of dollars spent, the variance would be in "squared dollars," a measure that is difficult to relate to; the standard deviation would be a number measured in good old familiar dollars.

TABLE 5.1.2 Finding the Sum of Squared Deviations

Data	Deviation	Squared Deviation
7	$7 - 4 = 3$	$3 \times 3 = 9$
2	$2 - 4 = -2$	$(-2) \times (-2) = 4$
1	-3	9
5	1	1
5	1	1
7	3	9
2	-2	4
1	-3	9
7	3	9
3	-1	1
Average $= 4$	Sum $= 0$	Sum $= 56$

Table 5.1.2 shows how this procedure works on our simple example. Dividing the sum of squared deviations (56) by $n - 1 = 10 - 1 = 9$, you get $56/9 = 6.222222222$, which is the variance. Taking the square root of 6.222222222, you get 2.494438258. Thus, rounding to three significant digits, the standard deviation is 2.49.[5]

The formula for the standard deviation puts the preceding procedure in mathematical shorthand. The standard deviation for a sample of data is denoted by the letter S, and the formula is:

■ The Standard Deviation for a Sample

$$S = \sqrt{\frac{\text{Sum of squared deviations}}{\text{Number of data items} - 1}}$$

$$= \sqrt{\frac{(X_1 - \bar{X})^2 + (X_2 - \bar{X})^2 + \cdots + (X_n - \bar{X})^2}{n - 1}}$$

$$= \sqrt{\frac{\sum_{i=1}^{n}(X_i - \bar{X})^2}{n - 1}}$$

Computing the standard deviation for our simple example using the formula produces the same result, 2.49:

$$S = \sqrt{\frac{\sum_{i=1}^{n}(X_i - \bar{X})^2}{n - 1}}$$

$$= \sqrt{\frac{56}{10 - 1}}$$

$$= \sqrt{6.222222222}$$

$$= 2.494438258$$

---

[5]Note that this answer, 2.49, does indeed appear to be a reasonable summary of the deviations, which range in size from 1 to 3.

Using a Calculator or a Computer

Of course, there is another, much simpler way to find the standard deviation: Use a calculator or a computer. This is how people *really* compute a standard deviation, by delegating the task of actual calculation to an electronic device. The steps and the formula you just learned were not a waste of time, however, since you now understand the basis for the number that will be computed for you automatically. That is, in interpreting a standard deviation, it is important to recognize it as a measure of typical (or *standard*) deviation size.

If your calculator has a Σ or a Σ+ key (a summation key), it can probably be used to find a standard deviation. Consult the calculator's instruction manual for details, which will likely proceed as follows: First, clear the calculator's storage registers to get it ready for a new problem. Then enter the data into the calculator, following each value by the summation key. You may now compute the standard deviation by hitting the appropriate key, probably labeled with an *S* or a sigma (σ).[6]

There are many different ways in which computers calculate a standard deviation, depending on which of the many available products you are using: spreadsheets, database programs, programming languages, or stand-alone statistical analysis programs. Consult the instruction manual for details.

Interpreting the Standard Deviation

The standard deviation has a simple, direct interpretation: It represents the variability of individuals within the data set by measuring how far a value typically is from the average of all values. Since it represents the typical deviation, you expect some data values to be closer to the average and others to be farther away. That is, you expect some deviations to be larger and some smaller than the *standard* deviation.

Figure 5.1.1 shows how to picture the standard deviation in terms of distance from the average value. Since the average indicates the center of the data, you would expect individuals to deviate to both sides of the average.

EXAMPLE

The Advertising Budget

Your firm spends $19 million per year on advertising, and top management is wondering if that figure is appropriate. Although there are many ways to decide this strategic number, it will always be helpful to understand your competitive position. Other firms in your industry, of size similar to yours, spend an average of $22.3 million annually. You can use the standard deviation as a way to place your difference (22.3 − 19 = $3.3 million) into perspective to see just how low your advertising budget is relative to these other firms.

---

[6]If your calculator has two standard deviation keys, one marked *n* and the other marked *n* − 1, choose the *n* − 1 key for now. The other key computes the *population* instead of the *sample* standard deviation, a distinction you will learn about later.

FIGURE 5.1.1   The number line with an average and a standard deviation indicated. Note that the average is a position on the number line (indicating an absolute number), whereas the standard deviation indicates a *distance* along the number line, namely, the typical distance from the average.

Here are the budgets, in millions of dollars, for the group of $n = 17$ similar firms:

$$8, 19, 22, 20, 27, 37, 38, 23, 23, 12, 11, 32, 20, 18, 23, 35, 11$$

You may verify that the average is $22.3 million (rounding $22.29411) and that the standard deviation is $9.18 million (rounding 9.177177 to three significant digits) for your peer group.

Since your difference from the peer group average ($3.3 million) is even smaller than the standard deviation ($9.18 million), you may conclude that your advertising budget is quite typical. Although your budget is smaller than the average, it is closer to the average than the typical firm in your peer group is.

To visualize your position with respect to the reference group, Figure 5.1.2 shows a histogram of your peer group, with the average and standard deviation indicated (note how effectively the standard deviation shows the typical extent of the data on either side of the average). Your firm, with a $19 million advertising budget, is indeed fairly typical compared to your peers. Although the difference of $3.3 million (between your budget and the peer group average) seems like a lot of money, it is small compared to the individual differences among your peers. Your firm is only slightly below average.

EXAMPLE

Customer Diversity

Your customers are not all alike; there are individual differences in size of order, product preference, yearly cycle, demands for information, loyalty, and so forth. Nonetheless, you probably have a "typical customer" profile in mind together with some feeling for the extent of the diversity.

You can summarize customer orders by reporting the average and the standard deviation:

Yearly total order, per customer:	
Average	$85,600
Standard deviation	$28,300

FIGURE 5.1.2   A histogram of the advertising budgets of your peer group of 17 firms, with the average and standard deviation indicated. Your firm's budget of $19 million is quite typical relative to your peers. In fact, you are not even one standard deviation away from the average.

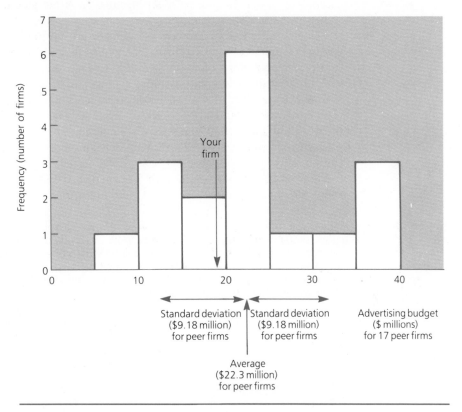

Thus, on average, each customer ordered $85,600 worth of orders last year. To indicate the diversity among customers, the standard deviation of $28,300 shows you that, *typically,* customers ordered approximately $28,300 more or less than the average value of $85,600. The *approximately* carries a lot of weight here: some customers may have been quite close to the average, whereas others were much more than $28,300 away from the average. The average indicates the typical size of yearly orders per customer, and the standard deviation indicates the typical deviation from average.

Note also that the standard deviation is in the same units of measurement as the average; in this example, both are measured in dollars. More precisely, the units of measurement are "dollars per year per customer." This matches the units of the original data set, which would be a list of dollars per year, with one number for each of your customers.

Interpreting the Standard Deviation for a Normal Distribution

When a data set is normally distributed, the standard deviation has a special interpretation. Approximately two thirds of the data values will be *within one standard deviation of the average,* on either side of the average, as shown in Figure 5.1.3.

For example, if your employees' abilities are normally distributed, then you may expect to find two thirds of them to be within one standard deviation either above or below the average. In fact, one third of them will be within one standard deviation above average, and one third of them will be within one standard deviation below average. The remaining one third of your employees would also divide up equally: one sixth (half of this one third) will be more than one standard deviation above the average, and one sixth of your employees will (unfortunately!) be more than one standard deviation below the average.

Figure 5.1.3 also shows that, for a normal distribution, we expect to find about 95% of the data *within two standard deviations from the average.*[7] This

---

FIGURE 5.1.3   When you are lucky enough to have a normal distribution, your data set is conveniently divided up according to number of standard deviations from the average. About two thirds of the data will be within one standard deviation from the average. About 95% of the data will be within two standard deviations from the average. Finally, nearly all (99.7%) of the data are expected to be within three standard deviations from the average.

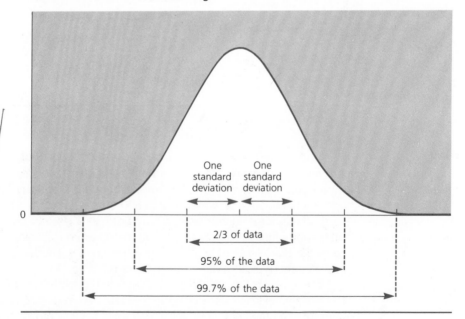

---

[7]Exactly 95% of the data values in a perfect normal distribution are actually within 1.96 standard deviations from the average. Since 1.96 is close to 2, we use "two standard deviations" as a convenient and close approximation.

fact will play a key role later on in the study of statistical inference, since error rates are often limited to 5%.

Finally, we expect nearly all of the data (99.7%) to be *within three standard deviations from the average.* This leaves only 0.3% of the data more extreme than this. In Figure 5.1.3 you can see how the normal distribution is nearly zero when you reach three standard deviations from the average.

What happens if your data set is not normally distributed? Then all bets are off, and these percentages do not apply. Unfortunately, since there are so many different kinds of skewed (or other nonnormal) distributions, there are no simple rules to replace these percentages for a normal distribution. Figure 5.1.4 shows an example of a skewed distribution. Instead of two thirds of the data being within one standard deviation from the average, you actually find about three fourths of the data here. Furthermore, most of these are to the left of the average (since the distribution is higher here).

EXAMPLE   **Stock Market Returns Vary from Day to Day**

Consider daily stock market prices, as measured by the Dow Jones Industrial Average at the close of each trading day from July 31 through October 9, 1987, and shown in Table 5.1.3. The Dow Jones Average is an average of the stock

FIGURE 5.1.4   When your distribution is skewed, there are no simple rules for finding the proportion of the data within one (or two or three) standard deviation from the average.

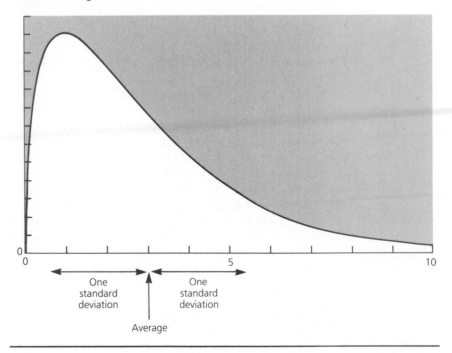

TABLE 5.1.3   Closing Stock Prices

Dow Jones Industrial Average	Date	Dow Jones Industrial Average	Date
2,572.07	July 31, 1987	2,561.38	
2,557.08		2,545.12	
2,546.72		2,549.27	
2,566.65		2,576.05	
2,594.23		2,608.74	
2,592.00		2,613.04	
2,635.84		2,566.58	
2,680.48		2,530.19	
2,669.32		2,527.90	
2,691.49		2,524.64	
2,685.43		2,492.82	
2,700.57		2,568.05	
2,654.66		2,585.67	
2,665.82		2,566.42	
2,706.79		2,570.17	
2,709.50		2,601.50	
2,697.07		2,590.57	
2,722.42		2,596.28	
2,701.85		2,639.20	
2,675.06		2,640.99	
2,639.35		2,640.18	
2,662.95		2,548.63	
2,610.97		2,551.08	
2,602.04		2,516.64	
2,599.49		2,482.21	October 9, 1987

This data set is from the *Daily Stock Price Record, New York Stock Exchange,* Standard & Poor's Corporation, 1987.

prices of 30 specially selected large industrial firms. One of the usual ways investors look at these data is as a graph of the index plotted against time, as shown in Figure 5.1.5.

Financial analysts and researchers often look instead at the *daily return,* which is the interest rate earned by investing in stocks for just one day. This is computed by taking the change in the index and dividing it by its value the previous day. For example, the first daily return, for August 3, is (2557.08 − 2572.07)/2572.07 = −.006, representing a downturn somewhat under 1%.[8] These daily returns represent, in a more direct way than the average itself, what is really happening in the market from day to day in a dynamic sense. We will focus our attention on these daily returns as a data set, shown in Table 5.1.4.

Figure 5.1.6 shows a histogram of these daily returns, indicating a normal distribution. The average daily return during this time was −0.0007, or approximately zero (an average downturn of seven hundredths of a percent). Thus, the market was heading, on average, neither higher nor lower during this time. The

---

[8]This is the return from July 31 through August 3. We will consider it to be a daily return, since the intervening two days were a weekend, with no trading.

FIGURE 5.1.5   The Dow Jones Industrial Average closing stock price, daily from July 31 to October 9, 1987.

standard deviation is 0.0117, indicating that the value of $1 invested in the market would change, on the average, by approximately $0.0117 each day in the sense that the value might go up or down by somewhat less or more than $0.0117.

The extreme values at either end of Figure 5.1.6 represent the largest daily up and down. On September 22, the market went up from 2492.82 to 2568.05, an upswing of 75.23 points, for a daily return of 0.030 (a gain of $0.030 per dollar invested the day before). On October 6, the market went down from 2640.18 to 2548.63, or 91.55 points, for a daily return of −0.035 (a loss of $0.035 per dollar invested the day before).

To be within one standard deviation (0.0117) of the average (−0.0007), a daily return would have to be between −0.0007 − 0.0117 = −0.0124 and −0.0007 + 0.0117 = 0.0110. Of the 49 daily returns, 32 fit this description. Thus, we have found that 32/49, or 65.3%, of daily returns are within one standard deviation of the average. This percentage is fairly close to the 2/3 (66.7%) you would expect for a perfect normal distribution. The 2/3 rule is working.

To be within two standard deviations of the average, a daily return would have to be between −0.0007 − (2 × 0.0117) = −0.0241 and −0.0007 + (2 × 0.0117) = 0.0227. Of the 49 daily returns, 47 fit this description (all except the two extreme observations we noted earlier). Thus, 47/49, or 95.9%, of daily returns are within two standard deviations of the average. This percentage is quite close to the 95% you would expect for a perfectly normal distribution.

TABLE 5.1.4   Daily Stock Market Returns

Dow Jones Industrial Average	Daily Return	Dow Jones Industrial Average	Daily Return
2572.07 (7/31/87)		2561.38	−0.015
2557.08 (8/3/87)	−0.006 = (2557.08 − 2572.07)/2572.07	2545.12	−0.006
2546.72 (8/4/87)	−0.004	2549.27	0.002
2566.65 (8/5/87)	0.008	2576.05	0.011
2594.23	0.011	2608.74	0.013
2592.00	−0.001	2613.04	0.002
2635.84	0.017	2566.58	−0.018
2680.48	0.017	2530.19	−0.014
2669.32	−0.004	2527.90	−0.001
2691.49	0.008	2524.64	−0.001
2685.43	−0.002	2492.82	−0.013
2700.57	0.006	2568.05	0.030
2654.66	−0.017	2585.67	0.007
2665.82	0.004	2566.42	−0.007
2706.79	0.015	2570.17	0.001
2709.50	0.001	2601.50	0.012
2697.07	−0.005	2590.57	−0.004
2722.42	0.009	2596.28	0.002
2701.85	−0.008	2639.20	0.017
2675.06	−0.010	2640.99	0.001
2639.35	−0.013	2640.18	−0.000
2662.95	0.009	2548.63	−0.035
2610.97	−0.020	2551.08	0.001
2602.04	−0.003	2516.64	−0.014
2599.49	−0.001	2482.21 (10/9/87)	−0.014

This example conforms to the normal distribution rules very closely. With other approximately normally distributed examples, you should not be surprised to find a larger difference from the 2/3 or the 95% you expect for a perfect normal distribution.

EXAMPLE   **The Stock Market Crash of 1987: 19 Standard Deviations!**

On Monday, October 19, 1987, the Dow Jones Industrial Average fell 508 points from 2246.74 (the previous Friday) to 1738.74. This represents a daily return of −0.2261; that is, the stock market lost 22.61% of its value. This unexpected loss in value, shown in Figure 5.1.7, was the worst since the "Great Crash" of 1929.

To get an idea of just how extreme this crash was in statistical terms, let's compare it to what you would have expected based on previous market behavior. For the baseline period, let's use the previous example, with its July 31 to October 9 time period, extending up to Friday one week before the crash.

For the baseline period, we found an average of −0.0007 and a standard deviation of 0.0117 for daily returns. How many of these standard deviations below this average does the loss of October 19 represent? The answer is

$$\frac{-0.2261 - (-0.0007)}{0.0117} = -19.26 \text{ standard deviations below the average}$$

FIGURE 5.1.6   A histogram of daily returns in stock prices. The average daily return is nearly zero, suggesting that ups and downs are about equally likely in the short term. The standard deviation, 0.0117, represents the size of typical day-to-day fluctuations. A dollar investment in the market would change in value by about a penny per day during this time.

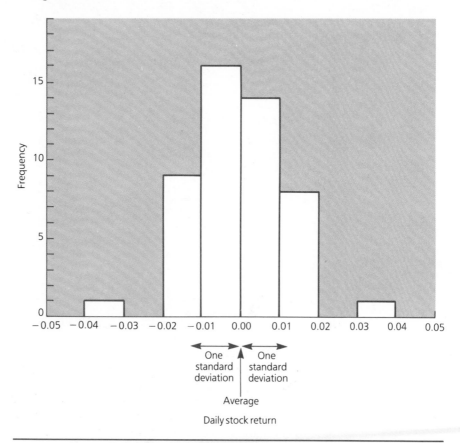

This shows how incredibly extreme the crash was. If daily stock returns were truly normally distributed (and if the distribution didn't change quickly over time), you would essentially *never* expect to see such an extreme result. We would expect to see daily returns more than one standard deviation away from the average fairly often (about one third of the time). We would see two standard deviations or more from time to time (about 5% of the time). We would see three standard deviations or more only very rarely—about 0.3% of the time or, roughly speaking, about once a year.[9] Even five standard deviations would be

---

[9]Something that happens only 0.3% of all days will happen about once a year for the following reasons. First, 0.3% expressed as a proportion is 0.003. Second, its reciprocal is 1/0.003 = 333, which means that it happens about every 333 days, or (very roughly) about once a year.

FIGURE 5.1.7   The Dow Jones Industrial Average closing stock price, daily from July 31 to December 31, 1987.

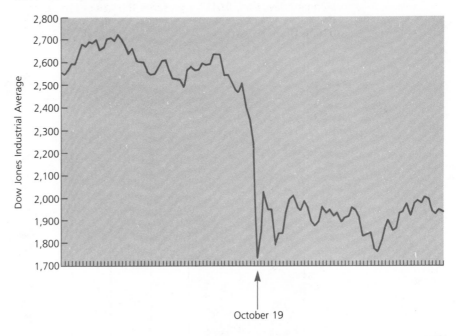

pretty much out of the question for a perfect normal distribution. To see 19.26 standard deviations is quite incredible indeed.

But we did see a daily return of 19.26 standard deviations below the average. This should remind you that stock market returns do *not* follow a perfect normal distribution. There is nothing wrong with the theory; it's just that the theory doesn't apply in this case. Although the normal distribution appears to apply most of the time to daily returns, the crash of 1987 should remind you of the need to check the validity of assumptions to protect yourself from special cases.

EXAMPLE

Market Volatility before and after the Crash

In the period following the crash of October 19, 1987, the market was generally believed to be in a volatile state. You can measure the extent of this volatility by using the standard deviation of daily returns, as defined in an earlier example. Here is a table of these standard deviations:

Standard Deviation	Time Period
0.0117	August 1 to October 9
0.0836	October 12 (1 week before) to October 26 (1 week after)
0.0209	October 27 to December 31, 1987

FIGURE 5.1.8   Daily returns from August 1 to December 31, 1987. Note how the market's volatility was larger after the crash than before.

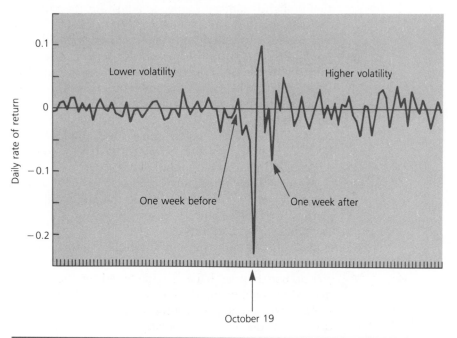

The standard deviation was about seven times higher during the period surrounding the crash (from one week before to one week after) than before this period. After the crash, the standard deviation was lower but remained at nearly double its earlier value (0.0209 compared to 0.0117). Apparently, the market got "back to business" to a large degree following the crash but still remained "nervous," as indicated by the volatility, which is measured by standard deviation.

You can see the heightened volatility in Figure 5.1.8. Aside from the wild gyrations of the market around October 19, the vertical swings of the graph are roughly double on the right as compared to the left. These volatilities were summarized using the standard deviations (roughly corresponding to vertical distances in the figure) in the preceding table.

The Sample and the Population Standard Deviations

There are actually two different (but related) kinds of standard deviation: the **sample standard deviation** (for a sample from a larger population, denoted S) and the **population standard deviation** (for an entire population, denoted σ, the lowercase Greek sigma).

Their names suggest their uses. If you have a sample of data selected at random from a larger population, then the sample standard deviation is appropriate. If, on the other hand, you have an entire population, then the population standard deviation should be used. The sample standard deviation is slightly larger in order to adjust for the randomness of sampling.

Some situations are ambiguous. For example, the salaries of all people who work for you might be viewed either as population data (based on the population of all people who work for you) or as sample data (viewing those who work for you, in effect, as a sample from all similar people in the population at large). Some of this ambiguity depends on how you view the situation, rather than on the data themselves. If you view the data as the entire universe of interest, then you are clearly dealing with a population. However, if you would like to generalize (for example, from your workers to similar workers in similar industries), you may view your data as a sample from a (perhaps hypothetical) population.

To resolve any remaining ambiguity, proceed as follows: *If in doubt, use the sample standard deviation.* Using the larger value is usually the careful, conservative choice since it ensures that you will not be systematically understating the uncertainty.

For computation, the only difference between the two methods is that you subtract 1 (i.e., divide by $n - 1$) for the sample standard deviation, but you do not subtract 1 (i.e., divide by N) for the population standard. This makes the sample standard deviation calculation slightly larger when the sample size is small, reflecting the added uncertainties of having a sample instead of the entire population.[10] There are also some conventional changes in notation: The sample average of the n items is denoted $\overline{X}$, whereas the population mean of the N items is denoted by the Greek letter μ (mu). The formulas are:

■ The Standard Deviation for a Sample

$$S = \sqrt{\frac{\text{Sum of squared deviations}}{\text{Number of data items} - 1}}$$

$$= \sqrt{\frac{(X_1 - \overline{X})^2 + (X_2 - \overline{X})^2 + \cdots + (X_n - \overline{X})^2}{n - 1}}$$

$$= \sqrt{\frac{\sum_{i=1}^{n}(X_i - \overline{X})^2}{n - 1}}$$

---

[10]It is also true that by dividing by $n - 1$ instead of n, the sample variance (the square of the standard deviation) is made "unbiased" (i.e., correct for the population, on the average). However, the sample standard deviation is still a "biased" estimator of the population standard deviation. Details of sampling from populations will be presented in Chapter 8.

■ **The Standard Deviation for a Population**

$$\sigma = \sqrt{\frac{\text{Sum of squared deviations}}{\text{Number of population items}}}$$

$$= \sqrt{\frac{(X_1 - \mu)^2 + (X_2 - \mu)^2 + \cdots + (X_N - \mu)^2}{N}}$$

$$= \sqrt{\frac{\sum_{i=1}^{N} (X_i - \mu)^2}{N}}$$

The smaller the number of items (N or n), the larger the difference between these two formulas. With 10 items, the sample standard deviation is 5.4% larger than the population standard deviation. With 25 items, there is a 2.1% difference, which narrows to 1.0% for 50 items and 0.5% for 100 items. Thus, with reasonably large amounts of data, there is little difference between the two methods.

5.2 The Range: Quick and Superficial

The **range** is the largest minus the smallest data value and represents the size or extent of the data. Here is the range of a small data set:

$$\text{Range of data set } (185, 246, 92, 508, 153) = \text{Largest} - \text{Smallest}$$
$$= 508 - 92$$
$$= 416$$

Note that the range is very quickly computed by scanning a list of numbers to pick out the smallest and largest and then subtracting. Back in the old days, before we had electronic calculators and computers, ease of computation led many people to use the range as a variability measure. Now that the standard deviation is more easily calculated, the range is not used as often.

When the extremes of the data (i.e., the largest and smallest values) are important, the range is a sensible measure of diversity. This might be the case when you are seeking to describe the extent of the data. This can be useful for two purposes: (1) to *describe* the total extent of the data or (2) to *search for errors* in the data. Since an extreme error made in recording the data will tend to turn up as an especially large (or small) value, the range will immediately seem too large, judging by common sense. This makes the range useful for *editing* the data, that is, for error checking.

On the other hand, because of its sensitivity to the extremes, the range is not very useful as a statistical measure of diversity in the sense of summarizing the data set as a whole. The range does not summarize the typical variability in the data but rather focuses too much attention on just two data values. The standard deviation is more sensitive to all of the data and therefore provides a better look at the big picture. In fact, the range will *always* be larger than the standard deviation.

EXAMPLE   **Employee Salaries**

Consider the salaries of employees working in an engineering department of a consumer electronics firm, as shown in Table 5.2.1. We will ignore the ID numbers and concentrate on the salary figures. The highest paid individual earns $44,500 per year (an engineering management position, head of the department), and the lowest paid individual earns just $16,500 (a very junior person with a promising future who has not yet completed basic engineering education). The range is $28,000 (44,500 − 16,500), representing the dollar amount separating the lowest and the highest paid people, as shown in Figure 5.2.1.

Note that the range was computed for the two extremes: those with the least and the most pay. The range does not pretend to indicate the typical variation in salary within the department; the standard deviation would be used to do that.

For a more complete analysis (and to satisfy your curiosity or to help you check your answers), the average salary within the department is $27,950, and the standard deviation (which more reliably indicates the *typical* variability in salary) is $8,581. This is the sample standard deviation, where these engineers are viewed as a sample of typical engineers doing this kind of work.

In summary, $28,000 (the range) separates the lowest and highest amounts. However, $8,581 (the standard deviation) indicates approximately how far individual people are from $27,950 (the average salary for this group).

EXAMPLE   **Duration of Hospital Stays**

Hospitals are now being run more like businesses than they were 10 years ago. Part of this is due to the more competitive atmosphere in medical care, with more health maintenance organizations (HMOs), who hire doctors as employees, supplementing traditional hospitals, whose doctors act more independently.

TABLE 5.2.1   Employee Salaries

Employee ID Number	Salary
918886653	$34,000
771631111	26,000
148609612	27,000
742149808	22,500
968454888	21,000
743594601	33,000
731866668	16,500
490731488	44,500
733401899	35,000
589246387	20,000

FIGURE 5.2.1 The range in salaries is $28,000 for the salary data (from $16,500 to $44,500) and indicates the width of the entire histogram.

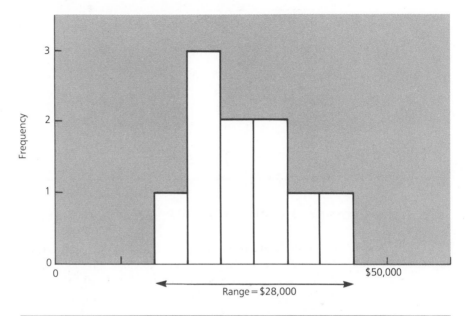

Range = $28,000

Another reason is that government reimbursement for medical care under the Medicare program currently pays a fixed amount depending on the diagnosis, rather than being based on the extent of treatment. This produces a strong incentive to limit, rather than expand, the amount of treatment necessary for a given person's illness.

One measure of the intensity of medical care is the number of days spent in the hospital. Table 5.2.2 shows a list of data representing the number of days spent last year by a sample of patients.[11] The range of this data set is 385, which is 386 − 1 and is impossible since there are only 365 (or 366) days in a year, and this data set is (supposed to be) for one year only. This illustrates the use of the range in editing a data set as a way of identifying errors before proceeding with the analysis. Examining the smallest and largest values is also useful for this purpose.

A careful examination of the original records indicated a typing error. The actual value, 286, was mistakenly transcribed as 386. The range for the corrected data set is 285 (that is, 286 − 1).

---

[11]This hypothetical data set is based on the experience and problems of a friend of mine at an economics research center, who spent weeks trying to get the computer to understand a large data tape of health care statistics as part of a study of the efficiency of health care delivery systems. Successful researchers, both in academia and business, often have to overcome many petty problems along the way toward a deeper understanding.

TABLE 5.2.2   Hospital Length of Stay for a Sample of Patients

(Patient Days Last Year)	
17	4
16	13
1	6
1	33
7	5
74	6
2	12
163	16
51	386
33	2
5	7
1	28
7	

■ 5.3 The Coefficient of Variation: A *Relative* Variability Measure

The **coefficient of variation,** defined as the standard deviation divided by the average, is a *relative* measure of variability as a percentage or proportion of the average. In general this is useful only when there are no negative numbers possible in your data set. The formula is:

■ **The Coefficient of Variation**

$$\text{Coefficient of variation} = \frac{\text{Standard deviation}}{\text{Average}}$$

For a sample:

$$\text{Sample coefficient of variation} = \frac{S}{\bar{X}}$$

For a population:

$$\text{Population coefficient of variation} = \frac{\sigma}{\mu}$$

Note that the standard deviation is the numerator, as is appropriate because the result is primarily an indication of variability.

For example, if the average spent by a customer per trip to the supermarket is $35.26 and the standard deviation is $14.08, then the coefficient of variation is $14.08/35.26 = 0.399$ or 39.9%. This means that, typically, the amount spent per shopping trip differs by about 39.9% from the average value. In absolute terms, this typical difference is $14.08 (the standard deviation), but it amounts to 39.9% (the coefficient of variation) relative to the average.

The coefficient of variation has *no measurement units.* It is a pure number, a proportion or percentage, whose measurement units have canceled each other in the process of dividing standard deviation by average. This makes the coefficient of variation useful in those situations where you don't care about the actual (absolute) size of the differences, and only the relative size is important.

Using the coefficient of variation, you may reasonably compare a large to a small firm to see which one has more variation on a "size-adjusted basis." Ordinarily, a firm that deals in hundreds of millions of dollars will have its sales vary on a similarly large scale, say, tens of millions. Another firm, with sales in the millions, might have its sales vary by hundreds of thousands. In each case, the variation is about 10% of the size of the average sales. The larger firm has a larger absolute variation (larger standard deviation), but both firms have the same relative or size-adjusted amount of variation (the coefficient of variation).

Note that the coefficient of variation can be larger than 100% even with positive numbers. This could happen with a very skewed distribution or with extreme outliers. It would indicate that the situation is *very* variable with respect to the average value.

EXAMPLE   **Uncertainty in Portfolio Performance**

Suppose you have invested $10,000 in 200 shares of XYZ Corporation stock selling for $50 per share. Your friend has purchased 100 shares of XYZ for $5,000. You and your friend expect the per-share price to grow to $60 next year, representing a 20% rate of return, (60 − 50)/50. You both agree that there is considerable risk in XYZ's marketing strategy, represented by a standard deviation of $9 in share price. This means that, although you expect the per-share price to be $60 next year, you wouldn't be surprised if it were approximately $9 larger or smaller than this.

You expect the value of your investment to grow to $12,000 next year ($60 × 200) with a standard deviation of $1,800 ($9 × 200; see Section 5.4 for further details). Your friend's investment is expected to grow to $6,000, with a standard deviation of $900 next year.

It looks as if your risk (standard deviation of $1,800) is double that of your friend ($900). This makes sense since your investment is twice as large in absolute terms. However, you are both investing in the same security, namely, XYZ stock. Thus, except for the size of your investments, your experiences will be identical. In a relative sense (relative to the size of the initial investment), your risks are identical. This is indeed the case if you compute the coefficient of variation (standard deviation of next year's value divided by its average or expected value). Your coefficient of variation is $1,800/$12,000 = 0.15, which matches your friend's coefficient of variation of $900/$6,000 = 0.15. Both of you agree that the uncertainty (or risk) is about 15% of the expected portfolio value next year.

EXAMPLE **Employee Productivity in Telemarketing**

Consider a telemarketing operation with 19 employees making phone calls to sell symphony tickets. Employees sell 23 tickets per hour, on the average, with a standard deviation of 6 tickets per hour. That is, you should not be at all surprised to hear of an employee selling approximately 6 tickets more or less than the average value (23).

Expressing the employee variability in relative terms using the coefficient of variation, you find that it is $6/23 = 0.261$, or 26.1%. This means that the variation of employee sales productivity is about 26.1% of the average sales level.

For the high-level analysis and strategy used by top management, the figure of 26.1% (coefficient of variation) may well be more useful than the figure of 6 tickets per hour (standard deviation). Top management can look separately at the level of productivity (23 tickets per employee per hour) and the variation in productivity (employees may typically be 26.1% above or below the average level).

The coefficient of variation is especially useful in making comparisons between situations of different sizes. Consider another telemarketing operation selling theater tickets, with an average of 35 tickets per hour and a standard deviation of 7. Since the theater ticket productivity is higher overall than the symphony ticket productivity (35 compared to 23, on average) you should not be surprised to see more variation (7 compared to 6). However, the coefficient of variation for the theater operation is $7/35 = 0.200$, or 20.0%. Compared to the 26.1% figure for the symphony, management can quickly conclude that the theater marketing group is actually *more* homogeneous, relatively speaking, than the symphony group.

■ 5.4 Effects of Adding to or Rescaling the Data

When a situation is changed in a systematic way, there is no need to recompute summaries such as typical value (average, median, mode), percentiles, or variability measures (standard deviation, range, coefficient of variation). A few basic rules show how to quickly find the summaries for a new situation.

If a fixed number is *added to* each data value, then this same number is added to the average, median, mode, and percentiles to obtain the corresponding summaries for the new data set. For example, adding a new access fee of $5 to accounts formerly worth $38, $93, $25, and $89 says that the accounts are now worth $43, $98, $30, and $94. The average value per account has jumped exactly $5, from $61.25 to $66.25. Rather than recompute the average for the new account values, you can simply add $5 to the old average. This rule applies to other measures; for example, the median rises by $5, from $63.50 to $68.50. However, the standard deviation and range are unchanged, since the data values are shifted but maintain the same dis-

TABLE 5.4.1   Effects of Adding to or Rescaling the Data

	Original Data	Add d	Multiply by c	Multiply then Add
	X	$X + d$	cX	$cX + d$
Average (similarly for median, mode, and percentiles)	$\overline{X}$	$\overline{X} + d$	$c\overline{X}$	$c\overline{X} + d$
Standard deviation (similarly for range)	S	S	$|c|S$	$|c|S$

tance from each other. The coefficient of variation does change, and may be easily computed from the standard deviation and the new average.

If each data value is *multiplied by* a fixed number, the average, median, mode, percentiles, standard deviation, and range are each multiplied by this same number to obtain the corresponding summaries for the new data set. The coefficient of variation is unaffected.[12]

These two effects act in combination if the data values are multiplied by a factor c and an amount d is then added; X becomes $cX + d$. The new average is $c \times$ (Old average) $+ d$ (likewise for the median, mode, and percentiles). The new standard deviation is $|c| \times$ (Old standard deviation), and the range is adjusted similarly (note that the added number, d, plays no role here).[13] The new coefficient of variation is easily computed from the new average and standard deviation.

Table 5.4.1 is a summary chart of these rules. The new coefficient of variation may be easily computed from the new standard deviation and average.

EXAMPLE

Uncertainty of Costs in Japanese Yen and in U.S. Dollars

Your firm's overseas production division has projected its costs for next year as follows:

Expected costs	325,700,000 Japanese yen
Standard deviation	50,000,000 Japanese yen

To complete your budget, it will be necessary to convert these into U.S. dollars. For simplicity, we will consider only business risk (represented by the standard deviation). A more comprehensive analysis would also consider exchange rate risk, which would allow for the risk of movements in the exchange rate.

---

[12]This assumes that the fixed number is positive. If it is negative, then make it positive before multiplying for the standard deviation and the range.

[13]Note that the standard deviation is multiplied by the *absolute value* of this factor so that it remains a positive number. For example, if $c = -3$, the standard deviation would be multiplied by 3.

Japanese yen are easily converted to U.S. dollars using the current exchange rate.[14] We will use a conversion factor of 0.007524 dollars per yen; that is, to convert amounts in yen to amounts in dollars, multiply by 0.007524. Multiplying both the average (expected) amount and the standard deviation by this conversion factor, you find the expected amount and risk in dollars (rounded to the nearest thousand):

| Expected costs | $2,451,000 |
| Standard deviation | $376,000 |

By using the basic rules, you were able to convert the summaries from yen to dollars without going through the entire budgeting process all over again in dollars instead of yen!

EXAMPLE

Total Cost and Units Produced

In cost accounting and in finance, a production facility often views costs as either *fixed* or *variable*. The fixed costs will apply regardless of how many units are produced, whereas the variable costs are charged on a per-unit basis. Fixed costs might represent rent and investment in production machinery, and variable costs might represent the cost of the production materials actually used.

Consider a shampoo manufacturing facility, with fixed costs of $1,000,000 per month and variable costs of $0.50 per bottle of shampoo produced. Based on a careful analysis of market demand, management has forecast next month's production at 1,200,000 bottles. Based on past experience with these forecasts, the firm recognizes an uncertainty of about 250,000 bottles. Thus, you expect to produce an average of 1,200,000 bottles of shampoo, with a standard deviation of 250,000 bottles.

Given this forecast of units to be produced, how do you forecast costs? Note that units are converted to costs by multiplying by $0.50 (the variable cost) and then adding $1,000,000 (the fixed cost). That is,

$$\text{Total cost} = \$0.50 \times \text{Units produced} + \$1,000,000$$

Using the appropriate rule, you find that the average (expected) cost and the standard deviation are

$$\text{Average cost} = \$0.50 \times 1,200,000 + \$1,000,000$$
$$= \$1,600,000$$
$$\text{Standard deviation of cost} = \$0.50 \times 250,000$$
$$= \$125,000$$

---

[14]This may be found, for example, by looking up "Foreign Exchange" in the table of contents on page 1 of *The Wall Street Journal*. We use the value reported on June 30, 1988.

Your budget of costs is complete. You expect $1,600,000, with a standard deviation (uncertainty) of $125,000.

The coefficient of variation of units produced is 250,000/1,200,000 = 20.8%. The coefficient of variation for costs is quickly computed as $125,000/$1,600,000 = 7.8%. Note that the relative variation in costs is much smaller due to the fact that the large fixed costs make the absolute level of variation seem smaller when compared to the larger cost base.

5.5 End-of-Chapter Materials

Summary

Variability (also called **diversity, uncertainty, dispersion,** and **spread**) is the extent to which data values differ from one another. Although measures of center (such as the average, median, or mode) indicate the typical *size* of the data values, a measure of variability will indicate *how close* to this central size measure the data values typically are. If all data values are identical, then the variability is zero. The more spread out things are, the larger the variability.

The **standard deviation** is the traditional choice for measuring variability, summarizing the typical distance from the average to a data value. The standard deviation indicates the extent of randomness of individuals about their common average. The **deviations** are the distances from each data value to the average. Positive deviations represent above-average individuals, and negative deviations indicate below-average individuals. The average of these deviations is always zero. The standard deviation indicates the typical size of these deviations (ignoring the minus signs) and is a number in the same unit of measurement as the original data (such as dollars, miles per gallon, or kilograms).

To find the sample standard deviation:

1 Find the deviations by subtracting the average from each data value.
2 Square these deviations, add them up, and divide the resulting sum by $n - 1$. This is the *variance.*
3 Take the square root. You now have the standard deviation.

When you have data for the entire population, you may use the **population standard deviation** (denoted by σ). Whenever you wish to generalize beyond the immediate data set to some larger population (either real or hypothetical), be sure to use the **sample standard deviation** (denoted by S). When in doubt, use the sample standard deviation. Here are their formulas:

$$S = \sqrt{\frac{\text{Sum of squared deviations}}{\text{Number of data items} - 1}}$$

$$= \sqrt{\frac{(X_1 - \bar{X})^2 + (X_2 - \bar{X})^2 + \cdots + (X_n - \bar{X})^2}{n - 1}}$$

$$= \sqrt{\frac{\sum_{i=1}^{n} (X_i - \bar{X})^2}{n - 1}}$$

$$\sigma = \sqrt{\frac{\text{Sum of squared deviations}}{\text{Number of population items}}}$$

$$= \sqrt{\frac{(X_1 - \mu)^2 + (X_2 - \mu)^2 + \cdots + (X_n - \mu)^2}{N}}$$

$$= \sqrt{\frac{\sum_{i=1}^{N} (X_i - \mu)^2}{N}}$$

Both formulas add up the squared deviations, divide, and then take the square root to undo the initial squaring of the individual deviations. For the sample standard deviation, you divide by $n - 1$ because the deviations are computed using the somewhat uncertain sample average instead of the exact population mean.

The **variance** is the square of the standard deviation. It provides the same information as the standard deviation but is more difficult to interpret since its unit of measurement is the square of the original data units (such as dollars squared, squared miles per squared gallon, or squared kilograms, whatever these things are). We therefore prefer the standard deviation for reporting variability measurement.

If your data follow a normal distribution, the standard deviation represents the approximate width of the middle two thirds of your cases. That is, about two thirds of your data values will be within one standard deviation from the average (either above or below). Approximately 95% will be within two standard deviations from the average, and about 99.7% will be within three standard deviations from average. However, don't expect these rules to hold for other (nonnormal) distributions.

The **range** is equal to the largest data value minus the smallest data value and represents the size or extent of the entire data set. The range may be used to describe the data and to help identify problems. However, the range is not very useful as a statistical measure of variability because it concentrates too much attention on the extremes rather than on the more typical data values. For most statistical purposes, the standard deviation is a better measure of variability.

The **coefficient of variation** is the standard deviation divided by the average and summarizes the *relative variability* in the data as a percentage of the average. The coefficient of variation has no measurement units and thus may be useful in comparing the variability of different situations on a size-adjusted basis.

When a fixed number is added to each data value, the average, median, percentiles, and mode all increase by this same amount; the standard deviation and range remain unchanged. When each data value is multiplied by a fixed number, the average, median, percentiles, mode, standard deviation, and range all change by this same factor, and the coefficient of variation remains unchanged.[15] When each data value is multiplied by a fixed number and then another fixed number is added, these two effects act in combination. The coefficient of variation can easily be computed after using these rules to find the average and standard deviation.

Key Words

variability, diversity, uncertainty, dispersion, spread 114
standard deviation 114
deviation 114
population standard deviation 127

sample standard deviation 127
variance 115
range 129
coefficient of variation 132

Questions

1 What is variability?
2 a. What is the traditional measure of variability?
  b. What other measures are also used?
3 a. What is a deviation from the average?
  b. What is the average of all of the deviations?
4 a. What is the standard deviation?
  b. What does the standard deviation tell you about the relationship between individual data values and the average?
  c. What are the measurement units of the standard deviation?
  d. What is the difference between the sample standard deviation and the population standard deviation?
5 a. What is the variance?
  b. What are the measurement units of the variance?
  c. Which is the more easily interpreted variability measure, the standard deviation or the variance? Why?
  d. Once you know the standard deviation, does the variance provide any additional real information about the variability?
6 If your data set is normally distributed, what proportion of the individuals do you expect to find:
  a. Within one standard deviation from the average?
  b. Within two standard deviations from the average?

---

[15]The standard deviation and range are multiplied by the *absolute value* of this fixed number so that it remains a positive number.

c. Within three standard deviations from the average?

d. More than one standard deviation from the average?

e. More than one standard deviation *above* the average? (Be careful!)

7 How would your answers to question 6 change if the data were not normally distributed?

8 a. What is the range?

b. What are the measurement units of the range?

c. For what purposes is the range useful?

d. Is the range a very useful statistical measure of variability? Why or why not?

9 a. What is the coefficient of variation?

b. What are the measurement units of the coefficient of variation?

10 Which variability measure is most useful for comparing variability in two different situations, adjusting for the fact that the situations have very different average sizes? Justify your choice.

11 When a fixed number is added to each data value, what happens to:

a. The average, median, and mode?

b. The standard deviation and range?

c. The coefficient of variation?

12 When each data value is multiplied by a fixed number, what happens to:

a. The average, median, and mode?

b. The standard deviation and range?

c. The coefficient of variation?

Problems

1 Planning an international trip for sightseeing, perhaps combined with business? There is a world of diversity in prices. Consider the price of a roll of film (100 ASA, 36 exposures) at various destinations:[16]

Location	Price of Roll of Film
Cairo	$2.95
Hong King	3.46
London	5.51
Mexico City	3.50
Munich	4.97
Paris	6.86
São Paulo	6.25
Tokyo	5.98

a. Find the average film price.

b. Find the standard deviation of film prices, viewing these locations as a sample of international destinations. What are the units of measurement?

c. Briefly summarize the interpretation of the standard deviation (from part *b*) in terms of the differences among these places.

d. Find the range. What are the units of measurement?

---

[16]Data are from "A Shopping Basket for the World Traveler," *Business Week*, October 19, 1987, p. 149.

  e. Briefly summarize the interpretation of the range (from part *d*) in terms of the differences among these places.
  f. Find the coefficient of variation. What are the units of measurement?
  g. Briefly summarize the interpretation of the coefficient of variation (from part *f*) in terms of the differences among these places.
  h. Find the variance. What are the units of measurement?
  i. Briefly summarize the interpretation of the variance (from part *h*) or indicate why there is no simple interpretation.
  j. Draw a histogram of this data set. Indicate the average, standard deviation, and range on your graph.

2 Consider the return on equity, expressed in terms similar to an interest rate, in percentage points per year, for the following major aerospace firms.[17] For these top firms in this industry group, there was definitely a variety of experiences. You may view these firms as a sample, indicating the performance of large aerospace firms in general during this time period.

Firm	Return on Equity (1987)
Boeing	9.6
United Technologies	13.8
Lockheed	20.8
Martin Marietta	25.4
McDonnell Douglas	10.5
General Dynamics	27.3
Northrop	10.2
Grumman	3.0
GenCorp	−18.6
Rohr Industries	6.9

  a. Find the standard deviation of the return on equity. What are the units of measurement?
  b. Briefly summarize the interpretation of the standard deviation (from part *a*) in terms of the differences among these firms.
  c. Find the range. What are the units of measurement?
  d. Briefly summarize the interpretation of the range (from part *c*) in terms of the differences among these firms.
  e. Find the coefficient of variation. What are the units of measurement?
  f. Briefly summarize the interpretation of the coefficient of variation (from part *e*) in terms of the differences among these firms.
  g. Find the variance. What are the units of measurement?
  h. Briefly summarize the interpretation of the variance (from part *g*) or indicate why there is no simple interpretation.
  i. Draw a histogram of this data set. Indicate the average, standard deviation, and range on your graph.

3 Consider the prices of a roll of film from problem 1, but expressed in French francs instead of U.S. dollars. Use the exchange rate listed in a recent issue of *The*

---

[17]Data are from "The Top 1000 U.S. Companies Ranked by Industry," *Business Week*, April 15, 1988, p. 233.

Wall Street Journal or another source. Based on your answers to problem 1 (that is, without recalculating from the data), compute:

a. The average price per roll in French francs.
b. The standard deviation.
c. The range.
d. The coefficient of variation.

4 The performance of mutual funds that invest in over-the-counter stocks has been quite varied. Consider the rate of return for 1986 for 25 funds, as shown in Table 5.5.1.

TABLE 5.5.1   Rate of Return for OTC Mutual Funds, 1986

−3.3%	9.2%	−2.4%
0.3	−0.8	8.0
13.9	−5.0	−7.2
9.7	3.2	−2.4
8.6	−5.0	20.4
2.2	9.5	10.3
2.3	0.0	−11.8
−6.9	7.3	−6.6
5.5		

Data are from "Returns Don't Measure up at Many Funds That Invest in Over-the-Counter Stocks," *The Wall Street Journal*, November 26, 1986, p. 23.

a. Find the average rate of return for these funds.
b. Find the population standard deviation, and briefly interpret this value.
c. How many of these mutual funds are within one standard deviation from the average? How does this compare to what you expect for a normal distribution?
d. How many of these mutual funds are within two standard deviations from the average? How does this compare to what you expect for a normal distribution?
e. How many of these mutual funds are within three standard deviations from the average? How does this compare to what you expect for a normal distribution?
f. Draw a histogram of this data set, and indicate limits of one, two, and three standard deviations on the graph. Interpret your answers to parts *c*, *d*, and *e* in light of the shape of the distribution.

5 Consider the number of executives for all Seattle corporations with 500 or more employees:[18]

12, 15, 5, 16, 7, 18, 15, 12, 4, 3, 22, 4, 12, 4, 6, 8, 4, 5, 6, 4, 22, 10, 11, 4, 7, 6, 10, 10, 7, 8, 26, 9, 11, 41, 4, 16, 10, 11, 12, 8, 5, 9, 18, 6, 5

a. Find the average number of executives per firm.
b. Find the (sample) standard deviation, and briefly interpret this value.
c. How many corporations are within one standard deviation from the average? How does this compare to what you expect for a normal distribution?
d. How many corporations are within two standard deviations from the average? How does this compare to what you expect for a normal distribution?

---

[18]Data are from *Pacific Northwest Executive*, April 1988, p. 20.

e. How many corporations are within three standard deviations from the average? How does this compare to what you expect for a normal distribution?

f. Draw a histogram of this data set and indicate limits of one, two, and three standard deviations on the graph. Interpret your answers to parts *c*, *d*, and *e* in light of the shape of the distribution.

6 Repeat problem 5 with the extreme outlier omitted, and write a paragraph comparing the results with and without the outlier.

7 All 18 people in a department have just received across-the-board pay raises of 5%. What has happened to:

a. The average salary for the department?

b. The standard deviation of salaries?

c. The range in salaries?

d. The coefficient of variation of salaries?

8 Based on a demand analysis forecast, a factory plans to produce 180,000 video game cartridges this quarter, on average, with an estimated uncertainty of 35,000 cartridges as the standard deviation. The fixed costs for this equipment are $72,000 per quarter, and the variable cost is $0.68 per cartridge produced.

a. What is the forecast expected total cost of the cartridges produced?

b. What is the uncertainty involved in this forecast of total cost, expressed as a standard deviation?

c. Find the coefficient of variation for the number of cartridges produced and for the total cost. Write a paragraph interpreting and comparing these coefficients of variation.

d. After the quarter is over, you find that the factory actually produced 210,000 cartridges. How many standard deviations above or below the average is this figure?

e. Suppose the firm actually produces 300,000 cartridges. How many standard deviations above or below the average is this figure? Would this be a surprise in light of the earlier forecast? Why or why not?

9 Your firm's total advertising budget has been set for the year. You (as marketing manager) expect to spend about $1,500,000 on TV commercials, with an uncertainty of $200,000 as the standard deviation. Your advertising agency collects a fee of 15% of this budget. Find the expected size of your agency's fee and its level of uncertainty.

10 You have been trying to control the weight of a chocolate and peanut butter candy bar by intervening in the production process. Table 5.5.2 shows the weights of two representative samples of candy bars from the day's production, one taken before and the other taken after your intervention.

a. Find the average weight of the candy bars before intervention.

b. Find the standard deviation of the weights before intervention.

c. Find the average weight of the candy bars after intervention.

d. Find the standard deviation of the weights after intervention.

e. Compare the standard deviations before and after your intervention, and write a paragraph summarizing what you find. In particular, have you been successful in reducing the variability in this production process?

11 Do people really drive at the speed limit? What variation in behavior, if any, is there from one state to another? Consider the percentage of vehicles exceeding 55 miles an hour for 1985, as shown in Table 5.5.3.

TABLE 5.5.2 Weight (in Ounces) for Two Samples of Candy Bars

Before Intervention	After Intervention	Before Intervention	After Intervention
1.62	1.60	1.68	1.69
1.71	1.71	1.66	1.59
1.63	1.65	1.64	1.66
1.62	1.64	1.70	1.68
1.63	1.63	1.66	1.59
1.69	1.65	1.71	1.57
1.64	1.74	1.63	1.62
1.63	1.75	1.65	1.75
1.62	1.66	1.70	1.72
1.70	1.73	1.64	1.63

TABLE 5.5.3 Speeding Drivers

State	Vehicles Exceeding 55 Miles per Hour	State	Vehicles Exceeding 55 Miles per Hour	State	Vehicles Exceeding 55 Miles per Hour
Arizona	56.4%	Montana	46.6%	Arkansas	40.2%
Rhode Island	54.0	Colorado	46.5	Delaware	40.1
Vermont	53.2	New York	45.6	Minnesota	39.2
New Hampshire	50.4	Louisiana	45.5	Iowa	39.1
Nevada	49.9	Texas	45.3	South Dakota	39.1
Michigan	49.8	Oklahoma	44.3	Idaho	37.8
California	49.7	Kansas	44.0	Illinois	37.0
Maine	49.7	Wisconsin	43.7	Connecticut	36.8
North Dakota	49.7	Nebraska	43.3	Pennsylvania	36.8
Massachusetts	48.5	Alabama	43.1	South Carolina	36.5
Missouri	47.7	Washington	43.1	North Carolina	34.2
Wyoming	47.7	Alaska	42.6	Kentucky	32.3
Florida	47.6	Ohio	42.6	Hawaii	31.1
New Mexico	47.4	Indiana	41.7	Virginia	29.5
Oregon	47.1	Utah	41.5	West Virginia	26.5
Mississippi	47.0	Georgia	40.7	Maryland	Not available
New Jersey	46.8	Tennessee	40.5		

Data are from "Adjusting the Speed Limit to Match Reality," *New York Times*, October 26, 1986, p. E5. Their source is the Federal Highway Administration, National Highway Traffic Safety Administration.

a. Summarize the behavior of motorists in a typical state by finding the average percentage of vehicles exceeding 55 mph.
b. Summarize the variation in motorists' behavior from state to state using the standard deviation of this data set. You may view this data set as a population consisting of all available information about this time period.
c. Draw a histogram of this data set. Indicate the average and standard deviation on this graph.

d. Write a paragraph summarizing what you have learned from examining and summarizing this data set.

12 For the yields of tax-exempt bonds (problem 1 in Chapter 3):
   a. For the standard deviation of the yield.
   b. Find the range.
   c. Find the coefficient of variation.
   d. Use these summaries to describe the extent of variability among these yields.

13 Using the data from problem 2 of Chapter 3, find the standard deviation and range to summarize the typical variability (or uncertainty) of the market response to stock buy-back announcements.

14 Using the data from problem 4 of Chapter 3, for the portfolio investments of Teachers Insurance & Annuity Association in broadcasting companies:
   a. Find the standard deviation of market value for these firms' stock in TIAA's portfolio.
   b. Find the range of these market values.
   c. Find the coefficient of variation.
   d. Interpret the variability based on these three summaries.
   e. How many market values are within one standard deviation of the average? How does this compare to what you would expect for a normal distribution?
   f. How many market values are within two standard deviations of the average? How does this compare to what you would expect for a normal distribution?

15 Summarize the variability in price of perfume in major European cities using the standard deviation, based on the data in problem 7 of Chapter 3.

16 Use the data set from problem 10 of Chapter 3 on poor quality in the production of electric motors.
   a. Find the standard deviation and range to summarize the typical batch-to-batch variability in quality of production.
   b. Remove the two outliers, and recompute the standard deviation and range.
   c. Compare the standard deviation and range values with and without the outliers. In particular, how sensitive is each of these summary measures to the presence of outliers?

17 Compute the standard deviation of the data from problem 2 of Chapter 4 to find the variability in spending levels from one regular customer to another for last month. Write a paragraph summarizing these differences.

18 How much variability in research and development expense is there from one firm to another in the food and beverage industry? Find and interpret the standard deviation and range for the data given in problem 3 of Chapter 4.

19 How much variability is there in loan fees for home mortgages? Find and interpret the standard deviation, range, and coefficient of variation for the data in problem 8 of Chapter 4.

Database Exercises

Please refer to the employee database in Appendix A.

1 For the annual salary levels:
   a. Find the range.

b. Find the standard deviation.

c. Find the coefficient of variation.

d. Compare these three summary measures. What do they tell you about typical salaries in this administrative division?

2 For the annual salary levels:

a. Construct a histogram, and indicate the average and standard deviation.

b. How many employees are within one standard deviation from the average? How does this compare to what you would expect for a normal distribution?

c. How many employees are within two standard deviations from the average? How does this compare to what you would expect for a normal distribution?

d. How many employees are within three standard deviations from the average? How does this compare to what you would expect for a normal distribution?

3 For the ages: Answer the parts of exercise 1.

4 For the ages: Answer the parts of exercise 2.

5 For the experience variable: Answer the parts of exercise 1.

6 For the experience variable: Answer the parts of exercise 2.

Projects

1 Find a data set of interest to you consisting of some quantity (for you to choose) measured for each firm in two different industry groups (with at least 15 firms in each group).

a. For each group:

(1) Summarize the variability using all of the techniques presented in this chapter that are appropriate to your data.

(2) Indicate these variability measures on a histogram and/or box plot of each data set.

(3) Write a paragraph summarizing what you have learned about this industry group by examining its variability.

b. For both groups, perform the following comparisons:

(1) Compare their standard deviations.

(2) Compare their coefficients of variation.

(3) Compare their ranges.

(4) Summarize what you have learned about how these industry groups relate to one another by comparing their variabilities. In particular, which variability measure is most helpful for your particular situation?

2 Find a data set consisting of at least 25 numbers relating to a firm or industry group of interest to you. Summarize the data using all of the techniques you have learned so far that are appropriate to your data. Use both numerical and graphical methods, and address both the typical value and the variability. Present your results as a two-page background report to management, beginning with an executive summary as the first paragraph.

Probability

How do you deal with uncertainty? By understanding how it works. *Probability* starts out by encouraging you to clarify your thinking in order to separate the truly uncertain things from the hard facts you are sure of. What exactly *is* the uncertain situation you're interested in? By what exact procedure is it determined? How likely are the various possibilities? Often there is some event that will either happen or won't happen: Will you get the contract? Will the customer send in the order form? Will they fix the machinery on time? In Chapter 6 you will learn about these kinds of situations, their combinations, and how uncertainty is reduced when you learn new information. In other situations you are interested in an uncertain *number* that has not yet been revealed: What will the announced earnings be? How high will the quarterly sales be? How much time will be lost due to computer trouble? In Chapter 7 you will see how to find a typical summary number, how to assess the risk (or variability) of the situation, and how to find the likelihoods of various scenarios based on an uncertain number.

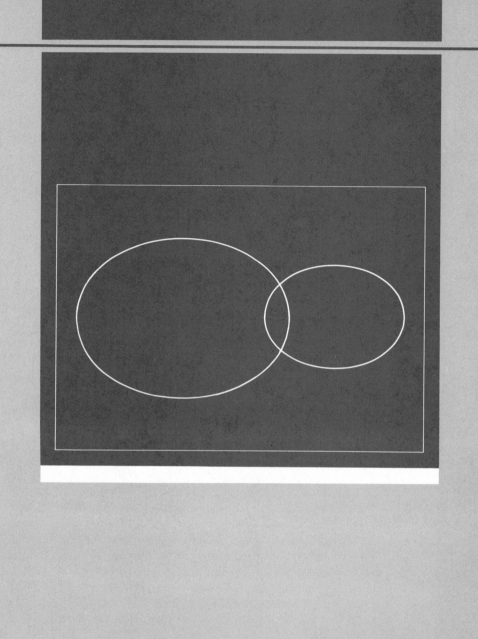

6 Probability
Understanding Random Situations

Our goal is to understand uncertain situations, at least to the greatest extent possible. Unfortunately, we will probably never be able to say "for sure" exactly what will happen in the future. However, by recognizing that some possibilities are more likely than others, and by quantifying (using numbers to describe) these relationships, you will find yourself in a much more competitive position than either those who have no idea what will happen or those who proceed by a "gut feeling" that has no real basis. The best policy is to combine an understanding of the probabilities with whatever wisdom and experience are available.

Here are some examples of uncertain situations:

1 Your division is just about to decide whether or not to introduce a new digital audio tape player into the consumer market. Although your marketing studies show that typical consumers like the product and feel that its price is reasonable, its success is hardly assured. Uncertainty comes from many factors. For example, what will the competition do? Will your suppliers provide quality components in a timely manner? Is there a flaw that hasn't been noticed yet? Will there be a recession or expansion in the economy? Will consumers spend real money on it, or do they just say that they will? Your firm will have to make the best decision it can based on the information available.

2 Your uncle, a farmer in Minnesota, writes to say that he thinks a drought is likely this year. Since he correctly predicted similar problems in 1988, you immediately purchase call options on corn and soybean futures on the Chicago Board of Trade. What will happen to your investment? It is quite speculative. If farmers have a good year, prices could fall and you could lose everything. On the other hand, if there is a serious drought, prices would rise and you would profit handsomely.

3 As manager of operations at a large chemical plant, you have many responsibilities. You must keep costs low while producing large quantities of products. Because some of these chemicals are poisonous, you have put a safety system into place. Still, despite your best efforts, you wonder: How likely is a major disaster during the next year? This is a very uncertain situation, and we do often hear about such disasters in the media. To properly understand the costs of safety and the potential benefits, you have decided to study the probability of failure in your plant.

4 Did you ever wonder about your chances of winning a sweepstakes? You would probably guess that it is a very improbable event. But how unlikely is it? An answer is provided by a newspaper article, which reports:

> The odds of winning the $10 million grand prize in the current Publishers Clearing House magazine sweepstakes mailing are 427,600,000 to 1. That is about 300 times more unlikely than getting struck by lightning, which is a mere 1.5 million–to–1 shot.[1]

How can you understand uncertain, random situations without being troubled by their imprecise nature? The best approach is to begin with solid, exact concepts. This can help you know "for sure" what is going on (to the greatest extent possible) even when you are analyzing a situation in which nothing is "for sure."

Such an approach establishes clear boundaries, starting with an exact description of the process of interest (the *random experiment*) together with a list of every outcome that could possibly result (the *sample space*). You may have a number of special cases to study that either happen or don't (e.g., "the project succeeded"); these are called *events*. The likelihood of an event happening is indicated by an exact number called its *probability*.

You may want to combine information about more than one event, for example, to see how likely it is that the reactor *and* the safety system will both fail. Or you may wish to keep your probabilities up to date by using *conditional probabilities* that reflect all available information. The easiest way to solve such probability problems is to first build a *probability tree* to organize your knowledge about a situation; this is much easier than trying to choose just the right combination of formulas. Some people also find *joint probability tables* and *Venn diagrams* useful in building intuition and solving problems.

---

[1]William P. Barrett, "Bank on Lightning, Not Mail Contests," *Seattle Times,* January 14, 1986, p. Dl.

■ 6.1 An Example: Is It behind Door Number 1, Door Number 2, or Door Number 3?

You are a contestant on a television game show, and the prize of your dreams (a trip to Hawaii, or perhaps a perfect grade on the midterm?) is behind either door number 1, door number 2, or door number 3. Behind the other two doors there is nothing. You can see all three closed doors, and you have no hints. While the crowd shouts its encouragement, you think it over, make up your mind, and tell everyone which door you choose. But before opening your choice of door, they tell you that they will first open a different door that does not have the prize behind it. After they do this, they offer you a chance to switch. There are now two doors left unopened: your choice and one other. Should you switch? The crowd goes wild, shouting encouragement and suggestions. Would you stay with your original choice or switch to the other door? Please think about it before looking at the answer in the following paragraphs.[2]

*   *   *   *   *

If you decided to stay with your original choice, you are in good company because nearly all students answer this way. Unfortunately, however, you are wrong, and your decision making abilities will definitely benefit from the study of probability.

If you decided to switch, congratulations.[3] You have *doubled* your chances of winning, from 1/3 to 2/3.

The principle at work here is that the switchers have made use of new information in an effective way, whereas those who didn't switch have not changed their chances at all. What is the new information? In order to open a door that is not yours and that does not have the prize behind it, the people running the contest have to know something about which door the prize is really behind. In their opening such a door, partial information is revealed to you.

Here's an informal explanation. Imagine having a twin who switches while you do not. Since there are just two doors left and the prize must be behind one of them, your twin will win every time that you do not. Since your overall chances of winning are unchanged at 1/3, it follows that your switching twin will win the remaining 2/3 of the time. For those of you who are not convinced, a detailed, formal solution will be presented as an example in Section 6.5.

Don't be discouraged if you didn't make the best choice. Instead, think about the powers you will develop by learning something about probability.

---

[2]A similar situation was described by B. Nalebuff, "Puzzles: Choose a Curtain, Duel-ity, Two Point Conversions, and More," *Journal of Economic Perspectives*, 1 (1987), pp. 157–63.

[3]Also, please write me a brief note describing why you decided to switch. I am curious about the different intuitive ways people use to get to the correct answer. Please send your note to Andy Siegel, Department of Management Science DJ-10, University of Washington, Seattle, Washington 98195. Thank you!

In fact, you should even feel optimistic, since your decisions will then be better than those of many others, who continue to "stand pat" in the face of new, important information.

■ 6.2 How Can You Analyze Uncertainty?

Our precise framework for studying random situations will begin by carefully identifying and limiting the situation. The result is a *random experiment* that produces one *outcome* from a list of possibilities (called the *sample space*) each time the experiment is run. There will usually also be a number of *events,* each of which either happens or doesn't happen, depending on the outcome.

The Random Experiment: A *Precise* Definition of a Random Situation

A **random experiment** is any well-defined procedure that produces an observable outcome that could not be perfectly predicted in advance. A random experiment must be well defined to eliminate any vagueness or surprise. It must produce a definite, observable outcome so that you know what happened after the random experiment is run. Finally, the outcome must not be perfectly predictable in advance since, if it were known with certainty, you would not really have a random situation.[4] Here are some examples of random experiments we will continue to discuss throughout this section:

1 From tomorrow's production, choose 15 frozen gourmet TV dinners according to a carefully specified random selection process, cook them, and record their quality as a whole number on a scale from 1 to 10. (The careful selection process ensures that the experiment is well-defined, and the outcome is the list of recorded measures of quality. Finally, the outcome is not known with certainty since, occasionally, problems do occur in any manufacturing process.)

2 The marketing department plans to select 10 representative consumers to form a focus group to discuss and vote on the design of a new reading lamp, choosing one of seven proposed designs. (The outcome is the selected design.)

3 A survey is designed to study family income in the area around a proposed new restaurant. A family is telephoned through random dialing, and its income is recorded.[5]

---

[4] In some cases, the outcome may seem perfectly predictable, such as whether class will meet tomorrow or whether IBM will still be a leader in computer technology in the year 2000. Feel free to still call these "random experiments" so long as there is any conceivable doubt about the out come, even if it is *nearly* certain.

[5] In order to be completely precise, you must specify what the outcome is in case nobody answers the telephone or they refuse to tell you their income. In this case, suppose you select a new number to dial and repeat the process until you get an income number. In this way, each time the random experiment is run you obtain an income figure as the outcome. Although this solves the immediate problem for probability, nonresponse remains a problem with statistical analysis because there is a group (the nonrespondents) for which you have no income information.

A complex situation usually contains many different random experiments; you are free to define the particular one (or ones) that will be most useful. For example, the selection of one TV dinner for quality inspection is a random experiment all by itself, producing just one quality number. The selection of all 15 TV dinners is also a random experiment—a larger one— producing a list of 15 quality numbers as its outcome.

Think of a random experiment as the arena in which things happen. By narrowing things down to a relatively small situation, you can think more clearly about the possible results.

The Sample Space: A List of What *Might* Happen

Each random experiment has a **sample space,** which is a list of *all possible outcomes* of the random experiment, prepared in advance without knowledge of what will happen when the experiment is run. Note that there is nothing random about the sample space. It is the (definite) list of things that might happen. This is an effective way to make a random situation more definite, and it will often help to clarify your thinking as well. Here are the sample spaces corresponding to the previous random experiments:

1 For the quality testing of TV dinners, the sample space is the collection of all possible lists of 15 numbers from 1 to 10. This sample space is too large to be presented in its entirety,[6] but here is how it might start and end:

1	1	1	1	1	1	1	1	1	1	1	1	1	1	1	(First list)
1	1	1	1	1	1	1	1	1	1	1	1	1	1	2	
1	1	1	1	1	1	1	1	1	1	1	1	1	1	3	
·	·	·	·	·	·	·	·	·	·	·	·	·	·	·	
·	·	·	·	·	·	·	·	·	·	·	·	·	·	·	
1	1	1	1	1	1	1	1	1	1	1	1	1	1	9	
1	1	1	1	1	1	1	1	1	1	1	1	1	1	10	
1	1	1	1	1	1	1	1	1	1	1	1	1	2	1	
1	1	1	1	1	1	1	1	1	1	1	1	1	2	2	
1	1	1	1	1	1	1	1	1	1	1	1	1	2	3	
·	·	·	·	·	·	·	·	·	·	·	·	·	·	·	
·	·	·	·	·	·	·	·	·	·	·	·	·	·	·	
10	10	10	10	10	10	10	10	10	10	10	10	10	10	9	
10	10	10	10	10	10	10	10	10	10	10	10	10	10	10	(Last list)

2 For the focus group choosing the design of a new reading lamp, the sample space is much smaller, consisting of the seven proposed designs:

---

[6]In fact, there are 1,000,000,000,000,000 lists (lines) in this sample space. This is 10^{15}, since there are 10 possibilities for the first TV dinner, times 10 for the second, and so forth through the 15th.

```
Design A
Design B
Design C
Design D
Design E
Design F
Design G
```

3 For the family income survey, the sample space is a list of all possible income values. Let's assume that income must be zero or a positive number and think of the sample space as a list of all nonnegative dollar amounts:

```
$0.00
$0.01
$0.02
  ·
  ·
  ·

$34,999.99
$35,000.00
$35,000.01
  ·
  ·
```

The Outcome: What Actually Happens

Each time a random experiment is run, it produces exactly one **outcome**. Since the sample space contains all possible outcomes, there cannot be any surprises: the outcome of a random experiment must be contained in the sample space.

Here are outcomes from one run of each of our random experiments:

1 For the quality testing of TV dinners, the outcome is a list of the quality measures for each of the 15 dinners tested:

$$7 \quad 8 \quad 7 \quad 7 \quad 6 \quad 7 \quad 7 \quad 5 \quad 7 \quad 8 \quad 7 \quad 7 \quad 8 \quad 6 \quad 8$$

2 For the focus group, after much discussion, the outcome is the selected design:

Design D

3 For the family income survey, after one "nobody home" and one "none of your business," you reached an individual who reported the family income (the outcome):

$36,500.00

Events: Either They Happen or They Don't

The formal definition of an **event** is any collection of outcomes specified in advance, before the random experiment is run. In practical terms, all that matters is that you can tell whether the event happened or didn't each time the random experiment is run. You may have many events (or just one) for a random experiment, each event corresponding to some feature of interest to you.

Here are some events for each of our random experiments:

1 For the quality testing of TV dinners, consider the event "all 15 dinners were of acceptable quality, that is, with scores of 5 and above." For example, the observed outcome:

$$7 \quad 8 \quad 7 \quad 7 \quad 6 \quad 7 \quad 7 \quad 5 \quad 7 \quad 8 \quad 7 \quad 7 \quad 8 \quad 6 \quad 8$$

clearly qualifies as "acceptable," so you could say that the event did happen. However, had the outcome been

$$6 \quad 8 \quad 5 \quad 5 \quad 7 \quad 7 \quad 8 \quad 4 \quad 7 \quad 6 \quad 8 \quad 7 \quad 7 \quad 7 \quad 6$$

instead, the event would *not* have "happened" since dinners were not all of acceptable quality.

To view this event in terms of the formal definition, as a collection of outcomes, you would have the following collection of all outcomes:

5	5	5	5	5	5	5	5	5	5	5	5	5	5	5	(First list)
5	5	5	5	5	5	5	5	5	5	5	5	5	5	6	
5	5	5	5	5	5	5	5	5	5	5	5	5	5	7	
5	5	5	5	5	5	5	5	5	5	5	5	5	5	8	
5	5	5	5	5	5	5	5	5	5	5	5	5	5	9	
5	5	5	5	5	5	5	5	5	5	5	5	5	5	10	
5	5	5	5	5	5	5	5	5	5	5	5	5	6	5	
5	5	5	5	5	5	5	5	5	5	5	5	5	6	6	
5	5	5	5	5	5	5	5	5	5	5	5	5	6	7	
.	.	.	.	.	.	.	.	.	.	.	.	.	.	.	
.	.	.	.	.	.	.	.	.	.	.	.	.	.	.	
.	.	.	.	.	.	.	.	.	.	.	.	.	.	.	
10	10	10	10	10	10	10	10	10	10	10	10	10	10	9	
10	10	10	10	10	10	10	10	10	10	10	10	10	10	10	(Last list)

Thus, the event "all are of acceptable quality" happens if and only if the actual outcome is in the list.

2 For the focus group, consider the event "the chosen design is easy to produce," which includes only the following designs:

Design A
Design B
Design C
Design F

Since the observed outcome, design D, is not in this list, this event "did not happen." Unfortunately, the focus group selected a design that is not easily produced.

3 For the family income survey, consider three different events:

First event:	Low income:	$10,000.00 to $24,999.99
Second event:	Middle income:	$25,000.00 to $44,999.99
Third event:	Qualifying income:	$20,000.00 or over

For the observed outcome, $36,500.00, you see that the first event did not happen, and the other two did happen. Thus, the selected family is "middle income" and has a "qualifying income" but is not "low income."

As you can see, there is nothing mysterious going on here. You have to be very careful in your definitions of the random experiment, the sample space, outcomes, and events in order to impose order upon an uncertain situation. However, in the end, events lead to reasonable, ordinary statements such as "Today's production passed quality inspection" or "Hey, Marge, I found another qualifying family!"

■ 6.3 How Likely Is an Event?

You know that each event either happens or doesn't happen every time the random experiment is run. This really doesn't say much. You want to know how *likely* the event is. This is provided by a number called the *probability of the event*. We will define this concept, indicate where the probability numbers come from, and show how the probability indicates the approximate proportion of time the event will occur when the random experiment is run many times.

Every Event Has a Probability

Every event has a number between 0 and 1, called its **probability**, which expresses how likely it is that the event will happen each time the random experiment is run. A probability of 0 indicates that the event essentially never happens, and a probability of 1 indicates that the event essentially always happens.[7] In general, the probability indicates approximately what proportion of the time the event is expected to happen:

---

[7]Due to mathematical technicalities, an event with probability 0 actually can happen. However, it cannot happen very often, and indeed, in technical language, we say that it "almost never happens." If you like to wonder about these things, consider, for example, the probability of pumping exactly 254,896.3542082947839478…barrels of oil tomorrow.

Probability	Interpretation
1.00	Always happens (essentially)
.95	Happens about 95% of the time: very likely
.50	Happens about half of the time
.37	Happens about 37% of the time
.02	Happens about 2% of the time (unlikely, but possible)
.00	Never happens (essentially)

Some care is needed in interpreting these numbers. If you have a one-shot situation that cannot be repeated (such as the probability that an old building will be successfully dynamited), a probability of 0.97 expresses a high likelihood of success with a small possibility of failure. However, it would be inappropriate to say, "we expect success about 97% of the time" unless you plan to repeat this exact procedure on many similar buildings in the future.

Another way to express likelihood is with *odds,* a positive number defined as the probability that the event happens divided by the probability that it does not happen:

■ The Odds

$$\text{Odds} = \frac{\text{Probability that the event happens}}{\text{Probability that the event does not happen}}$$

$$= \frac{\text{Probability}}{1 - \text{Probability}}$$

For example, a probability of 0.5 corresponds to odds of $0.5/(1 - 0.5) = 1$, sometimes stated as "odds of 1 to 1." A probability of 0.8 has odds of $0.8/(1 - 0.8) = 4$, or 4 to 1. Higher odds indicate higher probabilities and greater likelihood. Note that although the probability cannot be outside the range from 0 to 1, the odds can be any nonnegative number.

Where Do Probabilities Come From?

In textbooks, numbers to use as probabilities are often given along with other information about a problem. In real life, however, there are no tags attached saying, "By the way, the probability that the bolt will be defective and cause a problem is 0.003." How do we get the probability numbers to use in real life? There are three main ways: *relative frequency* (by experiment), *theoretical probability* (by formula), and *subjective probability* (by opinion.)

Relative Frequency and the Law of Large Numbers

Suppose you are free to run a random experiment as many times as you wish under the same exact circumstances each time, except for the randomness. The **relative frequency** of an event is the proportion of times the event occurs out of the number of times the experiment is run. It may be given either as a proportion (such as 0.148) or as a percentage (such as 14.8%). The formula for the relative frequency of an event is given by:

$$\text{Relative frequency of an event} = \frac{\text{Number of times the event occurs}}{\text{Number of times the random experiment is run}}$$

For example, if you interview 536 willing people and find 212 with qualifying incomes of $20,000.00 or over, the relative frequency is:

$$\frac{212}{536} = 0.396 \quad \text{or} \quad 39.6\%$$

For this relative frequency of 39.6% to make sense, the random experiment must be "find the income of a willing person" and the event of interest must be "income is $20,000.00 or over." With these definitions, it is clear that you have run the random experiment $n = 536$ times. There is another, different random experiment of interest here, namely, "find the incomes of 536 willing people"; however, the notion of relative frequency does not make sense for this larger random experiment because it has only been run once.

These are not trivial differences; managers often find this kind of careful "mental discipline" useful in dealing with more complex problems. The relative frequency and the probability of an event are similar but different concepts. The important difference is that the probability is an *exact number* whereas the relative frequency is a *random number*. This is because the probability of an event is a property of the basic situation (random experiment, sample space, event), whereas the relative frequency depends on the (random) outcomes that were produced when the random experiment was run n times.

Relative frequencies may be used as estimates (best guesses) of probability numbers when you have information from previous experience. For example, you might use this relative frequency (39.6% for qualified income) as an approximation to the true probability that a randomly chosen, willing person will have a qualifying income. You could then use this number, 0.396, as if it were a probability. Keep in mind, however, that there is a difference between the true (unknown) probability number and your best guess using the relative frequency approach.

The **law of large numbers** says that the relative frequency will be close to the probability if the experiment is run many times, that is, when n is large.

How close, typically, will the (random) relative frequency be to the (fixed) probability? The answer, which depends on how likely the event is and how many runs (n) are made, is provided in terms of a standard deviation in Table 6.3.1. For example, if an event has probability 0.75 and you run the random experiment $n = 100$ times, then you can expect the relative frequency to be approximately 0.04 above or below the true probability (0.75) on average.

Figures 6.3.1 and 6.3.2 show an example of how the relative frequency (the random line in each graph) approaches the probability (the fixed horizontal line at 0.25 in each graph). Note that the vertical scale has been en-

TABLE 6.3.1   Standard Deviation of the Relative Frequency

	Probability of 0.50	Probability of 0.25 or 0.75	Probability of 0.10 or 0.90
$n = 10$	0.16	0.14	0.09
25	0.10	0.09	0.06
50	0.07	0.06	0.04
100	0.05	0.04	0.03
1,000	0.02	0.01	0.01

FIGURE 6.3.1   The relative frequency of an event approximates its probability (0.25 in this case) and generally gets closer as n grows. With $n = 100$, you expect to be within approximately 0.04 of the probability.

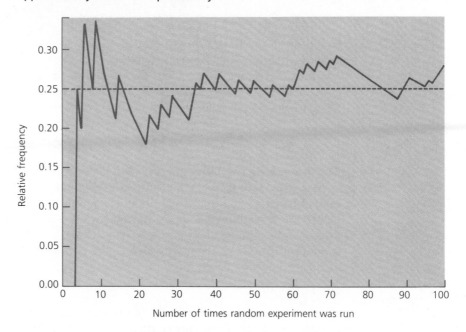

FIGURE 6.3.2   The relative frequency of an event, shown for n = 100 to 1,000 runs of a random experiment. Most of the time, the relative frequency will be within about 0.01 of the probability (0.25 in this example) when n = 1,000. Note the change in scale from the previous graph.

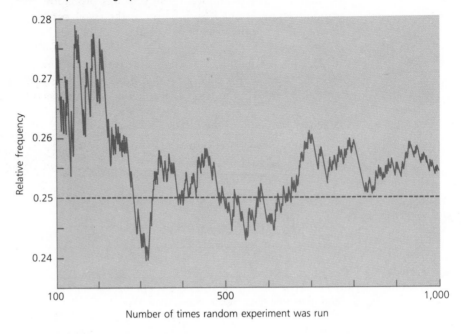

larged in Figure 6.3.2; this can be done because the relative frequency is closer to the probability for larger n.

Since the relative frequency is fairly close to the probability (at least for larger values of n) due to the law of large numbers, it is appropriate to use a relative frequency as a "best guess" of the probability based on available data.

Theoretical Probability

The **theoretical probability** is a probability number computed using an exact formula based on a mathematical theory or model. This approach can be used only with systems that can be described in mathematical terms. Most theoretical probability methods are too involved to be presented here. We will cover only the special case of the *equally likely* rule and, in later sections, special probability distributions such as the normal and the binomial.

The *Equally Likely* Rule

If all outcomes are equally likely, and this is a big "if," it is easy to find the probability of any event using theoretical probability. The probability is proportional to the number of outcomes represented by the event, according to the following formula:

If all outcomes are equally likely, then:

$$\text{Probability of an event} = \frac{\text{Number of outcomes in the event}}{\text{Total number of possible outcomes}}$$

EXAMPLE

Coin Tossing and Cards

Since a flipped coin is as likely to land "heads" as "tails," the probability of each of these events is 1/2. What about the three outcomes "heads," "tails," and "on edge"? Since there are three outcomes, does it follow that each of these has probability 1/3? Of course not, since the requirement that "all outcomes be equally likely" is violated here; the rule does not apply since the probability of a flipped coin landing on its edge is minuscule compared to the other two possibilities.

Since cards are generally shuffled before playing, which helps ensure randomness, the *equally likely* rule should apply to any situation in which you specify a property of one random card. For example, since 13 out of the 52 cards are hearts, the probability of receiving a heart is 0.25. Similarly, the probability of receiving an ace is 4/52 = 7.7%, and the probability of receiving a one-eyed jack is 2/52 = 3.8%.

EXAMPLE

Gender and Hiring

For another example, suppose that 15 equally qualified people have applied for a job and 6 are women. If the hiring choice is made from this group randomly (and, thus, without regard to gender), the probability that a woman will be chosen is 6/15 = 0.40 or 40%. This situation fits the *equally likely* rule if you view the random experiment as choosing one of these people and the event as "a woman is chosen." This event consists of 6 outcomes (the 6 women), and the probability is, then, 6 out of 15, the total number of possible job candidates (outcomes).

EXAMPLE

Defective Raw Materials

Suppose your supplier has a warehouse containing 83 automatic transmissions, of which 2 are defective. If one is chosen at random (without knowledge of which are defective), what is the probability that you will receive a defective part? The answer, by the *equally likely* rule, is 2 out of 83, or 2.4%.

Subjective Probability

A **subjective probability** is anyone's opinion of what the probability is for an event. While this may not seem very scientific, it is often the best you can do when you have no past experience (so you can't use relative frequency) and no theory (so you can't use theoretical probability). One way to improve the quality of a subjective probability is to use the opinion of an expert in that field, for example, an investment banker's opinion of the probability that a hostile takeover will succeed or an engineer's opinion of the feasibility of a new energy technology.

EXAMPLE   ### Settling a Lawsuit

Your firm has just been sued. Your first reaction is "Oh no!" but then you realize that firms get sued for various reasons all the time. So you sit down to review the details, which include claimed consequential damages of $5 million. Next you call a meeting of your firm's executives and lawyers to discuss strategy. So that you can choose the most effective strategy, it will help you to know how *likely* the various possible consequences are.

This is, of course, a probability situation. You are sitting right in the middle of a huge random experiment:

> Observe the progress of the lawsuit, and record the outcome in terms of (1) dollars spent (for fees and damages, if any) and (2) the resolution (dismissal, settlement without trial, judge trial, or jury trial).

Since so many lawsuits reach settlement without going to trial, you decide initially to consider the various possible costs of settlement. Three events of interest here would be:

1 Inexpensive settlement: less than $100,000.
2 Moderate settlement: $100,000 to $1,000,000.
3 Expensive settlement: over $1,000,000.

How will you find probabilities for these events? There have not been enough similar cases to rely on the relative frequency approach, even after consulting computerized legal databases to identify related lawsuits. There is no scientific theory that would give a formula for these probabilities, which rules out the theoretical·probability approach. This leaves only the avenue of subjective probability.

To find subjective probability values for these events, at the meeting it is decided to use the opinions of a legal expert who is familiar with this kind of litigation. After studying the particular details of the case and evaluating it with respect to a few previous similar cases and knowledge about the current "mood" in the legal system, your expert reports the following subjective probabilities:

1 Probability of inexpensive settlement: 0.10.
2 Probability of moderate settlement: 0.65.
3 Probability of expensive settlement: 0.15.

Note that these probabilities add up to 0.90, leaving a 10% chance of going to trial (i.e., *not* settling).

These subjective probabilities, representing your best assessment of the various likelihoods, tell you that there will probably be a moderate settlement. You are relieved that the likely dollar figure is substantially less than the $5 million mentioned in the initial papers. You can then use these probability numbers to help guide you in making the difficult decisions about the type and quantity of resources to bring forward in your defense.

Bayesian and Non-Bayesian Analysis

The methods of **Bayesian analysis** in statistics involve the use of subjective probabilities in a formal, mathematical way. Figure 6.3.3 (top) shows how a Bayesian analysis puts the observed data together with prior probabilities and a model (a mathematical description of the situation) to compute the results.

A non-Bayesian analysis is called a **frequentist analysis** and appears initially to be more objective since its calculations depend only on the observed data and the model. However, a more careful examination, shown in Figure 6.3.3 (bottom), reveals the hidden role that subjective opinions play by guiding the selection of the design (which produces the data) and the selection of a model.

FIGURE 6.3.3 The general approaches of the Bayesian and the frequentist (non-Bayesian) statisticians. Although both use prior subjective information, the Bayesian uses it in a direct way in computing the results. The frequentist, on the other hand, uses prior information in an informal way to set the stage for a seemingly more "objective" calculation.

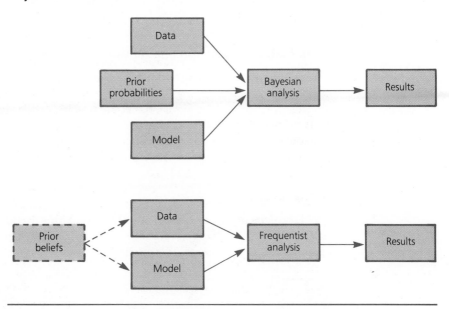

Bayesian analysis can be useful in complex statistical studies in business, especially when there is an expert available who has fairly reliable information that you want to include in the analysis along with the data. If this expert opinion can be used effectively in the design of the study and the choice of model, then there would be no need to use complex Bayesian calculations. However, if the situation is important enough and the expert opinion is precise enough to warrant special attention and care, then a Bayesian analysis should be considered.

■ 6.4 How Can You Combine Information about More than One Event?

There are two "big wins" you can get from understanding probability. The first one, which we have already covered, is appreciation of the concept of the likelihood of an event as a probability number and the corresponding mind-focusing activity of identifying the random experiment. This is a big step toward understanding a vague, uncertain situation. The second "big win" is the ability to consider *combinations of events* and to learn how to take information about the probabilities of some events and use it to find the probabilities of other events that are perhaps more interesting or important.

Keep in mind the objective: to combine the information you have with the basic rules of probability to obtain new, more useful information. Strictly speaking, this derived information is not really "new" since it logically follows from the old information. Rather, it represents a better presentation of the information you already have. The ability to quickly find these logical consequences will help you explore *what if* scenarios to guide your business decisions.

Venn Diagrams Help You See All the Possibilities

A **Venn diagram** is a picture that represents the universe of all possible outcomes (the sample space) as a rectangle with events indicated inside, often as circles or ovals, as in Figure 6.4.1. Each point inside the rectangle represents a possible outcome. Each time the random experiment is run, a point (outcome) is selected at random; if this point falls within an event's circle, then the event "happens"; otherwise the event does not happen.

Not an Event

The **complement** of an event is another event that happens only when the first event does *not* happen. Every event has a complement.[8] Here are some examples of complements of events:

---

[8]Please note the spelling. While every event has a *complement,* as defined here, only those events that are especially nice and well-behaved will deserve a *"compliment"* (spelled with an "i.")

Event	Complement of the Event
Successful product launch	Unsuccessful launch
Stock price went up	Stock price held steady or dropped
Production had acceptable quality	Production quality was not acceptable

When you think of an event as a collection of outcomes, the complementary event consists of all outcomes in the sample space that are *not* represented by the first event. This is illustrated by the Venn diagram in Figure 6.4.2.

FIGURE 6.4.1   A Venn diagram with two events, each indicated by a circle. Note that some points (outcomes) fall inside both circles, some fall outside both, and some fall within one but not the other. This is a convenient visual representation of all possibilities with two events.

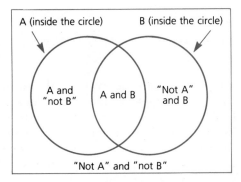

FIGURE 6.4.2   A Venn diagram with the complement "not A" indicated. The complement of A is an event that happens when (and only when) A does *not* happen.

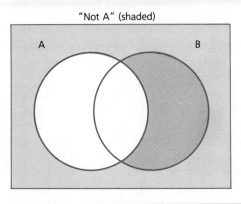

When constructing the complement of an event, be sure that you consider all possibilities. For example, the complement of "price went up" is *not* "price went down" because you must also include the possibility that the price remained steady.

The Complement (*not*) Rule

Since an event and its complement together represent all possible outcomes, with no duplication, the sum of their probabilities is 1. This leads to the following rule for an event we'll call A and its complement, called "not A":

$$\text{Probability of A} + \text{Probability of "not A"} = 1$$

This formula can be rewritten to determine the probability of the complement:

■ **The Complement Rule**

Probability of "not A" = 1 − Probability of A

For example, if the probability of a successful product launch is known to be 0.4, the probability of the complementary event "unsuccessful launch" is $1 - 0.4 = 0.6$.

The complement rule is the first illustration here of a method for getting "new" probability information (the probability of the complementary event) from facts that are already known (the probability of the event itself). If you're not impressed yet, please read on.

One Event *and* Another

Any two events can be combined to produce another event, called their **intersection**, which occurs whenever one event *and* the other event both happen as a result of a single run of the random experiment.

When you think of two events as collections of outcomes, their intersection is a new collection consisting of all outcomes contained in both collections, as illustrated in Figure 6.4.3.

For example, as manager of a business supplies firm, you may want to consider what you would do if a recession occurs next year and your competitors respond by lowering prices. The random experiment here is "at the end of next year, observe and record the state of the economy and the pricing policies of your competitors." The two events are "recession" (which will either occur or not occur) and "competitors lowered prices." Your current concern is with a new event, "recession *and* lower competitor prices." In order to formulate a policy, it will be helpful to consider how likely this new possibility is.

FIGURE 6.4.3   A Venn diagram with the intersection "A and B" indicated. This event happens when (and only when) A happens *and* B happens in a single run of the random experiment.

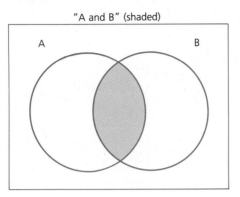

"A and B" (shaded)

The Intersection (*and*) Rules

To find the exact probability of this new event, the intersection of two other events, you will need *three* pieces of information. Just having the two probabilities (one for each event) is not enough; some indication of their relationship to each another is also needed. However, you can find *bounds* for the probability that both will happen, which let you say that this probability must fall between two numbers without specifying exactly what it is.

For example, based on the past experience of your repair shop, suppose the probability of a blown fuse is 6% and the probability of a broken wire is 4%. What is the probability of a blown fuse *and* a broken wire? You can't answer this based on the information given. It could be as small as 0% (if you never see an appliance with both problems) or as high as 4% (if every appliance with a broken wire also has a blown fuse).

In general, the probability of the intersection (A and B) cannot be larger than the smaller of the two probabilities. Also, it cannot be smaller than the sum of the probabilities of the events minus 1, because large events (with high probabilities) are forced to overlap within the sample space of total probability 1. Of course, the probability cannot be a negative number. Thus, some partial information about the probability of the intersection is provided by the following formulas, which are illustrated in Figure 6.4.4.

■ **The Intersection (*and*) Rules**

Probability of "A and B" ≤ Smaller of $\begin{cases} \text{Probability of A} \\ \text{Probability of B} \end{cases}$

Probability of "A and B" ≥ Larger of $\begin{cases} \text{Probability of A} + \text{Probability of B} - 1 \\ 0 \end{cases}$

FIGURE 6.4.4   The intersection rules for the probability of "A and B." The top diagram shows that this probability cannot be larger than the smaller of the two probabilities. The bottom diagram shows that when the events have large probabilities, the probability of "A and B" cannot be too small because of the forced overlap.

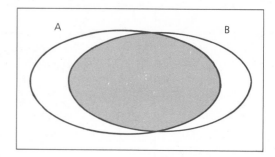

If these bounds are subtracted from 1, the above rules also give best- and worst-case scenarios for the complement of "A and B," which is the event "either A failed or B failed to happen."

For the appliance repair example, the first of the two formulas tells you that the probability of "blown fuse and broken wire" can be no larger than 4%, the smaller of the probabilities of the two events. The second formula tells you that it must be at least $0.06 + 0.04 - 1.00 = -0.90$, which really tells you nothing useful since you already know that the probability cannot be a negative number.

This last formula is useful only when the probabilities of the events are fairly large. For example, if the chances of convincing a new MBA student to join your firm is 75% and you think that there is an 85% chance that the firm will continue to expand, then there must be *at least* a $0.75 + 0.85 - 1.00 = 0.60$ or 60% chance that the student will join *and* your firm will continue to expand.

What if Both Events Can't Happen at Once?

Two events that cannot both happen at once are said to be **mutually exclusive events.** For example, you could not end the year with both "very good" and "very bad" profits. It is also impossible for your next recruit to be both a "male minority Ph.D." and a "female engineer with an MBA." Figure 6.4.5 shows a Venn diagram for two mutually exclusive events as two circles that do not overlap.

The Intersection (*and*) Rule for Mutually Exclusive Events

Since two mutually exclusive events cannot both happen at once, the probability of their intersection is 0. There is no problem with defining the inter-

FIGURE 6.4.5   A Venn diagram for two mutually exclusive events, which cannot both happen on a single run of the random experiment. Because the circles do not overlap, there are no points common to both events.

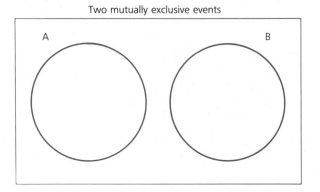

Two mutually exclusive events

section of two mutually exclusive events; this intersection is a perfectly valid event, but it can never happen. This implies that its probability is 0.

> ■ **The Intersection (*and*) Rule for Two Mutually Exclusive Events**
>
> Probability of "A and B" = 0

One Event *or* Another

Any two events can be combined to produce another event, called their **union**, which happens whenever either one event or the other event (or both events) happen as a result of a single run of the random experiment.[9]

When you think of two events as collections of outcomes, their union is a new collection consisting of all outcomes contained in either (or both) collections, as illustrated in Figure 6.4.6.

For example, suppose your labor contract is coming up for renegotiation soon, and you expect your workers to demand large increases in pay and benefits. With respect to management's most likely contract proposal, you want to know how likely the various consequences are so that you can plan ahead for contingencies. In particular, your workers might go on strike. Another possibility is a work slowdown. Either one would be a problem for you. The random experiment here is "wait and record labor's reaction to man-

---

[9]By convention, we will use the word *or* to signify "one or the other or both." Thus, you could say that the event "inflation or recession" happened not only during purely inflationary times or purely recessionary times, but also during those relatively rare time periods when both economic conditions prevailed.

FIGURE 6.4.6   A Venn diagram with the union "A or B" indicated. This event happens whenever either A happens, B happens, or both events happen in a single run of the random experiment.

"A or B" (sháded)

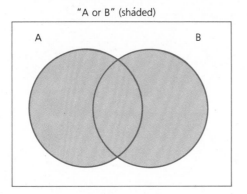

agement's contract proposal." The two events under consideration are "strike" and "slowdown." The union of these two events, "strike or slow-down," is clearly an important possibility since it represents a broad class of problem situations that will require your attention.

The Union (*or*) Rules

To find the exact probability of this new event, the union of two other events, you will again need *three* pieces of information; that is, some indication of the relationship between these two events is also needed. However, as with the intersection, you can find *bounds* for the probability that one or the other (or both) will happen, letting you say that this probability must fall between two numbers even though you can't specify it.

For example, consider an advertising campaign. For a particular TV advertisement, you have found there is a 35% chance that a typical person recalls seeing the ad and a 20% chance that the viewer is persuaded to raise his or her opinion of your product. The union of these two events, "recalls or is persuaded," represents those cases in which the ad has had some effect on the viewer. Based on just these two numbers, what can you say about the probability that a person either recalls or is persuaded? It could be as low as 35% (if all of those persuaded also recalled) or as high as 55% (if all of those who recalled were different from those persuaded).

In general, the probability of the union cannot be smaller than the larger of the two probabilities. Also, it cannot be larger than the sum of the probabilities. Of course, the probability cannot be larger than 1. Thus, some information about the probability of the union is provided by the following formulas, which are illustrated in Figure 6.4.7.

FIGURE 6.4.7   The union rules for the probability of "A or B." The diagram at the left shows that this probability cannot be smaller than the larger of the two probabilities because it contains each one. The diagram at the right shows that as the amount of overlap decreases, the probability of "A or B" gets closer to the sum of the probabilities, although it cannot be larger.

 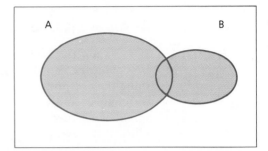

■ The Union (*or*) Rules

$$\text{Probability of ``A or B''} \geq \text{Larger of} \begin{cases} \text{Probability of A} \\ \text{Probability of B} \end{cases}$$

$$\text{Probability of ``A or B''} \leq \text{Smaller of} \begin{cases} \text{Probability of A + Probability of B} \\ 1 \end{cases}$$

For the advertising example, the first formula tells you that the probability of "recalls or was persuaded" is at least 35%, the larger of the probabilities of the two events. The second formula tells you that the probability can be no larger than 20% + 35% = 55%.

Don't be concerned if, in other situations, you find a number greater than 1 for the sum of the two probabilities (for example, 0.6 + 0.8 = 1.4). Since you already know that probabilities must be 1 or smaller, the second formula really provides no useful information in such a case.

The Union (*or*) Rule for Mutually Exclusive Events

If two events are mutually exclusive (i.e., they cannot both happen), you can find the exact probability of their union by adding their individual probabilities together. Knowing that they are mutually exclusive provides that extra piece of information that allows you to do more than simply specify bounds for the probability of their union.

Since two mutually exclusive events have no outcomes in common, when you add their probabilities, you count each outcome exactly once. Thus, the probability of their union is the sum of their individual probabilities:

■ **The Union (*or*) Rule for Two Mutually Exclusive Events**

Probability of "A or B" = Probability of A + Probability of B

Finding *or* from *and* and Vice Versa

If you know the probabilities of the three events A, B, and "A and B," the probability of "A or B" can be found. This probability is determined by summing the two probabilities of the basic events and subtracting the probability of their intersection. The subtraction represents those outcomes that would be counted *twice* otherwise, as illustrated in Figure 6.4.8. The probability of the event "A or B" is given by the following formula:

■ **Finding *or* from *and***

Probability of "A or B" = Probability of A + Probability of B

− Probability of "A and B"

FIGURE 6.4.8   A Venn diagram showing how the probability of "A or B" may be found. First add the probability of A and the probability of B. Then subtract the amount that has been counted twice, namely, the probability of the event "A and B."

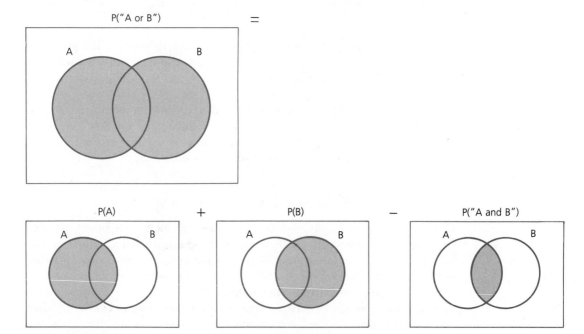

For example, based on the past experience in your repair shop, suppose the probability of a blown fuse is 6% and the probability of a broken wire is 4%. Suppose also that you know that 1% of appliances to be repaired come in with both a blown fuse *and* a broken wire. With these three pieces of information, you can easily find the probability that an appliance has one problem or the other (or both):

$$\text{Probability of “blown fuse or broken wire”} = 0.06 + 0.04 - 0.01$$
$$= 0.09$$

Thus, 9% of these appliances have one or the other problem (or both).

Using algebra, we can find a formula for the probability of "A and B" in terms of the probabilities of A, B, and "A or B":

■ **Finding *and* from *or***

Probability of "A and B" = Probability of A + Probability of B

− Probability of "A or B"

In fact, based on knowledge of any three of the four probabilities (for A, B, "A and B," and "A or B"), the remaining probability can be found.

When are these formulas useful? One application is to take known information about probabilities and use a formula to find the probability for another event, perhaps a more meaningful or useful one. Another application is to ensure that the information you are basing decisions on is logically consistent. Suppose, for example, that you have probabilities for A and for B from the relative frequency approach using past data, and you plan to use subjective probabilities for the events "A and B" and "A or B." You will want to make sure that the four resulting probabilities taken together satisfy the preceding formulas.

One Event *Given* Another: Reflecting Current Information

When you revise the probability of an event to reflect information that another event has occurred, the result is the **conditional probability** of the first event *given* the other event. (All of the ordinary probabilities you have learned about so far can be called **unconditional probabilities** if necessary to avoid confusion.) Here are some examples of conditional probabilities:

1 Suppose the home team has a 70% chance of winning the big game. Now introduce new information in terms of the event "the team is ahead at halftime." Depending on how this event turns out, the probability of winning should be revised. The probability of winning given that we are ahead at halftime would be larger, say, 85%. This 85% is the conditional probability of the event "win" given the event "ahead at halftime." The

probability of winning given that we are *behind* at halftime would be less than the 70% overall chance of winning, say, 35%. This 35% is the conditional probability of "win" given "behind at halftime."

2 Success of a new business project is influenced by many factors. To describe their effects, you could discuss the conditional probability of success given various factors, such as a favorable or unfavorable economic climate and actions by competitors. An expanding economy would increase the chances of success; that is, the conditional probability of success given an expanding economy would be larger than the (unconditional) probability of success.

The Rule for Finding a Conditional Probability Given Certain Information

To find the conditional probability of the event "success" given "expanding economy," you would proceed by computing, out of all "expanding economy" scenarios, the proportion that correspond to "success." This is the probability of "success and expanding economy" divided by the probability of "expanding economy."

This is the general rule for finding conditional probabilities. The conditional probability of A given B, provided the probability of B is positive, is:[10]

$$\text{Conditional probability of A given B} = \frac{\text{Probability of "A and B"}}{\text{Probability of B}}$$

It makes a difference whether you are determining the conditional probability of A given B (which is the probability for A updated to reflect B) or the conditional probability of B given A (which is the quite different probability of B updated to reflect A). For completeness, here is the formula for the other conditional probability.

$$\text{Conditional probability of B given A} = \frac{\text{Probability of "A and B"}}{\text{Probability of A}}$$

For example, if the probability of a blown fuse is 6%, the probability of a broken wire is 4%, and the probability of "blown fuse and broken wire" is 1%, you can compute the conditional probability of a broken wire given a blown fuse:

$$\begin{aligned}\text{Conditional probability of broken wire given blown fuse} &= \frac{\text{Probability of "broken wire and blown fuse"}}{\text{Probability of blown fuse}} \\ &= \frac{0.01}{0.06} \\ &= 0.17\end{aligned}$$

---

[10]Since you divide by the probability of B, the formula will not work if the event B has probability 0. In this special case, the conditional probability would be undefined. This is not a problem in practice since an event with probability 0 (essentially) never happens; hence, it doesn't really matter what happens "conditionally" on B.

In this case, having a blown fuse implies a greater likelihood that the wire is broken.

This conditional probability tells you that, out of all appliances you typically see that have a blown fuse, 17% also have a broken wire. Note how much greater this conditional probability is than the unconditional probability for a broken wire (4%). This happens because when you are given the fact that the fuse is blown, you are no longer talking about "all appliances" but are considering relatively few (6%) of them. The probability of "broken wire" is then revised from 4% to 17% to reflect this new information.

Figure 6.4.9 shows a Venn diagram for this situation. Note that the unconditional probabilities within each circle add up to the correct numbers (0.06 for blown fuse and 0.04 for broken wire). For the conditional probabiities, since you are assured (by the given information) that there is a blown fuse, this circle becomes the new sample space because no other outcomes are possible. Within this new sample space, the old probabilities must be divided by 0.06 (the unconditional probability of a blown fuse) so that they represent 100% of the new situation.

FIGURE 6.4.9   A Venn diagram for unconditional probabilities (top) and conditional probabilities (bottom) given a blown fuse. With the given information, only the "blown fuse" circle is relevant; thus, it becomes the entire sample space. Dividing the old probabilities by 0.06 (the probability of a blown fuse) gives you their conditional probabilities within the new sample space.

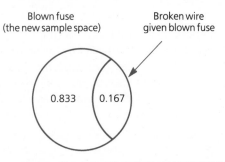

Conditional Probabilities for Mutually Exclusive Events

Since two mutually exclusive events cannot both happen, if you are given information that one has happened, it follows that the other did *not* happen. That is, the conditional probability of one event given the other is 0, provided the probability of the other event is not 0.

■ Conditional Probabilities for Two Mutually Exclusive Events

Conditional probability of A given B = 0

provided the probability of B is not 0.

Independent Events

Two events are said to be **independent events** if information about one does not change your assessment of the probability of the other. If information about one event *does* change your assessment of the probability of the other, the events are **dependent events.** For example, "being a smoker" and "getting cancer" are dependent events because we know that smokers are more likely to get cancer than nonsmokers. On the other hand, the events "your stock market portfolio will go up tomorrow" and "you will oversleep tomorrow morning" are independent events since your oversleeping will not affect the behavior of stock market prices.[11]

Formally, events A and B are independent if the probability of A is the same as the conditional probability of A given B.

Events A and B are independent if:

Probability of A = Conditional Probability of A given B

Events A and B are dependent if:

Probability of A ≠ Conditional Probability of A given B

There are several ways to find out whether two events are independent or dependent. You will usually need to use a formula; just "thinking hard" about whether they *should* be independent or not should be used only as a last resort when there is not enough information available to use the formulas. Following are three formulas. Use the formula that is easiest in terms of

---

[11]Unless, of course, you are a very powerful player in the financial markets and miss an important "power breakfast" meeting.

the information at hand, since all three methods must (by algebra) always give the same answer.[12]

Events A and B are independent if any of these formulas is true:

Probability of A = Conditional probability of A given B

Probability of B = Conditional probability of B given A

Probability of A and B = Probability of A × Probability of B

The third formula may be used to find the probability of "A and B" for two events that are known to be independent. However, this formula gives the wrong answer for dependent events.

EXAMPLE   Women in Executive Positions

For Seattle corporations with 500 or more employees, there are 468 executives, of whom 30 are women.[13] Using the relative frequency approach, you could say that the conditional probability of a person being a woman given that the person is an executive is 30/468 = 0.064 (i.e., 6.4% of executives are women). In the population at large, the (unconditional) probability of being a woman is 51.3%.[14] Since the probability of being a woman changes from 51.3% to only 6.4% when the extra information "is an executive" is given, these are *not* independent events. That is, "being a woman" and "being an executive" are dependent events. Note that this conclusion follows from the rules (given by the equations above) and the numbers, and *not* from pure thought about the situation.

The fact that these are dependent events expresses the historical fact that there have been gender differences in this time and place: men are more likely to be executives than are women (different probabilities of being an executive), and executives are more likely to be men than are people in the population at large (different probabilities of being male).

This probability analysis shows that there are gender differences, but it does not explain why. By looking at the percentages, a dependence, indicating gender differences, has clearly been found. These differences might be due to discrimination in hiring, a restricted supply of qualified job candidates, or some other reason; probability analysis will not (by itself) tell you which explanation is correct.

---

[12]There is just one technical difficulty to be considered: If one of the events has probability 0, it is not possible to compute the conditional probability of the other. Whenever one (or both) events has probability 0, we will declare them (automatically) independent of each other.

[13]Information is from "Seattle Corporations with 500 or More Employees," *Pacific Northwest Executive*, April 1988, p. 20.

[14]This is based on the total U.S. population of males (116,649,000) and of females (122,634,000), as reported in Bureau of the Census, *Statistical Abstract of the United States, 1987* (Washington, 1986), p. 14.

EXAMPLE **Market Efficiency**

Financial markets are said to be *efficient* if current prices reflect all available information. According to the theory of market efficiency, it is not possible to make special profits based on analyzing past price information, since this information is already reflected in the current price. Another conclusion is that prices must change randomly, since any systematic changes would be anticipated by the market.

One way to test market efficiency is to see whether there is any connection between yesterday's price change and today's price change. If the two events "price went up yesterday" and "price went up today" are independent, this would support the theory of market efficiency. In this case, knowing yesterday's price behavior would not help you predict the course of the market today.

On the other hand, if these events are dependent, then markets are not efficient. For example, if markets have "momentum" and tend to continue their upward or downward swings, then knowledge that the market went up yesterday would increase the likelihood of a rise today. This is incompatible with market efficiency, which holds that the markets would *anticipate* this further rise, and there would be no difference between the unconditional and the conditional probabilities.

The Intersection (*and*) Rule for Independent Events

As mentioned earlier, for independent events (and *only* for independent events) you can find the probability of "A and B" by simply multiplying the probabilities of the two events.

■ **The Intersection (*and*) Rule for Independent Events**

Probability of "A and B" = Probability of A × Probability of B

EXAMPLE **Risk Assessment for a Large Power Plant**

Large power plants present some risk due to the potential for disaster. Although this possibility is small, the news media remind you from time to time that disasters do happen. Suppose that the probability of overheating at your plant is 0.001 (one in a thousand) per day and the probability of failure of the backup cooling system is 0.000001 (one in a million). If you assume that these events are independent, the probability of "big trouble" (that is, the event "overheating and failure of backup cooling system") would be 0.001 × 0.000001 = 0.000000001 (one in a billion), which is a tolerably small likelihood for some people.

However, it may not be appropriate to assume that these events are independent. It may appear that there is no direct connection between failure of one system (causing overheating) and failure of the other (leaving you without backup cooling). However, independence is not determined by subjective thoughts but by looking at the probabilities themselves. It may well be that these are dependent events; for example, there might be a natural disaster (flood or earthquake) that causes *both* systems to fail. If the events are not independent, the "one in a billion" probability of "big trouble" would be wrong, and the actual probability could be much larger.

The Relationship between Independent and Mutually Exclusive Events

There is a big difference between *independent* and *mutually exclusive* events. In fact, two events that are independent *cannot* be mutually exclusive (unless one event has probability 0). Also, two events that are mutually exclusive cannot be independent (again, unless one event has probability 0). If one event (or both events) has probability 0, the events are independent *and* mutually exclusive.

■ 6.5 What's the Best Way to Solve Probability Problems?

There are two ways to solve probability problems: the hard way and the easy way. The hard way involves creative application of the right combination of the rules you have just learned. The easy way involves seeing the bigger picture by constructing a *probability tree* and reading the answers directly from the tree. Another useful method that helps you see what is going on is the construction of a *joint probability table*. A third method, already discussed, is the Venn diagram. Whether you use the easy way or the hard way, the answer will be the same.

Probability Trees

A **probability tree** is a picture indicating probabilities and conditional probabilities for combinations of two or more events. We will begin with an example of a completed tree and follow up with the details of how to construct the tree. Probability trees are closely related to *decision trees*, which are used in finance and other fields in business.

EXAMPLE **Software Support**

Software support is a demanding task. Some customers call to ask for advice on how to use the software. Others need help with problems they are having with it. Based on past experience as manager of software support, you have figured some probabilities for a typical support call and summarized your results in the probability tree shown in Figure 6.5.1.

Figure 6.5.1 includes a lot of information. Starting from the left, note that the probability of the event "irate caller" is 0.20 (that is, 20% of callers were irate, which says that 80% were not irate).

FIGURE 6.5.1   **Probability tree for the events "irate caller" and "was caller helped." The circled numbers are probabilities; the others are conditional probabilities.**

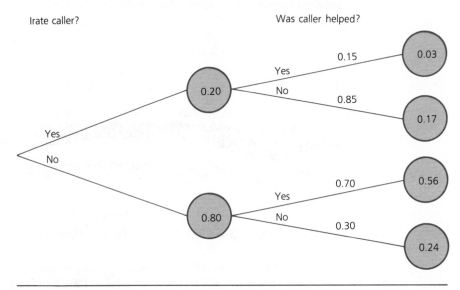

Some conditional probabilities are shown in the figure in the set of four branches directly under the heading "was caller helped?" Note that 15% of the irate callers were helped (this is the conditional probability of "helped" given "irate caller" and 85% of irate callers were not helped. Continuing down the remaining branches, we see that 70% of "not irate" callers were helped and 30% of these were not helped. We certainly seem to be doing a better job of helping nonirate callers (70% versus 15% help rates).

The circled numbers at the right in Figure 6.5.1 indicate the probabilities of various events formed using combinations of *and* and *not*. The probability that the caller is irate and is helped is 0.03. That is, 3% of all callers were both irate and helped. Next, 17% of callers were both irate and not helped; 56% of callers were not irate and were helped; and, finally, 24% of callers were both not irate and not helped.

From this tree you can find any probability of interest. For the event "irate caller," the probability is listed in the first column of circled numbers (0.20), with the probability of its complement, "not irate," just below. For the event "caller helped," the probability is found by adding the two circled probabilities at the right representing help: 0.03 + 0.56 = 0.59. The conditional probability for "caller helped" given "irate caller" is listed along that branch as 0.15. A little more work is required to find the conditional probability of "irate caller" given "caller helped." One solution is to use the definition of conditional probability:[15]

---

[15]This is the one formula you may still need from the last section. Probability trees do everything else for you!

$$\begin{aligned}\text{Conditional probability} \atop \text{of "irate caller"} \atop \text{given "caller helped"} &= \frac{\text{Probability of "irate caller and caller helped"}}{\text{Probability of "caller helped"}}\end{aligned}$$

$$= \frac{0.03}{0.03 + 0.56}$$

$$= 0.051$$

Thus, of all callers we helped, 5.1% were irate. The other way to find this conditional probability is to construct a new tree that begins with "was caller helped?" instead of "irate caller," since the *given* information must come first in order for the conditional probability to be listed in a probability tree.

Rules for Probability Trees

Constructing a probability tree consists of first drawing the basic tree, next recording all information given to you in the problem, and finally applying the fundamental rules to find the remaining numbers and complete the tree. Here are the rules for constructing a probability tree:

1 Probabilities are listed at each endpoint and circled. These add up to 1 (or 100%) at each level of the tree. For example, in Figure 6.5.1, at the first level is $0.20 + 0.80 = 1.00$, and at the second level is $0.03 + 0.17 + 0.56 + 0.24 = 1.00$. Use this rule if you have all but one circled probability in a column.

2 Conditional probabilities are listed along each branch (except perhaps for the first level) and add up to 1 (or 100%) for each group of branches radiating from a single point. For example, in the first branch of Figure 6.5.1 we have $0.15 + 0.85 = 1.00$, and at the second branch we have $0.70 + 0.30 = 1.00$. Use this rule if you have all but one conditional probability coming out from a single point.

3 The circled probability at a branch point times the conditional probability along a branch gives the circled probability at the end of the branch. For example, in Figure 6.5.1, for the upper-right branch line we have $0.20 \times 0.15 = 0.03$, for the next branch line we have $0.20 \times 0.85 = 0.17$, and similarly for the last two branch lines. Use this rule if you have all but one of the three numbers for a single branch line.

4 The circled probability at a branch point is the sum of the circled probabilities at the ends of all branches extending from it to the right. For example, in Figure 6.5.1, extending from the branch point labeled 0.20 are two branches ending with circled probabilities adding up to this number: $0.03 + 0.17 = 0.20$. Use this rule if you have all but one of the circled probabilities in a group consisting of one together with all of its branches.

Using these rules, if you know all but one of the probabilities for a particular branch or level, you can find the remaining probability. For reference, a generic probability tree is shown in Figure 6.5.2a, indicating the

FIGURE 6.5.2   a. A probability tree showing a variety of probabilities (in the circles) and conditional probabilities given A (along the branches). b. The generic Venn diagram, with the four basic probabilities indicated. These four probabilities are the same as the ending probabilities at the far right of a probability tree.

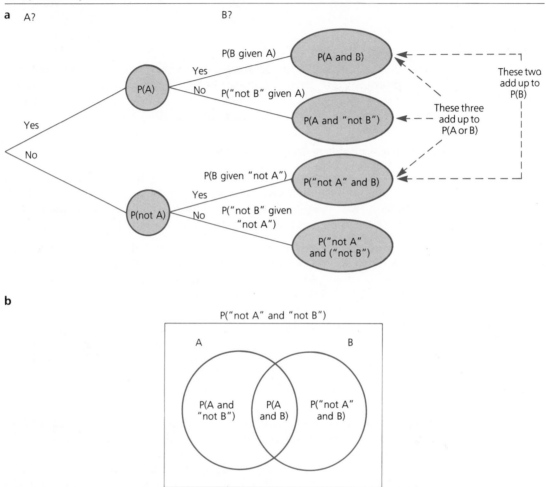

meanings of all numbers in the tree. The generic Venn diagram in Figure 6.5.2b is included for comparison.

EXAMPLE   **Drug Testing of Employees**

Your firm is considering mandatory drug testing of all employees. To assess the costs (resources for testing and possible morale problems) and benefits (a more productive work force), you have decided to study the probabilities of the various outcomes on a per-worker basis. The laboratory has provided you with some information, but not everything you need to know. Using a probability tree, you hope to compute the missing, helpful information.

The testing procedure is not perfect. You are told by the laboratory that if an employee uses drugs, the test will be "positive" with probability 0.90. Also, for employees who do not use drugs, the test will be "negative" (that is, "not positive") 95% of the time. Based on an informal poll of selected workers, you estimate that 8% of your employees use drugs.

Your basic probability tree for this situation is shown in Figure 6.5.3. The event "drug user" has been placed first since some of the initial information comes as a conditional probability given this information.

After recording the initial information, you have the tree in Figure 6.5.4. Note that 90% and 95% are conditional probabilities along the branches; the value 8% for drug users is an unconditional probability.

Although other problems may also provide three pieces of information from which to complete the tree, these items may well go in different places on the tree. For example, had you been given a probability (unconditional) for "test positive," you would not have been able to record it directly; you would have to make a note that the first and third circles at the far right add up to this number.

Next, apply the fundamental rules to complete the probability tree. This is like solving a puzzle, and there are many ways to do it that all lead to the right answer. For example, you might apply rule 1 to find that 0.92 goes below 0.08. Rule 2 also gives the conditional probabilities 0.10 and 0.05. Finally, rule 3 gives

FIGURE 6.5.3   Probability tree for the events "drug user" and "test positive" before any information is recorded.

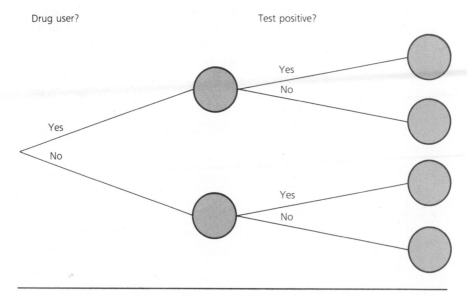

FIGURE 6.5.4   **The probability tree after the initial information has been recorded.**

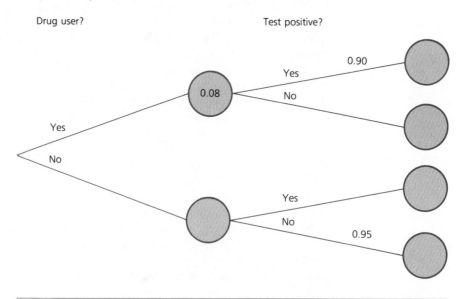

all of the probabilities for the ending circles. These results, which compose the completed tree, are shown in Figure 6.5.5.

It is now easy to make a Venn diagram, which is shown in Figure 6.5.6, using the results at the far right of the probability tree in Figure 6.5.5. Although you don't have to draw the Venn diagram to get answers, some people find the Venn diagram helpful.

You can now find any probability or conditional probability quickly and easily from the probability tree (Figure 6.5.5) or the Venn diagram (Figure 6.5.6). Here are some examples:

Probability of "drug user and test positive" = 0.072
Probability of "'not drug user' and test positive" = 0.046
Probability of "test positive" = 0.072 + 0.046 = 0.118
Conditional probability of "test positive" given "not drug user" = 0.05

Other conditional probabilities can be found through application of formulas, for example:

$$\begin{aligned}
\text{Conditional probability} \atop \text{of "drug user" given} \atop \text{"test positive"} &= \frac{\text{Probability of "drug user and test positive"}}{\text{Probability of "test positive"}} \\
&= \frac{0.072}{0.072 + 0.046} \\
&= \frac{0.072}{0.118} \\
&= 0.610
\end{aligned}$$

FIGURE 6.5.5   **The completed probability tree, after the fundamental rules have been applied.**

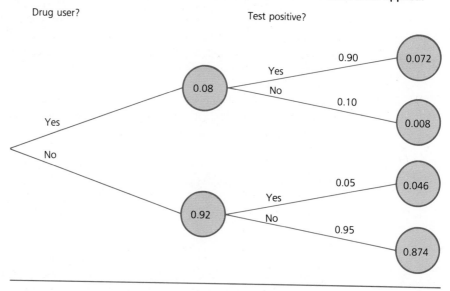

Drug user?

Test positive?

FIGURE 6.5.6   The Venn diagram for the employee drug testing example, with the four basic probabilities indicated.

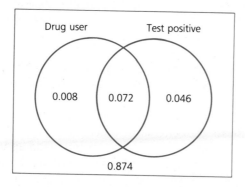

This conditional probability is especially interesting. Despite the apparent reliability of the drug testing procedure (90% positive for drug users and 95% negative for nonusers), there is a conditional probability of only 61% for "drug user" given "test positive." This means that, among all of your workers who test positive, only 61% will be drug users, and the remaining 39% will *not* be drug users.

This is a sobering thought indeed! Are you really ready to implement a procedure that includes 39% innocent people among those who test positive for drugs? Probability analysis has played an important role here in changing the initial information into other, more useful probabilities.

EXAMPLE

A Pilot Project Helps Predict Success of a Product Launch

Your firm is considering the introduction of a new product, and you have the responsibility of presenting the case to upper-level management. Two key issues are (1) whether or not to proceed with the project at all and (2) whether or not it is worthwhile to invest initially in a *pilot project* in a test market, which would cost less and provide some information as to whether the product is likely to succeed.

In getting your thoughts together, you have decided to assume the *what if* scenario that includes both the pilot project and the product launch. You also believe that the following probabilities are reasonable:

1 The probability that the product launch will succeed is 0.60.
2 The probability that the pilot project will succeed is 0.70. (This is slightly higher because the pilot project involves a more receptive market.)
3 The probability that either the pilot project or the product launch (or both) will succeed is 0.75.

To help you decide if the pilot project is worthwhile, you want to find out (1) the conditional probability that the product launch is successful given that the pilot project is successful and (2) the conditional probability that the product launch is successful given that the pilot project fails. In addition, for general background you also need (3) the probability that both the pilot project and the product launch succeed, and (4) the probability that they both fail.

All of these probabilities can be found by creative application of the basic formulas from Section 6.4. However, it can take a person a long time to determine the appropriate combination to use. It's easier to construct the probability tree and read off the answers.

Figure 6.5.7 shows the basic probability tree with the initial information recorded. Note that two of the three numbers have no immediate place in the tree, but you may record them on the side, as shown.

What to do next? Rule 1 for probability trees (or the complement rule) gives $1.00 - 0.70 = 0.30$ for the lower circle on the left. However, the circles on the right require more thought. If the top three numbers add up to 0.75 and two of them add up to 0.60, then the third number must be the difference, $0.75 - 0.60 = 0.15$, which goes in the second circle from the top (the probability of "successful pilot and 'not successful product launch'"). Now you can use rule 4 to find the probability for the top circle: $0.70 - 0.15 = 0.55$. You now have two of the top three circles on the right; since all three add up to 0.75, the remaining one must be $0.75 - 0.55 - 0.15 = 0.05$. At this point you can use the basic rules to complete the tree, as shown in Figure 6.5.8.

From this completed tree you can read off the required probabilities (and any other probabilities of interest to you). Here they are, with some brief discussion of the interpretation of the conditional probabilities:

1 The conditional probability that the product launch is successful given that the pilot project is successful is 0.786. If the pilot project were perfectly predictive

FIGURE 6.5.7   The initial probability tree, before the fundamental rules are applied.

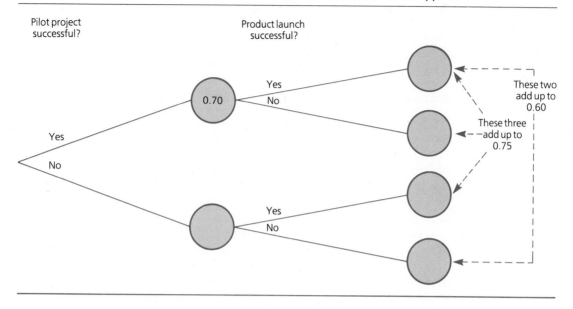

FIGURE 6.5.8   The completed probability tree, after the fundamental rules have been applied.

of success of the product launch, this number would be 1.00. With real-world imperfections, there is only a 78.6% chance of eventual success with the product following a successful pilot project.

2 The conditional probability that the product launch is successful given that the pilot project fails is 0.167. If the pilot project were perfectly predictive of later

success, then this number would be 0. However, here you find a 16.7% chance for success even if the pilot project fails.

3 The probability that both the pilot project and the product launch succeed is 0.55.

4 The probability that they both fail is 0.25.

EXAMPLE

Solution to "Is It behind Door Number 1, 2, or 3?"

We can now construct a probability tree for the example that was presented in Section 6.1. It is reasonable to assume that the prize is placed behind a random door (i.e., you have no clue as to which door it is) and that your guess is also random.[16] The probability tree for this situation is shown in Figure 6.5.9. This tree is a little different from those you have seen before, since there are *three* possibilities stemming from each branch. However, the fundamental rules for probability trees still hold true.

The basic numbers used to construct the tree are the probabilities of the prize being behind a given door (1/3) and the conditional probabilities of your guess (also 1/3—always the same conditional probability, since you don't know which door the prize is behind). Then, following the details of completing the tree, the answer is clear: Switching doubles your chances of winning from 1/3 to 2/3.

Joint Probability Tables

The **joint probability table** for two events gives you probabilities for the events, their complements, and combinations using *and*. Here is the joint probability table for the previous example of employee drug testing:

		Test positive?		
		Yes	No	
Drug user?	Yes	0.072	0.008	0.08
	No	0.046	0.874	0.92
		0.118	0.882	1

The numbers inside the table are the four circled numbers at the right of the probability tree. The numbers outside the table are totals, called *marginal probabilities,* and represent the probabilities of each event and its complement.

More generally, Figure 6.5.10 shows how to interpret the numbers in a generic joint probability table. Note that no conditional probabilities are given; they are easily computed using the basic formula.

---

[16]This assumption of random guessing is not necessary; in fact, you could always guess door 1, but the assumption simplifies the analysis.

FIGURE 6.5.9 The completed probability tree, after the fundamental rules have been applied.

Prize door	Your guess	Win if stay?	Win if switch?	They open door
		Yes (1/9)	No	2 or 3
		No	Yes (1/9)	3
		No	Yes (1/9)	2
		No	Yes (1/9)	3
		Yes (1/9)	No	1 or 3
		No	Yes (1/9)	1
		No	Yes (1/9)	2
		No	Yes (1/9)	1
		Yes (1/9)	No	1 or 2

Probability of winning: 1/3 (if stay)   2/3 (if switch)

■ 6.6 End-of-Chapter Materials

Summary

To understand random, unpredictable real-world situations, we begin by narrowing down the possibilities and carefully setting up an exact framework for the study of probability. A **random experiment** is any well-defined procedure that produces an observable outcome that could not be perfectly

FIGURE 6.5.10   The generic joint probability table.

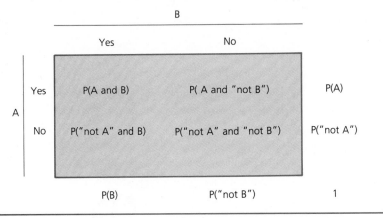

predicted in advance. Each random experiment has a **sample space,** which is a list of *all possible outcomes* of the random experiment, prepared in advance without knowing what will happen when the experiment is run. Each time a random experiment is run, it produces exactly one **outcome,** the result of the random experiment, describing and summarizing the observable consequences. An **event** either happens or does not happen each time the random experiment is run; formally, an event is any collection of outcomes specified in advance before the random experiment is run. There may be more than one event of interest for a given situation.

Associated with every event is a number between 0 and 1, called its **probability,** which expresses how likely it is that the event will happen each time the random experiment is run. If you run a random experiment many times, the **relative frequency** of an event is the proportion of times the event occurs out of the number of times the experiment is run. The **law of large numbers** says that the relative frequency (a random number) will be close to the probability (an exact, fixed number) if the experiment is run many times. Thus, a relative frequency based on past data may be used as an approximation to a probability value. A **theoretical probability** is computed using an exact formula based on a mathematical theory or model such as the *equally likely* rule; that is, if all outcomes are equally likely, then:

$$\text{Probability of an event} = \frac{\text{Number of outcomes in the event}}{\text{Total number of possible outcomes}}$$

A **subjective probability** is anyone's opinion (use an expert, if possible) of what the probability is for an event. The methods of **Bayesian analysis** in statistics involve the use of subjective probabilities in a formal, mathematical way. A non-Bayesian analysis is called a **frequentist analysis** and does not use subjective probabilities in its computations, although it is not totally objective, since opinions will have some effect on the choice of data and model (the mathematical framework.)

FIGURE 6.6.1   Venn diagrams provide an effective display of the meanings of the operations "not," "and," and "or," which define events in terms of other events.

The event A

The event "not A"

The event "A and B"

The event "A or B"

A **Venn diagram** is a picture that represents the universe of all possible outcomes (the sample space) as a rectangle with events indicated inside, often as circles or ovals, as in Figure 6.6.1. The **complement** of an event is another event that happens only when the first event does *not* happen. The complement rule is:

Probability of "not A" = 1 − Probability of A

The **intersection** of two events is an event that occurs whenever one event *and* the other event both happen as a result of a single run of the random experiment. The intersection (*and*) rules are:

$$\text{Probability of "A and B"} \leq \text{Smaller of} \begin{cases} \text{Probability of A} \\ \text{Probability of B} \end{cases}$$

$$\begin{array}{c}\text{Probability of}\\ \text{"A and B"}\end{array} \geq \text{Larger of} \begin{cases} \text{Probability of A} + \text{Probability of B} - 1 \\ 0 \end{cases}$$

Two events that cannot both happen at once are said to be **mutually exclusive events.** The rules for two mutually exclusive events are:

Probability of "A and B" = 0

Probability of "A or B" = Probability of A + Probability of B

The **union** of two events is an event that occurs whenever one event *or* the other event happens (or both events happen) as a result of a single run of the random experiment. The union (*or*) rules are:

$$\text{Probability of "A or B"} \geq \text{Larger of} \begin{cases} \text{Probability of A} \\ \text{Probability of B} \end{cases}$$

$$\text{Probability of "A or B"} \leq \text{Smaller of} \begin{cases} \text{Probability of A + Probability of B} \\ 1 \end{cases}$$

Based on knowledge of any three of the four probabilities (for A, B, "A and B," and "A or B"), the remaining probability can be found using one of the following formulas:

$$\text{Probability of "A or B"} = \text{Probability of A + Probability of B} \\ - \text{Probability of "A and B"}$$

$$\text{Probability of "A and B"} = \text{Probability of A + Probability of B} \\ - \text{Probability of "A or B"}$$

When you revise the probability of an event to reflect information that another event has occurred, the result is the **conditional probability** of that event *given* the other event. Ordinary (unrevised) probabilities are called **unconditional probabilities.** Conditional probabilities are found as follows (and are left undefined if the given information has probability 0):

$$\text{Conditional probability of A given B} = \frac{\text{Probability of "A and B"}}{\text{Probability of B}}$$

For two mutually exclusive events, the conditional probability is always 0 (unless it is undefined for technical reasons).

Two events are said to be **independent events** if information about one event does not change your assessment of the probability of the other event. If information about one event *does* change your assessment of the probability of the other, we say that the events are **dependent events.** Use any one of the following formulas to find out if two events are independent. Events A and B are independent if any of these formulas is true:

$$\text{Probability of A} = \text{Conditional probability of A given B}$$

$$\text{Probability of B} = \text{Conditional probability of B given A}$$

$$\text{Probability of "A and B"} = \text{Probability of A} \times \text{Probability of B}$$

The third formula may be used to find the probability of "A and B" for two events that are known to be independent but gives wrong answers for dependent events. Two independent events *cannot* be mutually exclusive unless one of the events has probability 0.

A **probability tree** is a picture indicating probabilities and some conditional probabilities for combinations of two or more events. One of the easiest ways to solve probability problems is to construct the probability tree and then read the answer. All probabilities and conditional probabilities may be found by adding up numbers from the tree or by applying the formula for a conditional probability. Here are the four rules used to construct and validate probability trees:

1 Probabilities are listed at each endpoint and circled. These add up to 1 (or 100%) at each level of the tree.
2 Conditional probabilities are listed along each branch (except perhaps for the first level) and add up to 1 (or 100%) for each group of branches coming out from a single point.
3 The circled probability at a branch point times the conditional probability along a branch gives the circled probability at the end of the branch (on the right).
4 The circled probability at a branch point is the sum of the circled probabilities at the ends of all branches coming out from it to the right.

The **joint probability table** for two events lists probabilities for the events, their complements, and combinations using *and.* Conditional probabilities can then be found by using the formula for a conditional probability.

Key Words

random experiment 154	Venn diagram 166
sample space 155	complement (not) 166
outcome 156	intersection (and) 168
event 157	mutually exclusive events 170
probability 158	union (or) 171
relative frequency 160	conditional probability 175
law of large numbers 160	unconditional probability 175
theoretical probability 162	independent events 178
subjective probability 163	dependent events 178
Bayesian analysis 165	probability tree 181
frequentist (non-Bayesian) analysis 165	joint probability table 190

Questions

1 a. What is a random experiment?
  b. Why does defining a random experiment help to focus your thoughts about an uncertain situation?
2 a. What is a sample space?
  b. Is there anything random or uncertain about a sample space?
3 a. What is an outcome?
  b. Must the outcome be a number?
4 a. What is an event?
  b. Can a random experiment have more than one event of interest?

5 a. What is a probability?

b. Which of the following has a probability number: a random experiment, a sample space, or an event?

c. If a random experiment is to be run just once, how can you interpret an event with a probability of 0.06?

6 a. What is the relative frequency of an event?

b. How is the relative frequency different from the probability of an event?

c. What is the law of large numbers?

7 a. Name the three main sources of probability numbers.

b What is the *equally likely* rule?

c. Are you allowed to use someone's guess as a probability number?

d. What is the difference between a Bayesian and a frequentist analysis?

8 What are mutually exclusive events?

9 a. What is the complement of an event?

b. What is the probability of the complement of an event?

10 a. What is the intersection of two events?

b. If you only know the probabilities of two events, what can you say about the probability of them both happening?

c. What is the probability of "one event and another" if you know:

(1) Their probabilities and the probability of "one event or the other"?

(2) Their probabilities and that they are independent?

(3) That they are mutually exclusive?

11 a. What is the union of two events?

b. If you only know the probabilities of two events, what can you say about the probability of either (or both) of them happening?

c. What is the probability of "one event or another" if you know:

(1) Their probabilities and the probability of "one event and the other"?

(2) That they are mutually exclusive?

12 a. What is the interpretation of conditional probability in terms of new information?

b. Is the conditional probability of A given B always the same number as the conditional probability of B given A?

c. How can you find the conditional probability from the probabilities of two events and the probability of their intersection?

d. What are the conditional probabilities for two independent events?

e. Is the conditional probability of A given B a probability about A or a probability about B?

13 a. What is the interpretation of independence of two events?

b. How can you tell whether two events are independent or not?

c. Under what conditions can two mutually exclusive events be independent?

14 a. What is a probability tree?

b. What are the four rules for probability trees?

15 What is a joint probability table?

16 What is a Venn diagram?

Problems

1 As a stock market analyst for a major brokerage house, you are responsible for knowing everything about the automotive companies. In particular, Ford is sched-

uled to release its net earnings for the past quarter soon, and you do not know what that number will be.

a. Describe the random experiment identified here.

b. What is the sample space?

c. What will the outcome tell you?

d. Based on everything you know currently, you have computed a dollar figure for net earnings that you feel is likely to be close to the actual figure to be announced. Identify precisely the event "the announced earnings are higher than expected" by listing the qualifying outcomes from the sample space.

e. You have an idea of the probability that the announced earnings will be higher than expected. What kind of probability is this if it is based not just on past experience but also on your opinion as to the current situation?

2 You are operations manager for a plant that produces copy machines. At the end of the day tomorrow, you will find out how many machines were produced and, of these, how many are defective.

a. Describe the random experiment identified here.

b. What is the sample space?

c. What will the outcome tell you?

d. Identify precisely the event "met the goal of 500 working (nondefective) machines with 5 or fewer defective machines" by listing the qualifying outcomes from the sample space.

e. In 22 of the past 25 days, this goal has been met. Find the appropriate relative frequency.

f. About how far away from the true, unknown probability of meeting the goal is the relative frequency from part *e*? (For simplicity, you may assume that these were independent runs of the same random experiment.)

3 You are responsible for a staff of 35 out of the 118 workers in a rug weaving factory. Next Monday a representative will be chosen from these 118 workers. Assume that the representative is chosen at random, without regard to whether he or she works for you.

a. What is the probability that one of your workers will be chosen?

b. What is the probability that the representative will not be one of yours?

4 You are responsible for scheduling a construction project to build a convention center. In order to avoid big trouble, it will be necessary for the concrete to be placed before July 27 and for the financing to be arranged before August 6. Based on your experience and that of others, using subjective probability, you have fixed probabilities of 0.83 and 0.91 for these two events, respectively.

a. Under these assumptions, what is the smallest possible value for the probability of the event "OK" (defined as achieving both goals)?

b. What is the largest possible value for the probability of the event "OK"?

c. What is the smallest possible value for the probability of the event "big trouble" (defined as not achieving both goals, that is, failing in at least one goal)?

d. What is the largest possible value for the probability of the event "big trouble"?

e. What is the smallest possible value for the probability of the event "made at least one goal"?

f. What is the largest possible value for the probability of the event "made at least one goal"?

g. Assume also that you have a 96% chance of meeting one deadline or the other (or both). Find the probability of "big trouble."

h. Are these events mutually exclusive? How do you know? (Assume information in part g).

i. Are these events independent? How do you know? (Assume information in part g).

5 Two divisions are cooperating in the production of a communications satellite. In order for the launch to be on time, both divisions must meet the deadline. You believe that each has a 90% chance of meeting the deadline.

a. In your worst-case scenario, what is the largest probability that the launch will have to be delayed due to a missed deadline?

b. In your best-case scenario, what is the smallest probability that the launch will have to be delayed due to a missed deadline?

c. Assuming the two divisions work independently (so that you have independent events), what is the probability that the launch will have to be delayed due to a missed deadline?

6 The probability of getting a big order currently under negotiation is 0.4. The probability of losing money this quarter is 0.5.

a. Assume that these are mutually exclusive events. Find the probability of getting the order or losing money.

b. Again assume that these are mutually exclusive events. Does this rule out the possibility that you fail to get the order and make money this quarter?

c. Now assume that the events "get the order" and "lose money" are independent (since the order will not show up in this quarter's financial statements). Find the probability of getting the order and losing money.

d. Now assume that the probability of getting the order and losing money is 0.1. Are the events "get the order" and "lose money" independent? How do you know?

7 Your firm has classified orders as either large or small in dollar amount and as either light or heavy in shipping weight. In the recent past, 28% of orders have been large dollar amounts, 13% of orders have been heavy, and 10% of orders have been large in dollar amounts and heavy in weight.

a. Complete a probability tree for this situation, with the first branch being the event "large dollar amount."

b. Construct the joint probability table for this situation.

c. Draw a Venn diagram for this situation.

d. Find the probability that an order is large in dollar amount or heavy (or both).

e. Find the probability that an order is for a large dollar amount and is not heavy.

f. Of the orders with large dollar amounts, what percentage are heavy? What conditional probability does this represent?

g. Of the heavy orders, what percentage are for large dollar amounts? What conditional probability does this represent?

h. Are the events "large dollar amount" and "heavy" mutually exclusive? How do you know?

i. Are the events "large dollar amount" and "heavy" independent? How do you know?

8 There are two locations in town (north and south) under consideration for a new restaurant, but only one location will actually become available. If it is in the north, the restaurant stands a 90% chance of surviving its first year. However, if it is built in the south, its chances of survival are only 65%. It is estimated that the chances of the northern location being available are 40%.

    a. Draw a probability tree for this situation, with the first branch being "location."
    b. Find the probability that the restaurant will survive its first year.
    c. Find the probability that the restaurant is built in the south and is successful.
    d. Find the probability that the restaurant is in the south given that it is successful.
    e. Find the probability of failure given that it is in the north.

9 The coming year is expected to be a good one with probability 0.70. Given that it is a good year, you expect that a dividend will be declared with probability 0.90. However, if it is not a good year, then a dividend will occur with probability 0.20.
    a. Draw a probability tree for this situation, with the most appropriate choice for the first branch.
    b. Find the probability that it is a good year and a dividend is issued.
    c. Find the probability that a dividend is issued.
    d. Find the conditional probability that it is a good year, given that a dividend is issued.

10 Your firm is considering the introduction of a new toothpaste. At a strategy session, it is agreed that a marketing study will be successful with probability 0.65. It is also agreed that the probability of a successful product launch is 0.40. However, given that the marketing study is successful, the probability of a successful product launch is 0.55.
    a. Draw the appropriate probability tree for this situation.
    b. Find the probability that the marketing study is successful and the product launch is successful.
    c. Given that the product launch succeeds, find the conditional probability that the marketing study was favorable.
    d. Find the conditional probability that the product launch is successful, given that the marketing study was not successful.
    e. Are the two events "marketing study successful" and "product launch successful" independent? How do you know?

11 You are a contestant on a TV game show with five doors. There is just one prize behind one door, randomly selected. After you choose, they deliberately open three doors (other than your choice) that do *not* have the prize. You have the opportunity to switch doors from your original choice to the other unopened door.
    a. What is the probability of getting the prize if you switch?
    b. What is the probability of getting the prize if you do not switch?

12 Consider a game in a gambling casino that pays off with probability 0.40. Yesterday 42,652 people played, and 17,122 won.
    a. Find the relative frequency of winning, and compare it to the probability.
    b. As the owner of a casino where many people play this game, how does the law of large numbers help you eliminate much of the uncertainty of gambling?
    c. As an individual who plays once or twice, does the law of large numbers help you limit the uncertainty? Why or why not?
    d. View a long-term investment in the stock market as a sequence of individual short-term "bets" that the market will go up, and discuss how the law of large numbers might make long-term investments less risky than short-term ones.

13 Your new firm is introducing two products, a bicycle trailer and a baby carriage for jogging. Your subjective probabilities of success for these products are 0.85 and 0.70, respectively. If the trailer is successful, you will be able to market the carriage to these customers; therefore, you feel that if the trailer is successful, the carriage will succeed with probability 0.80.

a. Draw a probability tree for this situation.

b. Find the probability that both products succeed.

c. Find the probability that neither product succeeds.

d. Find the probability that the trailer succeeds but the carriage does not.

e. In order for your firm to survive, at least one of the products must succeed. Find the probability that your firm will survive.

Database Exercises

Refer to the employee database in Appendix A.

1 View this database as the sample space of a random experiment in which an employee is selected at random. That is, each employee represents one outcome, and all possible outcomes are equally likely.

a. Find the probability of selecting a woman.

b. Find the probability that the salary is over $35,000.

c. Find the probability that the employee is at training level B.

d. Find the probability that the salary is over $35,000 and the employee is at training level B.

e. Find the probability that the salary is over $35,000 given that the employee is at training level B.

f. Is the event "salary over $35,000" independent of being at training level B? How do you know?

g. Find the probability that the salary is over $35,000 given that the employee is at training level C.

2 Continue to view this database as the sample space as in database exercise 1. Consider the two events "high experience (six years or more)" and "female."

a. Find the probabilities of these two events.

b. Find the probability of their intersection. What does this represent?

c. Draw a probability tree for these two events, where the first branch is for the event "female."

d. Find the conditional probability of high experience given female.

e. Find the conditional probability of being female given high experience.

f. Find the probability of being male without high experience.

g. Are the two events "female" and "high experience" independent? How do you know?

h. Are the two events "female" and "high experience" mutually exclusive? How do you know?

3 Continue to view this database as the sample space as in database exercise 1.

a. Are the two events "training level A" and "training level B" independent? How do you know?

b. Are the two events "training level A" and "training level B" mutually exclusive? How do you know?

Project

Choose a specific decision problem related to your business interests that depends on two uncertain events.

a. Select reasonable initial values for three probabilities.

b. Complete a probability tree.

c. Report two relevant probabilities and two relevant conditional probabilities, and interpret each one.

d. Write a paragraph discussing what you have learned about your decision problem from this project.

7

Random Variables
Working with Uncertain Numbers

Where do data sets really come from? You may view the numbers in a data set as observations of *random variables* resulting from a random experiment that produces numbers each time it is run. We associate a random variable with a population and view observations of the random variable as data. Here are some examples of random variables:

1 Next quarter's sales—a number that is currently unknown and that can take on one of a number of different values.
2 The number of defective machines produced next week.
3 The number of qualified people who will respond to your "help wanted" advertisement for a new full-time employee.
4 The value of your investment portfolio next year.
5 The reported income of the next family to respond to your information poll.

A **random variable** may be defined as a numerical result *in the abstract* of a random experiment. The value itself is called an **observation**. Thus, "next quarter's sales" is a random variable, and the actual future value $3,296,538 is an observation of this random variable. The pattern of probabilities for a random variable is called its **probability distribution.**

Many random variables have a mean and a standard deviation.[1] In addition, there is a probability for each event based on a random variable. There are two types of random variables: *discrete* and *continuous.* It is easier to work with a discrete random variable because you can make a list of all of its possible values. You will learn about two particular distributions that are especially useful: the *binomial distribution* (which is discrete) and the *normal distribution* (which is continuous).

---

[1] All of the random variables considered in this chapter have a mean and a standard deviation, although in theory there do exist random variables that have neither a mean nor a standard deviation.

The average of random numbers is itself a random number (after all, it is the result of a random experiment). Often, the average or total of many numbers will follow a nearly normal distribution, even if the original numbers follow some other distribution. This fact is the *central limit theorem*, which helps explain why the normal distribution is so important in statistics.

Since there are so many different types of situations in which data values can arise, there are many types of random variables. The *exponential* and the *Poisson* distributions provide a look at the tip of this iceberg.

■ 7.1 Discrete Random Variables

A random variable is **discrete** if you can list all possible values it can take on when it is observed.[2] A random variable is **continuous** if it can take on any value in a range (for example, any positive number). For some random variables, it is unclear whether they are discrete or continuous. For example, next quarter's sales might be $385,298.61, or $385,298.62, or $385,298.63, or a similar amount up to some very large number such as $4,000,000.00. Literally speaking, this is discrete (since you can list all the possible outcomes). However, from a practical viewpoint, since the dividing points are so close together and no single outcome is very likely, you may work with it as if it were continuous.

Here are some examples of discrete random variables:

1 The number of defective machines produced next week. The list of possible values is 0, 1, 2, ...
2 The number of qualified people who will respond to your "help wanted" advertisement for a new full-time employee. Again, the list of possible values is 0, 1, 2, ...
3 The resulting budget when a project is selected from four possibilities with costs of $26,000, $43,000, $54,000, and $83,000. The list of possible values is (in thousands of dollars) 26, 43, 54, and 83.

Such a list of possible values, together with the probability of each happening, is the probability distribution of the discrete random variable. These probabilities must be positive numbers (or 0) and must add up to 1. From this distribution, you can find the mean, the standard deviation, and the probability of any event based on the random variable.

EXAMPLE   **Profit under Various Economic Scenarios**

During a brainstorming session devoted to evaluation of your firm's future prospects, there was general agreement on the following simplified picture of what might happen in the future:

---

[2]Note the spelling of *discrete* when referring to random variables. It would be different to talk about a *discreet* one, which would know when to be quiet.

Economic Scenario	Profit ($ millions)	Probability
Great	10	0.20
Good	5	0.40
OK	1	0.25
Lousy	−4	0.15

This probability distribution can be easily used to find probabilities of all events concerning profit. The probability that the profit is $10 million, for example, is 0.20. The probability of making $5 million or more is found as follows: 0.20 + 0.40 = 0.60.

Finding the Mean and Standard Deviation

The **mean** or **expected value** of a discrete random variable is an exact number that summarizes it in terms of a typical value, in much the same way that the average summarizes a list of data.[3] The mean is denoted by the lowercase Greek letter μ (mu) or by $E(X)$ (read as "expected value of X") for a random variable X. The formula is:

■ Mean or Expected Value of X

$$\mu = E(X) = \text{Sum of (value times probability)}$$

$$= \sum XP(X)$$

If the probabilities were all equal, this would be the average of the values. In general, the mean of a random variable is a weighted average of the values using the probabilities as weights.

This mean profit in the preceding examples is

$$\text{Expected profit} = (10 \times 0.20) + (5 \times 0.40) + (1 \times 0.25) + (-4 \times 0.15)$$

$$= 3.65$$

Thus, the expected profit is $3.65 million. This number summarizes the various possible outcomes $(10, 5, 1, -4)$ using a single number that reflects their likelihoods.

The **standard deviation** of a discrete random variable indicates approximately how far you expect it to be from its mean. In many business situations, the standard deviation indicates the *risk* by showing just how

---

[3]In fact, the mean of a random variable is also called its average; however, we will use *mean* for random variables and *average* for data.

uncertain the situation is. The standard deviation is denoted by σ, which matches our use of σ as the population standard deviation. The formula is:

■ Standard Deviation of X

$$\sigma = \sqrt{\text{Sum of (squared deviation times probability)}}$$

$$= \sqrt{\sum (X - \mu)^2 P(X)}$$

Note that you would *not* get the correct answer by simply using the Σ key on your calculator, since this would not make proper use of the probabilities.

The standard deviation of profit for our example is

$$\sigma = \sqrt{[(10 - 3.65)^2 0.20] + [(5 - 3.65)^2 0.40] + [(1 - 3.65)^2 0.25] + [(-4 - 3.65)^2 0.15]}$$

$$= \sqrt{8.064500 + 0.729000 + 1.755625 + 8.778375}$$

$$= \sqrt{19.3275}$$

$$= 4.40$$

You may find it easier to calculate this value using the scheme shown in Table 7.1.1. The resulting standard deviation, $4.40 million, indicates that there is substantial risk involved here. Profit, expected to be $3.65 million, might easily be $4.40 million either above or below this figure.

Figure 7.1.1 shows the probability distribution, with the heights of the lines indicating the probability and the location of the lines indicating the amount of profit in each case. Also indicated is the expected value, $3.65 million, and the standard deviation, $4.40 million.

EXAMPLE **Evaluating Risk and Return**

Your job is to evaluate three different projects (X, Y, and Z) and make a recommendation to upper management. Each project requires an investment of $12,000 and pays off next year. Project X pays $14,000 for sure. Project Y pays

TABLE 7.1.1 Finding the Standard Deviation for a Discrete Random Variable

Profit	Probability	Deviation from Mean	Squared Deviation	Squared Deviation Times Probability
10	0.20	6.35	40.3225	8.064500
5	0.40	1.35	1.8225	0.729000
1	0.25	−2.65	7.0225	1.755625
−4	0.15	−7.65	58.5225	8.778375
			Sum:	19.3275
			Square root:	4.40

either \$10,000 or \$20,000 with probability 0.5 in each case. Project Z pays nothing with probability 0.98 and \$1,000,000 with probability 0.02. A summary is shown in Table 7.1.2.

The means are easily found: \$14,000 for X, $10,000 \times 0.50 + 20,000 \times 0.50 = \$15,000$ for Y, and $0 \times 0.98 + 1,000,000 \times 0.02 = \$20,000$ for Z. We could write these as follows:

$$E(X) = \mu_X = \$14,000$$

$$E(Y) = \mu_Y = \$15,000$$

$$E(Z) = \mu_Z = \$20,000$$

FIGURE 7.1.1 The probability distribution of future profits, with the mean (expected profits) and standard deviation (risk) indicated.

Standard deviation: \$4.40 million

Standard deviation: \$4.40 million

Expected profit: \$3.65 million

Profit (millions)

TABLE 7.1.2 Payoffs and Probabilities for Three Projects

Project	Payoff	Probability
X	14,000	1.00
Y	10,000	0.50
	20,000	0.50
Z	0	0.98
	1,000,000	0.02

Based only on these expected values, it would appear that Z is best and X is worst. However, these mean values don't tell the whole story. For example, although project Z has the highest expected payoff, it also involves considerable risk: 98% of the time there would be no payoff at all! The risks involved here are summarized by the standard deviations:

$$\sigma_X = \sqrt{(14{,}000 - 14{,}000)^2 \times 1.00} = \$0$$

$$\sigma_Y = \sqrt{(10{,}000 - 15{,}000)^2 \times 0.50 + (20{,}000 - 15{,}000)^2 \times 0.50} = \$5{,}000$$

$$\sigma_Z = \sqrt{(0 - 20{,}000)^2 \times 0.98 + (1{,}000{,}000 - 20{,}000)^2 \times 0.02} = \$140{,}000$$

These standard deviations confirm your suspicions. Project Z is indeed the riskiest—far more so than either of the others. Project X is the safest—a sure thing with no risk at all. Project Y involves a risk of $5,000.

Which project should be chosen? This question cannot be answered by statistical analysis alone. Although the expected value and the standard deviation provide helpful summaries to guide you in choosing a project, they do not finish the task. Generally, people prefer larger expected payoffs and lower risk. However, with the choices presented here, to achieve a larger expected payoff, you must take a greater risk. The ultimate choice of project will involve your (and your firm's) "risk versus return" preference to determine whether or not the increased expected payoff justifies the increased risk.[4]

What if you measure projects in terms of profit instead of payoff? Since each project involves an initial investment of $12,000, you can convert from payoff to profit by subtracting $12,000 from each payoff value in the probability distribution table:

$$\text{Profit} = \text{Payoff} - \$12{,}000$$

Using the rules from Section 5.4, which apply to summaries of random variables as well as to data, subtract $12,000 from each mean value and leave the standard deviation alone. Thus, without doing any detailed calculations, you come up with the following expected profits:

X: $2,000

Y: $3,000

Z: $8,000

The standard deviations of profits are the same as for payoffs, namely:

X: $0

Y: $5,000

Z: $140,000

---

[4]In your finance courses, you may learn about another factor that is often used in valuing projects, namely, the correlation (if any) between the random payoffs and the payoffs of a market portfolio. This helps measure the *diversifiable* and *nondiversifiable risk* of a project. Correlation (a statistical measure of association) will be presented in a later chapter.

■ 7.2 **The Binomial Distribution**

Percentages play a key role in business. When a percentage is arrived at by counting the number of times something happens out of the total number of possibilities, the number of occurrences might follow a *binomial distribution*. If so, there are a number of time-saving shortcuts available for finding the expected value, standard deviation, and probabilities of various events. Sometimes you will be interested in the percentage; at other times the number of occurrences will be more relevant. The binomial distribution can give answers in either case. Here are some examples for random variables that follow a binomial distribution:

1 The number of people who choose your laundry product as giving a "whiter, brighter wash," out of the three people asked.
2 The number of defective products out of 10 items produced.
3 The number of people who said they would buy your product, out of 200 interviewed.
4 The number of stocks that went up yesterday, out of all issues traded on major exchanges.
5 The number of female employees in a division of 75 people.
6 The number of Republican (or Democratic) votes cast in the next election.

Definition of Binomial Distribution and Proportion

Focus attention on a particular event. Each time the random experiment is run, either the event happens or it doesn't. These *two* possible outcomes gives us the *bi* in *binomial*. A random variable X, defined as the *number of occurrences* of a particular event out of n trials, has a **binomial distribution** if:

1 For each of the n trials, the event always has the same probability p of happening.
2 The trials are independent of one another.

The independence requirement rules out "peeking," as in the case of the distribution of people who order the special at a restaurant. If some people order the special because they see other customers obviously enjoying the rich, delicious combination of special aromatic ingredients, and say, "WOW! I'll have that too!," the number who order the special would *not* follow a binomial distribution. Choices have to be made independently in order to get a binomial distribution.

The **binomial proportion** f is the binomial random variable X expressed as a fraction of n:

■ **Binomial Proportion**

$$f = \frac{X}{n} = \frac{\text{Number of occurrences}}{\text{Number of trials}}$$

(Note that p is a fixed number, the probability of occurrence, whereas f is a random quantity based on the data.) For example, if you interviewed $n = 600$ shoppers, and found that $X = 38$ plan to buy your product, then the binomial proportion would be

$$f = \frac{X}{n} = \frac{38}{600} = 0.063, \quad \text{or} \quad 6.3\%$$

EXAMPLE   **A Whiter, Brighter Wash: The Hard Way to Compute**

This example shows the hard way to analyze a binomial random variable. Although it is not usually necessary to draw the probability tree, it will help you understand what is really going on. Furthermore, when the shortcuts to the procedure are presented later on, you will appreciate the time they save!

Suppose you have $n = 3$ people being interviewed. Each is independently shown two piles of folded laundry, one washed in our brand of detergent and the other in a competitor's brand, and asked, Which one is the whiter, brighter wash? Assume further that each person has probability $p = 0.60$ of choosing our brand.[5] At this point, you could construct a probability tree to analyze the whole situation, as shown in Figure 7.2.1a.

Note that the conditional probabilities along the branches are always 0.60 and 0.40, the probabilities for each individual since people decide independently and are not swayed by the others' choices. The number of people choosing our pile is listed at the far right in Figure 7.2.1a; for example, the second number from the top, 2, indicates that the first and second but not the third person chose our pile. To construct the probability distribution of the number of people who chose us, add up the probabilities for the different ways that each number could happen:

Number of People Who Chose Us, X	Percentage Who Chose Us, $f = X/n$	Probability
0	0.0%	0.064
1	33.3	0.288 (= 0.096 + 0.096 + 0.096)
2	66.7	0.432 (= 0.144 + 0.144 + 0.144)
3	100.0	0.216

This probability distribution is displayed in Figure 7.2.1b.

Now that you have the probability distribution, you can find all of the probabilities by adding the appropriate ones. For example, the probability that at least two people choose us is $0.432 + 0.216 = 0.648$. You can also use the formulas for the mean and standard deviation from Section 7.1 to find the mean value

---

[5]The probability p is usually given in textbook problems involving a binomial distribution. In real life, they arise just as other probabilities do: from relative frequency, theoretical probability, or subjective probability.

FIGURE 7.2.1 **a** A probability tree for three people each choosing a pile of laundry. There are eight combinations (the circles at the far right). In particular, there are three ways in which exactly two people would choose our brand: the second, third, and fifth circles from the top, giving a probability of 3 × 0.144 = 0.432. **b** The binomial probability distribution of the number of people who choose our brand as the "whiter, brighter wash."

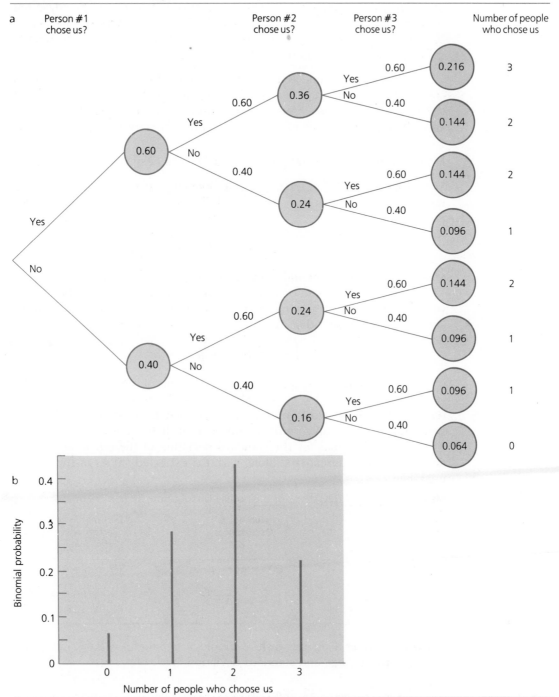

(1.80 people) and the standard deviation (0.849 people). However, *this would be too much work!* There is a much quicker formula for finding the mean, standard deviation, and probabilities. Although it was possible to compute directly in this small example, you will not usually be so lucky. For example, had you interviewed 10 people instead of 3, there would have been 1,024 probabilities at the right of the probability tree instead of the 8 in Figure 7.2.1.

Think of this example as a way of seeing the underlying situation and all combinations of choices, then simplifying to a probability distribution of the *number of occurrences.* Conceptually, this is the right way to view the situation. Now let's learn the easy way to compute the answers.

Finding the Mean and Standard Deviation the Easy Way

The mean number of occurrences in a binomial situation is $E(X) = np$, the number of possibilities times the probability of occurrence. The mean proportion is

$$E\left(\frac{X}{n}\right) = E(f) = p$$

which is the same as the individual probability of occurrence.[6]

This is what you would expect. For example, in a poll of a sample of 200 voters, if each has a 58% chance of being in favor of your candidate, on average, you would expect that

$$E\left(\frac{X}{n}\right) = E(f) = p = 0.58$$

or 58% of the sample will be in your favor. In terms of the number of people, you would expect $E(X) = np = 200 \times 0.58 = 116$ people out of the 200 in the sample to be in your favor. Of course, the actually observed number and percentage will probably randomly differ from these expected values.

There are formulas for the standard deviation of the binomial number and percentage, summarized along with the expected values in the following table:

Mean and Standard Deviation for a Binomial Distribution

	Number of Occurrences, X	Proportion or Percentage, $f = X/n$
Mean	$E(X) = \mu_X = np$	$E(f) = \mu_f = p$
Standard deviation	$\sigma_X = \sqrt{np(1-p)}$	$\sigma_f = \sqrt{\dfrac{p(1-p)}{n}}$

For the "whiter, brighter wash" example, $n = 3$ and $p = 0.60$. Using the formulas, the average and standard deviation are:

---

[6]You might have recognized X/n as the relative frequency of the event. The fact that $E(X/n)$ is equal to p says that, on average, the relative frequency of an event is equal to its probability.

	Number of Occurrences, X	Proportion or Percentage, $f = X/n$
Mean	$E(X) = np$	$E(f) = p$
	$= 3 \times 0.60$	$= 0.60$ or 60%
	$= 1.80$ people	
Standard deviation	$\sigma_X = \sqrt{np(1 - p)}$	$\sigma_f = \sqrt{\dfrac{p(1 - p)}{n}}$
	$= \sqrt{3 \times 0.60(1 - 0.60)}$	$= \sqrt{\dfrac{0.60(1 - 0.60)}{3}}$
	$= 0.849$ people	$= 0.283$ or 28.3%

The last number, 28.3%, representing the standard deviation of the percentage, is interpreted as *percentage points* rather than as a percentage of some number. That is, while the expected percentage is 60%, the actual observed percentage is typically about 28.3 percentage points above this value $(60 + 28.3 = 88.3\%)$ or below $(60 - 28.3 = 31.7\%)$. This is natural if you remember that a standard deviation is stated in the same units as the data, which are percentage points in the case of f.

EXAMPLE   **Recalling Advertisements**

Your company is negotiating with a marketing research firm to provide information on how your advertisements are doing with the American people. Selected people are to come in one day to watch TV programs and ads (for many products from many companies) and return the next day to answer questions. In particular, you plan to measure the *rate of recall*, which is the percentage of people who remember your ad the day after seeing it.

Before you contract with them to do the work, you are curious about how reliable and accurate the results are likely to be. Your budget allows 50 people to be tested. From your discussions with the research firm, it seems reasonable initially to assume that 35% of people will recall it, although you really don't know the exact proportion. Based on the assumption that it really is 35%, how accurate will the results be? That is, about how far from the estimate will the measured recall percentage be if the estimate is $p = 0.35$ with $n = 50$ for a binomial distribution? The answer is:

$$\sigma_f = \sqrt{\frac{p(1 - p)}{n}}$$

$$= \sqrt{\frac{0.35(1 - 0.35)}{50}}$$

$$= 0.0675 \quad \text{or} \quad 6.75\%$$

This says that the standard deviation of the result of the recall test (namely, the percentage of people tested who remembered the ad) is likely to differ from the true percentage for the entire population typically by about 7 percentage points in either direction (above or below).

You decide that the results need to be more accurate than that. The way to improve the precision of the results is to gather more information by increasing the sample size, n. Checking the budget and negotiating over the rates, you find that $n = 150$ is a possibility. With this larger sample, the standard deviation decreases to reflect the extra information:

$$\sigma_f = \sqrt{\frac{p(1 - p)}{n}}$$

$$= \sqrt{\frac{0.35(1 - 0.35)}{150}}$$

$$= 0.0389 \quad \text{or} \quad 3.89\%$$

You are disappointed that the extra cost didn't bring a greater improvement in the results. By tripling the size of the study, the accuracy didn't even double! This is due, technically, to the fact that it is the *square root* of n, rather than n itself, that is involved. Nevertheless, you decide that the extra accuracy is worth the cost.

Finding the Probabilities

Suppose you have a binomial distribution, you know the values of n and p, and you want to know the probability that X will be exactly equal to some number a. There is a formula for this probability that is useful for small to moderate n. When n is large, an approximation based on the *central limit theorem* (defined in a later section) will be easier. Here is the exact formula:[7]

---

[7] The notation $n!$ is read as "n factorial" and is the product of the numbers from 1 to n. For example, $4! = 1 \times 2 \times 3 \times 4 = 24$. (By convention, to get the correct answers, we define $0!$ to be 1.) Many calculators have a factorial key that works for values of n from 0 through 69. The notation

$$\binom{n}{a} = n!/[a!(n - a)!]$$

is the *binomial coefficient*, read aloud as "n choose a." It represents the number of different ways in which you could assign exactly a occurrences to the n possibilities. For example, with $n = 5$ and $a = 3$, the binomial coefficient is

$$\binom{5}{3} = \frac{5!}{3! \times (5 - 3)!} = \frac{120}{6 \times 2} = 10$$

Thus, there are 10 different ways (combinations) in which three out of five people could buy our product: the first three people could, or the first two and the fourth might, and so forth.

■ **Binomial Probability that X Equals a**

$$P(X = a) = \binom{n}{a} p^a (1 - p)^{(n-a)}$$

$$= \frac{n!}{a! \times (n - a)!} p^a (1 - p)^{(n-a)}$$

$$= \frac{1 \times 2 \times \cdots \times n}{[1 \times 2 \times \cdots \times a][1 \times 2 \times \cdots \times (n - a)]} p^a (1 - p)^{(n-a)}$$

By using this formula with each value of a from 0 to n (sometimes a lot of work), you can generate the entire probability distribution. From these values you can find any probability you want involving X by adding together the appropriate probabilities from this formula.

To see how to use the formula, suppose there are $n = 5$ possibilities with a success probability $p = 0.8$ for each one, and you want to find the probability of exactly $a = 3$ successes. The answer is

$$P(X = 3) = \binom{5}{3} 0.8^3 (1 - 0.8)^{(5-3)}$$

$$= \frac{5!}{3! \times (5 - 3)!} 0.8^3 \times 0.2^2$$

$$= \frac{1 \times 2 \times 3 \times 4 \times 5}{(1 \times 2 \times 3) \times (1 \times 2)} 0.512 \times 0.040$$

$$= 10 \times 0.02048$$

$$= 0.2048$$

This is the probability of *exactly* three successes. If you want the probability of *three or more* successes, you would have to compute the formula twice more: once for $a = 4$ and once for $a = 5$; the probability of three or more successes would be the total of these numbers. Without giving all the details, the answer is:

$$P(X \geq 3) = P(X = 3) + P(X = 4) + P(X = 5)$$

$$= 0.2048 + 0.4096 + 0.32768$$

$$= 0.94208$$

Thus, you have a 94.2% chance of achieving three or more successes out of these five.

EXAMPLE **How Many Major Customers Will Call Tomorrow?**

How many of your $n = 6$ major customers will call tomorrow? You are willing to assume that each one has a probability $p = 0.25$ of calling and that they call independently of one another. Thus, the number of major customers that will call tomorrow, X, follows a binomial distribution.

How many do you expect will call? That is, what is the expected value of X? The answer is $E(X) = n \times p = 1.5$ major customers. The standard deviation is $\sigma_X = \sqrt{6 \times 0.25 \times (1 - 0.25)} = 1.060660$, indicating that you can reasonably expect 1 or 2 more or less than the 1.5 you expect. Although this gives you an idea of what to expect, it doesn't tell you the chances that a given number will call. Let's compute the probabilities for this.

What is the probability that exactly $a = 2$ out of your $n = 6$ major customers will call? The answer is:

$$P(X = 2) = \binom{6}{2} 0.25^2 (1 - 0.25)^{(6-2)}$$

$$= 15 \times 0.0625 \times 0.316406$$

$$= 0.297$$

Here is the entire probability distribution of the number of major customers who will call you tomorrow, including all possibilities from 0 through $n = 6$:

$$P(X = 0) = \binom{6}{0} 0.25^0 (1 - 0.25)^6 = 1 \times 1 \times 0.177979 = 0.178$$

$$P(X = 1) = \binom{6}{1} 0.25^1 (1 - 0.25)^5 = 6 \times 0.25 \times 0.237304 = 0.356$$

$$P(X = 2) = \binom{6}{2} 0.25^2 (1 - 0.25)^4 = 15 \times 0.0625 \times 0.316406 = 0.297$$

$$P(X = 3) = \binom{6}{3} 0.25^3 (1 - 0.25)^3 = 20 \times 0.015625 \times 0.421875 = 0.132$$

$$P(X = 4) = \binom{6}{4} 0.25^4 (1 - 0.25)^2 = 15 \times 0.003906 \times 0.5625 = 0.0330$$

$$P(X = 5) = \binom{6}{5} 0.25^5 (1 - 0.25)^1 = 6 \times 0.000976 \times 0.75 = 0.00439$$

$$P(X = 6) = \binom{6}{6} 0.25^6 (1 - 0.25)^0 = 1 \times 0.000244 \times 1 = 0.000244$$

Note that the most likely outcomes are 1 or 2 calls, just as you suspected based on the average value of 1.5 calls.

From this probability distribution, you can compute any probability about the number of major customers who will call you tomorrow. It is highly unlikely that all six will call (0.000244 or 0.0244%, much less than a 1% chance). The probability that four or more will call is $0.0330 + 0.00439 + 0.000244 = 0.0376$. Your chances of spending a quiet day with no calls is 0.178. This probability distribution is shown in Figure 7.2.2.

FIGURE 7.2.2   The probability distribution of the number of major customers who call you tomorrow. These are binomial probabilities, with each vertical bar found using the formula based on $n = 6$ and $p = 0.25$. The number a is found along the horizontal axis.

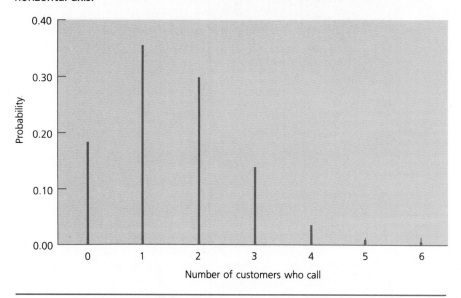

EXAMPLE

How Many Logic Analyzers to Schedule for Manufacturing?

You pay close attention to quality in your production facilities, but the logic analyzers you make are so complex that there are still some failures. In fact, based on past experience, about 97% of the finished products are in good working order. Today you will have to ship 17 of these machines. The question is: How many should you schedule for production to be reasonably certain that 17 working logic analyzers will be shipped?

It is reasonable to assume a binomial distribution for the number of working machines produced, with n being the number that you schedule and p being each one's probability (0.97) of working. Then you can compute the probability that 17 or more of the scheduled machines will work.

What happens if you schedule 17 machines, with no margin for error? You might think that the high (97%) rate would help you, but, in fact, the probability that all 17 machines will work (using $n = 17$ and $a = 17$) is just 0.596:

$$P(X = 17 \text{ working machines}) = \binom{17}{17}0.97^{17}0.03^{0}$$

$$= 1 \times 0.595826 \times 1$$

$$= 0.596$$

Thus, if you schedule the same number, 17, that you need to ship, you will be taking a big chance! There is only a 59.6% chance that you will meet the order, and a 40.4% chance that you will fail to ship the entire order in working condition. The probability distribution is shown in Figure 7.2.3.

It looks like you'd better schedule more than 17. What if you schedule $n = 18$ units for production? To find the probability that *at least* 17 working analyzers will be shipped, you'll need to find the probabilities for $a = 17$ and $a = 18$ and add them up:

$$P(X \geq 17) = P(X = 17) + P(X = 18)$$

$$= \binom{18}{17}0.97^{17}0.03^{1} + \binom{18}{18}0.97^{18}0.03^{0}$$

$$= 18 \times 0.595826 \times 0.03 + 1 \times 0.577951 \times 1$$

$$= 0.322 + 0.578$$

$$= 0.900$$

So if you schedule 18 for production, you have a 90% chance of shipping 17 good machines. It looks likely but you would still be taking a 10% chance of failure. This probability distribution is shown in Figure 7.2.4.

Similar tedious calculations reveal that if you schedule 19 machines for production, you have a 98.2% chance of shipping 17 good machines (9.2% + 32.9% + 56.1%). So, to be reasonably sure of success, you'd better schedule at least 19 machines to get 17 good ones!

FIGURE 7.2.3   **The probability distribution of the number of working logic analyzers produced *if you plan to produce only 17.* This is binomial, with $n = 17$ and $p = 0.97$.**

Number of working logic analyzers (17 scheduled)

FIGURE 7.2.4   The probability distribution of the number of working logic analyzers produced *if you plan to produce* 18. This is binomial, with *n* = 18 and *p* = 0.97.

Number of working logic analyzers (18 scheduled)

■ 7.3 The Normal Distribution

You already know from Chapter 3 how to tell if a data set is approximately normally distributed. Now it's time to learn how to compute probabilities for this familiar bell-shaped distribution. One reason the normal distribution is particularly useful is the fact that, given only a mean and a standard deviation, you can compute any probability of interest (provided that the distribution really is normal).

The **normal distribution,** a continuous distribution, is represented by the familiar bell-shaped curve shown in Figure 7.3.1a. Note that there is a normal distribution for each combination of a mean value and a standard deviation value. Just slide the curve to the right or left until the peak is centered above the mean value, then stretch it wider or narrower until the scale matches the standard deviation. Two different normal distributions are shown in Figure 7.3.1b.

Visualize Probabilities as the Area under the Curve

The bell-shaped curve gives you a guide for visualizing the probabilities for a normal distribution. You are more likely to see values occurring near the middle, where the curve is high. At the edges, where the curve is lower, values are not as likely to occur. Formally, it is the *area under the curve* that gives you the probability of being within a region, as illustrated in Figure 7.3.2.

FIGURE 7.3.1   a The normal distribution, with mean value μ and standard deviation σ. Note that the mean can be any number and the standard deviation can be any positive number. **b** Two different normal distributions. The one on the left has a smaller mean value (20) and a smaller standard deviation (5) than the other. The one on the right has mean 40 and standard deviation 10.

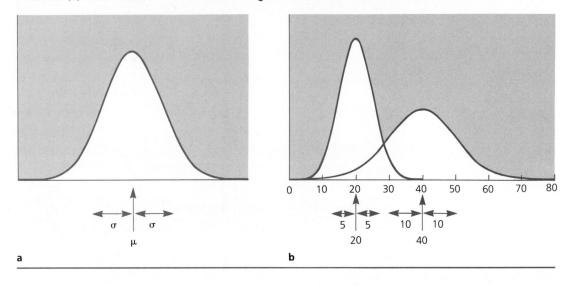

a

b

FIGURE 7.3.2   The probability that a normally distributed random variable is between any two values is equal to the area under the normal curve between these two values. You are more likely to see values in regions close to the mean.

FIGURE 7.3.3   The probability of falling within a region that is farther from the middle of the curve. Since the normal curve is lower here, the probability is smaller than that shown in Figure 7.3.2.

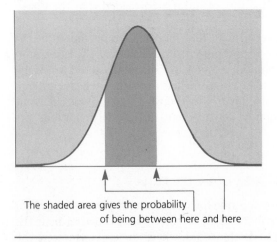

The shaded area gives the probability
of being between here and here

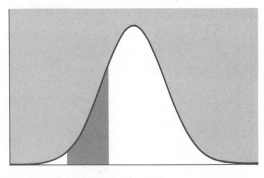

Note that a shaded strip near the middle of the curve will have a larger area than a strip of the same width located nearer to the edge. Compare Figure 7.3.2 to Figure 7.3.3 to see this.

The Standard Normal Distribution and Its Probabilities

The **standard normal distribution** is a normal distribution with mean $\mu = 0$ and standard deviation $\sigma = 1$. One way to compute probabilities for a normal distribution is to use tables that give probabilities for the standard one, since it would be impossible to keep different tables for each combination of mean and standard deviation. The standard normal distribution can represent any normal distribution, provided you think in terms of the *number of standard deviations above or below the mean* instead of the actual units (e.g., dollars) of the situation. The standard normal distribution is shown in Figure 7.3.4.

The **standard normal probability table,** shown in Table 7.3.1, gives the probability that a standard normal random variable is *less than* any given number. For example, the probability of being less than 1.38 is 0.9162, illustrated as an area in Figure 7.3.5. Doesn't it look like about 90% of the area? To find this number (0.9162), look up the value 1.38 in the standard normal probability table. While you're at it, look up 2.35 (to find 0.9906), 0 (to find 0.5000), and −0.82 (to find 0.2061). What is the probability corresponding to the value 0.36?

Solving Word Problems for Normal Probabilities

A typical word problem involving a normal distribution is a story involving some application to business that gives you a value for the mean and one for

FIGURE 7.3.4 The standard normal distribution with mean value $\mu = 0$ and standard deviation $\sigma = 1$. The standard normal distribution may be used to represent any normal distribution, provided you think in terms of the number of standard deviations above or below the mean.

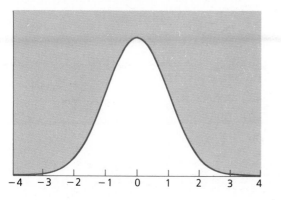

FIGURE 7.3.5 The probability that a standard normal random variable is *less than* 1.38 is 0.9162, as found in the standard normal probability table. This corresponds to the shaded region to the left of 1.38, which is 91.62% of the total area under the curve.

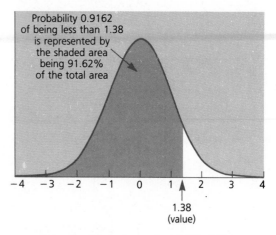

Probability 0.9162 of being less than 1.38 is represented by the shaded area being 91.62% of the total area

1.38
(value)

Using the standard normal probability table

TABLE 7.3.1 Standard Normal Probability Table

Probability 0.9162 of being less than 1.38 is represented by the shaded area being 91.62% of the total area

Using the standard normal probability table

1.38 (value)

Value	Probability	Value	Probability	Value	Probability	Value	Probability	Value	Probability	Value	Probability
-2.00	0.0228	-1.00	0.1587	0.00	0.5000	0.00	0.5000	1.00	0.8413	2.00	0.9772
-2.01	0.0222	-1.01	0.1562	-0.01	0.4960	0.01	0.5040	1.01	0.8438	2.01	0.9778
-2.02	0.0217	-1.02	0.1539	-0.02	0.4920	0.02	0.5080	1.02	0.8461	2.02	0.9783
-2.03	0.0212	-1.03	0.1515	-0.03	0.4880	0.03	0.5120	1.03	0.8485	2.03	0.9788
-2.04	0.0207	-1.04	0.1492	-0.04	0.4840	0.04	0.5160	1.04	0.8508	2.04	0.9793
-2.05	0.0202	-1.05	0.1469	-0.05	0.4801	0.05	0.5199	1.05	0.8531	2.05	0.9798
-2.06	0.0197	-1.06	0.1446	-0.06	0.4761	0.06	0.5239	1.06	0.8554	2.06	0.9803
-2.07	0.0192	-1.07	0.1423	-0.07	0.4721	0.07	0.5279	1.07	0.8577	2.07	0.9808
-2.08	0.0188	-1.08	0.1401	-0.08	0.4681	0.08	0.5319	1.08	0.8599	2.08	0.9812
-2.09	0.0183	-1.09	0.1379	-0.09	0.4641	0.09	0.5359	1.09	0.8621	2.09	0.9817
-2.10	0.0179	-1.10	0.1357	-0.10	0.4602	0.10	0.5398	1.10	0.8643	2.10	0.9821
-2.11	0.0174	-1.11	0.1335	-0.11	0.4562	0.11	0.5438	1.11	0.8665	2.11	0.9826
-2.12	0.0170	-1.12	0.1314	-0.12	0.4522	0.12	0.5478	1.12	0.8686	2.12	0.9830
-2.13	0.0166	-1.13	0.1292	-0.13	0.4483	0.13	0.5517	1.13	0.8708	2.13	0.9834
-2.14	0.0162	-1.14	0.1271	-0.14	0.4443	0.14	0.5557	1.14	0.8729	2.14	0.9838
-2.15	0.0158	-1.15	0.1251	-0.15	0.4404	0.15	0.5596	1.15	0.8749	2.15	0.9842
-2.16	0.0154	-1.16	0.1230	-0.16	0.4364	0.16	0.5636	1.16	0.8770	2.16	0.9846
-2.17	0.0150	-1.17	0.1210	-0.17	0.4325	0.17	0.5675	1.17	0.8790	2.17	0.9850
-2.18	0.0146	-1.18	0.1190	-0.18	0.4286	0.18	0.5714	1.18	0.8810	2.18	0.9854
-2.19	0.0143	-1.19	0.1170	-0.19	0.4247	0.19	0.5753	1.19	0.8830	2.19	0.9857
-2.20	0.0139	-1.20	0.1151	-0.20	0.4207	0.20	0.5793	1.20	0.8849	2.20	0.9861
-2.21	0.0136	-1.21	0.1131	-0.21	0.4168	0.21	0.5832	1.21	0.8869	2.21	0.9864
-2.22	0.0132	-1.22	0.1112	-0.22	0.4129	0.22	0.5871	1.22	0.8888	2.22	0.9868
-2.23	0.0129	-1.23	0.1093	-0.23	0.4090	0.23	0.5910	1.23	0.8907	2.23	0.9871
-2.24	0.0125	-1.24	0.1075	-0.24	0.4052	0.24	0.5948	1.24	0.8925	2.24	0.9875
-2.25	0.0122	-1.25	0.1056	-0.25	0.4013	0.25	0.5987	1.25	0.8944	2.25	0.9878
-2.26	0.0119	-1.26	0.1038	-0.26	0.3974	0.26	0.6026	1.26	0.8962	2.26	0.9881
-2.27	0.0116	-1.27	0.1020	-0.27	0.3936	0.27	0.6064	1.27	0.8980	2.27	0.9884
-2.28	0.0113	-1.28	0.1003	-0.28	0.3897	0.28	0.6103	1.28	0.8997	2.28	0.9887

0.9890	2.29	0.9015	1.29	0.6141	0.29	0.3859	−0.29	0.0985	−1.29	0.0110	−2.29
0.9893	2.30	0.9032	1.30	0.6179	0.30	0.3821	−0.30	0.0968	−1.30	0.0107	−2.30
0.9896	2.31	0.9049	1.31	0.6217	0.31	0.3783	−0.31	0.0951	−1.31	0.0104	−2.31
0.9898	2.32	0.9066	1.32	0.6255	0.32	0.3745	−0.32	0.0934	−1.32	0.0102	−2.32
0.9901	2.33	0.9082	1.33	0.6293	0.33	0.3707	−0.33	0.0918	−1.33	0.0099	−2.33
0.9904	2.34	0.9099	1.34	0.6331	0.34	0.3669	−0.34	0.0901	−1.34	0.0096	−2.34
0.9906	2.35	0.9115	1.35	0.6368	0.35	0.3632	−0.35	0.0885	−1.35	0.0094	−2.35
0.9909	2.36	0.9131	1.36	0.6406	0.36	0.3594	−0.36	0.0869	−1.36	0.0091	−2.36
0.9911	2.37	0.9147	1.37	0.6443	0.37	0.3557	−0.37	0.0853	−1.37	0.0089	−2.37
0.9913	2.38	0.9162	1.38	0.6480	0.38	0.3520	−0.38	0.0838	−1.38	0.0087	−2.38
0.9916	2.39	0.9177	1.39	0.6517	0.39	0.3483	−0.39	0.0823	−1.39	0.0084	−2.39
0.9918	2.40	0.9192	1.40	0.6554	0.40	0.3446	−0.40	0.0808	−1.40	0.0082	−2.40
0.9920	2.41	0.9207	1.41	0.6591	0.41	0.3409	−0.41	0.0793	−1.41	0.0080	−2.41
0.9922	2.42	0.9222	1.42	0.6628	0.42	0.3372	−0.42	0.0778	−1.42	0.0078	−2.42
0.9925	2.43	0.9236	1.43	0.6664	0.43	0.3336	−0.43	0.0764	−1.43	0.0075	−2.43
0.9927	2.44	0.9251	1.44	0.6700	0.44	0.3300	−0.44	0.0749	−1.44	0.0073	−2.44
0.9929	2.45	0.9265	1.45	0.6736	0.45	0.3264	−0.45	0.0735	−1.45	0.0071	−2.45
0.9931	2.46	0.9279	1.46	0.6772	0.46	0.3228	−0.46	0.0721	−1.46	0.0069	−2.46
0.9932	2.47	0.9292	1.47	0.6808	0.47	0.3192	−0.47	0.0708	−1.47	0.0068	−2.47
0.9934	2.48	0.9306	1.48	0.6844	0.48	0.3156	−0.48	0.0694	−1.48	0.0066	−2.48
0.9936	2.49	0.9319	1.49	0.6879	0.49	0.3121	−0.49	0.0681	−1.49	0.0064	−2.49
0.9938	2.50	0.9332	1.50	0.6915	0.50	0.3085	−0.50	0.0668	−1.50	0.0062	−2.50
0.9940	2.51	0.9345	1.51	0.6950	0.51	0.3050	−0.51	0.0655	−1.51	0.0060	−2.51
0.9941	2.52	0.9357	1.52	0.6985	0.52	0.3015	−0.52	0.0643	−1.52	0.0059	−2.52
0.9943	2.53	0.9370	1.53	0.7019	0.53	0.2981	−0.53	0.0630	−1.53	0.0057	−2.53
0.9945	2.54	0.9382	1.54	0.7054	0.54	0.2946	−0.54	0.0618	−1.54	0.0055	−2.54
0.9946	2.55	0.9394	1.55	0.7088	0.55	0.2912	−0.55	0.0606	−1.55	0.0054	−2.55
0.9948	2.56	0.9406	1.56	0.7123	0.56	0.2877	−0.56	0.0594	−1.56	0.0052	−2.56
0.9949	2.57	0.9418	1.57	0.7157	0.57	0.2843	−0.57	0.0582	−1.57	0.0051	−2.57
0.9951	2.58	0.9429	1.58	0.7190	0.58	0.2810	−0.58	0.0571	−1.58	0.0049	−2.58
0.9952	2.59	0.9441	1.59	0.7224	0.59	0.2776	−0.59	0.0559	−1.59	0.0048	−2.59
0.9953	2.60	0.9452	1.60	0.7257	0.60	0.2743	−0.60	0.0548	−1.60	0.0047	−2.60
0.9955	2.61	0.9463	1.61	0.7291	0.61	0.2709	−0.61	0.0537	−1.61	0.0045	−2.61
0.9956	2.62	0.9474	1.62	0.7324	0.62	0.2676	−0.62	0.0526	−1.62	0.0044	−2.62
0.9957	2.63	0.9484	1.63	0.7357	0.63	0.2643	−0.63	0.0516	−1.63	0.0043	−2.63
0.9959	2.64	0.9495	1.64	0.7389	0.64	0.2611	−0.64	0.0505	−1.64	0.0041	−2.64
0.9960	2.65	0.9505	1.65	0.7422	0.65	0.2578	−0.65	0.0495	−1.65	0.0040	−2.65
0.9961	2.66	0.9515	1.66	0.7454	0.66	0.2546	−0.66	0.0485	−1.66	0.0039	−2.66
0.9962	2.67	0.9525	1.67	0.7486	0.67	0.2514	−0.67	0.0475	−1.67	0.0038	−2.67
0.9963	2.68	0.9535	1.68	0.7517	0.68	0.2483	−0.68	0.0465	−1.68	0.0037	−2.68
0.9964	2.69	0.9545	1.69	0.7549	0.69	0.2451	−0.69	0.0455	−1.69	0.0036	−2.69
0.9965	2.70	0.9554	1.70	0.7580	0.70	0.2420	−0.70	0.0446	−1.70	0.0035	−2.70

TABLE 7.3.1 (Concluded)

Value	Probability	Value	Probability	Value	Probability	Value	Probability	Value	Probability	Value	Probability
-2.71	0.0034	-1.71	0.0436	-0.71	0.2389	0.71	0.7611	1.71	0.9564	2.71	0.9966
-2.72	0.0033	-1.72	0.0427	-0.72	0.2358	0.72	0.7642	1.72	0.9573	2.72	0.9967
-2.73	0.0032	-1.73	0.0418	-0.73	0.2327	0.73	0.7673	1.73	0.9582	2.73	0.9968
-2.74	0.0031	-1.74	0.0409	-0.74	0.2296	0.74	0.7704	1.74	0.9591	2.74	0.9969
-2.75	0.0030	-1.75	0.0401	-0.75	0.2266	0.75	0.7734	1.75	0.9599	2.75	0.9970
-2.76	0.0029	-1.76	0.0392	-0.76	0.2236	0.76	0.7764	1.76	0.9608	2.76	0.9971
-2.77	0.0028	-1.77	0.0384	-0.77	0.2206	0.77	0.7794	1.77	0.9616	2.77	0.9972
-2.78	0.0027	-1.78	0.0375	-0.78	0.2177	0.78	0.7823	1.78	0.9625	2.78	0.9973
-2.79	0.0026	-1.79	0.0367	-0.79	0.2148	0.79	0.7852	1.79	0.9633	2.79	0.9974
-2.80	0.0026	-1.80	0.0359	-0.80	0.2119	0.80	0.7881	1.80	0.9641	2.80	0.9974
-2.81	0.0025	-1.81	0.0351	-0.81	0.2090	0.81	0.7910	1.81	0.9649	2.81	0.9975
-2.82	0.0024	-1.82	0.0344	-0.82	0.2061	0.82	0.7939	1.82	0.9656	2.82	0.9976
-2.83	0.0023	-1.83	0.0336	-0.83	0.2033	0.83	0.7967	1.83	0.9664	2.83	0.9977
-2.84	0.0023	-1.84	0.0329	-0.84	0.2005	0.84	0.7995	1.84	0.9671	2.84	0.9977
-2.85	0.0022	-1.85	0.0322	-0.85	0.1977	0.85	0.8023	1.85	0.9678	2.85	0.9978
-2.86	0.0021	-1.86	0.0314	-0.86	0.1949	0.86	0.8051	1.86	0.9686	2.86	0.9979
-2.87	0.0021	-1.87	0.0307	-0.87	0.1922	0.87	0.8078	1.87	0.9693	2.87	0.9979
-2.88	0.0020	-1.88	0.0301	-0.88	0.1894	0.88	0.8106	1.88	0.9699	2.88	0.9980
-2.89	0.0019	-1.89	0.0294	-0.89	0.1867	0.89	0.8133	1.89	0.9706	2.89	0.9981
-2.90	0.0019	-1.90	0.0287	-0.90	0.1841	0.90	0.8159	1.90	0.9713	2.90	0.9981
-2.91	0.0018	-1.91	0.0281	-0.91	0.1814	0.91	0.8186	1.91	0.9719	2.91	0.9982
-2.92	0.0018	-1.92	0.0274	-0.92	0.1788	0.92	0.8212	1.92	0.9726	2.92	0.9982
-2.93	0.0017	-1.93	0.0268	-0.93	0.1762	0.93	0.8238	1.93	0.9732	2.93	0.9983
-2.94	0.0016	-1.94	0.0262	-0.94	0.1736	0.94	0.8264	1.94	0.9738	2.94	0.9984
-2.95	0.0016	-1.95	0.0256	-0.95	0.1711	0.95	0.8289	1.95	0.9744	2.95	0.9984
-2.96	0.0015	-1.96	0.0250	-0.96	0.1685	0.96	0.8315	1.96	0.9750	2.96	0.9985
-2.97	0.0015	-1.97	0.0244	-0.97	0.1660	0.97	0.8340	1.97	0.9756	2.97	0.9985
-2.98	0.0014	-1.98	0.0239	-0.98	0.1635	0.98	0.8365	1.98	0.9761	2.98	0.9986
-2.99	0.0014	-1.99	0.0233	-0.99	0.1611	0.99	0.8389	1.99	0.9767	2.99	0.9986
-3.00	0.0013	-2.00	0.0228	-1.00	0.1587	1.00	0.8413	2.00	0.9772	3.00	0.9987

the standard deviation. Then you are asked to find one or more probabilities of interest. Here is an example of such a word problem:

> The upper-management people at Simplified Technologies, Inc. have finally noticed that sales forecasts are usually wrong. Last quarter's sales were forecast as $18 million but came in at $21.3 million. Sales for the next quarter are forecast as $20 million, with a standard deviation (based on previous experience) of $3 million. Assuming a normal distribution centered at the forecast value, find the probability of a "really bad quarter," which is defined as sales lower than $15 million.

The beginning part sets the stage. The first numbers (18 and 21.3) describe past events but play no further role here. Instead, you should focus on the following facts:

> There is a normal distribution involved here.
> Its mean is $\mu = \$20$ million.
> Its standard deviation is $\sigma = \$3$ million.
> You are asked to find the probability that sales will be lower than $15 million.

The next step is to convert all of these numbers (except for the mean and standard deviation) into standardized numbers; this has to be done before you can look up the answer in the standard normal probability table. A **standardized number** is the number of standard deviations above the mean (or below the mean, if the standardized number is negative). This conversion is done as follows:

$$\text{Standardized number} = \frac{\text{Number} - \text{Mean}}{\text{Standard deviation}}$$

$$= \frac{\text{Number} - \mu}{\sigma}$$

In this example, the number $15 million is standardized as follows:

$$\frac{15 - \mu}{\sigma} = \frac{15 - 20}{3}$$

$$= -1.67$$

This tells you that $15 million is -1.67 standard deviations below the mean (the forecast value).[8] Your problem has now been reduced to finding a standard normal probability:

> Find the probability that a standard normal variable is less than -1.67.

From the table, you find the answer:

> The probability of a really bad quarter is 0.0475, or about 5%.

---

[8] You know that this is below the mean because the standardized number -1.67 is negative. The standardized number will be positive for any number above the mean. The standardized number for the mean itself is 0.

Whew! It seems that a really bad quarter is not very likely. However, a 5% chance is an outside possibility that should not be disregarded altogether.

Figures 7.3.6 and 7.3.7 show this probability calculation, both in terms of sales dollars and in terms of standardized sales numbers (standard deviations above or below the mean).

This was an easy problem, since the answer was found directly from the standard normal probability table. Here is a question that requires a little more care:

Continuing with the sales forecasting problem, find the probability of a "really good quarter," which is defined as sales in excess of $24 million.

The first step is to standardize the sales number: $24 million is $(24 - 20)/3 = 1.33$ standard deviations above the mean. Thus, you are asked to solve the following problem:

Find the probability that a standard normal variable *exceeds* 1.33.

Using the complement rule, we know that this probability is 1 minus the probability of being less than 1.33. Looking up 1.33 in the table, you find the answer:

Probability of a really good quarter $= 1 - 0.9082$

$= 0.0918$, or about 9%

This probability is illustrated, in standard numbers, in Figure 7.3.8.

FIGURE 7.3.6 The probability of a really bad quarter, that is, sales less than $15 million, is represented by the shaded area under the curve. This is based on the forecast of $20 million and the standard deviation of $3 million. The answer is found by first standardizing and then using the standard normal probability table.

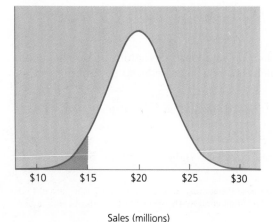

Sales (millions)

FIGURE 7.3.7 The probability of a really bad quarter, in terms of standardized sales numbers. This is the probability that sales will be more than 1.67 standard deviations *below* the mean. The answer is 0.0475.

−1.67

Standardized sales numbers

FIGURE 7.3.8   The probability of a really good quarter, in terms of standardized sales numbers. The shaded area is 1 minus the unshaded area under the curve, which may be looked up in the table. The answer is 0.0918.

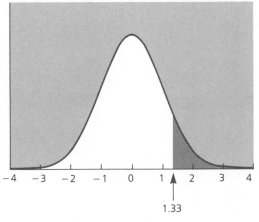

Standardized sales numbers

Here's another kind of problem:

Continuing with the sales forecasting problem, find the probability of a "typical quarter," which is defined as sales between $16 million and $23 million.

Begin by standardizing both of these numbers, to see that your task is to solve the following problem:

Find the probability that a standard normal is *between* −1.33 and 1.00.

To solve this kind of problem, look up each standardized number in the table, and find the difference between the probabilities for the answer. Be sure to subtract the smaller from the larger, so that your answer is a positive number and therefore a "legal" probability!

$$\text{Probability of a typical quarter} = 0.8413 - 0.0918$$

$$= 0.7495, \text{ or about } 75\%$$

This probability is illustrated, in standard numbers, in Figure 7.3.9.

Finally, here's yet another kind of problem:

Continuing with the sales forecasting problem, find the probability of a "surprising quarter," which is defined as sales either less than $16 million or more than $23 million.

This asks for the probability of *not* being between two numbers. Using the complement rule, you may simply take 1 minus the probability found in the

FIGURE 7.3.9   The probability of a typical quarter in terms of standardized sales numbers. The shaded area is found by looking up each standardized number in the table and then subtracting. Subtracting eliminates the *unshaded* area at the far left. The answer is 0.7495.

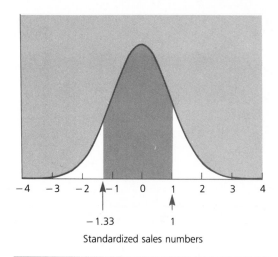

Standardized sales numbers

FIGURE 7.3.10   The probability of a surprising quarter, in terms of standardized sales numbers. The shaded area is found by looking up each standardized number in the table, finding the difference between the probabilities, and subtracting the result from 1. The answer is 0.2505.

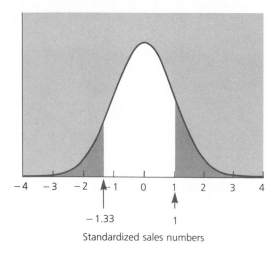

Standardized sales numbers

last example, which was the probability of being between these two values. The answer is therefore:

Probability of a surprising quarter = 1 − 0.7495

= 0.2505, or about 25%

This probability is illustrated, in standard numbers, in Figure 7.3.10.

The Four Different Probability Calculations

Following is a summary table of the four types of problems and how to solve them. The values *a* and *b* represent *standardized* numbers from the problem, found by subtracting the mean and dividing by the standard deviation. The table referred to is the standard normal probability table.

Computing Probabilities for a Normal Distribution

To Find the Probability of Being	Procedure
Less than *a*	Look up *a* in the table
More than *a*	Subtract above answer from 1
Between *a* and *b*	Look up *a* and *b* in the table, and subtract smaller probability from larger
Not between *a* and *b*	Subtract above answer from 1

You may be wondering if there is a difference between the two events "sales exceeded $22 million" and "sales were at least $22 million." The term *exceeded* means *more than*, whereas the term *at least* means *more than or equal to*. In fact, there is *no difference* between the probabilities of these two events; the difference between the probabilities is just a geometric line, which represents no area under the normal curve.

Be Careful: Things Need Not Be Normal!

If you have a normal distribution and you know the mean and standard deviation, you can find correct probabilities by standardizing and then using the standard normal probability table. Fortunately, if the distribution is only approximately normal, your probabilities will still be approximately correct.

However, if the distribution is very far from normal, then any probabilities you might compute based on the mean, the standard deviation, and the normal table could be very wrong indeed.

EXAMPLE

A Lottery (or Risky Project)

Consider a lottery (or a risky project, if you prefer) that pays back nothing 90% of the time, but pays $500 the remaining 10% of the time. The expected (mean) payoff is $50, and the standard deviation is $150 for this discrete random variable. Note that this does *not* represent a normal distribution; it's not even close because it's so discrete, with only two possible values.

What is the probability of winning at least $50? The correct answer is 10% because the *only* way to win anything at all is to win the full amount, $500, which is at least $50.

What if you assumed a normal distribution with this same mean ($50) and standard deviation ($150)? How far from the correct answer (10%) would you be? Very far away, because the probability that a normally distributed random variable exceeds its mean is 0.5 or 50%.

This is a big difference: 10% (the truth) versus 50% (computed by wrongly assuming a normal distribution). Figure 7.3.11 shows the large difference between the actual discrete distribution and the normal distribution with the same mean and standard deviation. Always be careful about assuming a normal distribution!

7.4 The Central Limit Theorem

There are two reasons that the normal distribution is so special. First, many data sets follow a normal distribution (although in business, we often have to work with logarithms of the data to eliminate skewness). Second, even when a distribution is not normal, the distribution of an *average* or a *sum* of numbers from this distribution will be closer to a normal distribution.

It is important to distinguish an *individual* measurement from an *average* or *sum* of measurements, which combines many individuals. Although the

FIGURE 7.3.11   The discrete distribution of the payoff and the normal distribution having the same mean ($50) and standard deviation ($150). These distributions and their probabilities are very different. The discrete distribution gives the correct answers; the assumption of normality is wrong in this case.

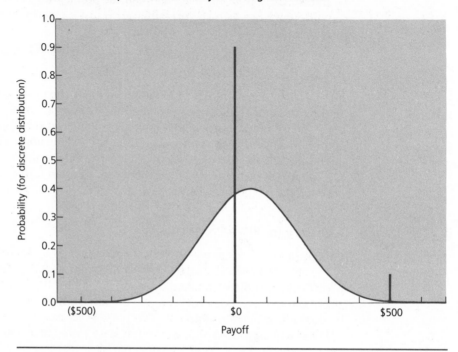

individuals retain whatever distribution they happen to have, the process of combining many individuals into an average or sum results in a more normal distribution.

To understand this, recognize that the process of getting a data set and computing the average is itself a random experiment, and the average is a random variable. Therefore, it makes sense to speak of the distribution of the average or the distribution of the sum as either having a normal distribution or not. Since we are dealing with probabilities and not statistics, we are free to imagine repeating the data-gathering process many times, producing multiple observations of the average. A histogram of these observations represents (approximately) its distribution.

The **central limit theorem** specifies that, for a data set consisting of n independent observations of a random variable representing a population, the following statements are true:

1 Distributions become more and more normal as n gets large, for both the *average* and the *sum*.
2 The means and standard deviations of the distributions of the average and the sum are as follows, where μ is the mean of the individuals and σ is the standard deviation of these individuals.

FIGURE 7.4.1   A histogram of sales of the largest 100 U.S. industrial corporations.

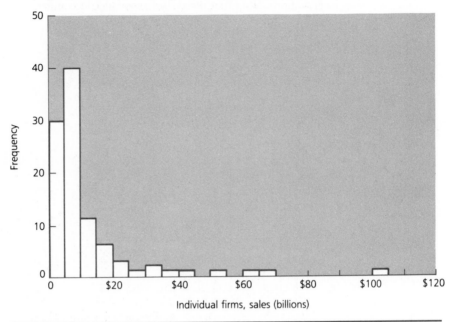

	Random Variable	
	Average	**Sum Total**
Mean	$\mu_{\bar{x}} = \mu$	$\mu_{sum} = n\mu$
Standard deviation	$\sigma_{\bar{x}} = \dfrac{\sigma}{\sqrt{n}}$	$\sigma_{sum} = \sigma\sqrt{n}$

The central limit theorem gives you all the information needed to compute probabilities for a sum or an average. If n is large enough, you may assume a normal distribution and use the standard normal probability tables.[9] To standardize the numbers, you may use the appropriate mean and standard deviation from the preceding table. Then all you have to do is remember how to compute probabilities for a normal distribution!

Figure 7.4.1 shows a histogram of sales of the top 100 U.S. industrial corporations.[10] As you can see, the distribution is quite skewed. Figure 7.4.2 shows the distribution of the *averages of 5 firms* taken from this list of 100

---

[9]How large is large enough? If the distribution of individuals is not too skewed, $n = 20$ is generally sufficient. However, if the distribution is extremely skewed or has large outliers, n may have to be much larger. If the distribution is fairly close to normal already, then n can be much smaller than 20, say, 10 or even 5.

[10]Data are from "The Fortune 500 Largest U.S. Industrial Corporations," *Fortune*, April 27, 1987, pp. 364–66.

FIGURE 7.4.2 A histogram of 100 averages of 5 firms taken from the 100 largest U.S. industrial corporations. Note that the skewness is reduced compared to the previous figure.

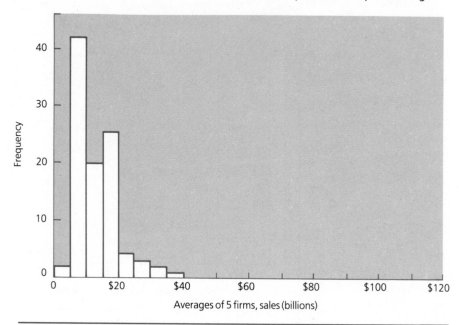

Averages of 5 firms, sales (billions)

(i.e., the average sales of 5 randomly selected firms was computed 100 times). The distribution is still skewed, but less so, and it is more normal than the distribution of the individual firms. Figures 7.4.3 and 7.4.4 use larger sample sizes, $n = 10$ and $n = 25$. Note how the means stay the same throughout, whereas the standard deviations get smaller according to the "divide by the square root of n" rule. Note also the progression in the figures from skewness to normality.

How does the central limit theorem work? The idea is that the extreme values in the data are averaged with each other. The long tail on the right of Figure 7.4.1, due to skewness, moves inward because the very large firms are averaged with some of the others. This explains the reduction in skewness.

Why does the distribution move toward a normal one? The complete answer relies on advanced mathematical statistics and will not be presented here. However, it is a general theoretical result, demanding only that σ be finite and nonzero.

EXAMPLE

How Much Do Shoppers Spend?

At your supermarket, the typical shopper spends $18.93 with a standard deviation of $12.52. You are wondering what would happen in a typical morning hour with 400 typical shoppers, assuming that each one shops independently.

FIGURE 7.4.3   A histogram of 100 averages of 10 firms. Note that the distribution is beginning to look more normal.

Averages of l0 firms, sales (billions)

FIGURE 7.4.4   A histogram of 100 averages of 25 firms. The distribution is now fairly normal, although some skewness remains.

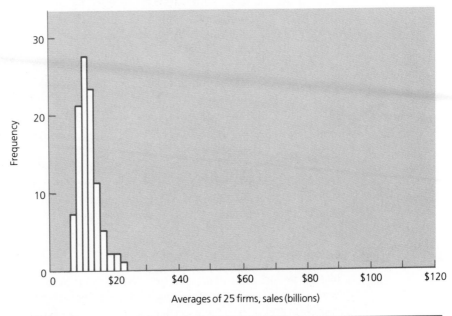

Averages of 25 firms, sales (billions)

Thus, $\mu = 18.93$, $\sigma = 12.52$, and $n = 400$. The central limit theorem can be used to tell you all about your total sales for the hour and, in particular, how likely it is that you will exceed \$8,000 in total sales for all 400 shoppers.

First, for the *total* sales for this hour, which is the sum of the purchases of all 400 shoppers, the expected value is:

$$\mu_{(total\ sales)} = n\mu$$

$$= 400 \times 18.93$$

$$= \$7,572.00$$

Next, you wonder how much variability you can expect in total sales. This is an *hour-to-hour* variability for total sales, as compared to the *shopper-to-shopper* variability of $\sigma = \$12.52$. The answer is:

$$\sigma_{(total\ sales)} = \sigma\sqrt{n}$$

$$= 12.52\sqrt{400}$$

$$= 12.52 \times 20$$

$$= \$250.40$$

In summary, for these 400 shoppers, you expect total sales of about \$7,572.00, with a standard deviation of \$250.40.

The central limit theorem also tells you that total sales will be approximately normally distributed. Since you have the mean and standard deviation, you can compute probabilities using the standard normal table. Note that the standard normal table would *not* apply to individual shoppers but (using the central limit theorem) would apply to total sales.

What is the probability that total sales will exceed \$8,000.00 for these 400 shoppers? First standardize this number using the appropriate mean and standard deviation (for total sales):

$$\text{Standardized total sales} = \frac{8,000 - \mu_{(total\ sales)}}{\sigma_{(total\ sales)}}$$

$$= \frac{8,000 - 7,572}{250.40}$$

$$= 1.71$$

Looking 1.71 up in the standard normal probability table, the final answer is found to be $1 - 0.9564 = 0.0436$, or about a 4% chance of exceeding \$8,000 in total sales. This probability is shown in Figure 7.4.5.

EXAMPLE

Consistency in Bubble Gum Production

It's OK if each individual piece of bubble gum isn't *exactly* 0.20 ounce, as promised on the package, so long as the average weight isn't too low (to avoid consumer and government lawsuits) or too high (to avoid unnecessary costs). In

FIGURE 7.4.5   The probability that total sales will exceed $8,000 is 0.0436. The mean and standard deviation were computed using the central limit theorem.

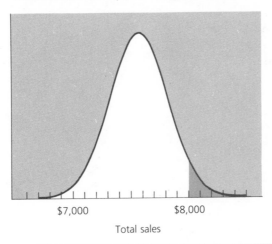

$7,000 $8,000

Total sales

your production facility, you know from experience that individual pieces of gum have a standard deviation of 0.052 ounce, representing variability about their mean value of 0.201 ounce. Any bags of 15 pieces that have an average weight per piece lower than 0.18 ounce will be rejected. What fraction of bags will be rejected this way?

We will assume that pieces are independently produced (which may not be reasonable, since a problem could affect a number of pieces at a time).

First you need to find the mean and standard deviation of the average of $n = 15$ pieces, where each piece has a mean weight of $\mu = 0.201$ ounce and a standard deviation of $\sigma = 0.052$.

$$\mu_{(average\ weight)} = \mu$$

$$= 0.201 \text{ ounce}$$

$$\sigma_{(average\ weight)} = \frac{\sigma}{\sqrt{15}}$$

$$= \frac{0.052}{3.872983}$$

$$= 0.013426 \text{ ounce}$$

Next convert 0.18 ounce to a standardized number:

$$\text{Standardized average weight limit} = \frac{0.18 - \mu_{(average\ weight)}}{\sigma_{(average\ weight)}}$$

$$= \frac{0.18 - 0.201}{0.013426}$$

$$= -1.56$$

FIGURE 7.4.6 The probability that the average weight per piece will be lower than 0.18 ounce is 0.0594. The mean and standard deviation were computed using the central limit theorem.

0.15   0.20   0.25

Average weight per piece of bubble gum

Finally, the probability of rejecting a bag is the probability that a standard normal variable is less than −1.56. From the standard normal probability table, the answer is 0.0594, meaning about 6% of the bags will be rejected. This probability is shown in Figure 7.4.6.

The Normal Approximation to the Binomial

Remember the binomial distribution? It is the number of times that something happens out of n independent tries. Since this number of times is a sum (in fact, it is the sum of observations of a random variable that is 1 if the event occurs and 0 otherwise), the central limit theorem tells you that a binomial distribution will be approximately normal provided n is large.[11] This fact will help you find probabilities for a binomial distribution when the numbers are too large to use the earlier formula. Since you learned how to find the mean and the standard deviation in Section 7.2, you already know enough to find these probabilities.

Here is convincing evidence of the binomial approximation to the normal. Suppose n is 100 and p is 0.10. The probability distribution, computed using the binomial formula, is shown in Figure 7.4.7. It certainly has the bell shape of a normal distribution. Although it is still discrete, with separate, individual bars, there are enough observations that the discreteness is not a dominant feature.

---

[11] It is also necessary that p be neither too close to 0 nor too close to 1; that is, with rare or nearly definite events, the approach to a normal distribution is much slower. The Poisson distribution, covered in a later section, is a good approximation to the binomial when n is large and p is close to 0.

FIGURE 7.4.7   The probability distribution of a binomial with $n = 100$ and $p = 0.10$ is fairly close to normal.

$$n = 100 \quad p = 0.1$$

Compare Figure 7.4.7 ($n = 100$) to Figure 7.4.8 ($n = 10$) to see that, with smaller n, the distribution is not as normal. Furthermore, the discreteness is more important when n is small.

EXAMPLE   **High- and Low-Speed Microprocessors**

We often don't have as much control over a manufacturing process as we would like. Such is the case with sophisticated microprocessor chips, such as those used in microcomputers, with 100,000 transistors placed on a 1/4-inch square of silicon. Despite careful controls, there is variation within the resulting chips: some will run at higher speeds than others.

In the spirit of the old software saying "It's not a bug, it's a feature!" the chips are sorted according to the speed at which they will actually run and priced accordingly (with the faster chips commanding a higher price). The catalog lists two products: 15 megahertz (slower) and 20 megahertz (faster).

Your machinery is known to produce the slow chips 80% of the time, on the average, and fast chips the remaining 20% of the time, with chips being slow or fast independently of one another. Today your goal is to ship 1,000 slow chips and 300 fast chips, perhaps with some chips left over. How many should you schedule for production?

FIGURE 7.4.8   The probability distribution of a binomial with $n = 10$ and $p = 0.10$ is not very
normal because n is not large enough.

$n = 10 \quad p = 0.1$

If you schedule 1,300 total chips, you expect 80% (1,040 chips) to be slow
and 20% (260 chips) to be fast. You would have enough slow ones, but not
enough fast ones, on average.

Since you know that you are limited by the number of fast chips, you compute 300/0.20 = 1,500. This tells you that if you schedule 1,500 chips, you can
expect 20% (300 chips) to be fast. So *on average* you would just meet the goal.
Unfortunately, this means that you have only about a 50% chance of meeting
the goal for fast chips!

Suppose you schedule 1,650 chips for production. What is the probability
that you will be able to meet the goal? To solve this, you first state it as a complete probability question:

> Given a binomial random variable (the number of fast chips produced) with
> $n = 1,650$ total chips produced and $p = 0.20$ probability that a chip is fast, find the
> probability that this random variable is at least 300 but less than 650.[12]

To solve this using the binomial distribution directly would require that you
compute the probability for 300, for 301, for 302, and so on until you got tired.
The central limit theorem allows you to solve it much faster using the standard

---

[12]This is because more than 1,650 − 1,000 = 650 fast chips would imply less than 1,000 slow
chips; thus, you would not be able to meet the goal for slow chips.

normal probability table. You will need to know the mean and standard deviation of the number of fast chips produced:

$$\mu_{\text{(number of fast chips)}} = np$$

$$= 1{,}650 \times 0.20$$

$$= 330$$

$$\sigma_{\text{(number of fast chips)}} = \sqrt{np(1 - p)}$$

$$= \sqrt{1{,}650 \times 0.20 \times 0.80}$$

$$= 16.24807$$

You also need to standardize the bounds on the number of fast chips needed, 300 and 650:

$$\text{Standardized lower number of fast chips} = \frac{300 - 330}{16.24807}$$

$$= -1.85$$

$$\text{Standardized upper number of fast chips} = \frac{650 - 330}{16.24807}$$

$$= 19.69464$$

Looking up these standardized values in the standard normal probability table, you find 0.0322 for -1.85 and note that 19.69464 is way off the end of the table, so you use the value 1.[13] Subtracting these numbers to find the probability of being between them, the answer is $1 - 0.0322 = 0.9678$. You conclude that if 1,650 chips are selected, you have a 96% chance of meeting the goal of shipping 300 fast chips and 1,000 slow ones.

One of the uses of probability is to help you understand what is happening "behind the scenes" in the real world. Let's see what might really be happening in an opinion poll by using a "what if" scenario analysis.

EXAMPLE   **Polling the Electorate**

Your telephone polling and research firm was hired to conduct an opinion poll to see if a new municipal bond initiative is likely to be approved by the voters in the next election. You decided to interview 800 randomly selected representative people who are likely to vote, and you found that 436 intend to vote in favor. Here's the "what-if": If the entire electorate were, in fact, evenly divided on the issue, what is the probability that you would expect to see this many or more of your sample in favor?

----

[13] This makes sense; the probability that a standard normal variable will be less than 19.69464 standard deviations above its mean is essentially 1, since this nearly always happens.

This is a binomial random variable with $n = 800$ and $X = 436$, so $f = 436/800 = 0.545$ or 54.5%. Let's assume that $p = 0.50$ (i.e., the entire electorate is evenly divided) and find the probability that you would observe a binomial proportion of at least 54.5%. This is found by standardizing 54.5% under these assumptions:

$$\mu_f = p = 0.50$$

$$\sigma_f = \sqrt{\frac{p(1 - p)}{n}}$$

$$= \sqrt{\frac{0.50 \times (1 - 0.50)}{800}}$$

$$= 0.0177$$

$$\text{Standardized value} = \frac{0.545 - \mu_f}{\sigma_f}$$

$$= \frac{0.045}{0.0177}$$

$$= 2.54$$

Using the normal probability tables, you find that the probability of seeing this large a margin in favor in the sample, assuming that the population is evenly divided, is $1 - 0.9945 = 0.0055$. This is very unlikely: a probability of about 0.5%.

You asked, what if the population were evenly divided and found the answer: A sample percentage of 54.5% or more is highly unlikely. The conclusion is that you have evidence against the "what-if" scenario of evenly divided voters. It looks good for the initiative!

7.5 Two Other Distributions: The Poisson and the Exponential

There are many other probability distributions that are useful in statistics. This section provides brief descriptions of two such distributions with an indication of how they might fit in with specialized business applications.

The Poisson Distribution

The Poisson distribution, like the binomial, is a counted number of times something happens. The difference is that there is no specified number n of possible tries. Here is one way that it can arise. If an event happens independently and randomly over time, and the average rate of occurrence is constant over time, then the number of occurrences in a fixed amount of time will follow the **Poisson distribution.**[14] The Poisson is a *discrete* distribution and depends only on the mean number of occurrences expected.

---

[14]Poisson is a French name, pronounced (more or less) "pwah-*soh*."

Here are some random variables that might follow a Poisson distribution:

1 The number of orders your firm receives tomorrow.
2 The number of people who apply for a job tomorrow to your human resources division.
3 The number of defects in a finished product.
4 The number of calls your firm receives next week for help concerning an "easy-to-assemble" toy.
5 A binomial number X when n is large and p is small.

The following figures show what the Poisson probabilities look like for a system expecting a mean of 0.5 occurrences (Figure 7.5.1), 2 occurrences (Figure 7.5.2), and 20 occurrences (Figure 7.5.3). Note from the bell shape of Figure 7.5.2 that the Poisson distribution is approximately normal when many occurrences are expected.

There are three important facts about a Poisson distribution. These facts, taken together, tell you how to find probabilities for a Poisson distribution when you know only its mean.

FIGURE 7.5.1 The Poisson distribution with 0.5 occurrences expected is a skewed distribution. There is a high probability, 0.607, that no occurrences will happen at all.

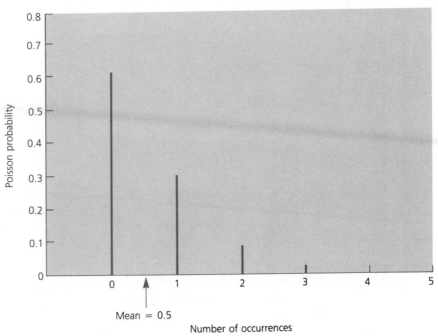

FIGURE 7.5.2   The Poisson distribution with two occurrences expected. The distribution is still somewhat skewed.

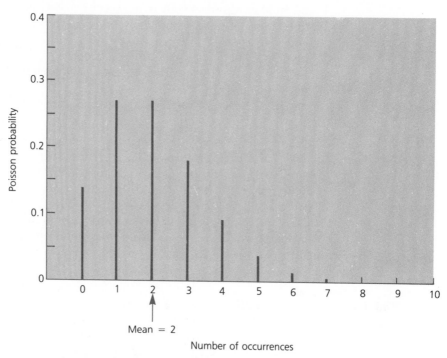

For a Poisson Distribution:

1 The standard deviation is always equal to the square root of the mean.
2 The exact probability that a Poisson random variable X with mean μ is equal to a is given by the formula:

$$P(X = a) = e^{-\mu}\frac{\mu^{a}}{a!}$$

where $e = 2.71828\ldots$
3 If the mean is large, then (based on the central limit theorem) the Poisson distribution is approximately normal.

EXAMPLE   ### How Many Warranty Returns?

Because your firm's quality is so high, you expect only 1.3 of your products to be returned, on average, each day for warranty repairs. What are the chances that no products will be returned tomorrow? That one will be returned? How about two? How about three?

FIGURE 7.5.3   The Poisson distribution with 20 occurrences expected. The distribution, although still discrete, is now fairly close to normal.

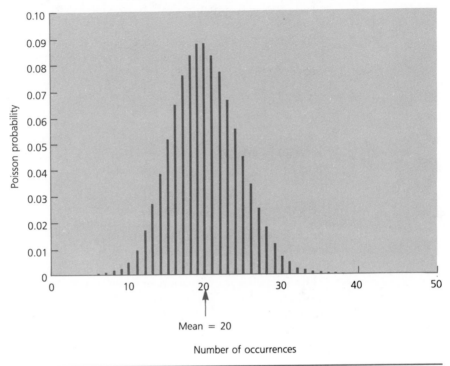

Since the mean (1.3) is so small, exact calculations are needed. Here are the details:

$$P(X = 0) = e^{-1.3} \times \frac{1.3^0}{0!} = 0.27253 \times \frac{1}{1} = 0.27253$$

$$P(X = 1) = e^{-1.3} \times \frac{1.3^1}{1!} = 0.27253 \times \frac{1.3}{1} = 0.35429$$

$$P(X = 2) = e^{-1.3} \times \frac{1.3^2}{2!} = 0.27253 \times \frac{1.69}{2} = 0.23029$$

$$P(X = 3) = e^{-1.3} \times \frac{1.3^3}{3!} = 0.27253 \times \frac{2.197}{6} = 0.099792$$

From these basic probabilities, you could also find the probability that two items *or fewer* will be returned by adding up the appropriate probabilities for 0, 1, and 2. The probability is, then, 0.27253 + 0.35429 + 0.23029 = 0.857, or 85.7%.

How Many Phone Calls?

Your firm handles 460 calls per day, on average. Assuming a Poisson distribution, find the probability that you will be overloaded tomorrow, with 500 or more calls received.

The mean is given. The standard deviation is $\sqrt{460} = 21.44761$. You may use the normal approximation because the mean (460) is so large. The standardized number of calls is

$$\frac{(500 - 460)}{21.44761} = 1.87$$

Using the standard normal probability table, the answer is a probability of $1 - 0.9693 = 0.0307$, so you may expect to be overloaded tomorrow with probability only about 3% (not very likely).

The Exponential Distribution

The **exponential distribution** is the very skewed continuous distribution shown in Figure 7.5.4. Its rise is vertical at 0, on the left, and it descends gradually, with a long tail on the right.

The following is a situation in which the exponential distribution is appropriate. If events happen independently and randomly with a constant rate over time, the *waiting time* between successive events follows an exponential distribution.[15]

Here are some examples of random variables that might follow an exponential distribution:

FIGURE 7.5.4　The exponential distribution is a very skewed distribution that is often used to represent waiting times between events.

The exponential distribution

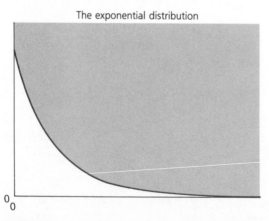

0
 0

---

[15]Note that this implies that the total number of events follows a Poisson distribution.

1 The time between customer arrivals at an auto repair shop.

2 The amount of time your copy machine works between visits by the repair people.

3 The length of time of a typical telephone call.

4 The time until a TV picture tube burns out.

The exponential distribution *has no memory* in the surprising sense that, after you have waited awhile without success for the next event, your average waiting time remaining until the next event is no shorter than it was when you started! This makes sense for waiting times, since occurrences are independent of one another and "don't know" that none have happened recently.

What does this property say about telephone calls? Suppose you are responsible for a switching unit for which the average call lasts five minutes. Consider all calls received at a given moment. On average, you expect them to last five minutes, with the individual durations following the exponential distribution. After one minute passes, some of these calls have ended. However, the calls that remain are all expected, on average, to last *five minutes more*. This is because the shorter calls have already been eliminated. While this may be difficult to believe, it has been confirmed (approximately) using real data.

The standard deviation of an exponential random variable is always equal to the square root of the mean. However, that by itself will not help you find the probabilities because the distribution is very different from a normal distribution.[16]

There is a relationship between the exponential and the Poisson distributions when events happen independently at a constant rate over time. The *number of events* in any fixed time period is Poisson, and the *waiting time between events* is exponential. This is illustrated in Figure 7.5.5. In fact, the

FIGURE 7.5.5   The relationship between the exponential and the Poisson distributions when events happen over time independently and at a constant rate.

---

[16]The probability that an exponential random variable X with mean μ is less than a is given by

$$P(X < a) = 1 - e^{-a/\mu}$$

distribution of the waiting time from any fixed time until the next event is exponential.

■ 7.6 End-of-Chapter Materials

Summary

A **random variable** is a numerical result *in the abstract* of a random experiment. A particular value taken on by a random variable is called an **observation**. The pattern of probabilities for a random variable is called its **probability distribution.** Random variables are either **discrete** (if you can list all possible outcomes) or **continuous** (if any number in a range is possible). Some random variables are literally discrete, but you can work with them as though they were continuous.

For a discrete random variable, the probability distribution is a list of the possible values together with their probabilities of occurrence. The mean or expected value and the standard deviation are computed as follows.

For a discrete random variable:

$$\mu = E(X) = \text{Sum of (value times probability)} = \sum XP(X)$$

$$\sigma = \sqrt{\text{Sum of (squared deviation times probability)}}$$

$$= \sqrt{\sum (X - \mu)^2 P(X)}$$

The interpretations are familiar. The **mean** or **expected value** indicates the typical or average value, and the **standard deviation** indicates the risk in terms of approximately how far from the mean you can expect to be.

A random variable X has a **binomial distribution** if it represents the *number of occurrences* of an event out of n trials, provided (1) for each of the n trials, the event always has the same probability p of happening, and (2) the trials are independent of one another. The **binomial proportion** is $f = X/n$, which also represents a percentage. The mean and standard deviation of a binomial or binomial proportion may be found as follows:

Mean and Standard Deviation for a Binomial Distribution

	Number of Occurrences, X	Proportion or Percentage, $f = X/n$
Mean	$E(X) = \mu_X = np$	$E(f) = \mu_f = p$
Standard deviation	$\sigma_X = \sqrt{np(1 - p)}$	$\sigma_f = \sqrt{\dfrac{p(1 - p)}{n}}$

The probability that a binomial random variable X is equal to some given number a (from 0 to n) is given by the formula below.

Binomial probability that X equals a:

$$P(X = a) = \binom{n}{a} p^a (1 - p)^{(n-a)}$$

$$= \frac{n!}{a! \times (n - a)!} p^a (1 - p)^{(n-a)}$$

$$= \frac{1 \times 2 \times \cdots \times n}{[1 \times 2 \times \cdots \times a][1 \times 2 \times \cdots \times (n - a)]} p^a (1 - p)^{(n-a)}$$

The notation $n!$ is n factorial, the product of the numbers from 1 to n, with $0! = 1$ by definition. The notation

$$\binom{n}{a} = n!/[a!(n - a)!]$$

is the *binomial coefficient,* read aloud as "n choose a."

The **normal distribution,** a continuous distribution, is represented by the familiar bell-shaped curve. The probability that a normal random variable will be between any two values is equal to the area under the normal curve between these two values. There is a normal distribution for each combination of a mean μ and a (positive) standard deviation σ. The **standard normal distribution** is a normal distribution with mean $\mu = 0$ and standard deviation $\sigma = 1$. You may think of the standard normal distribution as representing the number of standard deviations above or below the mean. The **standard normal probability table** gives the probability that a standard normal random variable is *less than* any given number.

To solve word problems involving normal probabilities, first identify the mean μ, standard deviation σ, and the probability asked for. Convert to a **standardized number** (the number of standard deviations above the mean, or below the mean if the standardized number is negative) by subtracting the mean and dividing by the standard deviation:

$$\text{Standardized number} = \frac{\text{Number} - \text{Mean}}{\text{Standard deviation}} = \frac{\text{Number} - \mu}{\sigma}$$

Finally, look up the standardized number or numbers in the standard normal probability table and use the following summary table (where a and b are standardized numbers) to find the final answer:

Computing Probabilities for a Normal Distribution

To Find the Probability of Being	Procedure
Less than a	Look up a in the table
More than a	Subtract above answer from 1
Between a and b	Look up a and b in the table, and subtract smaller probability from larger
Not between a and b	Subtract above answer from 1

The **central limit theorem** says that, for a data set consisting of n independent observations of a random variable representing a population, the following statements are true:

1 Distributions become more and more normal as n gets large, for both the *average* and the *sum*.
2 The means and standard deviations of the distributions of the average and the sum are as follows, where μ is the mean of the individuals and σ is the standard deviation of these individuals:

	Random Variable	
	Average	Sum Total
Mean	$\mu_{\overline{X}} = \mu$	$\mu_{\text{sum}} = n\mu$
Standard deviation	$\sigma_{\overline{X}} = \dfrac{\sigma}{\sqrt{n}}$	$\sigma_{\text{sum}} = \sigma\sqrt{n}$

Applying the central limit theorem, you can find probabilities for a sum or an average by using the standard normal probability table, finding the appropriate mean and standard deviation in the preceding summary table. In particular, binomial probabilities may be found (approximately) by using the standard normal probability table when n is large.

If occurrences happen independently and randomly over time, and the average rate of occurrence is constant over time, then the number of occurrences that happen in a fixed amount of time will follow the **Poisson distribution,** a discrete random variable. The standard deviation is the square root of the mean. If the mean is large, the Poisson distribution is approximately normal and the standard normal probability table may be used. Exact Poisson probabilities may be found using the following formula:

$$P(X = a) = e^{-\mu}\frac{\mu^{a}}{a!}$$

The **exponential distribution** is a very skewed continuous distribution useful for understanding such variables as waiting times and durations of telephone calls. It has no "memory," in the sense that after you have waited a while without success for the next event, your average waiting time until the next event is no shorter than it was when you started.

Key Words

random variable 203
observation 203
probability distribution 203
discrete random variable 204

continuous random variable 204
mean or expected value 205
standard deviation 205
binomial distribution 209

Questions

1 a. What is a random variable?
   b. What is the difference between a random variable and a number?

2 a. What is a discrete random variable?
   b. What is a continuous random variable?
   c. Give an example of a discrete random variable that is continuous for practical purposes.

3 a. What is the probability distribution of a discrete random variable?
   b. How do you find the mean of a discrete random variable? How do you interpret the result?
   c. How do you find the standard deviation of a discrete random variable? How do you interpret the result?

4 a. How do you tell if a random variable has a binomial distribution?
   b. What is a binomial proportion?
   c. What are n, p, X, and f?

5 For a binomial distribution:
   a. Why don't you just construct the probability tree to find the probabilities?
   b. How do you find the mean and the standard deviation?
   c. How do you find the probability that X is equal to some number?
   d. How do you find the exact probability that X is greater than or equal to some number?
   e. If n is a large number, how do you find the approximate probability that X is greater than or equal to some number?

6 a. What is a factorial?
   b. Find 3!, 0!, and 15!.
   c. What is a binomial coefficient? What does it represent in the formula for a binomial probability?
   d. Find the binomial coefficient "8 choose 5."

7 a. What is a normal distribution?
   b. Identify all of the different possible normal distributions.
   c. What does the area under the normal curve represent?
   d. What is the standard normal distribution? What is it used for?
   e. What numbers are found in the standard normal probability table?
   f. Find the probability that a standard normal random variable is less than -1.65.
   g. How do you standardize a number?

8 a. What is the central limit theorem?
   b. Does the central limit theorem specify that individual cases follow a normal distribution?
   c. How do you interpret the idea that the average has a normal distribution?
   d. What is the mean of a sum of independent observations of a random variable? What is its standard deviation?
   e. What is the mean of an average of independent observations of a random variable? What is its standard deviation?

9 a. What kinds of situations give rise to a Poisson distribution?
  b. Is the Poisson a discrete or a continuous distribution?
  c. What is the standard deviation of a Poisson distribution?
  d. How do you find probabilities for a Poisson distribution if the mean is large?
10 a. What kinds of situations give rise to an exponential distribution?
  b. What is meant by the fact that an exponential random variable has no memory?
  c. Can the standard normal probability table be used to find probabilities for an exponential distribution? Why or why not?

Problems

1 A call option on common stock is being evaluated. If the stock goes down, the option will expire worthless. If the stock goes up, the payoff depends on just how high the stock goes. For simplicity, the payoffs are modeled as a discrete distribution with the following probability distribution:

Payoff	Probability
$ 0	0.50
10	0.25
20	0.15
30	0.10

Even though options markets, in fact, behave more like a continuous random variable, this discrete approximation will give useful approximate results. Answer the following questions based on the discrete probability distribution given.
a. Find the mean, or expected value, of the option payoff.
b. Describe briefly what this expected value represents.
c. Find the standard deviation of the option payoff.
d. Describe briefly what this standard deviation represents.
e. Find the probability that the option will pay at least $20.
f. Find the probability that the option will pay less than $30.

2 The length of time a system is "down" (that is, broken) is described (approximately) by the following probability distribution:

Problem	Downtime (minutes)	Probability
Minor	5	0.60
Substantial	30	0.30
Catastrophic	120	0.10

Assume that these downtimes are exact. That is, there are three types of easily recognized problems that always take this long (5, 30, or 120 minutes) to fix.
a. What kind of probability distribution does this table represent?
b. Find the mean downtime.

   c. Find the standard deviation of the downtime.

   d. What is the probability that the downtime will be greater than 10 minutes, according to this table?

   e. What is the probability that the downtime is literally within one standard deviation of its mean? Is this about what you would expect for a normal distribution?

3 You can invest in just one of four projects on a lot of land you own. For simplicity, you have modeled the payoffs (as net present value in today's dollars) of the projects as discrete distributions. By selling the land you can make $60,000 for sure. If you build an apartment, you estimate a payoff of $130,000 if things go well (with probability 0.60) and $70,000 otherwise. If you build a single-family house, the payoff is $100,000 (with probability 0.6) and $60,000 otherwise. Finally, you could build a gambling casino which would pay very well—$500,000—but with a probability of just 0.10 since the final government permits are not likely to be granted; all will be lost otherwise.

   a. Find the expected payoff for each of these four projects. In terms of just the expected payoff, rank these projects in order from best to ‾ ⁻ ‥

   b. Find the standard deviation for each of these four projects. In terms of risk only, rank the projects from best to worst.

   c. Considering both the expected payoff and the risk involved, can any project or projects be eliminated from consideration entirely?

   d. How would you decide among the remaining projects? In particular, does any single project dominate the others completely?

4 It's been a bad day for the market, with 75% of securities losing value. You are evaluating a portfolio of 15 securities and will assume a binomial distribution for the number of securities that lost value.

   a. What assumptions are being made when you use a binomial distribution in this way?

   b. How many securities in your portfolio would you expect to lose value?

   c. What is the standard deviation of the number of securities in your portfolio that lose value?

   d. Find the probability that all 15 securities lose value.

   e. Find the probability that exactly 10 securities lose value.

   f. Find the probability that 13 or more securities lose value.

5 Your firm has decided to interview a random sample of 10 customers in order to determine whether or not to change a consumer product. Your main competitor has already done a similar but much larger study and has concluded that exactly 86% of consumers approve of the change. Unfortunately, your firm does not have access to this information (but you may use this figure in your computations here).

   a. What is the name of the probability distribution of the number of consumers who will approve of the change in your study?

   b. What is the expected *number* of people, out of the 10 you will interview, who will approve of the change?

   c. What is the standard deviation of the number of people, out of the 10 you will interview, who will approve of the change?

   d. What is the expected *percentage* of people, out of the 10 you will interview, who will approve of the change?

e. What is the standard deviation of the percentage of people, out of the 10 you will interview, who will approve of the change?

f. What is the probability that exactly eight of your interviewed customers will approve of the change?

g. What is the probability that eight or more of your interviewed customers will approve of the change?

6 A new project will be declared "successful" if you achieve a market share of 10% or more in the next two years. Your marketing department has considered all possibilities and decided that it expects the product to attain a market share of 12% in this time. However, this number is not certain. The standard deviation is forecast to be 3%, indicating the uncertainty in the 12% forecast as 3 percentage points. You may assume a normal distribution.

a. Find the probability that the new project is successful.

b. Find the probability that the new project fails.

c. Find the probability that the new project is wildly successful, defined as achieving at least a 15% market share.

d. To assess the precision of the marketing projections, find the probability that the attained market share falls close to the projected value of 12%, that is, between 11% and 13%.

7 A manufacturing plant has a fixed cost of $35,000 per month. This is known exactly due to long-term contracts. The variable cost depends somewhat on market prices and their fluctuations and is estimated to be $250 per item produced, with a standard deviation of $15 per item. Assume that exactly 150 items are scheduled for production next month.

a. Find the expected total cost.

b. Find the standard deviation of total cost. What does this represent?

c. Based only on the information given, is it possible to find the probability that the total cost will exceed $75,000? Why or why not?

d. If you assume a normal distribution for the cost, what is the probability that the total cost exceeds $75,000?

e. Again assuming a normal distribution, what is the probability that the total cost will be between $70,000 and $78,000?

8 A manufacturing process produces semiconductor chips with a known failure rate of 6.3%. Assume that chip failures are independent of one another. You will be producing 2,000 chips tomorrow.

a. What is the name of the probability distribution of the number of defective chips produced tomorrow?

b. Find the expected number of defective chips produced.

c. Find the standard deviation of the number of defective chips.

d. Find the probability that you will produce fewer than 135 defects.

e. Find the probability that you will produce more than 120 defects.

f. You just learned that you will need to ship 1,860 working chips out of tomorrow's production of 2,000. What are the chances that you will succeed? Will you need to increase the scheduled number produced?

g. If you schedule 2,100 chips for production, what is the probability that you will be able to ship 1,860 working ones?

9 A union strike vote is scheduled tomorrow, and it looks close. Assume that the number of votes to strike follows a binomial distribution. You expect 100 people to vote, and you have projected a probability of 0.53 that a typical individual will vote to strike.

a. Identify n and p for this binomial random variable.

b. Find the mean and standard deviation of the percentage who will vote to strike.

c. Find the probability that a strike will result.

10 Reconsider the previous problem and answer each part, but assume that 1,000 people will vote. (The probability for each one remains unchanged.)

11 Your customers' average order size is $2,601, with a standard deviation of $1,275. You are wondering what would happen if exactly 25 typical customers independently placed orders tomorrow.

a. Find the mean of tomorrow's total orders.

b. Find the standard deviation of tomorrow's total orders.

c. Next, assume that tomorrow's total orders follow a normal distribution. Why is this assumption reasonable, even if individual customer orders are somewhat skewed?

d. Find the probability that total orders will be at or above your break-even point of $60,000.

e. Find the probability of a truly amazing day, with total orders exceeding $75,000.

f. Find the probability of a typical day, with total orders between $60,000 and $70,000.

g. Find the probability of a surprising day, with total orders either below $55,000 or above $75,000.

h. What are the chances that tomorrow's average order per customer will be between $2,500 and $3,000?

12 You have a factory with 40 production machines that are essentially identical, each producing at a mean daily rate of 100 products with a standard deviation of 15. You may assume that they produce independently of one another. Consider the average daily production per machine tomorrow, which is a random variable.

a. Find the mean of this random variable. Compare it to the mean for a single machine.

b. Find the standard deviation of this random variable. Compare it to the standard deviation for a single machine.

c. What is the approximate probability distribution of this random variable? How do you know?

d. Find the probability that your average daily production per machine will be more than 102 products tomorrow.

e. Find the probability that your average daily production per machine will be between 97 and 103 products tomorrow.

13 If tomorrow is a typical day, your human resources division will expect to receive resumes in the mail from 175 job applicants. You may assume that applicants act independently of one another.
  a. What is the name of the probability distribution of the number of resumes received?
  b. What is the standard deviation of the number of resumes received?
  c. Find the approximate probability that you will receive more than 185 resumes.
  d. Find the approximate probability of a slow day, with just 160 resumes received.

14 A TV picture tube is expected to last for 20,000 hours before burnout.
  a. What is the name of the distribution often used for this kind of waiting time?
  b. Is the distribution skewed or symmetric?
  c. What is the standard deviation of the length of time until burnout?
  d. The tube has been working continuously for the past 8,500 hours and is still on. What is the expected time from now until burnout? (Be careful!)

Database Exercises

Refer to the employee database in Appendix A.

1 View each column as a collection of independent observations of a random variable.
  a. In each case, what kind of variable is represented, continuous or discrete? Why?
  b. Consider the event "annual salary is above $40,000." Find the value of the binomial random variable X that represents the number of times this event occurred. Also find the binomial proportion f and say what it represents.
  c. What fraction of employees are male? Interpret this number as a binomial proportion. What is n?

2 You have a position open and are trying to hire a new person. Assume that the mean and standard deviation of the new person's experience will follow a normal distribution with the mean and standard deviation of your current employees.
  a. Find the probability that the new person will have more than six years of experience.
  b. Find the probability that the new person will have less than three years of experience.
  c. Find the probability that the new person will have between four and seven years of experience.

3 Suppose males and females are equally likely and that the number of each gender follows a binomial distribution. (Note that the database contains *observations* of random variables, not the random variables themselves.)
  a. Find n and p for the binomial distribution of the number of males.
  b. Find n and p for the binomial distribution of the number of females.
  c. Find the observed value of X for the number of females.
  d. Use the normal approximation to the binomial distribution to find the probability of observing this many females (your answer to part c) or fewer in the database.

Projects

1 Choose a continuous random quantity that you might deal with in your current or future work as an executive. Model it as a normally distributed random variable, and estimate (i.e., guess) the mean and standard deviation. Identify three events of interest to you relating to this random variable, and compute their probabilities. Briefly discuss what you have learned.

2 Choose a discrete random quantity (taking on from 3 to 10 different values) that you might deal with in your current or future work as an executive. Estimate (i.e., guess) the probability distribution. Compute the mean and standard deviation. Identify two events of interest to you relating to this random variable, and compute their probabilities. Briefly discuss what you have learned.

3 Choose a binomial random quantity that you might deal with in your current or future work as an executive. Estimate (i.e., guess) the value of n and p. Compute the mean and standard deviation. Identify two events of interest to you relating to this random variable, and compute their probabilities. Briefly discuss what you have learned.

Statistical Inference

The real power of statistics comes from applying the concepts of *probability* to situations where you have *data.* The results, called *statistical inference,* give you exact probability statements about the world based on a set of data. Even a relatively small set of data will work just fine if you're careful. This is how, for example, those political and marketing polls can claim to know what "all Americans" think or do based on interviews of a carefully selected sample. One of the best ways to select a smaller representative sample from a larger group is to use a *random sample,* which will be covered in Chapter 8. The *confidence interval* provides an exact probability statement about an unknown quantity and will be presented in Chapter 9. When you need to decide between two possibilities, you can use *hypothesis testing* (in Chapter 10) to tell you what the data have to say about the situation. In an environment of uncertainty, where perfect answers are unavailable, statistical inference at least gives you answers that have some *known* error rates.

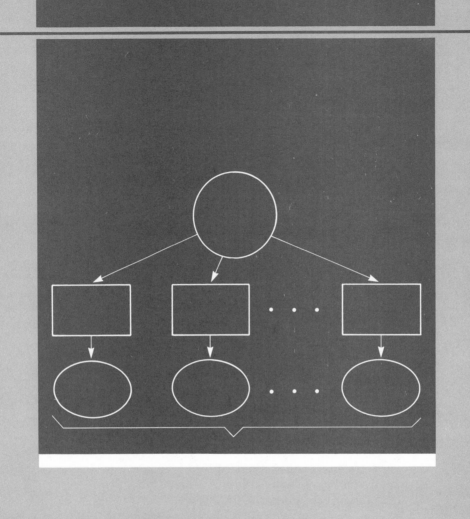

8

Random Sampling
Planning Ahead for
Data Gathering

It's 9:00 A.M. on Wednesday, and you've just read a memo from The Boss asking how your firm's customers would react to a new proposed discount pricing schedule. Your report will be needed in time for tomorrow's 10:00 meeting of the board of directors. What should you do? Some things are clear. For example, you will need to speak with some customers. Thinking it over, you decide that it will take 10 minutes just to interview one customer over the phone. With the time and people you can spare, and with 1,687 customers listed in your database, you could not possibly call every single one to get a reaction. What will you do?

The answer is, of course, that you will draw a *sample* from the *population* of all customers in the database. That is, you will call a manageable number of selected customers. Then you will cross your fingers and hope that the sample is *representative* enough of the larger population so that your report will convey facts needed at the board meeting. After all, the board is interested in how *all* customers would react, not just those in your smaller sample.

But how will you draw the sample? You might make a list of customers you need to talk with for other reasons and ask them for a reaction to the proposed discount schedule. However, you rightly reject this idea because this list is not representative, since it consists largely of "squeaky wheels" who require more hand-holding and are less self-sufficient than customers in general. Even worse, this group tends to place smaller orders of lower-tech equipment compared with your typical customers. To get a representative group of customers, you will need a different way of drawing a sample.

Random sampling will help you in two ways. First, it will ensure a representative sample (at least in an average sense) through selection without regard to any characteristic that might *bias* the sample and confuse the issue.[1] Second, by using a carefully controlled statistical procedure, you will also be able to describe approximately *how different* your results (from the sample) are from the characteristics of the population. Thus, through the use of random sampling, your survey results will be approximately correct (as compared to what you would find by interviewing all customers), and you will know if your results are close enough for comfort.

■ 8.1 Populations and Samples

The **population** is the collection of units (people, objects, or whatever) that you are interested in knowing about. A **sample** is a smaller collection of units selected from the population. Usually you have detailed information about individuals in the sample, but not for those in the population. There are many different ways a sample can be selected; naturally, some methods are much better than others for a given purpose. Here are some examples of populations and samples:

1 *The population:* the approximately 733,000 residents of Tulsa, Oklahoma, where your firm is considering opening a fast-food Mexican restaurant.
   a. A sample might be obtained by hiring people with clipboards to interview every 35th shopper they see at a local mall. Although this sample would tell you about some shoppers, you would have no information about the rest of the population.
   b. Another way to obtain a sample would be to interview (by telephone) every 2,000th person in the phone book. This systematic sample would tell you something about people who are at home to answer their telephones.
   c. Yet another way to draw a sample would be to interview customers as they leave a local McDonald's restaurant. This sample would tell you about a certain group of people who eat fast food.

2 *The population:* the 826 boxes of miscellaneous hardware that just arrived at your shipping dock. You will want to spot-check the invoice against the contents of selected boxes and also note any unacceptable items.
   a. A very convenient sample might be obtained by using the nearest 10 boxes and examining their contents. But this sample is hardly representative and, if your suppliers figured out your selection method, you could be taken advantage of.
   b. Another way to choose a sample would be to select three large, three medium, and three small boxes to examine. This seems to be an attempt to broaden the sampling method, but it also may not be representative of the boxes in general (which might be nearly all large boxes).

---

[1]This parenthetical qualification is needed because there may not be a sample that is *exactly* representative of the population. This would happen, for example, if each member of the population were unique.

c. Yet another way would be to use the invoice itself and select a random sample of the boxes listed. You would then find and open these boxes. This is an appropriate sample. By starting from the invoice, you are ensuring the correctness of this document. By choosing a random sample, your suppliers cannot guess beforehand which boxes you will examine.

3 *The population:* your suppliers (there are 598 of them). You are considering a new system that would involve paying a higher price for supplies in return for guarantees of higher quality and a faster response time.[2] The system would be worthwhile only if enough of your suppliers were interested.

a. One sample would be just your five key suppliers. Although it is good to include these important firms, you might want to include some of the others also.

b. A different sample could be obtained by delegating the selection to one of your workers with a memo that says, "Please get me a list of 10 suppliers for the just-in-time project." This method of delegating without control leaves you with an unknown quantity since you don't know the selection criterion used. You may suspect that the "quickest" or "most convenient" sample was used, and this may not be representative.

c. Yet another way to choose a sample would be to take your 5 key suppliers and include 10 more chosen by controlled delegation (say, in compliance with a memo reading "Please get me a list of 10 random nonkey suppliers, using the random number table." This would be a useful sample since it includes all of the most important players as well as a selection of the others.

How Do You Choose a Representative Sample?

The process of sampling is illustrated in Figure 8.1.1. From the larger population, a sample is chosen to be measured and analyzed in detail. We hope that the sample will be **representative**, meaning that each characteristic (and combination of characteristics) arises the same percentage of the time in the sample as in the population. A sample that is not representative in an important way is said to show **bias**. For example, if the sample has a much greater proportion of males than does the population, you could say that the sample shows a gender bias or that the sample is biased toward males.

Since each individual may be unique, there may be no sample that is completely representative. But how do you tell when a sample is representative enough? By deliberately *not* sampling based on any measurable characteristic, a randomly selected statistical sample will be free (on average) from bias and therefore representative (on average). Furthermore, the randomness introduced in a controlled way into a statistical sample will let you

---

[2]You may recognize this new system as relating to the "just-in-time" method of supplying a factory. Instead of having raw materials sit around in inventory, eating up real estate space and incurring interest costs on the money paid for them, these materials arrive in the right place at the factory just as they are needed.

FIGURE 8.1.1   A sample is a collection drawn from a larger population. This sample appears to be fairly representative but is not perfectly so because neither of the two open triangles were selected to be in the sample.

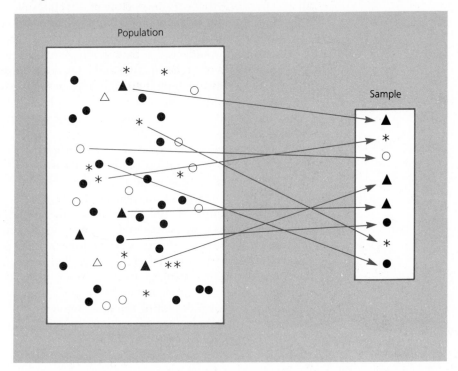

make probability statements about the results (beginning with specification of *confidence intervals,* discussed in the next chapter). Thus, a careful statistical sample will be nearly representative, *and* you will be able to compute just how representative it is.

Once you have carefully identified the most appropriate population for your purpose, the next step is to figure out how to access it. You keep track of the population by creating or identifying the **frame**, which tells you how to gain access to the population units by number. For our purposes, the frame consists of a list of population units numbered from 1 to N, where N is the number of units in the population. To access the 137th population unit, for example, you would locate it in the list to find information (such as name, serial number, or customer number) on how to measure it.

There are two basic kinds of samples. After a unit is chosen from the population to be in the sample, it is either put back (*replaced*) into the population so that it may be sampled again, or else it is not replaced. **Sampling without replacement** occurs if units cannot be chosen more than once in the sample, that is, if all units in the sample must be different. **Sampling with**

replacement takes place if a population unit can appear more than once in the sample. Note that these properties are determined by the *process* used to choose the sample, and not by the *results* of that process. For a small sample chosen from a large population, there is very little difference between these two methods. From now on in this book, we will work primarily with samples having distinct units chosen *without replacement.*

We will use the following standard notation for the number of units in the population (a property of the population) and for the number of units to be selected for the sample (which depends on how many you decide to select):

■ Notation for Number of Elementary Units

N = Size of population

n = Size of sample

A sample that includes the entire population (i.e., $n = N$) is called a **census**. But even if you could examine the entire population, you may well decide not to. When weighing costs against benefits, you may decide that it isn't worth the time and trouble to examine all units.

A Sample Statistic and a Population Parameter

A **sample statistic** (or just "statistic") is defined as any number computed from your sample data. Examples include the sample average, median, sample standard deviation, and percentiles. A statistic is a *random variable* because it is based on data obtained by random sampling, which is a random experiment. Therefore, a statistic is *known* and *random.*

A **population parameter** (or just "parameter") is defined as any number computed for the entire population. Examples include the population mean and population standard deviation. A parameter is a *fixed number* because no randomness is involved. However, you will not usually have data available for the entire population. Therefore, a parameter is *unknown* and *fixed.*

There is often a natural correspondence between statistics and parameters. For each population parameter (a number you would like to know but can't know exactly) there is a sample statistic computed from data that represents your best information about the unknown parameter. Such a sample statistic is called an **estimator** of the population parameter, and the actual number computed from the data is called an **estimate** of the population parameter. For example, the sample average is an estimator of the population mean, and, in a particular case, the estimate might be 18.3. The **error of estimation** is defined as the estimator (or estimate) minus the population parameter; it is usually unknown.

An **unbiased estimator** is neither systematically too high nor too low compared with the corresponding population parameter. This is a desirable property for an estimator. Technically, an estimator is unbiased if its mean value (the mean of its sampling distribution) is equal to the population parameter.

The central limit theorem, which states that the mean of $\overline{X}$ is μ, also tells you that $\overline{X}$ is an unbiased estimator of μ. Of course, for any *given* set of data, $\overline{X}$ will (usually) be too high or too low relative to the population mean, μ. If you were to repeat the sampling process many times, computing a new $\overline{X}$ for each sample, the results would average out to μ and thus would not be *systematically* too high or too low.

■ 8.2 The Random Sample

A **random sample** or **simple random sample** is selected such that (1) each population unit has an *equal probability of being chosen,* and (2) units are *chosen independently,* without regard to one another. By making population units equally likely to be chosen, random sampling is as fair and unbiased as possible. By ensuring independent selection, random sampling aims at gathering as much independent information as possible.[3] Because personal tastes and human factors are removed from the selection process, the resulting sample is more likely to be fair and representative than if you assigned someone to choose an "arbitrary" sample.

An equivalent way to define *random sample* is to say that of all possible samples that might have been chosen, one was chosen at random. This definition, however, is more difficult to work with since the number of samples can be huge. For example, there are 17,310,309,456,440 different samples of $n = 10$ units that could be chosen from a population of just $N = 100$ units.[4] However, this way of thinking about a random sample shows how fair it is, since random sampling does not favor any particular sample over the others.

Selecting a Random Sample

One way to choose a random sample is to use a table of random digits to represent the number of each selected population unit. The unit itself is then found with the help of the frame (this is the purpose of the frame: to go from a number to the actual population unit). A **table of random digits** is a list in which the digits 0 through 9 each occur with probability 1/10, inde-

---

[3]Although independence is a technical concept, it has important practical consequences as well. Here is an example to help you see the problems involved when units are *not* selected independently: In a hospital with 20 wards and 50 patients in each ward, you could select a sample (*not* a random sample) by choosing a ward at random and interviewing all patients in that ward. Note that each patient has an equal chance (1 in 20) of being interviewed. However, since patients are selected as a group instead of independently, your sample will not include important information about diversity within the hospital.

[4]In case you're interested, the formula for the number of distinct samples that could be chosen without replacement is $N!/[n!(N - n!)]$, which you may recognize as a part of the binomial probability formula.

pendently of each other. Here are the details of choosing a random sample of size n without replacement:

■ **Selecting a Random Sample without Replacement**

1 Establish a frame so that the members of the population are numbered from 1 through N.
2 Select a place to begin reading from the table of random digits. Ideally this is done randomly, for example, by tossing a coin.
3 Starting at the selected place, read the digits successively in the usual way (i.e., from left to right and continuing on the next line).
4 Organize these digits in groups whose size is the number of digits in the number N itself. For example, with a population of $N = 5,387$, read the random digits four at a time (since 5,387 has four digits). Or, if the population had $N = 3,163,298$ units, you would read the random digits in groups of seven.
5 Proceed as follows until you have a sample of n units:
  a. If the random number is between 1 and N and has not yet been chosen, include it in the sample.
  b. If the random number is 0 or is larger than N, discard it because there is no corresponding unit to be chosen.
  c. If the random number has already been chosen, discard it because you are sampling without replacement.

For example, let's choose a random sample of 9 customers from a list of 38 beginning wth 69506 in row 11, column 3 of Table 8.2.1, the Table of Random Digits. Since $N = 38$ has two digits, arrange the sequence of random digits in groups of two as follows: 69 50 61 96 10 01 47 99 23 38.... Ignore the first ones because 69, 50, 61, and 96 are all larger than $N = 38$. Consequently, the first sample number selected is 10. The rest of the selection is illustrated in Figure 8.2.1. When the number 10 comes up a second

---

FIGURE 8.2.1   Selecting a random sample without replacement of $n = 9$ units from a population of $N = 38$ units. The random digits are used in groups of two (since 38 has two digits) starting in row 11, column 3 of Table 8.2.1. Numbers are discarded for being either greater than 38 or smaller than 1. The number 10 is discarded the second time. Stop when you have found n units.

Start with random number table:
69506   19610   01479   92338   55140   81097   73071   61544   85356   51400

Arrange in groups of two (because 38 has two digits):
69 50 61 96 10 01 47 99 23 38 55 14 08 10 97 73 07 16 15 44 85 35 65 14 00

Eliminate numbers larger than 38 or smaller than 1:
10 01   23 38   14 08 10   07 16 15   35   14

Eliminate numbers previously listed:
10 01   23 38   14 08   07 16 15   35

Choose the first nine numbers:
10 1   23 38   14 8   7 16 15

TABLE 8.2.1 Table of Random Digits

	1	2	3	4	5	6	7	8	9	10
1	51449	39284	85527	67168	91284	19954	91166	70918	85957	19492
2	16144	56830	67507	97275	25982	69294	32841	20861	83114	12531
3	48145	48280	99481	13050	81818	25282	66466	24461	97021	21072
4	83780	48351	85422	42978	26088	17869	94245	26622	48318	73850
5	95329	38482	93510	39170	63683	40587	80451	43058	81923	97072
6	11179	69004	34273	36062	26234	58601	47159	82248	95968	99722
7	94631	52413	31524	02316	27611	15888	13525	43809	40014	30667
8	64275	10294	35027	25604	65695	36014	17988	02734	31732	29911
9	72125	19232	10782	30615	42005	90419	32447	53688	36125	28456
10	16463	42028	27927	48403	88963	79615	41218	43290	53618	68082
11	10036	66273	69506	19610	01479	92338	55140	81097	73071	61544
12	85356	51400	88502	98267	73943	25828	38219	13268	09016	77465
13	84076	82087	55053	75370	71030	92275	55497	97123	40919	57479
14	76731	39755	78537	51937	11680	78820	50082	56068	36908	55399
15	19032	73472	79399	05549	14772	32746	38841	45524	13535	03113
16	72791	59040	61529	74437	74482	76619	05232	28616	98690	24011
17	11553	00135	28306	65571	34465	47423	39198	54456	95283	54637
18	71405	70352	46763	64002	62461	41982	15933	46942	36941	93412
19	17594	10116	55483	96219	85493	96955	89180	59690	82170	77643
20	09584	23476	09243	65568	89128	36747	63692	09986	47687	46448
21	81677	62634	52794	01466	85938	14565	79993	44956	82254	65223
22	45849	01177	13773	43523	69825	03222	58458	77463	58521	07273
23	97252	92257	90419	01241	52516	66293	14536	23870	78402	41759
24	26232	77422	76289	57587	42831	87047	20092	92676	12017	43554
25	87799	33602	01931	66913	63008	03745	93939	07178	70003	18158
26	46120	62298	69126	07862	76731	58527	39342	42749	57050	91725
27	53292	55652	11834	47581	25682	64085	26587	92289	41853	38354
28	81606	56009	06021	98392	40450	87721	50917	16978	39472	23505
29	67819	47314	96988	89931	49395	37071	72658	53947	11996	64631
30	50458	20350	87362	83996	86422	58694	71813	97695	28804	58523
31	59772	27000	97805	25042	09916	77569	71347	62667	09330	02152
32	94752	91056	08939	93410	59204	04644	44336	55570	21106	76588
33	01885	82054	45944	55398	55487	56455	56940	68787	36591	29914
34	85190	91941	86714	76593	77199	39724	99548	13827	84961	76740
35	97747	67607	14549	08215	95408	46381	12449	03672	40325	77312
36	43318	84469	26047	86003	34786	38931	34846	28711	42833	93019
37	47874	71365	76603	57440	49514	17335	71969	58055	99136	73589
38	24259	48079	71198	95859	94212	55402	93392	31965	94622	11673
39	31947	64805	34133	03245	24546	48934	41730	47831	26531	02203
40	37911	93224	87153	54541	57529	38299	65659	00202	07054	40168
41	82714	15799	93126	74180	94171	97117	31431	00323	62793	11995
42	82927	37884	74411	45887	36713	52339	68421	35968	67714	05883
43	65934	21782	35804	36676	35404	69987	52268	19894	81977	87764
44	56953	04356	68903	21369	35901	86797	83901	68681	02397	55359
45	16278	17165	67843	49349	90163	97337	35003	34915	91485	33814
46	96339	95028	48468	12279	81039	56531	10759	19579	00015	22829
47	84110	49661	13988	75909	35580	18426	29038	79111	56049	96451
48	49017	60748	03412	09880	94091	90052	43596	21424	16584	67970
49	43560	05552	54344	69418	01327	07771	25364	77373	34841	75927
50	25206	15177	63049	12464	16149	18759	96184	15968	89446	07168

time, do not include it in the sample again (because you are choosing a sample without replacement); instead continue until $n = 9$ units are chosen.

Sampling by Shuffling the Population

Another way to choose a random sample from a population is easily implemented on a spreadsheet program such as Lotus® 1-2-3®. The idea here is to shuffle the population items into a completely random order and then select as many as you wish. This is just like shuffling a card deck and then dealing out as many cards as are needed.

In one column, list the numbers from 1 through N; there is usually a command (such as Data Fill) for doing this automatically. In the next column, use the random number function (such as @RAND) to place uniform random numbers from 0 to 1 alongside your first column. Next, convert these random number functions to solid numbers (using a command such as Range Value). Next, sort both columns in order according to the random number column. The result so far is that the population has been thoroughly shuffled into a random ordering. Finally, select the first n items from the shuffled population to determine your sample.

The resulting random sample has the same desirable properties attainable using the random number table.

EXAMPLE   ## Auditing

IBM reported sales of $34.276 billion and net earnings of $4.789 billion for 1986. The number of individual transactions must have been huge, and the reporting system must be carefully monitored in order for us to have faith in numbers like these. The auditors, the independent accounting firm Price Waterhouse, reported as follows:

> In our opinion, the accompanying consolidated financial statements . . . present fairly the financial position of International Business Machines Corporation . . . in conformity with generally accepted accounting principles consistently applied. Our examinations of these statements were made in accordance with generally accepted auditing standards and accordingly included such tests of the accounting records and such other auditing procedures as we considered necessary in the circumstances.[5]

An auditing problem like this one involves statistics because it requires analysis of large amounts of data about transactions. Although all large transactions are checked in detail, many auditors rely on statistical sampling as a way of spot-checking long lists of smaller transactions.[6]

Say a particular list of transactions (perhaps out of many such lists) has been generated and is numbered from 1 through 7,329. You have been asked to draw

---

[5]IBM, *1986 Annual Report*, p. 21.

[6]A review of the wide variety of techniques that can be used is provided by A. J. Wilburn, Marcel Dekker, *Practical Sampling for Auditors* (New York: 1984).

a random sample of 20 accounts starting from row 23, column 8 of the table of random digits. Arranging the random digits in groups of four and placing brackets around large numbers to be discarded, your initial list looks like this:

2387 0784 0241 [7592] 6232 [7742] 2762 [8957] 5874 2831 [8704] 7200 [9292] 6761 2017 4355 4877 [9933] 6020 1931 6691 3630 0803 [7459] 3939 0717 [8700] 0318 1584 6120...

Selecting the first $n = 20$ available numbers, you end up with a sample including the following transaction numbers:

2387, 784, 241, 6232, 2762, 5874, 2831, 7200, 6761, 2017, 4355, 4877, 6020, 1931, 6691, 3630, 803, 3939, 717, 318

Placing these numbers in order will make it easier to look up the actual transactions for verification. Your final ordered list of sample transactions is:

241, 318, 717, 784, 803, 1931, 2017, 2387, 2762, 2831, 3630, 3939, 4355, 4877, 5874, 6020, 6232, 6691, 6761, 7200

You would then look up these transactions in detail and verify their accuracy. The information learned by sampling from this list of transactions would be combined with other information learned by sampling from other lists and from complete examination of large, crucial transactions.

EXAMPLE   **A Pilot Study of Large Paper and Forest Products Firms**

You have a new product that is potentially very useful to paper and forest product companies. To formulate a marketing strategy in the early stages, you have decided to gather information about these firms. The problem is that the product is not yet entirely developed and you're not even sure how to gather the information! Therefore, you decide to run a **pilot study,** which is a small-scale version of a study designed to help you identify problems and fix them before the real study is run. For your pilot study, you have decided to use three of these firms, selected at random.

First you construct the frame, shown in Table 8.2.2.[7] Reading two digits at a time (since $N = 28$ has two digits), starting from row 39, column 3 in the table of random digits, and placing brackets around the large ones to be discarded, the initial list is:

[34], 13, [30], [32], [45], 24, [54], [64], [89], [34], [41], [73], 04, [78], [31], 26, [53], 10, 22, 03, ...

Selecting the first $n = 3$ available numbers, your sample will include firms with the following numbers:

13, 24, 4

---

[7]The list of firms is from "Investment Outlook Scoreboard," *Business Week*, December 28, 1987.

TABLE 8.2.2   The Frame

1	Avery International
2	Boise Cascade
3	Bowater
4	Champion International
5	Chesapeake
6	Consolidated Papers
7	Federal Paper Board
8	Fort Howard
9	Georgia-Pacific
10	Great Northern Nekoosa
11	International Paper
12	James River Corp. of Virginia
13	Jefferson Smurfit
14	Kimberly-Clark
15	Lawson Mardon Group
16	Longview Fibre
17	Louisiana-Pacific
18	Mead
19	Pentair
20	Potlatch
21	Scott Paper
22	Sonoco Products
23	Stone Container
24	Temple-Inland
25	Union Camp
26	Westvaco
27	Weyerhaeuser
28	Willamette Industries

Looking back at the frame to see which firms these are, and arranging them in alphabetical order, your sample of $n = 3$ firms for the pilot study will consist of Champion International, Jefferson Smurfit, and Temple-Inland.

8.3 The Sampling Distribution of a Statistic

Anything you measure based on a random sample of data will have a probability distribution called the **sampling distribution** of the statistic. Through understanding of this sampling distribution, you will be able to make the leap from information about a sample (what you already have) to information about the population (what you would like to know).

When you complete a survey of randomly selected consumers and find that, on average, they plan to spend $21.26 on groceries per trip, the number 21.26 may not look random to you. *But the result of your survey is random.* Let's be careful. The number 21.26 itself is not random. Instead, it's "the average spending on groceries per trip for these randomly selected consumers" that is the random variable. Looking at it this way, it is clear why it's random: Each time the random experiment is run, a new random sample of consumers would be interviewed, and the result would be different each time.

The way to *think* about a statistic can be very different from the way to *work* with one. To understand the concepts involved here, imagine repeating a study lots of times. This is necessary in order to see where randomness comes from; after all, if you just do the study once, the results will look like fixed numbers. But don't lose sight of the fact that, due to the constraints of real life, when you actually do a study, you (usually) just do it once. The idea of repeating it over and over is just a way of understanding the actual result by placing it in perspective along with all of the other possible results. With this in mind, examine the idea of a sampling distribution shown in Figure 8.3.1.

A Standard Error Is an *Estimated* Standard Deviation

Unfortunately, in real life you usually can't work directly with a sampling distribution because it is determined by properties of the entire population, and you have information only about a sample. Every (reasonable) distribu-

---

FIGURE 8.3.1　By *imagining* that the entire study is repeated many times, the *sampling distribution* of a statistic corresponds to the histogram of the statistic's values. In reality, of course, you just have one sample and one value of the statistic. This one value is interpreted with respect to all of the other outcomes that *might* have happened, as represented by the sampling distribution.

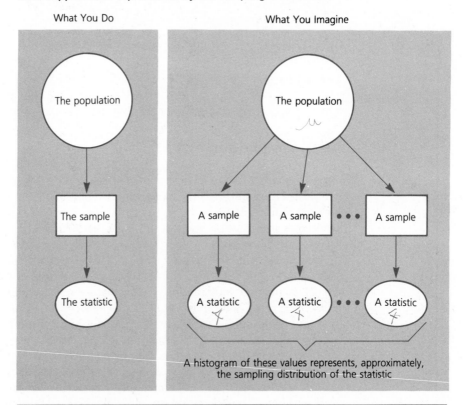

---

tion has a standard deviation, so the sampling distribution of any statistic has a standard deviation also. If you knew this standard deviation, you would know approximately how far the sample statistic is from its mean value (a population parameter). This would then help you know more about the population since, in addition to having a "best guess" (your statistic), you would have an indication of how good this guess is. Unfortunately, you don't know this standard deviation exactly because it depends on the population.

The solution is to use the sample information to guess, or estimate, the standard deviation of the sampling distribution of the statistic. The resulting approximation to the standard deviation of the statistic, based only on sample data, is called the **standard error of the statistic.** You interpret this standard error just as you would any standard deviation. The standard error indicates approximately how far the observed value of the statistic is from its mean. Literally, it indicates the standard *deviation* you would find if you took a very large number of samples, found the sample average for each one, and worked with these sample averages as a data set.

Why do we use two terms (standard deviation and standard error) since a standard error is just a kind of standard deviation? This is done primarily to emphasize that the *standard error* indicates the amount of uncertainty in a *summary number* (a statistic) representing the entire sample. By contrast, the term *standard deviation* is usually used to indicate the amount of variability among *individuals* (elementary units), specifically indicating how far individuals are typically from the average.

How Close Is the Sample Average to the Population Mean?

The sample average, $\overline{X}$, is a statistic since it is computed from the sample data. The **standard error of the average** (or just *standard error*, for short) estimates the sampling variability of the sample average, indicating approximately how far it is from the population mean. From the central limit theorem (Chapter 7), you know that the standard deviation of the sample average is $\sigma_{\overline{X}} = \sigma/\sqrt{n}$. In Chapter 7 we assumed that we knew population parameters such as σ because we were doing probability. Now that we are doing statistics again, σ is unknown, and so is the standard deviation of the sample average. But we have an estimate of the standard deviation: S, the standard deviation of the sample, from Chapter 5. If we replace σ with S, the result is an indication of the uncertainty in $\overline{X}$. Here are the standard deviation of $\overline{X}$ (which is exact) and the standard error of $\overline{X}$ (which is estimated and, therefore, only approximate).

■ **Standard Deviation of the Average**

$$\sigma_{\overline{X}} = \frac{\sigma}{\sqrt{n}}$$

■ Standard Error of the Average

$$S_{\bar{X}} = \frac{S}{\sqrt{n}}$$

This standard error indicates approximately how far the sample average, $\bar{X}$, is from the population mean, μ. Since $\bar{X}$ is often your best information about μ, this standard error tells you roughly how far off you are when you use the best available sample information (for example, average spending of 100 random consumers) in place of the *un*available population information (mean spending for the entire city). The standard error of the average is in the same measurement units (dollars, miles per gallon, people, or whatever) as the data values.

Note the difference between S and $S_{\bar{X}}$. The standard deviation, S, indicates approximately how far *individuals* are from the average, whereas the standard error, $S_{\bar{X}}$, indicates approximately how far the average, $\bar{X}$, is from the population mean, μ. This is illustrated in Figures 8.3.2 and 8.3.3. You would expect the sample average, $\bar{X}$, to be within two standard errors of the mean about 95% of the time. Following is a summary table to help you distinguish between variability of individuals and variability of averages, for both the population and a sample:

	For the Population	For a Sample
Variability of individuals	σ	S
Variability of $\bar{X}$, the average of n	$\sigma_{\bar{X}} = \sigma/\sqrt{n}$	$S_{\bar{X}} = S/\sqrt{n}$

Why should you ever look at more than one individual? Because individuals are more variable, more random, and less precise than the sample average. This is because the standard error is S divided by $\sqrt{n}$ and is thus smaller than S whenever n is 2 or more.

Why should you sample more rather than fewer individuals? Because the error $(\bar{X} - \mu)$ is typically smaller when information from more individuals is combined in a sample. The standard error indicates the approximate size of this error. Since the standard error gets smaller as n gets larger (all else equal), your information about the unknown μ improves as sample size grows because $\bar{X}$ will typically be closer to μ.

EXAMPLE

Shopping Trips

Suppose $n = 200$ randomly selected shoppers interviewed in a mall say that they plan to spend an average of $\bar{X} = \$19.42$ today with a standard deviation of $S = \$8.63$. This tells you that shoppers typically plan to spend about \$19.42, and that a typical *individual* shopper plans to spend about \$8.63 more or less

FIGURE 8.3.2   The sample average, $\overline{X}$, has less variability than individual X values. The standard error, $S_{\overline{X}}$, is smaller than the standard deviation, S, and would become even smaller (indicating greater precision of $\overline{X}$) for larger n than the sample of four used here.

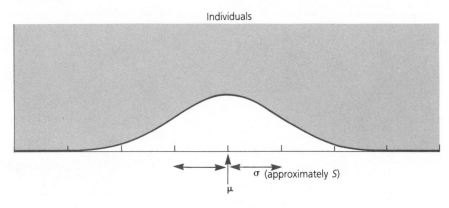

Individuals

σ (approximately S)

μ

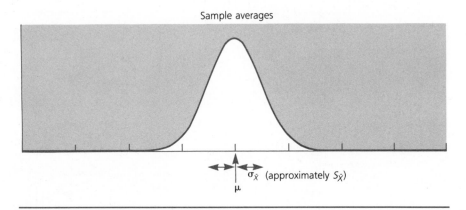

Sample averages

$\sigma_{\overline{X}}$ (approximately $S_{\overline{X}}$)

μ

than this amount. So far, this is no more and no less than a description of the individuals interviewed.

In fact, you can do more than just describe the sample data. You can say something about the unknown population mean, μ, which is the mean amount that *all* shoppers in the mall today plan to spend, including those you did not interview. The standard error is

$$S_{\overline{X}} = \frac{S}{\sqrt{n}}$$

$$= \frac{\$8.63}{\sqrt{200}}$$

$$= \frac{\$8.63}{14.14213562}$$

$$= \$0.610$$

FIGURE 8.3.3   The random experiments and histograms of the resulting data for individuals (left) and sample averages (right). Note how the standard error of the average is much smaller than the standard deviation (about 1/3 the size with sample size $n = 10$ used here). The standard deviation indicates the variability of *individuals* about their average, whereas the standard error indicates the variability of the sampling distribution of the sample average.

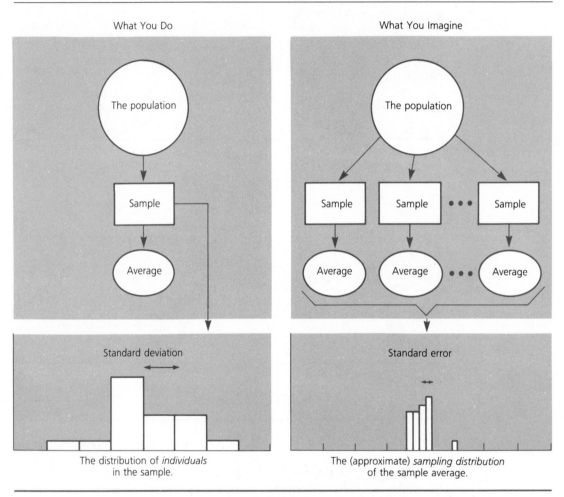

This tells you that when you use the sample average, $19.42, as an estimate of the unknown value μ for all shoppers, your error is only about $0.610. Note how much smaller the standard error ($0.610) is than the standard deviation ($8.63).

If you had interviewed only one person and (foolishly) tried to use the answer as an estimate of spending of all shoppers, your error would have been approximately $8.63. By going to the extra trouble of sampling $n = 200$ shoppers and combining this information by using the sample average, your error has been reduced—considerably—to approximately $0.610.

Correcting for Small Populations

When the population is small so that the sample is a major fraction of the population, the standard error formula should be reduced by applying the **finite-population correction factor** $\sqrt{(N - n)/N}$ to obtain the **adjusted standard error.**

When you sample nearly all of the population, your information about the population is very good. In fact, when you sample all of the population (so that $n = N$), your information is perfect and the standard error should be 0. The following formula is used to adjust the standard error to make it more accurate:[8]

■ **Adjusted Standard Error**

$$\text{(Finite-population correction factor)} \times \text{(Standard error)} = \sqrt{\frac{N - n}{N}} \times S_{\bar{x}}$$

$$= \sqrt{\frac{N - n}{N}} \times \frac{S}{\sqrt{n}}$$

When the sample size is close to the population size, the term $N - n$ is small and the adjusted standard error is also small, reflecting the high quality of this nearly complete sample. When the population size, N, is large, the finite-population correction factor is nearly 1 and thus will not change the standard error very much.[9]

You may be wondering why the population size, N, doesn't seem to matter for a large population, since the standard error depends only on the sample information, n and S. This is reasonable because the standard error reflects the randomness *in the sampling process* rather than any particular characteristic of the population. With a small sample from a large population, the sample values cannot "interfere" with each other very much due to nonreplacement, and sample properties (such as the variability in the average) will look pretty much the same even if you double the population size (holding its characteristics the same). On the other hand, with a small population, nonreplacement affects the sample more strongly by limiting the selection, an effect that changes with the population size. Figure 8.3.4 shows a situation in which it is reasonable that the sample values do not depend on the (large) population size.

---

[8]The theoretical justification for this formula may be found, for example, in W. G. Cochran, *Sampling Techniques,* 3rd ed. (New York: Wiley, 1977), Equation 2.20, p. 26; or in L. Kish, *Survey Sampling* (New York: Wiley, 1967), Equation 2.2.2, p. 41.

[9]When N is large and n is a small fraction of it, the finite-population correction factor reduces the standard error by approximately half of this fraction, that is, by $n/(2N)$. If, say, you are sampling 8% of a large population, then the correction will reduce the standard error by about 4%. (The exact correction in this case is 4.08%, quite close to the 4% approximation.)

FIGURE 8.3.4   When a small amount is sampled from a large population, the size of the population does not affect the standard error. The two urns are the same except for size. If a few balls are drawn at random from each one, the distributions of the number of black balls in the samples should be similar. Each sample is providing information about the percentage of black ones.

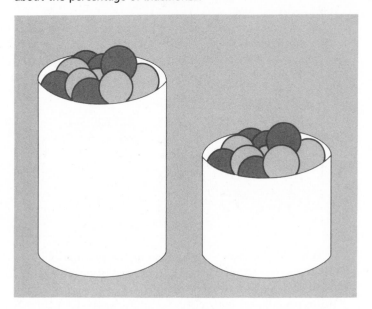

You may not always want to apply the finite-population correction factor, even in cases where you seem to be entitled to use it. Sometimes the population frame you sample from is not the population you are really interested in. If you are willing to assume that your frame represents a random sample from a much larger population, and you want to learn about this much larger population, then it is better not to use the correction factor. An **idealized population** might be defined as the much larger, sometimes imaginary, population that your actual population represents. When you are interested in the idealized population, you do not use the finite-population correction factor. On the other hand, if you just want to learn about the population frame and not go beyond it, then the correction factor will work to your advantage by expressing the lowering variability of this system.

For example, suppose from a list of 300 recent customers you have selected a random list of 50 to be interviewed about customer satisfaction. If you are only interested in the 300 recent customers on your list, you may feel free to reduce your initial standard error downward by 8.71%. However, if you wish to learn about *customers in general*, a potentially very large group that is represented by your convenient list of 300, you would not perform the adjustment. If you did (wrongly) adjust in this case, you would be deceiving yourself into thinking that the results are more precise than they really are.

When in doubt, the conservative, safe choice is *not* to use the finite-population correction factor.

<table>
<tr><td>EXAMPLE</td></tr>
</table>

Quality of the Day's Production

Of the 48 truckloads that left your factory today loaded with newly manufactured goods, you had 10 selected at random for detailed quality inspection. During inspection, a number from 1 to 20 is assigned to the shipment, with 20 being "perfect" and 1 being "@X%#!!!." As it turned out, the measurements were 19, 20, 20, 17, 20, 20, 15, 18, 20, and 15. The average for the day's sample is 18.4, and the standard deviation is 2.065591 for individual shipments. The (uncorrected) standard error is 0.653.

If you are interested in how close the day's sample average of 18.4 is to the *day's average* of all 48 shipments (which is unknown, since you only measured 10 truckloads), you may use the finite-population correction factor. In fact, you probably should use this factor because you have sampled a large portion (10/48 = 20.8%) of the population. The adjusted standard error is then:

$$\text{Adjusted standard error} = \sqrt{\frac{N-n}{N}} \times S_{\bar{x}}$$

$$= \sqrt{\frac{48-10}{48}} \times \frac{2.065591}{\sqrt{10}}$$

$$= 0.889757 \times 0.653197$$

$$= 0.581$$

The adjustment process has reduced the original standard error by about 11.0% (= 1 − 0.889757), from 0.653 to 0.581.

If, on the other hand, you are interested in how close the day's sample average of 18.4 is to the *quality in general* of your factory, you would not use the correction factor but would use the larger (uncorrected) standard error of 0.653. In essence, you would try to generalize to a very large *idealized population* of all of the truckloads that *might* have been produced today under the current conditions in your factory.

The Standard Error of a Binomial Proportion

The usual way to find a standard error is to take the standard deviation (which indicates the population variability) and substitute sample estimates (which you know) for population parameters (which you don't know). Consider an estimated percentage or proportion f for a binomial situation. The formula for the standard deviation σ_f involves the population proportion, p, which can be estimated by f itself (the sample proportion). Similarly, the formula for the standard deviation σ_X for a binomial count also involves substituting f for p. Here are the formulas for population standard deviations and the standard errors (estimated from sample data) for a binomial situation:[10]

	Standard Deviation (for the population)	Standard Error (estimated from a sample)
For f, a binomial proportion	$\sigma_f = \sqrt{\dfrac{p(1-p)}{n}}$	$S_f = \sqrt{\dfrac{f(1-f)}{n}}$
For X, a binomial count	$\sigma_X = \sqrt{np(1-p)}$	$S_X = \sqrt{nf(1-f)}$

The standard error S_f indicates the uncertainty or variability in the observed proportion, f, and is easily computed from information in the sample. Similarly, the standard error S_X indicates the uncertainty in the observed count, X. For example, if 8 machines out of 50 were defective, f would be 0.16 or 16%, and X would be 8.

EXAMPLE

A Consumer Survey

You have surveyed 937 people and found that 302, or 32.2%, of these would consider purchasing your product. You are wondering just how reliable these numbers are. In particular, how far are they from their values for the entire, much larger population? The standard error would provide a good answer.

You may assume that this is a binomial situation because you have selected people independently and randomly from the population. At this point, you know that $n = 937$, $X = 302$, and $f = 0.322$, or 32.2%. However, you don't know p, which is the percentage for the entire population (which you would like to know but can't). The standard error (the estimated standard deviation) may be used here because you do have an *estimate* of p, namely, the observed value of 0.322.

	Number of People, X	Proportion or Percentage $f = X/n$
Standard error (binomial distribution)	$S_X = \sqrt{nf(1-f)}$	$S_f = \sqrt{\dfrac{f(1-f)}{n}}$
	$= \sqrt{937 \times 0.322(1-0.322)}$	$= \sqrt{\dfrac{0.322(1-0.322)}{937}}$
	$= 14.3$ people	$= 0.0153$ or 1.53%

[10]Note that these formulas take you directly to the standard errors for a binomial situation. There is no need to first compute a standard deviation, S, and then divide by the square root of n, as you would do for a list of numbers (a nonbinomial situation).

The observed number, 302 people, is about 14.3 people away from (above or below) the unknown value you would expect, on the average, for this kind of study for this population. The observed proportion of people, 32.2%, is approximately 1.53 percentage points different from the unknown, true percentage in the entire population.

■ 8.4 Other Sampling Methods

The random sample is not the only way to select a sample from a population. There are many other methods, each with advantages and disadvantages. Some, such as the *stratified random sample*, use the principles of random sampling carefully. Others, such as *systematic sampling*, use very different methods and provide a fragile foundation, if any, for your statistical analysis.

One important consideration is to weigh the amount of hostile scrutiny the results will be subject to against the cost of obtaining the data. For an internal study in a friendly working environment, without much in the way of office politics (if there is such a place!), you may not need the rigor and care of a random sample. However, for an external study to be used by neutral or hostile parties, such as in a lawsuit, where people on the other side are likely to question your wisdom, it will be worth your while to pay attention to detail and use careful, randomized sampling methods.

The Stratified Random Sample

Sometimes a population contains clear, known, easily identified groups. If you choose a random sample from such a population as a whole, each segment or *stratum* may be under- or overrepresented in the sample as compared to the population.[11] This may contribute some extra randomness to the results since you would not be using the known information about these groups.

A **stratified random sample** is obtained by choosing a random sample separately from each of the strata (segments or groups) of the population. If the population is similar (homogeneous) within each stratum but differs markedly from one segment to another, stratification can increase the precision of your statistical analysis. Stratification can also make administration easier since you may be able to delegate the selection process to your field offices.

You are free to choose any sample size for each individual stratum. There is no requirement that you sample the same number from each stratum or that you allocate your sample size according to population percentages.

---

[11]*Stratum* is the singular and *strata* the plural for referring to segments or layers within a population. Perhaps you have seen stratified rock, with its pronounced layers.

This allows you to determine sample sizes according to costs and benefits. Some strata may be more costly to sample than others, and you will therefore tend to use smaller sample sizes for them. Some strata will be known to have more variability than others, and for these you will therefore tend to use larger samples.

Table 8.4.1 shows the details and notation for the population sizes, sample sizes, sample averages, and sample standard deviations for each stratum.

It remains to show how to combine the estimates from each stratum into an estimate for the entire population and how to obtain the standard error of the resulting estimate. Each stratum provides a random sample and a sample average. To find the stratified sampling estimate of the population mean, combine the sample averages using a weighted average based on the population size of each stratum. In this way, the larger segments of the population exert their rightful influence on the results. First multiply each sample average by the corresponding population size, then sum these and divide by the total population size.

■ Computing the Average for a Stratified Sample

$$\overline{X} = \frac{N_1\overline{X}_1 + N_2\overline{X}_2 + \cdots + N_L\overline{X}_L}{N_1 + N_2 + \cdots + N_L}$$

$$= \frac{\sum_{i=1}^{L} N_i\overline{X}_i}{N}$$

where N is the total population size $N_1 + N_2 + \cdots + N_L$.

How much variability is there in the resulting combined estimate? The answer, as always, is given by its standard error. This is found by combining the standard deviations from the individual strata in the following way. For each stratum, multiply the square of the population size by the square of the standard deviation and divide by the sample size. Add these up, take the square root, and divide by the total population size.

TABLE 8.4.1 Notation for Stratified Sampling

Stratum	Population Size	Sample Size	Sample Average	Sample Standard Deviation
1	N_1	n_1	$\overline{X}_1$	S_1
2	N_2	n_2	$\overline{X}_2$	S_2
.	.	.	.	.
.	.	.	.	.
.	.	.	.	.
L	N_L	n_L	$\overline{X}_L$	S_L

■ **Standard Error for a Stratified Sample**

$$S_{\bar{X}} = \frac{1}{N} \sqrt{\frac{N_1^2 S_1^2}{n_1} + \frac{N_2^2 S_2^2}{n_2} + \cdots + \frac{N_L^2 S_L^2}{n_L}}$$

$$= \frac{1}{N} \sqrt{\sum_{i=1}^{L} \frac{N_i^2 S_i^2}{n_i}}$$

If the population sizes for some strata are small, so that more than just a small fraction is sampled, then the finite-population correction factor may be applied, resulting in a more accurate standard error. For each stratum, multiply the population size by the square of the standard deviation and by the difference between the population and sample sizes, and then divide by the sample size. Add these up, take the square root, and divide by the total population size.

■ **Adjusted Standard Error for a Stratified Sample**

$$\begin{array}{c}\text{Adjusted} \\ \text{standard} \\ \text{error}\end{array} = \frac{1}{N} \sqrt{\frac{N_1(N_1 - n_1)S_1^2}{n_1} + \frac{N_2(N_2 - n_2)S_2^2}{n_2} + \cdots + \frac{N_L(N_L - n_L)S_L^2}{n_L}}$$

$$= \frac{1}{N} \sqrt{\sum_{i=1}^{L} \frac{N_i(N_i - n_i)S_i^2}{n_i}}$$

EXAMPLE

Adjusting for Sophistication of the Consumer

In order to develop a marketing strategy for your high-tech video and audio products, you need good information about potential customers. These people can be divided in a natural way into two groups according to whether they are sophisticated or naive about how the technology works. The sophisticated group wants to know detailed facts or "specs" on the products; the naive group needs information at a much more basic level.

To find out the dollar amount a typical potential consumer plans to spend on products like yours this year, you decide to use a stratified random sampling plan. This is reasonable because you expect sophisticated users to plan larger expenditures. By stratifying, you may be able to reduce the overall variability (of low and high expenditures) in the situation.

Your sampling frame, a list of names and addresses from a marketing firm, has 14,000 potential consumers. These have already been classified; there are 2,532 sophisticated and 11,468 naive consumers. You decide to select 200 sophisticated and 100 naive users for detailed interviews, concentrating on the sophisticated segment because of their larger expected purchases. The results came out as follows:

Stratum	Population Size	Sample Size	Sample Average	Sample Standard Deviation
Naive	$N_1 = 11,468$	$n_1 = 100$	$\bar{X}_1 = \$287$	$S_1 = \$83$
Sophisticated	$N_2 = 2,532$	$n_2 = 200$	$\bar{X}_2 = \$1,253$	$S_2 = \$454$

These estimates for the two strata are quite interesting in their own right. The results certainly confirm your suspicion that sophisticated users plan to spend more!

To come up with a single average value per potential consumer for the entire population, find the weighted average:

$$\bar{X} = \frac{N_1\bar{X}_1 + N_2\bar{X}_2}{N_1 + N_2}$$

$$= \frac{11,468 \times 287 + 2,532 \times 1,253}{11,468 + 2,532}$$

$$= \frac{6,463,912}{14,000}$$

$$= \$462$$

The resulting average, $462, is much closer to the naive expenditure of $287 than to the sophisticated expenditure of $1,253. This is because the naive segment is a much larger part of the population. Even though you sampled twice as much from the sophisticated segment, this simply increases your knowledge about them and (properly) does not increase the influence of this segment of the population.

How much uncertainty is involved in this estimate of $462 per person? The standard error is found to be

$$S_{\bar{X}} = \frac{1}{N}\sqrt{\frac{N_1^2 S_1^2}{n_1} + \frac{N_2^2 S_2^2}{n_2}}$$

$$= \frac{1}{14,000}\sqrt{\frac{11,468^2 \times 83^2}{100} + \frac{2,532^2 \times 454^2}{200}}$$

$$= \frac{1}{14,000}\sqrt{9,060,060,003 + 6,607,073,115}$$

$$= \$8.94$$

How can you be so precise as to know the population mean expenditure to within approximately $8.94 when the individual variation from one person to another is around $83 or $454 depending on the group? The answer is that you are estimating a *mean* and not the behavior of the individuals. In fact, looking just at the naive segment, which is most of your market here, the standard error is $83/10, or just above $8.

What have you gained by stratifying instead of sampling 300 at random from the entire population? You have controlled for much of the variation. Instead of having the large numbers (for sophisticated users) and the small numbers (for naive ones) lumped together in a single, highly variable sample, you have separated out this variation according to its known sources. As a result, your answers are much more precise. A careful calculation (details not presented here) suggests that without stratification, your standard error could have been three times larger than the $8.94 found in this case. And don't forget that a threefold reduction in standard error is ordinarily achievable only with a ninefold increase in the sample size (since $9 = 3^2$). By stratifying and sampling 300, you have achieved results comparable to a simple random sample of about 900. Stratification can be an important cost saver!

In other applications, stratification may help you more or less than in this example. Stratification will help you more when individuals are similar within each stratum but the strata are different from one another. That is to say, the strata do divide up the population into helpful, meaningful pieces.

If you recompute the standard error more carefully using the finite-population correction factor, you find that the standard error is reduced from $8.94 to $8.77. However, we will assume you decide to stick with the uncorrected, larger $8.94 to be conservative (so that you are not exaggerating the precision of your results) and because you are interested in possibly generalizing beyond the frame of 14,000 consumers to a much larger idealized population that your frame represents.

| EXAMPLE | ### The Price of a Typical Suit in a Department Store |

Consider a store with two departments: general sales (which sells budget suits) and top fashion (selling high-ticket, expensive clothing). The general sales department has a higher volume but a lower price per suit. The top fashion department has fewer customers but a higher price per suit. To summarize sales patterns in the store as a whole, management would like a single number that represents the price paid for a typical suit of clothes.

Figure 8.4.1 shows the basic situation: 90% of suits are bought in general sales (where suits cost $60), and 10% are from top fashion (where suits cost $450). At the top of the figure is shown a representative sample of 10 customers and the average price of $99.00 (which represents nine suits at $60 and one suit at $450).

At the bottom of Figure 8.4.1 are the results of an unrepresentative sample of one customer from each department. Taking a simple average of the

FIGURE 8.4.1   Careful stratified sampling methods can correct for the problems of unrepresentative sampling. The simple average for the unrepresentative sample, $255, is wrong. However, a weighted average for this same sample will give the correct answer, $99.

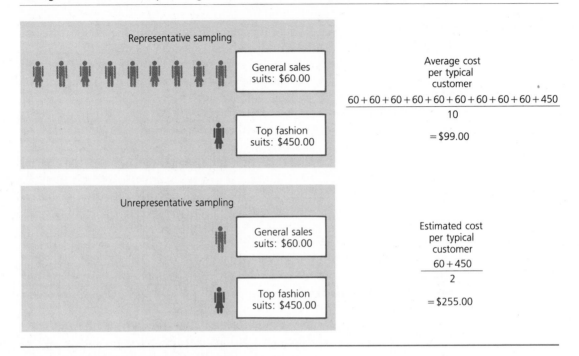

two suits, one at $60 and the other at $450, results in $255, which is clearly wrong. The problem is that the one customer in general sales actually represents much more of the population than does the one customer in top fashion.

Stratified sampling corrects this problem with the weighted average formula. Giving 90% of the weight to the general sales customer and the remaining 10% to the top fashion customer, the weighted average does indeed give the correct answer:[12]

$$\text{Weighted Average} = 0.90 \times \$60 + 0.10 \times \$450 = \$99$$

This shows why the average computed through the use of stratified sampling methods is correct. The weights in the weighted average reflect the importance in the population of each stratum in the sample.

---

[12]The weighted average was covered in Chapter 4.

The Systematic Sample

A **systematic sample** is obtained by selecting a single, random starting place in the frame and then taking units separated by a fixed interval. It is easy and convenient to select a sample by taking, say, every fifth unit from the frame, as illustrated in Figure 8.4.2. It is even possible to introduce some randomness to this sampling method by selecting the starting place at random. But this systematic sampling method has some serious problems because it is impossible to assess its precision.

FIGURE 8.4.2   A systematic sample is made through regular selection from the population. In this case, every fifth population unit is selected, beginning with number 3 of the frame.

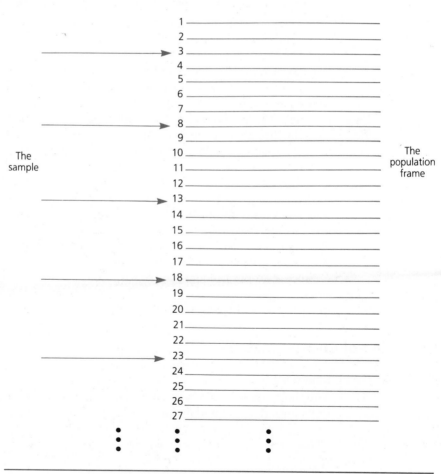

If you wish to select a systematic sample of n from a population of N, your interval between selected items will be N/n.[13] If you select the starting place as a random digit between 1 and N/n, the sample average will be a reasonable estimate of the population mean in the sense that it will be *unbiased*, that is, it will not be regularly too high or too low. This is the good news.

The bad news is that you cannot know *how good* your estimate is. When you ask, "What's the standard error?" the answer is, "Who knows? The sample is not sufficiently random." In the words of W. Edwards Deming (who is famous for, among other things, bringing quality to Japanese products):

> One method of sampling, used much in previous years, by me as well as by others, was to take a random start and every kth sampling unit thereafter (a patterned or systematic sample).... As there is no replication, there is no valid way to compute an unbiased estimate of the variance of an estimate made by this procedure.... The replicated method [random sampling] is so simple to apply that there is no point in taking a chance with an estimate that raises questions.[14]

One way in which systematic sampling can fail is when the list is ordered in an important, meaningful way. In this case, your random start determines how large your estimate will be so that a low starting number, for example, guarantees a low estimate.

A more serious failure of systematic sampling occurs if there is a repetitive pattern in the frame that matches your sampling interval. For example, if every 50th car that is produced gets special care and attention along the assembly line, and if you just happen to select every such 50th car to be in your systematic sample, your results will be completely useless in terms of representing the quality of *typical* cars.

So the reviews of systematic sampling are mixed. You might feel justified in using a systematic sample if (1) you are reasonably sure that there is no important ordering in the frame, (2) there are no important repetitive patterns in the frame, (3) you don't need to assess the quality of your estimate, and (4) you are sure that nobody will challenge your wisdom in selecting a systematic instead of a random sample.

Since a proper random sample will usually not cost very much more than a systematic sample, you may wonder why systematic samples are still used in some areas of business. So do I.

■ 8.5 End-of-Chapter Materials

Summary

Sampling is used to learn about a system that is too large and costly to study in its entirety. The **population** is the collection of units (people, objects, or

---

[13]If N/n is not a whole number, there are some small technical difficulties that require attention. See Chapter 4 of Kish, *Survey Sampling*, for a detailed discussion of this and other aspects of systematic sampling.

[14]W. Edwards Deming, *Sample Design in Business Research* (New York: Wiley, 1960), p. 98.

whatever) that you are interested in knowing about. A **sample** is a smaller collection of units selected from the population. A sample is **representative** if each characteristic (and combination of characteristics) arises the same percent of the time in the sample as in the population. A sample that is not representative in an important way is said to show **bias**. The **frame** tells you how to gain access to the population units by number from 1 to the population size, *N*. A sample is said to be chosen **without replacement** if units cannot be selected more than once to be in the sample. A sample is said to be chosen **with replacement** if a population unit can appear more than once in the sample. A sample that includes the entire population (*n* = *N*) is called a **census**.

A **statistic**, or **sample statistic,** is defined as any number computed from your sample data. A **parameter**, or **population parameter,** is defined as any number computed for the entire population. An **estimator** is a sample statistic used as a guess for the value of a population parameter. The actual number computed from the data is called an **estimate**. The **error of estimation** is defined as the estimator (or estimate) minus the population parameter and is usually unknown. An estimator is **unbiased** if it is correct on the average, that is, neither systematically too high nor too low, as compared to the corresponding population parameter. A **random sample** or **simple random sample** is selected such that (1) each population unit has an *equal probability of being chosen,* and (2) units are *chosen independently,* without regard to one another. A **table of random digits** is a list in which the digits 0 through 9 each occur with probability 1/10 independently of each other. Using such a table to select successive distinct population units is one way to select a random sample without replacement.

A **pilot study** is a small-scale version of a study, designed to help you identify problems and fix them before the real study is run.

Anything you measure, based on a random sample of data, will have a probability distribution called the **sampling distribution** of that statistic. The **standard error** of a statistic, an estimate of the standard deviation of its sampling distribution, indicates approximately how far from its mean value (a population parameter) the statistic is. The **standard error of the average** (or just *standard error,* for short) indicates approximately how far the (random, observed) sample average $\overline{X}$ is from the (fixed, unknown) population mean μ:

$$\text{Standard error} = S_{\overline{X}} = S/\sqrt{n}$$

The standard error gets smaller as the sample size *n* grows (all else equal), reflecting the greater information and precision achieved with a larger sample.

When the population is small, so that the sample is an important fraction of the population, the standard error formula should be reduced by applying the **finite-population correction factor** to obtain the **adjusted standard error** as follows:

(Finite-population correction factor) $\times$ (Standard error) $= \sqrt{\dfrac{N - n}{N}} \times S_{\overline{X}}$

$$= \sqrt{\dfrac{N - n}{N}} \times \dfrac{S}{\sqrt{n}}$$

An **idealized population** can be defined as the much larger, sometimes imaginary, population that your actual population represents. When you are interested in the idealized population, you do *not* use the finite-population correction factor. On the other hand, if you just want to learn about the population frame and not go beyond it, then the correction factor will work to your advantage by expressing the lower variability of this system. When in doubt, the safe choice is *not* to use the finite-population correction factor.

For a binomial distribution, the (population) standard deviations and the (sample) standard errors for both X (the number) and $f = X/n$ (the proportion) are as follows:

	Standard Deviation (for the population)	Standard Error (estimated from a sample)
f	$\sigma_f = \sqrt{\dfrac{p(1 - p)}{n}}$	$S_f = \sqrt{\dfrac{f(1 - f)}{n}}$
X	$\sigma_X = \sqrt{np(1 - p)}$	$S_X = \sqrt{nf(1 - f)}$

The standard error S_f indicates the uncertainty or variability in the observed proportion, f, and the standard error S_X indicates the uncertainty in the observed count, X.

A **stratified random sample** is obtained by choosing a random sample separately from each of the strata (segments or groups) of the population. If the population is similar within each stratum but differs markedly from one to another, stratification can increase the precision of your statistical analysis. For a population with L strata and N_i units in the ith stratum, denote the sample size by n_i, the sample average by $\overline{X}_i$, and the standard deviation by S_i. To combine these averages into a single number that reflects the entire population, take a weighted average. Here are formulas for this weighted average and its standard error:

$$\overline{X} = \frac{N_1 \overline{X}_1 + N_2 \overline{X}_2 + \cdots + N_L \overline{X}_L}{N_1 + N_2 + \cdots + N_L} = \frac{\displaystyle\sum_{i=1}^{L} N_i \overline{X}_i}{N}$$

$$S_{\overline{X}} = \frac{1}{N} \sqrt{\frac{N_1^2 S_1^2}{n_1} + \frac{N_2^2 S_2^2}{n_2} + \cdots + \frac{N_L^2 S_L^2}{n_L}} = \frac{1}{N} \sqrt{\sum_{i=1}^{L} \frac{N_i^2 S_i^2}{n_i}}$$

$$\text{Adjusted standard error} = \frac{1}{N} \sqrt{\frac{N_1(N_1 - n_1)S_1^2}{n_1} + \frac{N_2(N_2 - n_2)S_2^2}{n_2} + \cdots + \frac{N_L(N_L - n_L)S_L^2}{n_L}}$$

$$= \frac{1}{N} \sqrt{\sum_{i=1}^{L} \frac{N_i(N_i - n_i)S_i^2}{n_i}}$$

Use the adjusted standard error as a finite-population correction when you have sampled more than just a small fraction of any of the strata.

A **systematic sample** is obtained by selecting a single random starting place in the frame and then taking units separated by a regular interval. Although the sample average from a systematic sample is an unbiased estimator of the population mean (i.e., not regularly too high or too low), there are some serious problems with this technique. You cannot know how good the estimate is, since there is no reliable standard error for it. Problems can be particularly serious when population items are ordered in a meaningful way in the frame or when there is a repetitive pattern among population units in the frame. Since a proper random sample does not usually cost very much more than a systematic sample, you may wish to avoid using systematic samples.

Key Words

population 260	unbiased estimator 263
sample 260	random sample or simple random
representative 261	sample 264
bias 261	table of random digits 264
frame 262	pilot study 268
sampling without replacement 262	sampling distribution 269
sampling with replacement 262	standard error of a statistic 271
census 263	standard error of the average 271
sample statistic 263	finite-population correction factor 275
population parameter 263	adjusted standard error 275
estimator 263	idealized population 276
estimate 263	stratified random sample 279
error of estimation 263	systematic sample 285

Questions

1 a. What is a population?
  b. What is a sample? Why is sampling useful?
  c. What is a census? Would you always want to do a census if you had the resources?
2 a. What is a representative sample?
  b. What is a biased sample?
  c. How can a representative sample be chosen?
3 What is a frame? What is its role in sampling?
4 a. What is a random sample?
  b. Why is a random sample approximately representative?
  c. What is the difference between a random sample selected *with* and one selected *without* replacement?
  d. What is a table of random digits? How is it used in sample selection?
  e. What other method can be used to select a random sample using a spreadsheet program?
5 a. What is a pilot study?
  b. What can go wrong if you don't do a pilot study?
6 a. What is a statistic?
  b. What is a parameter?

7 a. What is an estimator?

b. What is an estimate?

c. A sample standard deviation is found to be 13.8. Is this number an estimator or an estimate of the population standard deviation?

d. What is the error of estimation? When you estimate an unknown number, do you know the size of this error or not?

8 a. What is the sampling distribution of a statistic?

b. What is the standard deviation of a statistic?

c. What is the standard error of a statistic?

d. What typically happens to the standard error as the sample size, n, increases?

9 a. What is the finite-population correction factor?

b. What is the adjusted standard error?

c. What is an idealized population?

d. In what way are your results more limited if you use the finite-population correction factor than if you don't?

10 a. What is a stratified random sample?

b. What are the benefits of stratification?

c. When is stratification most likely to be helpful?

11 a. What is a systematic sample?

b. What are the main problems with systematic samples?

c. Why is there no reliable standard error available for use with a sample average computed from a systematic sample?

Problems

1 Your automatic transmission factory has had some problems with quality. You have decided to gather information from tomorrow's production for careful evaluation. For each of the following sampling methods, say if the procedure is good, acceptable, or unreasonable. Give a reason for your choice.

a. The first 5 transmissions produced.

b. The 18 transmissions that are sitting outside the plant because they never worked.

c. Every 20th transmission produced.

d. A random sampling taken at the end of the day using the day's production as a frame.

e. All obviously defective transmissions together with a random sampling of the apparently normal ones.

2 You have chosen a sample of 25 supermarkets out of the 684 you have responsibility for. These 25 have been inspected, and the number of violations of company policy has been recorded. For each of the following quantities, state whether it is a statistic or a parameter.

a. The average number of violations among the 25 supermarkets you inspected.

b. The mean number of violations you would have recorded had you inspected all 684 supermarkets you are responsible for.

c. The variability from one supermarket to another in the population.

d. The variability from one supermarket to another, as measured by the standard deviation you computed.

e. The standard deviation of your sample average.

f. The standard error of your sample average.

3 Consider the net income as a percent of sales for industrial and farm equipment companies, as shown in Table 8.5.1.

TABLE 8.5.1   Net Income for Industrial and Farm Equipment Firms*

Firm	Net Income as a Percent of Sales
Caterpillar	1%
Dresser Industries	0
American Standard	6
Teledyne	7
Ingersoll-Rand	3
Cummins Engine	0
Black & Decker	0
Brunswick	6
TRINOVA	8
Dover	6
Foster Wheeler	2
Crane	3
Timken	0
Outboard Marine	1
Federal-Mogul	0
Fuqua Industries	5
Harnischfeger Industries	0
Tecumseh Products	6
Briggs & Stratton	5
York International	1
Eagle-Picher Industries	6
Cameron Iron Works	1
Roper	2
Coleman	3
Allied Products	4

*As listed in the Fortune 500, *Fortune,* April 27, 1987, pp. 398–99. Firms for which net income data were unavailable are omitted.

a. Construct a sampling frame, viewing this list as a population of large industrial and farm equipment firms.
b. Draw a random sample of 10 firms, starting from row 13, column 2 of the table of random digits.
c. Compute the sample average.
d. Compute the standard error of the average, both with and without use of the finite-population correction factor.
e. Write a paragraph explaining and interpreting the standard error.
f. Compute the population mean. (*Note:* In real life you usually can't do this!)
g. Write a brief paragraph explaining the relationship among the sample average, population mean, and standard error.

4 Consider the 10-year growth rate in earnings per share for the five largest furniture firms:

Firm	Growth in Earnings per Share*
Mohasco	2%
Leggett & Platt	17
Miller (Herman)	16
Hon Industries	15
Bassett Furniture Industries	3

*As included in the Fortune 500, *Fortune,* April 27, 1987, p. 398.

View this list as a (very small!) population with just $N = 5$ units. Consider drawing samples of size $n = 2$.

a. Make a list of all possible samples of size 2 that might be chosen. (*Hint:* There are 10 such samples.) For each sample, find the average.

b. Construct a histogram of the 10 sample averages from part a. This is the sampling distribution of the sample average.

c. Select a random sample of size 2 from the population by starting with the number in row 26, column 4 of the table of random digits. Find the sample average.

d. Indicate where the average (from part c) falls with respect to the sampling distribution (from part b).

e. Write a paragraph explaining how "drawing a random sample from the population and finding the average" gives essentially the same result as "drawing a number from the sampling distribution of the average."

5 Economists often make forecasts of future conditions. Consider three-month U.S. treasury bill rates for July 1, 1988, as predicted in December 1987 as part of a survey of economists, as shown in Table 8.5.2.

TABLE 8.5.2   Economic Forecasts*

Economist	Forecast of Rates on 7/1/88, as made in December 1987
Paul Boltz	6.40%
Philip Braverman	5.25
Kathleen Cooper	6.50
Robert Dederick	5.50
Lyle Gramley	5.80
Maury Harris	6.25
Richard Hoey	5.80
Stuart G. Hoffman	5.30
Lacy Hunt	6.60
Edward Hyman	5.50
Saul Hymans	5.70
David Jones	6.20
Samuel Kahan	6.50
Irwin Kellner	5.50
Thomas Lawler	6.20
Carol Leisenring	6.20
Alan Lerner	5.00
Mickey Levy	5.60
Donald Maude	5.60
William Melton	5.00
Lynn Michaelis	6.30
Harold Nathan	5.70
James Pate	6.20
Donald Ratajczak	5.86
David Resler	5.00
Alan Reynolds	5.90
Norman Robertson	6.25
Francis Schott	6.50
A. Gary Shilling	4.00
Allen Sinai	5.50
James Smith	4.90
Neal Soss	5.00
Donald Straszheim	5.75
David Wyss	5.00
Edward Yardeni	5.50

The Wall Street Journal, July 5, 1988, p. 2.

a. Find the average and the standard deviation. Briefly interpret these values.

b. Find the standard error of the average. Interpret this number carefully, by viewing this list as a random sample from a much larger list of economists that might have been selected.

c. Six months after these predictions were made, the actual closing rate for three-month treasury bills was recorded as 6.54%. Compare the average forecast to this actual outcome.

d. How many standard errors away from the sample average is the actual outcome (6.54%)? Would you ordinarily be surprised by such an extreme difference?

e. Explain why the forecast error (average forecast minus actual outcome) need not be approximately equal in size to the standard error. Do this by identifying the population mean and showing that the actual outcome is *not* the same object.

6 A random sample of 50 recent patient records at a clinic shows that the average billing per visit was $53.01 and the standard deviation was $16.48.

a. Find the standard error of the average and interpret it.

b. You feel that this standard error is too large for reasonable budgeting purposes. If the standard deviation were the same (which it would be, approximately), find the standard error you would expect to see for a sample of size 200.

7 Find the average and the standard error for the amounts that your regular customers spent on your products last month, viewing the data from problem 2 of Chapter 4 as a sample of customer orders.

8 Find the average and the standard error for the strength of cotton yarn used in a weaving factory, based on the data in problem 10 of Chapter 4.

9 Find the average and the standard error for the weight of candy bars before intervention, based on the data in problem 10 of Chapter 5.

10 From a list of the 729 people who went on a cruise, 25 were randomly selected for interview. Of these, 21 said that they were "very happy" with the accommodations.

a. What percent of the sample said that they were "very happy"?

b. If you had been able to interview all 729 people, approximately how different a percentage would you expect to find as compared to your answer to part a? To answer this, please indicate which statistical quantity you are using, and compute its value.

11 The accounts of a firm have been classified into 56 large accounts, 956 medium-sized accounts, and 16,246 small accounts. Each account has a *book value* (which is provided to you) representing the amount of money that is *supposed* to be in the account. Each account also has an *audit value* (which requires time and effort to track down) representing the amount of money that is *really* in the account. You are working with the auditors in preparing financial statements. The group has decided to examine all 56 large accounts, 15% of the medium-sized accounts, and 2% of the small accounts. The total error (book value minus audit value) was found to be $5,018 for the large accounts, $2,165 for the medium-sized accounts, and $10,792 for the small accounts. The standard deviations of the errors were $968, $152, and $73, respectively. (*Hint:* Do not confuse the *error*, which is measured for each account, with the *standard error* of an average.)

a. Find the sample average error per account in each of the three strata (groups) of accounts.

b. Combine these three averages to find the stratified sampling average estimate of the population mean error per account.

c. Find the standard error of your estimate in part b both with and without use of the finite-population correction factor. Why are the answers so different in this case?

d. Interpret the (corrected) standard error value in terms of the (unknown) population mean error per account.

12 A newspaper poll involved interviews with 1,487 people and found that 42.3% of those interviewed were in favor of the candidate in question. The election will be held in three weeks.

a. Approximately what percentage of the entire population would say they were in favor of the candidate, if they were interviewed under the same conditions?

b. Give at least two reasons why the actual outcome of the election could differ from this 42.3% by more than the standard error.

13 Randomly selected consumers in four cities have been interviewed as part of a study by a shoe retailer. Each consumer reported the number of pairs of shoes in his or her closet:

Population Size	Sample Size	Sample Average (number of pairs of shoes)	Sample Standard Deviation
3,638,815	200	13.77	13.57
6,899,665	200	12.72	12.11
9,608,853	250	8.79	12.34
709,212	200	10.43	14.99

a. Estimate the mean number of pairs of shoes for the population representing all four cities combined.

b. Find the standard error for your answer to part a.

c. Find the standard error with and without use of the finite-population correction factor, and compare. Why are they so similar?

Database Exercises

Please refer to the employee database in Appendix A. For now, view this database as the population of interest.

1 Show that this database is arranged in the form of a frame. In particular, how would you use it to gain access to population information for a particular employee?

2 Draw a random sample without replacement of 10 employees, using the table of random digits, starting in row 23, column 7.

a. List the employee numbers for your sample.

b. Find the average salary for your sample, and interpret this number.

c. Find the standard deviation of salary for your sample, and interpret this number.

d. Find the standard error of salary for your sample, and interpret this number. In particular, in what way is it different from the standard deviation found in the previous part of this exercise?

3 Continuing with the sample from the previous exercise:

a. Find the population mean for salary. (*Note:* In real life you usually cannot find the population mean. We are peeking "behind the scenes" here.)

b. Compare this population mean to the sample average for salary. In particular, how many standard errors apart are they?

c. Find the population standard deviation for salary, and interpret this number.

d. Compare this population standard deviation to the sample standard deviation for salary.

e. Find the population standard deviation for the average salary for a sample, and interpret this number. Compare it to the standard error from the sample salary data.

f. Arrange the numbers you have computed in a table where the columns are "population" and "sample" and the rows are "average and mean," "standard deviation of individuals," and "standard deviation and standard error of sample averages of 10 employees."

4 Do exercises 2 and 3 for the ages instead of the salaries.

5 Do exercises 2 and 3 for the experiences instead of the salaries.

6 Continuing with the sample from exercise 2:

a. Find the binomial X for the gender variable, and interpret it.

b. Find the standard error of X, and interpret it.

7 Continuing with the sample from the previous exercise:

a. Find the population mean for the binomial X.

b. How far is the observed X for your sample from its population mean?

c. How does this difference compare to the standard error of X?

8 Repeat the previous two exercises for the binomial proportion f in place of X.

Projects

1 Your library may have financial statements on file. Look at one, and select an important number (such as sales or earnings).

a. Identify a population of firms of interest to you, and create a sampling frame.

b. Select a random sample of 10 firms. Find the data for these firms from their financial statements.

c. Compute the average and the standard error.

d. Indicate (approximately) how far your average is from the mean value for *all* firms listed in your frame.

e. Write a paragraph summarizing what you have learned about statistics and about the firms in your population.

2 Your firm is planning the marketing strategy for a "new and improved" consumer product. Your advertising company has shown you five TV ads, and you must choose two of these. Having seen them, you feel that some ads appeal to women more than to men. Before committing $1.8 million to this campaign, your supervisor would like to know more about consumer reaction to these ads. Write a one-page memo to your supervisor suggesting how to go about gathering this needed information. Be sure to cover the following topics: random sample, stratified random sample, pilot study.

Confidence Intervals
Admitting that Estimates Are Not Exact

You've just completed interviews of representative potential customers. After showing them your next product and letting them sample it, you found out that 19.8% of them would like to buy the product within the next month. The standard error is 3.70% (using percentage points). So far, you know a lot about the people you interviewed, but what do you really know about the percentage of *all* potential customers? You remember the interpretation of the standard error (approximately how far the sample result, 19.8%, is from the population mean percentage for *all* potential customers), but now you need go further. Being "approximate" is not good enough. You would like to combine all you know about the unknown population percentage into a definite, authoritative, *exact* statement. The confidence interval is designed to do this. In this case, the confidence interval would be specified as:

> We are 95% sure that the percentage of all potential customers that would buy our product, if we could find that number, is somewhere between 12.6% and 27.1%.[1]

The objective is to get rid of as much uncertainty as possible and to make the statement as exact as possible. Probability is necessary in order to make an exact statement in the face of uncertainty. Statistics is needed in order to take advantage of the information in your sample data. This process of generalizing from sample data to make probability-based statements about the population is called **statistical inference.** In particular, a **confidence interval** is an interval computed from the data that has a *known probability* of including the (unknown) population parameter of

---

[1]Don't worry about where these numbers came from; the details are coming up soon. A careful explanation of what "95% sure" implies will follow in Section 9.3

interest. Thus, specifying the confidence interval is the best you can do under uncertainty: it is an exact probability statement in place of vague observations such as We're not sure, but... or It's probably pretty close.

Confidence intervals come in great variety: here is a brief preview of the coming attractions. You can choose the probability of the statement, called the **confidence level.** By tradition, this is set at 95%, but it is common to find 90%, 99%, and even 99.9% levels used. The trade-off for a higher confidence level is a larger, less useful interval. Depending on the question of interest, you may also decide whether the interval is two-sided (it's between this and that) or one-sided (it's at least as big as this). Finally, there are new standard errors that can be used for finding confidence intervals for comparing two different samples. As always, you must watch out for the technical assumptions lurking in the background, which, if not satisfied, will invalidate your confidence interval statements.

There is an approximate, all-purpose confidence interval statement that applies in many situations. Once you have estimated a population parameter using an appropriate unbiased estimator and found the appropriate standard error of this estimator, the confidence interval statement (in generic form) is as follows:

■ **Approximate Confidence Interval Statement**
We are 95% sure that the population parameter is somewhere between the estimator *minus* two standard errors and the estimator *plus* two standard errors.

You may remember that a normal variable will be within two standard deviations from the mean approximately 95% of the time; this is where these values come from (although somewhat indirectly) in this generic confidence interval statement.[2]

How widely applicable is the notion of confidence interval? Essentially every number you see reported in the newspapers, in your confidential strategic internal memos, and on television is an estimate of an important number. Essentially all estimators have their own "personal" standard errors, indicating their precision. Once you have these two numbers (estimate and standard error), you can use the approximate confidence interval statement. But there are some details and warnings to be observed for some cases, which follow.

---

[2]The exact figure for 95% probability for a normal distribution is actually ±1.960 standard deviations, but 2 is close enough for many purposes.

■ 9.1 The Confidence Interval for the Population Mean

We have just drawn a sample of data and computed the sample average, $\overline{X}$, in order to estimate the population mean. Let's pretend for a moment that we know the value of the (usually unknown) population mean, μ, so that the situation is as in Figure 9.1.1. The distance between the sample average and the population mean (the estimation error) is *the same* whether you measure it starting from one or from the other. This says that measuring in terms of standard errors from the population mean will give the same result as measuring in terms of standard errors from the sample average. This is no trivial result. Since the sample average is known, you can measure in terms of a *known* quantity (the standard error) from another *known* quantity (the sample average), and the same basic relationships hold as if you were measuring from the (unknown) population mean.

FIGURE 9.1.1   The sampling distribution of $\overline{X}$ is centered at μ. The distance between the sample average and the population mean (the error of estimation) is the same whether you measure starting from one or from the other. The confidence interval will be constructed by measuring from $\overline{X}$, which is known, instead of from μ, which is unknown.

Sampling distribution of $\overline{X}$

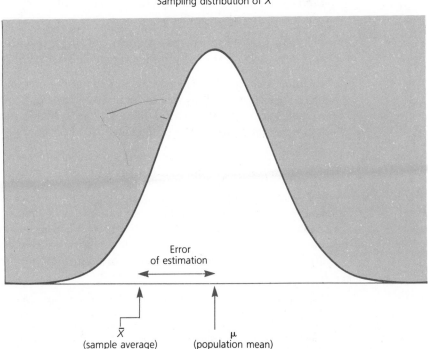

The intuitive reasoning behind the confidence interval goes as follows. Recall the fact that, for a normal distribution, the probability of falling within two standard deviations from the mean is approximately 0.95.[3] This leads to the following probability statement:

> The probability that the sample average is within 1.960 "standard deviations of the sample average" from the population mean is 0.95.

However, this statement involves measuring from the *unknown* population mean, μ. To avoid this problem, you can measure from the sample average, which leads to the following equivalent probability statement:

> The probability that the population mean is within 1.960 "standard deviations of the sample average" from the sample average is 0.95.

This statement still involves an unknown population parameter, since the standard deviation of the sample average is $\sigma_{\bar{X}} = \sigma/\sqrt{n}$. Statistics often proceeds by substituting what you know (an estimate) for what you don't know. The statement will still be approximately correct if you substitute the standard error $S_{\bar{X}} = S/\sqrt{n}$, which represents your best information about the standard deviation of the sample average. This leads to the following approximate probability statement:

> The probability that the population mean is within 1.960 *standard errors* from the sample average is *approximately* 0.95.

Unfortunately, this is only an approximate probability statement. To make it exact, we will use the *t*-table, discovered by Student and published in 1908.[4] By using the critical value from the *t*-table in place of 1.960, we obtain an *exact* probability statement instead of an approximate one:

> The probability that the population mean is within [critical value from the *t*-table] standard errors from the sample average is 0.95.

The price you pay for substituting the standard error (estimated from the data) for the unknown standard deviation is that the critical value from the *t*-table will be larger than 1.960, giving a wider, less precise interval. When the sample size, n, is small, this value will be larger than 1.960. When n is larger than 40, we will use 1.960 as an approximation.[5]

---

[3]You can verify from the normal probability tables that the probability is *exactly* 0.95 of being within 1.960 standard deviations.

[4]"Student" is the name used by W. S. Gossett, who was an executive at Guinness Brewery. He invented this important technique to help him in controlling and improving the brewing process.

[5]When an extra-careful analysis is required, you may want to use the slightly larger, exact critical *t*-value. Many computer programs automatically use this more careful approach.

To obtain a practical confidence interval from this probability statement, the final step is to change "probability 0.95" to "95% confidence." This is necessary because the confidence interval, in practice, is stated in terms of numbers instead of random variables.[6] The final confidence interval statement is as follows:

■ Exact Confidence Interval Statement

We are 95% sure that the population parameter is somewhere between the estimator minus t standard errors and the estimator plus t standard errors. In particular, we are 95% sure that μ is somewhere between

$$\bar{X} - tS_{\bar{X}} \quad \text{and} \quad \bar{X} + tS_{\bar{X}}$$

where t is taken from the t-table.

This reasoning also applies to a binomial situation, in which you are estimating the unknown probability of occurrence, p, after having observed X occurrences out of n trials. Remember from Chapter 7 that we use the sample proportion $f = X/n$ to estimate p and that the standard error of f is $S_f = \sqrt{f(1-f)/n}$. According to the exact confidence interval statement, using p as the population parameter and f as the estimator, your confidence interval is as follows:

■ Confidence Interval Statement for a Binomial Situation (n large)

In particular, we are 95% sure that p is somewhere between

$$f - tS_f \quad \text{and} \quad f + tS_f$$

where t is taken from the t-table.

The t-Table

The **t-table**, presented here as Table 9.1.1, can be used in many situations to find the multiplier for the confidence interval. Initially, the headings "confidence level" and "two-sided" at the top concern us the most. For constructing an ordinary two-sided 95% confidence interval, which is the most common case, use the featured column in the table. The one-sided case will be covered later in this chapter, and hypothesis testing will be covered in the next chapter.

In statistics, the general concept of **degrees of freedom** represents the number of independent pieces of information in your standard error. For the

---

[6]This subtle point will be considered further in Section 9.3.

TABLE 9.1.1 The *t*-Table

For One Sample: n	In General: Degrees of Freedom	80% 90%	90% 95%	95% 97.5%	98% 99%	99% 99.5%	99.8% 99.9%	99.9% 99.95%

Confidence Level:
Two-sided: 80%, 90%, 95%, 98%, 99%, 99.8%, 99.9%
One-sided: 90%, 95%, 97.5%, 99%, 99.5%, 99.9%, 99.95%

Hypothesis Test Level:
Two-sided: 0.20, 0.10, 0.05, 0.02, 0.01, 0.002, 0.001
One-sided: 0.10, 0.05, 0.025, 0.01, 0.005, 0.001, 0.0005

Critical Values

For One Sample: n	In General: Degrees of Freedom							
2	1	3.078	6.314	12.706	31.821	63.657	318.309	636.619
3	2	1.886	2.920	4.303	6.965	9.925	22.327	31.599
4	3	1.638	2.353	3.182	4.541	5.841	10.215	12.924
5	4	1.533	2.132	2.776	3.747	4.604	7.173	8.610
6	5	1.476	2.015	2.571	3.365	4.032	5.893	6.869
7	6	1.440	1.943	2.447	3.143	3.707	5.208	5.959
8	7	1.415	1.895	2.365	2.998	3.499	4.785	5.408
9	8	1.397	1.860	2.306	2.896	3.355	4.501	5.041
10	9	1.383	1.833	2.262	2.821	3.250	4.297	4.781
11	10	1.372	1.812	2.228	2.764	3.169	4.144	4.587
12	11	1.363	1.796	2.201	2.718	3.106	4.025	4.437
13	12	1.356	1.782	2.179	2.681	3.055	3.930	4.318
14	13	1.350	1.771	2.160	2.650	3.012	3.852	4.221
15	14	1.345	1.761	2.145	2.624	2.977	3.787	4.140
16	15	1.341	1.753	2.131	2.602	2.947	3.733	4.073
17	16	1.337	1.746	2.120	2.583	2.921	3.686	4.015
18	17	1.333	1.740	2.110	2.567	2.898	3.646	3.965
19	18	1.330	1.734	2.101	2.552	2.878	3.610	3.922
20	19	1.328	1.729	2.093	2.539	2.861	3.579	3.883
21	20	1.325	1.725	2.086	2.528	2.845	3.552	3.850
22	21	1.323	1.721	2.080	2.518	2.831	3.527	3.819
23	22	1.321	1.717	2.074	2.508	2.819	3.505	3.792
24	23	1.319	1.714	2.069	2.500	2.807	3.485	3.768
25	24	1.318	1.711	2.064	2.492	2.797	3.467	3.745
26	25	1.316	1.708	2.060	2.485	2.787	3.450	3.725
27	26	1.315	1.706	2.056	2.479	2.779	3.435	3.707
28	27	1.314	1.703	2.052	2.473	2.771	3.421	3.690
29	28	1.313	1.701	2.048	2.467	2.763	3.408	3.674
30	29	1.311	1.699	2.045	2.462	2.756	3.396	3.659
31	30	1.310	1.697	2.042	2.457	2.750	3.385	3.646
32	31	1.309	1.696	2.040	2.453	2.744	3.375	3.633
33	32	1.309	1.694	2.037	2.449	2.738	3.365	3.622
34	33	1.308	1.692	2.035	2.445	2.733	3.356	3.611
35	34	1.307	1.691	2.032	2.441	2.728	3.348	3.601
36	35	1.306	1.690	2.030	2.438	2.724	3.340	3.591
37	36	1.306	1.688	2.028	2.434	2.719	3.333	3.582
38	37	1.305	1.687	2.026	2.431	2.715	3.326	3.574
39	38	1.304	1.686	2.024	2.429	2.712	3.319	3.566
40	39	1.304	1.685	2.023	2.426	2.708	3.313	3.558
	Infinity Z	1.282	1.645	1.960	2.326	2.576	3.090	3.291

case of a single sample, the number of degrees of freedom is $n - 1$ (1 less than the number of observations) because the average is subtracted when the standard deviation is computed. For example, with $n = 10$ observations, you have 9 degrees of freedom and would use 2.262 from the t-table to form an ordinary two-sided 95% confidence interval. If $\sigma_{\overline{X}}$ is known exactly, use the t-value corresponding to an infinite number of degrees of freedom because you have perfect knowledge about the variability.

Where does the t-table come from? Statisticians define the t-*distribution* as the sampling distribution of $(\overline{X} - \mu)/S_{\overline{X}}$ when sampling from a normal distribution. For a large sample size (with many degrees of freedom), the denominator is nearly the same as $\sigma_{\overline{X}}$, and the t-distribution is nearly standard normal. This is why you find familiar numbers for the normal distribution (such as 1.960) at the bottom of the table. However, with smaller sample sizes the distribution is not normal. The effect of the denominator $S_{\overline{X}}$ is to spread out the t-distribution and give it longer tails than the normal. This is why the numbers are larger at the top of the table than at the bottom.

The Widely Used 95% Confidence Interval

Why are most confidence intervals computed at the 95% confidence level? One answer is that tradition has settled on this as a reasonable choice. The 95% level represents a compromise between trying to have as much confidence as possible and using a reasonably small interval.

The 100% confidence interval, unfortunately, is not very useful because it is too large. Consider the following exchange:

The Boss Jones, how much do you think a typical consumer will be willing to spend for our new brand of toothpaste?

Jones We estimate that the typical consumer will be willing to spend $1.35 per tube.

The Boss How exact is that estimate? What do we really believe?

Jones The analysis division is 100% sure that the typical consumer will be willing to spend between $0 and $35 million per tube.

Wait a minute! This is ridiculous. But the point is, to be 100% confident, you have to consider *every* remote, unrealistic possibility. By backing off from 100% to a confidence level that is still large but leaves some room for error, the result is a realistic and useful interval. Let's try it again:

The Boss Jones, how much do you think a typical consumer will be willing to spend for our new brand of toothpaste?

Jones We estimate that the typical consumer will be willing to spend $1.35 per tube.

The Boss How exact is that estimate? What do we really believe?

Jones The analysis division is 95% sure that the typical consumer will be willing to spend between $1.26 and $1.44 per tube.

Over the years, the 95% confidence level has emerged as a convenient, round number that is close but not too close to 100%. Other confidence levels are also used in practice, such as 90%, 99%, and even 99.9%; these will be considered after some examples.

| **EXAMPLE** | **Controlling the Average Thickness of Paper** |

The controls on the machinery in your paper factory have to be carefully adjusted so that the paper has the right thickness. Measurements of the thickness of selected sheets from an initial run of 0.004-inch paper are shown in Table 9.1.2.

Note that the average thickness was 0.004015 inch, which is about one third of a percent larger than the 0.004 inch that these sheets are supposed to be. Although some variation from the ideal has to be tolerated in nearly any process, your immediate concern is to determine the state of the machinery. You do not believe for a minute that the average, 0.004015 inch, represents the machinery output perfectly. The confidence interval will allow you to generalize from the 15 selected sheets you measured to the population, which, in this case, may be thought of as either the real population (all of the paper produced in the current run) or the idealized population (all of the paper the machine might produce under the current circumstances). This idealized population represents the current state of the machinery.

With a sample size $n = 15$, you have $n - 1 = 14$ degrees of freedom, for which the t-table value for a two-sided 95% confidence interval is 2.145. The confidence interval extends from

$$\overline{X} - t \times S_{\overline{X}} = 0.0040146667 - 2.145 \times 0.0000674986$$
$$= 0.00387$$

TABLE 9.1.2   Thicknesses of Selected Sheets of Paper (inches)

	0.00385
	0.00358
	0.00372
	0.00418
	0.00380
	0.00399
	0.00424
	0.00375
	0.00449
	0.00422
	0.00407
	0.00434
	0.00381
	0.00421
	0.00397
Average	0.0040146667
Standard deviation	0.0002614210
Standard error	0.0000674986
n	15

to

$$\bar{X} + t \times S_{\bar{X}} = 0.0040146667 + 2.145 \times 0.0000674986$$
$$= 0.00416$$

The final confidence interval statement is therefore:

> We are 95% sure that the machinery is currently producing paper with a mean thickness between 0.00387 inch and 0.00416 inch.

This confidence interval is illustrated in Figure 9.1.2. Your end result is now an exact probability statement about the general state of your machinery (or about the larger supply of paper from which you sampled) based on a small amount of sample data.

What can you do if the statement is not precise enough and you want to pin it down to a smaller interval than 0.00387 to 0.00416? You would have to do something to decrease your standard error, $S_{\bar{X}}$.[7] There are two ways to accomplish this. First, by increasing the sample size n, you will decrease the standard error if all other factors are held the same (because of the denominator in $S_{\bar{X}} = S/\sqrt{n}$). Second, if you can decrease the variability in the production process by finding the causes of important sources of variation and correcting them, then your standard error will decrease, even with the same sample size (because of the numerator in $S_{\bar{X}} = S/\sqrt{n}$).

EXAMPLE

Election Polling (a Binomial Situation)

The Wall Street Journal published results of a poll, 75 days before the 1988 presidential elections, showing that 57% had a favorable opinion of George Bush and 55% had a favorable opinion of Michael Dukakis.[8] Along with the results and

---

FIGURE 9.1.2   The confidence interval for mean paper thickness, based on a sample of $n = 15$ sheets with $\bar{X} = 0.004015$ inch and $S_{\bar{X}} = 0.0000675$ inch.

---

[7]Although you can decrease t somewhat, this is not likely to help very much unless your initial sample size was incredibly small.

[8]Results of a WSJ/NBC News poll as reported in "Poll, Swing Voters Depict Bush as Late Bloomer Who Has Come into His Own since Convention," *The Wall Street Journal*, August 25, 1988, p. 38.

analysis, the article included a look behind the scenes at some of the design and analysis of such a nationwide poll:

> The Wall Street Journal/NBC News poll was based on nationwide telephone interviews conducted Saturday, Sunday, and Monday with 2,185 adults aged 18 or older. There were 1,387 likely voters.
>
> The sample was drawn from a complete list of telephone exchanges in the country, chosen so that each region of the country was represented in proportion to its population. Households were selected by a method that gave all telephone numbers, listed and unlisted, a proportionate chance of being included. The results of the survey were weighted to adjust for variations in the sample relating to education, age, race, sex, and region.
>
> Chances are 19 out of 20 that if all adults in the United States had been surveyed using the same questionnaire, the findings would differ from these poll results by no more than 3 percentage points in either direction. The margin of error for subgroups may be larger.

The first paragraph gives the sample size, $n = 2,185$ adults. The second paragraph tells how the survey was designed. Some stratified sampling ideas have been used; in particular, they used a weighted averaging technique to adjust for the fact that education, age, and other variables in the sample may not match these levels in the larger population. The last paragraph pertains to confidence intervals.

The statement that "chances are 19 out of 20" says that the probability is 0.95, or 95% (since 19/20 = 0.95). The phrase "If all adults in the United States had been surveyed using the same questionnaire" is a careful definition of the *population,* not just in terms of the people but also in terms of their answers to the same questions used in the sample. The measure "3 percentage points in either direction" indicates the size of the confidence interval, as measured above and below any estimated percentage. Finally, the reference to the margin of error for subgroups correctly points out that a subgroup (for example, just the women or just the southwestern region) has a smaller sample size, n, and therefore may have a larger standard error and a wider confidence interval than the 3 percentage points mentioned earlier.

Now focus attention on the likely voters. There were $X = 1,387$ out of $n = 2,185$, indicating that only an estimated 63.5% of adults are considered likely to vote. This 63.5% is the exact percentage from the sample. What does it say about the population? Let's make a confidence interval statement. The standard error for this binomial situation is $S_f = \sqrt{f \times (1 - f)/n} = 1.03\%$, and the t-value for the two-sided 95% confidence interval from the t-table is 1.960 for $n = 2,185$. The confidence interval goes from[9]

$$f - t \times S_f = 63.5 - 1.960 \times 1.03 = 61.5\%$$

---

[9]Feel free to use either proportions or percentages when figuring a confidence interval for a binomial situation. Whichever you choose, be sure to use the same convention for both f and S_f. If you use 63.5% for f, then use 1.03% (in percentage points, *not* as a percentage of f) for its standard error. If you use 0.635 for f, then be sure to use 0.0103 for its standard error, S_f.

to

$$f + t \times S_f = 63.5 + 1.960 \times 1.03 = 65.5\%$$

The final confidence interval statement is therefore:

> We are 95% sure that, among all adults in the United States, some number between 61.5% and 65.5% were likely to vote as of the time this poll was done.

Your end result is now an exact probability statement about all adults in the United States, based on the exact results from a smaller sample. Or so it seems. If you want to be extra cautious in the inferences here, you may want to redefine the population to be all adults in the United States who could have been reached by telephone during the time of the survey and who were willing to communicate their views. Being even more careful, you might view the results in terms of whether people *describe* themselves as likely voters or not, rather than whether they really are likely to vote.

Other Confidence Levels

Although the most commonly used confidence level is 95%, other confidence levels are appropriate for use in special situations. The basic principle here is a trade-off of the size of the interval (a smaller interval suggests more precision and is therefore better) against the probability of including the population parameter (a higher probability of "being correct" is also better). In some situations you may need so much precision that you are willing to widen the interval in order to be correct more often. In other situations you may have a stronger need for a smaller interval and be willing to be wrong more often in order to achieve it. The standard 95% confidence level represents a common trade-off of these two factors, but it is not the only reasonable choice.

There is a tendency to prefer round numbers for confidence levels (avoiding confusing statements such as "being 92.649% confident," for example). The *t*-table presents values for constructing 90%, 95%, 99%, and 99.9% confidence intervals (in boldface at the top of the table) as well as a few other levels, which are listed primarily to help with one-sided intervals later on.

How much smaller is a confidence interval when you go for a lower confidence level? For a larger sample, the relative sizes of confidence intervals are shown in Figure 9.1.3.

EXAMPLE **Average Selling Price as Determined through Rebates**

You probably know about rebates. They can look a lot like a discount when you buy a product, but you need to put together a bunch of paperwork (such as the sales receipt; the label, which is permanently glued to the bottle; and your first-born child—just kidding), spend 25 cents to mail the letter, and, finally, wait a while to receive a check for 40 cents, which you have to cash at your bank.

FIGURE 9.1.3 The relative sizes of 90%, 95%, 99%, and 99.9% confidence intervals from a large sample. The more confidence you wish, the larger the interval must be in order to cover your demands.

One feature of rebates, from the manufacturer's point of view, is that they provide some useful information. Suppose your firm has a rebate program on a particular battery package with a list price of $2.99, and you would like to find out how much the public is *really* paying for these products after discounts and store sales. A carefully designed and randomized survey would provide good information about this, but it would not be justifiable on a cost basis just now. So you decide to analyze the sales receipts people have been sending in with their rebate requests.

First of all, what kind of sample is this? It's not random in any real sense of the word. Consumers who send in for rebates are not a representative cross section of all consumers. For example, they might be better organized (so that they can keep track of everything and send it in) and poorer (so that the rebate money is worth the trouble to them) than the public at large. Nonetheless, you decide that you want to know about the population of consumers who are likely to send in rebate requests, and you decide to view the ones you receive as a random sample from this idealized population.

So far, $n = 15,603$ receipts have been received and are available for analysis. The summary values are

Summary of Sales Receipts

n	15,603
Average sales price	$ 2.387
Standard deviation	$ 0.318
Standard error	$ 0.00255

Wow! Just look at the size of that standard error! It's so small because the sample is so large. Your estimate ($2.39) is *very* close to the population mean.

The 95% confidence interval, computed using $t = 1.960$, goes from $2.382 to $2.392. Evidently the mean price in your idealized population is within about half a penny from the estimated $2.387.

With precision like this, very little will be lost by making a statement at a much higher confidence level. For example, let's use the highest confidence level in the table. To achieve 99.9% confidence, use $t = 3.291$ in place of 1.960 to compute the confidence interval, which extends from

$$\overline{X} - t \times S_{\overline{X}} = 2.387 - 3.291 \times 0.00255 = \$2.379$$

to

$$\overline{X} + t \times S_{\overline{X}} = 2.387 + 3.291 \times 0.00255 = \$2.395$$

The final confidence interval statement is therefore:

> We are 99.9% sure that the mean purchase price for your batteries by consumers motivated to send in rebate requests is somewhere between $2.379 and $2.395.

Compare this to the 95% confidence interval. Although the 99.9% confidence interval is slightly larger, it is still very close to the estimated mean price (about a penny away from $2.387). Because the level of variability is low in this case (as measured by the standard error), you can make a very exact statement that is correct with very high probability.

EXAMPLE   Yield of a Manufacturing Process

Now that you have brought a new chemical processing facility into production, top management wants to know the dependable long-term capabilities of the system. The processes are delicate, and no matter how carefully things are controlled, there is still some variation from day to day and even from hour to hour in the amount produced. Let's construct a confidence interval for the long-term yield (viewing this number as the population mean) based on measured yields for a sample of time periods.

Table 9.1.3 shows the raw data, consisting of 12 measurements of the yield of the facility, together with the usual summary measures. As you can see, there is lots of variability here.

Because the variability is so high, you are concerned that the confidence interval will be larger than you would like. You have talked things over with others at work, and it seems that a 90% confidence interval would be acceptable.

The t-value for a two-sided 90% confidence interval with $n - 1 = 11$ degrees of freedom is 1.796. The confidence interval therefore extends from

$$\overline{X} - t \times S_{\overline{X}} = 60.3917 - 1.796 \times 5.4203 = 50.7$$

to

$$\overline{X} + t \times S_{\overline{X}} = 60.3917 + 1.796 \times 5.4203 = 70.1$$

TABLE 9.1.3 Yields of a Chemical Processing Facility (tons)

	71.7
	46.0
	103.9
	54.4
	43.3
	68.1
	73.4
	45.1
	45.6
	44.9
	77.8
	50.5
Average	60.3917
Standard deviation	18.7766
Standard error	5.4203
n	12

The final confidence interval statement is therefore:

We are 90% sure that the mean long-term yield of this highly variable process is somewhere between 50.7 and 70.1 tons.

Compared with the 95% confidence interval, which extends from 48.5 to 72.3 tons, this 90% interval is only slightly shorter. The effect is not dramatic. By being wrong an additional 5% of the time, you have gained only slightly more precision as compared to the standard 95% interval.

9.2 Assumptions Needed for Validity

How can you be sure that your confidence levels are accurate? That is, when you claim 95% confidence, how can you be sure that the population mean will really be in the interval with 95% probability? Some technical assumptions are required in order for the statistical theory to apply to your particular case. If the assumptions apply, your confidence intervals will be correctly specified. If the assumptions do not apply to a situation, the confidence statement may be wrong.

When we say that the confidence interval statement is correct, what are we really saying? Suppose you have a procedure for constructing a 95% confidence interval. If the procedure is correct and you imagine repeating it many times (constructing many confidence intervals), you would find that approximately 95% of the confidence intervals include the population mean. This does not ensure that the population mean will definitely be in your interval, just that it is very likely to be there.

When we say that the confidence interval statement is *wrong*, in the case of incorrect assumptions, what are we really saying? Simply that the probability of including the population mean is *not necessarily* equal to the 95% level (or other confidence level) that you claimed. Your procedure might claim to have 95% confidence, but in reality it may have a much smaller confidence level, even as low as 50%, 10%, or smaller. Such a confidence interval is nearly worthless even though it might *appear* to be just fine. On the other hand, your confidence level could actually be *larger* than the 95% you claimed, if the assumptions are not satisfied. Unfortunately, in some cases you don't know whether the true confidence level is higher or lower than your claimed 95%.

 The two **assumptions required for the confidence interval** are (1) random sampling and (2) a normal distribution. These must both be satisfied for the confidence statement to be valid. We will consider each assumption in turn.

Random Sampling

■ Assumption 1
The data set is a random sample from the population of interest.

The confidence interval is a statement about a population mean based on sample data. Naturally, there must be a strong relationship between your data and the population mean. A random sample ensures that your data represent the population and that each observation conveys new, independent information. Without a random sample, you would not be able to make exact probability statements about the results. If your sample consists only of your friends, for example, you cannot expect any confidence interval you compute to reflect a cross section of all of society.

One interpretation of this assumption is that you must select a random sample from a carefully identified population frame, as discussed in Chapter 8. Certainly, the result of such efforts will satisfy the assumption. But this assumption is not as restrictive as it might seem; there is an alternative way to satisfy the random sampling assumption using an idealized population.

If you have some data and would like to construct a confidence interval, but the data are not really a deliberately chosen, random sample from a precisely specified population, you could try to construct an idealized population. Ask yourself what your data do represent. If you can identify a larger group and are willing to "assume" that your data are a lot like a random sample from this larger group, then you may legitimately construct a confidence interval to tell you about the unknown mean of this idealized population.[10]

For example, suppose you have some data on people who have recently come in to apply for employment. Strictly speaking, this group is *not* a random sample from any population because no randomization has been applied in their selection. It is not enough to observe that they look like a

---

[10]However, if others disagree with you as to the identification of the idealized population, as the other side might in a lawsuit, then you have a problem. Since this is a conceptual problem, not a purely statistical problem, I can't help you.

random sample or that they look like a diverse group. The fact remains that, strictly speaking, they are not a random sample. However, if you are willing to view them as representatives of a larger population of people seeking employment and willing to take the time to try a firm like yours, then you may construct a confidence interval. This confidence interval goes beyond the particular people who applied for employment and tells you about others like them in your idealized population.

Here is an example to show how a confidence interval can fail if the data are not a random sample from the intended population.

EXAMPLE

Forecasting Interest Rates

Businesses depend on economic forecasts of future conditions as a way of dealing with uncertainty in the strategic planning process. These predictions are often viewed as the "best possible" information available. This may be so, yet how many of us know how dependable these forecasts really are? From time to time, *The Wall Street Journal* publishes past forecasts of selected economists together with the actual outcomes to see how well the predictions did the job.

A histogram of predictions of the three-month U.S. treasury bill interest rate at the end of 1985, as forecast six months in advance by 24 economists, is shown in Figure 9.2.1.[11] The two-sided 95% confidence interval based on these 24 forecasts extends from 6.93% to 7.64%, which includes the actual outcome of 7.08%. Is this what we should expect of a confidence interval, or were we just lucky here? The answer, unfortunately, is that we were just lucky.

Consider another set of forecasts. The histogram of predictions of the three-month U.S. treasury bill interest rate at the end of 1984, as forecast six months in advance by 22 economists, is shown in Figure 9.2.2.[12] The two-sided 95% confidence interval based on these 22 forecasts extends from 10.29% to 10.99% and *does not* include the actual outcome of 7.84%. In fact, the economists' predictions are disturbingly far from the actual outcome.

Should you be troubled by the fact that a confidence interval does not include its intended number? Not necessarily; after all, the intervals are only guaranteed to be right about 95% of the time. However, you should be surprised if the actual number is extremely far from the confidence interval. In this case the standard error is 0.167%, and the outcome of 7.84% (the intended number) is $(10.64 - 7.84)/0.167 = 16.8$ standard errors away from the sample average (10.64%). These 16.8 standard errors represent a very large distance and demand an explanation.

The explanation is simple. The random sampling assumption is not satisfied here; therefore, the confidence interval statement is not guaranteed to be cor-

---

[11]Data are from T. Herman and E. P. Foldessy, "Slight Drop in Interest Rates Seen in Early '86; Most Economists Surveyed Forecast Rise in Second Half," *The Wall Street Journal*, January 2, 1986, p. 2.

[12]Data are from T. Herman and E. P. Foldessy, "Interest Rates to Rise in '85 as Economy Emerges from Doldrums, According to Poll of Economists," *The Wall Street Journal*, January 2, 1985.

FIGURE 9.2.1   A histogram of forecasts of the three-month U.S. treasury bill interest rate, compared to the actual outcome at the end of <u>1985</u>. The economists' consensus was quite close to the actual future outcome in this case.

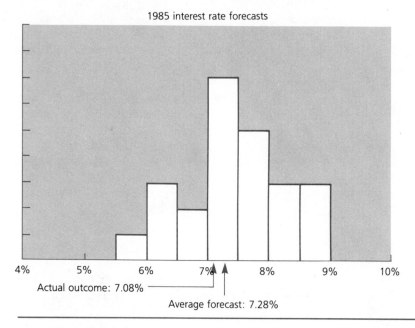

FIGURE 9.2.2   A histogram of forecasts of the three-month U.S. treasury bill interest rate, compared to the actual outcome at the end of <u>1984</u>. The economists' consensus was not as accurate in this case.

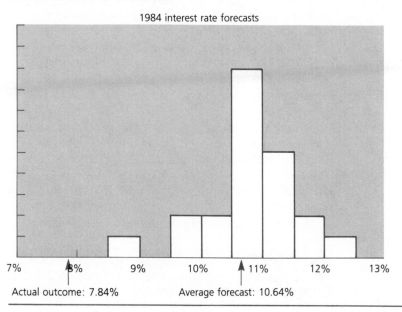

rect. We should have been more careful and skeptical in using the economists' predictions as an indication of the future.

What *do* these economic predictions represent? About the best we can do with predictions made by a sample of economists is to view them as a random sample from the *idealized population* of similar forecasts by top economists at the same time period. Our confidence interval, then, tells us about the mean consensus of this group of economists at this time. It does *not* tell us directly about the future rate because this future rate is *not* the mean of the population being sampled.

In between the forecasts and the actual outcome there was a sudden, unforeseen downward shift in interest rates. This is something that can and does happen in economics. However, in *statistics,* if your assumptions are satisfied, the correctness of your statements is guaranteed.

It often helps to clarify your thinking by separating the subject matter (in this case, economics) from the statistical principles. Then the best you can do is make a limited, exact statistical statement and interpret it according to the accepted ways of the subject matter.

Normal Distribution

■ Assumption 2
The quantity being measured is normally distributed.

The detailed theory behind the confidence interval is based on the assumption that the quantity being measured is normally distributed *in the population.* Such a simplifying assumption makes it possible to work out all of the equations and compute the *t*-table (which has already been done for you). Fortunately, in practice this requirement is much less rigid for two reasons.

First of all, you could never really tell whether the population is perfectly normal or not, since all you have is the sample with its randomness. In practice, therefore, you would look at a histogram of the data to see if the distribution is *approximately* normal, that is, not too skewed and with no extreme outliers.

Second, the central limit theorem often comes to the rescue. Since statistical inference is based primarily on the sample average, $\overline{X}$, what you need primarily is that the sampling distribution of $\overline{X}$ be approximately normal. The central limit theorem tells you that if n is large, $\overline{X}$ will be approximately normally distributed even if the individuals in the population (and the sample) are not.

Thus, the practical rule here may be summarized as follows:

■ Assumption 2 (in Practice)
Look at a histogram of the data. If it looks approximately normal, then you're OK (i.e., the confidence interval statement is approximately valid). If the his-

togram is slightly skewed, then you're OK provided the sample size is not too small. If the histogram is moderately skewed or has a very few moderate outliers, then you're OK provided the sample size is large. If the histogram is extremely skewed or has extreme outliers, then you may be in trouble.

What can you do if the normal distribution assumption is not satisfied at all, due, say, to extreme skewness? One approach is to transform the data (perhaps with logarithms) to bring about a normal distribution; keep in mind that the resulting confidence interval would then be for the mean of the population *logarithm* values. Another possibility is to use *nonparametric methods,* to be described in Chapter 16.

■ 9.3 Interpreting a Confidence Interval

What are you really communicating when you say that, based on weights from a sample of the day's production, you are 95% sure that the mean weight of all soap boxes produced today is between 15.93 and 16.28 ounces? It looks like a probability statement, but it must be interpreted carefully. The mean weight of all soap boxes produced today is some fixed, unknown number. It is either in the interval, or it isn't. In this light, where does the probability come from?

Which Event Has a 95% Probability?

In order for there to be a probability, there must be a random experiment. The probability refers to the entire *process* rather than just to the particular result. By saying that you are 95% sure that the population mean weight is between 15.93 and 16.28 ounces, you are making a statement about the exact numerical results based on the data. However, the 95% probability comes from the process itself, which views the numbers as *random.* A careful probability statement might be: "There is a 95% probability for the event 'the population mean weight is within the confidence interval' for the random experiment 'randomly choose some boxes and compute the confidence interval.'" Each time you collect data and compute a 95% confidence interval, you are performing a random experiment that has a probability for every event. The probability that the unknown population mean falls within the computed interval is 0.95.

This subtlety is partly a question of timing of information. You might reasonably say, There is a 55% chance that a stock market index will go up tomorrow. However, when tomorrow afternoon comes along and you see that the market did indeed go up, there is no remaining uncertainty or probability, the market did go up. Yet there *was* uncertainty before the fact. The one difference between this stock market example and the usual confidence interval statement is that when you compute a confidence interval you either include the population mean within the confidence interval or you don't, yet you may never know whether you did or not!

One useful way to interpret the 95% probability is to imagine repeating the sampling process over and over to obtain multiple confidence intervals, each one based on a different random sample. The notion of relative frequency and the law of large numbers (from Chapter 6) tell you that about 95% of these random, known intervals include the fixed, unknown population mean. This is illustrated in Figure 9.3.1. Note that each sample has its own average, $\overline{X}$, so some intervals are shifted to the right or left with respect to the others. Also, each one has its own standard error, $S_{\overline{x}}$, so some intervals are larger or smaller than others. Note that the confidence intervals that "missed" the population mean were still fairly close.

Your Lifetime Track Record

Of course, you ordinarily compute just *one* confidence interval for the population mean in a given situation. However, since many such studies will be independent of each other (since the sampling done for each study will ordinarily be chosen independently), you can interpret the meaning of "95% confidence" in terms of your lifetime track record. If you compute many 95% confidence intervals over your lifetime, and if the required assumptions are satisfied for each one, then approximately 95% of these confidence intervals will contain their respective population means.

FIGURE 9.3.1   Confidence intervals based on different random samples from a population. Usually you see only one (the one you computed, at the bottom). The others illustrate the meaning of "95% confidence": Of a large number of confidence intervals based on independent samples, approximately 95% will include the population mean.

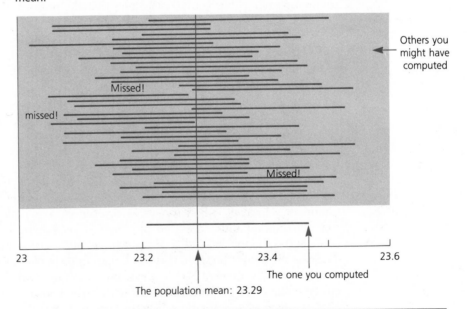

Looking back over your life from the golf course at the retirement home, you get that satisfying feeling that 95% of the time your confidence intervals were correct. Unfortunately, you also get that sinking feeling that 5% of them were wrong. And, to top things off, you may *never know* which cases were right and which were wrong! Such are the ways of statistical inference.

■ 9.4 One-Sided Confidence Intervals

In some cases it may not be necessary to specify that the population mean is probably *between* two confidence interval numbers. It may suffice to say that the population mean is *at least as large* as some number or (in other situations) to say that the population mean is *no larger than* some number. A **one-sided confidence interval** states with known confidence that the population mean is either *at least* or *no larger than* some computed number. If you are careful, constructing a one-sided confidence interval can provide a more effective statement than use of a two-sided interval would.

For example, you may be interested only in something being *big enough:* We are 95% sure that sales will be at least $560,000. Or you might be interested only in something being *small enough:* We are 95% sure that our defect rate is no larger than 1 in 10,000 units produced. Situations like these can benefit from a one-sided confidence interval statement.

Be Careful! You Can't Always Use a One-Sided Interval

There is one important criterion you must satisfy to use a one-sided confidence interval:

> ■ **Criterion for Using a One-Sided Confidence Interval**
> In order to use a one-sided interval, you must be sure that *no matter how the data had come out* you would still have used a one-sided interval on the same side ("at least" or "no larger than"). If, had the data come out different, you might have used a one-sided interval *on the other side,* you should use a two-sided confidence interval instead. If in doubt, use a two-sided interval.

Suppose your break-even cost is $18 per item produced, you have the basic data from a sample, and you are ready to compute a confidence interval. You might be tempted to proceed as follows: If the estimated cost is *high* (more than $18), you will state that you are 95% sure that costs are *at least...*, but if the estimated cost is *low* (less than $18) you will state instead that you are 95% sure that costs are *no more than....* Don't be tempted! Because switching the side of the interval based on the data is not allowed (by the preceding criterion), you should compute a two-sided interval instead (you are 95% sure that costs are between ... and ...). There are two good reasons for this. First of all, you are interested in both sides (sometimes one, sometimes the other). Second, switching sides of a one-sided confidence interval can invalidate your probability statement so that your true confidence level might be much lower than the 95% claimed.[13]

Computing the One-Sided Interval

To compute a one-sided interval, first find the t-value from Table 9.1.1 using the "one-sided" confidence level heading at the top. (The row is the same as for a two-sided interval since the number of degrees of freedom is still $n - 1$.) For example, to compute a 95% one-sided confidence interval with a sample size of $n = 23$, you would use $t = 1.717$. For a 99.9% one-sided confidence interval with $n = 35$ you would use $t = 3.348$.

Next, choose *one* of the following one-sided confidence interval statement types:

> We are 95% sure that the population mean is *at least as large* as $\overline{X} - t_{\text{one-sided}} \times S_{\overline{X}}$.

or

> We are 95% sure that the population mean is *not larger than* $\overline{X} + t_{\text{one-sided}} \times S_{\overline{X}}$.

An easy way to remember whether to add or subtract is to be sure that the sample average, $\overline{X}$, is included in your one-sided confidence interval (it should be, after all, since it is your best estimate of the population mean). Thus, when the one-sided interval extends upward to larger values ("at least") it must start *below* the sample average, and when the one-sided interval extends downward to smaller values ("no larger than") it must start *above* the sample average.

Figure 9.4.1 illustrates this and also compares one- and two-sided intervals. The beginning point of a *one-sided 95%* confidence interval is the same as one of the endpoints of a *two-sided 90%* confidence interval. The idea here is that there are two ways in which a two-sided interval might be wrong: Either the population mean is too big, or else it is too small. A one-sided interval sharing an endpoint with a two-sided interval can be wrong only half as often.

The one-sided confidence interval allows you to concentrate your attention on the most interesting cases. If you care only about errors on one side and don't care at all about errors on the other side, then the one-sided interval can begin *closer to the sample average* (and will therefore seem more precise) than a two-sided confidence interval. For example, for a large sample

---

[13]In the worst case of switching, you might end up with a 90% one-sided confidence interval when you are claiming 95% confidence. This happens if you switch sides according to whether $\overline{X}$ is above or below μ because you suffer from the 5% errors of *both* intervals, adding up to a total error rate of 10% instead of the 5% you thought you had.

FIGURE 9.4.1 Both kinds of one-sided confidence intervals are illustrated at the top. One-sided confidence intervals always include the sample average, starting from a point on one side and continuing indefinitely on the other. Note that the endpoint for the *95% one-sided* confidence interval is the same as one of the endpoints for the *90% two-sided* confidence interval.

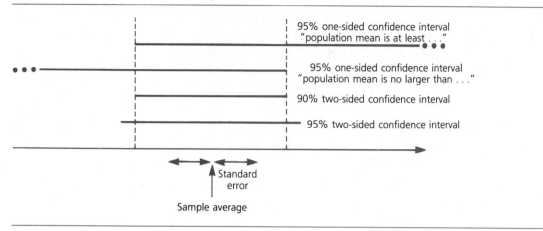

with an average of 19.0 and a standard error of 8.26, rather than saying, it's between 2.81 and 35.2, you could say instead that it's at least 5.41. Knowing that it's at least 5.41 provides more information than knowing it's at least 2.81. You can claim a stronger lower bound because you are not claiming any upper bound at all.

EXAMPLE   **The Savings of a New System**

You are evaluating a new automated production system and have decided to buy it if it can be demonstrated to save enough money per item produced. You have arranged for it to be installed on the premises so that you can try it out for a week. It will be programmed to produce a cross section of typical products, and the cost savings will be determined for each item produced.

What is the population here? It is an idealized population of all of the items the system *might* produce under conditions similar to the ones you tested under. Statistical inference can help you here by extending your information from the particular items you did produce to the mean of the much larger group of items that you might produce in the indefinite future under similar conditions.

Should a one-sided confidence interval be used here? Yes, because regardless of how the data come out, you are interested only in whether you will save enough money. Your final statement will be of the form: I am 95% sure that the mean cost savings per item produced over the long run will be *at least . . . .*

For a sample size of $n = 18$ items produced, with an average savings $\overline{X} = \$39.21$ and a standard error $S_{\overline{X}} = \$6.40$, the 95% one-sided confidence interval will extend indefinitely to larger values starting from

$$\overline{X} - t_{\text{one-sided}} \times S_{\overline{X}} = 39.21 - 1.740 \times 6.40 = 28.07$$

Therefore, your final one-sided confidence statement is:

> We are 95% sure that the mean cost savings are at least $28.07 per item produced.

Note that the one-sided confidence interval includes the sample average, $\overline{X} = \$39.21$, as it must. That is, the sample average of $39.21 satisfies the confidence interval statement by being at least as large as $28.07. It would have been wrong to have used the other endpoint. By using this way of checking as a guide, you will always make the correct one-sided statement.

To compute a one-sided confidence interval at a different level, simply substitute the appropriate t-value from the table. For example, the 99% one-sided confidence interval statement uses $t = 2.567$. Compared to the 95% interval statement, this is a weaker statement about cost savings that you are more confident about:

> We are 99% sure that the mean cost savings are at least $22.78 per item produced.

<table>
<tr><td>EXAMPLE</td><td>**Travel Costs**</td></tr>
</table>

In an effort to prepare a realistic travel budget, you have examined the costs of typical trips made in the recent past. In an effort to ensure that the budget will cover the demands of the coming year, you would like to arrive at a maximum dollar figure for mean cost per trip. This allows you to say that the mean cost *is no more than* this figure. Since you are only interested in this one side, you may use a one-sided confidence interval. You choose the 95% level of confidence.

Working from a list of 83 recent trips, you find that the average cost was $1,286 with a standard error of $71.03. The one-sided confidence interval will include all values from $0 (since you know the cost can't be negative) to the upper bound

$$\overline{X} + t_{\text{one-sided}} \times S_{\overline{X}} = 1,286 + 1.645 \times 71.03 = \$1,403$$

Here is your final one-sided confidence statement:

> We are 95% sure that the mean travel expense per trip is no larger than $1,403.

Checking to make sure that adding (instead of subtracting) is correct here, you note that the sample average ($1,286) is indeed within the confidence interval ($1,286 is no larger than $1,403).

This confidence interval is of limited use because the data are not really a random sample from the population of interest. You would like to predict *future* travel costs, but your sample data are from the past. The confidence interval takes past variability in travel costs into account, which is useful information for you. However, it does not (and cannot) take into account future trends in travel costs.

NOT ON MID-TERM

■ 9.5 Prediction Intervals

The confidence interval tells you where the *population mean* is, with known probability. This is fine if you are seeking a summary measure for a large population. If, on the other hand, you want to know about an *individual case,* this confidence interval is not appropriate. Instead, you need a much wider interval that reflects not just the estimated uncertainty $S_{\overline{X}} = S/\sqrt{n}$ of $\overline{X}$ (which may be very small when n is large) but also the estimated uncertainty S of an individual observation.

The **prediction interval** allows you to use data from a sample to predict a new observation with known probability, provided you obtain this additional observation in the same way as you obtained your past data. The situation is as follows. You have a random sample of n units from a population and have measured each one to obtain $X_1, X_2, \ldots, X_n$. You would now like to make a prediction about an *additional* unit randomly selected from the same population.

The uncertainty measure to use here is the **standard error for prediction,** a measure of variability of the distance between the sample average and the new observation. Two kinds of randomness are combined: for the sample average and for the new observation. This standard error for prediction is found by multiplying the standard deviation by the square root of $(1 + 1/n)$:

■ Standard Error for Prediction

$$S\sqrt{1 + \frac{1}{n}}$$

The standard error for prediction is even larger than the estimator S of the variability of individuals in the population. This is appropriate because the prediction interval must combine the uncertainty of individuals in the population (as measured by S) together with the uncertainty of the sample average (as measured by $S_{\overline{X}} = S/\sqrt{n}$).

Once you have an estimator ($\overline{X}$) and the standard error for prediction, you can form the prediction interval in much the same way as you form an ordinary confidence interval. The *t*-value is found in the table in just the same way for a given prediction confidence level and sample size n (not including the additional observation, of course). Only the standard error is different; be sure to use the standard error for prediction in place of the standard error of the average.

■ The Prediction Interval for a New Observation
Two-sided:

We are 95% sure that the new observation will be between
$\overline{X} - t \times S\sqrt{1 + 1/n}$ and $\overline{X} + t \times S\sqrt{1 + 1/n}$.

One-sided:

> We are 95% sure that the new observation will be at least
> $\overline{X} - t_{\text{one-sided}} \times S\sqrt{1 + 1/n}$.

or

> We are 95% sure that the new observation will be no larger than
> $\overline{X} + t_{\text{one-sided}} \times S\sqrt{1 + 1/n}$.

What does the figure 95% signify here? It is a probability according to the following random experiment: Get a sample, find the prediction interval, get a new observation, and see if the new observation falls in the interval. Note in particular that the 95% probability refers to drawing a new *sample* as well as a new observation. This is only natural; since one sample differs from another, the proportion of new observations that fall within the prediction interval will also vary from one sample to another. Averaged over the randomness of the initial sample, the resulting probability is 95% (or some other specified probability).

The following table summarizes when to use a prediction interval instead of a confidence interval.

When You Need to Learn About:	Use:
The population mean	Confidence interval
A new observation like the others	Prediction interval

EXAMPLE   ### How Long until Your Order Is Filled?

How long should you wait before ordering new supplies for production inventory? If you order too soon, you pay interest on the capital used to buy them while they sit around costing you rent for the warehouse space they occupy. If you order too late, then you risk being without necessary parts and bringing part of the production line to a halt.

The past eight times that your supplier has said, "They'll be there in two weeks," you made a note of how many business days it actually took for them to arrive. These numbers were as follows:

$$10, 9, 7, 10, 3, 9, 12, 5$$

The average is $\overline{X} = 8.125$ days, and the standard deviation is $S = 2.94897$. The standard error of the average is $S_{\overline{X}} = 1.04262$, but we do not need it. The standard error for prediction is

$$\text{Standard error for prediction} = S \times \sqrt{1 + \frac{1}{n}}$$

$$= 2.94897 \times \sqrt{1 + \frac{1}{8}}$$

$$= 2.94897 \times \sqrt{1.125}$$

$$= 2.94897 \times 1.06066$$

$$= 3.12786$$

For a two-sided 95% prediction interval, the t-value from the table for $n = 8$ is $t = 2.365$. The prediction interval extends from

$$\overline{X} - t \times (\text{Standard error for prediction}) = 8.125 - 2.365 \times 3.12786$$

$$= 0.728$$

to

$$\overline{X} + t \times (\text{Standard error for prediction}) = 8.125 + 2.365 \times 3.12786$$

$$= 15.52$$

You will be assuming that the delivery times are approximately normally distributed, that the $n = 8$ delivery times observed represent a random sample from the idealized population of "typical delivery times," and that the next delivery time is randomly selected from this same population. The final prediction interval statement is as follows:

We are 95% sure that the next delivery time will be somewhere between 0.7 and 15.5 days.

Why does this prediction interval extend over such a large range? This reflects the underlying uncertainty of the situation. In the past, based on your eight observations, the delivery times have been quite variable. Naturally, this makes exact predictions difficult.

If you merely want to be assured that the next delivery time will not be too late, you may construct a one-sided prediction interval using $t = 1.895$ from the one-sided 95% confidence column in the t-table. The upper limit is then

$$\overline{X} + t_{\text{one-sided}} \times (\text{Standard error for prediction}) = 8.125 + 1.895 \times 3.12786$$

$$= 14.05229$$

You may then make the following one-sided prediction interval statement:

We are 95% sure that the next delivery time will be no more than 14.1 days.

If you are willing to accept a 90% one-sided prediction interval, then the upper limit (using $t = 1.415$) would be

$$\overline{X} + t_{\text{one-sided}} \times (\text{Standard error for prediction}) = 8.125 + 1.415 \times 3.12786$$

$$= 12.55092$$

You would then make the following one-sided prediction interval statement:

> We are 90% sure that the next delivery time will be no more than 12.6 days.

■ 9.6 End-of-Chapter Materials

Summary

The process of generalizing from sample data to make probability-based statements about the population is called **statistical inference.** A **confidence interval** is a region computed from the data that has a known probability of including the (unknown) population parameter of interest. The probability that the population parameter is included within the confidence interval is called the **confidence level,** which is set by tradition at 95%, although levels of 90%, 99%, and 99.9% are also commonly used. The higher the confidence level, the larger (and usually less useful) the confidence interval. The approximate all-purpose confidence interval statement goes as follows:

> We are 95% sure that the population parameter is somewhere between the estimator *minus* two of the estimator's standard errors and the estimator *plus* two of its standard errors.

This is a restatement of the fact that, for a normal distribution, you expect to be within 1.960 (approximately 2) standard deviations from the mean with probability 0.95.

The two-sided 95% confidence interval statement for the population mean goes as follows:

> We are 95% sure that the population mean, μ, is somewhere between $\overline{X} - t \times S_{\overline{X}}$ and $\overline{X} + t \times S_{\overline{X}}$, where t is taken from the t-table.

For a binomial situation (n large), this leads to the following interval:

> We are 95% sure that p is somewhere between $f - tS_f$ and $f + tS_f$, where t is taken from the t-table.

To achieve a confidence level other than 95%, simply substitute the appropriate t-value in the interval statement. The **t-table** is used to adjust for the added uncertainty due to the fact that an estimator (the standard error) is being used in place of the unknown exact variability for the population. When you work with a single sample of size n, your **degrees of freedom** number is $n - 1$, which represents the number of independent pieces of information in your standard error (because the average is subtracted when the standard deviation is computed). If the standard error is known exactly, use the t-value for an infinite number of degrees of freedom.

The two **assumptions required for the confidence interval** statement to be valid are (1) the data are a random sample from the population of interest, and (2) the quantity being measured is normally distributed. The first assumption ensures that the data properly represent the unknown parameter, and the second assumption forms the basis for the probability calculations underlying the t-table. In practice, because the confidence interval is based largely on the sample average, $\overline{X}$, the central limit theorem allows you to relax assumption 2 so that even for a moderately skewed distribution, the assumption will be satisfied provided the sample size is large enough.

The reason we say 95% sure or 95% confident is that once the numbers have been computed for the confidence interval, they are not random anymore; the event that has probability 0.95 must include the randomness of the sampling process. The relative frequency interpretation is that if you were to repeat the sampling process over and over, computing a confidence interval each time, about 95% of the random, known intervals would include the fixed, unknown population mean. Similarly, your lifetime track record for confidence intervals computed under correct assumptions should include about 95% successes (that is, intervals containing the unknown parameter) and about 5% mistakes. However, you will not generally know which ones were right and which were wrong!

A **one-sided confidence interval** specifies with known confidence that the population mean is either *at least* or *no larger than* a computed number. You compute the endpoint of the one-sided confidence interval in the same way as for the two-sided interval, except for substituting the one-sided t-value for the two-sided value, and choosing the endpoint so that your one-sided interval includes the sample average, $\overline{X}$. To use a one-sided interval, you must be sure that *no matter how the data had come out* you would still have used a one-sided interval on the same side (above or below). Otherwise your confidence interval statement may not be valid. If in doubt, use a two-sided interval. The one-sided confidence interval statements take the following form:

> We are 95% sure that the population mean is *at least as large as* $\overline{X} - t_{\text{one-sided}} \times S_{\overline{X}}$.

or

> We are 95% sure that the population mean is *no larger than* $\overline{X} + t_{\text{one-sided}} \times S_{\overline{X}}$.

The **prediction interval** allows you to use data from a sample to predict a new observation with known probability, provided you obtain this additional observation in the same way as you obtained your data. The uncertainty measure to use is the **standard error for prediction,** $S \times \sqrt{1 + 1/n}$, a measure of variability of the distance between the sample average and the new observation. The prediction interval is then constructed in the same way as a confidence interval; simply substitute the standard error for prediction for the standard error of the average. The prediction interval formula for a new observation (two-sided) is:

We are 95% sure that the new observation will be between $\overline{X} - t \times S\sqrt{1 + 1/n}$ and $\overline{X} + t \times S\sqrt{1 + 1/n}$.

The prediction intervals for a new observation (one-sided) are:

We are 95% sure that the new observation will be at least $\overline{X} - t_{\text{one-sided}} \times S\sqrt{1 + 1/n}$.

or

We are 95% sure that the new observation will be no larger than $\overline{X} + t_{\text{one-sided}} \times S\sqrt{1 + 1/n}$.

Prediction intervals at levels other than 95% are available by selecting the appropriate t-value from the table. Remember that the confidence interval tells you about the population mean, whereas the prediction interval tells you about a new, single observation selected at random from the same population.

Key Words

statistical inference 297
confidence interval 297
confidence level 298
t-table 301
degrees of freedom 301

assumptions required for the
   confidence interval 311
one-sided confidence interval 317
prediction interval 321
standard error for prediction 321

Questions

1 What is statistical inference?

2 What does a confidence interval tell you about the population?

3 Which fact about a normal distribution leads to the factor 2 (or 1.960) in the generic confidence interval statement?

4 Why is it correct to say, "We are 95% sure that the population mean is between $15.85 and $19.36" but wrong to say, "The probability is 0.95 that the population mean is between $15.85 and $19.36"?

5 Why does the t-table give numbers larger than 1.960 for a two-sided 95% confidence interval?

6 a. How many degrees of freedom are there for a single sample of size n?
   b. What accounts for the degree of freedom lost?
   c. How many degrees of freedom should you use if the standard error is known exactly?

7 a. What confidence levels other than 95% are in common use?
   b. What would you do differently to compute a 99% confidence interval instead of a 95% interval?
   c. Which is larger, a two-sided 90% confidence interval or a two-sided 95% confidence interval?

8 a. Describe the two assumptions needed for the confidence interval statement to be valid.
   b. For each assumption, give an example of what could go wrong if it weren't satisfied.
   c. How does the central limit theorem help satisfy one of these assumptions?
   d. Under what circumstances would the central limit theorem not guarantee that the second assumption is satisfied?

9 a. What is the relative frequency interpretation of the correctness of a confidence interval?
   b. What is the "lifetime track record" interpretation of the correctness of many confidence intervals?

10 a. Why must a one-sided confidence interval always include the sample average?
   b. Must a one-sided confidence interval always include the population mean?

11 a. What additional criterion must be satisfied for a one-sided confidence interval to be valid (in addition to the two assumptions needed for a two-sided confidence interval).
   b. If in doubt, should you use a one-sided or a two-sided confidence interval?

12 a. What is the difference between a prediction interval and a confidence interval?
   b. Which type of interval should you use to learn about the mean spending habits of your typical customer?
   c. Which type of interval should you use to learn about the spending habits of an individual customer?

13 a. What is the standard error for prediction?
   b. Why is the standard error for prediction even larger than S?

14 a. What would you change in the computation of a two-sided 95% prediction interval to find a two-sided 99% prediction interval instead?
   b. What would you change in the computation of a two-sided 95% prediction interval to find a one-sided 95% prediction interval instead?
   c. What would you change in the computation of a two-sided 95% prediction interval to find a one-sided 90% prediction interval instead?

Problems

1 Find the appropriate t-value for each of the following situations:
   a. A two-sided 95% confidence interval based on the intensity of 14 flashlights.
   b. A one-sided 95% confidence interval based on 35 cost measurements.
   c. A two-sided 99.9% confidence interval based on people's responses in 1,859 tests of a new vaccine.

d. A one-sided 90% confidence interval based on the taste preferences of 23 restaurant diners.

e. A two-sided 99% confidence interval when the standard error is known exactly.

2 Table 9.6.1 shows the 1987 performance of stocks recommended by securities firms.

TABLE 9.6.1 Performance of Stocks Recommended by Securities Firms*

Firm	Performance
Thomson McKinnon	15.8%
Shearson Lehman	5.5
Prudential-Bache	4.7
Merrill Lynch	2.9
Drexel Burnham	2.5
A.G. Edwards	1.2
PaineWebber	0.4
E.F. Hutton	0.3
Dean Witter	−2.8
Kidder Peabody	−7.1

*From Dorfman, J.R., "Do Brokers' Stock Picks Perform Well?" *The Wall Street Journal*, February 5, 1988, p. 17.

a. Compute the average, and briefly describe its meaning.

b. Compute the standard deviation, and briefly describe its meaning.

c. Compute the standard error of the average, and briefly describe its meaning.

d. Find the two-sided 95% confidence interval for the mean performance of stocks recommended by similar brokerage firms during this time period, viewing the data set as a random sample from this idealized population.

e. Find the two-sided 90% confidence interval, and compare it to the 95% confidence interval.

f. Find the one-sided 99% confidence interval statement to the effect that the mean performance was *at least* as good as some number.

g. Suppose you decide that, had the data come out with an average performance loss, you would have used a one-sided confidence interval statement that the mean performance was *no larger than* some number (in place of your answer to part f). In this case, and using the same data table, is your answer to part f a valid confidence interval statement? Why or why not? If not, what should you do instead?

3 An election poll shows your favorite candidate ahead with 52.4% of the vote, based on interviews with 921 randomly selected people.

a. Find the two-sided 95% confidence interval for the percentage of the population in favor of your candidate.

b. Since this candidate has been your favorite for a long time now, and you want her to win, you are interested only in knowing that she has *at least* some percentage of the votes. In this case, would it be valid to make a one-sided confidence interval statement?

c. Find the one-sided 95% confidence interval that is appropriate, given the information in part b.

d. Find the similarly appropriate one-sided 90% confidence interval.

e. Write a brief paragraph describing how these confidence intervals shed important light on your candidate's chances. In particular, how much more do you know now as compared to knowing only the 52.4% figure?

4 A market survey has shown that people will spend an average of $2.34 each for your product next year, based on a sample survey of 400 people. The standard deviation of the sample was $0.72. Find the two-sided 95% confidence interval for next year's mean expenditure per person in the larger population.

5 A survey of your customers shows, to your surprise, that 42 out of 200 randomly selected customers were not satisfied with after-sale support and service.

   a. Find the summary statistics: the sample size, n; the sample percentage, f; and the standard error, S_f.

   b. Find the two-sided 95% confidence interval for the percent dissatisfied among *all* of your customers (i.e., not just those surveyed).

   c. Your population consists of 28,209 customers. Convert the percentages representing the endpoints of the confidence interval in part b to numbers of people in the population. State and interpret your result as a confidence interval for the population *number* of dissatisfied customers.

6 A sample of 93 coils of sheet steel showed that the average length was 101.37 meters, with a standard deviation of 2.67 meters.

   a. Interpret the standard deviation in words; in particular, what is it measuring the variability of?

   b. Find the standard error. Interpret this number in words, and distinguish it from the standard deviation you explained in part a.

   c. Find the two-sided 95% confidence interval for the mean length of coils in the larger population. Write a brief paragraph explaining its meaning.

   d. Find the two-sided 95% prediction interval for the length of the next coil to be produced. Write a brief paragraph explaining its meaning, and distinguish this prediction interval from the confidence interval you found for part c. In particular, why is the prediction interval so much wider than the confidence interval?

   e. Your integrity requires that you guarantee coils to be *at least* a certain length. Does this information make it appropriate for you to compute one-sided intervals? Why or why not?

   f. Find the appropriate one-sided 99% confidence interval, and explain its meaning.

   g. Find the appropriate one-sided 99% prediction interval, and explain its meaning.

7 As a basis for a brochure describing the speed of a new computer system, you have measured how long it takes the machine to complete a particular benchmark database program. Since the state of the disks in the database is constantly changing as records are added, changed, and deleted, there is some variation in the test results. Here are times, in minutes, for 14 independent repetitions of this testing procedure:

   5, 6, 8, 11, 5, 8, 11, 10, 6, 10, 5, 9, 5, 5

   a. Find the two-sided 95% confidence interval, and describe its meaning in terms of the long-run mean performance of the system.

   b. Find the appropriate one-sided 95% confidence interval, assuming you wish to show off how fast the system is (so that lower numbers are better).

   c. Find the appropriate one-sided 90% and one-sided 99% confidence intervals.

   d. Write a brief paragraph for an advertising brochure describing one (or more) of the preceding results. Be honest, but put your "best foot forward," and write in ordinary English. Include a technical footnote if necessary so that technically knowledgeable people can tell what you really did.

8 Samples of rock taken from various places in a proposed mine have been analyzed. For each sample, a "rate of return" number has been computed that represents the profit obtained (by selling the refined metal at the current market price) as a percentage of the cost of extraction. This measure reflects the difficulty in removing the ore, the difficulty in processing it, and the yield of the finished product, all in meaningful economic terms. You may assume that the samples were drawn at random and represent the conditions under which actual production would take place, if it is economically viable. Economic viability will require that the return be high enough to justify the costs of operation. For the 13 samples obtained, the rates of return were as follows:

8.1%, 6.2%, 19.8%, −4.3%, 5.1%, 0.2%, −10.4%, 11.8%, 2.0%, 4.7%, −3.2%, 8.9%, −6.2%

a. Find the summary statistics: n, the average, the standard deviation, and the standard error. Write a brief paragraph describing the situation as if you were explaining it to the board of directors.

b. Identify the population and the population mean. Why is the population mean important to the management and owners of the proposed mine?

c. Find the appropriate one-sided 99% confidence interval. Write a brief paragraph summarizing its meaning.

d. Write a brief paragraph outlining the situation and making recommendations on possible action to top management.

9 You are concerned about waste in the newspaper publishing process. Up to now, no measurements have been taken, although it is clear that frequent mistakes often require many pounds of newsprint to be thrown away. To judge the severity of the problem and to help you decide if action is warranted, you have begun collecting data. You will take action only if the amount of waste is large enough. So far, on 27 selected mornings, the weight of wastepaper has been recorded. The average is 273.1 pounds per day, with a standard deviation of 64.2 pounds.

a. Is it appropriate for you to compute a one-sided confidence interval for this situation? Why or why not?

b. Find the most useful one-sided 99% confidence interval. Why did you choose the side you did?

c. Express your confidence interval in terms of pounds per year, assuming operations continue 365 days per year.

d. Find a one-sided 99% prediction interval for tomorrow's waste. Compare and contrast this result to your confidence interval in part b.

10 So far at your new job, you have landed nine sales contracts with an average price of $3,782 and a standard deviation of $1,290.

a. Identify a reasonable idealized population that this sample represents.

b. If the distribution of sales prices is heavily skewed, would it be appropriate to construct the usual two-sided 95% confidence interval? Why or why not?

c. Assume now that the distribution of sales prices is only slightly skewed and not too different from a normal distribution. Compute the usual 95% confidence interval, and interpret it carefully in terms of your long-term prospects at this job. Be sure to address both the useful information and the limitations of the confidence interval in this situation.

d. Find the two-sided 90% prediction interval for the sales price of the next contract you land, assuming that conditions will remain essentially unchanged.

11 A random sample of 50 recent patient records at a clinic shows that the average billing per visit was $53.01 and the standard deviation was $16.48.
   a. Find the 95% confidence interval for the mean, and interpret it.
   b. Find the 99% confidence interval.
   c. Find the one-sided 95% confidence interval specifying *at least* some level of billing.

12 Find the 95% confidence interval for the amounts that your regular customers spent on your products last month, viewing the data from problem 2 of Chapter 4 as a random sample of customer orders.

13 Find the 95% confidence interval for the strength of cotton yarn used in a weaving factory based on the data in problem 10 of Chapter 4.

14 Find the 95% confidence interval for the weight of candy bars before intervention, based on the data in problem 10 of Chapter 5.

15 Find the one-sided 95% confidence interval for the weight of candy bars after intervention, based on the data in problem 10 of Chapter 5, indicating that the population mean weight is *no more than* some amount.

16 From a list of the 729 people who went on a cruise, 25 were randomly selected for interview. Of these, 21 said that they were very happy with the accommodations. Find the 95% confidence interval for the population percentage who would have said they were very happy with the accommodations.

Database Exercises

Refer to the employee database in Appendix A.

1 View this database as a population. Consider the following random sample of five employee numbers from this database: 24, 54, 27, 34, and 53.
   a. Find the average, standard deviation, and standard error for annual salary based on this sample.
   b. Find the 95% confidence interval for the population mean salary.
   c. Draw a graph in the style of Figure 9.1.2 indicating the sample average and confidence interval.

2 (Continue the previous problem, but look now at the entire population, which you can't usually do in real life.)
   d. Find the population mean and standard deviation, and compare them to the sample estimates.
   e. Draw a graph for this situation in the style of Figure 9.1.1. Be sure to use $\sigma_{\bar{x}}$ as the standard deviation of the sampling distribution.
   f. Is the population mean in the confidence interval in this case? Will it *always* be in the interval, for all random samples? Why or why not?

3 Repeat exercise 1, parts b and c, using a 99% confidence interval. Is the population mean annual salary in the interval?

4 Repeat exercise 1, parts b and c, using a 99.9% confidence interval. Is the population mean annual salary in the interval?

5 Repeat exercise 1 using a 95% confidence interval for a different random sample: employee numbers 4, 47, 45, 12, and 69. Also, answer the following:
   d. In real life, what (if anything) could you do about the fact that the population mean is not in the confidence interval?

    e. Also compute 99% and 99.9% intervals. At what confidence level (if any) is the confidence interval large enough to include the population mean?

6 Consider the following random sample of 15 employee numbers from this database: 66, 37, 56, 11, 32, 23, 53, 43, 55, 25, 7, 26, 36, 22, and 20.

    a. Find the percentage of women for this sample.

    b. Find the standard error for the percentage of women and interpret it.

    c. Find the 95% and 99% confidence intervals for the population percentage of women.

7 (Continue the previous problem, but look now at the entire population, which you can't usually do in real life.)

    d. Find the population percentage of women, and compare it to your sample estimate.

    e. Draw a graph for this situation in the style of Figure 9.1.1. Be sure to use σ_f as the standard deviation of the sampling distribution.

    f. Is the population mean in the confidence interval in this case?

8 Viewing the database in Appendix A as a random sample from a much larger population of employees:

    a. Find the 95% confidence interval for the population mean annual salary.

    b. Find the 95% confidence interval for the population mean age.

    c. Find the 95% confidence interval for the population mean experience.

    d. Find the 95% confidence interval for the population percentage of women.

    e. Find the 95% confidence interval for the population percentage who are advanced (at training level B or C).

9 Repeat the previous exercise using 99% confidence.

10 Viewing the database in Appendix A as a random sample from a much larger population of employees:

    a. Find the 95% one-sided confidence interval for the population mean annual salary specifying that salaries are *at least* some amount.

    b. Find the 99% one-sided confidence interval for part a.

    c. Find the 95% one-sided confidence interval for the population mean experience specifying that salaries are *at least* some amount.

    d. Find the 99% one-sided confidence interval for part c.

11 View the database in Appendix A as a random sample from the idealized population of potential employees you might hire next.

    a. Find the 95% prediction interval for the experience of your next hire. Why is this interval so much wider than the confidence interval for the population mean experience?

    b. Find the 95% prediction interval for the age of your next hire.

Projects

1 Obtain an estimated value and its standard error (either from data or by educated guess) for each of *two* situations important to your business interests. For each case, find a confidence interval, and write a sentence interpreting it. Explain your reasons if you use a confidence level other than 95% or if you use a one-sided confidence interval.

2 Obtain an estimated value and a standard deviation (either from data or by educated guess) for each of *two* situations important to your business interests. For each case, find a prediction interval, and write a sentence interpreting it. Explain your reasons if you use a prediction level other than 95% or if you use a one-sided prediction interval.

3 Find a report of an opinion poll in a newspaper. Write a paragraph summarizing one of their results. Be sure to mention sample size, the percentage, and the standard error. Compute your own two-sided 95% confidence interval. Compare your results to the margin of error, if this is reported in the newspaper article.

Hypothesis Testing
Deciding between Reality and Coincidence

Oh no. Not again. Your high-pressure sales contact is on the line, trying to sell you that miracle yield-enhancing additive to increase the productivity of your refinery. It looks like a good deal, but you're just not sure. You've been trying it out for a week (free, of course, for now), and—sure enough—the yield is up. But it's not up a whole lot, and, naturally, the process is variable, so it's hard to tell whether there's anything important going on or not. What you need is an objective assessment, but you know that what you'll get from your contact on the phone is just another sales pitch: "The yield is up, isn't it? Well, what did I tell you? If you sign up today, we'll throw in a free engraved pen-and-pencil set! Blah blah blah." So you give the secret signal to your secretary, who says that you're in a meeting just now and will call back later.

Here's what's troubling you. Sure, the yield is up. But even if you do nothing special at all, you know that the yield fluctuates from day to day and from week to week about its long-run mean value. So the yield is up for one of two reasons: either the additive is really working, or it's just a coincidence. After all, regardless of the additive, there's about a 50–50 chance that the week's yield would be higher than the long-term mean and about a 50–50 chance for it to be lower.

Look at it from the salesperson's point of view. Suppose for a moment that the additive is actually worthless and has no effect whatsoever on the yield. Next, convince managers at 100 different companies to try it out for a week. About 50 of these managers will find that their yield went down—no need to follow those up. But the other 50 or so will find slightly higher yields. Maybe some of these will even pay big money to continue using this worthless product.

What you need is a way of using the information gathered so far about the yield to help you determine if (on the one hand) it could reasonably be *just coincidence* that the yield was higher last week or if (on the other hand) you have convincing evidence that the additive really works. This is what hypothesis testing can help you do.

Hypothesis testing uses data to decide between two possibilities (called *hypotheses*).[1] It can tell you whether the results you're witnessing are just coincidence (and could reasonably be due to chance) or are likely to be real. Some people think of hypothesis testing as a way of using statistics to make decisions. Taking a broader view, an executive might look at hypothesis testing as *one component* of the decision-making process. Hypothesis testing by itself probably shouldn't be used to tell you whether to buy a product or not; nonetheless, it provides critically important information about how substantial and effective the product is.

■ 10.1 Hypotheses Are Not Created Equal!

A **hypothesis** is a statement about how the world is. It is a statement about the *population*. A hypothesis is not necessarily true; it can be either right or wrong, and you use the sample data to help you decide. When you know everything, there is no need for statistical hypothesis testing. When there is uncertainty, statistical hypothesis testing will help you learn as much as possible from the information available to you.

You will ordinarily work with a *pair* of hypotheses at a time. The data will help you decide which of the two will prevail. But the two hypotheses are not interchangeable; each one plays a different, special role.

The Null Hypothesis

The **null hypothesis,** denoted H_0, represents the *default* possibility that you will accept *unless you have convincing evidence to the contrary.* This is a very favored position. If your data are sketchy or too variable, you will end up accepting the null hypothesis because it has the "benefit of the doubt." In fact, you can end up accepting the null hypothesis without really proving anything at all, putting you in a fairly weak position. Thus, it can make an important difference which of your two hypotheses you refer to as the null hypothesis.

The null hypothesis is often the *more specific* hypothesis of the two. For example, the null hypothesis might claim that the population mean is exactly equal to some known reference value or that an observed difference is just due to random chance. To see that the hypothesis of random choice is

---

[1]The singular is one *hypothesis,* and the plural is two *hypotheses* (pronounced *"hypothesees"*).

indeed more specific, note that *non*random things can have very many different kinds of structure, but randomness implies a lack of structure.

The Research Hypothesis

The **research hypothesis,** denoted H_1, is to be accepted only if there is convincing statistical evidence that would rule out the null hypothesis as a reasonable possibility. The research hypothesis is also called the **alternative hypothesis.** Accepting the research hypothesis represents a much stronger position than accepting the null hypothesis because it requires convincing evidence.

People are often interested in establishing the research hypothesis as their hidden agenda, and they set up an appropriate null hypothesis solely for the purpose of refuting it. The end result would be to show that "it's not just random, and so here's my explanation..." This is an accepted way of doing research. Since people have fairly creative imaginations, the research community has found that by requiring that the null hypothesis of pure randomness be rejected before publication of a research finding, they can effectively screen many wild ideas that have no basis in fact. This does not *guarantee* that all research results are true, but it does screen out many incorrect ideas.

In deciding which hypothesis should be the research hypothesis, ask yourself, Which one has the *burden of proof*? That is, determine which hypothesis requires the more convincing evidence before you decide to believe in it. This one will be the research hypothesis. Don't neglect your own self-interest! Feel free to shift the burden of proof onto those trying to sell you things. Make them prove their claims!

What Will the Result Tell You?

There are two possible outcomes of a hypothesis test. By convention, they are described as follows:

FAIL TO REJECT

■ Results of a Hypothesis Test		
Either:	~~Accept~~ the null hypothesis, H_0. FTR	A weak conclusion; not a significant result.
Or:	Reject the null hypothesis, H_0, and accept the research hypothesis, H_1.	A strong conclusion; a significant result.

Note that we *never* speak of rejecting the research hypothesis. This is because of the favored status of the null hypothesis as default. Accepting the null hypothesis merely implies that you don't have enough evidence to decide against it.

It may help you to think of the hypotheses in terms of a criminal legal case. The null hypothesis is "innocent" and the research hypothesis is "guilty." Since our legal system is based on the principle of "innocent until proven guilty," this assignment of hypotheses makes sense. Accepting the null hypothesis of innocence says that there was not enough evidence to convict; it does not prove that the person is truly innocent. On the other hand, rejecting the null hypothesis and accepting the research hypothesis of guilt says that there is enough evidence to rule out innocence as a possibility and to convincingly establish guilt. We do not have to rule out guilt in order to find someone innocent, but we do have to rule out innocence in order to find someone guilty.

Examples of Hypotheses

Following are some examples of null and research hypotheses about the population. Note in each case that they cannot both be true, and that the data will be used to decide which one to accept.

1 *The situation:* A randomly selected group of 200 people view an advertisement, and the number of people who buy the product during the next week is recorded.
   The null hypothesis: The ad has no effect. That is, the percentage of buyers among those in the general population who viewed the ad is *exactly equal* to the baseline rate for those who did *not* view the ad in the general population. This baseline rate is known to be 19.3%, based on extensive past experience.
   The research hypothesis: The ad has an effect. That is, the percentage of buyers among those in the general population who viewed the ad is *different from* the baseline rate of 19.3% representing those buyers who did *not* view the ad in the general population.
   Discussion: Note that these hypotheses are statements about the general *population,* not about the 200 people in the sample. The sample evidence accumulated by observing the behavior of 200 randomly selected people will help decide which hypothesis to accept. Since the null hypothesis gives an exact value for the percentage, it is more specific that the research hypothesis, which specifies a large range (i.e., any percentage different from 19.3%). Also note that when you decide that an ad is effective, you will be making a strong statement since this is the research hypothesis. It is as if you are saying "OK. If this ad works as well as we all think it does, let's give it a chance to prove it to us. Or, on the other hand, if it will be a disaster to sales, let's find that out also."
2 *The situation:* You are evaluating the yield-enhancing additive described at the start of this chapter.
   The null hypothesis: The additive has no effect on the long-run yield, an amount known from past experience.

The research hypothesis: The additive has some effect on the long-run yield.

Discussion: The null hypothesis is more specific. Both hypotheses refer to the population (long-run yield) and not just to the particular results of last week (the sample). Your default is that the additive has no effect, and to convince you otherwise will require a conclusive demonstration. The burden of proof is on them (the manufacturers of the additive) to show effectiveness. It's not up to you to prove to them that it's *not* effective.

3 *The situation:* Your firm is being sued for gender discrimination, and you are evaluating the documents filed by the other side. They include a statistical hypothesis test, based on salaries of men and women, that finds a "highly significant difference" on average between men's and women's salaries.

The null hypothesis: Men's and women's salaries are equal except for random variation. That is, the actual salary differences between men and women are not unreasonably different from what you might get if you were to put all salaries into a hat, mix them up well, and deal them out to people without regard to gender.

The research hypothesis: The difference between men's and women's salaries is larger than random chance could reasonably account for.

Discussion: Note the use of an idealized population here. Since these employees are not a random sample in any real sense, the hypotheses refer to an idealized population that is identical in terms of the numbers of men and women and equal in terms of salaries, differing only in the random allocation of salaries to people. Your firm is in trouble since the null hypothesis has been rejected and the research hypothesis has been accepted. This is a strong conclusion that goes against you. But all is not necessarily lost. Don't forget that statistical methods generally tell you about the numbers only and not about *why* the numbers are this way. The salary differential might be due directly to gender discrimination, or it might be due to other factors, such as education, experience, and ability. A statistical hypothesis test that addresses only gender and salary cannot tell which factors are responsible.[2] Also, the hypothesis test results could be wrong, since errors can happen whenever statistical methods are used.

■ 10.2 Testing the Population Mean against a Known Reference Value

The simplest case of hypothesis testing involves testing the population mean against a known reference value. This **reference value** is a known, fixed number μ_0 that does not come from the sample data. The hypotheses are as follows:

---

[2]In a later chapter you will learn how *multiple regression* can adjust for other factors (such as education and experience) and can provide an *adjusted estimate* of the effect of gender on salary while holding these other factors constant.

$$H_0: \mu = \mu_0$$

The null hypothesis claims that the unknown population mean, μ, is *exactly equal* to the known reference value, μ_0.

$$H_1: \mu \neq \mu_0$$

The research hypothesis claims that the unknown population mean, μ, is *not equal* to the known reference value, μ_0.

This is a **two-sided test** because the research hypothesis includes values for the population mean μ on both sides (smaller and larger) of the reference value, μ_0.[3] Note that there are actually *three* different numbers involved here that have something to do with an average or mean value:

μ is the unknown population mean, which you are interested in learning about.

μ_0 is the known reference value you are testing against.

$\overline{X}$ is the known sample average you will use to decide which hypothesis to accept. Of these three numbers, this is the only one that is at all random because it is computed from the sample data. Note that $\overline{X}$ estimates, and hence represents μ.

The hypothesis test proceeds by comparing the two known numbers $\overline{X}$ and μ_0 against each other. If they are more different than random chance could reasonably account for, then the null hypothesis $\mu = \mu_0$ will be rejected because $\overline{X}$ provides information about the unknown mean, μ. If $\overline{X}$ and μ_0 are fairly close to each other, then the null hypothesis $\mu = \mu_0$ will be accepted. But how close is close? Where will we draw the line? Closeness must be based on $S_{\overline{X}}$, since this standard error tells you about the randomness in $\overline{X}$. Thus, if $\overline{X}$ and μ_0 are a sufficient number of standard errors apart, then you have convincing evidence against μ being equal to μ_0.

There are two different ways of carrying out the hypothesis test and getting the results. The first method uses confidence intervals, which were covered in the last chapter. This is the easier method because (a) you already know how to construct and interpret a confidence interval and (b) the confidence interval is directly meaningful because it is in the same units as your data (e.g., dollars, people, defect rates). The second method (based on the *t*-statistic) is more traditional but less intuitive since it requires that you calculate something new that is not in the same units as your data and that must be compared to the appropriate critical value from the *t*-table before you know the result.

---

[3]You will learn about *one-sided* hypothesis testing in Section 10.4.

It really doesn't matter which of the two methods (confidence interval or *t*-statistic) you use for hypothesis testing since they always give the same answer in the end. You may want to use the confidence interval method most of the time since it is quicker, easier, and provides more information about the situation. However, you will also want to know how to use the *t*-statistic method because it is so commonly used in practice. Since the two methods give the same result, either one may be called a *t-test*.

Using Confidence Intervals: The Easy Way

Here is how to test the null hypothesis H_0: $\mu = \mu_0$ against the research hypothesis H_1: $\mu \neq \mu_0$ based on a random sample from the population. First construct the 95% confidence interval based on $\overline{X}$ and $S_{\overline{X}}$ in the usual way (see Chapter 9). Then look to see whether the reference value, μ_0, is in the interval or not. If μ_0 is outside the confidence interval, it is not a reasonable value for the population mean, μ, and you will accept the research hypothesis; otherwise you will accept the null hypothesis. This is illustrated in Figure 10.2.1. There are a number of equivalent ways of describing the result of such a hypothesis test. Your decision in each case may be stated as indicated in Table 10.2.1.

Why does this method work? Remember that the confidence interval statement says that the probability that μ is in the (random) confidence interval is 0.95. Assume for a moment that the null hypothesis is true, so that $\mu = \mu_0$ exactly. Then the probability that μ_0 is in the confidence interval is also 0.95. This says that when the null hypothesis is true, you will make the correct decision in approximately 95% of all cases and be wrong only about

FIGURE 10.2.1   A hypothesis test for the population mean is decided based on the confidence interval. The question is whether or not the population mean could reasonably be equal to a given reference value. If the reference value is in the interval, then it is reasonably possible. If the reference value is outside the interval, then you would decide that it is not the population mean.

TABLE 10.2.1

If the reference value, μ_0, is in the confidence interval from $\overline{X} - tS_{\overline{X}}$ to $\overline{X} + tS_{\overline{X}}$, then:

Accept the null hypothesis, H_0.

Do not accept the research hypothesis, H_1.

The sample average, $\overline{X}$, is *not significantly different* from the reference value, μ_0.

The observed difference between the sample average, $\overline{X}$, and the reference value, μ_0, could reasonably be due to random chance alone.

The result is *not statistically significant*.

(All of the preceding statements are equivalent.)

If the reference value, μ_0, is *not* in the confidence interval from $\overline{X} - tS_{\overline{X}}$ to $\overline{X} + tS_{\overline{X}}$, then:

Accept the research hypothesis, H_1.

Reject the null hypothesis, H_0.

The sample average, $\overline{X}$, is *significantly different* from the reference value, μ_0.

The observed difference between the sample average, $\overline{X}$, and the reference value, μ_0, could not reasonably be due to random chance alone.

The result is *statistically significant*.

(All of the preceding statements are equivalent.)

5% of the time. In this sense you now have a decision-making process with exact, controlled probabilities. For a more detailed discussion of the various types of errors in hypothesis testing, see Section 10.3.

EXAMPLE

Does the "Yield-Increasing" Additive Really Work?

Recall the (supposedly) yield-increasing additive you were considering purchasing at the start of this chapter. Suppose that the basic facts of the matter are as shown in Table 10.2.2. Your data set consists of $n = 7$ observations of the yield taken while the additive was in use. Your population therefore should be all possible daily yields using the additive; in particular, the population mean, μ, should

TABLE 10.2.2 | Basic Facts for the "Yield-Increasing" Additive

Average daily yield over the past week	$\overline{X}$	39.6 tons
Standard error	$S_{\overline{X}}$	4.2 tons
Sample size	n	7 days
Your known mean daily long-term yield (without additive)	μ_0	32.1 tons

be the long-term mean yield achieved while using the additive (this is unknown and therefore not listed in the table). The sample average, $\overline{X}$, provides your best estimate of μ.

Indeed, it looks as if the additive is working well. The average daily yield achieved with the additive ($\overline{X} = 39.6$ tons) is 7.5 tons higher than the mean daily long-term yield ($\mu_0 = 32.1$ tons) you expect without the additive. This is no surprise. In hypothesis testing, the reference value is (almost) never *exactly* equal to the observed value ($\overline{X}$ here). The question is if they are more different than random chance alone would reasonably allow. A histogram of the data, with the sample average and the reference value indicated, is shown in Figure 10.2.2.

In preparation for hypothesis testing, you identify the hypotheses, which may be stated directly in terms of the known value, $\mu_0 = 32.1$ tons. (There is no reason to continue to use the symbolic notation μ_0 instead of its known value in the formal hypothesis statements.) The hypotheses are as follows:

$H_0: \mu = 32.1$ tons

The null hypothesis claims that the unknown long-term mean daily yield with the additive, μ, is exactly *equal* to the known reference value, $\mu_0 = 32.1$ tons (without the additive).

$H_1: \mu \neq 32.1$ tons

The research hypothesis claims that the unknown long-term mean daily yield with the additive, μ, is *not equal* to the known reference value, $\mu_0 = 32.1$ tons (without the additive).

FIGURE 10.2.2 A histogram of the seven yields obtained with the additive. The sample average summarizes the available data and is higher than the reference value. But is it significantly higher? The result of a hypothesis test will tell whether this sample histogram *could reasonably have come* from a population distribution whose mean is the reference value.

Next, to facilitate the hypothesis test, compute the confidence interval in the usual way using $t = 2.447$ from the t-table for $n - 1 = 6$ degrees of freedom:

> We are 95% sure that the long-term mean daily yield with the additive is somewhere between 29.3 and 49.9 tons.

Finally, to perform the actual hypothesis test, simply check whether the reference value, $\mu_0 = 32.1$ tons, is in the confidence interval or not.[4] It is in the interval because 32.1 is indeed between 29.3 and 49.9. That is, $29.3 \leq 32.1 \leq 49.9$ is a true statement. Your hypothesis test result is therefore as shown in Table 10.2.3.

The sample average daily yield with the additive, $\overline{X} = 39.6$ tons, is not significantly different from the long-term mean daily yield without the additive, $\mu_0 = 32.1$ tons. This result is inconclusive and ambiguous. You do not have convincing evidence in favor of the additive. When you next talk to the high-pressure sales contact who is trying hard to sell you the stuff, you'll have the confidence to say that *even though the yield is up, it is not up significantly,* and you are not yet convinced that the additive is worthwhile.

Does this test prove that the additive is ineffective? No. It *might* be effective; you just don't have convincing evidence one way or the other.

What else might be done to resolve the issue? Your sales contact might suggest that you use it for another month—free of charge, of course—to see if the additional information will be convincing enough. Or you might suggest this to your contact, if you have the nerve.

EXAMPLE   Employee Stock Ownership and Product Quality

There are many ways to achieve product quality. One way is to give employees more of a stake in the outcome of their work. According to this theory, em-

---

TABLE 10.2.3   Since the reference value, $\mu_0 = 32.1$ tons, is in the confidence interval from 29.3 to 49.9 tons:

Accept the null hypothesis, H_0: $\mu = 32.1$ tons.

Do *not* accept the research hypothesis, H_1: $\mu \neq 32.1$ tons.

The sample average yield, $\overline{X} = 39.6$, is *not significantly different* from the reference value, $\mu_0 = 32.1$.

The observed difference between the sample average yield, $\overline{X} = 39.6$, and the reference value, $\mu_0 = 32.1$, could reasonably be due to random chance alone.

The result is *not statistically significant.*

(All of the preceding statements are equivalent.)

---

[4] It would be silly to check whether $\overline{X}$ is in the interval or not, since, of course, $\overline{X}$ will always be in the confidence interval. The question here is if the known *reference value,* μ_0, is in the confidence interval.

ployees who own part of the company will have a direct payoff (higher dividend income or higher stock value) as a result of their high-quality products. This would give workers the incentive to improve quality on their own.

A study was conducted to find out how managers of 343 firms view the effectiveness of various kinds of employee relations programs.[5] Note that this study does not measure the effectiveness of these programs; instead it measures managers' *perceptions* of their effectiveness. Nonetheless, given that many managers have first-hand experience with how these plans work, these results should be interesting and useful.

Each of the 343 managers rated the effect of employee stock ownership on product quality using a scale from -2 to 2, where -2 signifies "large negative effect" and 2 signifies "large positive effect." The resulting average score was $\overline{X} = 0.35$, with a standard error of $S_{\overline{X}} = 0.14$:

Perceived Effect of Employee Stock Ownership on Product Quality (Scale from -2 to 2)

Average score	$\overline{X}$	0.35
Standard error	$S_{\overline{X}}$	0.14
Sample size	n	343

A reasonable question is, Do managers in general view employee stock ownership as a worthwhile technique for improving product quality? The answer will be found by performing a hypothesis test. Why not just use the fact that the average score was 0.35 to say that managers obviously consider it useful? Because this is a result for a *sample* of managers, and it may or may not represent the larger population of managers in general. In order to infer the views of managers in general based on the average from a sample, we will use a hypothesis test.

Since we will want to be convinced before concluding that employee stock ownership is viewed as worthwhile, this has the burden of proof and will be the research hypothesis. The null hypothesis will claim that ownership has no effect. If we define μ to be the mean score for the larger population of managers for firms similar to those sampled, the hypotheses are as follows:

$$H_0: \mu = 0$$

The null hypothesis claims that the unknown mean score, μ, that managers in general would give is exactly *equal* to the known reference value, $\mu_0 = 0$.

$$H_1: \mu \neq 0$$

The research hypothesis claims that the unknown mean score, μ, that managers in general would give is *not equal* to the known reference value, $\mu_0 = 0$.

[5]P. B. Voos, "Managerial Perceptions of the Economic Impact of Labor Relations Programs," *Industrial and Labor Relations Review* 40 (1987), pp. 195–208.

TABLE 10.2.4	Since the reference value, $\mu_0 = 0$, is not in the confidence interval from 0.08 to 0.62:
	Accept the research hypothesis, H_1: $\mu \neq 0$.
	Reject the null hypothesis, H_0: $\mu = 0$.
	The sample average score, $\overline{X} = 0.35$, is *significantly different* from the reference value, $\mu_0 = 0$.
	The observed difference between the sample average score, $\overline{X} = 0.35$, and the reference value, $\mu_0 = 0$, could not reasonably be due to random chance alone.
	The result is *statistically significant*.
	(All of the preceding statements are equivalent.)

Next, to facilitate the hypothesis test, compute the confidence interval in the usual way using $t = 1.960$ from the t-table:

We are 95% sure that the mean score for managers in general is somewhere between 0.08 and 0.62.

Finally, to perform the hypothesis test, simply check whether the reference value $\mu_0 = 0$ is in the interval or not. It is *not* in the interval because 0 is not between 0.08 and 0.62. Your t-test result is therefore as shown in Table 10.2.4.

Based on the reported opinions of managers, employee stock options have a *statistically significant positive effect* on product quality.[6] This result is conclusive. You do have convincing evidence that managers in general consider employee stock options to be effective in achieving product quality. Even though the score may be relatively small (0.35 on a scale from -2 to 2), the consensus of managers is that such options are indeed helpful.

Does this test absolutely prove that, if the larger population of managers were interviewed, the resulting mean score would be positive? Not really. Absolute proof is generally impossible in the presence of even a small amount of randomness. You have convincing evidence but not absolute proof. This says that you might be making an error in accepting the research hypothesis here (although it is not very likely). These ever-present errors will be discussed in Section 10.3.

EXAMPLE   **Pushing the Limits of Production (a Binomial Situation)**

One of the mysteries of producing electronic computer chips is that you can't tell for sure how good the results are until you test them. At that point, you find that some are unacceptable, others are fine, and some are especially good.

---

[6]You may claim a *positive* effect because (1) the result is statistically significant and (2) the effect as measured by $\overline{X}$ is positive (i.e., $\overline{X}$ is a positive number).

These especially good ones are separated and sold at a premium as "extra fast" because they process information more quickly than the others.

Your goal has been to improve the production process to the point where more than 10% of the long-run production can be sold as extra-fast chips. Based on a sample of 500 recently produced chips, you plan to perform a hypothesis test to see if the 10% goal has been exceeded, if you are far short, or if it's too close to call.

Because of recent improvements to the production process, you are hopeful. There were 58 extra-fast chips, giving an estimated rate of 11.6%, which exceeds 10%. But did you *significantly* exceed the goal, or were you just lucky? You'd like to know before celebrating.

Let's model this as a binomial situation in which each chip is either extra fast or not. The binomial probability p represents the probability of being extra fast. The sample size is $n = 500$, the observed count is $X = 58$, and the sample proportion is $f = 11.6\%$. The reference value is $p_0 = 10\%$.

Hypothesis testing for a binomial (with sufficiently large n) is really no different from testing with quantitative data. After all, in each case you have an estimate ($\overline{X}$ or f), a standard error ($S_{\overline{X}}$ or S_f), and a reference value (μ_0 or p_0). Here are the formal hypothesis statements for this binomial situation:

$$H_0: p = 10\%$$

The null hypothesis claims that extra-fast chips represent 10% of production.

$$H_1: p \neq 10\%.$$

The research hypothesis claims that the rate is different from 10%: either higher (Hooray! Time to celebrate!) or lower (Uh-oh, time to make some adjustments).

The 95% confidence interval is computed in the usual way for a binomial, based on the standard error $S_f = \sqrt{f(1 - f)/n} = 0.0143$ and 1.960 from the t-table. The interval is found to extend from 8.8% to 14.4%:

> You are 95% sure that extra-fast chips are being produced at a rate somewhere between 8.8% and 14.4% of total production.

Finally, to perform the hypothesis test, simply see whether the reference value $p_0 = 10\%$ is in the interval or not. It *is* in the interval because 10% is between 8.8% and 14.4%. Your t-test result is therefore as shown in Table 10.2.5.

The observed rate of production of extra fast chips is not statistically significantly different from 10%. You do not have enough information to tell whether the rate is conclusively either higher or lower. The result is inconclusive. Although 11.6% looked like a good rate (and actually exceeds the goal of 10%), it is not significantly different from the goal. Since 11.6% may be just randomly different

TABLE 10.2.5	Since the reference value, $p_0 = 10\%$, is in the confidence interval from 8.8% to 14.4%:

Accept the null hypothesis, H_0: $p = 10\%$.

Do not accept the research hypothesis, H_1: $p \neq 10\%$.

The sample proportion, $f = 11.6\%$, is *not significantly different* from the reference value, $p_0 = 10\%$.

The observed difference between the sample proportion, $f = 11.6\%$, and the reference value, $p_0 = 10\%$, could reasonably be due to random chance alone.

The result is *not statistically significant*.

(All of the preceding statements are equivalent.)

from the 10% goal, you do not have strong evidence that the goal has been reached.

Remember that you are doing statistical inference. You're not just interested in these particular 500 chips. You'd like to know about the long-run production rate for many more chips, with the machinery running as it is now. Statistical inference has told you that the rate is so close to 10% that you can't tell whether or not the goal has been reached yet.

You might decide to collect more data from tomorrow's production to see if the added information will allow you to show that the goal has been reached (by accepting the research hypothesis, you hope, with an observed *higher than* 10%). On the other hand, rather than just squeak by, you might want to hedge your bets by instituting some more improvements.

The *t*-Statistic: Another Way, Same Answer

Another way to carry out a two-sided test for a population mean is to first compute the *t*-statistic, which is defined as $(\overline{X} - \mu_0)/S_{\overline{X}}$, and then use the *t*-table to decide which hypothesis to accept. The answer will always be the same as from the confidence interval method, so it doesn't matter which method you use. The hypothesis testing procedure for comparing the population mean to a reference value based on $\overline{X}$ and $S_{\overline{X}}$ (using either method) is called **Student's *t*-test** or simply the ***t*-test**. The name *Student* was used by W. S. Gossett, chief brewer for Guinness, when he published the first paper to use the *t*-table (which he invented) in place of the normal probability table, correcting for the use of the sample standard deviation, S, in place of the unknown population standard deviation, σ, when the sample size, n, is small.[7]

---

[7]Student, "The Probable Error of a Mean," *Biometrika* 6 (1908), pp. 1–25.

In general, hypothesis tests proceed by first computing a number called a **test statistic** based on the data that provides the best information for discriminating between the two hypotheses. Next this test statistic (e.g., the t-statistic) is compared to the appropriate **critical value** taken from a standard table of critical values (e.g., the t-table) to determine which hypothesis should be accepted. In situations that are more complex than just testing a population mean, it can require some creative effort (1) to come up with a test statistic that uses the sample information most efficiently and (2) to find the appropriate critical value. Either this critical value is found by theory (as is the case with the t-table), or, increasingly in modern times, powerful computers are used to create a new, special critical value for each particular situation.

There are two different values referred to as t. The **critical t-value** is the number t_{table} found in the t-table and does not reflect the sample data in any way. The **t-statistic**, on the other hand, is the test statistic and represents how many standard errors there are separating μ_0 and $\overline{X}$:

■ The t-Statistic

$$t_{statistic} = \frac{\overline{X} - \mu_0}{S_{\overline{X}}}$$

The t-test uses both of these numbers, comparing the t-statistic computed from the data to the t-value found in the t-table. The result of the test is as stated in Table 10.2.6.

The *absolute value* of a number, denoted by enclosing the number between two vertical bars, is defined by removing the minus sign, if any. For example, $|3| = 3$, $|-17| = 17$, and $|0| = 0$. A useful rule of thumb is that if the t-statistic is larger in absolute value than 2, reject the null hypothesis; otherwise accept it. This would apply when n is larger than 40, using 2 as an approximation to the t-value of 1.960. It is thus easy to scan a column of t-statistics and tell which are significant. For example, 6.81, -4.97, 13.83, 2.46, and -5.81 are significant t-statistics, whereas 1.23, -0.51, 0.02, -1.86, and 0.75 are not significant t-statistics. (A negative value for the t-statistic tells you that the sample average, $\overline{X}$, is smaller than the reference value, μ_0.)

You might wonder what to do if the t-statistic is *exactly equal* to the t-value in the t-table. This would happen when μ_0 falls exactly at an endpoint of the confidence interval. How would you decide? Fortunately, this almost never happens. You might compute more decimal digits to decide, or you might conclude that your result is "significant, but just borderline."

Although the t-statistic may be easily compared to the value 2 (or to the more exact number from the t-table) to decide significance, remember that it is not in the same measurement units as the data. Since the measurement units in the numerator and denominator of the t-statistic cancel each other,

TABLE 10.2.6	If the *t*-statistic is *smaller* in absolute value than the *t*-value from the *t*-table ($|t_{\text{statistic}}| < t_{\text{table}}$):

Accept the null hypothesis, H_0.

Do *not* accept the research hypothesis, H_1.

The sample average, $\overline{X}$, is *not significantly different* from the reference value, μ_0.

The observed difference between the sample average, $\overline{X}$, and the reference value, μ_0, could reasonably be due to random chance alone.

The result is *not statistically significant*.

(All of the preceding statements are equivalent.)

If the *t*-statistic is *larger* in absolute value than the *t*-value from the *t*-table ($|t_{\text{statistic}}| > t_{\text{table}}$):

Accept the research hypothesis, H_1.

Reject the null hypothesis, H_0.

The sample average, $\overline{X}$, is *significantly different* from the reference value, μ_0.

The observed difference between the sample average, $\overline{X}$, and the reference value, μ_0, could *not* reasonably be due to random chance alone.

The result is *statistically significant*.

(All of the preceding statements are equivalent.)

the result is a pure number without measurement units. It represents the distance between $\overline{X}$ and μ_0 in *standard errors* rather than in dollars, miles per gallon, people, or whatever units your data set represents.

Other than this, there is nothing really different between the *t*-statistic and confidence interval approaches. To verify this, reconsider the preceding two examples.

For the example of the "yield-increasing" additive, the sample average is $\overline{X} = 39.6$ tons, the standard error is $S_{\overline{X}} = 4.2$ tons, the sample size is $n = 7$, and the reference value is $\mu_0 = 32.1$ tons. The reference value *is* in the confidence interval, which extends from 29.3 to 49.9. Based on this, you accept the null hypothesis. If you had computed the *t*-statistic instead, you would have found:

$$t_{\text{statistic}} = \frac{\overline{X} - \mu_0}{S_{\overline{X}}}$$

$$= \frac{39.6 - 32.1}{4.2}$$

$$= 1.785714$$

Since the absolute value of the t-statistic, 1.785714, is less than the t-table value of 2.447, you accept the null hypothesis. Thus, the t-statistic approach gives the same end result as the confidence interval approach.

For the example of the effect of employee stock ownership on product quality, the sample average score is $\overline{X} = 0.35$, the standard error is $S_{\overline{X}} = 0.14$, the sample size is $n = 343$, and the reference value is $\mu_0 = 0$. The reference value *is not* in the confidence interval, which extends from 0.08 to 0.62. Based on this, you accept the research hypothesis. Had you computed the t-statistic instead, you would have found:

$$t_{\text{statistic}} = \frac{\overline{X} - \mu_0}{S_{\overline{X}}}$$

$$= \frac{0.35 - 0}{0.14}$$

$$= 2.50$$

Since the absolute value of the t-statistic, 2.50, is greater than the t-table value of 1.960, you accept the research hypothesis. The t-statistic approach gives you the same end result as the confidence interval approach, as it always must do.

10.3 Interpreting a Hypothesis Test

Now that you know the mechanics involved in performing a hypothesis test and conventional ways to describe the result, it is time to learn the probability statement behind it all. Just as in the case of confidence intervals, since it is not possible to be correct 100% of the time, you end up with a statement involving the unknown population mean that is correct 95% (or 90%, or 99%, or 99.9%) of the time.

By convention, the formal details of hypothesis testing are set up in terms of the various *errors* that can be made. The result of a hypothesis test is acceptance of one of the hypotheses based on information from the sample data. You might be right and you might be wrong since the hypotheses are statements about the *population*, for which you have incomplete information. Generally, you will not know for sure if you are right or wrong in your choice. Of course, you hope that you are correct; however, depending on the situation, there may or may not be a useful probability statement to reassure you.

Each type of error is based on a different assumption about which hypothesis is *really* true. Of course, in reality, you won't ordinarily know which hypothesis is true, even after you've made a decision to accept one. However, to understand the results of your hypothesis test, it is helpful to put it in perspective with respect to all of the different ways the test could have come out.

Errors: Type I and Type II

If the null hypothesis is really true (even though, in reality, you won't know for sure if it is or not) but you wrongly decide to reject it and accept the research hypothesis instead, then you have committed a **type I error,** pronounced "type one error". The probability of a type I error occurring (when the null hypothesis is true) is controlled by convention at the 5% level:

$$P(\text{type I error when } H_0 \text{ is true}) = 0.05$$

It is possible to control the probability of a type I error because the null hypothesis is very specific, so there is an exact probability. For example, when you assume that the null hypothesis $H_0 : \mu = \mu_0$ is true, you are assuming that you know the value of the population mean. Once you know the population mean, probabilities can be easily calculated.

Testing at other levels (10%, 1%, or 0.1%, say) can be done by using a different t-value from the t-table—for example, by working with a different confidence interval (90%, 99%, or 99.9%, respectively). If you are not willing to be wrong 5% of the time when the null hypothesis is true, you might test at the 1% level instead (using the appropriate value in the t-table column with 2.576 at the bottom) so that your probability of committing a type I error (when the null hypothesis is true) would only be 1%.

If the research hypothesis is really true (even though, again, you won't usually know for sure if it is or not), but you wrongly decide to accept the null hypothesis instead, you have committed a **type II error.** The probability of a type II error occurring cannot be easily controlled:

$$P(\text{type II error when } H_1 \text{ is true}) \text{ is not easily controlled}$$

It is difficult to control the probability of a type II error because, depending on the true value of μ, this probability will vary.[8] Suppose μ is very close to μ_0. Then, due to randomness in the data, it will be very difficult to tell them apart. For example, suppose the null hypothesis claims that μ is 15.00000, but μ is actually 15.00001. Then, although the research hypothesis is technically true (since $15.00000 \neq 15.00001$), in practical terms you will have much trouble telling them apart and the probability of a type II error will be approximately 95%. On the other hand, if μ is far from 15, the probability of a type II error will be nearly 0, a pleasing situation. Thus, since the probability of a type II error depends so heavily on the true value of μ, it is difficult to control. These errors are illustrated in Figure 10.3.1.

Assumptions Needed for Validity

You may have already suspected that some assumptions must be satisfied for the results of the hypothesis test to be valid. Since the test can be done

---

[8]In principle, the probability can be computed for each value for μ. The resulting table or graph provides the basis for what is called the *power* of the test. This is basically a *what if* analysis, giving the type II error properties of the test under each possible value of μ.

FIGURE 10.3.1 Your decision to accept one of the two hypotheses may or may not be correct. Depending on which hypothesis is really true, there are two types of errors. Only the type I error is easily controlled, conventionally at the 5% level.

Your Decision

	Accept null hypothesis	Accept research hypothesis
Null hypothesis	Correct decision	Type I error (controlled at level 0.05 or other level)
Research hypothesis	Type II error (not easily controlled)	Correct decision

based on the confidence interval, the assumptions for hypothesis testing are the same as the assumptions needed for confidence intervals. The **assumptions for hypothesis testing** are (1) the data set is a random sample from the population of interest, and (2) either the quantity being measured is approximately normal, or else the sample size is large enough that the central limit theorem ensures that the sample average is approximately normally distributed.

What happens if these assumptions are not satisfied? Consider the probability of a type I error (wrongly rejecting the null hypothesis when it is actually true). This error probability will no longer be controlled at the low, manageable level of 5% (or other claimed level of your choice). Instead, the true error probability could be much higher or lower than 5%. A finding of significance then loses much of its prestige since the event "wrongly finding significance" is now a more common occurrence.

If the data set is not a random sample from the population of interest, there is essentially nothing that statistics can do for you because the required information is just not in the data.

Suppose your data set is a random sample, but the distribution is not normal. If your data distribution is so far from normal that you are concerned, you might try transforming the data (for example, using logarithms if all numbers are positive) to obtain a more normal distribution. If you decide to transform, note that you would no longer be testing the mean of the population but the mean of the *logarithm* of the population instead. Another solution would be to use a nonparametric test, to be explained in Chapter 16.

Hypotheses Have No Probabilities of Being True or False

Perhaps you've noticed that we have never said that a hypothesis is "probably" either true or false. We've always been careful either to accept or to reject a hypothesis, making a definite, exact decision each time. We talk about the errors we might make and *their* probabilities, but never about the probability of a hypothesis being true or false. The reason is simple:

There is nothing random about a hypothesis!

The null hypothesis is either true or false, depending on the value of the population mean, μ. There is no randomness involved in the population mean by itself. Similarly, the research hypothesis is also either true or false, and although you do not know which, there is no randomness involved in the hypothesis itself. The randomness comes only from the random sampling process, which gives you the data to help you decide.

Thus, your *decision* is known and random, just like a sample statistic, since it is based on the data. However, the true hypothesis is fixed but unknown, just like a population parameter.

Statistical Significance, Test Levels, and *p*-Values

By convention, a result is defined to be **statistically significant** if you accept the research hypothesis using a test at the 5% level, for example, based on a standard 95% confidence interval. Note that this is probably not the same use of the word *significant* that you are used to. Ordinarily, something "significant" has special importance. This is not necessarily so in statistics.

To illustrate, a lawyer once came to me deeply concerned because the other side in a lawsuit had found a *statistically significant difference* between measurements made on a door that had been involved in an accident and other, similar doors in the same building. Oh no! But after the special statistical meaning of the word *significant* was pointed out, the attorney was relieved to find that the other side had *not* shown that the door was extremely different from the others. They had only demonstrated that there was a *statistically detectable* difference. In fact, the difference was quite small. But with enough careful measurements, it was detectable! It was not just randomly different from the other doors (the null hypothesis); it was systematically different (the research hypothesis). Although the difference was statistically significant, it was not large enough to matter very much. The situation is analogous to snowflakes; each one is truly different from the others, yet for many purposes they are essentially identical.

The moral of this story is that you should not automatically be impressed when someone boasts of a "significant result." If the word is being used in its statistical sense, it only says that random chance has been ruled out. It still remains to examine the data to see if the effect is strong enough to be important to you. Statistical methods work only with the numbers; it is up to you to use knowledge from other fields to decide the importance and relevance of the statistical results.

There is another reason you should not be overly impressed by statistically significant results. Over your lifetime, approximately 5% of the test results you will see *for situations in which the null hypothesis is really true* will be significant. This implies that about 1 in every 20 uninteresting situations will be declared significant by mistake (i.e., by type I error). A pharmaceutical researcher once noticed that about 5% of the drugs being tested for a particularly difficult disease were found to have a significant effect. Since this is about the fraction of drugs that would be found *by mistake* to be effective, *even if none were in fact effective,* this observation suggests that the entire program might not be successful in finding a cure.

Depending on which column you use in the *t*-table, you can perform a hypothesis test at the 10%, 5%, 1%, or 0.1% level. This **test level** or **significance level** is the probability of a type I error when the null hypothesis is in fact true.[9] When you reject the null hypothesis and accept the research hypothesis, you may claim that your result is *significant* at the 10%, 5%, 1%, or 0.1% level, depending on the *t*-table column you used. The smaller the test level for which you can find significance, the more impressive the result. For example, finding a result that is significant at the 1% level is more impressive than finding significance at the 10% or 5% level; your type I error probability is smaller and your evidence against the null hypothesis is stronger. By convention, the following phrases may be used to describe your results:

Not significant	Not significant at the conventional 5% level
Significant	Significant at the conventional 5% level
Highly significant	Significant at the 1% level
Very highly significant	Significant at the 0.1% level

What should you do if you find significance at more than one level? Celebrate! Seriously, however, the smaller the level at which you find significance, the stronger your evidence is against the null hypothesis. You would therefore report only the *smaller* of the significance levels for which you find significance. For example, if you find significance at both the 5% and 1% levels, it would be sufficient to report only that your result is highly significant.

---

[9]In more general situations, including one-sided testing, the test level or significance level is defined more carefully as the *maximum* type I error probability, maximized over all possibilities included within the null hypothesis.

Whenever you find significance at one level, you will necessarily find significance at all *larger* levels.[10] Thus, a highly significant result (i.e., significant at the 1% level) must *necessarily* (i.e., provably, using mathematics) be significant at the 5% and 10% levels. However, it might or might not be significant at the 0.1% level.

The **p-value** is defined as the *smallest* level for which your test is significant and represents the *probability of observing a difference as extreme as your sample (or more so) if the null hypothesis were actually true*. If you find a p-value of 0.01, then, *if the null hypothesis were true*, the probability would be 1 in 100 of seeing a difference as large or larger than that observed in the sample. Thus, a small p-value is an indication of evidence *against* the null hypothesis. By convention, the p-value is reported (somewhat cryptically) within parentheses as follows:

$(p > 0.05)$	Not significant	Not significant at the conventional 5% level
$(p < 0.05)$	Significant	Significant at the conventional 5% level but not at the 1% level
$(p < 0.01)$	Highly significant	Significant at the 1% level but not at the 0.1% level
$(p < 0.001)$	Very highly significant	Significant at the 0.1% level

In some fields of study, you are permitted to report a result that is significant at the 10% level. This represents an error probability of 1 in 10 of rejecting a null hypothesis that is really true; many other fields consider this an unacceptably high error rate. However, some fields recognize that the unpredictability and variability of their data make it difficult to obtain a (conventionally) significant result at the 5% level. If you are working in such a field, you may use the following p-value statement as a possible alternative:

$(p < 0.1)$	Significant at the 10% level but not at the conventional 5% level

A p-value statement is often found inserted into text, as in "The style of music was found to have a significant effect ($p < 0.05$) on purchasing behavior." You may also see p-value statements included as footnotes either to text or to a table, as in "Productivity improved significantly as a result of the new exercise program."[11]

---

[10]Note that a *larger* level of significance is actually a *less* impressive result. For example, being significant at the 1% level is highly significant, whereas being significant at the (larger) 5% level is merely significant.

[11]($p < 0.05$)

◼ 10.4 **One-Sided Testing**

All of the tests we have done so far are two-sided tests because they test the null hypothesis H_0: $\mu = \mu_0$ against the research hypothesis H_1: $\mu \neq \mu_0$. This research hypothesis is two-sided because it allows for possible values for the population mean both above and below the reference value, μ_0.

However, you may not really be interested in testing whether the population mean is *different* from the reference value. You may have a special interest in it being *larger* (in some cases) or *smaller* (in other cases) than the reference value. For example, you might purchase a system only if possible long-term savings are *significantly larger* than some special number (the reference value, μ_0). Or you might be interested in claiming that your quality is high because the defect rate is *significantly smaller* than some impressively small number.

You don't need to use a one-sided test to be able to claim that the sample average is significantly larger or significantly smaller than the reference value; you can always use a two-sided test for this. If the two-sided test comes out significant (i.e., you accept the research hypothesis), then you may base your claim of significance on whether the sample average, $\overline{X}$, is larger than or smaller than the reference value:

■ Using a Two-Sided Test but Reporting a One-Sided Conclusion[12]	
If the two-sided test is significant and $\overline{X} > \mu_0$	The sample average, $\overline{X}$, is significantly larger than the reference value, μ_0
If the two-sided test is significant and $\overline{X} < \mu_0$	The sample average, $\overline{X}$, is significantly smaller than the reference value, μ_0

However, it may be advantageous to use a one-sided test. If you meet the requirements, you might be able to report a significant result using a one-sided test that would not be significant had you used a two-sided test. How is this possible? By focusing on just one side and ignoring the other, the one-sided test can better detect a difference on that side. The trade-off is that the one-sided test is incapable of detecting a difference, no matter how large, on the other side.

A **one-sided t-test** is set up with the null hypothesis claiming that μ is on one side of μ_0 and the research hypothesis claiming that it is on the other side. (We always include the case of $\mu = \mu_0$ in the null hypothesis, which is the default. This ensures that when you accept the research hypothesis and find significance, you have a stronger conclusion: either "significantly larger

---

[12]Remember, the *two*-sided conclusion would be "$\overline{X}$ is significantly different from μ_0."

than" or "significantly smaller than."[13]) The hypotheses for the two different kinds of one-sided tests are as follows:

■ **One-Sided Testing to See if μ Is Smaller than μ_0**

$$H_0: \mu \geq \mu_0$$

The null hypothesis claims that the unknown population mean, μ, is *at least as large* as the known reference value, μ_0.

$$H_1: \mu < \mu_0$$

The research hypothesis claims that the unknown population mean, μ, is *smaller* than the known reference value, μ_0.

■ **One-Sided Testing to See if μ Is Larger than μ_0**

$$H_0: \mu \leq \mu_0$$

The null hypothesis claims that the unknown population mean, μ, is *not larger* than the known reference value, μ_0.

$$H_1: \mu > \mu_0$$

The research hypothesis claims that the unknown population mean, μ, is *larger* than the known reference value, μ_0.

There is an important criterion you must satisfy before using a one-sided hypothesis test; it is essentially the same criterion that must be met for a one-sided confidence interval:

> In order to use a one-sided test, you must be sure that *no matter how the data had come out,* you would still have used a one-sided test on the same side ("larger than" or "smaller than") as you will use. If, had the data come out different, you might have used a one-sided test *on the other side* instead of the side you plan to use, you should use a two-sided test instead. If in doubt, use a two-sided test.

In particular, using a one-sided test can leave you open to criticism. Since the decision of what's interesting can be a subjective one, your decision to focus only on what's interesting to you may conflict with the opinions of others you want to convince. If you need to convince people who have a "hostile" attitude (for example, regulators or opposing lawyers), you should

---

[13]Technically speaking, the case of equality could be included in the research hypothesis. However, the mechanics of the test would be identical and significance would be found in exactly the same cases, but your conclusion would seem weaker.

consider using a two-sided test and giving the one-sided conclusion. On the other hand, if you need only convince "friendly" people, with interests similar to yours (for example, within your department or firm), and you satisfy the preceding criterion, you will want to take advantage of one-sided testing.

The guiding principle to help you through the details that follow is that the research hypothesis will be accepted only if there is convincing evidence against the null hypothesis. This says that you will accept the research hypothesis only when the sample average, $\overline{X}$, and the reference value, μ_0, have the same relationship as described in the research hypothesis *and* are far enough apart (namely, t_{table} or more standard errors apart, which represents the extent of reasonable variation from a mean value). The two different ways to implement a one-sided test, namely, using one-sided confidence intervals and the one-sided t-test, will now be described.

Using a One-Sided Confidence Interval

You can perform each of the one-sided tests using the one-sided confidence intervals you have learned about. Remember that there are two different one-sided confidence interval statements. You want to choose the one that matches the side of the claim of the research hypothesis. For example, if your research hypothesis is $H_1: \mu > \mu_0$, your one-sided confidence interval will consist of all values for μ that are *at least as large* as the appropriate computed number, $\overline{X} - t_{\text{table}} \times S_{\overline{X}}$, using the one-sided t-value from the t-table.

EXAMPLE   Launching a New Product

Suppose a break-even analysis for a new consumer product suggests that it will be successful if more than 23% of consumers are willing to try it. This 23% is the reference value, μ_0; it comes from a theoretical analysis, not from a random sample of data. To decide whether to launch the product or not, you have gathered some data from randomly selected consumers and have computed a one-sided confidence interval. Based just on the data, you expect 44.1% of consumers to try it ($\overline{X} = 44.1\%$), and your confidence interval statement is that you are 95% sure that *at least* 38.4% of consumers will be willing to try it. Since your break-even point, $\mu_0 = 23\%$, is well outside of this confidence interval (and, hence, it is *not* reasonable to suppose that the mean could be 23%), you do have convincing evidence that the population mean is greater than 23%. A summary of the situation is shown in Table 10.4.1.[14]

---

[14]Because this is a binomial situation, you may substitute f in place of $\overline{X}$, S_f in place of $S_{\overline{X}}$, p in place of μ, and p_0 in place of μ_0 throughout. To see that this example is also correct as stated here, note that $\overline{X} = f$ for the data set $X_1, X_2, \ldots, X_n$ where each number is either 0 or 1 according to the response of each consumer.

TABLE 10.4.1   Testing the Percentage of Consumers Who Are Willing to Try a New Product (Confidence Interval Approach)

Null hypothesis Research hypothesis	$H_0: \mu \leq \mu_0$ $H_1: \mu > \mu_0$	$H_0: \mu \leq 23\%$ $H_1: \mu > 23\%$
Average Standard error Sample size Reference value	$\overline{X}$ $S_{\overline{X}}$ n μ_0	44.1% 3.47% 205 23%
Confidence interval	$\overline{X} - t_{\text{table}} \times S_{\overline{X}}$	"We are 95% sure that population mean is at least 38.4%"
Decision	Accept H_1	"We expect significantly more than 23% of consumers to try our product"*

*Significant ($p < 0.05$) using a one-sided test.

The decision is made to accept H_1 because the reference value is not in the confidence interval (i.e., 23% is not "at least 38.4%").

Since the reference value, 23%, is so far below the confidence interval, you should try for a more impressive significance level. In fact, you can claim 99.9% certainty that the population mean is at least 33.4% using the t-table value 3.090 for this one-sided confidence interval. Since the reference value, 23%, is outside even this confidence interval, the result is very highly significant ($p < 0.001$).

How to Perform the Test

The preceding example demonstrated the ideas involved in executing a one-sided t-test. Table 10.4.2 shows a complete list of what to do in each case, including both types of conclusions (significant, not significant) and both types of one-sided hypothesis testing situations (looking for significantly larger, looking for significantly smaller). As always, the guiding principle is that it's significant if the reference value, μ_0, is *not* within the one-sided confidence interval matching the research hypothesis.

Figure 10.4.1 shows that in order for you to find $\overline{X}$ significantly larger than μ_0, the distance between them must be sufficiently large to ensure that it is not just due to random chance. Figure 10.4.2 gives the corresponding picture for a one-sided test on the other side.

The One-Sided t-Test: Another Way, Same Answer

Another way to carry out a one-sided t-test is to first compute the t-statistic and then use the one-sided critical values in the t-table to decide which hypothesis to accept. This procedure will always give you the same answer

FIGURE 10.4.1   Using a one-sided test to see if μ is larger than the reference value, μ_0. The one-sided confidence interval uses the same side as the research hypothesis (namely, those reasonably possible values of μ that are at least as large as the endpoint value of the interval). Only if the reference value, μ_0, is well below the sample average will you decide that the sample average is significantly larger.

FIGURE 10.4.2   Using a one-sided test to see if μ is smaller than the reference value, μ_0. The one-sided confidence interval uses the same side as the research hypothesis (namely, those reasonably possible values of μ that are smaller than or equal to the endpoint value of the interval). Only if μ_0 is well above the sample average will you decide that the sample average is significantly smaller.

you would find using the confidence interval approach. Recall that the t-statistic is

$$t_{\text{statistic}} = \frac{\overline{X} - \mu_0}{S_{\overline{X}}}$$

The t-statistic represents how far $\overline{X}$ is above μ_0 with respect to the randomness of the situation. Note that the t-statistic is positive whenever the sample

TABLE 10.4.2 One-Sided Testing to See if μ Is Larger than μ_0

The hypotheses being tested are H_0: $\mu \leq \mu_0$ against H_1: $\mu > \mu_0$.

The confidence interval statement is "We are 95% sure that the population mean is *at least* as large as $\overline{X} - t_{\text{table}} \times S_{\overline{X}}$."

If the reference value, μ_0, is in the confidence interval extending from $\overline{X} - t_{\text{table}} \times S_{\overline{X}}$ to all larger values:

Accept the null hypothesis, H_0.

Do *not* accept the research hypothesis, H_1.

The sample average, $\overline{X}$, is *not significantly larger* than the reference value, μ_0.

If $\overline{X}$ is larger than μ_0, the observed difference could reasonably be due to random chance alone.

The result is *not statistically significant*.

If the reference value, μ_0, is *not* in the confidence interval extending from $\overline{X} - t_{\text{table}} \times S_{\overline{X}}$ to all larger values:

Accept the research hypothesis, H_1.

Reject the null hypothesis, H_0.

The sample average, $\overline{X}$, is *significantly larger* than the reference value, μ_0.

The observed difference between the sample average, $\overline{X}$, and the reference value, μ_0, could *not* reasonably be due to random chance alone.

The result is *statistically significant*.

---

average, $\overline{X}$, exceeds the reference value, μ_0, and negative when the sample average is smaller than μ_0.

You use the same *t*-statistic for one- and two-sided testing. The difference is in how you proceed after computing it. Basically, you will find a significant result whenever it looks as if the research hypothesis might be true (i.e., $\overline{X}$ is either above or below μ_0, according to the claim of the research hypothesis) *and* the absolute value of the *t*-statistic is larger than the one-sided *t*-value from the *t*-table.

EXAMPLE **Launching a New Product, Revisited**

For the consumer product launch example considered earlier, the launch will be profitable only if more than 23% of consumers try the product. The appropriate facts and results are as shown in Table 10.4.3.

TABLE 10.4.2 **(concluded)** One-Sided Testing to See if μ Is Smaller than μ_0

The hypotheses being tested are H_0: $\mu \geq \mu_0$ against H_1: $\mu < \mu_0$.

The confidence interval statement is "We are 95% sure that the population mean is not larger than $\overline{X} + t_{table} \times S_{\overline{X}}$."

If the reference value, μ_0, is in the confidence interval extending from $\overline{X} + t_{table} \times S_{\overline{X}}$ to all smaller values:

Accept the null hypothesis, H_0.

Do *not* accept the research hypothesis, H_1.

The sample average, $\overline{X}$, is *not significantly smaller* than the reference value, μ_0.

If $\overline{X}$ is smaller than μ_0, the observed difference could reasonably be due to random chance alone.

The result is *not statistically significant*.

If the reference value, μ_0, is *not* in the confidence interval extending from $\overline{X} + t_{table} \times S_{\overline{X}}$ to all smaller values:

Accept the research hypothesis, H_1.

Reject the null hypothesis, H_0.

The sample average, $\overline{X}$, is *significantly smaller* than the reference value, μ_0.

The observed difference between the sample average, $\overline{X}$, and the reference value, μ_0, could *not* reasonably be due to random chance alone.

The result is *statistically significant*.

TABLE 10.4.3 Testing the Percentage of Consumers Who Are Willing to Try a New Product (*t*-Statistic Approach)

Null hypothesis	H_0: $\mu \leq \mu_0$	H_0: $\mu \leq 23\%$
Research hypothesis	H_1: $\mu > \mu_0$	H_1: $\mu > 23\%$
Average	$\overline{X}$	44.1%
Standard error	$S_{\overline{X}}$	3.47%
Reference value	μ_0	23%
t-statistic	$t_{statistic} = \dfrac{\overline{X} - \mu_0}{S_{\overline{X}}}$	$\dfrac{44.1 - 23}{3.47} = 6.08$
Critical value	$t_{one\text{-}sided}$	1.645
Decision	Accept H_1	"We expect significantly more than 23% of consumers to try our product"*

*Significant ($p < 0.05$) using a one-sided test.

The decision is made to accept H_1 because the data favor H_1 (i.e., 44.1% > 23%) and the absolute value of the t-statistic, 6.08, exceeds the t-table value, 1.645.

In the end, the result is the same (i.e., significant) whether you use the one-sided confidence interval or the one-sided t-test. In fact, since the t-statistic exceeds even the one-sided t-table value (3.090) for testing at level 0.001, you may claim a *very highly significant* result ($p < 0.001$).

How to Perform the Test

The preceding example showed the ideas involved in executing a one-sided t-test using the t-statistic. Table 10.4.4 shows a complete list of what to do in each case, including both types of conclusions (significant, not significant) and both types of one-sided hypothesis-testing situations (looking for significantly larger, looking for significantly smaller). Again, the guiding principle is that it's significant only if (1) the relationship between $\overline{X}$ and μ_0 supports the research hypothesis and (2) the absolute value of the t-statistic exceeds the one-sided t-value in the t-table.

EXAMPLE   ## Will Costs Go Down?

You have tested a new system that is supposed to reduce the *variable cost* or *unit cost* of production (i.e., the cost of producing each extra unit, ignoring fixed costs such as rent, which would be the same whether you produced the extra unit or not). Since the new system would involve some expenditures, you will be willing to use it only if you can be convinced that the variable cost will be less than $6.27 per unit produced.

Based on a careful examination of 30 randomly selected units that were produced using the new system, you found an average variable cost of $6.05. It looks as if your variable cost is, on average, less than the target of $6.27. But is it *significantly* less? That is, can you expect the long-run mean cost to be below $6.27, or is this just a random fluke of the particular 30 units you examined? Based on the information so far, you cannot say because you don't yet know how variable the process is. Is $6.05 less than $6.27? Yes, of course. Is $6.05 *significantly* less than $6.27? You can only tell by comparing the difference to the randomness of the process, using the standard error and the t-table.

So you go back and find the standard deviation, and then you compute the standard error, $0.12. Table 10.4.5 shows a summary of the situation and the results of a one-sided test (with both methods shown) of whether or not your costs are significantly lower than the required amount.

Using the confidence interval approach, you are 95% sure that the mean variable cost is less than $6.25. You are even more sure that it is less than the required amount, $6.27. Hence, the result is significant. Or you could simply note that the reference value ($6.27) is not in the confidence interval, which extends only up to $6.25.

TABLE 10.4.4 The One-Sided *t*-Test to See if μ Is *Larger* than μ_0

The hypotheses being tested are $H_0: \mu \leq \mu_0$ against $H_1: \mu > \mu_0$.

If $\overline{X} < \mu_0$ or $|t_{statistic}| < t_{table}$:

Accept the null hypothesis, H_0.

Do *not* accept the research hypothesis, H_1.

The sample average, $\overline{X}$, is *not significantly larger* than the reference value, μ_0.

If $\overline{X}$ is larger than μ_0, the observed difference could reasonably be due to random chance alone.

The result is *not statistically significant*.

If $\overline{X} > \mu_0$ and $|t_{statistic}| > t_{table}$:

Accept the research hypothesis, H_1.

Reject the null hypothesis, H_0.

The sample average, $\overline{X}$, is *significantly larger* than the reference value, μ_0.

The observed difference between the sample average, $\overline{X}$, and the reference value, μ_0, could *not* reasonably be due to random chance alone.

The result is *statistically significant*.

One-Sided Testing to See if μ Is *Smaller* than μ_0

The hypotheses being tested are $H_0: \mu \geq \mu_0$ against $H_1: \mu < \mu_0$.

If $\overline{X} > \mu_0$ or $|t_{statistic}| < t_{table}$:

Accept the null hypothesis, H_0.

Do *not* accept the research hypothesis, H_1.

The sample average, $\overline{X}$, is *not significantly smaller* than the reference value, μ_0.

If $\overline{X}$ is smaller than μ_0, the observed difference could reasonably be due to random chance alone.

The result is *not statistically significant*.

If $\overline{X} < \mu_0$ and $|t_{statistic}| > t_{table}$:

Accept the research hypothesis, H_1.

Reject the null hypothesis, H_0.

The sample average, $\overline{X}$, is *significantly smaller* than the reference value, μ_0.

The observed difference between the sample average, $\overline{X}$, and the reference value, μ_0, could *not* reasonably be due to random chance alone.

The result is *statistically significant*.

TABLE 10.4.5 **Testing the Long-Run Variable Cost**

Reference value	μ_0	$6.27
Null hypothesis	$H_0: \mu \geq \mu_0$	$H_0: \mu \geq \$6.27$
Research hypothesis	$H_1: \mu < \mu_0$	$H_1: \mu < \$6.27$
Average	$\bar{X}$	$6.05
Standard error	$S_{\bar{X}}$	$0.12
Sample size	n	30
Confidence interval	$\bar{X} + t_{table} \times S_{\bar{X}}$	"You are 95% sure that the long-run mean variable cost is less than $6.25"
t-statistic	$t_{statistic} = \dfrac{\bar{X} - \mu_0}{S_{\bar{X}}}$	$\dfrac{6.05 - 6.27}{0.12} = -1.833$
Critical value	t_{table}	1.699
Decision	Accept H_1	"Variable costs under the new system are significantly less than $6.27"*

*Significant ($p < 0.05$) using a one-sided test.

Using the t-statistic approach, you note that since the sample average favors the research hypothesis (6.05 < 6.27), and since the t-statistic is larger in absolute value than the critical value from the t-table ($|-1.833| = 1.833 > 1.699$), the result is significant.

You are entitled to use a one-sided test in this case because you are really interested in just that one side. If you can be convinced that the mean variable cost is less than $6.27, then the system is worth considering. If not, then you are not interested. By using a one-sided test in this way, you are admitting that, had the system been really bad, you would not have been able to say that "variable costs are significantly *more than* ..."; you would only be able to say that "they are *not significantly less.*"

Had you decided to use a two-sided test, which is valid but less efficient, you would actually have found that the result is *not* significant! The two-sided confidence interval extends from $5.80 to $6.30, which *does* contain the reference value. The t-statistic is still -1.833, but the two-sided t-value from the table is 2.045, which is now larger than the absolute value (1.833) of the t-statistic. Thus, this example shows that you can have a significant one-sided result but a nonsignificant two-sided result. This can happen only when the one-sided significance is borderline, passing the test with just a small margin, as in this example.

Should you buy the system? This is a business strategy question, not a statistical question. Use the results of the hypothesis test as one of your inputs, but consider all the other factors, such as availability of investment capital, personnel implications, and interactions with other projects. And don't forget this: Although hypothesis testing has led you to accept the research hypothesis that the variable costs are less than your threshold, this has *not* been absolutely proven; there is still room for error. You can't give a number for the probability that your hypothesis testing decision is wrong because you don't know which hypothesis is really true. The best you can say is that *if* the new system has variable costs of exactly $6.27, then you would wrongly decide significance (as you may have here) only 5% of the time.

Can You Create Value by Changing Your Firm's Name?

When a large firm changes its name, it's a major event. The budgets for advertising the change of name and for setting up the new image can be enormous. Why do firms do it? According to the theory of financial budgeting, firms should undertake only projects that increase the value of the firm to the owners, the shareholders. If it is reasonable for a firm to spend those resources to change its name, then you should observe an increase in the firm's value as measured by the price of its stock.

A study of the change in firm value around the time of the announcement of a name change might use a one-sided statistical hypothesis test to see if the stock price really did go up. One of the difficulties of measuring this kind of market price reaction is that the stock market as a whole responds to many forces, and the name change should be evaluated in light of what the stock price did compared to what it "should have done" based on the entire stock market during that time. So if the stock market was up, you would have to find the firm's stock up *an even larger percentage* than you would ordinarily expect on such a day before deciding that the announcement has had an effect.

This kind of *event study,* using an adjustment for large-scale market forces, involves computing an *abnormal return,* which represents the rate of return an investor would have received by holding the firm's stock, minus the rate of return the investor would have expected from an investment of similar risk (but involving no name change) during the same time period.

Thus, a positive abnormal return would show that the name change caused a price rise even larger than we would have expected in the absence of the name change. This could happen because the stock market was generally up and the firm's stock was up much more. Or it could happen because the stock market was down but the firm's stock was down less than expected given the market as a whole.

One study looked at 58 corporations that changed their names from 1981 to 1985.[15] The researchers reported their methods as follows:

> In order to test if [the abnormal return due to the name change] is different from zero, the test statistic employed is the ratio of the average abnormal returns...to their standard deviation.... This test statistic...is distributed standard normal if *n* is large enough.

They are saying that they have used a *t*-statistic to test the sample average against the reference value, $\mu_0 = 0$, of no abnormal returns due to a name

---

[15]D. Horsky and P. Swyngedouw, "Does It Pay to Change Your Company's Name? A Stock Market Perspective," *Marketing Science* 6 (1987), 320–35.

change. The "standard deviation" they refer to is the standard error of this estimated quantity. Since their sample size is large enough, the t-table values (for $n =$ infinity) are the same as the standard normal values.

The results of this study were given as follows:

> The mean abnormal return was found to be 0.61%, with a corresponding t-statistic... of 2.15. Thus, if the null hypothesis is that the residual returns are drawn from a population with a nonpositive mean, the one-sided null hypothesis can be rejected.

Since they have rejected the null hypothesis, they accept the research hypothesis. They have shown that the stock price rises significantly as a result of a name change. Does this say that you should rush out and change your firm's name as often as possible? Well, not really. They discuss the implications as follows:

> Our findings are that, for most of the firms, name changes are associated with improved performance, and that the greatest improvement tends to occur in firms that produce industrial goods and whose performance prior to the change was relatively poor.... Our findings do not support, however, the contention that the new name *per se* [i.e., by itself] will enhance demand for the firm's products. Rather, it seems that the act of a name change serves as a signal that other measures to improve performance such as changes in product offerings and organizational changes will be seriously and successfully undertaken.

Note that with a t-statistic of 2.15, they have found a significant result at the 5% level (since it exceeds 1.645). However, since the one-sided t-table value at the 1% level is 2.326, their result is significant but not highly significant.

■ 10.5 Testing Whether or Not a New Observation Comes from the Same Population

By now, you probably have the idea that if you can construct a confidence interval, you can do a hypothesis test. This is correct. Based on the prediction interval in Chapter 9 for a new observation (instead of for the population mean), you may now quickly test whether this new observation came from the same population as the sample data or not. The null hypothesis, H_0, claims that the new observation comes from the same normally distributed population as your sample, and the research hypothesis, H_1, claims that it does not. The data set is assumed to be a random sample.

The test is fairly simple, now that you know the basics of hypothesis testing and confidence intervals. Find the prediction interval (a special kind of confidence interval) based on the sample (but not using the new observation) using the *standard error for prediction*, $S\sqrt{1 + 1/n}$, as explained in Chapter 9. Then get the new observation. If the new observation is *not* in the interval, you will conclude that it is significantly different from the others.

If you want to use the t-test method, simply compute your t-statistic as the new observation minus the sample average, divided by the standard error for prediction. Then proceed just as before, comparing the t-statistic to the critical value from the *t*-table (with $n - 1$ degrees of freedom). The *t*-statistic for testing a new observation is

$$t_{\text{statistic}} = \frac{X_{\text{new}} - \bar{X}}{S \times \sqrt{1 + 1/n}}$$

If you want a one-sided test, to claim that the new observation is either significantly larger or significantly smaller than the average of the others, simply find the appropriate one-sided prediction interval or compare the *t*-statistic to the one-sided value in the *t*-table.

| EXAMPLE |

Is This System under Control?

You are scratching your head. Usually these art objects of molded porcelain that come out of the machine weigh about 30 pounds each. Of course, there is some variation; they don't all weigh *exactly* 30 pounds each—in fact, these "one-of-a-kind" objects are not supposed to be identical. But this is ridiculous! A piece just came out that weighs 38.31 pounds, way over the expected weight. You are wondering if the process has gone *out of control,* or if this is just a random occurrence to be expected every now and again. You would rather not adjust the machinery, since this involves shutting down the assembly line and finding the trouble; but if the line is out of control, the sooner you fix it, the better.

The null hypothesis claims that the system is still under control, that is, that the most recent piece is the same as the others except for the usual random variation. The research hypothesis claims that the system is out of control, and the most recent piece is significantly different from the others. Here is the information for the most recent piece as well as for a sample of ordinary pieces:

Sample size, *n*	19
Sample average, $\bar{X}$	31.52 pounds
Standard deviation, *S*	4.84 pounds
New observation, X_{new}	38.31 pounds

The standard error for prediction is

$$\text{Standard error for prediction} = S \times \sqrt{1 + \frac{1}{n}}$$

$$= 4.84 \times \sqrt{1 + \frac{1}{19}}$$

$$= 4.97$$

It would not be fair to use a one-sided test here because you would most certainly be interested in items that are greatly underweight as well as those that are overweight; either way, the system would be considered out of control. The two-sided prediction interval, based on the *t*-value of 2.101 from the *t*-table, extends from 31.52 − 2.101 × 4.97 = 21.1 to 31.52 + 2.101 × 4.97 = 42.0.

> We are 95% sure that a new observation, taken from the same population as the sample, will be somewhere between 21.1 and 42.0 pounds.

Since the new observation, at 38.31 pounds, is within this prediction interval, it seems to be within the range of reasonable variation. Although it is near the high end, it is *not significantly different* from the others.

The *t*-statistic is less (in absolute value) than the critical value, 2.101, confirming your decision to accept the null hypothesis:

$$t_{statistic} = \frac{38.31 - 31.52}{4.965735}$$

$$= 1.367$$

In retrospect, you probably should not have been surprised at a piece weighing 38.31 pounds. Since the sample standard deviation is 4.84 pounds, you expect individuals to be about this far from the average. This piece is not even two standard deviations away and is therefore (even according to this approximate rule) within the reasonable 95% region. This quick look is just an approximation; by using the standard error for prediction, your answer is exact because you took into account both the variation in your sample and the variation of the new observation in a mathematically correct way.

■ 10.6 Testing Two Samples

To test whether two samples are significantly different or not, on the average, all you need to know are (1) the appropriate standard error to use for evaluating the average difference and (2) its degrees of freedom. The problem will then be essentially identical to the methods you already know: you will be testing an observed quantity (the observed average difference) against a known reference value (zero, indicating no difference) using the appropriate standard error and critical value from the *t*-table.

You will see this method repeated over and over in statistics. Whenever you have an estimated quantity and its own standard error, you can easily construct confidence intervals and do hypothesis testing. The applications get more complex (and more interesting), but the methods are just the same as the procedures you already know. Let's generalize this method now to the two-sample case.

The Paired *t*-Test

The **paired *t*-test** is used to test whether two columns of numbers are different, on the average, *when there is a natural pairing between the two columns.*

This is appropriate, for example, for "before/after" studies, where you have a measurement for each person or thing both before and after some intervention (seeing an advertisement, taking a medication, adjusting the gears, etc.).

In fact, you already know how to do a paired t-test because it can be changed into a familiar one-sample problem by working with the *differences*, for example, "after" minus "before," instead of with the two samples individually. It is crucial that the data be paired; otherwise it would not be clear which pairs to find differences for.

It is not enough to have the averages and standard deviations for each of the two groups. This would lack any indication of the important information conveyed by the pairing of the observations. Instead, you will work with the average and the standard deviation of the *differences*.

A paired t-test can be very effective even when individuals show lots of variation from one to another. Since it concentrates on *changes*, it can ignore the (potentially confusing) variation in *absolute* levels of individuals. For example, individuals could be very different from one another, and yet the changes could be very similar (e.g., everyone receives a $100 pay raise). The paired t-test is not distracted by this individual variability in its methods to detect a systematic change.

Again, some assumptions are required for validity of the paired t-test. The first assumption is that the elementary units being measured are a random sample selected from the population of interest. Each elementary unit produces two measurements. Next, look at the data set consisting of the differences between these two sets of measurements. The second assumption is that these differences are (at least approximately) normally distributed.

EXAMPLE   **Reactions to Advertising**

An advertisement is being tested to determine if it is effective in creating the intended mood of relaxation. A sample of 15 people have been tested just before and just after viewing the ad. Their questionnaire included many items, but the one being considered now asked them to describe their current feelings on a scale from 1 (very tense) to 5 (completely relaxed). The results are shown in Table 10.6.1. (Note in particular that the average relaxation score increased by 0.67, going from 2.80 before to 3.47 after.)

This looks a lot like a two-sample problem, but it isn't. It's really a one-sample problem based on the *changes* in the relaxation scores. For example, person 1 went from a 3 to a 2, for a change of −1 in relaxation score (by convention, we compute the differences as "after" minus "before" so that increases end up as positive numbers and decreases as negatives). Computing the difference for each person, you end up with a familiar one-sample problem, as shown in Table 10.6.2.

You know exactly how to attack this kind of one-sample problem. Using the two-sided t-value of 2.145 from the t-table, together with a sample average of $\overline{X} = 0.6667$ and a standard error of $S_{\overline{X}} = 0.2702$, you find:

> You are 95% sure that the mean change in relaxation score for the larger population is somewhere between 0.087 and 1.25.

TABLE 10.6.1   Relaxation Scores

	Before	After
Person 1	3	2
Person 2	2	2
	2	2
	4	5
	2	4
	2	1
	1	1
	3	5
	3	4
	2	4
	5	5
	2	3
	4	5
	3	5
Person 15	4	4
Sample size	15	15
Average	2.8000	3.4667
Standard deviation	1.0823	1.5055

TABLE 10.6.2   Change in Relaxation Score

	(After − Before)
Person 1	−1
Person 2	0
	0
	1
	2
	−1
	0
	2
	1
	2
	0
	1
	1
	2
Person 15	0
Sample size	15
Average	0.6667
Standard deviation	1.0465
Standard error	0.2702

What is the reference value, μ_0, here? It is $\mu_0 = 0$ because a change of zero indicates *no effect* on relaxation in the population due to viewing the advertisement.

The hypothesis test merely involves seeing whether $\mu_0 = 0$ is in the confidence interval or not. It isn't, so the result is significant; that is, 0 is not a reasonable value for the change in the population based on your data:

Viewing of the advertisement resulted in a significant increase in relaxation ($p < 0.05$, two-sided test).

A two-sided test is needed here because it is also of interest to find out if an advertisement caused a significant *reduction* in relaxation. Having found significance with the two-sided test, you may state the result as a one-sided conclusion.

For completeness, here are the underlying hypotheses: The null hypothesis, H_0: $\mu = 0$, claims that the population mean change in relaxation from before to after is zero; that is, there is no change in mean relaxation. The research hypothesis, H_1: $\mu \neq 0$, claims that there *is* a change in mean relaxation from before to after.

The Unpaired t-Test

The **unpaired *t*-test** is used to test whether two *independent* columns of numbers are different, on the average. Such columns have no natural pairings. For example, you might have data on firms in each of two industry groups, or you might want to compare samples from two different production lines. These cases cannot be reduced to just a single column of numbers; you'll have to deal with both samples.

Once you find the appropriate standard error for this situation, the rest is easy. You will have an estimate (the difference between the two sample averages), its "personal" standard error, and the appropriate number of degrees of freedom. The rest, constructing the confidence interval and performing the hypothesis test, should be routine for you by now.

We have two samples, sample 1 and sample 2. The summary statistics for each sample will be denoted in a natural way, as shown in Table 10.6.3.

Here's what's new. The **standard error of the difference** indicates the sampling variability of the *difference* between the two sample averages. There are two different formulas: a large-sample formula, to be used whenever both sample sizes are 30 or larger, and a small-sample formula that is based on the assumption that the two populations have the same variability.[16] The large-sample formula works even when the variabilities are unequal by directly combining the two standard errors, $S_{(\bar{X}_1)}$ and $S_{(\bar{X}_2)}$. The small-sample formula includes a weighted average of the sample standard deviations to

TABLE 10.6.3   Notation for Two Samples

	Sample 1	Sample 2
Sample size	n_1	n_2
Average	$\bar{X}_1$	$\bar{X}_2$
Standard deviation	S_1	S_2
Standard error	$S_{(\bar{X}_1)}$	$S_{(\bar{X}_2)}$
Average difference		$\bar{X}_2 - \bar{X}_1$

---

[16]Solutions are available for the small-sample problem when variabilities are unequal, but they are more complex. One approach is presented in G. W. Snedecor and W. G. Cochran, *Statistical Methods*, 6th ed. (Ames: Iowa State University Press, 1976), p. 115.

estimate the population variability (assumed equal in the two populations). The small-sample standard error has $n_1 + n_2 - 2$ degrees of freedom: we start with the combined sample size, $n_1 + n_2$, and then subtract 1 for each sample average that was estimated. Here are formulas for the standard error of the difference for each case:

■ Standard Error of the Difference

Large-sample situation ($n_1 \geq 30$ and $n_2 \geq 30$):

$$S_{(\bar{X}_2 - \bar{X}_1)} = \sqrt{S^2_{(\bar{X}_1)} + S^2_{(\bar{X}_2)}} = \sqrt{\frac{S^2_1}{n_1} + \frac{S^2_2}{n_2}}$$

$$S_{(f_2 - f_1)} = \sqrt{S^2_{(f_1)} + S^2_{(f_2)}} \qquad \text{(for two binomials)}$$

Degrees of freedom = infinity

Small-sample situation (equal variabilities assumed):

$$S_{(\bar{X}_2 - \bar{X}_1)} = \sqrt{\frac{(n_1 - 1)S^2_1 + (n_2 - 1)S^2_2}{n_1 + n_2 - 2} \times \left(\frac{1}{n_1} + \frac{1}{n_2}\right)}$$

Degrees of freedom = $n_1 + n_2 - 2$

Be careful to use the correct variability measure for each formula, either the sample standard deviation or the standard error for the sample; the large-sample formula shows how to use either one. If, in the small-sample case, you are given the standard errors instead of the standard deviations, convert them to standard deviations by multiplying by the square root of the sample size for each sample. Note that in both formulas the standard deviations are squared before being combined.[17]

For the large-sample standard error formula, the estimated *variances* of the estimators X_1 and X_2 are added to derive the estimated variance of the difference. Taking the square root, you find the estimated standard deviation of the difference, which gives you the standard error of the difference.

For the small-sample standard error formula, the first fraction inside the square root sign combines the standard deviations using a weighted average (weighted according to the number of degrees of freedom for each one). The rest of the formula converts from the variation of *individuals* to the variation of the *average difference* by summing the reciprocal sample sizes, doing twice what you would do once to find an ordinary standard error.

The hypotheses being tested are $H_0: \mu_1 = \mu_2$ against $H_1: \mu_1 \neq \mu_2$. These may be written equivalently as $H_0: \mu_2 - \mu_1 = 0$ against $H_1: \mu_2 - \mu_1 \neq 0$.

---

[17]Thus, the *variances* are averaged here, as happens in so many formulas like this one. This has led theoretical statisticians to concentrate their attention on the variance. However, anyone who wants to interpret such numbers in their meaningful measurement units will have to take the square root. This is why we work with the standard deviation rather than with the variance in this book. Note that their information is equivalent because either may be converted to the other.

The assumptions needed in order for an unpaired two-sample *t*-test to be valid include the usual ones, plus one new one for the small-sample case only. First, each sample is assumed to be a random sample from its population (there are two populations here, with each sample representing one of them independently of the other). Second, each sample average is assumed to be approximately normally distributed, as we have required before. Finally, for the small-sample case only, it is also assumed that the *standard deviations are equal* in the two populations: $\sigma_1 = \sigma_2$. That is, the two populations differ (if at all) only in mean value and not in terms of the variability of individuals from the mean for their population.

EXAMPLE

Gender Discrimination and Salaries

Your firm is being sued for gender discrimination, and you are evaluating the documents filed by the other side. They have included a statistical hypothesis test, based on salaries of men and women, that finds a "highly significant difference," on average, between men's and women's salaries. Table 10.6.4 shows a summary of their results.

TABLE 10.6.4 Salaries Arranged by Gender

	Women	Men
	$21,100	$38,700
	29,700	30,300
	26,200	32,800
	23,000	34,100
	25,800	30,700
	23,100	33,300
	21,900	34,000
	20,700	38,600
	26,900	36,900
	20,900	35,700
	24,700	26,200
	22,800	27,300
	28,100	32,100
	25,000	35,800
	27,100	26,100
		38,100
		25,500
		34,000
		37,400
		35,700
		35,700
		29,100
Sample size	15	22
Average	$24,467	$33,095
Standard deviation	$ 2,806	$ 4,189
Standard error	$ 724	$ 893
Average difference	$8,628	

There are 15 women and 22 men in this department; the average yearly salaries are $24,476 for women and $33,095 for men. On average, men earn $8,628 more than women. This is a plain, clear fact. However, the issue is whether this difference is within the usual random variation or not. Essentially, no matter how you divide this group of 37 people into two groups of sizes 15 and 22, you will find different average salaries. The question is whether such a large difference as found here could reasonably be the result of a *random* allocation of salaries to men and to women, or if there is a need for some other explanation for the apparent inequity.

Each standard deviation ($2,806 for women, $4,189 for men) indicates that individuals within each group differ from their group average by roughly this amount. There is a bit more variation among the men than the women, but not enough to keep us from going ahead with a two-sample unpaired *t*-test.

The standard errors ($724 for women, $893 for men) indicate about how far the group averages are from the means for their respective idealized populations. For example, if you view these particular 15 women as a random sample from the idealized population of women in similar circumstances, then the average women's salary of $24,467 (random, due to the fact that only 15 have been examined) is approximately $724 away from the idealized population mean.

This is clearly a two-sample *unpaired* situation. Although you might want to subtract Mary's salary from Jim's, there is no systematic way to complete the process because these are really two separate, unpaired groups.

To evaluate the average difference of $8,628 to see if it could be reasonably due to randomness, you need its standard error and number of degrees of freedom. Here are computations for the small-sample formula:

$$S_{(\bar{X}_2 - \bar{X}_1)} = \sqrt{\frac{(n_1 - 1)S_1^2 + (n_2 - 1)S_2^2}{n_1 + n_2 - 2} \times \left(\frac{1}{n_1} + \frac{1}{n_2}\right)}$$

$$= \sqrt{\frac{(15 - 1)2,806^2 + (22 - 1)4,189^2}{15 + 22 - 2} \times \left(\frac{1}{15} + \frac{1}{22}\right)}$$

$$= \sqrt{\frac{(14)7,873,636 + (21)17,547,721}{35} \times (0.066667 + 0.045455)}$$

$$= \sqrt{13,678,087 \times 0.112121}$$

$$= \sqrt{1,533,603}$$

$$= 1,238$$

$$\text{Degrees of freedom} = n_1 + n_2 - 2 = 15 + 22 - 2 = 35$$

The 99.9% confidence interval is based on the *t*-value 3.591 from the *t*-table. Be sure to use the *degrees of freedom* column in the *t*-table since more than one sample is involved. The confidence interval extends from 8,628 − 3.591 × 1.238 to 8,628 + 3.591 × 1,238:

> You are 99.9% sure that the population mean salary difference is somewhere between $4,182 and $13,074.

This confidence interval does *not* include the reference value of 0, which would indicate no mean difference in salary between men and women in the population. Your hypothesis testing decision therefore is as follows:

> The average difference between men's and women's salaries is very highly significant ($p < 0.001$).

This result is also supported by the fact that the t-statistic is $8,628/1,238 = 6.97$, well above the t-table value of 3.591 for testing at the 0.001 significance level.

What can you conclude from this? First of all, the salary allocation between men and women is not just random. Well, it *could* be random, but only if you are willing to admit that a rare, 1 in 1,000 event has happened (this is the meaning of the significance level 0.001). Second, if the salary allocation is not random, there must be some other explanation. At this point, an individual may give his or her own favorite reason as though it were completely proven by the test result. However, it is one thing to say that there is a reason and another to be able to say *what* the reason is. Statistics has ruled out random chance as a reasonable possibility. That's all. If you want to propose a reason for the observed salary difference, you are entitled to do so, but don't expect the field of statistics to back you up. Having set the stage for an explanation, the field of statistics then exits, riding off into the sunset like the Lone Ranger.

So what might cause the salary difference? One explanation is that management, in its outdated, selfish, and illegal ways, has deliberately decided to pay people less if they are women than if they are men, looking only at the person's gender. However, it is not the only plausible explanation. The salary difference might be due to some other factor that (1) determines salary and (2) is linked to gender. In its defense, the firm might argue that it pays solely on the basis of *education and experience,* and it is not to be blamed for the fact that its pool of applicants consisted of better-educated and more experienced men as compared to the women. This argument basically shifts the blame from the firm to society in general.

This is a complicated issue. Fortunately (for the author!) the resolution of the question one way or the other will not be attempted in this book. It can be dodged by pointing out that it is not a statistical question and should be decided using expertise from another field of human endeavor. But stay tuned. This question will reappear in the chapter on multiple regression (with more data) in our continuing efforts to understand the interactions among gender, salary, education, and experience.

The field of statistics can be very helpful in providing exact answers in the presence of uncertainty, but the answers are limited in their scope and much further work and thought may be required before you reach a final explanation.

EXAMPLE   Your Productivity versus Theirs

You have a friendly rivalry going with the manager of the other division over employee productivity. Actually, it's not entirely friendly because you both report to the same boss, who allocates resources based on performance. You would not only like to have the higher productivity, you'd like it to be *significantly* higher so that there's no question about whose employees produce more.[18]

Here are summary measures of employee productivity in the two divisions:

	Your Division	Your Rival's Division
Sample size	53	61
Average	88.23	83.70
Standard deviation	11.47	9.21
Standard error	2.48	1.39
Average difference	4.53	

To evaluate the average difference of 4.53 to see if it could be reasonably due to randomness, you need its standard error. Following are computations for the large-sample formula, which is appropriate because both sample sizes are at least 30.

$$S_{(\bar{X}_2 - \bar{X}_1)} = \sqrt{S^2_{(\bar{X}_1)} + S^2_{(\bar{X}_2)}}$$
$$= \sqrt{1.58^2 + 1.18^2}$$
$$= \sqrt{2.48 + 1.39}$$
$$= \sqrt{3.87}$$
$$= 1.97$$

The 95% confidence interval is based on the *t*-value 1.960 from the *t*-table. The confidence interval extends from $4.53 - 1.960 \times 1.97$ to $4.53 + 1.960 \times 1.97$:

> You are 95% sure that the population mean productivity difference is somewhere between 0.67 and 8.39.

This confidence interval does *not* include the reference value of 0, which would indicate no mean difference in productivity between the two divisions in the (idealized) population. Thus, your hypothesis testing decision is as follows:

> The average difference between your employee productivity and that of your rival is statistically significant.

The *t*-statistic approach would, of course, have given the same answer. The *t*-statistic here is $4.53/1.97 = 2.30$, which exceeds the *t*-table critical value of 1.960.

The one-sided conclusion to a significant two-sided test may be used here. Because your division's productivity is higher, it follows that your division had *significantly higher productivity* than your rival's. Congratulations!

---

[18]In reality, even after the hypothesis test is done, there will still be *some* questions, because there is always some possibility of an error (type I or type II). What you hope to demonstrate is that the superior average productivity of your employees is not likely to be due to randomness alone.

■ 10.7 End-of-Chapter Materials

Summary

Hypothesis testing uses data to decide between two possibilities (called *hypotheses*); it is often used to distinguish structure from mere randomness and should be viewed as a helpful input to executive decision-making. A **hypothesis** is a statement about the population that may be either right or wrong; the data will help you decide which one (of two hypotheses) to accept as true. The **null hypothesis,** denoted H_0, represents the *default*, often a very specific case, such as pure randomness. The **research hypothesis** or **alternative hypothesis,** H_1, has the burden of proof, requiring convincing evidence against H_0 for its acceptance. Accepting the null hypothesis is a weak conclusion, whereas rejecting the null and accepting the research hypothesis is a strong conclusion and a significant result.

For testing whether or not the population mean, μ, is equal to a reference value, μ_0, the hypotheses are H_0: $\mu = \mu_0$ versus H_1: $\mu \neq \mu_0$. The **reference value,** μ_0, is a known, fixed number that does not come from the sample data. This is a **two-sided test** because the research hypothesis allows possible population mean values on both sides of the reference value. This test of a population mean is known as the *t*-**test** or **Student's** *t*-**test.** The outcome of the test is determined by checking if the sample average, $\overline{X}$, is farther from the reference value, μ_0, than random chance would allow if the population mean, μ, were actually equal to μ_0. Thus, the distance from $\overline{X}$ to μ_0 is compared to the standard error, $S_{\overline{X}}$, using the *t*-table. The test may be based either on the two-sided confidence interval (from Chapter 9) or on the *t*-**statistic,** defined as follows:

$$t_{\text{statistic}} = \frac{\overline{X} - \mu_0}{S_{\overline{X}}}$$

Here is how the two-sided *t*-test is decided, using your choice of the confidence interval approach or the *t*-statistic approach (which always give identical results):

- If the reference value, μ_0, is in the two-sided confidence interval, or (equivalently) $|t_{\text{statistic}}| < t_{\text{table}}$, then accept the null hypothesis, H_0. The sample average, $\overline{X}$, is *not significantly different* from μ_0. The observed difference between $\overline{X}$ and μ_0 could reasonably be just random. The result is *not statistically significant.*
- If the reference value, μ_0, is *not* in the two-sided confidence interval, or (equivalently) $|t_{\text{statistic}}| > t_{\text{table}}$, then accept the research hypothesis, H_1, and reject the null hypothesis, H_0. The sample average, $\overline{X}$, is *significantly different* from μ_0. The observed difference between $\overline{X}$ and μ_0 could *not* reasonably be just random. The result is *statistically significant.*

By deciding the hypothesis test in this way, you are accepting the null hypothesis ($\mu = \mu_0$) whenever μ_0 appears to be a reasonably possible value for

μ. When the null hypothesis is true, your probability of deciding correctly is equal to the confidence level (95% or other) for the column you used in the t-table.

Table 10.7.1 shows a summary of the situation for testing either the mean of a normal distribution or the probability of occurrence for a binomial distribution.

The t-statistic is an example of the general concept of a **test statistic,** which is the most helpful number that can be computed from your data for the purposes of deciding between two given hypotheses. The test statistic is compared to the appropriate **critical value** found in a standard statistical table; for example, a t-value found in the t-table is a **critical t-value.** A useful rule of thumb is that if the t-statistic is larger in absolute value than 2, you reject the null hypothesis; otherwise you accept it.

Depending on which is (in reality) the true hypothesis, there are two types of errors that you might make. The **type I error** is committed when the null hypothesis is true, but you reject it and declare that your result is statistically significant. The probability of committing a type I error (when the null hypothesis is true) is controlled by your choice of column in the t-table, conventionally the 5% level. The **type II error** is committed when the research hypothesis is true, but you accept the null hypothesis instead and declare the result *not* to be significant. The probability of committing a type II error (when the research hypothesis is true) is not easily controlled but can (depending on the true value of μ) be anywhere between 0 and the confidence level of the test (e.g., 95%). Note that each type of error is based on an assumption about which hypothesis is true. Since each hypothesis is either true or false depending on the population (*not* on the data), there is no notion of the probability of a hypothesis being true.

The **assumptions for hypothesis testing** are (1) the data set is a random sample from the population of interest, and (2) either the quantity being measured is approximately normal, or else the sample size is large enough

TABLE 10.7.1   Testing Either the Mean of a Normal Distribution or the Probability of Occurrence for a Binomial Distribution

	Normal	Binomial
Population mean	μ	p
Reference value	μ_0	p_0
Null hypothesis	$H_0: \mu = \mu_0$	$H_0: p = p_0$
Research hypothesis	$H_1: \mu \neq \mu_0$	$H_1: p \neq p_0$
Data	$X_1, X_2, \ldots, X_n$	X occurrences out of n trials
Estimator	$\overline{X}$	$f = X/n$
Standard error	$S_{\overline{X}} = S/\sqrt{n}$	$S_f = \sqrt{f(1-f)/n}$
Confidence interval	From $\overline{X} - tS_{\overline{X}}$ to $\overline{X} + tS_{\overline{X}}$	From $f - tS_f$ to $f + tS_f$
t-statistic	$t = (\overline{X} - \mu_0)/S_{\overline{X}}$	$t = (f - p_0)/S_f$

that the central limit theorem ensures that the sample average is approximately normally distributed.

The **test level** or **significance level** is the probability of accepting the research hypothesis when the null hypothesis is really true (i.e., committing a type I error). By convention, this level is set at 5% but may reasonably be set at 1% or 0.1% (or even 10% for some fields of study) by using the appropriate column in the t-table. The **p-value** is defined as the *smallest* test level for which your test is significant. The smaller the p-value, the more impressive the result in terms of evidence against the null hypothesis. A result is **statistically significant** ($p < 0.05$) if it is significant at the 5% level. Other terms used are *highly significant* ($p < 0.01$), *very highly significant* ($p < 0.001$), and *not significant* ($p > 0.05$).

A **one-sided test** is set up with the null hypothesis claiming that μ is on one side of μ_0 and the research hypothesis claiming that it is on the other side. To use a one-sided test, you must be sure that *no matter how the data had come out* you would still have used a one-sided test on the same side ("larger than" or "smaller than"). If in doubt, use a two-sided test; if it is significant, you are then entitled to state the *one*-sided conclusion. The test may be performed either by constructing the appropriate one-sided confidence interval (matching the claim of the research hypothesis) or by using the t-statistic. A significant result (accepting the research hypothesis) will be declared whenever the reference value μ_0 does *not* fall in the confidence interval. This will happen whenever $\overline{X}$ is on the side of μ_0 claimed in the research hypothesis and the absolute value of the t-statistic is larger than the t-value from the t-table.

For the one-sided t-test to see if μ is *larger* than μ_0, the hypotheses are $H_0: \mu \leq \mu_0$ and $H_1: \mu > \mu_0$. The confidence interval includes all values *at least* as large as $\overline{X} - t_{\text{table}} S_{\overline{X}}$.

> If μ_0 is in the confidence interval or (equivalently) either $\overline{X} < \mu_0$ or $|t_{\text{statistic}}| < t_{\text{table}}$, then accept the null hypothesis, H_0. The sample average, $\overline{X}$, is *not significantly larger* than μ_0. If $\overline{X}$ is larger than μ_0, the observed difference could reasonably be just random. The result is *not statistically significant.*
>
> If μ_0 is *not* in the confidence interval or (equivalently) both $\overline{X} > \mu_0$ and $|t_{\text{statistic}}| > t_{\text{table}}$, then accept the research hypothesis, H_1, and reject the null hypothesis, H_0. The sample average, $\overline{X}$, is *significantly larger* than μ_0. The observed difference could *not* reasonably be just random. The result is *statistically significant.*

For the one-sided t-test to see if μ is *smaller* than μ_0, the hypotheses are $H_0: \mu \geq \mu_0$ and $H_1: \mu < \mu_0$. The confidence interval includes all values *no larger* than $\overline{X} + t_{\text{table}} S_{\overline{X}}$.

> If μ_0 is in the confidence interval or (equivalently) either $\overline{X} > \mu_0$ or $|t_{\text{statistic}}| < t_{\text{table}}$, then accept the null hypothesis, H_0. The sample aver-

age, $\overline{X}$, is *not significantly smaller* than μ_0. If $\overline{X}$ is smaller than μ_0, the observed difference could reasonably be just random. The result is *not statistically significant.*

If μ_0 is *not* in the confidence interval or (equivalently) both $\overline{X} < \mu_0$ and $|t_{\text{statistic}}| > t_{\text{table}}$, then accept the research hypothesis, H_1, and reject the null hypothesis, H_0. The sample average, $\overline{X}$, is *significantly smaller* than μ_0. The observed difference could *not* reasonably be just random. The result is *statistically significant.*

Whenever you have an estimator (such as $\overline{X}$), the appropriate standard error for that estimator (such as $S_{\overline{X}}$), and a critical value from the appropriate table (such as the t-table), you may construct one- or two-sided confidence intervals (at various confidence levels) and perform one- or two-sided hypothesis tests (at various significance levels).

For the test of whether a new observation came from the same population as a sample, the null hypothesis claims that it did, and the research hypothesis claims otherwise. Using the standard error for prediction, $S\sqrt{1 + 1/n}$, to construct the prediction interval, accept the null hypothesis if the new observation falls within the interval, and accept the research hypothesis and declare significance otherwise. Or compute the t-statistic using the following equation, and compare it to the t-value in the t-table.

For testing a new observation

$$t_{\text{statistic}} = \frac{X_{\text{new}} - \overline{X}}{S \times \sqrt{1 + 1/n}}$$

Whichever method you choose (confidence interval or t-statistic), you have available all of the significance levels, p-value statements, and one- or two-sided testing procedures as before.

The **paired t-test** is used to test whether or not two samples have the same population mean value when there is a natural pairing between the two samples (for example, "before" and "after" measurements on the same people). By working with the differences ("after" minus "before"), we reduce such a problem to the familiar one-sample t-test, using $\mu_0 = 0$ as the reference value expressing the null hypothesis of no difference in means.

The **unpaired t-test** is used to test whether or not two samples have the same population mean value when there is *no* natural pairing between the two samples; that is, each is an independent sample from a different population. For a two-sided test, the null hypothesis claims that the mean difference is 0. To construct confidence intervals for the mean difference and to perform the hypothesis test, you need the **standard error of the difference** (which gives the estimated standard deviation of the sample average difference) and its degrees of freedom.

For a large-sample situation ($n_1 \geq 30$ and $n_2 \geq 30$):

$$S_{(\bar{X}_2 - \bar{X}_1)} = \sqrt{S^2_{(\bar{X}_1)} + S^2_{(\bar{X}_2)}} = \sqrt{\frac{S^2_1}{n_1} + \frac{S^2_2}{n_2}}$$

$$S_{(f_2 - f_1)} = \sqrt{S^2_{(f_1)} + S^2_{(f_2)}} \qquad \text{(for two binomials)}$$

Degrees of freedom = infinity

For a small-sample situation (assuming equal variabilities):

$$S_{(\bar{X}_2 - \bar{X}_1)} = \sqrt{\frac{(n_1 - 1)S^2_1 + (n_2 - 1)S^2_2}{n_1 + n_2 - 2} \times \left(\frac{1}{n_1} + \frac{1}{n_2}\right)}$$

Degrees of freedom = $n_1 + n_2 - 2$

Based on the average difference, its standard error, its number of degrees of freedom, and the reference value (0), you can construct confidence intervals and perform hypothesis tests in the usual way. Note that, in addition to the usual assumptions of random samples and normal distributions, the small-sample situation also requires that the population variabilities be equal ($\sigma_1 = \sigma_2$).

Key Words

hypothesis testing 336
hypothesis 336
null hypothesis 336
research hypothesis or
  alternative hypothesis 337
reference value 339
two-sided test 340
t-test or Student's t-test 348
test statistic 349
critical value 349
critical t-value 349
t-statistic 349

type I error 352
type II error 352
assumptions for hypothesis
  testing 353
statistically significant 354
test level or significance level 355
p-value 356
one-sided t-test 357
paired t-test 370
unpaired t-test 373
standard error of the difference 373

Questions

1 a. What is the purpose of hypothesis testing?
   b. How is the result of a hypothesis test different from a confidence interval statement?
2 a. What is a hypothesis? In particular, is it a statement about the population or the sample?
   b. How is the role of the null hypothesis different from that of the research hypothesis? Which one usually includes the case of pure randomness? Which one has the burden of proof? Which one has the benefit of the doubt?

c. Suppose you decide in favor of the null hypothesis. Is this a weak or a strong conclusion?

d. Suppose you decide in favor of the research hypothesis. Is this a weak or a strong conclusion?

e. "A null hypothesis can never be disproved." Comment.

3 a. Briefly describe the steps involved in performing a two-sided test concerning a population mean based on a confidence interval.

b. Briefly describe the steps involved in performing a two-sided test concerning a population mean based on the t-statistic.

4 a. What is Student's t-test?

b. Who was Student? What was his contribution?

5 a. What is the reference value? Does it come from the sample data? Is it known or unknown?

b. What is the t-statistic? Does it depend on the reference value?

c. Does the confidence interval change depending on the reference value?

6 a. What, in general, is a test statistic?

b. Which test statistic would you use for a two-sided t-test?

c. What, in general, is a critical value?

d. Which critical value would you use for a two-sided t-test?

7 a. What assumptions must be satisfied for a two-sided t-test to be valid?

b. Consider each assumption in turn. What happens if the assumption is not satisfied? What, if anything, can be done to fix the problem?

8 a. What is a type I error? Can it be controlled? Why or why not?

b. What is a type II error? Can it be controlled? Why or why not?

c. When, if ever, is it correct to say that "the null hypothesis is true with probability 0.95"?

d. What can you say about your lifetime track record in terms of correct decisions to accept true null hypotheses?

9 What p-value statement is associated with each of the following outcomes of a hypothesis test?

a. Not significant.

b. Significant.

c. Highly significant.

d. Very highly significant.

10 a. What is a one-sided test?

b. What are the hypotheses for a one-sided test?

c. When are you allowed to perform a one-sided test? What should you do if you're not sure if it's allowed?

d. If you perform a one-sided test when it's really not permitted, what is the worst that can happen?

e. Under what conditions are you permitted to make a one-sided statement based on a two-sided test?

11 a. How is a one-sided test performed based on a confidence interval?

b. How is a one-sided test performed based on the t-statistic?

12 Suppose you have an estimator and would like to test whether or not the population value equals 0. What do you need in addition to the estimated value?

13 What standard error would you use to test whether a new observation came from the same population as a sample? (Give both its name and the formula.)

14 a. What is a paired *t*-test?
   b. Identify the two hypotheses involved in a paired *t*-test.
   c. What is the "pairing" requirement? Give a concrete example.
   d. How is a paired *t*-test similar to and different from an ordinary *t*-test for just one sample?

15 a. What is an unpaired *t*-test?
   b. Identify the two hypotheses involved in an unpaired *t*-test.
   c. What is the "independence" requirement? Give a concrete example.
   d. How is an unpaired *t*-test similar to and different from an ordinary *t*-test for just one sample?
   e. When is each standard error appropriate? (Answer both in words and using a formula.)
   f. What new assumption is needed for the unpaired *t*-test to be valid for small samples? What can you do if this assumption is grossly violated?

16 a. Describe the general process of constructing confidence intervals and performing hypothesis tests using the rule of thumb when you have an estimator and its standard error.
   b. If you also know the number of degrees of freedom and can use the *t*-table, how would your answer change to be more exact?

Problems

1 Identify the null and research hypotheses for each of the following situations, using both words and mathematical symbols.
   a. To help your restaurant marketing campaign target the right age levels, you want to find out if there is a statistically significant difference, on the average, between the age of your customers and the age of the general population in town.
   b. To decide whether to launch a new product or not, you want to test whether a large enough percentage of the community would be interested in purchasing it. You will launch the product only if you find convincing evidence of demand.
   c. Part of the assembly line will have to be adjusted if the consistency of the injected plastic becomes too viscous as compared to a value your engineers consider reasonable. Based on recent measurements of the viscosity, should the equipment be adjusted or not? (You would adjust only if you are convinced that there is a need.)
   d. Some of your advertisements seem to get no reaction, as though they are being ignored by the public. You have arranged for a study to measure the public's awareness of your brand before and after viewing a TV show that includes the advertisement in question. You wish to see if the ad has a statistically significant effect.

2 Perform a two-sided hypothesis test at the 5% significance level for each of the following situations by first constructing the confidence interval and then indicating the result of the test.
   a. A random sample of 50 customers shows an average age of 33.6 years with a standard deviation of 16.2 years. Do your customers differ significantly from the mean age of 43.1 years for the community according to census records?

b. A survey of 400 randomly selected people in the community shows that 13.0% are willing to try your proposed new product. Does this percentage differ significantly from the 10% you figure is needed to justify going ahead with the product launch?

c. The average viscosity for 13 recent measurements was 51.22 with a standard error of 3.18. Does this differ significantly from the target viscosity of 56.00?

d. Your brand awareness, as measured on a scale from 1 to 5, was found to have increased an average of 0.68 points when 200 people were shown an advertisement and questioned before and after. The standard deviation of the increase was 1.39 points. Is this a significant change?

3 For each situation presented in problem 2, perform the test by using the t-statistic, and then indicate the result of the test.

4 For each situation presented in problem 2, perform a two-sided hypothesis test at the 1% level using your choice of method.

5 For each situation presented in problem 2, find the p-value (rounded to 0.05, 0.01, or 0.001) and indicate the extent of significance (e.g., "highly significant").

6 For each situation presented in problems 1 and 2, tell whether a one-sided test would be appropriate or not. If so, give the hypotheses and the result of a one-sided test. If not, give the one-sided result of a two-sided test for each appropriate situation.

7 A recent poll of 1,235 randomly sampled likely voters shows your favorite candidate ahead, with 52.1% in favor. There are two candidates. Use hypothesis testing to infer to the larger group of *all* likely voters.

a. Carefully identify the two-sided hypotheses.

b. Perform the hypothesis test at level 0.05, and give the result.

c. Make a careful, exact statement summarizing the result of the test and what it means.

d. Repeat parts b and c assuming that the percentage is 58.3% instead of 52.1%.

e. Explain why a one-sided test would be inappropriate here by showing that each of the three possible outcomes of a two-sided test would be of interest.

8 An example in this chapter showed that managers perceived employee stock ownership as having a significant positive effect on product quality. As part of that same study, managers were also asked to rate the effect of employee stock ownership on *unit labor cost*.[19] This effect, on a scale from -2 (large negative effect) to 2 (large positive effect) was 0.12 with a standard error of 0.11, based on a sample of 343 managers.

a. Find the 95% confidence interval, and state carefully what this represents. Keep in mind that these are opinions of randomly selected managers.

b. Is there a significant relationship between employee stock ownership and the unit cost of labor as perceived by managers? Why or why not?

c. Identify the null and research hypotheses.

d. Which hypothesis has been accepted? Is this a weak or a strong conclusion?

e. Has the accepted hypothesis been absolutely proven? If not, what type of error may have been made?

---

[19]P. B. Voos, *op. cit.*

9 The goal of your marketing campaign is for more than 25% of supermarket shoppers to recognize your brand name. A recent survey of 150 random shoppers found that 21.3% recognized your brand name.

a. It might be argued that the burden of proof is to show that more than 25% of shoppers recognize your brand name. Identify the appropriate one-sided hypotheses in this case, and perform the test at level 0.05.

b. On the other hand, it might be argued that you would be interested in knowing about all three possibilities: significantly more than 25% (indicating success), significantly less than 25% (indicating failure), and not significantly different from 25% (indicating that there is not enough information to say for sure). Identify the appropriate two-sided hypotheses in this case, and perform the test at level 0.05.

c. For the two-sided test, write a brief paragraph describing the result, the error that might have been made, and its implications for your marketing strategy.

10 You are supervising an audit to decide whether any errors in the recording of account transactions are "material errors" or not. In practical terms, for this situation involving 12,000 accounts, the *total error* is material only if it is larger than $5,000. The average error amount for 250 randomly selected accounts was found to be $0.25, and the standard deviation of the error amount was $193.05. You may assume that your reputation as an auditor is on the line, so you want to be fairly certain before declaring that the total error is not material.

a. Find the estimated total error based on your sample, and compare it to the material amount.

b. Identify the null and research hypotheses for a one-sided test, and explain why a one-sided test is appropriate here.

c. Find the appropriate one-sided 95% confidence interval statement.

d. Find the *t*-value.

e. Which hypothesis is accepted as a result of a one-sided test at the 5% level?

f. Write a brief paragraph explaining the results of this audit.

11 Dishwasher detergent is packaged in containers that claim a weight of 24 ounces. Although there is some variation from one package to another, your policy is to ensure that the mean weight for each day's production is slightly over 24 ounces. A random sample of 100 packages from today's production indicates an average of 24.23 ounces with a standard deviation of 0.15 ounces.

a. Find the *p*-value for a one-sided hypothesis test to check if the population mean weight is above the claimed weight.

b. Write a brief paragraph summarizing your test and its results.

c. Is your conclusion a strong one or a weak one? Why?

12 Do employees take more sick leave in the year before retirement? They may well have an incentive to do so if their accumulated paid sick leave (the number of days they are entitled to be away with full pay) is about to expire. Indeed, this appears to happen with government workers. One evaluation of this issue looked at statistics gathered by the U.S. General Accounting Office (GAO).[20] The study concluded:

> [What if] the bulge in sick days was just an aberration in the GAO sample rather than a real symptom of goofing off? In zeroing in on this question, we

[20]D. Seligman, "Sick in Washington," *Fortune*, March 28, 1988, p. 155.

note that the 714 retirees in the GAO sample averaged 30 sick days in their last year instead of the "expected" 14 days. So in a work year of 251 days (average for federal employees) the retirees were finding themselves indisposed 12.0% of the time instead of 5.6%. Could that happen by chance? The science of statistics tells us that the probability of any such swing in so large a sample is low. To be precise, one in 200,000.

a. Identify the population and the sample.
b. Identify the hypotheses being tested.
c. Identify the p-value that is mentioned here.
d. Which hypothesis has been rejected? Which has been accepted?
e. How significant (statistically) is the result?

13 Mutual funds that invest only in the securities of "socially aware" firms performed well in the first half of 1988. Although the mean rate of return for all mutual funds was 9.41%, the rate of return for these special funds was as shown in Table 10.7.2.

TABLE 10.7.2   Performance of Socially Aware Investment Funds

Ariel Growth	34.31%
Calvert Bond	4.60
Calvert Growth	8.50
Calvert Equity	13.20
Dreyfus Third Century	14.87
New Alternatives	18.89
Parnassus	36.45
Pax World	7.15
Pioneer	15.63
Pioneer II	17.19
Pioneer Bond	3.85
Pioneer III	26.72

C.W. Stevens, "Socially Aware Investing Turns Profitable," *The Wall Street Journal,* July 29, 1988, p. 27. Rates of return are for 1988 through July 14.

a. Could these funds reasonably represent a random sample of all mutual funds, or is there something special about their average return? Perform a hypothesis test in the usual way at the 5% level to resolve this issue.
b. Find the p-value for this test. In particular, is it highly significant?
c. Identify the underlying hypotheses and assumptions involved in part a.
d. Under these assumptions, the hypothesis test makes a clear and correct statement. However, are the assumptions realistic? Be sure to address independence (note that some of these funds are part of the same group).
e. Someone might claim that if you have lots of media reporters and analysts looking at the performance of every conceivable group of mutual funds, you are most likely to see the extremes (best and worst performance) reported. If there are 100 groups, then you might expect about 5 to be significantly different from the overall mean if you test each one at the 5% level. In light of this possibility, is the test from part a realistic, or should the result be viewed with some caution?

14 Your broker achieved a rate of return of 18.3% on your portfolio last year. For a sample of 25 other brokers in the area, according to a recent news article, the av-

erage rate of return was 15.2% with a standard deviation of 3.2% (as percentage points.)

a. To test whether your broker significantly outperformed this group, identify the idealized population and the hypotheses being tested. In particular, are you testing against a *mean* or against a *new observation?*

b. Find the standard error for prediction.

c. Find the two-sided 95% prediction interval for a new observation.

d. Did your broker outperform this group?

e. Did your broker *significantly* outperform this group?

f. Find the *t*-value and the *p*-value for this two-sided test.

15 Last year you received an average of 129.2 complaints (i.e., individual items to be fixed under warranty) per new car sold, with a standard deviation of 42.1 complaints based on 3,834 new cars sold. This year you have set up a quality assurance program to fix some of these problems before the car is delivered. So far this year, you have had an average of just 93.4 complaints per new car sold with a standard deviation of 37.7, based on 74 cars sold so far.

a. To see if your new quality assurance program is working, what hypothesis testing method would you use?

b. Identify the populations, samples, and hypotheses.

c. Perform a two-sided test at the 5% level, and report the results.

16 Why do firms change ownership? One possible reason for acquisitions is that the new owners expect to be able to manage the operations more efficiently than the current management. This theory leads to testable hypotheses. For example, it predicts that productivity should increase following a takeover and also that firms changing ownership should have lower productivity than firms in general. A study of this situation examined the productivity year by year for some firms that changed ownership and other firms that did not change owners.[21] In particular, they reported:

> These numbers display a very clear pattern. Plants that changed owners... tended to be less efficient...than nonchangers.... But the differences...[after the change] were declining in magnitude.... This signifies that the productivity of...changers relative to that of...nonchangers was both low and declining before the ownership change, and increasing (albeit still low) after the ownership change. With one exception, all of the productivity differences are *highly statistically significant.*

a. In the last line of the preceding quote, explain what is implied by "highly statistically significant."

b. Consider the comparison of average productivity of firms that changed ownership (at the time of the change) to average productivity of firms that did not change ownership. Identify all elements of this hypothesis testing situation, in particular: the hypotheses, the sample data, the type of test used, and the assumptions being made.

c. One result they reported was "at the time of ownership change, productivity level was 3.9% lower as compared to plants that did not change ownership. The

---

[21]F. Lichtenberg, "Productivity Improvements from Changes in Ownership," *Mergers & Acquisitions* 23 (1988), pp. 48–50.

t-statistic is 9.10." Perform a hypothesis test based on this information, and state your conclusion.

d. Why have they gone to the trouble of doing statistical hypothesis tests? What have they gained over and above simply observing and describing the productivity differences in their data?

17 Stress levels were recorded during a true answer and a false answer given by each of six people in a study of lie-detecting equipment, based on the idea that the stress involved in telling a lie can be measured. The results are shown in Table 10.7.3.

TABLE 10.7.3   Vocal Stress Level

Person	True Answer	False Answer
1	12.8	13.1
2	8.5	9.6
3	3.4	4.8
4	5.0	4.6
5	10.1	11.0
6	11.2	12.1

a. Was everyone's stress level higher during a false answer than during a true answer?

b. Find the average stress levels for true and for false answers. Find the average change in stress level.

c. Find the appropriate standard error for the average difference. In particular, is this a paired or an unpaired situation?

d. Find the 95% two-sided confidence interval for the mean difference in stress level.

e. Test to see if the average stress levels are significantly different. If they are significantly different, are they significantly higher or lower when a false answer is given?

f. Write a paragraph interpreting the results of this test. In particular, is this a conclusion about these six people or about some other group? Also, how can you find a significant difference when some individuals had higher stress and some had lower stress for the false answer?

18 A group of experts has rated your winery's two best vintages. Ratings are on a scale from 1 to 20, with higher numbers being better. The results are shown in Table 10.7.4.

TABLE 10.7.4   Wine-Tasting Scores

Expert	Chardonnay	Cabernet Sauvignon
1	17.8	16.6
2	18.6	19.9
3	19.5	17.2
4	18.3	19.0
5	19.8	19.7
6	19.9	18.8
7	17.1	18.9
8	17.3	19.5
9	18.0	16.2
10	19.8	18.6

a. Is this a paired or unpaired situation? Why?

b. Find the average rating for each vintage and the average difference in ratings.

c. Find the appropriate standard error for the average difference.

d. Find the 95% two-sided confidence interval for the mean difference in rating.

e. Test to see if the average ratings are significantly different. If they are significantly different, which vintage is superior?

f. Write a paragraph interpreting the results of this test.

19 To understand your competitive position, you have examined the reliability of your product as well as the reliability of your closest competitor's product. You have subjected each product to abuse that represents about a year's worth of wear-and-tear per day. Table 10.7.5 shows the data indicating how long each item lasted.

TABLE 10.7.5   Days until Failure

Your Products	Competitor's Products
1.0	0.2
8.9	2.8
1.2	1.7
10.3	7.2
4.9	2.2
1.8	2.5
3.1	2.6
3.6	2.0
2.1	0.5
2.9	2.3
8.6	1.9
5.3	1.2
	6.6
	0.5
	1.2

a. Find the average time to failure for your and your competitor's products. Find the average difference.

b. Find the appropriate standard error for this average difference. In particular, is this a paired or an unpaired situation? Why?

c. Find the two-sided 99% confidence interval for the mean difference in reliability.

d. Test at the 1% level if there is a significant difference in reliability between your products and your competitor's.

e. Find the p-value for the difference in reliability.

f. Write a brief paragraph, complete with footnote, that might be used in an advertising brochure showing off your products.

20 Child care is one of life's necessities for working parents. Monthly rates per child at a sample of family day-care centers in the North Seattle area are shown in Table 10.7.6. The Laurelhurst area is considered to be a highly desirable neighborhood, and real estate prices are higher in this area. Perform a one-sided hypothesis test at the 5% level to see if day-care prices are also higher in the Laurelhurst area.

21 Consider the weights for two samples of candy bars, before and after intervention, from problem 10 of Chapter 5.

a. Is this a paired or an unpaired situation?

b. Find the 95% confidence interval for the population mean difference in weight per candy bar.

c. Did intervention produce a significant change in weight? How do you know?

TABLE 10.7.6   Monthly Day-Care Rates in
                North Seattle

Laurelhurst Area	Non-Laurelhurst Area
400	500
625	425
440	300
550	350
600	550
500	475
	325
	350
	350

I am grateful to Ms. Colleen Bryant for
providing this data set.

22 Your Detroit division produced 135 defective parts out of the total production of
   983 last week. The Kansas City division produced 104 defectives out of 1,085 produced during the same time period.
   a. Find the percent defective for each division and compare them.
   b. Find the difference between these two percentages and interpret it.
   c. Find the standard error for this difference using the large-sample formula.
   d. Find the 95% confidence interval for the difference.
   e. Test to see if these two divisions differ in terms of quality of production, based
      on the defect rate.

23 You are analyzing the results of a consumer survey of a product, rated on a scale
   from 1 to 10. For the 130 consumers who described themselves as "outgoing," the
   average rating was 8.36, and the standard deviation was 1.82. For the 218 "shy"
   consumers, the average was 8.78, and the standard deviation was 0.91.
   a. Test to see if there is a significant difference between the ratings of outgoing
      and shy consumers.
   b. Report the test results using p-value notation.

24 Repeat the previous question for a different product. For 142 outgoing consumers,
   the average rating was 7.28, and the standard deviation was 2.18. For 277 shy consumers, the average rating was 8.78, and the standard deviation was 1.32.

Database Exercises

Refer to the employee database in Appendix A. View this data set as a random sample
from a much larger population of employees.

1 Is the average annual salary significantly different from $40,000?
2 You would like to claim that the population has significantly more than five years
  of experience. Can you support this claim?
3 Test to see if the gender ratio differs from 50%.
4 Test to see if the mean annual salary for men differs from that for women.
5 Test to see if the mean age for men differs from that for women.
6 Test to see if the average annual salary for training level A differs from that for levels B and C combined.
7 Test to see if the mean age for training level A differs from that for levels B and C
  combined.

Projects

1 Identify a decision process within your work or business interests that could be resolved based on data.
   a. Describe the null and research hypotheses.
   b. Compute (or use an educated guess for) an appropriate estimate and its standard
   error.
   c. Find a confidence interval.
   d. Test the hypothesis.
   e. Interpret and explain your results.

2 Find a news item (from a newspaper, a magazine, radio, or television) that reaches
a conclusion based on data.
   a. Identify the null and research hypotheses.
   b. Identify the population and the sample, to the extent that you can from the information given. Was any important information omitted?
   c. What was the result of their hypothesis test?
   d. Is their conclusion a weak one or a strong one?
   e. Discuss and interpret their claims.

PART

IV Regression and Time Series

■

At this point, you know the basics: how to look at data, compute and interpret probabilities, draw a random sample, and do statistical inference. Now it's a question of applying these concepts to see the relationships hidden within the more complex situations of real life. Chapter 11 shows you how statistics can summarize the relationship between two factors based on a bivariate data set with two columns of numbers. The *correlation* will tell you how strong the relationship is, and *regression* will help you predict one factor from the other. Perhaps the most important statistical method is *multiple regression*, covered in Chapter 12, which lets you use all of the factors you have available in order to predict (that is, reduce the uncertainty of) some important but unknown number. Since *communication* is such an important business skill, Chapter 13 will show you how to effectively tell others all about the useful things you have learned from a multiple regression analysis. While the basic concepts stay the same, new ways of applying statistical methods are needed for *time series analysis*, presented in Chapter 14, in order to extract the extra information contained in the time sequence of the observations.

Correlation and Regression
Measuring and Predicting Relationships

The world is filled with relationships: between attitude and productivity, between corporate strategy and market share, between government intervention and the state of the economy, between quantity and cost, between sales and earnings, and so on.

Up to now you have been concerned primarily with statistical summaries such as the average and variability, which are usually sufficient when you have *univariate* data (i.e., just *one* measurement, such as salary) for each elementary unit (e.g., employee). When you have *bivariate* data (e.g., salary and education) you can always study each measurement individually as though it were part of a univariate data set. But the real payoff comes from studying both measurements at once to see the relationship between the two.

There are three basic goals to keep in mind when studying relationships in bivariate data:

1 *Describing and understanding the relationship.* This is the most general goal, providing background information to help you understand how the world works. In studying a complex system, knowing which factors interact most strongly with each other (and which other ones do not affect one another) will help you gain the perspective necessary for long-range planning and other strategies..

2 *Forecasting and predicting a new observation.* Once you understand the relationship, you can use information about one of the measurements to help you do a better job of predicting the other. For example, if you know that orders are up this quarter, you can expect to see an increase in sales. If you have analyzed the relationship between orders and sales in the past, you may be able to come up with a good forecast of sales even if sales figures are unavailable.

3 *Adjusting and controlling a process.* When you *intervene* in a process (e.g., by adjusting the production level or providing an additive or service), you have to choose the extent of your intervention. If there is a direct relationship between intervention and result and you understand it, this knowledge can help you make the best possible adjustments.

Bivariate data can have many different kinds of structure; some are easy to work with, and others are more difficult. By exploring your data using a *scatterplot,* you can gain additional insights beyond the few conventional statistical summaries. There are two basic tools for summarizing bivariate data. *Correlation* analysis summarizes the strength of the relationship (if any) between the two factors. *Regression* analysis shows you how to predict or control one of the variables using the other one.

■ 11.1 Exploring Relationships Using Scatterplots and Correlations

Whenever you have bivariate data, you should draw a *scatterplot* so that you can really *see* the structure. Just as the histogram shows structure in univariate data (normal, skewed, outliers, etc.), the scatterplot will show you everything that is going on in bivariate data. If there are some problems in your data, such as outliers or other unexpected features, often the only way to uncover them is by looking at a scatterplot.

The *correlation* is a summary measure of the strength of the relationship. Like all statistical summaries, the correlation is both helpful and limited. If the scatterplot either shows a well-behaved *linear* relationship (to be defined soon) or shows no relationship at all, then the correlation provides an excellent summarization of the relationship. But if there are problems (to be defined soon) such as a *nonlinear* relationship, *unequal variability, clustering,* or *outliers* in the data, the correlation can be misleading.

By itself, the correlation is limited because its interpretation depends on the type of relationship in the data. This is why the scatterplot is so important: It will either confirm the usual interpretation of the correlation or show that there are problems with the data that render the correlation number misleading.

The Scatterplot Shows You the Relationship

A **scatterplot** displays each case (or elementary unit) using two axes to represent the two factors. If one variable is seen as causing, affecting, or influencing the other, then it is called X and defines the horizontal axis. The variable that might respond or be influenced is called Y and defines the ver-

TABLE 11.1.1   First-Quarter Performance

	Contacts	Sales
Bill	147	$126,300
Martha	223	182,518
Colleen	163	141,775
Gary	172	138,282

tical axis. If neither clearly influences or causes the other, you may choose either factor to be X and the other to be Y.

For the small bivariate data set in Table 11.1.1, the scatterplot is shown in Figure 11.1.1. Since we ordinarily think of effort influencing results, it is natural to display contacts made (effort) on the horizontal axis and the resulting sales on the vertical axis. Sometimes it's helpful to have the points labeled as in Figure 11.1.1; at other times these labels may cause too much clutter. A more conventional scatterplot for this data set is shown in Figure 11.1.2.

From either figure you can see information about each individual variable and about the relationship between variables. First, the distribution of the number of contacts (looking down at the horizontal scale) goes from about 150 to about 220, with a typical value of around 170. Second, the distribution of sales (looking at the vertical axis) goes from about $130,000 to about

FIGURE 11.1.1   The scatterplot displays one point for each row in your bivariate data set. Each point is labeled here to show where it came from. Martha's exceptional performance is highlighted to show her 223 contacts, which resulted in sales of $182,518 for the quarter.

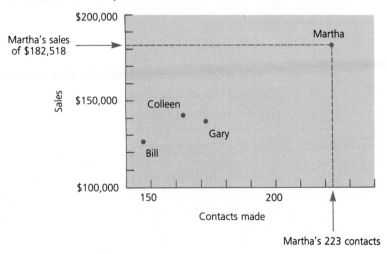

FIGURE 11.1.2   The scatterplot from the previous figure, without any extra information. You can see the distribution of contacts (along the horizontal axis), the distribution of sales (along the vertical axis), and the generally increasing relationship between contacts and sales (i.e., the points rise upward to the right).

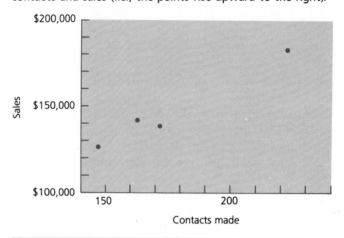

$180,000, with a typical value perhaps around $150,000. Finally, the relationship between contacts and sales appears to be a positive one: the pattern of points tilts upward and to the right. This tells you that those with more contacts (the data points to the right in the figure) also tended to have more sales (since these points are higher up in the figure). Although there appears to be such an increasing relationship overall, it does not apply to every case. This is typical of statistical analysis where you look for the trends of the "big picture," revealing patterns that are useful but usually not perfect.

Correlation Measures the Strength of the Relationship

The **correlation** or **correlation coefficient,** denoted r, is a pure number between −1 and 1 summarizing the strength of the relationship in the data. A correlation of 1 indicates a perfect straight-line relationship, with higher values of one variable associated with perfectly predictable higher values of the other. A correlation of −1 indicates a perfect negative straight-line relationship, with one variable *decreasing* as the other increases.

The usual interpretation of intermediate correlations between −1 and 1 is that the size (absolute value) of the correlation indicates the strength of the relationship, and the sign (positive or negative) indicates the direction (increasing or decreasing). The usual interpretation of a correlation of 0 is that there is no relationship, just randomness. However, these interpretations must be used with caution since curves (nonlinear structure) and outliers can distort the usual interpretation of the correlation. A quick look at the scatterplot will either confirm or rule out these nasty possibilities. Table 11.1.2 indicates how to interpret the correlation in each case. Remember that the correlation shows you how close the points are to being exactly on a tilted straight line. It does *not* tell you how steep that line is.

The Formula for the Correlation

The correlation is computed based on the data using a straightforward but time-consuming formula. Computers and many calculators can quickly compute the correlation for you. The formula is included in this section not so much for your use but rather to provide some insight into how it works.

The formula for the correlation coefficient is based on bivariate data consisting of the two measurements (X_1, Y_1) made on the first elementary unit through the measurements (X_n, Y_n) made on the last one. For example, X_1 might be sales of IBM and Y_1 might be net income of IBM; X_n could be sales of GM and Y_n net income of GM. Looking at each column of numbers separately, you could compute the usual sample standard deviation for just the X values to find S_X; similarly, S_Y represents the standard deviation of just the Y values.[1] The formula for the correlation is:

■ Formula for the Correlation Coefficient

$$r = \frac{\dfrac{1}{n-1} \displaystyle\sum_{i=1}^{n} (X_i - \bar{X})(Y_i - \bar{Y})}{S_X \times S_Y}$$

The terms in the numerator summation involve the interaction of the two variables and determine whether the correlation will be positive or negative. For example, if there is a strong positive (increasing) relationship, each term in the sum will be positive: if a point has a high X and a high Y, the product will be positive; if a point has a low X and a low Y, the product will again be positive because the two elements in the product will be negative (since X and Y are both below their respective averages), and a negative times a negative gives a positive number. Similarly, if there is a strong negative relationship, all terms in the sum in the numerator will be negative, resulting in a negative correlation.

---

[1] Note that S_X and S_Y are standard deviations representing the variability of *individuals* and should not be confused with standard errors $S_{\bar{X}}$ and $S_{\bar{Y}}$ representing the variability of the sample averages $\bar{X}$ and $\bar{Y}$, respectively.

TABLE 11.1.2   Interpreting the Correlation Coefficient

Correlation	Usual Interpretation	Some Other Possibilities
1	Perfect positive relationship. All data points must fall *exactly* on a line that tilts *upward* to the right.	None
Close to 1	Strong positive relationship. Data points bunch tightly, but with some random scatter, about a line that tilts *upward* to the right.	Data points fall exactly on an upward-sloping *curve* (nonlinear structure). Data points mostly have no relationship, but one *outlier* has distorted the correlation.
Close to 0 but positive	Slight positive relationship. Data points form a random cloud with a slight *upward* tilt toward the right.	*Clustering* has distorted the correlation.
0	*No relationship*, just a random cloud tilting neither up nor down toward the right.	Data points fall exactly on a *curve* tilting up on one side and down on the other. Data points fall exactly on a line, but one *outlier* has distorted the correlation. *Clustering* has distorted the correlation.
Close to 0 but negative	Slight negative relationship. Data points form a random cloud with a slight *downward* tilt toward the right.	Data points fall exactly on a downward-sloping *curve* (nonlinear structure).
Close to −1	Strong negative relationship. Data points bunch tightly, but with some random scatter, about a line that tilts *downward* to the right.	Data points mostly have no structure, but one *outlier* has distorted the correlation. *Clustering* has distorted the correlation.
−1	Perfect negative relationship. All data points must fall *exactly* on a line that tilts *downward* to the right.	None
Undefined	Data points fall exactly on a horizontal or vertical line.	Not enough data (less than $n = 2$ distinct pairs of X and Y values).

The denominator merely scales the numerator so that the resulting correlation will be an easily interpreted pure number between −1 and 1. Since the numerator involves the product of the two variables, it is reasonable to convert to a pure number through dividing by a product of terms involving these variables. If you did not divide, the numerator by itself would be difficult to interpret because its measurement units would be unfamiliar. For example, if X and Y are both measured as dollar amounts, the numerator would be in units of "squared dollars," whatever they are.

The numerator in the formula for the correlation coefficient, which is difficult to interpret due to its measurement units, is known as the **covariance** of X and Y. Although it is used occasionally (for example, in finance theory to describe the covariation of one stock market price with another), it is probably easier to use the correlation instead. The correlation and the covariance both represent the same information (provided you also know the individual standard deviations), but the correlation presents that information in a more accessible form.

Note also that the roles of X and Y are interchangeable in the formula; it is *symmetric* in X and Y. Thus, the correlation of X with Y is the same as the correlation of Y with X; it makes no difference which one comes first. This is true of correlation but not for regression (to be covered in Section 11.2).

The Various Types of Relationships

The following sections list the various types of relationships you might find when you look at a scatterplot of a bivariate data set. At least one example will be provided for each kind of relationship, together with the scatterplot, the correlation coefficient, and some discussion.

Linear Relationship

Some kinds of bivariate data sets are easier to analyze than others. Those with a *linear relationship* are the easiest. This relationship plays the same special role for bivariate data that the normal distribution plays for univariate data. A bivariate data set shows a **linear relationship** if the scatterplot shows points bunched randomly around a straight line.[2] The points might be tightly bunched and fall almost exactly on a line, or they might be wildly scattered, forming a cloud of points. But the relationship will not be strongly curved, will not be funnel-shaped, and will not have any extreme outliers.

EXAMPLE **Nielsen TV Ratings and People Meters**

You have probably heard of the Nielsen ratings for television shows. Because advertising rates are set based on the size of the TV audience, these ratings have a special importance to the TV networks and advertisers. Indeed, since a single 30-second advertisement can cost hundreds of thousands of dollars (plus pro-

---

[2] A bivariate data set is said to have a *bivariate normal distribution* if it shows a linear relationship and, in addition, each of the individual variables has a normal distribution. A more careful technical definition would also require that for each X value, the Y values be normally distributed with constant variation.

duction costs!), even a small change in the size of the viewer audience could have tremendous budgetary implications.

For about 30 years, the Nielsen ratings were based on a few thousand households that kept diaries in which they recorded details about their TV viewing. With the advent of inexpensive electronic equipment and computers, it became possible to use "people meters," which record the information automatically. The possible conversion from one system to the other is controversial because the numbers come out different between the two methods, and the stakes are huge. Consider:

> The problem is that initial people-meter tests suggest that fewer people may be watching some programs than diaries have indicated. Thus, advertising agencies, which place about $8 billion in advertising on network television annually, want to base new ad rates on people-meter ratings alone—and, they hope, wring price cuts from the networks.... The importance of the ratings is evident in a show like "Cosby," which commands an estimated $380,000 for a 30-second spot. In the two weeks ended Nov. 23, Nielsen people meters suggest that "Cosby" viewers included 20% fewer women ages 18 to 49 and 7% fewer men in the same age group than diaries show for that period.... For other programs, however, people meters suggest there are *more* viewers than diaries indicate.... Such disparities have big implications for negotiations between networks and advertisers over commercial fees.... Nielsen has been moving quickly on people meters in part because of competition from AGB Television Research Inc.[3]

Table 11.1.3 shows a bivariate data set consisting of the Nielsen index (one variable) and the people meter index (the other variable) measured for each of $n = 10$ TV shows (the elementary units).

TABLE 11.1.3   TV Ratings

	Nielsen Index	People Meters
The Cosby Show	27.4	24.4
Family Ties	27.2	25.5
Cheers	24.1	23.0
Moonlighting	22.7	20.2
Night Court	22.1	20.1
Growing Pains	18.3	17.5
Who's the Boss	17.5	16.1
Family Ties (Special)	17.5	13.3
Murder She Wrote	16.8	14.7
60 Minutes	16.5	13.6

P. Barnes and J. Lipman, "Networks and Ad Agencies Battle over Estimates of TV Viewership," *The Wall Street Journal,* January 1, 1987, p. 25. Their source is NBC. These were the 10 top shows from October 10 to October 23. One rating point represents 1% of the 97.7 million adults ages 25–54.

---

[3]P. Barnes and J. Lipman, "Networks and Ad Agencies Battle over Estimates of TV Viewership," *The Wall Street Journal,* January 1, 1987, p. 25.

FIGURE 11.1.3   A linear relationship in the scatterplot of two kinds of TV ratings for $n = 10$ top shows. Note the strong positive association, summarized by the high correlation of $r = 0.974$.

The scatterplot, shown in Figure 11.1.3, shows linear structure because the points could be described as being randomly scattered around a straight line. The relationship is positive because shows with higher Nielsen indexes generally have higher people meter ratings. The high correlation, $r = 0.974$, summarizes the fact that there is strong positive association but not a perfect relationship. There is some randomness, which could make a difference to the networks and advertisers.

EXAMPLE   **Mergers**

Investment bankers earn large fees for making arrangements and giving advice relating to mergers and acquisitions when one firm joins with or purchases another. Who are the big players? How many deals and how much money are involved to produce these huge fees? Some answers are provided by the bivariate data set in Table 11.1.4, which appeared around the time that some of the "stars" of First Boston left to go to work on their own.

The scatterplot, in Figure 11.1.4, shows a linear relationship, but one with substantially more scatter, or randomness, than in the previous example. There is a clear increasing trend, with the more successful firms being involved in more deals (toward the right) that involved more money (toward the top). The randomness involves substantial dollar amounts; for example, among firms involved with around 120 deals, the dollar amount of these deals differed by tens of billions of dollars. The correlation is $r = 0.790$, summarizing this strong increasing trend in the presence of noticeable randomness.

TABLE 11.1.4   Top Merger and Acquisition Advisors

	Number of Deals	Dollar Amount (millions)
Goldman Sachs	134	$63,465.0
First Boston	174	55,091.8
Morgan Stanley	120	42,336.3
Merrill Lynch	101	34,324.5
Shearson Lehman Brothers	164	25,631.7
Lazard Freres	44	24,251.5
Drexel Burnham Lambert	126	22,706.5
Salomon Brothers	76	21,859.7
Kidder Peabody	70	13,518.9
Dillon Read	42	11,167.8
Donaldson, Lufkin & Jenrette	47	7,750.1
Bankers Trust	41	5,525.7
PaineWebber	67	4,788.1
Allen & Co.	6	4,603.8
Bear Stearns	36	4,555.9

Data are from "Top Advisers for Mergers and Acquisitions," *The Wall Street Journal,* February 3, 1988, p. 1. Their source is IDD Information Services.

FIGURE 11.1.4   A linear relationship between the dollar amount and number of deals involved for the largest advisors for mergers and acquisitions. The correlation, $r = 0.790$, summarizes the strong increasing trend (successful advisors had lots of deals involving lots of money) partially obscured by randomness.

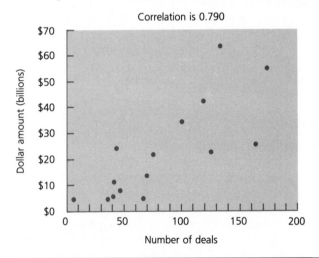

EXAMPLE   **Mortgage Rates and Fees**

When you take out a mortgage, there are many different kinds of costs. Usually the two largest are the *interest rate* (a yearly percentage that determines the size of your monthly payment) and the *loan fee* (a one-time percentage charged to

TABLE 11.1.5 Mortgage Costs

	Interest Rate	Loan Fee		Interest Rate	Loan Fee
Alaska USA FCU	10.25	2.00	Hallmark Mortgage	10.25	2.00
Amco Mortgage	10.125	1.95	Hoover Mortgage	10.125	2.00
American Builders	10.25	2.00	ICA Mortgage	10.25	2.00
ARCS Mortgage	10.20	2.00	Key Pacific Mortgage	10.25	2.00
Bay Mortgage	10.25	2.00	Metropolitan Federal	10.125	2.00
Bay Mortgage East	10.25	2.00	Mornet of WA	10.25	2.00
Benjamin Franklin	10.25	1.50	Mortgage Brokers	10.25	2.00
Cambelco Mortgage	10.125	2.00	Mt. Baker Bank	10.375	2.00
Cascade Pacific			Norwest Mortgage	10.25	2.50
Mortgage	10.125	2.00	Old Stone Bank	10.00	3.50
Cascade S&L	10.25	1.50	Olympic Savings		
Center Mortgage	10.125	2.50	Bank	10.25	2.00
Centrust Mortgage	10.50	1.125	Pacific First		
Chase Manhattan	10.875	2.00	Mortgage	10.25	2.50
Citifed Mortgage	10.25	2.00	Pacific R.E.		
Coast Exchange	10.25	2.00	Mortgage	10.375	2.00
Columbia Federal	10.50	2.00	Pioneer Federal		
Columbia Services	10.50	2.00	Savings	10.375	2.00
Commonwealth			Principal Financial	10.25	2.00
Mortgage	10.25	1.50	Pacific West		
Continental Mortgage	10.25	2.00	Mortgage	10.125	2.25
CrossLand Mortgage	10.25	2.75	Rainier Bank	10.50	2.00
Direct Mortgage			Seafirst Home		
Services	10.25	2.00	Loans	10.375	2.00
Family Savings	10.375	2.00	Sears Mortgage	10.25	2.00
Far West Mortgage	10.125	2.00	Summit Savings	10.50	2.00
First Fed Savings			Security Pacific N.B.	10.50	2.00
of WA	10.375	1.50	Shearson Lehman	10.375	1.50
First Interstate	10.375	2.00	Standard Green		
Fireman's Fund			Mortgage	10.25	1.625
Mortgage	10.125	2.25	Sterling Mortgage	10.125	2.00
First Mutual	10.25	2.00	U.S. Bankcorp		
First Union Mortgage	10.25	2.25	Mortgage	10.375	1.875
Fleet Mortgage Corp	10.375	2.50	United Pacific		
GMAC Mortgage	10.125	2.50	Mortgage	10.125	2.25
Goldome Rainier	9.875	3.375	University Fed.		
Great American Bank	10.50	1.50	Savings	10.25	2.00
Great NW Federal			University Mortgage	10.25	2.00
S&L	10.25	2.00	Valley Mortgage	10.25	2.00
Great Pacific			Washington Mutual	10.50	2.00
Mortgage	10.25	2.00	Weyerhaeuser	10.25	2.00
Great Western Bank	10.70	2.00	Willamette Financial	10.375	2.00

Data are from "How the Summer Rates," *Seattle Times,* July 3, 1988, p. D1. Their sources are *Scotsman Publishing's Electronic Bulletin* and the *Western Washington Bulletin.*

you at the time the loan is made). Some financial institutions let you "buy down" the interest rate by paying a higher initial loan fee, suggesting that there should be a relationship between these two costs. The relationship should be *negative* or *decreasing,* since a higher loan fee should go with a lower interest rate.

Table 11.1.5 shows a bivariate data set consisting of interest rates and loan fees for lenders of 30-year fixed-rate mortgage loans:

FIGURE 11.1.5   A decreasing linear relationship between interest rate and loan fee for mortgages. The correlation, −0.441, summarizes this decreasing relationship: higher fees tend to go with lower interest rates. Since the correlation is about midway between −1 and 0, this indicates substantial randomness in the data.

The scatterplot, in Figure 11.1.5, shows a linear relationship with substantial scatter and a *decreasing* association between loan fee and interest rate. The negative correlation, $r = -0.441$, confirms the decreasing relationship we had expected. The very substantial amount of randomness in the data is summarized by a correlation value about midway between −1 and 0.

Where did all the data go? There are 67 financial institutions in the bivariate data listing, but the number of points in the scatterplot looks much smaller than that. This is because some combinations are used by several institutions (for example, a loan fee of 2% with an interest rate of 10.25%). These overlapping data points look deceptively like just one point in a simple scatterplot such as Figure 11.1.5. By adding a little bit of extra randomness or "jitter" (just for purposes of *looking* at the data, not analyzing it!), you can separate these overlapping points and see your data more clearly.[4] The resulting "jittered" scatterplot is shown in Figure 11.1.6.

No Relationship

A bivariate data set shows **no relationship** if the scatterplot is just random, tilting neither upward nor downward as you move from left to right. The case of no relationship is a special linear relationship that is neither increas-

---

[4]For a general introduction to the many different techniques for looking at data (including jittering, on p. 135), see J. M. Chambers, W. S. Cleveland, B. Kleiner, and P. A. Tukey, *Graphical Methods for Data Analysis* (New York: Wadsworth, 1983).

FIGURE 11.1.6   The previous scatterplot with "jitter" added to separate the overlapping points and show the data set more clearly.

ing nor decreasing. Such a scatterplot may look like a cloud that is either circular or oval-shaped (the oval points either up and down or left to right; it is not tilted). In fact, by changing the scale for one or the other of your variables, you can make a data set with no relationship have either a circular or an oval-shaped scatterplot.

EXAMPLE

"Momentum" and the Stock Market

Does the stock market have "momentum"? That is, is the market likely to keep going up today because it went up yesterday? If there is a relationship between yesterday's market performance and today's, you would expect to find it in a scatterplot. After all, this is our best statistical tool for seeing the relationship, if any, between market behavior yesterday (one variable) and market behavior today (the other variable).

The bivariate data set consists of daily returns in the Dow Jones industrials, that is, the percent changes (increases or decreases) from one day to the next.[5] Although this seems to be a univariate time series, you can put essentially the same data in the two columns, offsetting the columns by one row so that today's close (on the left in the table) is in the same row as yesterday's close (on the right). This has been done in Table 11.1.6.

The scatterplot, in Figure 11.1.7, shows no relationship! There is a lot of random scatter but no trend either upward (which would have suggested momentum) or downward (which would have suggested that the market "overreacted" one

[5]The formula for daily return is (Today's price − Yesterday's price)/(Yesterday's price).

TABLE 11.1.6 Percent Change in the Dow Jones Industrial Stock Market Index

	Today	Yesterday
July 2, 1987	−0.29%	1.12%
	0.83	−0.29
	0.58	0.83
	−0.52	0.58
	0.20	−0.52
	−0.12	0.20
	1.16	−0.12
	0.10	1.16
	0.53	0.10
	0.52	0.53
	−0.89	0.52
	−0.80	−0.89
	0.09	−0.80
	0.07	0.09
	0.54	0.07
	0.35	0.54
	1.04	0.35
	0.78	1.04
	1.10	0.78
	0.18	1.10
	−0.58	0.18
	−0.41	−0.58
	0.78	−0.41
	1.07	0.78
	−0.09	1.07
	1.69	−0.09
	1.69	1.69
	−0.42	1.69
	0.83	−0.42
	−0.23	0.83
	0.56	−0.23
	−1.70	0.56
	0.42	−1.70
	1.54	0.42
	0.10	1.54
	−0.46	0.10
	0.94	−0.46
	−0.76	0.94
	−0.99	−0.76
	−1.33	−0.99
August 31, 1987	0.89	−1.33

day and then corrected itself the next) as you move from left to right in the picture. The correlation, $r = 0.0428$, is close to 0, confirming the lack of relationship.[6]

A scatterplot such as this one is consistent with the ideas of market efficiency and random walks. Market efficiency says that all information that is available

---

[6]A correlation coefficient such as this, computed for a time series and its own previous values, is called the *autocorrelation* of the series because it measures the correlation of the series with itself. You might say that this time series is not autocorrelated because the autocorrelation is close to zero.

FIGURE 11.1.7　There is no relationship between today's and yesterday's stock market performance. The correlation, $r = 0.0428$, is close to 0, summarizing the lack of relationship. If yesterday was a "good" day, then today's performance will look about the same as if yesterday had been a "bad" day.

or can be anticipated is immediately reflected in market prices. Since traders anticipate future changes in market prices, there can be no systematic relationships, and only randomness (i.e., a *random walk*) can remain. A random walk generates a time series of data with no relationship between previous behavior and the next step or change.[7]

By changing the scale of the horizontal or vertical axis, the cloud of points can be made to look more like a line. However, because the line is either *horizontal* or *vertical,* with no tilt, it still indicates no relationship. These cases are shown in Figures 11.1.8 and 11.1.9.

Nonlinear Relationship

Other kinds of bivariate data sets are not so simple to analyze. A bivariate data set has a **nonlinear relationship** if the scatterplot shows points bunched around a *curved* rather than a straight line. Since there are so many different kinds of curves that can be drawn, the analysis is more complex.

Correlation and regression analysis must be used with care on nonlinear data sets. For some problems you may want to transform one or both of the variables to obtain a linear relationship. This simplifies the analysis

---

[7]There is an entire book on this subject: B. G. Malkiel, *A Random Walk down Wall Street* (New York: W. W. Norton, 1981).

FIGURE 11.1.8 There is no relationship here, even though the scatterplot looks like a distinct line, because the line is horizontal, with no tilt. This is the same data set as in Figure 11.1.7, but with the Y scale expanded to flatten the appearance of the plot.

FIGURE 11.1.9 No relationship is apparent here either, although the scatterplot looks like a distinct line, because the line is vertical, with no tilt. In this case the X axis has been expanded from Figure 11.1.7.

(since correlation and regression are more easily applied to a linear relationship) provided the results are transformed back to the original data, if appropriate.[8]

---

[8]Transformations in regression will be considered further in Chapter 12.

EXAMPLE   ## Index Options

If you buy a *call option*, you have the right (but not the obligation) to buy some asset (it might be a lot of land, 100 shares of IBM stock, etc.) at a set price (the *strike price* or *exercise price*) whenever you want until the option expires. Businesses use options to hedge (i.e., reduce) risks at a much lower price compared to buying and perhaps later selling the asset itself. Options on stocks can be used either to reduce the risk of a portfolio or to create a portfolio of high risk with high expected return.

The higher the strike price, the less the option is worth. For example, an option to buy a candy bar for $2,000 is worthless, but an option to buy it at $0.25 would have some value. In fact, if candy bar prices are stable at $0.45, then the option would be worth $0.45 − $0.25 = $0.20. However, for most markets, uncertainty about the future adds to the value of the option. For example, on November 9, 1988, an option to buy IBM stock at a strike price of $125 anytime during the next two months, when the stock was trading at $120, was worth about $2.00 per share. Why would you want to buy stock at $125 through the option when you could buy it for $120 right now? You wouldn't, but you could hold on to the option and buy the stock for $125 when the market price for the stock rises to $135 (if it does). This market volatility (the *possibility* of a rise in prices) accounts for part of the value of an option.

So we expect to find a negative relationship between the *strike price* specified in the option contract and the *call price* at which the option contract itself is traded. Table 11.1.7 shows a bivariate data set for the most popular index options, based on Standard & Poor's 100 index.

The scatterplot, in Fig. 11.1.10, shows a nonlinear relationship. The relationship is clearly negative, since higher strike prices are associated with lower call prices; the correlation of $r = -0.962$ confirms a strong negative relationship. Since the relationship is nearly perfect and there is essentially no randomness, you might expect a correlation of −1. However, this could happen only if the points were exactly on a *straight line*. Since the points are exactly on a curve, the correlation must be different from −1.

TABLE 11.1.7   S&P 100 Index Call Options

Strike Price	Call Price
$230	$34.0000
245	19.2500
250	15.8750
255	11.6250
260	8.1250
265	5.2500
270	3.2500
275	1.8125
280	0.9375
285	0.5000

Data are from *The Wall Street Journal,* November 9, 1988, p. C15.

FIGURE 11.1.10   A nonlinear relationship between the price of an option and the strike price. You can see the expected negative relationship, but it is *nonlinear* because the line is curved. The correlation, $r = -0.962$, expresses a strong negative relationship. Due to the curvature, the correlation cannot be exactly -1 even though this is a perfect relationship, with no random scatter.

Strike price (option contract lets you buy at this price)

Advanced statistical methods, based on assumptions of an underlying normal distribution and a random walk for the stock price, have allowed analysts to compute an appropriate value for a call option price.[9] This complex and advanced theory is based on a careful computation of the expectation (mean value) of the random variable representing the option's ultimate payoff value.

EXAMPLE   ### Yield and Temperature

You can have a strong nonlinear relationship even if the correlation is *nearly zero!* This can happen if the strong relationship is neither increasing nor decreasing, as might happen if there is an optimal, or best possible, value. Consider the data taken as part of an experiment to find the temperature that produces the largest output yield for an industrial process, shown in Table 11.1.8.

The scatterplot, in Figure 11.1.11, shows a strong nonlinear relationship with some random scatter. The correlation, $r = -0.0155$, is essentially useless for summarizing this kind of nonlinear relationship: it can't decide whether the relationship is increasing or decreasing because it is doing both!

This scatterplot will be very useful to your firm, since it tells you that to maximize your output yield, you should set the temperature of the process at around 700 degrees. The yield falls off if the temperature is either too cold or too hot.

---

[9]An overview of the theory and practice of options is provided by J. C. Cox and M. Rubenstein, *Options Market* (Englewood Cliffs, N.J.: Prentice-Hall, 1985).

TABLE 11.1.8   Temperature and Yield for an
Industrial Process

Temperature	Yield
600	127
625	139
650	147
675	147
700	155
725	154
750	153
775	148
800	146
825	136
850	129

FIGURE 11.1.11   A nonlinear relationship between the output yield and the temperature of an industrial process. Although there is a strong relationship here, it is nonlinear. The correlation, $r = -0.0155$, merely tells you that, *overall*, the trend is neither up nor down.

This useful information has come to you from looking at the strong relationship between yield and temperature on the scatterplot.

Remember: A correlation value near zero might mean there is no relationship in your data, but it also might mean the relationship is nonlinear with no overall trend up or down.

Unequal Variability

Another technical difficulty that, unfortunately, arises quite often in business and economic data is that the vertical variability in a plot of the data may depend on where you are on the horizontal scale. When you measure large businesses (or other kinds of elementary units) you find lots of variability (perhaps millions or billions of dollars worth), but when you measure small businesses you might find variability only in the tens of thousands. A scatterplot is said to have **unequal variability** when the variability on the vertical axis changes dramatically as you move horizontally across the scatterplot.[10]

The problem with unequal variability is that the places with high variability, which represent the *least precise* information, tend to influence statistical summaries the most. So if you have a scatterplot with extremely unequal variability, the correlation coefficient (and other summaries of the relationship) will probably be unreliable.

This problem can often be solved by transforming the data, perhaps by using logarithms. It is fortunate that such a transformation, when applied to each variable, solves several problems. Not only will the variability be equalized, but the variables will also be more normally distributed in many cases. Logarithms (either natural base *e* or common base 10; pick one and stick with it) tend to work well with dollar amounts. The square root transformation often works well with count data, which are measures of the number of things or the number of times something happened.

EXAMPLE

Optical Cable

Many high-technology investments are risky: the methods are new and may not work perfectly, expensive equipment becomes obsolete relatively quickly, and the competition can be fierce. Nonetheless, billions of dollars have been invested in long-distance communications networks made of optical cable. If you were interested in this kind of investment, you would want to know how much it costs to install fiber-optic networks. This information for the dominant players in these ventures is shown in Table 11.1.9.

The scatterplot, in Figure 11.1.12, shows a generally increasing relationship: firms with larger investment dollars tended to produce more circuit miles. However, the variability is substantially unequal, as may be seen from the "funnel shape" of the data, opening out to the right. The smaller firms are crowded together at the lower left, indicating very little variability in circuit miles; the larger firms at the right show much greater variability in the circuit miles they achieve with these larger investments. Figure 11.1.13 indicates exactly which variabilities are unequal: the variabilities measured vertically, for circuit miles.

Could transformation take care of this unequal variability problem? Let's try natural logarithms. AT&T's investment, for example, is $1,300,000,000, so the logarithm is 21.0. Circuit miles for AT&T are 1,700,000,000, so the logarithm is 21.3. Results of taking the log of each data value are shown in Table 11.1.10.

---

[10]The technical words *heteroscedastic* (adjective) and *heteroscedasticity* (noun) also describe unequal variability.

TABLE 11.1.9　　Fiber-Optic Long-Distance Communications

	Investment (millions)	Circuit Miles* (millions)
AT&T	$1,300	1,700
MCI	500	650
GTE	130	110
United Telecommunications	2,000	1,200
Fibertrak	1,200	2,400
LDX Net	110	165
Electra Communications	40	72
Microtel	60	45
Litel Telecommunications	57	85
Lightnet	500	650
SoutherNet	90	50
RCI	90	87

*A *circuit mile* is defined as a length of cable capable of carrying one voice for one mile.

Data are from W. B. Johnston, "The Coming Glut of Phone Lines," *Fortune*, January 7, 1985, pp. 97–100. Their source is the Hudson Institute.

FIGURE 11.1.12　Unequal variability in the relationship between circuit miles and investment. The large players (to the right) show much more variability than the smaller players (at the left).

FIGURE 11.1.13　The scatterplot of circuit miles against investment, with the unequal variabilities clearly indicated.

The scatterplot, shown in Figure 11.1.14, shows a nice linear relationship between the logarithms of investment dollars and the logarithms of circuit miles. The scatterplot would have looked the same had you used common logarithms (base 10) or if you had transformed the "millions" numbers (such as $1,300) instead of the actual amounts (such as $1,300,000,000). The unequal variability problem has disappeared.

It is common for the correlation to increase (as it does here, from 0.820 untransformed to 0.957 for the logs) when a good transformation is used, but this may not always happen. However, it is generally true that because the correla-

TABLE 11.1.10   Fiber-Optic Long-Distance Communications

	Investment (logarithm of dollars)	Circuit Miles (logarithm)
AT&T	21.0	21.3
MCI	20.0	20.3
GTE	18.7	18.5
United Telecommunications	21.4	20.9
Fibertrak	20.9	21.6
LDX Net	18.5	18.9
Electra Communications	17.5	18.1
Microtel	17.9	17.6
Litel Telecommunications	17.9	18.3
Lightnet	20.0	20.3
SoutherNet	18.3	17.7
RCI	18.3	18.3

FIGURE 11.1.14   Transforming to a linear relationship between the natural logarithms of circuit miles and of investment dollars. By transforming in this way, the problem of unequal variability has been eliminated. This data set, on the log scale, has a linear relationship.

tion on the original scale is so sensitive to those few very large firms, the correlation number after transforming is a more *reliable* indication of the relationship.

Clustering

A bivariate data set is said to show **clustering** if there are separate, distinct groups in the scatterplot. This can be a problem if your data are clustered but you are not aware of it because the usual statistical summaries of the relationship are not sophisticated enough to respond to this kind of relationship. It is up to you to recognize clustering and to respond, for example, by separating the data set into two or more data sets, one for each cluster.

A typical problem with clustering is that within each cluster there is a clear relationship, but the correlation coefficient suggests that there is no relationship. Even worse, the correlation coefficient can suggest that the overall relationship is *opposite* to the relationship within each cluster! Always look at a scatterplot to see if you have this problem; the correlation alone can't tell you.

EXAMPLE　　Flower Bonds

U.S. Treasury bonds are among the least risky investments, in terms of the likelihood of your receiving the promised payments.[11] In addition to the primary market auctions by the treasury, there is an active secondary market in which all outstanding issues can be traded. You would expect to see an increasing relationship between the *coupon* of the bond, which indicates the size of its periodic payment (twice a year), and the current selling price. Table 11.1.11 shows a bivariate data set of coupons and bid prices for U.S. Treasury bonds maturing between 1994 and 1998.

TABLE 11.1.11　U.S. Treasury Bonds

Coupon Rate	Bid Price	Coupon Rate	Bid Price
7.000%	$ 92.94	12.625%	$119.06
9.000	101.44	8.875	100.38
7.000	92.66	10.500	108.50
4.125	94.50	8.625	99.25
13.125	118.94	9.500	103.63
8.000	96.75	11.500	114.03
8.750	100.88	8.875	100.38
12.625	117.25	7.375	92.06
9.500	103.34	7.250	90.88
10.125	106.25	8.625	98.41
11.625	113.19	8.500	97.75
8.625	99.44	8.875	99.88
3.000	94.50	8.125	95.16
10.500	108.31	9.000	100.66
11.250	111.69	9.250	102.31
8.375	98.09	7.000	88.00
10.375	107.91	3.500	94.53
11.250	111.97		

Data are from *The Wall Street Journal,* November 9, 1988, p. C19. The bid prices are listed per "face value" of $100 to be paid at maturity. Half of the coupon is paid every six months. For example, the first one listed pays $3.50 (half of the 7% coupon) every six months until maturity in 1994, at which time it pays an additional $100.

---

[11]However, there is still *interest rate risk* if you decide to sell the bond before maturity.

FIGURE 11.1.15 Clustering in the relationship between bid price and coupon payment for bonds. Pricing of an ordinary bond differs from that for a *flower bond,* so a separate relationship applies for each cluster. The overall correlation, $r = 0.867$, does not take the relationships within each cluster into account. The correlation for the cluster of ordinary bonds is much higher, at $r = 0.993$.

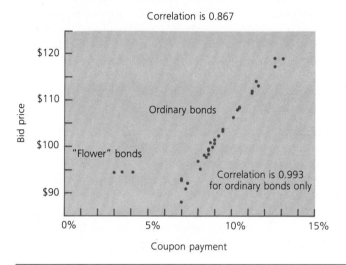

The scatterplot in Figure 11.1.15 shows clustering. The ordinary bonds form one cluster with a very strong linear relationship. After careful investigation, you would find out that the three special bonds in the cluster at the lower left are known as *flower bonds.* These three flower bonds form a cluster with a very different relationship between coupon and price. The overall correlation, $r = 0.867$, indicates the strength of the relationship among *all* of the data points in all clusters. The relationship among the ordinary bonds is very much stronger, with a correlation of $r = 0.993$, found by leaving the three flower bonds out of the calculation.

What might have happened if you had not identified the clusters? You might have mistakenly concluded that the relationship between coupon and price is merely "pretty strong," with a correlation of 0.867, instead of identifying the true relationship for ordinary bonds, which is "very strong," with a correlation of 0.993. If you were using this data set to compute prices or to decide which ordinary bonds to trade, your results would have been compromised by the presence of the flower bonds. Flower bonds are, in a sense, a different type of security altogether; it is somewhat confusing to have them listed alongside the others in bond price listings.

What are flower bonds, and why are they priced so differently? It is special tax treatment that makes them different. They are redeemable at par (that is, at face value) for payment of estate taxes. If you were very rich and about to die (so that estate taxes matter), you might be willing to pay about $94 per $100 worth of bonds. The rest of us probably would not have these in our portfolios.

According to the scatterplot (looking at the relationship for ordinary bonds), these bonds should be worth about $80 or less due to their low coupon payment. It is their estate tax value that pushes the price up so high.

Outliers

A data point in a scatterplot is a **bivariate outlier** if it does not fit the relationship of the rest of the data. An outlier can distort statistical summaries and make them very misleading. You should always watch out for outliers in bivariate data by looking at a scatterplot. If you can justify removing an outlier (for example, by finding that it should not have been there in the first place), then do so. Otherwise, if you have to leave it in, at least be aware of the problems it can cause.

An outlier can distort the correlation to make it seem that there is a strong relationship when, in fact, there is nothing but randomness and one outlier. An outlier can also distort the correlation to make it seem that there is *no* relationship when, in fact, there is a strong relationship and one outlier. How can you protect yourself from these traps? By looking at a scatterplot, of course.

EXAMPLE

Number Produced and Cost

Consider the number of items produced each week in a factory together with the total cost for that week. There should be a fairly strong relationship here. On high-volume weeks, lots of items will be produced, requiring lots of costly input materials. However, there can be surprises in the data. For the data set shown in Table 11.1.12, the correlation is negative, at $r = -0.623$. How could it be negative?

TABLE 11.1.12   Weekly Production

Number Produced	Cost
22	$ 3,470
30	3,783
26	3,856
31	3,910
36	4,489
30	3,876
22	3,221
45	4,579
38	4,325
3	14,131
30	3,589
38	3,999
41	4,158
27	3,666
28	3,885
31	3,574
37	4,495
32	3,814
41	4,430

FIGURE 11.1.16 An outlier has distorted the correlation. Instead of revealing a generally increasing relationship between number and cost, the correlation $r = -0.623$ suggests that there is a decreasing relationship, with higher production requiring a *lower* cost.

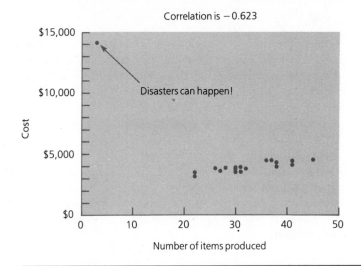

The scatterplot shown in Figure 11.1.16 has an extreme outlier. This explains the negative correlation even though the rest of the data show some positive association (this is difficult to tell because the outlier causes the rest of the data to be squashed together). Outliers should be investigated. In fact, what happened here is that there was a fire in the factory. Lots of the input materials were ruined, and these showed up as costs for that week. The output was low because production was halted at 11 A.M., and not even all of the production to that point could be used.

Is it permissible to omit the outlier? Probably so in this case. Certainly so if you are interested in the relationship for "ordinary" weeks and are willing to treat a disaster as a special case outside the usual circumstances. Indeed, if you omit the outlier, the correlation becomes strongly positive, at $r = 0.869$, indicating a fairly strong increasing relationship between inputs and outputs.

The data set without the outlier is shown in Figure 11.1.17. Note that, without the outlier present, the scale can be expanded, and more detail can be seen in the rest of the data.

Correlation Is Not Causation

We often think of correlation and causation as going together. This is reasonable because when one thing *causes* another, the two tend to be associated and therefore correlated (e.g., effort and results, inspection and quality, investment and return, environment and productivity).

FIGURE 11.1.17   The same data set with the outlier omitted to show the relationship for ordinary (i.e., nondisaster) weeks. The correlation is now a reasonably strong and positive $r = 0.869$, indicating an increasing relationship.

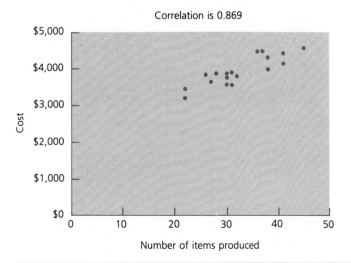

However, there can be correlation without causation. Think of it this way: The correlation is just a number that reveals whether large values of one variable tend to go with large (or with small) values of the other. The correlation cannot explain *why* the two are associated. Indeed, the correlation provides no sense of whether the investment is producing the return or vice versa! The correlation just indicates that the numbers seem to go together in some way.

One possible basis for correlation without causation is that there is some hidden, unobserved, "third factor" that makes one of the variables *seem* to cause the other when, in fact, each is being caused by the missing variable. The term **spurious correlation** refers to a high correlation that is actually due to some third factor. For example, you might find a high correlation between hiring new managers and building new facilities. Are the newly hired managers "causing" new plant investment? Or does the act of constructing new buildings "cause" new managers to be hired? Probably there is a third factor, namely, *high long-term demand* for the firm's products, that is causing both.

EXAMPLE   Apartment Rents and Vacancy Rates

The economic principle of supply and demand for rental space suggests that if you raise rents, fewer people will be able to afford to live in the building and the vacancy rate should go up. Table 11.1.13 shows a bivariate data set; let's see if it works out this way.

TABLE 11.1.13   The Apartment Market

	Vacancy Rate	Monthly Rent
Airport	4.8%	$378
Auburn	5.3	368
Ballard	1.3	348
Beacon Hill	4.9	391
Bellevue-East	4.2	463
Bellevue-West	3.6	581
Bothell/Juanita	4.4	483
Burien	3.5	363
Capitol Hill/Eastlake	5.0	395
Central	10.1	301
Des Moines	4.8	406
Downtown Seattle	8.3	449
Federal Way	4.5	403
First Hill	6.3	400
Greenlake/Wall	2.3	429
Kent	4.4	424
Kirkland	1.5	561
Madison/Leschi	0.4	572
Magnolia	1.4	443
Mercer Island	6.4	472
North King Co.	3.7	433
North Seattle	3.2	423
Queen Anne	3.3	428
Rainier Valley	15.7	341
Redmond	3.9	501
Renton	6.0	416
Riverton/Tukwila	4.7	381
University	4.3	430
West Seattle	3.9	355
White Center	6.1	381
King Country	4.7	428

Data are from *The Seattle Times*, October 18, 1987, p. E1. Their source is Cain and Scott.

The scatterplot shown in Figure 11.1.18 suggests a slight *negative* relationship, with substantial randomness. The correlation is $r = -0.472$. A negative correlation? That's absurd! You'd think that higher rents would drive tenants away and increase vacancy rates! However, there may not be any direct causation here; the negative correlation could be spurious. Both of these variables could be responding to a hidden third factor, namely, the desirability of the neighborhood. In the more desirable neighborhoods, the rents could be high and the vacancy rate low due to higher demand. In the less desirable neighborhoods, demand could be low, causing rents to be lower and vacancy rates to be higher.

■ 11.2 Regression: Prediction of One Thing from Another

Regression analysis is predicting one variable from the other. By convention, the variable being predicted is denoted Y, and the variable that helps with the prediction is X. It makes a big difference which one you denote as

FIGURE 11.1.18   Correlation without direct causation of vacancy rate by rental rate. There is
a negative relationship, $r = -0.472$, suggesting that higher rents go with *lower*
vacancy rates. This is explained by the missing "third factor," namely,
neighborhood desirability. The desirable neighborhoods have high rents and
low vacancy rates. The high rents are not "causing" the low vacancy rates any
more than the low vacancy rates "cause" high rents. The negative correlation
is *spurious*.

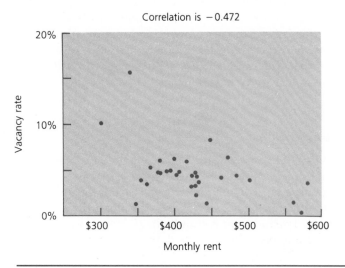

TABLE 11.2.1   Variables in Regression Analysis

	X	Y
Roles	Predictor	Predicted
	Independent variable	Dependent variable
	Explanatory variable	Explained variable
	Stimulus	Response
	Exogenous (from outside)	Endogenous (from inside)
Examples	Sales	Earnings
	Number produced	Cost
	Effort	Results
	Investment	Outcome
	Experience	Salary
	Temperature of process	Output yield

Y and which as *X*, since *X predicts Y* and *Y is predicted by X*. Table 11.2.1 shows
some of the standard ways used to refer to the role of each variable, together
with some examples.

A Straight Line Summarizes a Linear Relationship

Linear regression analysis is predicting one variable from the other when
the two have a linear relationship. Just as you use the average to summarize
a single variable, you can use a straight line to summarize a linear predic-

tive relationship between two variables. Just as there is variability about the average (for univariate data), there is also variability about the straight line (for bivariate data). Just like the average, the straight line is a useful but imperfect summary due to this randomness.

Figure 11.2.1 shows the straight line summary for the television ratings data, an example of a linear relationship given earlier in the chapter. Note how the line summarizes the increasing relationship. It captures the basic structure in the data, leaving the points to fluctuate randomly around it.

After a brief discussion of straight lines, you will be shown how to compute and interpret the regression line, how to measure how well it works, how to do inference about a population relationship based on a sample, and how to be careful in problematic situations.

Straight Lines

A straight line is described by two numbers, the *slope, b,* and the *intercept, a.* The **slope** indicates how steeply the line rises (or falls, if b is negative). As you move horizontally to the right exactly 1 unit (measured in X units), the line will rise (or fall, if $b < 0$) vertically a distance b units (measured in Y units). The **intercept** is simply the (vertical) value for Y when X is 0. In cases where it is absurd for X to be 0, the intercept should be viewed as a technical

FIGURE 11.2.1   The regression line summarizes the relationship between two measures of TV audience size. This line shows how to predict people meter ratings (Y) from the Nielsen index (X).

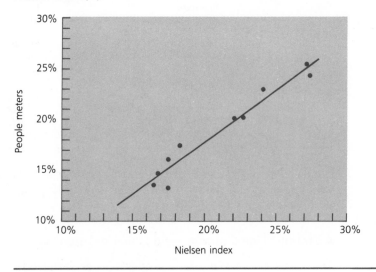

necessity for specifying the line and should not be interpreted directly.[12] The equation for a straight line is as follows:

■ **Equation for a Straight Line**

$$Y = \text{Intercept} + \text{Slope} \times X$$

$$= a + bX$$

The slope and intercept are illustrated in Figures 11.2.2, 11.2.3, and 11.2.4.

Finding a Line Based on Data

How should you find the best summary line to predict Y from X based on a bivariate data set? One approach is to find the line that has the smallest prediction error overall, in some sense. The conventional way to do this is to use the **least-squares line,** which has the smallest sum of squared vertical prediction errors compared to all other lines that could possibly be drawn. These prediction errors, the sum of whose squares is to be minimized, are shown in Figure 11.2.5, for the least-squares line, and in Figure 11.2.6, for a foolish choice of line, for the sales data from Table 11.1.1.

FIGURE 11.2.2   The straight line $Y = 3 + 0.5X$ starts at the intercept ($a = 3$), when X is 0, and rises 0.5 (one slope value, $b = 0.5$) for each distance of 1 moved to the right.

FIGURE 11.2.3   A line with negative slope. The straight line $Y = 4 - 0.5X$ starts at the intercept ($a = 4$), when X is 0, and falls 0.5 (since the slope value is negative, $b = -0.5$) for each distance of 1 moved to the right.

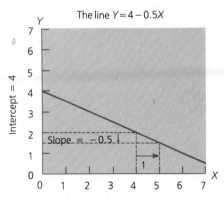

---

[12]It is possible to define the line in terms of the slope together with the value of Y at $\overline{X}$, so that the two numbers that specify the line are both always meaningful. However, this is rarely done at present.

FIGURE 11.2.4   An assortment of straight lines and their equations, showing the slope and intercept. The vertical line is the only one that cannot be written in the form $Y = a + bX$.

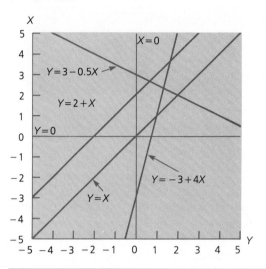

FIGURE 11.2.5   The least-squares line has the smallest sum of squared prediction errors of all possible lines. The prediction errors are measured vertically.

- The least-squares line
- Prediction errors are small
- Sum of squared errors is 53,445,498

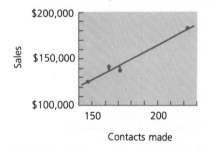

Contacts made

FIGURE 11.2.6   A foolish choice of line will have large prediction errors and will *not* be the least-squares line.

- A foolish line
- Prediction errors are large
- Sum of squared errors is 6,002,064,073

Contacts made

The least-squares line can easily be found. Computers and many calculators can automatically find the least-squares slope, b, and intercept, a. The slope is also called the **regression coefficient** of Y on X, and the intercept is also called the **constant term** in the regression. The slope, b, is found as the correlation, r, times the ratio of standard deviations, S_Y/S_X (which is in appropriate units of Y per X). The intercept, a, is determined so that the line goes through the most reasonable landmark, namely $(\overline{X},\overline{Y})$. The formulas are as follows:

■ **The Least-Squares Slope and Intercept**

$$\text{Slope} = b = r\frac{S_Y}{S_X}$$

$$\text{Intercept} = a = \overline{Y} - b\overline{X} = \overline{Y} - r\frac{S_Y}{S_X}\overline{X}$$

■ **The Least-Squares Line**

$$(\text{Predicted value of } Y) = a + bX$$

$$= \left(\overline{Y} - r\frac{S_Y}{S_X}\overline{X}\right) + r\frac{S_Y}{S_X}X$$

Don't expect to find all of the points on the line. Think of the line as summarizing the overall relationship in the data. Think of the data as the line together with randomness. Your **predicted value** for Y given a value of X will be the height of the line at X, which you find by using the equation of the least-squares line. You can find the predicted value either for a data point or for a new value of X. Each of your data points has a **residual**, which tells you how far the point is above (or below, if negative) the line. These residuals allow you to make adjustments, comparing actual values of Y to what you would expect them to be for corresponding values of X. The formula for the residual for the data point (X,Y) is

$$\text{Residual} = (\text{Actual } Y) - (\text{Predicted } Y) = Y - (a + bX)$$

EXAMPLE   **Fixed and Variable Costs**

Recall the production data from an earlier example, but with the outlier removed. Table 11.2.2 shows the data with X and Y indicated and summary statistics included. It is natural for X to be the number produced and Y to be the cost because a manager often needs to anticipate costs based on currently scheduled production.

The slope represents the *variable cost* (the marginal cost of producing one more item) and may be found from these summaries as follows:

$$\text{Variable cost} = b$$

$$= rS_Y/S_X$$

$$= 0.869193 \times 389.6131/6.5552$$

$$= \$51.66$$

TABLE 11.2.2   Weekly Production

	Number Produced, X	Cost, Y
	22	$3,470
	30	3,783
	26	3,856
	31	3,910
	36	4,489
	30	3,876
	22	3,221
	45	4,579
	38	4,325
	30	3,589
	38	3,999
	41	4,158
	27	3,666
	28	3,885
	31	3,574
	37	4,495
	32	3,814
	41	4,430
Average	$\bar{X} = 32.50$	$\bar{Y} = \$3{,}951.06$
Standard deviation	$S_X = 6.5552$	$S_Y = \$389.6131$
Correlation	$r = 0.869193$	

The other term, the intercept, represents the *fixed cost*. These are baseline costs such as rent that are incurred even if no items are produced. This intercept term may be found as follows:

$$\textit{Fixed cost} = a$$

$$= \bar{Y} - b\bar{X}$$

$$= 3{,}951.06 - 51.66 \times 32.5$$

$$= \$2{,}272$$

The least-squares line may be written as follows:

$$\text{Predicted cost} = \text{Fixed cost} + (\text{Variable cost})(\text{Number produced})$$

$$= \$2{,}272 + \$51.66(\text{Number produced})$$

The least-squares line is shown with the data in Figure 11.2.7.

You might use this estimated relationship to help with budgeting. If you anticipate the need to produce 36 of these items next week, you can predict your cost using the relationship in the past data as summarized by the least-squares line. Your forecast will be as follows:

$$\text{Predicted cost for producing 36 items} = a + b \times 36$$

$$= \$2{,}272 + \$51.66 \times 36$$

$$= \$4{,}132$$

FIGURE 11.2.7   The least-squares line summarizes the production cost data by estimating a
                 fixed cost (the intercept, a = $2,272) and a variable per-unit cost (the slope,
                 b = $51.66 per item produced).

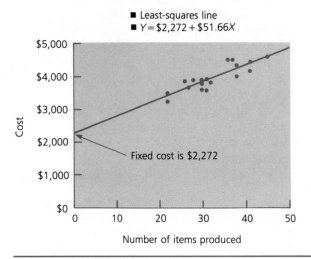

FIGURE 11.2.8   The least-squares line may be used to forecast, or predict, the expected value for
                 Y given a new value for X. In this case you are expecting to produce 36 items
                 next week. The least-squares line suggests that your expected cost will be
                 $4,132. Of course, the real cost will come in with some randomness, just like
                 the other points.

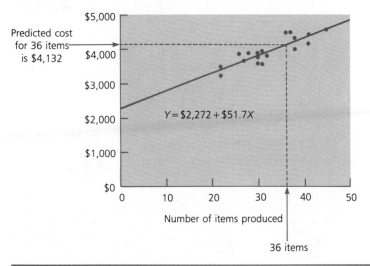

Your forecast cost is the height of the line at a production of 36 items, as shown
in Figure 11.2.8. Naturally you don't expect the cost to be exactly $4,132. How-
ever, you may reasonably expect the cost to just randomly differ from your best
guess of $4,132.

EXAMPLE   **Territory and Sales**

Your sales managers are a varied lot. Sure, some work harder than others, and some bring in more sales than others, but it's not so simple as that. Somebody assigned each one to a territory, and some territories provide more opportunity for business than others. In addition to just looking at how much each person sold (which is important, of course), you have decided to try to *adjust for territory size* to find out who is doing well and who is doing poorly. It might turn out that some of the good performers are not really doing well because you would expect higher sales for a territory that large. You also might discover some hidden talent: people with smaller sales levels who are above average for a territory that small. A regression analysis will help you make this adjustment. The data set is shown in Table 11.2.3.

The least-squares line is

$$\text{Expected sales} = \$1{,}371{,}744 + \$0.23675045(\text{Territory})$$

By inserting each sales manager's territory size into this equation, you find the expected sales based on territory size. For example, Anson's expected sales are $\$1{,}371{,}744 + 0.23675045 \times 4{,}956{,}512 = \$2{,}545{,}000$ (rounding the answer to the nearest thousand). Anson's actual sales (about \$2,687,000) are \$142,000 higher than his expected sales. Thus, Anson has a residual value of \$142,000, possibly indicating added value. The expected sales levels and residuals may be found for each sales manager and are shown in Table 11.2.4.

TABLE 11.2.3   Territory and Performance of Salespeople

	Territory (population size)	Sales (past year)
Anson	4,956,512	$2,687,224
Ashley	8,256,603	3,543,166
Jonathan	9,095,310	3,320,214
Rod	12,250,809	3,542,722
Nicholas	4,735,498	2,251,482
Clara	13,683,663	5,149,127
Brittany	3,580,058	2,024,809
Ian	2,775,820	1,711,720
Bonnie	4,637,015	3,260,464

TABLE 11.2.4   Territory, Actual Performance, Expected Performance, and Residuals

	Territory	Actual Sales	Expected Sales (rounded)	Residuals (rounded)
Anson	4,956,512	$2,687,224	$2,545,000	$142,000
Ashley	8,256,603	3,543,166	3,326,000	217,000
Jonathan	9,095,310	3,320,214	3,525,000	−205,000
Rod	12,250,809	3,542,722	4,272,000	−729,000
Nicholas	4,735,498	2,251,482	2,493,000	−241,000
Clara	13,683,663	5,149,127	4,611,000	538,000
Brittany	3,580,058	2,024,809	2,219,000	−195,000
Ian	2,775,820	1,711,720	2,029,000	−317,000
Bonnie	4,637,015	3,260,464	2,470,000	791,000

The residuals are interesting. The largest one, $791,000 indicates that Bonnie pulled in about $.79 million more in sales than you would have expected for a territory that size. Although her actual sales were not the highest, when you take account of the size of her territory (fairly small, actually), her results are very impressive. Another residual is fairly large, at $538,000, telling you that Clara's impressive sales of $5,149,127 (the highest of all) were not just due to her large territory. Indeed, she pulled in about $.5 million more than you would have expected for that territory size. However, the smallest residual, −$729,000, is negative, suggesting that Rod may not be pulling his weight. You would have expected about $.73 million more from him based on the size of his territory. The data, least-squares line, and notes on these three special managers are shown in Figure 11.2.9.

Be careful not to interpret these results too literally. Although these three special cases might well indicate two stars and a trouble spot, there could be other explanations. Perhaps Rod has had trouble because his territory is in a depressed area of the country, in which case his low adjusted total should not be attributed to his personal performance. Perhaps a more careful regression analysis could be done, taking other important factors into account.

How Useful Is the Line?

You have already seen that the least-squares line does not usually describe the data perfectly. It is a useful summary of the main trend, but it does not capture the random variation of the data points about the line. This raises

FIGURE 11.2.9   By comparing each data point to the regression line, you can evaluate performance after adjusting for some other factor. In this case, points above the line (with positive residuals) represent managers with higher sales than you would have expected for their size of territory. Points below the line indicate lower sales than expected.

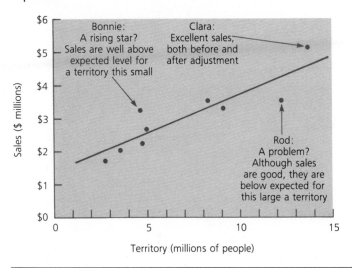

the question: How useful is the regression line? The answer is based on two important measures: the *standard error of estimate* (an absolute measure of how big the prediction errors are) and R^2 (a relative measure of how much has been explained).

The Standard Error of Estimate: How Large Are the Prediction Errors?

The **standard error of estimate,** denoted S_e here (but often denoted S in computer printouts) tells you approximately how large the prediction errors (residuals) are for your data set, in the same units as Y. How well can you predict Y? The answer is, to within about S_e above or below.[13] Since you usually want your forecasts and predictions to be as accurate as possible, you would be glad to find a *small* value for S_e. You can interpret S_e as a standard deviation in the sense that, if you have a normal distribution for the prediction errors, then you will expect about 2/3 of the data points to fall within a distance S_e either above or below the regression line. Also, about 95% of the data values should fall within $2S_e$, and so forth. This is illustrated in Figure 11.2.10 for the production cost example.

FIGURE 11.2.10   The standard error of estimate, S_e, indicates approximately how much error you make when you use the predicted value for Y (on the least-squares line) instead of the actual value of Y. You may expect about 2/3 of the data points to be within S_e above or below the least-squares line for a data set with a linear relationship, such as this one.

[13] A more careful, exact answer will be provided in a later section for predicting a new value of Y given a value for X.

The standard error of estimate may be found using the following formulas:

■ Standard Error of Estimate

$$S_e = S_Y \sqrt{(1 - r^2)\frac{n-1}{n-2}} \qquad \text{(for computation)}$$

$$= \sqrt{\left(\frac{1}{n-2}\right) \sum_{i=1}^{n} [Y_i - (a + bX_i)]^2} \qquad \text{(for interpretation)}$$

The first formula shows how S_e is computed by reducing S_Y according to the correlation and sample size. Indeed, S_e will usually be smaller than S_Y because the line $a + bX$ summarizes the relationship and therefore comes closer to the Y values than does the simpler summary, $\overline{Y}$. The second formula shows how S_e can be interpreted as the estimated standard deviation of the residuals: the squared prediction errors are averaged by dividing by $n - 2$ (the appropriate number of degrees of freedom when two numbers, a and b, have been estimated), and the square root undoes the earlier squaring, giving you an answer in the same measurement units as Y.

For the production cost data, the correlation was found to be $r = 0.869193$, the variability in the individual cost numbers is $S_Y = \$389.6131$, and the sample size is $n = 18$. The standard error of estimate is therefore

$$S_e = S_Y \sqrt{(1 - r^2)\frac{n-1}{n-2}}$$

$$= 389.6131 \sqrt{(1 - 0.869193^2)\frac{18-1}{18-2}}$$

$$= 389.6131 \sqrt{0.244503 \times \frac{17}{16}}$$

$$= 389.6131 \times \sqrt{0.259785}$$

$$= \$198.58$$

This tells you that, for a typical week, the actual cost was different from the predicted cost by about \$198.58. Although this least-squares line can help you predict the cost, you can't expect it to be closer than about \$198.58 to the truth, even for the data themselves.

R^2: How Much Is Explained?

R^2, pronounced "r squared" and also called the **coefficient of determination,** tells you how much of the variability of Y is explained by X.[14] It is found by

---

[14]Literally, R^2 is the proportion of the *variance* of Y that is explained by X. In order for technical details to work out properly, the variance rather than another variability measure must be used for defining R^2. The standard deviation would not work properly. Recall that the variance is simply the square of the standard deviation.

simply squaring the correlation, r (i.e., $R^2 = r^2$). This leaves $1 - R^2$ of the variation in Y unexplained. You usually want to see a big number for the R^2 value (close to but less than 1 or 100%). Ideally, you would like to explain 90% or more of the variation. Realistically, however, in many situations you will be lucky to explain even half of the variation.

For example, the correlation of the production cost data set is $r = 0.869193$. Thus, the R^2 value is

$$R^2 = 0.869193^2 = 0.755$$

This tells you that, based on the R^2 value, 75.5% of the variation in weekly cost is explained by the number produced each week. The remainder, 24.5% of the total cost variation, must be due to other causes.

Think of it this way: There is variation in cost from one week to another (summarized by S_Y). Some of this variation is due to the fact that production is higher in some weeks (resulting in a higher cost) and lower in others. Thus, the number produced "explains" part of the week-to-week variation in cost. But it doesn't explain all of this variation. There are other factors (such as occasional breakdowns, overtime, and mistakes) that also contribute to the variation in cost. The R^2 value tells you that 75.5% of the variation in cost is explained by the production level; the remaining 24.5% of the variation is still unexplained.

Confidence Intervals and Hypothesis Tests for Regression

Up to now you have been summarizing the *data:* estimating the strength of the relationship using the correlation coefficient, estimating the relationship using the least-squares line, and estimating the accuracy of the line using the standard error of estimate and R^2. Now it's time to go beyond merely summarizing the sample data and start doing statistical inference about the larger population you really want to understand. But what is the appropriate population to consider for a regression problem? The conventional answer is provided by the *linear model.*

The Linear Model Assumption Defines the Population

For statistical inference to be valid, the data set must be a random sample from the population of interest. As always, this ensures that the data set represents the population in an exact, controlled way. For simplicity, assume that the population has a linear relationship with randomness, as expressed by the **linear model,** which states that the observed value for Y is equal to the population relationship plus a random error that has a normal distribution:

> ■ **Linear Model for the Population**
>
> $$Y = (\alpha + \beta X) + \varepsilon$$
>
> $$= \text{Population relationship} + \text{randomness}$$
>
> where ε has a normal distribution with mean 0 and constant standard deviation σ.

The population relationship is given by two parameters: α is the population intercept (or constant term), and β is the population slope. Another population parameter, σ, indicates the amount of uncertainty in the situation. If your data were a census of the entire population, then your least-squares line would be the population relationship. Ordinarily, however, you use the least-squares intercept, a, as an *estimator* of α; the least-squares slope, b, as an *estimator* of β; and the standard error of estimate, S_e, as an *estimator* of σ. Of course, there are errors involved in this estimating since a, b, and S_e are based on a smaller sample and not on the entire population. Table 11.2.5 shows a summary of these population parameters and sample statistics.

The linear model is the basic assumption required for statistical inference in regression and correlation analysis. Confidence intervals and hypothesis tests based on the slope coefficient will assume that the linear model holds in the population. In particular, these confidence intervals and hypothesis tests will not be valid if the relationship is nonlinear or has unequal variability. It is up to you to watch for problems; if the linear model is not appropriate for your data, then the inferences from regression analysis could be wrong.

Standard Errors for the Slope and Intercept

You may suspect that there are standard errors lurking in the background, since there are population parameters and sample estimators. Once you know the standard errors and degrees of freedom, you will be able to con-

TABLE 11.2.5 Population Parameters and Sample Statistics

	Population (parameters: fixed and unknown)	Sample (estimators: random and known)
Intercept	α	a
Slope	β	b
Regression line	$Y = \alpha + \beta X$	$Y = a + bX$
Uncertainty	σ	S_e

struct confidence intervals and hypothesis tests using the familiar methods of Chapters 9 and 10.

The **standard error of the slope coefficient,** S_b, indicates approximately how far the estimated slope, b (the regression coefficient computed from the sample), is from the population slope, β, due to the randomness of sampling. The formula for S_b is as follows:

■ Standard Error of the Regression Coefficient

$$S_b = \frac{S_e}{S_X \sqrt{n-1}} \qquad \text{Degrees of freedom} = n - 2$$

This formula says that the uncertainty in b is proportional to the basic uncertainty (S_e) in the situation, but (1) S_b will be smaller when S_X is large (since the line is better defined when the X values are more spread out) and (2) S_b will be smaller when the sample size n is large (because there is more information). It is very common to see a term such as the square root of n in the denominator of a standard error formula, expressing the effect of additional information.

The degrees of freedom number for this standard error is $n - 2$, since two numbers, a and b, have been estimated to find the regression line.

For the production cost example (without the outlier!), the correlation is $r = 0.869193$, the sample size is $n = 18$, and the slope (variable cost) is $b = 51.66$ for the sample. The population is an idealized one: all of the weeks that might have happened under the same basic circumstances as the ones you observed. You might think of the population slope, β, as the slope you would compute if you had a lot more data. The standard error of b is

$$S_b = \frac{S_e}{S_X \sqrt{n-1}}$$

$$= \frac{198.58}{6.5552 \sqrt{18-1}}$$

$$= \frac{198.58}{27.0278}$$

$$= 7.35$$

The intercept term, a, was also estimated from the data. Therefore, it too has a standard error indicating its estimation uncertainty. The **standard error of the intercept term,** S_a, indicates approximately how far your estimate a is from α, the true population intercept term. This standard error, whose computation is shown below, also has $n - 2$ degrees of freedom.

> ■ **Standard Error of the Intercept Term**
>
> $$S_a = S_e \sqrt{\frac{1}{n} + \frac{\bar{X}^2}{S_X^2(n-1)}} \qquad \text{Degrees of freedom} = n - 2$$

This formula states that the uncertainty in a is proportional to the basic uncertainty (S_e), that it is small when the sample size n is large, that it is large when $\bar{X}$ is large (either positive or negative) with respect to S_X (because the data are far from the intercept itself), and that there is a $1/n$ baseline term because a would be the average of Y if $\bar{X}$ were 0.

For the production cost example, the intercept, $a = \$2,272$, indicates your estimated fixed costs. The standard error of this estimate is

$$\begin{aligned}
S_a &= S_e \sqrt{\frac{1}{n} + \frac{\bar{X}^2}{S_X^2(n-1)}} \\
&= 198.58 \sqrt{\frac{1}{18} + \frac{32.50^2}{6.5552^2(18-1)}} \\
&= 198.58 \sqrt{0.0555556 + \frac{1,056.25}{730.50}} \\
&= 198.58 \sqrt{1.5015} \\
&= 243.33
\end{aligned}$$

Confidence Intervals for Regression Coefficients

This should now be familiar material. You take an estimator (such as b), its own personal standard error (such as S_b), and the t-value from the t-table (for $n - 2$ degrees of freedom). The two-sided confidence interval extends from $b - tS_b$ to $b + tS_b$. The one-sided confidence interval claims either that the population slope, β, is at least $b - tS_b$ or that the population slope, β, is no more than $b + tS_b$ (using the one-sided t-values, of course). You may wish to reread the summary of Chapter 9 for a review of the basics of confidence intervals; the only difference here is that you are estimating a population *relationship* rather than just a population mean.

Similarly, inference for the population intercept term, α, is based on the estimator a and its standard error, S_a.

> ■ **Confidence Intervals**
>
> For the population slope, β:
>
> $$\text{From } b - tS_b \quad \text{to} \quad b + tS_b$$
>
> For the population intercept, α:
>
> $$\text{From } a - tS_a \quad \text{to} \quad a + tS_a$$

Variable Costs of Production

For the production cost data, the estimated slope is b = 51.66, the standard error is S_b = 7.35, and the two-sided t-table value for $n - 2$ = 16 degrees of freedom is 2.120 for 95% confidence. The 95% confidence interval for β extends from 51.66 − 7.35 × 2.120 = 36.08 to 51.66 + 7.35 × 2.120 = 67.24. Your confidence interval statement is as follows:

> You are 95% confident that the long-run (population) variable costs are somewhere between $36.08 and $67.24 per item produced.

As often happens, the confidence interval reminds you that the estimate ($51.66) is not nearly as exact as it appears. Viewing your data as a random sample from the population of production and cost experiences that might have happened under similar circumstances, you find that with just 18 weeks' worth of data, there is substantial uncertainty in the variable cost.

A one-sided confidence interval provides a reasonable upper bound that you might use for budgeting purposes. This reflects the fact that you don't know what the variable costs really are; you just have an *estimate* of them. In this example, the one-sided t-value from the table is 1.746, so your upper bound is 51.66 + 7.35 × 1.746 = 64.49. The one-sided confidence interval statement is:

> You are 95% confident that the long-run (population) variable costs are no greater than $64.49 per item produced.

Note that this bound ($64.49) is smaller than the upper bound of the two-sided interval ($67.24) because you are interested only in the upper side. That is, because you are not interested at all in the lower side, you can obtain an upper bound that is closer to the estimated value of $51.66.

Testing whether the Relationship Is Real or Coincidence

This chapter is about the relationship between X and Y. The correlation summarizes the strength of the relationship, and the regression equation exploits the relationship to predict Y from X. However, as often happens in statistics, you can summarize a relationship whether it is really there or not. It is the job of hypothesis testing to tell you if (on the one hand) the relationship that *appears* to be in your data could reasonably be pure coincidence or if (on the other hand) there is actually a significant association between X and Y.

The null hypothesis claims that there is *no relationship* between X and Y, that the apparent relationship in the data is just an artifact of the random pairing of X and Y values. The only way the linear model, $Y = \alpha + \beta X + \varepsilon$, can have Y *not* depend on X is if $\beta = 0$, so that X disappears and the linear model reduces to $Y = \alpha + \varepsilon$. Another way to say that there is no relationship is to say that X and Y are *independent* of each other.

The research hypothesis claims that there *is a relationship* between X and Y, not just randomness. This will happen whenever $\beta \neq 0$, so that the X term remains in the linear model for Y. Here are both hypotheses in mathematical form:

■ **Hypotheses for Testing Significance of a Relationship**

$H_0: \beta = 0$

$H_1: \beta \neq 0$

The test itself is performed in the usual way; again, there is nothing new here.[15] You might use the confidence interval approach and see whether the reference value, 0, is in the interval or not, deciding significance (accepting H_1) if it is not. Or you might construct the t-statistic b/S_b and compare it to the t-value from the table, deciding significance (H_1) if the absolute value of the t-statistic is larger.

For the variable production costs example, the confidence interval extends from \$36.08 to \$67.24. Since the reference value, 0, is not in this confidence interval, you may conclude that you do have significant variable costs. That is, based on your data, there is indeed a relationship between the number produced and the cost each week. The apparent association (higher numbers produced tend to cost more) could not reasonably be due to randomness alone.

Of course, the t-statistic approach gives the same answer. The t-statistic is $t = b/S_b = 51.66/7.35 = 7.03$. Since the absolute value of the t-statistic (7.03) is greater than the t-table value (2.120) with $n - 2 = 16$ degrees of freedom for testing at the 5% level, you would conclude that the slope (51.66) is indeed significantly different from 0.

Other Methods of Testing the Significance of a Relationship

There are other methods for testing the significance of a relationship. Although they may appear different at first glance, they always give the same answer as the method just described, based on the regression coefficient. These alternate tests are based on other statistics, for example, the correlation, r, instead of the slope coefficient, b. But since the basic question is the same (is there a relationship or not?), the answers will be the same also. This can be mathematically proven.

There are two ways to perform the significance test based on the correlation coefficient. You could look up the correlation coefficient in a special

---

[15]You may wish to review the summary of Chapter 10 to refresh your memory on the basics of hypothesis testing.

table, or else you could transform the correlation coefficient to find the t-statistic $t = r\sqrt{(n-2)/(1-r^2)}$, to be compared to the t-table value with $n - 2$ degrees of freedom. In the end the methods yield the same answer as testing the slope coefficient. In fact, the t-statistic defined from the correlation coefficient is the same number as the t-statistic defined from the slope coefficient ($t = b/S_b$).

This implies that you may conclude that there is significant correlation or that the correlation is not significant based on a test of significance of the regression coefficient, b. In fact, you may conclude that there is significant positive correlation if the relationship is significant and $b > 0$. Or, if the relationship is significant and $b < 0$, you may conclude that there is a significant negative correlation.

There is a significance test called the F-test for overall significance of a regression relationship. This test will be covered in the next chapter, on multiple regression. Although this test may also look different at first, in the end it is the same as testing the slope coefficient when you have just X and Y and are considering no other variables.

EXAMPLE   **Momentum in the Stock Market Revisited**

Earlier in the chapter, the stock market's daily percent changes were used as an example of the apparent lack of relationship between X = yesterday's change and Y = today's change. Let's now use regression to estimate the relationship between yesterday's and today's changes and then use hypothesis testing to see whether the relationship is significant or not. The data set, with least-squares line, is shown in Figure 11.2.11.

FIGURE 11.2.11   Daily percent changes (X = Yesterday and Y = Today) from 7/2 through 8/31/87. The least-squares line is nearly horizontal but has a slight tilt to it. Since the small tilt could be due to randomness, the hypothesis test concludes that there is no significant relationship between yesterday's and today's market performance.

Least=squares line: Today=0.00210+0.0423 (Yesterday)

The least-squares line is:

$$\text{Today} = 0.00209753 + 0.04231153 \times \text{Yesterday}$$

For example, on August 31, 1987, we have $X = -1.33\% = -0.0133$ and $Y = 0.89\% = 0.0089$. The predicted value for Y on this day is $0.00209753 + (0.04231153)(-0.0133) = 0.00153$.

Should you believe this prediction equation? It pretends to help you forecast today's market behavior based on yesterday's. The key is the slope coefficient, $b = 0.0423$, which says that only about 4.23% of yesterday's rise (or fall) will continue today, on average. However, how accurately has this coefficient been estimated? The answer is provided by the confidence interval based on the estimate ($b = 0.0423$), its standard error ($S_b = 0.1589$), and the t-table value ($t = 2.023$) with $41 - 2 = 39$ degrees of freedom:

> We are 95% sure that the population slope β is between -0.279 and 0.364.

This is a very wide interval; in fact, it contains 0, which would indicate no relationship. Thus, we conclude that since 0 is contained in the interval, the apparent slope is *not significant*. There is no significant association between yesterday's and today's market performance. You might also say that the slope coefficient is not significantly different from 0.

The t-statistic approach gives the same answer, of course. The standard error of the regression coefficient is $S_b = 0.1588875$, so the t-statistic is

$$t = b/S_b = 0.04231153/0.1588875 = 0.266$$

Such a small t-statistic is not significant (based on the t-table value of 2.023 for $41 - 2 = 39$ degrees of freedom).

Other Tests of a Regression Coefficient

In some applications you will want to test whether the slope is significantly different from some *reference value* β_0 representing an external standard for comparison. The reference value does not come from the same data set used for regression. For example, you might test to see whether your recent variable costs (the slope from a regression of $Y = \text{cost}$ on $X = \text{units produced}$) differ significantly from the budgeting assumptions (the reference value) you've used in the past.

The test of significance of the relationship between X and Y covered in the previous section is actually a test of whether the observed slope, b, is significantly different from the reference value $\beta_0 = 0$, which expresses the condition of no relationship. In this section we will allow β_0 to be nonzero. The test proceeds in the usual way. The hypotheses and results are as follows.

■ **Null and Research Hypotheses for Testing a Slope Coefficient**

Two-sided testing:

$$H_0: \beta = \beta_0$$

$$H_1: \beta \neq \beta_0$$

One-sided testing:

$$H_0: \beta \leq \beta_0$$

$$H_1: \beta > \beta_0$$

or

$$H_0: \beta \geq \beta_0$$

$$H_1: \beta < \beta_0$$

■ **Results of the Test**

If β_0 *is not* in the confidence interval for the slope, then the result is *significant*. For a two-sided test, use a two-sided interval and conclude that b is significantly different from β_0. If b is larger than β_0, you may conclude that it is significantly larger; otherwise it is significantly smaller. For a one-sided test, use a one-sided confidence interval and conclude that b is either significantly larger or significantly smaller than β_0, as appropriate.

If β_0 *is* in the confidence interval for the slope, then the result is *not significant*. For a two-sided test, use a two-sided interval and conclude that b is not significantly different from β_0. For a one-sided test, use a one-sided confidence interval and conclude that b is either not significantly larger or not significantly smaller than β_0, as appropriate.

Of course, the *t*-test may be used. The *t*-statistic is defined as follows:

$$t = \frac{b - \beta_0}{S_b}$$

Using the *t*-statistic, you would test these hypotheses about a population slope, β, just as you did in Chapter 10 for one- and two-sided testing of a population mean, μ.

For the variable production costs example, suppose your budgeting process assumes a variable cost of $100.00 per item produced. The 95% confidence interval computed earlier extends from $36.08 to $67.24 per unit. Since the reference value, $\beta_0 = \$100.00$, is not in the confidence interval, you may conclude that the estimated variable costs, $b = \$51.66$, are significantly different from your budgeting assumption. In fact, since the estimated costs are smaller, you may conclude that actual variable costs are *significantly under budget*.

Continuing this example, suppose your intelligence sources indicate that one of your competitors bids on projects based on a variable cost of $60.00 per item produced. Since this reference value, $\beta_0 = \$60.00$, is in the confidence interval for your variable costs, there is *no significant difference.* You may conclude that your variable costs do not differ significantly from your competitor's. Even though your estimated variable costs ($51.66) are lower, this might reasonably be due to random chance rather than to any actual cost advantage.

A New Observation: Uncertainty and the Confidence Interval

When you use regression to make a prediction about the value of a new observation, you want to know the uncertainty involved. You may even want to construct a confidence interval that you know has a 95% likelihood of containing the next observed value.

In this situation you know the value X_0, and you have predicted the value $a + bX_0$ for Y. There are now two sources of uncertainty that must be combined in order for you to find the standard error for this prediction. First of all, since a and b are estimated, the prediction $a + bX_0$ is uncertain. Second, there is always the randomness, ε, from the linear model (with standard error S_e) to be considered when you work with a single observation. The result of combining these uncertainties is the standard error of Y given X_0, denoted $S_{(Y|X_0)}$.[16] Following are the formula, together with its degrees of freedom, and the resulting confidence interval statement:

■ **Standard Error of a New Observation of Y given X_0**

$$S_{(Y|X_0)} = \sqrt{S_e^2\left(1 + \frac{1}{n}\right) + S_b^2(X_0 - \overline{X})^2} \qquad \text{Degrees of freedom} = n - 2$$

■ **Confidence Interval for a New Observation of Y Given X_0**

$$\text{From } (a + bX_0) - tS_{(Y|X_0)} \quad \text{to} \quad (a + bX_0) + tS_{(Y|X_0)}$$

The standard error depends on S_e (the basic uncertainty in the situation), on S_b (the uncertainty in the slope used for prediction), and on the distance from X_0 to $\overline{X}$. The standard error of a new observation will be smaller when X_0 is close to $\overline{X}$ because this is where you know the most. The standard error

---

[16]Note the use of the word *given;* this situation is similar to that of *conditional probability,* where you used additional information to update a probability. When you know the value X_0, you have additional information that can be used to decrease the uncertainty in Y from the (unconditional) standard deviation S_Y to the conditional standard error $S_{(Y|X_0)}$.

of a new observation will be large when X_0 is far from $\overline{X}$ because the information you have (the observed X values) is not near enough to the information you need (X_0). This behavior is shown in Figure 11.2.12 for the production cost data set.

For the production cost example, suppose you have scheduled $X_0 = 39$ units for production next week. Using the prediction equation, you have estimated the cost as $a + bX_0 = 2,272 + 51.66 \times 39 = \$4,287$. The uncertainty in this estimated cost for next week is

$$
\begin{aligned}
S_{(Y\,|\,X_0)} &= \sqrt{S_e^2\left(1 + \frac{1}{n}\right) + S_b^2(X_0 - \overline{X})^2} \\
&= \sqrt{198.58^2\left(1 + \frac{1}{18}\right) + 7.35^2(39 - 32.50)^2} \\
&= \sqrt{39{,}434 \times 1.055556 + 54.0225 \times 42.25} \\
&= \sqrt{43{,}907} \\
&= \$209.54
\end{aligned}
$$

The 95% confidence interval, using the t-value (2.120) from the t-table for $n - 2 = 16$ degrees of freedom, extends from $\$4,287 - 2.120 \times 209.54$ to $\$4,287 + 2.120 \times 209.54$. Therefore,

> You have 95% confidence that next week's production cost (forecast as $4,287 based on production of 39 units) will be somewhere between $3,843 and $4,731.

FIGURE 11.2.12 The confidence interval of a new observation for Y when X_0 is known depends on how far X_0 is from $\overline{X}$. The interval is smallest, indicating slightly greater precision, near $\overline{X}$, where you have the most information from the data.

Confidence interval for a new observation of Y

This confidence interval takes into account all of the statistical sources of error: the smallish sample size, the estimation of the least-squares line for prediction, and the estimated additional uncertainty of a new observation. If the linear model is an appropriate description of your cost structure, then the confidence interval will be correct. This statistical method, however, cannot and does not take into account other sources of error, such as a fire at the plant (such a large error could not reasonably come from the same normal distribution as the randomness in your data), an unforeseen shift in the cost structure, or the additional unforeseen costs of doubling or tripling production.

The Mean of Y: Uncertainty and the Confidence Interval

If you are interested in the *mean* value of Y at a given value X_0, you need the appropriate standard error, denoted $S_{(\text{predicted } Y|X_0)}$ (to be defined soon), in order to construct confidence intervals and perform hypothesis tests. This procedure is much like that of the previous section, where $S_{(Y|X_0)}$ was used for statistical inference involving a new observation of Y given X_0, except that the standard errors are different.

How do these two situations (mean of Y versus single observation of Y, given X_0) compare with each other? You use the *same estimated value* in both cases, namely, the predicted value $a + bX_0$ from the least-squares line. However, because individual observations are more variable than statistical summaries, $S_{(Y|X_0)}$ is larger than $S_{(\text{predicted } Y|X_0)}$. This is because an individual observation of Y (which is $\alpha + \beta X_0 + \varepsilon$ from the linear model) includes the random error term, ε, whereas the mean of Y (which is $\alpha + \beta X_0$) does not.

Think of it this way. After looking at incomes (X) and sporting goods expenditures (Y), you may find that you have a very good idea of how much a typical person who earns \$35,000 a year will spend on sporting goods, on average. This is the *average* amount spent on sporting goods by all people earning approximately \$35,000; it is well estimated in a large sample because it is an average value and will be close to the mean spent by all people in the population who earn around \$35,000. However, *individuals* differ substantially from one another (after all, not everyone plays racketball with clients at lunchtime). The variability of individuals is *not* averaged out in a large sample; it's still there no matter how large n is.

Given that X is equal to a known value, X_0, the mean value for Y is $\alpha + \beta X_0$. Note that this mean value is a population parameter because it is unknown and *fixed*, not random. The mean value for Y given X_0 is estimated by the predicted value $a + bX_0$, which is *random* because the least-squares estimates a and b are computed from the random sample of data. The extent of this randomness is summarized by the following formula for the standard error of the predicted value (the mean value) of Y given X_0.

■ **Standard Error of the Predicted (Mean) Value of Y given X_0**

$$S_{(\text{predicted } Y|X_0)} = \sqrt{S_e^2\left(\frac{1}{n}\right) + S_b^2(X_0 - \overline{X})^2} \qquad \text{Degrees of freedom} = n - 2$$

■ **Confidence Interval for the Predicted (Mean) Value of Y Given X_0**

$$\text{From } (a + bX_0) - tS_{(\text{predicted } Y|X_0)} \quad \text{to} \quad (a + bX_0) + tS_{(\text{predicted } Y|X_0)}$$

This standard error depends on S_e (the basic uncertainty in the situation), on S_b (the uncertainty in the slope used for prediction), and on the distance from X_0 to $\overline{X}$. It will be smaller when X_0 is close to $\overline{X}$ because this is where you know the most. The standard error of the predicted (mean) value will be large when X_0 is far from $\overline{X}$ because the information you have (the observed X values) is not near enough to the information you need (X_0). This behavior is shown in Figure 11.2.13 for the production cost data set.

Suppose you have set the production schedule at $X_0 = 39$ units for the indefinite future, and you want a good estimate of the long-term mean weekly production cost. Using the prediction equation, you have estimated this cost

FIGURE 11.2.13   The confidence interval of the predicted (mean) value Y when X_0 is known depends on how far X_0 is from $\overline{X}$. This interval is smaller than that for an individual observation of Y because of the extra randomness of individuals (compare to Figure 11.2.12).

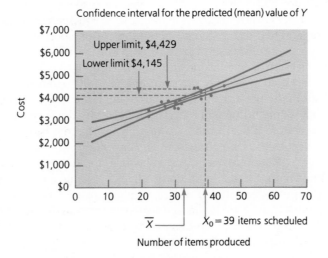

as $a + bX_0 = 2{,}272 + 51.66 \times 39 = \$4{,}287$. The uncertainty in this estimated long-term weekly cost is

$$
\begin{aligned}
S_{(Y \mid X_0)} &= \sqrt{S_e^2\left(\frac{1}{n}\right) + S_b^2(X_0 - \overline{X})^2} \\
&= \sqrt{198.58^2\left(\frac{1}{18}\right) + 7.35^2(39 - 32.50)^2} \\
&= \sqrt{39{,}434 \times 0.055556 + 54.0225 \times 42.25} \\
&= \sqrt{4{,}473.25} \\
&= \$66.88
\end{aligned}
$$

Note how much smaller this standard error is (\$66.88, for the mean) compared to the standard error for an individual week (\$209.54) from the previous section.[17]

The 95% confidence interval, using the t-value (2.120) from the t-table for $n - 2 = 16$ degrees of freedom, extends from $\$4{,}287 - 2.120 \times 66.88$ to $\$4{,}287 + 2.120 \times 66.88$. In other words,

> You have 95% confidence that the long-run mean weekly production cost (forecast as \$4,287, based on production of 39 units scheduled every week) will be somewhere between \$4,145 and \$4,429.

This confidence interval takes into account only the statistical error in estimating the predicted value, \$4,287, from the least-squares line based on this relatively small random sample of data. If the linear model is an appropriate description of your cost structure, the confidence interval will be correct. Again, however, this statistical method cannot take into account other, unforeseeable sources of error.

Regression Can Be Misleading

Although regression is one of the most powerful and useful methods of statistics, there are problems to watch out for. Since inference from a regression analysis is based on the linear model, the results may be invalid if the linear model fails to hold in the population. Your error rate might be much higher than the 5% claimed, your confidence may be much lower than the 95% you think you have, or your predictions might simply be worse than they would be if the problems were addressed.

Since you have a limited amount of data, you have little information about cases of which your data are unrepresentative. Since your regression is

---

[17]Due to round-off error, this result is off by a penny. If you use more precision in S_b (using 7.3472 instead of 7.35), you will find the more accurate answer, \$66.87.

based on the observed situation, it cannot necessarily anticipate the results of some intervention that produces a new situation with new dynamics. Furthermore, on a fairly technical note, it can make a big difference whether you are predicting Y from X or predicting X from Y.

These are some of the problems you should be aware of in order to make the best use of your own statistical analyses as well as those of others. Following is some further information about the pitfalls of regression.

The Linear Model May Be Wrong

Recall the linear model for the population:

$$Y = (\alpha + \beta X) + \varepsilon$$

$$= \text{(Population relationship)} + \text{Randomness}$$

where ε has a normal distribution with mean 0 and constant standard deviation. There are several ways in which this relationship might fail to hold in the population.

If the true relationship is *nonlinear,* the estimated straight line will not do a good job of predicting Y, as shown in Figures 11.2.14 and 11.2.15. Most computer programs will not object to using the least-squares estimation method in such situations, and few will even alert you to the problem. It's up to you to explore the data to discover trouble.

FIGURE 11.2.14 A nonlinear relationship cannot be well predicted by a line. Regression based on the linear model would predict *negative* stock index option prices at high strike prices, which is financially impossible.

The process of **extrapolation**, namely, predicting beyond the range of your data, is especially risky because you cannot protect yourself by exploring the data. Figure 11.2.16 illustrates the problem.

A single outlier can ruin everything, as in Figure 11.2.17. The linear model's assumption of a normal distribution for the randomness says that an outlier far from the population line is highly unlikely. The least-squares line will try hard to accommodate the outlier, and this interferes with its ability

---

FIGURE 11.2.15   Nonlinearity may involve a "threshold effect," again resulting in poor predictions. In this particular case, it looks like a clustering problem. You might get much better results by fitting a separate regression line to each cluster.

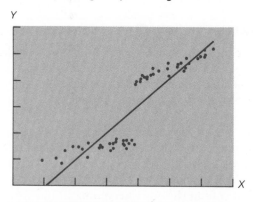

FIGURE 11.2.16   Extrapolating beyond the range of the data is risky. Although the population might follow a straight line, you don't have enough information to rule out other possibilities. The two curved lines shown are also nearly straight in the region where you have information, and they cannot be ruled out.

FIGURE 11.2.17   An outlier can seriously distort the results of a least-squares regression analysis. Your prediction ability for the typical cases is seriously harmed by the outlier's presence.

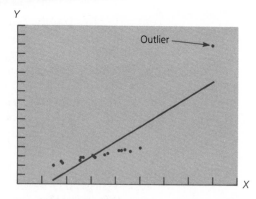

to predict the typical, non-outlier cases. So-called robust regression methods currently under development will provide some solutions to this problem.[18]

Finally, if there is *unequal variability* in your data, the inference will be unreliable. Too much importance will be given to the high-variability part of the data, and too little importance will be given to the more reliable low-variability part. There are two solutions to this problem: (1) Transform the data to equalize the variability and achieve a straight-line fit, or (2) use the advanced technique of *weighted* regression analysis to rebalance the importance of the observations.

Next, let's see what can go wrong in regression and its interpretation even when your data set *does* follow a linear model.

Predicting Intervention from Observed Experience Is Difficult

When you use regression to make predictions based on data, you are assuming that the new observation being predicted will arise from the same basic system that generated the data. If the system changes, either through its own evolution or due to an external intervention, the predictions may no longer apply.

For example, you might estimate a regression line to predict the dollar volume of new orders from the number of telephone calls answered in a department. The slope would give you an indication of the average value of each call. Should you undertake a marketing program to encourage customers to call? If you do this, by intervening in the system you may change the mixture of calls received. The marketing program may generate new calls that are primarily for information and are less likely to generate dollars immediately. You may very well experience an increase in orders through this campaign; the point is that the slope (based on past data) may not apply to the new system.

The Intercept May Not Be Meaningful

When regressing cost data (*Y*) on number of units produced (*X*), the intercept term gives you the fixed costs, which are very meaningful. But in other situations, the intercept term may have no useful meaning. You may still need it for technical reasons, in order to get your best predictions, but there may be no practical interpretation.

For example, consider a regression of salary (*Y*) on age (*X*). The slope indicates the incremental (extra) salary you can expect from an additional year of age, on average. Some kind of intercept term is needed to establish a baseline so that actual salaries can be predicted, for example, from the equation $a + bX$. Although a is useful here, its interpretation is difficult.

---

[18]See, for example, D. C. Hoaglin, F. Mosteller, and J. W. Tukey, *Understanding Robust and Exploratory Data Analysis* (New York: Wiley, 1983).

Literally, it is the expected salary you would pay a person whose age is $X = 0$: a newborn baby!

This is not really a problem. Just don't feel that you need to interpret a in these difficult cases.[19]

Explaining *Y* from *X* versus Explaining *X* from *Y*

It really does matter which of your variables is being predicted from the other: predicting Y from X is different from predicting X from Y, and each approach requires a different regression line. This seems reasonable because the errors are different in each case. For example, predicting productivity from experience involves making prediction errors in productivity units, whereas predicting experience from productivity involves making prediction errors in experience units. Of course, if all of your data points fall exactly on a line (so that the correlation is 1 or −1), this line will work for predicting either variable from the other.

However, in the usual case, there is some randomness or uncertainty, which tends to push your predicted values toward the average of the particular variable being predicted (either X or Y). In the extreme case, pure randomness, your best predictor of Y from X is $\overline{Y}$, and your best predictor of X from Y is $\overline{X}$. Remember the slope formula, $b = rS_Y/S_X$? This indicates that the line gets flatter (less steep) when there is more uncertainty (correlation, r, closer to 0).

Figures 11.2.18 and 11.2.19 show the two regression lines. Note that when the data points fall closer to a line, the two regression lines are closer together because the line is better defined by the data.

A Hidden "Third Factor" May Be Helpful

This last consideration is more of a suggestion for improvement than a problem. Although the least-squares line is the best way to predict Y from X, there is always the possibility that you could do a better job in predicting Y if you had more information. That is, perhaps X doesn't contain enough information about Y to do the best job, and maybe you could find another variable (a third factor) that would improve the predictions.

If you can substitute a different variable for X, you can perform another regression analysis to predict the same Y. A comparison of the R^2 terms (or the S_e terms) from each regression would provide some indication of which explanatory variable is most useful in predicting Y.

---

[19]One way around the problem is to use a so-called centercept instead of the intercept. The line would then be expressed as $Y = c + b(X - \overline{X})$. The centercept c is the expected value of Y for the most typical value of X, namely, $\overline{X}$, so interpretation is no problem. The slope is the same as before.

FIGURE 11.2.18 The two regression lines: one to predict Y from X (the usual procedure) and the other to predict X from Y. Since there is lots of randomness here, the lines are very different. Each one is close to predicting the average value ($\overline{X}$ or $\overline{Y}$) of the respective variable (i.e., a horizontal or vertical line).

FIGURE 11.2.19 The two regression lines are similar when there is less randomness and the data points are fairly close to a line. When the data points fall exactly on a line, the two regression lines will coincide.

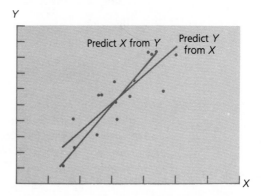

If you wish to combine the information in *two or more X* variables, you will need to use *multiple regression,* a very important method in business and research, which is the topic of the next chapter.

■ 11.3 End-of-Chapter-Materials

Summary

The three basic goals of bivariate data analysis of (X, Y) pairs are (1) describing and understanding the relationship, (2) forecasting and predicting a new observation, and (3) adjusting and controlling a process. *Correlation analysis* summarizes the strength of the relationship, and *regression analysis* is used to predict one variable from the other (usually Y from X).

Bivariate data are explored using the **scatterplot** of Y against X, providing a visual picture of the relationship in the data. The **correlation** or **correlation coefficient** (r) is a pure number between -1 and 1 summarizing the strength of the relationship. A correlation of 1 indicates a perfect straight-line relationship with upward tilt; a correlation of -1 indicates a perfect straight-line relationship with downward (negative) tilt. The correlation tells you how close the points are to being exactly on a tilted straight line, but it does not tell you how steep that line is. The formula for the correlation coefficient follows:

Formula for the Correlation Coefficient

$$r = \frac{\dfrac{1}{n-1}\sum_{i=1}^{n}(X_i - \bar{X})(Y_i - \bar{Y})}{S_X \times S_Y}$$

The **covariance** of X and Y is the numerator in the formula for the correlation coefficient. Because its measurement units are difficult to interpret, it is probably easier to work the correlation coefficient instead.

There are a number of relationships you might see when exploring a bivariate scatterplot. The easiest to analyze is a **linear relationship,** where the scatterplot shows points bunched randomly around a straight line with constant scatter. A scatterplot shows **no relationship** if it is just random, tilting neither upward nor downward as you move from left to right. There is a **nonlinear relationship** if the points bunch around a *curved* rather than a straight line. Since there are so many different kinds of curves that can be drawn, the analysis is more complex, but a transformation may help straighten out the relationship. You have the problem of **unequal variability** when the vertical variability changes dramatically as you move horizontally across the scatterplot. This causes correlation and regression analysis to be unreliable; these problems may be fixed by using either transformations or a so-called weighted regression. You have **clustering** if there are separate, distinct groups in the scatterplot; you may wish to analyze each group separately. A data point is a **bivariate outlier** if it does not fit with the relationship of the rest of the data; outliers can distort statistical summaries.

Correlation is not causation. The correlation coefficient summarizes the association in the numbers but cannot explain it. Correlation might be due to the X variable affecting Y, or the Y variable might affect X, or there might be a hidden third factor affecting both X and Y so that they seem associated. The term **spurious correlation** refers to a high correlation that is actually due to some third factor.

Regression analysis is predicting one variable from the other. **Linear regression analysis** is predicting one variable from the other using a straight line. The **slope**, b, is in measurement units of Y per unit X and indicates how steeply the line rises (or falls, if b is negative). The **intercept**, a, is the value for Y when X is 0. The equation for a straight line is:

Equation for a Straight Line

$$Y = \text{Intercept} + \text{Slope} \times X$$
$$= a + bX$$

The **least-squares line** has the smallest sum of squared vertical prediction errors of all possible lines and is used as the best predictive line based on data. The slope b is also called the **regression coefficient** of Y on X, and the intercept a is also called the **constant term** in the regression. The equations for the least-squares slope and intercept and the formula for the least-squares line follow.

Least-Squares Slope, Intercept, and Line

$$\text{Slope} = b = r\frac{S_Y}{S_X}$$

$$\text{Intercept} = a = \bar{Y} - b\bar{X} = \bar{Y} - r\frac{S_Y}{S_X}\bar{X}$$

Least-squares line:

$$\text{Predicted value of } Y = a + bX$$

$$= \left(\bar{Y} - r\frac{S_Y}{S_X}\bar{X}\right) + r\frac{S_Y}{S_X}X$$

The **predicted value** for Y given a value of X is found by substituting the value of X into the equation for the least-squares line. Each of the data points has a **residual**, a prediction error which tells you how far the point is above or below the line.

There are two measures of how useful the least-squares line is. The **standard error of estimate,** denoted S_e, tells you approximately how large the prediction errors (residuals) are for your data set *in the same units as Y.*

$$S_e = S_Y\sqrt{(1 - r^2)\frac{n - 1}{n - 2}} \qquad \text{(for computation)}$$

$$= \sqrt{\left(\frac{1}{n - 2}\right)\sum_{i=1}^{n}[Y_i - (a + bX_i)]^2} \qquad \text{(for interpretation)}$$

The R^2 value, also called the **coefficient of determination,** is the square of the correlation and tells you what percentage of the variability of Y is explained by X.

Confidence intervals and hypothesis tests for the regression coefficient require an assumption about the population. The **linear model** specifies that the observed value for Y is equal to the population relationship plus a random error that has a normal distribution. There are population parameters corresponding to the least-squares slope and intercept term computed from the sample:

Linear Model for the Population

$$Y = (\alpha + \beta X) + \varepsilon$$

$$= (\text{Population relationship}) + \text{Randomness}$$

where ε has a normal distribution with mean 0 and constant standard deviation σ.

Inference (use of confidence intervals and hypothesis tests) for the coefficients of the least-squares line is based on their standard errors (as always) using the t-table for $n - 2$ degrees of freedom. The **standard error of the slope coefficient,** S_b, indicates approximately how far the estimated slope, b (the regression coefficient computed from the sample), is from the population slope, β, due to the randomness of sampling. The **standard error of the intercept term,** S_a, indicates approximately how far the estimated a is from α, the true population intercept term.

Standard error of the regression coefficient

$$S_b = \frac{S_e}{S_X \sqrt{n - 1}}$$

Standard error of the intercept term

$$S_a = S_e \sqrt{\frac{1}{n} + \frac{\bar{X}^2}{S_X^2(n - 1)}}$$

Confidence interval for the population slope, β

From $b - tS_b$ to $b + tS_b$

Confidence interval for the population intercept, α

From $a - tS_a$ to $a + tS_a$

One way to test whether the apparent relationship between X and Y is real or just coincidence is to test β against the reference value $\beta_0 = 0$. There is a significant relationship if 0 is not in the confidence interval based on b and S_b or if the absolute value of $t = b/S_b$ exceeds the t-value in the t-table. This test is equivalent to testing significance of the correlation coefficient and is also the same as the F-test in multiple regression (see next chapter) when you have only one X variable. Of course, either coefficient (a or b) may be tested against any appropriate reference value using a one- or a two-sided test, as appropriate, and using the same methods you learned in Chapter 10 for testing a population mean.

For predicting a new observation of Y given that $X = X_0$, the uncertainty of prediction is estimated by the standard error $S_{(Y|X_0)}$, which also has $n - 2$ degrees of freedom. This allows you to construct confidence intervals and hypothesis tests for a new observation. An alternative formula gives the standard error for predicting the *mean* value of Y given X_0.

Standard error of a new observation of Y given X_0

$$S_{(Y|X_0)} = \sqrt{S_e^2\left(1 + \frac{1}{n}\right) + S_b^2(X_0 - \bar{X})^2}$$

Confidence interval for a new observation of Y given X_0

From $(a + bX_0) - tS_{(Y|X_0)}$ to $(a + bX_0) + tS_{(Y|X_0)}$

Regression analysis has its problems. If the linear model does not adequately describe the population, your predictions and inferences may be faulty. Exploring the data will help you determine if the linear model is appropriate by showing you problems such as nonlinearity, unequal variability, or outliers. The process of **extrapolation**, predicting beyond the range of the data, is especially risky because you cannot protect yourself by exploring the data.

Even if the linear model is appropriate, there are still problems. Since regression predicts based on past data, it cannot perfectly anticipate the effects of an intervention that changes the structure of a system. In some cases the intercept term, a, is difficult to interpret, although it may be a necessary part of the least-squares prediction equation. Be sure to choose carefully the variable you wish to predict, because predicting Y from X requires a different line than predicting X from Y, especially when there is substantial randomness in the data. Finally, there may be a third factor that would help you do a better job of predicting Y than using X alone; the next chapter will discuss this.

Key Words

scatterplot 398

correlation coefficient, r 400

covariance 403

linear relationship 403

no relationship 408

nonlinear relationship 411

unequal variability 416

clustering 418

bivariate outlier 421

spurious correlation 423

linear regression analysis 425

slope 426

intercept 426

least-squares line, $Y = a + bX$ 427

regression coefficient, b 428

constant term, a 428

predicted value 429

residual 429

standard error of estimate, S_e 434

coefficient of determination, R^2 435

linear model 436

standard error of the slope
  coefficient, S_b 438

standard error of the intercept
  term, S_a 438

extrapolation 451

Questions

1 What is new and different about analysis of bivariate data compared to univariate data?

2 Distinguish correlation and regression analysis.

3 Which activity (correlation or regression analysis) is involved in each of the following situations?

   a. Investigating to see whether there is any measurable connection between advertising expenditures and sales.

   b. Developing a system to predict portfolio performance based on changes in a major stock market index.

c. Constructing a budgeting tool to express costs in terms of the number of items produced.

d. Examining data to see how strong the connection is between employee morale and productivity.

4 For each of the following summaries, first indicate what the usual interpretation would be. Then indicate whether there are any other possibilities.

a. $r = 1$.

b. $r = 0.85$.

c. $r = 0$.

d. $r = -0.15$.

e. $r = -1$.

5 a. What is the covariance between X and Y?

b. Which is easier to interpret, the covariance or the correlation? Why?

6 Draw a scatterplot to illustrate each of the following kinds of structure in bivariate data. There is no need to work from data for this question; you may draw the points directly.

a. No relationship between X and Y.

b. Linear relationship with strong positive correlation.

c. Linear relationship with weak negative correlation.

d. Linear relationship with correlation -1.

e. Positive association with unequal variability.

f. Nonlinear relationship.

g. Clustering.

h. Positive association with an outlier.

7 a. If large values of X cause the Y values to be large, would you expect the correlation to be positive, negative, or zero? Why?

b. If you find a strong positive correlation, does this prove that large values of X cause the Y values to be large? If not, what other possibilities are there?

8 a. What is so special about the least-squares line that distinguishes it from all other lines?

b. How does the least squares line "know" that it is predicting Y from X instead of the other way around?

c. It is reasonable to summarize the "most typical" data value as having $\overline{X}$ as its X value and $\overline{Y}$ as its Y value. Show that the least-squares line passes through this most typical point.

d. Suppose the standard deviation of X and of Y are held fixed while the correlation decreases from one positive number to a smaller one. What happens to the slope coefficient, b?

9 Define the predicted value and the residual for a given data point.

10 For each of the following situations tell whether the predicted value or the residual would be most useful.

a. For budgeting purposes you need to know what number to place under "cost of goods sold" based on the expected sales figure for the next quarter.

b. You would like to see how your divisions are performing after adjusting for how well you expect them to do given the resources they consume.

c. To help you set the salary of a new employee, you want to know a reasonable pay figure for a person with the same experience.

d. As part of a payroll policy analysis report, you wish to show how much more (or less) each employee is paid compared to the expected salary for a person with the same experience.

11 Distinguish the standard error of estimate and the coefficient of determination.

12 a. Which is better, a lower or a higher value for R^2?

   b. Which is better, a lower or a higher value for S_e?

13 a. What is the linear model?

   b. Which two parameters define the population straight-line relationship?

   c. What sample statistics are used to estimate the three population parameters α, β, and σ?

14 Identify and write a formula for each of the following quantities, which are useful for accomplishing statistical inference.

   a. The standard error used for the regression coefficient.

   b. The standard error of the intercept term.

   c. The standard error of a new observation.

   d. The number of degrees of freedom for each of these standard errors.

15 Statistical inference in regression is based on the linear model. Name at least three problems that can arise when the linear model fails to hold.

16 What is extrapolation? Why is it especially troublesome?

17 Using a least-squares line, you have predicted that the cost of goods sold will rise to $8.33 million at the end of next quarter based on expected sales of $38.2 million. Your friend in the next office remarks, "Isn't it also true that a cost of goods sold of $8.33 million implies an expected sales level of $38.2 million?" Is this conclusion correct? Why or why not? (*Hint:* Which is X and which is Y in each case, and which is being predicted from the other?)

18 a. Give an example in which the intercept term, a, has a natural interpretation.

   b. Give an example in which the intercept term, a, does *not* have a natural interpretation.

Problems

1 Consider the following data set representing the ages (in years) and maintenance costs (in thousands of dollars per year) for five similar printing presses:

Age	Maintenance Cost
2	6
5	13
9	23
3	5
8	22

a. Draw a scatterplot of this data set. What kind of relationship do you see?

b. Find the correlation between age and maintenance cost. What do you learn from it?

c. Find the least-squares regression equation that predicts maintenance cost from the age of the machine. Draw this line on a scatterplot of the data.

d. What would you expect the annual maintenance to be for a press that is seven years old?

e. What is a typical size for the prediction errors?

f. How much of the variation in maintenance cost can be attributed to the fact that some presses are older than others?

g. Does age explain a significant amount of the variation in maintenance cost? How do you know?

h. Your conservative associate has suggested that you use $20,000 for planning purposes as the extra annual maintenance cost per additional year of life for each machine. Perform a hypothesis test at the 5% level to see if the extra annual cost is significantly different from your associate's suggestion.

2 A linear regression analysis has produced the following equation relating profits to hours of managerial time spent developing the past year's projects at a firm:

$$\text{Profits} = -\$957 + \$85 \times \text{Number of hours}$$

a. According to this estimated relationship, how large would the profits (or losses) be if no time were spent in planning?

b. On the average, an extra 10 hours spent planning resulted in how large an increase in project profits?

c. Find the break-even point, which is the number of hours for which the estimated profits would be zero.

d. If the correlation is $r = 0.351$, what percentage of the variation in profits is explained by the time spent?

e. How much of the variation in profits is left unexplained by the number of hours spent? Write a paragraph explaining how much faith you should have in this prediction equation and discussing other factors that might have an impact on profits.

3 Here are the second-quarter operating profits for six leading airlines in 1982 and 1983, in millions of dollars:

	Operating Profits	
	1982	1983
American	57.1	17.4
Pan American	46.5	−43.9
U.S. Air	38.4	40.0
United	37.3	22.4
Northwest	24.1	−5.2
Piedmont	13.3	18.6

Data are from *Business Week,* August 15, 1983, p. 31.

a. Draw a scatterplot of this data set, and comment on the relationship.

b. Find the correlation between 1982 and 1983 profits. Is there a strong relationship between profits in these two years?

c. Find R^2, and say what it represents.

d. Find the linear regression equation to predict 1983 profits from 1982 profits.

e. Find the predicted value and residual value for United Airlines. Say what each one represents.

f. Find the standard error of estimate. What does this measure?

g. Find the standard error of the regression coefficient.

h. Find the 95% confidence interval for the regression coefficient.

i. Test at the 5% level to see whether there is a significant relationship between profits in these two years or not.

4 Consider the number of deals and the total dollar amount of merger and acquisition activity for the top investment bankers, from Table 11.1.4.

a. Find the regression equation for predicting the dollar amount from the number of deals. What is the estimated dollar amount attributable to a single additional deal for these investment bankers?

b. Draw a scatterplot of the data set with the regression line.

c. Find the expected dollar amount for Goldman Sachs and the residual value. Interpret both of these values in business terms.

d. Find the standard error of the slope coefficient. What does this number indicate?

e. Find the 95% confidence interval for the expected marginal value of an additional deal to these firms (this is economics language for the slope).

f. Test at the 5% level to see if there is a significant relationship between the number of deals and the dollar amount.

g. Your investment banking firm is aiming to be in the top group next year, with 100 deals. Assuming that you will be "just like the big ones," compute a 95% confidence interval for the dollar amount you would expect to handle.

h. Test whether your firm, still assuming 100 deals next year, can expect to handle significantly more than $10 billion or not, using a one-sided test at the 5% level.

5 Consider the slightly scary topic of business failures. Table 11.3.1 shows data for each state on the number of failed businesses and the population.

TABLE 11.3.1 Business Failures by State

State	Failures	Population	State	Failures	Population
Alabama	607	4,021	Missouri	1,246	5,029
Alaska	176	521	Montana	194	826
Arizona	698	3,187	Nebraska	485	1,606
Arkansas	618	2,359	Nevada	362	936
California	10,257	26,365	New Hampshire	60	998
Colorado	2,654	3,231	New Jersey	981	7,562
Connecticut	308	3,174	New Mexico	357	1,450
Delaware	46	622	New York	1,866	17,783
District of			North Carolina	663	6,255
Columbia	61	626	North Dakota	94	685
Florida	2,792	11,366	Ohio	2,447	10,744
Georgia	955	5,976	Oklahoma	1,015	3,301
Hawaii	246	1,054	Oregon	1,141	2,687
Idaho	203	1,005	Pennsylvania	1,638	11,853
Illinois	3,388	11,535	Rhode Island	58	968
Indiana	1,236	5,499	South Carolina	235	3,347
Iowa	832	2,884	South Dakota	145	708
Kansas	1,575	2,450	Tennessee	1,213	4,762
Kentucky	972	3,726	Texas	4,892	16,370
Louisiana	1,389	4,481	Utah	580	1,645
Maine	80	1,164	Vermont	38	535
Maryland	453	4,392	Virginia	991	5,706
Massachusetts	685	5,822	Washington	1,634	4,409
Michigan	1,457	9,088	West Virginia	366	1,936
Minnesota	510	4,193	Wisconsin	1,424	4,775
Mississippi	470	2,613	Wyoming	274	509

Data are from U.S. Bureau of the Census, *Statistical Abstract of the United States, 1987,* 107th ed. (Washington: Bureau of the Census, 1986), pp. 22, 509. Data are for 1985.

a. Construct a scatterplot of business failures (Y) against population (X). Describe the relationship that you see. Does there appear to be some association?

b. Does the linear model appear to hold? Why or why not?
c. Find the logarithm of each data value, both for population and for business failures. You may choose either base 10 or base e, but use only one type.
d. Construct a scatterplot of the logarithms, and describe the relationship.
e. Find the equation of the regression line to predict the log of business failures from the log of population.
f. Find the two-sided 95% confidence interval for the slope coefficient of the log relationship.
g. Test at the 5% level to see whether there is a significant relationship between the logs of failures and of population. Explain why the result is reasonable.
h. If the slope for the logs were exactly 1, then business failures would be proportional to population. A value larger than 1 would say that large states have proportionately more failures, and a slope less than 1 would suggest that the smaller states have proportionately more failures. Test at the 5% level to see whether the population slope for the logs is significantly different from 1 or not, and briefly discuss your conclusion.

6 Consider the daily percent changes of McDonald's stock price and those of the Dow Jones Industrial Average for trading days in the month of July 1987, as shown in Table 11.3.2.

TABLE 11.3.2   Daily Changes in Stock Market Prices, July 1987

McDonald's	Dow Jones	McDonald's	Dow Jones
1.12%	0.47%	−0.58%	−1.35%
−0.29	1.41	−0.41	−1.14
0.83	0.70	0.78	2.08
0.58	0.69	1.07	3.17
−0.52	−0.69	−0.09	−0.66
0.20	−1.38	1.69	1.99
−0.12	−2.34	1.69	3.03
1.16	1.44	−0.42	−0.84
0.10	−0.24	0.83	1.48
0.53	0.47	−0.23	−0.63
0.52	−1.18	0.56	2.31
−0.89	−1.19	−1.70	−0.21
−0.80	0.72	0.42	−2.06
0.09	0.72	1.54	0.84
0.07	0.95	0.10	0.00
0.54	0.94	−0.46	−2.08
0.35	0.93	0.94	2.34
1.04	0.92	0.76	−0.21
0.78	0.92	−0.99	−1.67
1.10	0.45	−1.33	−2.33
0.18	0.23	0.89	1.08

a. Draw a scatterplot of McDonald's daily percent changes against the Dow Jones percent changes.
b. Describe the relationship you see in this scatterplot.
c. Find the correlation between these percent changes. Does this agree with your impression from the scatterplot?
d. Find the coefficient of determination (you may just square the correlation). Interpret this number as "variation explained." In financial terms, it represents the proportion of *nondiversifiable risk* in McDonald's. For example, if it were 100%, McDonald's stock would track the market perfectly, and diversification would introduce nothing new.

e. Find the proportion of *diversifiable risk*. This is just $1 - R^2$ (or 100% minus the percentage of nondiversifiable risk). This indicates the extent to which you can diversify away the risk of McDonald's stock by investing part of your portfolio in the Dow Jones Industrial stocks.

f. Find the regression equation to predict the percent change in McDonald's stock from the percent change in the Dow Jones Index. Identify the stock's so-called beta, a measure used by market analysts, which is equal to the slope of this line. According to the capital asset pricing model, stocks with large beta values tend to give larger expected returns (on average, over time) than stocks with smaller betas.

g. Find the 95% confidence interval for the slope coefficient.

h. Test at the 5% level to see whether or not the daily percent changes of McDonald's and of the Dow Jones Index are significantly associated.

i. Test at the 5% level to see whether the beta of McDonald's is significantly different from 1, which represents the beta of a highly diversified portfolio.

7 This problem continues the analysis of McDonald's and Dow Jones stock market data.

a. Find the 95% confidence interval for the percent change in McDonald's stock on a day in which the Dow Jones Index is unchanged.

b. Find the 95% confidence interval for the mean percent change in McDonald's stock for the idealized population of all days in which the Dow Jones Index is unchanged.

c. Find the 95% confidence interval for the percent change in McDonald's stock on a day in which the Dow Jones Index is up 1.5%.

d. Find the 95% confidence interval for the mean percent change in McDonald's stock for the idealized population of all days in which the Dow Jones Index is up 1.5%.

8 In the territory versus sales example (based on the data from Table 11.2.3), the least-squares line to predict sales based on the population of the territory was found to be:

$$\text{Expected sales} = \$1,371,744 + \$0.23675045(\text{Population})$$

a. Interpret the slope coefficient as a number with a simple and direct business meaning.

b. What proportion of the variation in sales from one agent to another is attributable to territory size? What proportion is due to other factors?

c. Does territory size have a significant impact on sales? How do you know?

d. Find the p-value for the significance of the slope coefficient.

9 Consider the earnings per share and the closing stock price of selected biotechnical firms with large market capitalization. Given the importance many analysts place on earnings per share, you might expect to find a strong correlation between earnings per share and share price. Of course, in a young field such as biotechnology, it may be too early to judge since the market price may depend more on the *expectation* of (random) future earnings than on the actual achieved earnings. Let's see how it comes out. The data are shown in Table 11.3.3.

a. Draw a scatterplot of the stock price against earnings per share.

b. Find the correlation coefficient. Does there appear to be a positive or a negative relationship between earnings and price?

c. Test at the 5% level to see if there is a significant link between earnings per share and stock price for these firms.

d. Test at the 10% level to see if there is a significant link between earnings per share and stock price for these firms.

TABLE 11.3.3 Biotechnical Stocks

	Earnings per share	Price (1/27/89)
Genentech	0.24	17.88
Alza	0.50	24.75
Amgen	0.09	37.00
Cetus	−0.22	11.38
Genetics Institute	−0.81	18.75
Biogen	−0.21	9.38
Centocor	0.21	17.00
Chiron	−0.97	15.00
Xoma	−1.00	15.00
Nova Pharmaceutical	−0.32	5.38
Immunex	0.02	11.75
Collagen	0.12	11.38
California Biotech	−0.87	5.25
Calgene	−0.66	6.38
DNA Plant Technology	−0.16	4.63
Repligen	−0.57	7.25
Imreg	−0.36	4.50
Celgene	−0.90	8.75
Cytogen	−1.10	3.63
Damon Biotech	−0.27	1.75

Data are from A. K. Naj, "Clouds Gather over the Biotech Industry; Firms Stumble on Regulation, Patent Problems," *The Wall Street Journal,* January 30, 1989, p. B1. Their source is IDD Information Services/Tradeline.

    e. Write a brief paragraph summarizing your findings so far.

    f. You are head of a biotech firm planning to go public soon (that is, to have your initial public offering of stock). Your earnings per share are $0.05. Based solely on this regression analysis, what stock price should you anticipate?

    g. Compute a two-sided 95% confidence interval for this anticipated stock price.

    h. Compute a two-sided 95% confidence interval for the mean anticipated stock price for the population of all such firms with earnings per share of $0.05.

10 Consider the circulation and the open line rate (price per line for an ad placed just once) for selected large newspapers shown in Table 11.3.4.

    a. Create a scatterplot of the open line rate against circulation.

    b. Find and interpret the correlation of open line rate with circulation. Is this correlation reasonable from a business standpoint?

    c. Find the regression equation to predict open line rate from circulation.

    d. Test to see if the association between the open line rate and circulation is statistically significant.

    e. Find the predicted and residual values for the *New York Times.* Interpret these values. In particular, is the open line rate higher or lower than what you would expect for a newspaper with this circulation?

11 In the previous problem, there is a possible outlier visible in the scatterplot. Let's test to see if it could reasonably be from the same population as the others by treating it as a new observation.[20]

---

[20]A more careful analysis would adjust for the fact that *The Wall Street Journal* cannot really be viewed as a random selection from an idealized population because it was selected, in part, based on the size of its difference from the others. An extensive treatment of outlier problems and solutions is provided by V. Barnett and T. Lewis, *Outliers in Statistical Data,* New York: Wiley, 1978.

TABLE 11.3.4   Newspaper Advertising Rates per Line

	Circulation	Open Line Rate
The Wall Street Journal	2,081,995	37.65
New York Daily News	1,374,858	18.48
USA Today	1,284,613	14.50
Los Angeles Times	1,057,536	14.61
New York Times	970,051	16.47
New York Post	963,069	16.07
Philadelphia Inquirer/News	828,236	13.82
Chicago Tribune	779,259	13.05
Washington Post	768,288	13.78
San Francisco Chronicle/Examiner	691,771	12.25
Chicago Sun-Times	663,693	10.53
Detroit News	657,015	14.18
Detroit Free Press	645,623	12.83
Long Island Newsday	533,384	7.81
Kansas City Times/Star	528,777	5.17
Miami Herald/News	514,702	11.08
Cleveland Plain Dealer	492,002	6.58
Milwaukee Journal	486,426	8.77
Houston Chronicle	443,592	6.03
Baltimore Sun	349,182	6.77

Data are from C. L. Bovée and W. F. Arens, *Contemporary Advertising,* 2nd ed. (Homewood, Ill.: Richard D. Irwin, 1986), p. 413.

    a. Remove *The Wall Street Journal* from the data set, and find the regression equation to predict the open line rate from circulation for the other newspapers.

    b. Find the two-sided 95% confidence interval for a new observation, with X_0 being the circulation of *The Wall Street Journal.*

    c. Test whether or not *The Wall Street Journal* is an outlier by seeing if its open line rate is in the confidence interval.

12 The *milline rate* in newspaper advertising is defined as the open line rate divided by the circulation, in millions. Thus, it is the cost per line of advertising per million circulation. This adjustment should take care of some of the differences in advertising rates due to circulation. That is, one explanation of the open line rate is that it is proportional to circulation. If it is just proportional, there should be nothing left in the milline rate to be explained by circulation. On the other hand, if there is an additional advantage or penalty to being big, the circulation should help explain the variation in milline rates. Let's use regression analysis to see if there is anything left in the milline rate to be explained by circulation, based on the data set in Table 11.3.5.

    a. Draw a scatterplot of milline rate against circulation.

    b. Find and interpret the correlation between circulation and milline rate.

    c. What percentage of the variation in milline rate is explained by circulation?

    d. Test to see if there is significant relationship between circulation and milline rate.

    e. Write a paragraph explaining and interpreting your results.

13 Your firm is having a quality problem with the production of plastic automotive parts: there are too many defectives. One of your engineers thinks that it's because the temperature of the process is not controlled carefully enough. Another engineer is sure that it's because the assembly line is being shut down too often for unrelated reasons. You have decided to analyze the problem and have come up with figures for the percent defective each day recently, the standard deviation of tem-

TABLE 11.3.5   Newspaper Advertising Rates per Line, Adjusted for Readership

	Circulation	Milline Rate
The Wall Street Journal	2,081,995	18.08
New York Daily News	1,374,858	13.43
USA Today	1,284,613	11.29
Los Angeles Times	1,057,536	13.81
New York Times	970,051	16.98
New York Post	963,069	16.69
Philadelphia Inquirer/News	828,236	16.69
Chicago Tribune	779,259	16.75
Washington Post	768,288	17.94
San Francisco Chronicle/Examiner	691,771	17.71
Chicago Sun-Times	663,693	15.87
Detroit News	657,015	21.58
Detroit Free Press	645,623	19.87
Long Island Newsday	533,384	14.64
Kansas City Times/Star	528,777	9.78
Miami Herald/News	514,702	21.53
Cleveland Plain Dealer	492,002	13.37
Milwaukee Journal	486,426	18.03
Houston Chronicle	443,592	13.59
Baltimore Sun	349,182	19.39

Data are from C. L. Bovée and W. F. Arens, *Contemporary Advertising*, 2nd ed. (Homewood, Ill.: Richard D. Irwin, 1986), p. 413.

TABLE 11.3.6   Defects and Possible Causes

Defect Rate	Temperature Variability	Stoppages
0.1%	11.94	5
0.1	9.33	4
8.4	21.89	0
0.0	8.32	1
4.5	14.55	0
2.6	12.08	8
3.2	12.16	0
0.0	12.56	2
0.0	10.10	2
5.2	13.08	2
4.9	17.19	0
0.1	10.76	1
6.8	13.73	3
4.8	12.42	2
0.0	12.83	2
0.9	5.78	5

perature measured hourly each day (as a measure of temperature control), and the number of assembly line stoppages each day. The raw data set is shown in Table 11.3.6.

a. Find the correlation of the defect rate with the temperature variability.
b. Find the correlation of the defect rate with stoppages.
c. Which possible cause, temperature variability or stoppages, accounts for more of the variation in defect rate from day to day? How do you know?

d. Test each of these correlations for statistical significance.

e. Draw a scatterplot of defect rate against stoppages. Write a brief paragraph interpreting the scatterplot and correlation.

f. Draw a scatterplot of defect rate against temperature variability. Write a brief paragraph interpreting the scatterplot and correlation.

g. Write a paragraph summarizing what you have learned and proposing a plan for action.

Database Exercises

Refer to the employee database in Appendix A.

1 Consider annual salary as the Y variable and experience as the X variable.
   a. Draw a scatterplot, and describe the relationship.
   b. Find the correlation coefficient. What does it tell you? Is it appropriate, compared to the scatterplot?
   c. Find the least-squares regression line to predict Y from X, and draw it on a scatterplot of the data.
   d. Find the standard error of estimate. What does it tell you?
   e. Find the standard error of the slope coefficient.
   f. Find the 95% confidence interval for the slope coefficient.
   g. Test at the 5% level to see if the slope is significantly different from 0. Interpret the result.
   h. Test at the 1% level to see if the slope is significantly different from 0.
   i. Test at the 5% level to see if the correlation coefficient is significantly different from 0.

2 a. What fraction of the variation in salaries can be explained by the fact that some employees have more experience than others?
   b. What salary would you expect for an individual with eight years of experience?
   c. Find the 95% confidence interval for the salary of a new individual (from the same population from which the data were drawn) who has eight years of experience.
   d. Find the 95% confidence interval for the mean salary for those individuals in the population who have eight years of experience.

3 a. What salary would you expect for an individual with three years of experience?
   b. Find the 95% confidence interval for the salary of a new individual (from the same population from which the data were drawn) who has three years of experience.
   c. Find the 95% confidence interval for the mean salary of those individuals in the population who have three years of experience.

4 a. What salary would you expect for an individual with no (zero years) experience?
   b. Find the 95% confidence interval for the salary of a new individual (from the same population from which the data were drawn) who has no experience.
   c. Find the 95% confidence interval for the mean salary of those individuals in the population who have no experience.

5 Repeat exercise 1 using annual salary as the Y variable and age as the X variable.

6 a. What fraction of the variation in salaries can be explained by the fact that some employees are older than others?
   b. What salary would you expect for a 42-year-old individual?
   c. Find the 95% confidence interval for the salary of a new individual (from the same population from which the data were drawn) who is 42 years old.

    d. Find the 95% confidence interval for the mean salary of all 42-year-olds in the population.

7 a. What salary would you expect for a 50-year-old individual?

    b. Find the 95% confidence interval for a new individual (from the same population from which the data were drawn) who is 50 years old.

    c. Find the 95% confidence interval for the mean salary of all 50-year-olds in the population.

8 Repeat exercise 1 using experience as the Y variable and age as the X variable.

9 a. What fraction of the variation in experience can be explained by the fact that some employees are older than others?

    b. How much experience would you expect for a 42-year-old individual?

    c. Find the 95% confidence interval for the experience of a new individual (from the same population from which the data were drawn) who is 42 years old.

    d. Find the 95% confidence interval for the mean experience of all 42-year-olds in the population.

10 a. How much experience would you expect for a 50-year-old individual?

    b. Find the 95% confidence interval for the experience of a new individual (from the same population from which the data were drawn) who is 50 years old.

    c. Find the 95% confidence interval for the mean experience of all 50-year-olds in the population.

11 Repeat exercise 1 using just the men, with annual salary as the Y variable and experience as the X variable.

12 Repeat exercise 1 using just the women, with annual salary as the Y variable and experience as the X variable.

Project

Find a bivariate data set relating to your work or business interests, with a sample size of $n = 15$ or more.

    a. Give your choice of dependent variable (Y) and independent variable (X), and briefly explain your reasons.

    b. Draw a scatterplot, and comment on the relationship.

    c. Compute the correlation coefficient, and briefly interpret it.

    d. Square the correlation coefficient, and briefly interpret it.

    e. Compute the least-squares regression equation, and draw the line on a scatterplot of your data.

    f. For two elementary units in your data set, compute predicted values for Y and residuals. Comment.

    g. Find a confidence interval for the slope coefficient.

    h. Test whether or not anything is being explained by your regression equation.

    i. Choose a value of X. Find the expected value of Y for this X. Find the confidence interval for the Y value of an individual with this X value. Find the confidence interval for the population mean Y value for individuals with this X value. Summarize and interpret these results.

    j. Comment on what you have learned by applying correlation and regression analysis to your data set.

Multiple Regression
Predicting One Factor from Several Others

The world is multivariate. In realistic business problems you have to consider data on more than just one or two factors. But don't despair; the next step, *multiple regression,* is a relatively easy procedure that will build on your ability to deal with the simpler cases of univariate and bivariate data. In fact, all of the basic ideas are in place already: average, variability, correlation, prediction, confidence intervals, and hypothesis tests.

Predicting a single Y variable from *two or more* X variables is called **multiple regression**. Predicting a single Y variable from a single X variable is called *simple regression* and was covered in the previous chapter. The goals for using multiple regression are the same as for simple regression. Here is a review of those goals with some examples:

1 *Describing and understanding the relationship.*
   a. Consider the relationship between salary (Y) and some basic characteristics of employees, such as gender (X_1, represented as 0 or 1 to distinguish male and female), years of experience (X_2), and education (X_3). Describing and understanding how these X factors influence Y would provide important evidence in a gender discrimination lawsuit. The regression coefficient for gender would give an estimate of how large the salary gap is between men and women *after adjustment* for age and experience. Even if your firm is not currently being sued, you might want to run such a multiple regression analysis so that any small problems can be fixed *before* they become large ones.
   b. If your firm makes bids on projects, then for the projects you win, you will have data available for the actual cost (Y), the estimated direct labor cost (X_1), the estimated materials cost (X_2), and supervisory function costs (X_3). Suppose you suspect your bids are unrealistically low. By figuring out the relationship between actual cost and the estimates made earlier during the bidding process, you will be able to tell which, if any, of the estimates are systematically too low or too high in terms of their contribution to the actual cost.

2 *Forecasting (predicting) a new observation.*

 a. An in-depth understanding of your firm's cost structure would be useful for many purposes. For instance, you would have a better idea of how much extra to budget during the rush season (e.g., for overtime). If the business is changing, you may be able to anticipate the effects of changes on your costs. One way to understand your cost structure is through multiple regression of costs (Y) on each potentially useful factor you can think of, such as the number of items produced (X_1), the number of workers (X_2), and the amount of overtime (X_3). Results of an analysis such as this can tell you much more than just "add a bunch for overtime." It can respond to hidden costs that tend to increase along with overtime, giving you the best predictions of actual cost based on the available information.

 b. Your firm's monthly sales (a time series) might be explained by an overall trend with seasonal effects. One way to analyze and forecast would be to use multiple regression to explain sales (Y) based on a trend (for example, $X_1 = 1, 2, 3, \ldots$, indicating months since the start) and a variable for each month (for example, X_2 would be 1 for January and 0 otherwise, X_3 would represent February, and so forth). You could use multiple regression to forecast sales several months ahead, as well as to understand your long-term trend and to see which months tend to be higher than others.

3 *Adjusting and controlling a process.*

 a. The wood pulp goes in one end, and paper comes flying out of the other, ready to be rolled and shipped. How do you control such a large piece of machinery? Just reading the instruction manual is often not good enough; it takes experience to get the thickness just right and to dry it sufficiently without wasting energy dollars. When this "experience" consists of data, a multiple regression analysis can help you find out which combination of adjustments (the X variables) produces the result (the Y variable) you want.

 b. "Hedging" in securities markets consists of setting up a portfolio of securities (often futures and options) that matches the risk of some asset as closely as possible. If you hold an inventory, you should consider hedging its risk. Banks use treasury futures and options contracts to hedge the interest rate risk of their deposit accounts and loans. Agricultural industries use hedging to decrease their risk due to commodity price fluctuations. The process of choosing a hedge portfolio may be accomplished using multiple regression analysis. Based on past data, you would attempt to explain the price movements of your asset (Y) by the price movements of securities (X_1, X_2, and so forth). The regression coefficients will tell you how much of each security to include in the hedge portfolio to get rid of as much risk as possible. You would be using multiple regression to adjust and control your risk exposure.

■ 12.1 Interpreting the Results of a Multiple Regression

Let p stand for the number of explanatory variables (X variables); this can be any manageable number.[1] Your elementary units are often called *cases;* they might be customers, firms, or items produced. The input data for a typical multiple regression analysis is shown in Table 12.1.1.

What will the computer output consist of, and how can you interpret it? First of all, we will provide an overview of the main results. A more detailed explanation will follow.

There will be an **intercept** or **constant term,** a, that gives the predicted value for Y when *all* X variables are 0. Also, there will be a **regression coefficient** for each X variable, indicating the effect of that X variable on Y after adjustment has been made for the other X variables; the regression coefficient b_j for the jth X variable indicates how much larger you expect Y to be for a case that is identical to another except for being one unit larger in X_j. Taken together, these regression coefficients give you the **prediction equation** or **regression equation,** predicted $Y = a + b_1 X_1 + b_2 X_2 + \cdots + b_p X_p$, which may be used for prediction or control. These coefficients $(a, b_1, b_2, \ldots, b_p)$ are traditionally computed using the method of least squares, which minimizes the sum of the squared prediction errors. The **prediction errors** or **residuals** are defined as $Y -$ (Predicted Y).

Just as for simple regression, with only one X, the **standard error of estimate,** S_e, indicates the approximate size of the prediction errors. Also as for simple regression, R^2 is the **coefficient of determination,** which indicates the percentage of the variation in Y that is "explained by" or "attributed to" all of the X variables.[2]

TABLE 12.1.1   Input Data for a Multiple Regression

	Y (dependent variable to be explained)	X_1 (first independent or explanatory variable)	X_2 (second independent or explanatory variable)		X_p (last independent or explanatory variable)
Case 1	10.9	2.0	4.7	$\cdots$	12.5
Case 2	23.6	4.0	3.4	$\cdots$	12.3
.	.	.	.	.	.
.	.	.	.	.	.
Case n	6.0	0.5	3.1	$\cdots$	7.0

---

[1] For technical reasons you must have at least one more case than you have X variables, that is, $n \geq p + 1$. For practical reasons you should have many more.

[2] However, it is not just the square of the correlation of Y with *one* of the X variables. Instead it is the square of r, the correlation of Y with the least-squares predictions (based on the regression equation), which uses *all* of the X variables.

Inference will begin with an overall test, called the **F-test,** to see if the X variables explain a significant amount of the variation in Y. If your regression is *not* significant, you are not permitted to go further. If the regression is significant, you may proceed with statistical inference using **t-tests for individual regression coefficients,** which show you whether an X variable has a significant impact on Y *holding all other* X *variables fixed.* Confidence intervals and hypothesis tests for an individual regression coefficient will be based on its standard error, of course. There is a standard error for each regression coefficient; these are denoted $S_{b_1}, S_{b_2}, \ldots, S_{b_p}$. Table 12.1.2 shows a list of the results of a multiple regression analysis.

EXAMPLE ### Magazine Ads

The price of advertising is different from one consumer magazine to another. What causes these differences in price? Probably something relating to the value of the ad to the advertiser. Magazines that reach more readers (all else equal) should be able to charge more for an ad. Also, magazines that reach a better-paid reading audience also should probably be able to charge more. Although there may be other important factors, let's look at these two together with one more, gender difference, to see if magazines charge more based on the percentage of men or women among the readers. Multiple regression will provide some answers and can help explain the impact of circulation, income, and gender on advertising prices.

Table 12.1.3 shows the multivariate data set to be analyzed. The page costs for a four-color, one-page ad run once will be the Y variable to be explained. The explanatory variables are X_1, circulation (actually the number of people who pay for a copy of each issue); X_2, percent male among the readership; and X_3, median income. The sample size is $n = 48$.

Table 12.1.4 shows the computer output from a multiple regression analysis from StatPad. Other statistical software packages will give much the same basic information, but perhaps without the explanations. These results will be interpreted in the following sections.

Regression Coefficients and the Regression Equation

The intercept or constant term, a, and the regression coefficients b_1, b_2, and b_3, are found by the computer using the method of least squares. Among all possible regression equations with various values for these coefficients, these are the ones that make the sum of squared prediction errors the smallest possible for these particular magazines. The regression equation, or prediction equation, is

$$\begin{aligned} \text{Predicted page costs} &= a + b_1 X_1 + b_2 X_2 + b_3 X_3 \\ &= -\$8{,}643 + 5.28(\text{Circulation}) - 11.00(\text{Percent male}) \\ &\quad + 1.22(\text{Median income}) \end{aligned}$$

TABLE 12.1.2 Results of a Multiple Regression Analysis

Name	Result	Description
Intercept or constant term	a	Predicted value for Y when every X is 0
Regression coefficients	$b_1, b_2, \ldots, b_p$	The effect of each X on Y, holding all other X variables constant
Prediction equation or regression equation	Predicted Y $= a + b_1 X_1 + b_2 X_2 + \cdots + b_p X_p$	Predicted value for Y given the values for the X variables
Prediction errors or residuals	$Y -$ Predicted Y	Error made by using the prediction equation instead of the actual value of Y for each case
Standard error of estimate	S_e	Approximate size of prediction errors (typical difference between actual Y and predicted Y from regression equation)
Coefficient of determination	R^2	Percentage of variability in Y explained by the X variables as a group
F-test	Significant or not significant	Tests whether the X variables, as a group, can predict Y better than just randomly; essentially a test to see if R^2 is larger than pure randomness would produce
t-tests for individual regression coefficients	Significant or not significant, for each X variable	Tests whether a particular X variable has an effect on Y, holding the other X variables constant; should only be performed if the F-test is significant
Standard errors of the regression coefficients	$S_{b_1}, S_{b_2}, \ldots, S_{b_p}$	Indicates the estimated sampling standard deviation of each regression coefficient; used in the usual way to find confidence intervals and hypothesis tests for individual regression coefficients
Degrees of freedom for standard errors of the regression coefficients	$n - p - 1$	Used to find the t-table value for confidence intervals and hypothesis tests for individual regression coefficients

TABLE 12.1.3 Advertising Costs and Characteristics of Magazines

	Y, Page Costs (color ad)	X_1, Circulation (thousands)	X_2, Percent Male	X_3 Median Income
Better Homes & Gardens	$73,820	8,000	22	$23,241
Business Week	35,140	845	72	30,884
Car & Driver	23,795	725	88	25,982
Cosmopolitan	28,980	2,250	17	22,785
Ebony	21,886	1,250	42	16,505
Family Circle	62,750	7,450	13	21,785
Field & Stream	33,760	2,000	79	24,337
Forbes	25,090	700	74	36,783
Fortune	30,040	670	71	35,204
Glamour	24,340	1,800	6	21,828
Golf Digest	26,625	1,025	82	32,949
Good Housekeeping	58,020	5,000	13	21,980
Harper's Bazaar	16,200	650	8	25,358
Hot Rod	20,400	850	78	23,056
House & Garden	25,430	1,000	19	23,726
House Beautiful	19,775	800	16	24,198
Ladies' Home Journal	48,000	5,000	12	21,583
Mademoiselle	16,280	1,000	9	23,660
McCalls	59,830	6,200	12	20,690
Mechanix Illustrated	24,815	1,600	81	22,568
Money	25,740	1,000	58	31,587
Motor Trend	21,905	750	84	23,878
Ms.	7,845	450	16	24,107
National Enquirer	26,500	4,637	40	19,969
National Geographic	95,575	8,400	55	26,294
National Lampoon	9,900	580	72	22,888
Newsweek	63,850	2,950	62	26,719
Outdoor Life	28,475	1,500	82	23,596
Parents Magazine	36,960	1,650	22	20,779
People	56,425	2,350	40	23,971
Playboy	55,710	5,000	78	24,051
Playgirl	7,220	650	36	19,329
Popular Mechanics	26,932	1,600	81	25,474
Popular Science	26,820	1,800	80	26,542
Reader's Digest	97,700	17,900	44	21,802
Redbook	42,675	3,800	11	22,794
Road & Track	18,775	630	89	28,093
Rolling Stone	17,770	700	66	24,074
Scientific American	24,000	720	68	29,531
Seventeen	19,250	1,500	9	21,251
Sports Illustrated	54,165	2,250	80	26,275
The Star	21,350	3,400	35	19,156
Time	85,870	4,400	56	26,908
True Story	13,435	1,400	18	14,325
TV Guide	77,400	17,345	45	20,461
U.S. News & World Report	42,510	2,050	63	26,998
Vogue	18,000	950	11	23,452
Woman's Day	60,435	7,125	8	21,910
Average	36,629	3,048	46.3	24,277
Standard deviation	22,973	3,756	29.1	4,271

Sample size: $n = 48$

Data are from C. L. Bovée and W. F. Arens, *Contemporary Advertising*, 2nd ed. (Homewood, Ill.: Richard D. Irwin, 1986), p. 430.

TABLE 12.1.4   Computer Printout for Multiple Regression Analysis of Magazine Ads

```
THE REGRESSION EQUATION IS:
        Page Costs
                = - 8,643
                +   5.2815  * Circulation
                -  10.9974  * Percent Male
                +   1.2226  * Median Income
The standard error of estimate:
                S = 13,129
        indicates the typical size of
        prediction errors in this data set.
The R-squared value:
                R2 = 0.694
        indicates the proportion of the
        variance of Page Costs that is
        explained by the regression model.

INFERENCE FOR Page Costs AT THE 5% LEVEL:
        The prediction equation DOES
        explain a significant proportion
        of the variation in Page Costs.
        F =   33.30  with
        3     and           44
        degrees of freedom
```

VARIABLE	effect on Page Costs COEFF	95% confidence interval FROM	TO	Hypothesis Test SIGNIFICANT?	std err of coeff STD ERR	t statistic t
Constant	-8,643	-33,414	16,129	No	12,291	-0.703
Circulation	5.28	4.21	6.35	Yes	0.530	9.958
Percent Male	-11.00	-166.58	144.58	No	77.197	-0.142
Median Income	1.22	0.14	2.30	Yes	0.535	2.283

The intercept, $a = -8,643$, suggests that the typical charge for a one-page color ad in a magazine with no paid subscribers, no men among its readership, and no income among its readers is $-$8,643$. This suggests that you would have to *pay* firms to advertise in such an absurd and useless place. However, there are no such magazines in this data set, so it may be best to view the intercept, a, as a possibly helpful step in getting the best predictions and not interpret it too literally.

Interpreting the Regression Coefficients

The regression coefficients are interpreted as the effect of each variable on page costs. In particular, they give you the average increase in page costs per increase of 1 in the X variable, where 1 means one unit of whatever that X variable measures.

The regression coefficient for circulation, $b_1 = 5.28$, indicates that, *all else equal,* a magazine with an extra 1,000 paid subscribers (since X_1 is given in thousands in the original data set) will charge an extra $5.28 (on average) for a one-page ad. You can also think of it as meaning that each extra subscriber is worth $0.00528, or about one-half cent per person. So if a different magazine had the same percent male readership and the same median income but 3,548 more subscribers, you would expect the page costs to be $5.28 \times 3.548 = \$18.73$ higher (on average) due to the larger readership.

The regression coefficient for percent male, $b_2 = -11.00$, indicates that, *all else equal,* a magazine with an extra 1% of male readers would charge $11.00 *less* (on average) for a full-page color ad. This suggests that women readers are more valuable than men readers. Statistical inference will confirm or deny this hypothesis by comparing this $-\$11.00$ effect to what you might find due to random coincidence.

The regression coefficient for income, $b_3 = 1.22$, indicates that, *all else equal,* a magazine with an extra dollar of median income among its readers would charge $1.22 more (on average) for a full-page ad. The sign (positive) is reasonable. If a magazine had the same total paid circulation and percent male readership but had a median income $4,000 higher, you would expect the page costs to be $1.22 \times 4,000 = \$4,880$ higher (on average) due to the higher income level.

Remember that regression coefficients indicate the effect of one X variable on Y while all other X variables are held constant. This should be taken literally. For example, the regression coefficient b_3 indicates the effect of median income on page costs, computed while holding circulation and percent male readership fixed. In this example, higher median income levels tend to result in higher page costs at fixed levels of circulation and of male readership (due to the fact that b_3 is a positive number).

What would the relationship be if the other variables, circulation and percent male, were *not* held constant? This may be answered by looking at the ordinary correlation coefficient, computed for just the two variables page costs and median income. In this case, higher median income is actually associated with *lower* page costs (the correlation of page costs with median income is negative: -0.011)! How can this be? One reasonable explanation is that magazines targeting a higher median income level cannot support a large circulation due to a relative scarcity of rich people in the general population. If this circulation decrease is large enough, it can offset the effect of higher income per reader.

Predictions and Prediction Errors

The prediction equation or regression equation is defined as: Predicted $Y = a + b_1 X_1 + b_2 X_2 + \cdots + b_p X_p$. For the magazine ads example, to find a predicted value for page costs based on the circulation, percent male readership, and median income for a magazine similar to those in the data set, substitute the X values into the prediction equation as follows:

$$\begin{array}{rl}
\text{Predicted} \\
\text{page costs} \end{array} = a + b_1 X_1 + b_2 X_2 + b_3 X_3$$

$$= -8{,}643 + 5.2815 \times X_1 - 10.9974 \times X_2 + 1.2226 \times X_3$$

$$= -8{,}643 + 5.2815(\text{Circulation}) - 10.9974(\text{Percent male})$$

$$+ 1.2226(\text{Median income})$$

For example, suppose you planned to launch a new magazine, *Popular Statistics,* that would reach a circulation of 900,000 with a readership that is 55% women and that has a median income of $20,000. Be sure to put these numbers into the regression equation *in the same form* as the original data set: $X_1 = 900$ (thousands circulation), $X_2 = 45$ (percent male), and $X_3 = 20{,}000$ (median income). The predicted value for this situation is:

$$\begin{array}{rl}
\text{Predicted page} \\
\text{costs for} = \\
\textit{Popular Statistics} \end{array} -8{,}643 + 5.2815(\text{Circulation})$$

$$- 10.9974(\text{Percent male}) + 1.2226(\text{Median income})$$

$$= -8{,}643 + 5.2815 \times 900 - 10.9974 \times 45$$

$$+ 1.2226 \times 20{,}000$$

$$= -8{,}643 + 4{,}753 - 495 + 24{,}452$$

$$= \$20{,}067$$

Of course, you would not expect page costs to be exactly $20,067 for two reasons. First of all, there is random variation even among the magazines you have data on, so the predictions are not perfect even for these. Second, predictions can only be useful to the extent that the predicted magazine is similar to the magazines in the original data set. For a new magazine, the advertising rates may be determined differently than for the well-established magazines used to compute the regression equation.

You can also use the equation to find the predicted page costs for the magazines in the original data set. The first magazine, *Better Homes & Gardens,* has $X_1 = 8{,}000$ (indicating a circulation of 8 million), $X_2 = 22$ (indicating 22% men among its readers), and $X_3 = 23{,}241$ (indicating a median annual income of $23,241 for its readers). The predicted value is

$$\begin{array}{rl}
\text{Predicted page} \\
\text{costs for } \textit{Better} = \\
\textit{Homes \& Gardens} \end{array} -8{,}643 + 5.2815(\text{Circulation}) - 10.9974(\text{Percent male})$$

$$+ 1.2226(\text{Median income})$$

$$= -8{,}643 + 5.2815 \times 8{,}000 - 10.9974 \times 22$$

$$+ 1.2226 \times 23{,}241$$

$$= -\$8{,}643 + \$42{,}252 - \$242 + \$28{,}414$$

$$= \$61{,}781$$

The residual, or prediction error, is defined as $Y -$ (Predicted Y). For a magazine in the original data set, this is the actual minus the predicted page costs. For *Better Homes & Gardens,* the actual page costs are \$73,820, compared to the predicted value of \$61,781. Thus, the prediction error is $73,820 - 61,781 = \$12,039$. A positive residual like this indicates that the actual page costs are *higher* than predicted—about \$12,000 higher for this magazine. For many of us \$12,000 is a lot of money; it is a good idea to look at some of the other prediction errors to see how well or poor the predictions are. How can *Better Homes & Gardens* charge so much more than we would expect? Basically because the prediction used only $p = 3$ of the many factors that influence the cost of advertising.

Table 12.1.5 shows the actual values and the predicted values (also called the *expected values* or *fitted values*) for page costs together with the prediction errors for each of the magazines in the original data set.[3]

How Good Are the Predictions?

This section will be primarily a review, since the standard error of estimate, S_e, and the coefficient of determination, R^2, have much the same interpretation for multiple regression as they had for simple regression in the previous chapter. The only difference is that your predictions are now based on more than one X variable. They are so similar because you are still predicting just one Y.

Typical Prediction Error: Standard Error of Estimate

Just as for simple regression, with only one X, the standard error of estimate indicates the approximate size of the prediction errors. For the magazine ads example, $S_e = \$13,129$. This tells you that actual page costs for these magazines are typically within about \$13,129 from the predicted page costs, in the sense of a standard deviation. That is, if the error distribution is normal, then you would expect about 2/3 of the actual page costs to be within S_e of the predicted page costs, about 95% to be within $2S_e$, and so forth.

The standard error of estimate, $S_e = \$13,129$, indicates the remaining variation in page costs after you have used the X variables (circulation, percent male, and median income) in the regression equation to predict page costs for each magazine. Compare this to the ordinary univariate standard deviation, $S_Y = \$22,973$ for the page costs, computed by ignoring all the other variables. This standard deviation, S_Y, indicates the remaining variation in page costs after you have used $\overline{Y}$ to predict the page costs for each

---

[3]These numbers differ slightly from the previous calculations because more significant digits were used for the regression coefficients. This is why the table shows a predicted value of \$61,783 instead of \$61,781 for *Better Homes & Gardens.* This round-off error is so small that it is not usually a problem.

TABLE 12.1.5 Predicted and Residual Values for Magazine Ads

	Page Costs (actual)	Page Costs (predicted)	Prediction Errors (residuals)
Better Homes & Gardens	$73,820	$ 61,783	$12,037
Business Week	35,140	32,789	2,351
Car & Driver	23,795	25,985	−2,190
Cosmopolitan	28,980	30,912	−1,932
Ebony	21,886	17,677	4,209
Family Circle	62,750	57,197	5,553
Field & Stream	33,760	30,807	2,953
Forbes	25,090	39,213	−14,123
Fortune	30,040	37,157	−7,117
Glamour	24,340	27,486	−3,146
Golf Digest	26,625	36,154	−9,529
Good Housekeeping	58,020	44,496	13,524
Harper's Bazaar	16,200	25,706	−9,506
Hot Rod	20,400	23,178	−2,778
House & Garden	25,430	25,438	−8
House Beautiful	19,775	24,992	−5,217
Ladies' Home Journal	48,000	44,021	3,979
Mademoiselle	16,280	25,468	−9,188
McCalls	59,830	49,267	10,563
Mechanix Illustrated	24,815	26,510	−1,695
Money	25,740	34,621	−8,881
Motor Trend	21,905	23,589	−1,684
Ms.	7,845	23,032	−15,187
National Enquirer	26,500	39,823	−13,323
National Geographic	95,575	67,265	28,310
National Lampoon	9,900	21,613	−11,713
Newsweek	63,850	38,924	24,926
Outdoor Life	28,475	27,227	1,248
Parents Magazine	36,960	25,235	11,725
People	56,425	32,637	23,788
Playboy	55,710	46,313	9,397
Playgirl	7,220	18,027	−10,807
Popular Mechanics	26,932	30,063	−3,131
Popular Science	26,820	32,436	−5,616
Reader's Digest	97,700	112,068	−14,368
Redbook	42,675	39,175	3,500
Road & Track	18,775	28,054	−9,279
Rolling Stone	17,770	23,763	−5,993
Scientific American	24,000	30,518	−6,518
Seventeen	19,250	25,163	−5,913
Sports Illustrated	54,165	34,486	19,679
The Star	21,350	32,351	−11,001
Time	85,870	46,879	38,991
True Story	13,435	16,068	−2,633
TV Guide	77,400	107,486	−30,086
U.S. News & World Report	42,510	34,501	8,009
Vogue	18,000	24,927	−6,927
Woman's Day	60,435	55,688	4,747

magazine. Note that $S_e = \$13,129$ is smaller than $S_Y = \$22,973$, indicating that your errors are typically smaller if you use the regression equation instead of just $\overline{Y}$ to predict page costs. This suggests that the X variables are helpful in explaining page costs.

Think of it this way. If you knew nothing, you would use the average page costs ($\overline{Y}$ = \$36,629) as your best guess, and you would be wrong by about S_Y = \$22,973. But if you knew the circulation, percent male readership, and median reader income, you could use the regression equation to find a prediction for page costs that would be wrong by only S_e = \$13,129. This reduction in prediction error (from \$22,973 to \$13,129) is one of the payoffs from running a regression analysis.

Percent Variation Explained: R^2

The coefficient of determination, R^2, indicates the percentage of the variation in Y that is explained by or attributed to all of the X variables.

For the magazine ads example, the coefficient of determination, R^2 = 0.694 or 69.4%, tells you that the explanatory variables (the X variables circulation, percent male, and median income) have explained 69.4% of the variation in page costs.[4] This leaves 30.6% of the variation unaccounted for and attributable to other factors. This is a fairly large R^2 number; many research studies find much smaller numbers yet still provide useful predictions. You usually want R^2 to be as large a value as possible, since higher numbers tell you that the relationship is a strong one. The highest possible value is R^2 = 100%, which happens only when all prediction errors are 0 and is usually a signal to look for a mistake somewhere.

Inference in Multiple Regression

The regression output so far is a fairly complete description of these particular (n = 48) magazines, but statistical inference will help you generalize to the idealized population of similar conceivable magazines. Rather than just observe that there is an average decrease in page costs of \$11.00 per percentage point increase in male readership, you can infer about a large population of similar magazines that could reasonably have produced this data, to see whether there is *necessarily* any connection between gender and page costs, or if the −\$11.00 regression coefficient could reasonably be just randomness. Could it be that this effect of percent male readership on page costs is just a random number, rather than indicating a systematic relationship? Statistical inference will provide an answer.

For reference, Table 12.1.6 shows the portion of the computer output from Table 12.1.4 that deals with statistical inference. We will discuss each item in the following sections, after indicating the population you will be inferring about.

---

[4]Technically, it is the *variance* (the squared standard deviation) of Y that is explained by the X variables.

TABLE 12.1.6   Statistical Inference for Magazine Ads

```
INFERENCE FOR Page Costs AT THE 5% LEVEL:
      The prediction equation DOES
      explain a significant proportion
      of the variation in Page Costs.
          F =   33.30  with
          3     and         44
          degrees of freedom
```

	effect on Page Costs	95% confidence interval		Hypothesis Test	std err of coeff	t statistic
VARIABLE	COEFF	FROM	TO	SIGNIFICANT?	STD ERR	t
Constant	−8,643	−33,414	16,129	No	12,291	−0.703
Circulation	5.28	4.21	6.35	Yes	0.530	9.958
Percent Male	−11.00	−166.58	144.58	No	77.197	−0.142
Median Income	1.22	0.14	2.30	Yes	0.535	2.283

Assumptions

For simplicity, assume that you have a random sample from a much larger population. Assume also that the population has a linear relationship with randomness, as expressed by the **multiple regression linear model,** which specifies that the observed value for Y is equal to the population relationship plus a random error that has a normal distribution. These random errors are also assumed to be independent from one case (elementary unit) to another.

■ **The Multiple Regression Linear Model for the Population**

$$Y = (\alpha + \beta_1 X_1 + \beta_2 X_2 + \cdots + \beta_p X_p) + \varepsilon$$

$$= \text{(Population relationship)} + \text{Randomness}$$

where ε has a normal distribution with mean 0 and constant standard deviation σ, and this randomness is independent from one case to another.

The population relationship is given by $p + 1$ parameters: α is the population intercept (or constant term), and $\beta_1, \beta_2, \ldots, \beta_p$ are the population regression coefficients, indicating the mean effect of each X on Y (in the population), holding all other X constant. A summary of population and sample quantities is shown in Table 12.1.7. If your data were a census of the entire population, then your least-squares regression coefficients would be the same as those in the population relationship. Ordinarily, however, you will use the least-squares intercept, a, as an *estimator* of α, and the least-

TABLE 12.1.7   Population and Sample Quantities in Multiple Regression

	Population (parameters: fixed and unknown)	Sample (estimators: random and known)
Intercept or constant	α	a
Regression coefficients	β_1	b_1
	β_2	b_2
	.	.
	.	.
	.	.
	β_p	b_p
Uncertainty in Y	σ	S_e

squares regression coefficients, $b_1, b_2, \ldots, b_p$, as *estimators* of $\beta_1, \beta_2, \ldots, \beta_p$, respectively. Of course, there are errors involved in estimating since the sample is much smaller than the entire population.

Is the Model Significant? The F-Test or R^2 Test

Inference begins with the F-test to see if the X variables explain a significant amount of the variation in Y. The F-test is used as a gateway to statistical inference: If it is significant, then there is a relationship, and you may proceed to investigate and explain it. If it is not significant, you might as well just have a bunch of unrelated random numbers; essentially nothing can be explained.

The null hypothesis for the F-test claims that there is *no* predictive relationship between the X variables and Y in the population. That is, Y is pure randomness and has no regard for the values of the X variables. Looking at the multiple regression linear model, this claim is equivalent to $Y = \alpha + \varepsilon$, which happens whenever *all* of the population regression coefficients are 0.

The research hypothesis for the F-test claims that there is some predictive relationship between the X variables and Y in the population. That is, Y is more than just pure randomness and must depend on at least one of the X variables. That is, the research hypothesis claims that *at least one* of the regression coefficients is not 0. Note that it is not necessary for every X variable to affect Y; it is enough for there to be just one.

■ **Hypotheses for the F-Test**

$$H_0: \beta_1 = \beta_2 = \cdots = \beta_p = 0$$

$$H_1: \text{At least one of } \beta_1, \beta_2, \ldots, \beta_p \neq 0$$

The easiest way to perform the F-test is to compare the R^2 value (the percent of the variation in Y that is explained by the X variables) to a table of R^2 values for the appropriate test level (5% or other). If the R^2 value is large enough, then the regression is significant; more than just a random amount of the variation in Y is explained. The table is indexed by n (the number of cases) and p (the number of X variables).

The traditional way of performing the F-test is harder to interpret, but it always gives the same result as the R^2 table. The F-test is traditionally done by computing the F-statistic and comparing it to the critical value in the F-table at the appropriate test level.[5] Two different degrees of freedom numbers are used: p (the number of X variables used to explain Y) and $n - p - 1$ (a measure of the randomness of the residuals *after* estimation of the $p + 1$ coefficients $a, b_1, \ldots, b_p$).

However, the F-statistic is an unnecessary complication because the R^2 value may be tested directly. Furthermore, R^2 is more directly meaningful than the F-statistic. Whether you use the F or the R^2 approach, your answer (significant or not) will be the same at each test level.

Why is the more complex F-statistic traditionally used when R^2, which is more directly meaningful, can be used instead? Perhaps it's just tradition, and perhaps it's because the F-tables have long been available. The use of a meaningful number (such as R^2) provides more insight into the situation and seems preferable, especially in the field of business.

■ Result of the F-Test (Decided Using R^2)

If the R^2 value is *smaller* than the critical value in the table, then the model is *not significant* (you accept the null hypothesis that the X variables *do not* help predict Y).

If the R^2 value is *larger* than the critical value in the table, then the model is *significant* (you reject the null hypothesis and accept the research hypothesis that the X variables *do* help predict Y).

Remember that the statistical meaning of *significant* is slightly different from its everyday usage. When you find a significant regression model, you know that the relationship between the X variables and Y is stronger than you would ordinarily expect from randomness alone. That is, you can tell that a relationship is there. It may or may not be a strong or useful relationship in any practical sense (you must look separately at this issue), but it is strong enough that it does not look purely random.

---

[5]In case you are curious, the F-statistic gets its name from Sir Ronald A. Fisher and is defined as the "explained mean square" divided by the "unexplained mean square." Large values of F suggest that the regression model is significant because you have explained a lot relative to the amount of unexplained randomness. Large values of R^2 also suggest significance. The link between F and R^2 is the fact that $F = (n - p - 1)[1/(1 - R^2) - 1]/p$ and $R^2 = 1 - 1/[1 + pF/(n - p - 1)]$, so that larger values of F go with larger values of R^2 and vice versa. This is why tests for large F are exactly equivalent to tests for large values of R^2.

For the magazine advertising cost example, the prediction equation *does* explain a significant proportion of the variation in page costs, as reported on the computer printout. This says that page costs does depend systematically on (at least one of) these factors and is not just random. You don't yet know which one or more of the X variables is responsible for this prediction of Y, but you know that there is at least one.

To verify that the regression equation is really significant, note that the coefficient of determination is $R^2 = 0.694$ or 69.4%. The R^2 table for testing at the 5% level with $n = 48$ magazines and $p = 3$ variables (see Table 12.1.8) shows the critical value 0.161 or 16.1%. In order for the equation to be significant at the conventional 5% level, the X variables would need to explain only 16.1% of the variation in page costs (Y). Since they explain more, the regression is significant.

Looking at the 1% and 0.1% R^2 tables (Tables 12.1.9 and 12.1.10) for $n = 48$ and $p = 3$, you find critical values of 0.225 (22.5%) and 0.306 (30.6%), respectively. Since the observed $R^2 = 69.4\%$ exceeds both of these, you may conclude that these X variables (circulation, percent male, and median income) have a *very highly significant* impact on Y (page costs). Using p-value notation, you could say that the regression is very highly significant ($p < 0.001$).[6]

Tables of Critical Values for Testing R^2

Tables 12.1.8 through 12.1.11 are used for testing whether the model is significant or not (the F-test). These tables are provided for test levels 0.05 (significant), 0.01 (highly significant), 0.001 (very highly significant), and 0.1. For each test level, your regression is significant if R^2 exceeds the value in the table for your number of X variables (p) and number of cases (n). For example, if you have run a regression with $p = 2$ explanatory X variables and $n = 35$ cases, then it is significant at level 0.05 if R^2 exceeds the critical value 0.171 (from the 5% table).

In practice, most computer programs will perform the F-test for you and report whether it is significant or not and, if so, at what level. These R^2 tables would not be needed in such cases. Their use is twofold: (1) to find significance when you have an R^2 value reported without significance test information, and (2) to show you how strongly the significance level depends on n and p. The critical R^2 value required for significance is smaller (less demanding) when n is larger because you have more information. However, the critical R^2 value required for significance is larger (more demanding) when p is larger because of the effort involved in estimating the extra regression coefficients.

---

[6]Note that the p in "p-value" stands for *probability* and is not the same p as used for the number of X variables, although the same letter is often used for both purposes.

If you have more than 50 cases, you may find critical values using the two multipliers at the bottom of the R^2 table according to the following formula:

■ **Critical Values for R^2 When $n > 50$**

$$\text{Critical value} = \frac{\text{Multiplier 1}}{n} + \frac{\text{Multiplier 2}}{n^2}$$

For example, with $n = 135$ cases and $p = 6$ explanatory X variables, to test at level 0.05 you would use the two multipliers 12.59 and -18.24 at the bottom of the $p = 6$ column in the 5% table. Using the formula, you would find the critical value for R^2 to be

$$\begin{aligned}
\text{Critical value} &= \frac{\text{Multiplier 1}}{n} + \frac{\text{Multiplier 2}}{n^2} \\
&= \frac{12.59}{135} + \frac{-18.24}{135^2} \\
&= 0.09326 - 0.00100 \\
&= 0.0923
\end{aligned}$$

If the R^2 for your data set (from the computer printout) exceeds this value (0.0923, or 9.23%), the F-test is significant; otherwise it is not.

Which Variables Are Significant? A *t*-Test for Each Coefficient

If the F-test is significant, you know that one or more of the X variables is helpful in predicting Y, and you may proceed with statistical inference using t-tests for individual regression coefficients to find out which one (or more) of the X variables is useful. These t-tests show you whether an X variable has a significant impact on Y, holding all other X variables fixed.

If the F-test is not significant, then you are *not* permitted to use t-tests on the regression coefficients. In rare cases, these t-tests can be significant even though the F-test is not. The F-test dominates in these cases, and you must conclude that nothing is significant. To do otherwise would raise your type I error rate above the claimed level (5%, for example).

The t-test for each coefficient is based on the estimated regression coefficient and its standard error and uses the t-table critical value for $n - p - 1$ degrees of freedom. The confidence interval for a particular population regression coefficient, say, the jth one, β_j, extends in the usual way:

■ **Confidence Interval for the jth Regression Coefficient, β_j**

From $b_j - tS_{b_j}$ to $b_j + tS_{b_j}$

where t is from the t-table for $n - p - 1$ degrees of freedom.

TABLE 12.1.8 R^2 Table: 5% Critical Values (Significant)

Number of Cases (n)	Number of X Variables (p)									
	1	2	3	4	5	6	7	8	9	10
3	0.994									
4	0.902	0.997								
5	0.771	0.950	0.998							
6	0.658	0.864	0.966	0.999						
7	0.569	0.776	0.903	0.975	0.999					
8	0.499	0.698	0.832	0.924	0.980	0.999				
9	0.444	0.632	0.764	0.865	0.938	0.983	0.999			
10	0.399	0.575	0.704	0.806	0.887	0.947	0.985	0.999		
11	0.362	0.527	0.651	0.751	0.835	0.902	0.954	0.987	1.000	
12	0.332	0.486	0.604	0.702	0.785	0.856	0.914	0.959	0.989	1.000
13	0.306	0.451	0.563	0.657	0.739	0.811	0.872	0.924	0.964	0.990
14	0.283	0.420	0.527	0.618	0.697	0.768	0.831	0.885	0.931	0.967
15	0.264	0.393	0.495	0.582	0.659	0.729	0.791	0.847	0.896	0.937
16	0.247	0.369	0.466	0.550	0.624	0.692	0.754	0.810	0.860	0.904
17	0.232	0.348	0.440	0.521	0.593	0.659	0.719	0.775	0.825	0.871
18	0.219	0.329	0.417	0.494	0.564	0.628	0.687	0.742	0.792	0.839
19	0.208	0.312	0.397	0.471	0.538	0.600	0.657	0.711	0.761	0.807
20	0.197	0.297	0.378	0.449	0.514	0.574	0.630	0.682	0.731	0.777
21	0.187	0.283	0.361	0.429	0.492	0.550	0.604	0.655	0.703	0.749
22	0.179	0.270	0.345	0.411	0.471	0.527	0.580	0.630	0.677	0.722
23	0.171	0.259	0.331	0.394	0.452	0.507	0.558	0.607	0.653	0.696
24	0.164	0.248	0.317	0.379	0.435	0.488	0.538	0.585	0.630	0.673
25	0.157	0.238	0.305	0.364	0.419	0.470	0.518	0.564	0.608	0.650

26	0.151	0.229	0.294	0.351	0.404	0.454	0.501	0.545	0.588	0.629
27	0.145	0.221	0.283	0.339	0.390	0.438	0.484	0.527	0.569	0.609
28	0.140	0.213	0.273	0.327	0.377	0.424	0.468	0.510	0.551	0.590
29	0.135	0.206	0.264	0.316	0.365	0.410	0.453	0.495	0.534	0.573
30	0.130	0.199	0.256	0.306	0.353	0.397	0.439	0.480	0.518	0.556
31	0.126	0.193	0.248	0.297	0.342	0.385	0.426	0.466	0.503	0.540
32	0.122	0.187	0.240	0.288	0.332	0.374	0.414	0.452	0.489	0.525
33	0.118	0.181	0.233	0.279	0.323	0.363	0.402	0.440	0.476	0.511
34	0.115	0.176	0.226	0.271	0.314	0.353	0.391	0.428	0.463	0.497
35	0.111	0.171	0.220	0.264	0.305	0.344	0.381	0.417	0.451	0.484
36	0.108	0.166	0.214	0.257	0.297	0.335	0.371	0.406	0.440	0.472
37	0.105	0.162	0.208	0.250	0.289	0.326	0.362	0.396	0.429	0.461
38	0.103	0.157	0.203	0.244	0.282	0.318	0.353	0.386	0.418	0.449
39	0.100	0.153	0.198	0.238	0.275	0.310	0.344	0.377	0.408	0.439
40	0.097	0.150	0.193	0.232	0.268	0.303	0.336	0.368	0.399	0.429
41	0.095	0.146	0.188	0.226	0.262	0.296	0.328	0.359	0.390	0.419
42	0.093	0.142	0.184	0.221	0.256	0.289	0.321	0.351	0.381	0.410
43	0.090	0.139	0.180	0.216	0.250	0.283	0.314	0.344	0.373	0.401
44	0.088	0.136	0.176	0.211	0.245	0.276	0.307	0.336	0.365	0.393
45	0.086	0.133	0.172	0.207	0.239	0.271	0.300	0.329	0.357	0.384
46	0.085	0.130	0.168	0.202	0.234	0.265	0.294	0.322	0.350	0.377
47	0.083	0.127	0.164	0.198	0.230	0.259	0.288	0.316	0.343	0.369
48	0.081	0.125	0.161	0.194	0.225	0.254	0.282	0.310	0.336	0.362
49	0.079	0.122	0.158	0.190	0.220	0.249	0.277	0.304	0.330	0.355
50	0.078	0.120	0.155	0.186	0.216	0.244	0.272	0.298	0.323	0.348
Multiplier 1	3.84	5.99	7.82	9.49	11.07	12.59	14.07	15.51	16.92	18.31
Multiplier 2	2.15	−0.27	−3.84	−7.94	−12.84	−18.24	−23.78	−30.10	−36.87	−43.87

TABLE 12.1.9 R^2 Table: 1% Critical Values (Highly Significant)

Number of Cases (n)	Number of X Variables (p)									
	1	2	3	4	5	6	7	8	9	10
3	1.000									
4	0.980	1.000								
5	0.919	0.990	1.000							
6	0.841	0.954	0.993	1.000						
7	0.765	0.900	0.967	0.995	1.000					
8	0.696	0.842	0.926	0.975	0.996	1.000				
9	0.636	0.785	0.879	0.941	0.979	0.997	1.000			
10	0.585	0.732	0.830	0.901	0.951	0.982	0.997	1.000		
11	0.540	0.684	0.784	0.859	0.916	0.958	0.985	0.997	1.000	
12	0.501	0.641	0.740	0.818	0.879	0.928	0.963	0.987	0.998	1.000
13	0.467	0.602	0.700	0.778	0.842	0.894	0.936	0.967	0.988	0.998
14	0.437	0.567	0.663	0.741	0.806	0.860	0.906	0.943	0.971	0.989
15	0.411	0.536	0.629	0.706	0.771	0.827	0.875	0.915	0.948	0.973
16	0.388	0.508	0.598	0.673	0.738	0.795	0.844	0.887	0.923	0.953
17	0.367	0.482	0.570	0.643	0.707	0.764	0.814	0.858	0.896	0.929
18	0.348	0.459	0.544	0.616	0.678	0.734	0.784	0.829	0.869	0.904
19	0.331	0.438	0.520	0.590	0.652	0.707	0.757	0.802	0.843	0.879
20	0.315	0.418	0.498	0.566	0.626	0.681	0.730	0.775	0.816	0.854
21	0.301	0.401	0.478	0.544	0.603	0.656	0.705	0.750	0.791	0.829
22	0.288	0.384	0.459	0.523	0.581	0.633	0.681	0.726	0.767	0.805
23	0.276	0.369	0.442	0.504	0.560	0.612	0.659	0.703	0.744	0.782
24	0.265	0.355	0.426	0.487	0.541	0.591	0.638	0.681	0.721	0.759
25	0.255	0.342	0.410	0.470	0.523	0.572	0.618	0.660	0.700	0.738

26	0.246	0.330	0.396	0.454	0.506	0.554	0.599	0.641	0.680	0.717
27	0.237	0.319	0.383	0.440	0.490	0.537	0.581	0.622	0.661	0.698
28	0.229	0.308	0.371	0.426	0.475	0.521	0.564	0.605	0.643	0.679
29	0.221	0.298	0.359	0.413	0.461	0.506	0.548	0.588	0.625	0.661
30	0.214	0.289	0.349	0.401	0.448	0.492	0.533	0.572	0.609	0.644
31	0.208	0.280	0.338	0.389	0.435	0.478	0.519	0.557	0.593	0.627
32	0.201	0.272	0.329	0.378	0.423	0.465	0.505	0.542	0.578	0.612
33	0.195	0.264	0.319	0.368	0.412	0.453	0.492	0.529	0.563	0.597
34	0.190	0.257	0.311	0.358	0.401	0.442	0.479	0.515	0.550	0.583
35	0.185	0.250	0.303	0.349	0.391	0.430	0.468	0.503	0.537	0.569
36	0.180	0.244	0.295	0.340	0.381	0.420	0.456	0.491	0.524	0.556
37	0.175	0.237	0.287	0.332	0.372	0.410	0.446	0.480	0.512	0.543
38	0.170	0.231	0.280	0.324	0.363	0.400	0.435	0.469	0.501	0.531
39	0.166	0.226	0.274	0.316	0.355	0.391	0.426	0.458	0.490	0.520
40	0.162	0.220	0.267	0.309	0.347	0.382	0.416	0.448	0.479	0.509
41	0.158	0.215	0.261	0.302	0.339	0.374	0.407	0.439	0.469	0.498
42	0.155	0.210	0.255	0.295	0.332	0.366	0.399	0.430	0.459	0.488
43	0.151	0.206	0.250	0.289	0.325	0.358	0.390	0.421	0.450	0.478
44	0.148	0.201	0.244	0.283	0.318	0.351	0.382	0.412	0.441	0.469
45	0.145	0.197	0.239	0.277	0.311	0.344	0.375	0.404	0.432	0.460
46	0.141	0.193	0.234	0.271	0.305	0.337	0.367	0.396	0.424	0.451
47	0.138	0.189	0.230	0.266	0.299	0.330	0.360	0.389	0.416	0.443
48	0.136	0.185	0.225	0.261	0.293	0.324	0.353	0.381	0.408	0.435
49	0.133	0.181	0.221	0.256	0.288	0.318	0.347	0.374	0.401	0.427
50	0.130	0.178	0.217	0.251	0.283	0.312	0.341	0.368	0.394	0.419
Multiplier 1	6.63	9.21	11.35	13.28	15.09	16.81	18.48	20.09	21.67	23.21
Multiplier 2	−5.81	−15.49	−25.66	−36.39	−47.63	−59.53	−71.65	−84.60	−97.88	−111.76

TABLE 12.1.10 R^2 Table: 0.1% Critical Values (Very Highly Significant)

Number of Cases (n)	Number of X Variables (p)									
	1	2	3	4	5	6	7	8	9	10
3	1.000									
4	0.998	1.000								
5	0.982	0.999	1.000							
6	0.949	0.990	0.999	1.000						
7	0.904	0.968	0.993	0.999	1.000					
8	0.855	0.937	0.977	0.995	1.000	1.000				
9	0.807	0.900	0.952	0.982	0.996	1.000	1.000			
10	0.761	0.861	0.922	0.961	0.985	0.996	1.000	1.000		
11	0.717	0.822	0.889	0.936	0.967	0.987	0.997	1.000	1.000	
12	0.678	0.785	0.856	0.908	0.945	0.972	0.989	0.997	1.000	1.000
13	0.642	0.749	0.822	0.878	0.920	0.952	0.975	0.990	0.997	1.000
14	0.608	0.715	0.790	0.848	0.894	0.930	0.958	0.978	0.991	0.998
15	0.578	0.684	0.759	0.819	0.867	0.906	0.938	0.962	0.980	0.992
16	0.550	0.654	0.730	0.790	0.840	0.881	0.916	0.944	0.966	0.982
17	0.525	0.627	0.702	0.763	0.813	0.856	0.893	0.923	0.949	0.968
18	0.502	0.602	0.676	0.736	0.787	0.831	0.869	0.902	0.930	0.953
19	0.480	0.578	0.651	0.711	0.763	0.807	0.846	0.880	0.910	0.935
20	0.461	0.556	0.628	0.688	0.739	0.784	0.824	0.859	0.890	0.917
21	0.442	0.536	0.606	0.665	0.716	0.761	0.801	0.837	0.869	0.897
22	0.426	0.517	0.586	0.644	0.694	0.739	0.780	0.816	0.849	0.878
23	0.410	0.499	0.567	0.624	0.674	0.718	0.759	0.795	0.829	0.859
24	0.395	0.482	0.548	0.605	0.654	0.698	0.739	0.775	0.809	0.839
25	0.382	0.466	0.531	0.587	0.635	0.679	0.719	0.756	0.790	0.821

26	0.369	0.452	0.515	0.570	0.618	0.661	0.701	0.737	0.771	0.802
27	0.357	0.438	0.500	0.553	0.601	0.644	0.683	0.719	0.753	0.784
28	0.346	0.425	0.486	0.538	0.585	0.627	0.666	0.702	0.735	0.767
29	0.335	0.412	0.472	0.523	0.569	0.611	0.649	0.685	0.718	0.750
30	0.325	0.401	0.459	0.510	0.555	0.596	0.634	0.669	0.702	0.733
31	0.316	0.389	0.447	0.496	0.541	0.581	0.619	0.654	0.686	0.717
32	0.307	0.379	0.435	0.484	0.527	0.567	0.604	0.639	0.671	0.702
33	0.299	0.369	0.424	0.472	0.515	0.554	0.590	0.625	0.657	0.687
34	0.291	0.360	0.414	0.460	0.503	0.541	0.577	0.611	0.643	0.673
35	0.283	0.351	0.404	0.450	0.491	0.529	0.564	0.598	0.629	0.659
36	0.276	0.342	0.394	0.439	0.480	0.517	0.552	0.585	0.616	0.646
37	0.269	0.334	0.385	0.429	0.469	0.506	0.540	0.573	0.604	0.633
38	0.263	0.326	0.376	0.420	0.459	0.495	0.529	0.561	0.591	0.620
39	0.257	0.319	0.368	0.411	0.449	0.485	0.518	0.550	0.580	0.608
40	0.251	0.312	0.360	0.402	0.440	0.475	0.508	0.539	0.569	0.597
41	0.245	0.305	0.352	0.393	0.431	0.465	0.498	0.529	0.558	0.586
42	0.240	0.298	0.345	0.385	0.422	0.456	0.488	0.518	0.547	0.575
43	0.235	0.292	0.338	0.378	0.414	0.447	0.479	0.509	0.537	0.564
44	0.230	0.286	0.331	0.370	0.406	0.439	0.470	0.499	0.527	0.554
45	0.225	0.280	0.324	0.363	0.398	0.431	0.461	0.490	0.518	0.544
46	0.220	0.275	0.318	0.356	0.391	0.423	0.453	0.482	0.509	0.535
47	0.216	0.269	0.312	0.349	0.383	0.415	0.445	0.473	0.500	0.526
48	0.212	0.264	0.306	0.343	0.377	0.408	0.437	0.465	0.491	0.517
49	0.208	0.259	0.301	0.337	0.370	0.401	0.429	0.457	0.483	0.508
50	0.204	0.255	0.295	0.331	0.363	0.394	0.422	0.449	0.475	0.500
Multiplier 1	10.83	13.82	16.27	18.47	20.52	22.46	24.32	26.12	27.88	29.59
Multiplier 2	−31.57	−54.02	−75.12	−96.26	−117.47	−138.94	−160.86	−183.33	−206.28	−229.55

TABLE 12.1.11 R^2 Table: 10% Critical Values

Number of Cases (n)	Number of X Variables (p)									
	1	2	3	4	5	6	7	8	9	10
3	0.976									
4	0.810	0.990								
5	0.649	0.900	0.994							
6	0.532	0.785	0.932	0.996						
7	0.448	0.684	0.844	0.949	0.997					
8	0.386	0.602	0.759	0.877	0.959	0.997				
9	0.339	0.536	0.685	0.804	0.898	0.965	0.998			
10	0.302	0.482	0.622	0.738	0.835	0.914	0.970	0.998		
11	0.272	0.438	0.568	0.680	0.775	0.857	0.925	0.974	0.998	
12	0.247	0.401	0.523	0.628	0.721	0.803	0.874	0.933	0.977	0.998
13	0.227	0.369	0.484	0.584	0.673	0.753	0.825	0.888	0.940	0.979
14	0.209	0.342	0.450	0.545	0.630	0.708	0.779	0.842	0.899	0.946
15	0.194	0.319	0.420	0.510	0.592	0.667	0.736	0.799	0.857	0.907
16	0.181	0.298	0.394	0.480	0.558	0.630	0.697	0.759	0.816	0.868
17	0.170	0.280	0.371	0.453	0.527	0.596	0.661	0.721	0.778	0.830
18	0.160	0.264	0.351	0.428	0.499	0.566	0.628	0.687	0.742	0.794
19	0.151	0.250	0.332	0.406	0.474	0.538	0.598	0.655	0.709	0.760
20	0.143	0.237	0.316	0.386	0.452	0.513	0.571	0.626	0.679	0.729
21	0.136	0.226	0.301	0.368	0.431	0.490	0.546	0.599	0.650	0.699
22	0.129	0.215	0.287	0.352	0.412	0.469	0.523	0.575	0.624	0.671
23	0.124	0.206	0.275	0.337	0.395	0.450	0.502	0.552	0.600	0.646
24	0.118	0.197	0.263	0.323	0.379	0.432	0.482	0.530	0.577	0.622
25	0.113	0.189	0.253	0.310	0.364	0.415	0.464	0.511	0.556	0.599

26	0.109	0.181	0.243	0.298	0.350	0.400	0.447	0.492	0.536	0.579
27	0.105	0.175	0.234	0.287	0.338	0.386	0.431	0.475	0.518	0.559
28	0.101	0.168	0.225	0.277	0.326	0.372	0.417	0.459	0.501	0.541
29	0.097	0.162	0.218	0.268	0.315	0.360	0.403	0.444	0.484	0.523
30	0.094	0.157	0.210	0.259	0.305	0.348	0.390	0.430	0.469	0.507
31	0.091	0.152	0.203	0.251	0.295	0.337	0.378	0.417	0.455	0.492
32	0.088	0.147	0.197	0.243	0.286	0.327	0.366	0.405	0.442	0.478
33	0.085	0.142	0.191	0.236	0.277	0.317	0.356	0.393	0.429	0.464
34	0.082	0.138	0.185	0.229	0.269	0.308	0.346	0.382	0.417	0.451
35	0.080	0.134	0.180	0.222	0.262	0.300	0.336	0.371	0.406	0.439
36	0.078	0.130	0.175	0.216	0.255	0.291	0.327	0.361	0.395	0.427
37	0.075	0.127	0.170	0.210	0.248	0.284	0.318	0.352	0.385	0.416
38	0.073	0.123	0.166	0.205	0.241	0.276	0.310	0.343	0.375	0.406
39	0.071	0.120	0.162	0.199	0.235	0.269	0.302	0.334	0.366	0.396
40	0.070	0.117	0.157	0.194	0.229	0.263	0.295	0.326	0.357	0.387
41	0.068	0.114	0.154	0.190	0.224	0.257	0.288	0.319	0.348	0.378
42	0.066	0.111	0.150	0.185	0.219	0.250	0.281	0.311	0.340	0.369
43	0.065	0.109	0.146	0.181	0.214	0.245	0.275	0.304	0.333	0.361
44	0.063	0.106	0.143	0.177	0.209	0.239	0.269	0.297	0.325	0.353
45	0.062	0.104	0.140	0.173	0.204	0.234	0.263	0.291	0.318	0.345
46	0.060	0.102	0.137	0.169	0.200	0.229	0.257	0.285	0.312	0.338
47	0.059	0.099	0.134	0.166	0.196	0.224	0.252	0.279	0.305	0.331
48	0.058	0.097	0.131	0.162	0.191	0.220	0.247	0.273	0.299	0.324
49	0.057	0.095	0.128	0.159	0.188	0.215	0.242	0.268	0.293	0.318
50	0.055	0.093	0.126	0.156	0.184	0.211	0.237	0.263	0.287	0.312
Multiplier 1	2.71	4.61	6.25	7.78	9.24	10.65	12.02	13.36	14.68	15.99
Multiplier 2	3.12	3.08	2.00	0.32	−1.92	−4.75	−7.59	−11.12	−14.94	−19.05

The *t*-test is significant if the reference value 0 (indicating no effect) is *not* in the confidence interval. There is nothing really new here; this is just the usual generic procedure for a two-sided test.

Alternatively, you could compare the *t*-statistic b_j/S_{b_j} to the *t*-table value, deciding significance if the absolute value of the *t*-statistic is larger. As you look down a column of *t*-values, one for each coefficient, there is an easy, approximate way to tell which coefficients are significant: these are the ones that are 2 or larger in absolute value, since the *t*-table value is approximately 2 for a test at the 5% level (provided *n* is large enough). As always, the *t*-statistic and the confidence interval approaches must always give the same result (significant or not) for each test.

What exactly is being tested here? The *t*-test for β_j decides whether or not X_j has a significant effect on Y in the population with all other X variables held constant. This is not a test for the correlation of X_j with Y, which would ignore all the other X variables. Rather, it is a test for the effect of X_j on Y after adjustment has been made for all other factors. In studies of salary designed to identify possible gender discrimination, it is common to adjust for education and experience. Although the men in a department might be paid more than women, on average, it is also important to see whether these differences can be explained by factors other than gender. By including all these factors in a multiple regression (by regressing Y = salary on X_1 = gender, X_2 = education, and X_3 = experience), the regression coefficient for gender will represent the effect of gender on salary after adjustment for education and experience.[7]

Here are the formulas for the hypotheses for the significance test of the *j*th regression coefficient:

■ **Hypotheses for the *t*-Test of the *j*th Regression Coefficient**

$$H_0: \beta_j = 0$$

$$H_1: \beta_j \neq 0$$

For the magazine advertising example, the *t*-test will have $n - p - 1 = 48 - 3 - 1 = 44$ degrees of freedom. The two-sided critical value from the

---

[7]The gender variable, X_1, might be represented as 0 for a woman and 1 for a man. In this case, the regression coefficient would represent the extra pay, on average, for a man compared to a woman with the same education and experience. If the gender variable were represented as 1 for a woman and 0 for a man, the regression coefficient would be the extra pay for a woman compared to a man with the same characteristics otherwise. Fortunately, the conclusions will be identical regardless of which representation is used.

TABLE 12.1.12   Multiple Regression Computer Printout

VARIABLE	effect on Page Costs COEFF	95% confidence interval FROM	95% confidence interval TO	Hypothesis Test SIGNIFICANT?	std err of coeff STD ERR	t statistic t
Constant	-8,643	-33,414	16,129	No	12,291	-0.703
Circulation	5.28	4.21	6.35	Yes	0.530	9.958
Percent Male	-11.00	-166.58	144.58	No	77.197	-0.142
Median Income	1.22	0.14	2.30	Yes	0.535	2.283

t-table is 1.960 (or, more accurately, 2.015).[8] Table 12.1.12 provides the appropriate information from the computer printout of Table 12.1.6.

Two of the X variables are significant because their 95% confidence intervals do not include 0. As we suspected originally, circulation has a lot to do with advertising costs. With such a high t-value, 9.958, the effect of circulation on page costs is very highly significant (holding percent male and median income constant). The effect of median income on page costs is also significant (holding circulation and percent male constant).

Evidently, the percentage of male readership does not significantly affect page costs (holding circulation and median income constant), since this t-test is not significant. It is possible that this percentage has an impact on page costs only through median income, which tends to be higher for males. Thus, after adjusting for median income, it is reasonable that the variable for percent male would provide no further information for determining page costs. Although the estimated effect of percent male is −$11.00, it is only randomly different from 0. Strictly speaking, you are not allowed to interpret this −$11.00 coefficient; since it is not significant, you have no "license" to explain it. It may *look* like −$11.00, but it is not distinguishable from $0.00; you can't even really tell if it is positive or negative!

The constant, a = −$8,643, is not significant. It is not significantly different from zero. No claim can be made as to whether the population parameter, α, is positive or negative, since it might reasonably be zero. In cost accounting applications, a often estimates the fixed cost of production. The confidence intervals and hypothesis tests would show you whether there is a significant fixed component in your cost structure or not.

Other Tests for a Regression Coefficient

You may also perform other tests with regression coefficients, just as you have with mean values. If there is a reference value for one of the regression

---

[8]Don't forget that using the t-value for an infinite number of degrees of freedom whenever there are more than 40 degrees of freedom is just an approximation. In this case the true t-table value is 2.015; 1.960 is just a convenient approximation.

coefficients (which does not come from the data), you may test whether the estimated regression coefficient differs significantly from the reference value or not. Simply see if the reference value is in the confidence interval, and decide "significantly different" if it is not, as usual. Or use the t-statistic $(b_j - \text{Reference value})/S_{b_j}$, deciding "significantly different" if its absolute value is larger than the t-table value for $n - p - 1$ degrees of freedom.

Suppose you had believed (before coming across this data set) that the additional cost per paid subscriber was $2.00 per thousand people. To test this assumption, use $2.00 as the reference value. Since the confidence interval, $4.21 to $6.35, excludes the reference value, you may conclude that the effect of paid circulation on ad costs, adjusting for percent male readership and median income, is significantly more than $2.00 per thousand. Note that this is a one-sided conclusion based on a two-sided test. The two-sided test is appropriate here because the estimate might have come out on the other side of $2.00.

One-sided confidence intervals may be computed in the usual way for one (or more) regression coefficients, giving you a one-sided statement about the population regression coefficient (or coefficients) of interest. Be sure to use the one-sided t-values from the t-table for $n - p - 1$ degrees of freedom, and be sure that your confidence interval for β_j includes the regression coefficient b_j.

For example, the regression coefficient for income is $b_3 = 1.22$, indicating that (all else equal) an extra dollar of median income would boost the price of a full-page ad by $1.22, on average. The standard error is $S_{b_3} = 0.535$, and the one-sided t-table value for $n - p - 1 = 44$ is $t = 1.645$, so the one-sided interval will extend upward from $b_3 - tS_{b_3} = 1.22 - 1.645 \times 0.535 = 0.3399$. Your conclusion is:

> You are 95% sure that an extra dollar of median income will boost the average page cost by at least $0.34.

The 34 cents defining the one-sided confidence bound is much lower than the estimated value of $1.22 because you have allowed for the random errors of estimation. By using a one-sided instead of a two-sided interval, you can claim 34 cents instead of the smaller value of 14 cents, which defines the lower endpoint of the two-sided interval.

One-sided tests may be done for regression coefficients in the usual way, provided you are only interested in *one side* of the reference value and would not change the side of interest had the estimates come out differently.

Which Variables Are Explaining the Most?

Which X variable or variables are explaining the most about Y? This is a good question. Unfortunately, there is no completely satisfying answer because relationships among the X variables can make it fundamentally impossible to decide precisely which X variable is really responsible for the behavior of the Y variable. The answer depends on how you view the situation (in particular, whether or not you can change the X variables individually). The answer also depends on how the X variables interrelate (or correlate) with each other. Following are two useful but incomplete answers to this tough question.

Comparing the Standardized Regression Coefficients

Since the regression coefficients $b_1, \ldots, b_p$ may all be in different measurement units, direct comparison is difficult; a small coefficient may actually be more important than a larger one. This is the classic problem of "trying to compare apples and oranges." The *standardized regression coefficients* eliminate this problem by expressing the coefficients in terms of a single, common set of statistically reasonable units so that comparison may at least be attempted.

The regression coefficient b_i indicates the effect of a change in X_i on Y with all of the other X variables unchanged. The measurement units of regression coefficient b_i are units of Y per unit of X_i. For example, if Y is the dollar amount of sales and X_1 is the number of people in the sales force, b_1 is in units of dollars of sales per person. Suppose that the next regression coefficient, b_2, is in units of dollars of sales per number of total miles traveled by the sales force. The question of which is more important to sales, staffing level or travel budget, cannot be answered by comparing b_1 to b_2 because dollars per person and dollars per mile are not directly comparable.

The **standardized regression coefficient,** found by multiplying the regression coefficient b_i by S_{X_i} and dividing it by S_Y, represents the expected change in Y (in standardized units of S_Y) due to an increase in X_i of one of its standardized units (i.e., S_{X_i}), with all other X variables unchanged.[9] The absolute values of the standardized regression coefficients may be compared, giving a rough indication of the relative importance of the variables.[10] Each standardized regression coefficient is in units of standard deviations of Y per standard deviation of X_i. These are just the ordinary sample standard deviations for each variable that you learned in Chapter 5. Use of these units is natural because they set the measurement scale according to the actual variation in each variable in your data set.

---

[9]Standardized regression coefficients are sometimes referred to as *beta coefficients*. We will avoid this term because it could easily be confused with the population regression coefficients (also β, or beta) and with the nondiversifiable component of risk in finance (which is called the *beta* of a stock and is an ordinary, unstandardized sample regression coefficient, where Y is the percent change in a market index and X is the percent change in the value of a stock certificate).

[10]Recall that the absolute value simply ignores any minus sign.

■ **Standardized Regression Coefficients**

$$b_i S_{X_i}/S_Y$$

Each regression coefficient is adjusted according to a ratio of ordinary sample standard deviations. The absolute values give a rough indication of the relative importance of each X variable.

To standardize the regression coefficients for the magazine ads example, you first need the standard deviation for each variable:

Standard Deviations			
Page Costs	**Circulation**	**Percent Male**	**Median Income**
$S_Y = 22{,}973$	$S_{X_1} = 3{,}756$	$S_{X_2} = 29.1$	$S_{X_3} = 4{,}271$

You also need the regression coefficients:

Regression Coefficients		
Circulation	**Percent Male**	**Median Income**
$b_1 = 5.28$	$b_2 = -11.00$	$b_3 = 1.22$

Finally, the standardized regression coefficients may be computed:

Standardized Regression Coefficients		
Circulation	**Percent Male**	**Median Income**
$b_1 S_{X_1}/S_Y$ $= 5.28 \times 3{,}756/22{,}973$ $= 0.863$	$b_2 S_{X_2}/S_Y$ $= -11.00 \times 29.1/22{,}973$ $= -0.014$	$b_3 S_{X_3}/S_Y$ $= 1.22 \times 4{,}271/22{,}973$ $= 0.227$

Here's the direct interpretation for one of these standardized coefficients: The value 0.863 for circulation says that an increase in circulation of one of its standard deviations (3,756) will result in an expected increase in page costs of 0.863 of its standard deviations (22,973). That is, an increase of 3,756 in circulation will result in an expected increase of 0.863 × 22,973 = $19,826 in page costs.

More importantly, these standardized regression coefficients may now be compared. The largest in absolute value is 0.863 for circulation, suggesting that this is the most important. Next is median income, with 0.227. The smallest absolute value is $|-0.014| = 0.014$ for percent male.

It would be wrong to compare the regression coefficients directly, without first standardizing. Note that percent male has the largest regression coefficient (in absolute value), $|-11.00| = 11.00$. However, because it is in different measurement units from the others, a direct comparison makes no sense.

The absolute values of the standardized regression coefficients may be compared, providing a *rough* indication of importance of the variables. Again, the results are not perfect because relationships among the X variables can make it fundamentally impossible to decide which X variable is really responsible for the behavior of the Y variable.

Comparing the Correlation Coefficients

You might not really be interested in the regression coefficients from a multiple regression, which represent the effects of each variable with all others fixed. If you simply want to see how strongly each X variable affects Y, allowing the other X variables to "do what comes naturally," you may compare the *absolute values of the correlation coefficients* for Y with each X in turn.

The correlation clearly measures the strength of the relationship (as was covered in Chapter 11), but why use the absolute value? Remember, a correlation near 1 or -1 indicates a strong relationship, and a correlation near 0 suggests no relationship. The absolute value of the correlation gives the *strength* of the relationship without indicating its *direction.*

Multiple regression *adjusts* or *controls* for the other variables, whereas the correlation coefficient does not.[11] If it is important that you adjust for the effects of other variables, then multiple regression is your answer. If you don't need to adjust, the correlation approach may meet your needs.

Here are the correlation coefficients of Y with each of the X variables for the magazine ads example. For example, the correlation of page costs with median income is -0.011.

Correlation with Page Costs		
Circulation	**Percent Male**	**Median Income**
0.806	−0.066	−0.011

In terms of the relationship to page costs, without adjustment for the other X variables, circulation has by far the highest absolute value of correlation, 0.806. Next in absolute value is percent male, with $|-0.066| = 0.066$. Median income has the smallest absolute value, 0.011. It looks as if only circula-

---

[11]There is an advanced statistical concept, the *partial correlation coefficient,* which is not covered in this book. It gives the correlation between two variables while controlling or adjusting for one or more additional variables.

tion is important in determining page costs. In fact, neither of the other two variables alone explains a significant amount of page costs.

The multiple regression gives a different picture because it controls for other variables. After adjusting for circulation, the multiple regression coefficient for median income indicates a significant effect on page costs. Here's how to interpret this: The adjustment for circulation controls for the fact that higher incomes go with smaller circulations. The circulation effect is removed, leaving only the pure income effect, which can be detected because it is no longer masked by the competing circulation effect.

Although the correlation coefficients indicate the *individual* relationships with Y, the standardized regression coefficients from a multiple regression can provide you with important additional information.

12.2 Pitfalls and Problems in Multiple Regression

Unfortunately, multiple regression does not always work out as well in real life as it does in the textbooks. This section includes a checklist of potential problems and some suggestions about how to fix them (when possible).

There are three main kinds of problems. Following is a quick overview of each; more details will follow.

1 The problem of **multicollinearity** arises when some of your explanatory (X) variables are too similar. Although they do a good job of explaining and predicting Y (as indicated by a high R^2 and a significant F-test), the individual regression coefficients are poorly estimated. This is because there is not enough information to decide which one (or more) of the variables is doing the explaining. One solution is to omit some of the variables in an effort to end the confusion. Another solution is to redefine some of the variables (perhaps using ratios) to distinguish them from one another.

2 The problem of **variable selection** arises when you have a long list of potentially useful explanatory X variables and you are trying to decide which ones to include in the regression equation. On one hand, if you have too many X variables, the unnecessary ones will degrade the quality of your results (perhaps due to multicollinearity). Some of the information in the data is wasted on the estimation of unnecessary parameters. On the other hand, if you omit a necessary X variable, your predictions will lose quality because helpful information is being ignored. One solution is to think hard about *why* each X variable is important and to make sure that each one you include is performing a (potentially) useful function. Another solution is to use an automated procedure that automatically selects the most useful variables for you.

3 The problem of **model misspecification** refers to the many different potential incompatibilities between your application and the multiple re-

gression linear model, which is the underlying basis and framework for a multiple regression analysis. Your particular application might or might not conform to the assumptions of the multiple regression linear model. By exploring the data, you can be alerted to some of the potential problems with nonlinearity, unequal variability, or outliers. However, you may or may not have a problem: even though the histograms of some variables may be skewed, and even though some scatterplots may be nonlinear, the multiple regression linear model might still hold. There is a *diagnostic plot* that helps you decide when the problem is serious enough to need fixing. A possible solution is creation of new X variables, constructed from the current ones, and/or transformation of some or all of the variables. Another serious problem arises if you have a *time series,* so that the independence assumption of the multiple regression linear model is not satisfied. The time series problem is complex; however, you may be able to do multiple regression using *percent changes* from one time period to the next in place of the original data.

Multicollinearity: Are the Explanatory Variables Too Similar?

When some of your explanatory (X) variables are similar to one another, you may have a *multicollinearity* problem because it is difficult for multiple regression to distinguish between the effect of one variable and the effect of another. The consequences of multicollinearity can be *statistical* or *numerical:*

1 *Statistical* consequences of multicollinearity include difficulties in testing individual regression coefficients due to inflated standard errors. Thus, you may be unable to declare an X variable significant even though (by itself) it has a strong relationship with Y.

2 *Numerical* consequences of multicollinearity include difficulties in the computer's calculations due to numerical instability. In extreme cases, the computer may try to divide by zero and thus fail to complete the analysis. Or, even worse, the computer may complete the analysis but then report meaningless, wildly incorrect numbers.[12]

Multicollinearity may or may not be a problem, depending on the purpose of your analysis and the extent of the multicollinearity. Small to moderate amounts of multicollinearity are usually not a problem. Extremely strong multicollinearity (for example, including the same variable twice) will always be a problem and may cause serious errors (numerical consequences). Fortunately, if your purpose is primarily to predict or forecast Y, strong multicollinearity may not be a problem because a careful multiple re-

---

[12]Dividing by zero is mathematically impossible; for example, 5/0 is undefined. However, due to small round-off errors made in computation, the computer may divide 5.0000000000968 by 0.0000000000327 instead. Instead of stopping and reporting trouble, the computer would use the inappropriate huge result of this division, 152,905,198,779.72.

gression program can still produce the best (least-squares) forecasts of Y based on all of the X variables. However, if you want to use the individual regression coefficients to explain how Y is affected by each X variable, then the statistical consequences of multicollinearity will probably cause trouble because these effects cannot be separated. Table 12.2.1 summarizes the impact of multicollinearity on the regression analysis.

How can you tell if you have a multicollinearity problem? One simple way is to look at the ordinary bivariate correlations of each pair of variables.[13] The *correlation matrix* is a table giving the correlation between every pair of variables in your multivariate data set. The higher the correlation coefficient between one X variable and another, the more multicollinearity you have. This is because a high correlation (close to 1 or to -1) indicates strong association and tells you that these two X variables are measuring something similar, bringing overlapping information to the analysis.

The primary statistical effect of multicollinearity is to *inflate the standard errors of some or all of the regression coefficients* (S_{b_i}). This is only natural: if two X variables contain overlapping information, it is difficult to compute the effect of each individually. A high standard error is the computer's way of saying, "I found the regression coefficient for you, but it's not very precise because I can't tell whether this variable or some other one is really responsible." The result is that the confidence intervals for the regression coefficients become larger, and the t-tests are less likely to be significant.

With strong multicollinearity, you may find a regression that is very highly significant (based on the F-test) but for which none of the t-tests of the individual X variables is significant. The computer is telling you that the X variables taken as a group explain a lot about Y, but it is impossible to single out any particular X variables as being responsible. Remember that the

TABLE 12.2.1   Effects of Multicollinearity in Regression

Extent of Multicollinearity	Effect on the Regression Analysis
Little	Not a problem
Moderate	Not usually a problem
Strong	Statistical consequences: Often a problem if you want to estimate effects of individual X variables (i.e., regression coefficients); may not be a problem if your goal is just to predict or forecast Y
Extremely strong	Numerical consequences: Always a problem; computer calculations may even be wrong due to numerical instability

[13]Unfortunately, a complete diagnosis of multicollinearity is much more difficult than this because the X variables must be considered all at once, not just two at a time. Full technical details may be found, for example, in D. A. Belsley, E. Kuh, and R. E. Welsch, *Regression Diagnostics: Identifying Influential Data and Sources of Collinearity* (New York: Wiley, 1980).

t-test for a particular variable X_i measures its effect with the others held fixed. Thus, the t-test for X_i measures only the *additional* information conveyed by X_i over and above that of the other variables. If some other variable is very similar, then X_i really isn't bringing significant new information into the regression.

One solution is to omit X variables that duplicate the information already available in other X variables. For example, if your X variables include three different size measures, consider either eliminating two of them or else combining them into a single size measure (for example, using their average).

Another solution is to redefine some of the variables so that each X variable has a clear, unique role in explaining Y. One common way to apply this idea to a group of similar X variables is to choose a single representative X variable (choose one or form an index from all of them) and express other variables as ratios (per-capita values can do this) with respect to your representative X variable. For example, you could explain sales (Y) using population (X_1) and total income (X_2) for each region; however, these variables are multicollinear (that is, population and total income are highly correlated). You could correct the problem by explaining sales (Y) using population (X_1) and per-capita income (the new X_2 variable). In effect, you would let population be the representative variable, indicating the overall size of the territory, and you would redefine income to convey new information (about how well off people are) instead of repeating old information (about how large the territory is).

EXAMPLE   ### Predicting Market Value from Sales, Employees, and Assets

What is the *market value* of a firm, and how is it determined? It is the total value of all outstanding common stock, easily found by multiplying the total shares outstanding by the current price per share. It is determined by supply and demand in the stock market. Financial theorists tell us that it represents the present value of the (uncertain, risky) future cash flows of the firm. But how does it relate to other features of a firm? Let's use multiple regression to find out.

Consider the information shown in Table 12.2.2 on market value (the Y variable, to be explained) and some explanatory X variables (the value of assets owned, yearly sales, number of employees) for the rubber products companies in the Fortune 500.

You should anticipate a multicollinearity problem with this data set because every X is basically a *size* variable. The X variables bring in similar, overlapping information; that is, large firms tend to be large in every aspect: market value, assets, sales, and employees. Small firms tend to be small in every aspect. Table 12.2.3 shows the multiple regression output.

Note that the regression is significant according to the F-test. Well over half ($R^2 = 59.2\%$) of the variation in market value is explained by the X variables

TABLE 12.2.2   Rubber Products Companies in the Fortune 500

	Market Value (millions), Y	Assets (millions), X_1	Sales (millions), X_2	Employees, X_3
Goodyear	$3,023	$8,610	$10,328	121,586
Firestone	1,386	2,593	3,712	55,000
GenCorp	1,949	2,119	3,099	26,700
Goodrich	1,319	1,820	2,553	11,914
Premark Intl	867	1,407	1,959	21,900
Dayco	254	511	911	4,000
Armstrong	191	521	800	7,505
Rubbermaid	1,969	579	795	6,103
Cooper	375	368	578	5,398
Dorsey	159	190	527	4,400
Danaher	252	741	524	6,950
Carlisle	314	322	466	4,949
Millipore	1,778	398	443	4,868
Standard Products	468	199	443	5,700
Lancaster Colony	267	250	423	5,100

Data are from "The Fortune 500," *Fortune,* April 27, 1987, pp. 355–83, 405.

TABLE 12.2.3   Regression Analysis of Rubber Products Companies

The regression equation:

Market value=451.8042-0.01004 × Assets+0.4698 × Sales-0.01693 × Employees

The standard error of estimate:

$$S=636.9899$$

indicates the typical size of prediction errors in this data set.
   The coefficient of determination:

$$R^2=0.592497$$

indicates the proportion of the variance of market value that is explained by the regression model.
   Inference for market value at the 5% level:

$$F=5.331237 \quad \text{(with 3 and 11 degrees of freedom)}$$

The prediction equation *does* explain a significant proportion of the variation in market value.

Variable	Coefficient (b_i)	95% Confidence Interval From	95% Confidence Interval To	Hypothesis Test Significant?	Standard Error (S_{b_i})	$t=b_i/S_{b_i}$
Constant	451.804	-81.149	984.758	No	242.146	1.866
Assets	-0.010	-1.940	1.920	No	0.877	-0.011
Sales	0.470	-1.176	2.116	No	0.748	0.628
Employees	-0.017	-0.078	0.044	No	0.028	-0.615

taken together as a group, and this is statistically significant at the 5% level.[14] However, due to multicollinearity, *no single X variable is significant.* Thus, market value is explained, but you can't say which *X* is doing the explaining.

Some useful information about multicollinearity is provided by the correlation matrix, Table 12.2.4, which lists the correlation between every pair of variables in the multivariate data set. Note the extremely high correlations among the *X* variables: 0.996 between assets and sales, 0.980 between sales and employees, and 0.979 between assets and employees. Such high correlations suggest that, at least with respect to the numbers, these three *X* variables are providing nearly identical information. No wonder the regression analysis can't tell them apart.

If you were to keep only one of the three *X* variables, you would find a significant regression with a significant *t*-test for that variable *regardless of which X variable you chose to keep.* That is, each one does a good job of explaining market value by itself.

If you want to retain all of the information contained in the three *X* variables, a good way to proceed is to keep one of them as your representative size variable and define the other two as ratios. Let's keep assets as the representative size variable because it indicates the fixed investment required by the firm. The other variables will now be replaced by the ratio of sales to assets (indicating the number of dollars of sales generated per dollar of assets) and the ratio of employees to assets (indicating the number of employees per million dollars of assets). Now assets is the clear size variable, and the others bring in new information about generation of sales by assets and efficiency in the use of employees. Table 12.2.5 shows the new data set.

Let's first check the correlation matrix, shown in Table 12.2.6, to look for multicollinearity problems.

These correlations look much better. The correlations among the *X* variables (-0.296, -0.109, and 0.647) are no longer extremely high. Although the correlation of 0.647 between sales/asset and employees/asset is statistically significant, it is not high enough to present a serious numerical problem.

What should you expect to see in the multiple regression results? The regression should still be significant, and the *t*-test for assets should now be significant

TABLE 12.2.4 Correlation Matrix for Rubber Products Companies

	Market Value, Y	Assets, X_1	Sales, X_2	Employees, X_3
Market value, Y	1.000	0.755	0.760	0.721
Assets, X_1	0.775	1.000	0.996	0.979
Sales, X_2	0.760	0.996	1.000	0.980
Employees, X_3	0.721	0.979	0.980	1.000

---

[14] The R^2 table for $n = 15$ firms and $p = 3$ explanatory X variables indicates that any R^2 value over 49.5% will be statistically significant. This is equivalent to the F-test based on the F-statistic of 5.33 reported in the printout.

TABLE 12.2.5   Defining New X Variables for Rubber Products Companies, Using Ratio to Assets

	Market Value (millions), Y	Assets (millions), X_1	Ratio of Sales to Assets, X_2	Ratio of Employees to Assets, X_3
Goodyear	$3,023	$8,610	1.200	14.121
Firestone	1,386	2,593	1.432	21.211
GenCorp	1,949	2,119	1.462	12.600
Goodrich	1,319	1,820	1.403	6.546
Premark Intl	867	1,407	1.392	15.565
Dayco	254	511	1.783	7.828
Armstrong	191	521	1.536	14.405
Rubbermaid	1,969	579	1.373	10.541
Cooper	375	368	1.571	14.668
Dorsey	159	190	2.774	23.158
Danaher	252	741	0.707	9.379
Carlisle	314	322	1.447	15.370
Millipore	1,778	398	1.113	12.231
Standard Products	468	199	2.226	28.643
Lancaster Colony	267	250	1.692	20.400

TABLE 12.2.6   Correlation Matrix for New X Variables for Rubber Products Companies

	Market Value, Y	Assets, X_1	Ratio of Sales to Assets, X_2	Ratio of Employees to Assets, X_3
Market value, Y	1.000	0.755	−0.399	−0.254
Assets, X_1	0.755	1.000	−0.296	−0.109
Ratio of sales to assets, X_2	−0.399	−0.296	1.000	0.647
Ratio of employees to assets, X_3	−0.254	−0.109	0.647	1.000

because it has no competing size variables. The uncertainty to be resolved is, knowing the assets, does it help you to know the sales ratio or the employee ratio in order to explain market value? Table 12.2.7 shows the results.

These results confirm our expectations: The regression (F-test) is significant, and the t-test for assets is also significant now that the strong multicollinearity has been eliminated. We have also found that the other two variables (sales per asset and employees per asset) are *not* significant.

Apparently, for this small ($n = 15$) group of large rubber products firms, much of the variation in market value can be explained by the level of assets. Furthermore, information about sales volume and about human resources (employees) contributes little, if any, additional insight into the market value of these successful firms. Perhaps analysis with a larger sample of firms would be able to detect the impact of these variables.

Variable Selection: Are You Using the Wrong Variables?

Statistical results depend heavily on the information you provide as data to be analyzed. In particular, you must use care in choosing the explanatory

TABLE 12.2.7   Regression Analysis Using New X Variables for Rubber Products Companies

The regression equation:

Market value=1,146.610+0.2919 × Assets-239.858(Sales per asset)
            -13.7035(Employees per asset)

The standard error of estimate:

$$S=624.1254$$

indicates the typical size of prediction errors in this data set.
The coefficient of determination:

$$R^2=0.608791$$

indicates the proportion of the variance of market value that is explained by the regression model.
Inference for market value at the 5% level:

$$F=5.705990 \quad \text{(with 3 and 11 degrees of freedom)}$$

The prediction equation *does* explain a significant proportion of the variation in market value.

| Variable | Coefficient (b_i) | 95% Confidence Interval | | Hypothesis Test Significant? | Standard error (S_{b_i}) | $t=b_i/S_{b_i}$ |
		From	To			
Constant	1146.610	-245.295	2538.517	No	632.410	1.813
Assets	0.292	0.111	0.473	Yes	0.082	3.557
Sales per asset	-239.858	-1300.53	820.820	No	481.918	-0.498
Employees per asset	-13.704	-93.977	66.570	No	36.472	-0.376

(X) variables for a multiple regression analysis. It is *not* a good idea to include too many X variables "just to be safe" or because "each one seems like it might have some effect." If you do so, you may have trouble finding significance for the regression (the F-test), or, due to multicollinearity caused by unnecessary variables, you may have trouble finding significance for some of the regression coefficients.

What happens when you include one extra, irrelevant X variable? Your R^2 will be slightly larger because a little more of Y can be explained by exploiting the randomness of this new variable.[15] However, the F-test of significance of the regression takes this increase into account, so this larger R^2 is not an advantage.

In fact, it is a slight to moderate *disadvantage* to include such an extra X variable. The estimation of an unnecessary parameter (the unneeded re-

---

[15]Although R^2 will always be either the same or larger, there is a similar quantity called *adjusted* R^2 that may be either larger or smaller when an irrelevant X variable is included. The adjusted R^2 will increase only if the X variable expolains more than a useless X variable would be expected to randomly explain. The adjusted R^2 may be computed from the (ordinary, unadjusted) R^2 value using the formula $1 - (n - 1)(1 - R^2)/(n - p - 1)$.

gression coefficient) leaves less information remaining in the standard error of estimate, S_e. For technical reasons, this leads to a less powerful F-test that is less likely to find significance when population X variables do in fact help explain Y.

What happens when you omit a necessary X variable? Important helpful information will be missing from the data set, and your predictions of Y will not be as good as if this X variable had been included. The standard error of estimate, S_e, will tend to be larger (indicating larger prediction errors), and R^2 will tend to be smaller (indicating that less of Y has been explained). Naturally, if a crucial X variable is omitted, you may not even find a significant F-test for the regression.

Your incentives here are to include just enough X variables (not too many, not too few) and to include the correct ones. If in doubt, you might include just a few of the X variables you are not sure of. There is a subjective method for achieving this (based on a prioritized list of X variables), and there are many different automatic methods.

Prioritizing the List of *X* Variables

One good way to proceed is to think hard about the problem, the data, and just what it is that you are trying to accomplish. Then produce a prioritized list of the variables as follows:

1 Select the Y variable you wish to explain, understand, or predict.
2 Select the single X variable that you feel is most important in determining or explaining Y. If this is difficult, because you feel that they are *all* so important, imagine that you are forced to choose.
3 Select the most important remaining X variable by asking yourself, "With the first variable taken into account, which X variable will contribute the most *new* information toward explaining Y?"
4 Continue selecting the most important remaining X variable in this way until you have a prioritized list of the X variables. At each stage, ask yourself, "With the X variables previously selected taken into account, which remaining X variable will contribute the most *new* information toward explaining Y?"

Next compute a regression with just those X variables from your list that you consider crucial. Also run a few more regressions including some (or all) of the remaining variables to see if they do indeed contribute toward predicting Y. Finally, choose the regression result you feel is most helpful.

Even though this procedure is fairly subjective (since it depends so heavily on your opinion), it has two advantages. First, when a choice is to be made between two X variables that are nearly equally good at predicting Y, you will have control over the selection (an automated procedure might make a less intuitive choice). Second, by carefully prioritizing your explanatory X variables, you gain further insight into the situation. By clarifying your thoughts, this exercise may be worth nearly as much as getting the multiple regression results!

Automating the Variable Selection Process

If you want the selection of variables to be done for you based on the data, instead of thinking hard about the situation, there are many different ways to proceed. Unfortunately, there is no single overall "best" answer to the automatic variable selection problem. Statistical research is still continuing on the problem. However, you can expect a good automatic method to provide you with a fairly short list of X variables that will do a fairly good job of predicting Y.

The best methods of automatic variable selection look at *all subsets* of the X variables. For example, if you have three explanatory X variables to choose from, then there are eight subsets to look at, as shown in Table 12.2.8.

TABLE 12.2.8	A List of All Possible Subsets of the X Variables When $p = 3$
1	None (just use $\overline{Y}$ to predict Y)
2	X_1
3	X_2
4	X_3
5	X_1, X_2
6	X_1, X_3
7	X_2, X_3
8	X, X_2, X_3

If you have 10 X variables, there will be 1,024 different subsets.[16] Even if you can compute that many regressions, how will you know which subset is best? A number of technical approaches have been suggested by statistical researchers based on formulas that trade off the additional information in a larger subset against the added difficulty in estimation.[17]

One widely used approach is called *stepwise selection*. At each step, a variable is either added to the list or removed from the list, depending on its usefulness. The process continues until the list stabilizes. This process is faster than looking at all subsets but may not work as well in some cases. Here are some further details of the stepwise selection procedure:

1 *Getting started.* Is there an X variable that is helpful in explaining Y? If not, stop now and report that no helpful X variable can be found. If there is a helpful one, put the most useful X variable on the list (this is the one with the highest absolute correlation with Y).

---

[16]The general formula is that 2^p subsets can be formed from p explanatory X variables.

[17]One good measure for choosing the best subset of X variables in regression is *Mallows' C_p statistic*. This and other approaches are discussed in N. R. Draper and H. Smith, *Applied Regression Analysis* (New York: Wiley, 1981), Chapter 6; and in G. A. F. Seber, *Linear Regression Analysis* (New York: Wiley, 1977), Chapter 12.

2 *Forward selection step.* Look at all of the X variables that are *not* on the list. In particular, look at the one that contributes the most *additional* explanation of Y. If it explains enough about Y, then include it on the list.

3 *Backward elimination steps.* Is there an X variable on the list that is no longer helpful (now that there are additional variables on the list)? If so, remove it, but be sure still to consider it for possible inclusion later on. Continue eliminating X variables until none can be eliminated from the list.

4 *Repeat until done.* Repeat steps 2 and 3 until no variable can be added to or dropped from the list.

The end result of the stepwise selection process is usually a fairly useful, fairly short list of explanatory X variables to use in multiple regression analysis to explain Y.

Model Misspecification: Does the Regression Equation Have the Wrong Form?

Even if you have a good list of X variables that contains the right information for explaining Y, there may still be problems. *Model misspecification* refers to all of the ways that the multiple regression linear model might fail to represent your particular situation. Here are some of the ways in which a regression model might be misspecified:

1 The expected response of Y to the X variables might be *nonlinear.* That is, the regression equation $a + b_1X_1 + b_2X_2 + \cdots + b_pX_p$ might not adequately describe the true relationship between Y and the X variables.

2 There might be *unequal variability* in Y. This would violate the assumption that the standard deviation, σ, in the multiple regression linear model is constant regardless of the values of the X variables.

3 There might be one or more *outliers* or *clusters,* which could seriously distort the regression estimates.

4 You might have a *time series,* in which case the randomness in the multiple regression linear model would not be independent from one time period to the next. In general, time-series analysis is complex (see Chapter 14). However, you may be able to work with a multiple regression using the *percent change* (from one time period to the next) in place of the original variables.

Some of these problems can be identified by exploring all of the possible scatterplots you can draw taking variables two at a time (for example, for $p = 3$ you would have six scatterplots: $[X_1, Y]$, $[X_2, Y]$, $[X_3, Y]$, $[X_1, X_2]$, $[X_1, X_3]$, $[X_2, X_3]$). For a complete analysis, all of these scatterplots should be at least briefly explored so that you are alerted to potential troubles. But keep in mind that these scatterplots may overstate the need for corrective action. For example, Y may show a curved relationship against X_1, yet this may not be a problem by itself.

Fortunately, there is a more direct method that often identifies serious problems. The *diagnostic plot* is a single scatterplot of residuals against predicted values that can point out most serious problems involving nonlinearity, unequal variability, and outliers. Thus, you may use all of the scatterplots of the basic variables as background information and then use the diagnostic plot as a basis for deciding whether or not to change the analysis.

Exploring the Data to See Nonlinearity or Unequal Variability

By looking at all of the scatterplots that can be made, one for each pair of variables, you can see much of the structure of the relationships among these variables. Often, useful insights into your situation can be made by looking at the data in this way. However, you still can't see *all* of the structure. For example, you would miss any combined effect of two variables on a third because you can see only two at a time.[18] Nonetheless, much useful background information can be obtained from the basic scatterplots.

Consider the earlier example of magazine ads, with page costs (Y) to be explained by circulation (X_1), percent male readership (X_2), and median income (X_3). Let's look at the scatterplots defined by each of the four variables against each of the others (Figures 12.2.1 through 12.2.6).

FIGURE 12.2.1 The scatterplot of Y (page costs) against X_1 (circulation) shows a strong increasing relationship. There are two possible outliers at the top right. Note that these are outliers only in terms of circulation, not in terms of page costs.

FIGURE 12.2.2 The scatterplot of Y (page costs) against X_2 (percent male) shows very little if any structure.

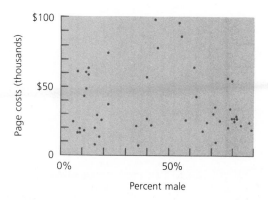

---

[18]Some computer systems can rotate a scatterplot in real time so that you can visually inspect the three-dimensional plot of three variables at once! A collection of techniques for exploring multivariate data is given in J. M. Chambers, W. S. Cleveland, B. Kleiner, and P. A. Tukey, *Graphical Methods for Data Analysis* (Boston: Duxbury Press, 1983).

FIGURE 12.2.3   The scatterplot of Y (page costs) against X_3 (median income) shows an unusual form of unequal variability. The variability of page costs is highest in the middle range of median income. This is because the high-circulation magazines (with higher page costs) tend to appeal to the middle-income group.

FIGURE 12.2.4   The scatterplot of X_1 (circulation) against X_2 (percent male) shows two possible outliers in the middle at the top. Note also the tendency for predominantly male publications to have relatively low circulations.

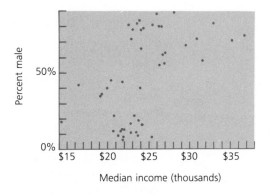

FIGURE 12.2.5   The scatterplot of X_1 (circulation) against X_3 (median income) shows that the high-circulation magazines tend to appeal to the middle-income group, but there is considerable variability within this group. The extremes (high-income and low-income) tend to have low circulations.

FIGURE 12.2.6   The scatterplot of X_2 (percent male) against X_3 (median income) shows clear gender differences in income level. Magazines appealing to a high-income readership tend to have more males among their readers; magazines appealing to a low-income readership tend to have more females. Middle-income magazines show large variability in terms of gender.

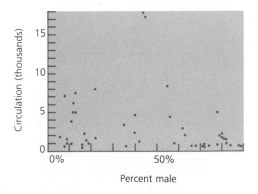

The correlation matrix is also helpful, since it gives a summary of the strength and direction of the association in each of these scatterplots, as shown in Table 12.2.9.

TABLE 12.2.9   Correlation Matrix for Magazine Ads Data Set

	Page Costs, Y	Circulation, X_1	Percent Male, X_2	Median Income, X_3
Page costs, Y	1.000	0.806	−0.066	−0.011
Circulation, X_1	0.806	1.000	−0.197	−0.267
Percent male, X_2	−0.066	−0.197	1.000	0.520
Median income, X_3	−0.011	−0.267	0.520	1.000

How would you summarize the results of this exploration of scatterplots and examination of correlations? The strongest association is between circulation and page costs (Figure 12.2.1); there is also strong association between median income and percent male (Figure 12.2.6). We also learn that the magazines with the largest circulation and the largest page costs tend to appeal to the middle-income group, leading to some unequal variability patterns (Figures 12.2.3 and 12.2.5). Also, there may be an outlier problem involving the two magazines (*Reader's Digest* and *TV Guide*) with the largest circulation (Figures 12.2.1, 12.2.4, and 12.2.5).

Is there a problem? The diagnostic plot will help you decide which problems (if any) require action and will show you whether the action works or not.

Using the Diagnostic Plot to Decide if You Have a Problem

The **diagnostic plot** for multiple regression is a scatterplot of the prediction errors (residuals) against the predicted values and is used to see if the predictions can be improved by fixing problems in your data.[19] The residuals, $Y − [a + b_1X_1 + b_2X_2 + \cdots + b_pX_p]$, are plotted on the vertical axis, and the predicted values, $a + b_1X_1 + b_2X_2 + \cdots + b_pX_p$, go on the horizontal axis. Because the methods for fixing problems are fairly complex (outlier removal, transformation, etc.), you fix a problem only if it is clear and extreme.

> Do not intervene unless the diagnostic plot shows you a clear and definite problem.

You read a diagnostic plot in much the same way you would read any bivariate scatterplot (see Chapter 11). Table 12.2.10 shows how to interpret what you find.

Why does it work this way? The residuals represent the *unexplained* prediction errors for Y that could not be accounted for by the multiple regression linear model involving the X variables. The predicted values represent the *current explanation*, based on the X variables. If there is any strong rela-

---

[19]The *predicted values* are also referred to as the *fitted values*.

TABLE 12.2.10 How to Interpret a Diagnostic Plot of Residuals against Predicted Values in Multiple Regression

Structure in the Diagnostic Plot	Interpretation
No relationship; just random, untilted scatter	Congratulations! No problems are indicated. Some improvements may still be possible, but the diagnostic plot cannot detect them.
Tilted linear relationship	Impossible by itself, since the least-squares regression equation should already have accounted for any purely linear relationship.
Tilted linear relationship with outlier(s)	The outlier(s) have distorted the regression coefficients and the predictions. The predictions for the well-behaved portion of the data can be improved if you feel that the outliers can be controlled (perhaps by transformation) or omitted.*
Curved relationship, typically U-shaped or inverted U-shaped	There is a nonlinear relationship in the data. Your predictions can be improved by either transforming, including an extra variable, or using nonlinear regression.
Unequal variability	Your prediction equation has been inefficiently estimated. Too much importance has been given to the less reliable portion of the data and too little to the most reliable part. This may be controlled by transforming Y (perhaps along with some of the X variables as well).

*A transformation should never be used *solely* to control outliers. However, when you transform a distribution to reduce extreme skewness, you may find that the former outliers are no longer outliers in the transformed data set.

tionship visible in the diagnostic plot, the current explanation can and should be improved by changing it to account for this visible relationship.

Shown in Figure 12.2.7 is the diagnostic plot for the example of magazine ads, with page costs (Y) explained by circulation (X_1), percent male readership (X_2), and median income (X_3). This is a tilted relationship with two outliers at the right. These outliers have corrupted the quality of the predictions for the rest of the data; there is real potential here for a better prediction equation if we can do something about the outliers.

Remember the outliers in the circulation (X_1) variable (see Figures 12.2.1, 12.2.4, and 12.2.5)? Before you consider omitting these two magazines (*Reader's Digest* and *TV Guide*,) you should explore to determine the nature of the outliers. Checking the source of the data, it seems that they are not errors. The histogram of circulation, shown in Figure 12.2.8, indicates extreme skewness. Although you don't necessarily have to transform X variables just because of skewness, the bigger problem of outliers might be solved by transforming to solve the smaller problem of skewness.

Figure 12.2.9 shows the histogram of the natural logarithm of circulation, $\log X_1$.[20] The outlier problem disappears when the logarithm transfor-

---

[20]For example, *Newsweek* has a circulation of 2,950 (in thousands). The natural logarithm of 2,950 is 7.9896.

FIGURE 12.2.7   This diagnostic plot shows some unexplained structure remaining in the residuals: note the upward tilt to most of the scatterplot, which is actually caused by the two outliers at the far right. This is the diagnostic plot for the multiple regression of the basic variables page costs (Y) as explained by circulation (X_1), percent male (X_2), and median income (X_3).

Fitted values (thousands)

FIGURE 12.2.8   In addition to the problem of outliers, the histogram of circulation (X_1) shows extreme skewness. A transformation may take care of both problems.

Circulation (thousands)

mation is used on the circulation value. You would not use a transformation *solely* to control outliers, nor would you need to transform *solely* to achieve a normal distribution for an X variable. However, because this transformation achieves *both* of these goals (outlier control and normal distribution), it is worth trying to determine if it will improve the regression results.

FIGURE 12.2.9   There are no outliers in the histogram of the *logarithm* of circulation. Apparently, *Reader's Digest* and *TV Guide* do not have unusually large circulations in terms of *percentage* difference from the other magazines. However, in terms of actual *numbers* of copies, they are unusually large.

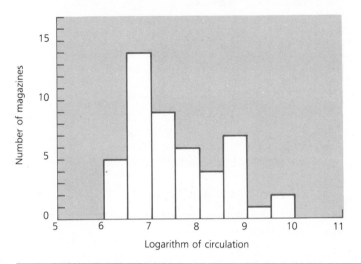

Table 12.2.11 shows the multiple regression results after the transformation to the log of circulation. The variables are now page costs (Y) explained by the natural log of circulation (the new X_1), percent male (X_2), and median income (X_3). There are several improvements: the R^2 value has improved (i.e., increased, indicating a better explanation) to 83.9% from 69.4%, and the standard error of estimate has improved (decreased, indicating smaller errors) from \$13,129 to \$9,535. It looks as if transforming circulation has been very useful in improving our understanding and prediction of page costs.

The diagnostic plot for this regression, shown in Figure 12.2.10, indicates that the outlier and tilting problems have been fixed: there are no outliers and no overall tilt. However, a new problem has emerged: *unequal variability* (also called heteroscedasticity). The residuals are much more variable (vertically) at the right than at the left in the scatterplot. This is not really a new problem; it was there all along but couldn't be seen until the larger problems (outliers and tilting) were fixed.

Why is this unequal variability an important problem? There are two main reasons. First, the regression estimates are inefficient because multiple regression does not "realize" that the smaller values (at the left in the diagnostic plot) are more accurate (since they are less variable) than the larger values at the right. The extra information in the data for smaller magazines is wasted, and the extra variability of the larger magazines is given too much attention. Second, your predicted values for the smaller magazines will contain unnecessary errors because multiple regression is

TABLE 12.2.11   Multiple Regression Output after Transforming to the Log of Circulation

```
THE REGRESSION EQUATION IS:
         Page Costs
                   =-184544.
                   +23811.48  * Log of Circulation
                   +32.15577  * Percent Male
                   +1.664740  * Median Income
The standard error of estimate:
             S =9535.197
             indicates the typical size of
             prediction errors in this data set.
The R-squared value:
             R2 =0.838715
             indicates the proportion of the
             variance of Page Costs that is
             explained by the regression model.

INFERENCE FOR Page Costs AT THE 5% LEVEL:
             The prediction equation DOES
             explain a significant proportion
             of the variation in Page Costs.
                F =76.26971  with
                3      and          44
                degrees of freedom
```

	effect on Page Costs	95% confidence interval		Hypothesis Test	std err of coeff	t statistic
VARIABLE	COEFF	FROM	TO	SIGNIFICANT?	STD ERR	t
Constant	-184544.	-218396.	-150691.	Yes	16797.24	-10.9865
Log of Circulation	23811.48	20629.32	26993.63	Yes	1578.931	15.08075
Percent Male	32.15577	-81.3015	145.6131	No	56.29568	0.571194
Median Income	1.664740	0.870878	2.458603	Yes	0.393901	4.226285

FIGURE 12.2.10   The diagnostic plot after transforming to the logarithm of circulation. The tilting and outlier problems have been fixed. However, unequal variability is now a problem. This is seen from the funnel shape opening outward to the right.

content to make these errors the same dollar size as for the larger magazines!

How can this unequal variability be controlled? A logarithm transformation of Y often works well in a case like this.[21] Since page costs (Y) and median income (X_3) are both measured in dollars, it would probably be best to transform both to logarithms for consistency. Since percent male is not in dollars, it need not be transformed.

TABLE 12.2.12 Multiple Regression Output after Transforming to the Log of Page Costs, Circulation, and Median Income

```
THE REGRESSION EQUATION IS:
        Log of Page Costs
            =-8.63341
            +0.641891   * Log of Circulation
            +0.001211   * Percent Male
            +1.395419   * Log of Median Income
The standard error of estimate:
            S =0.240554
        indicates the typical size of
        prediction errors in this data set.
The R-squared value:
            R2 =0.859367
        indicates the proportion of the
        variance of the Log of Page Costs that is
        explained by the regression model.

INFERENCE FOR Log Page Costs AT THE 5% LEVEL:
        The prediction equation DOES
        explain a significant proportion
        of the variation in Log of Page Costs.
            F =89.62431  with
            3      and           44
        degrees of freedom
```

VARIABLE	effect on Log Page COEFF	95% confidence interval FROM	TO	Hypothesis Test SIGNIFICANT?	std err of coeff STD ERR	t statistic t
Constant	-8.63341	-13.6771	-3.58967	Yes	2.502623	-3.44974
Log Circulation	0.641891	0.562247	0.721534	Yes	0.039517	16.24303
Percent Male	0.001211	-0.00164	0.004071	No	0.001419	0.853167
Log Median Income	1.395419	0.905965	1.884872	Yes	0.242858	5.745802

---

[21] If your Y variable, in another situation, contains both positive and negative values, transformation is difficult, and the logarithm cannot be used because it is undefined for zero or for negative values. In some situations you may be able to redefine Y so that it is always positive. For example, if Y is profit (Income − Expenses), you might consider using the ratio Income/Expenses instead. The logarithm would then be log (Income/Expenses) = log (Income) − log (Expenses) and may be thought of as representing profit on a percentage scale rather than an absolute dollar scale.

Table 12.2.12 shows the multiple regression results after transformation to the log of page costs, circulation, and median income. The variables are now the log of page costs (the new Y) explained by the log of circulation (the new X_1), percent male (X_2), and the log of median income (the new X_3). The R^2 value is up only slightly, indicating little improvement overall. The standard error of estimate is now on the log scale for page costs, and so is not directly comparable to the previous values.[22] The diagnostic plot will tell you whether these transformations have helped or not.

The diagnostic plot for this regression, shown in Figure 12.2.11, indicates that the unequal variability problem has been fixed by transforming to the logarithms of page costs, circulation, and median income.

Using Percent Changes to Model an Economic Time Series

One assumption of the multiple regression linear model is that the random component (ε) is independent from one data value to the next. When you have time-series data, this assumption is often violated because changes are usually small from one period to the next, yet there can be large changes over longer periods of time.

Another way to understand the problem is to recognize that many economic time series increase over time, for example, gross national product, disposable income, and your firm's sales (we hope!). A multiple regression of one such variable (Y) on the others (X variables) will have a high R^2 value, suggesting strong association. But if each series is *individually* increasing

---

FIGURE 12.2.11 This is a wonderful diagnostic plot: no further problems are detectable in the data. There is no apparent relationship after transformation to the log of page costs (Y), the log of circulation (X_1), and the log of median income (X_3). Only percent male (X_2) has been left untransformed.

Fitted values (log scale)

---

[22]Interpreting the results of a multiple regression when logarithms are used will be covered in a later section of this chapter.

over time, in its own particular way and without regard to the others, this is deceiving. You should really conclude that there is meaningful association only if the *pattern* of increases over time for *Y* can be predicted from those of the *X* variables.

One way to solve this problem is to work with the *percent changes* of each variable, defined by the proportion (Current − Previous)/Previous, which represents the one-period growth rate of that variable. You lose nothing by doing this because the forecasting problem may be equivalently viewed either as predicting the *change* from the current level of *Y* or as predicting the *future level* of *Y*.

Imagine a system that is more or less at equilibrium at each time period but that changes somewhat from one period to the next. What you really want to know is how to use information about the *X* variables to predict the next value of your *Y* variable. One problem is that your data set represents past history with *X* values that are not currently reasonable as possibilities. By working with the percent changes, you make the past history much more relevant to your current experience. In other words, although your firm's sales are probably much different from what they were five years ago, the percent change in sales from one year to the next may well be similar from year to year. Or, if you are using GNP (gross national product) to predict something, although you may never see the same GNP as we had 10 years ago, you might easily see the same (at least approximately) growth rate (percent change) in the GNP.

Think of it this way: A system in equilibrium may tend to change in similar ways through time, even though it may find itself in entirely different circumstances as time goes by.

You may find that your R^2 suffers when you use percent changes instead of the original data values. In some cases the regression will no longer be significant. This might "look bad" at first (after all, everybody likes large R^2 values), but a closer look often shows that the original R^2 was overoptimistic, and the smaller value is closer to the truth.

EXAMPLE Predicting Dividends from Sales of Nondurable and Durable Goods

How are dividends set by firms in the U.S. economy? If you are not careful, you might conclude that dividends respond in a very precise way to the level of sales of nondurable goods each year. If you are careful to use percent changes, then you will realize that dividends are not quite so simply explained.

Note that each of the columns in Table 12.2.13 shows a general increase over time. You should therefore expect to see strong correlations among these variables since high values of one are associated with high values of the others. This is indeed what you see in the correlation matrix, as shown in Table 12.2.14.

It would then be no surprise to find a very high R^2 value, suggesting that a whopping 98.9% of the variation in dividends is explained by sales of nondurables and durables. *But this would be wrong!* More precisely, in the historical

TABLE 12.2.13 Dividends, Sales of Nondurable Goods, and Sales of Durable Goods, 1976–1982

Year	Dividends (billions), Y	Sales of Nondurable Goods (billions), X_1	Sales of Durable Goods (billions), X_2
1976	$33.8	$436.0	$220.4
1977	38.2	473.1	249.4
1978	43.0	522.7	281.4
1979	48.1	589.2	307.5
1980	52.9	657.1	300.2
1981	61.3	712.4	326.2
1982	63.9	731.2	338.0

Data are from U.S. Department of Commerce, Bureau of Economic Analysis, *Business Statistics: 1986* (Washington: U.S. Government Printing Office, 1987), pp. 151, 188–89.

TABLE 12.2.14 Correlation Matrix for Dividends, Sales of Nondurable Goods, and Sales of Durable Goods

	Dividends, Y	Nondurables, X_1	Durables, X_2
Dividends, Y	1.000	0.994	0.955
Nondurables, X_1	0.994	1.000	0.951
Durables, X_2	0.995	0.951	1.000

TABLE 12.2.15 Yearly Percent Changes of Dividends, Sales of Nondurable Goods, and Sales of Durable Goods

Year	Dividends (yearly change), Y	Sales of Nondurable Goods (yearly change), X_1	Sales of Durable Goods (yearly change), X_2
1976	—	—	—
1977	13.0%	8.5%	13.2%
1978	12.6	10.5	12.8
1979	11.9	12.7	9.3
1980	10.0	11.5	−2.4
1981	15.9	8.4	8.7
1982	4.2	2.6	3.6

context it would be correct; however, it would not be nearly as useful in predicting future levels of dividends.

Table 12.2.15 shows the *percent changes* of these variables. For example, the 1977 value for dividends is $(38.2 − 33.8)/33.8 = 0.130$, or 13.0%. (Note that data are missing for 1976 because there is no previous year given in the original data set.) The correlation matrix in Table 12.2.16 shows a much more modest association among the changes in these variables from one year to the next. In fact, with such a small sample size ($n = 6$ for the percent changes), none of these pairwise correlations is even significant. The R^2 for the multiple regression

TABLE 12.2.16   Correlation Matrix for Percent Changes in Dividends, Sales of Nondurable Goods, and Sales of Durable Goods

	Dividends, Y	Nondurables, X_1	Durables, X_2
Dividends, Y	1.000	0.599	0.539
Nondurables, X_1	0.599	1.000	0.101
Durables, X_2	0.539	0.101	1.000

of the percent changes has been reduced to 59.1%, and the F-test is not significant. This suggests that changes in sales levels of nondurables and durables cannot be used to help understand changes in dividends from one year to the next.

Economically speaking, the regression analysis using percent changes makes more sense. The level of dividends in the economy is a complex process involving the interaction of many factors. Due to our tax system and the investors' apparent dislike of sudden changes in dividend levels, we should not expect dividends to be nearly completely explained merely by sales levels.

■ 12.3 Dealing with Nonlinear Relationships and Unequal Variability

The multiple regression techniques discussed so far are based on the multiple regression linear model, which has *constant variability*. If your data set does not have such a linear relationship, as indicated by the diagnostic plot covered earlier, you have three choices. The first two use multiple regression and will be covered in this section.

1 *Transform some or all variables.* By transforming one or more of the variables (for example, using logarithms) you may be able to obtain a new data set that has a linear relationship. Remember that logarithms can only be used to transform positive numbers. If your data set shows unequal variability, you may be able to correct the problem by transforming Y and (perhaps) also transforming some of the X variables.

2 *Introduce a new variable.* By introducing an additional, necessary X variable (for example X_1^2, the square of X_1), you may be able to obtain a linear relationship between Y and the new set of X variables. This method can work well when you are seeking an *optimal* value for Y, for example, to optimize profits or production yield. In other situations, you might use products of the variables (for example, defining $X_5 = X_1 \times X_2$) so that the regression equation can reflect the *interaction* between these two variables.

3 *Use nonlinear regression.* There may be an important nonlinear relationship, perhaps based on some theory, that must be estimated directly. The advanced methods of *nonlinear regression* can be used in these cases if both the form of the relationship and the form of the randomness are known.[23]

---

[23] An introduction to nonlinear regression is provided in N. R. Draper and H. Smith, *Applied Regression Analysis*, 2nd ed. (New York: Wiley, 1981), Chapter 10.

Transforming to a Linear Relationship: Interpreting the Results

There is a useful guideline for transforming your data. To keep things from getting too complicated, try to use the same transformation on all variables that are measured in the same units. For example, if you take the logarithm of sales (measured in dollars or thousands of dollars), you should probably also transform all other variables that measure dollar amounts in the same way. In this way dollar amounts for all appropriate variables will be measured on a percentage scale (this is what logarithms do) rather than on an absolute dollar scale.

■ **Consistency Guideline for Transforming Multivariate Data**
Variables that are measured in the same basic units should probably all be transformed in the same way.

When you transform some or all of your variables and then perform a multiple regression analysis, some of the results will require a new interpretation. This section will show you how to interpret the results when either (1) Y is left untransformed (that is, only some or all of the X variables are transformed) or (2) Y is transformed using the natural logarithm (regardless of whether none, some, or all of the X variables are transformed). The Y variable is special because it is the one being predicted, so transforming Y redefines the meaning of a prediction error.

Table 12.3.1 is a summary of the interpretation of the basic numbers on the computer output: the coefficient of determination, R^2, the standard error of estimate, S_e, the regression coefficients, b_i, and the significance test for b_i when you have used some transformations.[24] The procedure for producing predicted values for Y using the regression equation is also included.

The R^2 value has the same basic interpretation, regardless of how you transform the variables.[25] It tells you how much of the variability of your current Y (in whatever form, transformed or not) is explained by the current form of the X variables.

The standard error of estimate, S_e, has a different interpretation depending on whether Y is transformed or not. If Y is not transformed, the usual interpretation (the typical size of the prediction errors) still applies because Y itself is being predicted. However, if log Y is used in the regression analysis, then Y appears in the regression in percentage terms rather than as an absolute measurement. The appropriate measure of relative variability, from Chapter 5, is the *coefficient of variation* because the same percentage variability will be found at high predicted values of Y as at smaller values. The

---

[24]The relationships are easier to interpret if you use the *natural logarithm* for Y (to the base $e = 2.71828\ldots$, sometimes written "ln") instead of the logarithm to the base 10.

[25]We are assuming here that each transformation is "reasonable," in the sense that it does not change the relative ordering of the observations, and that it is a relatively "smooth" function.

TABLE 12.3.1 Interpreting a Multiple Regression When Transformation Has Been Used

	If Y Is Not Transformed:	If Natural Log of Y Is Used:
R^2	*Usual interpretation:* the percent of variability of Y explained by the (perhaps transformed) X variables	*Usual interpretation:* the percent of variability of (transformed) Y that is explained by the (perhaps transformed) X variables
S_e	*Usual interpretation:* approximate size of prediction errors of Y	*New interpretation:* The coefficient of variation of the prediction errors of Y is given by* $$\sqrt{2.71828^{(S_e^2)} - 1}$$
b_i	*Usual interpretation:* the expected effect of a unit change in (perhaps transformed) X_i on Y, all else equal	*Similar interpretation:* the expected effect of a unit change in (perhaps transformed) X_i on log Y. If X_i has also been transformed using logarithms, then b_i is also called the *elasticity* of Y with respect to X_i: the expected effect (in percentage points of Y) of a 1% change in X_i, all else equal
Significance test for b_i	*Usual interpretation:* Does X_i have an impact on Y, holding other X variables fixed?	*Usual interpretation:* Does X_i have an impact on Y, holding other X variables fixed?
Prediction of Y	*Usual procedure:* Use the regression equation to predict Y from the X variables, being sure to transform the X variables first	*New procedure:* Begin by using the regression equation to predict log Y from the X variables, being sure to transform the X variables first. Then find the predicted value for Y as follows:[†] $$2.71828^{[(1/2)S_e^2 + \text{Predicted value for log } Y]}$$

Warning: This coefficient of variation may not be reliable for values larger than around 1 (or 100%) since the extreme skewness in these cases makes estimation of means and standard deviations very difficult.

[†]This predicts the expected (i.e., average or mean) value of Y for the given values of the X variables. To predict the median value of Y instead, use the following, simpler formula:

$$2.71828^{(\text{Predicted value for log } Y)}$$

formula for this coefficient of variation in Table 12.3.1 is based on theory for the lognormal distribution.[26]

The regression coefficients, b_i, have their usual interpretation if Y is not transformed: they give the expected effect of an increase in X_i on Y, where the increase in X_i is one unit in whatever transformation was used on X_i. If Y is transformed, b_i indicates the change in *transformed Y*. If you have used both the logarithm of Y and the logarithm of X_i, then b_i has the special economic interpretation of *elasticity*. The **elasticity** of Y with respect to X_i is the expected *percentage* change in Y associated with a 1% increase in X_i, holding the other X variables fixed; the elasticity is estimated using the regression coefficient from a regression using the natural logarithms of both Y and X_i. Thus, an elasticity is just like a regression coefficient except that the changes are measured in percentages instead of the original units.

The significance test for a regression coefficient, b_i, retains its usual interpretation for any reasonable transformation. The basic question is, Does X_i have a detectable impact on Y (holding the other X values fixed), or does Y appear to behave just randomly with respect to X_i? Because the question has a yes or no answer, rather than a detailed description of the response, the basic question being tested is the same whether you use the logarithm transformation or not. Of course, the test proceeds in a different way in each case, and performance is best when you use the transformations that achieve a multiple regression linear model form for your data.

The predictions of Y change considerably depending on whether you transform Y or not. If Y is not transformed, the regression equation predicts Y directly. Simply take the appropriately transformed values for each X_i; multiply each by its regression coefficient, b_i; add them up; add a; and you have the predicted value for Y.

If Y is transformed using natural logarithms, there is a correction for the skewness of the untransformed Y. Using the appropriately transformed values of the X variables in the regression equation will get you a prediction of log Y. The new procedure for predicting (untransformed) Y given in the preceding table does two things. First, by exponentiating, the prediction of log Y is brought back to the original units of Y. Second, the skewness correction (based on S_e) inflates this value to reflect the fact that an average value is larger than a median or mode for this kind of a skewed distribution.

EXAMPLE

Magazine Ads Transformed and Interpreted

Table 12.3.2 shows the multiple regression results for the magazine ads example after transformation to the log of page costs, circulation, and median income.

---

[26]A random variable is said to have a *lognormal distribution* if the distribution of its logarithm is normal. There are several excellent technical references for this distribution, including N. L. Johnson and S. Kotz, *Continuous Univariate Distributions*—(New York: Wiley, 1970), Chapter 14; and J. Aitchison and J. A. C. Brown, *The Lognormal Distribution* (London: Cambridge University Press, 1957). The lognormal distribution is also very important in the theory of pricing of financial options.

TABLE 12.3.2 Multiple Regression Results Using the Logs of Page Costs, Circulation, and Median Income

```
THE REGRESSION EQUATION IS:
        Log of Page Costs
            =-8.63341
            +0.641891   * Log of Circulation
            +0.001211   * Percent Male
            +1.395419   * Log of Median Income
The standard error of estimate:
            S =0.240554
        indicates the typical size of
        prediction errors in this data set.
The R-squared value:
            R2 =0.859367
        indicates the proportion of the
        variance of the Log of Page Costs that is
        explained by the regression model.
INFERENCE FOR Log Page Costs AT THE 5% LEVEL:
        The prediction equation DOES
        explain a significant proportion
        of the variation in Log of Page Costs.
        F =89.62431   with
        3       and          44
        degrees of freedom
```

VARIABLE	effect on Log Page COEFF	95% confidence interval FROM	TO	Hypothesis Test SIGNIFICANT?	std err of coeff STD ERR	t statistic t
Constant	-8.63341	-13.6771	-3.58967	Yes	2.502623	-3.44974
Log Circulation	0.641891	0.562247	0.721534	Yes	0.039517	16.24303
Percent Male	0.001211	-0.00164	0.004071	No	0.001419	0.853167
Log Median Income	1.395419	0.905965	1.884872	Yes	0.242858	5.745802

The variables are now the log of page costs (the new Y), explained by the log of circulation (the new X_1), percent male (X_2), and the log of median income (the new X_3). Let's interpret these results.

The R^2 value, 85.9%, has its usual conceptual interpretation, even in terms of the untransformed variables. It tells you that 85.9% of the variation in page costs from one magazine to another can be accounted for by knowing the values of circulation, percent male, and median income of each magazine.[27] The concept of R^2 is the same whether you transform using logs or not, but the details are slightly different.

---

[27] The particular measure of variability used here is variance of page costs on the log scale, as explained by a multiple regression linear model using log circulation, percent male, and log median income.

The standard error of estimate, $S_e = 0.240554$, has a new interpretation. To make sense of this number (which literally indicates the typical size of prediction errors on the log scale), you use this equation:

$$\sqrt{2.71828^{(S_e^2)} - 1} = \sqrt{2.71828^{(0.240554)^2} - 1}$$
$$= \sqrt{2.71828^{0.057866} - 1}$$
$$= \sqrt{1.05957 - 1}$$
$$= 0.244 \quad \text{or} \quad 24.4\%$$

This tells you that your prediction error is typically 24.4% of the predicted value. For example, if your predicted page costs are $100,000, your variation is 24.4% of this, or $24,400, giving you a standard error of estimate for page costs that is applicable to such very large magazines. If your predicted page costs are $20,000, taking 24.4%, you find $4,882 as the appropriate standard error of estimate for these smaller magazines. It makes sense that the standard error of estimate should depend on the size of the magazine, because the large magazines have much more room for variability than the smaller ones.

The regression coefficient $b_1 = 0.642$, for log circulation, is an elasticity because the natural logarithm transformation was also used on Y. Thus, for every 1% increase in circulation, you expect a 0.642% increase in page costs. This suggests that there are some declining returns to scale in that you achieve less than a full 1% increase in page costs for a 1% increase in circulation. You might wonder whether these returns are significantly declining or if this $b_1 = 0.642$ is essentially equal to 1 except for randomness. The answer is found quickly by noting that the reference value, 1, is outside the confidence interval for b_1 (which extends from 0.562 to 0.722), implying that the returns to scale are indeed significantly declining.

Does circulation have a significant impact on page costs, holding percent male and median income fixed? The answer is yes, as given by the usual t-test for significance of b_1 in this multiple regression. This result may be tested simply by seeing whether the reference value (0) is in the confidence interval or not.

Finally, let's obtain a predicted value for Y for *Better Homes & Gardens*. This will differ slightly from the predicted value computed much earlier in this chapter and will be slightly better because the data did not follow a multiple regression linear model before transformation. There are two steps to predicting Y: first predict log Y directly from the regression equation, and then combine with S_e to obtain the predicted value.

The data values for *Better Homes & Gardens* are $X_1 = 8,000$ (indicating a circulation of 8 million paid subscribers), $X_2 = 22$ (indicating 22% men among its readers), and $X_3 = \$23,241$ (indicating the median annual income for its readers). Transforming the circulation and the median income values to logs in the regression equation, you find the predicted value for log (page costs) for *Better Homes & Gardens*:

$$\text{Predicted log(Page costs)} = -8.6334 + 0.6419 \times \text{log(Circulation)}$$
$$+ 0.001211(\text{Percent male}) + 1.3954$$
$$\times \text{log(Median income)}$$
$$= -8.6334 + 0.6419 \times \text{log(8,000)} + 0.001211$$
$$\times 22 + 1.3954 \times \text{log(23,241)}$$
$$= -8.6334 + 0.6419 \times 8.9872 + 0.001211 \times 22$$
$$+ 1.3954 \times 10.0537$$
$$= 11.1911$$

In order to find the predicted value for page costs, the next step is:

$$\text{Predicted page costs} = e^{[(1/2)S_e^2 + \text{Predicted value for log } Y]}$$
$$= 2.71828^{[(1/2)0.240554^2 + 11.1911]}$$
$$= 2.71828^{[(1/2)0.057866 + 11.1911]}$$
$$= 2.71828^{11.2200}$$
$$= \$74{,}610$$

This predicted value compares favorably with the actual page costs for this magazine, $73,820. However, we were lucky to be this close. The appropriate standard error for comparing the actual to the predicted value is 24.4% of $74,610, which is $18,205. If you compute the predicted page costs for other magazines, you will find that they are typically not nearly this close to the actual values. For an idea of how this compares to some of the other magazines, the relative prediction errors for the first five magazines in the list are -1.1%, 26.2%, 17.7%, -9.3%, and 52.0%. So it seems that 24.4% is a reasonable summary of the typical size of the errors.

Fitting a Curve with Polynomial Regression

Consider a nonlinear *bivariate* relationship. If the scatterplot of Y against X shows a curved relationship, you may be able to use multiple regression by first introducing a new X variable that is also curved with respect to X. The simplest choice is to introduce X^2, the square of the original X variable. You now have a *multivariate* data set with three variables: Y, X, and X^2. You are using **polynomial regression** when you predict Y using a single X variable together with some of its powers (X^2, X^3, etc.). Let's consider just the case of X with X^2.

With these variables, the usual multiple regression equation, $Y = a + b_1 X_1 + b_2 X_2$, becomes the *quadratic polynomial* $Y = a + b_1 X + b_2 X^2$.[28]

---

[28]The word *polynomial* refers to any sum of constants times nonnegative integer powers of a variable, for example, $3 + 5x - 4x^2 - 15x^3 + 8x^6$. The word *quadratic* indicates that no powers higher than 2 are used, for example, $7 - 4x + 9x^2$ or $9 - 3x^2$. Although higher powers can be used to model more complex nonlinear relationships, the results are often unstable when powers higher than 3 are used.

FIGURE 12.3.1   Quadratic polynomials can be used to model a variety of curved relationships. Here
is a selection of possibilities. Flipping any of these curves horizontally or vertically
still gives you a quadratic polynomial.

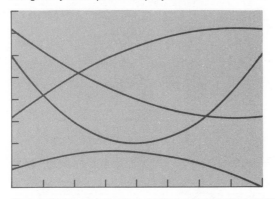

This is still considered a linear relationship because the individual terms
are added together. More precisely, you have a *linear* relationship between Y
and the pair of variables (X, X^2) you are using to explain the *nonlinear* relationship between Y and X.

At this point, you may simply compute the multiple regression of Y on
the two variables X and X^2 (so that the number of variables rises to $p = 2$
while the number of cases, n, is unchanged). All of the techniques you
learned earlier in this chapter can be used: predictions, residuals, R^2 and
S_e as measures of quality of the regression, testing of the coefficients, and
so forth.

Figure 12.3.1 shows some of the variety of curves that quadratic polynomials can produce. If your scatterplot of Y against X resembles one of these
curves, then the introduction of X^2 as a new variable will do a good job of
explaining and predicting the relationship.

EXAMPLE   **Optimizing the Yield of a Production Process**

Consider the data in Table 12.3.3, taken as part of an experiment to find the
temperature that produces the largest yield for an industrial process. This data
set could be very useful to your firm since it tells you that to maximize your output yield, you should set the temperature of the process at around 700 degrees.
The yield apparently falls off if the temperature is either too cold or too hot.

The scatterplot, shown in Figure 12.3.2 with the least-squares line, shows
how disastrous linear regression can be when it is inappropriately used to predict
a nonlinear relationship. There is an abundance of structure here that could be
used to predict yield from temperature and to determine the highest-yielding
temperature, but a straight line just isn't going to do it for you!

TABLE 12.3.3   Temperature and Yield for an
Industrial Process

Temperature, X	Yield, Y
600	127
625	139
650	147
675	147
700	155
725	154
750	153
775	148
800	146
825	136
850	129

FIGURE 12.3.2   The nonlinear relationship between output yield and the temperature of an industrial process is very badly described by the least-squares line. The predictions are unnecessarily far from the actual values.

Polynomial regression will correct this problem and also give you a good estimate of the optimal temperature that maximizes your yield. Table 12.3.4 shows the multivariate data set to use; note that only the last variable (the square of temperature) is new. Here is the prediction equation from multiple regression. It is graphed along with the data in Figure 12.3.3.

$$\text{Yield} = -712.10490 + 2.39119 \times \text{Temperature} - 0.00165$$
$$\times \text{Temperature}^2$$

TABLE 12.3.4 Creating a New Variable (Squared Temperature) in Order to Do Polynomial Regression

Yield, Y	Temperature, $X_1 = X$	Temperature squared, $X_2 = X^2$
127	600	360,000
139	625	390,625
147	650	422,500
147	675	455,625
155	700	490,000
154	725	525,625
153	750	562,500
148	775	600,625
146	800	640,000
136	825	680,625
129	850	722,500

FIGURE 12.3.3 The results of a quadratic polynomial regression to explain yield based on temperature and its square. The predictions are now excellent.

The coefficient of determination for this multiple regression is $R^2 = 0.969$, indicating that a whopping 96.9% of the variation of yield has been explained by temperature and its square (in fact, less than 1% had been explained by the straight line alone). The standard error of estimate is $S_e = 1.91$, indicating that yield may be predicted to within a few units (compared to the much larger value of 10.23 for the straight line).

How can you test whether the extra term (Temperature^2) was really necessary? The t-test for its regression coefficient ($b_2 = -0.00165$), based on a standard error of $S_{b_2} = 0.000104$ with 8 degrees of freedom, indicates that this

TABLE 12.3.5 Multiple Regression Results, Using Squared Temperature as a Variable in Order to Do Polynomial Regression

```
        S=1.907383
        R2 =0.969109
INFERENCE FOR Yield AT THE 5% LEVEL:
  The prediction equation DOES
explain a significant proportion
   of the variation in Yield.
      F =125.4877 with
           2 and 8
   degrees of freedom
```

VARIABLE	effect on Yield COEFF	95% confidence interval FROM	TO	Hypothesis Test SIGNIFICANT?	std err of coeff STD ERR	t statistic t
Constant	-712.104	-837.485	-586.723	Yes	54.37167	-13.0969
Temperature	2.391188	2.042414	2.739963	Yes	0.151246	15.80988
Temperature2	-0.00165	-0.00189	-0.00141	Yes	0.000104	-15.8402

term is *very highly significant*. Of course, this was obvious from the strong curvature in the scatterplot. Table 12.3.5 shows the computer output.

What is the best temperature to use in order to optimize yield? If the regression coefficient b_2 for your squared X variable is *negative* (as it is here), then the quadratic polynomial has a *maximum* value at $-b_1/2b_2$.[29] For this example, the temperature that achieves the highest yield is

$$\text{Optimal temperature} = -b_1/2b_2$$

$$= -2.39119/[2(-0.00165)]$$

$$= 724.6$$

A temperature setting of 725 degrees will be a good choice.

Modeling Interaction between Two X Variables

In the multiple regression linear model, each of the X variables is multiplied by its regression coefficient, and these are then added together with a to find the prediction $a + b_1 X_1 + \cdots + b_p X_p$. There is no allowance for interaction among the variables. Two variables are said to show **interaction** if a change in both of them causes an expected shift in Y that is different from the sum of the shifts in Y obtained by changing each X individually.

Many systems show interaction, especially if just the right combination of ingredients is required for success. For an extreme example, let $X_1 =$ gunpowder, $X_2 =$ heat, and $Y =$ reaction. A pound of gunpowder doesn't do

---

[29]If b_2 is positive, then there is a *minimum* value at the same place: $-b_1/2b_2$.

much by itself; neither does a lighted match all by itself. But put these together and they interact, causing a very strong explosion as the reaction. In business, you have interaction whenever "the whole is more (or less) than the sum of its parts."

One common way to model interaction in regression analysis is to use a *cross-product,* formed by multiplying one X variable by another to define a new X variable that is to be included along with the others in your multiple regression. This cross-product will represent the interaction of those two variables. Furthermore, you will be able to test for the existence of interaction by using the t-test for significance of the regression coefficient for the interaction term.

If your situation includes an important interaction, but you don't provide for it in the regression equation, then your predictions will suffer. For example, consider predicting sales (Y) from business travel (X_1, miles) and contacts (X_2, number of people seen) for a group of salespeople. The usual regression equation that would be used to predict sales, $a + b_1(\text{Miles}) + b_2(\text{Contacts})$, does not recognize the possibility of interaction between miles and contacts. The value of an additional mile of travel (by itself) is estimated as b_1, *regardless of the number of contacts seen.* Similarly, the value of an additional contact seen (by itself) is estimated as b_2, *regardless of the number of miles traveled.*

If you believed that there was some interaction between miles and contacts, so that salespeople with more contacts were able to make more productive use of their traveling miles, this model would be misspecified. One way to correct it would be to include a new X variable, the cross-product $X_3 = X_1 \times X_2 = \text{Contacts} \times \text{Miles}$. The resulting model is still a linear model and may be written in two equivalent ways:

$$\text{Predicted sales} = a + b_1(\text{Miles}) + b_2(\text{Contacts}) + b_3(\text{Miles} \times \text{Contacts})$$

$$= a + [b_1 + b_3(\text{Contacts})](\text{Miles}) + b_2(\text{Contacts})$$

This says that an extra mile of travel counts more toward sales when the number of contacts is larger (provided $b_3 > 0$). Conveniently, you can use the t-test of b_3 to see if this effect is significant; if it is not, then you can omit the extra variable, X_3, and use the regression analysis of Y on X_1 and X_2.

Another way in which interaction is modeled in regression analysis is to use transformation of some or all of the variables. Because logarithms convert multiplication to addition, the multiplicative equation with interaction

$$Y = A X_1^{b_1} X_2^{b_2}$$

is converted to a linear additive equation with no interaction by taking logs of all variables:

$$\log Y = \log A + b_1 \log X_1 + b_2 \log X_2$$

$$= a + b_1 \log X_1 + b_2 \log X_2$$

■ 12.4 Indicator Variables: Predicting from Categories

Multiple regression is based on arithmetic and therefore requires meaningful numbers (quantitative data). What can you do if your variables are not all quantitative? An **indicator variable** (also called a *dummy variable*) is a quantitative variable using only the values 0 and 1 that is used to represent qualitative categorical data. For example, you might have a gender variable, which would be 1 for women and 0 for men (or the other way around). You can use one or more indicator variables as predictor (X) variables in your multiple regression analysis.[30]

If a qualitative X variable encompasses just two categories (such as men/women, buy/browse, or defective/conforming), you may represent it directly as an indicator variable. You may decide arbitrarily which of the two categories will be represented as 1 and which will be 0 (the baseline). Although the choice is arbitrary at this point, you must remember which alternative you chose in order to interpret the results later on! Table 12.4.1 shows an example of a categorical variable that represents each person's gender, with the arbitrary choice of "woman" to be 1 and "man" to be 0.

If a qualitative X variable has more than two categories, you will need to use more than one indicator variable to replace it. First, select one of the categories to use as the baseline value against which the effects of the other categories will be measured. Do *not* use an indicator variable for the baseline category in the regression analysis because it will be represented by the constant term in the regression output. You will create a separate indicator variable for each of the nonbaseline categories. For each elementary unit (person, firm, or whatever) in the sample, you will have at most one value of 1 in the group of indicator variables; they will all be 0 if the elementary unit belongs to the baseline category. Remember the following rule:

TABLE 12.4.1   An Indicator Variable Representing Gender

Categorical Variable	Indicator Variable
Man	0
Man	0
Woman	1
Man	0
Woman	1
Woman	1
.	.
.	.
.	.

[30]If your response (Y) variable is qualitative, the situation is much more complex because the error term, ε, in the multiple regression linear model cannot have a normal distribution. If Y has only two categories, you might use the *logit model* (*multiple logistic regression*) or the *probit model*. If your Y variable has more than two categories, then the *multinomial logit model* or the *multinomial probit model* might be appropriate. Some helpful discussion is provided in J. Kmenta, *Elements of Econometrics* (New York: Macmillan, 1986), Section 11-5.

> ■ **Rule for Using Indicator Variables**
> The number of indicator variables used in multiple regression to replace a qualitative variable is *one less than* the number of categories. The remaining category defines the *baseline.* The baseline category is represented by the constant term in the regression output.

Which category should be the baseline? You may choose the one you are most interested in comparing the other categories against.[31] You should probably choose a category that occurs fairly frequently.

Here is an example of a categorical variable that represents the nature of each item in a sample processed by a firm's mailroom. Four categories were used: business envelope, oversize envelope, small box, and large box. Since the vast majority of cases were business envelopes, this was chosen for convenience to be the baseline category. This single qualitative variable (type of item) is to be used in a multiple regression analysis to help explain Y = Processing time. Table 12.4.2 shows the three indicator variables that would be created and used along with the other X variables.

Interpreting and Testing Regression Coefficients for Indicator Variables

Once the categorical X variables are replaced with indicator variables, the multiple regression can be performed in the usual way. Although the regression still has its usual interpretation, there are some special ways to think about the regression coefficients and their t-tests when you use indicator variables, as shown in Table 12.4.3. Remember that if X_i is an indicator vari-

TABLE 12.4.2 Using Three Indicator Variables to Represent Four Categories, Omitting "Business Envelope" as the Baseline Category

Categorical Variable: Type of Item	Indicator Variables		
	Oversize Envelope, X_1	Small Box, X_2	Large Box, X_3
Business envelope	0	0	0
Small box	0	1	0
Business envelope	0	0	0
Business envelope	0	0	0
Large box	0	0	1
Oversize envelope	1	0	0
Business envelope	0	0	0
Oversize envelope	1	0	0
Business envelope	0	0	0
.	.	.	.
.	.	.	.
.	.	.	.

---

[31]What if you need to compare against more than one category? One simple solution is to run *several* multiple regression analyses, each one with a different category as the baseline.

TABLE 12.4.3 Interpreting the Regression Coefficient for an Indicator Variable X_i

b_i	The regression coefficient b_i represents the *average difference* in Y between the category represented by X_i and the baseline category, holding all other X variables fixed. If b_i is a positive number, its category has a *higher* estimated average Y than the baseline category; if b_i is a negative number, then average Y for its category is *lower* than for the baseline (all else equal).
Significance test for b_i	In terms of the expected Y value, holding all other X variables fixed, is there any difference (other than randomness) between the category represented by X_i and the baseline category?

able, it represents just one category of the original qualitative variable (namely, the category where it is 1).

EXAMPLE

Estimating the Impact of Gender on Salary after Adjusting for Experience

Uh-oh. Your firm is worried about being sued for gender discrimination. There is a growing perception that males are being paid more than females in your department. A quick analysis of the 24 men and 26 women in the department shows that the average man was paid $4,214 more annually than the average woman. Furthermore, based on the standard error of $1,032, this is very highly statistically significant ($p < 0.001$).[32]

Does this imply discrimination against women? Well... not necessarily. The statistical results do summarize the salaries of the two groups and compare the difference against what would be expected due to randomness. Statistically, you may conclude that there are gender differences in salary that go well beyond randomness. However, statistics will not tell you the *reason* for these differences. Although there might be discrimination in hiring at your firm (either overt or subtle), there are other possibilities that could explain the gender differences. There may even be an economic basis for why men would be paid more in this particular situation.

At a meeting, someone suggests that the experience of your workers should also be considered as a possible explanation of the salary differences. The work of analyzing this possibility is delegated to you, and you decide to try multiple regression analysis as a way of understanding *the effect of gender on salary after adjusting for experience*. Multiple regression is the appropriate procedure because a regression coefficient is always adjusted for the other X variables. The regression coefficient for the indicator variable representing gender will give you the expected salary difference between a man and a woman with the same experience.

---

[32]This is the standard error of the difference for a two-sample, unpaired situation. So far, this is Chapter 10 material.

Your multiple regression variables are salary (Y), experience (X_1), and gender (X_2). Gender will be represented as an indicator variable with Female = 1 and Male = 0. Table 12.4.4 shows the multivariate data set.

First, here are the results of data exploration. The scatterplot of salary against experience in Figure 12.4.1 shows a strong relationship (correlation $r = 0.803$). Employees with more experience are generally compensated more. There is a hint of nonlinearity, perhaps a "saturation effect" or an indication of "diminishing returns," in which an extra year of experience counts less and less as experience is accumulated. In any case, you can expect experience to account for much of the variation in salary.

The scatterplot of salary against gender, in Figure 12.4.2, confirms the fact that men are generally paid higher. However, this plot is much clearer when redone as two *box plots,* one for each gender, as in Figure 12.4.3. There is a clear relationship between gender and salary, with men paid higher on average. Although there is some overlap between the two box plots, the average salary difference is very highly significant (using the two-sample, unpaired t-test from Chapter 10).

The relationship between gender and experience, shown in Figure 12.4.4, shows that men have more experience on average than women. The lower part of the plot for women is not missing; it indicates that 25% of the women have little or no experience.

So far, what have you learned? There is a strong relationship between all pairs of variables. Extra experience is compensated, and being female is associated with a lower salary and less experience.

One important question remains: When you *adjust* for experience (in order to compare a man's salary to a woman's with the same experience), is there a gender difference in salary? This information is not in the scatterplots because it involves all three variables simultaneously. The answer will be provided by the multiple regression. Table 12.4.5 shows the computer output.

The regression coefficient for gender, -488.08, indicates that the expected salary difference between a man and a woman with the same experience is $488.08, with the woman paid *less* than the man. This is because an increase of 1 in the indicator variable X_2 brings you from 0 (man) to 1 (woman) and results in a negative expected change ($-$488.08) in salary.

Note that the regression coefficient for gender is not significant. It's not even close! The t-test for significance of this coefficient is testing whether there is a difference between men and women at the same level of experience. This result tells you that, once experience is taken into account, there is no detectable difference between the average salary levels of men and women. The clear salary differences between men and women can be explained by differences in their experience. You have evidence that your firm may discriminate based on *experience* but not based solely on *gender.*

Does this analysis prove that there is no gender discrimination at your firm? Well . . . no. You may conclude only that there is no evidence of discrimination. Since accepting the null hypothesis (a finding of "not significant") leads to a

TABLE 12.4.4   Salary, Experience, and Gender for Employees

	Salary, Y	Experience (years), X_1	Gender (1 = Female, 0 = Male), X_2
	$39,700	16	0
	28,500	2	1
	30,650	2	1
	31,000	3	1
	33,700	25	0
	33,250	15	0
	35,050	16	1
	22,800	0	1
	36,300	33	0
	35,600	29	1
	32,350	3	1
	31,800	16	0
	26,900	0	1
	37,250	19	0
	30,450	1	1
	31,350	2	1
	38,200	32	0
	38,200	21	1
	28,950	0	1
	33,950	34	0
	34,100	8	1
	32,900	11	1
	30,150	5	1
	30,800	1	0
	31,300	11	1
	33,550	18	1
	37,750	44	0
	31,350	2	1
	27,350	0	1
	35,700	19	1
	32,250	7	0
	25,200	0	1
	35,900	15	1
	36,700	14	0
	32,050	4	1
	38,050	33	0
	36,100	19	0
	35,200	20	1
	34,800	24	0
	26,550	3	0
	26,550	0	1
	32,750	17	0
	39,200	19	0
	30,450	0	1
	38,800	21	0
	41,000	31	0
	29,900	6	0
	40,400	35	0
	37,400	20	0
	35,500	23	0
Average	33,313	13.98	52.0%
Standard deviation	4,188	11.87	

Sample size: $n = 50$

FIGURE 12.4.1 The scatterplot of salary against experience shows a strong increasing relationship. The more experienced employees are compensated accordingly.

FIGURE 12.4.2 The scatterplot of salary against gender is difficult to interpret because gender is an indicator variable. It's better to use box plots, as in the next figure.

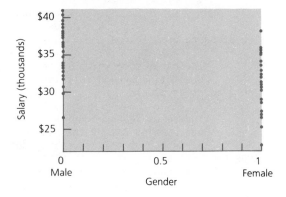

FIGURE 12.4.3 Box plots of salary, one for each gender, provide a better way of exploring the relationship between gender and salary. Men are paid more on average, although there is considerable overlap in salary levels.

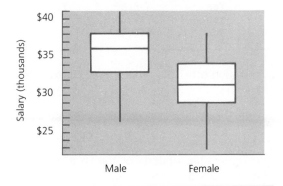

FIGURE 12.4.4 On average, men have more experience than women. These are box plots representing the relationship between gender and experience.

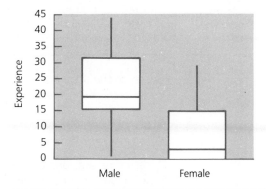

weak conclusion (as discussed in Chapter 10), it is difficult to prove the absence of discrimination.

Does this analysis show that there is no gender discrimination in society at large? No, because the data reflect only one department at one firm and are hardly representative of this larger group.

But isn't the lower experience level of women due to past societal discrimination? This may well be true, but it cannot be determined based on the statistical analysis just performed. This data set has no information about the possible

TABLE 12.4.5   Multiple Regression Results for Employee Salary, Experience, and Gender

```
THE REGRESSION EQUATION IS:
        Salary
            =   29776
            +   271.15 * Experience
                -488.08 * Gender
The standard error of estimate:
            S =2,538.76
        indicates the typical size of
        prediction errors in this data set.
The R-squared value:
            R2 =  64.7%
        indicates the proportion of the
        variance of Salary that is
        explained by the regression model.
INFERENCE FOR Salary AT THE 5% LEVEL:
        The prediction equation DOES
        explain a significant proportion
        of the variation in Salary.
            F = 43.1572 with
            2    and         47
        degrees of freedom
```

	effect on Salary	95% confidence interval		Hypothesis Test	std err of coeff	t statistic
VARIABLE	COEFF	FROM	TO	SIGNIFICANT?	STD ERR	t
Constant	29776	27867	31685	Yes	948.86	31.38
Experience	271.15	195.46	346.84	Yes	37.63	7.21
Gender	-488.08	-2269.06	1292.90	No	885.29	-0.55

causes of the apparent salary discrimination other than that it may be explained by differences in experience.

Separate regressions

A different approach to multiple regression analysis of multivariate data that includes a qualitative variable is to divide up the data set according to category and then perform a separate multiple regression for each category. For example, you might have two analyses: one for the men and another for the women. Or you might separately analyze the oil from the gas and from the nuclear power plants.

The use of indicator variables is just one step in the direction of separate regressions. With indicator variables you essentially have a different constant term for each category but the same values for each regression coefficient. With separate regressions, you have a different constant term *and* a different regression coefficient for each category.

12.5 **End-of-Chapter-Materials**

Summary

Predicting a single Y variable from *two or more* X variables is called **multiple regression.** The goals of multiple regression are (1) to describe and understand the relationship, (2) to forecast (predict) a new observation, and (3) to adjust and control a process.

The **intercept** or **constant term,** a, gives the predicted value for Y when *all* X variables are 0. The **regression coefficient** b_j, for the jth X variable, specifies the effect of X_j on Y after adjusting for the other X variables; b_j indicates how much larger you expect Y to be for a case that is identical to another except for being one unit larger in X_j. Taken together, these regression coefficients give you the **prediction equation** or **regression equation,** Predicted $Y = a + b_1X_1 + b_2X_2 + \cdots + b_pX_p$, which may be used for prediction or control. These coefficients $(a, b_1, b_2, \ldots, b_p)$ are traditionally computed using the method of *least squares,* which minimizes the sum of the squared prediction errors. The **prediction errors** or **residuals** are given by $Y - $ (Predicted Y).

There are two ways of summarizing how good the regression analysis is. The **standard error of estimate,** S_e, indicates the approximate size of the prediction errors. The **coefficient of determination,** R^2, indicates the percentage of the variation in Y that is "explained by" or "attributed to" the X variables.

Inference begins with the **F-test,** an overall test to see if the X variables explain a significant amount of the variation in Y. If your regression is *not* significant, you are not permitted to go further. If the regression is significant, you may proceed with statistical inference using **t-tests for individual regression coefficients.** Confidence intervals and hypothesis tests for an individual regression coefficient will be based on its standard error, $S_{b_1}, S_{b_2}, \ldots,$ or S_{b_p}. The critical value from the t-table will have $n - p - 1$ degrees of freedom.

Inference is based on the **multiple regression linear model,** which specifies that the observed value for Y is equal to the population relationship plus independent random errors that have a normal distribution:

Multiple Regression Linear Model for the
Population

$Y = (\alpha + \beta_1 X_1 + \beta_2 X_2 + \cdots + \beta_p X_p) + \varepsilon$

$= $ Population relationship + Randomness

where ε has a normal distribution with mean 0 and constant standard deviation σ, and this randomness is independent from one case to another

---

For each population parameter $(\alpha, \beta_1, \beta_2, \ldots, \beta_p, \sigma)$ there is a sample estimator $(a, b_1, b_2, \ldots, b_p, S_e)$.

The hypotheses of the F-test are as follows:

Hypotheses for the F-test

$H_0: \beta_1 = \beta_2 = \ldots = \beta_p = 0$

$H_1:$ At least one of $\beta_1, \beta_2, \ldots, \beta_p \neq 0$

The result of the F-test is given as follows:

If the R^2 value is *smaller* than the critical value in the table, the model is *not significant* (accept the null hypothesis that the X variables *do not* help to predict Y).

If the R^2 value is *larger* than the value in the table, the model is *significant* (reject the null hypothesis and accept the research hypothesis that the X variables *do* help to predict Y).

The confidence interval for an individual regression coefficient β_j is

Confidence Interval for Regression Coefficient β_j

From $b_j - tS_{b_j}$ to $b_j + tS_{b_j}$

---

where t is from the t-table for $n - p - 1$ degrees of freedom. The hypotheses for the t-test of the jth regression coefficient are

Hypotheses for the t-Test of Regression Coefficient β_j

$H_0: \beta_j = 0$

$H_1: \beta_j \neq 0$

There are two approaches to the difficult problem of deciding which X variables are contributing the most to a regression equation. The **standardized regression coefficient,** $b_i S_{X_i}/S_Y$, represents the expected change in Y due to a change in X_i, measured in units of standard deviations of Y per standard deviation of X_i, holding all other X variables constant. If you don't want to adjust for all other X variables (by holding them constant), you may compare the absolute values of the correlation coefficients for Y with each X instead.

There are some potential problems with a multiple regression analysis:

1 The problem of **multicollinearity** arises when some of your explanatory (X) variables are too similar to each other. The individual regression coefficients are poorly estimated because there is not enough information to decide *which one* (or more) of the variables is doing the explaining. You might omit some of the variables or redefine some of the variables (perhaps using ratios) to distinguish them from one another.

2 The problem of **variable selection** arises when you have a long list of potentially useful explanatory X variables and would like to decide which ones to include in the regression equation. With too many X variables the quality of your results will decline because information is being wasted in estimating unnecessary parameters. If one or more important X variables is omitted, your predictions will lose quality due to missing information. One solution is to include only those variables that are clearly necessary, using a prioritized list. Another solution is to use an automated procedure such as *all subsets* or *stepwise regression.*

3 The problem of **model misspecification** refers to the many different potential incompatibilities between your application and the multiple regression linear model. By exploring the data, you can be alerted to some of the potential problems with nonlinearity, unequal variability, or outliers. However, you may or may not have a problem: even though the histograms of some variables may be skewed, and even though some scatterplots may be nonlinear, the multiple regression linear model might still hold. The *diagnostic plot* can help you decide when the problem is serious enough to need fixing. Another serious problem arises if you have a time series; it may help to do multiple regression using the percent changes from one time period to the next in place of the original data values for each variable.

The **diagnostic plot** for multiple regression is a scatterplot of the prediction errors (residuals) against the predicted values and is used to decide whether you have any problems in your data that need to be fixed. Do not intervene unless the diagnostic plot shows you a clear and definite problem.

There are three ways of dealing with nonlinearity and/or unequal variability: (1) transform some or all variables, (2) introduce a new variable, or (3) use nonlinear regression. If you transform, each group of variables that is measured in the same basic units should probably be transformed in the same way. If you transform some of the X variables but do not transform Y, then most of the interpretation of the results of a multiple regression analysis remains unchanged. If you use the natural logarithm of Y, then R^2 and significance tests for individual regression coefficients retain their usual interpretation, individual regression coefficients have similar interpretations, and a new interpretation is needed for S_e.

The **elasticity** of Y with respect to X_i is the expected *percentage* change in Y associated with a 1% increase in X_i, holding the other X variables fixed; the elasticity is estimated using the regression coefficient from a regression analysis using the natural logarithm of both Y and X_i.

Another way to deal with nonlinearity is to use **polynomial regression** to predict Y using a single X variable together with some of its powers (X^2, X^3, etc.).

Two variables are said to show **interaction** if a change in both of them causes an expected shift in Y that is different from the sum of the shifts in

Y obtained by changing each X individually. Interaction is often modeled in regression analysis by using a *cross-product,* formed by multiplying one X variable by another, which defines a new X variable to be included along with the others in your multiple regression. Interaction can also be modeled by using transformations of some or all of the variables.

An **indicator variable** (also called a *dummy variable*) is a quantitative variable consisting only of the values 0 and 1 that is used to represent qualitative categorical data as an explanatory X variable. The number of indicator variables used in multiple regression to replace a qualitative variable is *one less* than the number of categories. The remaining category defines the *baseline.* The baseline category is represented by the constant term in the regression output.

Instead of using indicator variables, you might compute separate regressions for each category. This provides you with a more flexible model with different regression coefficients for each X variable for each category.

Key Words

multiple regression 471
intercept or constant term 473
regression cofficient 473
prediction equation or regression
  equation 473
prediction errors or residuals 473
standard error of estimate 473
coefficient of determination 473
F-test 474
t-tests for individual regression
  coefficients 474

multiple regression linear model 483
standardized regression coefficient 499
multicollinearity 502
variable selection 502
model misspecification 502
diagnostic plot 515
elasticity 527
polynomial regression 530
interaction 534
indicator variable 536

Questions

1 For multiple regression, answer the following:
  a. What are the three goals?
  b. What kind of data are necessary?
2 For the regression equation, answer the following:
  a. What is it used for?
  b. Where does it come from?
  c. What does the constant term tell you?
  d. What does a regression coefficient tell you?
3 Describe the two measures that tell you how helpful a multiple regression analysis is.
4 a. What does the result of the F-test tell you?
  b. What are the two hypotheses of the F-test?
  c. In order for the F-test to be significant, do you need a high or a low value of R^2? Why?
5 a. What is the t-test for an individual regression coefficient?
  b. In what way is such a test adjusted for the other X variables?

   c. If the *F*-test is not significant, are you permitted to go ahead and test individual regression coefficients?
6 a. How are the standardized regression coefficients computed?
   b. How are they useful?
   c. What are their measurement units?
7 a. What is multicollinearity?
   b. What are the harmful effects of extreme multicollinearity?
   c. How might moderate multicollinearity cause your *F*-test to be significant, even though none of your *t*-tests is significant?
   d. How can multicollinearity problems be solved?
8 a. If you want to be sure to get the best predictions, why not include among your *X* variables every conceivably helpful variable you can think of?
   b. How can a prioritized list help you solve the variable selection problem?
   c. Briefly describe two automatic methods for variable selection.
9 a. What is the multiple regression linear model?
   b. List three ways in which the multiple regression linear model might fail to hold.
   c. What scatterplot can help you spot problems with the multiple regression linear model?
10 a. What are the axes in the diagnostic plot?
   b. Why is it good to find *no* structure in the diagnostic plot?
11 Why should variables measured in the same basic units be transformed in the same way?
12 a. What is an elasticity?
   b. Under what circumstances will a regression coefficient indicate the elasticity of *Y* with respect to X_i?
13 How does polynomial regression help you deal with nonlinearity?
14 a. What is interaction?
   b. What can be done to include interaction terms in the regression equation?
15 a. What kind of variable should you create in order to include information about a *categorical* variable among your *X* variables? Please give the name of the variables, and indicate how they are created.
   b. For a categorical variable with four categories, how many indicator variables would you create?
   c. What does the regression coefficient of an indicator variable indicate?

Problems

1 For each of the following situations, identify the *Y* variable, the *X* variables, and the appropriate statistic or test.
   a. Your firm is wondering about the results of magazine advertising as part of an assessment of marketing strategy. For each ad, you have information on its cost, its size, and the number of inquiries it generated. In particular, you are wondering if the number of leads generated by an ad has any connection with its cost and size.
   b. It's budgeting time again, and you would like to know the expected payoff (in terms of dollars collected) of spending an extra dollar on collection of delinquent accounts, after adjusting for the size of the pool of delinquent accounts.
   c. In order to substantiate a claim of damages, you need to estimate the revenues your firm lost when the opening of the new lumber mill was delayed for three months. You have access to data for similar firms on their total assets, lum-

ber mill capacity, and revenues. For your firm, you know total assets and lumber mill capacity (if it had been working), but you wish to estimate the revenues.

d. Productivity is a concern. For each employee, you have data on productivity as well as other factors. You want to know how much these factors explain about the variation in productivity from one employee to another.

2 Table 12.5.1 shows data on Picasso paintings giving the price, area of canvas, and year for each one.

a. Find the regression equation to predict price from area and year.

b. Interpret the regression coefficient for area.

c. Interpret the regression coefficient for year.

d. What would you expect the sales price to be for a 1954 painting with an area of 4,000 square centimeters?

e. About how large are the prediction errors, in thousands of dollars, for these paintings?

f. What percentage of the variation in prices of Picasso paintings can be attributed to the size of the painting and the year in which it was painted?

g. Is the regression significant? Report the results of the appropriate test, and interpret its meaning.

h. Does area have significant impact on price, following adjustment for year? In particular, are larger paintings worth significantly more or significantly less on average than smaller paintings from the same year?

i. Does year have a significant impact on price, following adjustment for area? What does this tell you about older versus newer paintings?

TABLE 12.5.1   Price, Area, and Year for Picasso Paintings

Price (thousands)	Area (square cm.)	Year
$100	768	1911
50	667	1914
120	264	1920
400	1,762	1921
375	10,109	1921
28	945	1922
35	598	1923
750	5,256	1923
145	869	1932
260	7,876	1934
78	1,999	1940
90	5,980	1941
360	1,141	1943
150	5,520	1944
65	5,334	1944
58	1,656	1953
65	2,948	1956
95	3,510	1960
210	6,500	1963
32	1,748	1965
55	3,441	1968
80	7,176	1969
18	6,500	1969

Data are from E. Mayer, *International Auction Records,* vol. XVII (Caine, England: Hilmarton Manor Press, 1983), pp. 1056–58.

TABLE 12.5.2   Multiple Regression Results for Fast-Growth Firms

```
THE REGRESSION EQUATION IS:
   New Jobs =-144.764 + 0.099109*(New Firms) + 78.61557*(Pct Fast)
S  = 133.7854
R2 = 81.0%
```

VARIABLE	effect on New Jobs COEFF	95% confidence interval FROM	TO	Hypothesis Test SIGNIFICANT?	std err of coeff STD ERR	t statistic t
Constant	−144.76	−282.96	−6.57	Yes	68.6944	−2.11
New Firms	0.0991	0.0825	0.1157	Yes	0.0082	12.04
Pct Fast	78.62	20.04	137.19	Yes	29.1152	2.70

3 For the 50 states, consider a multiple regression analysis to explain the number of new jobs created, using the number of new firms created and the percentage of fast-growth companies. The variables used are "new jobs" (in thousands), "new firms" (actual number of firms), and "pct fast" (in percentage points, so that, for example, 3.15% is represented by the number 3.15). Multiple regression results are shown in Table 12.5.2.[33]

a. Approximately how much of the variation in new job creation from one state to another can be explained by the number of new firms and the percent of fast-growth firms?

b. Have "new firms" and "pct fast" explained a significant proportion of the variability in "new jobs"? How do you know?

c. Find the predicted value of "new jobs" and the residual value for Washington state, given that New jobs = 242 (thousand), New firms = 1,741, and Pct fast = 2.44% for this state.

d. What exactly does the regression coefficient 0.0991 for "new firms" tell you?

e. Does the percent of fast-growth firms seem to have an impact on job creation after adjustment for the number of new companies? How do you know?

f. Write a paragraph summarizing what you can learn about job growth from this multiple regression analysis.

4 Computers tend to slow down when they are overloaded. The *response time* is how long it takes from when you hit the ENTER key until the computer comes back with your answer. Naturally, when the computer is busier (either with users or with other work) you would expect it to take longer. This response time (in seconds) was measured at various times together with the number of users on the system and the load (the percent of the time that the machine is busy with high-priority tasks). The data is shown in Table 12.5.3.

a. Explore the data by commenting on the relationships in the three scatterplots you can produce by considering variables two at a time. In particular, do these relationships seem reasonable?

b. Compute the correlation matrix and compare it to the relationships you saw in the scatterplots.

---

[33]Data analyzed are from "Rating the States 1987: New Jobs, New Companies, and the Climate for Growth," *INC.*, October 1987. p. 77.

TABLE 12.5.3 Computer Response Time, Number of Users, and Load Level

Response Time	Users	Load
0.31	1	20.2%
0.69	8	22.7
2.27	18	41.7
0.57	4	24.6
1.28	15	20.0
0.88	8	39.0
2.11	20	33.4
4.84	22	63.9
1.60	13	35.8
5.06	26	62.3

c. Find the regression equation to predict response time from users and load. (You will probably need to use a computer for this and subsequent parts of this problem.)

d. To within approximately how many seconds can response time be predicted by users and load for this data set?

e. Is the F-test significant? What does this tell you?

f. Are the regression coefficients significant? Write a sentence for each variable, interpreting its adjusted effect on response time.

g. Note that the two regression coefficients are very different from each other. Compute the standardized regression coefficients to compare them, and write a sentence about the relative importance of users and load in terms of effect on response time.

5 Table 12.5.4 shows some of the results of a multiple regression analysis to explain money spent on home food-processing equipment (Y) based on income (X_1), education (X_2), and money spent on sporting equipment (X_3). All money variables represent total dollars for the past year; education is in years. There are 20 cases.

TABLE 12.5.4 Multiple Regression Results for Food-Processing Equipment

THE REGRESSION EQUATION IS:

$Y = -9.26 + 0.00137 X1 + 10.8 X2 + 0.00548 X3$

COLUMN	COEFFICIENT	ST. DEV. OF COEF.	T-RATIO = COEF/S.D.
	-9.26247	13.37258	-0.69264
X1	0.001373	0.000191	7.165398
X2	10.76225	0.798748	13.47389
X3	0.005484	0.025543	0.214728

S = 16.11

R-SQUARED = 94.2 PERCENT

a. How much would you expect a person to spend on food-processing equipment if they earn $25,000 per year, have 14 years of education, and spent $292 on sporting equipment last year?

b. How successful is the regression equation in explaining food-processing expenditures? In particular, which statistic in the results should you look at, and is it statistically significant?

c. To within approximately what accuracy (in dollars per year) can predictions of food-processing expenditures be made for the people in this study?

d. For each of the three X variables, state whether it has a significant effect on food-processing expenditures or not (after adjusting for the other X variables).

6 Consider the multiple regression printout shown in Table 12.5.5, which attempts to explain 1987 compensation of the top executives of 11 major fuel corporations based on the sales and the ROE (return on equity) of the firm.[34] For example, the data for Exxon consists of a compensation number of 1,207 (in thousands of dollars) for the chair of the board, a ROE number of 15.0 (in percentage points), and a sales number of 77,721 (in millions of dollars).

TABLE 12.5.5   Multiple Regression Results for Executive Compensation

THE REGRESSION EQUATION IS: Pay = 583.3609 + 0.0044 * Sales + 30.3880 * ROE.
    S =149.3560   R2 =0.770379
    F =13.42005 with 2 and 8 degrees of freedom

VARIABLE	effect on Pay COEFF	95% confidence interval FROM	95% confidence interval TO	Hypothesis Test SIGNIFICANT?	std err of coeff STD ERR	t statistic t
Constant	583.3609	389.5154	777.2064	Yes	84.06135	6.939704
ROE	30.38801	11.13718	49.63883	Yes	8.348146	3.640090
Sales	0.004369	-0.00038	0.009128	No	0.002063	2.117528

a. To within approximately how many dollars can you predict the compensation of the top executives of these firms based on sales and ROE?

b. Find the predicted salary and the residual prediction error for the top executive of Exxon, expressing both in dollars.

c. If ROE is interpreted as an indicator of the firm's performance, is there a significant link between performance and pay (adjusting for firm sales)? How do you know?

d. What exactly does the regression coefficient 30.38801 for ROE tell you?

e. How can it be that sales does not have a significant impact on pay (adjusting for ROE) despite its large t-statistic of 2.12?

7 In many ways, nonprofit corporations are run much like other businesses. Charity organizations with larger operations would be expected to have a larger staff, although some have more overhead than others. Table 12.5.6 shows the number of paid staff members of charity organizations as well as the amounts of money (in

---

[34]Data are from "Executive Compensation Scoreboard," *Business Week,* May 2, 1988, p. 76. The form of this analysis was suggested by Rolf R. Anderson, personal communication, 1989.

TABLE 12.5.6 Staff and Contribution Levels ($ millions) for Charities

Charity Organization	Staff	Public	Government	Other
Salvation Army	29,350	$473	$ 92	$300
American Red Cross	22,100	341	30	602
Planned Parenthood	8,200	67	106	101
CARE	7,087	45	340	12
Easter Seals	5,600	83	51	78
Association of Retarded Citizens	5,600	28	80	32
Volunteers of America	5,000	14	69	83
American Cancer Society	4,453	271	0	37
Boys Clubs	3,650	103	9	75
American Heart Association	2,700	151	1	27
UNICEF	1,652	67	348	48
March of Dimes	1,600	106	0	6
American Lung Association	1,500	80	1	17

Data are from G. Kinkead, "America's Best-Run Charities," *Fortune*, November 9, 1987, p. 146.

millions of dollars) raised from public donations, government payments, and other sources of income.

a. Find the regression equation to predict staff levels from the contributions of each type for these charities. (You will probably need to use a computer for this.)

b. How many additional paid staff members would you expect to see, on average, working for a charity that receives $5 million more from public donations than another charity (all else equal)?

c. To within approximately how many people can the regression equation predict the staffing levels of these charities from their revenue figures?

d. Find the predicted staffing level and its residual for the American Red Cross.

e. Does revenue from public donations have a significant impact on staffing level, holding other revenues fixed? How do you know?

f. What is the result of the *F*-test? What does it tell you?

8 Table 12.5.7 shows the levels of investment and the results obtained by the important players in fiber-optics cable for long-distance communications.

TABLE 12.5.7 Fiber-Optics Long-Distance Communications Firms

	Investment (millions)	Circuit miles* (millions)
AT&T	$1,300	1,700
MCI	500	650
GTE	130	110
United Telecommunications	2,000	1,200
Fibertrak	1,200	2,400
LDX Net	110	165
Electra Communications	40	72
Microtel	60	45
Litel Telecommunications	57	85
Lightnet	500	650
SoutherNet	90	50
RCI	90	87

Data are from W. B. Johnston, "The Coming Glut of Phone Lines," *Fortune*, January 7, 1985, pp. 97–100. Their source is the Hudson Institute.

*A *circuit mile* is defined as a length of cable capable of carrying one voice for one mile.

a. Find the regression equation to predict circuit miles from investment.
b. Draw the diagnostic plot of residual values against predicted values. What relationship, if any, do you see in the diagnostic plot? What corrective action is required?
c. Find the natural (base e) logarithm for each data value.
d. Find the regression equation to predict the log of circuit miles from the log of investment.
e. Draw the diagnostic plot for the regression using logarithms. Is any further corrective action needed? How do you know?
f. Exactly what does the regression coefficient tell you?
g. Find the two-sided 95% confidence interval for the regression coefficient (for the logs of both variables).
h. Do firms that spend more achieve significantly more circuit miles? How do you know?
i. For a regression such as this, using logs of both variables, a regression coefficient less than 1 suggests economies of scale, and a regression coefficient larger than 1 suggests extra expenses for larger projects. For this data set, what kind of economies of scale does the regression coefficient suggest? Are they statistically significant?

9 Setting prices is rarely an easy task. A low price usually results in higher sales, but there will be less profit per sale. A higher price produces higher profit per sale, but sales will be lower overall. Usually a firm wants to choose the price that will maximize the total profit, but there is considerable uncertainty about the demand. Table 12.5.8 shows hypothetical results of a study of profits in comparable test markets of equal sizes, where only the price was changed.

TABLE 12.5.8 Price and Profit in Test Markets

Price	Profit
$ 8	$ 6,486
9	10,928
10	15,805
11	13,679
12	12,758
13	9,050
14	5,702
15	−109

a. Find the regression equation of the form Profit $= a + b$(Price).
b. Test to see whether the regression coefficient (from part a) is significant or not. Is this result reasonable?
c. To within approximately how many dollars can profit be predicted from price in this way?
d. Examine a diagnostic plot to see if there is any further structure remaining that would help you explain profit based on price. Describe the structure that you see.
e. Create another X variable using the squared price values, and find the multiple regression equation to predict profit from price and squared price.
f. To within approximately how many dollars can profit be predicted from price using these two X variables?

g. Test to see whether a significant proportion of the variation in profit can be explained by price and squared price taken together.

h. Find the price at which the predicted profit is maximized. Compare this to the price at which the observed profit was the highest.

10 Table 12.5.9 shows the results of a multiple regression analysis designed to explain the salaries of chief executive officers based on the sales of their firm and the industry group.[35] The Y variable represents CEO salary (in millions of dollars). The X_1 variable is the firm's sales (in billions of dollars). X_2, X_3, and X_4 are indicator variables representing the industry groups aerospace, banking, and natural resources, respectively (the natural resources group includes the large oil companies). The indicator variable for the baseline group, automotive, has been omitted. There are $n = 49$ observations in this data set.

TABLE 12.5.9   Multiple Regression Results for CEO Salaries

```
THE REGRESSION EQUATION IS:
        Salary   = 931.8383
                 + 0.01493 * Sales
                 - 215.747 * Aerospace
                 - 135.550 * Bank
                 - 303.774 * Natural Resources
    S  = 401.8215
    R2 = 0.423469
```

VARIABLE	COEFF	STD ERR
Constant	931.8383	163.8354
Sales	0.014930	0.003047
Aerospace	-215.747	222.3225
Bank	-135.550	177.0797
Natural Resources	-303.774	187.4697

a. Do sales and industry group have a significant impact on CEO salary?

b. What is the estimated effect of an additional dollar of sales on CEO salary, adjusted for industry group?

c. Is the salary difference you estimated due to sales in part b statistically significant? What does this tell you in practical terms about salary differences?

d. According to the regression coefficient, how much more or less is the CEO of a bank paid compared to the CEO of an automotive firm of similar size?

e. Is the salary difference comparing banking to automotive that you estimated in part d statistically significant? What does this tell you in practical terms about salary differences?

11 Consider the page costs example used in Section 12.1.

a. Which X variable is the least helpful in explaining page costs? How do you know?

b. Rerun the regression analysis omitting this X variable.

c. Compare the following results without the X variable to the results with the X variable: F-test, R^2, regression coefficients, t-statistics.

---

[35]The data used are from "Executive Compensation Scoreboard," *Business Week*, May 2, 1988, p. 57.

TABLE 12.5.10   Interest Rates

Year	Federal Funds (overnight)	Treasury Bills (3-month)	Treasury Bonds (10-year)
1976	4.47%	4.49%	6.42%
1977	6.65	6.16	7.79
1978	10.25	9.25	9.14
1979	13.82	12.00	10.65
1980	19.44	14.62	12.29
1981	12.54	11.69	14.07
1982	8.79	8.01	10.26
1983	9.62	9.18	11.65
1984	7.95	7.67	11.13
1985	8.02	7.02	9.38
1986	5.87	5.27	7.59

Data are year-end annualized rates from N. L. Jacob and R. R. Pettit, *Investments,* 2nd ed. (Homewood, Ill.: Richard D. Irwin, 1988), p. 389. Their source is *Federal Reserve Bulletin,* various issues.

12 Consider the interest rates on securities with various terms to maturity, shown in Table 12.5.10.
   a. Find the regression equation to predict the long-term interest rate (Treasury bonds) from the two shorter-term rates.
   b. Create a new variable, "interaction," by multiplying the two shorter-term rates together. Find the regression equation to predict the long-term interest rate (Treasury bonds) from both of the shorter-term rates and the interaction.
   c. Test whether there is any interaction between the two shorter-term interest rates that would enter into the relationship between short-term and long-term interest rates.

Database Exercises

Refer to the employee database in Appendix A.

1 Consider the prediction of annual salary from age and experience.
   a. Find and interpret the regression equation and regression coefficients.
   b. Find and interpret the standard error of estimate.
   c. Find and interpret the coefficient of determination.
   d. Is the model significant? What does this tell you?
   e. Test each regression coefficient for significance, and interpret the results.
   f. Find and interpret the standardized regression coefficients.
   g. Examine the diagnostic plot, and report serious problems, if there are any.
2 Continue using predictions of annual salary based on age and experience.
   a. Find the predicted annual salary and prediction error for employee 33, and compare the result to the actual annual salary.
   b. Find the predicted annual salary and prediction error for employee 52, and compare the result to the actual annual salary.
   c. Find the predicted annual salary and prediction error for the highest-paid employee, and compare the result to the actual annual salary. What does this comparison tell you?

    d. Find the predicted annual salary and prediction error for the lowest-paid employee, and compare the result to the actual annual salary. What does this comparison tell you?

3 Consider the prediction of annual salary from age alone (as compared to exercise 1, where experience was also used as an X variable).

    a. Find the regression equation to predict annual salary from age.

    b. Using results from part a of exercise 1 and this exercise, compare the effect of age on annual salary with and without an adjustment for experience.

    c. Test whether age has a significant impact on annual salary with and without an adjustment for experience. Briefly discuss your results.

4 Now examine the effect of gender on annual salary, with and without adjusting for age and experience.

    a. Find the average annual salary for men and for women, and compare them.

    b. Test whether men are paid significantly more than women using a two-sided test at the 5% level. (You may wish to refer back to Chapter 10 for the appropriate test to use.)

    c. Find the multiple regression equation to predict annual salary from age, experience, and gender, using an indicator variable for gender.

    d. Examine and interpret the regression coefficient for gender.

    e. Does gender have a significant impact on annual salary after adjustment for age and experience?

    f. Compare and discuss your results from parts b and e of this exercise.

5 Now examine the effect of training level on annual salary, with and without adjusting for age and experience.

    a. Find the average annual salary for each of the three training levels, and compare them.

    b. Find the multiple regression equation to predict annual salary from age, experience, and training level, using indicator variables for training level. Omit the indicator variable for level A as the baseline.

    c. Examine and interpret the regression coefficient for each indicator variable for training level.

    d. Does training level appear to have a significant impact on annual salary after adjustment for age and experience?

    e. Compare and discuss the average salary differential between training levels A and C, both with and without adjusting for age and experience.

6 Consider predicting annual salary from age, experience, and an interaction term.

    a. Create a new variable, "interaction," by multiplying age by experience for each employee.

    b. Find the regression equation to predict annual salary from age, experience, and interaction.

    c. Test whether you have a significant interaction by using a t-test for the regression coefficient of the interaction variable.

    d. What is the average effect on annual salary of an extra year's experience for a 40-year-old employee?

    e. What is the average effect on annual salary of an extra year's experience for a 50-year-old employee?

    f. Interpret the interaction between age and experience by comparing your answers to parts d and e of this exercise.

Project

Find a multivariate data set relating to your work or business interests, with a sample size of $n = 25$ or more, for which the F-test is significant and at least one of the t-tests is significant.

a. Give your choice of dependent variable (Y), and briefly explain your reasons.

b. Examine and comment on the scatterplots defined by plotting Y against each X variable.

c. Compute and briefly interpret the correlation matrix.

d. Report the regression equation.

e. For two elementary units in your data set, compute predicted values for Y and residuals.

f. Interpret each regression coefficient and its confidence interval.

g. Which regression coefficients are significant? Which (if any) are not? Are these results reasonable?

h. Comment on what you have learned from multiple regression analysis about the effects of the X variables on Y.

Report Writing
Communicating the Results of a Multiple Regression

Communication is an essential management skill with many applications. You use communication strategies to motivate those who report to you, to convince your boss you've done a good job, to obtain resources needed for a new project, to persuade your potential customers, to bring your suppliers into line, and so on.

Statistical summaries can help you communicate the basic facts of a situation in the most objective and useful way.[1] They can help you make your point to an audience. You can gain their credibility because it is clear that you have gone to some trouble to carefully survey the entire situation so that you can present them with the "big picture." Here are some examples of reports that include statistical information:

1 *A market survey.* Your firm is in the process of deciding whether or not to go ahead and launch a new product. The market survey provides important background information about potential customers: their likes and dislikes, how much they might be willing to pay, what kind of support they expect, and so on. To help you understand these consumers, the report might include a multiple regression analysis to determine how eager they are to buy the product based on characteristics such as income and industry group. The purpose of the report is to provide background information for decision making. The audience is middle- and upper-level management, including those who will ultimately make the decision.

2 *Recommendations for improving a production process.* In the presence of anticipated domestic and international competition when your patent expires next year, you would like to remain in the market as a low-cost

---

[1]There are, of course, other uses for statistics. Consider, for example, D. Huff, *How to Lie with Statistics* (New York: Norton, 1954).

producer. This goal is reasonable because, after all, you have much more experience than anyone else. Based on data collected from actual operations, as well as experiments with alternative processes, the report summarizes the various approaches and their expected savings under various scenarios. There might be multiple regression results to identify the important factors and to suggest how to adjust them. The purpose of the report is to help reduce costs. The audience might be middle- and upper-level management, who would decide which suggestions to adopt.

3 *A review of hiring and compensation practices.* Either as part of a periodic review or in reaction to accusations of unfairness, your firm is examining its human resources practices. A multiple regression analysis might be used to explain salary by age, experience, gender, qualifications, and so on. By comparing official policies to the regression results, you can see whether the firm is effectively implementing its goals or not. By testing the regression coefficient for gender, you can see whether or not there is evidence of gender discrimination. The purposes of the study include helping the firm achieve its human resource management goals and, perhaps, defending the firm against accusations of discrimination. The audience might be middle- and upper-level management, who might make some adjustments in human resource management policies, or it might be the plaintiff and judge in a lawsuit.

4 *Determination of cost structure.* In order to control costs, it helps to know what they are. In particular, as demand and production go up and down, what component of your total cost can be considered fixed cost, and what, then, are the variable costs per unit of each item you produce? A multiple regression analysis can provide estimates of your cost structure based on actual experience. The purpose of the study is to understand and control costs. The audience consists of those managers responsible for budgeting and for controlling costs.

5 *Product testing.* Your firm, in your opinion, produces the best product within its category. One way to convince others of this is to report the statistical results from objective testing. Toothpaste firms have used this technique for years now ("...has been shown to be an effective decay-preventing dentifrice that can be of significant value..."). Various statistical hypothesis testing techniques might be used here, from an unpaired *t*-test to multiple regression. The purpose of the study is to prove superiority of your product. The audience consists of your potential customers. The form of the "report" might range from a quote on the package to a paragraph in the information brochure to a 200-page report filed with a government agency and made available upon request.

Let's assume that your primary consideration when using statistical results in a report is to *communicate.* Be kind to your readers, and explain what you have learned using language that is easy for them to understand. They will probably be more impressed with your work if they understand it than if they get lost in technical terminology and details.

Reports are written for various reasons and for various audiences. Once you have identified these, you will find that the writing is easier because you can picture yourself addressing your audience for a real purpose. Defining your purpose helps you narrow down the topic so that you can concentrate on the relevant issues. Identifying your audience helps you select the appropriate writing style and level of detail.

13.1 How to Organize Your Report

How you organize your report will depend on your purpose and the appropriate audience. In this section is an outline of the main parts of a statistical report, which you may modify to fit your particular purpose. There are six parts to this form of a typical report:

1 The *executive summary* is a paragraph at the very beginning that describes the most important facts and conclusions from your work.
2 The *introduction* consists of several paragraphs in which you describe the background, the questions of interest, and the data set you have worked with.
3 The *analysis and methods section* lets you interpret the data by presenting graphic displays, statistical summary numbers, and results, which you explain as you go along.
4 The *conclusion and summary* move back to the big picture to give closure, pulling together all of the important thoughts you would like your readers to remember.
5 A *reference* is a note indicating the material you have taken from an outside source and giving enough information so that your audience can locate it. You might have references appear as notes on the appropriate page of a section, or you might gather them together in their own section.
6 The *appendix* should contain all supporting material that is important enough to include but not important enough to appear in the text of your report.

In addition, you may also wish to include a *title page* and a *table of contents*. The **title page** goes first and includes the title of the report, the name and title of the person you prepared it for, your name and title (as the preparer), and the date. The **table of contents** goes after the executive summary, giving an outline of the report together with page numbers.

The best organization is straightforward and direct. Remember, your purpose is to make it easy for the reader to understand what you've done. Don't play games with your audience by keeping them in suspense until the last page. Instead, tell them all of the most important results at the start and fill in details later. Your readers will appreciate it because they are as pressed for time as you are. This strategy will also help your message reach those people who only read a part of your paper.

Use an outline in planning your report, perhaps with one line representing each paragraph. This is an excellent way to keep the big picture in mind as you work out the exact wording.

The Executive Summary Paragraph

The **executive summary** is a paragraph at the very beginning that describes the most important facts and conclusions from your work, omitting unnecessary details. Writing in straightforward nontechnical language, you should orient the reader to the importance of the problem and explain your contribution to its understanding and solution. You are, in essence, reducing the entire report to a single paragraph.

Some people, especially those who are technically oriented, may complain that their hundreds of pages of analysis have already been reduced to 15 pages of report, and that it would be impossible (and unfair) to reduce all of that precious work to a single paragraph. However, there are important people who will read no more than the executive summary, and if you want your message to reach them, you are doing yourself a favor by providing them the convenience of the executive summary.

Although the executive summary goes first, it is often easiest to write it last, after you have finished the rest of the report. Only at this time are you completely sure of just what it is you are summarizing!

The Introduction Section

The **introduction** consists of several paragraphs in which you describe the background, the questions of interest, and the data set you have worked with. Write in nontechnical language, as if to an intelligent person who knows very little about the details of the situation. After reading the executive summary and introduction, your reader should be completely oriented to the situation. All that remains are the details.

It's OK to repeat material from the executive summary. You may even want to take some of the sentences directly from the executive summary and use them as initial topic sentences for paragraphs in the introduction.

The Analysis and Methods Section

In the **analysis and methods** section you interpret the data by presenting graphic displays, statistical summary numbers, and results, explaining them as you go along. This is your chance to give some of the details that have been only hinted at in the executive summary and introduction.

Be selective. You should probably leave out much of the analysis you have actually done on the problem. A careful analyst will explore many avenues "just in case," in order to check assumptions and validate the basic approach. But many of these results belong in a separate folder, in which you keep an archive of everything you looked at. From this folder, select only those items that are important and helpful to the story you are telling in the report. For example, if a group of scatterplots had ordinary linear structure, you might include just one of these with a comment that the others were much the same. Choose the materials that most strongly relate to your purpose.

To help your reader understand your points, you will want to include each graph on the page of text that discusses it. Many computers can help you do this. An alternative is to use a reducing copy machine to enable you to paste a small graph directly on the page of text.

Here is a list of items you should consider including in the analysis and methods section, organized according to the four basic activities of statistics:

1 *Design.* If there are important aspects of how you obtained the data that could not be covered in the introduction, you can include them either here or in an appendix.

2 *Data exploration.* Tell your reader what you found in the data. You might want to include some graphs (histograms, box plots, or scatterplots) if they help the reader see what you're talking about. An extremely skewed histogram or a diagnostic plot with structure might be shown to justify using a transformation to help satisfy the underlying assumptions. If you have outlier trouble, now is your chance to mention it and justify how you dealt with it.

3 *Estimation.* Report the appropriate statistical summaries, and explain what they say about the business situation you are examining. These might be averages (indicating typical value), standard deviations (perhaps indicating risk), correlations (indicating strength of relationship), or regression coefficients (indicating the adjusted effect of one factor on another). You will also want to include measures of the uncertainty in these estimates so that your readers can assess the quality of the information you are reporting. These would include standard errors and confidence intervals for the estimates, whenever possible and appropriate, as well as R^2 and the standard error of estimate for a regression analysis.

4 *Hypothesis tests.* If appropriate, tell your reader whether or not the estimated effects are "really there" by testing them, for example, against the reference value 0. Once you find a statistically significant result, you have license to explain it. If an estimate is *not* statistically significant, you are *not* permitted to explain it.[2] By testing, you reassure your reader by showing that your claims have a solid foundation.

---

[2] For example, if a regression coefficient is computed as −167.35 but is not significantly different from 0, you really are not even sure that it is a negative number. Since the true effect (in the population) might be positive instead of negative, don't make the mistake of "explaining" why it is negative.

The Conclusion and Summary Section

By this point, your reader is somewhat familiar with the details of your project. The **conclusion and summary** section now moves back to the big picture to give closure, pulling together all of the important thoughts you would like your readers to remember. Whereas the executive summary primarily provides the initial orientation, the conclusion and summary can draw on the details you have provided in the intervening sections. Keep in mind that while some readers get here by reading your pages in order, others may flip directly here to see how it ends.

In particular, be sure to tell exactly what the analysis has revealed about the situation. Why did you go to all of the trouble? What made it worth all that time? How have your questions been answered?

Including References

Whenever you take text, data, or ideas from an outside source, it is necessary to give proper credit. A **reference** is a note indicating the kind of material you have taken from an outside source and giving enough information so that your reader can obtain a copy. You might have each note appear as a footnote on the same page as its text reference, or you might gather them together in their own section.

Be sure to provide enough information in your reference so that an interested person can actually find the information you used. It is not enough to just give the author's name or to say "U.S. Department of Commerce." A full reference will also include such details as the date, volume, page, and publisher. Even a statement such as "the 1990 sales figure is from the firm's annual reports" does not provide enough information because, for example, the sales figures for 1990 may be revised in 1991 and appear as a different number in the annual report a year or two later.

Here are examples of common types of references:

1 For *quoted text taken from a book,* your reference should include the author(s), the year published, the title, the place of publication, and the publisher, as well as the page number for this material. Here is a sample paragraph and footnote:

> In order to give credit where credit is due, as well as to avoid being accused of plagiarism, you should provide adequate references in your report. In the words of Siegel:
>
>> Whenever you take text, data, or ideas from an outside source, it is necessary to give proper credit. A **reference** is a note indicating the kind of material you have taken from an outside source and giving enough information so that your reader can obtain a copy.[1]

---

[1] This quote is from A. F. Siegel, *Practical Business Statistics* (Homewood, Ill.: Richard D. Irwin, 1990), p. 564.

2 For an *idea taken from a book,* explained in your own words and not as a direct quote, proceed as follows:

> As explained by Bovée and Arens, *combination rates* for newspaper advertising are often available when the same advertisement is placed in two related editions of a newspaper.[1] These might be the morning and evening editions of the same newspaper or else two different but related newspapers.

[1]This material is covered in C. L. Bovée and W. F. Arens, *Contemporary Advertising,* 2nd ed. (Homewood, Ill.: Richard D. Irwin, 1986), p. 413.

3 For *data taken from a magazine article,* your note should include the title of the article, the author (if given), the magazine, the date, and the page. If the data are attributed to another source, you should mention that source as well. For example:

> Some mutual funds were able to implement a low-risk strategy that attained a high return on your investment. For example, here are average total returns from 1984–1988 for some mutual funds that had "very low risk" strategies: Drexel Burnham (15.6% return), Eaton Vance Income Fund Boston (14.4% return), and Fidelity Puritan (14.9% return).[1] Of course, there is no guarantee that this exceptional performance will continue in the future.

[1]Data are from "The Best Return for the Least Risk: Our Mutual Fund Scoreboard Can Help You Pick a Winner," *Business Week,* February 20, 1989, p. 80. Their source is Morningstar, Inc.

4 For material you learned from an interview, letter, or telephone call, your reference is to a *personal communication.* Be sure to mention the person's name and title as well as the place and date of the communication. For example:

> One of the most important things about futures markets is that "they allow investors to hedge risks at a relatively low cost."[1] This allows you to change the risk-return characteristics of a portfolio to suit your individual preferences.

[1]Professor Avraham Kamara, Department of Finance, University of Washington, personal communication, 3/30/89.

If you would like more complete information about references, the *Chicago Manual of Style* is an excellent source for further details.[3]

The Appendix Section

The **appendix** contains all supporting material that is important enough to include but not important enough (perhaps due to space limitations) to be

[3]See "Documentation: References, Notes, and Bibliographies" in *The Chicago Manual of Style,* 13th ed. (Chicago: University of Chicago Press, 1982), Chapter 15.

included in the text of your report. This would include a listing of your data (if it fits on a few pages) and their source. You might also include, if appropriate, some details of the design of your study, some extra graphs and tables, and further technical explanation for statements in the report itself. For clarity, you might put material into different appendix sections: Appendix A, Appendix B, and so on.

Using an appendix is your way of keeping everyone happy. The casual reader's thoughts will not be interrupted, and the more technical reader will have easy access to important material. For example:

> Since the gender effect was not statistically significant, the multiple regression analysis was repeated after removing the gender variable. The results did not change in any meaningful way (details may be found in Appendix C).

■ 13.2 Hints and Tips

This section gives some hints and tips to help you save time in producing an effective report.

Think about Your Audience

Keep it brief. Remember that your readers probably don't have enough time to get things done either. You can do them a favor by selecting and including only the most important results, graphs, and conclusions. If you must include lots of technical materials, try placing them in an appendix.

Make it clear. Be sure to use straightforward language and to provide enough introduction and orientation so that your readers don't get left behind.

Look it over. Read your rough draft, putting yourself in the place of your reader. Try to forget that you have been living and breathing this project for weeks, and pretend you have only heard vague things about it. See if you have provided enough connections with everyday life to bring your reader into the subject.

What to Write First? Next? Last?

The order in which you do things can make a difference. You can't write the paper until you know what the results are. Many people write the introduction and executive summary *last* because only then do they know what they are introducing and summarizing.

Do the analysis first. Explore the data, look at the graphs, compute the estimates, and do the hypothesis tests. Perhaps even run the multiple regression with different X variables. This stage will produce a file folder filled with more material than you could ever use. Save it all, just in case you'll need to check something out later.

Next, select the most important results from your analysis file. Now that you know how things have turned out, you are ready to make an outline of the analysis and methods section. Perhaps you could also outline some conclusions at this point.

All that remains is to create paragraphs from the lines on your outline, decide what to place in the appendix, choose the references, and write the introduction and executive summary. After you've done this rough draft, read it over with your audience in mind, and make the final changes. If possible, ask a friend to read it over, too. Print it out. You're done!

Other Sources

There are many sources of information about good writing, covering language, style, and usage. For example:

1 Use a *dictionary* to check usage of a word you're not sure about. Computer word processors are often quicker for checking spelling.
2 Use a *thesaurus* to look for different words with a similar meaning. This can help you find just the right word or can help you avoid repeating the same term too many times. Many computer word processing programs have a built-in thesaurus.
3 There are a number of books available that are filled with advice for managers who need to write reports that might involve some technical material, for example, Lesikar's *Basic Business Communication*, Tichy's *Effective Writing for Engineers, Managers, and Scientists*, and Weisman's *Technical Correspondence.*[4]
4 For more details about writing conventions, consult the *Chicago Manual of Style*.

■ 13.3 Example: A Quick Pricing Formula for Customer Inquiries

An example of a report based on a multiple regression analysis, following the organization plan suggested earlier in this chapter, is presented on pages 568–74. Note how the practical meaning rather than the details is emphasized throughout.

---

[4]R. V. Lesikar, *Basic Business Communication* (Homewood, Ill.: Richard D. Irwin, 1988); H. J. Tichy, *Effective Writing for Engineers, Managers, and Scientists* (New York: Wiley, 1966); H. M. Weisman, *Technical Correspondence* (New York: Wiley, 1968).

A QUICK PRICING FORMULA FOR CUSTOMER INQUIRIES

Prepared for
Bonnie S. Wennerstrom, Vice President of Sales

Prepared by
Clara H. Siegel, Director of Research
Mount Olympus Design and Development Corporation
April 10, 1989

Executive Summary

We are losing potential customers because we cannot respond immediately with a price quotation. Our salespeople report that by the time we call back with a price quote the next day, many of these contacts have already made arrangements to work with one of our competitors. Our proposed solution is to create a quick pricing formula. Potential customers for routine jobs will be able to obtain an approximate price over the phone. This should help keep them interested in us while they wait for the exact quote the next day. Not only will they know if we're "in the ballpark," but this will also help us appear more responsive to customer needs.

Introduction

Preparing a price quotation currently requires three to six hours of engineering work. When our customers call us about a new job, they want to know the price range so that they can "comparison shop." In the past, when we had fewer competitors, this was not a problem. Even though our quality is superior, we are losing more and more jobs to competitors who can provide information more quickly.

We checked with Engineering and agree that the time delay is necessary if an exact quote is required. A certain amount of rough preliminary work is essential in order to determine the precise size of the layout and the power requirements, which, in turn, determine our cost.

We also checked with a few key customers. Although they do not require an exact price quote immediately, it would be a big help if we could give them a rough idea of the price during that initial contact. This would meet two of their needs: (1) They can be sure that we are competitive, and (2) this pricing information helps them with *their* design decisions because they can quickly evaluate several approaches.

Based on our own experience, we have created a formula that produces an approximate number for our cost remarkably quickly:

$$\text{Quick cost number} = \$1,356 + \$35.58(\text{Components}) + \$5.68(\text{Size})$$

The resulting "quick cost number" will, in most cases, differ from our own detailed cost computation by no more than \$200. A quick telephone quotation could be given by simply adding in the appropriate (confidential) markup, depending on the customer's discount class.

We assembled data from recent detailed quotations, taken from our own internal computerized records that support the detailed price quote that we routinely commit ourselves to for a period of seven days. The key variables we analyzed include:

1 The **cost** computed by Engineering. This is internal confidential material. This is the variable to be predicted; it is the only variable *not* available during the initial phone conversation.
2 The **number of components** involved. This is a rough indication of the complexity of the design and is nearly always provided by the customer during the initial contact.
3 The **layout size.** This is a very rough indication of the size of the actual finished layout. It is provided by the customer as an initial starting point.

Of the 72 quotations given this quarter, we selected 56 as representative of the routine jobs we see most often. The cases that were rejected either required a special chemical process or coating or else used exotic components for which we have no stable source. The data set is included in the appendix.

Analysis and Methods

This section begins with a description of our typical price quotations and continues with the cost prediction formula (using multiple regression methodology) and its interpretation.

Here is a profile of our most typical jobs. From the histograms in Figure 1, you can see that our typical price quote involves a cost somewhere between $3,000 and $5,000, with just a few above or below. The standard deviation of cost is $707, indicating the approximate error we would make if we were to (foolishly!) make quick quotes simply based on the average cost of $3,987. The number of components is typically 10 to 50, with just a few larger jobs. The layout size is typically anywhere from 200 to the low 300s. There are no outlier problems because all large or atypical jobs are treated separately as special cases, and the quick cost formula would not be appropriate.

Next, we considered the *relationship* between cost and each of the other variables. As you can see from the first two scatterplots in Figure 2, there is a very strong rela-

FIGURE 1   Histograms of the variables

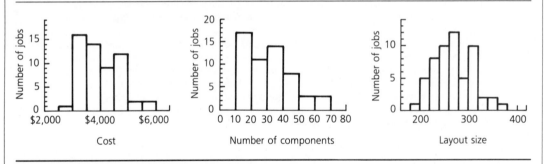

FIGURE 2   Scatterplots of the variables

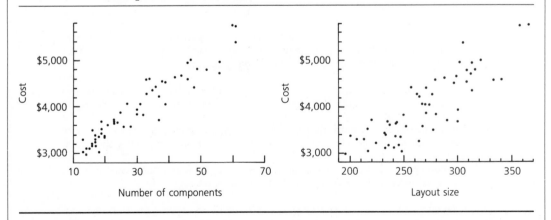

tionship between the number of components and our cost (the correlation is 0.949) and a strong relationship between the layout size and our cost (correlation 0.857). These strong relationships suggest that we will indeed be able to obtain a useful prediction of cost based on these variables. The number of components and the layout size are moderately related (correlation 0.760; the scatterplot is in the appendix). Because this relationship is not perfect, the layout size may be bringing useful additional information into the picture. Furthermore, the relationships appear to be linear, suggesting that regression analysis is appropriate.

A multiple regression analysis to predict cost based on the other variables (number of components and layout size) produced the following prediction equation:

$$\text{Predicted cost} = \$1,356 + \$35.58(\text{Components}) + \$5.68(\text{Size})$$

This predicted cost can be easily computed from the customer's information provided over the telephone and represents our best prediction of the detailed cost figure obtainable (in the least-squares sense) from a linear model of this type. This is the "quick cost number" we are proposing.

This prediction equation appears very reasonable. The estimated fixed cost of $1,356 should more than cover our usual overhead expenses. The estimated cost per component of $35.58 is somewhat larger than what you might expect because the best prediction includes other factors (such as labor) that also increase with the complexity of the design. The $5.68 per unit of layout size is again higher than our actual cost because the layout size number also represents information about other costly aspects of the design.

Here is an example of the use of the prediction equation. Consider a customer who inquires about a job involving about 42 components and a layout size of around 315. Our cost may be estimated as follows:

$$\text{Predicted cost} = \$1,356 + \$35.58 \times 42 + \$5.68 \times 315$$

$$= \$4,640$$

If this customer ordinarily receives a 20% markup (according to confidential records easily available on the computer), then the price quote might be found as follows:

$$\text{Quick price quote} = \$4,640 \times 1.2$$

$$= \$5,568$$

How accurate are these quick cost quotes? They should usually be within $200 of the detailed cost information (which is not immediately available) based on the standard error of estimate of $169.[1]

There are three approaches we might use to handle this remaining error. First, we could tell the customer that this number is only approximate and that the final figure will depend on the standard detailed cost calculation. Second, at the opposite extreme, we could give firm quotes instantly, perhaps after adding a few hundred dollars as a "safety margin." Finally, we could reserve the right to revise the quote but guarantee the customer that the price would not rise by more than some figure (perhaps $100).

How effective are number of components and layout size in predicting cost? Consider all of the variation in cost from one job to another; a very large fraction of this

---

[1] For the normal linear model, we would expect about 2/3 of the quick cost numbers for this data set to be within $169 of their respective detailed cost numbers. For similar jobs in the future, this error would be slightly higher due to uncertainties in the regression coefficients in the prediction equation. For *different* jobs in the future, it is difficult to tell the size of the error.

variation is explained by the number of components and the layout size (R-squared is 94.5%). This is extremely unlikely to have occurred by accident; the regression equation is very highly statistically significant.[2]

The average cost is $3,987. By using the prediction equation instead of this average cost, we reduce our error from $707 (the ordinary standard deviation of cost) to $169 (the standard error of estimate from the regression analysis).

Do we need both the number of components and the layout size in order to predict cost? Yes, because the additional contribution of each one (over and above the information provided by the other) is very highly statistically significant, according to the t-test of each regression coefficient.

We also checked for possible technical problems and didn't find any. For example, the diagnostic plot in the appendix shows no additional structure that could be used to improve the results further.

Conclusion and Summary

We can offer our customers better service by providing instant price quotations for our most typical design jobs using the following predicted cost equation:

$$\text{Predicted cost} = \$1,356 + \$35.58(\text{Components}) + \$5.68(\text{Size})$$

After adding markup and, perhaps, a few hundred dollars to cover the prediction error, we could provide instant quotes in several different formats:

1 Provide the quote as an *approximate* price only. Tell the customer that the actual price will depend on the standard detailed cost calculation available the next day. In effect, the customer bears all the risk of the price uncertainty.
2 Provide a *firm* quote. We might add a little extra for this purpose in order to shift the price uncertainty risk from the customer to us.
3 Compromise. Provide an *approximate* quote, but limit the customer's risk by "capping" the price change. For example, we might reserve the right to revise the price but promise not to raise it by more than $100. Consider also whether we should *lower* the price or not when the prediction is too high.

This predicted cost equation is based on our actual design experience and on conventional statistical methods. The multiple regression analysis is appropriate for our most typical design jobs, and the results are very highly statistically significant.

If we do implement a "quick price quote" policy, we should be aware of the following selection problem: As customers begin to "figure out" how we provide these quotes, they may bring unfairly complex layout problems to us. Since the prediction equation is based on our *typical* jobs, a serious change in the level of complexity could lead to incorrect pricing. We could respond by identifying the source of this additional complexity and updating our quick pricing model accordingly from time to time.

If this works well with customers, we might consider expanding the program to produce quick quotes on additional categories of design work.

---

[2]The p-value is less than 0.001, indicating the probability of finding such a strong predictive relationship if, in fact, there were just randomness, with no relationship.

References

The data used were taken from confidential internal corporate records in the system as of 4/6/89.

The statistical software used was StatPad, a trademark of Skyline Technologies, Inc.

An explanation of general statistical principles in business is provided in A. F. Siegel, *Practical Business Statistics* (Homewood, Ill.: Richard D. Irwin, 1990).

Appendix

Here is the data set that was analyzed. We included only routine designs, rejecting 16 designs that either required a special chemical process or coating or else used exotic components for which we have no stable source.

Number of Components	Layout Size	Cost	Number of Components	Layout Size	Cost
27	268	$4,064	42	288	$4,630
23	243	3,638	24	244	3,659
30	301	3,933	37	220	3,712
16	245	3,168	23	235	3,677
37	265	4,227	32	250	3,826
14	233	3,105	28	267	3,576
20	247	3,352	38	309	4,547
33	334	4,581	49	317	4,806
23	290	3,708	56	313	4,717
35	314	4,360	14	196	2,981
31	270	4,058	46	314	4,949
17	236	3,162	13	248	3,032
47	322	5,008	39	274	4,051
52	309	4,790	33	262	4,283
34	341	4,593	17	264	3,250
25	271	3,869	44	277	4,280
26	252	3,572	44	299	4,665
19	300	3,677	17	233	3,389
16	224	3,211	17	206	3,296
30	280	3,840	61	358	5,732
36	257	4,428	56	302	4,963
61	306	5,382	15	241	3,109
19	216	3,518	48	271	4,419
16	277	3,496	39	297	4,524
46	280	4,588	19	232	3,425
60	366	5,752	20	201	3,368
18	217	3,042	13	213	3,295
18	242	3,358	21	237	3,605

Here is the computer printout of the multiple regression analysis:

```
CORRELATIONS:

              Cost        Components      Size
Cost        1.           0.949313      0.856855
Components  0.949313     1.            0.759615
Size        0.856855     0.759615      1.
```

```
THE REGRESSION EQUATION:

   Cost          = 1356.148
                 + 35.57949  * Components
                 + 5.678224  * Size


   S =169.1943
   R2 =0.944757
INFERENCE FOR Cost AT THE 5% LEVEL:
        The prediction equation DOES
        explain a significant proportion
        of the variation in Cost.
            F =453.2050   with
            2      and        53
        degrees of freedom
```

VARIABLE	effect on Cost COEFF	95% confidence interval FROM	TO	Hypothesis Test SIGNIFICANT?	std err of coeff STD ERR	t statistic t
Constant	1356.148	983.1083	1729.189	Yes	185.9845	7.291728
Components	35.57949	30.55847	40.60051	Yes	2.503300	14.21303
Size	5.678224	3.916505	7.439943	Yes	0.878329	6.464801

Figure 3 shows the scatterplot of the two explanatory variables: number of components and layout size. The correlation is 0.760.

The diagnostic plot of cost prediction errors plotted against predicted cost (Figure 4) showed no structure, just a random scatter of data points. This suggests that there is no simple way to improve these predictions of cost based on the number of components and the layout size.

FIGURE 3 Scatterplot of number of components against layout size

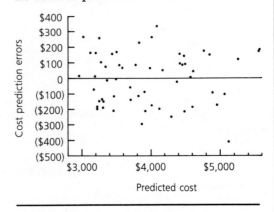

FIGURE 4 The diagnostic plot shows no obvious problems

■ 13.4 **End-of-Chapter Materials**

Summary

Communication is an essential management skill, and statistical summaries can help you communicate the basic facts of a situation in a direct and objective way. Be kind to your readers, and explain what you have learned using language that is easy for them to understand. Identifying your *purpose* helps you narrow down the topic so that you can concentrate on the relevant issues. Identifying your *audience* helps you select the appropriate writing style and level of detail.

The best organization is straightforward and direct. You want to make it quick and easy for your readers to hear your story. Develop an outline early on, perhaps with one line representing each paragraph of your paper. Here is one reasonable plan for organization:

1 The **executive summary** is a paragraph at the very beginning that describes the most important facts and conclusions from your work.
2 The **introduction** consists of several paragraphs in which you describe the background, the questions of interest, and the data set you have worked with.
3 The **analysis and methods** section lets you interpret the data by presenting graphic displays, summaries, and results, which you explain as you go along.
4 The **conclusion and summary** move back to the big picture to give closure, pulling together all of the important thoughts you would like your readers to remember.
5 A **reference** is a note indicating the kind of material you have taken from an outside source and giving enough information so that your reader can obtain a copy. You might have these appear on the appropriate page of a section, or you might gather them together in their own section.
6 The **appendix** contains all supporting material that is important enough to include but not important enough to appear in the text of your report.

In addition, you may also wish to include a *title page* and a *table of contents* page. The **title page** goes first, including the title of the report, the name and title of the person you prepared it for, your name and title (as the preparer), and the date. The **table of contents** goes after the executive summary, showing an outline of the report together with page numbers.

Do the analysis first. Next, select the most important results from your analysis file. Then make an outline of the analysis and methods section and conclusions. Create paragraphs from the entries in your outline, decide

what to place in the appendix, choose the references, and write the introduction and executive summary.

   Be brief and clear. Read over your material with your audience in mind.

Key Words

title page 561   analysis and methods 562
table of contents 561   conclusion and summary 564
executive summary 562   reference 564
introduction 562   appendix 565

Questions

1 What is the primary purpose of writing a report?

2 Why is it necessary to identify the purpose and audience of a report?

3 How can an outline help you?

4 Give some reasons why you might want to include statistical results in a report.

5 Should you leave key results out of the executive summary, ending it with a sentence like "We have examined these issues and have come up with some recommendations." Why or why not?

6 How can you use the executive summary and introduction to reach a diverse audience with limited time?

7 Is it OK to repeat material in the introduction that already appeared in the executive summary?

8 a. What kind of material appears in the analysis and methods section?
  b. Should you describe everything you have examined in the analysis and meth-
     ods section? Why or why not?

9 Should you assume that everyone who reads your conclusion is already familiar
with all of the details of the analysis and methods section?

10 a. Give two reasons for providing a reference when you make use of material from
      a book, magazine, or other source.
   b. How can you tell if you have provided enough information in a reference?
   c. How would you reference material from a telephone call or an interview with
      an expert?

11 a. What material belongs in the appendix?
   b. How can an appendix help you satisfy both the casual and the dedicated
      reader?

12 What can you do to help those in your audience who are short of time?

13 When is the best time to write the introduction and executive summary, first or
last? Why?

14 What is the relationship between the outline and the finished report?

15 How would you check the meaning of a word to be sure that you are using it
correctly?

16 How can you find synonyms for a given word? Why might you want to?

Problems

1 Your boss has just asked you to write a report. Identify the purpose and audience in each of the following situations:
   a. The firm is considering expansion of the shipping area. Background material is needed on the size of facilities at other firms.
   b. The new stereo system is almost ready to be shipped. It is clearly superior to everything else on the market. Your boss was contacted by a hi-fi magazine for some material to include in their "new products" column.
   c. Manufacturing equipment has been breaking down fairly often lately, and nobody seems to know why. Fortunately, information concerning the details of each breakdown is available.
   d. Your firm's bank is reluctant to lend any more money because they claim that your industry group's sales are too closely tied to the economy and are therefore too vulnerable to financial trouble in a recession. Your boss feels that data available for the firm's sales and for the U.S. gross national product might prove otherwise.

2 Fill in the blanks, using either *affect* or *effect*.
   a. The amount of overtime and the time of day had a significant _____ on accidents in the workplace.
   b. The amount of overtime and the time of day significantly _____ accidents in the workplace.
   c. Curiously, the amount of experience does not seem to _____ the productivity of these workers.
   d. Curiously, the amount of experience does not seem to have an _____ on the productivity of these workers.

3 Using your imagination, create an executive summary paragraph for a hypothetical report based on each of the situations in problem 1. (*Note:* Only one paragraph is required for each situation.)

4 For each of the following sentences, say which section (or sections) it might be located in.
   a. The scatterplot of defects against the rate of production shows a moderately strong relationship, with a correlation of 0.782, suggesting that our worst problems happen at those times of high demand, when we can least afford them.
   b. The third option, to sell the division to an independent outsider, should be held in reserve as a last resort, to be used only if the other two possibilities don't work out.
   c. These problems began five years ago, when the new power plant was installed, and have cost the firm at least $2 million over the past two years.
   d. Here is the data set, giving the prices for each product in each of the different markets.

5 Arrange selected information to form a proper reference for each of the following cases.
   a. The title of the article from *The Wall Street Journal* is "How a Money Manager Can Pull a Rabbit out of a Hat." It appeared on March 16, 1989, which was a

Thursday. It was on page Cl. It was written by James A. White, a staff reporter. The article is about how money managers can choose an evaluation method that makes them look good.

b. In order to be sure about a technical detail in a report about leasing and taxes, you have called an expert at the University of Washington. Professor Lawrence D. Schall confirms your suspicion that the laws are highly complex in this area and suggests that no simple approach to the problem will work in general.

c. You have been using a book called *Tools and Methods for the Improvement of Quality* as background reading for a report suggesting manufacturing improvements. The appropriate chapter is 8, and the authors are Howard Gitlow, Shelly Gitlow, Alan Oppenheim, and Rosa Oppenheim. The book was published in 1989 by Richard D. Irwin, Inc., located in Homewood, Illinois. The book is copyrighted and has ISBN number 0-256-05680-3. It is dedicated to "the never-ending improvement of the species."

6 What important information is missing from each of the following references?
  a. Personal communication, 1990.
  b. *Business Week*, p. 80.
  c. *Basic Business Communication* (Homewood, Ill.: Richard D. Irwin).
  d. James A. White, "Will the Real S&P 500 Please Stand Up? Investment Firms Disagree on Index," *The Wall Street Journal.*

Database Exercise

Refer to the employee database in Appendix A.

1 Write a 3–5-page report summarizing the relationship between gender and salary for these employees. Be sure to discuss the results of the following statistical analyses: (a) a two-sample *t*-test of male salaries against female salaries, and (b) a multiple regression to explain salary using age, experience, and an indicator variable for gender.

Project

Perform a multiple regression analysis using business data of your choice, and write up the results as a report to upper-level management, either as a background summary report or as a proposal for action. Your report should include 5–7 pages plus an appendix and should be based on the following format:

a. *Introduction:* Describe the background and questions of interest and the data set clearly as if to an intelligent person who knows nothing about the details of the situation.

b. *Analysis and Methods:* Analyze the data, presenting displays and results, explaining as you go along. Consider including some of each of the following:
  (1) *Explore* the data using histograms or box plots for each variable and using scatterplots for each pair of variables.

(2) Use a *transformation* (such as the logarithm) *only* if this would clearly help the analysis by dealing with a big problem in the diagnostic plot.

(3) Compute the *correlation* of each pair of variables, and interpret these values.

(4) Report the *multiple linear regression* to predict one variable (chosen appropriately) from the others. Comment on how good the regression analysis is both in terms of prediction accuracy (standard error of estimate) and how well it explains the relationship (coefficient of determination). In particular: Are your results reasonable? Are they statistically significant?

c. *Conclusion and summary:* What has this analysis told you about the situation? How have your questions been answered?

d. *Appendix:* List the data, with their source indicated (a photocopy of the data set is acceptable). (This does not count toward the page limit.)

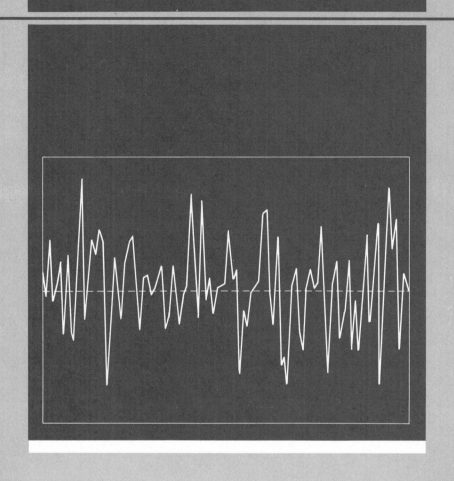

14 Time Series
Understanding Changes over Time

A time series is different from cross-sectional data because *ordering of the observations conveys important information.* In particular, you are interested in more than just a typical value to summarize the entire series (the average, for example) or even the variability of the series (as described by, say, the standard deviation). You would like to know *what is likely to happen next.* Such a forecast must carefully extend the most recent behavior with respect to the patterns over time, which are evident in past behavior. Here are some examples of time-series situations:

1 In order to prepare a budget for next quarter, you need a good estimate of the expected sales. This forecast will be the basis for predicting the other numbers in the budget, perhaps using regression analysis. By looking at a time series of actual quarterly sales for the past few years, you should be able to come up with a forecast that represents your "best guess" based on the overall trend in sales (up, hopefully) and taking into account any seasonal variation. For example, if there has always been a downturn from fourth quarter (which includes the holiday shopping season) to first quarter, you will want your forecast to reflect the usual seasonal pattern.

2 In order to decide whether to build that new factory or not, you need to know how quickly your market will grow. Analyzing the available time-series data on industry sales and prices will help you evaluate your chances for success. But don't expect to get exact answers. Predicting the future is a tricky and uncertain business, even with all of the computerized help you can get. Although time-series analysis will help you by providing a "reality check" to your decision making, substantial risk may still remain.

3 By constantly monitoring time-series data related to your firm, both internal (sales, cost, etc.) and external (industrywide sales, imports, etc.),

you will be in the best position to manage effectively. By anticipating future trends corresponding to those you spotted in the early stages, you will be ready to participate in growth areas or to move away from dead-end markets. By anticipating seasonal needs for cash, you can avoid the panic of having too little and the costs of having too much. By anticipating the need for inventory, you can avoid the losses due to unfilled orders (which help your competition) and the costs (interest and storage) of carrying too much. There is a tremendous amount of valuable information contained in these time-series data sets.

14.1 An Overview of Time-Series Analysis

Methods from previous chapters (confidence intervals and hypothesis tests, for example) must be modified before they will work with time series data. Why? Because the necessary assumptions are not satisfied. In particular, a time series is *not a random sample* from a population.[1] Tomorrow's price, for example, is likely to be closer to today's than to last year's price; successive observations are *not* independent of one another. If you go ahead and compute confidence intervals and hypothesis tests in the usual way, the danger is that your error rate might be much higher than the 5% you might claim. Time-series analysis requires specialized methods that take into account the dependence among observations. The basic ideas and concepts of statistical inference are the same, but the methods are adapted to a new situation.

The primary goal of time-series analysis is to create forecasts of the future. This requires a model to describe your time series. A **model** (also called a **mathematical model** or a **process**) is a system of equations that can produce an assortment of artificial time-series data sets. Here are the basic steps involved in forecasting:

1 Select a family of time-series models.
2 Estimate the particular model (within this chosen family) that produces artificial data matching the essential features (but not the quirks and exceptions) of the actual time-series data set.
3 Your **forecast** will be the expected (i.e., mean) value of the future behavior of the estimated model. Note that you can predict the future for a mathematical model by using a computer, even though the future of the actual series is unavailable.
4 The **forecast limits** are the confidence limits for your forecast (if the model can product them); if the model is correct, the future observation has a 95% probability, for example, of being within these limits. The limits are computed in the usual way from the standard error, which represents the variability of the future behavior of the estimated model.

---

[1] The exception is the *pure random noise process,* described in Section 14.3.

Following these steps does more than just produce forecasts. By selecting an appropriate model that produces data sets that "look like" your actual series, you gain insight into the patterns of behavior of the series. This kind of deeper statistical understanding of "how the world works" will be useful to you as background information in decision making.

Although we all want dependable forecasts of the future, don't expect forecasts to be exactly right. The forecast accuracy we would really like to have is probably impossible because the truly unexpected, by definition, cannot be foreseen.[2] However, the need for forecasts is so strong that people are willing to try anything that *might* lead to a slight improvement, and sophisticated statistical methods have been developed to help fill this need. Although the results may be the best we can come up with based on the available information, they still might not suit your real needs very well.

There are many different approaches to time-series analysis. The methods of time series analysis are varied and are still evolving. Following some examples of time-series data sets, we will discuss two of the most important methods for analyzing time series in business:

1 *Trend-seasonal analysis* is a direct, intuitive approach to estimating the basic components of a monthly or quarterly time series. These components include (1) the long-term trend; (2) the exactly repeating seasonal patterns; (3) the medium-term, wandering, cyclic ups and downs; and (4) the random, irregular "noise." Forecasts are obtained by imposing the usual seasonal patterns on the long-term trend.

2 *Box-Jenkins ARIMA processes* are flexible linear models that can precisely describe a wide variety of different time-series behaviors, including even the medium-term ups and downs of the so-called business cycle. Although these basic models are fairly simple to describe, their estimation requires extensive computer calculations. Forecasts and confidence limits are obtained by statistical theory based on the future behavior of the estimated model.

EXAMPLE

The Stock Market Is a Random Walk

Each day's closing value of a stock market index—for example, the Dow Jones Industrial Average—forms a time series of vital importance to many of us. Figure 14.1.1 shows a typical time-series graph, with the series itself plotted ver-

---

[2]For example, on January 2, 1985, *The Wall Street Journal* reported the forecasts of prominent economists together with the actual outcome. The average six-month-ahead forecast for the short-term U.S. Treasury bill interest rate was 10.64%. Six months later, the actual interest rate turned out to be 7.84%. When you consider that a difference of one quarter of a percentage point in interest rates is worth about $1,000 in present value to your typical first-time home purchaser, such a difference is worth huge amounts to industry and the economy. None of the economists, with all of their sophisticated forecasting methods, had expected such a steep plunge in interest rates.

tically as *Y* against time (in number of trading days), which is plotted horizontally as *X*.

What information would be lost if you were to draw a histogram of the Dow Jones index values, compute the average, or find an ordinary confidence interval? You would lose information about the *ordering* of the observations; you would be treating the index values as if they had been arranged in an arbitrary sequence. Figure 14.1.2 demonstrates that essential information is lost when a

FIGURE 14.1.1 A time-series plot of the Dow Jones Industrial Average, daily from July 31 through October 9, 1987.

Trading days since July 31, 1987

FIGURE 14.1.2 The results of randomly shuffling the order of the data in the time series from the preceding figure. Essential information is lost because all time trends disappear. Time-series analysis requires special methods that will *not* lose this important information.

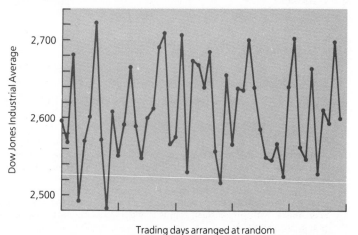

Trading days arranged at random

random ordering is used, showing why special time-series methods are needed that will take advantage of this important information. A good time-series method for stock market data should recognize that the stock market usually changes by a small amount each day (relative to the day before) as it wanders through its ups and downs.

The financial theory of efficient markets argues that the stock market should follow a *random walk*, in which the daily changes amount to unpredictable, random noise.[3] Figure 14.1.3 shows that the daily changes (today's value minus yesterday's value) in stock market price over this time period are indeed random.

The *random walk* model is included within the Box-Jenkins ARIMA framework as a special case of a series that "knows" only where it is but not how it got there.

EXAMPLE   Aerospace Orders Showed Steady Growth

The aerospace industry has enjoyed substantial growth over the past few decades. Table 14.1.1 shows the number of new orders for aerospace vehicles (aircraft, aircraft engines, missile and spacecraft engines, missiles, and spacecraft) placed each year from 1961 through 1986.

FIGURE 14.1.3   The daily changes in the Dow Jones Industrial Average, in proper order (no shuffling). This is basically a random series, supporting the *random walk* model for stock behavior.

[3]Because large investors act immediately on their available information, any *foreseeable* trends are already reflected in the stock price. The only changes that are possible are due to the *unforeseeable*, or randomness. A more careful analysis would work with the percent change rather than the change itself; this makes a difference only when a series has changed by an appreciable percentage of its value over the entire time period.

TABLE 14.1.1   Aerospace Vehicles

Year	New Orders	Year	New Orders
1961	13,418	1974	32,704
1962	14,963	1975	28,995
1963	17,637	1976	35,992
1964	17,970	1977	38,922
1965	22,213	1978	49,819
1966	27,233	1979	67,561
1967	26,900	1980	69,624
1968	27,168	1981	74,922
1969	22,005	1982	89,168
1970	21,161	1983	91,647
1971	21,553	1984	104,863
1972	23,842	1985	110,968
1973	27,044	1986	110,836

Data are from U.S. Department of Commerce, Bureau of Economic Analysis, *Business Statistics 1986* (Washington: U.S. Government Printing Office, 1987), p. 141.

FIGURE 14.1.4   Steady growth: the number of new orders for aerospace vehicles from 1961 to 1986.

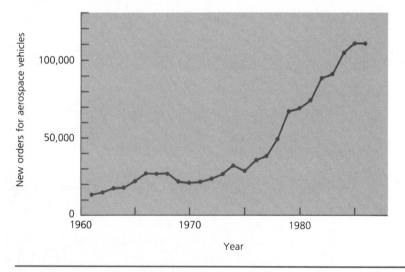

The time-series plot in Figure 14.1.4 shows overall steady growth, with increased orders nearly every year. The upward curvature suggests a constant growth rate, which would result in exponential growth. One way to estimate the rate of growth is to use the regression coefficient for predicting the logarithm of the time-series data (Y) from the time period (X). Table 14.1.2 shows the logarithms of the time-series values.

A time-series plot of the logarithms, Figure 14.1.5, shows a linear (i.e., straight-line) relationship, confirming the pattern of exponential growth at a constant rate for new orders.

TABLE 14.1.2   Aerospace Vehicles and Logarithms

Year, X	New Orders	Natural Logarithm of New Orders, Y
1961	13,418	9.50
1962	14,963	9.61
1963	17,637	9.78
1964	17,970	9.80
1965	22,213	10.01
1966	27,233	10.21
1967	26,900	10.20
1968	27,168	10.21
1969	22,005	10.00
1970	21,161	9.96
1971	21,553	9.98
1972	23,842	10.08
1973	27,044	10.21
1974	32,704	10.40
1975	28,995	10.27
1976	35,992	10.49
1977	38,922	10.57
1978	49,819	10.82
1979	67,561	11.12
1980	69,624	11.15
1981	74,922	11.22
1982	89,168	11.40
1983	91,647	11.43
1984	104,863	11.56
1985	110,968	11.62
1986	110,836	11.62

FIGURE 14.1.5   The logarithms of new orders show linear (straight-line) growth over time. This indicates that the orders have grown at a constant rate (i.e., exponential growth).

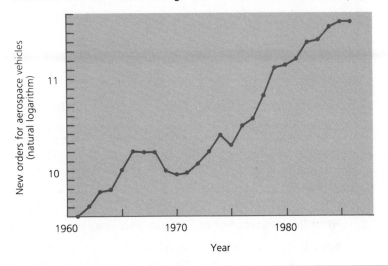

FIGURE 14.1.6 The logarithms of new orders for aerospace vehicles (*Y*) plotted against time (*X*), together with the least-squares regression line. The regression coefficient, a slope of 0.0832, is used to find the yearly growth rate of 8.7%.

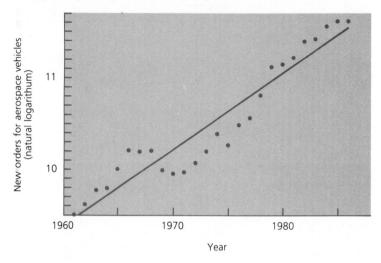

The estimated regression line is shown in Figure 14.1.6. The regression equation is

Predicted log of new orders = −153.723 + 0.083218 × Year

Each additional year adds the regression coefficient 0.083218 to the previous predicted log, so (using the exponential function to undo the logarithm) it *multiplies* the previous number of new orders by

$$e^{0.083218} = 2.71828^{0.083218} = 1.086779$$

By subtracting 1, we find that the estimated growth rate in new aerospace orders is 8.7% per year from 1961 through 1986:

Growth rate = 8.7%

Note that the data points are *not* randomly distributed about the regression line in Figure 14.1.6. A series that has this tendency, staying above the line for a while and then staying below for a while, is said to have *serial correlation*. Although the least-squares line is still a good estimator of growth, statistical inference (confidence intervals and hypothesis tests) would give incorrect results because serial correlation is not permitted in the linear regression model of Chapter 11.

EXAMPLE   Total Retail Sales Show Growth and Seasonal Variation

Table 14.1.3 shows the raw, unadjusted total U.S. retail sales, in millions, monthly from 1984 through 1986. The time-series plot of these sales figures, in Figure 14.1.7, shows steady overall growth with substantial variation (bumpiness)

TABLE 14.1.3   U.S. Retail Sales, Unadjusted

Year	Month	Sales (millions)	Year	Month	Sales (millions)
1984	January	$ 92,409	1985	July	$115,765
1984	February	93,202	1985	August	121,374
1984	March	103,815	1985	September	114,489
1984	April	104,055	1985	October	116,491
1984	May	111,246	1985	November	118,686
1984	June	111,725	1985	December	139,332
1984	July	106,319	1986	January	106,726
1984	August	110,574	1986	February	100,459
1984	September	103,433	1986	March	114,915
1984	October	108,960	1986	April	116,334
1984	November	112,732	1986	May	126,087
1984	December	130,903	1986	June	120,973
1985	January	98,806	1986	July	121,446
1985	February	95,645	1986	August	124,721
1985	March	110,204	1986	September	125,444
1985	April	113,207	1986	October	123,835
1985	May	120,491	1986	November	121,365
1985	June	115,131	1986	December	152,106

Data are from U.S. Department of Commerce, Bureau of Economic Analysis, *Business Statistics 1986* (Washington: U.S. Government Printing Office, 1987), p. 37.

FIGURE 14.1.7   U.S. retail sales, monthly from 1984 through 1986. Note the strong seasonal pattern that repeats each year, as well as the steady overall growth.

from one month to the next. A close look at this variation revelas that it is not just random but repeats itself fairly closely from one year to the next. The highest points are in December (just before the start of the next year); sales then drop to the lowest values, in January and February. This kind of seasonal pattern matches our perception of holiday season shopping patterns in the United States.

The government also provides *seasonally adjusted* sales figures, removing the predictable changes from one month to the next, as shown in Table 14.1.4. When the predictable seasonal patterns are removed from the series, the result is a much smoother indication of steady growth, as shown in Figure 14.1.8 (compare to previous figure). The remaining variation indicates fluctuations that were not consistent from one year to the next. These reflect changes that were not expected at that time of year.

TABLE 14.1.4   U.S. Retail Sales

| Year | Month | Sales (millions) | |
		Unadjusted	Adjusted for Seasonal Variation
1984	January	$ 92,409	$105,098
1984	February	93,202	105,079
1984	March	103,815	104,163
1984	April	104,055	106,264
1984	May	111,246	106,964
1984	June	111,725	108,686
1984	July	106,319	107,125
1984	August	110,574	106,620
1984	September	103,433	107,585
1984	October	108,960	108,623
1984	November	112,732	110,029
1984	December	130,903	109,835
1985	January	98,806	110,569
1985	February	95,645	111,839
1985	March	110,204	112,500
1985	April	113,207	114,511
1985	May	120,491	114,504
1985	June	115,131	114,163
1985	July	115,765	115,185
1985	August	121,374	116,904
1985	September	114,489	119,091
1985	October	116,491	115,711
1985	November	118,686	116,412
1985	December	139,332	117,389
1986	January	106,726	118,393
1986	February	100,459	117,590
1986	March	114,915	117,259
1986	April	116,334	118,113
1986	May	126,087	119,507
1986	June	120,973	119,605
1986	July	121,446	120,478
1986	August	124,721	121,839
1986	September	125,444	128,952
1986	October	123,835	122,121
1986	November	121,365	121,678
1986	December	152,106	127,613

Data are from U.S. Department of Commerce, Bureau of Economic Analysis, *Business Statistics 1986* (Washington: U.S. Government Printing Office, 1987), p. 38.

FIGURE 14.1.8   Seasonally adjusted U.S. retail sales, monthly from 1984 through 1986. The seasonal pattern has been eliminated, and the impression of steady growth has been enhanced. The remaining variation indicates changes that were not expected at that time of year.

TABLE 14.1.5   U.S. Treasury Bills

Year	Yield	Year	Yield
1961	2.38%	1974	7.89%
1962	2.78	1975	5.84
1963	3.16	1976	4.99
1964	3.55	1977	5.26
1965	3.95	1978	7.22
1966	4.88	1979	10.04
1967	4.32	1980	11.51
1968	5.34	1981	14.08
1969	6.68	1982	10.69
1970	6.46	1983	8.52
1971	4.35	1984	9.57
1972	4.07	1985	7.47
1973	7.04	1986	5.96

Data are from U.S. Department of Commerce, Bureau of Economic Analysis, *Business Statistics 1986* (Washington: U.S. Government Printing Office, 1987), pp. 65, 204. These are the rates on new issues of taxable three-month bills.

EXAMPLE

Interest Rates

One way the U.S. government raises cash is by selling securities. Treasury bills are short-term securities, with one year or less until the time they mature, at which time they pay back the initial investment plus interest. Table 14.1.5 shows yields (interest rates) on U.S. Treasury bills each year from 1961 through 1986.

FIGURE 14.1.9   Interest rates on three-month U.S. Treasury bills from 1961 through 1986 have shown an overall increasing trend with cyclic fluctuations. These cycles, however, have various lengths and are not expected to repeat exactly the way seasonal patterns do.

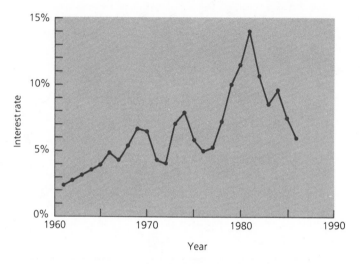

The time-series plot, in Figure 14.1.9, indicates a general rise in interest rates over this time period with substantial variation. There appears to be a cyclic pattern of rising and falling rates of increasing magnitude; however, use caution in interpreting this pattern. Because of government intervention, economists do not generally expect this pattern of massively increasing interest rates to continue.

Unlike the example of new aerospace orders, interest rates are not expected to continue growing in the future. Unlike the example of retail sales, the cycles of interest rates in Figure 14.1.9 do not show an exactly repeating pattern.

A time series that wanders about will often form trends and cycles that are not really expected to continue in the future. The Box-Jenkins ARIMA process approach (to be presented in Section 14.3) is especially well suited to this kind of time-series behavior because it takes into account the fact that a series will usually appear to produce cycles whenever it wanders about.

■ 14.2 Trend-Seasonal Analysis

Trend-seasonal analysis is a direct, intuitive approach to estimating the four basic components of a monthly or quarterly time series: the long-term trend, the seasonal patterns, the cyclic variation, and the irregular component. The basic time-series model expresses the numbers in the series as the product obtained by multiplying these basic components together.

> ■ **Trend-seasonal time-series model**
>
> Data = Trend × Seasonal × Cyclic × Irregular

Here are the definitions of these four components:

1 The long-term **trend** indicates the *very* long-term behavior of the time series, typically as a straight line or an exponential curve. This is useful in seeing the overall picture.

2 The exactly repeating **seasonal component** indicates the effects of the time of year. For example, heating demands are high in the winter months, sales are high in December, and agricultural sales are high at harvest time. Each time period during the year has its *seasonal index,* which indicates how much higher or lower this particular time usually is as compared to the others. For example, with quarterly data there would be a seasonal index for each quarter; an index of 1.235 for the fourth quarter says that sales are about 23.5% higher at this time compared to all quarters during the year. An index of 0.921 for the second quarter says that sales are 7.9% lower (since $1 - 0.921 = 0.079$) at this time.

3 The medium-term **cyclic component** consists of the gradual ups and downs that do *not* repeat each year and so are excluded from the seasonal component. Since they are gradual, they are not random enough to be considered part of the independent random error (the irregular component). The cyclic variation is especially difficult to forecast beyond the immediate future, yet it can be very important since basic business cycle phenomena (such as recessions) are considered to be part of the cyclic variation in economic performance.

4 The short-term, random **irregular component** represents the leftover, residual variation that can't be explained. It is the effect of those one-time occurrences that happen randomly, rather than systematically, over time. The best that can be done with the irregular component is to summarize how large it is (using a standard deviation, for example), to determine whether it changes over time, and to recognize that even in the best situation, a forecast can be no closer (on average) than the typical size of the irregular variation.

The four basic components of a time series (trend, seasonal, cyclic, and irregular components) can be estimated in different ways. Here is an overview of the **ratio-to-moving-average** method (to be presented in detail), which divides the series by a smooth moving average as follows:

1 A *moving average* is used to eliminate the seasonal effects by averaging over the entire year, reducing the irregular component and producing a combination of trend and cyclic components.

2 Dividing the series by the smoothed moving average series gives you the *ratio-to-moving-average,* which includes both seasonal and irregular val-

ues. Grouping by time of year and then averaging within groups, you find the *seasonal index* for each time of year. Dividing each series value by the appropriate seasonal index for its time of year, you find *seasonally adjusted* values.

3 A regression of the seasonally adjusted series (Y) on time (X) is used to estimate the *long-term trend* as a straight line over time.[4] This trend has no seasonal variation and leads to a seasonally adjusted forecast.

4 Forecasting may be done by *seasonalizing the trend.* Taking predicted values from the regression equation (the trend) for future time periods and then multiplying by the appropriate seasonal index, you get forecasts that reflect both the long-term trend and the seasonal behavior.

The advantages of the ratio-to-moving-average method are its easy computation and interpretation. The main disadvantage is that the model is not completely specified; therefore, measures of uncertainty (such as forecast limits) are not easily found.[5]

The following example of a time series exhibits all of these components. We will refer back to this example through the remainder of this section.

EXAMPLE   **Washington Water Power Company**

Table 14.2.1 shows the quarterly operating revenues as reported by Washington Water Power Company, an electric and natural gas utility serving eastern Washington and northern Idaho. This time series shows distinct seasonal patterns. Revenues are typically high in the first and fourth quarters, as can be seen in the time series plot of the data (Figure 14.2.1). Since the seasonal pattern is not repeated perfectly each year, there will be some cyclic and irregular behavior as well. Note also the long-term trend, represented by the general rise over time (except, perhaps, at the end of the series).

The results of a trend-seasonal analysis are shown in Figure 14.2.2. The trend is a straight line, the seasonal index repeats exactly each year, the cyclic component wanders erratically, and the irregular component is basically random. Because the cyclic and irregular components are small compared to the seasonal variations, they have been enlarged in Figure 14.2.3 to show that they really are cyclic and irregular. The computations for this analysis will be explained soon; at this point you should understand how the basic components relate to the original time series.

Trend and Cyclic: The Moving Average

Our objective is to identify the four basic components of a time series. We begin by averaging a year's worth of data at a time in order to eliminate the

---

[4]For example, this time variable, X, might consist of the numbers $1, 2, 3, \ldots$.

[5]In particular, the partially random structure of the cyclic component is not spelled out in detail. This problem is not solved by the multiple regression approach, which uses indicator variables to estimate seasonal indices.

TABLE 14.2.1   Washington Water Power Company

Year	Quarter	Operating Revenues[a] (thousands)
1980	1	$ 91,707
1980	2	63,048
1980	3	57,041
1980	4	78,667
1981	1	96,794
1981	2	74,949
1981	3	56,791
1981	4	89,127
1982	1	116,250
1982	2	71,998
1982	3	59,620
1982	4	98,985
1983	1	106,878
1983	2	71,800
1983	3	65,880
1983	4	94,254
1984	1	122,915
1984	2	92,079
1984	3	80,241
1984	4	118,075
1985	1	150,682
1985	2	96,967
1985	3	85,492
1985	4	126,312
1986	1	129,762
1986	2	82,597
1986	3	74,167
1986	4	103,340

Data are from Washington Water Power Company Annual Reports, 1980–1986.

seasonal component and reduce the irregular component. A **moving average** is a new series created by averaging nearby observations of a time series, then moving along to the next time period; this produces a less bumpy series. We average a full year at a time so that the seasonal components always contribute in the same way regardless of where in the year you are.

> Moving average = Trend × Cyclic

Here is how to find the moving average for quarterly data at a given time period. Start with the value at this time, add it to the values of its neighbors, then add *half* the values of the next neighbors, and divide by 4. Such a weighted average is needed so that the span is symmetric around the base time and still captures exactly a year of data.[6] If you have monthly data, av-

---

[6] By weighting the extremes by 1/2, you ensure that this quarter counts just the same in the moving average as the other quarters.

FIGURE 14.2.1   A time series plot of quarterly revenues of the Washington Water Power Company. Note the strong seasonal effects that repeat each year. You can also see an upward long-term trend throughout most of this time period, as well as some irregular behavior.

FIGURE 14.2.2   Quarterly revenues broken down into the four basic components: a straight-line trend, a seasonal index that repeats each year, a wandering cyclic component, and a random irregular component. These are shown on the same scale as the original series.

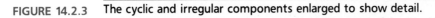

FIGURE 14.2.3   The cyclic and irregular components enlarged to show detail.

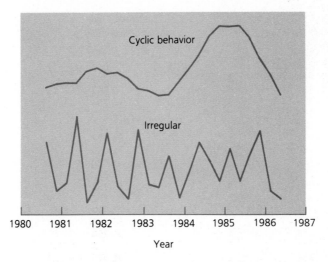

erage the series at the base time period together with the five nearest months on each side and half of the next one out on each side. The moving average is unavailable for the first two and last two quarters or, for a monthly series, for the first six and last six months.

For the Washington Water Power Company, the moving average of operating revenues for the third quarter of 1980 is given by [(1/2) × 91,707 + 63,048 + 57,041 + 78,667 + (1/2) × 96,794]/4 = 73,252. For the fourth quarter of 1980, the moving-average value is [(1/2) × 63,048 + 57,041 + 78,667 + 96,794 + (1/2) × 74,949]/4 = 75,375. The moving-average values are shown in Table 14.2.2 and are displayed in the time series plot of Figure 14.2.4.

Seasonal Index: The Average Ratio-to-Moving-Average Indicates Seasonal Behavior

To isolate the seasonal behavior, start by taking the ratio of the original data to the moving average (this is where the ratio-to-moving-average gets its name). The result will include the seasonal and irregular components because the moving average cancels out the trend and cyclic components in the data:

$$(\text{Seasonal})\,(\text{Irregular}) = \frac{\text{Data}}{\text{Moving average}}$$

TABLE 14.2.2   Washington Water Power Company Revenues with Moving Average

Year	Quarter	Operative Revenues (thousands)	Moving Average of Operating Revenues (thousands)
1980	1	$ 91,707	(unavailable)
1980	2	63,048	(unavailable)
1980	3	57,041	$ 73,252
1980	4	78,667	75,375
1981	1	96,794	76,832
1981	2	74,949	78,108
1981	3	56,791	81,847
1981	4	89,127	83,910
1982	1	116,250	83,895
1982	2	71,998	85,481
1982	3	59,620	85,542
1982	4	98,985	84,346
1983	1	106,878	85,103
1983	2	71,800	85,294
1983	3	65,880	86,708
1983	4	94,254	91,247
1984	1	122,915	95,577
1984	2	92,079	100,350
1984	3	80,241	106,798
1984	4	118,075	110,880
1985	1	150,682	112,148
1985	2	96,967	113,834
1985	3	85,492	112,148
1985	4	126,312	107,837
1986	1	129,762	104,625
1986	2	82,597	100,338
1986	3	74,167	(unavailable)
1986	4	103,340	(unavailable)

FIGURE 14.2.4   The moving average of operating revenues for Washington Water Power Company. The seasonal and irregular patterns have been eliminated, leaving only the trend and cyclic patterns.

Next, to eliminate the irregular component, you average these values for each season. The seasonal component will emerge because it is present each year, whereas the irregular will tend to be averaged away. The end results include a **seasonal index** for each time of the year, a factor that indicates how much larger or smaller this particular time period is compared to a typical period during the year. For example, a seasonal index of 1.30 for the first quarter indicates that the first quarter is generally 30% larger than a typical quarter. On the other hand, a third-quarter seasonal index of 0.74 would indicate that the third quarter is generally 26% lower.

$$\text{Seasonal index} = \text{Average of} \left(\frac{\text{Data}}{\text{Moving average}} \right) \text{for that season}$$

For the Washington Water Power Company, the first ratio-to-moving-average value is $57,041/73,252 = 0.77870$ for the third quarter of 1980. The third-quarter seasonal index is found by averaging these third-quarter ratios for all of the available years, as shown in Table 14.2.3.

Once each seasonal index has been found, it can be used throughout, even when the moving average is unavailable, because the seasonal pattern is exactly repeating, by definition. Table 14.2.4 shows the ratio-to-moving-average values and seasonal indexes for Washington Water Power Company. The typical yearly pattern is shown in Figure 14.2.5, and the repeating seasonal pattern is shown in Figure 14.2.6.

Seasonal Adjustment: The Series Divided by the Seasonal Index

On April 18, 1989, *The Wall Street Journal* reported a seasonally adjusted statistic on its front page:

> Paper and paperboard production in the United States fell in February to a seasonally adjusted annual rate of 76.8 million tons from a revised 77.4 million tons in January, the American Paper Institute reports.

TABLE 14.2.3 Computing the Third-Quarter Seasonal Index for Washington Water Power Company

Year	Third-Quarter Ratio-to-Moving-Average
1980	0.77870
1981	0.69387
1982	0.69697
1983	0.75979
1984	0.75133
1985	0.76163
1986	(unavailable)
Average	0.7404

TABLE 14.2.4 Washington Water Power Company Revenues and Seasonal Indexes

Year	Quarter	Operating Revenues (thousands)	Moving Average (thousands)	Ratio-to-Moving-Average	Seasonal Index
1980	1	$ 91,707	(unavailable)	(unavailable)	1.2952
1980	2	63,048	(unavailable)	(unavailable)	0.8727
1980	3	57,041	$ 73,252	0.77870	0.7404
1980	4	78,667	75,375	1.04367	1.0914
1981	1	96,794	76,832	1.25982	1.2952
1981	2	74,949	78,108	0.95956	0.8727
1981	3	56,791	81,847	0.69387	0.7404
1981	4	89,127	83,910	1.06217	1.0914
1982	1	116,250	83,895	1.38566	1.2952
1982	2	71,998	85,481	0.84227	0.8727
1982	3	59,620	85,542	0.69697	0.7404
1982	4	98,985	84,346	1.17357	1.0914
1983	1	106,878	85,103	1.25586	1.2952
1983	2	71,800	85,294	0.84179	0.8727
1983	3	65,880	86,708	0.75979	0.7404
1983	4	94,254	91,247	1.03295	1.0914
1984	1	122,915	95,577	1.28603	1.2952
1984	2	92,079	100,350	0.91758	0.8727
1984	3	80,241	106,798	0.75133	0.7404
1984	4	118,075	110,880	1.06489	1.0914
1985	1	150,682	112,148	1.34360	1.2952
1985	2	96,967	113,834	0.85183	0.8727
1985	3	85,492	112,248	0.76163	0.7404
1985	4	126,312	107,837	1.17132	1.0914
1986	1	129,762	104,625	1.24026	1.2952
1986	2	82,597	100,338	0.82319	0.8727
1986	3	74,167	(unavailable)	(unavailable)	0.7404
1986	4	103,340	(unavailable)	(unavailable)	1.0914

FIGURE 14.2.5 The seasonal indexes show that Washington Water Power Company operating revenues are typically highest in quarters 1 and 4 (the colder seasons) and lower during the rest of the year.

FIGURE 14.2.6 The seasonal component of Washington Water Power Company's operating revenues, extracted from the original series, is exactly repeating each year.

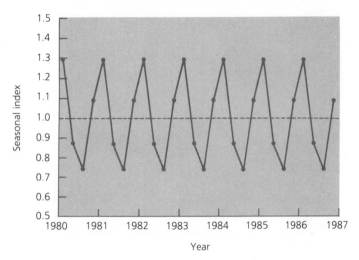

What is "seasonally adjusted," and how can there be a fall on a seasonally adjusted basis even though the actual value might have risen? **Seasonal adjustment** eliminates the expected seasonal component from a measurement (by dividing the series by the seasonal index for that period) so that one quarter or month may be directly compared to another (after seasonal adjustment) to reveal the underlying trends.

For retail sales, December is an especially good month. If sales are up in December as compared to November, it is no surprise; it is just the expected outcome. But if December sales are up even more than expected for this time of year, it may be time to bring out the champagne and visit that tropical island. To say, "December sales were higher than November's on a seasonally adjusted basis" is the same as saying, "December was up more than we expected." On the other hand, December sales could be way up but not as much as expected, so that December sales would actually be *down* on a seasonally adjusted basis.

To find a seasonally adjusted value, simply divide the original data value by the appropriate seasonal index for its month or quarter:

$$\text{Seasonally adjusted value} = \left(\frac{\text{Data}}{\text{Seasonal index}} \right) = \text{Trend} \times \text{Cyclic} \times \text{Irregular}$$

For the Washington Water Power Company, the seasonally adjusted revenues for first quarter of 1980 are the actual revenues (91,707, in thousands of dollars) divided by the first-quarter seasonal index (1.2952).

Seasonally adjusted
revenues for first   = \$91,707/1.2952 = \$70,805   (in thousands)
quarter 1980

Why is the seasonally adjusted result *smaller* than the actual revenues? Because revenues are generally higher in the first quarter compared to a typical quarter in the year. In fact, you expect first-quarter revenues to be approximately 29.5% higher (based on the seasonal index of 1.2952). Dividing by the seasonal index removes this expected seasonal fluctuation, reducing the first-quarter revenues to the status of a typical quarter.

In the next quarter (second quarter 1980), the seasonally adjusted revenue is 63,048/0.8727 = 72,245. Note that revenues fell sharply (from 91,707 to 63,048) from the first to the second quarter of 1980. However, on a seasonally adjusted basis, revenues actually *increased* from 70,805 to 72,245. This tells you that the drop, large as it seems, was actually smaller than you would expect for that time of year.

Note the large increase in revenues from the third to the fourth quarter of 1982 (from 59,620 to 98,985). On a seasonally adjusted basis, this was also a large increase (from 80,526 to 90,693). Seasonal adjustment confirms your impression that this is a "real" and not just a seasonal increase in revenues.

Table 14.2.5 shows the seasonally adjusted revenues for the entire time series. They are plotted in Figure 14.2.7 along with the original data. The seasonally adjusted series is somewhat smoother than the original data because the seasonal variation has been eliminated. However, some roughness remains because the irregular and cyclic components are present in the seasonally adjusted series, in addition to the trend.

Long-Term Trend and Seasonally Adjusted Forecast: The Regression Line

When a time series shows an upward or downward long-term linear trend over time, regression analysis can be used to estimate this trend and to forecast the future. Although this leads to a useful forecast, an even more careful and complex method (an *ARIMA process,* for example) would pay more attention to the cyclic component than the method presented here.

Here's how the regression analysis works. Use the time period as the X variable to predict the seasonally adjusted series as the Y variable.[7] The resulting regression equation will represent the long-term trend. By substituting future time periods as new X values, you will be able to forecast this long-term trend into the future.

---

[7]If your series shows substantial exponential growth rather than a linear relationship, as a new start-up firm might, you could use the *logarithm* of the seasonally adjusted series as your Y variable and then transform back your predicted values (see Chapter 12) to make the forecast.

TABLE 14.2.5 Washington Water Power Company Revenues and Seasonally Adjusted Revenues

Year	Quarter	Operating Revenues (thousands)	Seasonal Index	Seasonally Adjusted Revenues (thousands)
1980	1	$ 91,707	1.2952	$ 70,805
1980	2	63,048	0.8727	72,245
1980	3	57,041	0.7404	77,043
1980	4	78,667	1.0914	72,077
1981	1	96,794	1.2952	74,733
1981	2	74,949	0.8727	85,881
1981	3	56,791	0.7404	76,705
1981	4	89,127	1.0914	81,661
1982	1	116,250	1.2952	89,754
1982	2	71,998	0.8727	82,500
1982	3	59,620	0.7404	80,526
1982	4	98,985	1.0914	90,693
1983	1	106,878	1.2952	82,518
1983	2	71,800	0.8727	82,273
1983	3	65,880	0.7404	88,981
1983	4	94,254	1.0914	86,358
1984	1	122,915	1.2952	94,900
1984	2	92,079	0.8727	105,510
1984	3	80,241	0.7404	108,378
1984	4	118,075	1.0914	108,184
1985	1	150,682	1.2952	116,338
1985	2	96,967	0.8727	111,111
1985	3	85,492	0.7404	115,470
1985	4	126,312	1.0914	115,731
1986	1	129,762	1.2952	100,186
1986	2	82,597	0.8727	94,645
1986	3	74,167	0.7404	100,174
1986	4	103,340	1.0914	94,683

FIGURE 14.2.7 The seasonally adjusted series allows you to compare one quarter to another. By eliminating the *expected* seasonal changes, you have a clearer picture of where your business is heading.

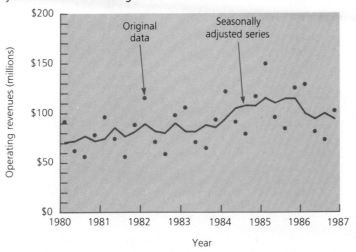

Be careful how you represent the time periods. It is important that the numbers you choose be evenly spaced.[8] One easy way to do this is to use the numbers 1, 2, 3,... to represent X directly in terms of number of time periods (quarters or months).

Table 14.2.6 shows the data for the regression analysis (last two columns) to detect the long-term trend for Washington Water Power Company.

The regression equation, estimated using least squares, is:

$$\text{Long-term trend} = 70,650.07 + 1,433.16(\text{Time period})$$

TABLE 14.2.6   Washington Water Power Company Revenues with Regression Variables to Find the Long-Term Trend

Year	Quarter	Operating Revenues (thousands)	Seasonally Adjusted Revenues (thousands), Y	Time Periods, X
1980	1	$ 91,707	$ 70,805	1
1980	2	63,048	72,245	2
1980	3	57,041	77,043	3
1980	4	78,667	72,077	4
1981	1	96,794	74,733	5
1981	2	74,949	85,881	6
1981	3	56,791	76,705	7
1981	4	89,127	81,661	8
1982	1	116,250	89,754	9
1982	2	71,998	82,500	10
1982	3	59,620	80,526	11
1982	4	98,985	90,693	12
1983	1	106,878	82,518	13
1983	2	71,800	82,273	14
1983	3	65,880	88,981	15
1983	4	94,254	86,358	16
1984	1	122,915	94,900	17
1984	2	92,079	105,510	18
1984	3	80,241	108,378	19
1984	4	118,075	108,184	20
1985	1	150,682	116,338	21
1985	2	96,967	111,111	22
1985	3	85,492	115,470	23
1985	4	126,312	115,731	24
1986	1	129,762	100,186	25
1986	2	82,597	94,645	26
1986	3	74,167	100,174	27
1986	4	103,340	94,683	28

---

[8]You would definitely *not* want to use 1984.1, 1984.2, 1984.3, 1984.4, 1985,... because these numbers are not evenly spaced. You might use 1984.125, 1984.375, 1984.625, 1984.875, 1985.125,... instead, which represents each time period as the halfway point of a quarter. The first quarter of 1980 is represented by its midpoint, 1980.125, which is halfway between the beginning (1980.000) and the end (1980.250), as found by averaging them: (1980.000 + 1980.250)/2 = 1980.125.

This suggests that Washington Water Power Company has grown at an average rate of $1,433 (in thousands) per quarter.[9]

It is easy to forecast this long-term trend by substituting the appropriate time period into the regression equation. For example, to find the trend value for the first quarter of 1987, use $X = 29$ to represent the next time period following the end of the series. The forecast is then:

$$\begin{aligned}
\text{Forecast trend value for first quarter 1987} &= \$70,650.07 + \$1,433.16(\text{Time period}) \\
&= \$70,650.07 + \$1,433.16 \times 29 \\
&= \$112,212 \text{ (in thousands)}
\end{aligned}$$

Table 14.2.7 shows the predicted values, giving the long-term trend values and their forecasts for two years beyond the end of the data. Figure 14.2.8 shows how this trend line summarizes the seasonally adjusted series and extends to the right by extrapolation to indicate the seasonally adjusted forecasts.

Forecast: The Seasonalized Trend

All you need to do now to forecast the future is to "seasonalize" the long-term trend by putting the expected seasonal variation back in. To do this, simply multiply the trend value by the appropriate seasonal index for the time period you are forecasting. This process is the *reverse* of seasonal adjustment. The resulting forecast includes the long-term trend and the seasonal variation.

Forecast = Trend × Seasonal index

To forecast the revenues of Washington Water Power Company for the first quarter of 1987, you would multiply the trend value of 112,212 (found by regression for the 29th time period) by the first-quarter seasonal index of 1.2952:

$$\text{Revenue forecast for first quarter 1987} = \$112,212 \times 1.2952 = \$145,337 \text{ (in thousands)}$$

Table 14.2.8 shows the forecasts for two years beyond the end of the data. Figure 14.2.9 shows how this seasonalized trend summarizes the series and extends to the right by extrapolation to provide reasonable forecasts that include the expected seasonal behavior of revenues.

---

[9]Since the revenue figures are in thousands, estimated growth has actually been $1,433,160 per quarter.

TABLE 14.2.7   Washington Water Power Company Revenues and Long-Term Trend Values

Year	Quarter	Operating Revenues (thousands)	Seasonally Adjusted Revenues (thousands), Y	Time Periods, X	Trend and Seasonally Adjusted Forecast (thousands), Predicted Y
1980	1	$ 91,707	$ 70,805	1	$ 72,083
1980	2	63,048	72,245	2	73,516
1980	3	57,041	77,043	3	74,950
1980	4	78,667	72,077	4	76,383
1981	1	96,794	74,733	5	77,816
1981	2	74,949	85,881	6	79,249
1981	3	56,791	76,705	7	80,682
1981	4	89,127	81,661	8	82,115
1982	1	116,250	89,754	9	83,548
1982	2	71,998	82,500	10	84,982
1982	3	59,620	80,526	11	86,415
1982	4	98,985	90,693	12	87,848
1983	1	106,878	82,518	13	89,281
1983	2	71,800	82,273	14	90,714
1983	3	65,880	88,981	15	92,147
1983	4	94,254	86,358	16	93,581
1984	1	122,915	94,900	17	95,014
1984	2	92,079	105,510	18	96,447
1984	3	80,241	108,378	19	97,880
1984	4	118,075	108,184	20	99,313
1985	1	150,682	116,338	21	100,746
1985	2	96,967	111,111	22	102,180
1985	3	85,492	115,470	23	103,613
1985	4	126,312	115,731	24	105,046
1986	1	129,762	100,186	25	106,479
1986	2	82,597	94,645	26	107,912
1986	3	74,167	100,174	27	109,345
1986	4	103,340	94,683	28	110,778
1987	1	(unavailable)	(unavailable)	29	112,212
1987	2			30	113,645
1987	3			31	115,078
1987	4			32	116,511
1988	1			33	117,944
1988	2			34	119,377
1988	3			35	120,811
1988	4			36	122,244

Should you believe these forecasts? Not necessarily. It depends on whether you believe that the recent cyclic downturn is permanent or not. This trend-seasonal analysis seems to indicate that it is temporary to a large extent. Unfortunately, you cannot always know these things for sure based only on the data available at the time.

FIGURE 14.2.8　The least-squares regression line used to predict the seasonally adjusted series from the time period can be extended to the right to provide seasonally adjusted forecasts.

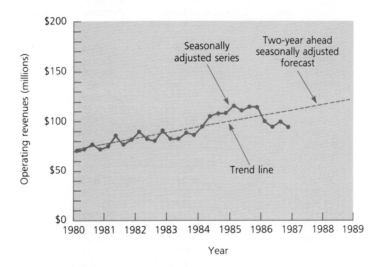

FIGURE 14.2.9　Forecasts are made by multiplying the trend line by the seasonal index. The result includes the trend and seasonal components but not the cyclic and irregular behavior of the series.

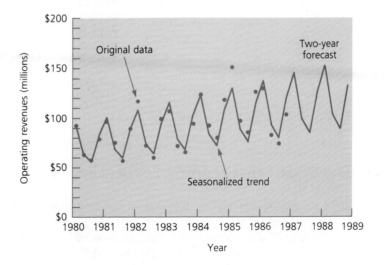

TABLE 14.2.8   Washington Water Power Company Revenues and Forecasts

Year	Quarter	Operating Revenues (thousands)	Trend and Seasonally Adjusted Forecast (thousands)	Seasonal Index	Forecast (thousands)
1980	1	$ 91,707	$ 72,083	1.2952	$ 93,363
1980	2	63,048	73,516	0.8727	64,158
1980	3	57,041	74,950	0.7404	55,491
1980	4	78,667	76,383	1.0914	83,366
1981	1	96,794	77,816	1.2952	100,788
1981	2	74,949	79,249	0.8727	69,161
1981	3	56,791	80,682	0.7404	59,736
1981	4	89,127	82,115	1.0914	89,623
1982	1	116,250	83,548	1.2952	108,212
1982	2	71,998	84,982	0.8727	74,164
1982	3	59,620	86,415	0.7404	63,980
1982	4	98,985	87,848	1.0914	95,880
1983	1	106,878	89,281	1.2952	115,637
1983	2	71,800	90,714	0.8727	79,167
1983	3	65,880	92,147	0.7404	68,224
1983	4	94,254	93,581	1.0914	102,137
1984	1	122,915	95,014	1.2952	123,062
1984	2	92,079	96,447	0.8727	84,169
1984	3	80,241	97,880	0.7404	72,469
1984	4	118,075	99,313	1.0914	108,393
1985	1	150,682	100,746	1.2952	130,487
1985	2	96,967	102,180	0.8727	89,172
1985	3	85,492	103,613	0.7404	76,713
1985	4	126,312	105,046	1.0914	114,650
1986	1	129,762	106,479	1.2952	137,912
1986	2	82,597	107,912	0.8727	94,175
1986	3	74,167	109,345	0.7404	80,957
1986	4	103,340	110,778	1.0914	120,907
1987	1	(unavailable)	112,212	1.2952	145,337
1987	2		113,645	0.8727	99,178
1987	3		115,078	0.7404	85,202
1987	4		116,511	1.0914	127,164
1988	1		117,944	1.2952	152,762
1988	2		119,377	0.8727	104,181
1988	3		120,811	0.7404	89,446
1988	4		122,244	1.0914	133,420

■ 14.3 Modeling Cyclic Behavior Using Box-Jenkins ARIMA Processes

The Box-Jenkins approach is one of the best methods we have for the important goals of *understanding* and *forecasting* a business time series. The resulting *ARIMA processes* are linear statistical models that can precisely describe many different time-series behaviors, including even the medium-term wandering of the so-called business cycle. Compared to the trend-seasonal approach of the previous section, the Box-Jenkins approach has a more solid statistical foundation but is somewhat less intuitive. As a result, you can obtain reliable statistical measures of uncertainty (a standard error for the forecast, for example) once you have found an appropriate model within the Box-Jenkins family.

Here's an outline of the steps involved "behind the scenes" when you use Box-Jenkins methods to help you understand what the forecasts and their confidence intervals represent:

1 A fairly simple process is chosen from the Box-Jenkins family of ARIMA processes that generates data with the same overall look as your series, except for randomness. This involves selecting a particular type of model and estimating the parameters from your data. The resulting model will tell you useful facts such as (a) the extent to which each observation influences the future and (b) the extent to which each observation brings useful new information to help you forecast.

2 The forecast for any time is the expected (i.e., average or mean) future value of the estimated process at that time. Imagine the universe of all reasonably possible future behaviors of your series, starting with your data and extending it into the future according to the model selected in step 1. The formula for the forecast quickly computes the average of all of these future scenarios.

3 The standard error of a forecast for any time is the standard deviation of all reasonably possible future values for that time.

4 The forecast limits extend above and below the forecast value such that (if the model is correct) there is a 95% chance, for example, that the future value for any time will fall within the forecast limits. They are constructed so that for each future time period, 95% of the reasonably possible future behaviors of your series fall within the limits. This assumes that your series will continue to behave similarly to the estimated process.

The **Box-Jenkins ARIMA processes** are a family of linear statistical models based on the normal distribution that have the flexibility to imitate the behavior of many different real time series by combining *autoregressive (AR) processes, integrated (I) processes,* and *moving-average (MA) processes.*[10] The result is a **parsimonious model,** that is, one that uses just a few estimated parameters to describe the complex behavior of a time series. Although the theory and computations involved are complex, the models themselves are fairly simple and are quickly calculated using a computer.

We will begin by reviewing the random noise process and then describe how each component of an ARIMA process adds structure and smoothness to the model. We will cover only some of the basics of these complex models.[11]

---

[10]The word *process* refers to any statistical procedure that produces time-series data.

[11]For further details, see C. R. Nelson, *Applied Time Series Analysis for Managerial Forecasting* (San Francisco: Holden-Day, 1973); or G. E. P. Box and G. M. Jenkins, *Time Series Analysis: Forecasting and Control* (San Francisco: Holden-Day, 1976).

A Random Noise Process Has No Memory: The Starting Point

A **random noise process** consists of a random sample (independent observations) from a normal distribution with constant mean and standard deviation. There are no trends because, due to independence, the observations "have no memory" of the past behavior of the series.

The model for random noise says that at time t the observed data, Y_t, will consist of a constant, μ (the long-term mean of the process), plus random noise, ε_t, with mean zero.

■ **The Random Noise Process**

Data = Mean value + Random noise

$$Y_t = \mu + \varepsilon_t$$

The long-term mean of Y is μ.

A random noise process tends to be basically flat (tilted neither up nor down), to be very irregular, and to have constant variability, as shown in Figure 14.3.1.

If you have a random noise process, the analysis is easy because the data form a random sample from a normal distribution—a situation you learned about in Chapters 9 and 10. The average is the best forecast for any future time period, and the ordinary prediction interval for a new observation gives you the forecast limits for any future value of the series.

Most business and economic time series data sets have some structure in addition to their random noise component. You may think of this structure in terms of the way each observation "remembers" the past behavior of the

---

FIGURE 14.3.1   A random noise process consists of independent observations from a normal distribution. It is basically flat and bumpy, with constant variability.

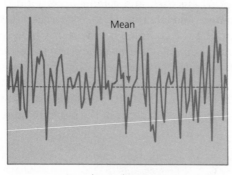

A random noise process

series. When this memory is strong, the series can be much smoother than a random noise process.

An Autoregressive (AR) Process Remembers Where It Was

An observation of an **autoregressive process** (the *AR* in ARIMA) consists of a linear function of the previous observation plus random noise.[12] Thus, an autoregressive process remembers where it was and uses this information in deciding where to go next.

The model for an autoregressive process says that at time t the data value Y_t consists of a constant, δ (delta), plus an autoregressive coefficient, φ (phi), times the previous data value, Y_{t-1}, plus random noise, ε_t. Note that this is a linear regression model that predicts the current level ($Y = Y_t$) from the previous level ($X = Y_{t-1}$). In effect, the series moves a proportion $(1 - \varphi)$ back toward its long-run mean and then moves a random distance from there. By increasing φ from 0 toward 1, you can make the process look smoother and less like random noise.[13] It is important that φ be less than 1 (in absolute value) in order that the process be stable.

■ The Autoregressive Process

Data = $\delta + \varphi$(Previous value) + Random noise

$$Y_t = \delta + \varphi Y_{t-1} + \varepsilon_t$$

The long-term mean value of Y is $\delta/(1 - \varphi)$.

Because it has memory, an autoregressive process can stay high for a while, then stay low for a while, and so on, thereby generating a cyclic pattern of ups and downs about a long-term mean value, as shown in Figure 14.3.2. The particular process shown here has $\varphi = 0.8$, so that $Y_t = 0.8Y_{t-1} + \varepsilon_t$, where ε has standard deviation 1 and is the same noise as in Figure 14.3.1.

Autoregressive models make sense for business data. They express the fact that where you go depends partly on where you are (as expressed by the autoregressive coefficient, φ) and partly on what happens to you along the way (as expressed by the random noise component).

Forecasting with an autoregressive process is done with predicted values from the estimated regression equation after going forward one unit in time, so that the predicted Y_{t+1} is $\hat{\delta} + \hat{\varphi}Y_t$. (The "hats" over the coefficients

---

[12]This is a *first-order* autoregressive process. In general, the observation might depend on *several* of the most recent observations, as determined by a multiple regression.

[13]If the coefficient, φ, is negative, the autoregressive process can actually be *more* bumpy than random noise because it tends to be alternatively high and low. We will assume that φ is positive so that an autoregressive process is smoother than random noise.

FIGURE 14.3.2 An autoregressive process evolves as a linear regression equation in which the current value helps predict the next value. Note that the series is less bumpy than pure noise (compare to Figure 14.3.1) and that it can stray from its long-term mean value for extended periods.

An autoregressive (AR) process

indicate that they are estimated from the data rather than the population values.) The forecast is a compromise between the most recent data value and the long-term mean value of the series. The further into the future you look, the closer to the long-term mean value your forecast will be because the process gradually "forgets" the distant past.

A Moving-Average (MA) Process Has a Limited Memory

An observation of a **moving-average process** (the *MA* in ARIMA) consists of a constant, μ (the long-term mean of the process), plus independent random noise minus a fraction of the previous random noise.[14] A moving-average process does not remember exactly where it was, but it does remember the random noise component of where it was. Thus, its memory is limited to one step into the future; beyond that it starts anew.

The model for a moving-average process says that at time t the data value, Y_t, consists of a constant, μ, plus random noise, ε_t, minus a fraction, θ (theta, the moving-average coefficient), of the previous random noise. By decreasing the coefficient, θ, from 0 to -1, you can make the process look less like random noise, but it will be only slightly smoother.[15]

---

[14]This is a *first-order* moving-average process. In general, the observation might depend on several of the most recent random noise components, and the limited memory could be several steps long.

[15]If the coefficient, θ, is positive, the moving-average process can actually be somewhat *more* bumpy than random noise because it tends to be alternately high and low. We will assume that θ is negative so that a moving-average process is somewhat smoother than random noise.

■ The Moving-Average Process

$$\text{Data} = \mu + \text{Random noise} - \theta(\text{Previous random noise})$$

$$Y_t = \mu + \varepsilon_t - \theta\varepsilon_{t-1}$$

The long-term mean value of Y is μ.

Because it has memory, a moving-average process can produce adjacent pairs of observations that are more likely to *both* be either high or low. However, because its memory is limited, the series is random again after only two steps. The result is a series that is not quite as random as a pure random noise series. Compare the moving-average process in Figure 14.3.3 to the pure random noise series of Figure 14.3.1 to see the decreased randomness. The particular process shown in Figure 14.3.3 has $\theta = -0.8$, so that $Y_t = \varepsilon_t + 0.8\varepsilon_{t-1}$, where ε has standard deviation 1 and is the same noise as in Figure 14.3.1. In fact, this series *is* a moving average of random noise.

Pure moving-average models have only limited applicability for business data because of their limited memory (as expressed by the moving-average coefficient, θ). They are best used in combination with autoregressive processes to permit a sharper focus on recent events than pure autoregressive processes allow.

Forecasting the next observation with a moving-average process is based on an estimate of the current random noise, $\hat{\varepsilon}_t$. Beyond the next observation, the best forecast is the estimated long-term mean, $\hat{\mu}$, because all but the immediate past has been forgotten.

FIGURE 14.3.3   A moving-average process remembers only part of the previous noise. The result is slightly less irregular than pure random noise (compare to Figure 14.3.1).
Two periods ahead, it becomes random again because it does not remember where it was.

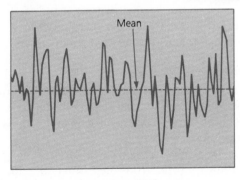

A moving-average (MA) process

The Autoregressive Moving-Average (ARMA) Process Combines AR and MA

An observation of an **autoregressive moving-average (ARMA) process** consists of a linear function of the previous observation plus independent random noise minus a fraction of the previous random noise. This combines an autoregressive process with a moving-average process.[16] An autoregressive moving-average process remembers both where it was and the random noise component of where it was. Thus, its memory combines that of the autoregressive process with that of the moving-average process. The result is an autoregressive process with an improved short-term memory.

The model for an autoregressive moving-average (ARMA) process says that at time t the data value, Y_t, consists of a constant, δ, plus an autoregressive coefficient, φ, times the previous data value, Y_{t-1}, plus random noise, ε_t, minus a fraction, θ, of the previous random noise. This is like a linear regression model except that the errors are not independent. As φ goes from 0 toward 1, and as θ goes from 0 to -1, the resulting process looks smoother and less like random noise. It is important that φ be less than 1 (in absolute value) in order that the process be stable.

■ **The Autoregressive Moving-Average (ARMA) Process**

Data = δ + φ(Previous value) + Random noise − θ(Previous random noise)

$$Y_t = \delta + \varphi Y_{t-1} + \varepsilon_t - \theta \varepsilon_{t-1}$$

The long-term mean value of Y is $\delta/(1 - \varphi)$.

Because of its memory, an ARMA process can stay high for a while, then stay low for a while, and so forth, generating a cyclic pattern of ups and downs about a long-term mean value, as shown in Figure 14.3.4. The particular process shown here has $\varphi = 0.8$ and $\theta = -0.8$, so that $Y_t = 0.8Y_{t-1} + \varepsilon_t + 0.8\varepsilon_{t-1}$ where ε has standard deviation 1 and is the same noise as in Figure 14.3.1. Since the purely autoregressive process (Figure 14.3.2) shares this same random noise, a comparison of Figures 14.3.2 and 14.3.4 shows the contribution of the moving-average term to the smoothness of this ARMA process.

The combination of autoregressive and moving-average processes is a powerful and useful one for business data. By adjusting the coefficients (φ and θ), you can choose a model to match any of a wide variety of cyclic and irregular time-series data sets.

Forecasting the next observation with an ARMA process is done by combining the predicted value from the estimated autoregression equation

---

[16]This is a *first-order* autoregressive moving-average process. In general, the observation might depend on several of the most recent observations and random noise components.

FIGURE 14.3.4   In an autoregressive moving-average (ARMA) process, both the current value and the current noise help determine the next value. The result is smoother due to the memory of the autoregressive process combined with the additional short-term (one-step-ahead) memory of the moving-average process.

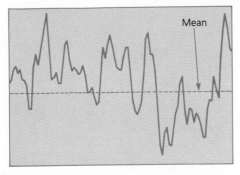

An autoregressive moving-average (ARMA) process

(predicted $Y_{t+1} = \hat{\delta} + \hat{\varphi} Y_t$, where "hats" again indicate estimates) with an estimate of the current random noise, ε_t. Beyond the next observation, the best forecast is based only on the previous forecast value. The further into the future you look, the closer to the long-term mean value, μ, your forecast will be because the process gradually forgets the distant past.

EXAMPLE   **Forecasting the Unemployment Rate Using an ARMA Process**

Table 14.3.1 shows the U.S. unemployment rate for all civilian workers, recorded by year from 1961 through 1986. This data set is graphed in Figure 14.3.5.

TABLE 14.3.1   Civilian Unemployment Rate

Year	Unemployment Rate	Year	Unemployment Rate
1961	6.7%	1974	5.6%
1962	5.5	1975	8.5
1963	5.7	1976	7.7
1964	5.2	1977	7.1
1965	4.5	1978	6.1
1966	3.8	1979	5.8
1967	3.8	1980	7.1
1968	3.6	1981	7.6
1969	3.5	1982	9.7
1970	4.9	1983	9.6
1971	5.9	1984	7.5
1972	5.6	1985	7.2
1973	4.9	1986	7.0

Data are from U.S. Department of Commerce, Bureau of Economic Analysis, *Business Statistics 1986* (Washington: U.S. Government Printing Office, 1987), p. 44.

FIGURE 14.3.5 The U.S. unemployment rate from 1961 through 1986. Note the degree of smoothness (this is obviously *not* just random noise) and the tendency toward cyclic behavior.

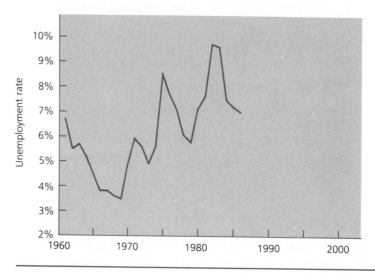

TABLE 14.3.2 Estimates of an ARMA Model Fitted to the Unemployment Rate Data

Coefficient	Estimate	Standard Error	t-ratio
Autoregression ($\hat{\varphi}$)	0.657	0.184	3.58
Moving average ($\hat{\theta}$)	−0.477	0.214	−2.23
Constant ($\hat{\delta}$)	2.159	0.289	7.47
Mean ($\hat{\delta}/(1 - \hat{\varphi})$)	6.293	0.842	7.47
Standard deviation of random noise	0.995		

An ARMA model was estimated for this data set, using the method of least squares, with the results as shown in Table 14.3.2.[17] Note that the autoregressive coefficient and the moving-average coefficient are both statistically significant, based on the *t*-ratio. This is an approximate test, and any *t*-ratio above 1.96 in absolute value is considered significant, provided the series is not too short.

---

[17] The goal of least-squares estimation is to make the random noise component as small as possible, so that as much as possible of the structure of the series is captured by the autoregressive and moving-average components of the model. When the noise is a random sample from a normal distribution, the powerful general method of maximum likelihood gives the same estimates as the method of least squares because of the exponentiated square term in the normal density function.

These results give us an ARMA model that produces time-series data that somewhat resemble the unemployment rate data, with the same kind of irregularity, smoothness, and cyclic behavior. This estimated ARMA model is as follows:

$$\text{Data} = 2.159 + 0.657(\text{Previous value}) + \text{Random noise}$$
$$+ \ 0.477(\text{Previous random noise})$$

$$Y_t = 2.159 + 0.657Y_{t-1} + \varepsilon_t + 0.477\varepsilon_{t-1}$$

This estimated model suggests that the unemployment rate does not change by large amounts from one year to the next, since each year's data value is generated taking the previous year's level into account. Literally, each year's data value is found by first moving $(1 - 0.657) = 34.3\%$ of the way from the current unemployment rate toward the long-run mean value of 6.293, then adding new random noise, and finally adding 47.7% of the previous random noise.

How closely do data from the estimated ARMA process mimic the unemployment rate? Figure 14.3.6 shows the actual unemployment rate together with two simulations created from the estimated ARMA process, starting at the same (6.7%) unemployment rate for 1961 but using different random noise. Think of these simulations as alternative scenarios of what might have happened instead of what actually did happen.

The real purpose of time-series analysis in business is to forecast. Table 14.3.3 shows forecasts of the unemployment rate, together with forecast limits, for the next 10 years as computed based on the estimated ARMA model. Figure 14.3.7

FIGURE 14.3.6   Two simulations from the estimated ARMA process together with the actual unemployment rate. Note how the artificial simulations have the same basic character as the real data in terms of smoothness, irregularities, and cycles. This ability to behave like the real series is an important feature of Box-Jenkins analysis.

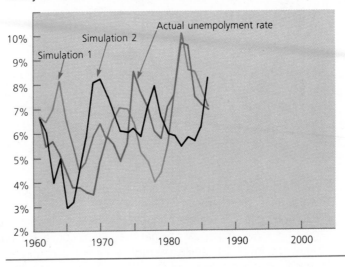

TABLE 14.3.3 Forecasts and Forecast Limits Given by the ARMA Model
Fitted to the Unemployment Rate Data

| Year | Forecast | 95% Forecast Limits | |
		Lower	Upper
1987	6.68%	4.73%	8.63%
1988	6.55	3.60	9.50
1989	6.46	3.18	9.75
1990	6.40	2.98	9.83
1991	6.37	2.89	9.84
1992	6.34	2.84	9.84
1993	6.32	2.81	9.84
1994	6.31	2.80	9.83
1995	6.31	2.79	9.83
1996	6.30	2.78	9.82

FIGURE 14.3.7 The unemployment rate, its 10-year-ahead forecast, and the 95% forecast limits, as computed based on the estimated ARMA model. The forecast says that the series, on average, will gradually forget that it is higher than its long-run mean. The forecast limits are wide enough to anticipate future cyclic and irregular behavior.

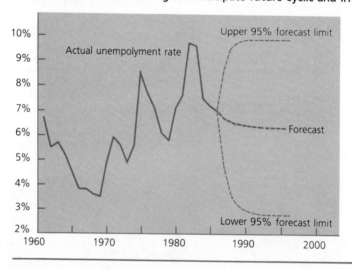

shows that the forecast heads gradually from the last series value (7.0% for 1986) toward the long-term mean value of 6.293%. This forecast, the best that can be done based only on the data and this ARMA model, says that *on average* we expect the series to gradually forget that it was above its long-term mean and to revert back down. Of course, we really expect it to continue its cyclic and irregular behavior; this is the reason that the 95% forecast limits are so wide.

FIGURE 14.3.8 The unemployment rate, its 10-year-ahead forecast, the 95% forecast limits, and three simulations of the future. The forecast represents the *average* of all such simulations at each future time. The forecast limits enclose 95% of all such simulations at each future time.

Figure 14.3.8 shows three simulations of the future, created from the estimated ARMA model using new, independent noise. The forecast represents the average of all such simulations of the future. The forecast limits enclose the middle 95% of all such simulations at each time period in the future.

A Pure Integrated (I) Process Remembers Where It Was and Then Moves at Random

Each observation of a **pure integrated (I) process,** also called a **random walk,** consists of a random step away from the current observation. This process knows where it is, but has forgotten how it got there. A random walk is said to be a **nonstationary process** because over time it tends to move farther and farther away from where it was. In contrast, the autoregressive, moving-average, and ARMA models each represent a **stationary process** because they tend to behave similarly over long time periods, staying relatively close to their long-run mean.

The model for a random walk says that at time t the data value, Y_t, consists of a constant, δ (the "drift" term), plus the previous data value, Y_{t-1}, plus random noise, ε_t. Although this looks just like an autoregressive model with $\varphi = 1$, its behavior is very different.[18] The drift term, δ, allows us to

---

[18]This is why we restricted φ to be smaller than 1 in absolute value in the definition of autoregressive and ARMA processes. Remember that autoregressive and ARMA models are stationary, but the random walk is not. For an ARMA process, the long-run mean $\delta/(1 - \varphi)$ is undefined if $\varphi = 1$ due to division by zero.

force the process to walk randomly upward on average over time (if $\delta > 0$) or downward (if $\delta < 0$). However, even if $\delta = 0$, the series will *appear* to have upward and downward trends over time.

■ The Pure Integrated (Random Walk) Process

Data = δ + Previous value + Random noise

$$Y_t = \delta + Y_{t-1} + \varepsilon_t$$

Over time, Y is not expected to stay close to any long-term mean value.

The easiest way to analyze pure integrated processes is to work with the series of *differences*,[19] $Y_t - Y_{t-1}$, which follow a random noise process.

■ The Pure Integrated (Random Walk) Process in Differenced Form

Data − Previous value = δ + Random noise

$$Y_t - Y_{t-1} = \delta + \varepsilon_t$$

Since there is no tendency to return to a long-run mean value, random walks can be deceptive, creating the appearance of trends where there really are none. The random walk in Figure 14.3.9 was created using $\delta = 0$, so there are *no real trends,* just random changes. The series did not "know" when it reached its highest point; it just continued at random in the same way from wherever it happened to be. The same random noise was used as in Figure 14.3.1, which represents the differences of the series in Figure 14.3.9.

Forecasting the next observation with a random walk is done by adding the estimated drift term, $\hat{\delta}$, to the current observation. For each additional time period you forecast into the future, an additional $\hat{\delta}$ is added. If there is no drift term (i.e., if you believe that $\delta = 0$), then the current value *is* the forecast of all future values. The forecast limits in either case will continue to widen over time (more than for ARMA processes) due to nonstationarity.

The random walk model is important on its own (as a stock market model, for example). It is also a key building block when used with ARMA models to create ARIMA models, with added flexibility to analyze more complex time-series data sets.

---

[19]For stock market and some other business data sets, it may be better to work with the *percent changes,* $(Y_t - Y_{t-1})/Y_{t-1}$. This is a variation on the idea of working with differences. Literally, percent changes are appropriate when the *logarithms* of the data follow a random walk with relatively small steps.

FIGURE 14.3.9   A pure integrated (I) process or random walk with no drift can appear to have trends when, in reality, there are none. The series remembers only where it is and takes totally random steps from there.

An integrated (I) process, or random walk, with no drift

The Autoregressive Integrated Moving-Average (ARIMA) Process Remembers Its Changes

If the changes or differences in a series are generated by an autoregressive moving-average (ARMA) process, then the series itself follows an **autoregressive integrated moving-average (ARIMA) process.** Thus, the *change* in the process consists of a linear function of the previous change, plus independent random noise, minus a fraction of the previous random noise.[20] This process knows where it is, remembers how it got there, and even remembers part of the previous noise component. Therefore, ARIMA processes can be used as a model for time-series data sets that are very smooth, changing direction slowly. These ARIMA processes are *nonstationary* due to the inclusion of an integrated component. Thus, over time, the series will tend to move farther and farther away from where it was.

The model for an autoregressive integrated moving-average process states that at time t the data value's change, $Y_t - Y_{t-1}$, consists of a constant, δ, plus an autoregressive coefficient, φ, times the previous change, $Y_{t-1} - Y_{t-2}$, plus random noise, ε_t, minus a fraction, θ, of the previous random noise. This is like a linear regression model in terms of the *differences*, except that the errors are not independent. As φ goes from 0 toward 1, and as θ goes from 0 to -1, the resulting process will be smoother. It is important that φ be less than 1 (in absolute value) in order that the process be stable.

---

[20]This is a *first-order* autoregressive integrated moving-average process. In general, the change might depend on several of the most recent changes and random noise components.

> ■ **The Autoregressive Integrated Moving-Average (ARIMA) Process in Differenced Form**
>
> Data change = δ + φ(Previous change) + Random noise
>
> − θ(Previous random noise)
>
> $$Y_t - Y_{t-1} = \delta + \varphi(Y_{t-1} - Y_{t-2}) + \varepsilon_t - \theta\varepsilon_{t-1}$$
>
> The long-term mean value of the *change* in Y is $\delta/(1 - \varphi)$. Over time, Y is not expected to stay close to any long-term mean value.

Figure 14.3.10 shows the ARIMA process created by summing (sometimes called *integrating*) the ARMA process of Figure 14.3.4. Since it shares the same random noise as the random walk of Figure 14.3.9, you can see how the autoregressive and moving-average components smooth out the changes while preserving the overall behavior of the series.

Forecasting with an ARIMA model is done by forecasting the changes of the ARMA model for the differences. Due to nonstationarity, the forecasts can tend indefinitely upward (or downward), and the forecast limits will widen as you extend your forecast further into the future.

When is differencing helpful? An ARIMA model (with differencing) will be useful for situations in which there is no tendency to return to a long-run mean value (for example, a stock's price, the U.S. GNP, the consumer price index, or your firm's sales). An ARMA model (which does not include differencing) will be useful for situations in which the series tends to stay near a long-term mean value (examples might include the unemployment rate, interest rates, changes in the price index, and your firm's debt ratio).

FIGURE 14.3.10   An autoregressive integrated moving-average (ARIMA) process remembers where it is, how it got there, and some of the previous noise. This results in a very smooth time-series model. Compare it to the random walk (with the same noise) in Figure 14.3.9.

An autoregressive integrated moving-Average (ARIMA) process

More advanced ARIMA models can be created to include the seasonal behavior of quarterly and monthly series. The idea is to include last year's value in addition to last month's value in the model equations.

14.4 End-of-Chapter Materials

Summary

A time series is different from cross-sectional data because the ordering of the observations conveys important information. Methods from previous chapters (confidence intervals and hypothesis tests, for example) must be modified before they will work with time-series data because a time series is usually not a random sample from a population.

The primary goal of time series analysis is to create forecasts, that is, to *predict the future*. These are based on a **model** (also called a **mathematical model** or a **process**), which is a system of equations that can produce an assortment of different artificial time-series data sets. A **forecast** is the expected (i.e., mean) value of the future behavior of the estimated model. Like all estimates, forecasts are usually wrong. The **forecast limits** are the confidence limits for your forecast (if the model can produce them); if the model is correct for your data, then the future observation has a 95% probability, for example, of being within these limits.

Trend-seasonal analysis is a direct, intuitive approach to estimating the four basic components of a monthly or quarterly time series: the long-term trend, the seasonal patterns, the cyclic variation, and the irregular component. The long-term **trend** indicates the *very* long-term behavior of the time series, typically as a straight line or an exponential curve. The exactly repeating **seasonal component** indicates the effects of the time of year. The medium-term **cyclic component** consists of the gradual ups and downs that do not repeat each year. The short-term, random **irregular component** represents the leftover, residual variation that can't be explained.

Trend-Seasonal Time-Series Model

Data = Trend × Seasonal × Cyclic × Irregular

The **ratio-to-moving-average** method divides the series by a smooth moving average as follows:

1 A **moving average** is a new series created by averaging nearby observations. We use a year of data in each average so that the seasonal component is eliminated.

$$\text{Moving average} = \text{Trend} \times \text{Cyclic}$$

2 Dividing the series by the smoothed moving average series produces the ratio-to-moving-average, a combination of seasonal and irregular values. Grouping by time of year and then averaging produces the **seasonal index** for each time of the year, indicating how much larger or smaller a particular time period is compared to a typical period during the year. **Seasonal adjustment** eliminates the expected seasonal component from an observation (by dividing the series by the seasonal index for that period) so that one quarter or month may be directly compared to another (after seasonal adjustment) to reveal the underlying trends.

$$\text{Seasonal} \times \text{Irregular} = \frac{\text{Data}}{\text{Moving average}}$$

$$\begin{matrix} \text{Seasonal} \\ \text{index} \end{matrix} = \text{Average of} \left(\frac{\text{Data}}{\text{Moving average}} \right) \text{for that season}$$

$$\begin{matrix} \text{Seasonally} \\ \text{adjusted value} \end{matrix} = \left(\frac{\text{Data}}{\text{Seasonal index}} \right) = \text{Trend} \times \text{Cyclic} \times \text{Irregular}$$

3 A regression of the seasonally adjusted series (Y) on time (X) is used to estimate the long-term trend as a straight line over time and to provide a seasonally adjusted forecast. This is appropriate only if the long-term trend in your series is linear.

4 Forecasting may be done by *seasonalizing the trend,* i.e., multiplying it by the appropriate seasonal index.

The **Box-Jenkins ARIMA processes** form a family of linear statistical models based on the normal distribution that have the flexibility to imitate the behavior of many different real time series by combining *autoregressive (AR) processes, integrated (I) processes,* and *moving-average (MA) processes.* The result is a **parsimonious model,** that is, one that uses just a few estimated parameters to describe the complex behavior of a time series. Here is an outline of the steps involved:

1 A process is selected from the Box-Jenkins family of ARIMA processes that generates data with the same overall look as your series, except for randomness.

2 The forecast at any time is the expected (i.e., average or mean) future value of the estimated process at that time.

3 The standard error of a forecast at any time is the standard deviation of the future value of the estimated process at that time.

4 The forecast limits extend above and below the forecast value, so that there is a 95% chance, for example, that the future value of the estimated process will fall within the forecast limits at any time. This assumes that the future behavior of the series will be similar to that of the estimated process.

A **random noise process** consists of a random sample (independent observations) from a normal distribution with constant mean and standard deviation. The average is the best forecast for any future time period, and the ordinary prediction interval for a new observation gives you the forecast limits for any future value of the series.

The Random Noise Process:

Data = Mean value + Random noise

$$Y_t = \mu + \varepsilon_t$$

The long-term mean of Y is μ.

An observation of an **autoregressive process** consists of a linear function of the previous observation plus independent random noise. Forecasting is done using predicted values from the estimated regression equation $\hat{\delta} + \hat{\varphi}Y_t$. The forecast is a compromise between the most recent data value and the long-term mean value of the series. The further into the future you look, the closer to the long-term mean value your forecast will be.

The Autoregressive Process

Data = δ + φ(Previous value) + Random noise

$$Y_t = \delta + \varphi Y_{t-1} + \varepsilon_t$$

The long-term mean value of Y is $\delta/(1 - \varphi)$.

An observation of a **moving-average process** consists of a constant, μ (the long-term mean of the process), plus independent random noise minus a fraction of the previous random noise.

The Moving-Average Process

Data = μ + Random noise − θ(Previous random noise)

$$Y_t = \mu + \varepsilon_t - \theta\varepsilon_{t-1}$$

where the long-term mean value of Y is μ. This produces a moving average of two observations at a time from a random noise process. Forecasting the next observation is based on an estimate of the current random noise, ε_t; beyond this, the best forecast is the estimated long-term mean.

An observation of an **autoregressive moving-average (ARMA) process** consists of a linear function of the previous observation, plus independent random noise, minus a fraction of the previous random noise. This combines an autoregressive with a moving-average process.

The Autoregressive Moving-Average (ARMA) Process

Data = δ + φ(Previous value) + Random noise
      − θ(Previous random noise)

$$Y_t = \delta + \varphi Y_{t-1} + \varepsilon_t - \theta\varepsilon_{t-1}$$

where the long-term mean value of Y is $\delta/(1 - \varphi)$. Forecasting the next observation is done by combining the predicted value from the estimated autoregression equation $\hat{\delta} + \hat{\varphi}Y_t$ with an estimate of the current random noise, $\hat{\varepsilon}_t$. Beyond this, the best forecast is based only on the previous forecast value. The further in the future you look, the closer to the long-term mean value your forecast will be.

An observation of a **pure integrated (I) process,** also called a **random walk,** consists of a random step away from the current observation. A random walk is said to be a **nonstationary process** because it tends to move farther and farther away from where it was. In contrast, the autoregressive, moving-average, and ARMA models are **stationary processes** because they tend to behave similarly over long time periods, staying relatively close to their long-run means. Forecasting the next observation with a random walk is done by adding an estimate of $\hat{\delta}$, the drift term, to the current observation for each additional period in the future.

Pure Integrated (Random Walk) Process

Data = δ + Previous value + Random noise

$Y_t = \delta + Y_{t-1} + \varepsilon_t$

Over time, Y is not expected to stay close to any long-term mean value.

Pure Integrated (Random Walk) Process in Differenced Form

Data − Previous value = δ + Random noise

$Y_t - Y_{t-1} = \delta + \varepsilon_t$

If the changes or differences of a series are generated by an autoregressive moving-average (ARMA) process, then the series follows an **autoregressive integrated moving-average (ARIMA) process.** These are nonstationary processes: over time, the series will tend to move farther and farther away from where it was. Forecasting with an ARIMA model is done by forecasting the changes of the ARMA model for the differences. Due to nonstationarity, the forecasts can tend indefinitely upward (or downward), and the forecast limits widen as you extend further into the future.

The Autoregressive Integrated Moving-Average (ARIMA) Process in Differenced Form:

Data change = δ + φ(Previous change) + Random noise

　　　　　　 − θ(Previous random noise)

$Y_t - Y_{t-1} = \delta + \varphi(Y_{t-1} - Y_{t-2}) + \varepsilon_t - \theta\varepsilon_{t-1}$

The long-term mean value of the *change* in Y is $\delta/(1 - \varphi)$. Over time, Y is not expected to stay close to any long-term mean value.

More advanced ARIMA models can be created to include the seasonal behavior of quarterly and monthly series.

Key Words

model, mathematical model, or process 582
forecast 582
forecast limits 582
trend-seasonal analysis 592
trend 593
seasonal component 593
cyclic component 593
irregular component 593
ratio-to-moving-average 593
moving average 595
seasonal index 599
seasonal adjustment 601
Box-Jenkins ARIMA processes 609

parsimonious model 609
random noise process 610
autoregressive (AR) process 611
moving-average (MA) process 612
autoregressive moving-average (ARMA) process 614
pure integrated (I) process or random walk 619
nonstationary process 619
stationary process 619
autoregressive integrated moving-average (ARIMA) process 621

Questions

1 a. How is a time series different from cross-sectional data?
  b. What information is lost when you look at a histogram for time series data?
2 a. What is a forecast?
  b. What are the forecast limits?
  c. What role does a mathematical model play in forecasting?
  d. Why doesn't trend-seasonal analysis produce forecast limits?
3 a. Name the four basic components of a monthly or quarterly time series, from the trend-seasonal approach.
  b. Carefully distinguish the cyclic and the irregular components.
4 a. How is the moving average different from the original series?
  b. For trend-seasonal analysis, why do we use exactly one year of data at a time in the moving average?
  c. Which components remain in the moving average? Which are reduced or eliminated?
5 a. How do you compute the ratio-to-moving-average? Which components does it represent?
  b. What do you do to the ratio-to-moving-average to produce a seasonal index? Why does this work?
  c. What does a seasonal index represent?
  d. How do you seasonally adjust a time-series value? How do you interpret the result?
6 a. How is a linear trend estimated in trend-seasonal analysis?
  b. What kind of forecast does the linear trend represent?
  c. What do you do to produce a forecast from the linear trend?
  d. Which components are represented in this forecast? Which are missing?

7 a. How is the flexibility of the Box-Jenkins ARIMA process approach helpful in time series analysis?

   b. What is parsimony?

   c. How does the forecast relate to the actual future behavior of the estimated process?

   d. How do the forecast limits relate to the actual future behavior of the estimated process?

8 a. Define the random noise process in terms of the relationship between successive observations.

   b. Comment on the following: If it's a random noise process, then special time-series methods aren't needed to analyze it.

   c. What are the forecast and forecast limits for a random noise process?

9 a. Define a first-order autoregressive process in terms of the relationship between successive observations.

   b. What are the X and Y variables in the regression model to predict the next observation in a first-order autoregressive process?

   c. Describe the forecasts of an autoregressive process in terms of the most recent data observation and the long-run mean value for the estimated model.

10 a. Define a first-order moving-average process in terms of the relationship between successive observations.

   b. What is a moving-average process a moving average of?

   c. Describe the forecasts two or more periods into the future of a first-order moving-average process in terms of the long-run mean value for the estimated model.

11 a. Define a first-order ARMA process in terms of the relationship between successive observations.

   b. What parameter value would you set equal to zero in an ARMA process in order to have an autoregressive process?

   c. What parameter value would you set equal to zero in an ARMA process in order to have a moving-average process?

   d. Describe the forecasts for the distant future based on an ARMA process.

12 a. Define a random walk in terms of the relationship between successive observations.

   b. Carefully distinguish a random noise process from a random walk.

   c. Comment on the following: If it's a random walk, then special time-series methods aren't needed to analyze it.

   d. What is the effect of the drift term in a random walk?

   e. Describe the forecasts for a random walk process.

13 Distinguish stationary and nonstationary time-series behavior.

14 For each of the following, say whether it is stationary or nonstationary:

   a. Autoregressive process.

   b. Random walk.

   c. Moving-average process.

   d. ARMA process.

15 a. Define a first-order ARIMA process in terms of the relationship between successive observations.
   b. What parameter values would you set equal to zero in an ARIMA process in order to have a random walk?
   c. How can you construct an ARMA process from an ARIMA process?
   d. Describe the forecasts for the distant future based on an ARIMA process.
16 What kind of additional terms are needed to include seasonal behavior in advanced ARIMA models?

Problems

1 For each of the following, tell whether or not you would expect it to have a strong seasonal component and why.
   a. Sales of colorful wrapping paper, recorded monthly.
   b. The number of air travelers to Hawaii from Chicago, recorded monthly.
   c. The S&P 500 stock market index, recorded daily. Assume that the stock market is efficient, so that any foreseeable trends have already been eliminated through the action of large investors attempting to profit from them.
2 Table 14.4.1 shows the quarterly sales of Caterpillar, Inc., a multinational company that designs, manufactures, and markets tractors, loaders, and other specialized vehicles.

TABLE 14.4.1   Quarterly Sales for Caterpillar, Inc.

Year	Sales (millions)
1984	$1,385
1984	1,827
1984	1,709
1984	1,655
1985	1,475
1985	1,639
1985	1,806
1985	1,805
1986	1,735
1986	1,989
1986	1,822
1986	1,775

From Caterpillar, Inc. annual reports, 1985 and 1986.

   a. Construct a time-series plot for this data set. Describe any trend and seasonal behavior that you see in the plot.
   b. Calculate the moving average (using one year of data at a time) for this time series. Construct a time-series plot with both the data and the moving average.

c. Find the seasonal index for each quarter. Do these values appear reasonable when you look at the time-series plot of the data?

d. Which is Caterpillar's worst quarter (1, 2, 3, or 4)? On average, how much lower are sales then compared to a typical quarter during the year?

e. Find the seasonally adjusted sales corresponding to each of the original sales values.

f. From first to second quarter of 1984, sales went up from 1,385 to 1,827. What happened on a seasonally adjusted basis?

g. From the fourth quarter of 1985 to the first quarter of 1986, Caterpillar's sales declined from 1,805 to 1,735. What happened on a seasonally adjusted basis?

h. Find the regression equation to predict the long-term trend in seasonally adjusted sales for each time period.

i. Compute the seasonally adjusted forecast for the second quarter of 1991.

j. Compute the forecast for the first quarter of 1992.

3 Table 14.4.2 shows the quarterly sales of Castle & Cooke, Inc., an international firm specializing in brand-name food products (Dole, Bumble Bee, A&W, etc.). The 1983 annual report claims that "the results by quarter are heavily influenced by seasonal factors which are inherent to the company's business."

TABLE 14.4.2 Quarterly Sales for Castle & Cooke, Inc.

Year	Sales (thousands)	Year	Sales (thousands)
1982	$453,491	1984	343,167
1982	343,669	1984	468,195
1982	387,988	1985	460,398
1982	435,642	1985	324,155
1983	352,004	1985	386,082
1983	284,030	1985	429,918
1983	320,867	1986	381,080
1983	404,634	1986	487,473
1984	402,120	1986	492,266
1984	306,606	1986	377,072

Data are from Castle & Cooke, Inc. annual reports, 1983–1986.

a. Construct a time-series plot for this data set. Do you agree that there are seasonal factors present here?

b. Calculate the moving average (using one year of data at a time) for this time series. Construct a time-series plot with both the data and the moving average.

c. Describe any cyclic behavior that you see in the moving average.

d. Find the seasonal index for each quarter. Do these values appear reasonable when you look at the time-series plot of the data?

e. Which is Castle & Cooke's best quarter (1, 2, 3, or 4)? On average, how much higher are sales then as compared to a typical quarter during the year?

f. Which is Castle & Cooke's worst quarter (1, 2, 3, or 4)? On average, how much lower are sales then as compared to a typical quarter during the year?

g. Find the seasonally adjusted sales corresponding to each of the original sales values. Construct a time-series plot of this seasonally adjusted series.

h. Describe the behavior of the seasonally adjusted series. In particular, identify any change in volatility over this time period.

4 Table 14.4.3 shows the quarterly sales of Deere & Co.

TABLE 14.4.3   Quarterly Sales for Deere & Co.

Year	Sales (millions)	Year	Sales (millions)	Year	Sales (millions)
1976	$ 632.7	1979	$ 909.5	1982	1,059.2
1976	899.8	1979	1,353.9	1982	1,254.8
1976	887.0	1979	1,408.5	1982	1,147.2
1976	714.3	1979	1,261.2	1982	1,147.0
1977	605.9	1980	1,114.8	1983	859.6
1977	1,011.7	1980	1,540.6	1983	1,010.8
1977	1,008.5	1980	1,368.1	1983	995.6
1977	977.9	1980	1,446.3	1983	1,101.9
1978	789.9	1981	1,074.6	1984	886.9
1978	1,119.2	1981	1,467.0	1984	1,242.7
1978	1,125.9	1981	1,471.3	1984	1,037.2
1978	1,120.0	1981	1,433.8	1984	1,232.4

From Deere & Co. annual reports, 1977–1984.

a. Construct a time-series plot for this data set. Describe the seasonal and cyclic behavior that you see, as well as any evidence of irregular behavior.

b. Which quarter (1, 2, 3, or 4) appears to be Deere's worst in terms of sales level, based on your plot in part a? Is this appropriate for the agriculture business?

c. Is the seasonal pattern (in your graph for part a) consistent across the entire time period? If not, when does it appear to break down? If Deere had diversified away somewhat from the agriculture business, how might this account for the patterns you see?

d. Calculate the moving average (using one year of data at a time) for this time series. Construct a time-series plot with both the data and the moving average.

e. Describe the cyclic behavior revealed by the moving average.

f. Find the seasonal index for each quarter. Do these values appear reasonable compared to the time-series plot of the data?

g. Find the seasonally adjusted sales corresponding to each of the original sales values. Construct a time series plot of this seasonally adjusted series.

h. Compare the plot of the seasonally adjusted series to the moving average you constructed earlier. Describe their similarities and differences. Why are they different?

i. Do you see an overall linear long-term trend up or down in Deere's sales data? Would it be appropriate to use a regression line for forecasting this series?

5 Based on past data, your firm's sales show a seasonal pattern. The seasonal index for November is 1.08, for December it is 1.38, and for January it is 0.84. Sales for November were $285,167.

a. Would you ordinarily expect an increase in sales from November to December in a typical year? How do you know?

b. Find November's sales, on a seasonally adjusted basis.

c. Take the seasonally adjusted November figure and seasonalize it using the December index to find the expected sales level for December.

d. Sales for December have just been reported as $430,106. Is this higher or lower than expected, based on November's sales?

e. Find December's sales, on a seasonally adjusted basis.

f. Were sales up or down from November to December, on a seasonally adjusted basis? What does this tell you?

g. Using the same method as in part c, find the expected level for January sales based on December's sales.

6 The number of diners per quarter eating at your après-ski restaurant has been examined using trend-seasonal analysis. The quarterly seasonal indexes are 1.45, 0.55, 0.72, and 1.26 for quarters 1, 2, 3, and 4, respectively. A linear trend has been estimated as 5,423 + 408(Quarter number), where the quarter number starts at 1 in the first quarter of 1987 and increases by 1 each successive quarter.

a. Find the seasonally adjusted forecast value for the first quarter of 1991.

b. Find the seasonally adjusted forecast value for the second quarter of 1991.

c. Why is the seasonally adjusted forecast larger in the second quarter, in which you would expect fewer skiers coming to dinner?

d. Find the forecast value for the first quarter of 1991.

e. Find the forecast value for the second quarter of 1991.

f. On a seasonally adjusted basis, according to this estimated linear trend, how many more diners do you expect to serve each quarter compared to the previous quarter?

g. Your strategic business plan includes a major expansion project when the number of diners reaches 70,000 per year. In which year will this first happen, according to your forecasts? (*Hint:* Compute and add the four forecasts for each year to find yearly totals for 1993 and 1994.)

7 Your seasonally adjusted monthly sales forecast is $382,190 + $4,011(Month number), where the month number is 1 for January 1987 and increases by 1 each month. The seasonal index for February sales is 0.923, and it is 1.137 for April. What you need now is a forecast for cost of goods sold in order to plan ahead for filling future orders. You have found that monthly sales have been a good predictor of monthly cost of goods sold and have estimated the following regression equation:

$$\text{Predicted cost of goods sold} = \$106,582 + 0.413(\text{Sales})$$

a. Find the seasonally adjusted forecast of monthly sales for February 1994.

b. Find the forecast of monthly sales for February 1994.

c. Find the forecast of cost of goods sold for February 1994.

d. Find the forecast of cost of goods sold for April 1995.

8 For each of the following, tell whether it is likely to be stationary or nonstationary and why.

   a. The price per share of IBM stock, recorded daily.

   b. The prime rate, recorded weekly. This is the interest rate that banks charge their best customers for their loans.

   c. The thickness of paper, measured five times per minute as it is being produced and rolled, assuming that the process is in control.

   d. The price of a full-page advertisement in *TV Guide,* recorded each year.

9 Table 14.4.4 shows basic computer results from a Box-Jenkins analysis of the daily percentage changes in the Dow Jones Industrial stock market index from July 31 to October 9, 1987.

TABLE 14.4.4   Results of a Box-Jenkins Analysis of Daily Percentage Changes in the Dow Jones Index

Coefficient	Estimate	Standard Error	t-ratio
Autoregression	−0.3724	1.7599	−0.21
Moving average	−0.4419	1.6991	−0.26
Constant	−0.000925	0.002470	−0.37
Mean	−0.000674	0.001799	−0.37
Standard deviation of random noise	0.011950		

   a. What kind of process has been estimated?

   b. Write the model in a way that shows how the next observation is determined from the previous one. Use the actual estimated coefficients.

   c. Which estimated coefficients are statistically significant?

   d. Using 0 in place of all estimated coefficients that are not statistically significant, write down the model that shows how the next observation is determined from the previous one. What kind of process is this?

   e. Write a brief paragraph summarizing your results as support for the random walk theory of market behavior.

10 Tables 14.4.5 and 14.4.6 show basic computer results from a Box-Jenkins analysis of yields on U.S. Treasury bills each year from 1961 through 1986.

TABLE 14.4.5   Basic Results of a Box-Jenkins Analysis of U.S. Treasury Bill Interest Rates

Coefficient	Estimate	Standard Error	t-ratio
Autoregression	0.6684	0.1644	4.07
Moving average	−0.7303	0.1484	−4.92
Constant	2.0104	0.4977	4.04
Mean	6.0640	1.501	4.04
Standard deviation of random noise	1.4596		

TABLE 14.4.6   Resulting Forecasts from a Box-Jenkins Analysis of
U.S. Treasury Bill Interest Rates

| Year | Forecast | 95% Forecast Limits | |
		Lower	Upper
1987	5.9751	3.1135	8.8367
1988	6.0044	1.0841	10.9248
1989	6.0241	0.4233	11.6248
1990	6.0372	0.1578	11.9165
1991	6.0459	0.0463	12.0456
1992	6.0518	−0.0009	12.1045
1993	6.0557	−0.0205	12.1319
1994	6.0583	−0.0283	12.1450
1995	6.0601	−0.0313	12.1514
1996	6.0613	−0.0322	12.1547

a. What kind of process has been fitted?

b. Write the model in a way that shows how the next observation is determined from the previous one.

c. Which estimated coefficients are statistically significant?

d. Draw a time-series plot of the original data, the forecasts, and the forecast limits.

e. Comment on these forecasts and forecast limits. In particular, explain the connection between the odd negative lower forecast limits and any pattern of unequal variability in the series itself. (*Hint:* If interest rates cannot be negative, can variability stay constant as the level of interest rates rises and falls?)

Projects

1 Select a firm of interest to you, and obtain at least three continuous years of quarterly sales figures from the firm's annual reports at your library.

a. Draw a time-series graph, and comment on the structure you see.

b. Compute the one-year moving average, draw it on your graph, and comment.

c. Compute the seasonal indexes, graph them, and comment.

d. Compute and graph the seasonally adjusted series, then comment on what you see. In particular, what new information have you gained through seasonal adjustment?

e. Compute the trend line, and seasonalize it to find forecasts for two years into the future. Graph these forecasts along with the original data. Comment on how reasonable these forecasts seem to you.

2 Find yearly data on a business or economic time series of interest to you for at least 20 continuous years. (This project requires access to compute software that can estimate ARIMA models.)

a. Graph this time series, and comment on the structure you see.

b. Does the series appear to be stationary or nonstationary? If it is extremely nonstationary (ending up far away from where it started, for example), graph the differences to see if they appear to be stationary.

c. Fit a first-order autoregressive process to your series (or to the differences, if the series was nonstationary). Based on the t-statistic, is the autoregressive coefficient significant?

d. Fit a first-order moving-average process to your series (or to the differences, if the series was nonstationary). Based on the t-statistic, is the moving-average coefficient significant?

e. Fit a first-order ARMA process to your series (or to the differences, if the series was nonstationary). Based on the t-statistic, which coefficients are significant?

f. Based on the results for these three models, which one do you select? You may want to exclude components that are not significant.

g. Now work with the original series (even if you have been using differences). Estimate your chosen model, including an integrated (I) component if you have been differencing, and find forecasts and forecast limits.

h. Graph the forecasts and forecast limits along with the original data, and comment.

i. Comment on the model selection procedure. (Keep in mind that the selection procedure is much more complicated when higher-order processes are used.)

V

Methods and Applications

The selected topics of these last four chapters will show you how the ideas and methods of statistics can be applied to some special situations. The *analysis of variance* (ANOVA for short) is a collection of methods that compare the extent of variability due to various sources in order to perform hypothesis tests for complex situations. Chapter 15 introduces these methods and shows how ANOVA can be used to test whether several samples come from similar populations or not. In Chapter 16, *nonparametric* statistical methods (based on ranks) will show you how to test hypotheses in some difficult situations, for example, when the distributions are not normal or the data are merely *ordinal* (ordered categories) instead of quantitative (meaningful numbers). When you have only *nominal* data (unordered categories), the special testing methods of *chi-squared analysis* (see Chapter 17) are needed because you can't do arithmetic or ranking on these categories. Finally, Chapter 18 covers the basic statistical methods of *quality control:* how to decide which problems to solve, how to manage when there is variability in production, and how to decide when to fix things and when to leave well enough alone.

ANOVA
Testing for Differences among Many Samples, and Much More

The **analysis of variance** (or **ANOVA**, for short) provides a general framework for statistical hypothesis testing based on careful examination of the different sources of variability in a complex situation. Here are some examples of situations in which ANOVA would be helpful:

1 In order to cut costs, you have tested five additives that claim to improve the yield of your chemical production process. You have run 10 production runs for each additive and another 10 using no additive. This is an example of a *one-way design,* since a single factor ("additive") appears at several different levels. The result is a data set consisting of six lists of yields. The usual variability from one run to another makes it difficult to tell whether any improvements were just due to luck or whether the additives were truly better than the others. What you need is a test of the following null hypothesis: These six lists are really all the same, and any differences are just random. You can't just use a *t*-test, from Chapter 10, because you have more than two samples.[1] Instead, the one-way analysis of variance will tell you whether there are any significant (i.e., systematic or nonrandom) differences among these additives. If significant differences exist, you may examine them in detail. Otherwise, you may conclude that there are no detectable systematic differences among the additives.

2 It occurs to you that you could run *combinations* of additives for the situation just described. With five additives, there are $2^5 = 32$ possible combinations (including no additives), and you have run each combina-

---

[1]You might consider using an unpaired *t*-test to compare the additives two at a time. However, there are 15 such tests, and this *group* of tests is no longer valid because the probability of error is no longer controlled. In particular, assuming validity of the null hypothesis of no differences, the probability of wrongly declaring *some pair* of yields to be significantly different could be much higher than the 5% error rate that applies to an *individual* test. The F-test will keep the error rate at 5%, and you may use modified *t*-tests if the F-test is significant.

tion twice.[2] This is an example of a *factorial design* with five factors (the additives) each at two levels (either used or not used). The analysis of variance for this data set would indicate (*a*) whether or not each additive has a significant effect on yield and (*b*) whether there are any significant interactions resulting from combinations of additives.

3 As part of a marketing study, you have tested three types of media (newspaper, radio, and television) in combination with two types of ads (direct and indirect approach). Each person in the study was exposed to one combination, and a score was computed reflecting the effectiveness of the advertising. This is an example of a *two-way design* (the factors are "media" and "type of ad"). The analysis of variance will tell you (*a*) whether the media types have significantly different effectiveness, (*b*) whether the two types of ads have significantly different effectiveness, and (*c*) whether there are any significant interactions between media and type of ad.

The analysis of variance uses an **F-test** based on the **F-statistic,** a ratio of two variance measures, to perform each hypothesis test.[3] The numerator represents the variability due to the special, interesting effect being tested, and the denominator represents a baseline measure of randomness. If the ratio is larger than the value in the *F*-table, the effect is significant.

The **one-way analysis of variance,** in particular, is used to test whether or not the averages from several different situations are significantly different from one another. This is the simplest kind of analysis of variance. Although more complex situations require more complicated calculations, the general ANOVA idea remains the same: to test significance by comparing one source of variability (the one being tested) against another source of variability (the underlying randomness of the situation).

■ 15.1 Using Box Plots to Look at Many Samples at Once

Since the purpose of the analysis of variance is only to test hypotheses, it is up to you to remember to explore your data. You should examine statistical summaries (average and standard deviation, for example) and histograms or box plots for each list of numbers in your data set. The analysis of variance might tell you that there are significant differences, but you would also have to examine ordinary statistical summaries to actually see those estimated differences.

---

[2]It is a good idea to run each case more than once, if you can afford it, because you will then have more information about the variability in each situation.

[3]Recall that the variance is the square of the standard deviation. This is the accepted way to proceed with ANOVA. Had the history of statistics developed differently, we might be comparing ratios of standard deviations to tables containing the square roots of our current *F*-tables. However, the variance method is firmly established by tradition, and we will use it here.

Box plots are particularly well suited to the task of comparing several distributions because unnecessary details are omitted, allowing you to concentrate on the essentials. Here is a checklist of things to look for when using box plots or histograms to compare similar measurements across a variety of situations:

1 Do the box plots look reasonable? You might as well spot trouble *before* you spend a lot more time working with the data set. For example, you might discover that you've called up the wrong data set. (Do the numbers seem to be much too big or too small? Are these last year's data?) You might also spot some outliers that could be examined and, if they are errors, corrected.

2 Do the centers (medians) appear different from one box plot to another? This provides an initial, informal assessment for which the analysis of variance will provide an exact, formal answer. Also, do the centers show any patterns of special interest?

3 Is the variability reasonably constant from one box plot to another? This is important because the analysis of variance will assume that these variabilities are equal in the population. If, for example, the higher boxes (with larger medians) are systematically wider (indicating more variability), then the analysis of variance may give incorrect answers.[4]

EXAMPLE

Comparing the Quality of Your Suppliers' Products

Your firm currently purchases the same electronic components from three different suppliers, and you are concerned. Although some of your associates contend that this arrangement allows your firm to get the good prices and fast delivery times, you are troubled by the fact that products must be designed to work with the *worst* combination of components that might be installed. The overriding concern is with costs and benefits. In particular, would the firm be better off negotiating an exclusive contract with just one supplier to obtain faster delivery of high-quality components at a higher price? As part of the background information on this question, you have been looking at the quality of components delivered by each supplier.

The data set has just arrived. You had asked your firm's QA (quality assurance) department to check out 20 components from each supplier (randomly selected from recent deliveries). They actually tested 21 components for each, but not all produced a reliable measurement. The quality score is a composite of several different measurements, on a scale of 0 to 100, indicating the extent of

---

[4]This problem of unequal variability can often be fixed by transforming the original data values, for example, using logarithms if all of your data values are positive numbers. Examine the box plots of the transformed data to see if the problem has been fixed. If the analysis of variance finds significant differences on the log scale, you would conclude that the original groups also show significant differences. Thus, the interpretation of the results of an analysis of variance remains much the same even when you transform, provided that you use the same transformation on all of your data.

TABLE 15.1.1   Quality Scores for Suppliers' Products

	Amalgamated	Bipolar	Consolidated
	75	94	90
	72	87	86
	87	80	92
	77	86	75
	84	80	79
	82	67	94
	84	86	95
	81	82	85
	78	86	86
	97	82	92
	85	72	92
	81	77	85
	95	87	87
	81	68	86
	72	80	92
	89	76	85
	84	68	93
	73	86	89
		74	83
		86	
		90	
Average	$\bar{X}_1 = 82.055556$	$\bar{X}_2 = 80.666667$	$\bar{X}_3 = 87.684211$
Standard deviation	$S_1 = 7.124706$	$S_2 = 7.598245$	$S_3 = 5.228688$
Sample size	$n_1 = 18$	$n_2 = 21$	$n_3 = 19$

agreement with the specifications of the component and your firm's needs. Higher scores are better, and a score of 75 or higher is sufficient for many applications. Table 15.1.1 shows the data set, together with some basic statistical summaries.

On average, Consolidated has the highest quality score (87.7), followed by Amalgamated (82.1), and finally Bipolar (80.7). The box plots in Figure 15.1.1 also suggest that Consolidated's products are generally higher in quality than the others, although there is considerable overlap and the highest-quality component actually came from Amalgamated (with a score of 97). Much additional information is also provided by these box plots: no component achieved perfect quality (a score of 100), and the variability is similar from one supplier to another (as indicated by the size of each box).

Although Consolidated appears to have the highest quality, you wonder if that could just be due to the random selection of these particular components. If you could examine many more components from each supplier, would Consolidated still be the best, on average? The analysis of variance provides an answer without requiring the prohibitive cost of obtaining more data.

■ 15.2 The *F*-Test Tells You if the Averages Are Significantly Different

The *F*-test for the one-way analysis of variance will tell you whether the averages of several independent samples are significantly different from one an-

FIGURE 15.1.1 Box plots of the quality of components purchased from each of your three suppliers. Amalgamated and Bipolar are quite similar (although the downside appears worse for Bipolar). Consolidated appears to have consistently higher quality, although there is considerable overlap in the distribution of these quality scores.

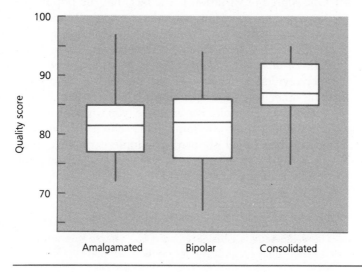

other. This replaces the unpaired t-test (from Chapter 10) when you have more than two samples and gives the identical result when you have exactly two samples.

The Data Set and Sources of Variation

The data set for the one-way analysis of variance consists of k independent univariate samples, each one with the same measurement units (e.g., dollars or miles per gallon). The sample sizes may be different from one sample to another; this is permitted. The data set will then be of the form in Table 15.2.1.

TABLE 15.2.1 Data Set for One-Way ANOVA

	Sample 1	Sample 2	$\cdots$	Sample k
	$X_{1,1}$	$X_{2,1}$	$\cdots$	$X_{k,1}$
	$X_{1,2}$	$X_{2,2}$		$X_{k,2}$
	$\cdot$	$\cdot$	$\cdot$	$\cdot$
	$\cdot$	$\cdot$	$\cdot$	$\cdot$
	$\cdot$	$\cdot$	$\cdot$	$\cdot$
	X_{1,n_1}	X_{2,n_2}	$\cdots$	X_{k,n_k}
Average	$\bar{X}_1$	$\bar{X}_2$		$\bar{X}_k$
Standard deviation	S_1	S_2	$\cdots$	S_k
Sample size	n_1	n_2		n_k

One way to identify sources of variation is to ask the question, Why are these data values different from one another? There are two sources of variation here, so there are two answers:

1 One source of variation is the fact that the populations may be different from one another. For example, if sample 2 involves a particularly effective treatment, then the numbers in sample 2 will generally be different (higher) than the numbers in the other samples. This source is called the *between-sample variability*. The larger the between-sample variability, the more evidence you have of differences from one population to another.

2 The other source of variation is the fact that there is (usually) diversity within every sample. For example, you wouldn't expect all of the numbers in sample 2 to be the same. This source is called the *within-sample variability*. The larger the within-sample variability, the more random your situation is and the harder it is to tell whether the populations are actually different or not.

■ Sources of Variation for a One-Way Analysis of Variance
Between-sample variability (from one sample to another)
Within-sample variability (inside each sample)

For the supplier quality example, the two sources of variation are (1) the possibly different quality levels of the three suppliers and (2) the possibly different quality scores on different components from the same supplier.

The *F*-test will be based on a ratio of measures of these sources of variation. But first we will consider the foundations of this hypothesis test.

The Assumptions

The assumptions underlying the *F*-test in the one-way analysis of variance provide a solid framework for an exact probability statement based on observed data.

■ Assumptions for a One-Way Analysis of Variance

1 The data set consists of *k* random samples from *k* populations.
2 Each population has a normal distribution, and the standard deviations of the populations are identical, so that $\sigma_1 = \sigma_2 = \cdots = \sigma_k$. This allows you to use standard statistical tables for hypothesis testing.

Note that there are no assumptions about the mean values of the normal distributions in the populations. The means are permitted to take on any values; the hypotheses will deal with them.

For the supplier quality example, the assumptions are that the QA department's data represent three random samples, one from the population of quality scores of each supplier. Furthermore, the distribution of quality scores is assumed to be normal for each supplier, and all three suppliers are assumed to have the same variability (population standard deviation) of quality score. The box plots examined earlier suggest that the assumptions about normal distributions and equal variability are reasonable and roughly satisfied by this data set.

The Hypotheses

The null hypothesis for the F-test in the one-way analysis of variance claims that the k populations (represented by the k samples) all have the same mean value. The research hypothesis claims that they are *not* all the same, that is, at least two population means are different.

■ Hypotheses for a One-Way Analysis of Variance
Null Hypothesis:

$$H_0: \mu_1 = \mu_2 = \cdots = \mu_k \quad \text{(the means are all equal)}$$

Research Hypothesis:

$$H_1: \mu_i \neq \mu_j \quad \text{for at least one pair of populations}$$
$$\text{(the means are } not \text{ all equal)}$$

Because the standard deviations are assumed to be equal in all of the populations, the null hypothesis is actually claiming that *the populations are identical* to each other. The research hypothesis claims that some differences exist, regardless of the number of populations that actually differ. That is, the research hypothesis includes the cases in which just one population is different from the others, in which several are different, and in which all are different.

For the supplier quality example, the null hypothesis claims that the three suppliers have identical quality characteristics: their components have the same distribution of quality scores (the same normal distribution with the same mean and standard deviation). The research hypothesis claims that there are some supplier differences in terms of mean quality level (they might all three be different, or two might be the same with the third one either higher or lower).

The F-Statistic

The F-statistic for a one-way analysis of variance is the ratio of variability measures for the two sources of variation: the between-sample variability divided by the within-sample variability. Think of the F-statistic as measuring how many times more variable the sample averages are compared to what you would expect if they were just randomly different. The F-test is performed by computing the F-statistic and comparing it to the value in the F-table. There are several computations involved.

Because the null hypothesis claims that all population means are equal, we will need an estimate of this mean value that combines all of the information from the samples. The **grand average** is the average of all of the data values from all of the samples combined. It may also be viewed as a *weighted average* of the sample averages, where the larger samples have more weight.

■ **The Total Sample Size, n, and the Grand Average, $\overline{X}$**

$$n = n_1 + n_2 + \cdots + n_k$$

$$= \sum_{i=1}^{k} n_i$$

$$\overline{X} = \frac{n_1 \overline{X}_1 + n_2 \overline{X}_2 + \cdots + n_k \overline{X}_k}{n}$$

$$= \frac{\sum_{i=1}^{k} n_i \overline{X}_i}{n}$$

For the supplier quality example, the total sample size and grand average are as follows:

$$n = n_1 + n_2 + \cdots + n_k$$

$$= 18 + 21 + 19$$

$$= 58$$

$$\overline{X} = \frac{n_1 \overline{X}_1 + n_2 \overline{X}_2 + \cdots + n_k \overline{X}_k}{n}$$

$$= \frac{18 \times 82.055556 + 21 \times 80.666667 + 19 \times 87.684211}{58}$$

$$= \frac{4{,}837}{58}$$

$$= 83.396552$$

The **between-sample variability** measures how different the sample averages are from one another. This would be zero if the sample averages were all identical, and it would be large if they were very different. It is basically a measure of the variability of the sample averages.[5] Here is the formula:

■ **The Between-Sample Variability for One-Way Analysis of Variance**

$$\text{Between-sample variability} = \frac{n_1(\overline{X}_1 - \overline{X})^2 + n_2(\overline{X}_2 - \overline{X})^2 + \cdots + n_k(\overline{X}_k - \overline{X})^2}{k - 1}$$

$$= \frac{\sum_{i=1}^{k} n_i(\overline{X}_i - \overline{X})^2}{k - 1}$$

Degrees of freedom $= k - 1$

The degrees of freedom number expresses the fact that you are measuring the variability of k averages. One degree of freedom is lost (as for an ordinary standard deviation) because the grand average was estimated.

For the supplier quality example, the between-sample variability (with $k - 1 = 3 - 1 = 2$ degrees of freedom) is computed as follows:

Between-sample
   variability

$$= \frac{n_1(\overline{X}_1 - \overline{X})^2 + n_2(\overline{X}_2 - \overline{X})^2 + \cdots + n_k(\overline{X}_k - \overline{X})^2}{k - 1}$$

$$= [18(82.055556 - 83.396552)^2 + 21(80.666667 - 83.396552)^2$$
$$+ 19(87.684211 - 83.396552)^2]/(3 - 1)$$

$$= \frac{32.369 + 156.498 + 349.296}{2}$$

$$= \frac{538.163}{2}$$

$$= 269.08$$

The **within-sample variability** measures how variable each sample is. Because the samples are assumed to have equal variability, there is only one measure of within-sample variability. This would be zero if each sample consisted of its sample average repeated many times, and it would be large if each sample contained a wide diversity of numbers. The square root of the

---

[5]The formula for the between-sample variability may be viewed as the result of replacing all data values by their sample averages, combining all of these to form one large data set, computing the ordinary sample standard deviation, squaring to get the variance, and multiplying by the scaling factor $(n - 1)/(k - 1)$.

within-sample variability provides an estimator of the population standard deviations. Here is the formula:

■ The Within-Sample Variability for One-Way Analysis of Variance

$$\text{Within-sample variability} = \frac{(n_1 - 1)(S_1)^2 + (n_2 - 1)(S_2)^2 + \cdots + (n_k - 1)(S_k)^2}{n - k}$$

$$= \frac{\sum\limits_{i=1}^{k}(n_i - 1)(S_i)^2}{n - k}$$

Degrees of freedom $= n - k$

The degrees of freedom number expresses the fact that you are measuring the variability of all n data values about their sample averages but have lost k degrees of freedom because k different sample averages were estimated.

For the supplier quality example, the within-sample variability (with $n - k = 58 - 3 = 55$ degrees of freedom) is computed as follows:

Within-sample
  variability

$$= \frac{(n_1 - 1)(S_1)^2 + (n_2 - 1)(S_2)^2 + \cdots + (n_k - 1)(S_k)^2}{n - k}$$

$$= \frac{(18 - 1)(7.124706)^2 + (21 - 1)(7.598245)^2 + (19 - 1)(5.228688)^2}{58 - 3}$$

$$= \frac{17 \times 50.7614 + 20 \times 57.7333 + 18 \times 27.3392}{55}$$

$$= \frac{862.944 + 1,154.667 + 492.105}{55}$$

$$= \frac{2,509.716}{55}$$

$$= 45.63$$

The F-statistic is the ratio of these two variability measures, indicating the extent to which the sample averages differ from one another (the numerator) with respect to the overall level of variability in the samples (the denominator).

■ **The F-Statistic for One-Way Analysis of Variance**

$$F = \frac{\text{Between-sample variability}}{\text{Within-sample variability}}$$

Degrees of freedom = $k - 1$ (numerator) and $n - k$ (denominator)

Note that the F-statistic has *two* numbers for degrees of freedom. It inherits the degrees of freedom of both of the variability measures it is based on.

For the supplier quality example, the F-statistic (with 2 and 55 degrees of freedom) is computed as follows:

$$F = \frac{\text{Between-sample variability}}{\text{Within-sample variability}}$$

$$= \frac{269.08}{45.63}$$

$$= 5.897$$

This tells you that the between-sample variability (due to differences among suppliers) is 5.897 times the within-sample variability. That is, there is 5.897 times as much variability among suppliers as you would expect, based only on the variability of individual suppliers. Is this large enough to indicate significant supplier differences? A statistical table is needed.

The F-Table

The **F-table** is a list of critical values for the distribution of the F-statistic when the null hypothesis is true, so that the F-statistic exceeds the F-table value a controlled percentage of the time (5%, for example) when the null hypothesis is true. To find the critical value, use your numbers of degrees of freedom to find the row and column in the F-table corresponding the level you are testing at (e.g., 5%). Tables 15.2.2 through 15.2.5 give F-table critical values for testing at the 5%, 1%, 0.1%, and 10% levels, respectively.

For the supplier quality example, the degrees of freedom are 2 (for between-sample variability) and 55 (for within-sample variability). The critical value for testing at the usual 5% level, found in the F-table, is somewhere between 3.316 and 3.150 (these are the respective values for 30 and for 60 within-sample degrees of freedom, which bracket the unlisted value for 55 degrees of freedom). For testing at the 1% level, the critical value is between 5.390 and 4.977.

The Result of the F-Test

The F-test is performed by comparing the F-statistic (computed from your data) to the critical value from the F-table. The result is *significant* if the

TABLE 15.2.2   *F*-Table: Level 5% Critical Value

Denominator Degrees of Freedom ($n - k$ for within-sample variability in one-way ANOVA)	Numerator Degrees of Freedom ($k - 1$ for between-sample variability in one-way ANOVA)																
	1	2	3	4	5	6	7	8	9	10	12	15	20	30	60	120	Infinity
1	161.45	199.50	215.71	224.58	230.16	233.99	236.77	238.88	240.54	241.88	243.91	245.95	248.01	250.10	252.20	253.25	254.32
2	18.513	19.000	19.164	19.247	19.296	19.330	19.353	19.371	19.385	19.396	19.413	19.429	19.446	19.462	19.479	19.487	19.496
3	10.128	9.552	9.277	9.117	9.013	8.941	8.887	8.845	8.812	8.786	8.745	8.703	8.660	8.617	8.572	8.549	8.526
4	7.709	6.944	6.591	6.388	6.256	6.163	6.094	6.041	5.999	5.964	5.912	5.858	5.803	5.746	5.688	5.658	5.628
5	6.608	5.786	5.409	5.192	5.050	4.950	4.876	4.818	4.772	4.735	4.678	4.619	4.558	4.496	4.431	4.398	4.365
6	5.987	5.143	4.757	4.534	4.387	4.284	4.207	4.147	4.099	4.060	4.000	3.938	3.874	3.808	3.740	3.705	3.669
7	5.591	4.737	4.347	4.120	3.972	3.866	3.787	3.726	3.677	3.637	3.575	3.511	3.445	3.376	3.304	3.267	3.230
8	5.318	4.459	4.066	3.838	3.687	3.581	3.500	3.438	3.388	3.347	3.284	3.218	3.150	3.079	3.005	2.967	2.928
9	5.117	4.256	3.863	3.633	3.482	3.374	3.293	3.230	3.179	3.137	3.073	3.006	2.936	2.864	2.787	2.748	2.707
10	4.965	4.103	3.708	3.478	3.326	3.217	3.135	3.072	3.020	2.978	2.913	2.845	2.774	2.700	2.621	2.580	2.538
12	4.747	3.885	3.490	3.259	3.106	2.996	2.913	2.849	2.796	2.753	2.687	2.617	2.544	2.466	2.384	2.341	2.296
15	4.543	3.682	3.287	3.056	2.901	2.790	2.707	2.641	2.588	2.544	2.475	2.403	2.328	2.247	2.160	2.114	2.066
20	4.351	3.493	3.098	2.866	2.711	2.599	2.514	2.447	2.393	2.348	2.278	2.203	2.124	2.039	1.946	1.896	1.843
30	4.171	3.316	2.922	2.690	2.534	2.421	2.334	2.266	2.211	2.165	2.092	2.015	1.932	1.841	1.740	1.683	1.622
60	4.001	3.150	2.758	2.525	2.368	2.254	2.167	2.097	2.040	1.993	1.917	1.836	1.748	1.649	1.534	1.467	1.389
120	3.920	3.072	2.680	2.447	2.290	2.175	2.087	2.016	1.959	1.910	1.834	1.750	1.659	1.554	1.429	1.352	1.254
Infinity	3.841	2.996	2.605	2.372	2.214	2.099	2.010	1.938	1.880	1.831	1.752	1.666	1.571	1.459	1.318	1.221	1.000

TABLE 15.2.3   *F*-Table: Level 1% Critical Values

Denominator Degrees of Freedom ($n - k$ for within-sample variability in one-way ANOVA)	Numerator Degrees of Freedom ($k - 1$ for between-sample variability in one-way ANOVA)																
	1	2	3	4	5	6	7	8	9	10	12	15	20	30	60	120	Infinity
1	4052.2	4999.5	5403.4	5624.6	5763.7	5859.0	5928.4	5891.1	6022.5	6055.8	6106.3	6157.3	6208.7	6260.6	6313.0	6339.4	6365.9
2	98.501	98.995	99.159	99.240	99.299	99.333	99.356	99.374	99.388	99.399	99.416	99.432	99.449	99.466	99.482	99.491	99.499
3	34.116	30.816	29.456	28.709	28.236	27.910	27.671	27.488	27.344	27.228	27.051	26.871	26.689	26.503	26.315	26.220	26.125
4	21.197	18.000	16.694	15.977	15.522	15.207	14.976	14.799	14.659	14.546	14.374	14.198	14.020	13.838	13.652	13.558	13.463
5	16.258	13.274	12.060	11.392	10.967	10.672	10.455	10.289	10.158	10.051	9.888	9.722	9.553	9.379	9.202	9.112	9.021
6	13.745	10.925	9.780	9.148	8.746	8.466	8.260	8.102	7.976	7.874	7.718	7.559	7.396	7.229	7.057	6.969	6.880
7	12.246	9.547	8.451	7.847	7.460	7.191	6.993	6.840	6.719	6.620	6.469	6.314	6.155	5.992	5.823	5.737	5.650
8	11.258	8.649	7.591	7.006	6.632	6.371	6.178	6.029	5.911	5.814	5.667	5.515	5.359	5.198	5.032	4.946	4.859
9	10.561	8.021	6.992	6.422	6.057	5.802	5.613	5.467	5.351	5.257	5.111	4.962	4.808	4.649	4.483	4.398	4.311
10	10.044	7.559	6.552	5.994	5.636	5.386	5.200	5.057	4.942	4.849	4.706	4.558	4.405	4.247	4.082	3.996	3.909
12	9.330	6.927	5.953	5.412	5.064	4.821	4.640	4.499	4.388	4.296	4.155	4.010	3.858	3.701	3.535	3.449	3.361
15	8.683	6.359	5.417	4.893	4.556	4.318	4.142	4.004	3.895	3.805	3.666	3.522	3.372	3.214	3.047	2.959	2.868
20	8.096	5.849	4.938	4.431	4.103	3.871	3.699	3.564	3.457	3.368	3.231	3.088	2.938	2.778	2.608	2.517	2.421
30	7.562	5.390	4.510	4.018	3.699	3.473	3.304	3.173	3.067	2.979	2.843	2.700	2.549	2.386	2.208	2.111	2.006
60	7.077	4.977	4.126	3.649	3.339	3.119	2.953	2.823	2.718	2.632	2.496	2.352	2.198	2.028	1.836	1.726	1.601
120	6.851	4.786	3.949	3.480	3.174	2.956	2.792	2.663	2.559	2.472	2.336	2.191	2.035	1.860	1.656	1.533	1.381
Infinity	6.635	4.605	3.782	3.319	3.017	2.802	2.639	2.511	2.407	2.321	2.185	2.039	1.878	1.696	1.473	1.325	1.000

TABLE 15.2.4   *F*-Table: Level 0.1% Critical Values

Numerator Degrees of Freedom ($k - 1$ for between-sample variability in one-way ANOVA)

Denominator Degrees of Freedom ($n - k$ for within-sample variability in one-way ANOVA)	1	2	3	4	5	6	7	8	9	10	12	15	20	30	60	120	Infinity
1	405284	500000	540379	562500	576405	585937	592873	598144	602284	605621	610668	615764	620908	626099	631337	633972	636629
2	998.50	999.00	999.17	999.25	999.30	999.33	999.36	999.38	999.39	999.40	999.42	999.43	999.45	999.47	999.48	999.49	999.50
3	167.03	148.50	141.11	137.10	134.58	132.85	131.58	130.62	129.86	129.25	128.32	127.37	126.42	125.45	124.47	123.97	123.47
4	74.137	61.246	56.177	53.436	51.712	50.525	49.658	48.996	48.475	48.053	47.412	46.761	46.100	45.429	44.746	44.400	44.051
5	47.181	37.122	33.202	31.085	29.752	28.834	28.163	27.649	27.244	26.917	26.418	25.911	25.395	24.869	24.333	24.060	23.785
6	35.507	27.000	23.703	21.924	20.803	20.030	19.463	19.030	18.688	18.411	17.989	17.559	17.120	16.672	16.214	15.981	15.745
7	29.245	21.689	18.772	17.198	16.206	15.521	15.019	14.634	14.330	14.083	13.707	13.324	12.932	12.530	12.119	11.909	11.697
8	25.415	18.494	15.829	14.392	13.485	12.858	12.398	12.046	11.767	11.540	11.194	10.841	10.480	10.109	9.727	9.532	9.334
9	22.857	16.387	13.902	12.560	11.714	11.128	10.698	10.368	10.107	9.894	9.570	9.238	8.898	8.548	8.187	8.001	7.813
10	21.040	14.905	12.553	11.283	10.481	9.926	9.517	9.204	8.956	8.754	8.445	8.129	7.804	7.469	7.122	6.944	6.762
12	18.643	12.974	10.804	9.633	8.892	8.379	8.001	7.710	7.480	7.292	7.005	6.709	6.405	6.090	5.762	5.593	5.420
15	16.587	11.339	9.335	8.253	7.567	7.092	6.741	6.471	6.256	6.081	5.812	5.535	5.248	4.950	4.638	4.475	4.307
20	14.818	9.953	8.098	7.095	6.460	6.018	5.692	5.440	5.239	5.075	4.823	4.562	4.290	4.005	3.703	3.544	3.378
30	13.293	8.773	7.054	6.124	5.534	5.122	4.817	4.581	4.393	4.239	4.000	3.753	3.493	3.217	2.920	2.759	2.589
60	11.973	7.767	6.171	5.307	4.757	4.372	4.086	3.865	3.687	3.541	3.315	3.078	2.827	2.555	2.252	2.082	1.890
120	11.378	7.321	5.781	4.947	4.416	4.044	3.767	3.552	3.379	3.237	3.016	2.783	2.534	2.262	1.950	1.767	1.543
Infinity	10.827	6.908	5.422	4.617	4.103	3.743	3.475	3.266	3.097	2.959	2.742	2.513	2.266	1.990	1.660	1.447	1.000

TABLE 15.2.5 *F*-Table: Level 10% Critical Values

Numerator Degrees of Freedom ($k - 1$ for between-sample variability in one-way ANOVA)

Denominator Degrees of Freedom ($n - k$ for within-sample variability in one-way ANOVA)	1	2	3	4	5	6	7	8	9	10	12	15	20	30	60	120	Infinity
1	39.863	49.500	53.593	55.833	57.240	58.204	58.906	59.439	59.858	60.195	60.705	61.220	61.740	62.265	62.794	63.061	63.328
2	8.526	9.000	9.162	9.243	9.293	9.326	9.349	9.367	9.381	9.392	9.408	9.425	9.441	9.458	9.475	9.483	9.491
3	5.538	5.462	5.391	5.343	5.309	5.285	5.266	5.252	5.240	5.230	5.216	5.200	5.184	5.168	5.151	5.143	5.134
4	4.545	4.325	4.191	4.107	4.051	4.010	3.979	3.955	3.936	3.920	3.896	3.870	3.844	3.817	3.790	3.775	3.761
5	4.060	3.780	3.619	3.520	3.453	3.405	3.368	3.339	3.316	3.297	3.268	3.238	3.207	3.174	3.140	3.123	3.105
6	3.776	3.463	3.289	3.181	3.108	3.055	3.014	2.983	2.958	2.937	2.905	2.871	2.836	2.800	2.762	2.742	2.722
7	3.589	3.257	3.074	2.961	2.883	2.827	2.785	2.752	2.725	2.703	2.668	2.632	2.595	2.555	2.514	2.493	2.471
8	3.458	3.113	2.924	2.806	2.726	2.668	2.624	2.589	2.561	2.538	2.502	2.464	2.425	2.383	2.339	2.316	2.293
9	3.360	3.006	2.813	2.693	2.611	2.551	2.505	2.469	2.440	2.416	2.379	2.340	2.298	2.255	2.208	2.184	2.159
10	3.285	2.924	2.728	2.605	2.522	2.461	2.414	2.377	2.347	2.323	2.284	2.244	2.201	2.155	2.107	2.082	2.055
12	3.177	2.807	2.606	2.480	2.394	2.331	2.283	2.245	2.214	2.188	2.147	2.105	2.060	2.011	1.960	1.932	1.904
15	3.073	2.695	2.490	2.361	2.273	2.208	2.158	2.119	2.086	2.059	2.017	1.972	1.924	1.873	1.817	1.787	1.755
20	2.975	2.589	2.380	2.249	2.158	2.091	2.040	1.999	1.965	1.937	1.892	1.845	1.794	1.738	1.677	1.643	1.607
30	2.881	2.489	2.276	2.142	2.049	1.980	1.927	1.884	1.849	1.819	1.773	1.722	1.667	1.606	1.538	1.499	1.456
60	2.791	2.393	2.177	2.041	1.946	1.875	1.819	1.775	1.738	1.707	1.657	1.603	1.543	1.476	1.395	1.348	1.291
120	2.748	2.347	2.130	1.992	1.896	1.824	1.767	1.722	1.684	1.652	1.601	1.545	1.482	1.409	1.320	1.265	1.193
Infinity	2.706	2.303	2.084	1.945	1.847	1.774	1.717	1.670	1.632	1.599	1.546	1.487	1.421	1.342	1.240	1.169	1.000

F-statistic is *larger* because this indicates greater differences among the sample averages.

If the *F*-statistic is *smaller* than the critical value from the *F*-table:

Accept the null hypothesis, H_0.

Do *not* accept the research hypothesis, H_1.

The sample averages are *not significantly different* from each other.

The observed differences among the sample averages could reasonably be due to random chance alone.

The result is *not statistically significant*.

(All of the above statements are equivalent to one another.)

If the *F*-statistic is *larger* than the critical value from the *F*-table:

Accept the research hypothesis, H_1.

Reject the null hypothesis, H_0.

The sample averages are *significantly different* from each other.

The observed differences among the sample averages could *not* reasonably be due to random chance alone.

The result is *statistically significant*.

(All of the above statements are equivalent to one another.)

To test the supplier quality example at the 5% level, the *F*-statistic (5.897) is compared to the *F*-table critical value (somewhere between 3.316 and 3.150). Since the *F*-statistic is larger, the result is significant:

There are significant differences among your suppliers in terms of average quality level ($p < 0.05$).

To test supplier quality at the 1% level, the *F*-statistic (5.897) is compared to the *F*-table critical value (somewhere between 5.390 and 4.977). Since the *F*-statistic is larger, the result is *highly* significant, a stronger result than before:

The supplier differences are highly significant ($p < 0.01$).

■ 15.3 The Least-Significant-Difference Test: Which Pairs Are Different?

What if you want to know *which* sample averages are significantly different from others? The *F*-test doesn't give you this information; it merely tells you whether or not there are differences. There are a number of different solutions to this problem. The method presented here, the **least-significant-difference test,** is based on *t*-tests for the average difference between pairs of samples.

There is a strict rule that must be obeyed in order that the probability of a type I error remain at a low rate of 5% (or other chosen level). The problem is that there are many *t*-tests (one for each pair of samples), and even though the *individual* error rate for each one remains at 5%, the *group* error rate, for all pairs, can be much higher.[6]

■ Strict Requirement for Testing Individual Pairs

If your *F*-test is not significant, you may *not* test particular samples to see if they are different from each other. The *F*-test has already told you that there are *no* significant differences whatsoever. If the *F*-test is not significant, but some *t*-test appears to be significant, the *F*-test overrides; the *t*-test is not really significant.

If your *F*-test is significant, you may go ahead and test all of the samples against one another to find out which particular pairs of samples are different.

The *t*-test for deciding whether or not two particular samples are different is based on three numbers:

1 The *average difference* between those samples, found by subtracting one average from the other (it doesn't matter which you subtract from which, as long as you remember how you did it).
2 The *standard error* for this average difference.
3 The number of *degrees of freedom,* which is $n - k$ regardless of which groups are being compared because the standard error uses the information from all of the samples.

The standard error is computed as follows:

■ Standard Error for the Average Difference between Two Samples

$$\text{Standard error} = \sqrt{(\text{Within-sample variability})\left(\frac{1}{n_i} + \frac{1}{n_j}\right)}$$

when n_i and n_j are the sample sizes of the two samples being compared.

Note that this standard error may change depending on which pairs of samples you are comparing. This is because the variability of the sample averages being compared depends on the sample sizes.

---

[6]The group error rate is the probability that *any one or more* of the *t*-tests wrongly declares significance when, in fact, there are no population mean differences.

The test then proceeds using the t-table in the usual way, either by constructing a confidence interval for the population mean difference and seeing if it includes the reference value 0 (for no difference) or else by computing the t-statistic (dividing the average difference by the standard error) and comparing the result to the t-table value.

For the supplier quality example, there are three pairs of suppliers to be compared: Amalgamated to Bipolar, Amalgamated to Consolidated, and Bipolar to Consolidated. Are you permitted to test these pairs against each other? Yes, because the F-test shows that there are significant differences in mean quality score from one supplier to another.

Here are the calculations for comparing Amalgamated to Bipolar, using the approximate t-table value of 1.960 for $n - k = 58 - 3 = 55$ degrees of freedom:[7]

$$\text{Average difference} = 80.667 - 82.056 = -1.389$$

$$\text{Standard error} = \sqrt{(\text{Within-sample variability})\left(\frac{1}{n_2} + \frac{1}{n_1}\right)}$$

$$= \sqrt{(45.63)\left(\frac{1}{21} + \frac{1}{18}\right)}$$

$$= \sqrt{45.63 \times 0.103175}$$

$$= \sqrt{4.708}$$

$$= 2.170$$

The 95% confidence interval for the population mean difference extends from

$$-1.389 - 1.960 \times 2.170 = -5.64$$

to

$$-1.389 + 1.960 \times 2.170 = 2.86$$

The t-statistic is

$$t = -\frac{1.389}{2.170} = -0.640$$

Bipolar has a lower quality score than Amalgamated, −1.389 points difference on average, but the difference is *not statistically significant*. You are 95% sure that the difference is somewhere between −5.64 and 2.86. Because this confidence interval includes the possibility of zero difference, you accept the null hypothesis that there is no difference in the population mean qual-

---

[7]This t-table value, 1.960, is for an infinite number of degrees of freedom and is often used as an approximation when the number of degrees of freedom is 40 or more. Slightly different answers will be obtained if the more exact value, 2.004, is used.

ity scores of Amalgamated and Bipolar. You could also perform the t-test by observing that the t-statistic (-0.640) is smaller in magnitude than the t-table value of 1.960.

However, Consolidated *does* have significantly higher quality than either Amalgamated or Bipolar. Here are the calculations for comparing Amalgamated to Consolidated:

$$\text{Average difference} = 87.684 - 82.056 = 5.628$$

$$\text{Standard error} = \sqrt{(45.63)\left(\frac{1}{19} + \frac{1}{18}\right)} = 2.222$$

The 95% confidence interval for the population mean difference extends from

$$5.628 - 1.960 \times 2.222 = 1.27$$

to

$$5.628 + 1.960 \times 2.222 = 9.98$$

$$t = \frac{5.628}{2.222} = 2.533$$

The computations for comparing Bipolar to Consolidated are:

$$\text{Average difference} = 87.684 - 80.667 = 7.017$$

$$\text{Standard error} = \sqrt{(45.63)\left(\frac{1}{19} + \frac{1}{21}\right)} = 2.139$$

The 95% confidence interval for the population mean difference extends from

$$7.017 - 1.960 \times 2.139 = 2.82$$

to

$$7.017 + 1.960 \times 2.139 = 11.21$$

$$t = \frac{7.017}{2.139} = 3.281$$

Here is a summary of what the analysis of variance has told you about the quality of these three suppliers:

1 There are significant differences among the suppliers. The F-test decided that their population mean quality scores are not all identical.
2 Consolidated has significantly superior quality compared to each of the other suppliers (based on the least-significant-difference test).
3 The other two suppliers, Amalgamated and Bipolar, are not significantly different from each other in terms of average quality level.

■ 15.4 More Advanced ANOVA Designs

When your data set has more structure than just a single collection of samples, the analysis of variance can often be adapted to help answer the more complex questions that can be asked.

In order for ANOVA to be the appropriate analysis, your data set should still consist of a collection of samples with one basic measurement for each elementary unit, just as it was for the one-way analysis of variance. What's new is that there is now some structure or pattern to the arrangement of these samples. For example, while salary data for the four groups "white male," "white female," "minority male," and "minority female" could be analyzed using one-way ANOVA to see whether salaries differ significantly from one group to another, a two-way ANOVA would also allow you to ask questions about a gender difference and a racial difference.

You will still need to satisfy the basic assumptions. First, each sample is assumed to be a random sample from the population to which you wish to generalize. Second, each population is assumed to follow a normal distribution and the standard deviations of these populations are assumed to be identical.

There is another way to look at the kind of data structure needed in order for ANOVA to be appropriate: you need a multivariate data set in which exactly one variable is quantitative (the basic measurement) and all others are qualitative. The qualitative variables, taken together, define the grouping of the quantitative observations into samples.

Variety Is the Spice of Life

There is tremendous diversity in the world of ANOVA because there are many different ways the samples might relate to one another. What distinguishes one kind of analysis from another is the *design,* that is, the way in which the data were collected. When using advanced ANOVA, it's up to you to be sure that the computer uses an ANOVA model that is appropriate for your data; in many cases there's no way the computer could choose the correct model based only on the data set. Here are some highlights of these more advanced ANOVA methods.

Two-Way ANOVA

When your samples form a table, with rows for one factor and columns for another, you may ask three basic kinds of questions: (1) Does the first factor make any difference? (2) Does the second factor make any difference? and (3) Does the effect of the first factor depend on the second factor, or do the two factors act independently of one another? The first two questions refer to the *main effects* of each factor by itself, while the third question refers to the *interaction* of the factors with one another.

Here is an example for which two-way ANOVA would be appropriate. The first factor is *shift,* indicating whether the day shift, the night shift, or the swing shift was on duty at the time the part was manufactured. The second factor is *supplier,* indicating which of your four suppliers provided the raw materials. The measurement is the overall *quality score* of the manufactured product. The first question concerns the main effect of shift: Do the quality scores differ significantly from one shift to another? The second question concerns the main effect of supplier: Do the quality scores differ significantly from one supplier to another? The third question concerns the interaction of shift with supplier, for example: Do the quality scores for the three shifts show different patterns depending on which supplier's raw materials are being used?

For a concrete example of interaction, suppose that the night shift's quality scores are usually higher than for the other shifts, except that the night crew has trouble working with raw materials from one particular supplier (and the other shifts have no such trouble).

Three-Way and More

When there are three or more factors defining your samples, the analysis of variance still examines the *main effects* of each factor (to see if it makes a difference) and the *interactions* among factors (to see how the factors relate to one another). What's new is that there are more kinds of interactions, each to be examined separately, than for just a two-way ANOVA with only two factors. There are *two-way interactions* which consider the factors two at a time, *three-way interactions* which consider combinations of three factors at once, and so forth up until you look at the highest-level interaction of all factors at once.

Analysis of Covariance (ANCOVA)

The analysis of covariance combines regression analysis with ANOVA. For example, in addition to the basic data for ANOVA, you might have an important additional quantitative variable. Instead of either doing ANOVA while ignoring this additional variable, or doing regression while ignoring the groups, ANCOVA will do both at once. You may think of the analysis either in terms of the relationship between separate regression analyses performed for each sample, or in terms of an ANOVA that has been adjusted for differences in the additional variable.

Multivariate Analysis of Variance (MANOVA)

When you have more than one quantitative response variable, you may use the multivariate analysis of variance to study the differences in all responses from one sample to another. If, for example, you had three quantitative ratings measured for each finished product (How nice does it look? How well does it work? How noisy is it?) then you could use MANOVA to see whether these measures differ significantly according to the main effects of shift (day, night, or swing) and supplier.

How to Read an ANOVA Table

The general form of the traditional ANOVA table is shown in Table 15.4.1. While such a table is useful for testing hypotheses about your population means (once you know how to read it!), it has two serious deficiencies. First, it tells you nothing in terms of the original measurements; you will need to examine a separate table of average values to find out, for example, whether quality was higher for the day or the night shift. Second, most of the ANOVA table has no direct practical interpretation: for many applications only the first (source of variation) and last (p-value) columns are useful; the others are merely computational steps along the way to the p-values which give you the results of the significance tests. Nonetheless, it is traditional to report this table to substantiate your claims of statistical significance in ANOVA.

Each hypothesis is tested using an F-test, which compares the mean square for that source of variation (which is large when that source of variation makes a difference in your quantitative measurement) to the error mean square, asking the question How much stronger than purely random is this particular source? To find out whether that source of variation (the ith one, say) has a significant effect or not, compare the computed F-value (F_i) in the table to the F-table value with numerator degrees of freedom (df_i) for that source and denominator degrees of freedom (df_e) for the error. Or else look directly at the p-value (p_i) and decide "significant" if it is small enough, for example, if $p < 0.05$.

| EXAMPLE | **The Effect of Price Changes and Product Type on Grocery Sales** |

We expect sales to go up when an item is temporarily "on sale" at a lower price than usual. If the product is one that consumers can easily stock up on at home, you would expect to see even higher sales than for a more perishable or less fre-

TABLE 15.4.1   General Form of the Traditional ANOVA Table

Source of Variation	Sum of Squares	Degrees of Freedom	Mean Square	F-Value	p-Value
Source 1	SS_1	df_1	$MS_1 = SS_1/df_1$	$F_1 = MS_1/MS_e$	p_1
Source 2	SS_2	df_2	$MS_2 = SS_2/df_2$	$F_2 = MS_2/MS_e$	p_2
.	.	.	.	.	.
.	.	.	.	.	.
.	.	.	.	.	.
Source k	SS_k	df_k	$MS_k = SS_k/df_k$	$F_k = MS_k/MS_e$	p_k
Error or residual	SS_e	df_e	$MS_e = SS_e/df_e$		

quently consumed product. These questions are addressed in a study by Litvack, Calantone, and Warshaw.[8] They used a two-way ANOVA with the following basic structure:

> The first factor is defined by the two *product types:* stock-up and nonstock-up items. Stock-up items are those that consumers can easily buy in quantity and store at home, such as dog food, tissues, and canned fish. Nonstock-up items included mustard, cheese, and breakfast cereals.
>
> The second factor is defined by the three *price manipulations:* lowered 20%, unchanged, and raised 20% as compared to the usual price at each store.
>
> The measurement is defined as the change in sales, in number of units sold per $1 million of grocery sales for each store. Note that by dividing in this way, they have adjusted for the different sizes of one store as compared to another, making it appropriate to analyze smaller and larger grocery stores together.

The change in sales was measured for a variety of products of each type and a variety of price manipulations, resulting in an ANOVA table like Table 15.4.2. The p-value 0.5694 for product type indicates *no significant differences* on average between stock-up items and nonstock-up items. This is somewhat surprising, because we expected to find a difference; however, please read on for further results. The p-value 0.0001 for price manipulation shows that there are *very highly significant differences* on average among lowered, unchanged, and raised prices; that is, the price change had a significant impact on sales.

The interaction term is highly significant ($p = 0.0095$ is less than 0.01). This says that a product's sales reaction to price depended on whether it was a stock-up item or a nonstock-up item. That is, stock-up items reacted differently to price changes than the others did.

How can it be that the main effect for product type was not significant, but the interaction of product type with price manipulation was significant? Remember that the main effect looks only at the *average* for each item type, while the interaction looks at all combinations of product type and pricing manipulation.

Although The ANOVA table provides useful results for significance tests, much important information is missing. In particular: What was the effect of a

TABLE 15.4.2   ANOVA Table for Product and Price Effects on Sales

Source of Variation	Sum of Squares	Degrees of Freedom	Mean Square	*F*-Value	*p*-Value
Product type	0.469	1	0.469	0.32	0.5694
Price manipulation	33.284	2	16.642	11.50	0.0001
Interaction:					
Product type × Price manipulation	13.711	2	6.856	4.74	0.0095
Error or residual	377.579	261	1.447		

[8]D. S Litvack, R. J. Calantone, and P. R. Warshaw, "An Examination of Short-Term Retail Grocery Price Effects," *Journal of Retailing* 61 (1985), pp. 9–25.

20% price reduction on sales of a typical stock-up item? The answer to such practical questions cannot be found in the ANOVA table! To answer questions like this, you will need to examine the average values, as shown in Table 15.4.3 and displayed in Figure 15.4.1. Each average represents 12 products and 4 stores. Note that sales of stock-up items (on the left in the figure) are *not* uniformly higher or lower than for nonstock-up items (on the right); this helps explain why the main effect for product type was not significant. Note also that sales went way up only when prices were lowered for stock-up items; this happened only when the right combination of both factors was present and is therefore part of the interaction term which is indeed significant. It is also clear that sales dropped off when prices were raised and were highest when prices were lowered, leading to the significant main effect for price manipulation.

Don't be fooled or intimidated into thinking that an ANOVA table (such as Table 15.4.2) is supposed to tell the whole story. If it's not already provided to you, be sure to ask to see the average values (such as Table 15.4.3 and Figure 15.4.1) so that you can understand what's really going on!

TABLE 15.4.3   Percent Change in Standardized Sales

| | Price Manipulation | | |
Product Type	Lowered 20%	Unchanged	Raised 20%
Stock-up	54.95	1.75	−24.10
Nonstock-up	10.55	6.95	−7.60

FIGURE 15.4.1   The average change in sales for the six combinations of product type with price manipulation. The ANOVA table tests hypotheses about the six population means that these averages represent.

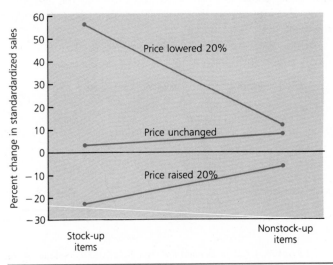

EXAMPLE

Jokes in the Workplace

What kinds of jokes are unacceptable in the workplace? Why do some people take offense at some kinds of jokes while others do not? These matters were studied using ANOVA by Smeltzer and Leap.[9] As an executive, these issues may involve you beyond your personal appreciation for humor because "joking may impact on civil and human rights litigation and on the quality of work life."

The study involved a three-way ANOVA. The three factors were gender (male or female), race (black or white), and experience (inexperienced with less than one full year or experienced). Considering all combinations of these three factors, each with two categories, there are 8 different types of employees (male black inexperienced, male black experienced, male white inexperienced, and so forth). Let's look at how the 165 people in their study each rated 5 sexist jokes on a 7-point scale indicating how inappropriate these jokes were in the workplace.

The ANOVA results are shown in Table 15.4.4. The sums of squares, the mean squares, and the residual results are not needed. All of the usual hypothesis tests can be performed using the p-values provided.

Of the main effects, only race is significant. This says that whites and blacks had different opinions, overall, on the appropriateness of sexist jokes in the workplace. As always, the ANOVA table doesn't tell you which group felt they were more appropriate; you would have to examine the average responses for each group to find this out. The differences were not large (5.4 for whites as compared to 4.36 for blacks, according to the study), but they are highly unlikely to be this different due to random chance alone.

Of the two-way interactions, only gender × race is significant. This indicates that the difference in attitudes between men and women depended on whether they were black or white. The three-way interaction was not significant, indicating that there are no further detailed distinctions among attitudes that are discernible in this data set.

TABLE 15.4.4 ANOVA Table for Appropriateness of Sexist Jokes in the Workplace

Source of Variation	Degrees of Freedom	F-Value	p-Value
Main effects			
Gender	1	2.83	0.09
Race	1	15.59	0.0001
Experience	1	0.54	0.46
Two-way interactions			
Gender × Race	1	6.87	0.009
Gender × Experience	1	0.00	1.0
Race × Experience	1	2.54	0.11
Three-way interaction			
Gender × Race × Experience	1	1.44	0.23

[9]L. R. Smeltzer and T. L. Leap, "An Analysis of Individual Reactions to Potentially Offensive Jokes in Work Settings," *Human Relations* 41 (1988), pp. 295–304.

■ 15.5 End-of-Chapter Materials

Summary

The **analysis of variance** (or **ANOVA** for short) provides a general framework for statistical hypothesis testing based on careful examination of the different sources of variability in a complex situation. The analysis of variance uses an **F-test** based on the **F-statistic**, a ratio of two variance measures, to perform each hypothesis test. The numerator represents the variability due to that special, interesting effect being tested, and the denominator represents a baseline measure of randomness. If the ratio is larger than the value in the F-table, the effect is significant. The **one-way analysis of variance,** in particular, is used to test whether the averages from several different situations are significantly different from one another or not.

Don't forget to explore your data. Box plots help you compare several distributions at once, so that you can see the structure in your data, identify problems (if any), and check assumptions required for the analysis of variance, such as normal distributions and equal variability.

The data set for the one-way analysis of variance consists of k independent univariate samples, each using the same measurement units. The one-way analysis of variance compares two sources of variation:

Between-sample variability (from one sample to another).
Within-sample variability (inside each sample).

There are two assumptions that must be satisfied for the result of a one-way analysis of variance to be valid:

1 The data set consists of k random samples from k populations.
2 Each population has a normal distribution, and the standard deviations of the populations are identical, so that $\sigma_1 = \sigma_2 = \cdots = \sigma_k$.

The null hypothesis claims that there are no differences from one sample to another, and the research hypothesis claims that some differences exist:

$$H_0: \mu_1 = \mu_2 = \cdots = \mu_k \quad \text{(the means are all equal)}$$

$$H_1: \mu_i \neq \mu_j \quad \text{for at least one pair of populations (the means are } not \text{ all equal)}$$

The **grand average** is the average of all of the data values from all of the samples combined:

$$\overline{X} = \frac{n_1 \overline{X}_1 + n_2 \overline{X}_2 + \cdots + n_k \overline{X}_k}{n}$$

$$= \frac{\sum_{i=1}^{k} n_i \overline{X}_i}{n}$$

The **between-sample variability** measures how different the sample averages are from one another, and the **within-sample variability** measures how variable each sample is:

$$\text{Between-sample variability} = \frac{n_1(\overline{X}_1 - \overline{X})^2 + n_2(\overline{X}_2 - \overline{X})^2 + \cdots + n_k(\overline{X}_k - \overline{X})^2}{k - 1}$$

$$= \frac{\sum\limits_{i=1}^{k} n_i(\overline{X}_i - \overline{X})^2}{k - 1}$$

Degrees of freedom $= k - 1$

$$\text{Within-sample variability} = \frac{(n_1 - 1)(S_1)^2 + (n_2 - 1)(S_2)^2 + \cdots + (n_k - 1)(S_k)^2}{n - k}$$

$$= \frac{\sum\limits_{i=1}^{k} (n_i - 1)(S_i)^2}{n - k}$$

Degrees of freedom $= n - k$

The F-statistic is the ratio of these two variability measures, indicating the extent to which the sample averages differ from one another (the numerator) with respect to the overall level of variability in the samples (the denominator).

$$F = \frac{\text{Between-sample variability}}{\text{Within-sample variability}}$$

Degrees of freedom $= k - 1$ (numerator)   and $n - k$ (denominator)

The **F-table** is a list of critical values for the distribution of the F-statistic such that the F-statistic exceeds the F-table value a controlled percentage of the time (5%, for example) when the null hypothesis is true. The F-test is performed by comparing the F-statistic (computed from your data) to the critical value from the F-table.

The F-test only tells you whether or not there are differences. If the F-test finds significance, the **least-significant-difference test** may be used to compare each pair of samples to see which ones are significantly different from each other. This test is based on the average difference for the two groups being compared, the standard error of this average difference, and the number of degrees of freedom $(n - k)$:

$$\text{Standard error} = \sqrt{(\text{Within-sample variability})\left(\frac{1}{n_i} + \frac{1}{n_j}\right)}$$

where n_i and n_j are the sizes of the two samples being compared.

There are many advanced ANOVA techniques, including two-way and higher designs. In order for ANOVA to be the appropriate analysis, your data set should consist of a collection of samples, with one basic measurement for each elementary unit, just as it was for the one-way analysis of variance.

Remember that the ANOVA table does not tell the whole story; always ask to see the average values so that you can understand what's really going on.

Key Words

analysis of variance (ANOVA) 639
F-test 640
F-statistic 640
one-way analysis of variance 640
grand average 646

between-sample variability 646
within-sample variability 647
F-table 649
least-significant-difference test 655

Questions

1 Explain in what sense the analysis of variance involves actually analyzing variance—in particular, what variances are analyzed and why?
2 a. What kind of data set should be analyzed using the one-way analysis of variance?
  b. Why shouldn't you use the unpaired t-test instead of the one-way analysis of variance?
3 Name and interpret the two sources of variation in the one-way analysis of variance.
4 Which assumption helps the data be representative of the population?
5 What assumptions are required concerning the distribution of each population?
6 Do the sample sizes have to be equal in the one-way analysis of variance?
7 a. State the hypotheses for the one-way analysis of variance.
  b. Is the research hypothesis very specific about the nature of any differences?
8 Describe and give a formula for each of the following quantities, which are used in performing a one-way analysis of variance:
  a. Total sample size, n.
  b. Grand average, $\overline{X}$.
  c. Between-sample variability and its degrees of freedom.
  d. Within-sample variability and its degrees of freedom.
  e. F-statistic and its degrees of freedom.
  f. F-table.
9 When may you use the least-significance-difference test to compare individual pairs of samples? When is this not permitted?
10 Why can the standard error of the average difference be a different number depending on which samples you are comparing?

Problems

1 Three advertisements have been tested, each one using a different random sample of consumers from the same city. Scores indicating the effectiveness of the advertisement were analyzed, and the results were as follows:

	Ad 1	Ad 2	Ad 3
Average	63.2	68.1	53.5
Standard deviation	7.9	11.3	9.2
Sample size (consumers)	101	97	105

a. Which advertisement appears to have the highest effectiveness? Which appears to have the lowest?

b. Find the total sample size, n, the grand average, $\overline{X}$, and the number of samples, k.

c. Find the between-sample variability and its degrees of freedom.

d. Find the within-sample variability and its degrees of freedom.

2 Refer to the data for problem 1.

a. Find the F-statistic and its numbers of degrees of freedom.

b. Interpret the F-statistic in terms of how many times more volatile one source of variability is than another.

c. Find the critical value from the F-table at the 5% level.

d. Report the result of the F-test at the 5% level.

e. Summarize what this test has told you about any differences among these ads for consumers in general in this city.

3 Refer to the data for problem 1.

a. Find the critical value from the F-table at the 0.1% level, and report the result of the F-test at this level.

b. Summarize what this test has told you about any differences among these ads for consumers in general in this city.

4 Refer to the data for problem 1.

a. Find the average difference between the effectiveness of ad 1 and that of ad 2.

b. Find the standard error for this average difference.

c. How many degrees of freedom does this standard error have?

d. Find the 99.9% confidence interval for the population mean difference in effectiveness between ad 1 and ad 2.

e. Are the effectiveness scores of ad 1 and ad 2 very highly significantly different? How do you know?

5 Refer to the data for problem 1.

a. Find the average difference and its standard error for *every* pair of advertisements.

b. Test every pair of advertisements at the 1% level, and report the results.

6 Three companies are trying to sell you their additives to reduce waste in a chemical manufacturing process. You're not sure their products are appropriate because your process is different from the industry standard (it's a proprietary trade secret). You have arranged to get a small supply of each additive, provided free, for testing purposes. Here are the summaries of the waste measurements when each additive was used, all else kept equal:

	Sludge Away	Cleen Up	No Yuk
Average	245.97	210.92	240.45
Standard deviation	41.05	43.52	35.91
Sample size (batches)	10	10	10

a. Which additive appears to leave the highest amount of waste? Which appears to leave the lowest?

b. Find the total sample size, n, the grand average, $\overline{X}$, and the number of samples, k.

c. Find the between-sample variability and its degrees of freedom.

d. Find the within-sample variability and its degrees of freedom.

7 Refer to the data for problem 6.

a. Find the F-statistic and its numbers of degrees of freedom.

b. Interpret the F-statistic in terms of how many times more volatile one source of variability is than another.

c. Find the critical value from the F-table at the 5% level.

d. Report the result of the *F*-test at the 5% level.

e. Summarize what this *F*-test has told you about the comparative abilities of these additives to reduce waste.

8 Refer to the data for problem 6. Would it be appropriate to use the least-significant-difference test to find out whether Cleen Up has significantly lower waste than Sludge Away (at the 5% level)? Why or why not?

9 Refer to the data for problem 6.

a. Find the critical value from the *F*-table at the 10% level, and report the result of the *F*-test at this level.

b. Summarize what this *F*-test has told you about the comparative abilities of these additives to reduce waste.

10 Refer to the data for problem 6. Select the two additives with the largest average difference in waste, and answer the following. (Use the least-significant-difference test method for this problem, even if you feel that it is not appropriate to do so.)

a. Find the size of the average difference for this pair.

b. Find the standard error of this average difference.

c. How many degrees of freedom does this standard error have?

d. Find the two-sided 90% confidence interval for the mean difference.

e. Based on the average difference, the standard error, the degrees of freedom, and the *t*-table, do these two additives appear to be significantly different at the 10% test level?

f. Can you conclude that the two additives are really significantly different at the 10% level? Why or why not? (Be careful. You may wish to consider the result of the *F*-test from the previous problem.)

11 In an attempt to regain control of your time, you have been recording the time required, in minutes, to respond to each telephone call for the day. Before you make changes (such as referring certain types of calls to subordinates), you would like to have a better understanding of the situation. Grouping calls by type, the results for call lengths were as follows:

Information	Sales	Service	Other
0.6	5.1	5.2	6.3
1.1	1.7	2.9	1.2
1.0	4.4	2.6	3.1
1.9	26.6	1.2	2.5
3.8	7.4	7.0	3.0
1.6	1.4	14.2	2.6
0.4	7.0	8.4	0.8
0.6	3.9	0.6	
2.2	3.1	26.7	
12.3	1.2	7.7	
4.2	1.9	4.8	
2.8	17.3	7.2	
1.4	7.8	2.7	
	4.3	3.4	
	3.4	13.3	
	1.3		
	2.0		

a. Draw box plots on the same scale for these four types of calls, and describe the structure you see.

b. Compute the average and standard deviation for each type of call.

   c. Which type of call appears to have the highest average length? Which has the lowest?

   d. Are the assumptions of normal distribution and equal variability for the one-way analysis of variance satisfied for this data set? Why or why not?

   e. Find the logarithm of each data value, and draw box plots for these logarithms.

   f. Is the assumption of equal variability better satisfied using logarithms than using the original data?

12 Refer to the data for problem 11. Continue using the logarithms of the lengths of calls.

   a. Find the total sample size, n, the grand average, $\overline{X}$, and the number of samples, k.

   b. Find the between-sample variability and its degrees of freedom.

   c. Find the within-sample variability and its degrees of freedom.

13 Refer to the data for problem 11. Continue using the logarithms of the lengths of calls.

   a. Find the F-statistic and its numbers of degrees of freedom.

   b. Find the critical value from the F-table at the 5% level.

   c. Report the result of the F-test at the 5% level.

   d. Summarize what this test has told you about any differences among these types of calls.

14 Refer to the data for problem 11. Continue using the logarithms of the lengths of calls.

   a. Find the average difference and its standard error for every pair of types of calls.

   b. Which pairs of types of calls are significantly different from each other, in terms of average logarithm of length?

15 Use multiple regression with indicator variables, instead of one-way ANOVA, to test whether the quality data in Table 15.1.1 show significant differences from one supplier to another. (You may wish to review the material on indicator variables from Chapter 12.)

   a. Create the Y variable by listing all quality scores in a single, long column. Do this by stacking Amalgamated's scores on top of Bipolar's on top of Consolidated's.

   b. Create two indicator variables, one for Amalgamated and one for Bipolar.

   c. Run a multiple regression analysis.

   d. Compare the F-statistic from the multiple regression to the F-statistic from the one-way ANOVA. Comment.

   e. Compare the regression coefficients for the indicator variables to the average differences in quality scores from one supplier to another. Comment.

   f. Do these two methods—multiple regression and one-way ANOVA—give different answers, or are they in complete agreement? Why do you think it works this way?

16 Which is better: competition or cooperation? And does the answer depend on whether the participants share the same values? A study by Cosier and Dalton sheds light on these issues.[10] One of their ANOVA tables provides the basis for Table 15.5.1

   a. The average performance was higher for the cooperation group than for the competition group. Was it significantly higher? How do you know?

---

[10]R. A. Cosier and D. R. Dalton, "Competition and Cooperation: Effects of Value Dissensus and Predisposition to Help," *Human Relations* 41 (1988), pp. 823–39.

TABLE 15.5.1 Effects of Competition-Cooperation and Value Dissensus on Performance

Source of Variation	Sum of Squares	Degrees of Freedom	Mean Square	F-Value	p-Value
Competition – cooperation (A)	3,185.77	1	3,185.77	4.00	0.049682
Value dissensus (B)	58.04	1	54.04	0.07	0.792174
A × B	424.95	1	424.95	0.53	0.469221
Error	51,729.98	65	795.85		
Total	55,370.49	68			

b. The average performance was higher when value dissensus was low. Does value dissensus have a significant impact on performance? How do you know?

c. Is the interaction significant? What does this tell you?

17 Are prices really higher in department stores as compared to off-price stores? Kirby and Dardis[11] examined prices of 20 items (shirts, pants, etc.) for 13 weeks and found that prices are indeed 40% higher in department stores. The ANOVA table, adapted from their report, is shown in Table 15.5.2.

TABLE 15.5.2 Analysis of Variance for Prices by Store Type, Item, and Week

Source of Variation	Sum of Squares	Degrees of Freedom	Mean Square	F-Value	p-Value
Store type (A)	1,794,577,789	1	1,794,577,789	1,121.52	0.000000
Item (B)	25,726,794,801	19	1,354,041	864.21	0.000000
Week (C)	246,397,563	12	2,053,313	12.83	0.000000
Two-way interaction					
A × B	970,172,936	19	510,617	31.91	0.000000
A × C	69,197,628	12	5,766,469	3.60	0.000027
B × C	320,970,292	228	140,776	0.88	0.884253
Three-way interaction					
A × B × C	264,279,428	228	115,912	0.72	0.998823
Residual	1,664,128,185	1040	1,600,123		
Total	31,056,518,626	1559			

a. Are the higher prices (40% higher at department stores on average) significantly higher? How do you know?

b. What kind of ANOVA is this?

c. Identify the three factors in this analysis. How many categories are there for each one?

d. What does the p-value for main effect B tell you?

e. Are there significant differences in pricing from one week to another? How do you know?

f. Consider the interaction between type of store and item. Is it significant? What does this tell you?

g. Consider the interaction between type of store and week. Is it significant? What does this tell you?

h. Consider the interaction between item and week. Is it significant? What does this tell you?

---

[11] G. H. Kirby and R. Dardis, "Research Note: A Pricing Study of Women's Apparel in Off-Price and Department Stores," *Journal of Retailing* 62 (1986), pp. 321–30.

i. Usually we only examine p-values to see if they are small enough to declare significance. However, the three-way interaction p-value appears suspiciously large, suggesting that there may be significantly *less* randomness than was expected for this model. Which technical assumption of hypothesis testing may not be satisfied here?

Database Exercises

Refer to the employee database in Appendix A.

1 Break down the annual salaries into three groups according to training level (A, B, or C).
  a. Draw a box plot to compare these three groups. Comment on what you see.
  b. Find the average for each training level, and comment.
  c. Find the between-sample and the within-sample variabilities and their respective degrees of freedom.
  d. Find the F-statistic and its numbers of degrees of freedom.
  e. Perform the F-test at level 0.05, and report the results.
  f. Report the results of the least-significant-difference test, if appropriate.
  g. Summarize what you have learned about the database from this problem.
2 Answer the parts of exercise 1 using age in place of annual salary.
3 Answer the parts of exercise 1 using experience in place of annual salary.

Projects

1 Find a quantity of interest to you, and look up its value for at least 10 firms in each of at least three industry groups. You should thus have at least 30 numbers.
  a. Draw box plots, one for each industry group, and summarize your data set. Be sure to use the same scale, to facilitate comparison.
  b. Find the average and standard deviation for each industry group.
  c. Comment on whether the assumptions for the one-way analysis of variance appear to be (1) satisfied, (2) somewhat satisfied, or (3) not at all satisfied by your data. Correct any serious problem, if possible, by transforming.
  d. Find the between-sample variability and its degrees of freedom.
  e. Find the within-sample variability and its degrees of freedom.
  f. Find the F-statistic and its numbers of degrees of freedom.
  g. Find the appropriate critical value in the F-table at your choice of significance level.
  h. Perform the F-test, and report the results.
  i. If the F-test is significant, perform the least-significant-difference test for each pair of industry groups, and summarize any differences you find.
2 From your library, choose a few scholarly journals in a business field of interest to you (the reference librarian may be able to help you). Skim the articles in several issues to locate one that uses the analysis of variance. Write a page summarizing the following:
  a. What is the main question being addressed?
  b. What kind of data have been analyzed? How were they obtained?
  c. Find a hypothesis test that has performed. Identify the null and research hypotheses. State the results of the test.

Nonparametrics
Testing with Ordinal Data
or Nonnormal Distributions

Have you been at all troubled by the assumptions required for statistical inference? Perhaps you should be. In particular, it should be disturbing that the population distribution is required to be *normal* when this can be so difficult to verify based on sample data. Sure, the central limit theorem helps you sometimes, but when your sample size is not large enough or when you have strong skewness or outliers, it would be nice if you had an alternative. You do.

Nonparametric methods are statistical procedures for hypothesis testing that do not require a normal distribution (or any other particular shape of distribution) because they are based on counts or ranks (the smallest observation has rank 1, the next is 2, then 3, etc.) instead of the actual data values. These methods still require that you have a random sample from the population, to ensure that your data provide useful information. Because they are based on ranking and do not require computing sums of data values, many nonparametric methods work with *ordinal data* as well as with quantitative data. Here is a summary of two nonparametric approaches:

■ The Nonparametric Approach Based on Counts

1 Count the number of times some event occurs in the data set.
2 Use the binomial distribution to decide whether this count is reasonable or not under the null hypothesis.

> ### ■ The Nonparametric Approach Based on Ranks
>
> 1 Create a new data set using the rank of each data value. The **rank** of a data value indicates its position after you order the data set. For example, the data set (35, 95, 48, 38, 57) would become (1, 5, 3, 2, 4) because 35 is the smallest (it has rank 1), 95 is the largest (with rank 5), 48 is the third smallest (rank 3), etc.
> 2 Ignore the original data, and concentrate on the rank ordering.
> 3 Use statistical formulas and tables created especially for testing ranks.

Parametric methods are statistical procedures that require a completely specified model. Most of our statistical inference so far has required parametric models (including t-tests, regression tests, and the F-test). For example, the linear model for regression specifies the prediction equation as well as the exact form of the random noise. By contrast, *non*parametric methods are more flexible and do not require an exact specification of the situation.

The biggest surprise about nonparametric methods is a pleasant one: you lose very little when you fail to take advantage of a normal distribution (when you have one), and you can win very big when your distribution is not normal. Thus, using a nonparametric method is like taking out an insurance policy: you pay a small premium, but you will receive a lot if problems do arise.

One way to measure the effectiveness of different statistical tests is in terms of their efficiency. One test is said to be more **efficient** than another if it makes better use of the information in the data.[1] Thus, nonparametric methods are nearly as efficient as parametric ones (when you have a normal distribution) and can be much more efficient (when you don't). Here is a summary of the advantages of the nonparametric approach:

> ### ■ Advantages of Nonparametric Testing
>
> 1 No need to assume normality; can be used even if the distribution is not normal.
> 2 Avoids many problems of transformation; can be used even if data cannot easily be transformed to be normal and, in fact, gives the same result whether you transform or not.
> 3 Can even be used to test ordinal data because ranks can be found based on the natural ordering.
> 4 Can be much more efficient than parametric methods when distributions are not normal.

---

[1] The formal definition of *efficiency* is stated in terms of the relative work (sample sizes) required for the tests to give similar results.

There is only one disadvantage of nonparametric methods, and it is relatively small:

> ■ **Disadvantage of Nonparametric Testing**
> Less statistically efficient than parametric methods when distributions are normal; however, this efficiency loss is often slight.

In this chapter, you will learn about the one-sample problem (testing the median), as well as the paired and unpaired two-sample problems (testing for a difference).

■ 16.1 Testing the Median against a Known Reference Value

On the one hand, when you have an ordinary univariate sample of data from a population, you might use the average and standard error to test a hypothesis about the population mean (the t-test). And this is fine if the distribution is normal.

On the other hand, the nonparametric approach, because it is based on the rank ordering of the data, tests the population *median*. The median is the appropriate summary because it is defined in terms of ranks (remember that the median has rank $(1 + n)/2$ for a sample of size n).

How can we get rid of the normal distribution assumption? It's easy once you realize that half of the population is below the median and half is above, if the population distribution is continuous.[2] There is a binomial probability distribution inherent here, since the data set is a random sample of independent observations. Using probability language from Chapters 6 and 7, the number of data values below the population median is the number of "below-median" events that occur in n independent trials, where each event has probability $1/2$. Therefore:

> The number of sample data values below a continuous population's median follows a binomial distribution where $p = 0.5$ and n is the sample size.

The Sign Test

The *sign test* makes use of this binomial distribution. To test whether or not the population median could reasonably be \$65,536, for example, you could see how many sample values fall below \$65,536 and determine if this is a

---

[2] You will soon see how to adapt the test to a noncontinuous population.

reasonable observation from a binomial distribution. The **sign test** decides whether the population median is equal to a given reference value based on the number of sample values that fall below that reference value. No arithmetic is performed on the data values, only comparing and counting. Here is the procedure:

■ The Sign Test

1. Count the number of data values that are *different* from the reference value, θ_0. This number is m, the **modified sample size.**
2. Find the limits in the table for this modified sample size.
3. Count how many data values fall below the reference value, θ_0, and compare this number to the limits in the table.[3]
4. If the count from step 3 falls *outside* the limits of the table, the difference is statistically significant. If it falls *at or within* the limits, the difference is not statistically significant.

The Hypotheses

First assume that the population distribution is continuous. The null hypothesis for the sign test claims that the population median, θ, is exactly equal to some specified reference value, θ_0. (As usual, this reference value is assumed to be known precisely and was not computed from the current data set.) The research hypothesis claims the contrary: the population median is not equal to this reference value.

■ Hypotheses for the Sign Test for the Median of a Continuous Population Distribution

$$H_0: \theta = \theta_0$$

$$H_1: \theta \neq \theta_0$$

where θ is the (unknown) population median and θ_0 is the (known) reference value being tested.

In general, even if the distribution is not continuous, the sign test will decide whether your reference value, θ_0, divides the population exactly in half or not:[4]

---

[3] If you prefer, you may count how many fall *above* the reference value. The result of the test will be the same.

[4] This is slightly different from θ_0 being the median. For example, the (very small) population consisting of the numbers (11, 12, 13, 13, 14) has a median of 13. However, there are two values below but just one above 13. Thus, the null hypothesis of the sign test specifies *more* than just that the population median be θ_0.

> ■ **Hypotheses for the Sign Test in General**
>
> H_0: The probability of being above θ_0 is equal to the probability of being below θ_0 in the population
>
> H_1: These probabilities are not equal
>
> where θ_0 is the (known) reference value being tested.

The Assumption

There is an assumption required for validity of the sign test. One of the strengths of this nonparametric method is that so little is required for it to be valid.

> ■ **Assumption Required for the Sign Test**
> The data set is a random sample from the population of interest.

Table 16.1.1 lists the ranks for the sign test. If m is larger than 100, you would find the table values for level 0.05 by rounding $(m - 1.96\sqrt{m})/2$ and $(m + 1.96\sqrt{m})/2$ to the nearest whole numbers. For example, for $m = 120$ these formulas give 49.3 and 70.7, which round to the table values 49 and 71. For level 0.01, you would round $(m - 2.576\sqrt{m})/2$ and $(m + 2.576\sqrt{m})/2$.

EXAMPLE

Comparing Local to National Family Income

Your upscale restaurant is considering franchises in new communities. One of the ways you screen is by looking at *median* family income, because the *mean* family income might be high due to just a few families. A survey of one community estimated the median family income as $70,547, and you are wondering whether this is significantly higher than the national median family income of $27,735.[5] It certainly *appears* that this community has a higher median income, but with a sample of only 25 families, you would like to be careful before coming to a conclusion. Table 16.1.2 shows the data set, indicating those families with incomes below $27,735.

---

[5]As reported for 1985 in Bureau of the Census, *Statistical Abstract of the United States, 1987* (Washington, 1986), p. 437.

TABLE 16.1.1   Ranks for the Sign Test

Modified Sample Size, *m*	5% Test Level			1% Test Level		
	Sign Test Is Significant if Number Is Either:			Sign Test Is Significant if Number Is Either:		
	Less than	or	More than	Less than	or	More than
6	1		5	—		—
7	1		6	—		—
8	1		7	1		7
9	2		7	1		8
10	2		8	1		9
11	2		9	1		10
12	3		9	2		10
13	3		10	2		11
14	3		11	2		12
15	4		11	3		12
16	4		12	3		13
17	5		12	3		14
18	5		13	4		14
19	5		14	4		15
20	6		14	4		16
21	6		15	5		16
22	6		16	5		17
23	7		16	5		18
24	7		17	6		18
25	8		17	6		19
26	8		18	7		19
27	8		19	7		20
28	9		19	7		21
29	9		20	8		21
30	10		20	8		22
31	10		21	8		23
32	10		22	9		23
33	11		22	9		24
34	11		23	10		24
35	12		23	10		25
36	12		24	10		26
37	13		24	11		26
38	13		25	11		27
39	13		26	12		27
40	14		26	12		28
41	14		27	12		29
42	15		27	13		29
43	15		28	13		30
44	16		28	14		30
45	16		29	14		31
46	16		30	14		32
47	17		30	15		32
48	17		31	15		33
49	18		31	16		33
50	18		32	16		34
51	19		32	16		35
52	19		33	17		35
53	19		34	17		36
54	20		34	18		36
55	20		35	18		37

TABLE 16.1.1 *(Concluded)*

Modified Sample Size, *m*	5% Test Level		1% Test Level	
	Sign Test Is Significant if Number Is Either:		Sign Test Is Significant if Number Is Either:	
	Less than	or More than	Less than	or More than
56	21	35	18	38
57	21	36	19	38
58	22	36	19	39
59	22	37	20	39
60	22	38	20	40
61	23	38	21	40
62	23	39	21	41
63	24	39	21	42
64	24	40	22	42
65	25	40	22	43
66	25	41	23	43
67	26	41	23	44
68	26	42	23	45
69	26	43	24	45
70	27	43	24	46
71	27	44	25	46
72	28	44	25	47
73	28	45	26	47
74	29	45	26	48
75	29	46	26	49
76	29	47	27	49
77	30	47	27	50
78	30	48	28	50
79	31	48	28	51
80	31	49	29	51
81	32	49	29	52
82	32	50	29	53
83	33	50	30	53
84	33	51	30	54
85	33	52	31	54
86	34	52	31	55
87	34	53	32	55
88	35	53	32	56
89	35	54	32	57
90	36	54	33	57
91	36	55	33	58
92	37	55	34	58
93	37	56	34	59
94	38	56	35	59
95	38	57	35	60
96	38	58	35	61
97	39	58	36	61
98	39	59	36	62
99	40	59	37	62
100	40	60	37	63

TABLE 16.1.2	Incomes of Sampled Families	
	$ 39,465	$137,414
	80,806	16,477*
	267,525	5,921*
	163,819	187,445
	58,525	83,414
	25,479*	36,346
	29,341	19,605*
	96,270	156,681
	85,421	138,933
	56,240	70,547
	14,706*	81,802
	54,348	78,464
	7,081*	

*Income below $27,735.

Your reference value is $\theta_0 = \$27,735$, a number that is not from the data set itself. Here are the steps involved in performing the sign test:

1 All 25 families have incomes different from this reference value, so the modified sample size is $m = 25$, the same as the actual sample size.
2 The limits from the table for testing at the 5% level are 8 and 17 for $m = 25$.
3 There are six families with income below the reference value.
4 Since the number 6 falls outside the limits (i.e., it is less than 8), you reject the null hypothesis and conclude that the result is statistically significant:

> The observed median family income of $70,547 for this community is significantly different from the national median family income of $27,735.

Your suspicions have been confirmed: this is indeed an upscale community. The median family income in the community is significantly higher than the national median.[6]

■ 16.2 Testing for Differences in Paired Data

When your data set consists of *paired* observations, arranged as two columns, you can create a single sample that represents the changes or the differences between them. This is appropriate, for example, for before/after studies, where you have a measurement for each person or thing both before and after some intervention (seeing an advertisement, taking a medication, adjusting the gears, etc.). That is how the paired *t*-test worked in Chapter 10. Here we will illustrate the nonparametric solution.

Use the Sign Test on the Differences

The nonparametric procedure for testing whether two columns of values are significantly different, the **sign test for the differences,** applies the sign test

---

[6]This is the one-sided conclusion to a two-sided test, as described in Chapter 10.

(from the previous section) to a single column representing the differences between the two columns. The reference value, θ_0, will be 0, representing "no net difference" in the population. The sign test will then determine whether the changes are balanced (so that there are as many increases as decreases, except for randomness) or systematically different (for example, significantly more increases than decreases).

Table 16.2.1 shows how the data set for a typical application would look. In some applications, column 1 (X) would represent "before" and column 2 (Y) "after." It is important that there be a natural pairing so that each row represents two observations (in the same measurement units) for the *same* person or thing. Here is how to perform the test:

■ **The Sign Test for the Differences**

1 Count the number of data values that change between columns 1 and 2. This number is *m*, the modified sample size.
2 Find the limits in the table for this modified sample size.
3 Count how many data values went down (that is, have a smaller value in column 2 compared to column 1), and compare this count to the limits in the table.[7]
4 If this count falls outside the limits from the table, then the two samples are *significantly different*. If it falls at or within the limits, then the two samples are *not statistically different*.

Note that only the direction (up or down) of the change matters (from column 1 to column 2), not the actual size of the change. This implies that you can use this test on ordinal as well as on quantitative data. But some sense of ordering is required so that you can know the direction (up or down) of the change.

The Hypotheses

The null hypothesis claims that just as many units go up (comparing the paired data values X and Y) as down in the population. Any net movement

TABLE 16.2.1   Paired Observations

Elementary Units	Column 1	Column 2
1	X_1	Y_1
2	X_2	Y_2
.	.	.
.	.	.
.	.	.
n	X_n	Y_n

---

[7]If you prefer, you may count how many went *up* instead. The result of the test will be the same.

up or down in the sample would just be random under this hypothesis. The research hypothesis claims that the probabilities of going up and down are different.

■ **Hypotheses for the Sign Test for the Differences**

H_0: The probability of $X < Y$ equals the probability of $Y < X$. That is, the probability of going up equals the probability of going down.

H_1: The probability of $X < Y$ is *not* equal to the probability of $Y < X$. The probabilities of going up and down are unequal.

The Assumption

As with other, similar tests, there is an assumption required for validity of the sign test for the differences.

■ **Assumption Required for the Sign Test for the Differences**
The data set is a random sample from the population of interest. Each elementary unit in this population has both values X and Y measured for it.

EXAMPLE   **Rating Two Advertisements**

Two advertisements were shown to each member of a group of 17 people. Each ad was scored by each person on a scale from 1 to 5 indicating the creativity of the advertisement. The results are shown in Table 16.2.2.

TABLE 16.2.2   Level of Creativity

Ad 1	Ad 2
4	2
2	4
4	5
4	4
4	4
2	5
3	3
4	5
3	5
5	4
3	4
3	5
4	5
5	5
4	5
5	4
2	5

1 The number of data values that went either up or down (from ad 1 to ad 2) is 13. That is, 13 people gave different scores to the two ads, and the remaining 4 gave the same score to both. Thus, the modified sample size is $m = 13$.

2 The limits in the table for testing at the 5% level at $m = 13$ are 3 and 10.

3 Three people gave ad 2 a lower score than ad 1. This is within the limits of the table (you would have to find either *less than 3* or *more than 10* such people for the result to be significant).

4 You therefore accept the null hypothesis that the creativity ratings for these two ads are similar.

The result is not significant. Even though only 3 out of 17 people rated ad 1 higher in creativity, this could reasonably be due to random chance and not to any particular quality of the advertisements.

16.3 Testing to See if Two Unpaired Samples Are Significantly Different

Now suppose that you have two independent (unpaired) samples and want to test whether they could have come from populations with the same distribution or not. On the one hand, the unpaired t-test from Chapter 10 assumes that the distributions are normal (with the same standard deviation for small samples) and then tests whether the means are identical. On the other hand, the nonparametric approach assumes only that you have two random samples from two populations and then tests whether the populations' distributions are identical. Table 16.3.1 shows how a typical data set with two unpaired samples would look.

The Procedure Is Based on the Ranks of *All* of the Data

The procedure is first to *put both samples together* and define an overall set of ranks. If one sample has systematically smaller values than the other, its ranks will be smaller, too. By comparing the overall ranks of one sample to those of the other sample, you can test whether they are systematically or just randomly different.

TABLE 16.3.1 Two Unpaired Samples

Sample 1 (n₁ observations from population 1)	Sample 2 (n₂ observations from population 2)
$X_{1,1}$	$X_{2,1}$
$X_{1,2}$	$X_{2,2}$
.	.
.	.
.	.
X_{1,n_1}	X_{2,n_2}

Note: The two sample sizes, n_1 and n_2, may be different.

There are several different ways to get the same basic answer to this problem. The **Wilcoxon rank-sum test** and the **Mann-Whitney U-test** are two different ways to compute the same result of a nonparametric test for two unpaired samples; they both lead to the same conclusion. The Wilcoxon rank-sum test is based on the sum of the overall ranks in one of the samples, and the Mann-Whitney U-test is based on the number of ways you can find a value in one sample that is bigger than a value in the other sample.

An easier approach is to work with the *average* rank of the two samples. This test is algebraically equivalent to the others and makes clear the main idea of what is happening with many nonparametric methods: although you work with the ranks instead of the data values, the basic ideas of statistics remain the same.[8] Here's how to perform this test:

■ The Nonparametric Test for Two Unpaired Samples

1 Put both samples together, and sort them to obtain the *overall ranks*. If you have repeated numbers (ties), use the average of their ranks so that equal numbers are assigned equal ranks.

2 Find the average overall rank for each sample, $\overline{R}_1$ and $\overline{R}_2$.

3 Find the difference between these average overall ranks, $\overline{R}_2 - \overline{R}_1$.

4 Find the standard error for the average difference in the ranks:[9]

$$(n_1 + n_2) \sqrt{\frac{n_1 + n_2 + 1}{12n_1n_2}}$$

5 Divide the average difference (from step 3) by its standard error (from step 4) to find the test statistic:

$$\text{Test statistic} = \frac{\overline{R}_2 - \overline{R}_1}{(n_1 + n_2) \sqrt{\dfrac{n_1 + n_2 + 1}{12n_1n_2}}}$$

6 If the test statistic is larger than 1.960 in magnitude, the two samples are *significantly different*. If the test statistic is smaller than 1.960 in magnitude, the two samples are *not significantly different*.[10]

---

[8]For example, here is the formula to express the average difference in ranks in terms of the U-statistic: $(n_1 + n_2)(U - n_1n_2/2)/(n_1n_2)$. The Mann-Whitney U-statistic is defined as $n_1n_2 + n_1(n_1 + 1)/2$ minus the sum of the overall ranks in one of the samples.

[9]This standard error is exact. There is no need for estimation because it can be computed directly from the properties of randomly shuffled ranks under the null hypothesis.

[10]To use a different test level, you would substitute the appropriate t-table value with an infinite number of degrees of freedom in place of 1.960 here. For example, to test at the 1% level, use 2.576 in place of 1.960.

The Hypotheses

The null hypothesis claims that the two samples were drawn from populations with the *same distribution;* the research hypothesis claims that these population distributions are different.

■ **Hypotheses for Testing Two Unpaired Samples**

H_0: The two samples come from populations with the same distribution

H_1: The two samples come from populations with different distributions

---

The Assumptions

There are assumptions required for validity of the test for two unpaired samples. In addition to the usual requirement of random sampling, in order to use the *t*-table value with an infinite number of degrees of freedom, the sample sizes must be large enough.

■ **Assumptions Required for Testing Two Unpaired Samples**

1 Each sample is a random sample from its population.
2 More than 10 elementary units have been chosen from each population, so that $n_1 > 10$ and $n_2 > 10$.

EXAMPLE   **Fixed-rate and Adjustable-rate Mortgage Applicants**

The bank is planning a marketing campaign for home equity loans. Some people in the meeting feel that variable-rate mortgages appeal more to the lower-income applicants because they can qualify for a larger loan amount and therefore can afford to buy a more expensive house. Others feel that the higher risk of a variable-rate mortgage appeals more to the higher-income applicants because they have a larger "cushion" to use in case their payments go up in the future. Which group is correct? You have just compiled some data on the incomes of recent mortgage applicants, which are shown in Table 16.3.2.

Note the outlier ($240,000). This alone would call into question the use of a two-sample *t*-test. You called to check and found that the number is correct. Should you delete the outlier? Probably not, because it really does represent a high-income family applying for a fixed-rate loan, and this is useful information to you.

TABLE 16.3.2   Incomes of Mortgage Applicants

Fixed-Rate	Variable-Rate
$ 34,000	$37,500
25,000	86,500
41,000	36,500
57,000	65,500
79,000	21,500
22,500	36,500
30,000	99,500
17,000	36,000
36,500	91,000
28,000	59,500
240,000	31,000
22,000	88,000
57,000	35,500
68,000	72,000
58,000	
49,500	

FIGURE 16.3.1   Although the highest income is in the fixed-rate group, it appears that incomes are actually higher in general for the variable-rate group. However, there is considerable overlap in income scores between these two groups. The presence of the large outlier would be a problem for a two-sample t-test, but it is no problem for a nonparametric test.

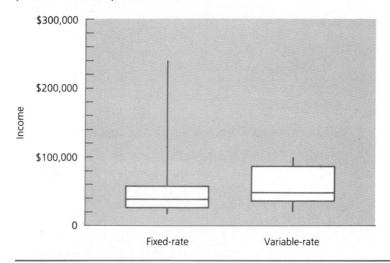

Here comes nonparametrics to the rescue! Because it works with ranks instead of the actual data values, it wouldn't matter if the highest income were $1 trillion; it would still be treated as simply the largest value.

A look at this two-sample data set using box plots is provided in Figure 16.3.1. This figure suggests that the variable-rate group has higher incomes, but this is unclear due to the considerable overlap between the two groups.

TABLE 16.3.3 Initial Database before Sorting

Income	Mortgage Type	Income	Mortgage Type
$ 34,000	Fixed	$49,500	Fixed
25,000	Fixed	37,500	Variable
41,000	Fixed	86,500	Variable
57,000	Fixed	36,500	Variable
79,000	Fixed	65,500	Variable
22,500	Fixed	21,500	Variable
30,000	Fixed	36,500	Variable
17,000	Fixed	99,500	Variable
36,500	Fixed	36,000	Variable
28,000	Fixed	91,000	Variable
240,000	Fixed	59,500	Variable
22,000	Fixed	31,000	Variable
57,000	Fixed	88,000	Variable
68,000	Fixed	35,500	Variable
58,000	Fixed	72,000	Variable

You will have to rank-order *all* of the income data. To do this, create a new database structure with one column for income (listing *both* columns of the original data set) and another as mortgage type, as shown in Table 16.3.3.

Now you are ready to sort the database in order by income; the results are shown in Table 16.3.4. You will want to indicate the mortgage type along with each income level in the sorting process; this is an easy task on a computer spreadsheet. After sorting, list the ranks as the numbers 1, 2, 3, and so forth.

If you have ties (two or more income levels that are the same), use the average rank for these levels. For example, in Table 16.3.4 the income level $36,500 occurs three times (at ranks 12, 13, and 14), so the average rank for $36,500, $(12 + 13 + 14)/3 = 13$, is listed for all three occurrences. There are two incomes at $57,000, so the average rank, $(18 + 19)/2 = 18.5$, is listed for both.

At this point you are ready to compute the average ranks. From the column of ranks, first select only the numbers representing fixed-rate mortgages and compute their average rank:

$$\frac{1 + 3 + 4 + 5 + 6 + 7 + 9 + 13 + 16 + 17 + 18.5 + 18.5 + 20 + 23 + 25 + 30}{16} = \frac{216}{16}$$

$$= 13.50$$

Next calculate the average rank for variable-rate mortgages:

$$\frac{2 + 8 + 10 + 11 + 13 + 13 + 15 + 21 + 22 + 24 + 26 + 27 + 28 + 29}{14} = \frac{249}{14}$$

$$= 17.7857$$

Table 16.3.5 shows what has been accomplished. The original income figures are listed in the original order, and the ranks have been assigned. Note that our outlier ($240,000) has the highest rank (30) but that its *rank* is not an outlier.

TABLE 16.3.4 Database after Sorting Income, Then Including Ranks

Income	Mortgage Type	Ranks by Income (ties, in bold, have been averaged)
$ 17,000	Fixed	1
21,500	Variable	2
22,000	Fixed	3
22,500	Fixed	4
25,000	Fixed	5
28,000	Fixed	6
30,000	Fixed	7
31,000	Variable	8
34,000	Fixed	9
35,500	Variable	10
36,000	Variable	11
36,500	Fixed	**13**
36,500	Variable	**13**
36,500	Variable	**13**
37,500	Variable	15
41,000	Fixed	16
49,500	Fixed	17
57,000	Fixed	**18.5**
57,000	Fixed	**18.5**
58,000	Fixed	20
59,500	Variable	21
65,500	Variable	22
68,000	Fixed	23
72,000	Variable	24
79,000	Fixed	25
86,500	Variable	26
88,000	Variable	27
91,000	Variable	28
99,500	Variable	29
240,000	Fixed	30

Note also that (as was suggested by the box plots) the apparently lower income level corresponding to fixed-rate mortgages has a lower average rank.

But are incomes for fixed-rate and variable-rate applicants different? That is, are these average ranks (13.50 and 17.79) significantly different? The standard error of the average difference in the ranks is needed next:

$$\text{Standard error} = (n_1 + n_2) \sqrt{\frac{n_1 + n_2 + 1}{12 n_1 n_2}}$$

$$= (16 + 14) \sqrt{\frac{16 + 14 + 1}{12 \times 16 \times 14}}$$

$$= (30) \sqrt{\frac{31}{2,688}}$$

$$= (30) \times 0.10739$$

$$= 3.2217$$

TABLE 16.3.5   Income and Ranks for Mortgage Applicants

Fixed-Rate		Variable-Rate	
Income	Rank	Income	Rank
$ 34,000	9	$37,500	15
25,000	5	86,500	26
41,000	16	36,500	13
57,000	18.5	65,500	22
79,000	25	21,500	2
22,500	4	36,500	13
30,000	7	99,500	29
17,000	1	36,000	11
36,500	13	91,000	28
28,000	6	59,500	21
240,000	30	31,000	8
22,000	3	88,000	27
57,000	18.5	35,500	10
68,000	23	72,000	24
58,000	20		
49,500	17		
Average rank	$\overline{R}_1 = 13.50$		$\overline{R}_2 = 17.7857$

Sample sizes: $n_1 = 16$, $n_2 = 14$.

The test statistic is the difference in ranks divided by the standard error:

$$\text{Test statistic} = \frac{\text{Average difference in ranks, } \overline{R}_2 - \overline{R}_1}{\text{Standard error}}$$

$$= \frac{17.7857 - 13.5000}{3.2217}$$

$$= \frac{4.2857}{3.2217}$$

$$= 1.3303$$

Because the magnitude of this test statistic (you would now ignore a minus sign, if any), 1.3303, is less than 1.960, the two samples are not significantly different. The observed differences between incomes of fixed-rate and variable-rate mortgage applicants are *not* statistically significant.

16.4 End-of-Chapter Materials

Summary

Nonparametric methods are statistical procedures for hypothesis testing that do not require a normal distribution (or any other particular shape of distribution) because they are based on counts or ranks instead of the actual data values. Many nonparametric methods work with ordinal data as well as with quantitative data. To use the nonparametric approach based on counts:

1 Count the number of times some event occurs in the data set.
2 Use the binomial distribution to decide whether this count is reasonable or not under the null hypothesis.

To use the nonparametric approach based on ranks:

1 Create a new data set using the rank of each data value. The **rank** of a data value indicates its position after you order the data set. For example, the data set (35, 95, 48, 38, 57) would become (1, 5, 3, 2, 4) because 35 is the smallest (it has rank 1), 95 is the largest (with rank 5), 48 is ranked as the third-smallest (rank 3), etc.
2 Ignore the original data values, and concentrate only on the rank ordering.
3 Use statistical formulas and tables created especially for testing ranks.

Parametric methods are statistical procedures that require a completely specified model, as do most of the methods considered before this chapter. One issue is the efficiency of nonparametric tests as compared to parametric ones. One test is said to be more **efficient** than another if it makes better use of the information in the data. Nonparametric tests have many advantages:

1 There is no need to assume a normal distribution.
2 Many problems of transformation are avoided. In fact, the test gives the same result whether you transform or not.
3 Even ordinal data can be tested because ranks can be found based on the natural ordering.
4 Such tests can be much more efficient than parametric methods when distributions are not normal.

The only disadvantage of nonparametric testing is that it is less statistically efficient than parametric methods when distributions are normal; however, the efficiency lost is often slight.

The **sign test** decides whether the population median is equal to a given reference value based on the number of sample values that fall below that reference value. Instead of assuming a normal distribution, the theory is based on the fact that the number of sample data values below a continuous population's median follows a binomial distribution, where $p = 0.5$ and n is the sample size.

To perform the sign test:

1 Count the number of data values that differ from the reference value, θ_0. This number is m, the **modified sample size.**
2 Find the limits in the table for m.
3 Count how many data values fall below the reference value, and compare this number to the limits in the table.
4 If the count from step 3 falls outside the limits from the table, the difference is statistically significant. If it falls at or within the limits, the difference is not statistically significant.

The hypotheses for the sign test for the median of a continuous population distribution are:

$$H_0: \theta = \theta_0$$

$$H_1: \theta \neq \theta_0$$

where θ is the (unknown) population median and θ_0 is the (known) reference value being tested.

The hypotheses for the sign test in general are:

H_0: The probability of being above θ_0 is equal to the probability of being below θ_0 in the population

H_1: These probabilities are not equal

where θ_0 is the (known) reference value being tested. The data set is assumed to be a random sample from the population of interest.

When you have paired observations ("before and after," for example), you may apply the sign test to the differences or changes. This nonparametric procedure for testing whether the two columns are significantly different is called the **sign test for the differences.** The procedure is as follows:

1 Count the number of data values that differ between columns 1 and 2. This number is m, the *modified sample size.*
2 Find the limits in the table for m.
3 Count how many data values went down (that is, have a smaller value in column 2 than in column 1), and compare this count to the limits in the table.
4 If this count falls outside the limits from the table, then the two samples are significantly different. If it falls at or within the limits, then the two samples are not statistically different.

The hypotheses for the sign test for the differences are:

H_0: The probability of $X < Y$ equals the probability of $Y < X$. That is, the probability of going up equals the probability of going down.

H_1: The probability of $X < Y$ is not equal to the probability of $Y < X$. The probabilities of going up and down are unequal.

The data set is assumed to be a random sample from the population of interest, where each elementary unit in this population has both X and Y values measured for it.

If you have two independent (unpaired) samples and wish to test for differences, there is a nonparametric procedure that substitutes for the unpaired t-test.

The **Wilcoxon rank-sum test** and the **Mann-Whitney U-test** are two different ways to compute the same result of a nonparametric test for two unpaired samples. The Wilcoxon rank-sum test is based on the sum of the overall ranks in one of the samples, and the Mann-Whitney U-test is based on the number of ways you can find a value in one sample that is bigger than a value in the other sample. An easier approach is to work with the *average rank* of the two samples:

1 Put both samples together, and sort them to obtain the overall ranks. In case of ties, use the average of their ranks.
2 Find the average overall rank for each sample, $\bar{R}_1$ and $\bar{R}_2$.
3 Find the difference between these overall ranks, $\bar{R}_2 - \bar{R}_1$.
4 Find the standard error for the average difference in the ranks:

$$\text{Standard error} = (n_1 + n_2)\sqrt{\frac{n_1 + n_2 + 1}{12n_1n_2}}$$

5 Divide the difference from step 3 by its standard error from step 4 to find the test statistic:

$$\text{Test statistic} = \frac{\bar{R}_2 - \bar{R}_1}{(n_1 + n_2)\sqrt{\dfrac{n_1 + n_2 + 1}{12n_1n_2}}}$$

6 If the test statistic is larger than 1.960 in magnitude, the two samples are significantly different. If the test statistic is smaller than 1.960 in magnitude, the two samples are not significantly different.

The hypotheses for testing two unpaired samples are:

H_0: The two samples come from populations with the same distribution

H_1: The two samples come from populations with different distributions

The assumptions that must be satisfied for testing two unpaired samples are:

1 Each sample is a random sample from its population.
2 More than 10 elementary units have been chosen from each population, so that $n_1 > 10$ and $n_2 > 10$.

Key Words

Questions

1. a. What is a nonparametric statistical method?
   b. For the nonparametric approach based on counts, what is being counted? What probability distribution is used to make the decision?
   c. For the nonparametric approach based on ranks, what information is disregarded from the data set? What is substituted in its place?

2. a. What is a parametric statistical method?
   b. Name some parametric methods you have used.

3. a. List the advantages of nonparametric testing over parametric methods, if any.
   b. List the disadvantages, if any, of nonparametric testing compared to parametric methods. How serious are these shortcomings?

4. a. How should you interpret the statement: One test is more efficient than another?
   b. If the distribution is normal, which would be more efficient, a parametric test or a nonparametric test?
   c. If the distribution is far from normal, which would be likely to be more efficient, a parametric test or a nonparametric test?

5. a. For a continuous population, which measure of typical value is the sign test concerned with?
   b. What probability distribution does this test rely on?
   c. Suppose the population is discrete and an appreciable fraction of the population is *equal* to its median. How do the hypotheses for the sign test change as compared to the case of a continuous population?

6. a. Can the sign test be used with quantitative data? Why or why not?
   b. Can the sign test be used with ordinal data? Why or why not?
   c. Can the sign test be used with nominal data? Why or why not?

7. a. What assumption must be met for the sign test to be valid?
   b. What assumption is not required for the sign test but would be required for a *t*-test to be valid?

8. Describe the similarities and differences between the sign test and the *t*-test.

9. a. What kind of data set is appropriate for the sign test for the differences?
   b. What hypotheses are being tested?
   c. What assumption is required?

10. a. Can the sign test for the differences be used with quantitative data? Why or why not?
    b. Can the sign test for the differences be used with ordinal data? Why or why not?
    c. Can the sign test for the differences be used with nominal data? Why or why not?

11. Describe the similarities and differences between the sign test for the differences and the paired *t*-test.

12. a. Describe the data set consisting of two unpaired samples.
    b. What hypotheses would ordinarily be tested for such data?

13. a. What is the difference (if any) between the Wilcoxon rank-sum test and the Mann-Whitney *U*-test?
    b. What is the relationship between the Wilcoxon rank-sum test, the Mann-Whitney *U*-test, and the test based on the difference between the average overall ranks in each sample?

14 a. What happens if there is an outlier in one of the samples in a test of two un-paired samples? For each case (very large or very small outlier), say what the rank of the outlier would be.

   b. Which statistical method (nonparametric or parametric) is more sensitive to an outlier? Why?

15 a. Can the nonparametric test for two unpaired samples be used with quantitative data? Why or why not?

   b. Can the nonparametric test for two unpaired samples be used with ordinal data? Why or why not?

   c. Can the nonparametric test for two unpaired samples be used with nominal data? Why or why not?

16 Describe the similarities and differences between the nonparametric test for two unpaired samples and the unpaired t-test.

Problems

1 For each of the following situations, say whether parametric or nonparametric methods would be preferred. Give a reason for your choice, and indicate how seri-ous a problem it would be to use the other method.

   a. Your data set consists of bond ratings, of which AAA is a higher grade than AA, which is higher than A, and so on.

   b. Your data set consists of profits as a percentage of sales, and there is an outlier due to one firm that is involved in a serious lawsuit. You feel that the outlier must be left in because this lawsuit represents one of the risks of this industry group.

   c. Your data set consists of the weights of faucet washers being produced by a manu-facturing system that is currently under control. The histogram looks very much like a normal distribution.

2 Consider the profits of the building materials firms in the Fortune 500:

Firm	Profits (as a percentage of sales)
American Standard	−1
Owens-Illinois	−2
Owens-Corning Fiberglas	7
USG	4
Manville	−59
Corning Glass Works	10
Nortek	1
Norton	7
Lafarge	7
Certainteed	4
National Gypsum	−7
Anchor Glass	−1
Calmat	9
Southdown	9

Data are from *Fortune*, April 24, 1989, pp. 380–81.

a. Draw a histogram of these profit percentages. Describe the distribution.

b. Find the average and the median. Explain why they are either similar or different.

c. Use the *t*-test to see if the mean profit (for the idealized population of similar firms operating under similar circumstances) is significantly different from the reference value -5% (i.e., a 5% loss). (Use the *t*-test for now, even if you feel it is inappropriate.)

d. Use the sign test to see whether the median profit of this idealized population differs significantly from a 5% loss.

e. Compare these two testing approaches to this data set. In particular, which of these two tests (*t*-test or sign test) is appropriate here? Are both appropriate? Why?

3 Consider the profits of the aerospace firms in the Fortune 500:

Firm	Profits (as a percentage of sales)
United Technologies	4
Boeing	4
McDonnell Douglas	2
Rockwell International	7
Allied-Signal	4
Lockheed	6
General Dynamics	4
Textron	3
Northrop	2
Martin Marietta	6
Grumman	2
Gencorp	3
Sequa	4
Colt Industries	5
Sundstrand	−5
Rohr Industries	4
Kaman	3

Data are from *Fortune,* April 24, 1989, p. 380.

a. Draw a histogram of these profit percentages. Describe the distribution.

b. Find the average and the median. Explain why they are either similar or different.

c. Use the *t*-test to see if the mean profit (for the idealized population of similar firms operating under similar circumstances) is significantly different from zero. (Use the *t*-test for now, even if you feel it is inappropriate.)

d. Use the sign test to see whether the median profit of this idealized population is significantly different from zero.

e. Compare these two testing approaches to this data set. In particular, which of these two tests (*t*-test or sign test) is appropriate here? Are both appropriate? Why?

4 Of the 35 people in your sales force, more than half have productivity above the national median. The exact numbers are 23 above and 12 below. Are you just lucky, or is your sales force significantly more productive than the national median? How do you know?

5 Last year your department handled a median of 63,821 calls per day (this is the median of the total calls handled each day during the year). So far this year, more than half of the days have had total calls above this level (there were 15 days above and only 9 days below). Do you have the right to claim that you are overloaded compared to last year? Explain why or why not.

6 An advertisement is being tested to see if it is effective in creating the intended mood of relaxation. A sample of 15 people were tested just before and just after viewing the ad. Their questionnaire included many items, but the one being considered now is: Please describe your current feeling on a scale from 1 (very tense) to 5 (completely relaxed). The results are as follows:

| | Relaxation Scores | |
Person	Before	After
1	3	2
2	2	2
	2	2
	4	5
	2	4
·	2	1
·	1	1
·	3	5
	3	4
	2	4
	5	5
	2	3
	4	5
	3	5
15	4	4

a. How many people reported higher relaxation after viewing the ad than before? How many reported lower relaxation? How many were unchanged?

b. Find the modified sample size.

c. Perform the nonparametric sign test for the differences.

d. Briefly summarize this result in terms of the effect (if any) of the advertisement.

7 Stress levels were recorded during a true answer and a false answer given by each of six people in a study of lie-detecting equipment, based on the idea that the stress involved in telling a lie can be measured:

| | Vocal Stress Level | |
Person	True Answer	False Answer
1	12.8	13.1
2	8.5	9.6
3	3.4	4.8
4	5.0	4.6
5	10.1	11.0
6	11.2	12.1

a. Was everyone's stress level higher during a false answer than during a true answer?

b. How many had more stress during a true answer? During a false answer?

c. Find the modified sample size.

d. Use the nonparametric sign test for the differences to tell whether there is a significant difference in stress level between true and false answers.

8 Your human resources department has referred 26 employees for alcohol counseling. While the work habits of 15 improved, 4 actually got worse, and the remaining 7 were unchanged. Use the sign test for the differences to tell whether the counseling program is effective or not.

9 Use the data sets from problems 2 and 3, on profit as a percent of sales for building materials firms and for aerospace firms.

a. Find the median profit for each industry group, and compare them.

b. Combine the two data sets into a single column of profit percentages next to a column indicating industry group.

c. Sort the profit percentages, carrying along the industry group information. List the ranks in a third column, averaging appropriately when there are ties.

d. List the overall ranks for each industry group.

e. Find the average rank for each industry group; also find the difference between these average ranks.

f. Find the appropriate standard error for this difference in average rank.

g. Find the test statistic for the nonparametric test for two unpaired samples.

h. What is your conclusion from this test regarding profits in these two industry groups?

10 Your firm is being sued for gender discrimination, and you are evaluating the documents filed by the other side. Here is their data set:

Salaries	
Women	Men
$21,100	$38,700
29,700	30,300
26,200	32,800
23,000	34,100
25,800	30,700
23,100	33,300
21,900	34,000
20,700	38,600
26,900	36,900
20,900	35,700
24,700	26,200
22,800	27,300
28,100	32,100
25,000	35,800
27,100	26,100
	38,100
	25,500
	34,000
	37,400
	35,700
	35,700
	29,100

a. Draw box plots for this data set on the same scale, and comment on their appearance.

b. Use a nonparametric method to test whether these salary distributions are significantly different.

c. Briefly summarize your conclusions based on the result of this test.

11 To understand your competitive position, you have examined the reliability of your product as well as the reliability of your closest competitor's product. You have subjected each product to abuse that represents about a year's worth of wear and tear per day. Here is the data indicating how long each item lasted:

Days until Failure	
Your Products	Competitor's Products
1.0	0.2
8.9	2.8
1.2	1.7
10.3	7.2
4.9	2.2
1.8	2.5
3.1	2.6
3.6	2.0
2.1	0.5
2.9	2.3
8.6	1.9
5.3	1.2
	6.6
	0.5
	1.2

a. Find the median time to failure for your and your competitor's products. Find the difference in medians.

b. Find the nonparametric test statistic to determine whether your reliability differs significantly from your competitor's.

c. State the result of this nonparametric test.

d. Write a brief paragraph, complete with footnote, that might be used in an advertising brochure showing off your products.

Database Exercises

Refer to the employee database in Appendix A.

1 Use a nonparametric test to see whether the median age of employees differs significantly from 40 years.

2 Use a nonparametric test to see whether the median experience of employees differs significantly from three years.

3 Use a nonparametric test to see whether the distribution of annual salaries for men differs significantly from the distribution for women.

Projects

1 Find a univariate data set related to your work or business interests, and select a reasonable reference value to test against.
   a. Draw a histogram of your data, and comment on its appearance.
   b. Perform the t-test, and report the conclusion.
   c. Perform the sign test, and report the conclusion.
   d. Compare your two test results. If they are different, tell which one should be believed (if an appropriate choice can be made).

2 Continue with the same data set from the previous project, but insert a single, additional data value that is an extreme outlier. Repeat parts a–d of the previous project for this new data set. Also:
   e. Write a paragraph describing your experience of how the t-test and the sign test each respond to an outlier.

3 Find two unpaired univariate data sets related to your work or business interests. It should make sense to test whether the two samples are significantly different.
   a. Draw box plots for your data on the same scale, and comment on their appearance.
   b. Write down the null and research hypotheses for the appropriate nonparametric test.
   c. Perform the appropriate nonparametric test, and report the conclusion.
   d. Write a paragraph summarizing what the test result has told you about this business situation.

17

Chi-Squared Analysis
Testing for Patterns in Qualitative Data

How can you do statistical inference on qualitative data, where each observation gives you a category (such as a color or an energy source) instead of a number? You already know the answer for two cases. First, if you have *attribute data* (i.e., qualitative data with just two categories), the binomial distribution and its normal approximation can provide you with confidence intervals and hypothesis tests for the population percentage. Second, if you have *ordinal data* (with a natural ordering), the nonparametric methods of Chapter 16 can be used. However, if you have *nominal data* (with no natural ordering) and more than two categories (or more than one variable), you will need other methods. Here are some examples:

1 No manufacturing process is perfect, and yours is no exception. When defects occur, they are grouped into categories of assignable causes. The overall percent defective is an *attribute variable* and may be analyzed with the binomial distribution (if you can assume independence). The percent of the defective items can be computed for each assignable cause. You would find a percent due to a bad chip, the percent due to a bad soldering connection, the percent due to a bad circuit board, and so on. As these percentages fluctuate from week to week, you would like to know whenever the system goes out of control, changing more than just randomly from its state before.

2 Opinion polls are a useful source of information for many of us. In addition to the political details provided by the media's polls, many firms use polls to learn how their customers (actual and potential) feel about how things are and how they might be. This information is useful in planning strategy for marketing and new product introduction. Many opinion polls produce qualitative data, such as the categories "yes," "no," and "no opinion." Another type of qualitative data would result

from the selection of a preferred product from a list of leading brands. You might use statistical inference to compare the opinions of two groups of people and test whether they differ significantly. Or you might test a single group against a known standard.

The **chi-squared tests** provide hypothesis tests for qualitative data, where you have categories instead of numbers. With nominal qualitative data, you can only count (since ordering and arithmetic cannot be done). Chi-squared tests are therefore based on counts that represent the number of items in the sample falling into each category. The **chi-squared statistic** measures the difference between the *actual* counts and the *expected* counts (assuming validity of the null hypothesis) as follows:

■ The Chi-Squared Statistic

$$\text{Chi-squared statistic} = \text{Sum of } \frac{(\text{Observed count} - \text{Expected count})^2}{\text{Expected count}}$$

$$= \sum \frac{(O_i - E_i)^2}{E_i}$$

where the sum extends over all categories or combinations of categories. The definition of *expected count* will depend on the particular form of the null hypothesis being tested.

Based on the chi-squared statistic as a measure of how close the data set conforms to the null hypothesis, the chi-squared test can decide whether the null hypothesis is a reasonable possibility or not.

■ 17.1 Summarizing Qualitative Data by Using Counts and Percentages

Here is a typical qualitative data set, given in the usual way as a list of measurements for each elementary unit in the sample. The elementary units here are people who came to an auto showroom, and the measurement is the type of vehicle they are looking for:

Pickup, Economy car, Economy car, Family sedan, Pickup, Economy car, Sports car, Economy car, Family sedan, Pickup, Economy car, Family sedan, Van, Van, Economy car, Family sedan, Pickup, Sports car, Family sedan, Family sedan, Economy car, Van, Economy car, Family sedan, Sports car, Economy car, Economy car, Van, Van, . . .

Because a list like this goes on and on, you will probably want to work with a summary table of counts (frequencies) or percentages. This preserves the information from the data while presenting it in a more useful way in a smaller space. An example is shown in Table 17.1.1.

TABLE 17.1.1   Vehicle Desired

Type	Count (frequency)	Percent of Total
Family sedan	187	(187/536 =) 34.9%
Economy car	206	38.4
Sports car	29	5.4
Van	72	13.4
Pickup	42	7.8
Total	536	100.0%

TABLE 17.1.2   Responses to the Question on General Motors Cars

	Baby Boomers	Non–Baby Boomers	Overall
Agree	52%	39%	42%
Disagree	43	53	51
Not sure	5	8	7
Total	100%	100%	100%

Some of the numbers in this table were calculated using an estimate of 20.3% for the percent of baby boomers in the adult population.

Summary tables of counts or percentages are also helpful for analysis of *bivariate* qualitative data, where you have more than one measurement. When *Business Week* investigated Americans' feelings about General Motors, they worked with Louis Harris & Associates to ask several questions of each person responding.[1] Two qualitative variables were:

1 The answer to the question: "Some people have argued that General Motors cars all look alike. Do you agree?" Answers were classified as "Agree," "Disagree," or "Not sure."
2 A classification by age and education into one of two groups: baby boomer or non–baby boomer. The definition of baby boomer was "age 18 to 39 with at least some college education."

Since each person provides a category as a response to each of these variables, the actual results of the poll looked something like this, person by person:

Disagreeing Baby boomer, Agreeing Non–baby boomer, Disagreeing Baby boomer, Not sure Non–baby boomer, . . .

The results for the 1,250 adults polled are summarized, in part, in Table 17.1.2.

Whenever you see a table of counts or percentages, it may help to imagine the underlying qualitative data set it came from. The next step is to test various hypotheses about these counts and percentages.

---

[1]"BW/Harris Poll: Americans Are Still Sold on General Motors,"*Business Week,* March 16, 1987, p. 108.

■ 17.2 Testing if Population Percentages Are Equal to Known Reference Values

You already know how to test a single percentage against a reference value using the binomial distribution (see Chapter 10). However, another method is needed for testing an entire table of percentages against another table of reference values. A common application of such a test is to find out whether your recent experience (summarized by counts and percentages) is typical relative to your past experience (the reference values).

The Chi-Squared Test for Equality of Percentages

The **chi-squared test for equality of percentages** is used to determine whether a table of *observed* counts or percentages could reasonably have come from a population with known percentages (the reference values). Here is a summary of the situation and its solution:

■ The Chi-Squared Test for Equality of Percentages

The data: A table indicating the count for each category for a single qualitative variable.

The hypotheses:

H_0: The population percentages are equal to a set of known, fixed reference values

H_1: The population percentages are not equal to this set of reference values; at least one category is different

The expected counts: For each category, multiply the population reference proportion (the percentage divided by 100) by the sample size, n.

The assumptions:

1 The data set is a random sample from the population of interest.
2 At least five counts are expected in each category.

The chi-squared statistic:

$$\text{Chi-squared statistic} = \text{Sum of } \frac{(\text{Observed count} - \text{Expected count})^2}{\text{Expected count}}$$

$$= \sum \frac{(O_i - E_i)^2}{E_i}$$

Degrees of freedom: Number of categories minus 1.

The chi-squared test result: Significant if the chi-squared statistic is larger than the value from Table 17.2.1; not significant otherwise.

TABLE 17.2.1   Critical Values for Chi-Squared Tests

Degrees of Freedom	10% Level	5% Level	1% Level	0.1% Level
1	2.706	3.841	6.635	10.828
2	4.605	5.991	9.210	13.816
3	6.251	7.815	11.345	16.266
4	7.779	9.488	13.277	18.467
5	9.236	11.071	15.086	20.515
6	10.645	12.592	16.812	22.458
7	12.017	14.067	18.475	24.322
8	13.362	15.507	20.090	26.124
9	14.684	16.919	21.666	27.877
10	15.987	18.307	23.209	29.588
11	17.275	19.675	24.725	31.264
12	18.549	21.026	26.217	32.909
13	19.812	22.362	27.688	34.528
14	21.064	23.685	29.141	36.123
15	22.307	24.996	30.578	37.697
16	23.542	26.296	32.000	39.252
17	24.769	27.587	33.409	40.790
18	25.989	28.869	34.805	42.312
19	27.204	30.144	36.191	43.820
20	28.412	31.410	37.566	45.315
21	29.615	32.671	38.932	46.797
22	30.813	33.924	40.289	48.268
23	32.007	35.172	41.638	49.728
24	33.196	36.415	42.980	51.179
25	34.382	37.652	44.314	52.620
26	35.563	38.885	45.642	54.052
27	36.741	40.113	46.963	55.476
28	37.916	41.337	48.278	56.892
29	39.087	42.557	49.588	58.301
30	40.256	43.773	50.892	59.703
31	41.422	44.985	52.191	61.098
32	42.585	46.194	53.486	62.487
33	43.745	47.400	54.776	63.870
34	44.903	48.602	56.061	65.247
35	46.059	49.802	57.342	66.619
36	47.212	50.998	58.619	67.985
37	48.363	52.192	59.893	69.346
38	49.513	53.384	61.162	70.703
39	50.660	54.572	62.428	72.055
40	51.805	55.758	63.691	73.402
41	52.949	56.942	64.950	74.745
42	54.090	58.124	66.206	76.084
43	55.230	59.304	67.459	77.419
44	56.369	60.481	68.710	78.749
45	57.505	61.656	69.957	80.077
46	58.641	62.830	71.201	81.400
47	59.774	64.001	72.443	82.720
48	60.907	65.171	73.683	84.037
49	62.038	66.339	74.919	85.351
50	63.167	67.505	76.154	86.661

TABLE 17.2.1 *(Concluded)*

Degrees of Freedom	10% Level	5% Level	1% Level	0.1% Level
51	64.295	68.669	77.386	87.968
52	65.422	69.832	78.616	89.272
53	66.548	70.993	79.843	90.573
54	67.673	72.153	81.069	91.872
55	68.796	73.311	82.292	93.167
56	69.919	74.468	83.513	94.461
57	71.040	75.624	84.733	95.751
58	72.160	76.778	85.950	97.039
59	73.279	77.931	87.166	98.324
60	74.397	79.082	88.379	99.607
61	75.514	80.232	89.591	100.888
62	76.630	81.381	90.802	102.166
63	77.745	82.529	92.010	103.442
64	78.860	83.675	93.217	104.716
65	79.973	84.821	94.422	105.988
66	81.085	85.965	95.626	107.258
67	82.197	87.108	96.828	108.526
68	83.308	88.250	98.028	109.791
69	84.418	89.391	99.228	111.055
70	85.527	90.531	100.425	112.317
71	86.635	91.670	101.621	113.577
72	87.743	92.808	102.816	114.835
73	88.850	93.945	104.010	116.091
74	89.956	95.081	105.202	117.346
75	91.061	96.217	106.393	118.599
76	92.166	97.351	107.583	119.850
77	93.270	98.484	108.771	121.100
78	94.374	99.617	109.958	122.348
79	95.476	100.749	111.144	123.594
80	96.578	101.879	112.329	124.839
81	97.680	103.010	113.512	126.083
82	98.780	104.139	114.695	127.324
83	99.880	105.267	115.876	127.565
84	100.980	106.395	117.057	129.804
85	102.079	107.522	118.236	131.041
86	103.177	108.648	119.414	132.277
87	104.275	109.773	120.591	133.512
88	105.372	110.898	121.767	134.745
89	106.469	112.022	122.942	135.978
90	107.565	113.145	124.116	137.208
91	108.661	114.268	125.289	138.438
92	109.756	115.390	126.462	139.666
93	110.850	116.511	127.633	140.893
94	111.944	117.632	128.803	142.119
95	113.038	118.752	129.973	143.344
96	114.131	119.871	131.141	144.567
97	115.223	120.990	132.309	145.789
98	116.315	122.108	133.476	147.010
99	117.407	123.225	134.642	148.230
100	118.498	124.342	135.807	149.449

If the chi-squared statistic is *larger* than the critical value from the chi-squared table for the appropriate number of degrees of freedom, you have evidence that the observed counts are very different from those expected for your reference percentages. You would then reject the null hypothesis and accept the research hypothesis, concluding that the observed sample percentages are *significantly different* from the reference values.

If the chi-squared statistic is *smaller* than the critical value from the chi-squared table, then the observed data are not very different from what you would expect based on the reference percentages. You would accept the null hypothesis and conclude that the observed sample percentages are *not significantly different* from the reference values.

As a rule of thumb, there should be at least five counts expected in each category because the chi-squared test is an approximate, not an exact, test. The approximation is close enough for practical purposes when this rough guideline is followed, but it may be in error when you have too few expected counts in some category. The risk is that your type I error probability will not be controlled at the 5% level (or other chosen level).

EXAMPLE

Quality Problems Categorized by Their Causes

As part of your firm's commitment to total quality control, defects are carefully monitored because this provides useful information for quality improvement. Each defective component is checked to see whether the problem is a bad chip, a bad soldering joint, or a bad circuit board. Based on past data from this assembly line, you know what percentages to expect (the reference percentages) when the process is under control. By comparing the current results to these reference percentages, you can test whether the process is currently under control or not.[2]

Table 17.2.2 shows the data set, representing the problems from the previous week. Table 17.2.3 shows the reference values, based on the past year's experience when the assembly line seemed to be working properly. Although the chip problems are very close to the reference value (16.0% observed chip defects in the past week compared to the reference value of 15.2%), the others are fairly different (70.0% compared to 60.5% for a bad soldering joint, for example). The question is whether these differences are significant or not. That is, could the defect rates have reasonably been produced by sampling from a population whose percentages correspond to the reference values? Or are the differences so great that they could not reasonably be due to random chance alone? The chi-squared test for equality of percentages will provide an answer. Here are the hypotheses:

H_0: The process is still in control (the observed defect rates are equal to the reference values)

H_1: The process is not in control (the observed defect rates are not equal to the reference values)

---

[2]Of course, you would also, separately, keep a close eye on the overall percent defective. The analysis here helps you identify trouble due to a specific cause. The topic of quality control will be covered in Chapter 18.

TABLE 17.2.2   The Observed Data: Defective Components from
the Previous Week

Problem	Observed Count (frequency)	Percent of Total
Chip	8	(8/50 =) 16.0%
Solder	35	70.0
Board	7	14.0
Total	50	100.0%

TABLE 17.2.3   The Reference Values: Defective
Components from the Previous
Year When "in Control"

Problem	Percent of Total
Chip	15.2%
Solder	60.5
Board	24.3
Total	100.0%

TABLE 17.2.4   The Expected Counts: Hypothetical Numbers
of Defective Components to Match
"in Control" Reference Percentages

Problem	Expected Count
Chip	(0.152 × 50 =) 7.60
Solder	30.25
Board	12.15
Total	50.0

Table 17.2.4 shows the table of expected counts, found by multiplying the reference percentages (15.2%, 60.5%, and 24.3%) by the sample size, $n = 50$. Note that it's perfectly all right for the expected counts to include a decimal part; this is necessary so that the computed percentages give you the reference percentages exactly. Note also that the total expected count matches the total actual count, namely, the sample size, $n = 50$.

As for the assumptions, this data set is sampled from the idealized population of all components that would be built under similar circumstances. Thus, your actual experience is viewed as a random sample from this idealized population of what *might* have happened. The second assumption is also satisfied because all expected counts are at least 5 (that is, 7.6, 30.3, and 12.2 are all 5 or larger). Note that this assumption is checked by looking at the *expected*, not the *observed*, counts.

The chi-squared statistic is computed by combining the observed and expected counts for all categories as follows (be sure to omit the total because it is not a category):

$$\text{Chi-squared statistic} = \sum \frac{(\text{Observed count} - \text{Expected count})^2}{\text{Expected count}}$$

$$= \frac{(8 - 7.60)^2}{7.60} + \frac{(35 - 30.25)^2}{30.25} + \frac{(7 - 12.15)^2}{12.15}$$

$$= \frac{0.1600}{7.60} + \frac{22.5625}{30.25} + \frac{26.5225}{12.15}$$

$$= 0.0211 + 0.7459 + 2.1829$$

$$= 2.950$$

The number of degrees of freedom is 1 less than the number of categories. There are three categories here (chip, solder, and board); therefore,

$$\text{Degrees of freedom} = 3 - 1 = 2$$

Looking in the chi-squared table for 2 degrees of freedom, the critical value for testing at the 5% level is 5.991. Since the chi-squared statistic (2.950) is smaller, you accept the null hypothesis. It is reasonably possible that the assembly line is producing defects that match the "in control" reference proportions and that the discrepancy is just due to the usual random chance for a sample of size 50. You do not have convincing evidence that the process is out of control, so you accept the possibility that it is still in control.

> The observed percentages are not significantly different from the reference percentages. Based on this, there is no evidence that the process has gone out of control.

■ 17.3 Testing for Association between Two Qualitative Variables

Now suppose you have *two* qualitative variables; that is, your data set consists of *bivariate qualitative data*. After you have examined each variable separately by examining counts and percentages, you may be interested in the *relationship* (if any) between these two variables. In particular, you may be interested in whether there is any relationship at all between the two. Here are some applications for such a test:

1 One variable represents the favorite recreational activity of each person (from a list including sports, reading, TV, etc.). The other variable is each person's favorite breakfast cereal. By understanding the relationship between these two variables, you are better equipped to plan marketing strategy. If you are in cereals, this would help you decide what kind of ma-

terial to put on cereal boxes. If you are in recreation, this would help you decide which cereal companies to approach about joint marketing plans.

2 One variable represents the cause of the defective component. The other variable represents the manager in charge when the component was produced. The relationship, if any, will help you focus your efforts where they will do the most good by identifying the specific managers who should devote more attention to solving the problems. If a cause shows up for all managers, you have a systematic problem and should look at the larger system (not the individual managers) for a solution. If a cause shows up for just one manager, you could begin by delegating its solution to that manager.

The Meaning of Independence

Two qualitative variables are said to be **independent** if knowledge about the value of one variable does not help you predict the other; that is, the *probabilities* for one variable are the same as the *conditional probabilities* given the other variable. Each variable has its own population percentages, which represent the probabilities of occurrence for each category. The **conditional population percentages** are the probabilities of occurrence for one variable when you restrict attention to just one category of the other variable. These restricted population percentages represent the conditional probabilities for one variable given this category of the other.

For example, suppose the population percentage of "paint-flake" defects is 3.1% overall. When Jones is the manager on duty, however, the conditional population percentage of paint-flake defects is 11.2%. In this case, knowledge about one variable (the particular manager) helps you predict the outcome of the other (the defect type) because 3.1% and 11.2% are different. Paint-flake defects are more likely when Jones is on duty and less likely when someone else is in charge. Therefore, these two variables are *not independent*.

You should note that the real-life situation is somewhat more involved than this example because you have to work with *sample percentages* as estimates of population probabilities; you won't be able to just look at the percentages and see if they are different, because they will (nearly) always be different due to random chance. The chi-squared test for independence will tell you when the differences go *beyond* what is reasonable due to random chance alone.

The Chi-Squared Test for Independence

The **chi-squared test for independence** is used to decide whether two qualitative variables are independent or not, based on a table of observed counts from a bivariate qualitative data set. It is computed from a table that gives the counts you would expect if the two variables were independent. Here is a summary of the situation and its solution:

■ The Chi-Squared Test for Independence

The data: A table indicating the counts for each combination of categories for two qualitative variables, summarizing a bivariate data set.

The hypotheses:

H_0: The two variables are independent of one another. That is, the probabilities for either variable are equal to the conditional probabilities given the other variable.

H_1: The two variables are associated; they are not independent of one another. There is at least one category of one variable whose probability is not equal to the conditional probability given some category of the other variable.

The expected table: For each combination of categories, one for each variable, multiply the count for one category by the count for the other category, and then divide by the total sample size, n:

$$\text{Expected count} = \frac{\left(\begin{array}{c}\text{Count for category} \\ \text{for one variable}\end{array}\right)\left(\begin{array}{c}\text{Count for category} \\ \text{for other variable}\end{array}\right)}{n}$$

The assumptions:

1 The data set is a random sample from the population of interest.
2 At least five counts are expected in each combination of categories.

The chi-squared statistic:

$$\text{Chi-squared statistic} = \sum \frac{(\text{Observed count} - \text{Expected count})^2}{\text{Expected count}}$$

where the sum extends over all combinations of categories.

Degrees of freedom:

$$\left(\begin{array}{c}\text{Number of categories} \\ \text{for first variable}\end{array} - 1\right)\left(\begin{array}{c}\text{Number of categories} \\ \text{for second variable}\end{array} - 1\right)$$

The chi-squared test result: Significant association if the chi-squared statistic is larger than the table value; no significant association otherwise.

If the chi-squared statistic is larger than the critical value from the chi-squared table (Table 17.2.1), you have evidence that the observed counts are very different from those that would be expected if the variables were independent. You would reject the null hypothesis of independence and accept the research hypothesis. You would conclude that the variables show *significant association,* that is, they *are not independent* of each other.

If the chi-squared statistic is smaller than the critical value from the chi-squared table, then the observed data are not very different from what you would expect if the variables were independent of each other in the population. You would accept the null hypothesis of independence. You would conclude that the variables do not show significant association. This is a weak conclusion because the null hypothesis of independence has been accepted; you *accept* independence, but you have *not proven* independence.

Why is the expected table computed this way? Remember from probability theory (Chapter 6) that when two events are independent, the probability that they will *both* occur is equal to the product of their probabilities. The equation that defines the expected count expresses independence, in effect, by multiplying these probabilities.[3]

EXAMPLE **Is Your Market Segmented?**

You are trying to set strategy for a marketing campaign for a new product line consisting of three rowing machines. The basic model is made of industrial-strength chrome with black plastic fittings and a square seat. The designer model comes in a variety of colors and with a sculpted seat. The complete model adds a number of accessories to the designer model (computerized display, running water, sound effects, etc.).

To help your team write the information brochure and press releases, you need to know which model each type of customer will prefer so that you don't go overboard[4] about how practical a model is when your market actually consists of impulsive types.

A marketing firm has gathered data in a small test market. For each purchase, two qualitative variables were recorded. One is the model (basic, designer, or complete), and the other is the type of consumer (summarized for this purpose as either practical or impulsive). Table 17.3.1 shows the data set, presented as a table of counts for these $n = 221$ customers. For example, of the 221 purchases, 22 were basic machines purchased by practical customers.

---

[3] If you divide both sides of the equation for the expected count by n, it is easier to see this. The result is:

$$\frac{\text{Expected count}}{n} = \frac{\left(\begin{array}{c}\text{Count for category}\\\text{for one variable}\end{array}\right)}{n} \times \frac{\left(\begin{array}{c}\text{Count for category}\\\text{for other variable}\end{array}\right)}{n}$$

Since dividing by n gives you a proportion that estimates the probability, the equation states that the probability of a combination of a particular category for one variable with a particular category for the other variable is equal to the product of these probabilities. This is the same as the definition of independence for probabilities (see Chapter 6).

[4] Sorry about the pun.

The *overall percentages,* obtained by dividing each count by the total sample size, n, indicate what percent fall into each category of each variable and each combination of categories (one category for each variable). From Table 17.3.2, you see that your largest group of sales is designer models to impulsive shoppers (39.8% of all sales.) The next largest group is complete models to practical shoppers (24.4% of total sales.) Looking at the totals by model type (the right-most column) you see that the basic model is the slowest seller (only 21.3% of all rowing machines sold were the basic model). This may be because your customers are upscale and able to pay more to get the higher-end models (that's good news—congratulations!).

The *percentages by model,* obtained by dividing each count by the total count for that model, indicate the percentages of each type of customer for each model. These are the *conditional sample percentages given the model* and estimate the corresponding conditional population percentages (the conditional probabilities). This shows you the customer profile for each type of machine. From Table 17.3.3, you can see that the basic model is purchased in roughly equal proportions by each type of customer (46.8% practical versus 53.2% impulsive). The designer model's customers are almost exclusively impulsive, whereas the complete model's customers are much more likely to be practical than impulsive.

The *percentages by customer type,* obtained by dividing each count by the total count for that customer type, indicate the percentages of each model type

TABLE 17.3.1   Counts: Rowing Machine Purchases

	Practical	Impulsive	Total
Basic	22	25	47
Designer	13	88	101
Complete	54	19	73
Total	89	132	221

TABLE 17.3.2   Overall Percentages: Rowing Machine Purchases

	Practical	Impulsive	Total
Basic	(22/221 =) 10.0%	11.3%	21.3%
Designer	5.9	39.8	45.7
Complete	24.4	8.6	33.0
Total	40.3%	59.7%	100.0%

TABLE 17.3.3   Percentages by Model: Rowing Machine Purchases

	Practical	Impulsive	Total
Basic	(22/47 =) 46.8%	53.2%	100.0%
Designer	12.9	87.1	100.0
Complete	74.0	26.0	100.0
Total	40.3%	59.7%	100.0%

TABLE 17.3.4   Percentages by Customer Type: Rowing Machine Purchases

	Practical	Impulsive	Total
Basic	(22/89 =) 24.7%	18.9%	21.3%
Designer	14.6	66.7	45.7
Complete	60.7	14.4	33.0
Total	100.0%	100.0%	100.0%

bought by each type of customer. These are the *conditional sample percentages given the customer type* and estimate the corresponding conditional population percentages (the conditional probabilities). This gives you a profile of the model preferences for each customer type. From Table 17.3.4, you can see that practical customers strongly prefer the complete model (60.7% of them purchased it), and impulsive shoppers strongly prefer the designer model (66.7% of them purchased it). However, you should not ignore the other choices (such as basic model purchases by practical consumers) since they still represent a sizable minority fraction of your market.

Do these two variables look like they are independent? No. We have already noted several facts that indicate some kind of relationship between customer type and model preference. For example, looking at the table of percentages by customer type, you see that although 33.0% of all customers purchased complete units, a much larger percentage (60.7%) of practical customers purchased these units. If they were independent, you would expect the practical consumers to show the same buying patterns as anyone else. Knowledge of customer *does* seem to help you predict the model purchased, suggesting that the two factors are not independent.

If they were independent, the percentages by customer type would be the same in all three columns: practical shoppers and impulsive shoppers would have the same model purchase profile as all shoppers together. Similarly, if they were independent, the percentages by model would be the same for all four rows: the basic model, the designer model, and the complete model would have the same customer profile as that for all models together.

The *expected table* (obtained by multiplying the total count for each customer type by the total count for each model type and then dividing by total sample size, $n = 221$) indicates the counts you would expect if customer type were independent of model purchased. Table 17.3.5 shows that the expected table keeps the same total count for each customer type as was actually

TABLE 17.3.5   Expected Counts: Rowing Machine Purchases

	Practical	Impulsive	Total
Basic	(89 × 47/221 =) 18.93	28.07	47.00
Designer	40.67	60.33	101.00
Complete	29.40	43.60	73.00
Total	89.00	132.00	221.00

observed (89 practical and 132 impulsive). The model purchases are also the same (47 basic, 101 designer, and 73 complete). But the counts inside the table have been rearranged to show what you would expect (on average) assuming independence.

Note that you would expect 40.67 purchases of designer machines by practical consumers (based on 89 practical shoppers and 101 designer machines sold out of the 221 total). However, you actually sold only 13 (from the original table of counts), far fewer than the 40.67 expected under the assumption of independence.

Are model purchases independent of customer type? Are the differences between the original observed counts and these expected counts greater than would be reasonable due to random chance if they were, in fact, independent? The chi-squared test will decide.

The hypotheses are as follows:

H_0: Customer type is independent of the model purchased.

H_1: Customer type is not independent of the model purchased.

The null hypothesis claims that customers have the same preferences (percent of each model purchased) regardless of their type (practical or impulsive). The research hypothesis claims that these preferences are different.

Let's check the assumptions. Is the data set a random sample from the population of interest? Not really, but it may be close enough. This depends in part on how carefully the marketing study was designed, that is, how representative the test market is of your overall customers. Keep in mind that statistical inference can generalize only to the larger population (real or idealized) that is *represented* by your sample. For now, let's assume it is a random sample of purchases in cities similar to your test area, in stores like those that were included in the test. The second assumption is satisfied because every entry in the expected table is 5 or greater.

The chi-squared statistic is the sum of (Observed − Expected)^2/Expected; Table 17.3.6 shows these values (note that the row and column of totals are omitted). The chi-squared statistic is the sum of these values:

$$\text{Chi-squared statistic} = \sum \frac{(\text{Observed count} - \text{Expected count})^2}{\text{Expected count}}$$

$$= 0.50 + 18.83 + 20.58 + 0.34 + 12.69 + 13.88$$

$$= 66.8$$

TABLE 17.3.6   (Observed − Expected)^2/Expected: Rowing Machine Purchases

	Practical	**Impulsive**
Basic	([22 − 18.93]^2/18.93 =) 0.50	0.34
Designer	18.83	12.69
Complete	20.58	13.88

The number of degrees of freedom is 2 because there are three categories of rowing machines and two categories of customers:

$$\text{Degrees of freedom} = (3 - 1)(2 - 1)$$
$$= 2 \times 1$$
$$= 2$$

Looking in the chi-squared table for 2 degrees of freedom at the 5% test level, you find the critical value 5.991. Because the chi-squared statistic (66.8) is larger than this critical value, there is significant association between these qualitative variables. In fact, because it is so much larger, let's test at the 0.1% level. This critical value (still with 2 degrees of freedom) is 13.816. The chi-squared statistic (66.8) is still much higher. Your conclusion is therefore:

> The association between customer type and model purchased is very highly significant ($p < 0.001$).

Because, assuming independence, the probability that you would see data with this much association or more is so small ($p < 0.001$), you have very strong evidence against the null hypothesis of independence. You may now plan the marketing campaign with some assurance that the different models really do appeal differently to different segments of the market.

■ 17.4 End-of-Chapter Materials

Summary

Qualitative data are summarized using counts and percentages. The **chi-squared tests** provide hypothesis tests for qualitative data, where you have categories instead of numbers. The **chi-squared statistic** measures the difference between the *actual* counts and the *expected* counts (based on the null hypothesis).

$$\text{Chi-squared statistic} = \sum \frac{(\text{Observed count} - \text{Expected count})^2}{\text{Expected count}}$$

where the sum extends over all categories or combinations of categories. The definition of *expected count* will depend on the particular form of the null hypothesis being tested.

The **chi-squared test for equality of percentages** is used to decide whether a table of observed counts or percentages (summarizing a single qualitative variable) could reasonably have come from a population with known percentages (the reference values). The hypotheses are:

> H_0: The population percentages are equal to a set of known, fixed reference values.

H_1: The population percentages are not equal to this set of reference values. At least one category is different.

The assumptions are:

1 The data set is a random sample from the population of interest.
2 At least five counts are expected in each category.

For the chi-squared statistic,

$$\text{Chi-squared statistic} = \sum \frac{(\text{Observed count} - \text{Expected count})^2}{\text{Expected count}}$$

the expected count for each category is the population reference percentage multiplied by the sample size, n, and the degrees of freedom equal the number of categories minus 1.

If the chi-squared statistic is larger than the critical value from the chi-squared table at the appropriate degrees of freedom, you have evidence that the observed counts are very different from those expected for your reference percentages. You would reject the null hypothesis and accept the research hypothesis. The observed sample percentages are significantly different from the reference values.

If the chi-squared statistic is smaller than the critical value from the chi-squared table, then the observed data are not very different from what you would expect based on the reference percentages. You would accept the null hypothesis. The observed sample percentages are *not* significantly different from the reference values.

When you have *bivariate qualitative data*, you may wish to test whether the two variables are associated or not. Two qualitative variables are said to be **independent** if knowledge about the value of one variable does not help you predict the other; that is, the probabilities for one variable are the same as the conditional probabilities given the other variable. The **conditional population percentages** are the probabilities of occurrence for one variable when you restrict attention to just one category of the other variable. Your sample data set provides estimates of these population percentages and conditional population percentages.

One way to summarize bivariate qualitative data is to use *overall percentages*, which give you the relative frequency of each *combination* of categories, one for each variable. Another approach is to use the *percentages by one of the variables* to obtain a profile of estimated conditional probabilities for the other variable *given* each category of the first variable.

The **chi-squared test for independence** is used to decide whether two qualitative variables are independent or not, based on a table of observed counts from a bivariate qualitative data set. It is computed from a table that gives the counts you would expect if the two variables were independent. The hypotheses are:

H_0: The two variables are independent of one another. That is, the probabilities for either variable are equal to the conditional probabilities given the other variable.

H_1: The two variables are associated; they are not independent of one another. There is at least one category of one variable whose probability is not equal to the conditional probability given some category for the other variable.

The expected table is constructed as follows: For each combination of categories, one for each variable, multiply the count for one category by the count for the other category, then divide by the total sample size, n:

$$\text{Expected count} = \frac{\left(\begin{array}{c}\text{Count for category} \\ \text{for one variable}\end{array}\right)\left(\begin{array}{c}\text{Count for category} \\ \text{for other variable}\end{array}\right)}{n}$$

The assumptions are:

1 The data set is a random sample from the population of interest.
2 At least five counts are expected in each combination of categories.

The Chi-Squared Statistic:

$$\text{Chi-squared statistic} = \text{sum of } \frac{(\text{Observed count} - \text{Expected count})^2}{\text{Expected count}}$$

$$\begin{array}{c}\text{Degrees of} \\ \text{freedom}\end{array} = \left(\begin{array}{c}\text{Number of categories} \\ \text{for first variable}\end{array} - 1\right)\left(\begin{array}{c}\text{Number of categories} \\ \text{for second variable}\end{array} - 1\right)$$

If the chi-squared statistic is larger than the critical value from the chi-squared table, you have evidence that the observed counts are very different from those that would be expected if the variables were independent. You would reject the null hypothesis of independence and accept the research hypothesis, concluding that the variables show significant association.

If the chi-squared statistic is smaller than the critical value from the chi-squared table, the observed data are not very different from what you would expect if they were independent in the population. You would accept the null hypothesis of independence and conclude that the variables do not show significant association. This is a weak conclusion because the null hypothesis of independence has been accepted; you *accept* independence, but have *not proven* independence.

Key Words

chi-squared tests 702
chi-squared statistic 702
chi-squared test for equality
  of percentages 704

independent 710
conditional population percentages 710
chi-squared test for independence 710

Questions

1 For what kind of variables are chi-squared tests useful?
2 a. What does the chi-squared statistic measure, in terms of the relationship between the observed data and the null hypothesis?

b. Do you reject the null hypothesis for large or for small values of the chi-squared statistic? Why?

3 What is the purpose of the chi-squared test for equality of percentages?

4 a. For what kind of data set is the chi-squared test for equality of percentages appropriate?

b. What are the reference values for this test?

c. What are the hypotheses?

d. How are the expected counts obtained? What do they represent?

e. What assumptions are required in order that this test be valid?

5 a. For the chi-squared test for equality of percentages, what do you conclude if the chi-squared statistic is *larger* than the value in the chi-squared table?

b. What do you conclude if the chi-squared statistic is *smaller* than the value in the chi-squared table?

6 a. What is meant by independence of two qualitative variables?

b. What is the relationship between conditional probabilities and independence of qualitative variables?

7 What is the purpose of the chi-squared test for independence?

8 a. For what kind of data set is the chi-squared test for independence appropriate?

b. What are the reference values for this test, if any?

c. What are the hypotheses?

d. How are the expected counts obtained? What do they represent?

e. What assumptions are required in order that this test be valid?

9 a. For the chi-squared test for independence, what do you conclude if the chi-squared statistic is *larger* than the value in the chi-squared table?

b. What do you conclude if the chi-squared statistic is *smaller* than the value in the chi-squared table?

10 Why is it much more difficult to establish independence than it is to establish dependence (lack of independence)?

Problems

1 a. If an observed count is 3 and the expected count is 8.61, is there any problem with going ahead with a chi-squared test?

b. If an observed count is 8 and the expected count is 3.29, is there any problem with going ahead with a chi-squared test?

2 For each potential customer entering an auto showroom, the type of vehicle desired is recorded. Table 17.4.1 shows data for the past week, together with percentages for the past year at this time:

TABLE 17.4.1   Vehicle Desired

Type	This Week's Count	Last Year's Percentages
Family sedan	187	25.8%
Economy car	206	46.2
Sports car	29	8.1
Van	72	12.4
Pickup	42	7.5
Total	536	100.0%

a. Find the percentages for last week's vehicles.

b. Compare last week's percentages to last year's percentages. Describe any differences you see in terms that would be useful to an automobile salesperson.

c. Assuming last year's percentages continued to apply, how many of these 536 people would you expect to be looking for an economy car? Compare this to the observed number of such people.

d. Find the expected count for each type of vehicle, assuming last year's percentages still apply.

e. Find the chi-squared statistic, viewing last year's percentages as exact.

f. Discuss the assumptions required for the chi-squared test to be valid. In particular, what population are you inferring about?

g. How many degrees of freedom are there for this chi-squared test?

h. Find the appropriate chi-squared table value for the 5%, 1%, and 0.1% levels.

i. Perform the chi-squared test at each of these levels, and report the results.

j. State your conclusions (with a p-value), discussing any shifts in consumer preferences.

3 Last year at this time, your firm's incoming telephone calls followed the percentages shown in Table 17.4.2.

TABLE 17.4.2   Incoming Calls

Type	Count (first day of the month)	Percent of Total (this month last year)
Reservation	53	33.2%
Information	54	38.1
Service request	28	12.5
Cancellation	18	9.7
Other	7	6.5
Total	160	100.0%

a. Find the percentages for the first day of this month, and compare them to last year's percentages for this month.

b. Find the expected number of calls of each type for the first day of this month, assuming the population percentages are given by last year's total for the month.

c. Find the chi-squared statistic and the number of degrees of freedom.

d. Report the results of the chi-squared test at the 5% level.

e. Summarize what the chi-squared test has told you about any change in the pattern of calls compared to last year at this time.

4 Out of 267 roller skates randomly selected for close examination, 5 were found to have a loose rivet, and 12 were not cleaned according to specifications.

a. Using the formula for computing an expected count, how many roller skates would you expect to have *both* problems if the problems are independent?

b. Find the estimated probability of a loose rivet, using the relative frequency.

c. Similarly, find the estimated probability of a cleaning problem.

d. Use the probability formula from Chapter 6 to find the estimated probability of a loose rivet *and* a cleaning problem, assuming they are independent, using your estimated probabilities from parts b and c.

e. Convert your probability from part d to an expected count by multiplying it by the sample size.

f. Compare your answers to parts a (from the expected count formula) and e (from the independence formula). Comment on why they both came out this way.

5 Your firm is considering expansion to a nearby city. A survey of employees in that city, asked to respond to the question "Will business conditions in this area get better, stay the same, or get worse?" produced the data set shown in Table 17.4.3.

TABLE 17.4.3   Survey Responses Regarding Future Business Conditions

	Managers	Other Employees	Total
Better	23	185	
Same	37	336	
Worse	11	161	
Not sure	15	87	
Total			

a. Fill in the "Total" row and column.
b. Find the table of overall percentages. Interpret these as estimates of probabilities in the population. In particular, what probabilities do they represent?
c. Find the table of percentages by type of employee. Interpret these as estimates of probabilities in the population. In particular, what probabilities do they represent?
d. Find the table of percentages by response. Interpret these as estimates of probabilities in the population. In particular, what probabilities do they represent?
e. Does the response *appear* to be independent of the employee's classification? Why or why not?

6 Refer to the data for problem 5.
a. What does the null hypothesis of independence claim, in practical terms, for this situation?
b. How many managers responding "Worse" would you expect to find in this sample if response were independent of employee classification?
c. Find the table of expected counts, assuming independence.
d. Find the chi-squared statistic.
e. How many degrees of freedom does the chi-squared test have?

7 Refer to the data for problem 5.
a. Find the critical value from the chi-squared table for the 5% level, and report the result of the chi-squared test.
b. Find the critical value from the chi-squared table for the 1% level, and report the result of the chi-squared test.
c. Find the critical value from the chi-squared table for the 0.1% level, and report the result of the chi-squared test.
d. State your conclusions (with p-value), and discuss the results in practical terms.

8 Consider the results of a small opinion poll concerning the chances of another stock market crash in the next 12 months comparable to the crash of 1987, shown in Table 17.4.4.
a. Fill in the "Total" row and column.
b. Find the table of overall percentages. Interpret these as estimates of probabilities in the population. In particular, what probabilities do they represent?

TABLE 17.4.4 Responses to the Opinion Poll on the Chances of Another Big Crash in the Stock Market

	Stockholders	Nonstockholders	Total
Very likely	18	26	
Somewhat likely	41	65	
Not very likely	52	68	
Not likely at all	19	31	
Not sure	8	13	
Total			

Results of a much larger poll for this and related questions appeared in a Business Week/Harris Poll, *Business Week*, November 9, 1987, p. 36.

    c. Find the table of percentages by type of person (stockholder/nonstockholder). Interpret these as estimates of probabilities in the population. In particular, what probabilities do they represent?

    d. Find the table of percentages by response. Interpret these as estimates of probabilities in the population. In particular, what probabilities do they represent?

    e. Does the response *appear* to be independent of the stockholder/nonstockholder classification? Why or why not?

9 Refer to the data for problem 8.

    a. What does the null hypothesis of independence claim, in practical terms, for this situation?

    b. How many stockholders responding "Very likely" would you expect to find in this sample if response were independent of stockholder/nonstockholder classification?

    c. Find the table of expected counts, assuming independence.

    d. Find the chi-squared statistic.

    e. How many degrees of freedom does the chi-squared test have?

10 Refer to the data for problem 8.

    a. Find the critical value from the chi-squared table for the 5% level, and report the result of the chi-squared test.

    b. Find the critical value from the chi-squared table for the 1% level, and report the result of the chi-squared test.

    c. Find the critical value from the chi-squared table for the 0.1% level, and report the result of the chi-squared test.

    d. State your conclusions (with p-value), and discuss the results in practical terms.

Database Exercises

Refer to the employee database in Appendix A.

1 Do training levels A, B, and C have approximately the same number of employees, except for randomness? (To answer this, test whether the percentage of employees at each training level differs significantly from the proportions 1/3, 1/3, and 1/3 for the three levels.)

2 Is there evidence of gender discrimination in training level? To answer this, proceed as follows:

    a. Create a table of counts for the two qualitative variables "gender" and "training level."

b. Compute the overall percentage table, and comment briefly.

c. Compute a table of percentages by gender, and comment.

d. Compute a table of percentages by training level, and comment.

e. Is it appropriate to use the chi-squared test for independence on this data set? Why or why not?

f. Omit training level C, restricting attention only to those employees at training levels A and B for the rest of this exercise. Compute the expected table.

g. Still omitting training level C, compute the chi-squared statistic.

h. Still omitting training level C, report the results of the chi-squared test for independence at the 5% level. Comment on these results.

Projects

1 Obtain data for a single (univariate) qualitative variable relating to your work or business interests, together with a list of reference percentages for comparison.

a. Summarize these observations in a table of counts.

b. Summarize these observations in a table of percentages.

c. Compare the percentages for the data to your reference percentages, and comment on the similarities and differences.

d. Find the table of expected counts, assuming that your reference percentages are correct for the population.

e. List the [(Observed − Expected)^2/Expected] values for each category. Find the largest and smallest values in this list, and explain why these particular categories are smallest and largest by comparing the observed and expected percentages for these categories.

f. Find the chi-squared statistic.

g. Perform the chi-squared test, and find the p-value.

h. Comment on what the chi-squared test has told you about this business situation.

2 Obtain data for two qualitative variables (a bivariate data set) relating to your work or business interests.

a. Summarize these observations in a table of counts.

b. Summarize these observations in a table of overall percentages, and comment.

c. Summarize these observations in a table of percentages by one of your variables. Comment on the profiles of the other variable.

d. Repeat the previous part using percentages by the other variable.

e. What does the null hypothesis of independence claim for this situation? Is it a reasonable possibility, in your opinion?

f. Find the table of expected counts, assuming that your two variables are independent.

g. List the [(Observed − Expected)^2/Expected] values for each combination of categories. Find the largest and smallest values in this table, and explain why these particular combinations of categories are smallest and largest by comparing the observed and expected counts for these categories.

h. Find the chi-squared statistic.

i. Perform the chi-squared test, and find the p-value.

j. Comment on what the chi-squared test has told you about this business situation.

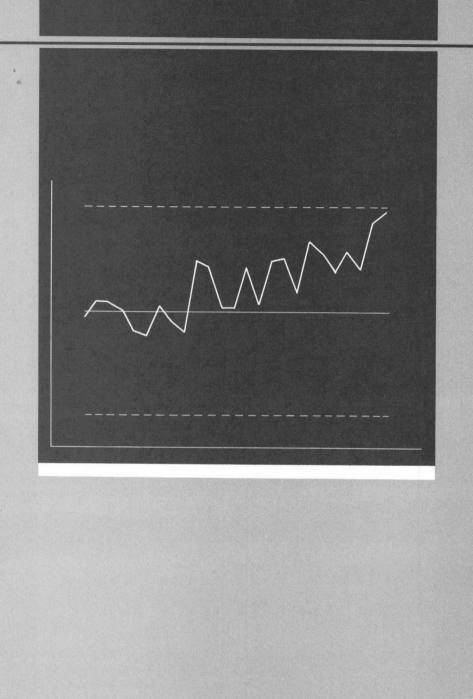

18

Quality Control
Recognizing and Managing Variation

Statistical quality control is the use of statistical methods for evaluating and improving the results of any activity. Whether the activity involves production or service, it can be monitored so that problems can be discovered and corrected before they become more serious. Statistics is well suited for this task because good management decisions must be based, in part, on *data*. Here are some examples to indicate the variety of ways that statistical quality control can be used to enhance the firm's bottom line:

1 Firms don't like it very much when a customer returns merchandise. In addition to losing the sale you thought you had, this customer might not be saying good things about your firm's products. But why not view this problem as an opportunity? By collecting data on the various reasons for returning the product, you obtain a wealth of information that is useful in a variety of areas. Analyzing this list will show you how to improve product quality by directing your attention to the most important problems. In addition, you may learn more about your customers. Such a proprietary database could be useful in marketing and sales efforts, as well as in the design of new products.

2 Your package indicates that 16 ounces of dishwasher detergent are contained in every box. If you could do it inexpensively, you'd like to be sure that every box had *exactly* 16 ounces. However, the costs would be prohibitive. Some level of variation from one box to another will be tolerated, and you want to control this level of variation. One goal is to avoid public relations trouble by making sure that no boxes are seriously underweight and that, on average, you have at least 16 ounces per box. Another goal is to hold costs down by not allowing too much extra in the boxes. By collecting and analyzing the net weights of these boxes (either every one or a random sample from each batch), you can moni-

tor the process and its level of variability. When everything seems to be under control, you can leave the process alone. When you detect a problem, you can fix it by adjusting or replacing the machinery. Proper monitoring can even allow you to fix a problem before it occurs by enabling you to spot a trend that, if continued, will soon cause real trouble.

3 The accounts receivable department has a very important function: to convert your firm's sales into cash. Any problems you might have with accounts receivable translate directly into lost value, for example, cash you would have received if the file hadn't been held up three weeks waiting for an internal review. And don't forget that cash received later is worth less due to the time value of money. By collecting data on the progress of a sample of normal and problem accounts, you can tell whether or not you have the process of bill collection "under control." By analyzing problems that show up over and over, you can identify those parts of this system that need to be redesigned. Perhaps you need a few extra workers over here. Or maybe different steps could take place simultaneously—"in parallel"—so that one group doesn't have to wait for another group to finish before doing its work.

Quality control looks good on the cost-benefit scale. The costs of setting up a program of statistical quality control are typically small compared to the money saved as a result. When production of defective items is eliminated, you save because inspection of every item is unnecessary. You also save the cost of either reworking or junking defective items. Finally, the reputation for quality and dependability will help you land the contracts you need at favorable prices.

But don't expect statistical methods to do everything for you. They can only provide information; it's up to you to make good use of it. They might tell you that something funny probably happened around 10:30 A.M. because the packages are getting significantly heavier, but it's still up to you and your workers to adjust the machines involved.

And don't expect statistical methods to do the impossible. The capabilities of the system itself must be considered. If a drill bit is so old and worn out that it is incapable of drilling a smooth hole, no amount of statistical analysis by itself will correct the problem. Although a good quality control program will help you get the most out of what is available, you may discover that some modernization is necessary before acceptable results can be achieved.

The four basic activities of statistics all play important roles in quality control. The *design* phase involves identification of particular processes to look at and measurements to take. The other three activities are often assisted by a *control chart* to display the data. The *exploration* phase involves checking the data for particular kinds of problems in the process. The *estimation* phase involves characterizing the current state of the process and how well it's performing. The *hypothesis testing* phase involves deciding whether the process should be adjusted or left alone.

W. Edwards Deming brought statistical quality control methods to the Japanese in the 1950s and continues to help firms around the world with their quality control programs. Here are Deming's 14 points for managing continued improvement in quality, which summarize how a company should go about improving quality:[1]

1 *Create constancy of purpose toward improvement of product and service,* with the aim to become competitive, to stay in business, and to provide jobs.

2 *Adopt a new philosophy.* We are in a new economic age, created by Japan. We can no longer live with commonly accepted styles of American management, nor with commonly accepted levels of delays, mistakes, or defective products.

3 *Cease dependence on inspection to achieve quality.* Eliminate the need for inspection on a mass basis by building quality into the product in the first place.

4 *End the practice of awarding business on the basis of price tag.* Instead, minimize total cost.

5 *Improve constantly and forever the system of production and service to improve quality and productivity,* and thus constantly decrease costs.

6 *Institute training on the job.*

7 *Institute supervision:* the aim of supervision should be to help people and machines and gadgets do a better job. Supervision of management is in need of overhaul, as well as supervision of production workers.

8 *Drive out fear,* so that everyone may work effectively for the company.

9 *Break down barriers between departments.* People in research, design, sales, and production must work as a team to foresee problems of production and use that may be encountered with the product or service.

10 *Eliminate slogans, exhortations, and targets for the work force which ask for zero defects and new levels of productivity.* Such exhortations only create adversarial relationships. The bulk of the causes of low productivity belong to the system and thus lie beyond the power of the work force.

11 *Eliminate work standards that prescribe numerical quotas for the day.* Substitute aids and helpful supervision.

12 *Remove the barriers that rob the hourly worker of the right to pride of workmanship.* The responsibility of supervisors must be changed from sheer numbers to quality. This means abolishment of the annual rating, or merit rating, and management by objective.

13 *Institute a vigorous program of education and training.*

14 *Put everybody in the company to work to accomplish the transformation.*

[1] These 14 points are reprinted from *The ESB Journal,* Spring 1989, published by the Educational Service Bureau of Dow Jones & Co., Inc. Further discussion of these points may be found, for example, in W. Edwards Deming, *Out of the Crisis* (Cambridge, Mass.: MIT Center for Advanced Engineering Studies, 1986); and in H. Gitlow, S. Gitlow, A. Oppenheim, and R. Oppenheim, *Tools and Methods for the Improvement of Quality* (Homewood, Ill.: Richard D. Irwin, 1989).

■ 18.1 **Processes and Causes of Variation**

A **process** is any business activity that takes inputs and transforms them into outputs. A manufacturing process takes raw materials and turns them into products. Restaurants have processes that take food and energy and transform them into ready-to-eat meals. Offices have a variety of processes that transform some kind of information (perhaps papers with basic information) into other information (perhaps computerized records or paychecks).

A process can be made up of other processes, called *subprocesses,* each of which is a process in its own right. For example, airplane production might be viewed as a single process that takes various inputs (metal, plastic, wire, computerized information) and transforms them into airplanes. This enormous process consists of many subprocesses (for example, assembling the fuselage, connecting the wires to the cabin lights, testing the wing flaps). Each of these subprocesses consists of further subprocesses (placing one rivet, soldering one wire, checking the maximum extension). You are free to focus on whatever level of detail you want in order to achieve your purpose. The methods of statistical process control are adaptable to essentially any process or subprocesses.

Statistical process control is the use of statistical methods to monitor the functioning of a process so that you can adjust or fix it when necessary and can leave it alone when it's working properly. The goal is to detect problems and fix them *before* defective items are produced. By using sampled data to keep a process in a state of statistical control, you can ensure high-quality production without inspecting every single item!

Nearly every process shows some variation among its results. Some variations are small and unimportant, such as the exact number of chocolate chips varying by a few from one cookie to another. Other variations are more crucial, such as a metal box getting squashed and resembling a modern-art sculpture instead of what the customer wanted.

The difference between "what you wanted" and "what you got" could be due to any number of causes. Some of these causes are easier to find than others. Sometimes you find out the cause even before you get the data (for example, because you could smell the smoke). Some causes require some detective work to discover what (say, a machine that needs adjustment) and why (perhaps an employee needs new glasses). Yet other causes are not even worth the effort of investigation (such as, Why did the tape machine use an extra tiny fraction of an inch more for this box than for that one?).

Any time you could reasonably find out why a problem occurred, you have an **assignable cause of variation.** Note that you may not actually know the cause; it is enough that you could reasonably find it out without too much expense. Here are some examples of assignable causes and possible solutions:

1 Dust gets into the "clean room" and interferes with the production of microchips and disk drives. Possible solutions include checking the cleaning

apparatus, replacing filters and seals as needed, and reviewing employee procedures for entering and leaving the area.

2 Clerks fill out the forms incorrectly, placing the totals in the wrong boxes. Possible solutions include training the clerks, redesigning the forms, and doing both.

All causes of variation that would not be worth the effort to identify are grouped together as **random causes of variation.**[2] These causes should be viewed as defining the basic randomness of the situation, so that you know what to expect when things are in control and so that you don't expect too much. Here are some examples of variation due to random causes:

1 The bottle-filling machinery is accurate to a fraction of a drop of soda. Even when it is adjusted properly, there is still some small amount of variation in liquid from one bottle to the next.

2 The number of corn flakes in a cereal box varies from one box to the next. There is no reason to control this variability, provided it falls within acceptable limits and the total weight is close enough to the net weight promised on the package.

When you have identified and eliminated all of the assignable causes of variation, so that only random causes remain, your process is said to be **in a state of statistical control,** or, simply, **in control.** When a process is in control, all you have to do is monitor it to see if it stays in control. When a process goes *out of control,* there is an assignable cause and, therefore, a problem to be fixed.

Quality control programs are no longer completely internal to a company. More and more firms are demanding that their suppliers prove (by providing control charts) that the products they are buying were produced when the system was in control. If you are having problems with a supplier, you may want to consider this possibility.

The Pareto Diagram Shows Where to Focus Attention

Suppose you have examined a group of defective components and have classified each one according to the cause of the defect. The **Pareto diagram** displays the causes of the various defects in order from most to least frequent so that you can focus attention on the most important problems. In addition to showing the number and percentage of defectives due to each cause, the diagram indicates the *cumulative* percentage so that you can easily tell, for example, the percentage for the two (or three, or four) biggest problems combined.

---

[2]This is not exactly the same as the strict statistical definition of the word *random.* See, for example, the definition of *random sample* in Chapter 8. However, the Statistical Division of the American Society for Quality Control, in *Glossary and Tables for Statistical Quality Control* (Milwaukee, Wis.: American Society for Quality Control, 1983), p. 29, defines *random or chance causes* as follows: "Factors, generally numerous and individually of relatively small importance, which contribute to variation, but which are not feasible to detect or identify."

Here's how to create a Pareto diagram:

1 Begin with the number of defects (the frequency) for each problem cause. Find the total number of defects and the percentage of defects for each cause.
2 Sort the causes in descending order by frequency so that the biggest problems come first in the list.
3 Draw a bar graph of these frequencies.
4 Find the cumulative percentage for each cause by adding its percentage to all percentages above it in the list.
5 Draw a line (on top of the bar graph) indicating these cumulative percentages.
6 Add labels to the diagram. Indicate the name of each problem cause underneath its bar. On the left, indicate the vertical scale in terms of the *number* of defects. On the right, indicate the *cumulative percentage* of defects.

For example, consider problems encountered in the production of small consumer electronics components, as shown in Table 18.1.1. This same data set, sorted and with percentages computed, is shown in Table 18.1.2. The Pareto diagram, shown in Figure 18.1.1, indicates that the biggest problem is with power supplies, representing about twice the number of defects due to the next most important problem, which involves the plastic case. Looking at the cumulative percentage line, you see that these two major problems account for a large majority (85.9%) of the defects. The three biggest problems together account for nearly all (97.2%) of the defects.

TABLE 18.1.1 Defect Causes, with Frequency of Occurrence

Cause of Problem	Number of Cases
Solder joint	37
Plastic case	86
Power supply	194
Dirt	8
Shock (was dropped)	1
Total	326

TABLE 18.1.2 Defect Causes Sorted by Frequency with Percentage of Occurrence and Cumulative Percentages

Cause of Problem	Number of Cases	Percent	Cumulative Percent
Power supply	194	59.5%	59.5%
Plastic case	86	26.4	85.9
Solder joint	37	11.3	97.2
Dirt	8	2.5	99.7
Shock (was dropped)	1	0.3	100.0
Total	326	100.0%	

FIGURE 18.1.1   The Pareto diagram for causes of defects in the production of small consumer electronics components. The bars show the importance (frequency) of each cause; for example, 86 or 26.4% of the problems involved the plastic case. The line shows the cumulative percent of the most important causes; for example, the top two causes (power supply and plastic case) together accounted for 85.9% of defects.

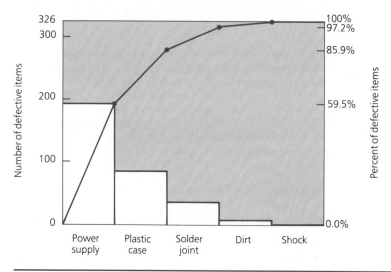

In a Pareto diagram, the tallest bars will always be at the left (indicating the most frequent problems), and the shortest bars will be at the right. The line indicating the cumulative percentage will always go upward and will tend to level off toward the right.

One useful function of the Pareto diagram is to introduce some objectivity into the discussion of what to do about quality. Rather than having employees choose problems to solve based just on what they know and on what they enjoy doing, the Pareto diagram helps you concentrate their attention on those problems that are most crucial to the company.

■ 18.2 Control Charts and How to Read Them

Once you have selected one of the many processes you are responsible for as a manager and have chosen one of the many possible measurements that can be made on that process, you will want to understand this information in order to know when to act and when *not* to act. A **control chart** displays successive measurements of a process together with a *center line* and *control limits*, which are computed to help you decide whether the process is in control or not. If you decide that the process is not in control, the control chart will help you identify the problem so that you can fix it.

All four basic activities of statistics are involved in the use of control charts for quality control. The *design* phase involves selecting the process and measurements to examine for producing the control chart. Once you have a control chart, the other three activities come into play. The *exploration* phase involves looking at the chart in order to spot patterns, trends, and exceptions that tell you how the process is working and what it is likely to do in the future. The *estimation* phase involves computing summaries of the process, some of which are displayed in the control chart. Finally, the *hypothesis testing* phase involves using data (the measurements) to decide whether the process is in control or not. Here are the hypotheses being tested:

H_0: The process is in control

H_1: The process is not in control

Note that the default (the null hypothesis) is that the process is assumed to be in control. By setting it up this way, you ensure that the process will not be adjusted unless there is convincing evidence that there is a problem. Making adjustments can be very expensive due to lost production time, the cost of making the adjustments, and the possibility that adjusting will *add to* the variability of the system. You don't want to make adjustments unless you really need to. As they say, "If it ain't broke, don't fix it!"

The **false alarm rate** is how often you decide to fix the process when there really isn't any problem; this is the same concept as the type I error in hypothesis testing. Conventional control charts use a factor of three standard errors instead of two because the conventional 5% type I error rate of statistical hypothesis testing is unacceptably high for most quality control applications.[3]

The rest of this section will show you how to read a generic control chart. The details of how to construct the various types of control charts will be presented beginning in Section 18.3.

The Control Limits Show if a Single Observation Is out of Control

For a process that is in control, you should expect to see a plot that stays within the control limits, as shown in Figure 18.2.1. All observations are within the control limits; no observation falls outside. Although there is variation from one item to the next, the chart shows no clear patterns. The process is varying randomly within the control limits.

---

[3]From Chapter 10, on hypothesis testing, recall that the *t*-table value for two-sided testing at the 5% level is 1.96, or approximately 2. By using 3 instead of 1.96, the theoretical false alarm rate is reduced from 5% way down to 0.27% for large samples.

FIGURE 18.2.1   This control chart shows a process that is in control. The measurements fluctuate randomly within the control limits.

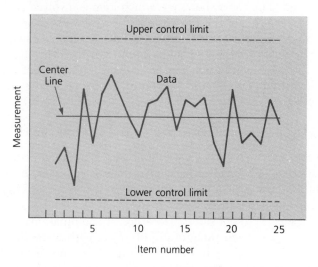

FIGURE 18.2.2   This process is not in control. The 16th measurement is outside the control limits (it is above the upper limit). An investigation of the circumstances of this particular item's production may help you avoid this kind of problem in the future.

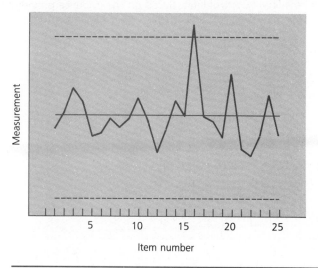

If any measurement falls outside of the control limits, either above the upper control limit or below the lower limit, you have evidence that the process is not in control. An example is shown in Figure 18.2.2. In statistical terms, you reject the null hypothesis that the process is in control and accept the research hypothesis that the process is not in control. In practical terms, you have a problem, and the control chart will help guide you toward a solution. The chart shows you which item is involved so that you can investigate by looking at the records for this item and talking with those responsible. You might quickly find an obvious assignable cause (such as a broken drill bit or an overheated solder bath). On the other hand, you might find that further investigation and testing are required before the problem can be identified. Or it could be the rare case of a false alarm, with no fixing needed.

How to Spot Trouble Even within the Control Limits

One way in which you can spot a process that is out of control is to look for points that fall outside the control limits. However, even if all points are within the control limits, it still may be clear from looking at the chart that the process is not in control.

The idea is to consider the nature of combinations of points within the control limits. Even though all points are within the limits, if they tend to fall suspiciously close to one of the limits (as shown in Figure 18.2.3) or if they are moving systematically toward a limit (as shown in Figure 18.2.4), you would decide that the process is no longer in control.[4]

FIGURE 18.2.3   Even though all points are within the control limits, there is a troublesome pattern here. Note that a sequence of 11 points (items 12 through 22) fall close to, but inside, the lower control limit. Based on the evidence provided by the entire chart, you would decide that the process is not in control.

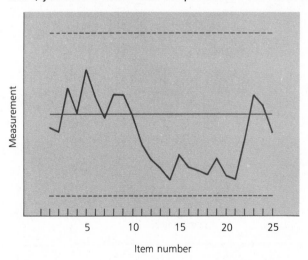

---

[4]A collection of rules for deciding whether such a process is in control or not is given in Gitlow et al., *op cit.*, pp. 190–94. In particular, you could decide that the process is not in control if eight or more consecutive points fall on one side of the center line or if eight or more consecutive points form a sequence that is always moving either upward or downward.

FIGURE 18.2.4 Even though all points are within the control limits, there is a troublesome trend here. Note that the sequence has a steady drift upward. There is no need to wait for the trend to continue through the upper control limit. You should decide *now* that the process is not in control.

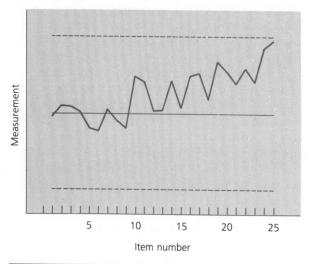

A sudden jump to another level in a control chart (such as occurred in Figure 18.2.3) suggests that there was an abrupt change in the process. Perhaps something fell into the gears and is slowing them down, or maybe a new worker just took charge and hasn't learned the system yet.

A gradual drift upward or downward (as in Figure 18.2.4) suggests that something is progressively wearing out. Perhaps some component of the machinery has worn through its hard outer shell and has begun to slowly disintegrate, or maybe the chemical bath has begun to reach the end of its useful life and should be replaced.

Part of your job in interpreting control charts is to be a detective. By exploring the data and looking at the trends and patterns, you learn what kinds of things to look for in order to fix the problem and get the process back into control.

■ 18.3 Charting a Quantitative Measurement with $\overline{X}$ and R Charts

For charting a quantitative measurement, it is conventional to choose a fairly small sample size (for example, $n = 4$ or $n = 5$ are common choices) and then chart the results of many successive samples. Each point on the control chart will then represent a summary (perhaps center or variability) for the n individual observations. It is advisable to choose a small n because the process may change quickly and you would like to detect the change before very many defects are produced.

Perhaps the most common ways of charting a quantitative measurement are the $\bar{X}$ and R charts. The **$\bar{X}$ chart** displays the *average* of each sample together with the appropriate center line and control limits so that you can monitor the level of the process. The **R chart** displays the *range* (the largest value minus the smallest) for each sample together with center line and control limits so that you can monitor the variability of the process. These charts and others like them (including the percentage chart) are due to W. A. Shewhart.

Why is the range sometimes used in quality control charts instead of the (statistically) more conventional standard deviation as a measure of variability? Because the range is easier to compute. Back when computers were not widely available, this was an important advantage because it meant that workers could construct their own charts by hand. Although (as was shown in Chapter 5) the standard deviation is better than the range as a measure of variability, with small sample sizes (such as $n = 4$ or 5) the range is nearly as good as the standard deviation.

There are two ways to find the control limits and center line for each of these charts, depending on whether or not you have an external standard (from past experience, for example). If you don't have an external standard, the limits are computed based only on the data. If you do have an external standard, the limits are based only on this standard. Table 18.3.1 shows how to compute the center line and the control limits for the $\bar{X}$ and $\bar{R}$ charts. The multipliers $A, A_2, D_1, D_2, D_3,$ and D_4 are given in Table 18.3.2. The symbol $\bar{\bar{X}}$ is the average of all of the sample averages, and $\bar{R}$ is the average of the ranges for all of the samples.

For example, suppose there is no standard given, and the sample summaries are as shown in Table 18.3.3. With sample size $n = 4$, you will need the table values $A_2 = 0.729$, $D_3 = 0$, and $D_4 = 2.282$. For the $\bar{X}$ chart, the center line and control limits will be as follows:

Center line: $\qquad\qquad\qquad\qquad\qquad \bar{\bar{X}} = 21.84$

Lower control limit: $\qquad \bar{\bar{X}} - A_2\bar{R} = 21.84 - (0.729)(1.20) = 20.97$

Upper control limit: $\qquad \bar{\bar{X}} + A_2\bar{R} = 21.84 + (0.729)(1.20) = 22.71$

TABLE 18.3.1 Finding the Center Line and Control Limits for $\bar{X}$ and R Charts

		Center Line	Control Limits
$\bar{X}$ chart	Standard given (μ_0 and σ_0)	μ_0	From $\mu_0 - A\sigma_0$ to $\mu_0 + A\sigma_0$
	No standard given	$\bar{\bar{X}}$	From $\bar{\bar{X}} - A_2\bar{R}$ to $\bar{\bar{X}} + A_2\bar{R}$
R chart	Standard given (σ_0)	$d_2\sigma_0$	From $D_1\sigma_0$ to $D_2\sigma_0$
	No standard given	$\bar{R}$	From $D_3\bar{R}$ to $D_4\bar{R}$

TABLE 18.3.2 Multipliers to Use for Constructing $\overline{X}$ and R Charts

| Sample Size, n | Chart for Averages ($\overline{X}$ Chart): Factors for Control Limits | | Charts for Ranges (R chart) | | | | |
	A	A_2	Factor for Central Line, d_2	D_1	D_2	D_3	D_4
2	2.121	1.880	1.128	0	3.686	0	3.267
3	1.732	1.023	1.693	0	4.358	0	2.574
4	1.500	0.729	2.059	0	4.698	0	2.282
5	1.342	0.577	2.326	0	4.918	0	2.114
6	1.225	0.483	2.534	0	5.078	0	2.004
7	1.134	0.419	2.704	0.204	5.204	0.076	1.924
8	1.061	0.373	2.847	0.388	5.306	0.136	1.864
9	1.000	0.337	2.970	0.547	5.393	0.184	1.816
10	0.949	0.308	3.078	0.687	5.469	0.223	1.777
11	0.905	0.285	3.173	0.811	5.535	0.256	1.744
12	0.866	0.266	3.258	0.922	5.594	0.283	1.717
13	0.832	0.249	3.336	1.025	5.647	0.307	1.693
14	0.802	0.235	3.407	1.118	5.696	0.328	1.672
15	0.775	0.223	3.472	1.203	5.741	0.347	1.653
16	0.750	0.212	3.532	1.282	5.782	0.363	1.637
17	0.728	0.203	3.588	1.356	5.820	0.378	1.622
18	0.707	0.194	3.640	1.424	5.856	0.391	1.608
19	0.688	0.187	3.689	1.487	5.891	0.403	1.597
20	0.671	0.180	3.735	1.549	5.921	0.415	1.585
21	0.655	0.173	3.778	1.605	5.951	0.425	1.575
22	0.640	0.167	3.819	1.659	5.979	0.434	1.566
23	0.626	0.162	3.858	1.710	6.006	0.443	1.557
24	0.612	0.157	3.895	1.759	6.031	0.451	1.548
25	0.600	0.153	3.931	1.806	6.056	0.459	1.541

These values are from ASTM-STP 15D, American Society for Testing and Materials.

TABLE 18.3.3 Summaries of Measurements for Eight Samples of $n = 4$ Components Each

Sample Identification Number	Sample Average, $\overline{X}$	Sample Range, R
1	22.3	1.8
2	22.4	1.2
3	21.5	1.1
4	22.0	0.9
5	21.1	1.1
6	21.7	0.9
7	22.1	1.5
8	21.6	1.1
Average	$\overline{\overline{X}} = 21.84$	$\overline{R} = 1.20$

For the R chart, these values are as follows:

Center line: $\bar{R} = 1.20$

Lower control limit: $D_3\bar{R} = (0)(1.20) = 0$

Upper control limit: $D_4\bar{R} = (2.282)(1.20) = 2.74$

Now suppose that there is a standard given in addition to the data in Table 18.3.3, so that you know (say, from past experience) that $\mu_0 = 22.00$ and $\sigma_0 = 0.50$. With sample size $n = 4$, you will need the table values $A = 1.500$, $d_2 = 2.059$, $D_1 = 0$, and $D_2 = 4.698$. For the $\bar{X}$ chart, the center line and control limits will be as follows:

Center line: $\mu_0 = 22.00$

Lower control limit: $\mu_0 - A\sigma_0 = 22.00 - (1.500)(0.50) = 21.25$

Upper control limit: $\mu_0 + A\sigma_0 = 22.00 + (1.500)(0.50) = 22.75$

For the R chart, these values are as follows:

Center line: $d_2\sigma_0 = (2.059)(0.50) = 1.03$

Lower control limit: $D_1\sigma_0 = (0)(0.50) = 0$

Upper control limit: $D_2\sigma_0 = (4.698)(0.50) = 2.35$

| EXAMPLE | **Net Weight of Dishwasher Detergent** |

From each batch of 150 boxes of dishwasher detergent, 5 boxes are selected at random and the contents weighed. This information is then summarized in a control chart, which is examined to see whether the process needs to be adjusted or not. Measurements and summaries (average, largest, smallest, and range) are shown in Table 18.3.4 for 25 samples of 5 boxes each.

Since some of the packing equipment is fairly new, no outside standard is available. Here are the center line and control limits for the $\bar{X}$ and R charts, using the table entries for sample size $n = 5$. For the $\bar{X}$ chart:

Center line: $\bar{\bar{X}} = 16.093$

Lower control limit: $\bar{\bar{X}} - A_2\bar{R} = 16.093 - (0.577)(0.263) = 15.941$

Upper control limit: $\bar{\bar{X}} + A_2\bar{R} = 16.093 + (0.577)(0.263) = 16.245$

For the R chart:

Center line: $\bar{R} = 0.263$

Lower control limit: $D_3\bar{R} = (0)(0.263) = 0$

Upper control limit: $D_4\bar{R} = (2.114)(0.263) = 0.556$

TABLE 18.3.4 Net Weights of Sampled Boxes of Dishwasher Detergent, with Sample Summaries

Sample Identification Number	Individual Measurements within Each Sample (net weight, in ounces)					Sample Summaries			Range, R
	1	2	3	4	5	Average, $\overline{X}$	Largest	Smallest	
1	16.12	16.03	16.25	16.19	16.24	16.166	16.25	16.03	0.22
2	16.11	16.10	16.28	16.18	16.16	16.166	16.28	16.10	0.18
3	16.16	16.21	16.10	16.09	16.04	16.120	16.21	16.04	0.17
4	15.97	15.99	16.34	16.18	16.02	16.100	16.34	15.97	0.37
5	16.21	16.00	16.14	16.12	16.10	16.114	16.21	16.00	0.21
6	15.77	16.11	16.01	16.02	16.17	16.016	16.17	15.77	0.40
7	16.02	16.29	16.08	15.96	16.11	16.092	16.29	15.96	0.33
8	15.83	16.08	16.25	16.14	16.15	16.090	16.25	15.83	0.42
9	16.16	15.90	16.08	15.98	16.09	16.042	16.16	15.90	0.26
10	16.08	16.10	16.13	16.03	16.03	16.074	16.13	16.03	0.10
11	15.90	16.16	16.15	15.99	16.07	16.054	16.16	15.90	0.26
12	16.09	16.05	16.07	15.98	15.95	16.028	16.09	15.95	0.14
13	15.98	16.18	16.08	16.08	16.07	16.078	16.18	15.98	0.20
14	16.23	16.05	16.10	16.07	16.16	16.122	16.23	16.05	0.18
15	15.96	16.20	16.35	16.11	16.08	16.140	16.35	15.96	0.39
16	16.00	16.04	16.02	16.03	16.09	16.036	16.09	16.00	0.09
17	16.12	16.12	15.95	15.98	16.10	16.054	16.12	15.95	0.17
18	16.30	16.05	16.10	16.09	16.07	16.122	16.30	16.05	0.25
19	16.11	16.15	16.25	16.03	16.05	16.118	16.25	16.03	0.22
20	15.85	16.06	15.96	16.20	16.25	16.064	16.25	15.85	0.40
21	15.94	15.88	16.02	16.06	16.10	16.000	16.10	15.88	0.22
22	16.15	16.15	16.21	15.95	16.13	16.118	16.21	15.95	0.26
23	16.10	16.17	16.24	16.00	15.87	16.076	16.24	15.87	0.37
24	16.22	16.34	16.40	16.07	16.12	16.230	16.40	16.07	0.33
25	16.32	15.97	15.88	16.03	16.27	16.094	16.32	15.88	0.44
						$\overline{\overline{X}} = 16.093$			$\overline{R} = 0.263$

The $\overline{X}$ and R charts (both shown in Figure 18.3.1) show a process that is in control. All observations in each chart fall within the control limits. There are no clear nonrandom patterns (such as an upward or downward trend or too many successive points falling too close to a limit). Does observation 24, at the right in the $\overline{X}$ chart, look suspicious to you because it's so close to the upper control limit? Perhaps it does, but because it's still within the limits, you would do better to resist the temptation to mess with the packaging process until the evidence is more clear. With a single isolated point near (but within) the control limits, you would still decide that the process is in control; but feel free to remain suspicious and to look for further evidence, clues, and patterns that would show that the process needs adjustment.

Figure 18.3.2 shows how this kind of control chart technology might be implemented on the shop floor for this example. This form, available from the American Society for Quality Control, allows you to record background information, measurements, summaries, and control charts all in one place.

FIGURE 18.3.1   The $\bar{X}$ and R charts for 25 samples of five boxes of dishwasher detergent. The process is in control because all points fall within the control limits, and the plots indicate randomness, with no clear trends or patterns.

■ 18.4 Charting the Percent Defective

Suppose that items are inspected and then classified as either defective or not. This is not a quantitative measurement, so a new control chart is needed. For each group of items, the *percent defective* can be computed and charted to give an idea of how widespread the problem is.

The **percentage chart** displays the percent defective together with the appropriate center line and control limits so that you can monitor the rate at which the process produces defective items. The control limits are set at three standard deviations, assuming a binomial distribution for the number of defective items. There is a rule of thumb to use for deciding on a sample size:

> ■ **Selecting the Sample Size, *n*, for a Percentage Chart**
> You should expect at least five defective items in a sample.

This says that the sample size, n, will be much larger for the percentage chart than for the $\bar{X}$ and R charts. For example, if you expect 10% defective items, your sample size should be at least $n = 5/0.10 = 50$. If you expect

FIGURE 18.3.2 The background information, measurements, summaries, and control charts for the dishwasher detergent weights, as they might be recorded on the shop floor.

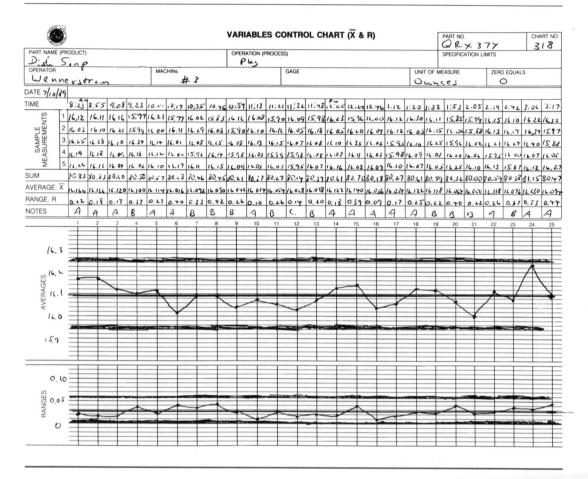

only 0.4% defectives, your sample size should be at least $n = 5/0.004 = 1,250$.

If you are fortunate enough to essentially *never* produce a defective item, don't despair. Although you can't find a sample size that satisfies this rule, you are nonetheless obviously in great shape. Congratulations on your dedication to quality.

Table 18.4.1 shows how to compute the center line and the control limits for the percentage chart. No special table of multipliers is needed because, as you may already have noticed, these formulas use the standard deviation of a binomial distribution. Recall that f is the observed proportion or percentage in one sample. The symbol $\bar{f}$ represents the average of all of the sample proportions.

TABLE 18.4.1 Finding the Center Line and Control Limits for the Percentage Chart

	Center Line	Control Limits
Standard given (p_0)	p_0	From $p_0 - 3\sqrt{\dfrac{p_0(1 - p_0)}{n}}$ to $p_0 + 3\sqrt{\dfrac{p_0(1 - p_0)}{n}}$
No standard given	$\bar{f}$	From $\bar{f} - 3\sqrt{\dfrac{\bar{f}(1 - \bar{f})}{n}}$ to $\bar{f} + 3\sqrt{\dfrac{\bar{f}(1 - \bar{f})}{n}}$

TABLE 18.4.2 Summaries of Measurements for 12 Samples of $n = 500$ Items Each

Sample Identification Number	Number of Defective Items, X	Sample Percentage, f
1	10	2.0%
2	11	2.2
3	10	2.0
4	12	2.4
5	7	1.4
6	14	2.8
7	13	2.6
8	11	2.2
9	6	1.2
10	12	2.4
11	11	2.2
12	13	2.6
Average	10.8333	$\bar{f} = 2.1667\%$

For example, suppose there is no standard given, and the sample summaries are as shown in Table 18.4.2. With sample size $n = 500$, the center line and control limits for the percentage chart will be as follows:

Center line:

$$\bar{f} = 0.021667 \quad \text{or} \quad 2.1667\%$$

Lower control limit:

$$\bar{f} - 3\sqrt{\frac{\bar{f}(1 - \bar{f})}{n}} = 0.021667 - 3\sqrt{\frac{0.021667(1 - 0.021667)}{500}}$$

$$= 0.021667 - (3)(0.006511)$$

$$= 0.0021 \quad \text{or} \quad 0.21\%$$

Upper control limit:

$$\bar{f} + 3\sqrt{\frac{\bar{f}(1 - \bar{f})}{n}} = 0.021667 + (3)(0.006511)$$

$$= 0.0412 \quad \text{or} \quad 4.12\%$$

Now suppose that there is a standard given in addition to the data in Table 18.4.2, so that you know (say, from past experience) that the process produces defective items at a rate of $p_0 = 2.30\%$. With sample size $n = 500$, the center line and control limits for the percentage chart will be as follows:

Center line:

$$p_0 = 0.0230 \quad \text{or} \quad 2.30\%$$

Lower control limit:

$$p_0 - 3\sqrt{\frac{p_0(1 - p_0)}{n}} = 0.0230 - 3\sqrt{\frac{0.0230(1 - 0.0230)}{500}}$$

$$= 0.0230 - (3)(0.0067039)$$

$$= 0.0029 \quad \text{or} \quad 0.29\%$$

Upper control limit:

$$p_0 + 3\sqrt{\frac{p_0(1 - p_0)}{n}} = 0.0230 + (3)(0.0067039)$$

$$= 0.0431 \quad \text{or} \quad 4.31\%$$

EXAMPLE **Filling out Purchase Orders**

When purchase orders are entered into the computer and processed, errors are sometimes found that require special attention to correct them. Of course, "special attention" is expensive, and you would like the percentage of problems to be small. In order to keep an eye on this problem, you regularly look at a percentage chart.

For each batch of 300 purchase orders, the percent of errors is recorded, as shown in Table 18.4.3. You are not using any standard for the percentage chart, so the center line and control limits are as follows:

Center line:

$$\bar{f} = 0.0515 \quad \text{or} \quad 5.15\%$$

Lower control limit:

$$\bar{f} - 3\sqrt{\frac{\bar{f}(1 - \bar{f})}{n}} = 0.0515 - 3\sqrt{\frac{0.0515(1 - 0.0515)}{300}}$$

$$= 0.0515 - (3)(0.012760)$$

$$= 0.0132 \quad \text{or} \quad 1.32\%$$

Upper control limit:

$$\bar{f} + 3\sqrt{\frac{\bar{f}(1 - \bar{f})}{n}} = 0.0515 + (3)(0.012760)$$

$$= 0.0898 \quad \text{or} \quad 8.98\%$$

TABLE 18.4.3　Summaries of Errors in 25 Batches of
$n = 300$ Purchase Orders

Batch Identification Number	Number of Errors, X	Sample Percentage, f
1	5	1.7 %
2	11	3.7
3	7	2.3
4	14	4.7
5	5	1.7
6	11	3.7
7	11	3.7
8	10	3.3
9	14	4.7
10	8	2.7
11	5	1.7
12	16	5.3
13	12	4.0
14	9	3.0
15	13	4.3
16	17	5.7
17	20	6.7
18	30	10.0
19	23	7.7
20	25	8.3
21	35	11.7
22	24	8.0
23	22	7.3
24	23	7.7
25	16	5.3
Average	15.44	$\bar{f} = 5.15\%$

The percentage chart (Figure 18.4.1) shows that the processing of purchase orders is *not* in control. Two batches (18 and 21) are outside the upper control limit due to excessive errors. Furthermore, the entire right-hand side of the chart appears to have a higher percentage than the left side. It appears that the process was in control, at a low error rate, but then some problem began around batch number 16 or 17 that increased the error rate.

The control chart has done its job: to alert you to problems and provide clues to help you solve them. Yes, there is a problem. The clue is a high error rate starting around batch 16 or 17.

An investigation of what was happening around the time of production of batch 16 shows that work began at that time on a new investment project. There were so many purchase orders to process that extra help was hired. Apparently the higher error rates were due initially to the strain on the system (due to the large volume of purchase orders) and the fact that the new employees had not yet learned the system. Although the error rate does drop at the end of the chart (on the right), it still may be somewhat high. It may well be time to institute a quick course of further training for the new people in order to bring the error rate back down to a lower level.

FIGURE 18.4.1 The processing of purchase orders is not in control and needs some attention. Batches 18 and 21 are above the upper control limit, and there appears to have been a shift in level around batch number 16 or 17.

18.5 End-of-Chapter Materials

Summary

Statistical quality control is the use of statistical methods for evaluating and improving the results of any activity. A **process** is any business activity that takes inputs and transforms them into outputs. A process can be made up of other processes, called *subprocesses,* each of which is a process in its own right. **Statistical process control** is the use of statistical methods to monitor the functioning of a process so that you can adjust or fix it when necessary and can leave it alone when it's working properly. Any time you could reasonably find out why a problem occurred, you have an **assignable cause of variation.** All causes of variation that would not be worth the effort to identify are grouped together as **random causes of variation.** When you have identified and eliminated all of the assignable causes of variation, so that only random causes remain, your process is said to be **in a state of statistical control** or, simply, **in control.**

The **Pareto diagram** displays the causes of the various defects in order from most to least frequent so that you can focus attention on the most important problems. The tallest bars will always be at the left (indicating the most frequent problems) and the shortest bars will be at the right. The line indicating the cumulative percentage will always go upward and will tend to level off toward the right.

A **control chart** displays successive measurements of a process together with a *center line* and *control limits,* which are computed to help you decide whether the process is in control or not. If you decide that the process is *not* in control, the control chart helps you identify the problem so that you can fix it. The hypotheses being tested are:

H_0: The process is in control

H_1: The process is not in control

The **false alarm rate** is how often you decide to fix the process when there really isn't any problem. This is the same concept as the type I error in hypothesis testing. Conventional control charts use a factor of three standard errors instead of two because the conventional 5% type I error rate of statistical hypothesis testing is unacceptably high for most quality control applications. A process that is in control will usually have a control chart plot that stays within the control limits. If any measurement falls outside of the control limits, either above the upper control limit or below the lower limit, you would decide that the process is not in control. A sudden jump to another level in a control chart or a gradual drift upward or downward can also indicate a process that is not in control, even if all points fall within the control limits.

It is conventional, for charting a quantitative measurement, to choose a fairly small sample size ($n = 4$ or $n = 5$ are common choices) and then chart the results of many successive samples. The $\bar{X}$ **chart** displays the *average* of each sample together with the appropriate center line and control limits so that you can monitor the level of the process. The R **chart** displays the *range* (the largest value minus the smallest) for each sample together with center line and control limits so that you can monitor the variability of the process.

The **percentage chart** displays the percent defective together with the appropriate center line and control limits so that you can monitor the rate at which the process produces defective items. The sample size required is much larger than for charting a quantitative measurement. A common rule of thumb is that you should expect at least five defective items in a sample.

Key Words

Questions

1 a. What is statistical quality control?
  b. Why are statistical methods so helpful for quality control?

2 a. What is a process?
   b. What is the relationship between a process and its subprocesses?
   c. What is statistical process control?
3 Can statistical process control be applied to business activities in general, or is it restricted to manufacturing?
4 Why should you monitor a process? Why not just inspect the results and throw away the defective ones?
5 a. What is an assignable cause of variation?
   b. What is a random cause of variation?
6 a. What do we mean when we say that a process is in a state of statistical control?
   b. What should you do when a process is not in control?
   c. What should you do when a process appears to be in control?
7 a. What information is displayed in a Pareto diagram?
   b. What makes the Pareto diagram useful as a management tool?
8 a. What is a control chart?
   b. Explain how control charts help you perform the four basic activities of statistics.
   c. What hypotheses are being tested when you use control charts?
   d. What is the false alarm rate? Is it conventional to set it at 5%?
9 a. Describe a typical control chart for a process that is in control.
   b. Describe three different ways in which a control chart could tell you that the process is not in control.
10 a. What is the purpose of the $\overline{X}$ chart?
   b. What is a typical sample size?
   c. How would you find the center line if you had no standard?
   d. How would you find the center line if you did have a standard?
   e. How would you find the control limits if you had no standard?
   f. How would you find the control limits if you did have a standard?
11 a. What is the purpose of the R chart?
   b. What is a typical sample size?
   c. How would you find the center line if you had no standard?
   d. How would you find the center line if you did have a standard?
   e. How would you find the control limits if you had no standard?
   f. How would you find the control limits if you did have a standard?
12 a. What is the purpose of the percentage chart?
   b. How large should the sample size be?
   c. How would you find the center line if you had no standard?
   d. How would you find the center line if you did have a standard?
   e. How would you find the control limits if you had no standard?
   f. How would you find the control limits if you did have a standard?

Problems

1 For each of the following situations, tell whether a Pareto diagram, an $\overline{X}$ chart, an R chart, or a percentage chart would be the most helpful. Give a reason for your choice.
   a. Your workers all want to be helpful, but they can't seem to agree on which problems to solve first.
   b. Some of the engines come off the line with too much oil, and others come off with too little. Something has to be done to control the differences from one to the next.

c. The gears being produced are all pretty much the same size in each batch, but they tend to be consistently too large compared to the desired specification.

d. Management would like to track the rate at which defective candy coatings are produced.

e. You would like to understand the limits of variation of the machinery so that you can set it to fill each bottle just a tiny bit more than the amount claimed on the label.

f. Usually you pay the bills on time, but a small fraction of them slip through the system and are paid late with a penalty. You'd like to keep an eye on this to see if things are getting worse.

2 A tractor manufacturing plant has been experiencing problems with the division that makes the transmissions. A Pareto diagram, shown in Figure 18.5.1, has been constructed based on recent experience.

a. What is the most important problem, in terms of the number of transmissions affected? What percent of all difficulties does this problem represent?

b. What is the next most important problem? What percent does it represent?

c. What percent of defective transmissions do the top two problems, taken together, represent?

d. What percent of problems do the top three problems together represent?

e. Write a paragraph, as if to your supervisor, summarizing the situation and recommending action.

3 A candy manufacturer has observed the frequency of various types of problems that occur in the production of small chocolates with a hard candy coating. The basic data set is shown in Table 18.5.1.

a. Arrange the problems in order from most to least frequent, and create a table showing number of cases, percent of total problem cases, and cumulative percent.

b. Draw a Pareto diagram for this situation.

FIGURE 18.5.1   **Pareto diagram for defective transmissions.**

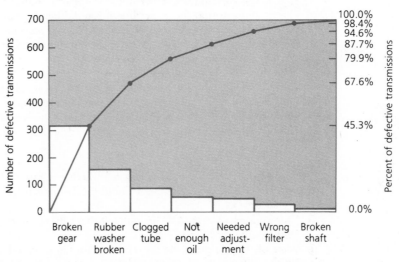

TABLE 18.5.1   Frequency of Occurrence of Various Problems in
Candy Manufacturing

Cause of Problem	Number of Cases
Miscellaneous	22
Not enough coating	526
Squashed	292
Too much coating	89
Two stuck together	57

c. What is the most important problem, in terms of the number of candies affected? What percent of all difficulties does this problem represent?

d. What is the next most important problem? What percent does it represent?

e. What percent of defective candies do the top two problems, taken together, represent?

f. Write a paragraph, as if to your supervisor, summarizing the situation and recommending action.

4 A firm specializing in the processing of rebate certificates has tabulated the frequency of occurrence of various types of problems, as shown in Table 18.5.2.

TABLE 18.5.2   Frequency of Occurrence of Various Problems in
Processing Rebate Certificates

Cause of Problem	Number of Cases
Blank	53
Illegible	528
Two numbers transposed	184
Wrong place on form	330

a. Arrange the problems in order from most to least frequent, and create a table indicating the number of cases, percent of total problem cases, and cumulative percent.

b. Draw a Pareto diagram for this situation.

c. What is the most important problem, in terms of the number of certificates affected? What percent of all difficulties does this problem represent?

d. What is the next most important problem? What percent does it represent?

e. What percent of defective certificates do the top two problems, taken together, represent?

f. Write a paragraph, as if to your supervisor, summarizing the situation and recommending action.

5 Consider the $\overline{X}$ chart shown in Figure 18.5.2 showing the average number of chocolate chips per cookie.

a. Describe in general terms what you see in the chart.

b. Decide whether this process is in control or not. Give a reason for your answer.

c. What action, if any, is warranted?

6 Find the center line and control limits for each of the following situations.

a. $\overline{X}$ chart, sample size $n = 6$, $\overline{\overline{X}} = 56.31$, $\overline{R} = 4.16$, no standard given.

b. R chart, sample size $n = 6$, $\overline{\overline{X}} = 56.31$, $\overline{R} = 4.16$, no standard given.

c. $\overline{X}$ chart, sample size $n = 3$, $\overline{\overline{X}} = 182.3$, $\overline{R} = 29.4$, no standard given.

FIGURE 18.5.2 An $\overline{X}$ chart for the number of chocolate chips per cookie.

d. R chart, sample size $n = 3$, $\overline{\overline{X}} = 182.3$, $\overline{R} = 29.4$, no standard given.

e. $\overline{X}$ chart, sample size $n = 5$, $\overline{\overline{X}} = 108.3$, $\overline{R} = 13.8$, standards are $\mu_0 = 100.0$ and $\sigma_0 = 5.0$.

f. R chart, sample size $n = 5$, $\overline{\overline{X}} = 108.3$, $\overline{R} = 13.8$, standards are $\mu_0 = 100.0$ and $\sigma_0 = 5.0$.

g. $\overline{X}$ chart, sample size $n = 8$, standards are $\mu_0 = 2.500$ and $\sigma_0 = 0.010$.

h. R chart, sample size $n = 8$, standards are $\mu_0 = 2.500$ and $\sigma_0 = 0.010$.

7 Consider the data set shown in Table 18.5.3, representing the thicknesses of a protective coating.

a. Find the average, $\overline{X}$, and the range, R, for each sample.

b. Find the overall average, $\overline{\overline{X}}$, and the average range, $\overline{R}$.

c. Find the center line for the $\overline{X}$ chart.

d. Find the control limits for the $\overline{X}$ chart.

e. Draw the $\overline{X}$ chart.

f. Comment on what you see in the $\overline{X}$ chart. In particular, is this process in control? How do you know?

g. Write a paragraph, as if to your supervisor, summarizing the situation and defending the action you feel is appropriate.

8 Continue with the data set in Table 18.5.3, representing the thicknesses of a protective coating.

a. Find the center line for the R chart.

b. Find the control limits for the R chart.

c. Draw the R chart.

d. Comment on what you see in the R chart. In particular, is the variability of this process in control? How do you know?

9 Mr. K. R. Wood, president of Broccoli Enterprises, is interested in the data shown in Table 18.5.4, representing the lengths of broccoli trees after cutting.

TABLE 18.5.3 Thicknesses of a Protective Coating: 25 Samples of Three Items Each

Sample Identification Number	Individual Measurements within Each Sample		
	1	2	3
1	12.51	12.70	12.57
2	12.60	12.53	12.39
3	12.40	12.81	12.56
4	12.44	12.57	12.60
5	12.78	12.61	12.58
6	12.75	12.43	12.61
7	12.53	12.51	12.68
8	12.64	12.49	12.51
9	12.57	12.74	12.81
10	12.70	12.87	12.95
11	12.74	12.80	12.86
12	12.90	12.83	12.91
13	13.05	13.00	13.02
14	12.88	12.88	13.11
15	13.03	12.85	13.05
16	12.96	12.88	12.95
17	12.91	12.75	13.01
18	12.95	13.03	12.89
19	13.17	12.81	13.17
20	13.17	13.05	12.97
21	12.95	13.04	12.80
22	13.04	13.25	12.95
23	13.12	13.07	13.11
24	12.83	13.13	13.31
25	13.24	13.18	13.13

a. Find the average, $\overline{X}$, and the range, R, for each sample.

b. Find the overall average, $\overline{\overline{X}}$, and the average range, $\overline{R}$.

c. Find the center line for the $\overline{X}$ chart.

d. Find the control limits for the $\overline{X}$ chart.

e. Draw the $\overline{X}$ chart.

f. Comment on what you see in the $\overline{X}$ chart. In particular, is this process in control? How do you know?

g. Write a paragraph summarizing the situation and defending the action you feel is appropriate.

10 Continue with the data set in Table 18.5.4, representing the lengths of broccoli trees after cutting.

a. Find the center line for the R chart.

b. Find the control limits for the R chart.

c. Draw the R chart.

d. Comment on what you see in the R chart. In particular, is the variability of this process in control? How do you know?

11 Find the center line and control limits for each of the following situations.

a. Percentage chart, sample size $n = 300, f = 0.0731$.

b. Percentage chart, sample size $n = 450, f = 0.1683$.

TABLE 18.5.4 Lengths of Trees of Broccoli: 20 Samples of Four Stems Each

Sample Identification Number	Individual Measurements within Each Sample			
	1	2	3	4
1	8.60	8.47	8.44	8.51
2	8.43	8.42	8.62	8.46
3	8.65	8.32	8.65	8.51
4	8.39	8.54	8.50	8.41
5	8.49	8.53	8.61	8.46
6	8.63	8.46	8.64	8.54
7	8.47	8.63	8.54	8.55
8	8.52	8.50	8.31	8.63
9	8.35	8.43	8.51	8.61
10	8.31	8.65	8.46	8.40
11	8.58	8.43	8.55	8.45
12	8.28	8.57	8.58	8.48
13	8.45	8.52	8.52	8.54
14	8.38	8.48	8.41	8.57
15	8.56	8.60	8.58	8.51
16	8.39	8.47	8.59	8.41
17	8.53	8.58	8.54	8.42
18	8.78	8.52	8.46	8.50
19	8.48	8.49	8.74	8.59
20	8.46	8.47	8.70	8.32

    c. Percentage chart, sample size $n = 800$, $f = 0.0316$, standard is $p_0 = 0.0350$.

    d. Percentage chart, sample size $n = 1,500$, standard is $p_0 = 0.01$.

12 Consider the data set shown in Table 18.5.5, summarizing recent numbers of errors in batches of 500 invoices.

    a. Find the percentage, f, for each batch.

    b. Find the average percentage, $\bar{f}$.

    c. Find the center line for the percentage chart.

    d. Find the control limits for the percentage chart.

    e. Draw the percentage chart.

    f. Comment on what you see in the percentage chart. In particular, is this process in control? How do you know?

    g. Write a paragraph, as if to your supervisor, summarizing the situation and defending the action you feel is appropriate.

13 No matter how closely the production process is monitored, some chips will work faster than others and be worth more in the marketplace. The goal is to make this number as high as possible, and improvements are being implemented continually. Consider the data set shown in Table 18.5.6, summarizing the number of memory chips that worked properly at the highest speed for each of 25 batches of 1,000 chips.

TABLE 18.5.5 Summaries of Defective Invoices in 25 Batches of
$n = 500$

Batch Identification Number	Number of Errors, X
1	58
2	57
3	60
4	64
5	57
6	53
7	53
8	74
9	40
10	54
11	56
12	54
13	60
14	51
15	54
16	47
17	52
18	50
19	62
20	56
21	60
22	67
23	50
24	60
25	67

a. Find the center line for the percentage chart.
b. Find the control limits for the percentage chart.
c. Draw the percentage chart.
d. Comment on what you see in the percentage chart. In particular, is this process in control? How do you know?
e. For the particular case of high-speed memory chips here, does the control chart show good or bad news?
f. Write a paragraph, as if to your supervisor, summarizing the situation.

14 Consider the data set shown in Table 18.5.7, indicating hourly summaries of the temperature for a baking oven measured four times per hour.
a. Draw an $\overline{X}$ and an R chart for each day.
b. For each day, summarize the charts. In particular, was the process in control? How do you know?
c. For each day, tell what action is appropriate.
d. A new product requires that the temperature be constant to within plus or minus 10 degrees. Based on the "in control" control charts from part a, do you think that these ovens can be used for this purpose? Why or why not?

TABLE 18.5.6   Number of Highest-Speed Memory Chips for 25 Batches of 1,000 Chips Each

Batch Identification Number	Number of Highest-Speed Chips, X	Percent of Highest-Speed Chips, f
1	75	0.075
2	61	0.061
3	62	0.062
4	70	0.070
5	60	0.060
6	56	0.056
7	61	0.061
8	65	0.065
9	54	0.054
10	71	0.071
11	84	0.084
12	84	0.084
13	110	0.110
14	71	0.071
15	103	0.103
16	103	0.103
17	80	0.080
18	90	0.090
19	84	0.084
20	88	0.088
21	111	0.111
22	118	0.118
23	147	0.147
24	136	0.136
25	123	0.123
Average	86.68	0.08668

15 Find the probability that a particular set of eight consecutive points will fall on one side of the center line for a process that is in control. (*Hints:* For a process that is in control, assume that the probability is 0.5 that a point is on the same side as the first point, and these are independent. You may therefore compute the probability for a binomial distribution with $p = 0.5$ and $n = 7$. You would use $n = 7$ instead of $n = 8$ because the first point of the sequence is free to fall on either side, so the situation is really determined by the seven other points.)

TABLE 18.5.7 Average and Range of Temperatures Taken Four Times per Hour

Time	Monday $\bar{X}$	Monday R	Tuesday $\bar{X}$	Tuesday R	Wednesday $\bar{X}$	Wednesday R
12:00	408.65	30.74	401.07	25.23	402.92	31.96
1:00	401.57	24.81	405.97	32.72	407.28	9.11
2:00	395.52	21.93	401.70	34.56	399.61	22.85
3:00	402.25	35.91	402.06	38.15	398.43	38.52
4:00	405.04	28.68	403.35	31.03	389.97	12.16
5:00	404.12	38.18	407.82	34.93	402.37	18.39
6:00	404.44	18.16	400.30	30.56	406.29	48.44
7:00	407.19	14.14	403.69	17.97	407.77	32.63
8:00	407.43	21.56	399.72	14.11	398.22	19.30
9:00	412.60	25.29	394.77	28.89	408.42	19.11
10:00	413.40	14.32	400.82	37.26	402.91	28.52
11:00	407.26	39.70	401.96	33.30	391.20	20.08
12:00	402.97	32.92	399.94	16.43	398.59	13.29
1:00	387.44	21.89	401.01	16.95	401.72	35.90
2:00	414.39	14.34	399.67	30.34	394.37	12.32
3:00	401.25	18.62	401.67	29.53	409.59	32.91
4:00	400.43	27.96	413.30	12.62	421.97	40.38
5:00	399.31	25.93	412.47	45.47	394.58	48.70
6:00	403.14	37.57	406.62	43.65	407.01	25.75
7:00	403.07	33.52	421.90	21.75	403.40	63.81
8:00	403.66	45.69	429.67	24.30	404.93	82.12
9:00	404.05	40.52	422.75	25.79	391.82	67.03
10:00	399.00	39.77	422.56	15.28	393.96	84.53
11:00	410.18	37.71	424.39	16.64	421.68	92.92

Projects

1 Obtain some qualitative data relating to quality showing how frequently different situations have occurred. Possible sources include your firm, a local business, your own experiences, or the library. Draw the Pareto diagram, and describe what you see. Write a one-page summary of the situation for management.
2 Obtain some quantitative data relating to quality. Possible sources include your firm, a local business, your own experiences, or the library. The data set should consist of at least 10 samples of from 3 to 20 observations each. Draw the $\bar{X}$ and R charts, then describe what you see. Write a one-page summary of the situation for management.

Employee Database

Following are the employee records of an administrative division as of January 6, 1990:

Employee Number[1]	Annual Salary	Gender	Age (years)	Experience (years)	Training Level[2]
1	$32,368	F	42	3	B
2	53,174	M	54	10	B
3	52,722	M	47	10	A
4	53,423	M	47	1	B
5	50,602	M	44	5	B
6	49,033	M	42	10	A
7	24,395	M	30	5	A
8	24,395	F	52	6	A
9	43,124	M	48	8	A
10	23,975	F	58	4	A
11	53,174	M	46	4	C
12	58,515	M	36	8	C
13	56,294	M	49	10	B
14	49,033	F	55	10	B
15	44,884	M	41	1	A
16	53,429	F	52	5	B
17	46,574	M	57	8	A
18	58,968	F	61	10	B
19	53,174	M	50	5	A
20	53,627	M	47	10	B
21	49,033	M	54	5	B
22	54,981	M	47	7	A
23	62,530	M	50	10	B
24	27,525	F	38	3	A
25	24,395	M	31	5	A
26	56,884	M	47	10	A
27	52,111	M	56	5	A
28	44,183	F	38	5	B
29	24,967	F	55	6	A
30	35,423	F	47	4	A
31	41,188	F	35	2	B
32	27,525	F	35	3	A
33	35,018	M	39	1	A
34	44,183	M	41	2	A
35	35,423	M	44	1	A

Employee Number[1]	Annual Salary	Gender	Age (years)	Experience (years)	Training Level[2]
36	49,033	M	53	8	A
37	40,741	M	47	2	A
38	49,033	M	42	10	A
39	56,294	F	44	6	C
40	47,180	F	45	5	C
41	46,574	M	56	8	A
42	52,722	M	38	8	C
43	51,237	M	58	2	B
44	53,627	M	52	8	A
45	53,174	M	54	10	A
46	56,294	M	49	10	B
47	49,033	F	53	10	B
48	49,033	M	43	9	A
49	55,549	M	35	8	C
50	51,237	M	56	1	C
51	35,200	F	38	1	B
52	50,175	F	42	5	A
53	24,352	F	35	1	A
54	27,525	F	40	3	A
55	29,606	F	34	4	B
56	24,352	F	35	1	A
57	47,180	F	45	5	B
58	49,033	M	54	10	A
59	53,174	M	47	10	A
60	53,429	F	45	7	B
61	53,627	M	47	10	A
62	26,491	F	46	7	A
63	42,961	M	36	3	B
64	53,174	M	45	5	A
65	37,292	M	46	0	A
66	37,292	M	47	1	A
67	41,188	F	34	3	B
68	57,242	F	45	7	C
69	53,429	F	44	6	C
70	53,174	M	50	10	B
71	44,138	F	38	2	B

[1]These numbers were assigned for the sole purpose of giving each employee a unique number.
[2]The training is offered from time to time and is voluntary (it is not a job requirement). Employees who have not taken either training course are coded as "A". They become "B" after the first training course, and they change to "C" after the second and final course.

Answers to Selected Problems

Chapter 1

Problems

6 a. Exploring the data.
 c. Hypothesis testing.

Chapter 2

Problems

8 a. An employee.
 b. Multivariate.
 c. Salary and years of experience are quantitative; others are qualitative.
 d. Education is ordinal qualitative because the natural ordering HS, BA, MBA corresponds to more and more education.
 e. Cross-sectional.

Database Exercises

1 a. Multivariate.
 d. Ordinal.
2 For gender:
 a. No.
 b. Yes.
 c. No.
 d. Yes.

■ Chapter 3

Problems

1 a.

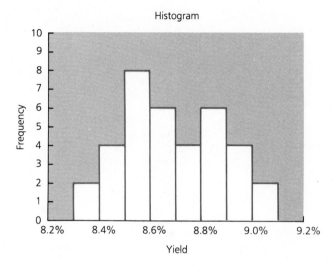

b. Mid to high 8%s.
c. Approximately normal.

8 a.

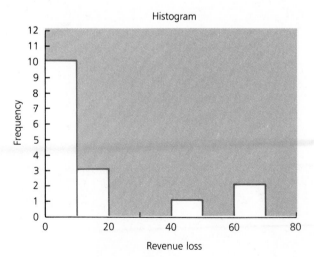

b. Skewed.

Database Exercises

2 a.

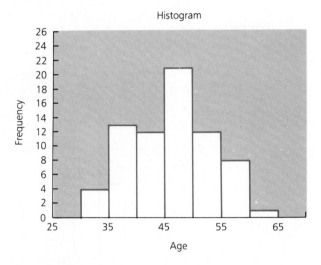

Histogram

b. Approximately normal.
c. Typical age is in high 40s; most employees are within about 10 years of this typical age. Strong concentration near the middle with relatively few older and younger employees.

■ Chapter 4

Problems

1 a. 15.6.
 b. 14.
 e. 6, 24.5.
 f. 0, 34.
 g.

Box plot

h.

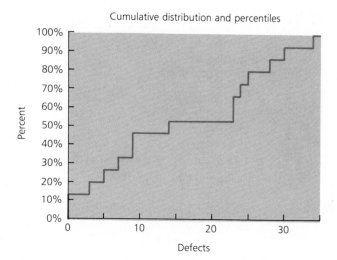

Cumulative distribution and percentiles

i. 30.
j. 86.7th percentile.
5 14.6%.

Database Exercises

1 a. $45,141.50.
b. $49,033.00.
c.

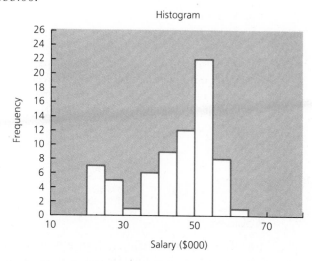

Histogram

$52,500.00.
d. Average is lowest, median is next, and mode is highest. This is expected for a skewed distribution with a long tail towards low values.

■ Chapter 5

Problems

1 a. $4.935.
  b. $1.465, dollars.
  c. A typical location differs from the average price by approximately $1.465 per roll.
  d. $3.91, dollars.
  e. The total difference in price, from the cheapest to the most expensive location, is $3.91 per roll.
  f. 0.297 or 29.7%, none.
  g. A typical location differs from the average price by approximately 29.7%.
  h. 2.148, squared dollars.
  i. No simple interpretation because measurement units are not directly understandable.
5 a. 10.4.
  b. 7.187, a typical firm of this type had approximately 7.187 more or fewer executives than the average.
  c. 38. This is somewhat more than the 30 we would expect (67% of 45) for a normal distribution.

Database Exercises

1 a. $38,555.00.
  b. $10.805.85.
  c. 0.239 or 23.9%.
  d. The highest paid employee earns $38,555.00 more than the lowest paid employee. A typical employee earns approximately $10,805.85 more or less than the average salary. A typical employee earns approximately 23.9% more or less than the average salary. These summaries tell you about variation in salary.

■ Chapter 6

Problems

1 a. Wait until the earnings figure is released, then observe it.
  b. All dollar amounts; including positive, negative, and zero.
  c. Ford's earnings for the past quarter.
  d. All dollar amounts that exceed your computed dollar figure.
  e. Subjective probability.
3 a. 0.297.

4 a. 0.74.
b. 0.83.
c. 0.17.
d. 0.26.
e. 0.91.
f. 1.
g. 0.22.
h. No, since the probability of meeting both deadlines is 0.78, which is not zero.
i. No, since the probability of meeting both deadlines, 0.78, is not equal to the product of the probabilities, $0.83 \times 0.91 = 0.755$.

8 a.

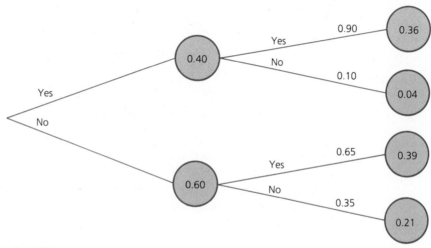

b. 0.75.
c. 0.39.
d. 0.52.
e. 0.10.

Database Exercises

1 a. 0.394.
b. 0.817.
e. 0.917.

■ Chapter 7

Problems

1 a. 8.5.
c. 10.14.
e. 0.25.

4 b. 11.25.
   c. 1.68.
   d. 0.0134.
   f. 0.236.
6 a. 0.748.
7 a. $72,500.
   b. $2,250.
   d. 0.133.
11 a. $65,025.
   b. $6,375.
   d. 0.785.

Database Exercises

1 b. 52.

■ Chapter 8

Problems

1 a. Unreasonable; not representative.
2 a. Statistic.
   b. Parameter.
3 b. Brunswick, Black & Decker, Dover, Crane, TRINOVA, Briggs & Stratton, Fuqua Industries, Ingersoll-Rand, Cummins Engine, American Standard.
   c. 4.2.
   d. 0.651, 0.841.

Database Exercises

2 a. 14, 53, 62, 38, 70, 40, 24, 17, 59, 26.
6 a. 5, the number of female employees (also 5 for the number of males).
   b. 1.581, indicating that in a sample of 10 with 5 women, we expect this number (5) to be approximately 1.581 from what we would have expected on average in such a sample.

■ Chapter 9

Problems

1 a. 2.160.
2 a. 2.34%, typical performance.

b. 5.9798, approximate difference (percentage points) between individual firms and the average.

c. 1.8910, approximate difference (percentage points) between the average (2.34%) and the mean for the (idealized) population of similar brokerage firms.

d. From -1.938 to 6.618.

d. From -1.126 to 5.806; smaller interval than the 95% interval.

f. At least as large as -2.995.

g. No, you must either use the same one side regardless of the data, or else use the two-sided interval.

3 a. From 49.2% to 55.6%.

Database Exercises

1 a. $35,139.20, $12,269.35, $5,487.02.

b. From $19,905.03 to $50,373.36.

Chapter 10

Problems

1 a. $H_0: \mu = \mu_0$, claiming that the mean age of your customers (μ) is equal to the mean age in town (μ_0).

$H_1: \mu \neq \mu_0$, claiming that the mean age of your customers (μ) is *not* equal to the mean age in town (μ_0).

2 a. Yes, since the reference value, 43.1, is not in the confidence interval from 29.1 to 38.1.

3 a. Significant because the t-statistic, -4.15, exceeds the t-table value of 1.960 in absolute value.

5 a. Very highly significant ($p < 0.001$).

6 a. Not appropriate. One-sided result of two-sided test: your customers are very highly significantly younger than 43.1 years old, on average.

17 b. 8.5, 9.2, 0.7.

c. 0.26458, paired.

d. From 0.020 to 1.380.

e. Significantly different. Significantly higher stress for false answers, on average (t-statistic is -2.646).

19 a. 4.475, 2.360, 2.115.

b. 1.007, unpaired. No natural pairing since different objects are being tested.

c. From -0.691 to 4.921.

d. Not significant at level 0.01 (t-statistic is 2.101).

e. Significant ($p < 0.05$).

Database Exercises

1 a. Yes, (95% confidence interval is from \$42,627 to \$47,655; *t*-statistic is 4.009).

■ Chapter 11

Problems

1 a.

Linear relationship.
b. 0.985. Strong increasing relationship.
c. Predicted cost = −1.065 + 2.753 × Age.

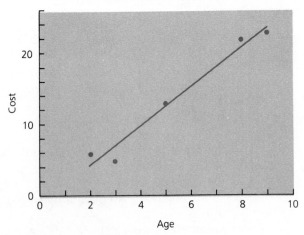

Data, with least-squares line

d. 18.20.
e. 1.725.

    f. 96.9%.

    g. Yes. Confidence interval for slope (from 1.853 to 3.653) does not include zero; t-statistic is 9.734.

    h. Significantly different. Reference value (20) is not in 95% confidence interval (from 1.853 to 3.653).

Database Exercises

2 a. 30.4%.

    b. $49,284.86.

    c. $31,284 to $67,286 (standard error is $9,184.02).

    d. $46,570 to $52,000 (standard error is $1,385.14).

■ Chapter 12

Problems

1 a. Y is the number of leads. X_1 is the cost. X_2 is the size. The F-test.

2 a. Price = 8344.004 + 0.026259 × area − 4.26698 × year.

    b. Each additional square centimeter of area results in an average price increase of $26.26, holding year constant.

    c. Each additional year is expected to *subtract* $4,266.98 from the price, holding area constant; more recent paintings apparently have less value.

    d. $111,348.

    e. $153,110.

    f. 28.2%.

    g. Yes. The F-test is significant ($R^2 = 0.282$ with $n = 23$ and $p = 2$ exceeds the table value of 0.259). Thus area and year taken together do explain a significant fraction of variation in price from one painting to another.

    h. Yes. Significantly more.

    i. Yes. Newer paintings are worth less than older ones.

6 b. $1,381,000, −$174,153.

Database Exercises

1 a. Salary = 22380.64 + 300.5515 × Age + 1579.259 × Experience.

    b. 8,910.19.

    c. 0.3395.

    e. Experience is significant; age is not.

    f. 0.203458 for age, 0.473715 for experience.

2 a. 35,681.41, −663.419, predicted is below actual of 35,018.

■ Chapter 13

Problems

1 a. Purpose: assist with decision making by providing analysis of competitors' positions. Audience: top management.
2 a. Effect.
   b. Affects.
3 a. Analysis and methods.
4 a. J. A. White, "How a Money Manager Can Pull a Rabbit out of a Hat," *The Wall Street Journal,* March 16, 1989, p. C1.
5 a. Name, title, place.

■ Chapter 14

Problems

2 b. Starting at third quarter 1984: 1,655.25, 1,643.00,...
   c. First quarter: 0.924562.
   e. Starting at first quarter 1984: 1,498.01, 1,764.89,...
   h. Long-term trend = 1,562.06 + 23.1442 × (time period).
   i. 2,256.39.
   j. 2,150.37.
5 b. 264,044.
   c. 364,380.
6 a. 12,359.
   d. 17,921.

■ Chapter 15

Problems

1 b. $n = 303$, $\overline{X} = 61.4073$, $k = 3$.
   c. 5,617.30, 2.
   d. 91.0060, 300.
4 b. 1.3562.
16 a. Yes. Significant main effect (A) with $p < 0.05$.

Database Exercises

1 b. 41,011, 48,387, 53,927.
   c. between: 797,916,214, 2; within: 96,732,651, 68.

Chapter 16

Problems

2 d. Significantly different.
6 b. 10.
  c. Not significant.
10 b. Test statistic = 4.5319; average difference in ranks = 16.4258 (don't forget ties!); standard error = 3.6245.

Chapter 17

Problems

2 c. 247.63.
  e. 29.49.
6 d. 5.224.

Chapter 18

Problems

1 a. Pareto diagram.
  b. R chart.
6 a. 56.31, 54.301, 58.319.
7 b. 12.842, 0.208.
  c. 12.842.
  d. 12.629, 13.055.
8 a. 0.208.
  b. 0, 0.535.
11 a. 0.0280, 0.1182.
  c. 0.0155, 0.0545.

Statistical Tables

TABLE C-1 Standard Normal Probability Table

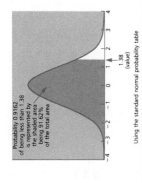

Probability 0.9162 of being less than 1.38 is represented by the shaded area of the total area being 91.62% of the total area

1.38 (value)

Using the standard normal probability table

Value	Probability	Value	Probability	Value	Probability	Value	Probability	Value	Probability	Value	Probability
-2.00	0.0228	-1.00	0.1587	0.00	0.5000	0.00	0.5000	1.00	0.8413	2.00	0.9772
-2.01	0.0222	-1.01	0.1562	-0.01	0.4960	0.01	0.5040	1.01	0.8438	2.01	0.9778
-2.02	0.0217	-1.02	0.1539	-0.02	0.4920	0.02	0.5080	1.02	0.8461	2.02	0.9783
-2.03	0.0212	-1.03	0.1515	-0.03	0.4880	0.03	0.5120	1.03	0.8485	2.03	0.9788
-2.04	0.0207	-1.04	0.1492	-0.04	0.4840	0.04	0.5160	1.04	0.8508	2.04	0.9793
-2.05	0.0202	-1.05	0.1469	-0.05	0.4801	0.05	0.5199	1.05	0.8531	2.05	0.9798
-2.06	0.0197	-1.06	0.1446	-0.06	0.4761	0.06	0.5239	1.06	0.8554	2.06	0.9803
-2.07	0.0192	-1.07	0.1423	-0.07	0.4721	0.07	0.5279	1.07	0.8577	2.07	0.9808
-2.08	0.0188	-1.08	0.1401	-0.08	0.4681	0.08	0.5319	1.08	0.8599	2.08	0.9812
-2.09	0.0183	-1.09	0.1379	-0.09	0.4641	0.09	0.5359	1.09	0.8621	2.09	0.9817
-2.10	0.0179	-1.10	0.1357	-0.10	0.4602	0.10	0.5398	1.10	0.8643	2.10	0.9821
-2.11	0.0174	-1.11	0.1335	-0.11	0.4562	0.11	0.5438	1.11	0.8665	2.11	0.9826
-2.12	0.0170	-1.12	0.1314	-0.12	0.4522	0.12	0.5478	1.12	0.8686	2.12	0.9830
-2.13	0.0166	-1.13	0.1292	-0.13	0.4483	0.13	0.5517	1.13	0.8708	2.13	0.9834
-2.14	0.0162	-1.14	0.1271	-0.14	0.4443	0.14	0.5557	1.14	0.8729	2.14	0.9838
-2.15	0.0158	-1.15	0.1251	-0.15	0.4404	0.15	0.5596	1.15	0.8749	2.15	0.9842
-2.16	0.0154	-1.16	0.1230	-0.16	0.4364	0.16	0.5636	1.16	0.8770	2.16	0.9846
-2.17	0.0150	-1.17	0.1210	-0.17	0.4325	0.17	0.5675	1.17	0.8790	2.17	0.9850
-2.18	0.0146	-1.18	0.1190	-0.18	0.4286	0.18	0.5714	1.18	0.8810	2.18	0.9854
-2.19	0.0143	-1.19	0.1170	-0.19	0.4247	0.19	0.5753	1.19	0.8830	2.19	0.9857
-2.20	0.0139	-1.20	0.1151	-0.20	0.4207	0.20	0.5793	1.20	0.8849	2.20	0.9861
-2.21	0.0136	-1.21	0.1131	-0.21	0.4168	0.21	0.5832	1.21	0.8869	2.21	0.9864
-2.22	0.0132	-1.22	0.1112	-0.22	0.4129	0.22	0.5871	1.22	0.8888	2.22	0.9868
-2.23	0.0129	-1.23	0.1093	-0.23	0.4090	0.23	0.5910	1.23	0.8907	2.23	0.9871
-2.24	0.0125	-1.24	0.1075	-0.24	0.4052	0.24	0.5948	1.24	0.8925	2.24	0.9875
-2.25	0.0122	-1.25	0.1056	-0.25	0.4013	0.25	0.5987	1.25	0.8944	2.25	0.9878
-2.26	0.0119	-1.26	0.1038	-0.26	0.3974	0.26	0.6026	1.26	0.8962	2.26	0.9881
-2.27	0.0116	-1.27	0.1020	-0.27	0.3936	0.27	0.6064	1.27	0.8980	2.27	0.9884
-2.28	0.0113	-1.28	0.1003	-0.28	0.3897	0.28	0.6103	1.28	0.8997	2.28	0.9887
-2.29	0.0110	-1.29	0.0985	-0.29	0.3859	0.29	0.6141	1.29	0.9015	2.29	0.9890
-2.30	0.0107	-1.30	0.0968	-0.30	0.3821	0.30	0.6179	1.30	0.9032	2.30	0.9893

TABLE C-1 (Continued)

Value	Probability	Value	Probability	Value	Probability	Value	Probability	Value	Probability
-2.31	0.0104	-1.31	0.0951	0.31	0.3783	1.31	0.6217	2.31	0.9896
-2.32	0.0102	-1.32	0.0934	0.32	0.3745	1.32	0.6255	2.32	0.9898
-2.33	0.0099	-1.33	0.0918	0.33	0.3707	1.33	0.6293	2.33	0.9901
-2.34	0.0096	-1.34	0.0901	0.34	0.3669	1.34	0.6331	2.34	0.9904
-2.35	0.0094	-1.35	0.0885	0.35	0.3632	1.35	0.6368	2.35	0.9906
-2.36	0.0091	-1.36	0.0869	0.36	0.3594	1.36	0.6406	2.36	0.9909
-2.37	0.0089	-1.37	0.0853	0.37	0.3557	1.37	0.6443	2.37	0.9911
-2.38	0.0087	-1.38	0.0838	0.38	0.3520	1.38	0.6480	2.38	0.9913
-2.39	0.0084	-1.39	0.0823	0.39	0.3483	1.39	0.6517	2.39	0.9916
-2.40	0.0082	-1.40	0.0808	0.40	0.3446	1.40	0.6554	2.40	0.9918
-2.41	0.0080	-1.41	0.0793	0.41	0.3409	1.41	0.6591	2.41	0.9920
-2.42	0.0078	-1.42	0.0778	0.42	0.3372	1.42	0.6628	2.42	0.9922
-2.43	0.0075	-1.43	0.0764	0.43	0.3336	1.43	0.6664	2.43	0.9925
-2.44	0.0073	-1.44	0.0749	0.44	0.3300	1.44	0.6700	2.44	0.9927
-2.45	0.0071	-1.45	0.0735	0.45	0.3264	1.45	0.6736	2.45	0.9929
-2.46	0.0069	-1.46	0.0721	0.46	0.3228	1.46	0.6772	2.46	0.9931
-2.47	0.0068	-1.47	0.0708	0.47	0.3192	1.47	0.6808	2.47	0.9932
-2.48	0.0066	-1.48	0.0694	0.48	0.3156	1.48	0.6844	2.48	0.9934
-2.49	0.0064	-1.49	0.0681	0.49	0.3121	1.49	0.6879	2.49	0.9936
-2.50	0.0062	-1.50	0.0668	0.50	0.3085	1.50	0.6915	2.50	0.9938
-2.51	0.0060	-1.51	0.0655	0.51	0.3050	1.51	0.6950	2.51	0.9940
-2.52	0.0059	-1.52	0.0643	0.52	0.3015	1.52	0.6985	2.52	0.9941
-2.53	0.0057	-1.53	0.0630	0.53	0.2981	1.53	0.7019	2.53	0.9943
-2.54	0.0055	-1.54	0.0618	0.54	0.2946	1.54	0.7054	2.54	0.9945
-2.55	0.0054	-1.55	0.0606	0.55	0.2912	1.55	0.7088	2.55	0.9946
-2.56	0.0052	-1.56	0.0594	0.56	0.2877	1.56	0.7123	2.56	0.9948
-2.57	0.0051	-1.57	0.0582	0.57	0.2843	1.57	0.7157	2.57	0.9949
-2.58	0.0049	-1.58	0.0571	0.58	0.2810	1.58	0.7190	2.58	0.9951
-2.59	0.0048	-1.59	0.0559	0.59	0.2776	1.59	0.7224	2.59	0.9952
-2.60	0.0047	-1.60	0.0548	0.60	0.2743	1.60	0.7257	2.60	0.9953
-2.61	0.0045	-1.61	0.0537	0.61	0.2709	1.61	0.7291	2.61	0.9955
-2.62	0.0044	-1.62	0.0526	0.62	0.2676	1.62	0.7324	2.62	0.9956
-2.63	0.0043	-1.63	0.0516	0.63	0.2643	1.63	0.7357	2.63	0.9957
-2.64	0.0041	-1.64	0.0505	0.64	0.2611	1.64	0.7389	2.64	0.9959
-2.65	0.0040	-1.65	0.0495	0.65	0.2578	1.65	0.7422	2.65	0.9960
-2.66	0.0039	-1.66	0.0485	0.66	0.2546	1.66	0.7454	2.66	0.9961
-2.67	0.0038	-1.67	0.0475	0.67	0.2514	1.67	0.7486	2.67	0.9962
-2.68	0.0037	-1.68	0.0465	0.68	0.2483	1.68	0.7517	2.68	0.9963
-2.69	0.0036	-1.69	0.0455	0.69	0.2451	1.69	0.7549	2.69	0.9964
-2.70	0.0035	-1.70	0.0446	0.70	0.2420	1.70	0.7580	2.70	0.9965

z	Area	z	Area	z	Area	z	Area	z	Area	z	Area
-2.71	0.0034	-1.71	0.0436	-0.71	0.2389	0.71	0.7611	1.71	0.9564	2.71	0.9966
-2.72	0.0033	-1.72	0.0427	-0.72	0.2358	0.72	0.7642	1.72	0.9573	2.72	0.9967
-2.73	0.0032	-1.73	0.0418	-0.73	0.2327	0.73	0.7673	1.73	0.9582	2.73	0.9968
-2.74	0.0031	-1.74	0.0409	-0.74	0.2296	0.74	0.7704	1.74	0.9591	2.74	0.9969
-2.75	0.0030	-1.75	0.0401	-0.75	0.2266	0.75	0.7734	1.75	0.9599	2.75	0.9970
-2.76	0.0029	-1.76	0.0392	-0.76	0.2236	0.76	0.7764	1.76	0.9608	2.76	0.9971
-2.77	0.0028	-1.77	0.0384	-0.77	0.2206	0.77	0.7794	1.77	0.9616	2.77	0.9972
-2.78	0.0027	-1.78	0.0375	-0.78	0.2177	0.78	0.7823	1.78	0.9625	2.78	0.9973
-2.79	0.0026	-1.79	0.0367	-0.79	0.2148	0.79	0.7852	1.79	0.9633	2.79	0.9974
-2.80	0.0026	-1.80	0.0359	-0.80	0.2119	0.80	0.7881	1.80	0.9641	2.80	0.9974
-2.81	0.0025	-1.81	0.0351	-0.81	0.2090	0.81	0.7910	1.81	0.9649	2.81	0.9975
-2.82	0.0024	-1.82	0.0344	-0.82	0.2061	0.82	0.7939	1.82	0.9656	2.82	0.9976
-2.83	0.0023	-1.83	0.0336	-0.83	0.2033	0.83	0.7967	1.83	0.9664	2.83	0.9977
-2.84	0.0023	-1.84	0.0329	-0.84	0.2005	0.84	0.7995	1.84	0.9671	2.84	0.9977
-2.85	0.0022	-1.85	0.0322	-0.85	0.1977	0.85	0.8023	1.85	0.9678	2.85	0.9978
-2.86	0.0021	-1.86	0.0314	-0.86	0.1949	0.86	0.8051	1.86	0.9686	2.86	0.9979
-2.87	0.0021	-1.87	0.0307	-0.87	0.1922	0.87	0.8078	1.87	0.9693	2.87	0.9979
-2.88	0.0020	-1.88	0.0301	-0.88	0.1894	0.88	0.8106	1.88	0.9699	2.88	0.9980
-2.89	0.0019	-1.89	0.0294	-0.89	0.1867	0.89	0.8133	1.89	0.9706	2.89	0.9981
-2.90	0.0019	-1.90	0.0287	-0.90	0.1841	0.90	0.8159	1.90	0.9713	2.90	0.9981
-2.91	0.0018	-1.91	0.0281	-0.91	0.1814	0.91	0.8186	1.91	0.9719	2.91	0.9982
-2.92	0.0018	-1.92	0.0274	-0.92	0.1788	0.92	0.8212	1.92	0.9726	2.92	0.9982
-2.93	0.0017	-1.93	0.0268	-0.93	0.1762	0.93	0.8238	1.93	0.9732	2.93	0.9983
-2.94	0.0016	-1.94	0.0262	-0.94	0.1736	0.94	0.8264	1.94	0.9738	2.94	0.9984
-2.95	0.0016	-1.95	0.0256	-0.95	0.1711	0.95	0.8289	1.95	0.9744	2.95	0.9984
-2.96	0.0015	-1.96	0.0250	-0.96	0.1685	0.96	0.8315	1.96	0.9750	2.96	0.9985
-2.97	0.0015	-1.97	0.0244	-0.97	0.1660	0.97	0.8340	1.97	0.9756	2.97	0.9985
-2.98	0.0014	-1.98	0.0239	-0.98	0.1635	0.98	0.8365	1.98	0.9761	2.98	0.9986
-2.99	0.0014	-1.99	0.0233	-0.99	0.1611	0.99	0.8389	1.99	0.9767	2.99	0.9986
-3.00	0.0013	-2.00	0.0228	-1.00	0.1587	1.00	0.8413	2.00	0.9772	3.00	0.9987

TABLE C-2 Table of Random Digits

	1	2	3	4	5	6	7	8	9	10
1	51449	39284	85527	67168	91284	19954	91166	70918	85957	19492
2	16144	56830	67507	97275	25982	69294	32841	20861	83114	12531
3	48145	48280	99481	13050	81818	25282	66466	24461	97021	21072
4	83780	48351	85422	42978	26088	17869	94245	26622	48318	73850
5	95329	38482	93510	39170	63683	40587	80451	43058	81923	97072
6	11179	69004	34273	36062	26234	58601	47159	82248	95968	99722
7	94631	52413	31524	02316	27611	15888	13525	43809	40014	30667
8	64275	10294	35027	25604	65695	36014	17988	02734	31732	29911
9	72125	19232	10782	30615	42005	90419	32447	53688	36125	28456
10	16463	42028	27927	48403	88963	79615	41218	43290	53618	68082
11	10036	66273	69506	19610	01479	92338	55140	81097	73071	61544
12	85356	51400	88502	98267	73943	25828	38219	13268	09016	77465
13	84076	82087	55053	75370	71030	92275	55497	97123	40919	57479
14	76731	39755	78537	51937	11680	78820	50082	56068	36908	55399
15	19032	73472	79399	05549	14772	32746	38841	45524	13535	03113
16	72791	59040	61529	74437	74482	76619	05232	28616	98690	24011
17	11553	00135	28306	65571	34465	47423	39198	54456	95283	54637
18	71405	70352	46763	64002	62461	41982	15933	46942	36941	93412
19	17594	10116	55483	96219	85493	96955	89180	59690	82170	77643
20	09584	23476	09243	65568	89128	36747	63692	09986	47687	46448
21	81677	62634	52794	01466	85938	14565	79993	44956	82254	65223
22	45849	01177	13773	43523	69825	03222	58458	77463	58521	07273
23	97252	92257	90419	01241	52516	66293	14536	23870	78402	41759
24	26232	77422	76289	57587	42831	87047	20092	92676	12017	43554
25	87799	33602	01931	66913	63008	03745	93939	07178	70003	18158
26	46120	62298	69126	07862	76731	58527	39342	42749	57050	91725
27	53292	55652	11834	47581	25682	64085	26587	92289	41853	38354
28	81606	56009	06021	98392	40450	87721	50917	16978	39472	23505
29	67819	47314	96988	89931	49395	37071	72658	53947	11996	64631
30	50458	20350	87362	83996	86422	58694	71813	97695	28804	58523
31	59772	27000	97805	25042	09916	77569	71347	62667	09330	02152
32	94752	91056	08939	93410	59204	04644	44336	55570	21106	76588
33	01885	82054	45944	55398	55487	56455	56940	68787	36591	29914
34	85190	91941	86714	76593	77199	39724	99548	13827	84961	76740
35	97747	67607	14549	08215	95408	46381	12449	03672	40325	77312
36	43318	84469	26047	86003	34786	38931	34846	28711	42833	93019
37	47874	71365	76603	57440	49514	17335	71969	58055	99136	73589
38	24259	48079	71198	95859	94212	55402	93392	31965	94622	11673
39	31947	64805	34133	03245	24546	48934	41730	47831	26531	02203
40	37911	93224	87153	54541	57529	38299	65659	00202	07054	40168
41	82714	15799	93126	74180	94171	97117	31431	00323	62793	11995
42	82927	37884	74411	45887	36713	52339	68421	35968	67714	05883
43	65934	21782	35804	36676	35404	69987	52268	19894	81977	87764
44	56953	04356	68903	21369	35901	86797	83901	68681	02397	55359
45	16278	17165	67843	49349	90163	97337	35003	34915	91485	33814
46	96339	95028	48468	12279	81039	56531	10759	19579	00015	22829
47	84110	49661	13988	75909	35580	18426	29038	79111	56049	96451
48	49017	60748	03412	09880	94091	90052	43596	21424	16584	67970
49	43560	05552	54344	69418	01327	07771	25364	77373	34841	75927
50	25206	15177	63049	12464	16149	18759	96184	15968	89446	07168

TABLE C-3 The *t*-Table

Confidence Level:							
Two-sided	80%	90%	95%	98%	99%	99.8%	99.9%
One-sided	90%	95%	97.5%	99%	99.5%	99.9%	99.95%

Hypothesis Test Level:							
Two-sided	0.20	0.10	0.05	0.02	0.01	0.002	0.001
One-sided	0.10	0.05	0.025	0.01	0.005	0.001	0.0005

For One Sample: n	In General: Degrees of Freedom				Critical Values			
2	1	3.078	6.314	12.706	31.821	63.657	318.309	636.619
3	2	1.886	2.920	4.303	6.965	9.925	22.327	31.599
4	3	1.638	2.353	3.182	4.541	5.841	10.215	12.924
5	4	1.533	2.132	2.776	3.747	4.604	7.173	8.610
6	5	1.476	2.015	2.571	3.365	4.032	5.893	6.869
7	6	1.440	1.943	2.447	3.143	3.707	5.208	5.959
8	7	1.415	1.895	2.365	2.998	3.499	4.785	5.408
9	8	1.397	1.860	2.306	2.896	3.355	4.501	5.041
10	9	1.383	1.833	2.262	2.821	3.250	4.297	4.781
11	10	1.372	1.812	2.228	2.764	3.169	4.144	4.587
12	11	1.363	1.796	2.201	2.718	3.106	4.025	4.437
13	12	1.356	1.782	2.179	2.681	3.055	3.930	4.318
14	13	1.350	1.771	2.160	2.650	3.012	3.852	4.221
15	14	1.345	1.761	2.145	2.624	2.977	3.787	4.140
16	15	1.341	1.753	2.131	2.602	2.947	3.733	4.073
17	16	1.337	1.746	2.120	2.583	2.921	3.686	4.015
18	17	1.333	1.740	2.110	2.567	2.898	3.646	3.965
19	18	1.330	1.734	2.101	2.552	2.878	3.610	3.922
20	19	1.328	1.729	2.093	2.539	2.861	3.579	3.883
21	20	1.325	1.725	2.086	2.528	2.845	3.552	3.850
22	21	1.323	1.721	2.080	2.518	2.831	3.527	3.819
23	22	1.321	1.717	2.074	2.508	2.819	3.505	3.792
24	23	1.319	1.714	2.069	2.500	2.807	3.485	3.768
25	24	1.318	1.711	2.064	2.492	2.797	3.467	3.745
26	25	1.316	1.708	2.060	2.485	2.787	3.450	3.725
27	26	1.315	1.706	2.056	2.479	2.779	3.435	3.707
28	27	1.314	1.703	2.052	2.473	2.771	3.421	3.690
29	28	1.313	1.701	2.048	2.467	2.763	3.408	3.674
30	29	1.311	1.699	2.045	2.462	2.756	3.396	3.659
31	30	1.310	1.697	2.042	2.457	2.750	3.385	3.646
32	31	1.309	1.696	2.040	2.453	2.744	3.375	3.633
33	32	1.309	1.694	2.037	2.449	2.738	3.365	3.622
34	33	1.308	1.692	2.035	2.445	2.733	3.356	3.611
35	34	1.307	1.691	2.032	2.441	2.728	3.348	3.601
36	35	1.306	1.690	2.030	2.438	2.724	3.340	3.591
37	36	1.306	1.688	2.028	2.434	2.719	3.333	3.582
38	37	1.305	1.687	2.026	2.431	2.715	3.326	3.574
39	38	1.304	1.686	2.024	2.429	2.712	3.319	3.566
40	39	1.304	1.685	2.023	2.426	2.708	3.313	3.558
Infinity		1.282	1.645	1.960	2.326	2.576	3.090	3.291

TABLE C-4 R² Table: 5% Critical Values (Significant)

Number of Cases (n)	Number of X Variables (p)									
	1	2	3	4	5	6	7	8	9	10
3	0.994									
4	0.902	0.997								
5	0.771	0.950	0.998							
6	0.658	0.864	0.966	0.999						
7	0.569	0.776	0.903	0.975	0.999					
8	0.499	0.698	0.832	0.924	0.980	0.999				
9	0.444	0.632	0.764	0.865	0.938	0.983	0.999			
10	0.399	0.575	0.704	0.806	0.887	0.947	0.985	0.999		
11	0.362	0.527	0.651	0.751	0.835	0.902	0.954	0.987	1.000	
12	0.332	0.486	0.604	0.702	0.785	0.856	0.914	0.959	0.989	1.000
13	0.306	0.451	0.563	0.657	0.739	0.811	0.872	0.924	0.964	0.990
14	0.283	0.420	0.527	0.618	0.697	0.768	0.831	0.885	0.931	0.967
15	0.264	0.393	0.495	0.582	0.659	0.729	0.791	0.847	0.896	0.937
16	0.247	0.369	0.466	0.550	0.624	0.692	0.754	0.810	0.860	0.904
17	0.232	0.348	0.440	0.521	0.593	0.659	0.719	0.775	0.825	0.871
18	0.219	0.329	0.417	0.494	0.564	0.628	0.687	0.742	0.792	0.839
19	0.208	0.312	0.397	0.471	0.538	0.600	0.657	0.711	0.761	0.807
20	0.197	0.297	0.378	0.449	0.514	0.574	0.630	0.682	0.731	0.777
21	0.187	0.283	0.361	0.429	0.492	0.550	0.604	0.655	0.703	0.749
22	0.179	0.270	0.345	0.411	0.471	0.527	0.580	0.630	0.677	0.722
23	0.171	0.259	0.331	0.394	0.452	0.507	0.558	0.607	0.653	0.696
24	0.164	0.248	0.317	0.379	0.435	0.488	0.538	0.585	0.630	0.673
25	0.157	0.238	0.305	0.364	0.419	0.470	0.518	0.564	0.608	0.650
26	0.151	0.229	0.294	0.351	0.404	0.454	0.501	0.545	0.588	0.629
27	0.145	0.221	0.283	0.339	0.390	0.438	0.484	0.527	0.569	0.609
28	0.140	0.213	0.273	0.327	0.377	0.424	0.468	0.510	0.551	0.590
29	0.135	0.206	0.264	0.316	0.365	0.410	0.453	0.495	0.534	0.573
30	0.130	0.199	0.256	0.306	0.353	0.397	0.439	0.480	0.518	0.556

31	0.126	0.193	0.248	0.297	0.342	0.385	0.426	0.466	0.503	0.540
32	0.122	0.187	0.240	0.288	0.332	0.374	0.414	0.452	0.489	0.525
33	0.118	0.181	0.233	0.279	0.323	0.363	0.402	0.440	0.476	0.511
34	0.115	0.176	0.226	0.271	0.314	0.353	0.391	0.428	0.463	0.497
35	0.111	0.171	0.220	0.264	0.305	0.344	0.381	0.417	0.451	0.484
36	0.108	0.166	0.214	0.257	0.297	0.335	0.371	0.406	0.440	0.472
37	0.105	0.162	0.208	0.250	0.289	0.326	0.362	0.396	0.429	0.461
38	0.103	0.157	0.203	0.244	0.282	0.318	0.353	0.386	0.418	0.449
39	0.100	0.153	0.198	0.238	0.275	0.310	0.344	0.377	0.408	0.439
40	0.097	0.150	0.193	0.232	0.268	0.303	0.336	0.368	0.399	0.429
41	0.095	0.146	0.188	0.226	0.262	0.296	0.328	0.359	0.390	0.419
42	0.093	0.142	0.184	0.221	0.256	0.289	0.321	0.351	0.381	0.410
43	0.090	0.139	0.180	0.216	0.250	0.283	0.314	0.344	0.373	0.401
44	0.088	0.136	0.176	0.211	0.245	0.276	0.307	0.336	0.365	0.393
45	0.086	0.133	0.172	0.207	0.239	0.271	0.300	0.329	0.357	0.384
46	0.085	0.130	0.168	0.202	0.234	0.265	0.294	0.322	0.350	0.377
47	0.083	0.127	0.164	0.198	0.230	0.259	0.288	0.316	0.343	0.369
48	0.081	0.125	0.161	0.194	0.225	0.254	0.282	0.310	0.336	0.362
49	0.079	0.122	0.158	0.190	0.220	0.249	0.277	0.304	0.330	0.355
50	0.078	0.120	0.155	0.186	0.216	0.244	0.272	0.298	0.323	0.348
Multiplier 1	3.84	5.99	7.82	9.49	11.07	12.59	14.07	15.51	16.92	18.31
Multiplier 2	2.15	−0.27	−3.84	−7.94	−12.84	−18.24	−23.78	−30.10	−36.87	−43.87

TABLE C-5 R^2 Table: 1% Critical Values (Highly Significant)

Number of Cases (n)	Number of X Variables (p)									
	1	2	3	4	5	6	7	8	9	10
3	1.000									
4	0.980	1.000								
5	0.919	0.990	1.000							
6	0.841	0.954	0.993	1.000						
7	0.765	0.900	0.967	0.995	1.000					
8	0.696	0.842	0.926	0.975	0.996	1.000				
9	0.636	0.785	0.879	0.941	0.979	0.997	1.000			
10	0.585	0.732	0.830	0.901	0.951	0.982	0.997	1.000		
11	0.540	0.684	0.784	0.859	0.916	0.958	0.985	0.997	1.000	
12	0.501	0.641	0.740	0.818	0.879	0.928	0.963	0.987	0.998	1.000
13	0.467	0.602	0.700	0.778	0.842	0.894	0.936	0.967	0.988	0.998
14	0.437	0.567	0.663	0.741	0.806	0.860	0.906	0.943	0.971	0.989
15	0.411	0.536	0.629	0.706	0.771	0.827	0.875	0.915	0.948	0.973
16	0.388	0.508	0.598	0.673	0.738	0.795	0.844	0.887	0.923	0.953
17	0.367	0.482	0.570	0.643	0.707	0.764	0.814	0.858	0.896	0.929
18	0.348	0.459	0.544	0.616	0.678	0.734	0.784	0.829	0.869	0.904
19	0.331	0.438	0.520	0.590	0.652	0.707	0.757	0.802	0.843	0.879
20	0.315	0.418	0.498	0.566	0.626	0.681	0.730	0.775	0.816	0.854
21	0.301	0.401	0.478	0.544	0.603	0.656	0.705	0.750	0.791	0.829
22	0.288	0.384	0.459	0.523	0.581	0.633	0.681	0.726	0.767	0.805
23	0.276	0.369	0.442	0.504	0.560	0.612	0.659	0.703	0.744	0.782
24	0.265	0.355	0.426	0.487	0.541	0.591	0.638	0.681	0.721	0.759
25	0.255	0.342	0.410	0.470	0.523	0.572	0.618	0.660	0.700	0.738
26	0.246	0.330	0.396	0.454	0.506	0.554	0.599	0.641	0.680	0.717
27	0.237	0.319	0.383	0.440	0.490	0.537	0.581	0.622	0.661	0.698
28	0.229	0.308	0.371	0.426	0.475	0.521	0.564	0.605	0.643	0.679
29	0.221	0.298	0.359	0.413	0.461	0.506	0.548	0.588	0.625	0.661
30	0.214	0.289	0.349	0.401	0.448	0.492	0.533	0.572	0.609	0.644

31	0.208	0.280	0.338	0.389	0.435	0.478	0.519	0.557	0.593	0.627
32	0.201	0.272	0.329	0.378	0.423	0.465	0.505	0.542	0.578	0.612
33	0.195	0.264	0.319	0.368	0.412	0.453	0.492	0.529	0.563	0.597
34	0.190	0.257	0.311	0.358	0.401	0.442	0.479	0.515	0.550	0.583
35	0.185	0.250	0.303	0.349	0.391	0.430	0.468	0.503	0.537	0.569
36	0.180	0.244	0.295	0.340	0.381	0.420	0.456	0.491	0.524	0.556
37	0.175	0.237	0.287	0.332	0.372	0.410	0.446	0.480	0.512	0.543
38	0.170	0.231	0.280	0.324	0.363	0.400	0.435	0.469	0.501	0.531
39	0.166	0.226	0.274	0.316	0.355	0.391	0.426	0.458	0.490	0.520
40	0.162	0.220	0.267	0.309	0.347	0.382	0.416	0.448	0.479	0.509
41	0.158	0.215	0.261	0.302	0.339	0.374	0.407	0.439	0.469	0.498
42	0.155	0.210	0.255	0.295	0.332	0.366	0.399	0.430	0.459	0.488
43	0.151	0.206	0.250	0.289	0.325	0.358	0.390	0.421	0.450	0.478
44	0.148	0.201	0.244	0.283	0.318	0.351	0.382	0.412	0.441	0.469
45	0.145	0.197	0.239	0.277	0.311	0.344	0.375	0.404	0.432	0.460
46	0.141	0.193	0.234	0.271	0.305	0.337	0.367	0.396	0.424	0.451
47	0.138	0.189	0.230	0.266	0.299	0.330	0.360	0.389	0.416	0.443
48	0.136	0.185	0.225	0.261	0.293	0.324	0.353	0.381	0.408	0.435
49	0.133	0.181	0.221	0.256	0.288	0.318	0.347	0.374	0.401	0.427
50	0.130	0.178	0.217	0.251	0.283	0.312	0.341	0.368	0.394	0.419
Multiplier 1	6.63	9.21	11.35	13.28	15.09	16.81	18.48	20.09	21.67	23.21
Multiplier 2	−5.81	−15.49	−25.66	−36.39	−47.63	−59.53	−71.65	−84.60	−97.88	−111.76

TABLE C-6 R^2 Table: 0.1% Critical Values (Very Highly Significant)

Number of Cases (n)	Number of X Variables (p)									
	1	2	3	4	5	6	7	8	9	10
3	1.000									
4	0.998	1.000								
5	0.982	0.999	1.000							
6	0.949	0.990	0.999	1.000						
7	0.904	0.968	0.993	0.999	1.000					
8	0.855	0.937	0.977	0.995	1.000	1.000				
9	0.807	0.900	0.952	0.982	0.996	1.000	1.000			
10	0.761	0.861	0.922	0.961	0.985	0.996	1.000	1.000		
11	0.717	0.822	0.889	0.936	0.967	0.987	0.997	1.000	1.000	
12	0.678	0.785	0.856	0.908	0.945	0.972	0.989	0.997	1.000	1.000
13	0.642	0.749	0.822	0.878	0.920	0.952	0.975	0.990	0.997	1.000
14	0.608	0.715	0.790	0.848	0.894	0.930	0.958	0.978	0.991	0.998
15	0.578	0.684	0.759	0.819	0.867	0.906	0.938	0.962	0.980	0.992
16	0.550	0.654	0.730	0.790	0.840	0.881	0.916	0.944	0.966	0.982
17	0.525	0.627	0.702	0.763	0.813	0.856	0.893	0.923	0.949	0.968
18	0.502	0.602	0.676	0.736	0.787	0.831	0.869	0.902	0.930	0.953
19	0.480	0.578	0.651	0.711	0.763	0.807	0.846	0.880	0.910	0.935
20	0.461	0.556	0.628	0.688	0.739	0.784	0.824	0.859	0.890	0.917
21	0.442	0.536	0.606	0.665	0.716	0.761	0.801	0.837	0.869	0.897
22	0.426	0.517	0.586	0.644	0.694	0.739	0.780	0.816	0.849	0.878
23	0.410	0.499	0.567	0.624	0.674	0.718	0.759	0.795	0.829	0.859
24	0.395	0.482	0.548	0.605	0.654	0.698	0.739	0.775	0.809	0.839
25	0.382	0.466	0.531	0.587	0.635	0.679	0.719	0.756	0.790	0.821
26	0.369	0.452	0.515	0.570	0.618	0.661	0.701	0.737	0.771	0.802
27	0.357	0.438	0.500	0.553	0.601	0.644	0.683	0.719	0.753	0.784
28	0.346	0.425	0.486	0.538	0.585	0.627	0.666	0.702	0.735	0.767
29	0.335	0.412	0.472	0.523	0.569	0.611	0.649	0.685	0.718	0.750
30	0.325	0.401	0.459	0.510	0.555	0.596	0.634	0.669	0.702	0.733

31	0.316	0.389	0.447	0.496	0.541	0.581	0.619	0.654	0.686	0.717
32	0.307	0.379	0.435	0.484	0.527	0.567	0.604	0.639	0.671	0.702
33	0.299	0.369	0.424	0.472	0.515	0.554	0.590	0.625	0.657	0.687
34	0.291	0.360	0.414	0.460	0.503	0.541	0.577	0.611	0.643	0.673
35	0.283	0.351	0.404	0.450	0.491	0.529	0.564	0.598	0.629	0.659
36	0.276	0.342	0.394	0.439	0.480	0.517	0.552	0.585	0.616	0.646
37	0.269	0.334	0.385	0.429	0.469	0.506	0.540	0.573	0.604	0.633
38	0.263	0.326	0.376	0.420	0.459	0.495	0.529	0.561	0.591	0.620
39	0.257	0.319	0.368	0.411	0.449	0.485	0.518	0.550	0.580	0.608
40	0.251	0.312	0.360	0.402	0.440	0.475	0.508	0.539	0.569	0.597
41	0.245	0.305	0.352	0.393	0.431	0.465	0.498	0.529	0.558	0.586
42	0.240	0.298	0.345	0.385	0.422	0.456	0.488	0.518	0.547	0.575
43	0.235	0.292	0.338	0.378	0.414	0.447	0.479	0.509	0.537	0.564
44	0.230	0.286	0.331	0.370	0.406	0.439	0.470	0.499	0.527	0.554
45	0.225	0.280	0.324	0.363	0.398	0.431	0.461	0.490	0.518	0.544
46	0.220	0.275	0.318	0.356	0.391	0.423	0.453	0.482	0.509	0.535
47	0.216	0.269	0.312	0.349	0.383	0.415	0.445	0.473	0.500	0.526
48	0.212	0.264	0.306	0.343	0.377	0.408	0.437	0.465	0.491	0.517
49	0.208	0.259	0.301	0.337	0.370	0.401	0.429	0.457	0.483	0.508
50	0.204	0.255	0.295	0.331	0.363	0.394	0.422	0.449	0.475	0.500
Multiplier 1	10.83	13.82	16.27	18.47	20.52	22.46	24.32	26.12	27.88	29.59
Multiplier 2	−31.57	−54.02	−75.12	−96.26	−117.47	−138.94	−160.86	−183.33	−206.28	−229.55

TABLE C-7 R^2 Table: 10% Critical Values

Number of Cases (n)	\multicolumn{10}{c}{Number of X Variables (p)}									
	1	2	3	4	5	6	7	8	9	10
3	0.976									
4	0.810	0.990								
5	0.649	0.900	0.994							
6	0.532	0.785	0.932	0.996						
7	0.448	0.684	0.844	0.949	0.997					
8	0.386	0.602	0.759	0.877	0.959	0.997				
9	0.339	0.536	0.685	0.804	0.898	0.965	0.998			
10	0.302	0.482	0.622	0.738	0.835	0.914	0.970	0.998		
11	0.272	0.438	0.568	0.680	0.775	0.857	0.925	0.974	0.998	
12	0.247	0.401	0.523	0.628	0.721	0.803	0.874	0.933	0.977	0.998
13	0.227	0.369	0.484	0.584	0.673	0.753	0.825	0.888	0.940	0.979
14	0.209	0.342	0.450	0.545	0.630	0.708	0.779	0.842	0.899	0.946
15	0.194	0.319	0.420	0.510	0.592	0.667	0.736	0.799	0.857	0.907
16	0.181	0.298	0.394	0.480	0.558	0.630	0.697	0.759	0.816	0.868
17	0.170	0.280	0.371	0.453	0.527	0.596	0.661	0.721	0.778	0.830
18	0.160	0.264	0.351	0.428	0.499	0.566	0.628	0.687	0.742	0.794
19	0.151	0.250	0.332	0.406	0.474	0.538	0.598	0.655	0.709	0.760
20	0.143	0.237	0.316	0.386	0.452	0.513	0.571	0.626	0.679	0.729
21	0.136	0.226	0.301	0.368	0.431	0.490	0.546	0.599	0.650	0.699
22	0.129	0.215	0.287	0.352	0.412	0.469	0.523	0.575	0.624	0.671
23	0.124	0.206	0.275	0.337	0.395	0.450	0.502	0.552	0.600	0.646
24	0.118	0.197	0.263	0.323	0.379	0.432	0.482	0.530	0.577	0.622
25	0.113	0.189	0.253	0.310	0.364	0.415	0.464	0.511	0.556	0.599
26	0.109	0.181	0.243	0.298	0.350	0.400	0.447	0.492	0.536	0.579
27	0.105	0.175	0.234	0.287	0.338	0.386	0.431	0.475	0.518	0.559
28	0.101	0.168	0.225	0.277	0.326	0.372	0.417	0.459	0.501	0.541
29	0.097	0.162	0.218	0.268	0.315	0.360	0.403	0.444	0.484	0.523
30	0.094	0.157	0.210	0.259	0.305	0.348	0.390	0.430	0.469	0.507

31	0.091	0.152	0.203	0.251	0.295	0.337	0.378	0.417	0.455	0.492
32	0.088	0.147	0.197	0.243	0.286	0.327	0.366	0.405	0.442	0.478
33	0.085	0.142	0.191	0.236	0.277	0.317	0.356	0.393	0.429	0.464
34	0.082	0.138	0.185	0.229	0.269	0.308	0.346	0.382	0.417	0.451
35	0.080	0.134	0.180	0.222	0.262	0.300	0.336	0.371	0.406	0.439
36	0.078	0.130	0.175	0.216	0.255	0.291	0.327	0.361	0.395	0.427
37	0.075	0.127	0.170	0.210	0.248	0.284	0.318	0.352	0.385	0.416
38	0.073	0.123	0.166	0.205	0.241	0.276	0.310	0.343	0.375	0.406
39	0.071	0.120	0.162	0.199	0.235	0.269	0.302	0.334	0.366	0.396
40	0.070	0.117	0.157	0.194	0.229	0.263	0.295	0.326	0.357	0.387
41	0.068	0.114	0.154	0.190	0.224	0.257	0.288	0.319	0.348	0.378
42	0.066	0.111	0.150	0.185	0.219	0.250	0.281	0.311	0.340	0.369
43	0.065	0.109	0.146	0.181	0.214	0.245	0.275	0.304	0.333	0.361
44	0.063	0.106	0.143	0.177	0.209	0.239	0.269	0.297	0.325	0.353
45	0.062	0.104	0.140	0.173	0.204	0.234	0.263	0.291	0.318	0.345
46	0.060	0.102	0.137	0.169	0.200	0.229	0.257	0.285	0.312	0.338
47	0.059	0.099	0.134	0.166	0.196	0.224	0.252	0.279	0.305	0.331
48	0.058	0.097	0.131	0.162	0.191	0.220	0.247	0.273	0.299	0.324
49	0.057	0.095	0.128	0.159	0.188	0.215	0.242	0.268	0.293	0.318
50	0.055	0.093	0.126	0.156	0.184	0.211	0.237	0.263	0.287	0.312
Multiplier 1	−2.71	4.61	6.25	7.78	9.24	10.65	12.02	13.36	14.68	15.99
Multiplier 2	3.12	3.08	2.00	0.32	−1.92	−4.75	−7.59	−11.12	−14.94	−19.05

TABLE C-8   *F*-Table: Level 5% Critical Value

Denominator Degrees of Freedom ($n - k$ for within-sample variability in one-way ANOVA)	Numerator Degrees of Freedom ($k - 1$ for between-sample variability in one-way ANOVA)																
	1	2	3	4	5	6	7	8	9	10	12	15	20	30	60	120	Infinity
1	161.45	199.50	215.71	224.58	230.16	233.99	236.77	238.88	240.54	241.88	243.91	245.95	248.01	250.10	252.20	253.25	254.32
2	18.513	19.000	19.164	19.247	19.296	19.330	19.353	19.371	19.385	19.396	19.413	19.429	19.446	19.462	19.479	19.487	19.496
3	10.128	9.552	9.277	9.117	9.013	8.941	8.887	8.845	8.812	8.786	8.745	8.703	8.660	8.617	8.572	8.549	8.526
4	7.709	6.944	6.591	6.388	6.256	6.163	6.094	6.041	5.999	5.964	5.912	5.858	5.803	5.746	5.688	5.658	5.628
5	6.608	5.786	5.409	5.192	5.050	4.950	4.876	4.818	4.772	4.735	4.678	4.619	4.558	4.496	4.431	4.398	4.365
6	5.987	5.143	4.757	4.534	4.387	4.284	4.207	4.147	4.099	4.060	4.000	3.938	3.874	3.808	3.740	3.705	3.669
7	5.591	4.737	4.347	4.120	3.972	3.866	3.787	3.726	3.677	3.637	3.575	3.511	3.445	3.376	3.304	3.267	3.230
8	5.318	4.459	4.066	3.838	3.687	3.581	3.500	3.438	3.388	3.347	3.284	3.218	3.150	3.079	3.005	2.967	2.928
9	5.117	4.256	3.863	3.633	3.482	3.374	3.293	3.230	3.179	3.137	3.073	3.006	2.936	2.864	2.787	2.748	2.707
10	4.965	4.103	3.708	3.478	3.326	3.217	3.135	3.072	3.020	2.978	2.913	2.845	2.774	2.700	2.621	2.580	2.538
12	4.747	3.885	3.490	3.259	3.106	2.996	2.913	2.849	2.796	2.753	2.687	2.617	2.544	2.466	2.384	2.341	2.296
15	4.543	3.682	3.287	3.056	2.901	2.790	2.707	2.641	2.588	2.544	2.475	2.403	2.328	2.247	2.160	2.114	2.066
20	4.351	3.493	3.098	2.866	2.711	2.599	2.514	2.447	2.393	2.348	2.278	2.203	2.124	2.039	1.946	1.896	1.843
30	4.171	3.316	2.922	2.690	2.534	2.421	2.334	2.266	2.211	2.165	2.092	2.015	1.932	1.841	1.740	1.683	1.622
60	4.001	3.150	2.758	2.525	2.368	2.254	2.167	2.097	2.040	1.993	1.917	1.836	1.748	1.649	1.534	1.467	1.389
120	3.920	3.072	2.680	2.447	2.290	2.175	2.087	2.016	1.959	1.910	1.834	1.750	1.659	1.554	1.429	1.352	1.254
Infinity	3.841	2.996	2.605	2.372	2.214	2.099	2.010	1.938	1.880	1.831	1.752	1.666	1.571	1.459	1.318	1.221	1.000

TABLE C-9   *F*-Table: Level 1% Critical Values

Denominator Degrees of Freedom ($n - k$ for within-sample variability in one-way ANOVA)	Numerator Degrees of Freedom ($k - 1$ for between-sample variability in one-way ANOVA)																
	1	2	3	4	5	6	7	8	9	10	12	15	20	30	60	120	Infinity
1	4052.2	4999.5	5403.4	5624.6	5763.7	5859.0	5928.4	5891.1	6022.5	6055.8	6106.3	6157.3	6208.7	6260.6	6313.0	6339.4	6365.9
2	98.501	98.995	99.159	99.240	99.299	99.333	99.356	99.374	99.388	99.399	99.416	99.432	99.449	99.466	99.482	99.491	99.499
3	34.116	30.816	29.456	28.709	28.236	27.910	27.671	27.488	27.344	27.228	27.051	26.871	26.689	26.503	26.315	26.220	26.125
4	21.197	18.000	16.694	15.977	15.522	15.207	14.976	14.799	14.659	14.546	14.374	14.198	14.020	13.838	13.652	13.558	13.463
5	16.258	13.274	12.060	11.392	10.967	10.672	10.455	10.289	10.158	10.051	9.888	9.722	9.553	9.379	9.202	9.112	9.021
6	13.745	10.925	9.780	9.148	8.746	8.466	8.260	8.102	7.976	7.874	7.718	7.559	7.396	7.229	7.057	6.969	6.880
7	12.246	9.547	8.451	7.847	7.460	7.191	6.993	6.840	6.719	6.620	6.469	6.314	6.155	5.992	5.823	5.737	5.650
8	11.258	8.649	7.591	7.006	6.632	6.371	6.178	6.029	5.911	5.814	5.667	5.515	5.359	5.198	5.032	4.946	4.859
9	10.561	8.021	6.992	6.422	6.057	5.802	5.613	5.467	5.351	5.257	5.111	4.962	4.808	4.649	4.483	4.398	4.311
10	10.044	7.559	6.552	5.994	5.636	5.386	5.200	5.057	4.942	4.849	4.706	4.558	4.405	4.247	4.082	3.996	3.909
12	9.330	6.927	5.953	5.412	5.064	4.821	4.640	4.499	4.388	4.296	4.155	4.010	3.858	3.701	3.535	3.449	3.361
15	8.683	6.359	5.417	4.893	4.556	4.318	4.142	4.004	3.895	3.805	3.666	3.522	3.372	3.214	3.047	2.959	2.868
20	8.096	5.849	4.938	4.431	4.103	3.871	3.699	3.564	3.457	3.368	3.231	3.088	2.938	2.778	2.608	2.517	2.421
30	7.562	5.390	4.510	4.018	3.699	3.473	3.304	3.173	3.067	2.979	2.843	2.700	2.549	2.386	2.208	2.111	2.006
60	7.077	4.977	4.126	3.649	3.339	3.119	2.953	2.823	2.718	2.632	2.496	2.352	2.198	2.028	1.836	1.726	1.601
120	6.851	4.786	3.949	3.480	3.174	2.956	2.792	2.663	2.559	2.472	2.336	2.191	2.035	1.860	1.656	1.533	1.381
Infinity	6.635	4.605	3.782	3.319	3.017	2.802	2.639	2.511	2.407	2.321	2.185	2.039	1.878	1.696	1.473	1.325	1.000

TABLE C-10   F-Table: Level 0.1% Critical Values

Denominator Degrees of Freedom ($n - k$ for within-sample variability in one-way ANOVA)	Numerator Degrees of Freedom ($k - 1$ for between-sample variability in one-way ANOVA)																
	1	2	3	4	5	6	7	8	9	10	12	15	20	30	60	120	Infinity
1	405284	500000	540379	562500	576405	585937	592873	598144	602284	605621	610668	615764	620908	626099	631337	633972	636629
2	998.50	999.00	999.17	999.25	999.30	999.33	999.36	999.38	999.39	999.40	999.42	999.43	999.45	999.47	999.48	999.49	999.50
3	167.03	148.50	141.11	137.10	134.58	132.85	131.58	130.62	129.86	129.25	128.32	127.37	126.42	125.45	124.47	123.97	123.47
4	74.137	61.246	56.177	53.436	51.712	50.525	49.658	48.996	48.475	48.053	47.412	46.761	46.100	45.429	44.746	44.400	44.051
5	47.181	37.122	33.202	31.085	29.752	28.834	28.163	27.649	27.244	26.917	26.418	25.911	25.395	24.869	24.333	24.060	23.785
6	35.507	27.000	23.703	21.924	20.803	20.030	19.463	19.030	18.688	18.411	17.989	17.559	17.120	16.672	16.214	15.981	15.745
7	29.245	21.689	18.772	17.198	16.206	15.521	15.019	14.634	14.330	14.083	13.707	13.324	12.932	12.530	12.119	11.909	11.697
8	25.415	18.494	15.829	14.392	13.485	12.858	12.398	12.046	11.767	11.540	11.194	10.841	10.480	10.109	9.727	9.532	9.334
9	22.857	16.387	13.902	12.560	11.714	11.128	10.698	10.368	10.107	9.894	9.570	9.238	8.898	8.548	8.187	8.001	7.813
10	21.040	14.905	12.553	11.283	10.481	9.926	9.517	9.204	8.956	8.754	8.445	8.129	7.804	7.469	7.122	6.944	6.762
12	18.643	12.974	10.804	9.633	8.892	8.379	8.001	7.710	7.480	7.292	7.005	6.709	6.405	6.090	5.762	5.593	5.420
15	16.587	11.339	9.335	8.253	7.567	7.092	6.741	6.471	6.256	6.081	5.812	5.535	5.248	4.950	4.638	4.475	4.307
20	14.818	9.953	8.098	7.095	6.460	6.018	5.692	5.440	5.239	5.075	4.823	4.562	4.290	4.005	3.703	3.544	3.378
30	13.293	8.773	7.054	6.124	5.534	5.122	4.817	4.581	4.393	4.239	4.000	3.753	3.493	3.217	2.920	2.759	2.589
60	11.973	7.767	6.171	5.307	4.757	4.372	4.086	3.865	3.687	3.541	3.315	3.078	2.827	2.555	2.252	2.082	1.890
120	11.378	7.321	5.781	4.947	4.416	4.044	3.767	3.552	3.379	3.237	3.016	2.783	2.534	2.262	1.950	1.767	1.543
Infinity	10.827	6.908	5.422	4.617	4.103	3.743	3.475	3.266	3.097	2.959	2.742	2.513	2.266	1.990	1.660	1.447	1.000

TABLE C-11   *F*-Table: Level 10% Critical Values

Denominator Degrees of Freedom ($n - k$ for within-sample variability in one-way ANOVA)	Numerator Degrees of Freedom ($k - 1$ for between-sample variability in one-way ANOVA)																
	1	2	3	4	5	6	7	8	9	10	12	15	20	30	60	120	Infinity
1	39.863	49.500	53.593	55.833	57.240	58.204	58.906	59.439	59.858	60.195	60.705	61.220	61.740	62.265	62.794	63.061	63.328
2	8.526	9.000	9.162	9.243	9.293	9.326	9.349	9.367	9.381	9.392	9.408	9.425	9.441	9.458	9.475	9.483	9.491
3	5.538	5.462	5.391	5.343	5.309	5.285	5.266	5.252	5.240	5.230	5.216	5.200	5.184	5.168	5.151	5.143	5.134
4	4.545	4.325	4.191	4.107	4.051	4.010	3.979	3.955	3.936	3.920	3.896	3.870	3.844	3.817	3.790	3.775	3.761
5	4.060	3.780	3.619	3.520	3.453	3.405	3.368	3.339	3.316	3.297	3.268	3.238	3.207	3.174	3.140	3.123	3.105
6	3.776	3.463	3.289	3.181	3.108	3.055	3.014	2.983	2.958	2.937	2.905	2.871	2.836	2.800	2.762	2.742	2.722
7	3.589	3.257	3.074	2.961	2.883	2.827	2.785	2.752	2.725	2.703	2.668	2.632	2.595	2.555	2.514	2.493	2.471
8	3.458	3.113	2.924	2.806	2.726	2.668	2.624	2.589	2.561	2.538	2.502	2.464	2.425	2.383	2.339	2.316	2.293
9	3.360	3.006	2.813	2.693	2.611	2.551	2.505	2.469	2.440	2.416	2.379	2.340	2.298	2.255	2.208	2.184	2.159
10	3.285	2.924	2.728	2.605	2.522	2.461	2.414	2.377	2.347	2.323	2.284	2.244	2.201	2.155	2.107	2.082	2.055
12	3.177	2.807	2.606	2.480	2.394	2.331	2.283	2.245	2.214	2.188	2.147	2.105	2.060	2.011	1.960	1.932	1.904
15	3.073	2.695	2.490	2.361	2.273	2.208	2.158	2.119	2.086	2.059	2.017	1.972	1.924	1.873	1.817	1.787	1.755
20	2.975	2.589	2.380	2.249	2.158	2.091	2.040	1.999	1.965	1.937	1.892	1.845	1.794	1.738	1.677	1.643	1.607
30	2.881	2.489	2.276	2.142	2.049	1.980	1.927	1.884	1.849	1.819	1.773	1.722	1.667	1.606	1.538	1.499	1.456
60	2.791	2.393	2.177	2.041	1.946	1.875	1.819	1.775	1.738	1.707	1.657	1.603	1.543	1.476	1.395	1.348	1.291
120	2.748	2.347	2.130	1.992	1.896	1.824	1.767	1.722	1.684	1.652	1.601	1.545	1.482	1.409	1.320	1.265	1.193
Infinity	2.706	2.303	2.084	1.945	1.847	1.774	1.717	1.670	1.632	1.599	1.546	1.487	1.421	1.342	1.240	1.169	1.000

TABLE C-12 Ranks for the Sign Test

Modified Sample Size, m	5% Test Level			1% Test Level		
	Sign Test Is Significant if Number Is Either:			Sign Test Is Significant if Number Is Either:		
	Less than	or	More than	Less than	or	More than
6	1		5	—		—
7	1		6	—		—
8	1		7	1		7
9	2		7	1		8
10	2		8	1		9
11	2		9	1		10
12	3		9	2		10
13	3		10	2		11
14	3		11	2		12
15	4		11	3		12
16	4		12	3		13
17	5		12	3		14
18	5		13	4		14
19	5		14	4		15
20	6		14	4		16
21	6		15	5		16
22	6		16	5		17
23	7		16	5		18
24	7		17	6		18
25	8		17	6		19
26	8		18	7		19
27	8		19	7		20
28	9		19	7		21
29	9		20	8		21
30	10		20	8		22
31	10		21	8		23
32	10		22	9		23
33	11		22	9		24
34	11		23	10		24
35	12		23	10		25
36	12		24	10		26
37	13		24	11		26
38	13		25	11		27
39	13		26	12		27
40	14		26	12		28
41	14		27	12		29
42	15		27	13		29
43	15		28	13		30
44	16		28	14		30
45	16		29	14		31
46	16		30	14		32
47	17		30	15		32
48	17		31	15		33
49	18		31	16		33
50	18		32	16		34
51	19		32	16		35
52	19		33	17		35

TABLE C-12 *(Concluded)*

Modified Sample Size, m	5% Test Level		1% Test Level	
	Sign Test Is Significant if Number Is Either:		Sign Test Is Significant if Number Is Either:	
	Less than	or More than	Less than	or More than
53	19	34	17	36
54	20	34	18	36
55	20	35	18	37
56	21	35	18	38
57	21	36	19	38
58	22	36	19	39
59	22	37	20	39
60	22	38	20	40
61	23	38	21	40
62	23	39	21	41
63	24	39	21	42
64	24	40	22	42
65	25	40	22	43
66	25	41	23	43
67	26	41	23	44
68	26	42	23	45
69	26	43	24	45
70	27	43	24	46
71	27	44	25	46
72	28	44	25	47
73	28	45	26	47
74	29	45	26	48
75	29	46	26	49
76	29	47	27	49
77	30	47	27	50
78	30	48	28	50
79	31	48	28	51
80	31	49	29	51
81	32	49	29	52
82	32	50	29	53
83	33	50	30	53
84	33	51	30	54
85	33	52	31	54
86	34	52	31	55
87	34	53	32	55
88	35	53	32	56
89	35	54	32	57
90	36	54	33	57
91	36	55	33	58
92	37	55	34	58
93	37	56	34	59
94	38	56	35	59
95	38	57	35	60
96	38	58	35	61
97	39	58	36	61
98	39	59	36	62
99	40	59	37	62
100	40	60	37	63

TABLE C-13   Critical Values for Chi-Squared Tests

Degrees of Freedom	10% Level	5% Level	1% Level	0.1% Level
1	2.706	3.841	6.635	10.828
2	4.605	5.991	9.210	13.816
3	6.251	7.815	11.345	16.266
4	7.779	9.488	13.277	18.467
5	9.236	11.071	15.086	20.515
6	10.645	12.592	16.812	22.458
7	12.017	14.067	18.475	24.322
8	13.362	15.507	20.090	26.124
9	14.684	16.919	21.666	27.877
10	15.987	18.307	23.209	29.588
11	17.275	19.675	24.725	31.264
12	18.549	21.026	26.217	32.909
13	19.812	22.362	27.688	34.528
14	21.064	23.685	29.141	36.123
15	22.307	24.996	30.578	37.697
16	23.542	26.296	32.000	39.252
17	24.769	27.587	33.409	40.790
18	25.989	28.869	34.805	42.312
19	27.204	30.144	36.191	43.820
20	28.412	31.410	37.566	45.315
21	29.615	32.671	38.932	46.797
22	30.813	33.924	40.289	48.268
23	32.007	35.172	41.638	49.728
24	33.196	36.415	42.980	51.179
25	34.382	37.652	44.314	52.620
26	35.563	38.885	45.642	54.052
27	36.741	40.113	46.963	55.476
28	37.916	41.337	48.278	56.892
29	39.087	42.557	49.588	58.301
30	40.256	43.773	50.892	59.703
31	41.422	44.985	52.191	61.098
32	42.585	46.194	53.486	62.487
33	43.745	47.400	54.776	63.870
34	44.903	48.602	56.061	65.247
35	46.059	49.802	57.342	66.619
36	47.212	50.998	58.619	67.985
37	48.363	52.192	59.893	69.346
38	49.513	53.384	61.162	70.703
39	50.660	54.572	62.428	72.055
40	51.805	55.758	63.691	73.402
41	52.949	56.942	64.950	74.745
42	54.090	58.124	66.206	76.084
43	55.230	59.304	67.459	77.419
44	56.369	60.481	68.710	78.749
45	57.505	61.656	69.957	80.077
46	58.641	62.830	71.201	81.400
47	59.774	64.001	72.443	82.720
48	60.907	65.171	73.683	84.037
49	62.038	66.339	74.919	85.351
50	63.167	67.505	76.154	86.661

TABLE C-13 *(Concluded)*

Degrees of Freedom	10% Level	5% Level	1% Level	0.1% Level
51	64.295	68.669	77.386	87.968
52	65.422	69.832	78.616	89.272
53	66.548	70.993	79.843	90.573
54	67.673	72.153	81.069	91.872
55	68.796	73.311	82.292	93.167
56	69.919	74.468	83.513	94.461
57	71.040	75.624	84.733	95.751
58	72.160	76.778	85.950	97.039
59	73.279	77.931	87.166	98.324
60	74.397	79.082	88.379	99.607
61	75.514	80.232	89.591	100.888
62	76.630	81.381	90.802	102.166
63	77.745	82.529	92.010	103.442
64	78.860	83.675	93.217	104.716
65	79.973	84.821	94.422	105.988
66	81.085	85.965	95.626	107.258
67	82.197	87.108	96.828	108.526
68	83.308	88.250	98.028	109.791
69	84.418	89.391	99.228	111.055
70	85.527	90.531	100.425	112.317
71	86.635	91.670	101.621	113.577
72	87.743	92.808	102.816	114.835
73	88.850	93.945	104.010	116.091
74	89.956	95.081	105.202	117.346
75	91.061	96.217	106.393	118.599
76	92.166	97.351	107.583	119.850
77	93.270	98.484	108.771	121.100
78	94.374	99.617	109.958	122.348
79	95.476	100.749	111.144	123.594
80	96.578	101.879	112.329	124.839
81	97.680	103.010	113.512	126.083
82	98.780	104.139	114.695	127.324
83	99.880	105.267	115.876	127.565
84	100.980	106.395	117.057	129.804
85	102.079	107.522	118.236	131.041
86	103.177	108.648	119.414	132.277
87	104.275	109.773	120.591	133.512
88	105.372	110.898	121.767	134.745
89	106.469	112.022	122.942	135.978
90	107.565	113.145	124.116	137.208
91	108.661	114.268	125.289	138.438
92	109.756	115.390	126.462	139.666
93	110.850	116.511	127.633	140.893
94	111.944	117.632	128.803	142.119
95	113.038	118.752	129.973	143.344
96	114.131	119.871	131.141	144.567
97	115.223	120.990	132.309	145.789
98	116.315	122.108	133.476	147.010
99	117.407	123.225	134.642	148.230
100	118.498	124.342	135.807	149.449

TABLE C-14 Multipliers to Use for Constructing $\overline{X}$ and R Charts

Sample Size, n	Chart for Averages ($\overline{X}$ Chart): Factors for Control Limits		Charts for Ranges (R chart)				
			Factor for Central Line,	Factors for Control Limits			
	A	A_2	d_2	D_1	D_2	D_3	D_4
2	2.121	1.880	1.128	0	3.686	0	3.267
3	1.732	1.023	1.693	0	4.358	0	2.574
4	1.500	0.729	2.059	0	4.698	0	2.282
5	1.342	0.577	2.326	0	4.918	0	2.114
6	1.225	0.483	2.534	0	5.078	0	2.004
7	1.134	0.419	2.704	0.204	5.204	0.076	1.924
8	1.061	0.373	2.847	0.388	5.306	0.136	1.864
9	1.000	0.337	2.970	0.547	5.393	0.184	1.816
10	0.949	0.308	3.078	0.687	5.469	0.223	1.777
11	0.905	0.285	3.173	0.811	5.535	0.256	1.744
12	0.866	0.266	3.258	0.922	5.594	0.283	1.717
13	0.832	0.249	3.336	1.025	5.647	0.307	1.693
14	0.802	0.235	3.407	1.118	5.696	0.328	1.672
15	0.775	0.223	3.472	1.203	5.741	0.347	1.653
16	0.750	0.212	3.532	1.282	5.782	0.363	1.637
17	0.728	0.203	3.588	1.356	5.820	0.378	1.622
18	0.707	0.194	3.640	1.424	5.856	0.391	1.608
19	0.688	0.187	3.689	1.487	5.891	0.403	1.597
20	0.671	0.180	3.735	1.549	5.921	0.415	1.585
21	0.655	0.173	3.778	1.605	5.951	0.425	1.575
22	0.640	0.167	3.819	1.659	5.979	0.434	1.566
23	0.626	0.162	3.858	1.710	6.006	0.443	1.557
24	0.612	0.157	3.895	1.759	6.031	0.451	1.548
25	0.600	0.153	3.931	1.806	6.056	0.459	1.541

These values are from ASTM-STP 15D, American Society for Testing and Materials.

StatPad

A statistical analysis worksheet for Lotus 1-2-3

Reference Manual and Tutorial

Prepared by

Andrew F. Siegel

and

Mildred M. Siegel

Copyright © 1988, 1990 Skyline Technologies, Inc.

1 WHAT IS STATPAD?

StatPad[1] is a statistical computer program which extends Lotus 1-2-3[2] (release 2.01) by giving it the ability to perform the basic functions needed in a first course in statistics at the MBA level. StatPad was designed to make statistical analysis as accessible, painless, and easy to interpret as possible by bringing basic statistical power into the environment where business data is often found, namely within a Lotus 1-2-3 worksheet. Whenever possible, the analysis is guided by choices from a menu, and the results consist of graphs, explanatory text, and computational results which become part of the worksheet.

StatPad will perform all aspects of basic statistics: design using a random sample, exploration through graphic representations of data, estimation with summaries and confidence intervals (both one- and two-sided at various confidence levels), hypothesis testing (both one- and two-sided at various test levels), normal and binomial probability calculations, multiple regression analysis, and trend seasonal time series analysis.

BOX PLOT

HISTOGRAM

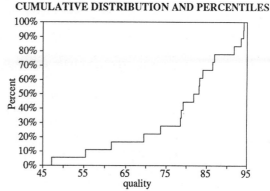
CUMULATIVE DISTRIBUTION AND PERCENTILES

---

[1] *StatPad* is a trademark of Skyline Technologies, Inc.

[2] Lotus and 1-2-3 are registered trademarks of Lotus Development Corporation.

2 HOW TO USE THIS MANUAL

2.1 Overview: how to use StatPad

To run StatPad, all you need to do is to get into Lotus 1-2-3, retrieve (/File Retrieve) the file *StatPad.wk1*, then hit (ALT) (S) to activate StatPad. You might start by selecting the INPUT function to put in some data, then select UNIVAR ONE-SAMPLE analysis to gain access to statistical analysis.

Here is a short list of areas where StatPad differs from 1-2-3. It will get you started. If you run into difficulty, think about looking up the relevant section in "How to interact with StatPad" in Section 4, or in the Tutorial, Section 7.

First, StatPad operates within Lotus 1-2-3, and uses a hierarchical menu structure similar to Lotus 1-2-3.

StatPad must be present (using /File Retrieve) on your Lotus 1-2-3 worksheet before you enter your data.

To start StatPad, HOLD down (ALT) while you PRESS (S).

The Input command will name your range automatically so that it corresponds to the numbers you type in. When you try to analyze a column of numbers that has not yet been given a range name, StatPad will prompt you for the range name and then allow you to point to the data before continuing with the analysis.

When StatPad asks you where to place the results, use the arrow keys to put the highlighted area where you want it. In particular, try to avoid writing on top of parts of the worksheet you want to keep!

Generally, StatPad expects your data to be present in the worksheet before you begin statistical analysis. You may find StatPad's INPUT function a helpful way to enter data; also see Section 4.2, "Bringing your data into the worksheet".

Note: Charts of the StatPad commands, in Section 5, show the chains of commands which lead to the statistical results you are aiming for. With each chart there is a brief description of the type of data needed for these statistical analyses.

WARNINGS: **do not insert or delete** entire rows or columns, or reset all range names, or use columns FA through IV, or begin a range name with an underline "_", or operate on any range name which begins with "_". **Do not** use range names that are also Lotus macro commands, such as *return*, *quit*, or *blank* (a complete list may be found in the Lotus reference manual).

2.2 If you are experienced in the use of Lotus 1-2-3

Since StatPad operates within Lotus 1-2-3 and uses a similar menu system, you should be able to get the StatPad program on your system and running quickly. Section 3, "How to Install StatPad" lists the hardware and software you need to get started.

Section 4, "How to Interact with StatPad" covers what you need to know in order to run StatPad. It would be worthwhile to look it over.

Examine the Charts of the StatPad command menus in Section 5. They show the chains of commands which lead to the statistical results you are aiming for. With each chart there is a brief description of the type of data needed to carry out each statistical analysis.

A glossary of terms used in the StatPad menus is included in Section 6.

If you run into difficulty, you can look up specific subjects in the tutorial (Section 7) which works through each menu item step-by-step.

The above material should be sufficient for getting started on StatPad, if you are comfortable with 1-2-3.

2.3 If you are still learning 1-2-3

Installing StatPad is straightforward, even for the student who isn't completely versed in 1-2-3. First you will want to check the hardware and software requirements in Section 3.1. The installation directions are in Section 3.2.

"How to interact with StatPad", Section 4, contains what you need to know to actually run the program.

In addition, there is a tutorial (Section 7) which will take you through each StatPad menu, giving the nature of the data you need to use, showing ways of bringing the data onto your worksheet, indicating the procedure to follow, and then illustrating what the result will look like on your computer screen.

2.4 Conventions used in this manual

These conventions are used in the instructions that follow:

TYPE   Type in the words shown in capital letters.
                       Used for letters and numbers.

PRESS   Press the indicated named keys.

SELECT   Choose the commands from the menus of StatPad or Lotus 1-2-3.
                       This can be done in either of two ways:

                              (1) Type the first letter of the command.
                              -- or --
                              (2) Move the cursor to the command by using the arrow
                              keys on the alphanumeric pad. Then PRESS ⎡ENTER ↵ ⎤.

3 HOW TO INSTALL STATPAD

3.1 Computer and software needed to run StatPad

COMPUTER: StatPad should run on any IBM PC, XT, AT, PS/2, or compatible, that runs Lotus 1-2-3 release 2.01.

SOFTWARE: Lotus 1-2-3 (Release 2.01) and StatPad.

MEMORY: You will need at least 512K of RAM memory (which is fairly standard these days).

GRAPHICS HARDWARE: You will need graphics hardware to generate displays of statistical data. Graphics standards such as VGA, EGA, and Hercules (or compatible) produce good graphic images. Once your graphics hardware has been installed into your Lotus 1-2-3 program (as specified in the Lotus 1-2-3 manuals) StatPad will be able to draw graphs on your computer.

StatPad works through Lotus 1-2-3. Please refer to your Lotus manual (or systems helper) for details such as how to tell 1-2-3 about your graphics hardware, and how to print out your graphs and the results of your analyses.

3.2 Installation

Copy the file *StatPad.wk1* onto the disk or subdirectory that contains your other Lotus 1-2-3 worksheet files.

If you plan on using the tutorial (Section 7), then copy *.* from your StatPad disk onto the disk or subdirectory that contains your other 1-2-3 worksheet files. This will also copy the data files that are used with the tutorial. These data files are:

```
DATABOOK.WK1
DATACATA.WK1
DATADIET.WK1
DATAFIBR.WK1
DATAFOOD.WK1
DATAPHON.WK1
DATAPLUM.WK1
DATASALE.WK1
DATASCHL.WK1
```

Always work with a copy of StatPad (it's not copy-protected), and keep your original disk safely stored away.

To copy files to a hard disk, first change directories to your 1-2-3 files directory. Then put your StatPad disk in the A drive and:

Hard disk:

To copy **StatPad file.**	**TYPE**	Copy a:StatPad.wk1
	PRESS	[ENTER ⏎]

To copy data **files.**	**TYPE**	Copy a:data*.wk1
	PRESS	[ENTER ⏎]

If you have 2 floppy disk drives but no hard disk, put your StatPad disk in the A drive, your worksheet files disk in the B drive, and:

Floppy disks:

To copy **StatPad file.**	**TYPE**	Copy a:StatPad.wk1 b:
	PRESS	[ENTER ⏎]

To copy data **files.**	**TYPE**	Copy a:data*.wk1 b:
	PRESS	[ENTER ⏎]

4 HOW TO INTERACT WITH STATPAD

4.1 Beginning a session with StatPad

A Bringing StatPad into your worksheet

1. Let's assume that you have already copied the file *StatPad.wk1* onto your worksheet-files disk or the worksheet-files subdirectory of your hard disk.

2. Begin by loading Lotus 1-2-3 in the usual manner.

3. Use the "/FILE RETRIEVE StatPad" commands to bring StatPad's statistical capabilities into the worksheet.

4. Move to a blank area of the worksheet, for example by hitting the TAB key (→).

5. HOLD DOWN (ALT) WHILE YOU PRESS (S) to activate StatPad and display the opening menu.

B Saving a StatPad session

1. Use the "/FILE SAVE" commands to save your worksheet exactly as it is at any time complete with data, results, and StatPad itself. Be sure to give a new name for the file to be saved.

2. You may now either continue your work, retrieve a different worksheet, retrieve StatPad to begin a new session, or quit Lotus 1-2-3.

C Continuing with a worksheet with StatPad already on it

1. Load 1-2-3 in the usual manner.

2. Use the "/FILE RETRIEVE" commands to retrieve the worksheet you were working on, giving the same name it was saved as.

3. You will find yourself in the same part of the worksheet you were in when you saved. You may move to a blank area of the worksheet or to the area containing the data you are interested in if necessary.

4. HOLD (ALT) WHILE YOU PRESS (S) to activate StatPad and display the opening StatPad menu. Because StatPad was saved with your worksheet, it is immediately available to you when you return to your worksheet.

4.2 Bringing your data into the worksheet

Note that StatPad must be retrieved into your worksheet first.
Your data is then brought in afterwards.

There are several ways to bring data into the statistical worksheet: typing in the data, using StatPad's convenient INPUT function, bringing data in from another Lotus worksheet, and importing data from a text file.

A Typing in the data

You may type your data into the Lotus worksheet as you usually do, without invoking StatPad.

B Using StatPad's INPUT function

Select INPUT from StatPad's opening menu (see below for more information about the menus). StatPad will ask you for a range name and for data values.

StatPad will automatically label the column of values, place the numbers you type into this range, and name the range for future use.

Note INPUT works only with numbers; it will not work with text. As a result, you may be sure that your data values will be interpreted properly by worksheet formulas and StatPad. This avoids the problem that a space before a number (e.g., " 10") becomes a string in a worksheet cell with the value zero. With INPUT you are guaranteed that your numbers will be interpreted properly.

Section 7.3(B) of the tutorial demonstrates the Input function in detail.

C Using data from another Lotus worksheet

You can extract data values from a preexisting worksheet, and bring these numbers into a worksheet that already has StatPad on it. It isn't necessary to name and define the range(s) when importing them, because the first time you try to use them StatPad will initiate a routine to help you names and define these ranges.

The first two steps are not necessary if you wish to bring in an entire worksheet of data that does not contain StatPad.

1. /FILE RETRIEVE your data worksheet (be sure to save your work-in-progress first, if any).

2. Use /FILE EXTRACT VALUES in order to save your selected data using a temporary filename.

3. Use /FILE RETRIEVE to bring in StatPad or a worksheet with StatPad on it if necessary.

4. Move your cursor to the top left corner of where you would like the data to be brought in.

5. /FILE COMBINE COPY ENTIRE will bring in the data from the temporary file you created in Step 2. Or you may give the name of an entire worksheet that does not contain StatPad. Or you may use /FILE COMBINE COPY NAMED/SPECIFIED-RANGE in order to bring in just one range of numbers[3].

D Using data from a text file

If your data set is in a text file, you might try the /FILE IMPORT NUMBERS command to bring pure numbers into the worksheet.

If text is interspersed with numbers, then the /FILE IMPORT TEXT command combined with the advanced /DATA PARSE command may be necessary.[4]

Please see your Lotus manual or systems expert for further details.

4.3 StatPad's menu system

The heart of StatPad's ease of use is the menu system which asks you about your data and provides choices to you to help guide the analysis. (Section 4.1.A gives instructions for bringing the opening StatPad menu up onto the screen.)

You use StatPad's menu system in exactly the same way that you use the Lotus menu system (which comes up when you hit the "/" key).

You may select a menu item in either of two ways:

1. Use the cursor keys (the left and right arrows) to highlight your selection. As you pass over each possibility, further information about that selection is provided about it in the second line of the menu. When you have made your selection, PRESS the ENTER key.

    OR

2. TYPE the first letter of your selection. For example, you could select HISTOGRAM from a menu by typing H.

---

[3] Be careful with /FILE COMBINE COPY NAMED/SPECIFIED-RANGE. If you bring in formulas (instead of numbers) that refer to cells that are not part of that range, the results may not be what you would like.

[4] If you use Lotus's /DATA PARSE command to create a Format-Line, 1-2-3 will automatically insert a new row into the worksheet. When you are done, please use /WORKSHEET DELETE ROW to eliminate this extra row. This is the exception to the rule "never delete rows or columns when you use StatPad". It is necessary here in order to eliminate the inserted row that would otherwise cause trouble.

StatPad's menu system is *hierarchical*, just like the Lotus menu system. This means that each selection you make will bring a new menu (or request for information) to the screen, until you have supplied all the information needed to obtain the statistical result. Note, to return to a previous menu level, PRESS the ESCAPE key. This can be done repeatedly to go back several menu levels.

All of the StatPad menus have STOP as an option. Select this when you want to leave the StatPad menu system and return the control of the spreadsheet to yourself. You will find that StatPad's results remain in the worksheet, just where you put them. You might stop in order to perform some ordinary Lotus 1-2-3 function such as moving the cursor, or correcting a number. You can then reactivate StatPad by HOLDING (ALT) WHILE YOU PRESS (S).

4.4 Statistical variables and range names

StatPad likes to have each statistical variable arranged as a single column of numbers in the worksheet with no blank cells or labels within the range of data. You may, of course, include a descriptive label at the top, above the data range.

A descriptive range name is needed for each variable. Lotus allows this name to have up to 15 characters; spaces are permitted but the name must be typed the same way each time (except that upper and lower case letters are interchangeable).

There are three ways to affix range names to the variables:

1. Type in your data using StatPad's INPUT function, which automatically names the range for you.

2. Use the Lotus /RANGE NAME CREATE command to name your range. You might use this, for example, after inserting or deleting some data in order to be sure that the range includes only the single column of *numbers* you wish to analyze.

3. Wait to name the range until StatPad needs to use this variable. When StatPad asks for "Range name for a column of data", and you enter the proposed data name, StatPad will respond that this range does not exist and ask if you want to point to the range. When you point it out, StatPad will then name it for you automatically.

    A quick way to select the column of data is to move to the top of the column and hit the period (.) key, then PRESS (End) and down (↓). The entire column will then be selected.

Be careful: a blank space before a data value will change it from a number to a label, which will be interpreted as zero.

4.5   Results and where to put them

When answers have been generated, StatPad will ask you where to place the results, and will highlight the cells on the screen where it proposes to put the results, while asking "RESULTS HERE?" at the top of the screen. You may reply as follows:

1.   If you would like the results to go in the selected area, replacing and destroying the current contents of any of these highlighted cells, simply hit (ENTER ↵).

2.   If you would like to move the highlighted area to a different place, use the cursor keys (up, down, left, right to move one cell; tab, shift tab; PgUp, or PgDn to move an entire screenful) to position the results where you want them, then hit (ENTER ↵).

4.6   Printing a graph

After you have generated and examined a graph on the screen:

PRESS   (ENTER ↵)   This will bring up new menu:
                                                   CONTINUE PRINT STOP

This menu gives you the following choices:

CONTINUE   To return to StatPad and continue with statistical analysis.

PRINT   To save the graph so it can be printed later.

STOP   To stop statistical analysis, and return to your worksheet in
                          LOTUS 1-2-3.

If you select PRINT, you will be asked "NAME TO SAVE GRAPH UNDER?" Your graph will be saved as a ".PIC" file under the name you assigned to it and may be printed later, for example, using Lotus Printgraph.

If you want to modify a graph that is on your screen before saving it, perhaps naming the axes and adding titles, first hit (ENTER ↵) to bring up the CONTINUE PRINT STOP menu, then:

SELECT   STOP   To return to 1-2-3

SELECT   /GRAPH etc.   To modify axes & titles

SELECT   /GRAPH SAVE   To save as a .PIC file

A graph can be saved as a .PIC file for printing either with the StatPad PRINT command or with the 1-2-3 /GRAPH SAVE command. However, it *cannot* be saved properly with the 1-2-3 /GRAPH NAME CREATE command.

4.7 Ending a session with StatPad

To leave StatPad, select STOP from the main StatPad menus. This returns you to 1-2-3.

If you wish to save your work, give the file a meaningful name which relates to the kind of data you have been analyzing, and use the /FILE SAVE (Type name, PRESS [ENTER ←]) REPLACE commands.[5]
You are now in 1-2-3 and may continue spreadsheet work or use /QUIT to leave 1-2-3.

4.8 What *not* to do when working with StatPad

Because StatPad lives within the 1-2-3 worksheet, it is possible to inadvertently make some change to the worksheet that could cause StatPad to stop working. This section contains a short list of actions to avoid.

A Don't reset, change, or delete the special range names

StatPad uses a lot of range names to keep track of things (like which part of the program does what), and where the internal data may be found. All of these range names start with the underline character "_". Consequently, your range names will appear at the start (and StatPad's range names will appear at the end) of any list of range names.

StatPad will be unable to function if you interfere with the special range names in any way. Never reset the range names. Generally, it's fine to work with your own range names (that don't begin with "_") and to create and delete them. However, you should avoid using range names that are also Lotus macro commands, such as *return*, *quit*, or *blank* (a complete list may be found in the Lotus 1-2-3 reference manual).

B Don't insert or delete rows or columns

Because StatPad lives in the same worksheet you are operating in (at the extreme right-hand side of it) serious trouble may result if you insert or delete any rows or columns in the worksheet. As an alternative, try using 1-2-3's /RANGE ERASE command to delete unwanted data or results, and feel free to /COPY and to /MOVE in order to reposition material within the worksheet. Of course it's OK to type in, modify, and erase data in existing cells.[6]

---

[5] NOTE: If you happen to save the file with your current work on it *without renaming it*, the file will be saved as *StatPad.wk1*. If this should happen, you may use /RANGE ERASE to remove the new material and "clean up" this copy of StatPad for re-use.

[6] Note that 1-2-3's /DATA PARSE FORMAT-LINE CREATE command will insert a new row into the worksheet. When you are done parsing, you may delete this extra row in order to restore the worksheet to its earlier form.

C Don't use the extreme right-hand side of the worksheet

StatPad reserves all rights to the range from cell FA1 to cell IV8192. This leaves you 156 columns (A to EZ) and 8192 rows (1 to 8192) to work in, and so should not be a problem.

D Don't change the argument separator

You probably weren't thinking of doing it, but please don't use /WORKSHEET GLOBAL DEFAULT OTHER INTERNATIONAL PUNCTUATION because this changes the punctuation rules for StatPad's program and might cause it to fail.

4.9 Troubleshooting

If things are not going perfectly well for you, please look at the items in this list before trying more drastic measures.

A Dealing with an error

When the ERROR message flashes in the upper right-hand side of the screen, count to 10 slowly, then read the message (if any), and finally hit ENTER to clear the error. Sometimes it may be helpful to hit ESC a few times also.

If more than a minute has gone by with no output, and you suspect trouble, you can interrupt StatPad by hitting CONTROL BREAK (i.e. HOLD down the CONTROL key Ctrl while you PRESS the BREAK key Break). This may need to be repeated a few times.

As a very last resort, you may need to restart the computer. See your systems expert for further details. This technique should not ordinarily be necessary.

B Be sure all data entries are numbers

StatPad will usually detect an empty cell within a range of data and ask you to fix it. However, it is too time-consuming for the program to also check for cells that should contain numbers but actually contain labels (i.e. text). When StatPad calls on one of Lotus's internal functions with this range, it could cause an error or be interpreted as a zero. The exception to this rule is with StatPad's random sampling: you may select a random sample from a column of data consisting of text such as firm names (which are not numbers, but will still work just fine).

C Save your worksheet often

If something goes wrong, it is always comforting to have a recent (5-minutes old?) copy of your worksheet made using the /FILE SAVE command. Be sure to save it under a meaningful name so that the StatPad file is unchanged and will be available for a new problem.

D Error messages

Here is an explanation of the error messages you may see while using StatPad.

2000 or less, please; please hit ENTER

In order to select a random sample as a list of numbers, the population size you specify cannot be larger than 2,000.

Must be 1 to 15; please hit ENTER

In order to use Multivar, you must have between 1 and 15 explanatory X variables. Please see Section 7.8 (A) for a review of appropriate data for a multiple regression analysis.

Must be 3 to 100; please hit ENTER

In order to use Univar Many sample, you must have between 3 and 100 columns of data to analyze.

Must be one column of data. Hit ENTER to continue

You have specified a range name that is two or more columns wide. StatPad requires that each statistical variable be in a single column. If your two (or more) columns represent more than one statistical variable, then give each column its own individual name.

Must have same number of data values; please hit ENTER

In order to use Bivar or Multivar, you must have the same number of data values in each range.

Need 2 full years of data; please hit ENTER

In order to perform Time series analysis, you must have at least two full years of data, either monthly or quarterly.

Percentage must be positive and less than 100; please hit ENTER

When computing percentiles for a normal distribution (using *Probability* from the opening menu) you must specify the probability as a percentage that is bigger than 0 and smaller than 100. That is, numbers like 5, 15, 85, and 99.9 would be OK. However, numbers like 238, 0, 100, or -57 are not allowed here.

Probability must be between 0 and 1; please hit ENTER

In order to compute binomial probabilities, the probability for each case that you specify must be a number between 0 and 1 and cannot be either 0 or 1.

Range '(name)' does not exist; please hit ENTER

You have specified a name that is not an assigned range name for a column of data. If you have misspelled it, then select "Change" and provide the correct spelling. If you would like to assign the range name at this time, then select "Point" and highlight the column of numbers you wish to analyze. Do *not* highlight the title, if any, at the top of the column. Or you could select "Stop" to return to 1-2-3 so that you may look around in the worksheet and think about the problem you're working on.

Sample size is too big; please hit ENTER

In order to draw a random sample from a population, the sample size you specify cannot be larger than the population size because StatPad uses sampling without replacement. Try again using a smaller number for the sample size.

Standard deviation must be positive; please hit ENTER

When computing probabilities for a normal distribution, you may specify any number for the mean, but you must choose a positive number for the standard deviation. Try again and use a positive standard deviation.

There are blank cells in your range. Please fix; please hit ENTER

> You have specified a range for analysis that includes one or more blank cells. Select "Stop" to return to 1-2-3 from StatPad so that you can fix the problem. Hint: use 1-2-3's /RANGE NAME CREATE command to highlight the range of cells that 1-2-3 has assigned to this name; it may be different from what you thought. The safest way to redefine a range in 1-2-3 is first to /RANGE NAME DELETE it and then to use /RANGE NAME CREATE to re-specify it. Or, after /RANGE NAME DELETE, you might go directly into StatPad; the first time you try to work with this range name StatPad will allow you to point to your data.

TROUBLE. It's not OK to insert or delete rows or cols. Please hit ENTER. Please hit ENTER and load a fresh copy of StatPad

> Something has happened so that StatPad can no longer function. Remember that StatPad is part of your worksheet; if you insert or delete rows or columns, then StatPad will be affected also. It's perfectly OK to use /RANGE ERASE on your part of the worksheet and to /MOVE and /COPY within this area. But don't use /WORKSHEET INSERT or /WORKSHEET DELETE![7]

---

[7] Also note that when you create a "Format-Line" with /DATA PARSE FORMAT-LINE CREATE, a new row is automatically inserted into the worksheet. If you are very careful, you may delete this extra row when you are done and StatPad will still function.

5 OVERVIEW AND CHARTS OF STATPAD MENU COMMANDS

Charts of all StatPad menus are collected together in this section. Before each chart is a brief paragraph describing the type of data needed and/or the nature of the results expected.

The charts show the selections you need to make to generate specific statistical results. They let you know which choices you will be called on to make to arrive at the results. They orient you to the analyses that can be carried out for each type of data and situation.

The Tutorial (Section 7) works through each of the command charts in detail. It illustrates the menu commands, and the numerical and graphic statistical results you will see. Several minor menu lines have been omitted from the command charts, but are explained in the tutorial.

5.1 Univariate one-sample data

Requires a single column of numbers.

In a univariate data set, one variable only is measured for each elementary unit of the sample. The data set consists of a single column of numbers. Some examples of univariate one-sample data are: the cost of living in the 10 largest major American cities, heights of mountains in the Presidential Range of New Hampshire, or today's closing prices of the most active stocks on the New York Stock Exchange.

5.2   Univariate two- and many-sample data

Requires two (or more) columns of numbers.

In univariate two- (and many-sample) data, one variable is measured for each item of two (or more) independent samples. The data set consists of two or more columns of numbers. It is not necessary that the data sets contain the same number of values, only that they be measured in the same units. However, when two samples *do* have the same number of data values, you have the option to perform a *paired* analysis which would be appropriate, for example, with "before and after" measurements on the same individuals.

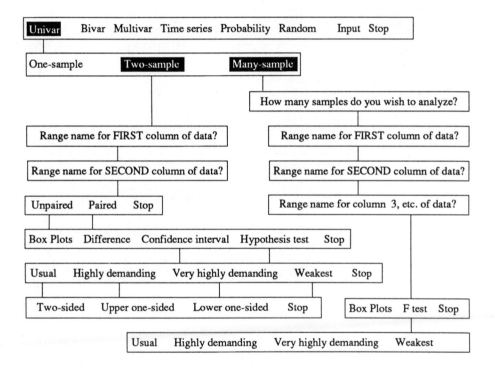

5.3 Bivariate data

Requires two columns of numbers with the same number of rows in each.

In a bivariate data set two variables are measured for each elementary unit of the sample, and one variable is to be predicted from the other. The data set consists of two columns of numbers with the same number of entries. Each variable can be measured in a different unit (for example, salary dollars and years of experience for employees). The two variables must contain the same number of data values.

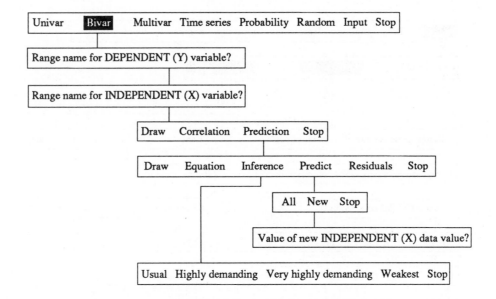

5.4 Multivariate data

Requires two or more columns of numbers with the same number of rows in each.

In a multivariate data set, 3 or more variables are measured for each elementary unit of the sample, and one variable is to be predicted from the others. The data set consists of two or more columns of numbers with the same number of entries. Each variable can be measured in a different unit (for example, salary dollars, productivity level, and years of experience for employees). All variables in a multivariate data set must contain the same number of data values.

5.5 Time series

Requires a single column with at least two full years of quarterly or monthly observations.

In a trend-seasonal time series analysis, a single variable is measured for each successive time period (either monthly or quarterly). The data set consists of a single column of numbers. For example: monthly ice-cream sales or quarterly freight miles.

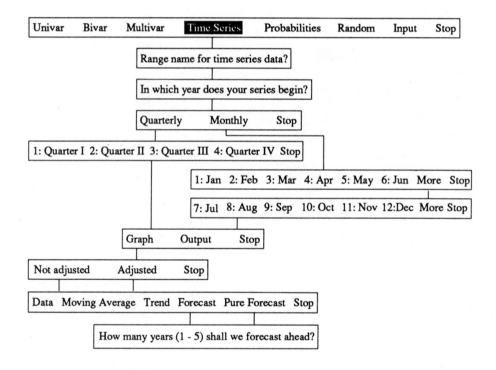

5.6 Normal probability calculations

Requires the mean (any number) and the standard deviation (any positive number) which define the normal distribution; also one or two numbers to define either the event for which you want the probability or the percentage for which you want the percentile.

After you provide values for the mean and standard deviation of a normal distribution, you can find the probability of being less than, more than, between, or not between numbers of your choosing; percentiles are also available. For example, StatPad could find the probability that sales will exceed $65,000 if you are willing to assume that the sales amount follows a normal distribution with mean $60,000 and standard deviation $10,000. Or you could find the 75th percentile, which is the sales level such that the probability of being less is 0.75.

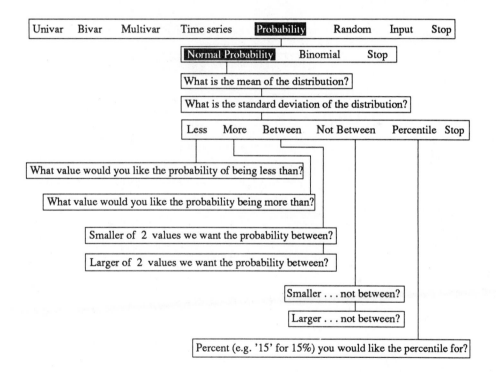

5.7 Binomial probability calculations

Requires the number of repetitions or cases (a positive whole number) and the probability for each case (a positive number less than 1) which define the binomial distribution; also one or two numbers to define the event for which you want the probability.[8]

After you provide values for the number of cases and the probability of success for each one, you can find the probability of the number of successes being equal to, more than, less than, between, or not between whole numbers of your choosing. It is necessary that the cases be independent of each other and that the cases always have the same probability of success. For example, you can find the probability that 8 or more of the 10 machines you manufacture today will work properly, assuming each has a 97% chance of working.

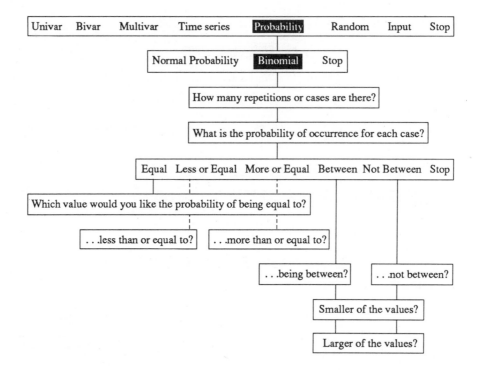

---

[8] The binomial distribution also requires that the cases be *independent* of one another. Otherwise the results may not be applicable to your situation.

5.8   Generating random samples

Requires *either* a sample size number and a range name for a column of text, *or* two numbers: the population size (2,000 or less) and the sample size.

A random sample is then chosen for you so that each unit of the population has the same chance of being selected and units are selected independently of one another.

If you specify a range name, then StatPad will randomly select from this list. For example, you could select 15 from a list of 273 employee names. If you specify only the population size, then StatPad will produce a list of numbers randomly selected from 1 to this number. For example, you could select 23 random numbers between 1 and 200. In either case you have the option either to leave the sample in random order or to have it put in order (either alphabetical or numerical, as appropriate).

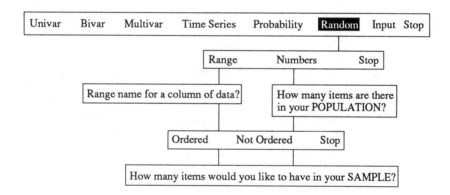

5.9 Typing in data (Input)

Requires a name (8 characters or less) and a list of numbers to be typed in as a column.

The Input function, which makes it easy to type in a list of data and give it a name, is discussed in Section 4.2 and in the Tutorial, Section 7.3(A).

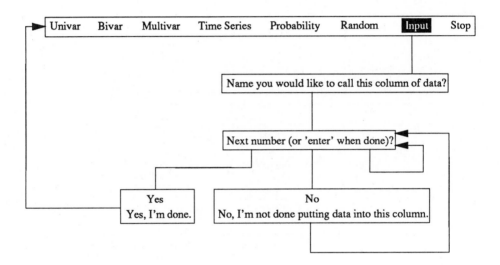

6 GLOSSARY OF TERMS USED IN STATPAD MENUS

Bivar

Bivar is short for *bivariate data*, which is two related columns. Two variables are measured for each elementary unit, and one is to be predicted from the other(s). For example, you might have sales (one column) and earnings (the other column) for 23 different firms. Or you might have salary and years of experience for a number of employees.

Box plot

A **box plot** is a picture of the five-number summary of a univariate data set (a single column of numbers) showing the smallest, the lower quartile (25th percentile), the median (50th percentile), the upper quartile (75th percentile) and the largest. Box plots provide a convenient way to compare two or more samples side by side.

CDF

The **CDF** or **cumulative distribution function** is a display of the percentiles of a univariate data set (a single column of numbers). The percentages are displayed on the vertical axis and the data values (the percentile value for each percentage) are displayed on the horizontal axis. For example, to find the 90th percentile, find 90% on the vertical axis, move horizontally until you hit the graph,[9] then move down to find the 90th percentile.

Confidence Interval

This is a **confidence interval** for a univariate data set (a single column of numbers) representing a random sample from a large population. You may set the probability that the (fixed but unknown) population mean is within the (random but known) confidence interval at either 95% (the standard) or 99%, 99.9%, or 90%. You also may choose either the usual two-sided or a one-sided interval. Confidence intervals are also provided for the mean difference between two samples and for regression coefficients with bivariate and multivariate data.

Describe

The **describe** command will produce a collection of summary measures for a univariate data set (a single column of numbers) including the average, the trimmed average, the

---

[9] If you hit a flat portion, move halfway across.

median, the standard deviation, the interquartile range (IQR), the range, the largest, the upper quartile, the lower quartile, the smallest, the standard error of the average, and the number of cases. Only one of these measures (the standard error of the average) requires that the data set be a random sample from a population; the other summaries are purely descriptive.

Highly demanding (interval)

This selection will set the confidence level at 99%. Also see *interval* in this glossary.

Histogram

The **histogram** for a univariate data set (a single column of numbers) is a bar chart which shows the frequency of occurrence of your data values. From the histogram, you can observe the approximate center of your data set, its variability, the pattern symmetry or skewness, and any outliers that might be present.

Input

The **input** command on the opening menu is an easy way to type a column of data into the worksheet and give it a name.

Interval

This is a **confidence interval** for a univariate data set (a single column of numbers) representing a random sample from a large population. You may set the probability that the (fixed but unknown) population mean is within the (random but known) confidence interval at either 95% (the standard) or 99%, 99.9%, or 90%. You also may choose either the usual two-sided or a one-sided interval. Confidence intervals are also provided for the mean difference between two samples and for regression coefficients with bivariate and multivariate data.

Lower one-sided (interval)

This selection will result in a confidence interval of the form "We are ___% sure that the population mean is *less* than ___". Also see *interval* in this glossary.

Many-sample

In a univariate **many-sample** analysis, numbers from three or more samples are compared. Each sample is represented by one column of data, and the same variable must be measured for each sample. For example, you might compare productivity measures (the variable) for employees (the individuals) in each of four plants (the samples). You would arrange the employee productivity measures into four columns, one for each plant.

Multivar

Multivar is short for *multivariate data*, which is three or more related columns. Two or more variables are measured for each elementary unit, and one variable is to be predicted from the other(s). For example, you might have sales (one column), earnings (a second column), and number of employees (a third column) for 31 different firms. Or you might have salary, age, and experience for a number of employees.

One-sample

A univariate **one-sample** data set is a single column of numbers representing a statistical variable measured for a number of elementary units. For example, a list of employee salaries.

Percentiles

For a sample of data, a **percentile** is a number, in the same units as the data, chosen so that a specified percentage of the entire data set is smaller than this number. For example, if the 35th percentile of employee salaries were \$27,805, then approximately 35% of employees have salaries less than \$27,805. Given a data value, you can find its percentile ranking (e.g., \$35,000 is the 47th percentile). Or, given a percentage, you can find the percentile (data value) at that ranking (e.g., the 65th percentile is \$43,830).

For a distribution, a **percentile** is a number such that the probability of observing a smaller value is equal to a specified percentage. For example, if the 90th percentile of Sales were \$58,000, then the probability that the observed value of Sales will be smaller than \$58,000 is 0.90 or 90%.

Probability

The **probability** of an event is a number, between 0 and 1, which indicates the likelihood it has of occurring. StatPad can compute probabilities for the normal distribution and for the binomial distribution.

Random

In a **random** sample each item of the population has an equal chance of being selected and items are chosen independently of one another. Equivalently, every different sample has the same chance of being selected. StatPad chooses a random sample *without replacement* so that an item from the population cannot be chosen more than once to be included in the sample.

Test

Hypothesis testing for a univariate data set (a single column of numbers) decides whether the (unknown) population mean differs from some given, fixed value. The result tells whether the (observed) sample average differs *significantly* from the given, fixed value or not. The data set must be a random sample from the population of interest.

Time series

A trend-seasonal **time-series** analysis starts with successive monthly or quarterly observations (a single column of numbers). The series is analyzed in terms of the long-term trend, the repeating seasonal fluctuations, the medium-term wandering cycles, and the random irregular component.

Two-sample

In a univariate **two-sample** data, numbers from two samples are compared. Each sample is represented by one column of data, and the same variable must be measured for each sample. For example, you might compare productivity measures (the variable) for employees (the individuals) in each of two plants (the samples). If there is a natural pairing between your two samples (for example, before and after measures for the same individuals) then you should choose the *paired* analysis option. For example, comparing advertising recall measures before and after viewing a television segment would give you paired data.

Two-sided (interval)

This selection will result in a confidence interval of the form "We are ___% sure that the population mean is *between* ___ and ___". Also see *interval* in this glossary.

Univar

Univar is short for *univariate data*, which is a single column of numbers. A single variable is measured for each elementary unit. For example, a list of employee salaries. Or a list of prices of common stock.

Upper one-sided (interval)

This selection will result in a confidence interval of the form "We are ___% sure that the population mean is *larger* than ___". Also see *interval* in this glossary.

Usual (interval)

This selection will set the confidence level at 95%. Also see *interval* in this glossary.

Very highly demanding (interval)

This selection will set the confidence level at 99.9%. Also see *interval* in this glossary.

Weakest (interval)

This selection will set the confidence level at 90%. Also see *interval* in this glossary.

7 TUTORIAL

7.1 Who is the tutorial for?

This tutorial is for anyone who wants a step-by-step explanation of the StatPad statistical analysis system. It will help you become fluent by walking you through the computer keystrokes needed to generate statistical results and graphs.

Data sets for the tutorial exercises are on the original StatPad disk, and can be readily copied from there.

7.2 Starting and leaving StatPad

This section will show you the basic procedures for getting your system set up, beginning a session, ending a session, and dealing with possible problems ("troubleshooting") that you may encounter. You will examine the opening screens, which contain brief instructions for using StatPad and warnings about actions to avoid because they may interfere with the program's operation. You then go to an unoccupied part of the worksheet, activate the first StatPad menu and examine the choices there. Then, you will save your worksheet under another name and leave StatPad.

A Bringing StatPad into your worksheet

Before you begin, you need to be sure you have copied StatPad onto the disk or subdirectory where you save your 1-2-3 worksheets.

1. Start your computer in your usual way.

2. Bring 1-2-3 up on your screen. (Refer to your Lotus manual or system consultant if necessary).

3. Bring StatPad on your worksheet.

Retrieve StatPad	**PRESS**	/̄
	SELECT	FILE
	SELECT	RETRIEVE
	SELECT	STATPAD.WK1

You now see the first StatPad screen which contains brief information about the program and instructions for activating StatPad. Note the warnings at the bottom of the screen. The screen will look like this:

StatPad
Instruction
Screen.

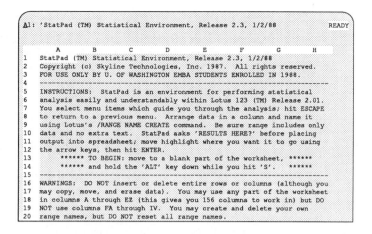

```
A1: 'StatPad (TM) Statistical Environment, Release 2.3, 1/2/88          READY

         A        B        C        D        E        F        G        H
1   StatPad (TM) Statistical Environment, Release 2.3, 1/2/88
2   Copyright (c) Skyline Technologies, Inc. 1987.  All rights reserved.
3   FOR USE ONLY BY U. OF WASHINGTON EMBA STUDENTS ENROLLED IN 1988.
4   ----------------------------------------------------------------------
5   INSTRUCTIONS:  StatPad is an environment for performing statistical
6   analysis easily and understandably within Lotus 123 (TM) Release 2.01.
7   You select menu items which guide you through the analysis; hit ESCAPE
8   to return to a previous menu.  Arrange data in a column and name it
9   using Lotus's /RANGE NAME CREATE command.  Be sure range includes only
10  data and no extra text.  StatPad asks 'RESULTS HERE?' before placing
11  output into spreadsheet; move highlight where you want it to go using
12  the arrow keys, then hit ENTER.
13       ****** TO BEGIN: move to a blank part of the worksheet,  ******
14       ****** and hold the 'ALT' key down while you hit 'S'.    ******
15  ----------------------------------------------------------------------
16  WARNINGS:  DO NOT insert or delete entire rows or columns (although you
17  may copy, move, and erase data).  You may use any part of the worksheet
18  in columns A through EZ (this gives you 156 columns to work in) but DO
19  NOT use columns FA through IV.  You may create and delete your own
20  range names, but DO NOT reset all range names.
```

The instructions continue, so:

**Continue on
to second
instruction
screen**

PRESS   PgDn

StatPad
Instruction
Screen:
Continued

```
A21: '------------------------------------------------------------------READY

         A        B        C        D        E        F        G        H
21  ----------------------------------------------------------------------
22  GETTING DATA INTO StatPad:  Statpad's main menu includes an 'INPUT'
23  function that allows you to easily type new data into the worksheet and
24  name it automatically.  If you have data in a worksheet file already,
25  you may bring it into StatPad using Lotus's /FILE COMBINE COPY ENTIRE
26  command.  If you have data in a standard text file, you may be able to
27  bring it in using Lotus's /FILE IMPORT NUMBERS command.  Please see
28  your Lotus manual for further details.
29  ----------------------------------------------------------------------
30  PLEASE:  Tell your instructor if you have any problems or suggestions.
31  ----------------------------------------------------------------------
32      Skyline Technologies, Inc.
33      4244 University Way NE, Box 95529
34      Seattle, Washington 98145
35  ----------------------------------------------------------------------
```

These two screens give a condensation of some of the main features of the
StatPad program. StatPad is now resident within your worksheet but you have
not yet activated the program.

B Activating StatPad and examining the opening menu

To activate StatPad, HOLD (ALT) while you PRESS (S). But first you want to move to an unoccupied part of the worksheet:

Move to free part of worksheet.	**PRESS**	(Home)
	PRESS	(→)
Activate StatPad.	**HOLD** (ALT)	while you **PRESS** (S).

You now see the first StatPad menu:

StatPad
Opening
Menu.

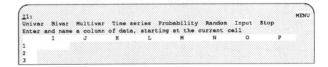

The StatPad menu system starts out by asking you to indicate either the kind of data you are using or the type of action (calculation or input) you want to make. With this information StatPad can display the menu of statistical procedures that is appropriate to your task.

Note the opening menu line: the selections are:

Univariate: to analyze a single column of numbers that is already in the worksheet, (e.g., salaries of 27 employees),

Bivariate: to analyze two columns of numbers in order to predict one from the other, (e.g., salary and years of experience for 27 employees, to see how experience affects salary),

Multivariate: to analyze two or more columns of numbers in order to predict one from the other(s), (e.g., salary, years of experience, and age for 27 employees, to see how experience and age together affect salary),

Time Series: to analyze quarterly or monthly observations in terms of the long-term trend, the repeating seasonal fluctuations, the medium-term wandering cycles, and the random irregular component, (e.g., quarterly sales of an ice-cream factory),

Probabilities: to determine the likelihood of the occurrence of various events for a normal or a binomial distribution, (e.g., to find the probability that sales will exceed $60 million assuming a normal distribution with mean $55 million and standard deviation $12 million; or to find the probability that more than 10 of the 35 consumers you will interview will be aware of your product assuming each one has a 25% chance of being aware of it),

Random: to generate a random sample from a population either as numbers or as a list from a column of numbers or words, (e.g., to select a random sample of 50 items from the day's production of 843 items),

Input: to type in a column of data and give it a name, (e.g., to type in today's closing prices of a group of stocks).

In the following tutorials we will work out problems relevant to each of these statistical topics.

C   Leaving StatPad

You can leave StatPad from any main menu by selecting STOP

Exiting from StatPad	SELECT	STOP

You are now back in 1-2-3. StatPad is still resident on your 1-2-3 worksheet even though it isn't activated now. If there were data on your worksheet you could save and rename it now with /FILE SAVE (giving a new filename).

D   Troubleshooting

What if StatPad wasn't one of the choices available to you when you tried to retrieve the file? Either you haven't yet copied the file *StatPad.wk1* to the disk or directory where you keep your worksheet files, or else 1-2-3 is not looking there for its files. The solution is to copy this file into the right place.

Here's how to find out where 1-2-3 is actually looking for your worksheet files:

Check 1-2-3's file directory	SELECT	/ FILE DIRECTORY
	Prompt	*Enter current directory: ...*

You will see, at the top of the screen, the disk and directory where 1-2-3 looks for worksheet files on your computer. Now you can copy the file *StatPad.wk1* to the right place and try again with /FILE RETRIEVE.

If this doesn't work, try checking with your systems consultant.

7.3   Bringing data into the worksheet

Note that StatPad must be retrieved to your worksheet first.
Your data is then brought in afterwards.

StatPad uses named ranges of data for its statistical analysis. These ranges need to be organized as *single columns* of data which will be numbers in most cases. This section covers several ways of putting data onto the worksheet: typing in the data, using StatPad's INPUT command, copying data from another 1-2-3 worksheet, and importing data from a text file. This section ends with a discussion of how to give a range name to an unnamed column of data without leaving the StatPad menu sequence you are working in.

A   Typing in the data

Please note that when you are typing in data to use with StatPad it is easiest when StatPad has already been retrieved into your worksheet but not yet activated (with ⟨ALT⟩ ⟨S⟩) *before* you type in the numbers.

Here is a list of the steps involved:

1.   Start 1-2-3.

2.   Retrieve the file *StatPad.wk1* (Section 7.2 A), or another worksheet which already has StatPad on it.

3.   Move to a free area of the worksheet.

4.   Type your data as one column of numbers on the 1-2-3 worksheet.

5.   You have a choice of how to name this data set:

   (a) You may wait until you are ready to use the data. StatPad will allow you to point to your data set if you use a new range name that StatPad does not recognize (further details given in 7.3 F).

   (b) You may define and name your data right now in 1-2-3 with the / RANGE NAME CREATE commands, being sure to specify only the *numbers* in your single column of data.

6.   Now that your data is in the worksheet, you may start the StatPad command system by HOLDING ⟨ALT⟩ while you PRESS ⟨S⟩. (Section 7.2 B)

Naming and defining a column of data in StatPad: Sometimes you might not get around to naming and defining a range until you're ready to use it. When you are in StatPad and are asked "range name for a column of data", just type in the range name you want for the data and then follow the prompts which will direct you in pointing to the data range. Here are the prompts and responses for step 5(a) above: naming and defining a column of data in StatPad.

Prompt	*Range name for a column of data*
TYPE	testing (or other appropriate range name for your data)

Prompt   *Range 'testing' does not exist; please hit ENTER*

PRESS   ENTER ←

Menu   *Point Change Stop*

Here is the explanation for this new menu:

Point	Select this one to point to your data to name this range
Change	Select this one to specify a different range name (e.g., to correct the spelling)
Stop	Stop statistical analysis, return to 1-2-3's ready mode

Let's point to the data this time:

PRESS   ENTER ← to select Point

Prompt   *testing*   *Enter range: ...*

The prompt shows the range name you chose and asks you to enter the range. You can use the arrow keys to move to the first cell of your range (the first number at the top of your column of data). Then indicate the cells of the range with the following key sequence.

PRESS   Period ▫

PRESS   End

PRESS   Down ↓

PRESS   ENTER ←

You now have a named range. You use this name in answer to StatPad prompts, just as you do with 1-2-3 prompts.

B   Using the Input command

The INPUT command makes it easy for you to type your numbers into a single column. The range will be automatically named for you, and will also be labelled at the top.

Below is the menu chart showing the commands you will be using.

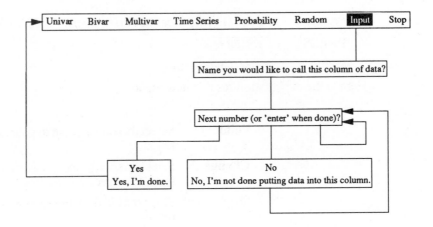

Move to a free area of the worksheet and then start the StatPad program with ⟨ALT⟩ ⟨S⟩. If necessary, refer back to Section 7.2(A) "Bringing StatPad into the worksheet" and 7.2(B) "Activating StatPad". Here is a summary of the steps to the StatPad opening menu:

1. Run 1-2-3.

2. Retrieve the file *StatPad.wk1* or another worksheet file that includes StatPad. (Section 7.2 A)

3. Move to a free area of the worksheet (e.g., cell I1).

4. Activate StatPad. (HOLD ⟨ALT⟩ while you PRESS ⟨S⟩.) (Section 7.2 B).

This brings up the opening StatPad menu:

Input:
StatPad
Opening
Menu

```
I1:                                                          MENU
Univar  Bivar  Multivar  Time series  Probability  Random  Input  Stop
Enter and name a column of data, starting at the current cell
        I       J       K       L       M       N       O       P
1
2
3
```

(1) INPUT is the 7th command on the opening StatPad menu.
Select the INPUT command from the opening StatPad menu in one of the following ways:

To begin the Input process TYPE the letter "I",

OR

PRESS the <u>RIGHT</u> ARROW key 6 times to highlight INPUT and then PRESS ⌷ ENTER ↵ ⌷.

(2) The input menu that comes up next asks you to name the data range which will contain your numerical values.

Input: Name
for a Column
of Data

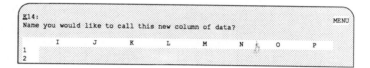

Use "bookcost" for your range name. The column of numbers you will be typing in represent the average retail price of new books. They will be used in the next section of the tutorial (analysis of univariate one-sample data).

Specify the range name:	**TYPE**	Bookcost
	PRESS	⌷ ENTER ↵ ⌷

(3) The next menu asks you to enter the numbers:

Entering the data values	*Prompt*	*Next number (or 'enter' when done)?*
	TYPE	A number from the following list
	PRESS	⌷ ENTER ↵ ⌷ after each number.

39	39	50
35	19	25
23	11	22
31	33	55

When you have entered the entire data set, your screen will look like this:

Input: Screen
Display, Entered
Bookcost Data

```
I14:                                                           READY
Next number (or 'enter' when done)?

          I     J     K     L     M     N     O     P
 1   bookcost
 2        39
 3        35
 4        23
 5        31
 6        39
 7        19
 8        11
 9        33
10        50
11        25
12        22
13        55
14
```

(4) Ending the INPUT process:

| **To conclude the input routine** | *Prompt* | Next number (or 'enter' when done)? |
| | **PRESS** | (ENTER ←) |

Input: Ending
Data Entry

```
I14:                                                            MENU
Yes  No
Yes - I'm done putting data into this column
          I     J     K     L     M     N     O     P
 1   bookcost
 2        39
 3        35
 4        23
 5        31
 6        39
 7        19
 8        11
 9        33
10        50
11        25
12        22
13        55
14
```

| **StatPad now checks that you are really done** | *Prompt* | Yes No |
| | **PRESS** | (ENTER ←) to Select "Yes" - I'm done putting data in this column" |

You now return to the opening StatPad menu.

Note that if you were not finished entering your data when you pressed (ENTER ←), you could select "No, I'm not done", and continue entering the rest of your data.

You can save your worksheet as *bookcost.wk1*. It now contains a univariate one-sample data set in addition to the StatPad system. You can use it later for statistical analyses. First, select **STOP**, then:

Saving the	**SELECT**	/ FILE SAVE
worksheet		
	Prompt	*Enter save file name: ...*
	TYPE	bookcost
	PRESS	ENTER ↵

The next section explains how to handle some difficulties you might encounter with the INPUT menus or with your columns of data. After that, we will consider a different way to get data into your StatPad worksheet, namely, by retrieving data ranges from another Lotus 1-2-3 worksheet.

C Troubleshooting the Input command

(1) If you try to enter a letter instead of a number, or a number with a space in it (e.g. "4 5"), StatPad will not enter these in your column of data, but will ask if you are done entering data or not. You may SELECT NO, and continue with data entry.

(2) If you make a numerical mistake in entering a data value, fix it in 1-2-3 (you cannot correct it within INPUT). Here is how to do this:

(a) Finish entering your data with INPUT, then SELECT STOP to return to 1-2-3 and put in the correct value(s). You may then return to StatPad by HOLDING ALT while you PRESS S.

Note that you can change the values of the cells of the existing range, but if you add any additional data values you will need to rename your range since it is already defined by the number of cells you filled with the INPUT function. Your data set may be renamed by using 1-2-3's /RANGE NAME CREATE command, giving the range name, and then using the arrow keys to adjust the highlighted range appropriately.[10]

D Using data from another Lotus worksheet

Sometimes you need a data set which is on another 1-2-3 worksheet. In this section we describe how to import such data into your StatPad worksheet.

The data for the Tutorial exercises is on your original StatPad disk, which contains several worksheets with data sets applicable to the various statistical problems we will work through in the tutorial. If you have not already done so, copy them to where 1-2-3 looks for worksheet files. The filenames all begin with "data".

---

[10] When you use 1-2-3's /RANGE NAME CREATE command to change a range name that already exists, any formulas (even in other cells) that use this range name will change so that they operate on the new range. If you are in this situation and do not want to change these formulas, you may first use the /RANGE NAME DELETE command to delete the range name before you define it using /RANGE NAME CREATE.

Directions for copying these data sets onto your directory or disk:

If you have a hard disk, change directories to your 1-2-3 files directory. Then put your StatPad disk in the A drive and:

Hard disk:

To copy data files.	**TYPE**	Copy a:data*.wk1
	PRESS	[ENTER ←]

If you have 2 floppy disk drives but no hard disk, put your StatPad disk in the A drive, your worksheet files disk in the B drive, and:

Floppy disks:

To copy data files.	**TYPE**	Copy a:data*.wk1 b:
	PRESS	[ENTER ←]

The data you will use in this exercise is found on the worksheet, *datafood.wk1*. The column of data is labeled "Foodcost" and the first number is in cell A2.

Here is a summary of the steps you will take in transferring the column of data from *datafood.wk1* to your final worksheet, which will be called *foodcost.wk1*:

(1) Retrieve StatPad (or a worksheet containing StatPad), but do not activate it yet (or choose STOP if StatPad is already active). The transfer of data uses 1-2-3 menus, not StatPad menus.

(2) Bring the data into a free part of this worksheet using /FILE COMBINE COPY.

(3) You may name the range either at this point, or else wait to do this when StatPad asks for a range name for a column of data. The steps are worked out in Section 7.3 (F). We will wait and define the range in StatPad the first time we need to use this data set, in Section 7.4 (G, H).

(4) Label it on your worksheet (if it is not already labelled) for convenient recognition.

(5) Save the worksheet, naming it *foodcost.wk1*. This will then be a worksheet containing StatPad and the univariate one-sample data set, to be used in the Section 7.4 of the tutorial.

Here are the directions:

Retrieve StatPad	**SELECT**	/ FILE RETRIEVE
	SELECT	Bookcost.wk1 (if you did the INPUT tutorial) **OR** StatPad.wk1
Move to free part of worksheet	**PRESS**	Tab →|
Bring in data file	**SELECT**	/ FILE
	SELECT	COMBINE
	SELECT	COPY
	SELECT	ENTIRE-FILE
	Prompt	*Name of file to combine: ...*
	SELECT	DATAFOOD.WK1
Save and rename file	**SELECT**	/ FILE SAVE
	Prompt	*Enter save file name:...*
	TYPE	Foodcost
	PRESS	ENTER ←
	Prompt	*Cancel Replace*
	SELECT	REPLACE

You now have the univariate one-sample data set, Foodcost, on the worksheet with StatPad. If you did the INPUT tutorial, the data set Bookcost is on the same worksheet, now saved as *foodcost.wk1*. Both data sets will be used in Section 7.4, statistical analysis with univariate one-sample data.

Note: be careful using the /FILE COMBINE COPY ENTIRE-FILE command to bring in a very large worksheet or a worksheet that already contains StatPad. You might use /FILE COMBINE COPY NAMED/SPECIFIED-RANGE instead to bring in a smaller collection of cells.

E   Using data from a text file

If your data set is in a text file, as might be created by a word processor using its "save unformatted" command, you might try the /FILE IMPORT NUMBERS command to bring them into the worksheet.

If text is interspersed with numbers, then the /FILE IMPORT TEXT command combined with the advanced /DATA PARSE command may be useful.[11]

Please see your Lotus manual or systems expert for further details.

F   Naming your column of data in StatPad

Sometimes you might not get around to naming and defining a range until you're ready to use it. When this occurs, you can give it a range name without leaving the StatPad menu sequence you were working in. When you are in StatPad and are asked *"range name for a column of data?"*, just type in the range name you want for the data and then follow the directions which will guide you in pointing to the data range. Here are the prompts you will encounter the first time you ask StatPad to analyze a range name that has not yet been named:

Name Asked For	*Prompt*	*Range name for column of data*
	TYPE	Sales (or other appropriate range name for your data)
Finding Range is Unnamed	*Prompt*	*Range 'sales' does not exist; please hit ENTER*
	PRESS	(ENTER ←)
Choices	*Menu*	*Point Change Stop*

Here is the explanation of the choices on this new menu:

Point	Select this one to point to your data to name this range
Change	Select this one to specify a different range name
Stop	Stop statistical analysis, return to ready mode

---

[11] If you use Lotus's /DATA PARSE command to create a Format-Line, 1-2-3 will automatically insert a new row into the worksheet. When you are done, please use /WORKSHEET DELETE ROW to eliminate this extra row. This is the exception to the rule "never delete rows or columns when you use StatPad". It is necessary here in order to eliminate the inserted row that would otherwise cause trouble.

**Naming
Data Set**

SELECT *Point*

Prompt *Sales Enter range: ...*

The prompt shows the range name you chose and asks you to enter the range. Use the arrow keys to move to the first cell of your range (the first number at the top of your column of data). Then indicate the cells of the range with the following key sequence.

**MOVE
CURSOR** Use arrow keys to move cursor to first cell of column of data

PRESS Period $\boxed{.}$

PRESS $\boxed{\text{End}}$

PRESS Down $\boxed{\downarrow}$

PRESS $\boxed{\text{ENTER} \leftarrow}$

You now have a named range. You may use this name in answer to StatPad prompts. After the range is named you are returned to the StatPad menu you had been working in.

7.4 Statistical analysis of univariate one-sample data

A Appropriate data

Requires a single column of numbers. For example, salaries of a sample of employees.

Univariate, bivariate and multivariate data: Data sets are measurements of individual items called **elementary units**; these could be people or vegetables or ingots. The characteristic measured is called a variable. Depending on how many variables are measured for each elementary unit, the data set is considered to be **univariate** (one variable is measured), **bivariate** (two variables are measured for each elementary unit), or **multivariate** (more than two).

Characteristics of samples for univariate one-sample analyses: The way a data set was formed can make it suitable or unsuitable for some of these procedures:

Two of the procedures for univariate one-sample data require that the data be a random sample drawn from a large population because they involve statistical inference about the population. These procedures are: interval (confidence interval) and test (hypothesis test).

More information about the samples used in this tutorial exercise: Your worksheet *foodcost.wk1* contains two univariate data sets. Here is some information about these data sets:

The data set *bookcost* is a random sample drawn from a larger list of average retail prices of newly published hardcover books listed by subject.[12] The actual data is presented in the table below. The subjects (or fields of interest) are the elementary units, and the cost is the variable. The rounded values for this data set are also on your StatPad disk in the file *databook.wk1*.

New Books and New Editions Published, and Imports, By Subject.	
Average Retail Prices: 1986	
Agriculture	39
Art	35
Biography	23
Business	31
General reference	39
Home Economics	19
Juvenile	11
Language	33
Medicine	50
Poetry and Drama	25
Religion	22
Technology	55

The data set *foodcost* which was imported from another worksheet in Section 7.3 (D) is from a hypothetical sample of 35 households randomly selected in a given city. The values listed are the dollar amounts spent on food by these consumers during the previous week. A single variable has been measured, so we are dealing with a univariate data set. The elementary units are the individual families, and the variable is each family's weekly outlay for food. The values for this data set are on your StatPad disk in the file *datafood.wk1*.

---

[12] Data are from Table No. 383 of U.S. Bureau of the Census, *Statistical Abstract of the United States*: 1989 (109th edition.) Washington, DC, 1989

Dollar amounts spent on food by randomly selected consumers.		
$54.50	15.92	32.50
35.50	22.83	47.00
58.45	21.19	28.50
92.00	23.50	22.00
39.00	34.67	22.00
50.89	34.00	77.00
136.50	106.00	81.50
22.17	29.00	61.70
32.00	65.00	11.50
29.07	57.00	18.36
52.00	60.26	21.50
44.35	25.50	

B StatPad menus

Below is the menu chart showing the commands you will be using. The fourth menu line lists the statistical graphs you will be generating and procedures you will be performing.

Univariate
One-Sample
Data: Menu
Command Chart

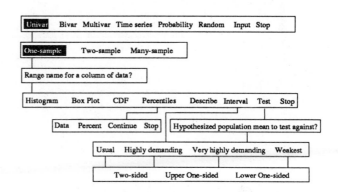

We assume that you are in 1-2-3 and have a worksheet with StatPad and either the data from Sections 7.3 (B) and (D), as saved in *foodcost.wk1*, or with some of your own data already entered. If not, please use Section 7.2 to bring in StatPad, and Section 7.3 to bring in your data, or substitute data of your own. Here's how to retrieve your worksheet file into 1-2-3:

Bring in a worksheet with	**SELECT**	/ FILE
data and StatPad	**SELECT**	RETRIEVE
	SELECT	FOODCOST.WK1

Your screen should show the two data sets, *bookcost* and *foodcost* in the two columns at the left of the screen. Move around the worksheet if necessary (perhaps Home, then tab →).

Activate StatPad	**HOLD** ALT while you **PRESS** S

This brings up the StatPad opening menu. The selection UNIVAR (abbreviation for "univariate data") is the first menu choice, and the cursor is on it. Your screen will look like this:

Univariate
One-Sample:
Opening Menu,
Book & Food
Cost Data

```
J2: (F2) 54.5                                                      MENU
Univar  Bivar  Multivar  Time series  Probability  Random  Input  Stop
Analyze one kind of measurement: one-sample, two-sample or many-sample
         I        J        K        L        M        N        O        P
  1   bookcost foodcost
  2       39     54.50
  3       35     35.50
  4       23     58.45
  5       31     92.00
  6       39     39.00
  7       19     50.89
  8       11    136.50
  9       33     22.17
 10       50     32.00
 11       25     29.07
 12       22     52.00
 13       55     44.35
 14             15.92
 15             22.83
 16             21.19
 17             23.50
 18             34.67
 19             34.00
 20            106.00
```

The opening cursor is on Univar:

Choose Univariate	**SELECT**	UNIVAR
Data	**PRESS**	ENTER ←

The second StatPad menu comes up. You have the choice of one-sample, two-samples or many samples. Although you have two data sets, each one is a single sample of values for the elementary unit it describes and should be analyzed one at a time. So, you want to choose ONE-SAMPLE. It is the first menu choice and the cursor is on it, so:

Univariate
One-Sample: Second
Menu

```
J2: (F2) 54.5                                                          MENU
One-sample  Two-sample  Many-sample  Stop
Histogram, summary, confidence interval, hypothesis test
        I      J      K      L      M      N      O      P
 1  bookcost foodcost
 2      39    54.50
 3      35    35.50
 4      23    58.45
 5      31    92.00
 6      39    39.00
 7      19    50.89
 8      11   136.50
 9      33    22.17
10      50    32.00
11      25    29.07
12      22    52.00
13      55    44.35
14            15.92
15            22.83
16            21.19
17            23.50
18            34.67
19            34.00
20           106.00
```

The cursor is on One-sample:

Select   **PRESS**   ⌜ENTER ←⌝
One-sample

You are now asked for the range name for a column of data

Specify Range   **TYPE**   bookcost
Name for Data
                       PRESS   ⌜ENTER ←⌝

Univariate
One-Sample:
Prompt for
Range Name

```
J2: (F2) 54.5                                                          MENU
range name for a column of data? bookcost
        I      J      K      L      M      N      O      P
 1  bookcost foodcost
 2      39    54.50
 3      35    35.50
 4      23    58.45
```

The next menu lists the procedures (graphs and computations) which can be performed with this kind of data. Here is your screen with the cursor highlighting "Histogram":

Univariate
One-Sample:
Statistical Procedures
Menu.

```
J2: (F2) 54.5                                                    MENU
Histogram  Box plot  CDF  Percentiles  Describe  Interval  Test  Stop
Display the data in frequency form
        I        J        K        L        M        N        O        P
1  bookcost foodcost
2        39    54.50
3        35    35.50
4        23    58.45
```

C Histogram

We assume you are in StatPad with your data if not, please use Section 7.3 to bring in your data.

If you are not looking at the menu that starts "Histogram....", Activate StatPad with (ALT) (S), and Select *Univariate* and *One-sample*, and enter your range name at the prompt.

Now you can draw a histogram of the *bookcost* data:

Draw   **SELECT**   Histogram
Histogram

Univariate,
One-Sample:
Histogram of
Average Cost of
Hardcover Books.

The table of data values for *bookcost* is in section 7.4(A). You can compare the histogram with the data values there. When you are done examining the histogram, return to StatPad by pressing (ENTER ↵).

Exit from Histogram	**PRESS**	ENTER ↵

You now see the menu that follows all graphs: **Continue Print Stop**

> If you choose **continue,** you will be returned to the Statistical Procedures menu in StatPad

> If you choose **print,** StatPad will let you to save your histogram as a .PIC file (in the same directory as your 1-2-3 files) for printing later, e.g., with Lotus Printgraph.

> If you choose "**Stop**" you are returned to your 1-2-3 worksheet.

Save the histogram for printing later.

Save histogram for printing later	**SELECT**	Print
	Prompt	*Name to save graph under (8 characters or less, no period)?*

You are now asked for a name to save the graph under. Use "bookhist". The .PIC extension will be added automatically.

Give Name for Graph	**TYPE**	bookhist
	PRESS	ENTER ↵

When you press the ENTER ↵, it ends the saving-for-printing procedure and StatPad brings you back again to the statistical procedures menu.

Drawings of the box plot and the cumulative distribution function of bookcost are done by the same method used for making its histogram.

D Box plot

The box plot is a diagrammatic representation of the five-number summary, which consists of the median, the quartiles and the extremes of the distribution. The quartiles are the sides of the box; the median is a line drawn within the box. Lines extending from the box terminate at the highest and lowest value of the distribution.

We assume you are in StatPad with your data if not, please use Section 7.3 to bring in your data.

If you are not looking at the menu that starts "Histogram....", please activate StatPad with (ALT) (S), and Select *Univariate* and *One-sample*, and enter your range name at the prompt.

Now you can draw a box-plot of the *bookcost* data:

Draw Box Plot   **SELECT**   Box Plot

You are asked to wait while StatPad draws the box plot, and then your screen will look like this:

Univariate
One-Sample:
Box-Plot,
Average Cost
of Hardcover
Books

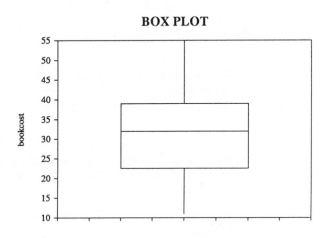

To leave the box plot you press (ENTER ←), as you did for the histogram.

Exit Box Plot   **PRESS**   (ENTER ←)

You again have the menu which gives you the choice of saving your graph for printing later or continuing with the analysis. This time continue:

Return   to   **SELECT**   Continue
Statistical
Procedures
Menu

E Cumulative distribution function

The cumulative distribution function presents a stepwise display which links each data value with the percentage of data values which are less than or greater than that value.

We assume you are in StatPad with your data if not, please use Section 7.3 to bring in your data.

If you are not looking at the menu that starts "Histogram....", please activate StatPad with ALT S, and Select *Univariate* and *One-sample*, and enter your range name at the prompt.

Now you can draw the cumulative distribution function of the *bookcost* data:

This time, from the statistical analyses menu select CDF, the cumulative distribution function.

Draw the cumulative distribution function

SELECT   CDF

Univariate
One-Sample:
Cumulative
Distribution
Function, Book Cost
Data

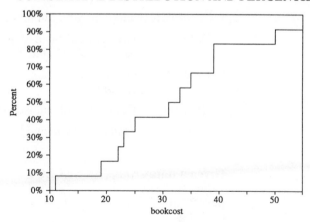

CUMULATIVE DISTRIBUTION AND PERCENTILES

Exit CDF

PRESS   ENTER ↵

SELECT   Continue

You are back in the StatPad analysis menu. Next, we will determine some percentiles.

F Percentiles

A percentile divides a data set into two groups of a desired size, where one group contains the data values larger than the percentile and the other group includes those that are smaller than the percentile. For example, a salary in the 75th percentile has 25% of salaries larger than itself, and 75% smaller.

With StatPad's Percentile function you can evaluate both the percentile of a given data value, and also the numerical value which corresponds to a given percentile.

We assume you are in StatPad with your data if not, please use Section 7.3 to bring in your data.

If you are not looking at the menu that starts "Histogram....", please activate StatPad with (ALT) (S), and Select *Univariate* and *One-sample*, and enter your range name at the prompt.

PERCENTILES is the fourth choice on the statistical procedures menu line.

Select Percentiles	**TYPE**	P

You now have the menu: *Data Percent Continue Stop*

Here are the explanations of your choices in this menu:

Data:	Given a data value (or a number in the same measurement units as the data set), find the percent that gives its percentile ranking
Percent:	Given a percentage, find the percentile (data value) at that ranking
Continue:	Continue with statistical analysis for this data set
Stop:	Stop statistical analysis, return to ready mode

Given a data value, find the percentile ranking	**SELECT**	Data

You are asked to *Please type number for which you want a percentile ranking:* You can choose any number, we used 31 in this example:

Indicate a number	**TYPE**	31
	PRESS	⎡ ENTER ↵ ⎤

Univariate
One-Sample:
Percentile,
Data Value
Menu

```
J2: (P2) 54.5                                                    READY
Please type number for which you want a percentile ranking: 31

        I      J      K      L      M      N      O      P
1   bookcost foodcost
2       39    54.50
3       35    35.50
4       23    58.45
```

Now you will see the message **"Results here?"**. Note that the cursor is now larger.
It has the footprint that will be occupied by the result when it is placed on your
screen. Any values which are covered by the large cursor will be erased in the
process. Move the large cursor with the arrow keys so that it doesn't overlap your
data ranges, and is where you want the results to be placed.

Position cursor	**PRESS**	ARROW KEYS as needed
and place result		
	PRESS	[ENTER ↵]

Univariate
One-Sample:
Percentile, Percentile
Ranking from Data
Value

```
L4:                                                              MENU
Data  Percent  Stop
Given a data value, find its percentile ranking
        I      J      K      L      M      N      O      P
1   bookcost foodcost         for bookcost:
2       39    54.50              31  is the
3       35    35.50              50  th percentile
4       23    58.45
```

You see that 31 is the 50th percentile. After your results are placed into the
worksheet you are returned to the percentile menu. Choose "percent" this time.

Given a	**SELECT**	Percent
percentage,		
find the data		
value		

Now you are asked *Percent (e.g. '15' for 15%) you would like the percentile for?*
We used 75 in the example. You can use any number interesting to this data set.

Provide a	**TYPE**	75
percent		
	PRESS	[ENTER ↵]

You again get the message **"Results here?"**

Position cursor   **PRESS**   ARROW KEYS as appropriate
and place result

                           PRESS   [ENTER ←]

Your screen will look something like this:

Univariate
One-Sample:
Percentile, Data
Value from
Percentage

```
L8:                                                                    MENU
Data  Percent  Continue  Stop
Given a percentage, find the percentile (data value) at that ranking
        I       J         K        L        M          N        O        P
1   BOOKCOST FOODCOST           for bookcost:
2        39     54.50                31  is the
3        35     35.50                50  th percentile
4        23     58.45
5        31     92.00           for bookcost:
6        39     39.00                75 th percentile
7        19     50.89                is       39
8        11    136.50
```

You are now back in the menu "Data Percent Continue Stop". Select "Continue" to return to the statistical results menu and continue with univariate one-sample analysis.

G Describe

The DESCRIBE command presents a table of summaries, including measures of center and variability to describe the data set. Only one of these measures, the *standard error of the average*, requires that the data set be a random sample from a large and relatively unknown population. The other measures in this display are applicable as descriptions of any list of numbers.

We assume you are in StatPad with your data if not, please use Section 7.3 to bring in your data.

If you are not looking at the menu that starts "Histogram....", please activate StatPad with [ALT] [S], and Select *Univariate* and *One-sample*, and enter your range name at the prompt.

Now you can display a description of the *bookcost* data:

Describe the   **SELECT**   Describe
Data:
Bookcost

You will see the message **"Results here?"**. Note that the cursor is now larger. It has the footprint that will be occupied by the result when it is placed on your screen. Any values which are covered by the cursor will be erased in the process. Move the cursor with the arrow keys so that it doesn't overlap your data ranges, and is where you want the results to be placed.

Position cursor   **PRESS**   ARROW KEYS as appropriate
for result

                 PRESS   `ENTER ←`

Univariate
One-Sample:
Descriptive summary
of Average Cost of
Hardcover Books

```
Summary of bookcost
Average:            31.83333
Trimmed average:     30.875
Median:                  32
Std. deviation:    12.79796
IQR:                   16.5
Range:                   44
Largest:                 55
Upper quartile:          39
Lower quartile:        22.5
Smallest:                11
Std. error of avg:3.694453
Number of cases:         12
```

The following illustration is included to show how your screen might look after the DESCRIBE results are put on the computer screen with the data sets and the percentile results.

Univariate One
Sample: Description
and Percentiles,
Average Cost of
Hardcover Books

```
L7:                                                                    MENU
Histogram  Box plot  CDF  Percentiles  Describe  Interval  Test  Stop
Display the data in frequency form
         I       J       K      L       M       N       O       P
1    bookcost foodcost         for bookcost:
2        39    54.50               31  is the
3        35    35.50               50 th percentile
4        23    58.45         for bookcost:
5        31    92.00               75 th percentile
6        39    39.00               is       39
7        19    50.89
8        11   136.50         Summary of bookcost
9        33    22.17         Average:        31.83333
10       50    32.00         Trimmed average:  30.875
11       25    29.07         Median:               32
12       22    52.00         Std. deviation: 12.79796
13       55    44.35         IQR:                16.5
14             15.92         Range:                44
15             22.83         Largest:              55
16             21.19         Upper quartile:       39
17             23.50         Lower quartile:     22.5
18             34.67         Smallest:             11
19             34.00         Std. error of avg:3.694453
20            106.00         Number of cases:      12
```

<u>Changing to a new data set in StatPad and naming and defining the set.</u>

The next statistical procedures will require a random sample from a large population, so we will use the data set *foodcost*. (See Section 7.4 A). One way to change data sets is to select STOP to leave StatPad, then reactivate it with `ALT` `S`, select UNIVAR and ONE-SAMPLE, and provide the new range name. Another way is to stay in StatPad and use the `Esc` key to escape to the previous menu level:

1.   Press escape to go to previous menu.

2.   Select One-sample.

3.   Type in the range name for the new data set.

4.   Follow the prompts (if necessary) to name this range.

The steps for this are stated below:

You are starting from the Statistical procedures menu ("Histogram ..."):

To change data sets	**PRESS**	Esc
	Menu	*One-sample Two-sample Many-sample* *Stop*
	SELECT	One-sample
	Prompt	*range name for a column of data?*
	TYPE	foodcost

The data set *foodcost* was imported from another worksheet in Section 7.3 (D), "Using data from another Lotus worksheet". At that time we said that we would name it when we needed to use it, which is now.

Naming a data set in StatPad	*Prompt*	*Range 'foodcost' does not exist; please hit ENTER*
	PRESS	ENTER ⏎
	Prompt	*Point Change Stop*

Here is the explanation of the choices on this new menu:

Point   Select this one to point to your data to name this range

Change   Select this one to specify a different range name

Stop   Stop statistical analysis, return to ready mode

Continued: Naming data set in StatPad	**SELECT**	Point
	Prompt	*foodcost Enter range: ...*
	PRESS	ARROW KEYS to move cursor to first cell of column of data
	PRESS	Period ⟨.⟩
	PRESS	End
	PRESS	Down ⬇
	PRESS	ENTER ⏎

You are now returned to the Statistical Procedures menu.

H   Confidence interval

The confidence interval is computed so that there is a designated probability, (typically 95%) that the unknown population mean can be found within its bounds. The calculation   can be made for a one-sided as well as the usual two-sided confidence intervals.

The data used for this procedure must be a random sample from a population with a relatively normal distribution. We will be using the data range *foodcost*, which satisfies these conditions.

We assume you are in StatPad with your data. If not, please use Section 7.3 to bring in your data. We will be using *foodcost* for our data set. It can be found as the file *datafood.wk1*.

If you are not looking at the menu that starts "Histogram....", Activate StatPad with (ALT) (S), and Select *Univariate* and *One-sample*, and enter your range name at the prompt. You may refer to Section 7.3 (F) for further directions if you need to provide a range name and point to your data.

You now have *foodcost* as a named range. The Statistical Procedures menu (beginning with "Histogram...") of the Univariate One-sample menu sequence is on your screen. INTERVAL is the sixth procedure listed on this menu. You will determine the 95% confidence interval for the unknown population mean, based on the sample data in the data set, *foodcost*.

Begin	**SELECT**	Interval
Confidence		
Interval		
Computation		

The menu that comes up asks you to specify the level of confidence you would like for your result. The choices are:

Usual	95% certain that the population mean falls within the calculated confidence interval
Highly demanding	99% certain that the population mean falls within the calculated confidence interval
Very highly demanding	99.9% certain ...
Weakest	90% certain ...

Choose	**95%**	**SELECT**	Usual
certainty			

The next menu gives you the choice of a two-sided or a one-sided confidence interval.

Two-sided	The USUAL interval, extending equally to both sides of the estimate
Upper one-sided	Extending indefinitely at the UPPER end, bounded only on the other side
Lower one-sided	Extending indefinitely at the LOWER end, bounded only on the other side
Stop	Stop statistical analysis, return to ready mode

For now, select the two-sided confidence interval:

Choose the two-sided interval	**SELECT**	Two-sided

Now you are asked **"Results here?"** Move the cursor to a position where it won't erase your data ranges or other cell contents which you want to save, when it places the results.

Position cursor for result	**PRESS**	**ARROW KEYS as needed**
	PRESS	ENTER ←

The illustration that follows shows the 95% two-sided confidence level for *foodcost* together with the description of that data set.

Univariate
One-Sample:
Confidence Interval,
Food Cost Data

```
L7:                                                                    MENU
Histogram  Box plot  CDF  Percentiles  Describe  Interval  Test  Stop
Display the data in frequency form
        J         K         L         M         N        O         P         Q
 1   foodcost         Confidence interval
 2     54.50            for foodcost:
 3     35.50          We are 95% sure that
 4     58.45          the population mean is
 5     92.00          between        35.16691
 6     39.00                  and    54.25365
 7     50.89
 8    136.50                          Summary of foodcost
 9     22.17                          Average:           44.71028
10     32.00                          Trimmed average:      40.07
11     29.07                          Median:               34.67
12     52.00                          Std. deviation:    27.78159
13     44.35                          IQR:                  34.56
14     15.92                          Range:                  125
15     22.83                          Largest:              136.5
16     21.19                          Upper quartile:      57.725
17     23.50                          Lower quartile:      23.165
18     34.67                          Smallest:              11.5
19     34.00                          Std. error of avg:4.695946
20    106.00                          Number of cases:         35
```

You might want to take the time now to evaluate confidence intervals for other levels of confidence, as well as one-sided upper and lower confidence intervals. You can easily do that on your own.

StatPad returns you to the statistical procedures menu. Since the next exercise, hypothesis testing, uses the same data set you are all set to continue.

I Hypothesis test

In brief, you are testing the population mean against a hypothesized population mean which you specify. The result of the test lets you know whether or not you should accept the null hypothesis that the true population mean equals the value you tested it against. You may also think of the results as telling you whether the sample average is significantly different from the hypothesized population mean, or if the difference could reasonably be due to random chance alone.

The assumptions made in order for the *t*-test to be valid are that the data represent a random sample from a fairly normally distributed population. To satisfy these assumptions we are using the data set, *datafood.wk1*. A description of this data set can be found in Section 7.4 (A).

We assume you are in StatPad with your data if not, please use Section 7.3 to bring in your data. The data we will be using can be found on the file *datafood.wk1*.

If you are not looking at the menu that starts "Histogram....", please activate StatPad with (ALT) (S), and Select *Univariate* and *One-sample*, and enter your range name at the prompt. TEST is the seventh procedure listed on this menu line.

Begin	**SELECT**	Test
Hypothesis		
Testing		

The next menu that comes up reads: *Hypothesized population mean to test against?* We are using the value 45.

Specify	**TYPE**	45
hypothesized		
population		
mean		

The menu that now appears gives you choices of the test level you would like to use:

Usual	The standard; incorrectly decides significance only 1
(5% level)	time in 20.

Highly Demanding (1% level)	More demanding than the standard; wrong only 1 time in 100.
Very Highly Demanding (0.1% level)	Much more highly demanding than the standard; wrong only 1 in 1,000.
Weakest (10% level)	Weaker than the standard; wrong 1 in 10 on average.

Choose significance level	SELECT	Usual

Your next menu choice is between a two-sided test or an upper- or lower- one-sided test. Here are the explanations of the entries on this menu:

Two-sided	The USUAL, when both ABOVE AND BELOW hypothesized value are relevant.
Upper one-sided	Used when only ABOVE the hypothesized value is relevant.
Lower one-sided	Used when only BELOW the hypothesized value is relevant.
Stop	Stop statistical analysis, return to ready mode

Since both sides of this distribution are relevant, choose two-sided.

Choose one- or two-sided	SELECT	Two-sided

Now you are asked "**Results here?**" Move the cursor to a position where it doesn't encroach on your data ranges or other cell contents which you want to save.

Position cursor for result	PRESS	**ARROW KEYS as needed**
	PRESS	(ENTER ↵)

You can repeat the *t*-test using 30 for your hypothesized population mean.

The figure below shows the two *t*-tests for the data set, *foodcost*, with hypothesized population means which give an acceptance and a rejection of the null hypothesis. The description of this data set is also included.

Univariate
One-Sample:
Hypothesis tests,
Food Cost Data

```
Q19:                                                              MENU
Histogram  Box plot  CDF  Percentiles  Describe  Interval  Test  Stop
Display the data in frequency form
        J        K         L          M        N      O       P          Q
1    foodcost  Testing foodcost                   Summary of foodcost
2       54.50  at the 5% level                    Average:        44.71028
3       35.50  Sample mean:    44.71028           Trimmed average:   40.07
4       58.45  IS NOT                             Median:           34.67
5       92.00  significantly different            Std. deviation:  27.78159
6       39.00  from the population mean           IQR:              34.56
7       50.89  hypothesized as:      45           Range:             125
8      136.50  (t-test)                           Largest:         136.5
9       22.17  t:     -0.06169                    Upper quartile:  57.725
10      32.00  df:         34                     Lower quartile:  23.165
11      29.07            Testing foodcost         Smallest:         11.5
12      52.00            at the 5% level          Std. error of avg:4.695946
13      44.35            Sample mean:    44.71028 Number of cases:    35
14      15.92            IS
15      22.83            significantly different
16      21.19            from the population mean
17      23.50            hypothesized as:    30
18      34.67            (t-test)
19      34.00            t:     3.132549
20     106.00            df:         34
```

You might try other significance levels, and one-sided analyses using the *t*-test on your own.

7.5 Statistical analysis of univariate two-sample data

A Appropriate data

Requires two columns of numbers in the same measurement units to be compared. For example, salaries for two groups of employees.

A data set is considered to be **univariate** if only one variable is measured for each elementary unit of each sample.

Characteristics of samples for univariate two-sample analyses: one variable is measured for two samples. It is not necessary that these samples contain the same number of values, only that they are measured in the same units. However, when they *do* have the same number of data values, and there is a natural pairing, you should run a paired analysis.

In order for the standard error, confidence intervals, and hypothesis tests to be statistically valid, your data set should be a random sample from a large population.

Information about the data used in this tutorial exercise: Two data sets are used in this section: The phone data set consists of two unpaired samples. The diet data set is made up of paired samples.

A software company is wondering whether it needs to increase the number of employees in its telephone answering division. Specifically, they would like to know whether more time is required to service technical assistance phone calls than is needed with general assistance. The table below shows a hypothetical random sample of the time, measured in minutes, required for these two types of telephone calls. The elementary unit is the phone call. The variable for both samples is the time in minutes for the individual calls. Note that the two samples contain different numbers of data values, and are both measured in the same units. The worksheet file *dataphon.wk1* contains the two lists of data values for the (unpaired) analyses of the telephone data.

Unpaired data: Telephone call durations.

TIME REQUIRED TO HANDLE TELEPHONE CALLS (MINUTES)	
General Assistance	Technical Assistance
7.99	15.29
19.44	2.66
18.70	11.70
1.43	9.23
4.70	0.95
10.17	17.89
1.39	2.13
0.96	8.35
1.04	7.83
14.57	1.05
15.74	8.50
1.11	11.84
11.89	2.95
10.35	1.54
5.38	26.21
3.47	17.90
4.56	
5.99	
9.14	
2.83	

A company which runs a weight loss program is interested in whether the changes found in the weight of its clients is a real change and not reflecting random changes alone. They have weights of 16 clients measured before and after a 4-week program, and want to analyze these to see whether there is a statistically significant difference. Here we have paired data for a random sample of clients. Note that both columns are measured in the same units, and contain the same number of data values. The variable for both of these samples is the weight of the subject. The elementary unit is the subject, who supplies both a before and an after weight. The worksheet file *datadiet.wk1* has the numerical values for the analyses of paired data. These worksheets are on your original StatPad disk.

Paired data: Weight of dieters, before and after 4-week diet.

WEIGHT BEFORE AND AFTER 4-WEEK DIET (Pounds)	
Before	After

178	158
124	132
104	98
115	95
167	152
212	215
165	165
151	130
133	130
217	219
118	111
135	126
215	224
162	164
213	196
178	161

B StatPad menus

Below is the menu chart showing the commands for both the two- and the many-sample univariate menus. We will be using only the two-sample commands.

Univariate
Two-Sample
Data: Menu
Command
Chart

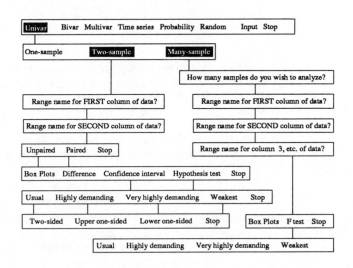

Data worksheets for the examples in the tutorial (except for the INPUT command) are included on your original StatPad disk. The worksheets have names which begin with "data" and end with an abbreviation of the subject matter of the elementary units of the data set. They contain columns of numbers only, no text.

The worksheets needed for the univariate two-sample tutorial are titled *dataphon.wk1* and *datadiet.wk1*. Check that these two worksheets are in your 1-2-3 file directory. You will be importing them on your current worksheet for the statistical analysis of univariate two-sample data.

Import your data onto a worksheet which already has StatPad on it. Follow the method given in Section 7.3 (D), "Importing data from another Lotus worksheet". The two columns of data on *dataphon.wk1* are "general" on the left, and "technical" on the right. Then activate StatPad. A description of this data set, and a table of the values is in Section 7.5 (A)

Activate StatPad.	**HOLD** (ALT)	while you **PRESS** (S)
Access to Univariate	**SELECT**	Univar
Two-sample Procedures	**SELECT**	Two-sample
Menu	*Prompt*	*range name for FIRST column of data?*
	TYPE	general

If you didn't name your range before, StatPad calls attention to this and gives you choices of what to do about it. Please refer to Section 7.3(F) of this tutorial, if necessary, to define your range name without leaving StatPad.

StatPad now asks you to enter the range name for the second column of data; please do this, pointing to the range if necessary. When this is completed, if your columns have equal numbers of data values, you will be at the menu *Paired Unpaired Stop*. You will arrive directly at the statistical procedures menu if they have unequal numbers of data points. StatPad bypasses the Paired menu in this case, since the two samples of *dataphon* have unequal numbers of data values.

Continued: Access to Statistical	*Prompt*	*range name for SECOND column of data?*
Procedures Menu	**TYPE**	technical
	PRESS	(ENTER ↵)

This brings you to the statistical procedures menu for unpaired univariate two-sample data. It lists: *Box plots Difference Confidence interval Hypothesis test Stop*. We start from here to carry out the analysis of these samples.

Repeat the above procedures using the paired samples from the worksheet file *datadiet.wk1*. It is a good idea to save the worksheet with these two data sets on it. You might rename it as *Unitwo* for univariate two-sample analysis.

Rename and Save Worksheet	**SELECT**	Stop (to leave StatPad)
	SELECT	/ FILE SAVE
	TYPE	Unitwo
	PRESS	ENTER ←

C Box plot

A box plot is a picture of the five-number summary for a data set: the smallest and largest values, the upper and lower quartiles and the median. It is a good way to compare the measures of center and variability of two samples.

We assume you are in StatPad with your data if not, please use Sections 7.5 (A) and (B) for information about the data sets, and Section 7.3 to bring in your data.

If you are not looking at the menu that starts "Box Plots....", please activate StatPad with ALT S, and Select *Univariate* and *Two-sample*, then enter your range names at the prompt.

Now draw a box-plot of the *phone* data:

Draw Box Plots	**SELECT**	Box Plots
	Prompt	*Units of measurement? (e.g. dollars or mpg)*
	TYPE	Minutes

Your screen shows box plots for the random samples, *general* and *technical*.

Univariate
Two-Sample
Unpaired: Box
Plot, Telephone
Data

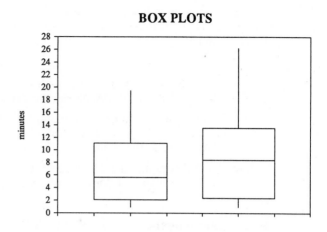

BOX PLOTS

| **Exit from Box** | **PRESS** | ENTER ← |
| Plot | | |

You now see the menu: **Continue   Print   Stop**

See Section 4.6 "Printing a Graph", which has directions for saving the graph to be printed later. For now, select "Continue", to return to the statistical procedures menu.

Return to	**SELECT**	Continue
Statistical		
Procedures		
Menu		

You may generate box plots for the diet data on your own. PRESS the ESCAPE key, then select *two-sample* from the menu *One-sample Two-sample Many-sample Stop*. At the prompt "Enter Range Name", type the range names for your diet data ranges, "before" and "after", and continue as above.

When you are through, you will be back at the statistical procedures menu where you can look at the average difference of the two samples of your data set.

D   Difference

This command computes the **difference** between the averages of your two columns of numbers and also reports the standard error of this difference (which is different depending on whether the analysis is paired or unpaired). The standard error is statistically appropriate only if your data sets arise as a random sample from a large population.

We assume you are in StatPad with your telephone and diet problems data also in the worksheet. If not, please use Section 7.3 to bring in your data.

If you are not looking at the menu that starts "Box Plots....", please activate StatPad with (ALT) (S), and Select *Univariate* and *Two-sample*, and enter your range names at the prompt.

First you will compute the difference for the unpaired telephone data, then follow with the diet samples, for comparison with paired data.

| **Determine the Difference between two samples** | **SELECT** | Difference |

You are asked "**Results here?**" Move the cursor to a position where it doesn't encroach on your data ranges or other cell contents which you want to keep.

| **Position cursor for result** | **PRESS** | **ARROW KEYS as appropriate** |
| | **PRESS** | (ENTER ←) |

Your result will look like this on the screen:

Univariate
Two-Sample
Unpaired: Difference,
Telephone Data

```
L11:                                                              MENU
Box plots  Difference  Confidence interval  Hypothesis test  Stop
Find the average difference between these two groups
        I       J       K       L       M       N       O       P
 1   Phone call times
 2   ------------------
 3   General  Technical
 4      7.99    15.29        The average difference:
 5     19.44     2.66           general
 6     18.70    11.70            minus
 7      1.43     9.23          tech
 8      4.70     0.95          is equal to:    -1.58375
 9     10.17    17.89          with (unpaired) standard
10      1.39     2.13            error         2.230029
11      0.96     8.35
```

You then returned to the procedures menu. You may continue with analysis of the paired diet data by pressing {Esc}, selecting *Two-sample* and entering the range names. From there the process is the same as above, except that you will get the menu line, **UNPAIRED PAIRED STOP** because the samples have the same numbers of data values. Select *Paired*.

The next figure shows the results of this analysis of the average difference for the data set, *datadiet*, with the ranges *before* and *after* treated as paired samples.

Univariate
Two-Sample Paired:
Difference, Dieter's
Weights

```
L9:                                                                    MENU
Box plots  Difference  Confidence interval  Hypothesis test  Stop
Find the average difference between these two groups
          I       J      K       L       M       N       O       P
1    WEIGHT BEFORE AND AFTER
2       4-WEEK DIET              The average difference:
3    Weight in pounds              Before
4    -------------------           minus
5     Before   After              After
6       178     158               is equal to:      6.9375
7       124     132               with (paired) standard
8       104      98                 error        2.590799
9       115      95
10      167     152
11      212     215
12      165     165
13      151     130
14      133     130
15      217     219
16      118     111
17      135     126
18      215     224
19      162     164
20      213     196
```

E Confidence interval

For comparing two samples of data, the usual confidence interval is for the *mean population difference* between the two groups.

We assume you are in StatPad with your telephone and diet problems data. If not, please use Section 7.3 to bring in these data sets.

If you are not looking at the menu that starts "Box Plots....", please activate StatPad with (ALT) (S), select *Univariate* and *Two-sample*, and enter your range names at the prompts.

Begin Confidence Interval Procedure	**SELECT**	Confidence interval

The next menu asks you to specify the level of confidence you need in your result (95%, 99%, 99.9%, or 90%).

Choose 95% confidence	**SELECT**	Usual

The next menu gives you the choice of a two-sided or a one-sided (upper or lower) confidence interval. For this exercise select the two-sided confidence interval:

Choose the usual interval	**SELECT**	Two-sided

Now you are asked "**Results here?**" Move the cursor to a position where it doesn't encroach on your data ranges or other cell contents which you want to save.

Position cursor for result	**PRESS**	**ARROW KEYS AS NEEDED**
	PRESS	ENTER ↵

Your screen will look like this:

Univariate
Two-Sample
Unpaired:
Confidence Interval,
Telephone Data

```
K3:                                                           MENU
Box plots  Difference  Confidence interval  Hypothesis test  Stop
Confidence interval for unknown population mean difference, from sample data
        I       J       K       L       M       N       O       P
1
2   General   Tech
3      7.99   15.29              Confidence interval for
4     19.44    2.66              general
5     18.70   11.70                minus
6      1.43    9.23              tech:
7      4.70    0.95                (unpaired)
8     10.17   17.89              We are 95% sure that
9      1.39    2.13              the population mean
10     0.96    8.35              difference is
11     1.04    7.83              between         -6.11574
12    14.57    1.05                      and     2.948243
13    15.74    8.50
```

If you already imported the data from *datadiet.wk1* you can repeat the confidence interval determination with the paired data in that data set. PRESS ESCAPE, select *Two-sample*, and provide the range names, then select PAIRED when the *PAIRED UNPAIRED STOP* menu appears. After that you follow the directions above to obtain the confidence interval.

The illustration below shows the confidence interval results for the paired diet data from the samples, *before* and *after*. The 95% confidence interval for the mean weight loss in the population from which these individuals were randomly selected extends from 1.42 to 12.46 pounds.

Univariate
Two-Sample
Paired Samples:
Confidence
Interval, Diet
Data

```
L12:                                                                    MENU
Box plots  Difference  Confidence interval  Hypothesis test  Stop
Confidence interval for unknown population mean difference, from sample data
        I        J        K        L        M        N        O        P
1   WEIGHT BEFORE AND AFTER
2      4-WEEK DIET                  Confidence interval for
3   Weight in pounds                   Before
4   --------------------               minus
5      Before    After                After:
6        178      158                  (paired)
7        124      132                We are 95% sure that
8        104       98                the population mean
9        115       95                difference is
10       167      152                between        1.415367
11       212      215                        and   12.45963
12       165      165
13       151      130
14       133      130
15       217      219
16       118      111
17       135      126
18       215      224
19       162      164
20       213      196
```

After these results appear on your screen, the StatPad procedures menu returns, and you are positioned to carry out hypothesis tests on your data set.

F Hypothesis test

The hypothesis test for two-sample data determines whether the difference in population mean values could reasonably be zero or not. You may also think of it as deciding whether the sample averages are significantly different from one another, or if such a difference could reasonably be due to random chance alone. Your data should be for a random sample from a population in order for statistical hypothesis testing to be valid.

We assume you are in StatPad with your telephone and diet problems data. If not, please use Section 7.3 to bring in your data.

If you are not looking at the menu that starts "Box Plots....", please activate StatPad with (ALT) (S), select *Univariate* and *Two-sample*, and enter your range names at the prompts.

The method for carrying out the hypothesis test is similar to that for the confidence interval, as can be seen from the menu chart in Section 7.5 (B).

Begin   **SELECT**   Hypothesis test
Hypothesis
Testing

The menu that comes up asks you to specify the level of significance you need in your result (

Usual (5% level)	The standard; incorrectly decides significance only 1 time in 20.
Highly Demanding (1% level)	More demanding than the standard; wrong only 1 time in 100.
Very Highly Demanding (0.1% level)	Much more highly demanding than the standard; wrong only 1 in 1,000.
Weakest (10% level)	Weaker than the standard; wrong 1 in 10 on average.

Choose the 5% level	**SELECT**	Usual

The new menu gives you the choice of a two-sided or a one-sided hypothesis test

Two-sided	The USUAL, when both ABOVE AND BELOW hypothesized value are relevant.
Upper one-sided	Used when only ABOVE the hypothesized value is relevant.
Lower one-sided	Used when only BELOW the hypothesized value is relevant.
Stop	Stop statistical analysis, return to ready mode

For this exercise select the two-sided confidence interval:

Choose the usual interval	**SELECT**	Two-sided

Now you are asked "**Results here?**" Move the cursor to a position where it doesn't encroach on your data ranges or other cell contents which you want to save.

Position cursor for result	**PRESS**	**ARROW KEYS as needed**
	PRESS	ENTER ↵

The hypothesis test of unpaired phone data shows that there is no significant difference in the average time of these general and technical calls.

Univariate
Two-Sample
Unpaired: Hypothesis
Test, Telephone Data

```
L13:                                                                    MENU
Box plots  Difference  Confidence interval  Hypothesis test  Stop
Test whether population means are identical (i.e. have zero difference)
         I        J         K         L         M         N        O        P
1
2    General   Tech
3      7.99    15.29              Testing at the 5% level:
4     19.44     2.66              The population mean for
5     18.70    11.70              general
6      1.43     9.23              IS NOT
7      4.70     0.95              significantly different
8     10.17    17.89              from the population mean
9      1.39     2.13              for tech
10     0.96     8.35              (unpaired t-test)
11     1.04     7.83              t:      -0.71019
12    14.57     1.05              df:         34
13    15.74     8.50
```

If you already imported the data from *datadiet.wk1* you can repeat the hypothesis test using this paired data set. PRESS ESCAPE, select *Two-sample*, enter the range names, and then select PAIRED when the *PAIRED UNPAIRED STOP* menu appears. After that follow the directions above to perform the hypothesis test.

The illustration below shows the results for the hypothesis test made on the diet data. The average weight loss is statistically significant.

Univariate
Two-Sample Paired:
Hypothesis Test, Diet
Data

```
L14:                                                                    MENU
Box plots  Difference  Confidence interval  Hypothesis test  Stop
Test whether population means are identical (i.e. have zero difference)
         I        J         K         L         M         N        O        P
1    Weight in pounds
2    --------------------
3    Before    After
4      178      158              Testing at the 5% level:
5      124      132              The population mean for
6      104       98              before
7      115       95              IS
8      167      152              significantly different
9      212      215              from the population mean
10      165      165              for after
11      151      130              (paired t-test)
12      133      130              t:      2.677745
13      217      219              df:         15
14      118      111
15      135      126
16      215      224
17      162      164
18      213      196
19      178      161
```

In the hypothesis test of the paired diet data the population mean of the *before* sample was found to be significantly different from the population mean for the *after* sample. Thus there *is* significant weight reduction, in the sense that the average reduction could not reasonably be due to random chance alone.

7.6 Statistical analysis of univariate many-sample data

A Appropriate data

Requires three or more columns of numbers, all in the same measurement units, to be compared. For example, salaries of four groups of employees.

In a **univariate** data set only one variable is measured for each elementary unit of the sample.

Characteristics of data used in univariate many-sample analyses: In univariate many-sample analysis, the same variable is measured for each of the independent samples. The samples can be made up of different numbers of data values, but they must be measured in the same units. The statistical procedures available with univariate many-sample data include box plots (which display the data) and the F-test (which tests to see if the groups are different on average from one another). In order for the F-test to be valid, your data should arise as random samples from large populations.

Information about the samples used in this tutorial exercise:
A company which manufactures rope and twine has found variations in the strength of the product produced by individual machines in their factories. They have taken samples from three of these machines and would like to find out whether there are real (as opposed to merely random) differences between the tensile strength of the fibers produced by these three machines or whether the differences they see can be attributed to randomness alone. The three samples are found in your worksheet *datafibr.wk1* as three columns of numbers, so they can be imported readily onto your StatPad worksheet. The variable is the breaking strength of the fiber being examined here. The elementary unit is the fiber being manufactured by the machine. The three samples in the data set are of fiber produced by machines A, B and C. Below is the table of data values.

BREAKING STRENGTH OF FIBERS PRODUCED BY THREE MACHINES (A, B, AND C) in POUNDS		
A	B	C
17.7	16.6	16.9
13.8	10.7	18.8
11.3	10.9	18.1
14.4	13.6	27.8
18.8	10.9	26.1
11.5	12.8	16.0
12.3	10.3	14.3
15.2	15.1	28.7
21.8	10.2	25.0
13.3	10.4	16.9
10.1	12.6	20.6
11.8	14.2	25.0
17.8	12.0	18.7
18.3	12.9	21.1
13.4	12.3	24.4
14.5	12.4	15.0
15.9		20.0
25.2		20.7
		28.3
		16.9
		17.4

B StatPad menus

Section 7.5 (B) contains the same command chart shown below. It is repeated here to emphasize the differences in the analyses which are appropriate for two-sample and more-than-two-sample data sets.

Univariate
Many-Sample
Data: Menu
Command Chart

Import your data onto a worksheet which already has StatPad on it. Follow the
method given in Section 7.3 (D), "Importing data from another Lotus worksheet".
The three columns of data on *datafibr.wk1* are "A", "B", and "C", going from left
to right. Next, activate StatPad. A description of this data set, and a table of the
values is in Section 7.6 (A)

Activate StatPad	**HOLD** (ALT)	while you **PRESS** (S).
Access to Univariate Many-sample Statistical Procedures Menu	**SELECT**	Univar
	SELECT	Many-sample
	Prompt	*How many samples do you wish to analyze?*
	TYPE	3
	PRESS	(ENTER ↵)

You are asked for the range name for your FIRST column of data. Then you will
be asked for the SECOND, and the THIRD. If you have not named your ranges,
StatPad will direct you in naming them now, and return you to the next menu in
this process. Name your ranges: A, B and C. If you need more help, you can refer
to Section 7.3 (F) for a brief tutorial on naming ranges in StatPad.

The directions below are for already named ranges. If you are naming the ranges in StatPad, the sequence will be the same, interrupted only for the naming procedure.

Continued:	*Prompt*	*Range name for column 1 of data?*
Access to		
Statistical	**TYPE**	A
Procedures		
Menu.	**PRESS**	(ENTER ←)
	Prompt	*Range name for column 2 of data?*
	TYPE	B
	PRESS	(ENTER ←)
	Prompt	*Range name for column 3 of data?*
	TYPE	C
	PRESS	(ENTER ←)
	Prompt	*Units of measurement? (e.g. dollars or mpg)*
	TYPE	POUNDS
	PRESS	(ENTER ←)

This brings you to the statistical procedures menu for univariate, many-sample data. It lists: *Box plots F-test Stop*. The next section of the tutorial draws the box plots for these samples.

C Box Plots

A box plot is a picture of the five-number summary for a data set. The five-number summary is composed of the smallest and largest values, the upper and lower quartiles and the median. It is used here to compare the measures of center and variability of the three samples.

We assume you are in StatPad with your data if not, please use Section 7.3 to bring in your data. Here we use the three columns of data values found in the worksheet *datafibr.wk1,* on your StatPad disk.

If you are not looking at the menu that reads: *Box plots F-test Stop*, please activate StatPad with (ALT) (S), select *Univariate* and *Many-sample*, and follow the prompts to this menu. If you would like more detailed directions, see Section 7.6 (B).

Now, we draw box plots of the *fiber* data:

Draw Box   **SELECT**   Box Plots
Plots

Univariate
Many-Sample:
Box Plots, Fiber
Data

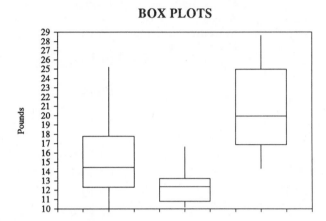

BOX PLOTS

Your screen shows box plots for the three samples A, B and C, going from left to right. (If you wanted to rank the samples in the order of size of their medians, you could specify the ranges in the order "b, a, c" the next time you use Univar Many-sample).

Exit from Box   **PRESS**   ENTER ↵
Plot Graph

You now have the menu: **Continue   Print Stop**

See Section 4.6 "Printing a Graph", which has directions for saving the graph to be printed later. For now, select "Continue", to return to the statistical procedures menu.

Return to   **SELECT**   Continue
Statistical
Procedures
Menu

You are now back at the procedures menu and can proceed with the F-test for the three samples of your univariate many-sample data.

D *F*-Test

The *F*-test is a one-way analysis of variance (ANOVA) test to determine if the samples in your many-sample data set are significantly different from each other on average. It measures how different the group averages are from each other as compared to how much randomness there is within each sample, and determines whether the differences are statistically significant or could reasonably be due to randomness alone.

If you completed the previous exercises you have already imported the univariate many-sample data needed to carry out an *F*-test, and are at the statistical procedures menu.

If you are not looking at the menu that reads: **Box plots F-test Stop,** please activate StatPad with (ALT) (S), select *Univariate* and *Many-sample*, and follow the prompts to this menu. Or see Section 7.6 (B) for a description of the menus and prompts leading to this menu.

Perform *F*-Test	SELECT	F-test

The menu that now appears gives you the choice of how demanding you would like the test level to be: (5%, 1%, 0.1%, or 10%). Choose the usual 5% level for now:

Choose the 5% level of significance.	SELECT	Usual

Now you are asked "**Results here?**" Move the cursor to a position where it doesn't encroach on your data ranges or other cell contents which you want to save.

Position cursor for result	PRESS PRESS	ARROW KEYS as needed [ENTER ↵]

Evidently there are significant differences among these machines. Your screen looks like this:

Univariate
Many-Sample:
F-Test, Fiber
Data

```
I16: 17.8                                                           MENU
Box plots  F-test  Stop
One way Analysis Of Variance (ANOVA) test to see if groups are different.
            I      J      K     L     M      N      O      P
 1   Breaking strength in pounds
 2   --------------------------------
 3        A      B      C
 4      17.7   16.6   16.9        The population means for
 5      13.8   10.7   18.8                A
 6      11.3   10.9   18.1                B
 7      14.4   13.6   27.8                C
 8      18.8   10.9   26.1        ARE
 9      11.5   12.8    16         significantly different
10      12.3   10.3   14.3        from each other
11      15.2   15.1   28.7        at test level 5%
12      21.8   10.2    25            F =   24.25671
13      13.3   10.4   16.9            with          2
14      10.1   12.6   20.6            and          52
15      11.8   14.2    25            degrees of freedom
16      17.8    12    18.7
17      18.3   12.9   21.1
18      13.4   12.3   24.4
19      14.5   12.4    15
20      15.9          20
```

7.7 Statistical analysis of bivariate data

A Appropriate data

Requires two columns of numbers, same number of rows in each, where each row represents two measurements on the same object. For example, age and salary for 53 employees.

A data set is **bivariate** when two variables have been measured for each elementary unit of the sample.

Characteristics of data used in bivariate analysis: In bivariate analysis the two variables can be measured in different units, for example, weight and height of children. Before you perform regression analysis, you will need to decide which variable should be predicted from the other. In order for statistical inference to be valid, the data must be random sample from a large population.

Information about the data used in this tutorial exercise: A mail-order firm based in the East is planning to expand to the West. They can do a good job of predicting catalog sales in the East, but have less experience so far in the West. We will use regression to help them predict sales in the West based on their prediction of Eastern sales. Below is a chart showing the two samples of predictions. The two columns of figures are on the worksheet *datacata.wk1* which can be found on your original StatPad disk.

Table showing the eastern and western sales generated by a number of mail-order catalogs.

Total Sales per Catalog (Thousands)	
EAST	WEST
223	214
161	104
211	171
189	143
223	211
226	165
114	104
118	64
230	185
205	184
193	146
154	117
58	15
211	168
176	103
80	32

B StatPad menus

Below is a menu chart showing the commands you will be using and the statistical procedures which are applicable for a bivariate data set.

Bivariate
Data: Menu
Command
Chart

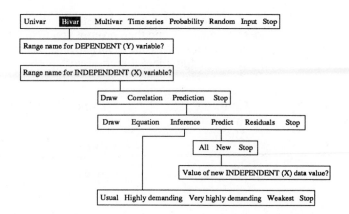

A word about DEPENDENT and INDEPENDENT VARIABLES: You will notice in the chart that after you have selected bivariate you will be asked for the range name of your dependent variable. In general, the DEPENDENT variable is to be predicted, and is usually the one that is responding to the situation. The INDEPENDENT variable is the one helping to do the prediction, and is usually the source the other is responding to.

For the mail-order catalog example (Section 7.7 A) the firm understands the eastern sales and would like to use this knowledge in order to predict the western sales. Therefore "western sales" is the dependent variable being predicted, and "eastern sales" is the independent variable.

We assume you are in StatPad with your data. If not, please refer to Section 7.3 (D) to bring in your data. You will find the data set in the worksheet *datacata.wk1* on your original StatPad disk.

Activate StatPad	**HOLD** ALT	while you **PRESS** S
Begin Bivariate Analysis	**SELECT**	Bivar
	Prompt	*range name for DEPENDENT (Y) variable?*
	TYPE	West
	PRESS	ENTER ↵

If you did not name your range before this, StatPad will tell you that "Range 'West' does not exist ...", and then prompt you to name the range, which you can do with *Point* without leaving the bivariate analysis menus. You may see Section 7.3 (F) if you would like more direction with the naming.

Continue Bivariate Analysis	*Prompt*	*Range name for INDEPENDENT (X) variable?*
	TYPE	East
	PRESS	ENTER ↵

This brings you to the first statistical procedures menu (the prediction function has an additional statistical procedures menu). The choices here are: *Draw Correlation Prediction Stop*. In the next section, we begin by drawing a scatterplot of the data.

If you want to rename and save your worksheet with the imported data and StatPad on it, you may *Stop* StatPad, then use /FILE SAVE and provide an appropriate name (for example, *Bivar* for bivariate data, or *Catalog* for the subject matter). Then use (ALT) (S) to reactivate StatPad.

C Draw

The DRAW function constructs the scatter plot of the catalog data, plotting West's sales on the *Y*-axis, against and East's sales on the *X*-axis.

To get started, if you did not do Section 7.7(B), you will need to run 1-2-3, retrieve a worksheet with StatPad, and import onto it the data set *datacata.wk1* which can be found on your original StatPad disk. Then activate *StatPad*, select *Bivar*, and answer the prompts by giving the range names to be used. You will then be at the Bivariate statistical procedures menu. Now draw the scatterplot, which has a linear increasing structure with some randomness:

Construct   **SELECT**   Draw
Scatter Plot

Bivariate
Data: Scatter
plot of
Catalog data

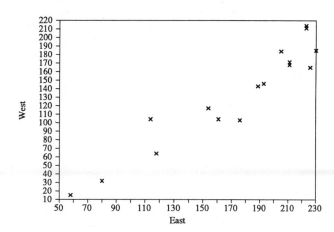

Leave the   **PRESS**   (ENTER ←)
Scatter Plot

Return to Statistical Procedures Menu	**SELECT**	Continue

From the procedures menu you are in position carry out the correlation analysis.

D Correlation

The correlation measures the strength of the association between the dependent and independent variable of a bivariate data set.

The correlation is a number from -1 to 1. A correlation value near 1 indicates a strong relationship in which large values of one variable are associated with large values of the other. A correlation value near −1 also indicates a strong relationship, except that large values of one variable are associated with *small* values of the other. A correlation value near 0 often indicates a weak relationship in which large values of one variable are associated with *both* small and large values of the other; however, there might be a more complex nonlinear relationship.

To get started: if you just drew the scatterplot of the bivariate data, you are already at the statistical procedures menu. Otherwise, you will need to run 1-2-3, retrieve a worksheet with StatPad, and import the data set *datacata.wk1* onto it. Then activate *StatPad*, select *Bivar*, answer the prompts by providing the range names to be used. You will then be at the first bivariate statistical procedures menu. Further directions for this are in Section 7.7(B). Now find the correlation as follows:

Determine Correlation	**SELECT**	Correlation

Now you are asked "**Results here?**" Move the cursor to a position where it doesn't encroach on your data ranges or other cell contents which you want to save.

Position cursor for result	**PRESS**	**ARROW KEYS as needed**
	PRESS	[ENTER ↵]

Your screen will look like this:

Bivariate:
Correlation, Catalog
Data

```
L5:                                                                        MENU
Draw  Correlation  Prediction  Stop
Compute the correlation
      I       J       K       L       M       N       O       P
1     East    West
2     223     214             Correlation is:   0.950931
3     161     104             for East
4     211     171             and West
5     189     143
6     223     211
7     226     165
8     114     104
9     118      64
10    230     185
11    205     184
12    193     146
13    154     117
14     58      15
15    211     168
16    176     103
17     80      32
```

The next option on the menu is PREDICTION.

E Prediction

The prediction command has a statistical procedures menu of its own. It performs regression/prediction analysis, draws the straight line which comes closest to the data, predicts values of Y from given values of X, and determines the residuals (prediction errors). It also does statistical inference: significance tests and confidence intervals.

To get started: if you just determined the correlation of the bivariate data set, you are already at the statistical procedures menu. Otherwise, you will need to run 1-2-3, retrieve a worksheet with StatPad on it, and import the data set *datacata.wk1* onto it, or use your own data. Then activate *StatPad* with (ALT) (S), select *Bivar*, and answer the prompts by providing range names. You will then be at the Bivariate procedures menu. Further directions for this are in Section 7.7(B). Now bring up the predictions menu:

Prediction   **SELECT**   Prediction
Menu

This brings up the prediction menu for bivariate data:

Draw Equation Inference Predict Residuals Stop

1 Draw

The *DRAW* command will draw a scatter plot of the data with the least squares line:

| **Draw least squares line** | SELECT | Draw |

| Bivariate: Least Squares Line, Catalog Data | | |

Data, with least squares line

| **Exit from graph** | PRESS | |

| **Return to prediction menu** | SELECT | Continue |

2 Equation

Next you will find the regression EQUATION for your data together with the standard errors, the standard error of estimate S, and the R-squared value.

| **Find regression equation** | SELECT | Equation |

Bivariate
Data:
Prediction,
Regression
Equation,
Catalog Data

```
L18:                                                                    MENU
Draw Equation Inference Predict Residuals Stop
Find the prediction equation
     I       J      K      L      M      N      O      P
1    East    West          The least squares
2    223     214           prediction equation is
3    161     104           West = a + b (East)
4    211     171           where a is:    -47.9577
5    189     143           and  b is:    1.043767
6    223     211           standard errors:
7    226     165             for a:       16.43745
8    114     104             for b:       0.090763
9    118      64           The standard error of estimate:
10   230     185                          S =19.15065
11   205     184           indicates the typical size of
12   193     146           prediction errors.
13   154     117           The R-squared value:
14    58      15                          R2 =0.904271
15   211     168           indicates the proportion of the
16   176     103           variance of West that is
17    80      32           explained by East.
```

You then return to the prediction menu, and from there may perform statistical
inference.

3 Inference

The next prediction procedure is *inference,* which provides significance tests
and confidence intervals as appropriate.

If you are not looking at the menu: *Draw Equation Inference Predict Residuals
Stop,* see the opening paragraphs of this section (Section 7.7 E), to bring you
there.

Significance tests and confidence intervals	**SELECT**	Inference

The menu that now appears gives you the choice of test level (for hypothesis
testing: 5%, 1%, 0.1%, or 10%) and confidence level (for confidence intervals:
95%, 99%, 99.9%, or 90% respectively).

Specify test level 5% and confidence level 95%	**SELECT**	Usual

Now you are asked **"Results here?"** Move the cursor to a position where it
doesn't encroach on your data ranges or other cell contents which you want to
save.

Position cursor for result	PRESS	ARROW KEYS as needed
	PRESS	ENTER ↵

There are several results presented here. The *F*-test shows that the regression is significant, i.e., a significant amount of the variation in Western catalog sales is explained by the Eastern sales levels. You may also find the 95% confidence interval for the regression coefficient (1.047), which extends from 0.854 to 1.240. You also see the results of hypothesis tests, the standard error for each coefficient, and its *t*-statistic.

Bivariate
Data:
Prediction,
Inference,
Catalog Data

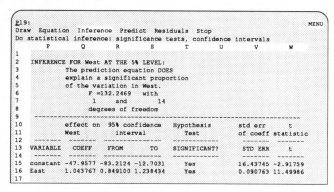

After the inference results are placed on your screen, you are again returned to the prediction menu. The next option there is to generate numerical prediction values.

4 Predict

The PREDICTION command predicts West's sales from East's sales, either for the sample data values or for other numbers that you provide.

If you are not looking at the menu: *Draw Equation Inference Predict Residuals Stop,* see the opening paragraphs of this section (Section 7.7 E) to bring you there.

From the bivariate prediction menu:

Predict Western Sales	SELECT	Predict

This brings up the menu: **All New Stop**

All	Compute predicted values for all data points
New	Compute west for a new value of east

Stop   Stop statistical analysis, return to ready mode

Predict for all   **SELECT**   All
of East's values

Here is the list of predicted values from all of your data points.

Bivariate: Prediction,
All Values, Catalog
Sales

```
I1:                                                                  MENU
All  New  Stop
Compute predicted values for all data points
         I        J        K        L        M        N        O        P
1                                   Predicted
2                                   West
3                                   from
4        East     West              East
5        223      214               184.8024
6        161      104               120.0888
7        211      171               172.2772
8        189      143               149.3143
9        223      211               184.8024
10       226      165               187.9337
11       114      104               71.03175
12       118      64                75.20682
13       230      185               192.1088
14       205      184               166.0146
15       193      146               153.4894
16       154      117               112.7824
17       58       15                12.58075
18       211      168               172.2772
19       176      103               135.7453
20       80       32                35.54364
```

You are now back at the prediction menu line. Select PREDICT and then NEW, to compute West for a new value of East.

Predict West   **SELECT**   Predict
for a new value
of East   **SELECT**   New

                Prompt   *Value of east?*

                TYPE   275

Now you are asked "**Results here?**" Move the cursor to a position where it doesn't encroach on your data ranges or other cell contents which you want to save.

Position   **PRESS**   **ARROW KEYS as needed**
cursor for
result   **PRESS**   ENTER ↵

Bivariate:
Prediction,
New Value,
Catalog Data

```
L6:                                                              MENU
Draw  Equation  Inference  Predict  Residuals  Stop
Get numerical predictions
          I       J      K      L        M       N      O      P
 1      East    West
 2                          When East
 3      223     214        is:          275
 4      161     104        We expect West
 5      211     171        to be: 239.0783
 6      189     143
 7      223     211
 8      226     165
 9      114     104
10      118      64
11      230     185
12      205     184
13      193     146
14      154     117
15       58      15
16      211     168
17      176     103
18       80      32
```

5 Residuals

The last computation in the prediction function is for the RESIDUALS, which compute the vertical prediction errors from the least squares line for the data values.

If you are not looking at the menu: **Draw Equation Inference Predict Residuals Stop**, see the opening paragraphs of this section (Section 7.7 E), to bring you there.

Determine prediction errors	**SELECT**	Residuals

Now you are asked "**Results here?**" Move the cursor to a position where it doesn't encroach on your data ranges or other cell contents which you want to save.

Position cursor for result	**PRESS**	**ARROW KEYS as needed**
	PRESS	ENTER ↵

StatPad computes the prediction error for each data value.

Bivariate: Residuals,
Catalog Data

```
Q1:                                                                    MENU
Draw  Equation  Inference  Predict  Residuals  Stop
Compute the prediction error for each data value
       I         J         K         L         M         N         O         P
 1                                  Residuals of
 2                                  West
 3        East      West            from
 4                                  East
 5        223       214             29.19755
 6        161       104            -16.0888
 7        211       171             -1.27723
 8        189       143             -6.31434
 9        223       211             26.19755
10        226       165            -22.9337
11        114       104             32.96824
12        118        64            -11.2068
13        230       185             -7.10882
14        205       184             17.98537
15        193       146             -7.48941
16        154       117             4.217530
17         58        15             2.419242
18        211       168             -4.27723
19        176       103            -32.7453
20         80        32             -3.54364
```

This is the end of the analysis of bivariate data. Leave StatPad and return to 1-2-3 using the *Stop* prompt of any StatPad menu.

7.8 Statistical analysis of multivariate data

A Appropriate data

Requires two or more columns of numbers, same number of rows in each, where each row represents measurements of the same object. For example, salary, age, and experience for 53 employees.

A data set is **multivariate** when more than two variables have been measured for each elementary unit of the sample.

Characteristics of data used in multivariate analysis: In multivariate analysis the variables can be measured in different units, for example the weight, height, and verbal ability of children. StatPad provides *correlation analysis*, showing you the associations between each pair of variables, and *multiple regression analysis*, allowing you to predict one variable (the dependent variable) from the others (the independent, predictor, or explanatory variables). In order for statistical inference (confidence intervals and hypothesis tests) to be valid, the data must be a random sample from a large population.

Information about the data used in this tutorial exercise: A company that manufactures plumbing fixtures is reevaluating production and expansion strategies and needs to understand the fixed cost of production and the variable costs of manufacturing each of the items in their line. They have gathered data for the past 13 weeks, to be found on the worksheet *dataplum.wk1* on your original StatPad disk. It is there as three columns of numbers. The first is the total cost, the next the number of sinks, and the last is the number of bathtubs. A chart of this data follows:

COST OF PRODUCTION (DOLLARS) AND NUMBER OF ITEMS PRODUCED FOR EACH OF THE PAST 13 WEEKS.		
COST	SINKS	TUBS
$19,843	105	54
19,690	98	55
19,662	96	59
19,520	101	54
19,350	97	57
19,420	97	56
18,788	100	50
19,557	100	55
19,492	86	63
20,214	103	55
19,601	99	55
19,075	95	56
19,528	87	63

B StatPad menus

Following is a chart showing the commands you will be following and the statistical procedures you will be using to analyze multivariate data.

Note that you are asked to specify the variables: the *dependent variable* is to be predicted by your independent or *predictor variables*. In this example, it is natural to consider predicting the total cost (dependent variable) from the number of sinks and the number of tubs (predictor variables).

We assume you are in StatPad with your data if not, please use Section 7.3 (D) to bring in your data. You will find the data set in the worksheet *dataplum.wk1* on your original StatPad disk.

Activate StatPad	**Hold** (ALT)	while you **PRESS** (S)
Begin Multivariate Analysis	**SELECT**	Multivar
	Prompt	*Range name for DEPENDENT variable Y to be predicted?*
	TYPE	Cost
	PRESS	(ENTER ←)

If you did not name your range before this, StatPad will tell you that "Cost does not exist", and then prompt you to name the range, without leaving the multivariate analysis menus. It will do the same with any other unnamed ranges. You can see Section 7.3 (F) for more direction with the naming.

Continue Multivariate Analysis	*Prompt*	*How many predictor variables? (1 to 15)*
	TYPE	2
	PRESS	(ENTER ←)
	Prompt	*Range name for predictor variable 1?*
	TYPE	Sinks
	PRESS	(ENTER ←)
	Prompt	*Range name for predictor variable 2?*
	TYPE	Bathtubs
	PRESS	(ENTER ←)

The next menu to come up lists the statistical procedures available with multivariate data.

Graph Correlation Prediction Stop

Graph	Draw a bivariate plot for EACH PAIR of variables
Correlation	Compute correlations for all pairs of variables as a table or matrix
Prediction	Perform multiple regression/prediction analysis

The PREDICTION command brings up a menu with these procedures:

Equation Inference Fitted and residuals Diagnose Stop

Equation	Find the prediction (regression) equation, S (standard error of estimate), and R-squared (percent variance explained by the regression equation)
Inference	Do statistical inference: significance tests and confidence intervals
Fitted and residuals	Compute predicted values (fitted values) and prediction errors (residuals)
Diagnose	Draw a plot of residuals against predicted values to help you look for further structure

If you want to rename and save your worksheet with the imported data and StatPad on it, select STOP, use /FILE SAVE, provide an appropriate name (for example *Multivar* for multivariate data or *plumbing* for the subject matter). Then you can reactivate StatPad with (ALT) (S), select *Multivar*, and provide your range names.

C Graph

The graph command will draw a bivariate scatter plot for each pair of variables. The first one is of total costs and the number of sinks manufactured with 13 points, one for each week.

We assume you are in StatPad with your data sets named and looking at the menu that begins "*Graph Correlation...* ". If you see the menu "Equation Inference ..." please hit (Esc) once. Otherwise, please use Section 7.3 (D) to bring in your data. You will find the data set in the worksheet, *dataplum.wk1*, on your original StatPad disk, or use your own data. Section 7.8 (B) discusses the menus for multivariate data.

Draw Scatter Plot   SELECT   Graph

Multivariate:
Scatter Plot, Total
Costs and
Number of Sinks
Produced

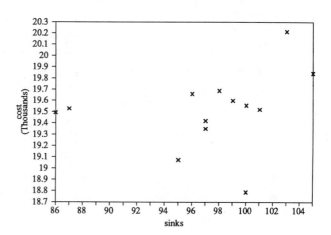

| Leave This | **PRESS** | ENTER ↵ |
| Graph | | |

This brings up the menu: **Next graph   Print   Continue   Stop**

Next graph	Show the next graph
Print	Save this graph as a .PIC file for printing later, then show the next graph
Continue	Continue statistical analysis without showing any of the remaining graph(s)
Stop	Show the next graph

Whether you select NEXT GRAPH or PRINT, StatPad will draw each possible scatter plot of your data samples. You may skip the remaining graph(s) with CONTINUE. With PRINT you can save the graph for printing later. The *prompts* will direct you, and Section 4.6 has more detailed directions for printing a graph.

| **Continue** | **SELECT** | Next Graph |
| **Scatter Plot** | | |

Multivariate:
Scatter Plot,
Total Costs and
Number of
Bathtubs
Produced

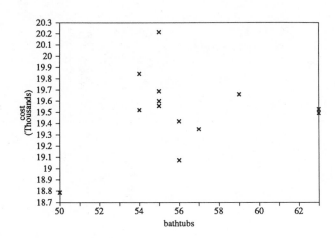

Leave This   **PRESS**   ENTER ←
Graph

Continue   **SELECT**   Next Graph
Scatter Plot

Multivariate:
Scatter Plot of
Sinks and
Bathtubs
Produced

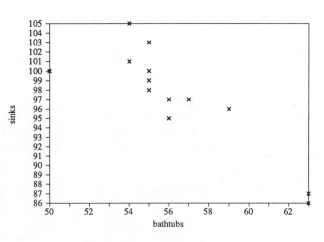

| **Leave This Graph** | **PRESS** | ENTER ← |

When all the graphs have been drawn, the menu that comes up does not include NEXT GRAPH.

| **Continue Multivariate Analysis** | **SELECT** | Continue |

You are now at the multivariate statistical procedures menu and can compute the correlation matrix.

D Correlation

The correlation command computes a table (the "correlation matrix") showing the correlations for all pairs of variables.

We assume you are in StatPad with your data sets named and looking at the menu that begins "*Graph Correlation...*"

If not, please use Section 7.3 (D) to bring in your data. You will find the data set in the worksheet, *dataplum.wk1*, on your original StatPad disk, or use your own data. Section 7.8 (B) discusses the menus for multivariate data.

| **Compute Correlations** | **SELECT** | Correlation |

Now you are asked "**Results here?**" Move the cursor to a position where it doesn't encroach on your data ranges or other cell contents which you want to save.

| **Position cursor for result** | **PRESS** | **ARROW KEYS as needed** |
| | **PRESS** | ENTER ← |

Multivariate:
Correlations,
Plumbing Data

```
L7:                                                                   MENU
Graph  Correlation  Prediction  Stop
Compute correlations for all pairs of variables
       I      J      K        L        M        N        O        P
 1    COST   SINKS BATHTUBS
 2                              CORRELATIONS:
 3    19,843    105    54              cost      sinks    bathtubs
 4    19,690     98    55   cost          1   0.263048  0.194923
 5    19,662     96    59   sinks  0.263048          1  -0.86300
 6    19,520    101    54   bathtubs 0.194923 -0.86300        1
 7    19,350     97    57
 8    19,420     97    56
 9    18,788    100    50
10    19,557    100    55
11    19,492     86    63
12    20,214    103    55
13    19,601     99    55
14    19,075     95    56
15    19,528     87    63
```

You are now back at the statistical procedures menu.

E Prediction

The PREDICTION command performs multiple regression/prediction analysis to predict one variable (the dependent variable you entered first) from the others.

We assume you are in StatPad with your data sets named and looking at the menu that begins "*Graph Correlation...*"

If not, please use Section 7.3 (D) to bring in your data. You will find the data set in the worksheet, *dataplum.wk1*, on your original StatPad disk, or use your own data. Section 7.8 (B) discusses the menus for multivariate data.

Perform   **SELECT**   Prediction
multiple
regression
analysis

When you select PREDICTION you get a menu listing these procedures for multiple regression analysis:

Equation Inference Fitted and residuals Diagnose Stop

Equation	Find the prediction (regression) equation, S (standard error of estimate), and R-squared (percent variance explained by the regression equation)
Inference	Do statistical inference: significance tests and confidence intervals
Fitted and residuals	Compute predicted values (fitted values) and prediction errors (residuals)

> **Diagnose**   Draw a plot of residuals against predicted values to help you look for further structure

These will now be described in turn.

1 Equation

We assume you are in StatPad with your data sets named and looking at the menu that begins "*Equation Inference...*"

If not, the beginning of this section, 7.8(E) orients you to arrive at this menu.

> **Derive the**   **SELECT**   Equation
> **prediction**
> **equation**

Now you are asked "**Results here?**" Move the cursor to a position where it doesn't encroach on your data ranges or other cell contents which you want to save.

> **Position**   **PRESS**   **ARROW KEYS as needed**
> **cursor for**
> **result**   **PRESS**   ⌈ ENTER ← ⌉

The results will look like this on your screen:

Multivariate:
Prediction/
Regression
Equation
Plumbing Data

```
L16:                                                                    MENU
Equation  Inference  Fitted and residuals  Diagnose  Stop
Find the prediction (regression) equation, s, and r-squared
           I       J        K        L        M        N        O        P
 1       COST    SINKS BATHTUBS
 2                                    THE REGRESSION EQUATION IS:
 3      19,843    105      54              cost
 4      19,690     98      55                   =367.5280
 5      19,662     96      59                   +105.3693  * sinks
 6      19,520    101      54                   +158.1629  * bathtubs
 7      19,350     97      57 The standard error of estimate:
 8      19,420     97      56                   S =181.7679
 9      18,788    100      50              indicates the typical size of
10      19,557    100      55              prediction errors in this data set.
11      19,492     86      63 The R-squared value:
12      20,214    103      55                   R2 =0.766756
13      19,601     99      55              indicates the proportion of the
14      19,075     95      56              variance of cost that is
15      19,528     87      63              explained by the regression model.
16
```

2 Inference

In this section on inference for multiple regression of multivariate data, you will be performing significance tests and computing confidence intervals.

We assume you are in StatPad and looking at the menu that begins *"Equation Inference..."*

If not, the beginning of this section, 7.8(E), orients you to arrive at this menu.

| **Using Statistical Inference** | **SELECT** | Inference |

The menu that now appears gives you the choice of how demanding you would like the test level to be: (5%, 1%, 0.1%, and 10%).

| **Choose 5% level** | **SELECT** | Usual |

Now you are asked **"Results here?"** Move the cursor to a position where it doesn't encroach on your data ranges or other cell contents which you want to save.

| **Position cursor for result** | **PRESS** | **ARROW KEYS as needed** |
| | **PRESS** | ENTER ↵ |

Multivariate: Prediction, Inference for Cost, Plumbing Data

```
S20:                                                              MENU
Equation  Inference  Fitted and residuals  Diagnose  Stop
Do statistical inference: significance tests, confidence intervals
        L       M       N       O       P       Q       R       S
 1  INFERENCE FOR cost AT THE 5% LEVEL:
 2          The prediction equation DOES
 3          explain a significant proportion
 4          of the variation in cost.
 5              F =16.43678  with
 6                  2      and      10
 7              degrees of freedom
 8  ----------------------------------------------------------------
 9          effect on  95% confidence   Hypothesis    std err      t
10          cost       interval         Test          of coeff  statistic
11  -------  -------  -----------------  -------------  -------  -------
12  VARIABLE  COEFF   FROM         TO    SIGNIFICANT?   STD ERR     t
13  -------  -------  -----------------  -------------  -------  -------
14  constant 367.5280 -7077.71 7812.772  No             3341.521 0.109988
15  sinks    105.3693 63.36814 147.3705  Yes            18.85067 5.589684
16  bathtubs 158.1629 93.72327 222.6026  Yes            28.92136 5.468724
17
```

INTERPRETATION OF RESULTS: The constant term indicates the estimated *fixed cost* of production. The regression coefficient for "sinks" indicates the estimated additional *variable cost* per sink produced. The regression coefficient for "tub" indicates the estimated additional *variable cost* per tub produced.

3 Fitted and residuals

This command computes the values predicted (fitted) by the least squares regression equation, as well as the prediction errors (residuals).

We assume you are in StatPad with your data sets named and looking at the menu that begins *"Equation Inference..."*

If not, the beginning of this section, 7.8(E), orients you to arrive at this menu.

Compute predicted values and residuals	**SELECT**	Fitted & Residuals

Now you are asked **"Results here?"** Move the cursor to a position where it doesn't encroach on your data ranges or other cell contents which you want to save.

Position cursor for result	**PRESS**	**ARROW KEYS as needed**
	PRESS	ENTER ←

The predicted fitted values, and the residuals are shown here:

Multivariate:
Prediction,
Fitted and
Residuals
Plumbing Data

```
M2: 'resi-                                                                MENU
Equation  Inference  Fitted and residuals  Diagnose  Stop
Compute fitted values (predicted values) and errors (residuals)
       I        J       K        L        M        N        O        P
1     COST   SINKS BATHTUBS
2                                         resi-     fitted
3    19,843    105      54               duals     values
4    19,690     98      55              -129.108 19972.10
5    19,662     96      59               297.3136 19392.68
6    19,520    101      54              -152.599 19814.59
7    19,350     97      57               -30.6313 19550.63
8    19,420     97      56              -253.642 19603.64
9    18,788    100      50               -25.4800 19445.48
10   19,557    100      55               -24.6101 18812.61
11   19,492     86      63               -46.4250 19603.42
12   20,214    103      55                98.44184 19393.55
13   19,601     99      55               294.4669 19919.53
14   19,075     95      56               102.9442 19498.05
15   19,528     87      63              -159.741 19234.74
16                                        29.07250 19498.92
17
```

4 Diagnose

The **diagnose** command draws a plot of the prediction errors (residuals) against the predicted (fitted) values to see if there is any structure present which was not already explained by the regression equation. This is designed to help you see when the regression equation is not doing a complete job of explaining all of the nonrandom structure in your data set.

We assume you are in StatPad with your data sets named and looking at the menu that begins *"Equation Inference..."*

If not, the beginning of this section, 7.8(E), orients you to arrive at this menu.

Draw graph to   **SELECT**   Diagnose
look for
additional
structure

This graph of the residuals plotted against the fitted values will come up. This particular plot looks fairly random and does not show any of the problems (nonlinearity or unequal variability) that would warrant further action.

Multivariate:
Prediction,
Diagnose,
Scatter Plot of
Fitted and
Residuals

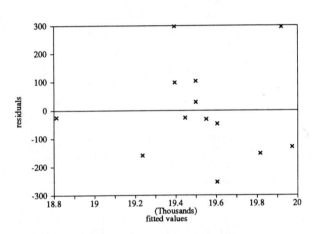

Exit from   **PRESS**   [ENTER ←]
graph

Return to   **SELECT**   Continue
prediction
menu

Return to   **PRESS**   [Esc] [Esc] [Esc]
Opening Menu

Instead of returning to the Opening Menu, you could return to 1-2-3 by PRESSING STOP on any menu. From there you could save this worksheet under an appropriate name, and then erase the data sets and the results from this tutorial section with / RANGE ERASE. StatPad is still, of course, on your worksheet, so you can import data for the next tutorial section and then reactivate StatPad.

7.9   Statistical analysis of time series data

A   Appropriate data

Requires a single column with at least two full years of quarterly or monthly observations.

In a trend-seasonal time series analysis, a single variable is measured for each successive time period (either monthly or quarterly). The data set consists of a single column of numbers. For example: monthly ice-cream sales or quarterly freight miles. The series is analyzed in terms of the long-term trend, the repeating seasonal fluctuations, the medium-term wandering cycles, and the random irregular component.

More information about the data used in this tutorial exercise: We will examine the quarterly sales of an entrepreneurial startup firm specializing in specialty foods. This business shows strong seasonality (sales are typically lowest in the summer months) and this firm has shown a healthy growth rate.

SPECIALTY FOOD CORPORATION QUARTERLY SALES, 1984-1987		
YEAR	QUARTER	SALES
1984	First	99
1984	Second	93
1984	Third	83
1984	Fourth	134
1985	First	136
1985	Second	121
1985	Third	82
1985	Fourth	143
1986	First	135
1986	Second	122
1986	Third	92
1986	Fourth	148
1987	First	153
1987	Second	140
1987	Third	125
1987	Fourth	198

B StatPad menus

The menu chart for trend-seasonal time series analysis is shown below. Note that hitting (Esc) will allow you to move to a higher menu level from the *Graph* ... or from the *Not Adjusted* ... menu so that you can easily explore all of the possibilities.

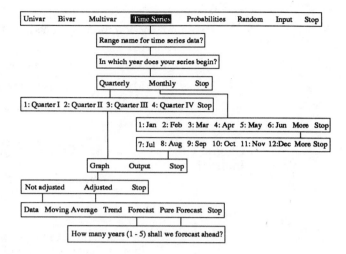

We assume you are in StatPad with your data if not, please use Section 7.3 (D) to bring in your data. You will find the data set in the worksheet *datasale.wk1* on your original StatPad disk. Then:

Activate   **HOLD** ALT   while you **PRESS** Ⓢ
StatPad

Begin   **SELECT**   Time Series
Time-Series
Analysis   *Prompt*   *range name for time series data?*

                      TYPE   Sales

If you did not name your range before this, StatPad will tell you that "*Range 'Sales' does not exist ...*", and then prompt you to name the range by pointing to it, without leaving the time-series analysis menus. You can see Section 7.3(F) for more direction with the naming.

                      Prompt   *In which year does your series begin?*

                      TYPE   1984

                      PRESS   ENTER ↵

Now you specify whether the measurements were made on a quarterly or a monthly schedule; the menu is: **Quarterly Monthly Stop**

Quarterly	This is a time series of quarterly observations
Monthly	This is a time series of monthly observations
Stop	Stop statistical analysis, return to ready mode

Choose Time Interval

SELECT	Quarterly
Prompt	*1: Quarter I 2: Quarter II 3: Quarter III 4: Quarter IV Stop*

If your data set is monthly, the prompt will show you the months January through June. If your monthly series begins in a month from July through December, you will first need to select *More* from this menu of months before making your selection. Selecting *More* again brings back the other months.

Specify Beginning Quarter

SELECT	1: Quarter I

This brings you to the statistical procedures menu for time series data: **Graph Output Stop**

Graph	Display the results graphically
Output	Place the numerical results into the spreadsheet
Stop	Stop statistical analysis, return to ready mode

If you wish to both look at graphs *and* place the output into the worksheet, after working with one choice you may hit (Esc) (twice) to return to this *Graph Output Stop* menu and choose the other.

C Graphing the data, moving average, trend, and forecast

The *Graph* command will allow you to examine various plots of the series, the moving average, and the forecast, either for the raw series or on a seasonally-adjusted basis.

We assume you are in StatPad with your data if not, please follow the steps in the previous section (7.9 B). You should now be looking at the menu *"Graph Output Stop"*. Now select graph:

Display   **SELECT**   Graph
graph

When you select **Graph** you will be asked if you want the data seasonally adjusted or not. Here are the choices:

Not Adjusted	Display results including the seasonal differences of the raw data
Adjusted	Display results on a seasonally adjusted basis

If you want to look at both the raw series *and* the seasonally-adjusted series, it's easy to move back and forth. After choosing one and looking at graphs, hit (Esc) to return to this *"Not Adjusted Adjusted"* menu and choose the other.

After you make this choice between seasonally adjusted or nonadjusted data, the statistical procedures menu for graphing the data will come up. Your screen will look like this:

Time Series:
Statistical
Procedures
Menu for
Graphing
Data

```
I1: 'Quarterly                                                        MENU
Data   Moving average   Trend   Forecast   Pure forecast   Stop
Display the series
       I          J        K        L        M        N        O        P
 1     Quarterly
 2     1984-1987
 3     ---------
 4     Sales
 5         99
 6         93
 7         83
 8        134
 9        136
```

Here are the choices of graphs:

Data	Display the series
Moving Average	Display the series with the smoothed series
Trend	Display the series with the seasonalized trend
Forecast	Display the future forecast (one to five years of seasonalized trend) with the series
Pure Forecast	Display the future forecast (one to five years of seasonalized trend) without the series
Stop	Stop statistical analysis, return to ready mode

The next section will look at all of these graphs on a raw (nonadjusted) basis; the section after that will look at all of these graphs on a seasonally adjusted basis.

1 Not seasonally adjusted

Graphs of the raw (unadjusted) series include all of the predictable seasonal fluctuations. That is, they show you the actual numbers you expect to see in each time period. In this section we will select "Not adjusted" and then look at each of the graphs.

We assume you are in StatPad looking at the menu "*Not Adjusted Adjusted Stop*". If you are looking at the menu "*Data Moving average ...*" please hit [Esc] once. Otherwise, please follow the directions above in Sections 7.9 B and C. Now select *Not Adjusted* and draw the first graph (the sales data series):

Choose not adjusted   **SELECT**   Not adjusted

Graph the series   **SELECT**   Data
**(not   seasonally
adjusted)**

Time Series:
Sales Data
Values, Not
Seasonally
Adjusted

The graph displays the three years of the data values of the series. There is an upward trend, a very strong seasonal pattern, as well as some other variation from year to year. Note that the dates on the horizontal axis should be interpreted as follows: 1.985 (in thousands) is the year 1985.

Exit from the graph	**PRESS**	ENTER ↵
Return to graph menu	**SELECT**	Continue

From here, you can proceed with the other graphs on this menu in any order for the unadjusted series, or you could hit Esc to switch to the seasonally-adjusted series. For now, let's continue with the rest of the graphs of the unadjusted series.

The **moving average** "smooths" your series by averaging a full year's worth of data at each point (the previous and the future half year) to eliminate the seasonal and random components and show you the trend and cyclic components of your series.

Graph the moving average	**SELECT**	Moving Average

Time Series: Sales
Data with Moving
Average, Not
Seasonally
Adjusted

raw and smoothed series

Exit from graph	**PRESS**	ENTER ↵
Return to graph menu	**SELECT**	Continue

The **trend** graph shows you your series with the seasonalized trend, after eliminating the cyclic and random components of the series. Note how the seasonalized trend below captures the upward trend and the seasonal variation, but does not try to include every detail.

Graph the seasonalized trend	SELECT	Trend

Time Series:
Sales Data with
Trend, Not
Seasonally
Adjusted

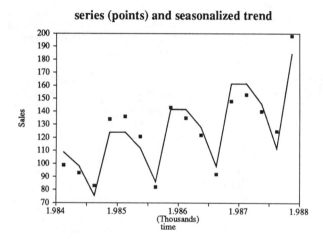

series (points) and seasonalized trend

Exit from graph	**PRESS**	ENTER ↵
Return to graph menu	**SELECT**	Continue

The **forecast** graph shows you your series with the seasonalized trend extended one to five years into the future. This forecast includes the trend and seasonal components, but not the cyclic and random ones. Let's look at the three-year-ahead forecast for the sales data:

Graph the forecast	SELECT	Forecast
	Prompt	*how many years (1-5) shall we forecast ahead?*
	TYPE	3
	PRESS	ENTER ↵

Here is a graph of the series with the three-year forecast. Note how the forecast extends the upward trend and the expected seasonal components (but not the cyclic and random details) into the future.

Time Series:
Sales Data with
Forecast, Not
Seasonally
Adjusted

series (points) and forecast

| **Exit from graph** | **PRESS** | ENTER ← |
| **Return to graph menu** | **SELECT** | Continue |

The **pure forecast** graph shows you the forecast only, without showing the time series it came from. Let's look at the three-year-ahead forecast for the sales data:

Graph the pure forecast	**SELECT**	Pure forecast
	Prompt	*how many years (1-5) shall we forecast ahead?*
	TYPE	3
	PRESS	ENTER ←

Here is a graph of the three-year forecast. Because the series is omitted, the vertical scale can be enlarged so that more detail can be shown.

Time Series: Pure
Forecast of Sales,
Not Seasonally
Adjusted

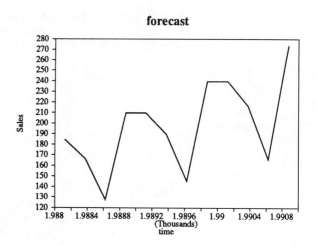

forecast

| Exit from graph | **PRESS** | ENTER ↵ |
| **Return to graph menu** | **SELECT** | Continue |

The next section will show you how to create these graphs on a seasonally-adjusted basis. In preparation, please return to the *"Not Adjusted Adjusted"* menu:

| **Return to seasonal adjustment menu** | **PRESS** | Esc |

2 Seasonally adjusted

The process of **seasonal adjustment** removes the predictable swings throughout the year so that you can see how well you *really* did. For example, your sales might be up 18% from the third to the fourth quarter. However, if sales have consistently risen about 25% from the third to fourth quarter in previous years, the 18% rise is no cause for celebration; in fact, it is a poor showing. The seasonally adjusted performance would actually show a downturn in sales, reflecting the fact that the rise was less than expected for this time of year.

Graphs of the seasonally-adjusted series do not include any of the predictable seasonal fluctuations. Therefore they do not show you the actual numbers you expect to see in each time period, but rather express them as they would be in a "typical" time of year rather than at some particular season. Both the series itself and its forecasts will look "smoother" because the seasonal fluctuations have been eliminated. In this section we will select "adjusted" and then look at each of the graphs.

We assume you are in StatPad looking at the menu "*Not Adjusted   Adjusted Stop*". If you are looking at the menu "*Data   Moving average ...*" please hit (Esc) once. Otherwise, please follow the directions above in Sections 7.9 B and introduction to C. Now select *Adjusted* and produce the graphs for the seasonally adjusted series:

Choose seasonally adjusted	**SELECT**	Adjusted
Graph the seasonally adjusted series	**SELECT**	Data

Here is a graph of the seasonally adjusted series. Note that the strong repeating seasonal pattern has been removed.

Time Series: Sales Data, Seasonally Adjusted

Exit from the graph	**PRESS**	(ENTER ←)
Return to graph menu	**SELECT**	Continue
Graph the Moving Average	**SELECT**	Moving average

Here is a graph of the seasonally adjusted series with the moving average. The adjusted series includes the random component whereas the moving average does not. They both include the trend and cyclic components.

Time Series:
Sales Data with
Moving
Average,
Seasonally
Adjusted

Exit from graph	PRESS	⌐ ENTER ↵ ⌐
Return to graph menu	SELECT	Continue
Graph the trend	SELECT	Trend

Here is a graph of the seasonally adjusted series and the trend. The trend has *not* been "seasonalized" and will be shown either as a straight line or an exponential curve.

Time Series:
Sales Data with
Trend,
Seasonally
Adjusted

Exit from graph	**PRESS**	⌐ENTER ←⌐
Return to graph menu	**SELECT**	Continue
Graph forecast	**SELECT**	Forecast
	Prompt	*How many years (1-5) shall we forecast ahead?*
	TYPE	3

Here is a graph of the seasonally adjusted series and the (unseasonalized) forecast. Note how the forecast extends the very smooth long-term behavior of the series into the future.

Time Series:
Sales Data with
Forecast,
Seasonally
Adjusted

series (points) and forecast
Seasonally adjusted

Exit from graph	**PRESS**	⌐ENTER ←⌐
Return to graph menu	**SELECT**	Continue
Graph the pure forecast	**SELECT**	Pure Forecast
	Prompt	*How many years (1-5) shall we forecast ahead?*
	TYPE	3

Here is a graph of the (unseasonalized) forecast by itself. Because the series is not shown, the vertical scale can be enlarged to show more detail.

Time Series: Pure
Forecast of Sales,
Seasonally
Adjusted

| **Exit from graph** | **PRESS** | ENTER ← |
| **Return to graph menu** | **SELECT** | Continue |

The next section will show you how to bring the numerical output these graphs are based on into the worksheet. In preparation, please return to the *"Graph Output Stop"* menu:

| **Return to seasonal adjustment menu** | **PRESS** | Esc |
| **Return to Graph/Output menu** | **PRESS** | Esc |

D   Output

In this exercise you will display on your screen the numerical values for the graphic results presented above, and these results will become part of your worksheet.

If you are continuing either from Section 7.9(C) or from 7.9(B), you are in StatPad with your data and are now looking at the menu that begins *"Graph Output Stop"*. Otherwise, please follow the directions in Section 7.9(B) to get here.

Display the numerical results	**SELECT**	Output
	Prompt	*RESULTS HERE? ...*

It is important to know where your data range is on the worksheet because this output requires a fairly large block of cells. Any values which are covered by the large cursor will be erased when the results are placed in the worksheet. Use your arrow keys, (PgUp), (PgDn), tab ⊣, and/or shift tab ⊢ to move the cursor so it doesn't cover any cells that contain information you need.

Position cursor for result	**PRESS**	**ARROW KEYS as needed**
	PRESS	(ENTER ↵)

Here are some comments on the output, which is shown below. The *time* column indicates precisely the middle of the specified period (for example, the first number 1986.125 represents the middle of the first quarter of 1986) so that graphs can be drawn properly. The next column is your original data series. The *smooth* column is the moving average, which cannot be computed for the first and last half-year of your series because it needs to average a half-year on either side of each time period. The *seasonal index* repeats exactly each year; the first value of 1.129 says that the first quarter is generally 12.9% higher than a typical quarter during the year. The *seasonally-adjusted* series is found by dividing the original series by the appropriate seasonal index. The *exponential trend* is the exponential curve that best fits the seasonally-adjusted series; if a linear (straight-line) trend fits better, StatPad will use it instead. The trend is extended five years into the future. Finally, the *seasonalized trend & forecast* is constructed by multiplying the appropriate seasonal index by the trend, and is extended five years into the future.

Time Series Output for Sales Data						
time	sales	smooth	seasonal index	seasonally adjusted	exponential trend	seasonalized trend & forecast
1984.125	99		1.124	88.09	96.84	108.83
1984.375	93		0.983	94.64	100.08	98.34
1984.625	83	106.88	0.728	113.95	103.42	75.33
1984.875	134	115.00	1.161	115.42	106.88	124.08
1985.125	136	118.38	1.124	121.02	110.45	124.12
1985.375	121	119.38	0.983	123.13	114.14	112.16
1985.625	82	120.38	0.728	112.58	117.95	85.91
1985.875	143	120.38	1.161	123.17	121.89	141.51
1986.125	135	121.75	1.124	120.13	125.96	141.56
1986.375	122	123.63	0.983	124.15	130.17	127.92
1986.625	92	126.50	0.728	126.31	134.52	97.98
1986.875	148	131.00	1.161	127.48	139.02	161.40
1987.125	153	137.38	1.124	136.14	143.66	161.45
1987.375	140	147.75	0.983	142.47	148.46	145.89
1987.625	125		0.728	171.62	153.42	111.75
1987.875	198		1.161	170.55	158.55	184.07
1988.125			1.124		163.85	184.14
1988.375			0.983		169.32	166.39
1988.625			0.728		174.98	127.45
1988.875			1.161		180.83	209.94
1989.125			1.124		186.87	210.01
1989.375			0.983		193.11	189.77
1989.625			0.728		199.56	145.36
1989.875			1.161		206.23	239.43
1990.125			1.124		213.12	239.51
1990.375			0.983		220.24	216.43
1990.625			0.728		227.60	165.78
1990.875			1.161		235.21	273.07
1991.125			1.124		243.07	273.16
1991.375			0.983		251.19	246.84
1991.625			0.728		259.58	189.07
1991.875			1.161		268.26	311.44
1992.125			1.124		277.22	311.54
1992.375			0.983		286.48	281.52
1992.625			0.728		296.05	215.63
1992.875			1.161		305.95	355.20

7.10 Normal probability calculations

A Appropriate data

Requires the mean (any number) and the standard deviation (any positive number) which define the normal distribution; also one or two numbers to define either the event for which you want the probability or the percentage for which you want the percentile.

After you provide values for the mean and standard deviation of a normal distribution, you can find the probability of being less than, more than, between, or not between numbers of your choosing; percentiles are also available. For example, StatPad could find the probability that sales will exceed $65,000 if you are willing to assume that the sales amount follows a normal distribution with mean $60,000 and standard deviation $10,000. Or you could find the 75th percentile, which is the sales level such that the probability of being less is 0.75.

Information about the situation used in this tutorial exercise: The problem you will be considering concerns the total quantity of radioactive waste produced by a pharmaceutical research and development laboratory. By computing various probabilities based on the assumption of a normal distribution, the firm will be in a better position to negotiate a waste-removal contract.[13]

To carry out normal probability analysis, the parameters you need are the mean and standard deviation of the distribution. For the waste-removal situation they are (based on limited past experience and some expert opinion) as follows:

Mean	1.6 gallons
Standard deviation:	0.47 gallons

---

[13] You should be aware that if you do *not* have a normal distribution, then the probabilities computed for the normal distribution might not be correct for your situation.

B StatPad menus

The menu chart below shows the information you will be asked for and the analyses you can perform.

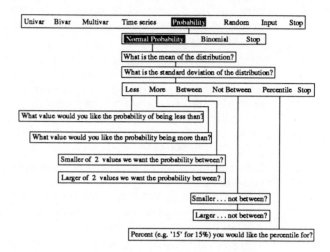

We assume that you have StatPad on your worksheet, and have activated it with ⌈ALT⌉ ⌈S⌉ so that you are looking at the opening menu "*Univar Bivar ...*". If not, please refer to Section 7.2 to see how to get here. Now begin normal probability analysis:

Begin Normal Probability Analysis	**SELECT**	Probability
	SELECT	Normal probability
	Prompt	*What is the mean of the distribution?*
	TYPE	1.6
	PRESS	⌈ ENTER ← ⌉
	Prompt	*What is the standard deviation of the distribution?*
	TYPE	0.47
	PRESS	⌈ ENTER ← ⌉

This brings you to the statistical procedures menu for normal probability analysis. You will carry out these analyses in the sections below. The menu is:

Less   More   Between   Not between   Percentile   Stop

Less	Find the probability of being LESS than some number
More	Find the probability of being MORE than some number
Between	Find the probability of being BETWEEN two numbers
Not Between	Find the probability of NOT being between two numbers
Percentile	Find the value (percentile), given the probability (percentage) of being less.

C   Finding probabilities: less, more, between, not between

StatPad provides probabilities of four types of events for a normal distribution: the probability of being less than some number, more than some number, between two numbers, or not between two numbers. You may select any of these from the menu in any order. Let's perform each of these calculations in turn.

We assume that you are looking at the statistical procedures menu which begins "*Less More ...*" . If not, please refer back to the previous section (7.10 B) to get started with normal probability.

Begin by finding the probability that less than 2 gallons of waste is produced:

Determine Probability of being less than 2 gallons	**SELECT**	Less
	Prompt	*What value would you like the probability of being less than?*
	TYPE	2
	PRESS	(ENTER ←)
	Prompt	*RESULTS HERE? ...*
Position cursor for result	**PRESS**	**ARROW KEYS as needed**
	PRESS	(ENTER ←)

Your screen will look like this, showing the answer 0.803.

Normal
Probability:
Being Less than
a Fixed Value

```
I7:                                                                    MENU
Less    More    Between    Not between    Percentile  Stop
Find the probability of being LESS than some number
        I        J        K         L        M        N        O        P
1    The probability that
2      a normal distribution
3      with mean:        1.6
4      and st. dev.:     0.47
5      is less than:     2
6      is equal to:    0.802633
7
8
```

You now return to the normal probability procedures menu "*Less More...*". Here's how to find the probability that more than 1.5 gallons will be produced:

Determine Probability of being more than 1.5 gallons	**SELECT**	More
	Prompt	*What value would you like the probability of being more than?*
	TYPE	1.5
	PRESS	ENTER ↵
	Prompt	*RESULTS HERE? ...*
Position cursor for result	**PRESS**	**ARROW KEYS as needed**
	PRESS	ENTER ↵

Your screen will look like this, showing the answer 0.584.

Normal
Probability:
Being More than
a Fixed Value

```
I7:                                                                    MENU
Less    More    Between    Not between    Percentile  Stop
Find the probability of being MORE than some number
        I        J        K         L        M        N        O        P
1    The probability that
2      a normal distribution
3      with mean:        1.6
4      and st. dev.:     0.47
5      is more than:     1.5
6      is equal to:    0.584245
7
8
```

You now return to the normal probability procedures menu "*Less More...*". Here's how to find the probability that the amount will be between 1 and 1.5 gallons:

Determine Probability of Being Between 1.0 and 1.5 gallons	**SELECT**	Between
	Prompt	*Smaller of two values we want the probability between?*
	TYPE	1
	PRESS	ENTER ↵
	Prompt	*Larger of two values we want the probability between?*

	TYPE	1.5
	PRESS	[ENTER ←]
	Prompt	*RESULTS HERE? ...*
Position cursor	PRESS	**ARROW KEYS as needed**
for result		
	PRESS	[ENTER ←]

Your screen will look like this, showing the answer 0.315.

Normal Probability: Being Between Two Values

```
I8:                                                              MENU
Less   More   Between   Not between   Percentile  Stop
Find the probability of being BETWEEN two numbers
          I      J      K      L      M      N      O      P
1    The probability that
2    a normal distribution
3    with mean:         1.6
4    and st. dev.:      0.47
5    is between:          1
6            and:        1.5
7    is equal to:   0.314882
8
```

You now return to the normal probability procedures menu "*Less More ...*". Here's how to find the probability that the amount will *not* be between 1.5 and 2.0 gallons:

Determine	SELECT	Not between
Probability of NOT		
Being Between 1.5	*Prompt*	*Smaller of two values we want the prob. of not being between?*
and 2 gallons		
	TYPE	1.5
	PRESS	[ENTER ←]
	Prompt	*Larger of two values we want the prob. of not being between?*
	TYPE	2
	PRESS	[ENTER ←]
	Prompt	*RESULTS HERE? ...*
Position cursor	PRESS	**ARROW KEYS as needed**
for result		
	PRESS	[ENTER ←]

Your screen will look like this, showing the answer 0.613.

Normal
Probability: Not
Being Between
Two Values

```
I8:                                                              MENU
Less    More    Between    Not between    Percentile  Stop
Find the probability of NOT being between two numbers
           I        J       K         L         M        N      O       P
1     The probability that
2       a normal distribution
3       with mean:        1.6
4       and st. dev.:     0.47
5       is not between:   1.5
6                and:     2
7       is equal to:   0.613121
8
```

D Finding percentiles

Finding a **percentile** solves the inverse of a probability problem: You specify the probability and StatPad finds the event with that probability. You might use it to find the 98th percentile: this is the number such that the probability of being smaller is 0.98.

We assume that you are looking at the statistical procedures menu which begins *"Less More ..."* . If not, please refer back to section (7.10 B) to get started with normal probability.

We will now compute the 80th percentile, which will tell you the amount of waste such that the probability of having this amount or less is 80%. Please note that the percentage should be entered as a number *without* the percent sign.

Find the 80th Percentile	SELECT	Percentile
	Prompt	*Percent (e.g. '15' for 15%) you would like the percentile for?*
Value	TYPE	80
	PRESS	[ENTER ←]
	Prompt	*RESULTS HERE? ...*
Position cursor for result	PRESS	**ARROW KEYS as needed**
	PRESS	[ENTER ←]

Your screen will look like this, showing that the 80th percentile is 1.995. That is, the probability of having 1.995 gallons or less is 0.80.

Normal
Probability:
Percentile

```
17:                                                                    MENU
Less    More    Between    Not between    Percentile  Stop
Find the value, given the probability of being less
        I       J       K       L       M       N       O       P
1
2              For a normal distribution
3                with mean              1.6
4                and st. dev.:          0.47
5                the          80 th
6                percentile is    1.995484
7
8
```

7.11 Binomial probability

A Appropriate data

Requires the number of repetitions or cases (a positive whole number) and the probability for each case (a positive number less than 1) which define the binomial distribution; also one or two numbers to define the event for which you want the probability.[14]

After you provide values for the number of cases and the probability for a binomial distribution, you can find the probability of being equal, less than or equal, more than or equal, between two numbers, or not between numbers of your choosing. For example, you can find the probability that 8 or more of the 10 machines you manufacture today will work properly, assuming each has a 97% chance of working.

Information about the situation used in this tutorial exercise: The problem you will be considering concerns a producer of wheat harvesters who has found that the machines have a 92% chance of working right the first time. They are planning to manufacture 35 harvesters tomorrow.

---

[14] The binomial distribution also requires that the cases be *independent* of one another. Otherwise the results may not be applicable to your situation.

B StatPad menus

Here is a chart of the commands you will use in calculating binomial probabilities:

Binomial
Probability:
Command Chart

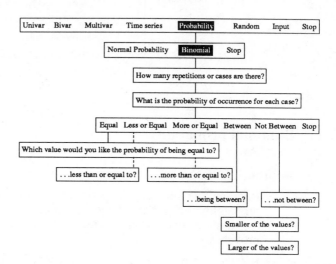

We assume that you have StatPad on your worksheet, and have activated it. If not,

Activate StatPad.	**HOLD** ⟨ALT⟩	while you **PRESS** ⟨S⟩

Begin Binomial Probability Analysis	**SELECT**	Probability
	SELECT	Binomial
	Prompt	*How many repetitions or cases are there?*
	TYPE	35
	PRESS	⟨ ENTER ↵ ⟩
	Prompt	*What is the probability (between 0 and 1) for each case?*
	TYPE	0.92
	PRESS	⟨ ENTER ↵ ⟩

The binomial probability procedures menu comes up:

Equal Less or equal More or equal Between Not between Stop

Equal	Find the probability of being EQUAL to some number
Less or equal	Find the probability of being LESS than OR EQUAL TO some number
More or equal	Find the probability of being MORE than OR EQUAL TO some number
Between	Find the probability of being BETWEEN two numbers
Not between	Find the probability of NOT being between two numbers
Stop	Stop statistical analysis, return to ready mode

In the following sections you will compute each of these binomial probabilities for the 35 wheat harvesters, each of which has an independent 92% chance of working right the first time.

C Finding probabilities: equal, less or equal, more or equal, between, not between

StatPad provides probabilities of five types of events for a binomial distribution. You may select any of these from the menu in any order. Let's perform each of these calculations in turn.

We assume that you are looking at the statistical procedures menu which begins *"Equal Less or equal ..."* . If not, please refer back to the previous section (7.11 B) to get started with binomial probability.

Begin by finding the probability that exactly 34 of the 35 harvesters will work right the first time:

Find Probability of Exactly 34	SELECT	Equal
	Prompt	*What value would you like the probability of being equal to?*
	TYPE	34
	PRESS	(ENTER ←)
	Prompt	*RESULTS HERE? ...*
Position cursor for result	**PRESS**	**ARROW KEYS as needed**
	PRESS	(ENTER ←)

Your screen will look like this, showing that the probability is 0.164 that exactly 34 will work right the first time.

Binomial Probability: Being Equal to a Given Value

```
I7:                                                                   MENU
Equal    Less or equal    More or equal    Between    Not between    Stop
Find the probability of being EQUAL to some number
          I        J        K        L        M        N        O        P
1    The probability that
2      a binomial distribution
3        with # cases:        35
4        and rate:          0.92
5      is exactly             34
6      is equal to:     0.164416
7
8
```

You now return to the binomial procedures menu "*Equal Less or equal ...*". Here's how to find the probability that 34 *or fewer* harvesters will work properly:

Find Probability of 34 or Less	**SELECT**	Less or Equal
	Prompt	*Value you want the probability of being LESS THAN OR EQUAL TO?*
	TYPE	34
	PRESS	ENTER ←
	Prompt	*RESULTS HERE? ...*
Position cursor for result	**PRESS**	**ARROW KEYS as needed**
	PRESS	ENTER ←

Your screen will look like this, showing that the probability is 0.946 that 34 or less will work right the first time.

Binomial Probability: Being Less than or Equal to a Given Value

```
J9:                                                                   MENU
Equal    Less or equal    More or equal    Between    Not between    Stop
Find the probability of being LESS than OR EQUAL TO some number
          I        J        K        L        M        N        O        P
1
2          The probability that
3            a binomial distribution
4              with # cases:        35
5              and rate:          0.92
6          is less than or equal to
7                                   34
8          is equal to:     0.945977
9
10
```

You now return to the binomial procedures menu "*Equal Less or equal ...*". Here's how to find the probability that 34 *or more* harvesters will work properly:

| **Find Probability of 34 or More** | **SELECT** | More or Equal |
| | *Prompt* | *Value you want the probability of being MORE THAN OR EQUAL TO?* |

	TYPE	34
	PRESS	[ENTER ←]
	Prompt	*RESULTS HERE? ...*
Position cursor for result	PRESS	**ARROW KEYS as needed**
	PRESS	[ENTER ←]

Your screen will look like this, showing that the probability is 0.218 that 34 or more will work properly:

Binomial Probability: Being More than or Equal to a Given Value

```
I8:                                                              MENU
Equal    Less or equal    More or equal    Between    Not between    Stop
Find the probability of being MORE than OR EQUAL TO some number
         I      J      K      L      M      N      O      P
1    The probability that
2    a binomial distribution
3       with # cases:      35
4       and rate:        0.92
5    is more than or equal to
6                          34
7    is equal to:    0.218438
8
9
```

You are returned to the binomial procedures menu "*Equal   Less or equal ...*". Here's how to find the probability that the number of working harvesters will be *between* 32 and 34 (that is, either 32 or 33 or 34 will work):

Find Probability of being between 32 and 34	SELECT	Between
	Prompt	*Smaller of two values we want the probability between?*
	TYPE	32
	PRESS	[ENTER ←]
	Prompt	*Larger of two values we want the probability between?*
	TYPE	34
	PRESS	[ENTER ←]
	Prompt	*RESULTS HERE? ...*
Position cursor for result	PRESS	**ARROW KEYS as needed**
	PRESS	[ENTER ←]

Your screen will look like this, showing that the probability is 0.640 that the number that work properly will be between 32 and or 34 (that is, either 32, 33, or 34):

Binomial
Probability:
Being Between
Two Values

```
I8:                                                                    MENU
Equal    Less or equal     More or equal     Between     Not between    Stop
Find the probability of being BETWEEN two numbers
         I       J        K         L         M         N        O       P
1    The probability that
2    a binomial distribution
3      with # cases:        35
4      and rate:           0.92
5    is between            32
6      and                 34
7    is equal to:     0.639948
8
9
```

You now return to the binomial procedures menu "*Equal Less or equal ...*". Here's how to find the probability that the number of working harvesters will *not be between* 31 and 33 (that is, either 0, 1, 2, ..., 30, 30, or 34, or 35 will work):

Find Probability of NOT being Between 31 and 33	**SELECT**	Not Between
	Prompt	*Smaller of values we want the probability of NOT being between?*
	TYPE	31
	PRESS	ENTER ↵
	Prompt	*Larger of values we want the probability of not being between?*
	TYPE	33
	PRESS	ENTER ↵
	Prompt	*RESULTS HERE? ...*
Position cursor for result	**PRESS**	**ARROW KEYS as needed**
	PRESS	ENTER ↵

Your screen will look like this, showing that the probability is 0.363 that the number of working harvesters will *not* be 31, 32, or 33:

Binomial
Probability: Not
Being Between
Two Values

```
I9:                                                                    MENU
Equal    Less or equal     More or equal     Between     Not between    Stop
Find the probability of NOT being between two numbers
         I       J        K         L         M         N        O       P
1
2            The probability that
3            a binomial distribution
4              with # cases:        35
5              and rate:           0.92
6            is NOT between         31
7              and                  33
8            is equal to:     0.362740
9
10
```

7.12   Choosing random samples for analysis

A   Appropriate data

Requires *either* a sample size number and a range name for a column of text, *or* two numbers: the population size (2,000 or less) and the sample size.

A random sample is then chosen for you so that each unit of the population has the same chance of being selected and units are selected independently of one another.

If you specify a range name, then StatPad will randomly select from this list. For example, you could select 15 from a list of 273 employee names. If you specify only the population size, then StatPad will produce a list of numbers randomly selected from 1 to this number. For example, you could select 23 random numbers between 1 and 200. In either case you have the option either to leave the sample in random order or to have it put in order (either alphabetical or numerical, as appropriate).

Information about the data used in this Tutorial exercise: The data set you will be drawing random samples from has as its units, the per capita dollar amount spent for public elementary and secondary school education by state for 1988.[15] Below is a table of the data values. The numerical values and list of states are also in the worksheet, *dataschl.wk1*, which is on your original StatPad disk.

Per Capita Expenditures for Elementary and Secondary Schools by State, 1988.							
AL	$504	IL	$626	MT	$782	RI	$693
AK	1,547	IN	652	NE	609	SC	591
AZ	570	IA	655	NV	674	SD	594
AR	455	KS	729	NH	627	TN	542
CA	686	KY	566	NJ	940	TX	751
CO	757	LA	599	NM	792	UT	715
CT	907	ME	755	NY	922	VT	845
DE	722	MD	731	NC	624	VA	682
DC	759	MA	720	ND	625	WA	832
FL	642	MI	747	OH	673	WV	717
GA	558	MN	799	OK	591	WI	756
HI	598	MS	531	OR	756	WY	1561
ID	622	MO	567	PA	729		

---

[15] Table No. 229. Public Elementary and Secondary School Estimated Finances , by State, 1988. U.S. Bureau of the Census, *Statistical Abstract of the United States: 1989* (109th edition.) Washington, DC, 1989.

B StatPad menus

Following is a chart showing the commands you will be using to choose a random sample.

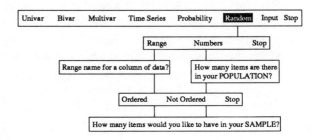

We assume you are in StatPad with your data if not, please use Section 7.3 (D) to bring in your data. You will find the data set in the worksheet *dataschl.wk1* on your original StatPad disk.

Activate StatPad.	**HOLD** (ALT)	while you **PRESS** Ⓢ

The opening StatPad menu now appears.

Choose a Random Sample	**SELECT**	Random

A menu now appears: **RANGE NUMBERS STOP.**

Range	Will select a random sample from a column of data (text or numbers).
Numbers	Will select a random sample from the numbers 1 through your population size (2,000 or less).
Stop	Stop statistical analysis; return to ready mode

These two choices will be worked through in the next sections.

C Range

If you are not at the menu line reading : "**Range Numbers....**", please see section 7.12(B).

Now select a random sample of 10 school expenditures from the column of numbers headed "school":

Choose a sample from a range of text or numbers	**SELECT**	Range
	Prompt	*range name for a column of data?*
	TYPE	School
	PRESS	ENTER ←

If you did not name your range before this, StatPad will tell you that *"Range 'School' does not exist ..."*, and then prompt you to name the range, without leaving the random analysis menus. You can see Section 7.3(F) if you would like more direction with the naming.

The next menu asks if you want the results ordered (sorted numerically) or not.

| **Ordered** | Put sample in order (alphabetic or numeric) |
| **Not Ordered** | Leave sample in random order |

Choose an ordered sample for now:

Choose sample sorted numerically	**SELECT**	Ordered
	Prompt	*How many items would you like to have in your SAMPLE?*
	TYPE	.10
	PRESS	ENTER ←
	Prompt	*RESULTS HERE? ...*
Position cursor for result	**PRESS**	**ARROW KEYS as needed**
	PRESS	ENTER ←

Random
Sample:
Ordered
Random
Sample of
Data Values

```
L1: 'Random                                                           MENU
Univar  Bivar  Multivar  Time series  Probability  Random  Input  Stop
Analyze one kind of measurement: one-sample, two-sample or many-sample
        I       J       K       L       M       N       O       P
1           Per capita          Random
2           expenditures        sample of
3       --------------------         10
4       State   School       from
5       AL        504        School
6       AK      1,547        with
7       AZ        570                51
8       AR        455        items:
9       CA        686                504
10      CO        757                591
11      CT        907                591
12      DE        722                594
13      DC        759                626
14      FL        642                673
15      GA        558                720
16      HI        598                751
17      ID        622                922
18      IL        626              1,561
19      IN        652
20      IA        655
```

After your random sample is placed into the worksheet, you then return to the opening StatPad menu.

D Numbers

If you are looking at the StatPad opening menu ("**Univar Bivar ...**"), please select **Random**. Otherwise, please see section 7.12(B) to get to the menu line "**Range Numbers ...**".

Now select a sample of 10 random numbers from 1 to 51 (the population size).

Choose a sample of numbers	SELECT	Numbers
	Prompt	*How many items are there in your POPULATION?*
	TYPE	51
	PRESS	ENTER ←

The next menu asks if you want the results ordered (sorted numerically) or not.

Ordered	Put sample in numerical order
Not Ordered	Leave sample in random order

Choose an unordered sample for now:

Leave sample in random order	SELECT	Not Ordered
	Prompt	*How many items would you like to have in your SAMPLE?*

TYPE	10
PRESS	[ENTER ↵]
Prompt	*RESULTS HERE? ...*
Position **PRESS**	**ARROW KEYS as needed**
cursor for	
result **PRESS**	[ENTER ↵]

Your list of random numbers will look something like this. Each one may be different, since a new random sample is chosen each time within the same session of 1-2-3.

Random
Sample: Not
Ordered, List
of Random
Numbers

```
K1: 'Numbers                                                        MENU
Univar  Bivar  Multivar  Time series  Probability  Random  Input  Stop
Analyze one kind of measurement: one-sample, two-sample or many-sample
        I       J       K       L       M       N       O       P
 1    School          Numbers
 2
 3      504           Random
 4     1547           sample of
 5      570                10
 6      455           from
 7      686           population
 8      757           with
 9      907                51
10      722           items:
11      759                15
12      642                 3
13      558                25
14      598                49
15      622                38
16      626                43
17      652                31
18      655                14
19      729                39
20      566                 8
```

Glossary

A

adjusted standard error 275

Used when the population is small, so that the sample is an important fraction of the population, and found by applying the finite-population correction factor to the standard error formula:

(Finite-population correction factor) ×

(Standard error)

$$= \sqrt{\frac{N - n}{N}} \times S_{\bar{x}} = \sqrt{\frac{N - n}{N}} \times \frac{S}{\sqrt{n}}$$

analysis and methods 562

The section of a report that lets you interpret the data by presenting graphic displays, summaries, and results, explaining as you go along.

analysis of variance (ANOVA) 639

A general framework for statistical hypothesis testing based on careful examination of the different sources of variability in a complex situation.

appendix 565

The section of a report that contains all supporting material important enough to include but not important enough to appear in the text of the report.

assignable cause of variation 728

The basis for *why* a problem occurred, any time this can be reasonably determined.

assumptions for hypothesis testing 353

(1) The data set is a random sample from the population of interest, and (2) the quantity being measured is approximately normal.

assumptions for the confidence interval 310

(1) The data are a random sample from the population of interest, and (2) the quantity being measured is approximately normal.

autoregressive (AR) process 611

A process in which each observation consists of a linear function of the previous observation plus independent random noise.

autoregressive integrated moving-average (ARIMA) process 621

A process in which the changes or differences are generated by an autoregressive moving-average (ARMA) process.

autoregressive moving-average (ARMA) process 614

A process in which each observation consists of a linear function of the previous observation, plus independent random noise, minus a fraction of the previous random noise.

average 72

The most common method for finding a typical value for a list of numbers, found by adding up all the values and then dividing by the number of items; also called the *mean*.

B

Bayesian analysis 165

Statistical methods involving the use of subjective probabilities in a formal, mathematical way.

between-sample variability 646

Used for ANOVA, a measure of how different the sample averages are from one another.

biased sample 261

A sample that is not representative in an important way.

bimodal distribution 47

Identified by the presence of two clear and separate groups in a histogram.

binomial distribution 209

The distribution of a random variable X that represents the number of occurrences of an event out of n trials, provided (1) for each of the n trials, the event always has the same probability p of happening, and (2) the trials are independent of one another.

binomial proportion 209

The proportion $f = X/n$, which also represents a percentage.

bivariate data 18

Data sets that have exactly two pieces of information recorded for each item.

Box-Jenkins ARIMA process 609

One of a family of linear statistical models based on the normal distribution that have the flexibility to imitate the behavior of many different real time series by combining autoregressive (AR) processes, integrated (I) processes, and moving-average (MA) processes.

box plot 93

A plot displaying the five-number summary as a graph.

C

census 263

A sample that includes the entire population, so that $n = N$.

central limit theorem 230

A rule stating that for n independent observations of a random variable representing a population, (1) the sampling distributions become more and more normal as n gets large, for both the average and the sum, and (2) the means and standard deviations of the distributions of the average and the sum are as follows, where μ is the mean of the individual random variable and σ is the standard deviation of these individuals:

$$\mu_{\bar{X}} = \mu \qquad \mu_{\text{sum}} = n\mu$$

$$\sigma_{\bar{X}} = \frac{\sigma}{\sqrt{n}} \qquad \sigma_{\text{sum}} = \sigma\sqrt{n}$$

chi-squared statistic 702

A measure of the difference between the actual counts and the expected counts (assuming validity of the null hypothesis).

chi-squared test for equality of percentages 704

A test used to determine whether a table of observed counts or percentages (summarizing a single qualitative variable) could reasonably have come from a population with known percentages (the reference values).

chi-squared test for independence 710

A test used to determine whether two qualitative variables are independent or not, based on a table of observed counts from a bivariate qualitative data set.

chi-squared tests 702

Tests that provide hypothesis tests for qualitative data, where you have categories instead of numbers.

clustering 418

Occurs in bivariate data when there are separate, distinct groups in the scatterplot; you may wish to analyze each group separately.

coefficient of determination, R^2 (bivariate data) 435

The square of the correlation, an indication of what percentage of the variability of Y is explained by X.

coefficient of determination, R^2 (multiple regression) 473

A measure that indicates the percentage of the variation in Y that is explained by or attributed to the X variables.

coefficient of variation 132

The standard deviation divided by the average, summarizing the relative variability in the data as a percentage of the average.

complement (NOT) 166

An alternative event that happens only when an event does *not* happen.

conclusion and summary 564

The section of a report that moves back to the "big picture" to give closure, pulling together all of the important thoughts you would like your readers to remember.

conditional population percentages for two qualitative variables 710

The probabilities of occurrence for one variable when you restrict attention to just one category of the other variable.

conditional probability 175

The probability of an event, revised to reflect information that another event has occurred (the probability of event A *given* event B).

confidence interval 297

An interval computed from the data that has a known probability of including the (unknown) population parameter of interest.

confidence level 298

The probability of including the population parameter within the confidence interval, set by tradition at 95%, although levels of 90%, 99%, and 99.9% are also used.

constant term, *a* (bivariate data) 428

The intercept of the least-squares line.

continuous quantitative variable 21

Any quantitative variable that is not discrete, that is, not restricted to a simple list of possible values.

continuous random variable 204

A random variable for which any number in a range is a possible value.

control chart 731

A display of successive measurements of a process together with a center line and control limits, which are computed to help you decide whether the process is in control or not.

correlation coefficient, *r* 400

A pure number between −1 and 1 summarizing the strength of the relationship.

correlation matrix 504

A table giving the correlation between every pair of variables in your multivariate data set.

covariance of *X* and *Y* 403

The numerator in the formula for the correlation coefficient.

critical *t*-value 349

A *t*-value found in the *t*-table and used for the *t*-test.

critical value 349

The appropriate value from a standard statistical table against which the test statistic is compared.

cross-sectional data 24

A data set for which the order of recording is not relevant.

cumulative distribution function 97

A plot of the data specifically designed to display the percentiles by plotting the percentages against the data values.

cyclic component 593

The medium-term component of a time series, consisting of the gradual ups and downs that do not repeat each year.

D

data set 17

A set consisting of some basic measurement or measurements for each item, with the same piece or pieces of information recorded for each one.

degrees of freedom 301

The number of independent pieces of information in the standard error.

dependent events 178

Events for which information about one of them changes your assessment of the probability of the other.

designing the study 9

The phase that involves planning the details of data gathering, perhaps using a random sample from a larger population.

detailed box plot 94

A display of the box plot with outliers, which are labeled separately, along with the most extreme observations that are not outliers.

deviation 114

The distance from a data value to the average.

diagnostic plot (multiple regression) 515

A scatterplot of the prediction errors (residuals) against the predicted values, used to decide whether you have any problems in your data that need to be fixed.

discrete quantitative variable 20

A variable that can only take on values from a list of possible numbers (such as 0 or 1, or the list $0, 1, 2, 3, \ldots$).

discrete random variable 204

A random variable for which you can list all possible outcomes.

E

efficient test 674

A test that makes better use of the information in the data compared to some other test.

elasticity of Y with respect to X_i 527

The expected percentage change in Y associated with a 1% increase in X_i, holding the other X variables fixed; estimated using the regression coefficient from a regression analysis using the logarithms of both Y and X_i.

elementary units 17

Measurements of individual items or things that make up a data set, which may be people, households, firms, cities, TV sets, or just about anything of interest.

error of estimation 263

The estimator (or estimate) minus the population parameter; it is usually unknown.

estimate 263

The actual number computed from the data.

estimating an unknown quantity 10

The best educated guess possible based on the available data.

estimator 263

A sample statistic used as a guess for the value of a population parameter.

event 157

Any collection of outcomes specified in advance, before the random experiment is run; it either happens or does not happen for each run of the experiment.

executive summary 562

A paragraph at the very beginning of a report that describes the most important facts and conclusions from your work.

expected value or mean of a random variable 205

The typical or average value for a random variable.

exploring the data 9

Looking at your data set from many angles, describing it, and summarizing it.

exponential distribution 244

A very skewed continuous distribution useful for understanding waiting times and the duration of telephone calls, for example.

extrapolation 451

Predicting beyond the range of the data; it is especially risky because you cannot protect yourself by exploring the data.

extremes 92

The smallest and largest values, which are often of interest.

F

F-statistic 640

The basis of the *F*-test in the analysis of variance, it is a ratio of two variance measures used to perform each hypothesis test.

F-table 649

A list of critical values for the distribution of the *F*-statistic when the null hypothesis is true, so that the *F*-statistic exceeds the critical value a controlled percentage of the time (5%, for example) when the null hypothesis is true.

F-test (ANOVA) 640

A test based on the *F*-statistic and used in the analysis of variance to perform each hypothesis test.

F-test (multiple regression) 474

An overall test to see if the X variables explain a significant amount of the variation in Y or not.

false alarm rate, for quality control 732

How often you decide to fix the process when there really isn't any problem.

finite-population correction factor 275

Used to reduce the standard error formula when the population is small, so that the sample is an important fraction of the population:

(Finite-population correction factor) $\times$

(Standard error)

$$= \sqrt{\frac{N - n}{N}} \times S_{\bar{X}} = \sqrt{\frac{N - n}{N}} \times \frac{S}{\sqrt{n}}$$

five-number summary 93

A list of special, landmark summaries of a data set: the smallest, lower quartile, median, upper quartile, and largest.

forecast, for time series 582

The expected (i.e., mean) value of the future behavior of the estimated model.

forecast limits 582

The confidence limits for your forecast (if the model can produce them); if the model is correct for your data, then the future observation has a 95% probability, for example, of being within these limits.

frame 262

A scheme that tells you how to gain access to the population units by number from 1 to the population size, N.

frequentist (non-Bayesian) analysis 165

An analysis that does not use subjective probabilities in its computations, although it is not totally objective since opinions will have some effect on the choice of data and model (the mathematical framework).

G

grand average, for ANOVA 646

The average of all of the data values from all of the samples combined.

H

histogram 34

A display of frequencies as a bar chart rising above the number line, indicating how often the various values occur in the data set.

hypothesis 336

A statement about the population that may be either right or wrong; the data will help you decide which one (of two hypotheses) to accept as true.

hypothesis testing 11, 336

The use of data to decide between two (or more) different possibilities in order to resolve an issue in an ambiguous situation; it is often used to distinguish structure from mere randomness and should be viewed as a helpful input to executive decision making.

I

idealized population 276

The much larger, sometimes imaginary, population that your sample represents.

independence of two qualitative variables 710

A relationship between two qualitative variables where knowledge about the value of one does not help you predict the other; that is, the probabilities for one variable are the same as the conditional probabilities *given* the other variable.

independent events 178

Two events for which information about one does not change your assessment of the probability of the other.

indicator variable 536

Also called a *dummy variable,* a quantitative variable that takes on only the values 0 and 1 and is used to represent qualitative categorical data as an explanatory X variable.

interaction, for multiple regression 534

A relationship between two X variables and Y in which a change in both of them causes an expected shift in Y that is different from the sum of the shifts in Y obtained by changing each X individually.

intercept, *a* 426

The value for Y when X is 0.

intercept or constant term, for multiple regression 473

The predicted value for Y when all X variables are 0.

intersection (*and*) 168

An event that happens whenever one event *and* another event both happen as a result of a single run of the random experiment.

introduction 562

Several paragraphs near the beginning of a report in which you describe the background, the questions of interest, and the data set you have worked with.

irregular component 593

The short-term, random component of a time series representing the leftover, residual variation that can't be explained.

J

joint probability table 190

A table listing the probabilities for two events, their complements, and combinations using *and.*

L

law of large numbers 160

A rule stating that the relative frequency (a random number) will be close to the probability (an exact, fixed number) if the experiment is run many times.

least-squares line, $Y = a + bX$ 427

The line with the smallest sum of squared vertical prediction errors of all possible lines, used as the best predictive line based on the data.

least-significant-difference test, for one-way ANOVA 655

Used only if the F-test finds significance, a test to compare each pair of samples to see which ones are significantly different from each other.

linear model 437

A model specifying that the observed value for Y is equal to the population relationship plus a random error that has a normal distribution.

linear regression analysis, for bivariate data 425

Predicting one variable from the other using a straight line.

linear relationship, in bivariate data 403

A scatterplot showing points bunched randomly around a straight line with constant scatter.

list of numbers 32

The simplest kind of data set, representing some kind of information (a single statistical variable) measured on each item of interest (each elementary unit).

logarithm 44

Often used to transform skewness into symmetry because it stretches the scale near zero, spreading out all of the small values that had been bunched together.

M

Mann-Whitney U-test 684

A nonparametric test for two unpaired samples.

mean 72

The most common method for finding a typical value for a list of numbers, found by adding up all the values and then dividing by the number of items; also called the *average*.

mean or expected value of a random variable 205

The typical or average value for a random variable.

median 80

The middle value, with half of the data items larger and half smaller.

mode 87

The most common category; the value listed most often in the data set.

model, mathematical model, or process (time series) 582

A system of equations that can produce an assortment of different artificial time-series data sets.

model misspecification 502

Refers to the many different potential incompatibilities between your application and the multiple regression linear model. By exploring the data, you can be alerted to some of the potential problems with nonlinearity, unequal variability, or outliers. However, you may or may not have a problem: even though the histograms of some variables may be skewed and even though some scatterplots may be nonlinear, the multiple regression linear model might still hold. The diagnostic plot can help you decide when the problem is serious enough to need fixing.

modified sample size, for the sign test 676

The number m of data values that are different from the reference value, θ_0.

moving-average (MA) process 612

A process in which each observation consists of a constant, μ (the long-term mean of the process), plus independent random noise, minus a fraction of the previous random noise.

moving average 595

A new time series created by averaging nearby observations.

multicollinearity 502

A problem that arises when some of your explanatory (X) variables are too similar. The individual regression coefficients are poorly estimated because there is not enough information to decide which one (or more) of the variables is doing the explaining.

multiple regression 471

Predicting a single Y variable from two or more X variables.

multiple regression linear model 483

A model specifying that the observed value for Y is equal to the population relationship plus independent random errors that have a normal distribution.

multivariate data 19

Data sets that have three or more pieces of information recorded for each item.

mutually exclusive events 170

Two events that cannot both happen at once.

N

no relationship, in bivariate data 408

Indicated by a scatterplot that is just random, tilting neither upward nor downward as you move from left to right.

nominal data 23

Categories of a qualitative variable that do not have a natural, meaningful order.

nonlinear relationship, in bivariate data 411

Revealed by a plot in which the points bunch around a curved rather than a straight line.

nonparametric methods 673

Statistical procedures for hypothesis testing that do not require a normal distribution (or any other particular shape of distribution) because they are based on counts or ranks instead of the actual data values.

nonstationary process 619

A process that, over time, tends to move farther and farther away from where it was.

normal distribution (data) 37

A particular, idealized, smooth bell-shaped histogram with all of the randomness removed.

normal distribution (random variable) 219

A continuous distribution represented by the familiar bell-shaped curve.

null hypothesis 336

Denoted H_0, the default hypothesis, often indicating a very specific case, such as pure randomness.

number line 33

A straight line, usually horizontal, with the scale indicated by numbers below it.

O

observation of a random variable 203

The actual value assumed by a random variable.

one-sided confidence interval 317

Specification of an interval with known confidence such that the population mean is either no less than or no larger than some computed number.

one-sided t-test 357

A t-test set up with the null hypothesis claiming that μ is on one side of μ_0 and the research hypothesis claiming that it is on the other side.

one-way analysis of variance 640

Used to test whether or not the averages from several different situations are significantly different from one another.

ordinal data 22

Categories of a qualitative variable that have a natural, meaningful order.

outcome 156

The result of a run of a random experiment, describing and summarizing the observable consequences.

outlier 50, 93, 421

A data value that doesn't seem to belong with the others because it is either far too big or far too small.

P

p-value 356

The smallest level for which your test is significant.

paired t-test 370

Used to test whether or not two samples have the same population mean value when there is a natural pairing between the two samples (for example, "before" and "after" measurements on the same people).

parametric methods 674

Statistical procedures that require a completely specified model.

Pareto diagram 729

A display of the causes of the various defects, in order from most to least frequent, so that you can focus attention on the most important problems.

parsimonious model, for time series 609

A model that uses just a few estimated parameters to describe the complex behavior of a time series.

percentage chart, for quality control 740

A display of the percent defective, together with the appropriate center line and control limits, so that you can monitor the rate at which the process produces defective items.

percentile 91

Summary measures expressing ranks as percentages from 0 to 100, rather than from 1 to n, so that the 0th percentile is the smallest number, the 100th percentile is the largest, the 50th percentile is the median, and so on.

pilot study 268

A small-scale version of a study, designed to help you identify problems and fix them before the real study is run.

Poisson distribution 240

The distribution of a discrete random variable for which occurrences happen independently and randomly over time and the average rate of occurrence is constant over time.

polynomial regression 530

A way to deal with nonlinearity in which Y is predicted using a single X variable together with some of its powers (X^2, X^3, etc.).

population 260

The collection of units (people, objects, or whatever) that you are interested in knowing about.

population parameter 263

Any number computed for the entire population.

population standard deviation 127

Denoted by σ, a variability measure for the entire population.

predicted value, for bivariate data 429

The prediction for Y given a value of X, found by substituting the value of X into the least-squares line.

prediction equation or regression equation, for multiple regression 473

Predicted $Y = a + b_1 X_1 + b_2 X_2 + \cdots + b_p X_p$, which may be used for prediction or control.

prediction errors or residuals, for multiple regression 473

Given by $Y - (\text{Predicted } Y)$.

prediction interval 321

Allows you to use data from a sample to predict a new observation, with known probability, pro-

vided you obtain this additional observation in the same way as you obtained your data.

probability 12

The likelihood of each of the various potential future events, based on a set of assumptions about how the world works.

probability distribution 203

The pattern of probabilities for a random variable.

probability of an event 153

A number between 0 and 1 that expresses how likely it is that the event will happen each time the random experiment is run.

probability tree 181

A picture indicating probabilities and some conditional probabilities for combinations of two or more events.

process, for quality control 728

Any business activity that takes inputs and transforms them into outputs.

pure integrated (I) process 619

A process in which each additional observation consists of a random step away from the current observation; also called a *random walk*.

Q

qualitative variable 22

A variable that indicates which of several nonnumerical categories an item falls into.

quantitative variable 20

A variable whose data are recorded as meaningful numbers.

quartiles 92

The 25th and 75th percentiles.

R

R^2 473

See coefficient of determination

R chart, for quality control 736

A display of the range (the largest value minus the smallest) for each sample, together with center line and control limits, so that you can monitor the variability of the process.

random causes of variation 729

All causes of variation that would not be worth the effort to identify.

random experiment 154

Any well-defined procedure that produces an observable outcome that could not be perfectly predicted in advance.

random noise process 610

A random sample (independent observations) from a normal distribution with constant mean and standard deviation.

random sample or simple random sample 264

A sample selected so that (1) each population unit has an equal probability of being chosen, and (2) units are chosen independently, without regard to one another.

random variable 203

A numerical result in the abstract of a random experiment.

random walk 619

An observation of a pure integrated (I) process that consists of a random step away from the previous observation.

range 129

The largest data value minus the smallest data value, representing the size or extent of the entire data set.

rank 80, 674

Used extensively in nonparametric statistical methods, an indication of a data value's position after you have ordered the data set. Each of the numbers $1, 2, 3, \ldots, n$ is associated with the data values so that the smallest has rank 1, the next smallest has rank 2, and so forth up to the largest, which has rank n.

ratio-to-moving-average 593

A method that divides a series by a smooth moving average for the purpose of performing trend-seasonal analysis on a time series.

reference 564

A note in a report indicating the kind of material you have taken from an outside source and giving enough information so that your reader can obtain a copy.

reference value 339

Denoted by μ_0, a known, fixed number that does not come from the sample data that the mean is tested against.

regression analysis 425

Predicting one Y variable from one or more other X variables.

regression coefficient, b, of Y on X, for bivariate data 428

The slope of the least-squares line.

regression coefficient, for multiple regression 473

The coefficient b_j, for the jth X variable, indicating the effect of X_j on Y after adjusting for the other X variables; b_j indicates how much larger you expect Y to be for a case that is identical to another except for being one unit larger in X_j.

relative frequency 160

For a random experiment run many times, the (random) proportion of times the event occurs out of the number of times the experiment is run.

representative sample 261

A sample in which each characteristic (and combination of characteristics) arises the same percent of the time as in the population.

research hypothesis or alternative hypothesis 337

Denoted by H_1, the hypothesis that has the burden of proof, requiring convincing evidence against H_0 before you will accept it.

residual, for bivariate data 429

The prediction error for each of the data points that tells you how far the point is above or below the line.

S

sample 260

A smaller collection of units selected from the population.

sample space 155

A list of all possible outcomes of a random experiment, prepared in advance without knowing what will happen when the experiment is run.

sample standard deviation 127

A variability measure used whenever you wish to generalize beyond the immediate data set to some larger population (either real or hypothetical).

sample statistic 263

Any number computed from your sample data.

sampling distribution 269

The probability distribution of anything you measure, based on a random sample of data.

sampling with replacement 262

A scheme in which a population unit can appear more than once in the sample.

sampling without replacement 262
A scheme in which a unit cannot be selected more than once to be in the sample.

scatterplot 398
A display for exploring bivariate data, Y against X, giving a visual picture of the relationship in the data.

seasonal adjustment 601
Eliminating the expected seasonal component from an observation (by dividing the series by the seasonal index for that period) so that one quarter or month may be directly compared to another to reveal the underlying trends.

seasonal component 593
The exactly repeating component of a time series that indicates the effects of the time of year.

seasonal index 599
An index for each time of the year, indicating how much larger or smaller this particular time period is as compared to a typical period during the year.

sign test 676
Used to decide whether the population median is equal to a given reference value based on the number of sample values that fall below that reference value.

sign test for the differences 680
A test applied to the differences or changes when you have paired observations (before/after measurements, for example); a nonparametric procedure for testing whether the two columns are significantly different.

skewed distribution 41
A distribution that is neither symmetric nor normal because the data values trail off more suddenly on one side and more gradually on the other.

slope, *b* 426
A measurement in units of Y per unit X that indicates how steeply the line rises (or falls, if b is negative).

spurious correlation 423
Refers to a high correlation that is actually due to some third factor.

standard deviation 114
The traditional choice for measuring variability, summarizing the typical distance from the average to each data value.

standard deviation of a random variable 205
An indication of the risk in terms of how far from the mean you can typically expect the random variable to be.

standard error for prediction 321
The uncertainty measure to use for prediction, $S \times \sqrt{1 + 1/n}$, a measure of variability of the distance between the sample average and the new observation.

standard error of a statistic 271
An estimate of the standard deviation of a statistic's sampling distribution, indicating approximately how far from its mean value (a population parameter) the statistic is.

standard error of estimate, S_e, for bivariate data 434
A measure of approximately how large the prediction errors (residuals) are for your data set in the same units as Y.

standard error of estimate, S_e, for multiple regression 473
Indicates the approximate size of the prediction errors.

standard error of the average 271
Indicates approximately how far the (random, observed) sample average, $\overline{X}$, is from the (fixed, unknown) population mean, μ: Standard error = $S_{\overline{X}} = S/\sqrt{n}$.

standard error of the difference 373
A measure that is needed to construct confidence intervals for the mean difference and to perform the hypothesis test, it gives the estimated standard deviation of the sample average difference.

standard error of the intercept term, S_a, for bivariate data 438
Indicates approximately how far the estimate a is from α, the true population intercept term.

standard error of the slope coefficient, S_b, for bivariate data 438
Indicates approximately how far the estimated slope, b (the regression coefficient computed

from the sample), is from the population slope, β, due to the randomness of sampling.

standard normal distribution 221

A normal distribution with mean $\mu = 0$ and standard deviation $\sigma = 1$.

standard normal probability table 221

A table giving the probability that a standard normal random variable is less than any given number.

standardized number 225

The number of standard deviations above the mean (or below the mean, if the standardized number is negative), found by subtracting the mean and dividing by the standard deviation.

standardized regression coefficient 499

The coefficient $b_i S_{(X_i)}/S_Y$, representing the expected change in Y due to a change in X_i, measured in units of standard deviations of Y per standard deviation of X_i, holding all other X variables constant.

state of statistical control (in control) 729

The state of a process after all of the assignable causes of variation have been identified and eliminated, so that only random causes remain.

stationary process 619

Processes such as the autoregressive, moving-average, and ARMA models, which tend to behave similarly over long time periods, staying relatively close to their long-run mean.

statistical inference 297

The process of generalizing from sample data to make probability-based statements about the population.

statistical process control 728

The use of statistical methods to monitor the functioning of a process so that you can adjust or fix it when necessary and leave it alone when it's working properly.

statistical quality control 725

The use of statistical methods for evaluating and improving the results of any activity.

statistically significant 354

A result that is significant at the 5% level ($p < 0.05$). Other terms used are *highly significant* ($p < 0.01$), *very highly significant* ($p < 0.001$), and *not significant* ($p > 0.05$).

statistics 7

The art and science of collecting and understanding data.

stem-and-leaf histogram 57

A histogram in which the bars are constructed by stacking numbers one on top of another.

stratified random sample 279

Obtained by choosing a random sample separately from each of the strata (segments or groups) of the population.

subjective probability 163

Anyone's opinion (use an expert, if possible) of what the probability is for an event.

summarization 71

Using one or more selected or computed values to represent the data set.

systematic sample 285

A sample obtained by selecting a single random starting place in the frame, then taking units separated by a fixed, regular interval. Although the sample average from a systematic sample is an unbiased estimator of the population mean (that is, it is not regularly too high or too low), there are some serious problems with this technique.

T

t-statistic 349

One way to perform the *t*-test: $t = (\overline{X} - \mu_0)/S_{\overline{X}}$.

t-table 301

The table used to adjust for the added uncertainty due to the fact that an estimator (the standard error) is being used in place of the unknown exact variability for the population.

t-test or Student's t-test 348

The hypothesis test for a mean.

t-tests for individual regression coefficients, for multiple regression 474

If the regression is significant, a method for proceeding with statistical inference for regression coefficients.

table of contents 561

The section of a report that follows the executive summary, showing an outline of the report together with page numbers.

table of random digits 266

A list in which the digits 0 through 9 each occur with probability 1/10, independently of each other.

test level or significance level 355

The probability of wrongly accepting the research hypothesis when, in fact, the null hypothesis is true (i.e., committing a type I error). By convention this level is set at 5%, but it may reasonably be set at 1% or 0.1% (or even 10% for some fields of study) by using the appropriate column in the *t*-table.

test statistic 349

The most helpful number that can be computed from your data for the purpose of deciding between two given hypotheses.

theoretical probability 162

A number computed using an exact formula based on a mathematical theory or model, such as the *equally likely* rule.

time-series data 24

Data values that are recorded in a meaningful sequence.

title page 561

The first page of a report, including the title of the report, the name and title of the person you prepared it for, your name and title (as the preparer), and the date.

transformation 44

Replacing each data value by a different number (such as its logarithm) to facilitate statistical analysis.

trend, for time series 593

The *very* long-term behavior of the time series, typically displayed as a straight line or an exponential curve.

trend-seasonal analysis 592

A direct, intuitive approach to estimating the four basic components of a monthly or quarterly time series: the long-term trend, the seasonal patterns, the cyclic variation, and the irregular component.

two-sided test 340

A test for which the research hypothesis allows possible population values on either side of the reference value

type I error 352

Committed when the null hypothesis is true, but you reject it and declare that your result is statistically significant.

type II error 352

Committed when the research hypothesis is true, but you accept the null hypothesis instead and declare the result *not* to be significant.

U

unbiased estimator 263

An estimator that is correct on the average, so that it is systematically neither too high nor too low compared to the corresponding population parameter.

unconditional probability 175

Ordinary (unrevised) probabilities.

unequal variability, in bivariate data 416

A problem that occurs when the variability in the vertical direction changes dramatically as you move horizontally across the scatterplot; this causes correlation and regression analysis to be unreliable. These problems may be fixed by using either transformations or a so-called weighted regression.

union (or) 171

An event that happens whenever one event *or* an alternative event happens (or both events happen) as a result of a single run of the random experiment.

univariate data 18

Data sets that have just one piece of information recorded for each item.

unpaired t-test 373

Used to test whether two samples have the same population mean value or not, when there is no natural pairing between the two samples (i.e., each is an independent sample from a different population).

V

variability, diversity, uncertainty, dispersion, or spread 114

The extent to which data values differ from one another.

variable 18

A piece of information recorded for every item (its cost, for example).

variable selection 502

The problem that arises when you have a long list of potentially useful explanatory X variables and would like to decide which ones to include in the regression equation. With too many X variables, the quality of your results will decline because information is being wasted in estimating unnecessary parameters. If one or more important X variables is omitted, your predictions will lose quality due to missing information.

variance 115

The square of the standard deviation, it provides the same information as the standard deviation but is more difficult to interpret since its units of measurement are the squared values of the original data units (such as dollars squared, squared miles per squared gallon, or squared kilograms, whatever these things are).

Venn diagram 166

A picture that represents the universe of all possible outcomes (the sample space) as an outer rectangle with events indicated inside, often as circles or ovals.

W

weighted average 75

A measure similar to the average, except that it allows you to give a different importance or *weight* to each data item.

Wilcoxon rank-sum test 684

A way to compute the result of a nonparametric test for two unpaired samples.

within-sample variability, for ANOVA 647

An overall measure of how variable each sample is.

X

$\bar{X}$ **chart, for quality control** 736

A display of the average of each sample, together with the appropriate center line and control limits, so that you can monitor the level of the process.

Index